# Collins

# STUDENT WORLD
# ATLAS

Collins
An imprint of HarperCollins Publishers
Westerhill Road
Bishopbriggs
Glasgow
G64 2QT

© HarperCollins Publishers 2012
Maps © Collins Bartholomew Ltd 2012

First published 2005, reprinted 2005
Second edition 2007
Third edition 2009, reprinted 2009, 2010 (twice)
Fourth edition 2012
ISBN 978-0-00-792674-9

Imp 001

The contents of this edition of the Collins Student
World Atlas are believed correct at the time of
printing. Nevertheless the publishers can accept
no responsibility for errors or omissions, changes
in the detail given, or for any expense or loss thereby
caused.

Printed and bound in Hong Kong

British Library Cataloguing in Publication Data.
A catalogue record for this book is available from
the British Library.

All mapping in this atlas is generated from Collins
Bartholomew digital databases. Collins
Bartholomew, the UK's leading independent
geographical information supplier, can provide a
digital, custom, and premium mapping service to
a variety of markets.
For further information:
Tel: +44 (0) 208 307 4515
e-mail: collinsbartholomew@harpercollins.co.uk

visit our website at: www.collinsbartholomew.com

**www.collinseducation.com**

# Contents

i Title
ii Contents

## MAP SKILLS

iii Map symbols and Map types
iv Graphs and statistics
1 Projections
2 Latitude and longitude
3 Map scale
4–5 Satellite images
6–7 Introducing GIS

## UNITED KINGDOM

8–9 **United Kingdom** Counties
10–11 **United Kingdom** Southeast England
12–13 **United Kingdom** Wales and Southwest England
14–15 **United Kingdom** Northern England
16–17 **United Kingdom** Northern Ireland and Southern Scotland
18–19 **United Kingdom** Northern Scotland
20–21 **United Kingdom** Climate
22 **United Kingdom** Relief
23 **United Kingdom** Rock types
24–25 **United Kingdom** Population and Migration
26–27 **United Kingdom** Economic activity
28 **United Kingdom** Energy
29 **United Kingdom** Tourism
30–31 **United Kingdom** Transport
32–33 **London 2012**

## EUROPE

34–35 **Europe** Relief
35 Physical regions, Countries, European Union
36 **Europe** Climate
37 **Europe** Population
38 **Europe** Economic activity
39 **Europe** Tourism and Environment
40 **Scandinavia**
41 **Ireland**
42 **Netherlands, Belgium and Luxembourg**
43 **Rotterdam–Europoort**
44 **France**
45 **France** Regions, Population, Energy, Trade
46 **Poland**
47 **Poland** Regions, Population, Minerals and Energy, Conservation
48 **Spain and Portugal**
49 **Spain** Regions, Population, Tourism and Water management

## EUROPE continued

50 **Italy**
51 **Italy** Regions, Earthquakes and Volcanoes, Pollution
52–53 **Mediterranean Basin**
54–55 **Central Europe**
56–57 **Southeast Europe**
58–59 **Russian Federation**

## NORTH AMERICA

60 **North America** Relief, Physical regions
61 **North America** Climate
62–63 **Canada**
63 **North America** Countries
64–65 **United States of America**
66 **United States** Population
67 **United States** Economic activity, Trade
68–69 **San Francisco**
70–71 **Mexico and the Caribbean**

## SOUTH AMERICA

72–73 **South America**
72 **South America** Physical regions
73 **South America** Countries
74 **South America** Climate
75 **South America** Land cover, Population, Trade
76–77 **Brazil** São Paulo
78 **Brazil** Population, Rio de Janeiro
79 **Brazil** Economic activity, Trade
80–81 **Rondônia**

## AFRICA

82 **Africa** Relief, Physical regions
83 **Africa** Climate
84–85 **Northern Africa**
84 **Africa** Countries
86 **Southern Africa**
87 **Kenya**
88 **Kenya** Population, Tourism
89 **Kenya** Economic activity, Nairobi, Trade

## ASIA

90–91 **Asia** Relief
91 **Asia** Physical regions, Countries
92 **Asia** Climate
93 **Asia** Monsoon

## ASIA continued

94–95 **Middle East**
94 **Middle East** Oil
96–97 **Pakistan, India, Bangladesh and Myanmar**
97 **India and Bangladesh** Population
98 **India and Bangladesh** Literacy, Economic activity, Tourism, Trade
99 **Bangladesh** Rainfall, Flood Control
100–101 **China**
102–103 **China** Population, Economic Activity, Trade
104–105 **Southeast Asia**
106 **Japan**
107 **Japan** Economic activity and Trade, Population, Energy, Tectonics

## OCEANIA

108–109 **Pacific Ocean**
110–111 **Australia and New Zealand**
111 **Australia and New Zealand** Climate
112 **The Arctic Ocean and Antarctic**

## WORLD

113 **World** International organizations
114–115 **World** Countries
116–117 **World** Relief
118–119 **World** Tectonics
120–121 **World** Climate, Vegetation
122 **World** Agriculture
123 **World** LEDCs and MEDCs
124–125 **World** Population
126–127 **World** Urbanization
128 **World** Birth rates, Death rates, Infant mortality rate
129 **World** Life expectancy, Literacy, Doctors
130 **World** Human Development Index, Access to safe water, Nutrition
131 **World** HIV/AIDS, Poverty, Aid
132–133 **World** Environmental issues
134–135 **World** Climate change
136 **World** Fuel production and Energy
137 **World** Gross National Income, Employment, Trade
138–139 **World** Ecological footprint
140–141 **World** Tourism
142 **World** Communications
143 **World** Air transport
144–151 **World** Statistics
152–170 **Dictionary of geographical terms**

171–195 **Index**

## Map Symbols

Symbols are used, in the form of points, lines or areas, on maps to show the location of and information about specific features. The colour and size of a symbol can give an indication of the type of feature and its relative size.

The meaning of map symbols is explained in a key shown on each page. Symbols used on reference maps are shown below.

### Relief and physical features

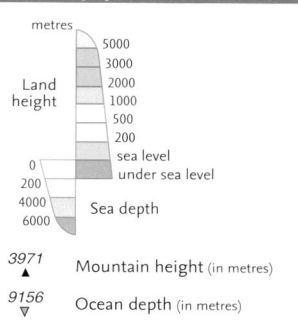

3971 ▲ Mountain height (in metres)

9156 ▽ Ocean depth (in metres)

☐ Permanent ice (ice cap or glacier)

### Water features

~ River

···· Intermittent river

~ Canal

◯ Lake / Reservoir

Intermittent lake

Marsh

### Communications

── Railway

══ Motorway

── Road

········· Ferry

⊕ Main airport

✦ Regional airport

### Administration

── International boundary

── Internal boundary

─ ─ Disputed boundary

······· Ceasefire line

### Settlement

☁ Urban area

| National capital | Population classification |
|---|---|
| ■ PARIS | Over 10 000 000 |
| ▣ ATHENS | 1 000 000 – 10 000 000 |
| ☐ SKOPJE | 500 000 – 1 000 000 |
| ☐ NICOSIA | 100 000 – 500 000 |

| Other city or town | Population classification |
|---|---|
| ● İstanbul | Over 10 000 000 |
| ● İzmir | 1 000 000 – 10 000 000 |
| ○ Antalya | 500 000 – 1 000 000 |
| ○ Split | 100 000 – 500 000 |
| ○ Dubrovnik | 10 000 – 100 000 |
| ○ Bar | 0 – 10 000 |

## Map Types

Many types of map are included in the atlas to show different information. The type of map, its symbols and colours are carefully selected to show the theme of each map and to make them easy to understand. The main types of map used are explained below.

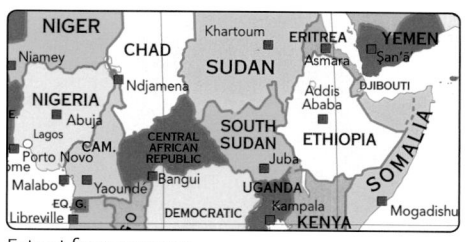

Extract from page 115

**Political maps** provide an overview of the size and location of countries in a specific area, such as a continent. Coloured squares indicate national capitals. Coloured circles represent other cities or towns.

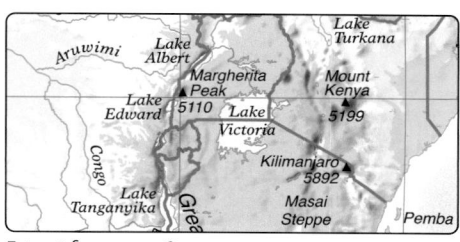

Extract from page 82

**Physical or relief maps** use colour to show oceans, seas, rivers, lakes, and the height of the land. The names and heights of major landforms are also indicated.

Extract from page 100

**Physical/political maps** bring together the information provided in the two types of map described above. They show relief and physical features as well as country borders, major cities and towns, roads, railways and airports.

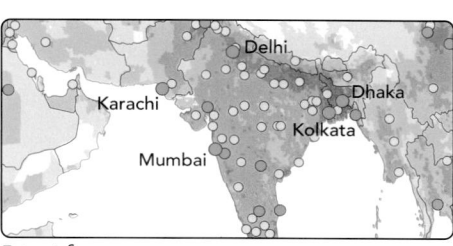

Extract from page 125

**Distribution maps** use different colours, symbols, or shading to show the location and distribution of natural or man-made features. In this map, symbols indicate the distribution of the world's largest cities.

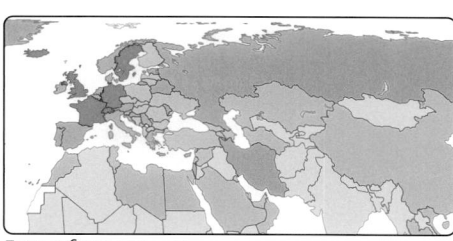

Extract from page 142

**Graduated colour maps** use colours or shading to show a topic or theme and a measure of its intensity. Generally, the highest values are shaded with the darkest colours. In this map, colours are used to show the number of telephone lines per 100 people.

Extract from page 36

**Isoline maps** use thin lines to show the distribution of a feature. An isoline passes through places of the same value. Isolines may show features such as temperature (isotherm), air pressure (isobar) or height of land (contour). The value of the line is usually written on it. On either side of the line the value will be higher or lower.

# Graphs and Statistics

## Climate Statistics and Tables

Throughout this atlas there are sets of **climatic statistics** (numbers showing temperatures and rainfall) for many different places. These statistics are set out in **climatic tables** like the one below for Vancouver, Canada:

| Vancouver | Jan | Feb | Mar | Apr | May | Jun | Jul | Aug | Sep | Oct | Nov | Dec |
|---|---|---|---|---|---|---|---|---|---|---|---|---|
| Temperature - max. (°C) | 5 | 7 | 10 | 14 | 18 | 21 | 23 | 23 | 18 | 14 | 9 | 6 |
| Temperature - min. (°C) | 0 | 1 | 3 | 4 | 8 | 11 | 12 | 12 | 9 | 7 | 4 | 2 |
| Rainfall - (mm) | 218 | 147 | 127 | 84 | 71 | 64 | 31 | 43 | 91 | 147 | 211 | 224 |

a   On the top line in the table are the name of the place and the months of the year.

b   On the next two lines is information about the average maximum (highest) and minimum (lowest) temperatures for each month.

c   On the bottom line is information about the average amount of rainfall for each month.

We can use this information to draw climatic graphs and understand what the climate is like in these places.

## Climate Graph

A **climatic graph** is a graph of the average temperatures and average rainfall of a place for the twelve months of the year. Look at this example of a climatic graph for Vancouver, which has been drawn from the climatic table shown on the left:

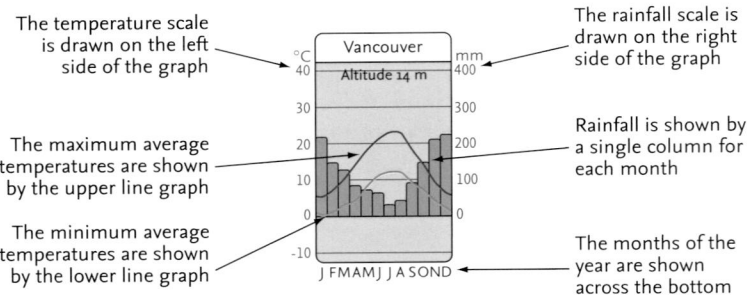

The temperature scale is drawn on the left side of the graph

The maximum average temperatures are shown by the upper line graph

The minimum average temperatures are shown by the lower line graph

The rainfall scale is drawn on the right side of the graph

Rainfall is shown by a single column for each month

The months of the year are shown across the bottom

## Data Represented Graphically

### Simple line graph:

World communication equipment, 2000 – 2010

### Simple pie:

Caribbean tourist arrivals by country of destination, 2010

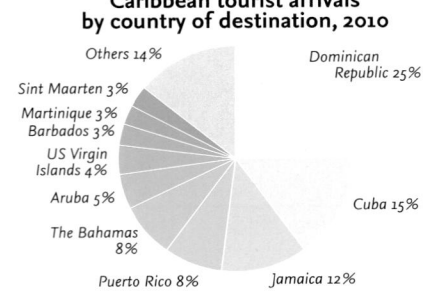

Caribbean total : 16 547 541 tourists

### Clustered columns:

Tourist arrivals

### Simple bars:

World's top 10 tourist destinations, 2010

### Donut pie:

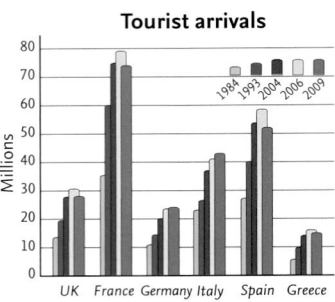

### Horizontal bars:

Poverty in developing countries, by region

### Ranking table:

Largest countries by population, 2011

| Country and continent | Population |
|---|---|
| **China** Asia | 1 332 079 000 |
| **India** Asia | 1 241 492 000 |
| **United States of America** N America | 313 085 000 |
| **Indonesia** Asia | 242 326 000 |
| **Brazil** S America | 196 655 000 |
| **Pakistan** Asia | 176 745 000 |
| **Nigeria** Africa | 162 471 000 |
| **Bangladesh** Asia | 150 494 000 |
| **Russian Federation** Asia/Europe | 142 836 000 |
| **Japan** Asia | 126 497 000 |
| **Mexico** N America | 114 793 000 |
| **Philippines** Asia | 94 852 000 |
| **Vietnam** Asia | 88 792 000 |
| **Ethiopia** Africa | 84 734 000 |
| **Egypt** Africa | 82 537 000 |
| **Germany** Europe | 82 163 000 |
| **Iran** Asia | 74 799 000 |
| **Turkey** Asia | 73 640 000 |
| **Thailand** Asia | 69 519 000 |
| **Dem. Rep. of the Congo** Africa | 67 758 000 |

### 100% stacked bars:

Primary energy supply

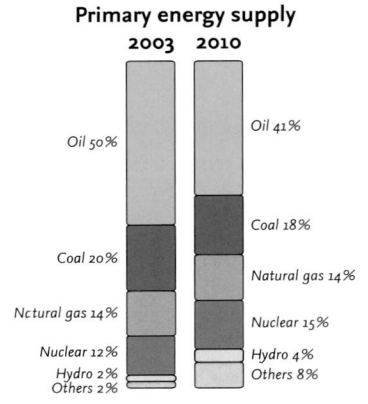

### Split donuts:

Exports, 2009   Imports, 2009

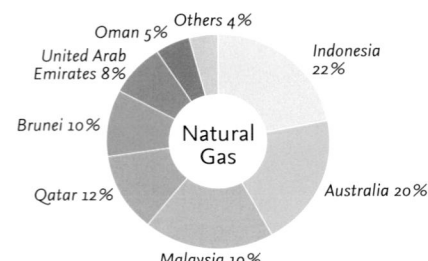

Because the Earth is a sphere and maps are flat, map makers (cartographers) have developed different ways of showing the Earth's surface on a flat piece of paper. These methods are called map projections, because they are based on the idea of the Earth's surface being 'projected' onto a piece of paper.

There are many types of map projection, but none of them show the Earth with perfect accuracy. Every map projection must stretch or distort the surface to make it fit onto a flat map. As a result, either shape, area, direction or distance will be distorted. The amount of distortion increases away from the point at which

the globe touches the piece of paper onto which it is projected. Areas of increasing distortion are shown in red on the diagrams below. Map projections are carefully chosen in this atlas to show the area of the Earth's surface as accurately as possible. The three main types of map projection used are explained below.

## Cylindrical Projections

 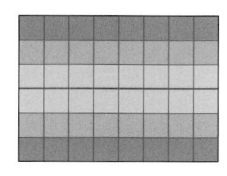

Cylindrical projections are constructed by projecting the surface of the globe or sphere (Earth) onto a cylinder that just touches the outside edges of that globe. Two examples of cylindrical projections are Mercator and Times.

**Mercator Projection** (see pages 104-105 for an example of this projection)

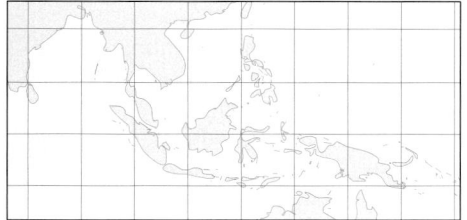

The Mercator cylindrical projection is useful for areas near the equator and to about 15 degrees north or south of the equator, where distortion of shape is minimal. The projection is useful for navigation, since directions are plotted as straight lines.

**Eckert IV** (see pages 114-115 for an example of this projection)

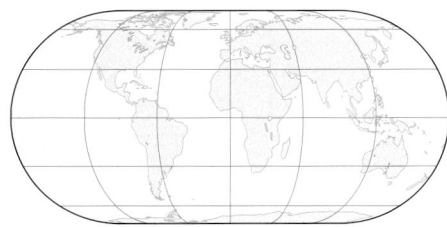

Eckert IV is an equal area projection. Equal area projections are useful for world thematic maps where it is important to show the correct relative sizes of continental areas. Ecker IV has a straight central meridian but all others are curved which help suggest the spherical nature of the earth.

## Conic Projections

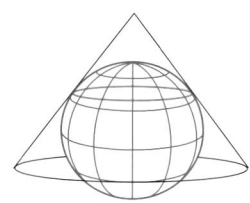 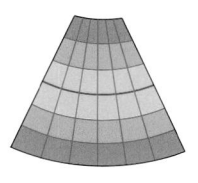

Conic projections are constructed by projecting the surface of a globe or sphere (Earth) onto a cone that just touches the outside edges of that globe. Examples of conic projections are Conic Equidistant and Albers Equal Area Conic.

**Conic Equidistant Projection** (see pages 58-59 for an example of this projection)

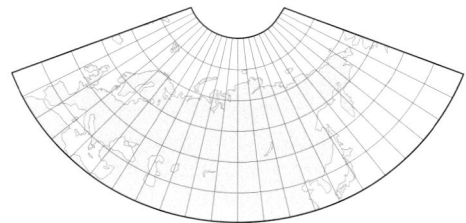

Conic projections are best suited for areas between 30° and 60° north and south of the equator when the east-west distance is greater than the north-south distance (such as Canada and Europe). The meridians are straight and spaced at equal intervals.

**Lambert Conformal** (see pages 62-63 for an example of this projection)

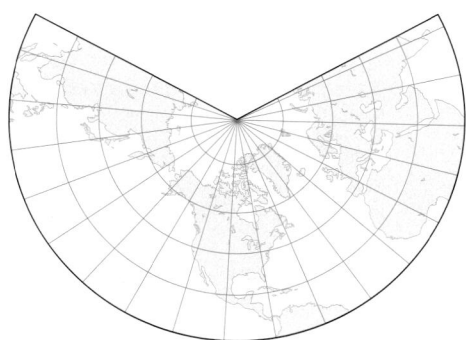

Lambert's Conformal Conic projection maintains an exact scale along one or two standard parallels (lines of latitude). Angles between locations on the surface of the earth are correctly shown. Therefore, it is used for aeronautical charts and large scale topographic maps in many countries. It is also used to map areas with a greater east-west than north-south extent.

## Azimuthal Projections

 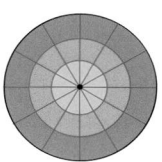

Azimuthal projections are constructed by projecting the surface of the globe or sphere (Earth) onto a flat surface that touches the globe at one point only. Some examples of azimuthal projections are Lambert Azimuthal Equal Area and Polar Stereographic.

**Polar Stereographic Projection** (see page 112 for an example of this projection)

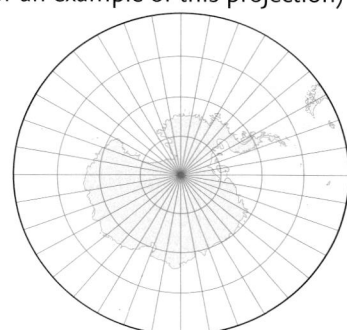

Azimuthal projections are useful for areas that have similar east-west and north-south dimensions such as Antarctica and Australia.

**Lambert Azimuthal Equal Area** (see pages 110-111 for an example of this projection)

This projection is useful for areas which have similar east-west, north-south dimensions such as Australia.

# Latitude and Longitude

## Latitude

Latitude is distance, measured in degrees, north and south of the equator. Lines of latitude circle the globe in an east-west direction. The distance between lines of latitude is always the same. They are also known as parallels of latitude. Because the circumference of Earth gets smaller toward the poles, the lines of latitude are shorter nearer the poles.

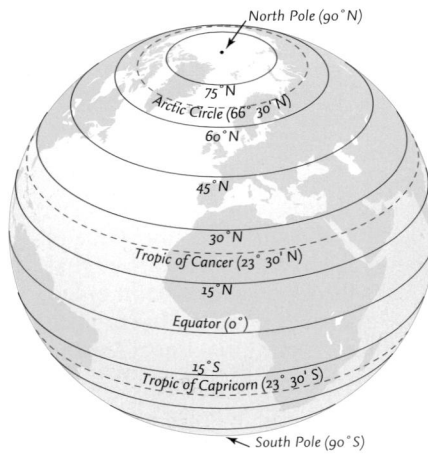

All lines of latitude have numbers between 0° and 90° and a direction, either north or south of the equator. The equator is at 0° latitude. The North Pole is at 90° north and the South Pole is at 90° south. The 'tilt' of Earth has given particular importance to some lines of latitude. They include:
• the Arctic Circle at 66° 30' north
• the Antarctic Circle at 66° 30' south
• the Tropic of Cancer at 23° 30' north
• the Tropic of Capricorn at 23° 30' south

The Equator also divides the Earth into two halves. The northern half, north of the Equator, is the **Northern Hemisphere.** The southern half, south of the Equator, is the **Southern Hemisphere.**

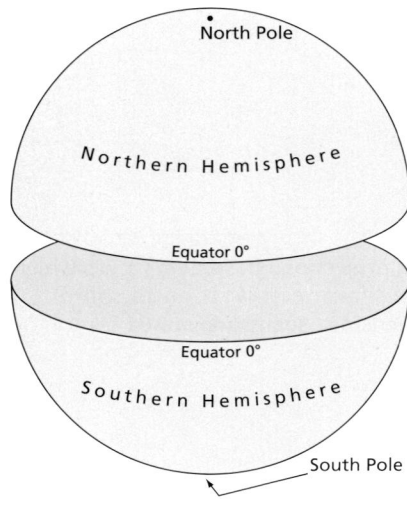

## Longitude

Longitude is distance, measured in degrees, east and west of the Greenwich Meridian (prime meridian). Lines of longitude join the poles in a north-south direction. Because the lines join the poles, they are always the same length, but are farthest apart at the equator and closest together at the poles. These lines are also called meridians of longitude.

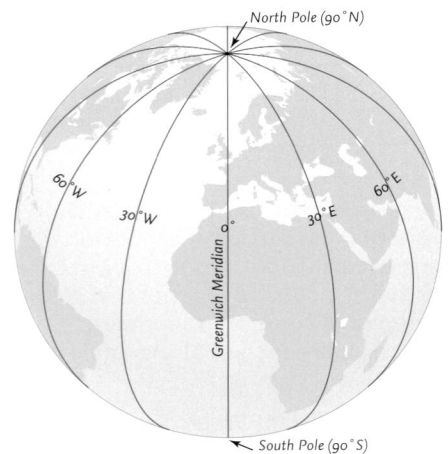

Longitude begins along the Greenwich Meridian (prime meridian), at 0°, in London, England. On the opposite side of Earth is the 180° meridian, which is the International Date Line. To the west of the prime meridian are Canada, the United States, and Brazil; to the east of the prime meridian are Germany, India and China. All lines of longitude have numbers between 0° and 180° and a direction, either east or west of the prime meridian.

The Greenwich Meridian and the International Date Line can also be used to divide the world into two halves. The half to the west of the Greenwich Meridian is the **Western Hemisphere.** The half to the east of the Greenwich Meridian is the **Eastern Hemisphere.**

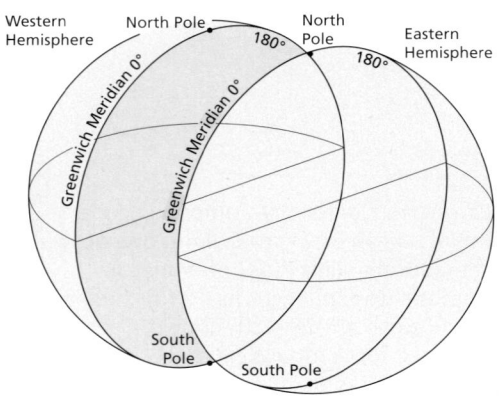

## Finding Places

When lines of latitude and longitude are drawn on a map, they form a grid, which looks like a pattern of squares. This pattern is used to find places on a map. Latitude is always stated before longitude (e.g., 42°N 78°W).

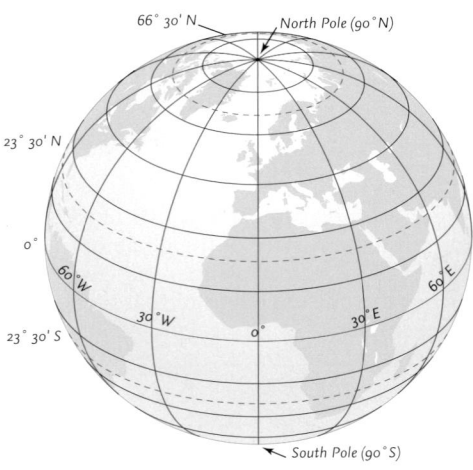

By stating latitude and then longitude of a place, it becomes much easier to find. On the map (below) point A is easy to find as it is exactly latitude 58° North of the Equator and longitude 4° West of the Greenwich Meridian (58°N 4°W).

To be even more accurate in locating a place, each degree of latitude and longitude can also be divided into smaller units called **minutes** ('). There are 60 minutes in each degree. On the map (below) Halkirk is one half (or 30/60ths) of the way past latitude 58°N, and one-half (or 30/60ths) of the way past longitude 3°W. Its latitude is therefore 58 degrees 30 minutes North and its longitude is 3 degrees 30 minutes West. This can be shortened to 58°30'N 3°30'W. Latitude and longitude for all the places and features named on the maps are included in the index.

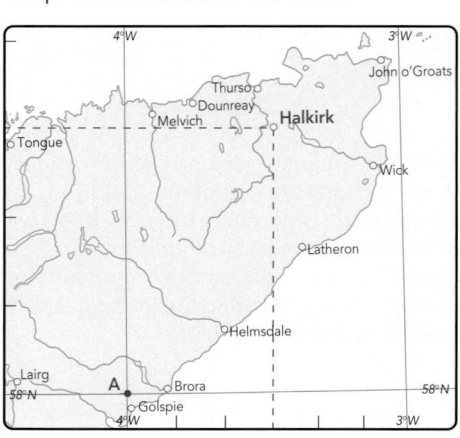

## Scale

To draw a map of any part of the world, the area must be reduced, or 'scaled down,' to the size of a page in this atlas, a foldable road map, or a topographic map. The scale of the map indicates the amount by which an area has been reduced.

The scale of a map can also be used to determine the actual distance between two or more places or the actual size of an area on a map. The scale indicates the relationship between distances on the map and distances on the ground.

Scale can be shown
- **using words:** for example, 'one centimetre to one kilometre' (one centimetre on the map represents one kilometre on the ground), or 'one centimetre to 100 kilometres' (one centimetre on the map represents 100 kilometres on the ground).
- **using numbers:** for example, '1 : 100 000 or 1/100 000' (one centimetre on the map represents 100 000 centimetres on the ground), or '1 : 40 000 000 or 1/40 000 000' (one centimetre on the map represents 40 million centimetres on the ground). Normally, the large numbers with centimetres would be converted to metres or kilometres.
- **as a line scale:** for example,

## Scale and Map Information

The scale of a map also determines how much information can be shown on it. As the area shown on a map becomes larger and larger, the amount of detail and the accuracy of the map becomes less and less.

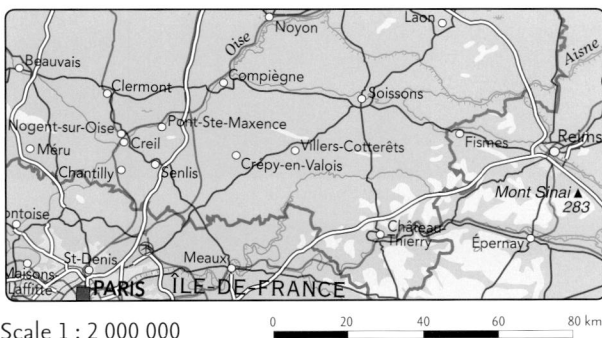

Scale 1 : 2 000 000

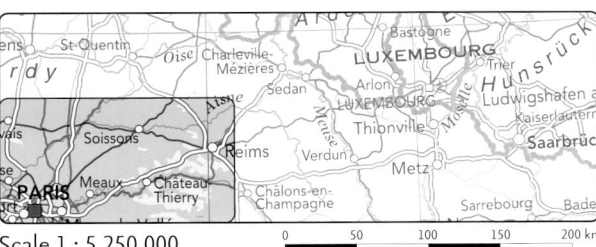

Scale 1 : 5 250 000

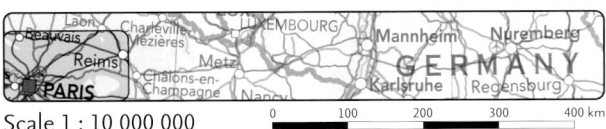

Scale 1 : 10 000 000

## Measuring Distance

The instructions below show you how to determine how far apart places are on the map, then using the line scale, to determine the actual distance on the ground.

To use the line scale to measure the straight-line distance between two places on a map:
1. place the edge of a sheet of paper on the two places on a map,
2. on the paper, place a mark at each of the two places,
3. place the paper on the line scale,
4. measure the distance on the ground using the scale.

To find the distance between Calgary and Regina, line up the edge of a piece of paper between the two places and mark off the distance.

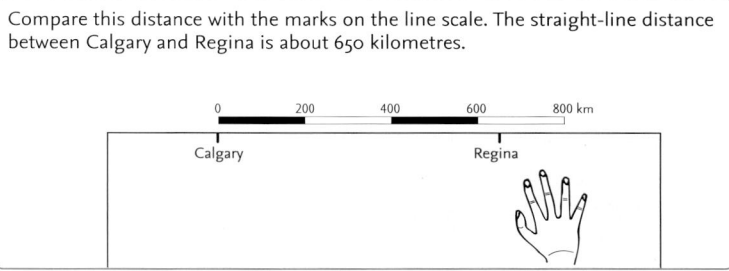

Compare this distance with the marks on the line scale. The straight-line distance between Calgary and Regina is about 650 kilometres.

Often, the road or rail distance between two places is greater than the straight-line distance. To measure this distance:
1. place the edge of a sheet of paper on the map and mark off the start point on the paper,
2. move the paper so that its edge follows the bends and curves on the map (Hint: use the tip of your pencil to pin the edge of the paper to the curve as you pivot the paper around each curve),
3. mark off the end point on the sheet of paper,
4. place the paper on the line scale and read the actual distance following a road or railroad.

To find the distance by road between Calgary and Regina, mark off the start point, then twist the paper to follow the curve of the road through Medicine Hat, Swift Current, Moose Jaw, and then into Regina. The actual distance is about 750 kilometres.

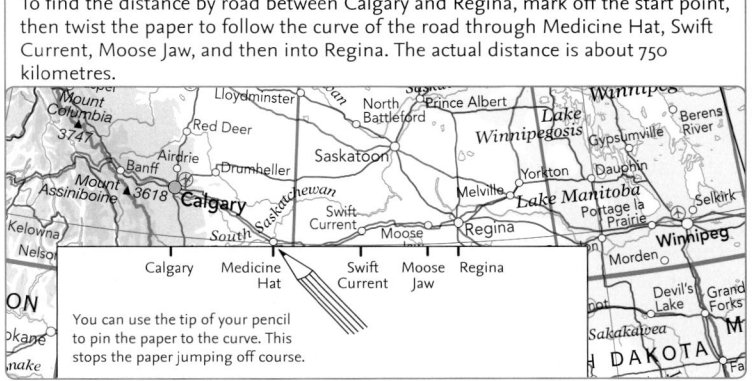

# Satellite Images

## Creating Satellite Images

Images captured by a large number of Earth-observing satellites provide unique views of the Earth. The science of gathering and interpreting such images is known as remote sensing. Geographers use images taken from high above the Earth to determine patterns, trends and basic characteristics of the Earth's surface. Satellites are fitted with different kinds of scanners or sensors to gather information about the Earth. The most well known satellites are Landsat and SPOT.

Satellite sensors detect electromagnetic radiation –X-rays, ultraviolet light, visible colours and microwave signals. This data can be processed to provide information on soils, land use, geology, pollution and weather patterns. Colours can be added to this data to help understand the images. In some cases this results in a 'false-colour' image where red areas represent vegetation and built-up areas show as blue/grey. Examples of satellite images are included in this atlas to illustrate geographical themes.

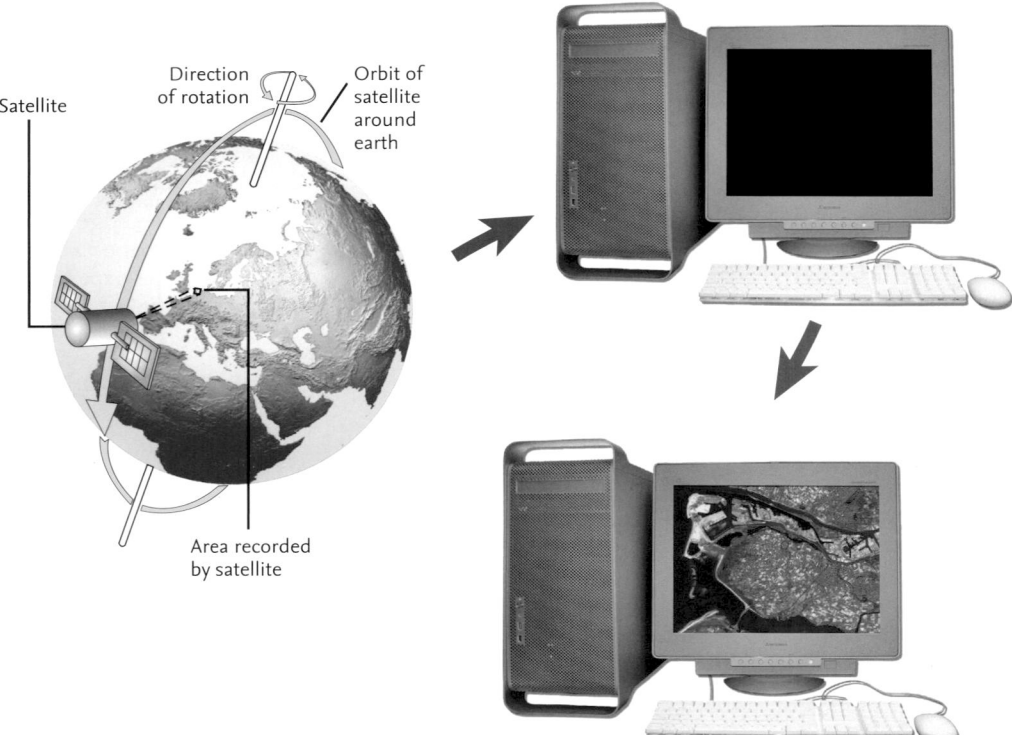

Satellite

Direction of rotation

Orbit of satellite around earth

Area recorded by satellite

## Receding Waters

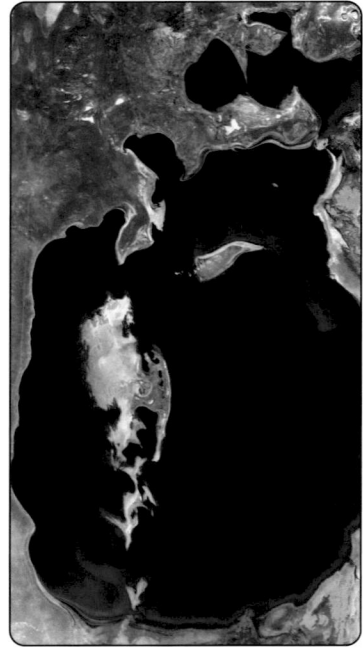

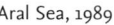

Aral Sea, 1989

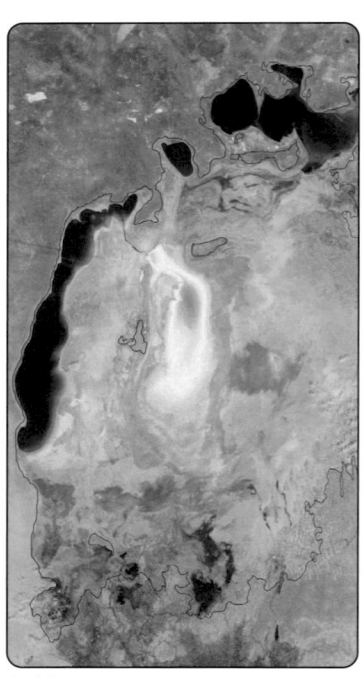

Aral Sea, 2009

The Aral Sea was once the world's fourth largest lake. Today, due to the diversion of the water from its feeder rivers for the irrigation of farmland, it is much smaller. The diversion process began in the 1960s and by 1989, Landsat imagery (above left) showed that the northern and southern half of the sea had become virtually separated. Since then the southern section further separated into eastern and western lobes and by 2009 virtually nothing remained of the southern half of the sea. The deterioration of the northern sea has slowed down but recovery of the southern sea is probably impossible.

## Natural Hazards

Kitakami River before tsunami, January 16, 2011

Kitakami River after tsunami, March 14, 2011

This pair of ASTER false-colour images, taken before and after the tsunami that struck northeast Japan in March 2011, show the devastating effect natural hazards can have in a short space of time. The March image shows how the water from the ocean spilled over the banks both north and south of the river Kitakami. Cropland and settlements close to the ocean appear to have disappeared.  Only rugged peaks rising above the flood plains escaped inundation.

## Urban Clusters

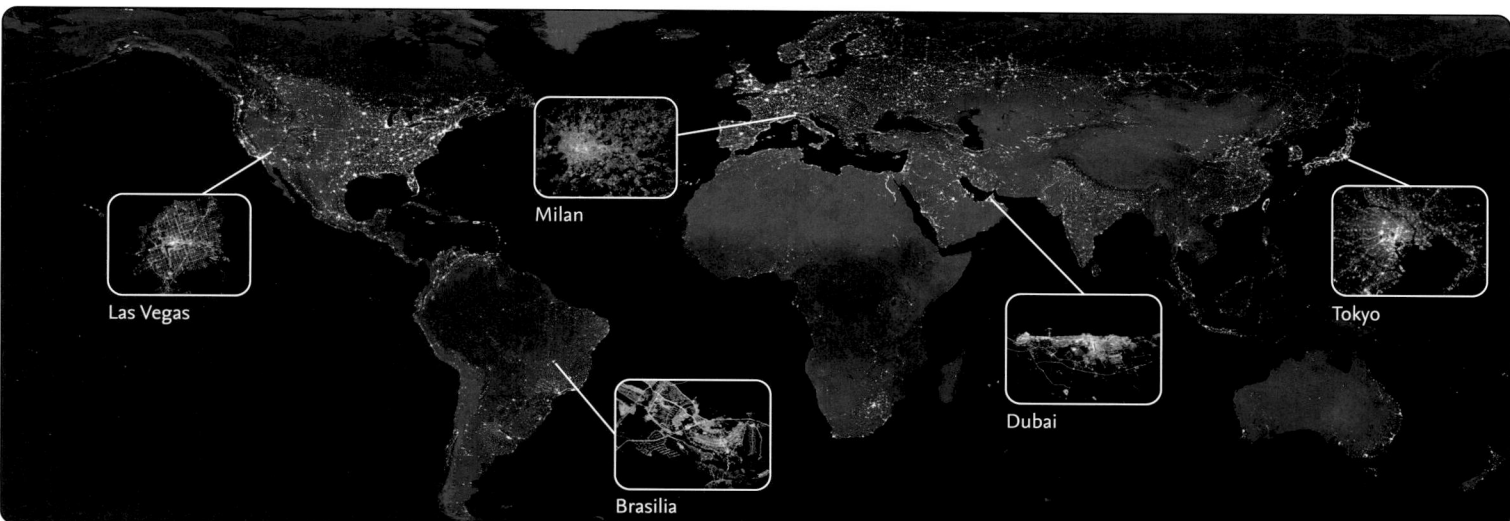

The World at Night

This image of Earth shows the most urbanized areas by mapping the locations of permanent lights on the Earth's surface. Cities tend to grow along coastlines and transportation networks so the underlying outlines of the continents are still visible. Many areas, such as deserts, dense forests and high mountains, are poorly lit or completely dark. Insets of some major cities show the brightest areas are at the heart of a city.

## City Growth

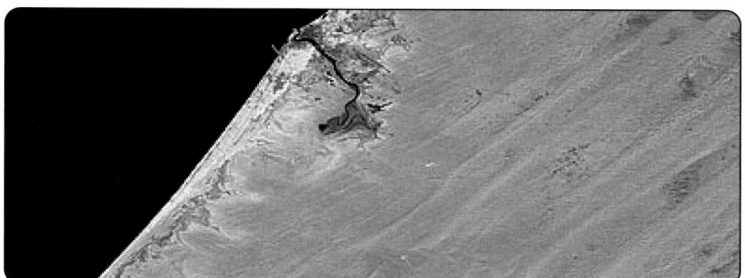

Dubai, 1973

Dubai, 2002

Dubai, 2008

The emergence of Dubai as a major metropolis and tourist destination is evident in these images. In the bottom image, captured in 2008, artificial islands shaped like palm trees stretch along the shore. Inland, irrigated vegetation stands out in red against the tan-coloured desert. In the top image, taken in 1973, the number and density of roads and buildings is far less than in 2008.

## Climate Change

Larsen Ice Shelf, January 31, 2002

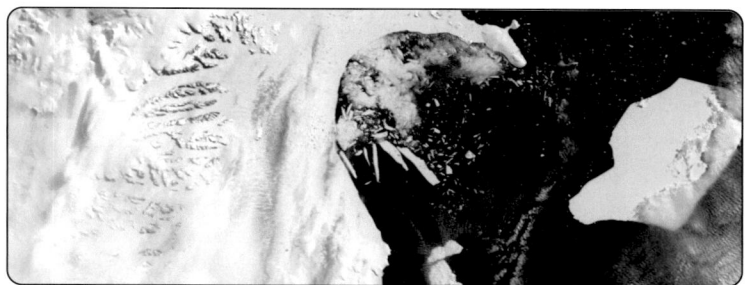

Larsen Ice Shelf, February 23, 2002

Larsen Ice Shelf, March 17, 2002

This series of images shows how a large floating ice mass in Antarctica shattered and separated from the continent over a period of 35 days. An area of 3250 square kilometres disintegrated to form drifting icebergs in the Weddell Sea. This event is attributed to strong climate warming in the region.

# Introducing GIS

## What is GIS?

GIS stands for **Geographic Information System.** A GIS is a set of tools which can be used to collect, store, retrieve, modify and display spatial data. Spatial data can come from a variety of sources including existing maps, satellite imagery, aerial photographs or data collected from GPS (Global Positioning System) surveys.

GIS links this information to its real world location and can display this in a series of layers which you can then choose to turn off and on or to combine. GIS is often associated with maps, however there are 3 ways in which a GIS can be applied to work with spatial information, and together they form an intelligent GIS:

> **1. The Database View** – the geographic database (or Geodatabase) is a structured database which stores and describes the geographic information.
>
> **2. The Map View** – a set of maps can be used to view data in different ways using a variety of symbols and layers as shown on the illustration on the right.
>
> **3. The Model View** – A GIS is a set of tools that create new geographic datasets from existing datasets. These tools take information from existing datasets, apply rules and write results into new datasets.

## Why use GIS?

A GIS can be used in many ways to help people and businesses solve problems, find patterns, make decisions or to plan for future developments. A map in a GIS can let you find places which contain some specific information and the results can then be displayed on a map to provide a clear simple view of the data.

For example you might want to find out the number of houses which are located on a flood plain in an area prone to flooding. This can be calculated and displayed using a GIS and the results can then be used for future planning or emergency provision in the case of a flood.

A company could use a GIS to view data such as population figures, income and transport in a city centre to plan where to locate a new business or where to target sales. Mapping change is also possible within a GIS. By mapping where and how things move over a period of time, you can gain insight into how they behave. For example, a meteorologist might study the paths of hurricanes to predict where and when they might occur in the future.

### GIS USERS

| | |
|---|---|
| The National Health Service | Environmental Agencies |
| The Police | Councils |
| Estate Agents | Supermarkets |
| Government Agencies | Insurance Companies |
| Schools | Banks |
| Emergency Services | Holiday Companies |
| The Military | Mapping Agencies |

## GIS Layers

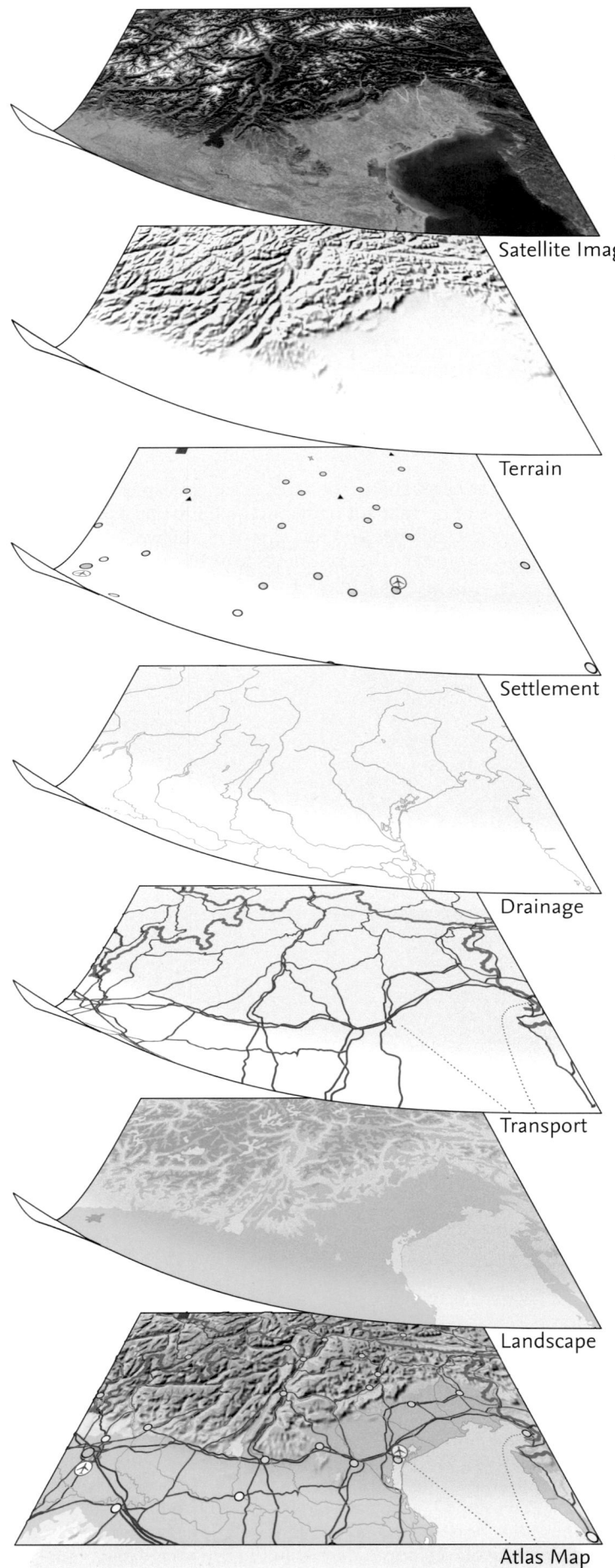

Satellite Image

Terrain

Settlement

Drainage

Transport

Landscape

Atlas Map

## Terrain

This map shows the relief of the country, and highlights the areas which are hilly in contrast to flatter areas. Relief can be represented in a variety of ways - contours and area colours can both show the topography. This terrain map uses shading which makes the hilly areas obvious.

## Energy Sources

This map illustrates the location of energy sources in the UK using point symbols. Each point symbol contains coordinate information and represents the different types of energy sources, for example the blue triangles show the location of wind farms. Points can be used to represent a variety of features such as banks, schools or shopping centres.

## Transportation

Roads shown here have been split into two categories, Motorways in green and Primary Roads in red, and these have been attributed with their road number. This is a road network using linear symbols. Rivers and railways could also be shown like this.

## Land Use

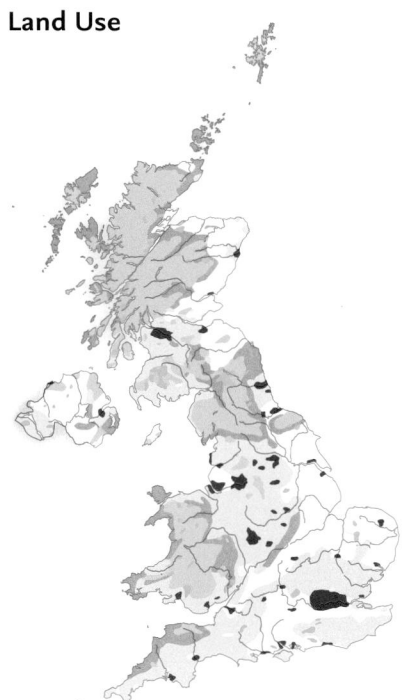

This Land Use map illustrates the different ways in which the land is used in areas across the UK. Each area is coloured differently depending on the type of land use. Areas in yellow are dominated by farms which grow crops, whereas urban areas are shown in red and forests in green. This map is used to show agricultural land use, but a similar map could be used to show different types of soils for example.

## Regional Migration

Graphs can be used on maps as a type of point symbol, and are an effective way of representing changes over time. This map has been divided into the regions of Britain and shows the number of people moving in and out of each region. The orange bar shows the number of people (in thousands) moving into an area, and the green bar shows the number of people moving out.

## Population Distribution

Population distribution can be shown on a map by using different colours for each category. This map uses 3 categories and each shows the number of people in a square kilometre. The yellow areas contain less than 10 people per square km; the light orange areas have 10 – 150, whilst the dark orange areas contain over 150 people per square km. The dark orange areas therefore have the highest population density.

# United Kingdom Counties

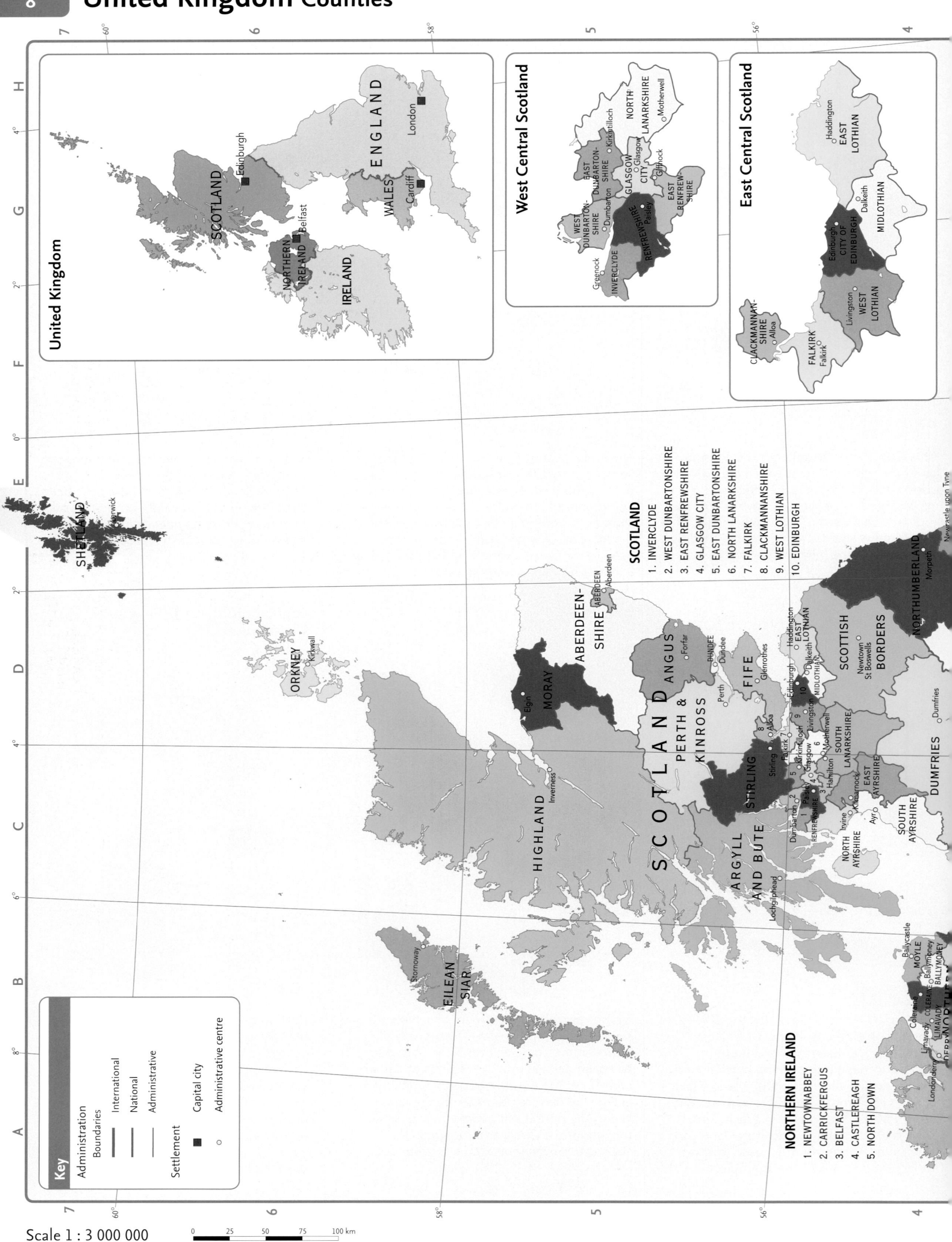

**United Kingdom**

SCOTLAND
Edinburgh

ENGLAND
London

NORTHERN
IRELAND
Belfast

WALES
Cardiff

IRELAND

**West Central Scotland**

NORTH
LANARKSHIRE
Motherwell

WEST
DUNBARTON-
SHIRE
Dumbarton

EAST
DUNBARTON-
SHIRE
Kirkintilloch

GLASGOW
CITY
Glasgow
Giffnock

EAST
RENFREW-
SHIRE

RENFREWSHIRE
Paisley

Greenock
INVERCLYDE

**East Central Scotland**

Haddington
EAST
LOTHIAN

Dalkeith
MIDLOTHIAN

Edinburgh
CITY OF
EDINBURGH

Livingston
WEST
LOTHIAN

CLACKMANNAN-
SHIRE
Alloa

FALKIRK
Falkirk

**Key**

Administration
Boundaries
International
National
Administrative

Settlement
■ Capital city
○ Administrative centre

SHETLAND
Lerwick

ORKNEY
Kirkwall

HIGHLAND
Inverness

EILEAN
SIAR
Stornoway

ARGYLL
AND BUTE
Lochgilphead

MORAY
Elgin

ABERDEEN-
SHIRE
ABERDEEN
Aberdeen

ANGUS
Forfar

PERTH &
KINROSS
Perth
DUNDEE
Dundee

FIFE
Glenrothes

STIRLING
Stirling

SCOTLAND

SCOTTISH
BORDERS
Newtown
St Boswells

NORTHUMBERLAND
Morpeth

Newcastle upon Tyne

Dumfries

DUMFRIES

SOUTH
LANARKSHIRE
Hamilton

EAST
AYRSHIRE
Kilmarnock

NORTH
AYRSHIRE
Irvine

SOUTH
AYRSHIRE
Ayr

Haddington
EAST LOTHIAN
Edinburgh
Dalkeith
MIDLOTHIAN
Livingston
Alloa
Falkirk
Motherwell
Glasgow
Dumbarton

**SCOTLAND**
1. INVERCLYDE
2. WEST DUNBARTONSHIRE
3. EAST RENFREWSHIRE
4. GLASGOW CITY
5. EAST DUNBARTONSHIRE
6. NORTH LANARKSHIRE
7. FALKIRK
8. CLACKMANNANSHIRE
9. WEST LOTHIAN
10. EDINBURGH

**NORTHERN IRELAND**
1. NEWTOWNABBEY
2. CARRICKFERGUS
3. BELFAST
4. CASTLEREAGH
5. NORTH DOWN

Ballycastle
MOYLE
COLERAINE
Coleraine
Ballymoney
BALLYMONEY
LIMAVADY
Limavady
Londonderry
NORTH

Scale 1 : 3 000 000

0    25    50    75    100 km

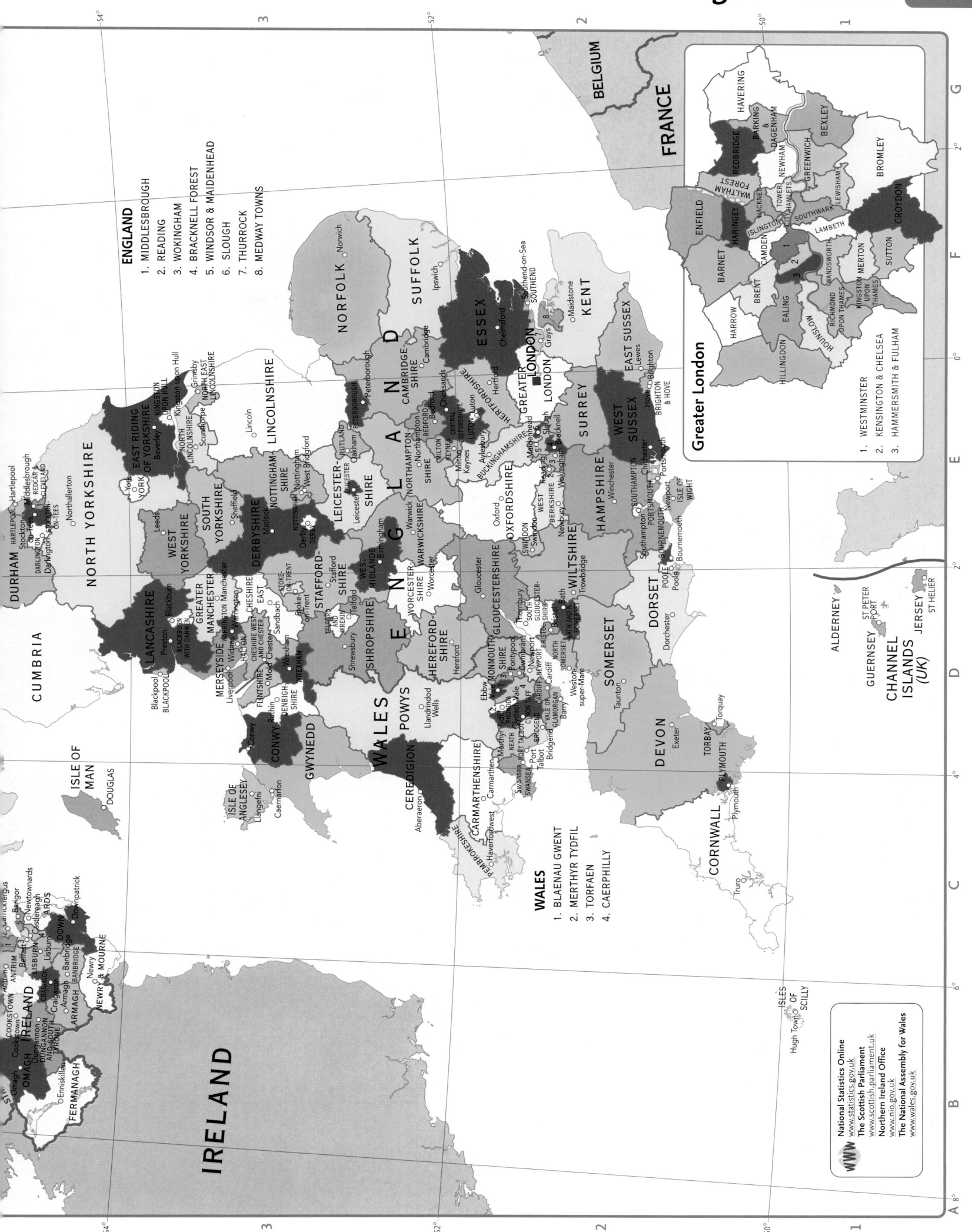

**ENGLAND**
1. MIDDLESBROUGH
2. READING
3. WOKINGHAM
4. BRACKNELL FOREST
5. WINDSOR & MAIDENHEAD
6. SLOUGH
7. THURROCK
8. MEDWAY TOWNS

**WALES**
1. BLAENAU GWENT
2. MERTHYR TYDFIL
3. TORFAEN
4. CAERPHILLY

**Greater London**
1. WESTMINSTER
2. KENSINGTON & CHELSEA
3. HAMMERSMITH & FULHAM

National Statistics Online
www.statistics.gov.uk
The Scottish Parliament
www.scottish.parliament.uk
Northern Ireland Office
www.nio.gov.uk
The National Assembly for Wales
www.wales.gov.uk

Conic Equidistant projection

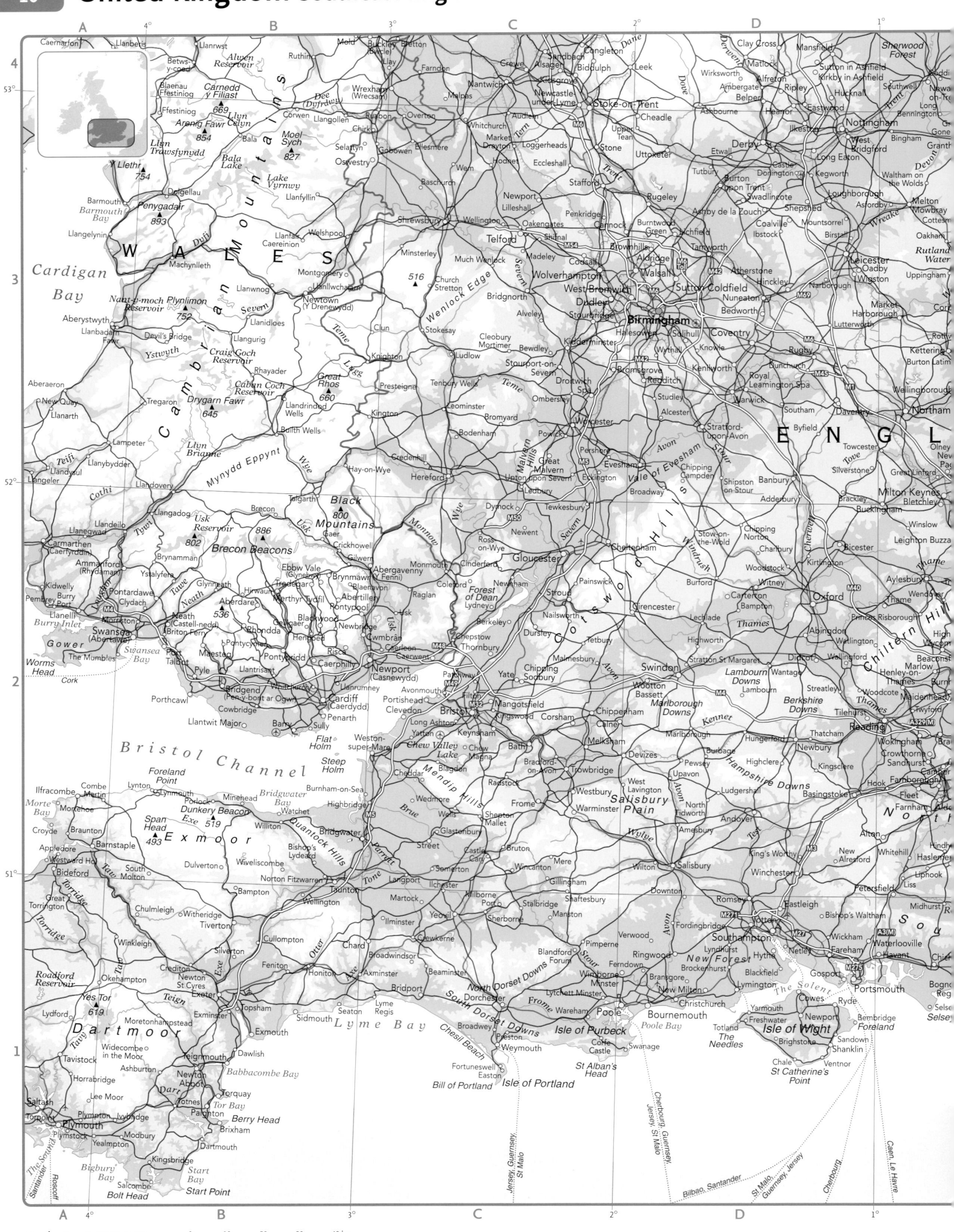

Scale 1 : 1 200 000

0   10   20   30   40 km

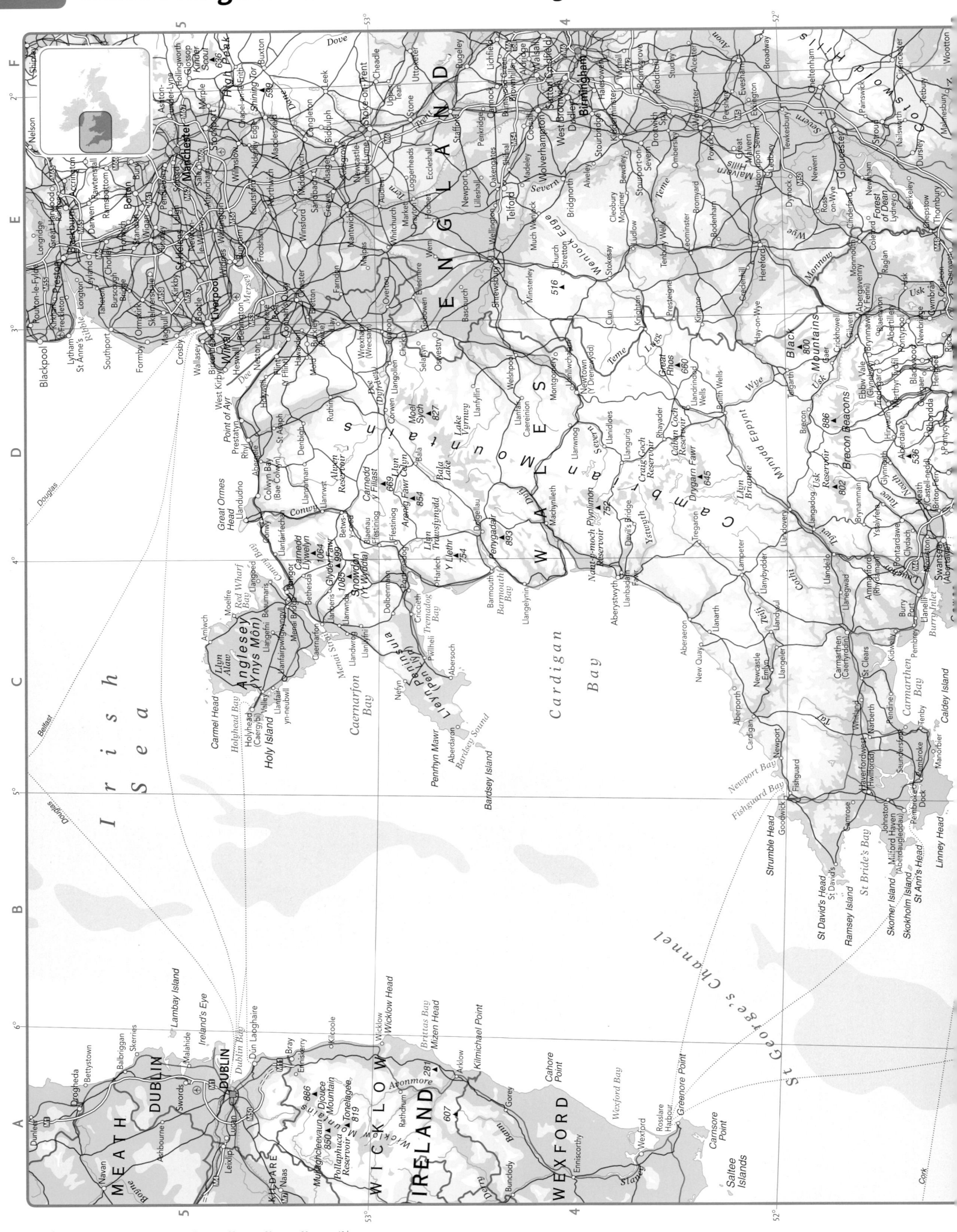

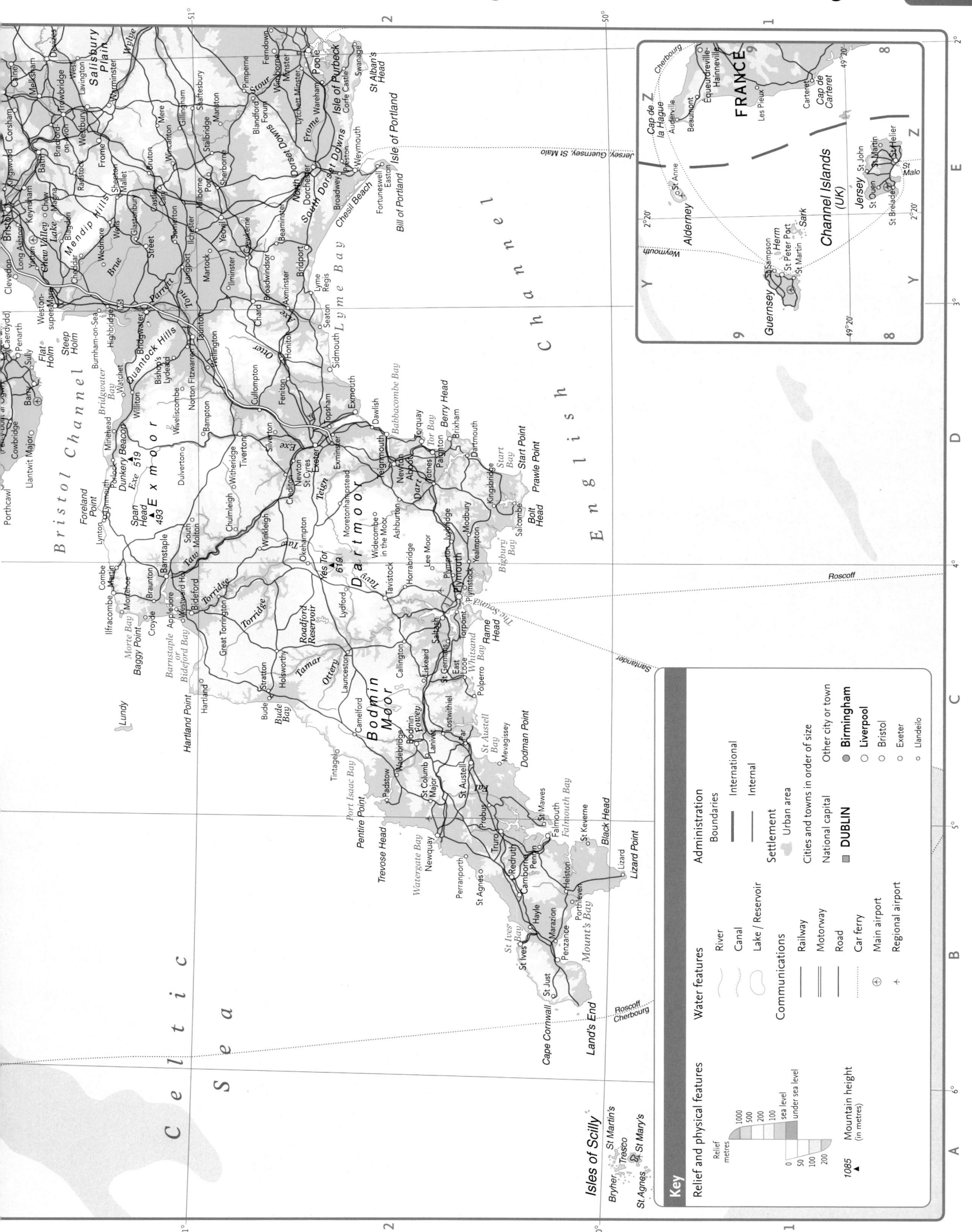

## Key

**Relief and physical features**

Relief
metres

1000
500
200
100
50
0
sea level
under sea level

1085 ▲ Mountain height
(in metres)

**Water features**

River
Canal
Lake / Reservoir

**Communications**

Railway
Motorway
Road
Car ferry
⊕ Main airport
✦ Regional airport

**Administration**

Boundaries
—— International
—— Internal

**Settlement**

▮ Urban area

Cities and towns in order of size

National capital ▮ DUBLIN
Other city or town ● Birmingham
○ Liverpool
○ Bristol
○ Exeter
○ Llandeilo

Conic Equidistant projection

0   10   20   30   40 km

**Key**

**Relief and physical features**

Relief
metres
1000
500
200
100
sea level
0
50
100
200
under sea level

▲ 1085  Mountain height (in metres)

**Water features**

~~~ River

═══ Canal

⬭ Lake / Reservoir

**Communications**

──── Railway

═══ Motorway

──── Road

········ Car ferry

⊕ Main airport

✈ Regional airport

**Administration**

Boundaries

━━━ International

──── Internal

**Settlement**

▨ Urban area

Cities and towns in order of size

National capital · Other city or town

■ **DUBLIN** · ● **Manchester**

○ Liverpool

○ Belfast

○ Carlisle

○ Keswick

*North Sea*

*North York Moors*

*Vale of Pickering*

*Yorkshire Wolds*

*Bridlington Bay*

*Holderness*

*Mouth of the Humber*

*Spurn Head*

*Lincolnshire Wolds*

*The Wash*

*Sherwood Forest*

*Holland Fen*

*West Fen*

*East Fen*

ENGLAND

Conic Equidistant projection

Scale 1 : 1 200 000

0   10   20   30   40 km

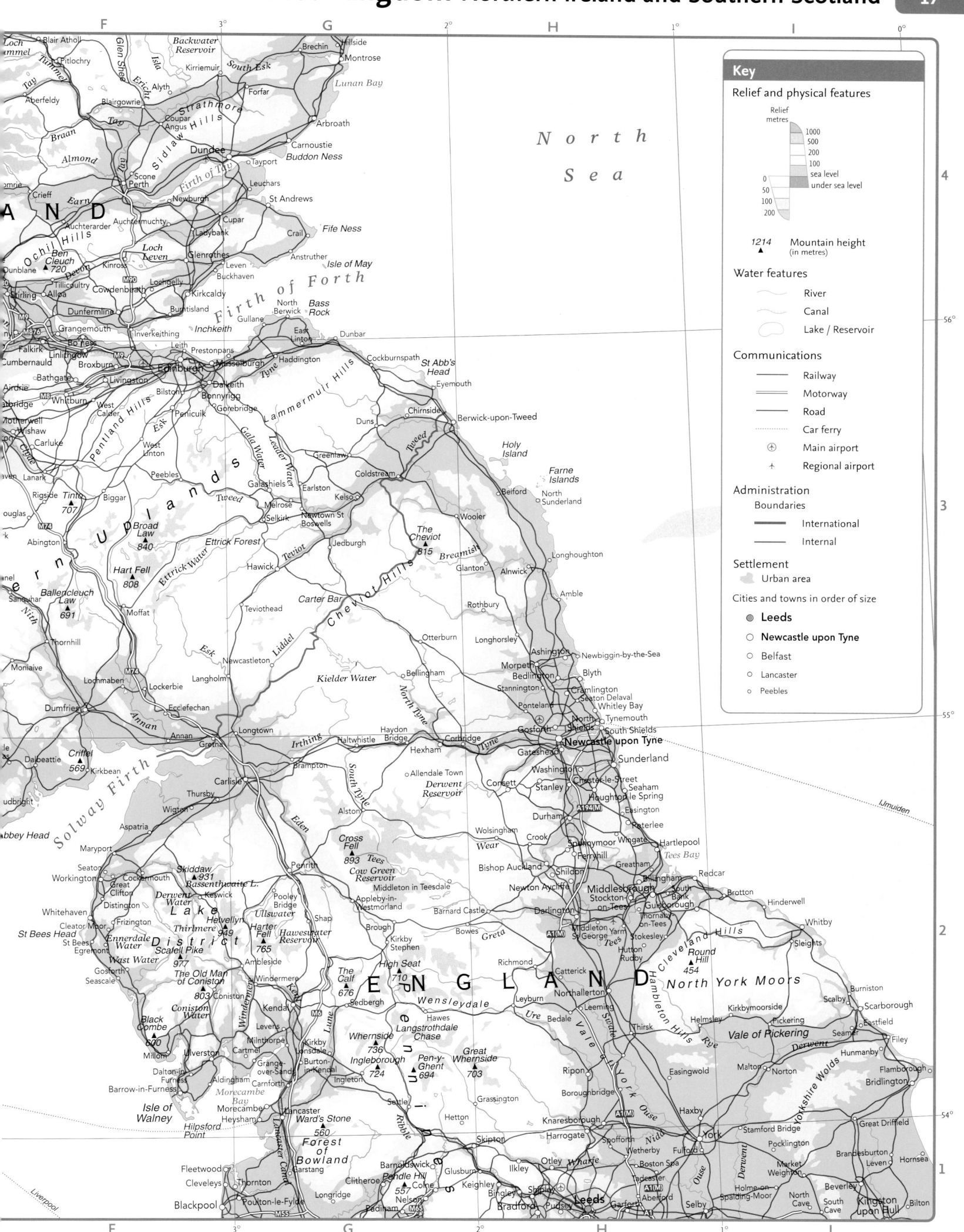

**Key**

**Relief and physical features**

Relief metres
1000
500
200
100
sea level
0
50
100
200
sea level
under sea level

1214 ▲ Mountain height (in metres)

**Water features**

~~~ River
=== Canal
Lake / Reservoir

**Communications**

Railway
Motorway
Road
Car ferry
⊕ Main airport
✈ Regional airport

**Administration**

Boundaries
International
Internal

**Settlement**

Urban area

Cities and towns in order of size

⦿ Leeds
○ Newcastle upon Tyne
○ Belfast
○ Lancaster
○ Peebles

*North Sea*

*Conic Equidistant projection*

**Key**

**Relief and physical features**

Relief
metres
1000
500
200
100
0 sea level
50
100 under sea level
200

▲ 1344 Mountain height
(in metres)

**Water features**

~ River

~ Canal

⬭ Lake / Reservoir

**Communications**

— Railway

— Road

···· Car ferry

⊕ Main airport

✦ Regional airport

**Settlement**

Urban area

Cities and towns in order of size

○ Aberdeen

○ Inverness

○ Kirkwall

Cape Wrath

Kyle of Durness

Kinlochbervie
Loch Inchard
Loch Laxford
Foinaven
915

Butt of
Lewis
Port Ness

Handa Island

Scourie

Loch Mo

Muirneag
248
Tolsta Head

Flannan Isles

West
Loch Roag
Great
Bernera
Isle of Lewis

Broad
Bay

Point of
Stoer

Loch
Assynt

Ben More
Assynt
998

Callanish
Stornoway
Eye
Peninsula

Lochinver

Canisp
846

Mealasta
Island
Loch
Langavat

Kebock Head

Rubha
Coigeach

Cul Mòr
849

Scarp
North Harris

Summer
Isles

Loch
Lurgainn

Taransay

Tirga Mòr
679

Clisham
799

Shiant Islands

Greenstone Point

Ullapool

St Kilda

Tarbert

South Harris
Scalpay

Rubha
Reidh

Gruinard
Bay

Loch Broom

Pabbay
Berneray
Boreray

Loch
Langavat

East Loch Tarbert

Rodel

Rubha
Hunish

Gairloch
Gair Loch

Fionn
Loch

An Teallach
1062

Beinn
Dearg
1084

Sound of Harris

Loch Maree

Sgurr Mòr
1110

North Uist
Lochmaddy

Uig

Loch Ewe

Loch
Fannich

WESTER

Le
Lui

Sound of Monach

Loch
Snizort

L. Dunvegan

Rona

Loch Torridon

Torridon

ROSS

Reser

Monach Islands

The
Storr
719

Sound of Raasay

Shieldaig

Benbecula
Balivanich

Portree
Raasay

Inner Sound

Loch
Monar

Carn Eighe
1183

South
Uist

Skye

L. Bracadale

Scalpay

Kyle of
Lochalsh

A'Chraaig
1120

Loch
Cluanie

Loch
Morar

Cuillin Hills
Sgurr
Alasdair
993
Blaven
928

Lochboisdale

Soay

Loch Eishort

Ladhar
Bheinn
1020

Loch
Quoich

Garry

Loch Logie

Glen Moriston

Augu

Glen Garry

Eriskay

Sound of Sleat

Ardvasar

Canna

Sound of Barra

Rum

Mallaig
Loch Neb

Arisaig

Loch Morar

Loch Arkaig

Loch Lochy

Barra

Castlebay

Eigg

Loch
Beoraid

Ben
Nevis
1344

Stob Choi
Claurigh
1177

Vatersay

Sound
of Arisaig

Sgurr
Dhomhnuill
888

Eilean
Shona

Loch Shiel

Fort William

L
Tr

Pabbay
Sandray

Muck

Loch
Leven

Kinlochleve

Mingulay

Point of
Ardnamurchan

Glen Coe
Bidean
nam Bian
1150

Ranr
Mo

Berneray

Coll

Morvern

Loch Linnhe

1108

Meall a
Bhuiridh

Tobermory

Tiree

Loch
Arienas

Mull

**ATLANTIC**

**OCEAN**

*Outer Hebrides*

*The Minch*

*Little Minch*

*Cuillin Sound*

Scale 1 : 1 200 000

0  10  20  30  40 km

9° · A · 8° · B · 7° · C · 6° · D · 5°

Conic Equidistant projection

# 1 Annual Rainfall and Winds

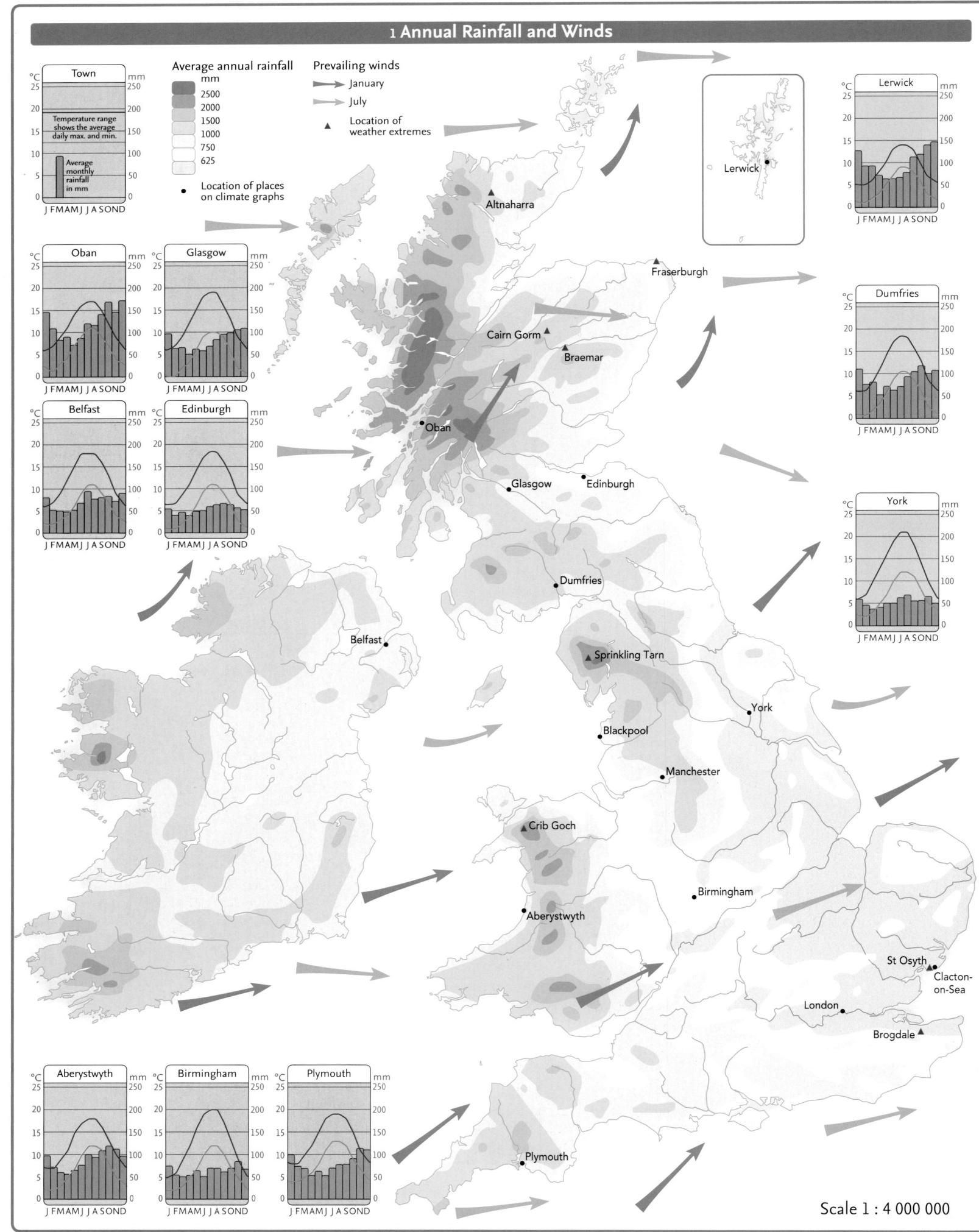

°C / Town / mm
25 — 250
20 — 200
15 — Temperature range shows the average daily max. and min. — 150
10 — 100
5 — Average monthly rainfall in mm — 50
0
J F M A M J J A S O N D

Average annual rainfall
mm
2500
2000
1500
1000
750
625

Prevailing winds
→ January
→ July
▲ Location of weather extremes
• Location of places on climate graphs

Oban
Glasgow
Belfast
Edinburgh
Lerwick
Dumfries
York
Aberystwyth
Birmingham
Plymouth

Altnaharra
Fraserburgh
Cairn Gorm ▲
Braemar ▲
Oban
Glasgow
Edinburgh
Dumfries
Belfast
Sprinkling Tarn ▲
York
Blackpool
Manchester
Crib Goch ▲
Aberystwyth
Birmingham
St Osyth ▲
Clacton-on-Sea
London
Brogdale ▲
Plymouth

Scale 1 : 4 000 000

## 2 Temperature and Currents

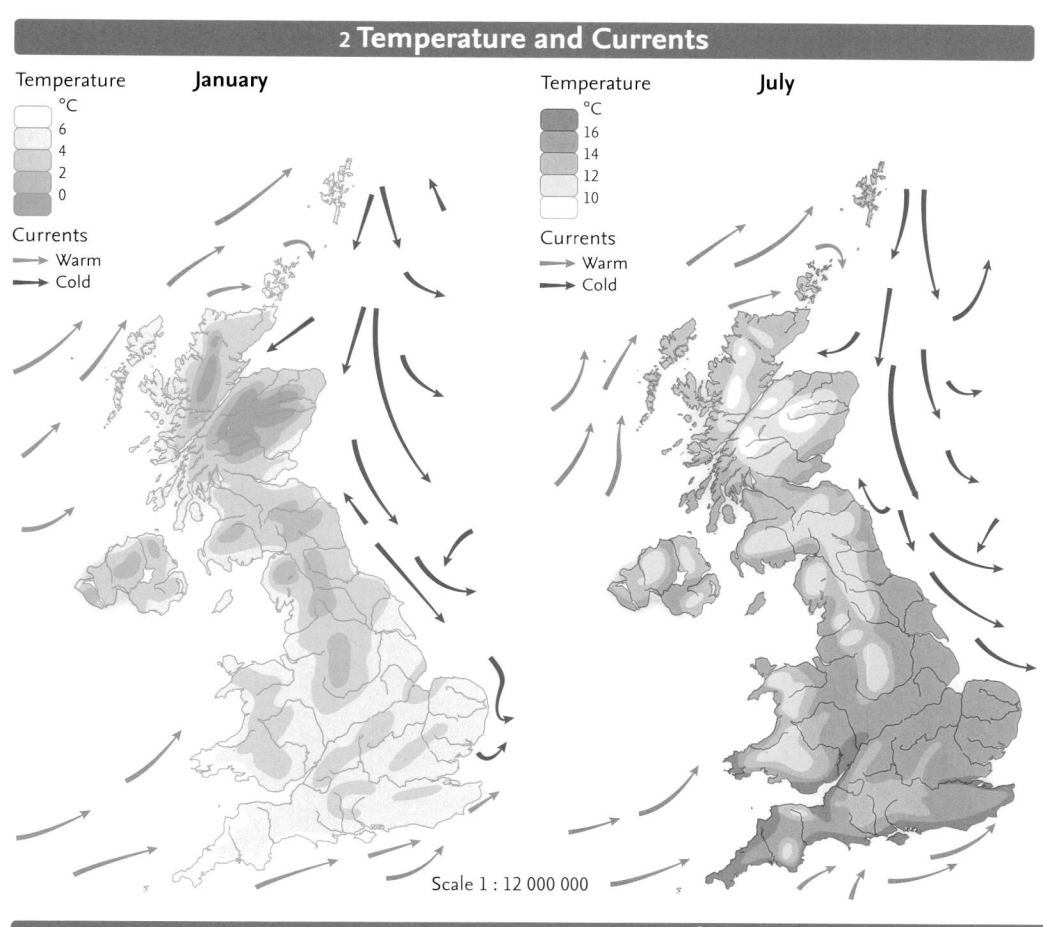

**January**

Temperature °C
- 6
- 4
- 2
- 0

Currents
- → Warm
- → Cold

**July**

Temperature °C
- 16
- 14
- 12
- 10

Currents
- → Warm
- → Cold

Scale 1 : 12 000 000

## 3 Weather Extremes

### Temperature

|  | Value | Location | Date |
|---|---|---|---|
| Highest | 38.5° | Brogdale, Kent | 10th August 2003 |
| Lowest | -27.2° | Braemar, Aberdeenshire | 10th January 1982 & 11th February 1895 |
|  |  | Altnaharra, Highlands | 30th December 1995 |

### Rainfall

|  | Value | Location | Date |
|---|---|---|---|
| Highest in 1 year | 6 528mm | Sprinkling Tarn, Cumbria | 1954 |
| Lowest annual average | 513mm | St Osyth, Essex |  |
| Highest annual average | 4 000mm | Crib Goch, Gwynedd |  |

### Winds

|  | Value | Location | Date |
|---|---|---|---|
| Strongest low-level gust | 123 knots | Fraserburgh, Aberdeenshire | 13th February 1989 |
| Strongest high-level gust | 150 knots | Cairn Gorm, Highland | 20th March 1986 |

 **Met Office** www.metoffice.gov.uk
**BBC Weather** www.bbc.co.uk/weather
**UK Climate Impacts Programme** www.ukcip.org.uk

## 4 Climate Statistics

### Aberystwyth

|  | Jan | Feb | Mar | Apr | May | Jun | Jul | Aug | Sep | Oct | Nov | Dec |
|---|---|---|---|---|---|---|---|---|---|---|---|---|
| Temperature - max. (°C) | 7 | 7 | 9 | 11 | 15 | 17 | 18 | 18 | 16 | 13 | 10 | 8 |
| Temperature - min. (°C) | 2 | 2 | 3 | 5 | 7 | 10 | 12 | 12 | 11 | 8 | 5 | 4 |
| Rainfall - (mm) | 97 | 72 | 60 | 56 | 65 | 76 | 99 | 93 | 108 | 118 | 111 | 96 |

### Belfast

|  | Jan | Feb | Mar | Apr | May | Jun | Jul | Aug | Sep | Oct | Nov | Dec |
|---|---|---|---|---|---|---|---|---|---|---|---|---|
| Temperature - max. (°C) | 6 | 7 | 9 | 12 | 15 | 18 | 18 | 18 | 16 | 13 | 9 | 7 |
| Temperature - min. (°C) | 2 | 2 | 3 | 4 | 6 | 9 | 11 | 11 | 9 | 7 | 4 | 3 |
| Rainfall - (mm) | 80 | 52 | 50 | 48 | 52 | 68 | 94 | 77 | 80 | 83 | 72 | 90 |

### Birmingham

|  | Jan | Feb | Mar | Apr | May | Jun | Jul | Aug | Sep | Oct | Nov | Dec |
|---|---|---|---|---|---|---|---|---|---|---|---|---|
| Temperature - max. (°C) | 5 | 6 | 9 | 12 | 16 | 19 | 20 | 20 | 17 | 13 | 9 | 6 |
| Temperature - min. (°C) | 2 | 2 | 3 | 5 | 7 | 10 | 12 | 12 | 10 | 7 | 5 | 3 |
| Rainfall - (mm) | 74 | 54 | 50 | 53 | 64 | 50 | 69 | 69 | 61 | 69 | 84 | 67 |

### Blackpool

|  | Jan | Feb | Mar | Apr | May | Jun | Jul | Aug | Sep | Oct | Nov | Dec |
|---|---|---|---|---|---|---|---|---|---|---|---|---|
| Temperature - max. (°C) | 7 | 7 | 9 | 11 | 15 | 17 | 19 | 19 | 17 | 14 | 10 | 7 |
| Temperature - min. (°C) | 1 | 1 | 2 | 4 | 7 | 10 | 12 | 12 | 10 | 8 | 4 | 2 |
| Rainfall - (mm) | 78 | 54 | 64 | 51 | 53 | 59 | 61 | 78 | 86 | 93 | 89 | 87 |

### Clacton-on-Sea

|  | Jan | Feb | Mar | Apr | May | Jun | Jul | Aug | Sep | Oct | Nov | Dec |
|---|---|---|---|---|---|---|---|---|---|---|---|---|
| Temperature - max. (°C) | 6 | 6 | 9 | 11 | 15 | 18 | 20 | 20 | 18 | 15 | 10 | 7 |
| Temperature - min. (°C) | 2 | 2 | 3 | 5 | 8 | 11 | 13 | 14 | 12 | 9 | 5 | 3 |
| Rainfall - (mm) | 49 | 31 | 43 | 40 | 40 | 45 | 43 | 43 | 48 | 48 | 55 | 50 |

### Dumfries

|  | Jan | Feb | Mar | Apr | May | Jun | Jul | Aug | Sep | Oct | Nov | Dec |
|---|---|---|---|---|---|---|---|---|---|---|---|---|
| Temperature - max. (°C) | 6 | 6 | 8 | 11 | 14 | 17 | 19 | 18 | 16 | 13 | 9 | 7 |
| Temperature - min. (°C) | 1 | 1 | 2 | 3 | 6 | 9 | 11 | 10 | 9 | 6 | 3 | 1 |
| Rainfall - (mm) | 110 | 76 | 81 | 53 | 72 | 63 | 71 | 93 | 104 | 117 | 100 | 107 |

### Edinburgh

|  | Jan | Feb | Mar | Apr | May | Jun | Jul | Aug | Sep | Oct | Nov | Dec |
|---|---|---|---|---|---|---|---|---|---|---|---|---|
| Temperature - max. (°C) | 6 | 7 | 9 | 11 | 14 | 17 | 18 | 18 | 16 | 13 | 9 | 7 |
| Temperature - min. (°C) | 1 | 1 | 2 | 4 | 6 | 9 | 11 | 11 | 9 | 7 | 3 | 2 |
| Rainfall - (mm) | 54 | 40 | 47 | 39 | 49 | 50 | 59 | 63 | 66 | 63 | 56 | 52 |

### Glasgow

|  | Jan | Feb | Mar | Apr | May | Jun | Jul | Aug | Sep | Oct | Nov | Dec |
|---|---|---|---|---|---|---|---|---|---|---|---|---|
| Temperature - max. (°C) | 6 | 7 | 9 | 12 | 15 | 18 | 19 | 19 | 16 | 13 | 9 | 7 |
| Temperature - min. (°C) | 0 | 0 | 2 | 3 | 6 | 9 | 10 | 10 | 9 | 6 | 2 | 1 |
| Rainfall - (mm) | 96 | 63 | 65 | 50 | 62 | 58 | 68 | 83 | 95 | 98 | 105 | 108 |

### Lerwick

|  | Jan | Feb | Mar | Apr | May | Jun | Jul | Aug | Sep | Oct | Nov | Dec |
|---|---|---|---|---|---|---|---|---|---|---|---|---|
| Temperature - max. (°C) | 5 | 5 | 6 | 8 | 10 | 13 | 14 | 14 | 13 | 10 | 7 | 6 |
| Temperature - min. (°C) | 1 | 1 | 2 | 3 | 5 | 7 | 9 | 9 | 8 | 6 | 3 | 2 |
| Rainfall - (mm) | 127 | 93 | 93 | 72 | 64 | 64 | 67 | 78 | 113 | 119 | 140 | 147 |

### London

|  | Jan | Feb | Mar | Apr | May | Jun | Jul | Aug | Sep | Oct | Nov | Dec |
|---|---|---|---|---|---|---|---|---|---|---|---|---|
| Temperature - max. (°C) | 8 | 8 | 11 | 13 | 17 | 20 | 23 | 23 | 19 | 15 | 11 | 9 |
| Temperature - min. (°C) | 2 | 2 | 4 | 5 | 8 | 11 | 14 | 13 | 11 | 8 | 5 | 3 |
| Rainfall - (mm) | 52 | 34 | 42 | 45 | 47 | 53 | 38 | 47 | 57 | 62 | 52 | 54 |

### Manchester

|  | Jan | Feb | Mar | Apr | May | Jun | Jul | Aug | Sep | Oct | Nov | Dec |
|---|---|---|---|---|---|---|---|---|---|---|---|---|
| Temperature - max. (°C) | 6 | 7 | 9 | 12 | 15 | 18 | 20 | 20 | 17 | 14 | 9 | 7 |
| Temperature - min. (°C) | 1 | 1 | 3 | 4 | 7 | 10 | 12 | 12 | 10 | 8 | 4 | 2 |
| Rainfall - (mm) | 69 | 50 | 61 | 51 | 61 | 67 | 65 | 79 | 74 | 77 | 78 | 78 |

### Oban

|  | Jan | Feb | Mar | Apr | May | Jun | Jul | Aug | Sep | Oct | Nov | Dec |
|---|---|---|---|---|---|---|---|---|---|---|---|---|
| Temperature - max. (°C) | 6 | 7 | 9 | 11 | 14 | 16 | 17 | 17 | 15 | 12 | 9 | 7 |
| Temperature - min. (°C) | 2 | 1 | 3 | 4 | 7 | 9 | 11 | 11 | 9 | 7 | 4 | 3 |
| Rainfall - (mm) | 146 | 109 | 83 | 90 | 72 | 87 | 120 | 116 | 141 | 169 | 146 | 172 |

### Plymouth

|  | Jan | Feb | Mar | Apr | May | Jun | Jul | Aug | Sep | Oct | Nov | Dec |
|---|---|---|---|---|---|---|---|---|---|---|---|---|
| Temperature - max. (°C) | 8 | 8 | 10 | 12 | 15 | 18 | 19 | 19 | 18 | 15 | 11 | 9 |
| Temperature - min. (°C) | 4 | 4 | 5 | 6 | 8 | 11 | 13 | 13 | 12 | 9 | 7 | 5 |
| Rainfall - (mm) | 99 | 74 | 69 | 53 | 63 | 53 | 70 | 77 | 78 | 91 | 113 | 110 |

### York

|  | Jan | Feb | Mar | Apr | May | Jun | Jul | Aug | Sep | Oct | Nov | Dec |
|---|---|---|---|---|---|---|---|---|---|---|---|---|
| Temperature - max. (°C) | 6 | 7 | 10 | 13 | 16 | 19 | 21 | 21 | 18 | 14 | 10 | 7 |
| Temperature - min. (°C) | 2 | 2 | 3 | 5 | 7 | 10 | 12 | 12 | 11 | 8 | 5 | 4 |
| Rainfall - (mm) | 59 | 46 | 37 | 41 | 50 | 50 | 62 | 68 | 55 | 56 | 65 | 50 |

**Blackpool** °C / mm
J F M A M J J A S O N D

**Manchester** °C / mm
J F M A M J J A S O N D

**Clacton-on-Sea** °C / mm
J F M A M J J A S O N D

**London** °C / mm
J F M A M J J A S O N D

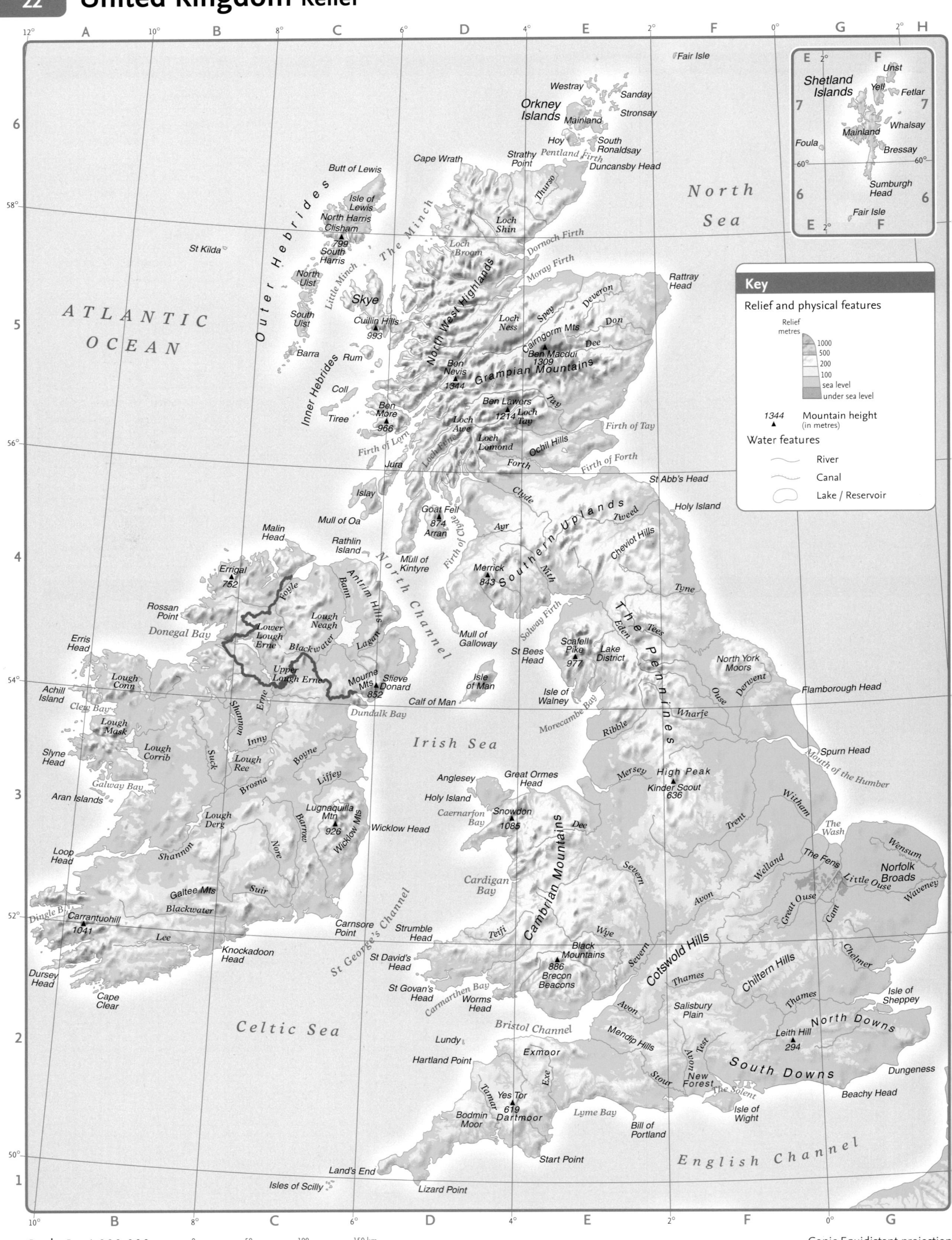

Scale 1 : 4 000 000

0   50   100   150 km

Conic Equidistant projection

**Key**

Relief and physical features

Relief
metres
1000
500
200
100
sea level
under sea level

1344 ▲  Mountain height
(in metres)

Water features

River

Canal

Lake / Reservoir

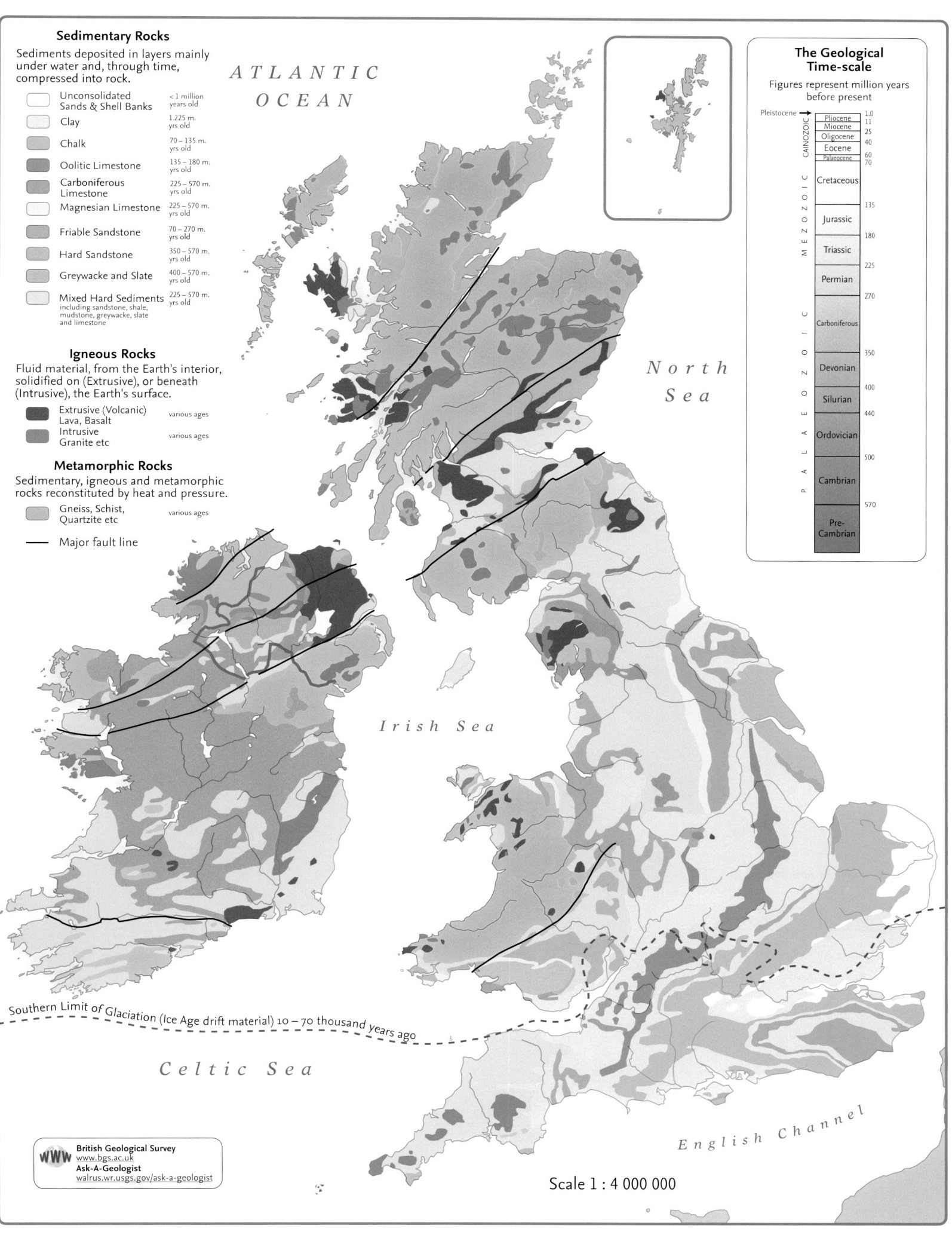

**Sedimentary Rocks**

Sediments deposited in layers mainly under water and, through time, compressed into rock.

| | | |
|---|---|---|
| | Unconsolidated Sands & Shell Banks | < 1 million years old |
| | Clay | 1.225 m. yrs old |
| | Chalk | 70 – 135 m. yrs old |
| | Oolitic Limestone | 135 – 180 m. yrs old |
| | Carboniferous Limestone | 225 – 570 m. yrs old |
| | Magnesian Limestone | 225 – 570 m. yrs old |
| | Friable Sandstone | 70 – 270 m. yrs old |
| | Hard Sandstone | 350 – 570 m. yrs old |
| | Greywacke and Slate | 400 – 570 m. yrs old |
| | Mixed Hard Sediments including sandstone, shale, mudstone, greywacke, slate and limestone | 225 – 570 m. yrs old |

**Igneous Rocks**

Fluid material, from the Earth's interior, solidified on (Extrusive), or beneath (Intrusive), the Earth's surface.

| | | |
|---|---|---|
| | Extrusive (Volcanic) Lava, Basalt | various ages |
| | Intrusive Granite etc | various ages |

**Metamorphic Rocks**

Sedimentary, igneous and metamorphic rocks reconstituted by heat and pressure.

| | | |
|---|---|---|
| | Gneiss, Schist, Quartzite etc | various ages |
| —— | Major fault line | |

ATLANTIC OCEAN

North Sea

Irish Sea

Celtic Sea

English Channel

Southern Limit of Glaciation (Ice Age drift material) 10 – 70 thousand years ago

**The Geological Time-scale**

Figures represent million years before present

| | | |
|---|---|---|
| Pleistocene → | | |
| | Pliocene | 1.0 |
| | Miocene | 11 |
| CAINOZOIC | Oligocene | 25 |
| | Eocene | 40 |
| | Palaeocene | 60 |
| | | 70 |
| | Cretaceous | |
| MESOZOIC | | 135 |
| | Jurassic | |
| | | 180 |
| | Triassic | |
| | | 225 |
| | Permian | |
| | | 270 |
| | Carboniferous | |
| | | 350 |
| | Devonian | |
| PALAEOZOIC | | 400 |
| | Silurian | |
| | | 440 |
| | Ordovician | |
| | | 500 |
| | Cambrian | |
| | | 570 |
| | Pre-Cambrian | |

**British Geological Survey**
www.bgs.ac.uk
Ask-A-Geologist
walrus.wr.usgs.gov/ask-a-geologist

Scale 1 : 4 000 000

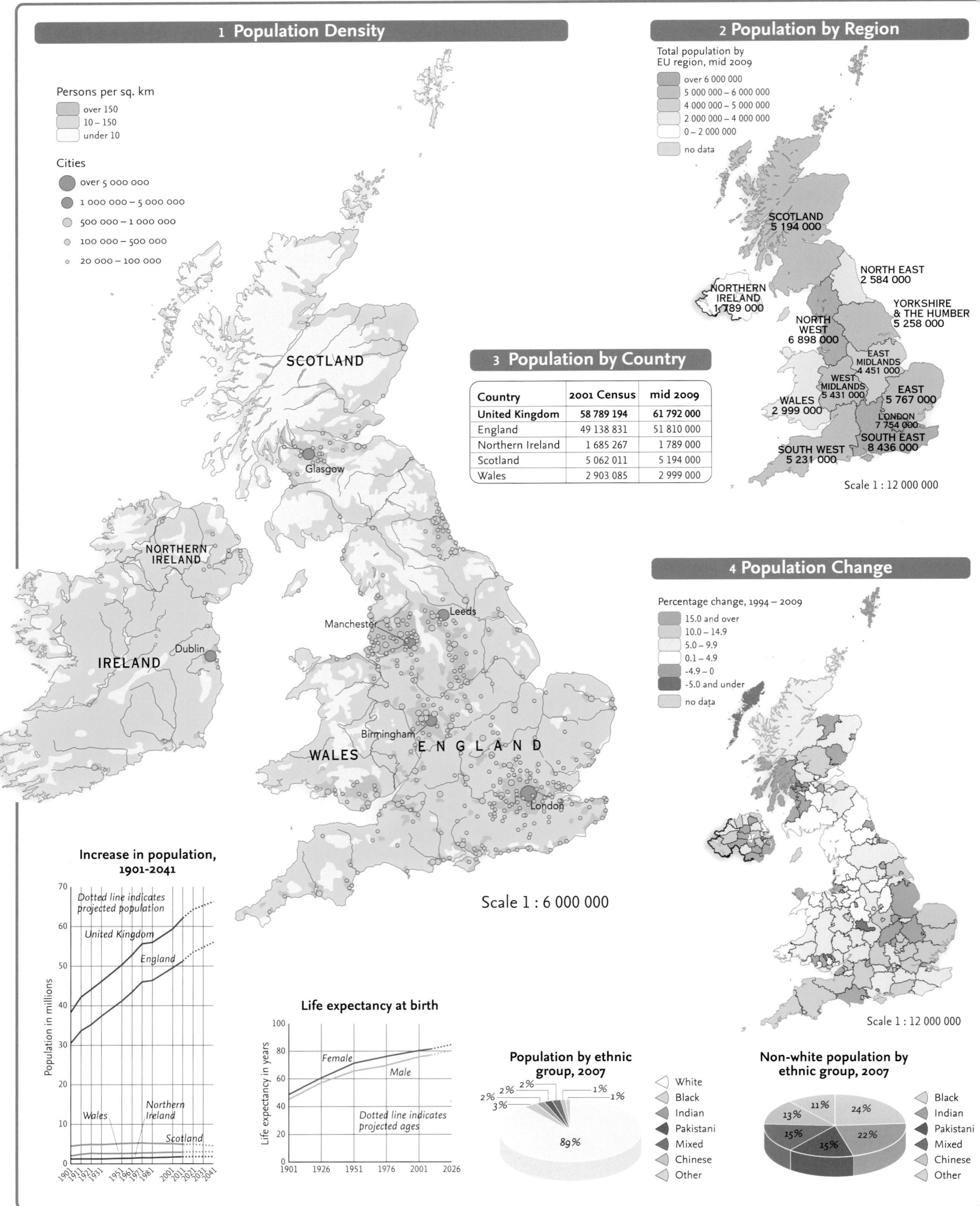

## 1 Population Density

Persons per sq. km
- over 150
- 10 – 150
- under 10

Cities
- over 5 000 000
- 1 000 000 – 5 000 000
- 500 000 – 1 000 000
- 100 000 – 500 000
- 20 000 – 100 000

SCOTLAND

Glasgow

NORTHERN IRELAND

IRELAND

Dublin

Leeds

Manchester

Birmingham

WALES

E N G L A N D

London

Scale 1 : 6 000 000

## 2 Population by Region

Total population by EU region, mid 2009
- over 6 000 000
- 5 000 000 – 6 000 000
- 4 000 000 – 5 000 000
- 2 000 000 – 4 000 000
- 0 – 2 000 000
- no data

SCOTLAND 5 194 000

NORTHERN IRELAND 1 789 000

NORTH EAST 2 584 000

NORTH WEST 6 898 000

YORKSHIRE & THE HUMBER 5 258 000

EAST MIDLANDS 4 451 000

WEST MIDLANDS 5 431 000

WALES 2 999 000

EAST 5 767 000

LONDON 7 754 000

SOUTH WEST 5 231 000

SOUTH EAST 8 436 000

Scale 1 : 12 000 000

## 3 Population by Country

| Country | 2001 Census | mid 2009 |
|---|---|---|
| United Kingdom | 58 789 194 | 61 792 000 |
| England | 49 138 831 | 51 810 000 |
| Northern Ireland | 1 685 267 | 1 789 000 |
| Scotland | 5 062 011 | 5 194 000 |
| Wales | 2 903 085 | 2 999 000 |

## 4 Population Change

Percentage change, 1994 – 2009
- 15.0 and over
- 10.0 – 14.9
- 5.0 – 9.9
- 0.1 – 4.9
- -4.9 – 0
- -5.0 and under
- no data

Scale 1 : 12 000 000

### Increase in population, 1901-2041

Dotted line indicates projected population

United Kingdom

England

Wales

Northern Ireland

Scotland

Population in millions

1901 1911 1921 1931 1941 1951 1961 1971 1981 1991 2001 2011 2021 2031 2041

### Life expectancy at birth

Female

Male

Dotted line indicates projected ages

Life expectancy in years

1901 1926 1951 1976 2001 2026

### Population by ethnic group, 2007

- White
- Black
- Indian
- Pakistani
- Mixed
- Chinese
- Other

89%
3%
2% 2% 2%
1% 1%

### Non-white population by ethnic group, 2007

- Black
- Indian
- Pakistani
- Mixed
- Chinese
- Other

24%
22%
15%
15%
13%
11%

## 5 Population under 16

Percentage, mid 2009

- 22.0 and over
- 21.0 – 21.9
- 20.0 – 20.9
- 19.0 – 19.9
- under 19.0
- no data

Scale 1 : 12 000 000

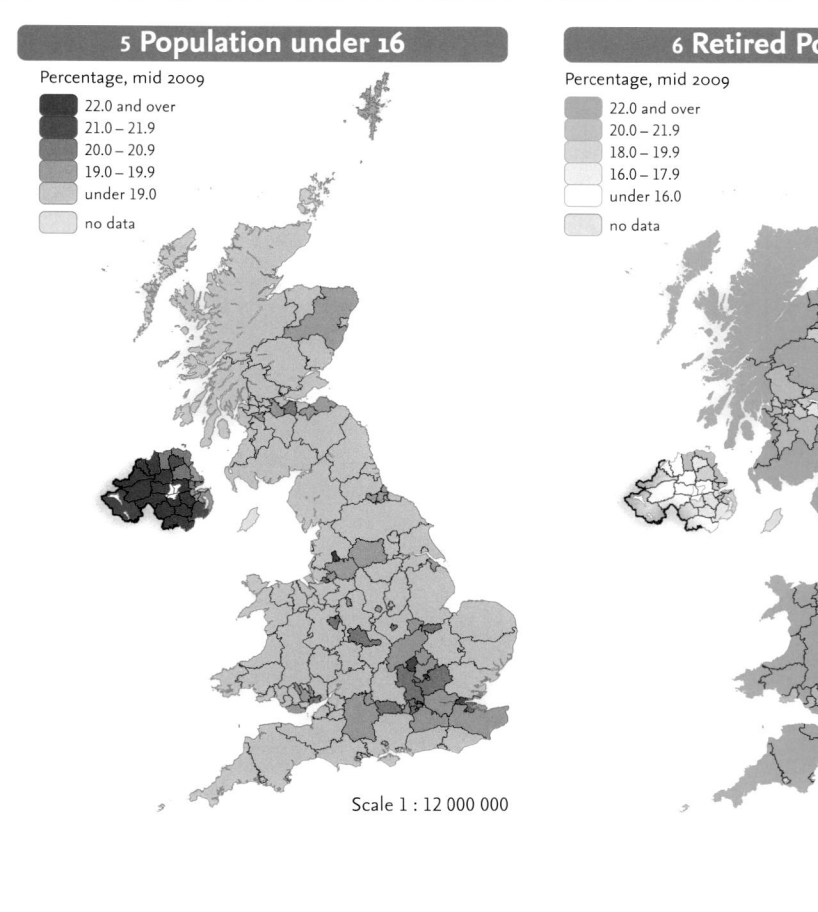

## 6 Retired Population

Percentage, mid 2009

- 22.0 and over
- 20.0 – 21.9
- 18.0 – 19.9
- 16.0 – 17.9
- under 16.0
- no data

Scale 1 : 12 000 000

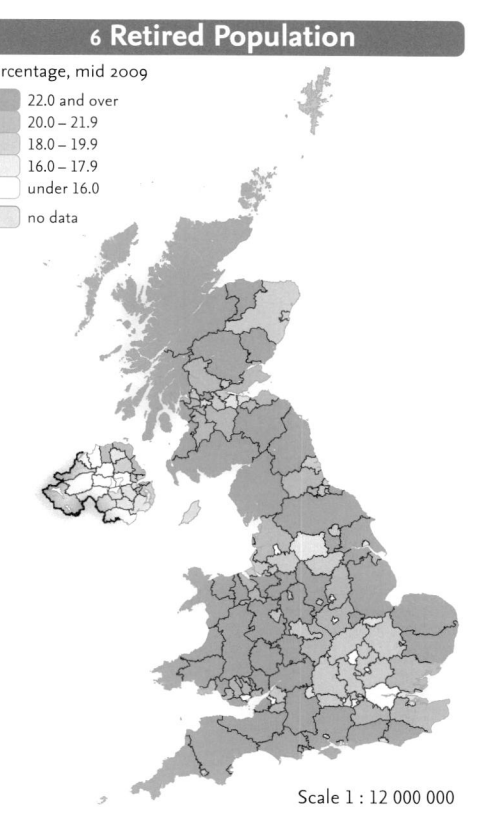

## 7 Population Structure

### Population by age group

1981
1991
2001
2011 projected
2021 projected
2031 projected

### UK

Male    Female

Each full square represents 1% of the total population

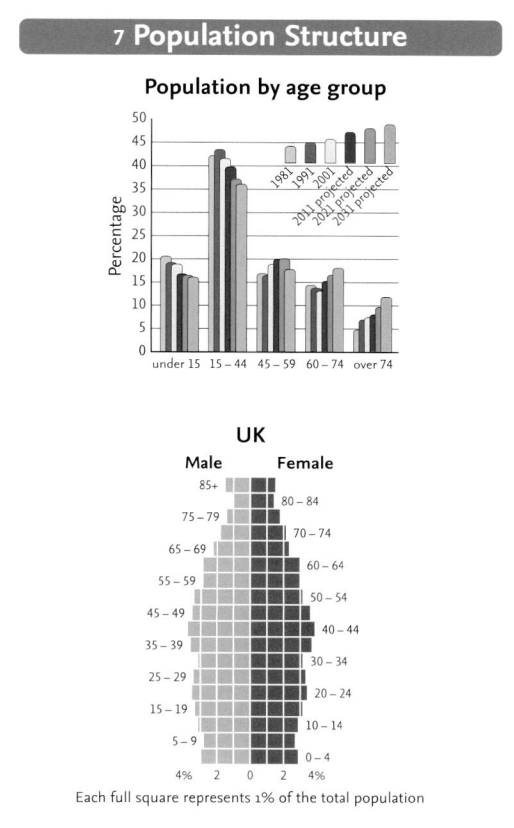

## 8 Internal Migration

Number of people moving, 2010 (in thousands)

IN    OUT

Scale 1 : 10 000 000

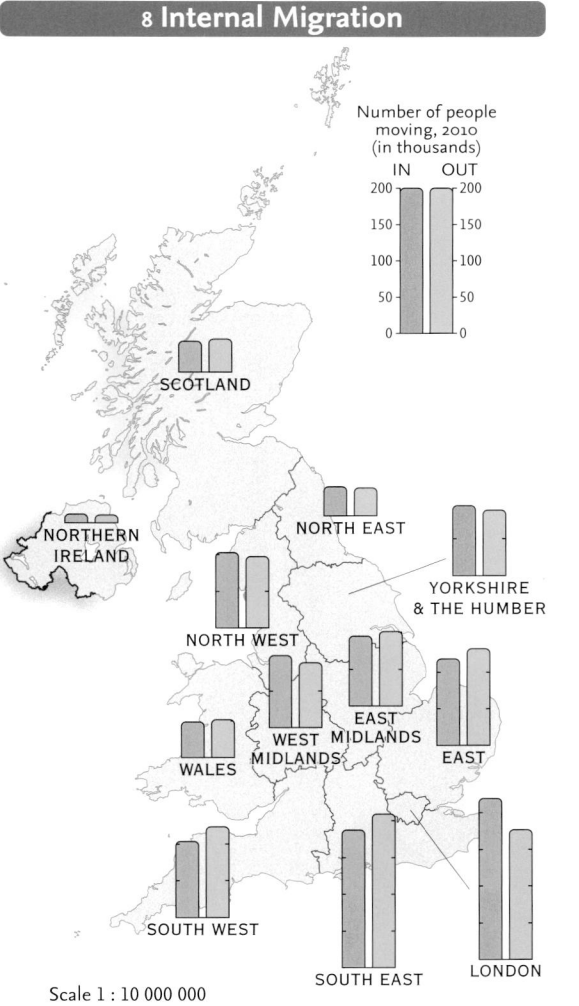

## 9 International Migration

### Reason for international immigration, 2009

- 40%
- 23%
- 12%
- 15%
- 10%

Legend:
- Formal study
- Definite job
- Looking for work
- Accompany/join
- Other

### Reason for international emigration, 2009

- 34%
- 27%
- 13%
- 22%
- 6%

Legend:
- Formal study
- Definite job
- Looking for work
- Accompany/join
- Other

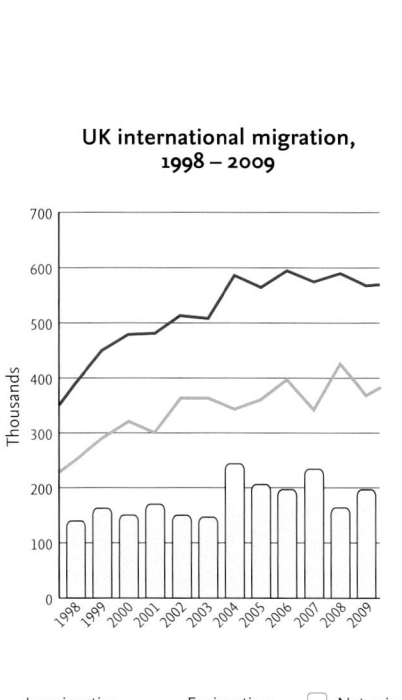

### UK international migration, 1998 – 2009

Thousands

— Immigration    — Emigration    ☐ Net migration

### UK net international migration, 2005 – 2009

Thousands

A8

British    European Union    Common-wealth    Other foreign

A8 - The 8 Central and Eastern European countries that joined the EU in May 2004 (A8 countries).

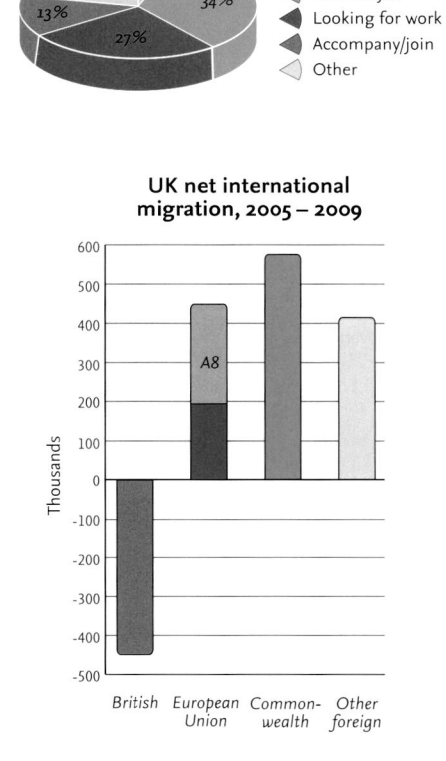

## 1 Employment by Region

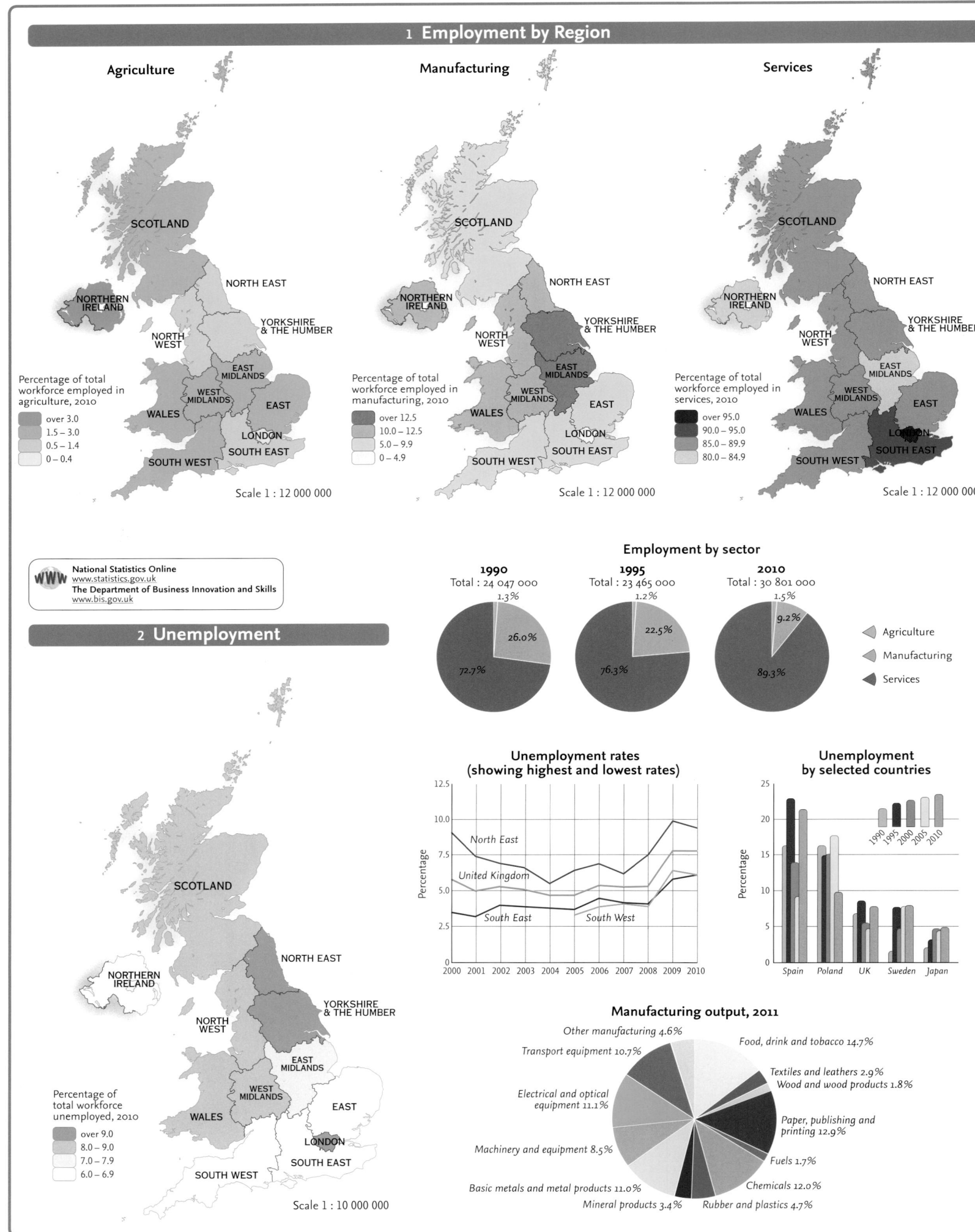

### Agriculture

Percentage of total workforce employed in agriculture, 2010
- over 3.0
- 1.5 – 3.0
- 0.5 – 1.4
- 0 – 0.4

Scale 1 : 12 000 000

### Manufacturing

Percentage of total workforce employed in manufacturing, 2010
- over 12.5
- 10.0 – 12.5
- 5.0 – 9.9
- 0 – 4.9

Scale 1 : 12 000 000

### Services

Percentage of total workforce employed in services, 2010
- over 95.0
- 90.0 – 95.0
- 85.0 – 89.9
- 80.0 – 84.9

Scale 1 : 12 000 000

**National Statistics Online**
www.statistics.gov.uk
**The Department of Business Innovation and Skills**
www.bis.gov.uk

### Employment by sector

**1990**
Total : 24 047 000
- 1.3%
- 26.0%
- 72.7%

**1995**
Total : 23 465 000
- 1.2%
- 22.5%
- 76.3%

**2010**
Total : 30 801 000
- 1.5%
- 9.2%
- 89.3%

- Agriculture
- Manufacturing
- Services

## 2 Unemployment

Percentage of total workforce unemployed, 2010
- over 9.0
- 8.0 – 9.0
- 7.0 – 7.9
- 6.0 – 6.9

Scale 1 : 10 000 000

### Unemployment rates (showing highest and lowest rates)

North East
United Kingdom
South East        South West

Percentage

2000 2001 2002 2003 2004 2005 2006 2007 2008 2009 2010

### Unemployment by selected countries

Percentage

1990 1995 2000 2005 2010

Spain   Poland   UK   Sweden   Japan

### Manufacturing output, 2011

- Other manufacturing 4.6%
- Transport equipment 10.7%
- Electrical and optical equipment 11.1%
- Machinery and equipment 8.5%
- Basic metals and metal products 11.0%
- Mineral products 3.4%
- Rubber and plastics 4.7%
- Chemicals 12.0%
- Fuels 1.7%
- Paper, publishing and printing 12.9%
- Wood and wood products 1.8%
- Textiles and leathers 2.9%
- Food, drink and tobacco 14.7%

## 3 Land Use

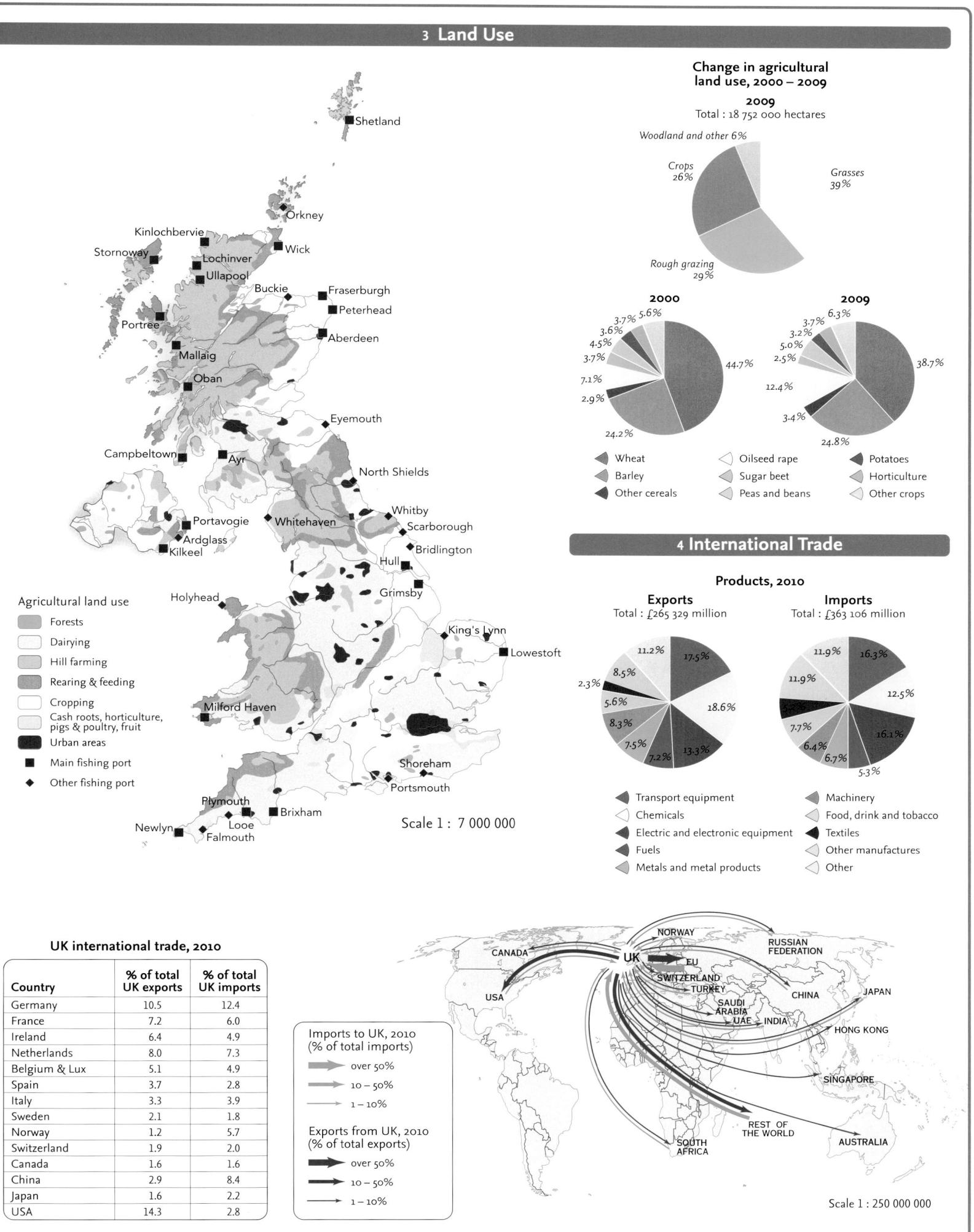

Shetland

Orkney
Kinlochbervie
Stornoway
Wick
Lochinver
Ullapool
Buckie
Portree
Fraserburgh
Peterhead
Aberdeen
Mallaig
Oban
Eyemouth
Campbeltown
Ayr
North Shields
Portavogie
Whitehaven
Whitby
Ardglass
Scarborough
Kilkeel
Bridlington
Hull
Holyhead
Grimsby
King's Lynn
Lowestoft
Milford Haven
Shoreham
Portsmouth
Plymouth
Looe
Brixham
Newlyn
Falmouth

Scale 1 : 7 000 000

### Agricultural land use

- Forests
- Dairying
- Hill farming
- Rearing & feeding
- Cropping
- Cash roots, horticulture, pigs & poultry, fruit
- Urban areas
- ■ Main fishing port
- ◆ Other fishing port

### Change in agricultural land use, 2000 – 2009

**2009**
Total : 18 752 000 hectares

- Woodland and other 6%
- Crops 26%
- Grasses 39%
- Rough grazing 29%

**2000**

- 5.6%
- 3.7%
- 3.6%
- 4.5%
- 3.7%
- 7.1%
- 2.9%
- 24.2%
- 44.7%

**2009**

- 6.3%
- 3.7%
- 3.2%
- 5.0%
- 2.5%
- 12.4%
- 3.4%
- 24.8%
- 38.7%

- Wheat
- Barley
- Other cereals
- Oilseed rape
- Sugar beet
- Peas and beans
- Potatoes
- Horticulture
- Other crops

## 4 International Trade

### Products, 2010

**Exports**
Total : £265 329 million

- 11.2%
- 17.5%
- 8.5%
- 2.3%
- 5.6%
- 18.6%
- 8.3%
- 7.5%
- 7.2%
- 13.3%

**Imports**
Total : £363 106 million

- 11.9%
- 16.3%
- 11.9%
- 12.5%
- 5.2%
- 16.1%
- 7.7%
- 6.4%
- 6.7%
- 5.3%

- Transport equipment
- Chemicals
- Electric and electronic equipment
- Fuels
- Metals and metal products
- Machinery
- Food, drink and tobacco
- Textiles
- Other manufactures
- Other

### UK international trade, 2010

| Country | % of total UK exports | % of total UK imports |
|---|---|---|
| Germany | 10.5 | 12.4 |
| France | 7.2 | 6.0 |
| Ireland | 6.4 | 4.9 |
| Netherlands | 8.0 | 7.3 |
| Belgium & Lux | 5.1 | 4.9 |
| Spain | 3.7 | 2.8 |
| Italy | 3.3 | 3.9 |
| Sweden | 2.1 | 1.8 |
| Norway | 1.2 | 5.7 |
| Switzerland | 1.9 | 2.0 |
| Canada | 1.6 | 1.6 |
| China | 2.9 | 8.4 |
| Japan | 1.6 | 2.2 |
| USA | 14.3 | 2.8 |

**Imports to UK, 2010 (% of total imports)**

- over 50%
- 10 – 50%
- 1 – 10%

**Exports from UK, 2010 (% of total exports)**

- over 50%
- 10 – 50%
- 1 – 10%

NORWAY
CANADA
RUSSIAN FEDERATION
UK
EU
SWITZERLAND
USA
TURKEY
CHINA
JAPAN
SAUDI ARABIA
UAE
INDIA
HONG KONG
SINGAPORE
REST OF THE WORLD
SOUTH AFRICA
AUSTRALIA

Scale 1 : 250 000 000

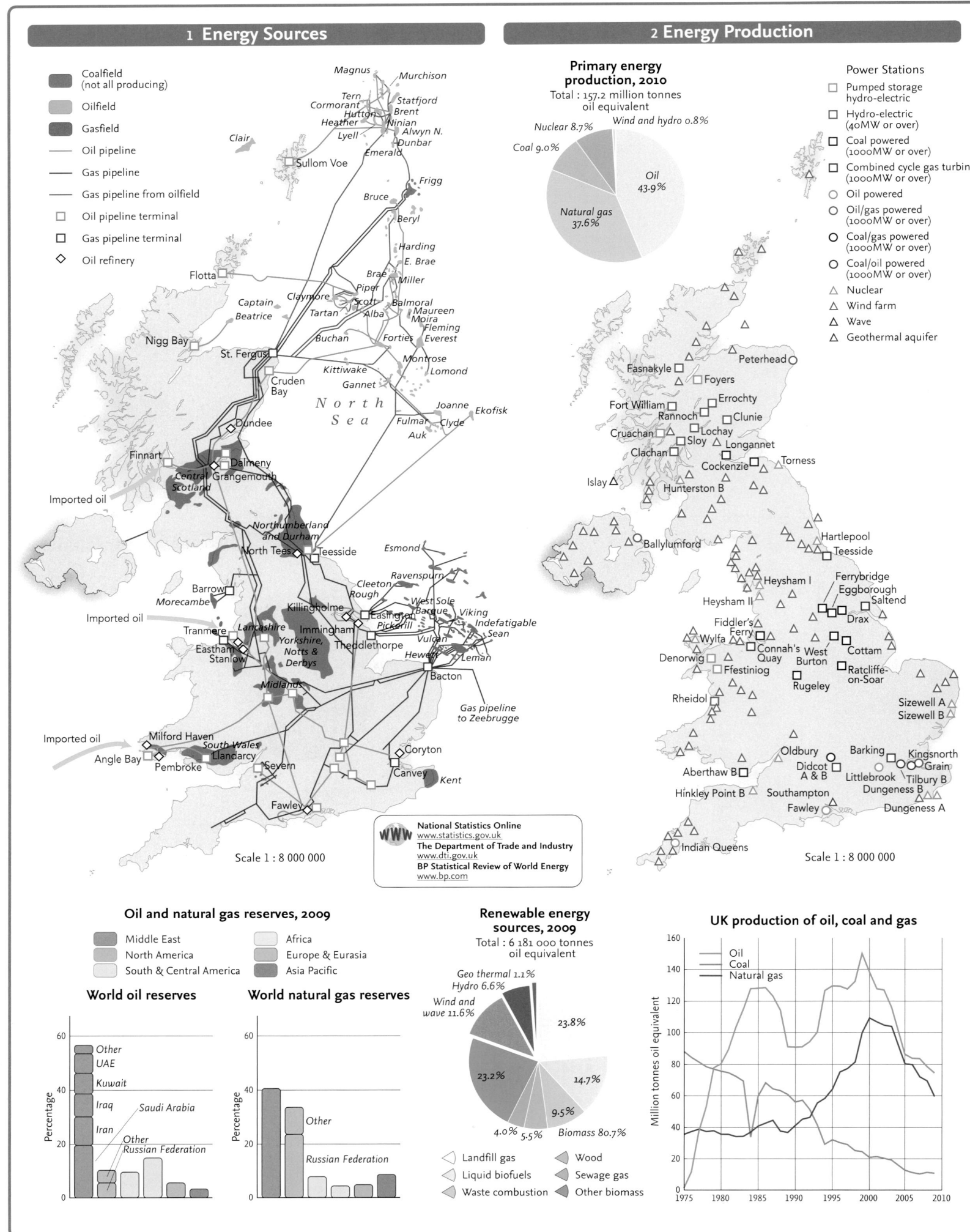

## 1 Energy Sources

Coalfield (not all producing)
Oilfield
Gasfield
Oil pipeline
Gas pipeline
Gas pipeline from oilfield
Oil pipeline terminal
Gas pipeline terminal
Oil refinery

*North Sea*

Magnus
Murchison
Tern
Cormorant
Hutton
Heather
Lyell
Statfjord
Brent
Ninian
Alwyn N.
Dunbar
Emerald
Clair
Sullom Voe
Frigg
Bruce
Beryl
Harding
E. Brae
Brae
Piper
Scott
Miller
Balmoral
Maureen
Moira
Fleming
Everest
Captain
Beatrice
Claymore
Tartan
Alba
Buchan
Forties
Flotta
Nigg Bay
St. Fergus
Cruden Bay
Kittiwake
Gannet
Montrose
Lomond
Joanne
Ekofisk
Fulmar
Clyde
Auk
Dundee
Finnart
Dalmeny
Central Scotland
Grangemouth
Imported oil
Northumberland and Durham
North Tees
Teesside
Esmond
Ravenspurn
Cleeton
Rough
West Sole
Barque
Viking
Indefatigable
Sean
Barrow
Morecambe
Killingholme
Lancashire
Immingham
Yorkshire, Notts & Derbys
Theddlethorpe
Vulcan
Hewett
Leman
Tranmere
Eastham
Stanlow
Midlands
Easington
Pickerill
Bacton
Gas pipeline to Zeebrugge
Imported oil
Milford Haven
South Wales
Llandarcy
Pembroke
Angle Bay
Severn
Coryton
Canvey
Kent
Fawley

Scale 1 : 8 000 000

National Statistics Online
www.statistics.gov.uk
The Department of Trade and Industry
www.dti.gov.uk
BP Statistical Review of World Energy
www.bp.com

## 2 Energy Production

**Primary energy production, 2010**
Total : 157.2 million tonnes oil equivalent

Nuclear 8.7%
Wind and hydro 0.8%
Coal 9.0%
Oil 43.9%
Natural gas 37.6%

Power Stations
Pumped storage hydro-electric
Hydro-electric (40MW or over)
Coal powered (1000MW or over)
Combined cycle gas turbine (1000MW or over)
Oil powered
Oil/gas powered (1000MW or over)
Coal/gas powered (1000MW or over)
Coal/oil powered (1000MW or over)
Nuclear
Wind farm
Wave
Geothermal aquifer

Peterhead
Fasnakyle
Foyers
Errochty
Fort William
Rannoch
Clunie
Cruachan
Lochay
Longannet
Clachan
Sloy
Torness
Islay
Cockenzie
Hunterston B
Ballylumford
Hartlepool
Teesside
Heysham I
Ferrybridge
Heysham II
Eggborough
Saltend
Fiddler's Ferry
Drax
Wylfa
Connah's Quay
Cottam
Denorwig
West Burton
Ffestiniog
Ratcliffe-on-Soar
Rugeley
Rheidol
Sizewell A
Sizewell B
Oldbury
Barking
Kingsnorth
Aberthaw B
Didcot A & B
Littlebrook
Grain
Hinkley Point B
Southampton
Tilbury B
Dungeness B
Fawley
Dungeness A
Indian Queens

Scale 1 : 8 000 000

## Oil and natural gas reserves, 2009

Middle East
North America
South & Central America
Africa
Europe & Eurasia
Asia Pacific

**World oil reserves**

Other
UAE
Kuwait
Iraq
Iran
Saudi Arabia
Other
Russian Federation

Percentage

**World natural gas reserves**

Other
Russian Federation

Percentage

## Renewable energy sources, 2009
Total : 6 181 000 tonnes oil equivalent

Geo thermal 1.1%
Hydro 6.6%
Wind and wave 11.6%
23.8%
23.2%
14.7%
9.5%
4.0%
5.5%
Biomass 80.7%

Landfill gas
Liquid biofuels
Waste combustion
Wood
Sewage gas
Other biomass

## UK production of oil, coal and gas

Oil
Coal
Natural gas

Million tonnes oil equivalent

1975  1980  1985  1990  1995  2000  2005  2010

## 1 Tourist Attractions

National Park

Area of Outstanding Natural Beauty (England, Wales & N. Ireland)
National Scenic Areas (Scotland)

Heritage Coast (England and Wales)
Preferred Conservation Zone (Scotland)

Long distance footpath

▲ World Heritage Site

● Major tourist attractions
(over 1 million visitors)

○ Other tourist attractions

St Kilda ▲ St Kilda

### Top 12 tourist attractions in London, 2010

| Attraction | Visitors |
|---|---|
| British Museum | 5 842 138 |
| Tate Modern | 5 061 172 |
| National Gallery | 4 954 914 |
| Natural History Museum | 4 647 613 |
| Science Museum | 2 751 902 |
| Victoria and Albert Museum | 2 629 065 |
| National Maritime Museum | 2 419 802 |
| Tower of London | 2 414 541 |
| St Paul's Cathedral | 1 892 467 |
| National Portrait Gallery | 1 819 442 |
| Tate Britain | 1 665 291 |
| British Library | 1 454 612 |

### London

### 2 International Tourism

**Visitors to UK, 2010**

France, Germany, USA, Ireland, Spain, Netherlands, Italy, Belgium, Poland, Australia

**Visitors to UK, distribution by area, 2010**

London, England, Scotland, Wales, Northern Ireland, Day trips

In 2009 tourism was worth £115.4 billion
to the UK economy.

### 3 Domestic Tourism

**Holiday trips by region, 2009**

England, Scotland, Wales, Northern Ireland

**Holiday destinations by region, 2009**

Country of destination

England, N Ireland, Scotland, Wales

Country of Residence

UK, England, N Ireland, Scotland, Wales

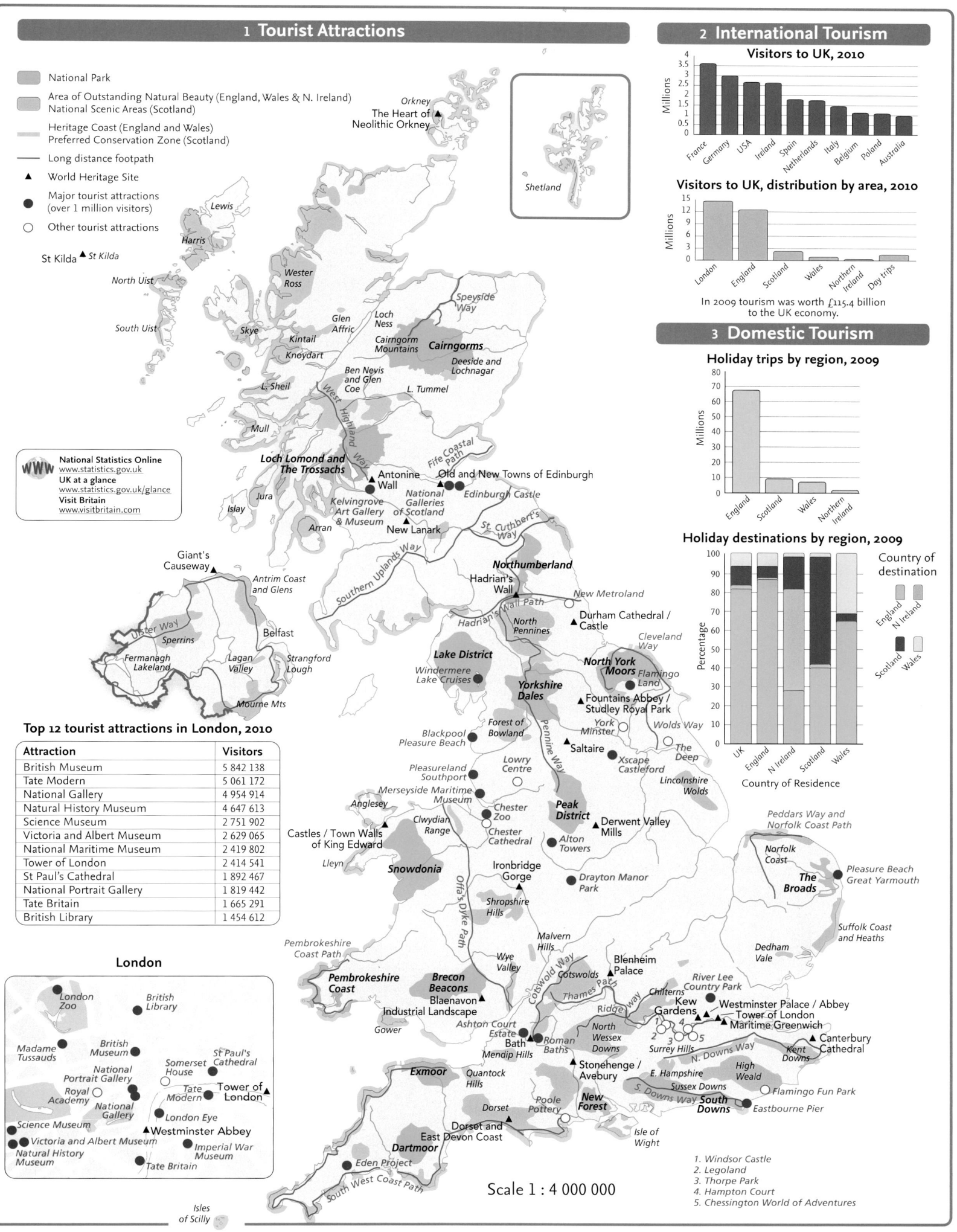

The Heart of Neolithic Orkney

Orkney

Shetland

Lewis

Harris

North Uist

South Uist

Wester Ross

Skye

Glen Affric

Loch Ness

Speyside Way

Kintail

Knoydart

Cairngorm Mountains

Cairngorms

Ben Nevis and Glen Coe

Deeside and Lochnagar

L. Sheil

West Highland Way

L. Tummel

Mull

Loch Lomond and The Trossachs

Islay

Jura

Arran

Kelvingrove Art Gallery & Museum

Antonine Wall

National Galleries of Scotland

New Lanark

Old and New Towns of Edinburgh

Edinburgh Castle

Fife Coastal Path

St. Cuthbert's Way

Southern Uplands Way

Giant's Causeway

Antrim Coast and Glens

Ulster Way

Sperrins

Belfast

Fermanagh Lakeland

Lagan Valley

Strangford Lough

Mourne Mts

Northumberland

Hadrian's Wall

Hadrian's Wall Path

New Metroland

Durham Cathedral / Castle

North Pennines

Cleveland Way

Lake District

Windermere Lake Cruises

North York Moors

Flamingo Land

Yorkshire Dales

Fountains Abbey / Studley Royal Park

Forest of Bowland

York Minster

Wolds Way

Blackpool Pleasure Beach

Saltaire

The Deep

Lowry Centre

Xscape Castleford

Pleasureland Southport

Merseyside Maritime Museum

Lincolnshire Wolds

Anglesey

Chester Zoo

Peak District

Clwydian Range

Chester Cathedral

Derwent Valley Mills

Castles / Town Walls of King Edward

Alton Towers

Lleyn

Snowdonia

Ironbridge Gorge

Drayton Manor Park

Peddars Way and Norfolk Coast Path

Norfolk Coast

The Broads

Pleasure Beach Great Yarmouth

Shropshire Hills

Offa's Dyke Path

Suffolk Coast and Heaths

Pembrokeshire Coast Path

Malvern Hills

Wye Valley

Dedham Vale

Pembrokeshire Coast

Brecon Beacons

Blaenavon Industrial Landscape

Gower

Cotswolds

Cotswold Way

Blenheim Palace

River Lee Country Park

Chilterns

Kew Gardens

Westminster Palace / Abbey
Tower of London
Maritime Greenwich

Thames Path

Ridgeway

North Wessex Downs

Surrey Hills

N. Downs Way

Canterbury Cathedral

Kent Downs

Ashton Court Estate

Bath

Roman Baths

Mendip Hills

Stonehenge / Avebury

E. Hampshire

High Weald

Exmoor

Quantock Hills

New Forest

Sussex Downs

S. Downs Way

South Downs

Flamingo Fun Park

Eastbourne Pier

Dorset

Poole Pottery

Isle of Wight

Dartmoor

Dorset and East Devon Coast

Eden Project

South West Coast Path

Isles of Scilly

Scale 1 : 4 000 000

1. Windsor Castle
2. Legoland
3. Thorpe Park
4. Hampton Court
5. Chessington World of Adventures

**London**

London Zoo

British Library

Madame Tussauds

British Museum

National Portrait Gallery

Somerset House

St Paul's Cathedral

Royal Academy

National Gallery

Tate Modern

Tower of London

Science Museum

London Eye

Victoria and Albert Museum

Westminster Abbey

Natural History Museum

Imperial War Museum

Tate Britain

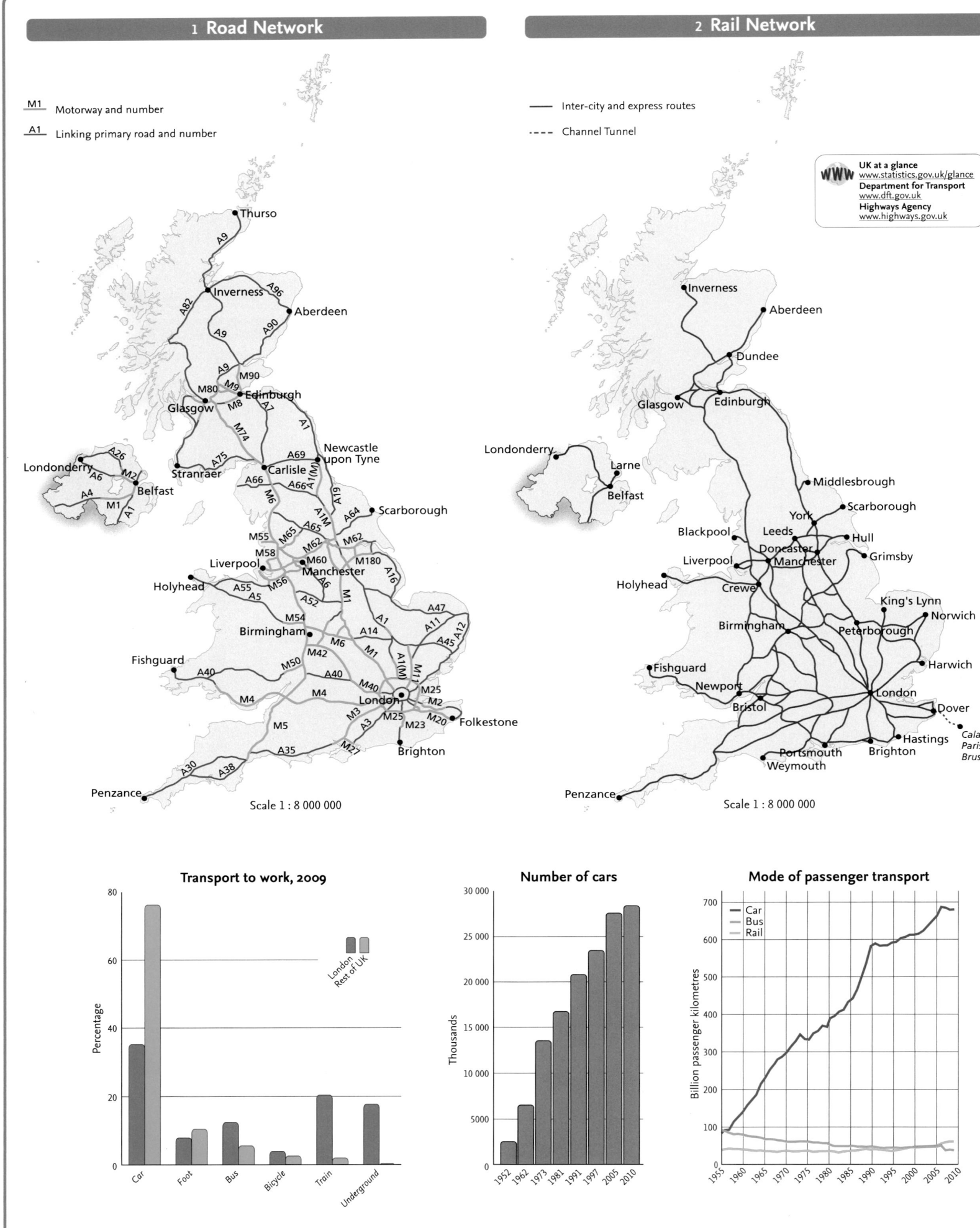

## 1 Road Network

M1 — Motorway and number

A1 — Linking primary road and number

## 2 Rail Network

—— Inter-city and express routes

---- Channel Tunnel

**WWW** UK at a glance
www.statistics.gov.uk/glance
Department for Transport
www.dft.gov.uk
Highways Agency
www.highways.gov.uk

Scale 1 : 8 000 000

Scale 1 : 8 000 000

**Transport to work, 2009**

London
Rest of UK

Percentage

Car, Foot, Bus, Bicycle, Train, Underground

**Number of cars**

Thousands

1952, 1962, 1973, 1981, 1991, 1997, 2005, 2010

**Mode of passenger transport**

Car
Bus
Rail

Billion passenger kilometres

1955, 1960, 1965, 1970, 1975, 1980, 1985, 1990, 1995, 2000, 2005, 2010

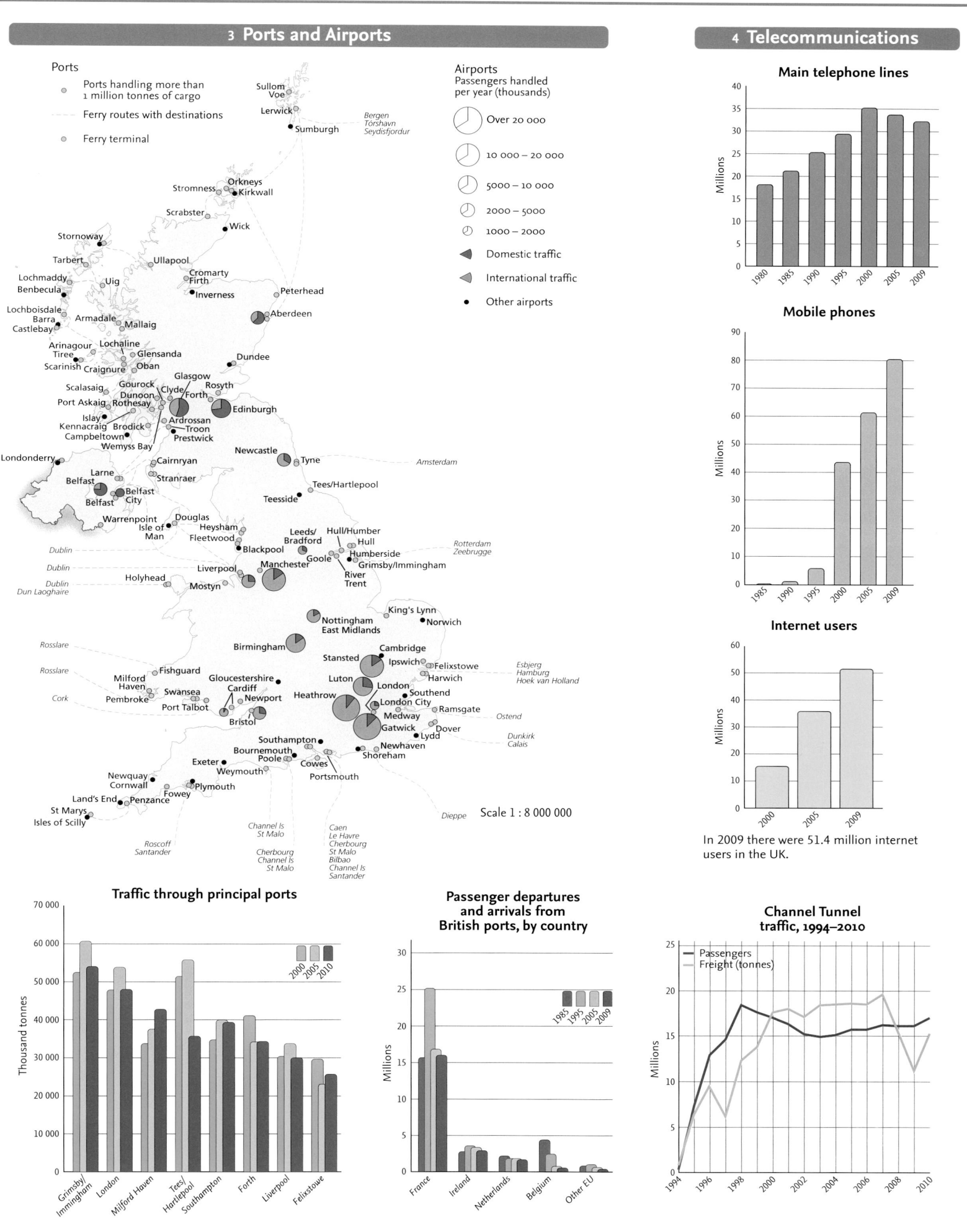

## 3 Ports and Airports

**Ports**

- Ports handling more than 1 million tonnes of cargo
- - - - Ferry routes with destinations
- Ferry terminal

**Airports**
Passengers handled per year (thousands)

- Over 20 000
- 10 000 – 20 000
- 5000 – 10 000
- 2000 – 5000
- 1000 – 2000
- Domestic traffic
- International traffic
- Other airports

Scale 1 : 8 000 000

## 4 Telecommunications

**Main telephone lines**
(Millions)

**Mobile phones**
(Millions)

**Internet users**
(Millions)

In 2009 there were 51.4 million internet users in the UK.

**Traffic through principal ports**
Thousand tonnes
2000 2005 2010
Grimsby/Immingham, London, Milford Haven, Tees/Hartlepool, Southampton, Forth, Liverpool, Felixstowe

**Passenger departures and arrivals from British ports, by country**
Millions
1985 1995 2005 2009
France, Ireland, Netherlands, Belgium, Other EU

**Channel Tunnel traffic, 1994–2010**
Millions
— Passengers
— Freight (tonnes)
1994–2010

# London 2012

## 1 Olympic Venues

In 2005 London won the bid to host the 2012 Olympic games. London previously hosted the Olympics in 1908 and in 1948, however, the size of the event in 2012 is enormous compared to the two previous games.

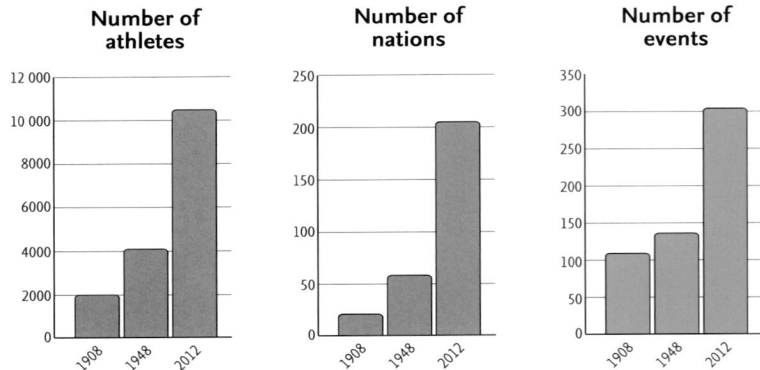

Number of athletes
12 000
10 000
8000
6000
4000
2000
0
1908
1948
2012

Number of nations
250
200
150
100
50
0
1908
1948
2012

Number of events
350
300
250
200
150
100
50
0
1908
1948
2012

**WWW** The Olympic Games www.olympic.org
London 2012 www.london2012.com

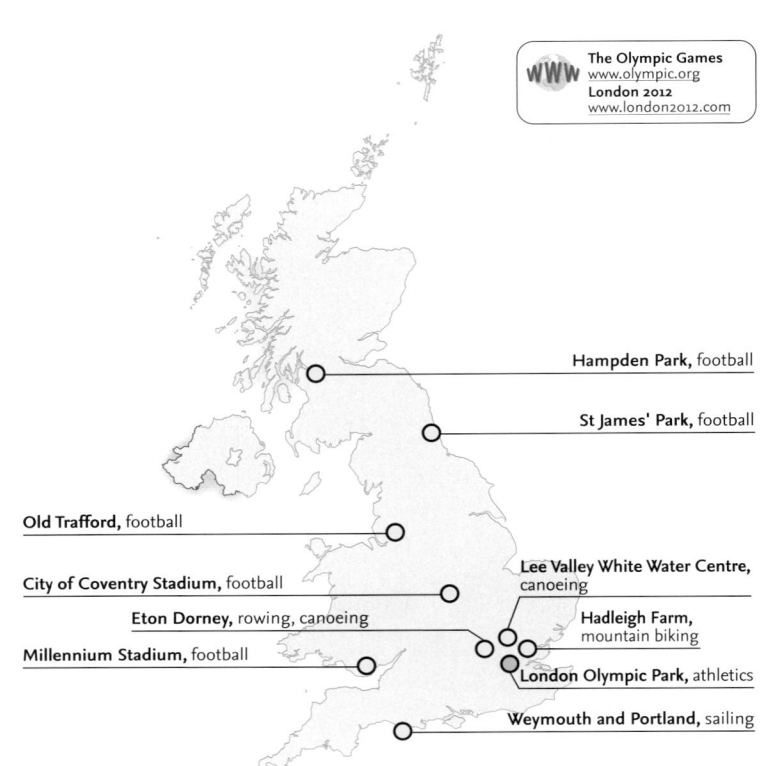

Hampden Park, football
St James' Park, football
Old Trafford, football
Lee Valley White Water Centre, canoeing
City of Coventry Stadium, football
Eton Dorney, rowing, canoeing
Hadleigh Farm, mountain biking
Millennium Stadium, football
London Olympic Park, athletics
Weymouth and Portland, sailing

### How will London cope with such a huge event?

The Olympics is more than a sporting event. It is important that the planning of the games considers the effect on the environment and the benefits it will bring to the city not only in 2012 but for years after the games are over.

## 2 London Venues

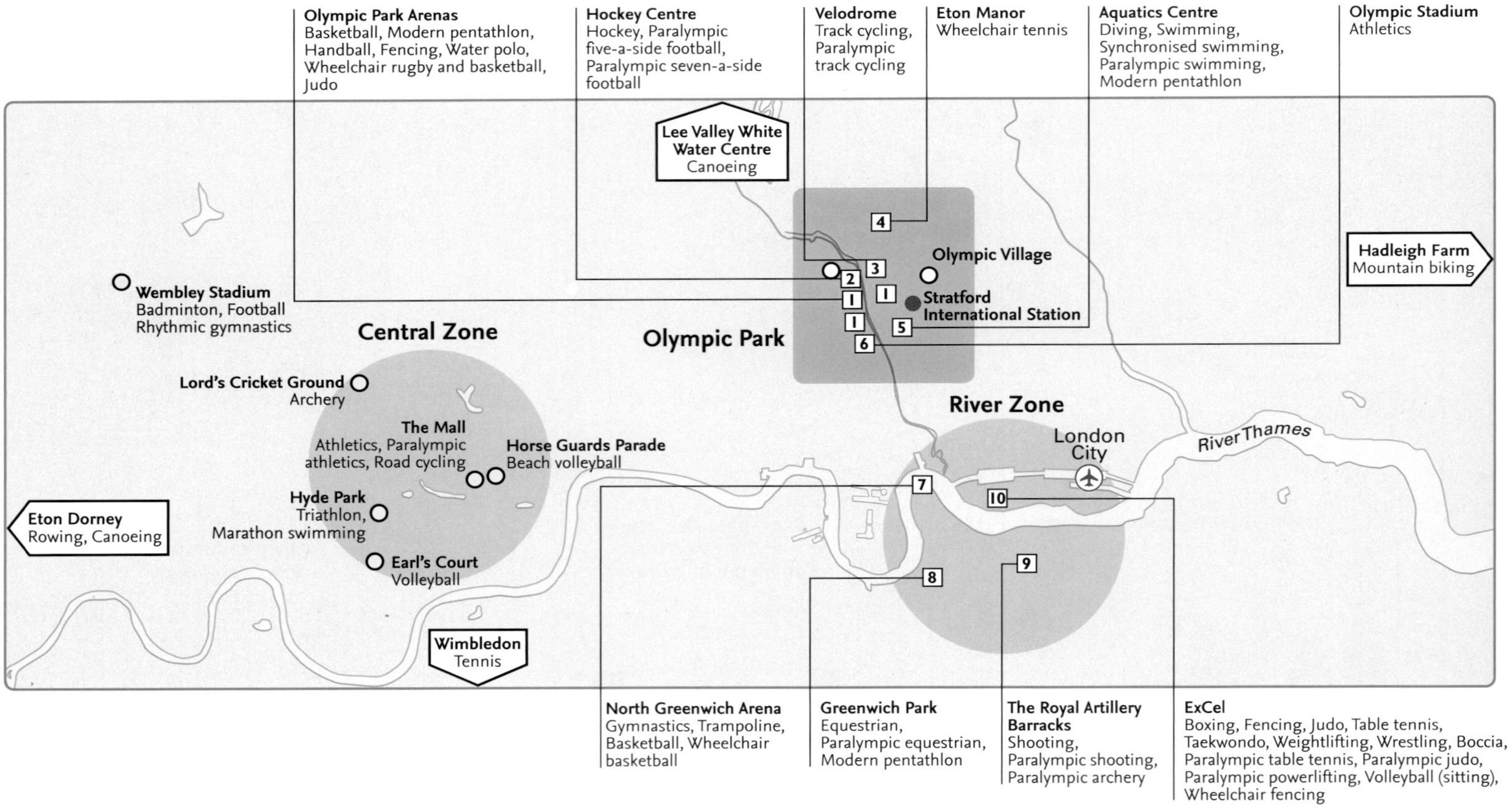

Olympic Park Arenas
Basketball, Modern pentathlon, Handball, Fencing, Water polo, Wheelchair rugby and basketball, Judo
Hockey Centre
Hockey, Paralympic five-a-side football, Paralympic seven-a-side football
Velodrome
Track cycling, Paralympic track cycling
Eton Manor
Wheelchair tennis
Aquatics Centre
Diving, Swimming, Synchronised swimming, Paralympic swimming, Modern pentathlon
Olympic Stadium
Athletics
Lee Valley White Water Centre
Canoeing
Olympic Village
Stratford International Station
Hadleigh Farm
Mountain biking
Wembley Stadium
Badminton, Football
Rhythmic gymnastics
Central Zone
Olympic Park
Lord's Cricket Ground
Archery
The Mall
Athletics, Paralympic athletics, Road cycling
Horse Guards Parade
Beach volleyball
River Zone
London City
River Thames
Hyde Park
Triathlon, Marathon swimming
Eton Dorney
Rowing, Canoeing
Earl's Court
Volleyball
Wimbledon
Tennis
1
2
3
4
5
6
7
8
9
10
North Greenwich Arena
Gymnastics, Trampoline, Basketball, Wheelchair basketball
Greenwich Park
Equestrian, Paralympic equestrian, Modern pentathlon
The Royal Artillery Barracks
Shooting, Paralympic shooting, Paralympic archery
ExCel
Boxing, Fencing, Judo, Table tennis, Taekwondo, Weightlifting, Wrestling, Boccia, Paralympic table tennis, Paralympic judo, Paralympic powerlifting, Volleyball (sitting), Wheelchair fencing

## Olympic Numbers

**4**
Billion viewers expected for the opening ceremony

**5**
Number of venues to remain in use after the games

**80 000**
Number of seats available for the opening and closing ceremonies

**7000**
Number of sponsors

**625**
Millions of pounds Londoners will contribute to staging the Olympics

**2.5**
Square kilometres covered by the Olympic Park

**5000**
Paid employees at the London 2012 Organising Committee at Games-time

**2000**
Kilometres of underground electric cable put down to avoid using pylo

## 3 Stratford Area

## 4 Olympic Park

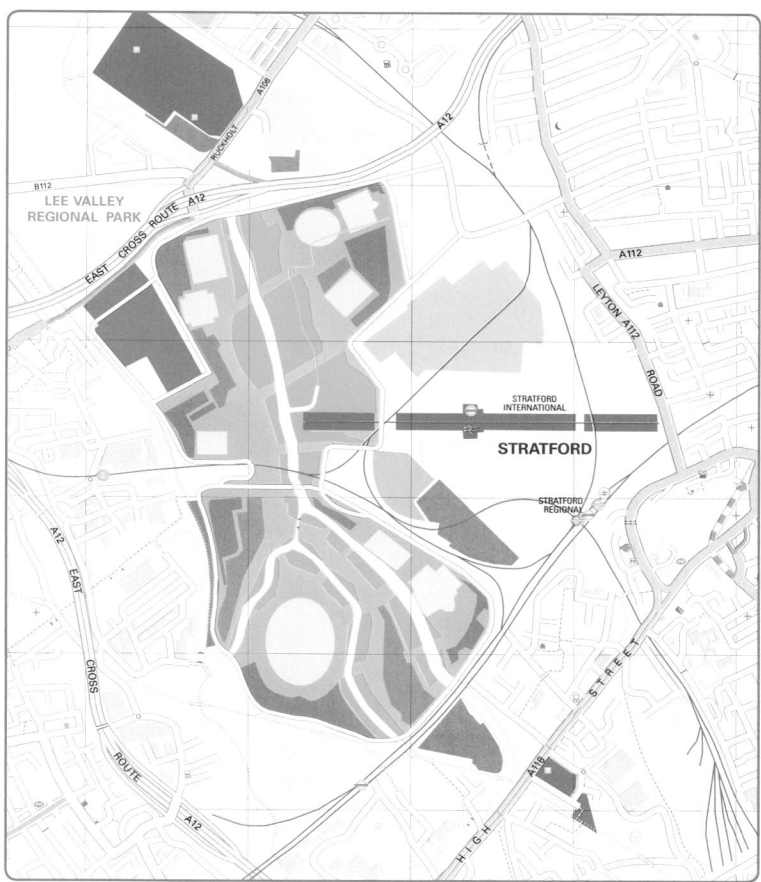

Olympic Park land use

| | |
|---|---|
| Green space | Transport mall |
| Servicing area | Media |

Common domain · Athletes' village · Spectator services
Arenas · Entrance · Sponsors' village

## 5 Planning

**Sustainability** is at the heart of the planning for 2012, and will focus on 5 key issues:
• combating climate change
• reducing waste
• enhancing biodiversity
• promoting inclusion
• improving healthy living

### Issues to consider
• Existing facilities for competitors and spectators
• New facilities and infrastructure for competitors and spectators
• Media facilities
• Ease of access
• Parking facilities
• Emergency services
• Catering facilities

The central location for the Olympics will be the Olympic Park, in the Lea Valley. By creating this park most of the venues and facilities can be centralised and within walking distance of each other.

### After the games

When the games are over the Olympic Park will be used as an urban park, the largest created in Europe for 150 years. It will extend from Hertfordshire to the Thames estuary and will restore wetland habitats and native species will be planted to provide a home for wildlife. Sports facilities and playing fields built for the games will be adapted for use by the local community. Some will be removed and relocated elsewhere in the UK.

Accommodation use during the Olympics will be converted into homes for key workers and amenities such as cafes, restaurants and shops will be available for the local community.

The development and upgrading of Stratford Regional station will improve access to the area and the creation of cycleways, canal towpaths and walkways will give the community access to open space.

Economically, the area will attract new business opportunities and create employment.

---

**9000**
Planned number of houses to be built around Olympic Park after the games

**3000**
Plants are being planted in the Olympic Park wetlands area

**20**
Percent of electricity requirements expected to use renewable energy sources

**100**
Million pounds to be spent on the upgrade of Stratford Regional station

**220**
Number of buildings demolished for the building of Olympic Park

**2000**
Number of newts relocated from the Olympic Park to the Waterworks Nature Reserve

**50 000**
Tonnes of contaminated soil on the site washed for reuse

**8.35**
Kilometres of waterways within or close to the Olympic Park, much of which is being restored

0    250    500    750    1000 km

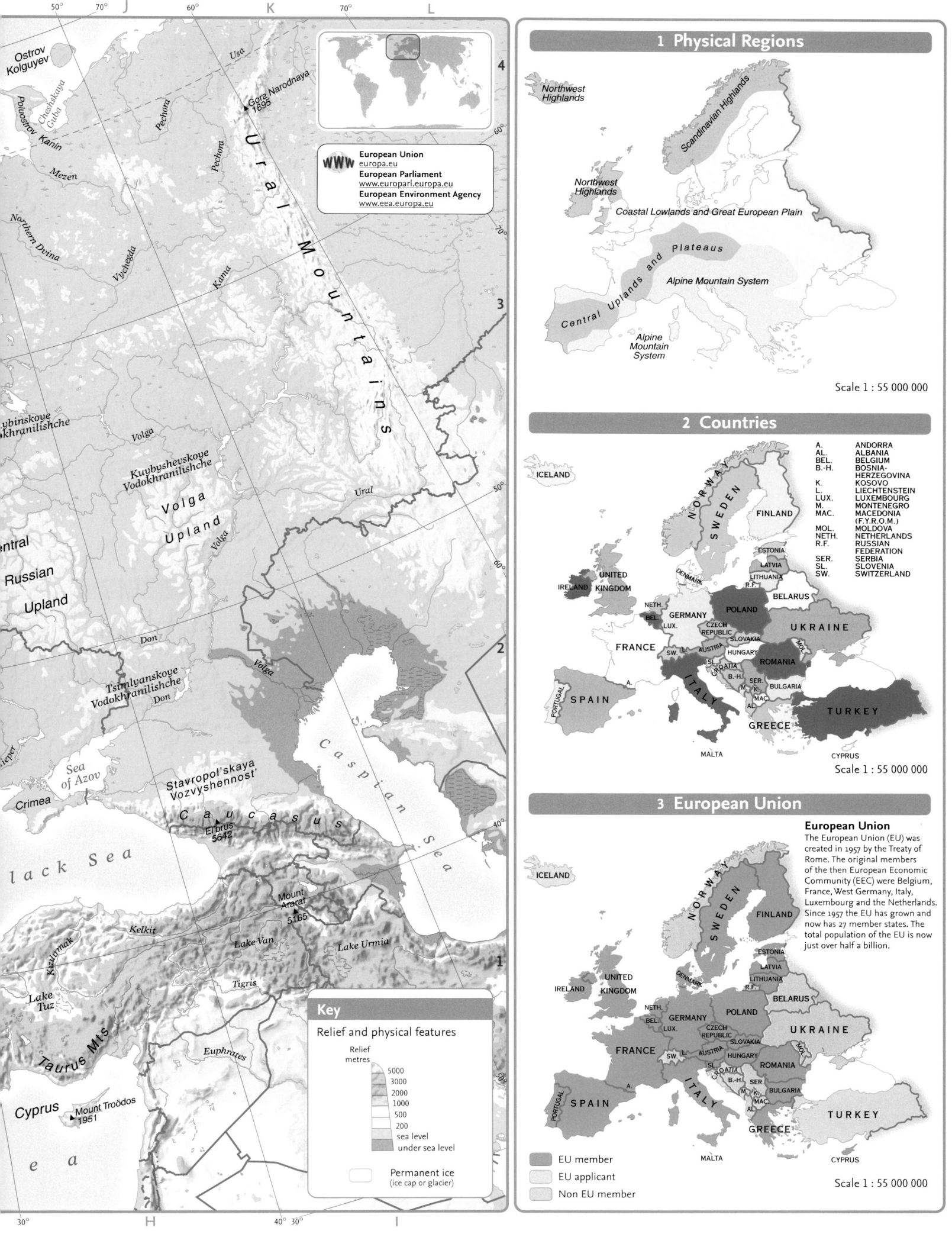

## 1 Physical Regions

Scale 1 : 55 000 000

## 2 Countries

| A. | ANDORRA |
| AL. | ALBANIA |
| BEL. | BELGIUM |
| B.-H. | BOSNIA-HERZEGOVINA |
| K. | KOSOVO |
| L. | LIECHTENSTEIN |
| LUX. | LUXEMBOURG |
| M. | MONTENEGRO |
| MAC. | MACEDONIA (F.Y.R.O.M.) |
| MOL. | MOLDOVA |
| NETH. | NETHERLANDS |
| R.F. | RUSSIAN FEDERATION |
| SER. | SERBIA |
| SL. | SLOVENIA |
| SW. | SWITZERLAND |

Scale 1 : 55 000 000

## 3 European Union

**European Union**

The European Union (EU) was created in 1957 by the Treaty of Rome. The original members of the then European Economic Community (EEC) were Belgium, France, West Germany, Italy, Luxembourg and the Netherlands. Since 1957 the EU has grown and now has 27 member states. The total population of the EU is now just over half a billion.

EU member
EU applicant
Non EU member

Scale 1 : 55 000 000

**Key**

Relief and physical features

Relief metres
5000
3000
2000
1000
500
200
sea level
under sea level

Permanent ice (ice cap or glacier)

European Union
europa.eu
European Parliament
www.europarl.europa.eu
European Environment Agency
www.eea.europa.eu

Conic Equidistant projection

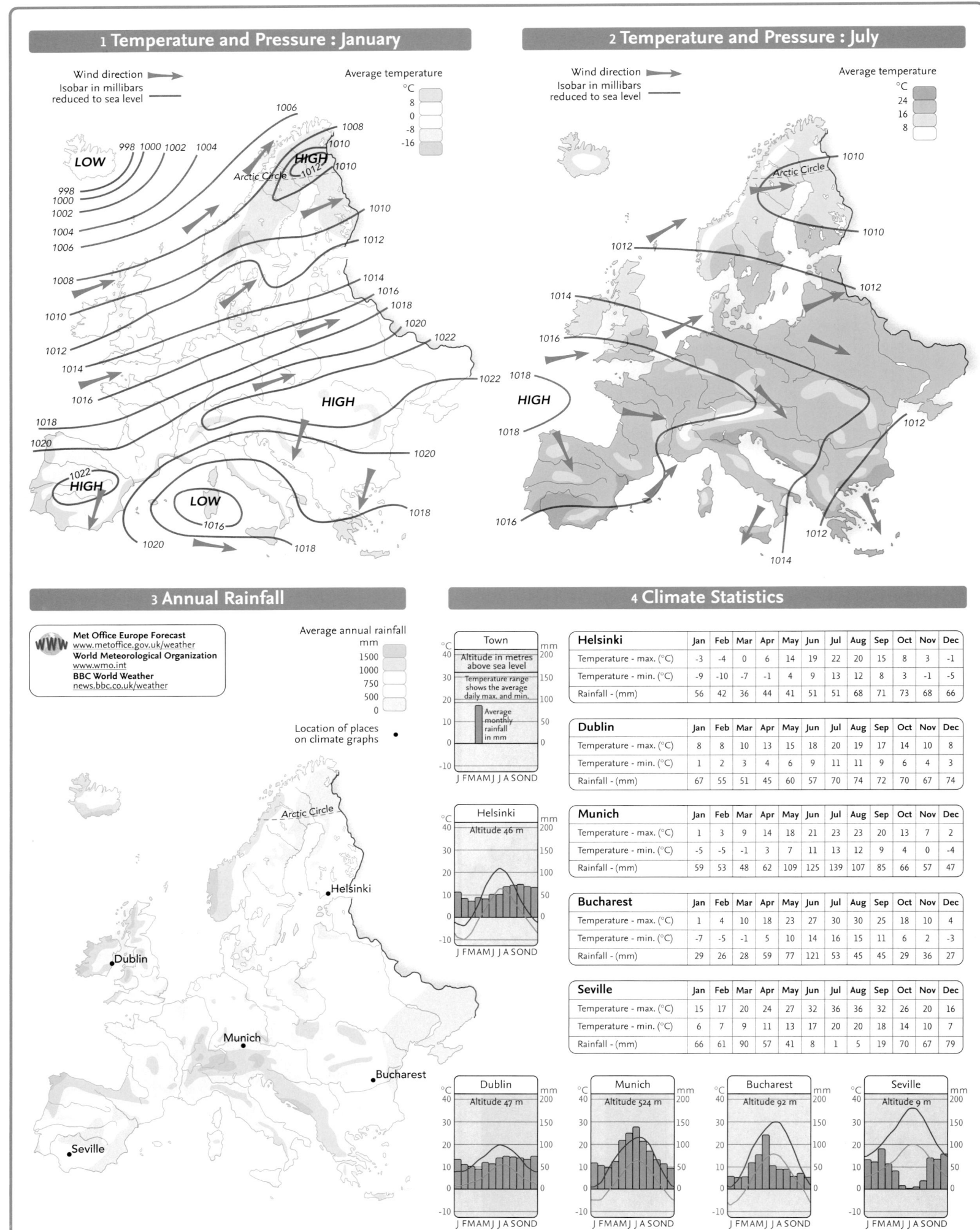

## 1 Temperature and Pressure : January

Wind direction →
Isobar in millibars
reduced to sea level ———

Average temperature
°C
8
0
-8
-16

## 2 Temperature and Pressure : July

Wind direction →
Isobar in millibars
reduced to sea level ———

Average temperature
°C
24
16
8

## 3 Annual Rainfall

WWW
**Met Office Europe Forecast**
www.metoffice.gov.uk/weather
**World Meteorological Organization**
www.wmo.int
**BBC World Weather**
news.bbc.co.uk/weather

Average annual rainfall
mm
1500
1000
750
500
0

Location of places
on climate graphs •

## 4 Climate Statistics

| Helsinki | Jan | Feb | Mar | Apr | May | Jun | Jul | Aug | Sep | Oct | Nov | Dec |
|---|---|---|---|---|---|---|---|---|---|---|---|---|
| Temperature - max. (°C) | -3 | -4 | 0 | 6 | 14 | 19 | 22 | 20 | 15 | 8 | 3 | -1 |
| Temperature - min. (°C) | -9 | -10 | -7 | -1 | 4 | 9 | 13 | 12 | 8 | 3 | -1 | -5 |
| Rainfall - (mm) | 56 | 42 | 36 | 44 | 41 | 51 | 51 | 68 | 71 | 73 | 68 | 66 |

| Dublin | Jan | Feb | Mar | Apr | May | Jun | Jul | Aug | Sep | Oct | Nov | Dec |
|---|---|---|---|---|---|---|---|---|---|---|---|---|
| Temperature - max. (°C) | 8 | 8 | 10 | 13 | 15 | 18 | 20 | 19 | 17 | 14 | 10 | 8 |
| Temperature - min. (°C) | 1 | 2 | 3 | 4 | 6 | 9 | 11 | 11 | 9 | 6 | 4 | 3 |
| Rainfall - (mm) | 67 | 55 | 51 | 45 | 60 | 57 | 70 | 74 | 72 | 70 | 67 | 74 |

| Munich | Jan | Feb | Mar | Apr | May | Jun | Jul | Aug | Sep | Oct | Nov | Dec |
|---|---|---|---|---|---|---|---|---|---|---|---|---|
| Temperature - max. (°C) | 1 | 3 | 9 | 14 | 18 | 21 | 23 | 23 | 20 | 13 | 7 | 2 |
| Temperature - min. (°C) | -5 | -5 | -1 | 3 | 7 | 11 | 13 | 12 | 9 | 4 | 0 | -4 |
| Rainfall - (mm) | 59 | 53 | 48 | 62 | 109 | 125 | 139 | 107 | 85 | 66 | 57 | 47 |

| Bucharest | Jan | Feb | Mar | Apr | May | Jun | Jul | Aug | Sep | Oct | Nov | Dec |
|---|---|---|---|---|---|---|---|---|---|---|---|---|
| Temperature - max. (°C) | 1 | 4 | 10 | 18 | 23 | 27 | 30 | 30 | 25 | 18 | 10 | 4 |
| Temperature - min. (°C) | -7 | -5 | -1 | 5 | 10 | 14 | 16 | 15 | 11 | 6 | 2 | -3 |
| Rainfall - (mm) | 29 | 26 | 28 | 59 | 77 | 121 | 53 | 45 | 45 | 29 | 36 | 27 |

| Seville | Jan | Feb | Mar | Apr | May | Jun | Jul | Aug | Sep | Oct | Nov | Dec |
|---|---|---|---|---|---|---|---|---|---|---|---|---|
| Temperature - max. (°C) | 15 | 17 | 20 | 24 | 27 | 32 | 36 | 36 | 32 | 26 | 20 | 16 |
| Temperature - min. (°C) | 6 | 7 | 9 | 11 | 13 | 17 | 20 | 20 | 18 | 14 | 10 | 7 |
| Rainfall - (mm) | 66 | 61 | 90 | 57 | 41 | 8 | 1 | 5 | 19 | 70 | 67 | 79 |

Town
Altitude in metres above sea level
Temperature range shows the average daily max. and min.
Average monthly rainfall in mm

Helsinki — Altitude 46 m

Dublin — Altitude 47 m

Munich — Altitude 524 m

Bucharest — Altitude 92 m

Seville — Altitude 9 m

Scale 1 : 40 000 000

0   400   800   1200   1600 km

Conic projection

## 1 Population Density

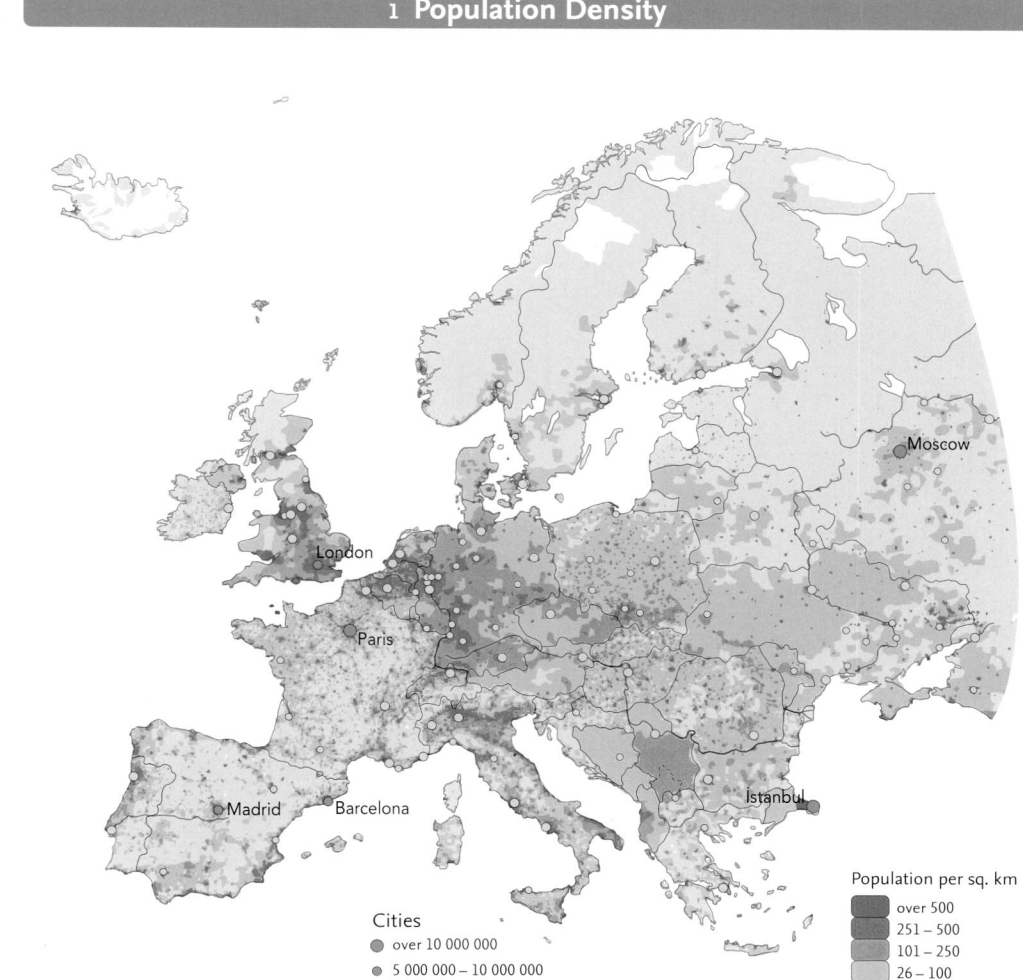

Scale 1 : 35 000 000

### Cities
- ● over 10 000 000
- ● 5 000 000 – 10 000 000
- ○ 1 000 000 – 5 000 000
- ○ 500 000 – 1 000 000

### Population per sq. km
- over 500
- 251 – 500
- 101 – 250
- 26 – 100
- 1 – 25
- less than 1

## 2 City Populations

| City | Country | Population |
|---|---|---|
| İstanbul | Turkey | 11 164 000 |
| Paris | France | 10 777 000 |
| Moscow | Russian Federation | 10 641 000 |
| London | United Kingdom | 8 693 000 |
| Madrid | Spain | 6 213 000 |
| Barcelona | Spain | 5 315 000 |
| St Petersburg | Russian Federation | 4 561 000 |
| Berlin | Germany | 3 489 000 |
| Rome | Italy | 3 375 000 |
| Athens | Greece | 3 283 000 |
| Milan | Italy | 2 980 000 |
| Lisbon | Portugal | 2 907 000 |
| Kiev | Ukraine | 2 894 000 |
| Birmingham | United Kingdom | 2 337 000 |
| Naples | Italy | 2 292 000 |
| Manchester | United Kingdom | 2 287 000 |
| Bucharest | Romania | 1 947 000 |
| Brussels | Belgium | 1 941 000 |
| Minsk | Belarus | 1 905 000 |
| Hamburg | Germany | 1 818 000 |
| Vienna | Austria | 1 753 000 |
| Warsaw | Poland | 1 720 000 |
| Budapest | Hungary | 1 711 000 |
| Turin | Italy | 1 678 000 |
| Leeds | United Kingdom | 1 575 000 |
| Marseille | France | 1 524 000 |
| Lyon | France | 1 523 000 |
| Kharkiv | Ukraine | 1 446 000 |
| Oporto | Portugal | 1 407 000 |
| Munich | Germany | 1 401 000 |

**WWW** EUROSTAT
epp.eurostat.ec.europa.eu
**United Nations Population Information Network**
www.un.org/popin

## 3 Population under 15

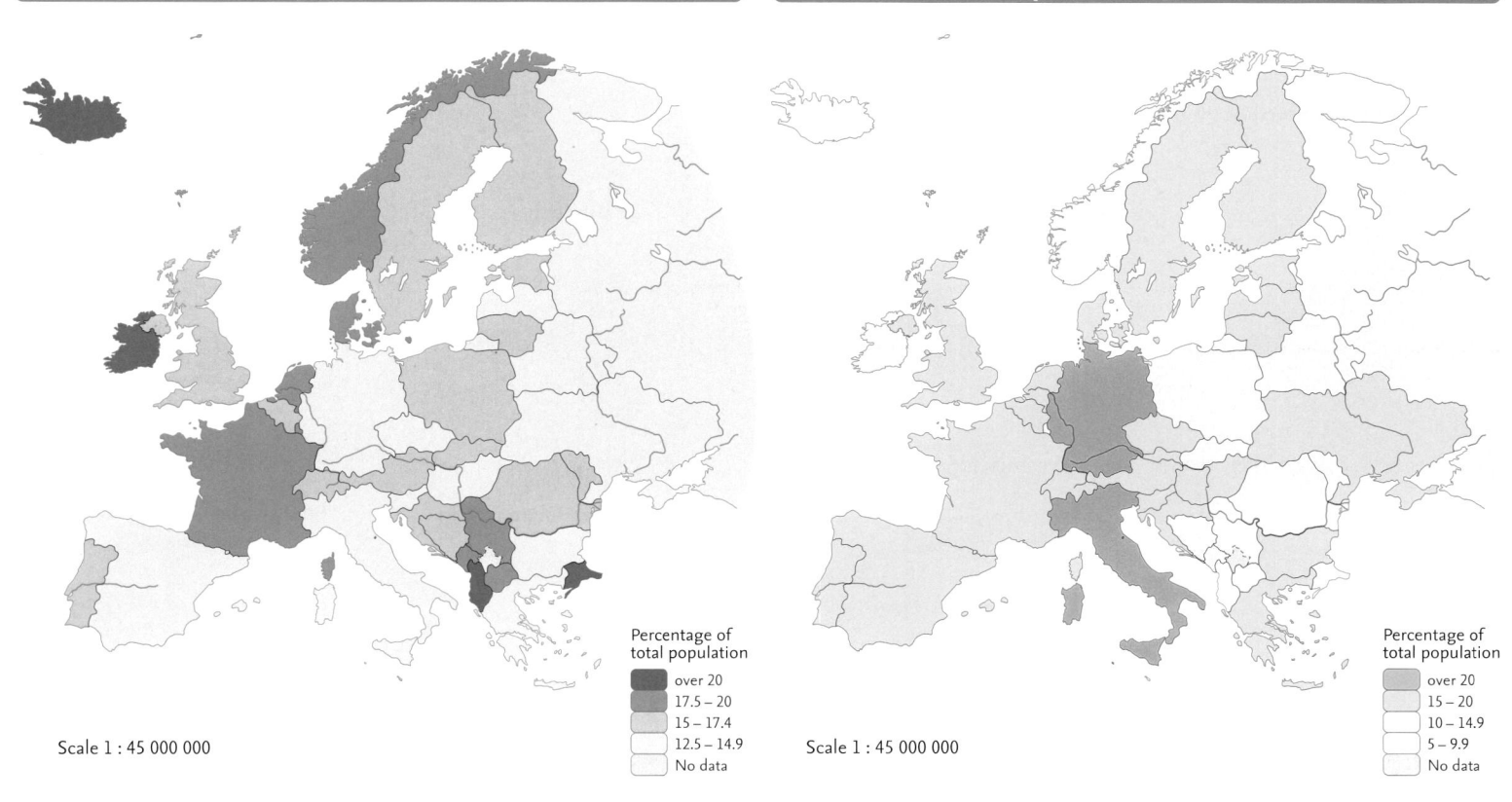

### Percentage of total population
- over 20
- 17.5 – 20
- 15 – 17.4
- 12.5 – 14.9
- No data

Scale 1 : 45 000 000

## 4 Population 65 and over

### Percentage of total population
- over 20
- 15 – 20
- 10 – 14.9
- 5 – 9.9
- No data

Scale 1 : 45 000 000

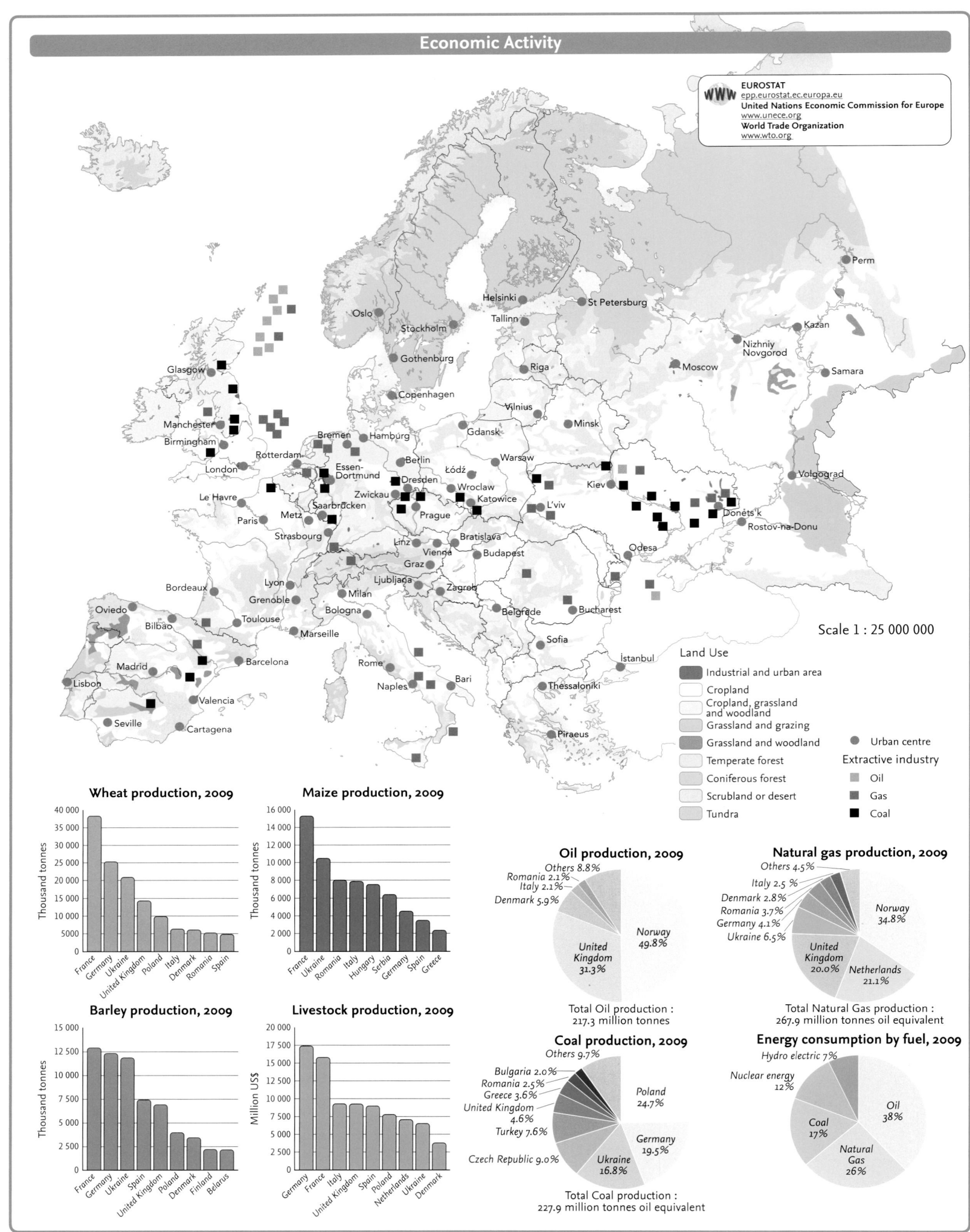

## Economic Activity

EUROSTAT
epp.eurostat.ec.europa.eu
United Nations Economic Commission for Europe
www.unece.org
World Trade Organization
www.wto.org

Scale 1 : 25 000 000

**Land Use**

- Industrial and urban area
- Cropland
- Cropland, grassland and woodland
- Grassland and grazing
- Grassland and woodland
- Temperate forest
- Coniferous forest
- Scrubland or desert
- Tundra
- Urban centre

**Extractive industry**

- Oil
- Gas
- Coal

### Wheat production, 2009

Thousand tonnes

France, Germany, Ukraine, United Kingdom, Poland, Italy, Denmark, Romania, Spain

### Maize production, 2009

Thousand tonnes

France, Ukraine, Romania, Italy, Hungary, Serbia, Germany, Spain, Greece

### Barley production, 2009

Thousand tonnes

France, Germany, Ukraine, Spain, United Kingdom, Poland, Denmark, Finland, Belarus

### Livestock production, 2009

Million US$

Germany, France, Italy, United Kingdom, Spain, Poland, Netherlands, Ukraine, Denmark

### Oil production, 2009

- Others 8.8%
- Romania 2.1%
- Italy 2.1%
- Denmark 5.9%
- Norway 49.8%
- United Kingdom 31.3%

Total Oil production :
217.3 million tonnes

### Natural gas production, 2009

- Others 4.5%
- Italy 2.5%
- Denmark 2.8%
- Romania 3.7%
- Germany 4.1%
- Ukraine 6.5%
- Norway 34.8%
- United Kingdom 20.0%
- Netherlands 21.1%

Total Natural Gas production :
267.9 million tonnes oil equivalent

### Coal production, 2009

- Others 9.7%
- Bulgaria 2.0%
- Romania 2.5%
- Greece 3.6%
- United Kingdom 4.6%
- Turkey 7.6%
- Czech Republic 9.0%
- Poland 24.7%
- Germany 19.5%
- Ukraine 16.8%

Total Coal production :
227.9 million tonnes oil equivalent

### Energy consumption by fuel, 2009

- Hydro electric 7%
- Nuclear energy 12%
- Oil 38%
- Coal 17%
- Natural Gas 26%

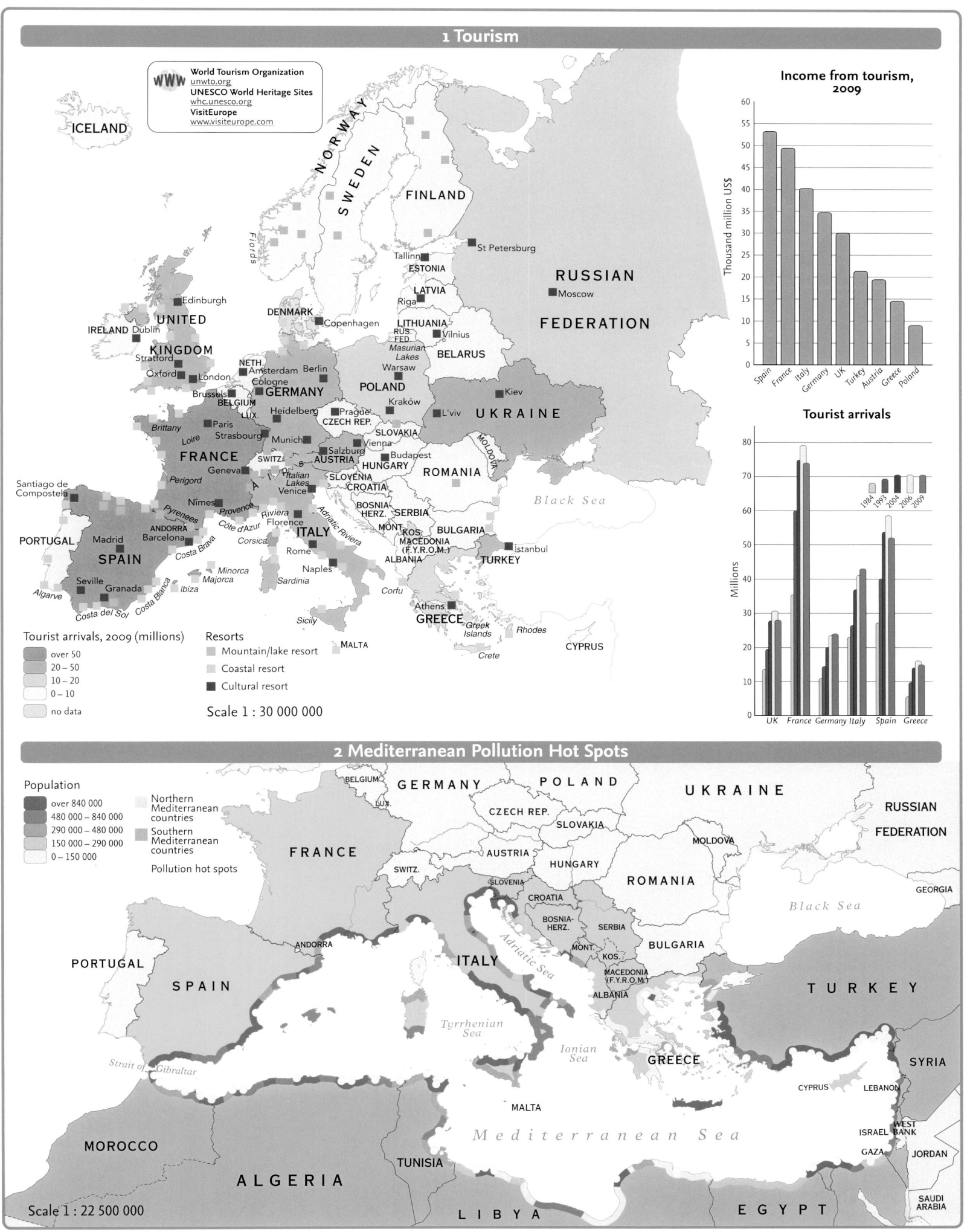

## 1 Tourism

World Tourism Organization
unwto.org
UNESCO World Heritage Sites
whc.unesco.org
VisitEurope
www.visiteurope.com

ICELAND

NORWAY
SWEDEN
FINLAND
Fjords

St Petersburg
Tallinn
ESTONIA
LATVIA
Riga

RUSSIAN
FEDERATION
Moscow

Edinburgh
UNITED
IRELAND Dublin
KINGDOM
Stratford
Oxford
London
Brussels
Brittany
FRANCE
Loire
Paris
Strasbourg

DENMARK
Copenhagen

LITHUANIA
RUS.
FED.
Vilnius
Masurian
Lakes
BELARUS
Warsaw

NETH.
Amsterdam Berlin
Cologne
GERMANY
BELGIUM
LUX.
Heidelberg
Prague
CZECH REP.
Munich
Salzburg
SWITZ.
AUSTRIA
Vienna
Geneva
Italian
Lakes
Venice
Budapest
HUNGARY
SLOVENIA
CROATIA

POLAND
Kraków

UKRAINE
Kiev
L'viv

MOLDOVA
ROMANIA

Black Sea

Santiago de
Compostela
PORTUGAL
Madrid
SPAIN
Seville Granada
Algarve
Costa del Sol
Costa Blanca
Ibiza
Perigord
Pyrenees
Nîmes
Provence
Côte d'Azur
Riviera
Florence
ITALY
Rome
Corsica
Minorca
Majorca
Sardinia

Naples

ANDORRA
Barcelona
Costa Brava

Adriatic Riviera
BOSNIA
HERZ.
MONT.
SERBIA
KOS.
MACEDONIA
(F.Y.R.O.M.)
ALBANIA

BULGARIA

TURKEY
İstanbul

Corfu
Athens
GREECE
Greek
Islands
Crete
Sicily
MALTA
Rhodes
CYPRUS

**Tourist arrivals, 2009 (millions)**
- over 50
- 20 – 50
- 10 – 20
- 0 – 10
- no data

**Resorts**
- Mountain/lake resort
- Coastal resort
- Cultural resort

Scale 1 : 30 000 000

### Income from tourism, 2009

Thousand million US$

Spain, France, Italy, Germany, UK, Turkey, Austria, Greece, Poland

### Tourist arrivals

Millions

1984 1993 2004 2006 2009

UK France Germany Italy Spain Greece

## 2 Mediterranean Pollution Hot Spots

**Population**
- over 840 000
- 480 000 – 840 000
- 290 000 – 480 000
- 150 000 – 290 000
- 0 – 150 000

- Northern Mediterranean countries
- Southern Mediterranean countries

Pollution hot spots

BELGIUM
LUX.
GERMANY
POLAND
CZECH REP.
SLOVAKIA
UKRAINE

FRANCE
SWITZ.
AUSTRIA
HUNGARY
SLOVENIA
CROATIA
BOSNIA-
HERZ.
MONT.
KOS.
SERBIA
MACEDONIA
(F.Y.R.O.M.)
ALBANIA
MOLDOVA
ROMANIA
BULGARIA

RUSSIAN
FEDERATION

Black Sea
GEORGIA

PORTUGAL
SPAIN
ANDORRA
ITALY
Adriatic Sea
Tyrrhenian
Sea
Ionian
Sea
GREECE
TURKEY

Strait of Gibraltar
MOROCCO
ALGERIA
TUNISIA
MALTA

Mediterranean Sea

LIBYA

CYPRUS
SYRIA
LEBANON
ISRAEL WEST BANK
GAZA
JORDAN
EGYPT
SAUDI
ARABIA

Scale 1 : 22 500 000

ICELAND

Straumnes
Horn
Grímsey
Rifstangi
Arctic Circle
Fontur
Siglufjörður
Öxarfjörður
Ísafjörður
Reiphólsfjöll
881
Sauðárkrókur
Akureyri
Seyðisfjörður
Egilsstaðir
ICELAND
Hofsjökull
1763
Snæfell
1833
Breiðdalsvík
Borgarnes
Bárðarbunga
2009 Sviahnúkar
1719
Faxaflói
Akranes
Vatnajökull
Höfn
Vesturhorn
REYKJAVÍK
Hekla
1491
Hvannadalshnúkur
2119
Keflavík
Eyjafjallajökull
1666
Vestmannaeyjar
Vík
Kötlutangi
Surtsey
Skaftárós

North Cape
Magerøya
Porsangerhalvøya
Sørøya
Hammerfest
Seiland
Vadsø
Lopphavet
Varangerfjorden
Kirkenes
Ringvassøya
Kvaløya
Tromsø
Iešjávri
Inarijärvi
Nikel'
Zapolyarnyy
Andøya
Senja
Jiehkkevárri
1833
Murmansk
Kola
Lapland
Harstad
Altaelva
Narvik
Muonioälven
Taivaskero
807
Ivalo
Lotta
Lovozero
Kiruna
Muonio
Kittilä
Monchegorsk
Kirovsk
Akkajaure
Sarektjåkka
2090
Torneälven
Sodankylä
Kemijoki
Lokan
tekojärvi
Ozero
Apatity
Kolvitskoye
Bodø
Kalixälven
Saittanulkki
337
Pello
Kemijärvi
Kandalaksha
Glomfjord
Jokkmokk
Övertorneå
Ylitornio
Rovaniemi
Kuusamo
Snøtinden
1594
Vuollerim
Haparanda
Tornio
Simojärvi
RUSSIAN
Ozero
Pyaozero
Louhki
Mo i Rana
Hornavan
Boden
Kemi
Taivalkoski
Mosjøen
Okstindan
1915
Norra
Storfjället
1792
Uddjaure
Älvsbyn
Luleå
Piteå
Oulu
Muhos
Kiantajärvi
FEDERATION
Ozero
Topozero
Vega
Storavan
Sorsele
Vindelälven
Jörn
Raahe
Hyrynsalmi
Brønnøysund
Storuman
Marsfjället
1589
Storuman
Skellefteå
Kalajoki
Oulainen
Oulujärvi
Kajaani
Reboly
Ozero
Leksozero
Vikna
Limingen
Malgomaj
Vilhelmina
Robertsfors
Kokkola
Haapajärvi
Kiuruvesi
Nurmes
Lieksa
Namsos
Tunnsjøen
Åsele
Lycksele
Umeå
Vännäs
Jakobstad
Iisalmi
Pielinen
Snåsa
Flåsjön
Nykarleby
Lestijärvi
Silinjärvi
Höytiäinen
Steinkjer
Strömsund
Örnsköldsvik
Vaasa
Lappajärvi
Kuopio
Outokumpu
Verdalsøra
Kallsjön
Hammerdal
Sollefteå
Lapua
Keitele
Kallavesi
Joensuu
Frøya
Stjørdalshalsen
Järpen
Storsjön
Indalsälven
Härnösand
Laihia
Kurikka
Alavus
Suonenjoki
Varkaus
Pyhäselkä
Orivesi
Smøla
Hitra
Trondheim
Løkken
Syarna
1761
Östersund
Brunflo
Kramfors
Närpes
Seinäjoki
Jyväskylä
Pieksämäki
Sortavala
Kristiansund
Støren
Røros
Bräcke
Timrå
Näsijärvi
Ylöjärvi
Päijänne
Mikkeli
Pihlajavesi
Molde
Åndalsnes
Storskrymten
1985
Hede
Ånge
Sundsvall
Brämön
Kankaanpää
Pori
Tampere
Kuohijärvi
Heinola
Saimaa
Imatra
Svetogorsk
Ålesund
Galdhøpiggen
2470
Fåmunden
Österdalälven
Sveg
Ljusdal
Hudiksvall
Rauma
Ylöjärvi
Valkeakoski
Hämeenlinna
Lahti
Lappeenranta
Vyborg
Måløy
Volda
Stranda
Otta
Iggesund
Söderhamn
Uusikaupunki
Forssa
Riihimäki
Kouvola
Hamina
Florø
Sandane
Gudbrandsdalen
Lillehammer
Rena
Älvdalen
Mora
Bollnäs
Rättvik
Turku
Hyvinkää
Järvenpää
Førde
Høyanger
Valdres
Gjøvik
Elverum
Siljan
Falun
Sandviken
Södra
Kvarken
Åland
Islands
Salo
Espoo
Vantaa
Kirkkonummi
St Petersburg
Sestroretsk
Bergen
Voss
Harteigen
1690
Hønefoss
Hamar
Borlänge
Gävle
Mariehamn
HELSINKI
Gulf of Finland
Kronstadt
Bømlo
Mosvatnet
Drammen
Kongsvinger
Ludvika
Avesta
Narva
Haugesund
Kongsberg
Lillestrøm
Fagersta
Sala
Uppsala
TALLINN
Rakvere
Tosno
Karmøy
Rjuvbrokkene
1443
OSLO
Ski
Arvika
Västerås
Enköping
Märsta
Täby
Norrtälje
Luga
Stavanger
Horten
Askim
Moss
Karlstad
Karlskoga
Arboga
Eskilstuna
STOCKHOLM
Kärdla
Haapsalu
ESTONIA
Lake
Peipus
RUSSIAN
Sandnes
Tønsberg
Sarpsborg
Kristinehamn
Örebro
Mälaren
Södertälje
Hiiumaa
Tartu
Sira
Skien
Fredrikstad
Åmål
Säffle
Kumla
Katrineholm
Finspång
Nynäshamn
Oxelösund
Saaremaa
Pärnu
Viljandi
Valka
Lake
Pskov
FEDERATION
Lindesnes
Porsgrunn
Larvik
Halden
Vänern
Lidköping
Mariestad
Motala
Linköping
Norrköping
Fårö
Kuressaare
Pskov
Ostrov
Arendal
Kristiansand
Vänersborg
Uddevalla
Trollhättan
Lilla Edet
Skara
Skövde
Falköping
Alingsås
Jönköping
Sommen
Tranås
Eksjö
Västervik
Visby
Gotland
Ventspils
Gulf
of Riga
Talsi
Valmiera
Opochka
Skagen
Hjørring
Brønderslev
Aalborg
Gothenburg
Borås
Kinna
Nässjö
377
Oskarshamn
Öland
Visby
Kuldīga
LATVIA
Rēzekne
Thisted
Frederikshavn
Läsø
Falkenberg
Bolmen
Värnamo
Växjö
Nybro
Kalmar
Liepāja
RIGA
Daugava
Daugavpils
Jutland
Struer
Skive
Hobro
Randers
Grenå
Halmstad
Ängelholm
Åsnen
Karlshamn
Ventspils
Mazeikiai
Jelgava
Rokiškis
Holstebro
Viborg
Ringkøbing
Herning
Silkeborg
Hässleholm
Kristianstad
Karlskrona
Klaipėda
Šiauliai
Panevėžys
Kupiškis
DENMARK
Århus
Vejle
Hillerød
Helsingør
Garždai
LITHUANIA
Kėdainiai
Esbjerg
Kolding
Holbæk
COPENHAGEN
Malmö
Lund
Ystad
Bornholm
(Denmark)
Rønne
Courland
Lagoon
Sovetsk
Ribe
Haderslev
Nyborg
Fyn
Slagelse
Køge
Zealand
Trelleborg
Nakskov
Møn
Kaliningrad
RUS. FED.
Kaunas
VILNIUS
BELARUS
Barysaw
Tønder
Flensburg
Schleswig
Lolland
Nykøbing
Falster
Rügen
Baltiysk
Chernyakhovsk
Hrodna
MINSK
North
Frisian
Islands
Fehmarn
Kiel
Sassnitz
Stralsund
Słupsk
Lębork
Gdynia
Elbląg
Olsztyn
Shchuchyn
Masty
East
Frisian
Islands
Wilhelmshaven
Bremerhaven
Emden
Norderstedt
Lübeck
HAMBURG
Neumünster
Rostock
GERMANY
Schwerin
Swinoujście
Koszalin
Słupsk
Szczecinek
Gdańsk
POLAND
Malbork
Ostróda
Choinice
Szczytno
Hrodna
Stowbtsy
Asipovichy

Norwegian
Sea
Arctic Circle
NORWAY
SWEDEN
FINLAND
DENMARK
Skagerrak
Kattegat
Baltic Sea
Gulf of Bothnia
Lake Ladoga
Sognefjorden

Scale 1 : 7 500 000

0   100   200   300 km

Conic Equidistant projection

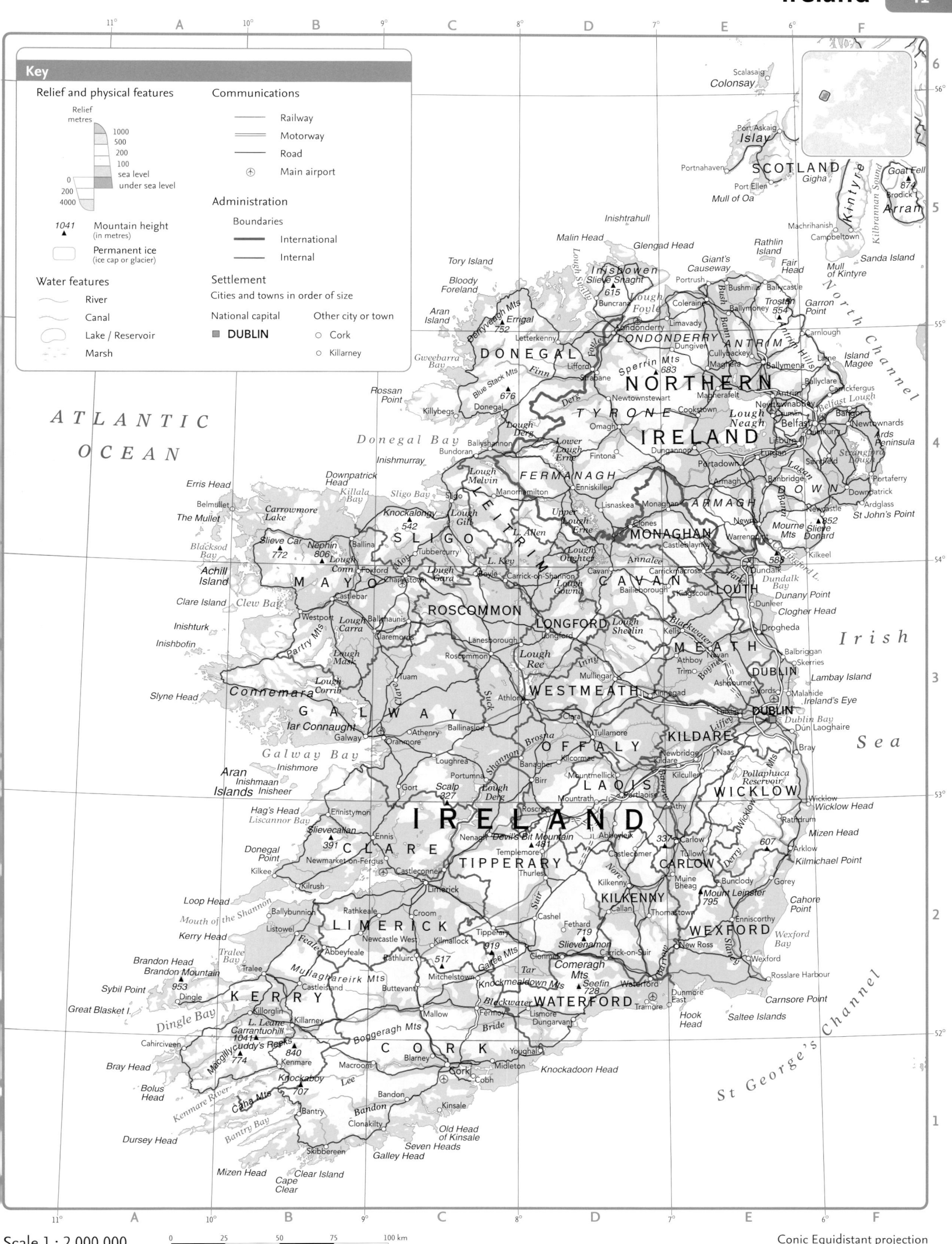

**Key**

Relief and physical features

Relief metres
1000
500
200
100
sea level
under sea level
0
200
4000

1041 ▲ Mountain height (in metres)

Permanent ice (ice cap or glacier)

Water features

River
Canal
Lake / Reservoir
Marsh

Communications

Railway
Motorway
Road
⊕ Main airport

Administration

Boundaries
International
Internal

Settlement

Cities and towns in order of size

National capital          Other city or town
■ DUBLIN                 ○ Cork
                          ○ Killarney

Scale 1 : 2 000 000

0    25    50    75    100 km

Conic Equidistant projection

**Key**

**Relief and physical features**

Relief
metres
5000
3000
2000
1000
500
200
0 sea level
200 under sea level
4000
6000

818 ▲ Mountain height
(in metres)

**Water features**

River
Canal
Lake / Reservoir
Marsh

**Communications**

Railway
Motorway
Road
⊕ Main airport

**Administration**
Boundaries

International
Internal

**Settlement**
Cities and towns in order of size

National capital | Other city or town
■ **PARIS** | ● **Rotterdam**
■ **AMSTERDAM** | ○ **Saarbrücken**
□ THE HAGUE | ○ Antwerp
□ LUXEMBOURG | ○ Leuven

Scale 1 : 2 000 000

0    20    40    60    80 km

Conic Equidistant projection

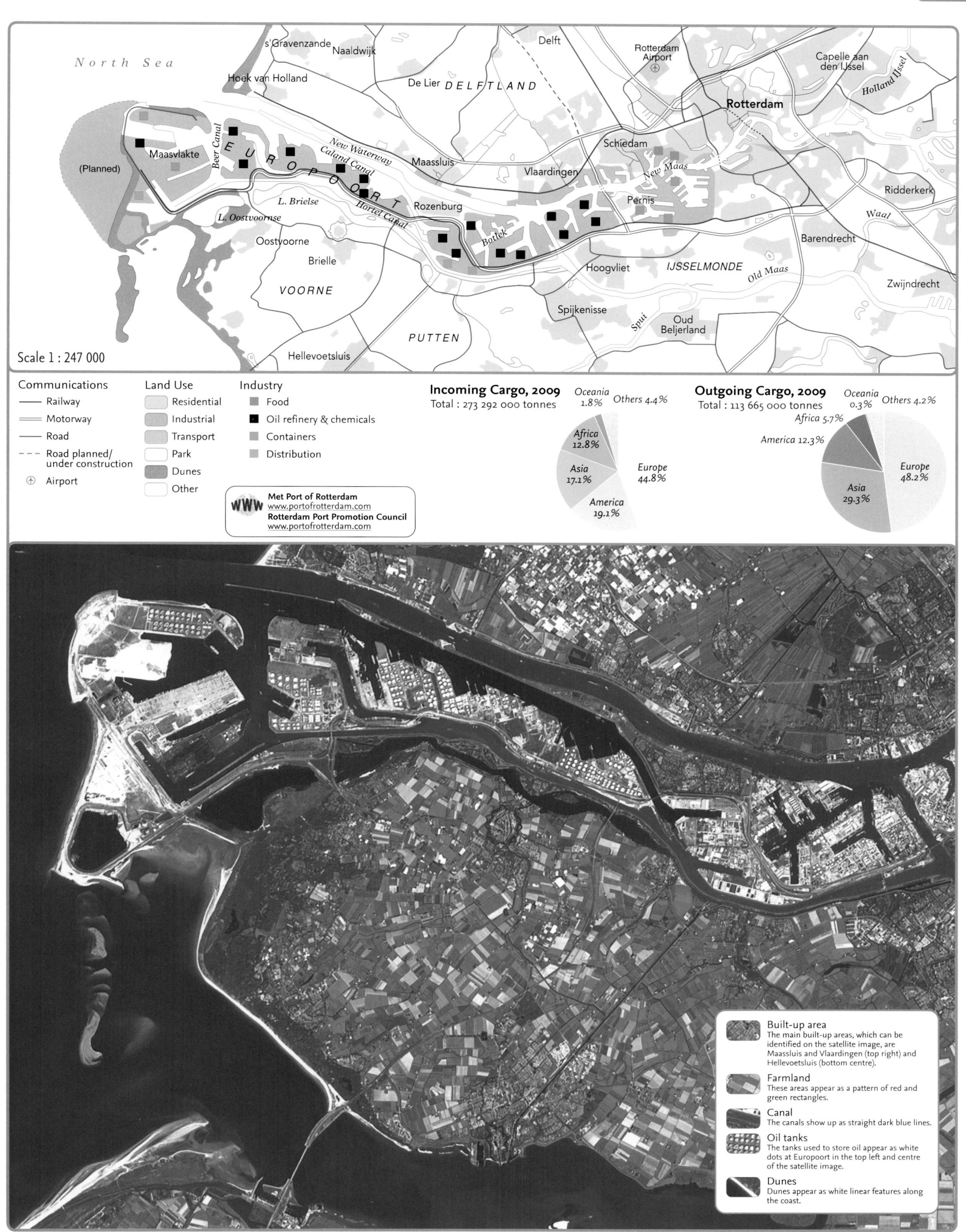

Scale 1 : 247 000

**Communications**
— Railway
═ Motorway
— Road
--- Road planned/ under construction
⊕ Airport

**Land Use**
Residential
Industrial
Transport
Park
Dunes
Other

**Industry**
■ Food
■ Oil refinery & chemicals
Containers
Distribution

www Met Port of Rotterdam
www.portofrotterdam.com
**Rotterdam Port Promotion Council**
www.portofrotterdam.com

**Incoming Cargo, 2009**
Total : 273 292 000 tonnes

Oceania 1.8%   Others 4.4%
Africa 12.8%
Asia 17.1%
Europe 44.8%
America 19.1%

**Outgoing Cargo, 2009**
Total : 113 665 000 tonnes

Oceania 0.3%   Others 4.2%
Africa 5.7%
America 12.3%
Asia 29.3%
Europe 48.2%

**Built-up area**
The main built-up areas, which can be identified on the satellite image, are Maassluis and Vlaardingen (top right) and Hellevoetsluis (bottom centre).

**Farmland**
These areas appear as a pattern of red and green rectangles.

**Canal**
The canals show up as straight dark blue lines.

**Oil tanks**
The tanks used to store oil appear as white dots at Europoort in the top left and centre of the satellite image.

**Dunes**
Dunes appear as white linear features along the coast.

## Key

### Relief and physical features

Relief
metres

5000
3000
2000
1000
500
200
sea level
0
under sea level
200
4000
6000

4808 ▲ Mountain height (in metres)

Permanent ice (ice cap or glacier)

### Water features

River
Intermittent river
Canal
Lake / Reservoir
Marsh

### Communications

Railway
Motorway
Road
Main airport

### Administration

Boundaries
International

### Settlement

Cities and towns in order of size

National capital

■ PARIS
■ LONDON
□ BERN
□ ANDORRA LA VELLA

Other city or town

● Marseille
○ Genoa
○ St-Étienne
○ Roscoff

AUS. AUSTRIA
LIECH. LIECHTENSTEIN

Scale 1 : 5 250 000

0    50    100    150    200 km

Lambert Conformal Conic projection

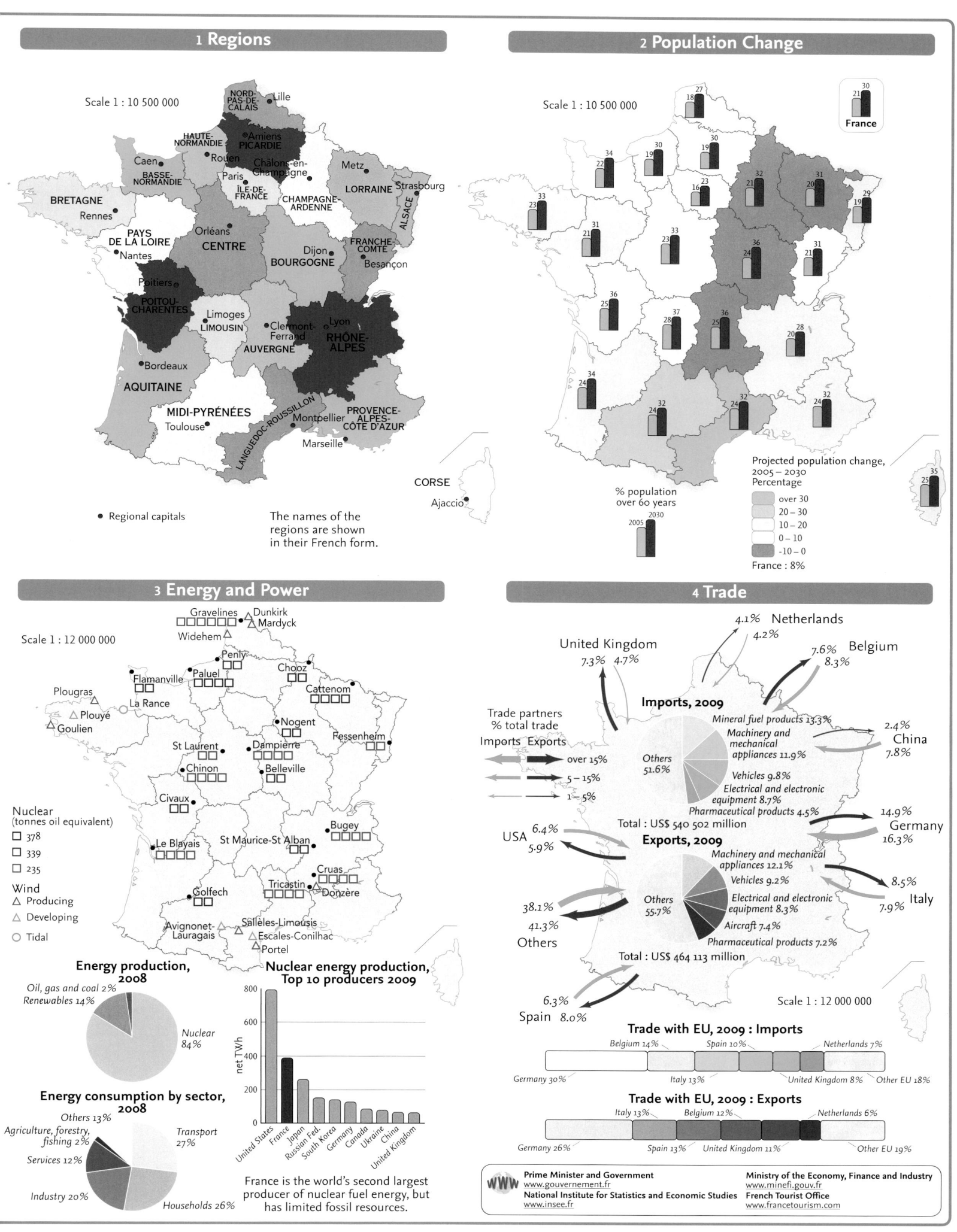

## 1 Regions

Scale 1 : 10 500 000

NORD-PAS-DE-CALAIS
Lille

HAUTE-NORMANDIE
Amiens
PICARDIE
Caen
Rouen
Châlons-en-Champagne
Metz
BASSE-NORMANDIE
Paris
LORRAINE
Strasbourg
BRETAGNE
ÎLE-DE-FRANCE
CHAMPAGNE-ARDENNE
ALSACE
Rennes
PAYS DE LA LOIRE
Orléans
CENTRE
Dijon
BOURGOGNE
FRANCHE-COMTÉ
Nantes
Besançon
Poitiers
POITOU-CHARENTES
Limoges
LIMOUSIN
Clermont-Ferrand
Lyon
RHÔNE-ALPES
AUVERGNE
Bordeaux
AQUITAINE
MIDI-PYRÉNÉES
Montpellier
PROVENCE-ALPES-CÔTE D'AZUR
Toulouse
LANGUEDOC-ROUSSILLON
Marseille

CORSE
Ajaccio

- Regional capitals

The names of the regions are shown in their French form.

## 2 Population Change

Scale 1 : 10 500 000

France

Projected population change,
2005 – 2030
Percentage

% population over 60 years

over 30
20 – 30
10 – 20
0 – 10
-10 – 0

2005   2030

France : 8%

## 3 Energy and Power

Scale 1 : 12 000 000

Gravelines   Dunkirk
Mardyck
Widehem
Penly
Flamanville   Paluel   Chooz
Plougras
La Rance   Cattenom
Plouyé
Goulien   Nogent
Fessenheim
St Laurent   Dampierre
Chinon   Belleville
Civaux
Bugey
Le Blayais   St Maurice-St Alban
Golfech   Cruas
Tricastin   Donzère
Avignonet-Lauragais   Salleles-Limouzis
Escales-Conilhac
Portel

Nuclear
(tonnes oil equivalent)
☐ 378
☐ 339
☐ 235

Wind
△ Producing
△ Developing
◯ Tidal

### Energy production, 2008

Oil, gas and coal 2%
Renewables 14%
Nuclear 84%

### Energy consumption by sector, 2008

Others 13%
Agriculture, forestry, fishing 2%
Services 12%
Industry 20%
Households 26%
Transport 27%

### Nuclear energy production, Top 10 producers 2009

net TWh

United States
France
Japan
Russian Fed.
South Korea
Germany
Canada
Ukraine
China
United Kingdom

France is the world's second largest producer of nuclear fuel energy, but has limited fossil resources.

## 4 Trade

Netherlands 4.1% / 4.2%
United Kingdom 7.3% / 4.7%
Belgium 7.6% / 8.3%

Trade partners
% total trade

Imports   Exports
over 15%
5 – 15%
1 – 5%

### Imports, 2009

Mineral fuel products 13.3%
Machinery and mechanical appliances 11.9%
Vehicles 9.8%
Electrical and electronic equipment 8.7%
Pharmaceutical products 4.5%
Others 51.6%

Total : US$ 540 502 million

China 2.4% / 7.8%
Germany 14.9% / 16.3%
Italy 8.5% / 7.9%

USA 6.4% / 5.9%

### Exports, 2009

Machinery and mechanical appliances 12.1%
Vehicles 9.2%
Electrical and electronic equipment 8.3%
Aircraft 7.4%
Pharmaceutical products 7.2%
Others 55.7%

Total : US$ 464 113 million

Others 38.1% / 41.3%

Spain 6.3% / 8.0%

Scale 1 : 12 000 000

### Trade with EU, 2009 : Imports

Germany 30%   Belgium 14%   Italy 13%   Spain 10%   United Kingdom 8%   Netherlands 7%   Other EU 18%

### Trade with EU, 2009 : Exports

Germany 26%   Italy 13%   Spain 13%   Belgium 12%   United Kingdom 11%   Netherlands 6%   Other EU 19%

www
Prime Minister and Government
www.gouvernement.fr
National Institute for Statistics and Economic Studies
www.insee.fr
Ministry of the Economy, Finance and Industry
www.minefi.gouv.fr
French Tourist Office
www.francetourism.com

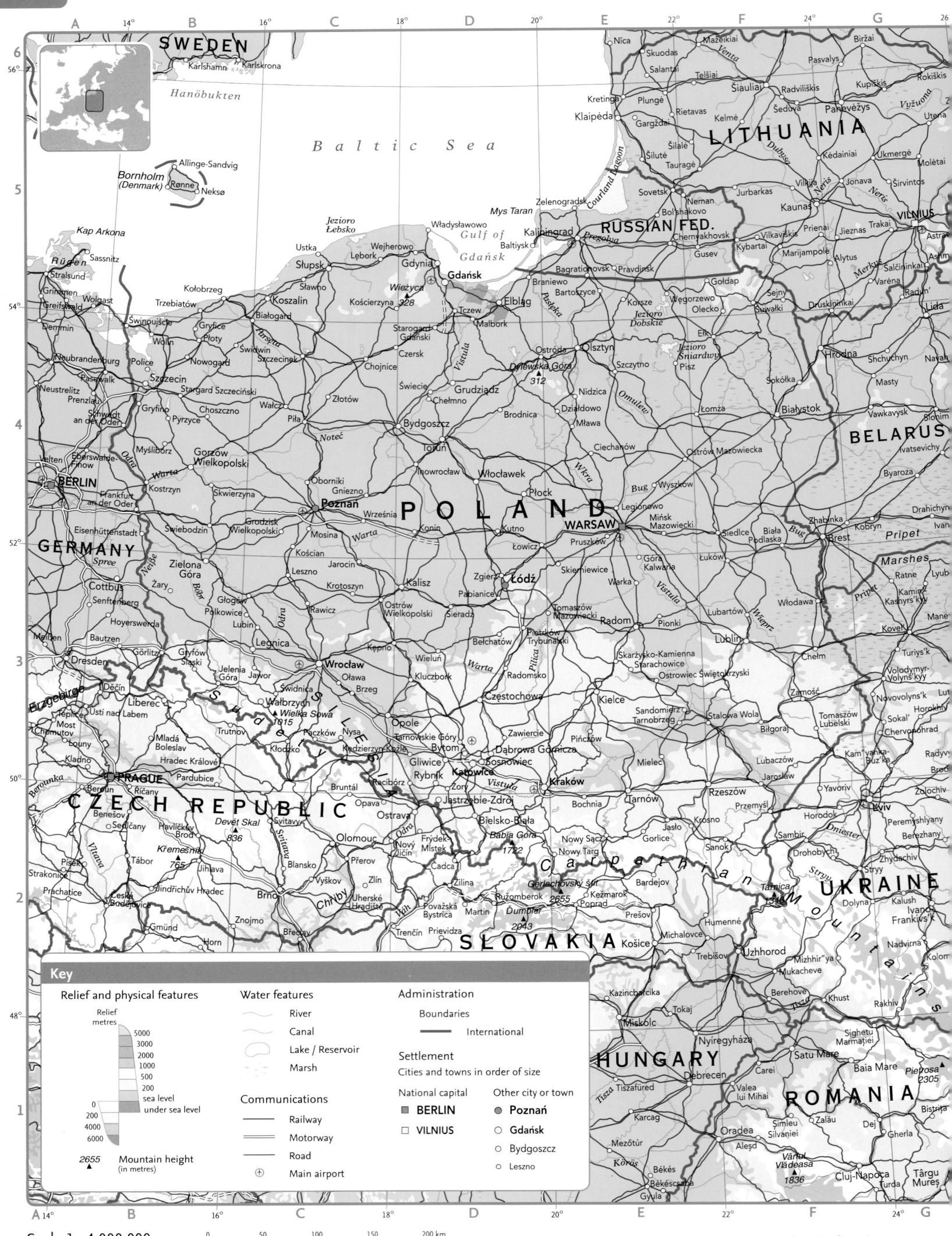

## Key

### Relief and physical features

Relief
metres
5000
3000
2000
1000
500
200
sea level
0
under sea level
200
4000
6000

2655 ▲ Mountain height
(in metres)

### Water features

～ River
～ Canal
◯ Lake / Reservoir
～ Marsh

### Communications

Railway
Motorway
Road
⊕ Main airport

### Administration

Boundaries
International

### Settlement

Cities and towns in order of size

National capital
■ BERLIN
□ VILNIUS

Other city or town
● Poznań
◯ Gdańsk
◦ Bydgoszcz
◦ Leszno

Scale 1 : 4 000 000

0    50    100    150    200 km

Lambert Conformal Conic projection

## 1 Regions

ZACHODNIOPOMORSKIE
• Szczecin

Gdańsk
POMORSKIE

WARMIŃSKO-MAZURSKIE
• Olsztyn

Bydgoszcz
KUJAWSKO-POMORSKIE

PODLASKIE
• Białystok

• Gorzów Wielkopolski

• Poznań
WIELKOPOLSKIE

MAZOWIECKIE
• Warsaw

LUBUSKIE

• Łódź
ŁÓDZKIE

DOLNOŚLĄSKIE
• Wrocław

Lublin
LUBELSKIE

OPOLSKIE
Opole

ŚLĄSKIE
• Kielce
ŚWIĘTOKRZYSKIE

• Katowice

• Kraków
MAŁOPOLSKIE

• Rzeszów
PODKARPACKIE

• Regional capitals

The names of the regions are shown in their Polish form.

Scale 1 : 8 000 000

## 2 Population

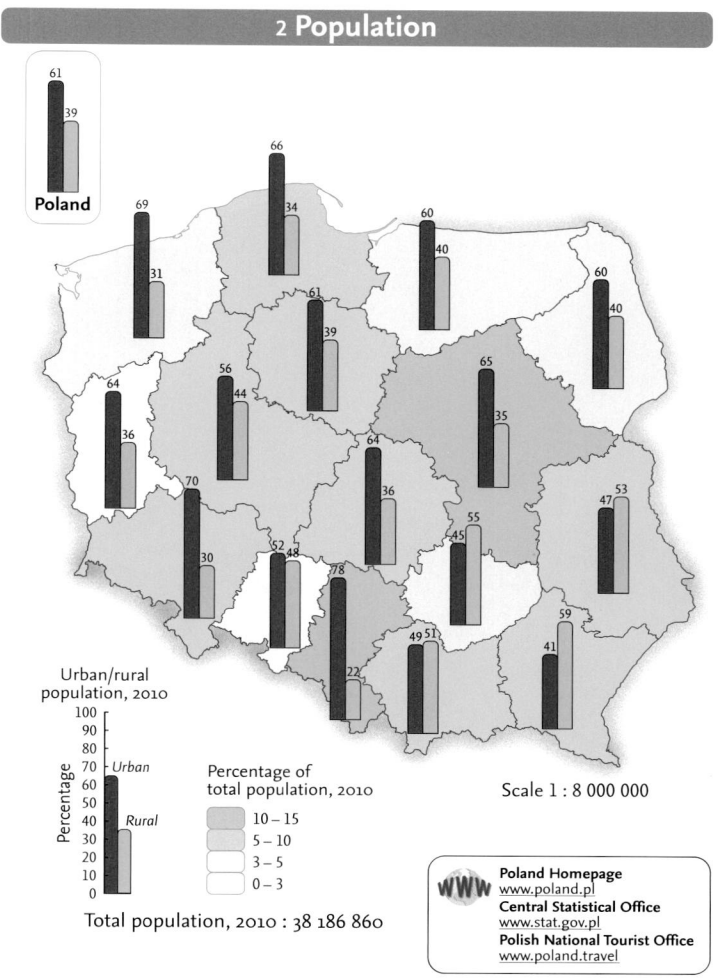

61 39
Poland

Urban/rural population, 2010

Percentage
Urban
Rural

Percentage of total population, 2010
10 – 15
5 – 10
3 – 5
0 – 3

Scale 1 : 8 000 000

Total population, 2010 : 38 186 860

WWW Poland Homepage
www.poland.pl
Central Statistical Office
www.stat.gov.pl
Polish National Tourist Office
www.poland.travel

## 3 Minerals and Energy

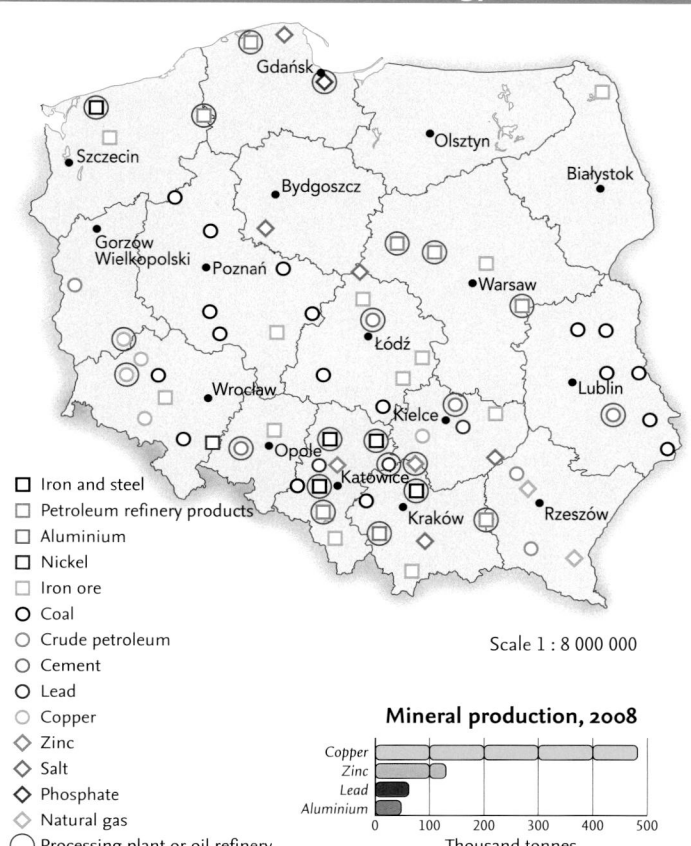

• Szczecin
Gdańsk
• Olsztyn
• Białystok
• Bydgoszcz
Gorzów Wielkopolski
• Poznań
• Warsaw
• Łódź
• Wrocław
• Lublin
• Kielce
• Opole
Katowice
• Kraków
• Rzeszów

☐ Iron and steel
☐ Petroleum refinery products
☐ Aluminium
☐ Nickel
☐ Iron ore
○ Coal
○ Crude petroleum
○ Cement
○ Lead
○ Copper
◇ Zinc
◇ Salt
◇ Phosphate
◇ Natural gas
○ Processing plant or oil refinery

Scale 1 : 8 000 000

### Mineral production, 2008

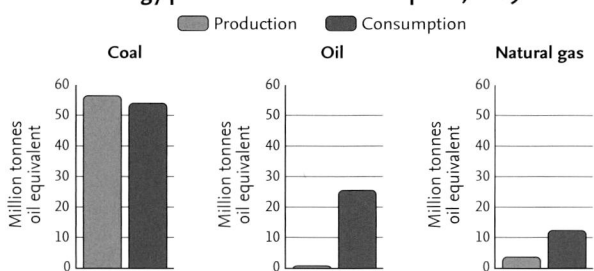

Copper
Zinc
Lead
Aluminium

0   100   200   300   400   500
Thousand tonnes

### Energy production and consumption, 2009

Production   Consumption

**Coal**
Million tonnes oil equivalent
60 50 40 30 20 10 0

**Oil**
Million tonnes oil equivalent
60 50 40 30 20 10 0

**Natural gas**
Million tonnes oil equivalent
60 50 40 30 20 10 0

## 4 Conservation

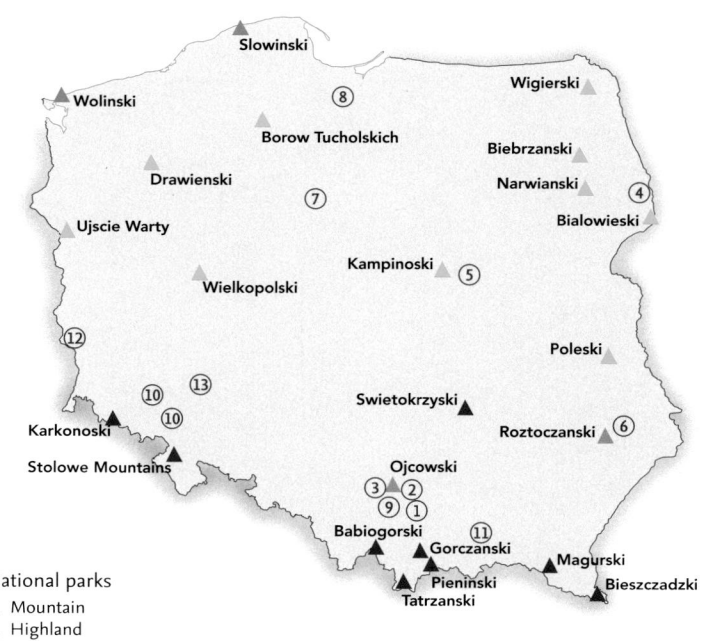

Slowinski
Wolinski
Wigierski
Borow Tucholskich
Biebrzanski
Drawienski
Narwianski
Ujscie Warty
Bialowieski
Kampinoski
Wielkopolski
Poleski
Karkonoski
Swietokrzyski
Roztoczanski
Stolowe Mountains
Ojcowski
Babiogorski
Gorczanski
Magurski
Pieninski
Bieszczadzki
Tatrzanski

National parks
▲ Mountain
▲ Highland
▲ Lowland/forest/lake
▲ Coastal

Scale 1 : 8 000 000

World Heritage sites
① Wieliczka Salt Mine
② Cracow's Historic Centre
③ Auschwitz Birkenau
④ Belovezhskaya Pushcha / Bialowieza Forest
⑤ Historic Centre of Warsaw
⑥ Old City of Zamosc
⑦ Medieval Town of Torun
⑧ Castle of the Teutonic Order in Malbork
⑨ Kalwaria Zebrzydowska: the Mannerist Architectural and Park Landscape Complex and Pilgrimage Park
⑩ Churches of Peace in Jawor and Swidnica
⑪ Wooden Churches of Southern Little Poland
⑫ Muskauer Park / Park Muzakowski
⑬ Centennial Hall in Wrocław

## Key

**Relief and physical features**

Relief metres

5000
3000
2000
1000
500
200
0 sea level
under sea level
200
4000
6000

▲ 3482  Mountain height (in metres)

**Water features**

River
Intermittent river
Canal
Lake / Reservoir
Marsh

**Communications**

Railway
Motorway
Road
⊕ Main airport

**Administration**

Boundaries
International

**Settlement**

Cities and towns in order of size

National capital
■ **MADRID**
□ ANDORRA LA VELLA

Other city or town
● Barcelona
○ Seville
○ Pamplona
○ Benidorm

Scale 1 : 5 250 000

0   50   100   150   200 km

Lambert Conformal Conic projection

## 1 Regions

Santiago de Compostela
GALICIA
Oviedo · ASTURIAS · CANTABRIA · Santander
PAÍS VASCO
Vitoria-Gasteiz · NAVARRA · Pamplona
Logroño · LA RIOJA
CASTILLA Y LEÓN
Valladolid
Zaragoza · ARAGÓN · CATALUÑA
Barcelona
MADRID · Madrid
ILLES BALEARS
Toledo
EXTREMADURA · CASTILLA-LA MANCHA · VALENCIA · Valencia
Palma de Mallorca
Mérida
Murcia · MURCIA
ANDALUCÍA
Seville

Scale 1 : 12 000 000

ISLAS CANARIAS
Santa Cruz de Tenerife
Las Palmas de Gran Canaria

• Regional capitals

The names of the regions are shown in their Spanish form.

## 2 Population Change and Internal Migration

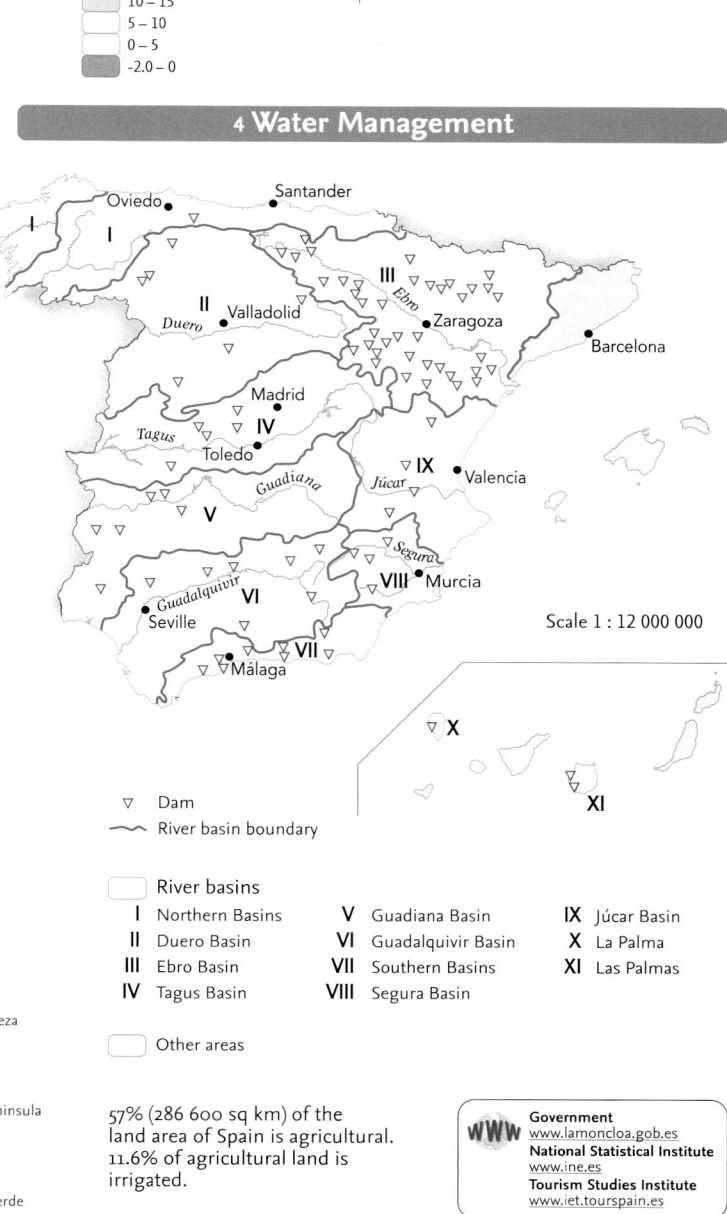

Main population movement, 2008
→ over 10 000 people
→ 7500 – 10 000 people
→ 3500 – 7500 people

ASTURIAS · CANTABRIA · PAÍS VASCO · NAVARRA
GALICIA · LA RIOJA
CASTILLA Y LEÓN
ARAGÓN · CATALUÑA
MADRID
EXTREMADURA · CASTILLA-LA MANCHA · VALENCIA
ILLES BALEARS
ANDALUCÍA
MURCIA

Scale 1 : 12 000 000

ISLAS CANARIAS

Population change, 1998 – 2008
Percentage
over 20
15 – 20
10 – 15
5 – 10
0 – 5
-2.0 – 0

## 3 Tourism

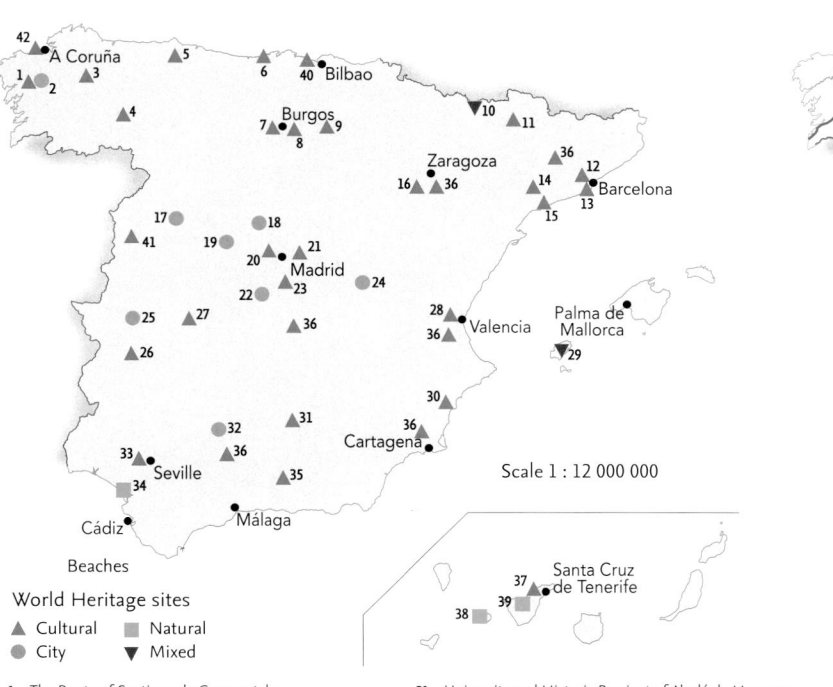

42 A Coruña
1
2
3
5
6 · 40 · Bilbao
4
7 · Burgos · 9
8
10
11
Zaragoza
16 · 36 · 36
14
15
36
12
Barcelona
13
17
41 · 18
19
20 · 21
22 · Madrid · 23
24
25 · 27
26
28 · Valencia
36
Palma de Mallorca
29
30
32 · 31
36
33 · 36
34 · Seville
35
Cádiz
Málaga
Cartagena

Scale 1 : 12 000 000

Santa Cruz de Tenerife
37
39
38

Beaches

World Heritage sites
▲ Cultural   ■ Natural
● City        ▼ Mixed

1  The Route of Santiago de Compostela
2  Santiago de Compostela (Old Town)
3  Roman Walls of Lugo
4  Las Médulas
5  Monuments of Oviedo and the Kingdom of the Asturias
6  Cave of Altamira and Paleolithic Cave Art of Northern Spain
7  Burgos Cathedral
8  Archaeological Site of Atapuerca
9  San Millan Yuso and Suso Monasteries
10 Pyrenees - Mount Perdu
11 Catalan Romanesque Churches of the Vall de Boi
12 Works of Antoni Gaudi
13 The Palau de la Musica Catalana and the Hospital de Sant Pau, Barcelona
14 Poblet Monastery
15 The archaeological ensemble of Tarraco
16 Mudejar Architecture of Aragón
17 Old City of Salamanca
18 Old Town of Segovia, including its aqueduct
19 Old Town of Ávila, including its Extra Muros churches
20 Monastery and Site of the Escorial, Madrid
21 University and Historic Precinct of Alcalá de Henares
22 Historic City of Toledo
23 Aranjuez Cultural Landscape
24 Historic Walled Town of Cuenca
25 Old Town of Cáceres
26 Archaeological Ensemble of Mérida
27 Royal Monastery of Santa Maria de Guadalupe
28 "La Lonja de la Seda" of Valencia
29 Ibiza, Biodiversity and Culture
30 The Palmeral of Elche
31 Renaissance Monumental Ensembles of Úbeda and Baeza
32 Historic Centre of Córdoba
33 Cathedral, the Alcazar and Archivo de Indias, Seville
34 Doñana National Park
35 Alhambra, Generalife and Albayzin, Granada
36 Rock-Art of the Mediterranean Basin on the Iberian Peninsula
37 San Cristóbal de la Laguna
38 Garajonay National Park
39 Teide National Park
40 Vizcaya Bridge
41 Prehistoric Rock Art Sites in the Côa Valley and Siega Verde
42 Tower of Hercules

## 4 Water Management

Oviedo · Santander
I · I
II · Valladolid
III
Duero · Ebro · Zaragoza
Barcelona
Madrid
Tagus · IV
Toledo
Guadiana · Júcar · IX
V · Valencia
VIII · Murcia
VI · Segura
Guadalquivir
Seville
VII
Málaga
X
XI

Scale 1 : 12 000 000

▽ Dam
⌒ River basin boundary

River basins
I    Northern Basins        V    Guadiana Basin       IX  Júcar Basin
II   Duero Basin            VI   Guadalquivir Basin    X   La Palma
III  Ebro Basin             VII  Southern Basins       XI  Las Palmas
IV   Tagus Basin            VIII Segura Basin

Other areas

57% (286 600 sq km) of the land area of Spain is agricultural. 11.6% of agricultural land is irrigated.

WWW  Government
www.lamoncloa.gob.es
National Statistical Institute
www.ine.es
Tourism Studies Institute
www.iet.tourspain.es

**Key**

Administration

Boundaries

International

Settlement

Cities and towns in order of size

National capital

**ROME**

□ **SARAJEVO**

□ BERN

□ SAN MARINO

Other city or town

● **Milan**

○ **Genoa**

○ Venice

○ Ragusa

**Key**

Relief and physical features

Relief metres

5000
3000
2000
1000
500
200
sea level
under sea level
0
200
4000
6000

Water features

River

Canal

Lake / Reservoir

Communications

Railway

Motorway

Road

4808 ▲ Mountain height (in metres)

Main airport

Permanent ice (ice cap or glacier)

Scale 1 : 5 250 000

0    50    100    150    200 km

Lambert Conformal Conic projection

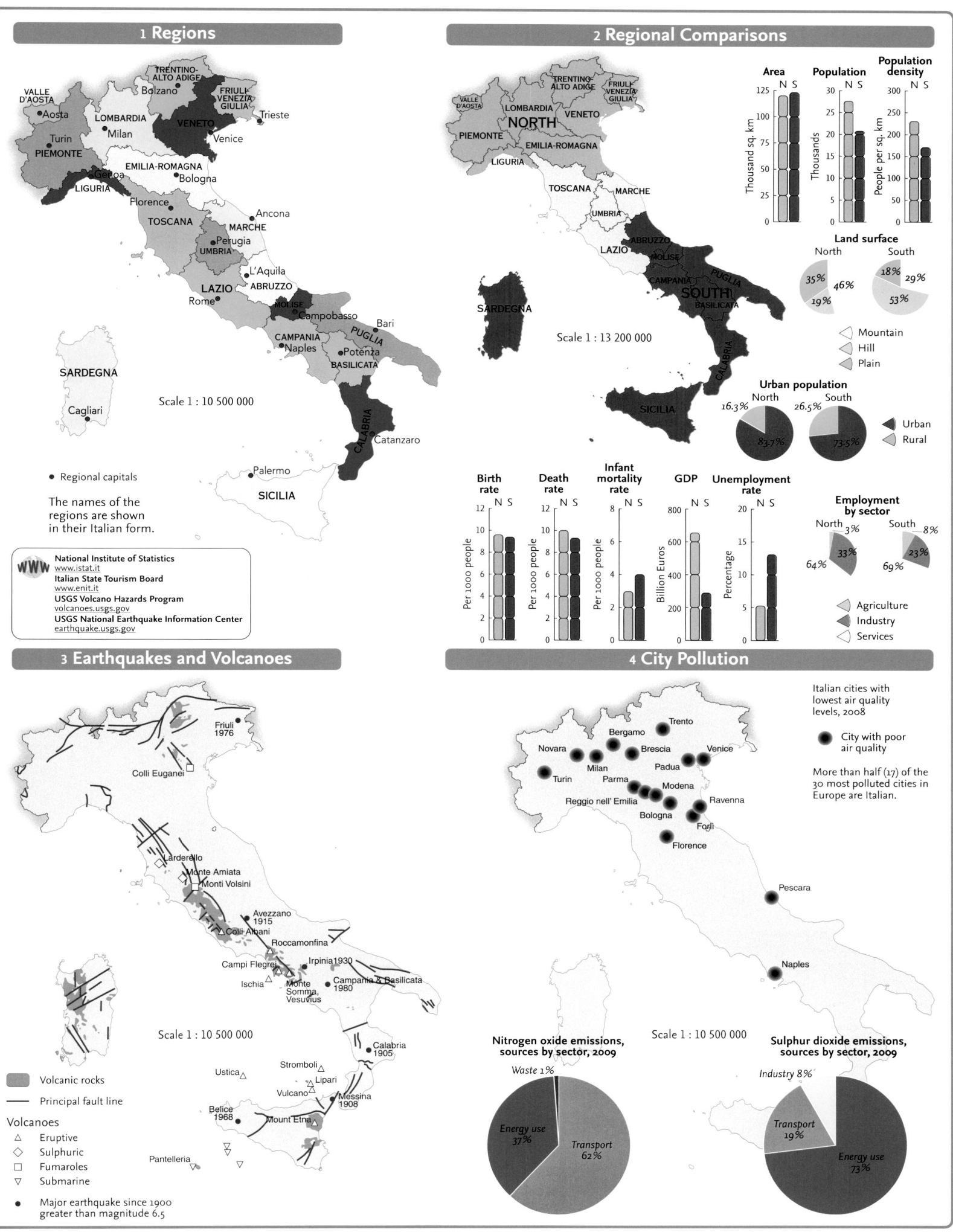

## 1 Regions

## 2 Regional Comparisons

## 3 Earthquakes and Volcanoes

## 4 City Pollution

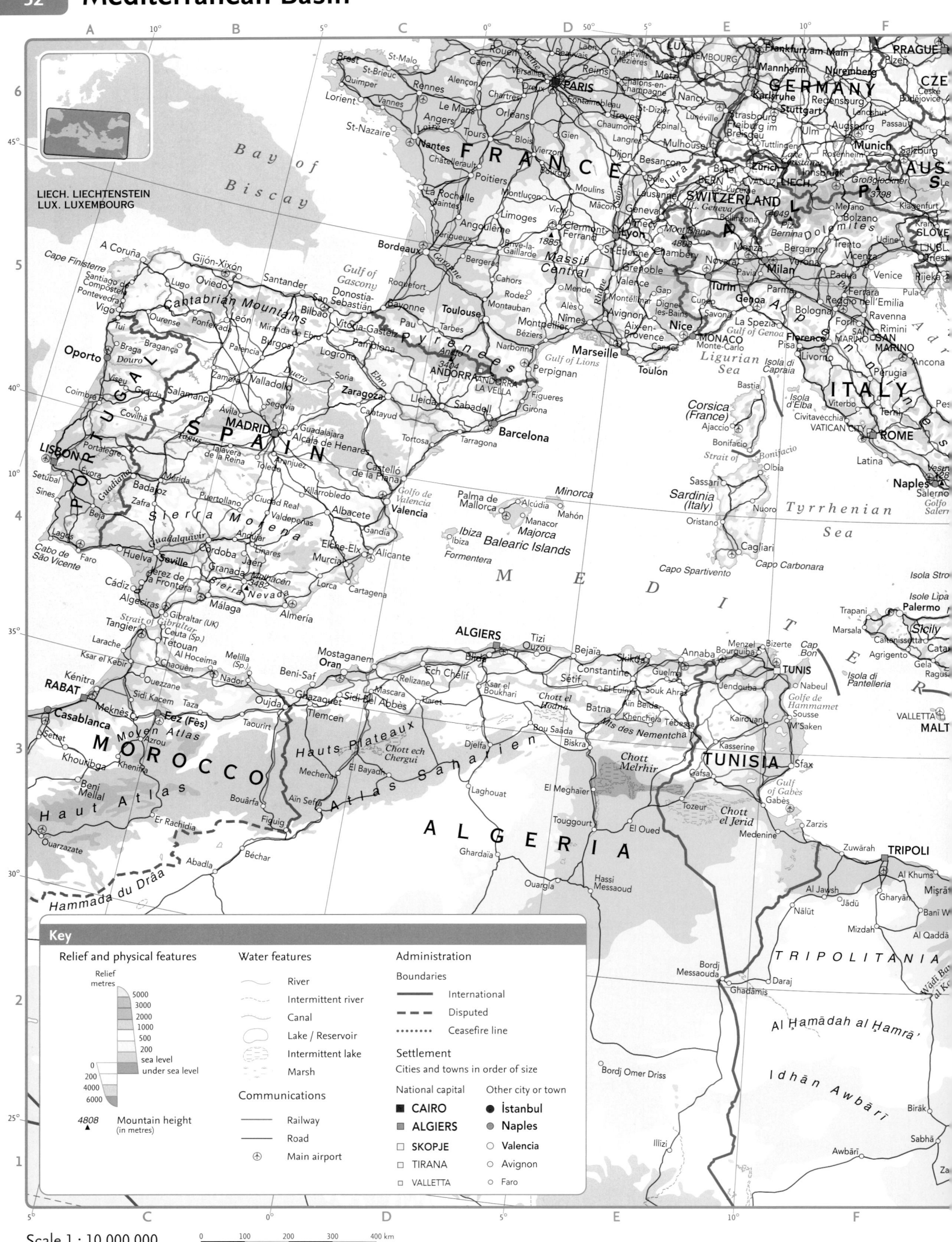

## Key

### Relief and physical features

Relief metres

5000
3000
2000
1000
500
200
sea level
under sea level

0
200
4000
6000

▲ 4808   Mountain height
(in metres)

### Water features

〜 River

〜 Intermittent river

〜 Canal

Lake / Reservoir

Intermittent lake

Marsh

### Communications

Railway

Road

✈ Main airport

### Administration

Boundaries

——— International

– – – Disputed

········· Ceasefire line

### Settlement

Cities and towns in order of size

National capital

■ CAIRO
■ ALGIERS
□ SKOPJE
□ TIRANA
□ VALLETTA

Other city or town

● İstanbul
● Naples
○ Valencia
○ Avignon
○ Faro

Scale 1 : 10 000 000

0   100   200   300   400 km

0    50    100    150    200 km

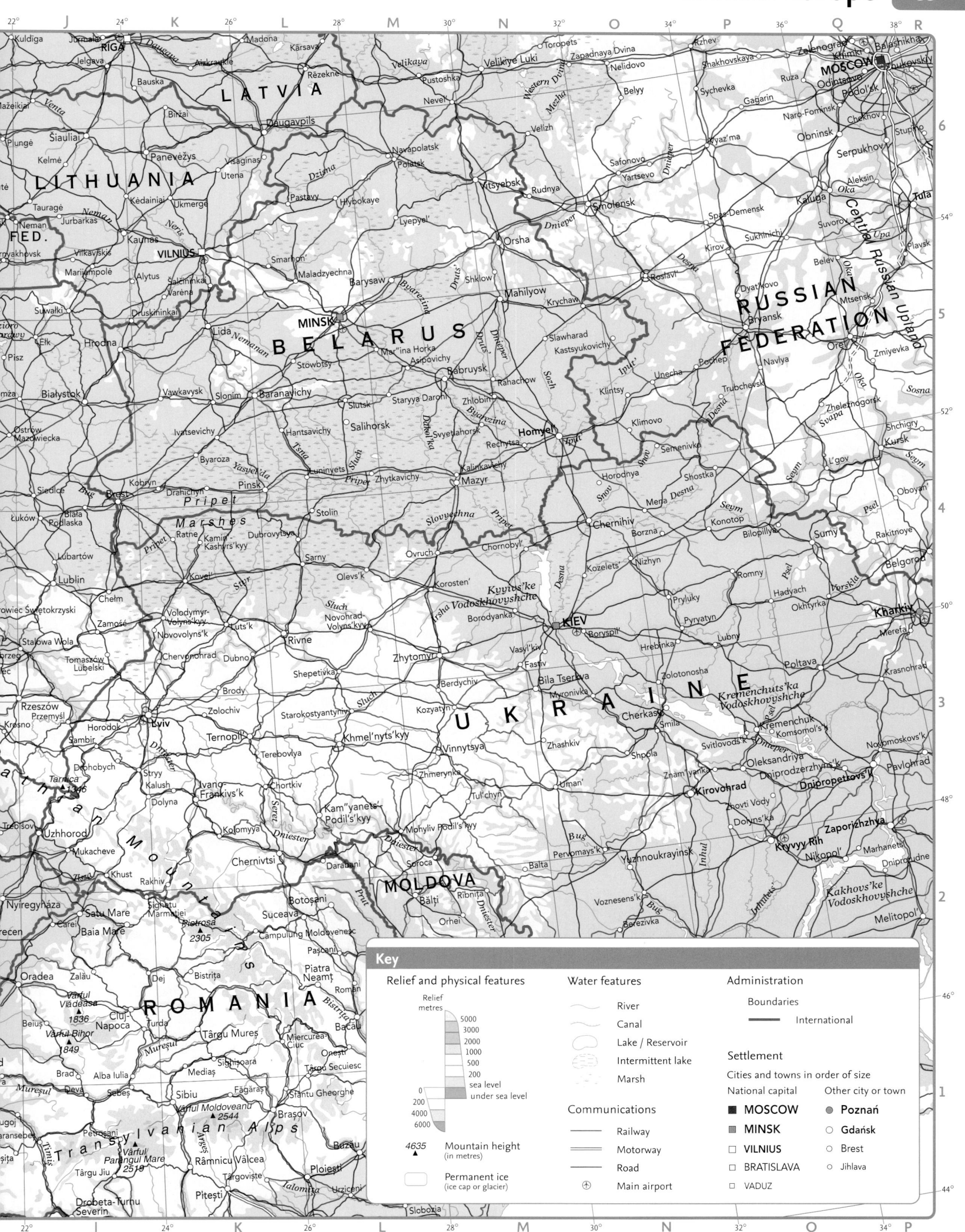

**Key**

**Relief and physical features**

Relief
metres
5000
3000
2000
1000
500
200
sea level
under sea level
0
200
4000
6000

4635 ▲ Mountain height
(in metres)

Permanent ice
(ice cap or glacier)

**Water features**

~~~ River

~~~ Canal

Lake / Reservoir

Intermittent lake

Marsh

**Communications**

Railway

Motorway

Road

⊕ Main airport

**Administration**

Boundaries

International

**Settlement**

Cities and towns in order of size

National capital          Other city or town

■ MOSCOW                ● Poznań

■ MINSK                   ○ Gdańsk

□ VILNIUS                 ○ Brest

□ BRATISLAVA             ○ Jihlava

□ VADUZ

Conic Equidistant projection

## Key

### Relief and physical features

Relief
metres

5000
3000
2000
1000
500
200
sea level
0
200
4000
6000
under sea level

▲ 3917   Mountain height
(in metres)

### Water features

~~~~~ River

-·-·- Intermittent river

~~~ Canal

⬭ Lake / Reservoir

⬭ Intermittent lake

Marsh

### Communications

—— Railway

═══ Motorway

—— Road

⊕ Main airport

### Administration

Boundaries

—— International

- - - Disputed

····· Ceasefire line

### Settlement

Cities and towns in order of size

National capital    Other city or town

▣ **ATHENS**     ● İstanbul

▢ SARAJEVO    ◓ Bursa

▢ NICOSIA     ○ Antalya

              ○ Split

              ○ Dubrovnik

Scale 1 : 5 000 000

0   50   100   150   200 km

**MOLDOVA**

Comrat
Cahul
Artsyz
Tatarbunary
Bolhrad
Reni İzmayil
aila
rşova
ernavodă
Tulcea
Babadag
*Danube Delta*
Sulina

**UKRAINE**

Odesa
Bijhorod-Dnistrovs'kyy
Skadovs'k
Armyans'k
Chornomors'ke
Krasnoperekops'k
Henicheś'k
Novooleksiyivka

*Sea of Azov*

**RUSSIAN FEDERATION**

Primorsko-Akhtarsk
Tikhoretsk
Timashevsk
Slavyansk-na-Kubani
Temryuk
*Kuban'*
Krymsk
Anapa
**Krasnodar**
*Tshchikskove Vodokhranilishche*
Maykop
Khadyzhensk
Psebay

**Crimea**

Dzhankoy
Nyzhn'ohirs'kyy
Kerch

Yevpatoriya
Simferopol'
Feodosiya
Sudak
Sevastopol'
Yalta

Novorossiysk
*Caucasus*
Tuapse
Sochi
Gagra
**GEORGIA**
Sokhumi

Constanța
Mangalia
rich
Kavarna
*Nos Kaliakra*
rna

*B l a c k   S e a*

ğneada Burnu

Sinop
İnebolu
Bafra
Samsun
Terme
Rize

Zonguldak
Bartın
Kastamonu
Boyabat
Vezirköprü
*Yeşilırmak*
Ordu
Giresun
Trabzon

Ereğli
Karabük
*Devrez*
Tosya
Osmancık
Merzifon
Niksar
Gümüşhane
Şebinkarahisar
Bayburt

ray
Sarıyer
Beykoz
Kandıra
*Bosporus*
İzmit
Adapazarı
Düzce
Bolu
Gerede
*Köroğlu Tepesi 2400*
Mudurnu
Beypazarı
Çankırı
*Kızılırmak*
Çorum
Turhal
*Yeşilırmak*
Amasya
Tokat
Suşehri
*Kızıl Dağı 3025*
Zara
Erzincan

**İstanbul**
Kadıköy
**Bakırköy**
**Kartal**
Körfez
Yalova
Gölcük
Geyve
Göynük
*Sakarya*
Bilecik
İnegöl
Bozüyük
Eskişehir
*Porsuk*
Polatlı
**Keçiören**
Etimesgut
**ANKARA**
**Çankaya**
Kırıkkale
*Delice*
Yozgat
Akdağmadeni
Sivas
Divriği
Tunceli
*Keban Barajı*

*Sea of Marmara*
andırma
İafakemalpaşa
**Bursa**
*Uludağ 2493*
Susurluk
alikesir
Simav
Kütahya
Tavşanlı
Sivrihisar
Yunak
Kaman
Kırşehir
Boğazlıyan
Şarkışla
Kangal
Arapgir
Elazığ

Demirci
Eski Gediz
Emirdağ
*Sakarya*
Cihanbeyli
*Kızılırmak*
Pınarbaşı

isar
hisar
Uşak
Banaz
Afyon
**T U R K E Y**
*Lake Tuz*
Avanos
Nevşehir
Kayseri
*Erciyes Dağı 3917*
Malatya
Ergani

Salihli
Alaşehir
*Gediz*
Sandıklı
Akşehir
Aksaray
Göksun
Elbistan
Adıyaman
Siverek

demiş
lın
Nazilli
iyükmenderes
Civril
*Gelincik Dağı 2799*
*A n a t o l i a*
*Eğirdir Gölü*
Bor
Niğde
*Demirkazık Tepe 3756*
Kahramanmaraş
*Atatürk Barajı*
Viranşehir

Denizli
Dinar
Isparta
Eğirdir
*Beyşehir Gölü*
Karapınar
Ereğli
*Medetsiz Tepe 3524*
Kozan
Kadirli
Gaziantep
Nizip
Birecik
Şanlıurfa

Muğla
Burdur
Korkuteli
*Geyik Dağ 2877*
Karaman
*T a u r u s   M o u n t a i n s*
Ceyhan
Kozan
Osmaniye
Kilis
Akçakale

as
Yatağan
Marmaris
Dalaman
Serik
Karaman
Seydişehir
Seyhan
**Adana**
Tarsus
Mersin
İskenderun
İskenderun Körfezi
Antakya
*Euphrates*
*Batın*

Rhodes
Fethiye
Kaş
Elmalı
*3073*
**Antalya**
Manavgat
Ermenek
Mut
Erdemli
Kırıkhan
**Aleppo**
*Buhayrat al Asad*
Ar Raqqah

*Antalya Körfezi*
Alanya
Silifke
Anamur
Samandağı
İdlib
Madınat ath Thawrah

Lindos

*Rhodes*

*Cape Apostolos Andreas*

Latakia
Jablah
Bāniyās
**Hamāh**
*J. an Nuşayrīyah*

Aigialousa
Kyrenia
Famagusta
**S Y R I A**

*Cape Arnauti*
Polis
**NICOSIA**
*Mount Troödos 1951*
**CYPRUS**
Larnaca
Tartūs
Homs
Tadmur

Paphos
Limassol

Tripoli
*Qornet es Saouda 3088*
Al Qaryatayn

*S E A*

**LEBANON**
**BEIRUT**
Zahlé
An Nabk
Sab' Ābār

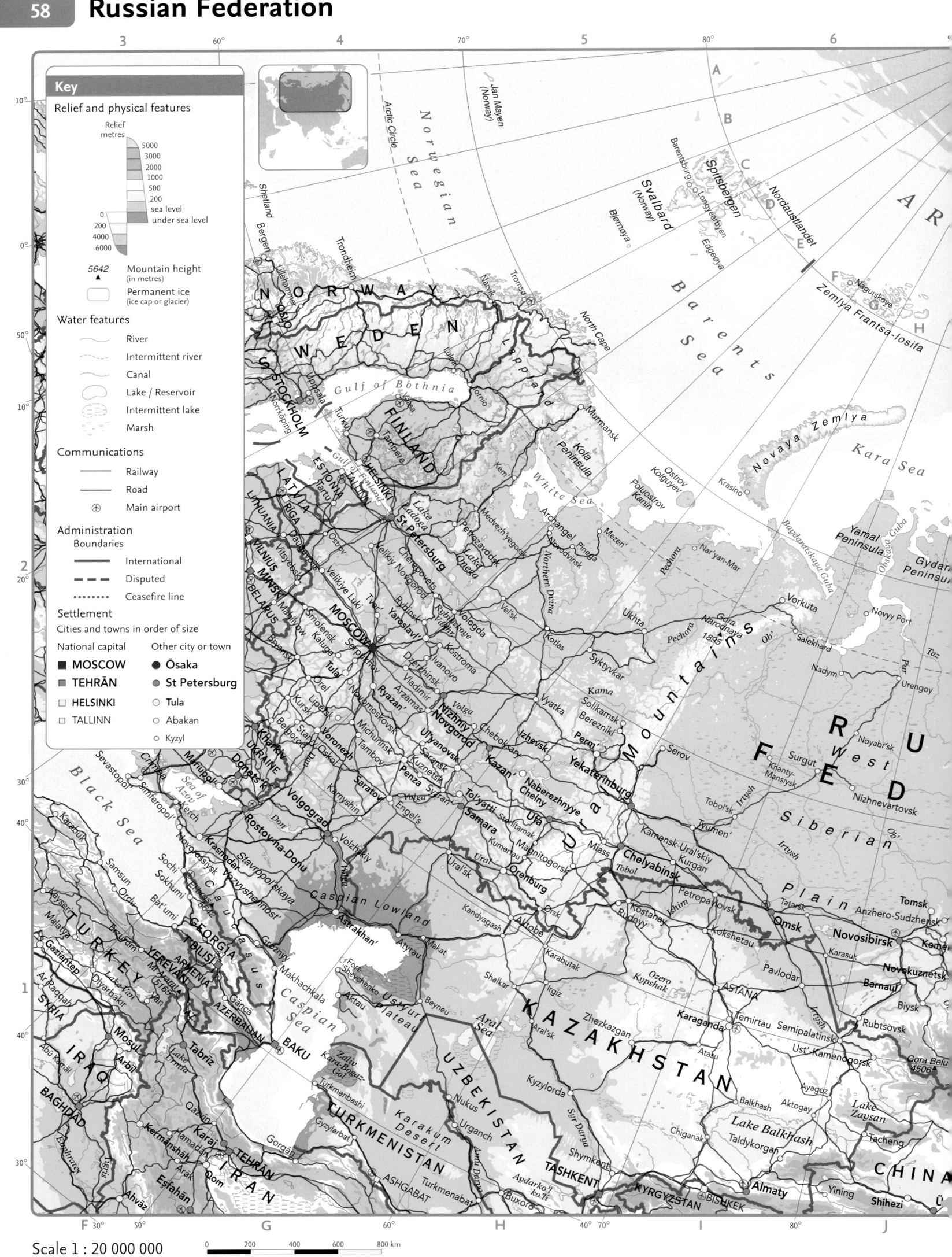

**Key**

Relief and physical features

Relief
metres

5000
3000
2000
1000
500
200
0 sea level
under sea level
200
4000
6000

5642 ▲ Mountain height (in metres)

Permanent ice (ice cap or glacier)

Water features

~ River

Intermittent river

Canal

Lake / Reservoir

Intermittent lake

Marsh

Communications

Railway

Road

⊕ Main airport

Administration
Boundaries

International

Disputed

Ceasefire line

Settlement
Cities and towns in order of size

National capital        Other city or town

■ MOSCOW          ● Ōsaka

■ TEHRĀN           ● St Petersburg

□ HELSINKI          ○ Tula

□ TALLINN           ○ Abakan

                    ○ Kyzyl

Scale 1 : 20 000 000

0    200   400   600   800 km

ARCTIC OCEAN

Ostrov
Komsomolets

Ostrov Oktyabr'skoy
Revolyutsii

Severnaya
Zemlya

Ostrov Bol'shevik

Proliv Vil'kitskogo

J K L M N

Severnaya
Zemlya

Taymyr Peninsula

Gory Byrranga

North Siberian Lowland

Ozero
Taymyr

Khatangskiy Zaliv

Nordvik

Ust'-Olenek

Olenek

Olenekskiy
Zaliv

Tiksi

Bulun

New Siberia Islands

Ostrov
Novaya Sibir'

Ostrov
Kotel'nyy

Ostrov Bol'shoy
Lyakhovskiy

Laptev
Sea

East Siberian Sea

Wrangel Island

Proliv Longa

Chukchi
Sea

Point
Hope

Arctic Circle

Kotzebue

Seward
Peninsula

Norton Sound

Nome

St Lawrence
Island

Cape
Romanzof

Nunivak
Island

U.S.A.

Bering
Strait

Chukotskiy
Poluostrov

Iul'tin

Anadyrskiy
Zaliv

St Matthew I.

Bering

Sea

Pyasina

Popigay

Anabar

Kheta

Khatanga

Kotuy

Yanskiy
Zaliv

Yana

Kazach'ye

Srednekolymsk

Verkhoyansk

Adycha

Khrebet Cherskogo

Mama

Gora Pobeda
3003

El'ginskiy

Indigirka

Kolyma

Bol'shoy Anyuy

Omolon

Matvy Anyuy

Ambarchik

Beluga

Anadyr'

Velikaya

Seymchan

Omsukchan

Susuman

Strelka

Palatka

Magadan

Okhotsk

Kamenskoye

Gizhiga

Zaliv
Shelikhova

Penzhinskaya Guba

Palana

Korekskiy Khrebet

Olyutorskiy
Zaliv

Karaginskiy
Zaliv

Ust'-Kamchatsk

Kamchatka

Sopka
Klyuchevskaya 4750

Petropavlovsk-
Kamchatskiy

Peninsula

Sea
of
Okhotsk

Ozernovskiy

Severo-Kuril'sk

Indika

Noril'sk

Gory Kamen'
1678

Ozero
Khantayskoye

Nizhnyaya Tunguska

Tembenchi

Tura

Taymura

Podkamennaya Tunguska

S I B E R I A N

Siberia

Central

Siberian

Plateau

Chunya

Vilyuy

Markha

Nyurba

Chernyshevskiy

Mirnyy

Verkhnevilyuysk

Vilyuy

Olenek

Muna

Olenek

Olenek

Lena

Verkhoyanskiy Khrebet

Aldan

Allakh-Yun'

Yakutsk

Ust'-Maya

Maya

Aldan

Lena

Lena

Uchur

Khrebet Dzhugdzhur

Ayan

Okha

Shantarskiye
Ostrova

Uda

Sakhalin

Aleksandrovsk-
Sakhalinskiy

Tatarskiy Proliv

Poronaysk

Uglegorsk

Yuzhno-Sakhalinsk

Korsakov

Kuril'sk
Administered
by Rus Fed
Claimed by Japan

Kuril Islands

Wakkanai

Asahi-
dake
2290

Asahikawa

Hokkaido

Kushiro

Yeniseysk

Angara

Achinsk

Kansk

Krasnoyarsk

Nizhneudinsk

Abakan

Zapadnyy Sayan

Vostochnyy Sayan

R A T I O N

Lena

Vitim

Olëkma

Stanovoy Khrebet

Tynda

Zeya

Skovorodino

Svobodnyy

Blagoveshchensk

Amur

Komsomol'sk-
na-Amure

Khabarovsk

Amur

Sikhote-Alin'

Sapporo

Hakodate

Hachinohe

Aomori

Ust'-Ilimsk

Ust'-Kut

Bratsk

Lena

Lake
Baikal

Kachug

Usol'ye-
Sibirskoye

Irkutsk

Ulan-Ude

Sretensk

Chita

Karymskoye

Argun'

Baykal'

Nizhneudinsk

Kyzyl

Hövsgöl
Nuur

Uvs
Nuur

Aangom

Hovd

MONGOLIA

Altay

Bayanhongor

Arvayheer

ULAN BATOR

Javarthushuu

Choybalsan

Kyakhta

Yablonovyy Khrebet

Borzya

Hulun Buir

Hulun Nur

Da Hinggan Ling

CHINA

Bei'an

Fuyu

Daqing

Qiqihar

Ulanhot

Nianji

Jiamusi

MANCHURIA

Harbin

Mudanjiang

Jixi

Lake
Khanka

Ussuriysk

Vladivostok

Nakhodka

Yichun

Jilin

Changchun

Tongliao

Yanji

Ch'ŏngjin

Kimch'aek

NORTH
KOREA

P'YŎNGYANG

JAPAN

Akita

Sendai

Niigata

TOKYO

Yokohama

Kyoto

Osaka

Nagoya

Sea of
Japan
(East Sea)

Shenyang

Fushun

Anshan

Dandong

Chifeng

Xilinhot

G o b i

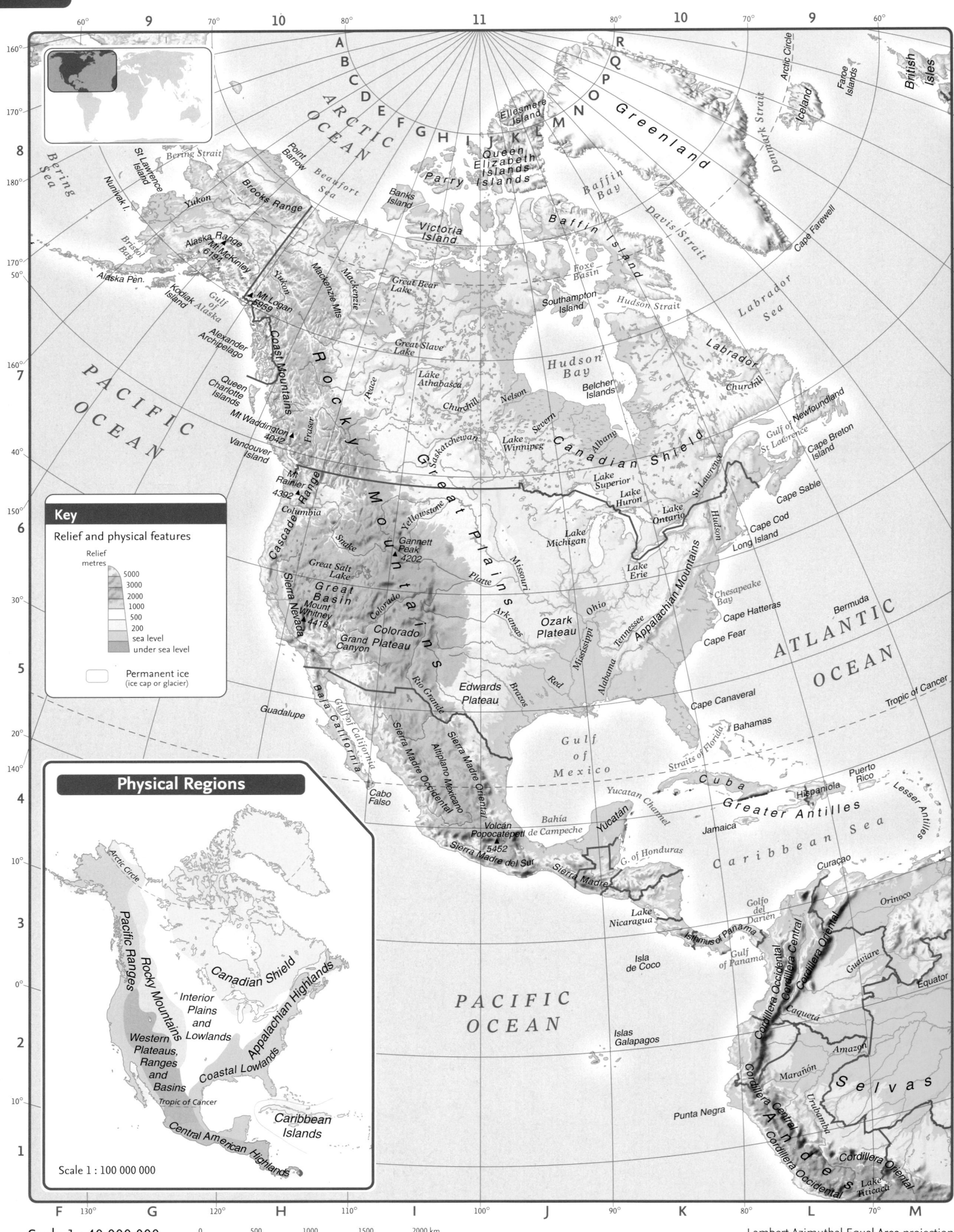

**Key**

Relief and physical features

Relief
metres
5000
3000
2000
1000
500
200
sea level
under sea level

Permanent ice
(ice cap or glacier)

**Physical Regions**

Pacific Ranges
Rocky Mountains
Interior Plains and Lowlands
Canadian Shield
Appalachian Highlands
Western Plateaus, Ranges and Basins
Coastal Lowlands
Central American Highlands
Caribbean Islands

Scale 1 : 100 000 000

Scale 1 : 40 000 000

0    500    1000    1500    2000 km

Lambert Azimuthal Equal Area projection

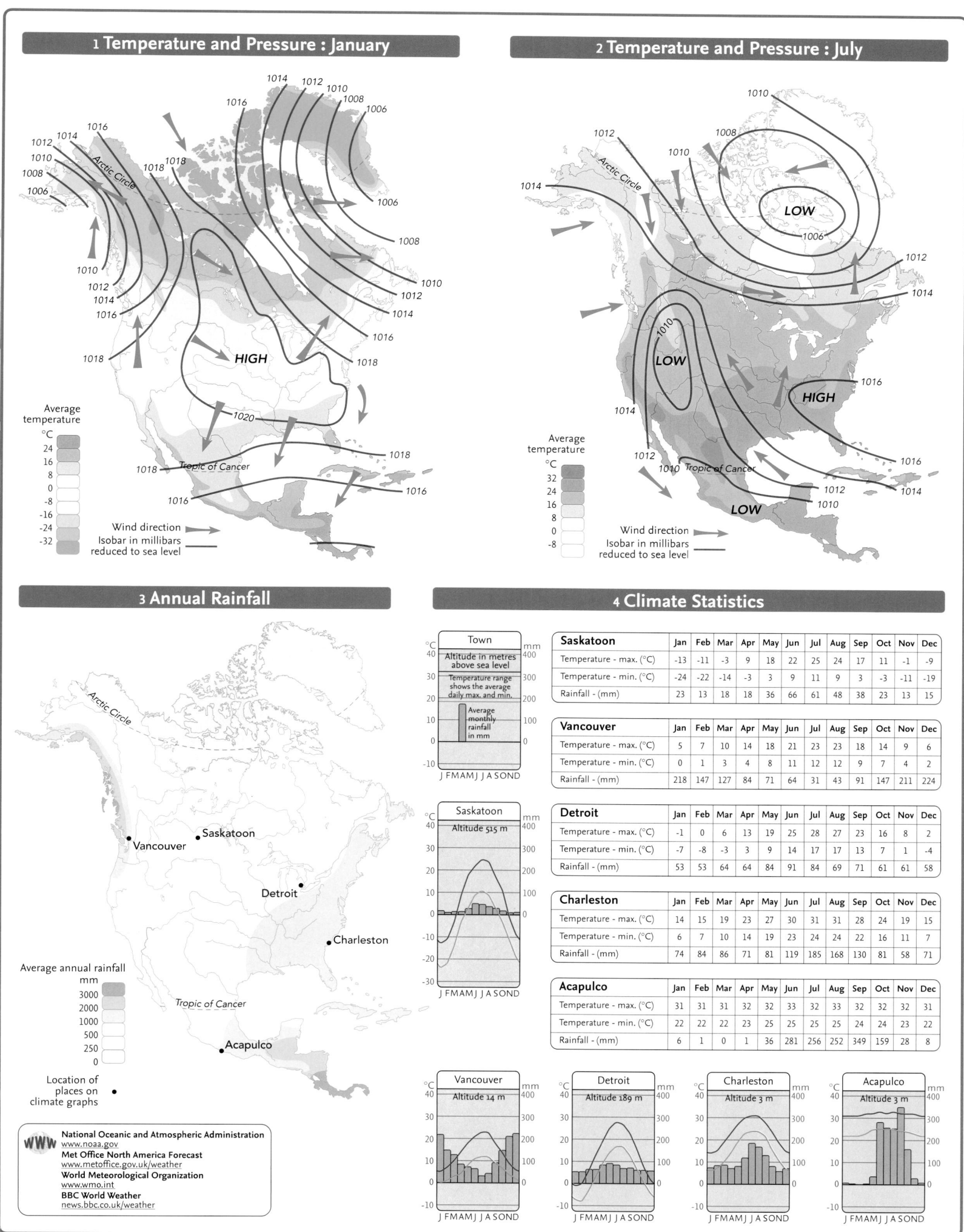

## 1 Temperature and Pressure : January

HIGH

Average temperature
°C
24
16
8
0
-8
-16
-24
-32

Wind direction
Isobar in millibars reduced to sea level

## 2 Temperature and Pressure : July

LOW

LOW

HIGH

LOW

Average temperature
°C
32
24
16
8
0
-8

Wind direction
Isobar in millibars reduced to sea level

## 3 Annual Rainfall

Arctic Circle

Vancouver
Saskatoon
Detroit
Charleston
Tropic of Cancer
Acapulco

Average annual rainfall
mm
3000
2000
1000
500
250
0

Location of places on climate graphs •

wWw National Oceanic and Atmospheric Administration
www.noaa.gov
Met Office North America Forecast
www.metoffice.gov.uk/weather
World Meteorological Organization
www.wmo.int
BBC World Weather
news.bbc.co.uk/weather

## 4 Climate Statistics

Town
Altitude in metres above sea level
Temperature range shows the average daily max. and min.
Average monthly rainfall in mm

| Saskatoon | Jan | Feb | Mar | Apr | May | Jun | Jul | Aug | Sep | Oct | Nov | Dec |
|---|---|---|---|---|---|---|---|---|---|---|---|---|
| Temperature - max. (°C) | -13 | -11 | -3 | 9 | 18 | 22 | 25 | 24 | 17 | 11 | -1 | -9 |
| Temperature - min. (°C) | -24 | -22 | -14 | -3 | 3 | 9 | 11 | 9 | 3 | -3 | -11 | -19 |
| Rainfall - (mm) | 23 | 13 | 18 | 18 | 36 | 66 | 61 | 48 | 38 | 23 | 13 | 15 |

| Vancouver | Jan | Feb | Mar | Apr | May | Jun | Jul | Aug | Sep | Oct | Nov | Dec |
|---|---|---|---|---|---|---|---|---|---|---|---|---|
| Temperature - max. (°C) | 5 | 7 | 10 | 14 | 18 | 21 | 23 | 23 | 18 | 14 | 9 | 6 |
| Temperature - min. (°C) | 0 | 1 | 3 | 4 | 8 | 11 | 12 | 12 | 9 | 7 | 4 | 2 |
| Rainfall - (mm) | 218 | 147 | 127 | 84 | 71 | 64 | 31 | 43 | 91 | 147 | 211 | 224 |

| Detroit | Jan | Feb | Mar | Apr | May | Jun | Jul | Aug | Sep | Oct | Nov | Dec |
|---|---|---|---|---|---|---|---|---|---|---|---|---|
| Temperature - max. (°C) | -1 | 0 | 6 | 13 | 19 | 25 | 28 | 27 | 23 | 16 | 8 | 2 |
| Temperature - min. (°C) | -7 | -8 | -3 | 3 | 9 | 14 | 17 | 17 | 13 | 7 | 1 | -4 |
| Rainfall - (mm) | 53 | 53 | 64 | 64 | 84 | 91 | 84 | 69 | 71 | 61 | 61 | 58 |

| Charleston | Jan | Feb | Mar | Apr | May | Jun | Jul | Aug | Sep | Oct | Nov | Dec |
|---|---|---|---|---|---|---|---|---|---|---|---|---|
| Temperature - max. (°C) | 14 | 15 | 19 | 23 | 27 | 30 | 31 | 31 | 28 | 24 | 19 | 15 |
| Temperature - min. (°C) | 6 | 7 | 10 | 14 | 19 | 23 | 24 | 24 | 22 | 16 | 11 | 7 |
| Rainfall - (mm) | 74 | 84 | 86 | 71 | 81 | 119 | 185 | 168 | 130 | 81 | 58 | 71 |

| Acapulco | Jan | Feb | Mar | Apr | May | Jun | Jul | Aug | Sep | Oct | Nov | Dec |
|---|---|---|---|---|---|---|---|---|---|---|---|---|
| Temperature - max. (°C) | 31 | 31 | 31 | 32 | 32 | 33 | 32 | 33 | 32 | 32 | 32 | 31 |
| Temperature - min. (°C) | 22 | 22 | 22 | 23 | 25 | 25 | 25 | 25 | 24 | 24 | 23 | 22 |
| Rainfall - (mm) | 6 | 1 | 0 | 1 | 36 | 281 | 256 | 252 | 349 | 159 | 28 | 8 |

Saskatoon
Altitude 515 m

Vancouver
Altitude 14 m

Detroit
Altitude 189 m

Charleston
Altitude 3 m

Acapulco
Altitude 3 m

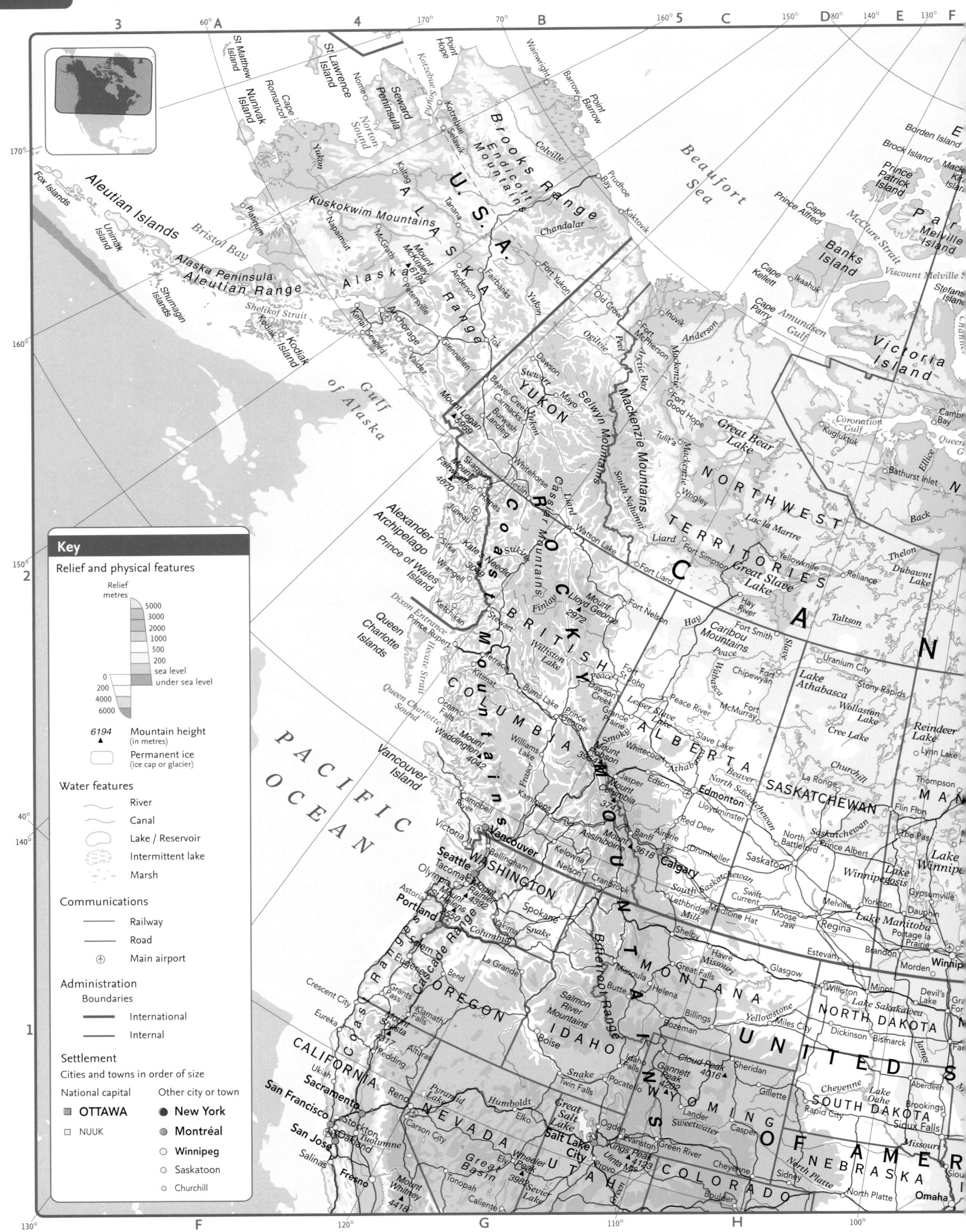

**Key**

**Relief and physical features**

Relief
metres
5000
3000
2000
1000
500
200
sea level
0
under sea level
200
4000
6000

▲ 6194   Mountain height
(in metres)

Permanent ice
(ice cap or glacier)

**Water features**

River
Canal
Lake / Reservoir
Intermittent lake
Marsh

**Communications**

Railway
Road
⊕ Main airport

**Administration**

Boundaries
International
Internal

**Settlement**

Cities and towns in order of size
National capital          Other city or town
■ **OTTAWA**              ● **New York**
□ NUUK                    ● **Montréal**
                          ○ **Winnipeg**
                          ○ Saskatoon
                          ○ Churchill

Scale 1 : 17 000 000

0    200    400    600    800 km

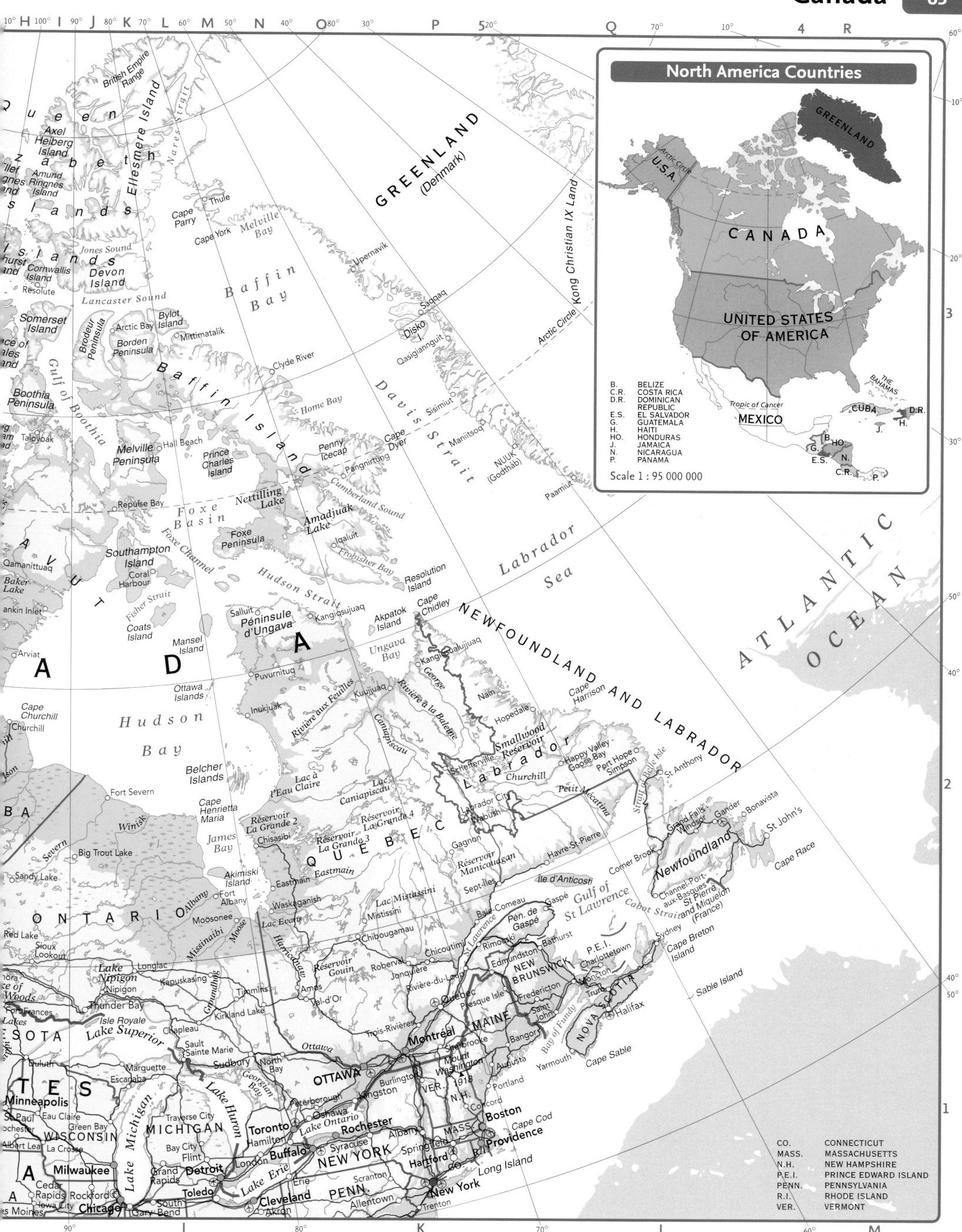

## North America Countries

GREENLAND

U.S.A.

C A N A D A

UNITED STATES
OF AMERICA

MEXICO

THE
BAHAMAS

CUBA          D.R.

Tropic of Cancer

| B. | BELIZE |
| C.R. | COSTA RICA |
| D.R. | DOMINICAN REPUBLIC |
| E.S. | EL SALVADOR |
| G. | GUATEMALA |
| H. | HAITI |
| HO. | HONDURAS |
| J. | JAMAICA |
| N. | NICARAGUA |
| P. | PANAMA |

Scale 1 : 95 000 000

GREENLAND
(Denmark)

Kong Christian IX Land

Arctic Circle

British Empire Range

Axel Heiberg Island

Amund Ringnes Island

Ellesmere Island

Nares Strait

Queen Elizabeth Islands

Devon Island

Cornwallis Island

Cape Parry

Cape York

Melville Bay

Jones Sound

Lancaster Sound

Thule

Upernavik

Sadqaq

Disko

Qasigiannguit

Somerset Island

Brodeur Peninsula

Arctic Bay

Bylot Island

Borden Peninsula

Boothia Peninsula

Gulf of Boothia

Taloyoak

Melville Peninsula

Hall Beach

Prince Charles Island

Baffin Island

Baffin Bay

Clyde River

Home Bay

Davis Strait

Penny Icecap

Cape Dyer

Pangnirtung

Cumberland Sound

Sisimiut

Maniitsoq

NUUK
(Godthåb)

Paamiut

Repulse Bay

Foxe Basin

Nettilling Lake

Amadjuak Lake

Foxe Channel

Foxe Peninsula

Iqaluit

Frobisher Bay

Resolution Island

NUNAVUT

Qamanittuaq

Baker Lake

Southampton Island

Coral Harbour

Fisher Strait

Coats Island

Mansel Island

Hudson Strait

Labrador Sea

Rankin Inlet

Arviat

C A N A D A

Salluit

Kangiqsujuaq

Akpatok Island

Cape Chidley

Péninsule d'Ungava

Ungava Bay

NEWFOUNDLAND AND LABRADOR

Cape Churchill

Churchill

Hudson Bay

Ottawa Islands

Puvurnituq

Inukjuak

Kangiqsualujjuaq

Nain

Rivière aux Feuilles

Kuujjuaq

George

Rivière à la Baleine

Hopedale

Belcher Islands

Fort Severn

Caniapiscau

Lac à l'Eau Claire

Cape Harrison

Smallwood Reservoir

Happy Valley-Goose Bay

Port Hope Simpson

St Anthony

Strait of Belle Isle

Labrador

Cape Henrietta Maria

Réservoir La Grande 2

Lac Caniapiscau

Réservoir La Grande 4

Schefferville

Churchill

Petit Mécatina

Winisk

James Bay

Chisasibi

Réservoir La Grande 3

Labrador City

Wabush

Bonavista

Severn

Big Trout Lake

Akimiski Island

Eastmain

Eastmain

QUEBEC

Gagnon

Réservoir Manicouagan

Grand Falls-Windsor

Gander

St John's

Sandy Lake

Fort Severn

Fort Albany

Waskaganish

Lac Mistassini

Sept-Îles

Havre-St-Pierre

Île d'Anticosti

Corner Brook

Newfoundland

Cape Race

ONTARIO

Albany

Moosonee

Missinaibi

Moose

Mistissini

Chibougamau

Gagnon

Baie-Comeau

Pén. de Gaspé

Gaspé

Gulf of St Lawrence

Channel-Port-aux-Basques

St Pierre and Miquelon (France)

Cabot Strait

Red Lake

Sioux Lookout

Lake Nipigon

Longlac

Nipigon

Kapuskasing

Hearst

Timmins

Réservoir Gouin

Roberval

Amos

Val-d'Or

Chicoutimi

Jonquière

Rimouski

Rivière-du-Loup

NEW BRUNSWICK

Bathurst

P.E.I.

Charlottetown

Cape Breton Island

Sydney

Sable Island

Woods

Lake of the Woods

Fort Frances

Thunder Bay

Isle Royale

Chapleau

Kirkland Lake

Sault Sainte Marie

Georgian Bay

North Bay

Sudbury

Ottawa

Trois-Rivières

Québec

Presque Isle

Edmundston

Fredericton

Saint John

Moncton

Truro

NOVA SCOTIA

Halifax

MINNESOTA

Duluth

Marquette

Escanaba

Lake Superior

Lake Huron

Peterborough

OTTAWA

Burlington

Mount Washington 1918

MAINE

VER.

N.H.

Augusta

Portland

Bay of Fundy

Yarmouth

Cape Sable

Minneapolis

St Paul

Eau Claire

Green Bay

Traverse City

Bay City

Flint

WISCONSIN

MICHIGAN

Toronto

Hamilton

Lake Ontario

Rochester

Oshawa

Syracuse

Albany

Springfield

Concord

Boston

MASS.

Cape Cod

ATLANTIC OCEAN

Rochester

La Crosse

Grand Rapids

London

Buffalo

NEW YORK

Hartford

CO.

R.I.

Providence

Long Island

Albert Lea

Cedar Rapids

Rockford

Iowa City

South Bend

Gary

Chicago

Detroit

Toledo

Lake Erie

Erie

Cleveland

Akron

PENN.

Scranton

Allentown

Trenton

New York

Milwaukee

Lake Michigan

UNITED STATES

Des Moines

| CO. | CONNECTICUT |
| MASS. | MASSACHUSETTS |
| N.H. | NEW HAMPSHIRE |
| P.E.I. | PRINCE EDWARD ISLAND |
| PENN. | PENNSYLVANIA |
| R.I. | RHODE ISLAND |
| VER. | VERMONT |

Lambert Conformal Conic projection

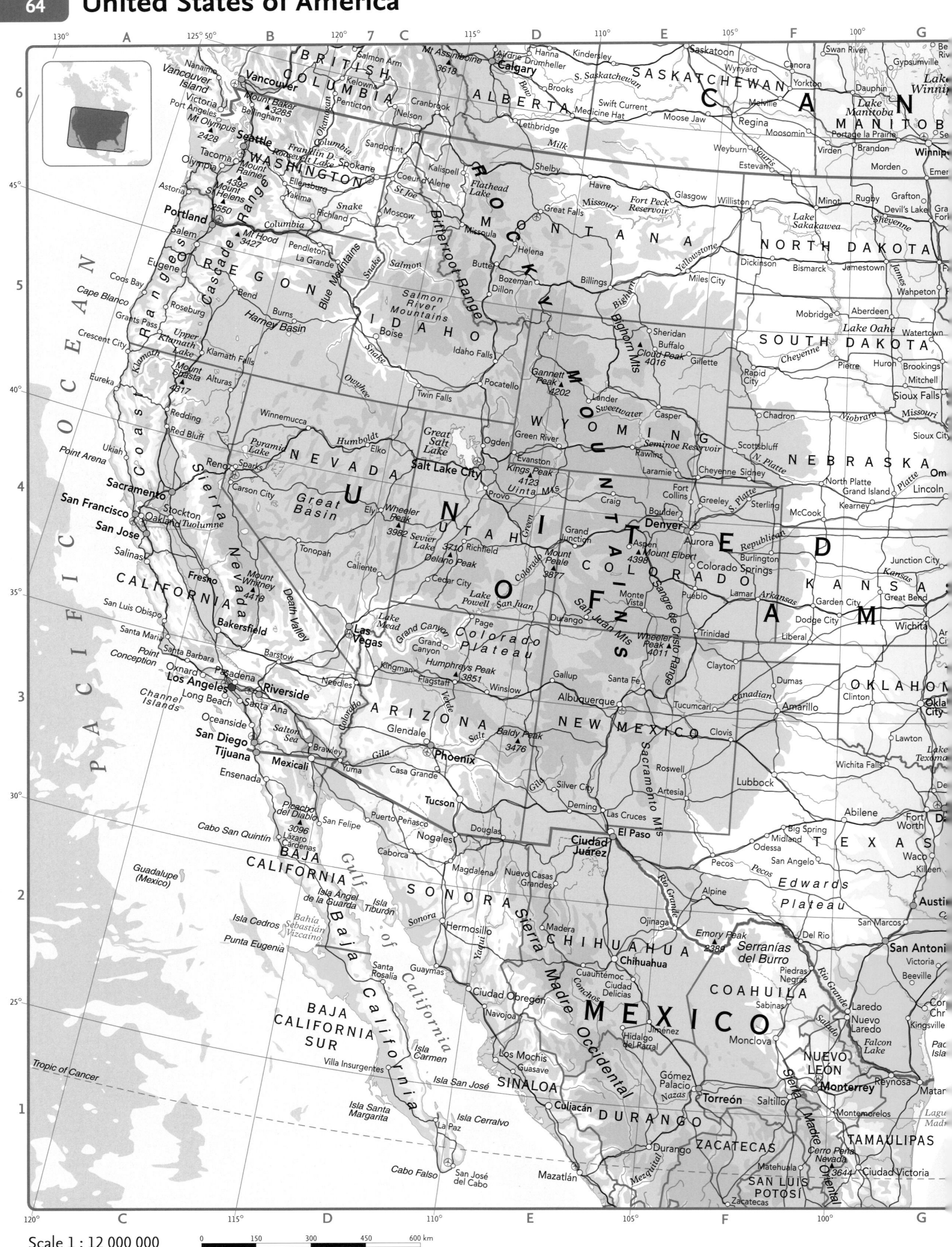

Scale 1 : 12 000 000

0   150   300   450   600 km

## 1 Population Density

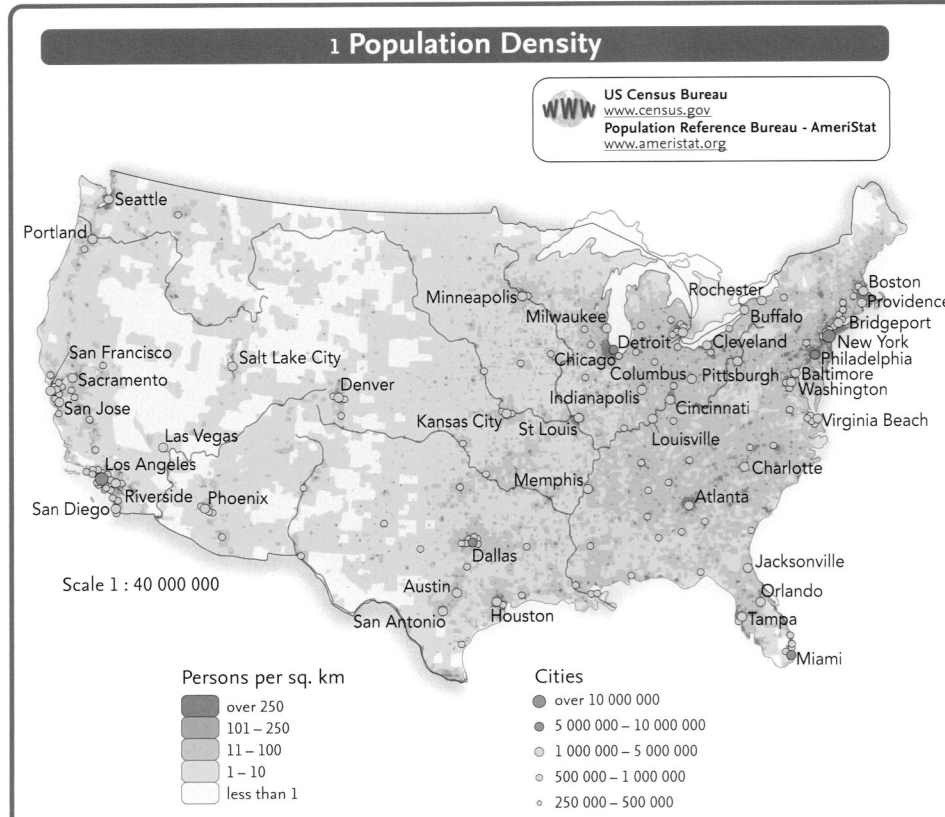

US Census Bureau
www.census.gov
Population Reference Bureau - AmeriStat
www.ameristat.org

Scale 1 : 40 000 000

**Persons per sq. km**
- over 250
- 101 – 250
- 11 – 100
- 1 – 10
- less than 1

**Cities**
- over 10 000 000
- 5 000 000 – 10 000 000
- 1 000 000 – 5 000 000
- 500 000 – 1 000 000
- 250 000 – 500 000

## 2 State Comparisons

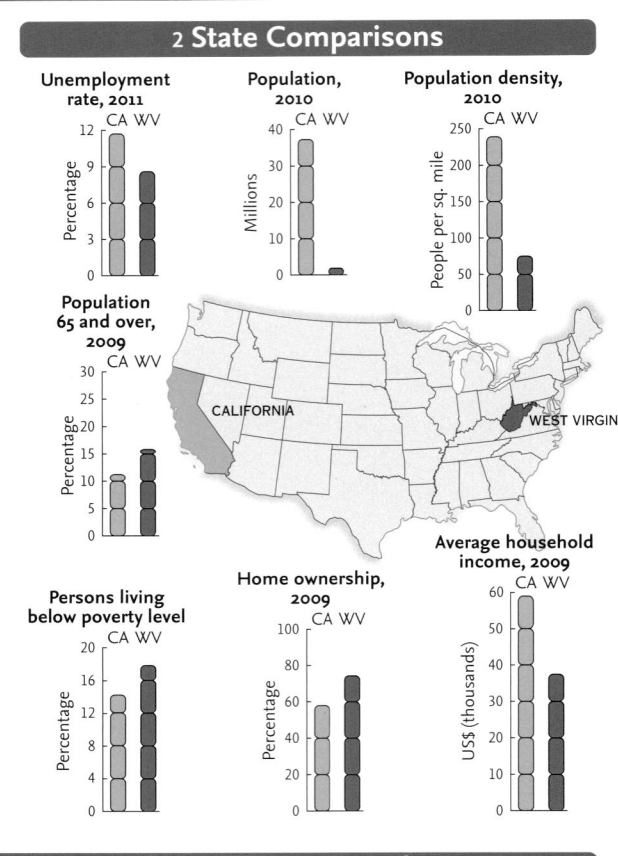

Unemployment rate, 2011

Population, 2010

Population density, 2010

Population 65 and over, 2009

Average household income, 2009

Persons living below poverty level

Home ownership, 2009

CALIFORNIA

WEST VIRGINIA

## 3 Main Urban Agglomerations

| Urban agglomeration | 1980 | 1990 | 2000 | 2015 (projected) |
|---|---|---|---|---|
| New York | 15 601 000 | 16 086 000 | 17 846 000 | 19 968 000 |
| Los Angeles | 9 512 000 | 10 883 000 | 11 814 000 | 13 165 000 |
| Chicago | 7 216 000 | 7 374 000 | 8 333 000 | 9 513 000 |
| Miami | 3 122 000 | 3 969 000 | 4 946 000 | 5 967 000 |
| Philadelphia | 4 540 000 | 4 725 000 | 5 160 000 | 5 833 000 |
| Dallas | 2 468 000 | 3 219 000 | 4 172 000 | 5 145 000 |
| Atlanta | 1 625 000 | 2 184 000 | 3 542 000 | 4 886 000 |
| Houston | 2 424 000 | 2 922 000 | 3 849 000 | 4 789 000 |
| Boston | 3 281 000 | 3 428 000 | 4 049 000 | 4 773 000 |
| Washington | 2 777 000 | 3 376 000 | 3 949 000 | 4 635 000 |
| Detroit | 3 807 000 | 3 703 000 | 3 909 000 | 4 363 000 |
| Phoenix | 1 422 000 | 2 025 000 | 2 934 000 | 3 840 000 |
| San Francisco | 2 656 000 | 2 961 000 | 3 236 000 | 3 683 000 |

## 4 Population Growth

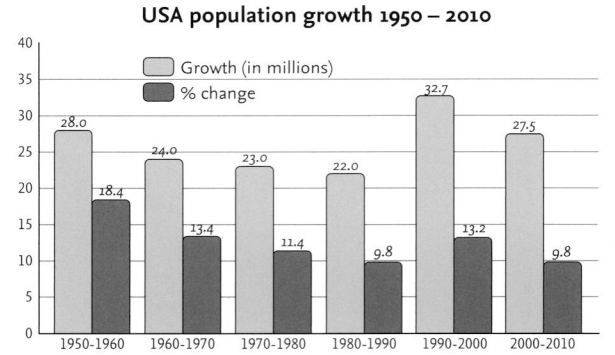

**USA population growth 1950 – 2010**

- Growth (in millions)
- % change

1950-1960: 28.0, 18.4
1960-1970: 24.0, 13.4
1970-1980: 23.0, 11.4
1980-1990: 22.0, 9.8
1990-2000: 32.7, 13.2
2000-2010: 27.5, 9.8

## 5 Population Change

Midwest 4.7%

Northeast 4.1%

West 14.2%

South 13.3%

Population change, 2000 – 2010
Percentage
- over 30
- 20 – 30
- 10 – 20
- 0 – 10
- -10 – 0

Scale 1 : 40 000 000

## 6 Immigration

**Immigration into USA by country, 2010**
Total : 1 042 625

Caribbean, Mexico, Africa, Europe, China, India, Philippines, Vietnam, Colombia, South Korea

## 7 Economic Activity

Seattle
□○

Minneapolis/St Paul
○○
Milwaukee ○ Detroit ○○
Chicago □○○ Cleveland ○○
Buffalo
New York
□○○○
Pittsburgh
Indianapolis ○ ○○ Philadelphia
□○
San Francisco/Oakland □□□○○◆
Silicon Valley
Kansas City
□○
St Louis
□□
Baltimore
□○
Washington
□○
Los Angeles
□□□○○
Atlanta
□○
Dallas
□□○
Birmingham
Houston
□○
New Orleans
□○
Miami ◆

Scale 1 : 40 000 000

• Major industrial centre

**Manufacturing industry**
□ Metal working
□ Oil refinery
□ Shipbuilding
□ Aircraft manufacturing
□ Car manufacturing
□ Mechanical engineering

○ Electrical engineering
○ Publishing / Paper
○ Chemicals
○ Textiles
○ Food processing

**Service industry**
◆ Banking and finance
◆ Tourism

## 8 Silicon Valley

Berkeley
Oakland
San Francisco
Oakland
San Francisco
Bay
Hayward
San Francisco
San Mateo ✱
Fremont ✱
Redwood City ✱✱✱
Stanford ✱ Palo Alto ✱✱
Milpitas ✱✱✱✱
✱✱✱✱ Mountain View ✱✱✱✱ Sunnyvale Santa Santa Clara
✱✱✱ Clara ✱✱✱✱✱
✱✱✱ Cupertino ✱✱✱ San Jose
✱✱✱✱✱
✱✱✱ ✱✱✱✱
Scotts Valley
✱
Santa Cruz Gilroy

PACIFIC
OCEAN

——— Extent of Silicon Valley
✱ IT company
▨ Built-up area

Scale 1 : 1 200 000

WWW **Department of Commerce**
www.commerce.gov
**US Trade and Development Agency**
www.ustda.gov
**UN Commodity Trade Statistics**
comtrade.un.org

## 9 Trade

CANADA
UNITED KINGDOM
IRELAND
RUSSIAN FEDERATION
NETHERLANDS
BELGIUM
SWITZERLAND
FRANCE
GERMANY
SOUTH KOREA
ITALY
JAPAN
USA
ISRAEL
CHINA
SAUDI ARABIA
HONG KONG
MEXICO
INDIA
NIGERIA
THAILAND
MALAYSIA
VENEZUELA
SINGAPORE
OTHERS
BRAZIL
AUSTRALIA

Scale 1 : 175 000 000

**Imports to USA, 2010**
**(% of total imports)**
→ over 15%
→ 5 – 15%
→ 1 – 5%

**Exports from USA, 2010**
**(% of total exports)**
→ over 15%
→ 5 – 15%
→ 1 – 5%

### Import commodities, 2010

Mineral fuels 18.4% | Machinery 13% | Pharmaceutical products 3.2%
| Others 42.5%
Electrical and electronic equipment 13.4% | Vehicles 9.5%

### Export commodities, 2010

Machinery 14.3% | Vehicles 7.8% | Aircraft 6.2%
| Others 53.6%
Electrical and electronic equipment 11.8% | Mineral fuels 6.3%

# San Francisco

HAYWARD FAULT
CALAVERAS FAULT
SAN ANDREAS FAULT

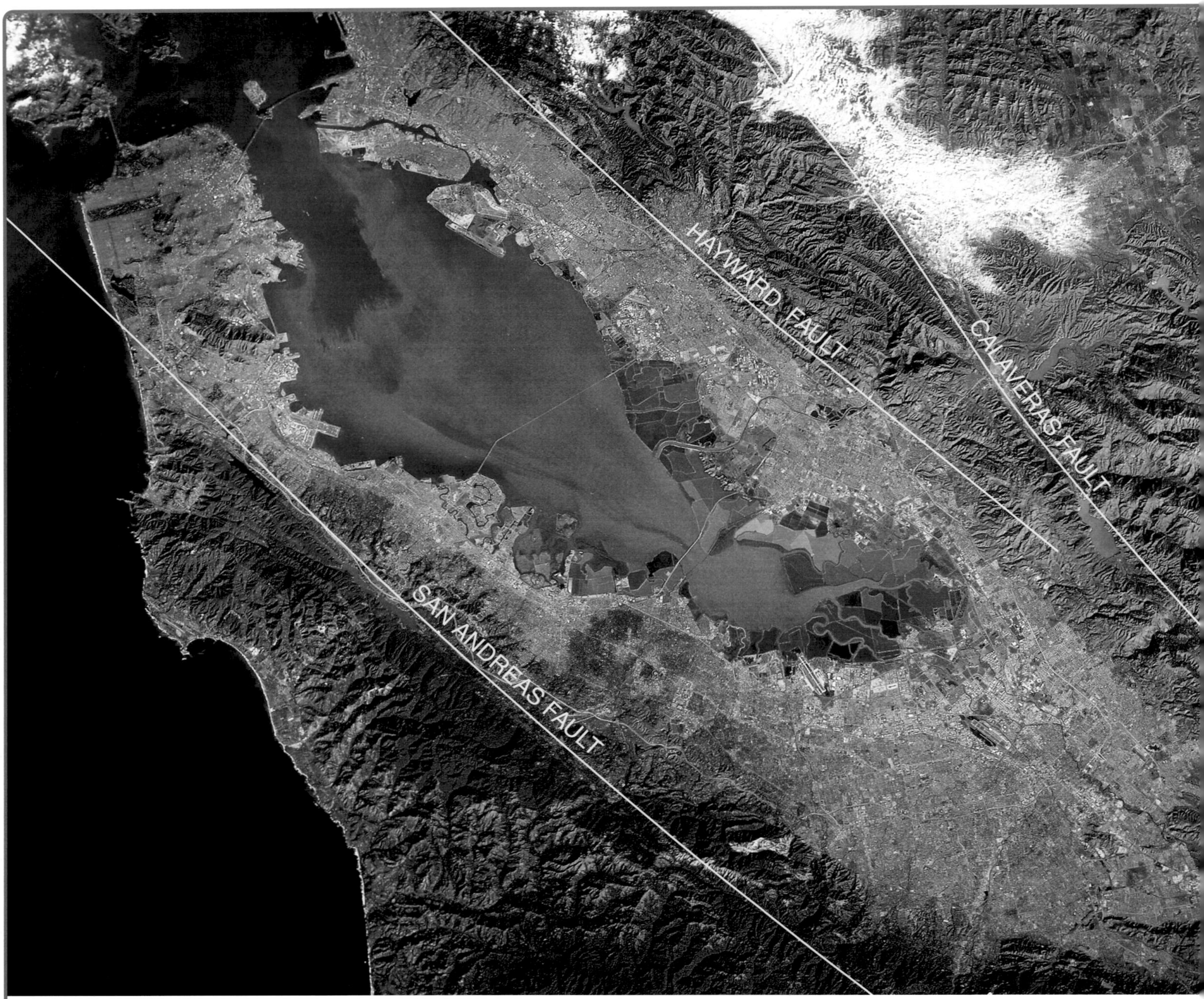

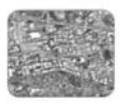

Built-up area

The built up area shown as blue/green on the satellite image surrounds San Francisco Bay and extends south to San Jose. Three bridges link the main built up areas across San Francisco Bay.

Woodland

Areas of dense woodland cover much of the Santa Cruz Mountains to the west of the San Andreas Fault Zone. Other areas of woodland are found on the ridges to the east of San Francisco Bay.

Marsh / Salt Marsh

Areas of dark green on the satellite image represent marshland in the Coyote Creek area and salt marshes between the San Mateo and Dumbarton Bridges.

Reservoir / lake

Lakes and reservoirs stand out from the surrounding land. Good examples are the Upper San Leandro Reservoir east of Piedmont and the San Andreas Lake which lies along the fault line.

Airport

A grey blue colour shows San Francisco International Airport as a flat rectangular strip of land jutting out into the bay.

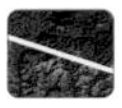

Main fault line

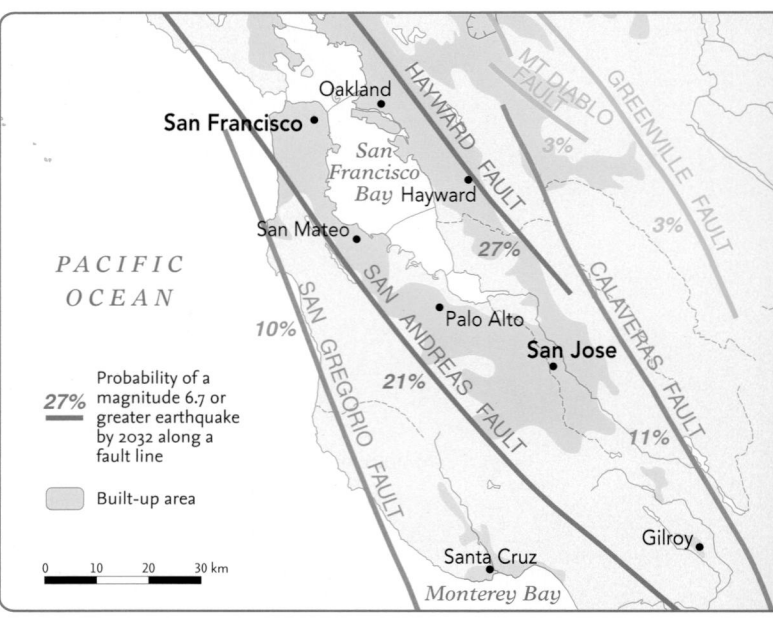

## Fault Lines in the San Francisco Bay Region

Oakland
San Francisco
San Francisco Bay
Hayward
San Mateo
PACIFIC OCEAN
Palo Alto
San Jose
HAYWARD FAULT
MT DIABLO FAULT
GREENVILLE FAULT
CALAVERAS FAULT
SAN ANDREAS FAULT
SAN GREGORIO FAULT
3%
3%
27%
10%
21%
11%
27% Probability of a magnitude 6.7 or greater earthquake by 2032 along a fault line
Built-up area
0 10 20 30 km
Gilroy
Santa Cruz
Monterey Bay

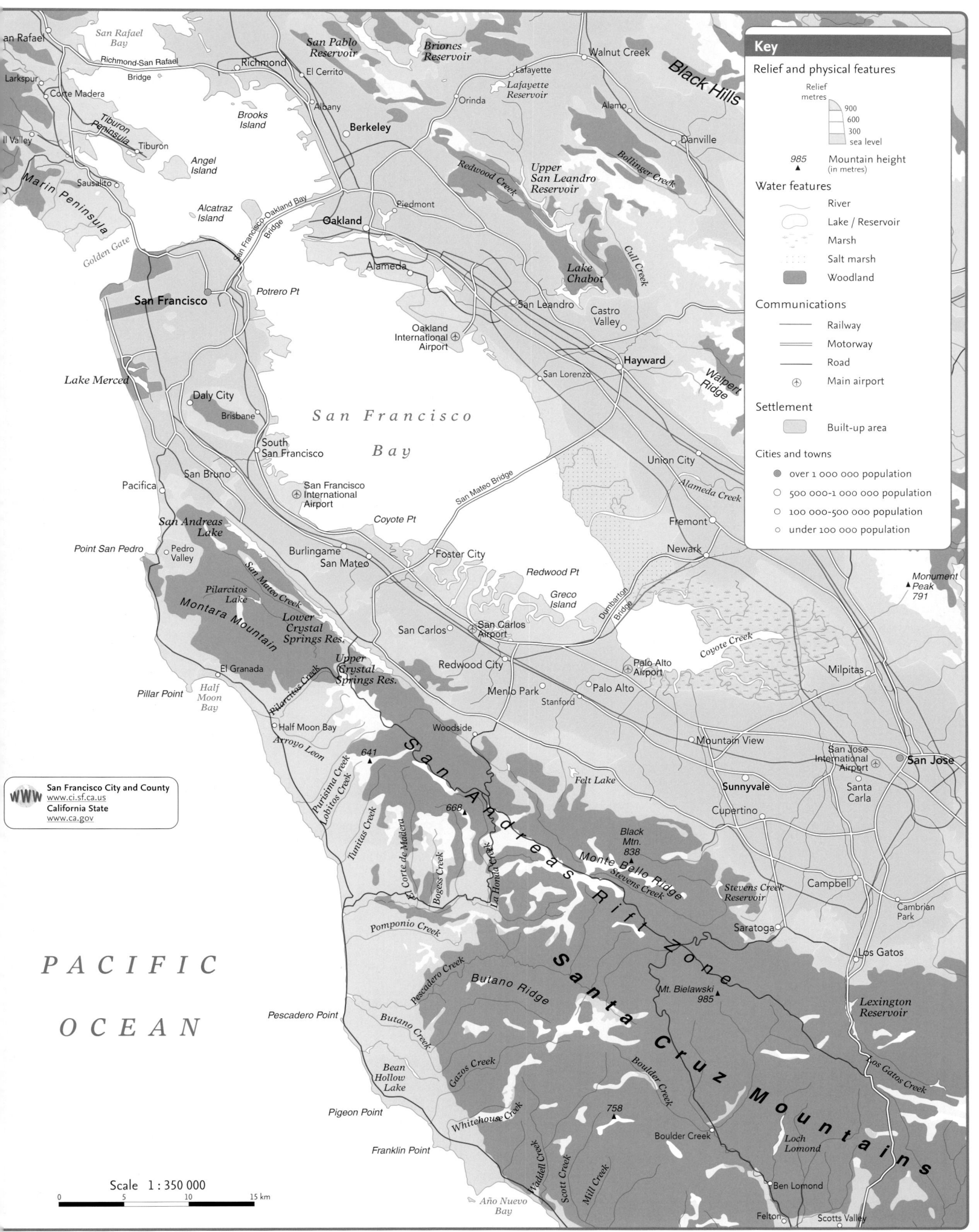

**Key**

**Relief and physical features**

Relief
metres
900
600
300
sea level

985 ▲ Mountain height
(in metres)

**Water features**

River
Lake / Reservoir
Marsh
Salt marsh
Woodland

**Communications**

Railway
Motorway
Road
⊕ Main airport

**Settlement**

Built-up area

**Cities and towns**

● over 1 000 000 population
○ 500 000–1 000 000 population
○ 100 000–500 000 population
○ under 100 000 population

San Francisco City and County
www.ci.sf.ca.us
California State
www.ca.gov

PACIFIC

OCEAN

Scale 1 : 350 000

0    5    10    15 km

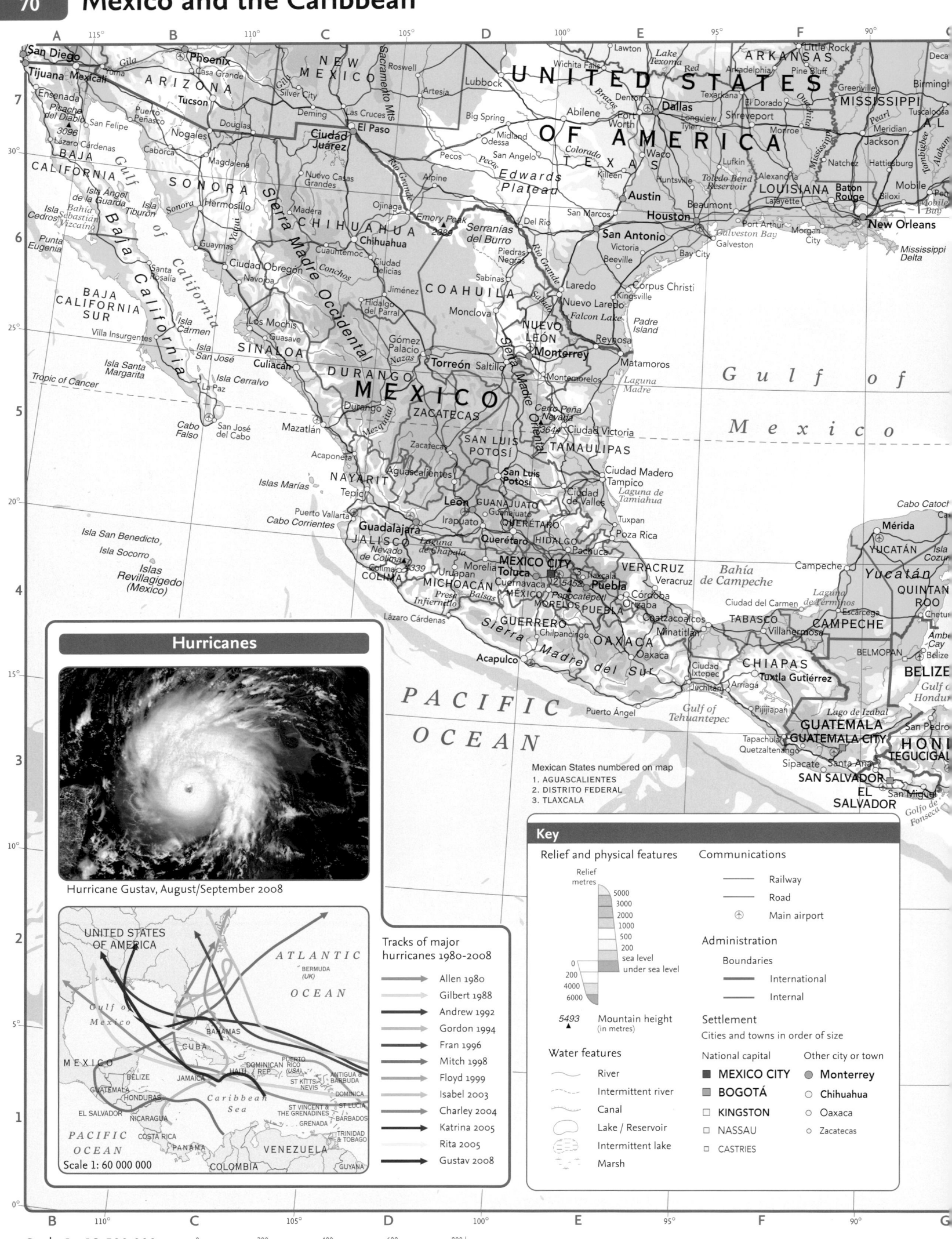

## Hurricanes

Hurricane Gustav, August/September 2008

UNITED STATES OF AMERICA

*ATLANTIC*

BERMUDA
(UK)

*OCEAN*

*Gulf of Mexico*

BAHAMAS

CUBA

MEXICO

BELIZE

GUATEMALA

JAMAICA

HAITI

DOMINICAN REP.

PUERTO RICO (USA)

ANTIGUA & BARBUDA

ST KITTS & NEVIS

DOMINICA

HONDURAS

*Caribbean Sea*

ST VINCENT & THE GRENADINES

ST LUCIA

BARBADOS

EL SALVADOR

NICARAGUA

GRENADA

TRINIDAD & TOBAGO

*PACIFIC OCEAN*

COSTA RICA

PANAMA

VENEZUELA

COLOMBIA

GUYANA

Scale 1: 60 000 000

### Tracks of major hurricanes 1980-2008

- Allen 1980
- Gilbert 1988
- Andrew 1992
- Gordon 1994
- Fran 1996
- Mitch 1998
- Floyd 1999
- Isabel 2003
- Charley 2004
- Katrina 2005
- Rita 2005
- Gustav 2008

Mexican States numbered on map
1. AGUASCALIENTES
2. DISTRITO FEDERAL
3. TLAXCALA

## Key

### Relief and physical features

Relief metres

5000
3000
2000
1000
500
200
0 sea level
200 under sea level
4000
6000

5493 ▲ Mountain height (in metres)

### Water features

- River
- Intermittent river
- Canal
- Lake / Reservoir
- Intermittent lake
- Marsh

### Communications

— Railway
— Road
⊕ Main airport

### Administration

Boundaries

— International
— Internal

### Settlement

Cities and towns in order of size

National capital

■ MEXICO CITY
■ BOGOTÁ
□ KINGSTON
□ NASSAU
□ CASTRIES

Other city or town

● Monterrey
○ Chihuahua
○ Oaxaca
○ Zacatecas

Scale 1 : 13 500 000

0  200  400  600  800 km

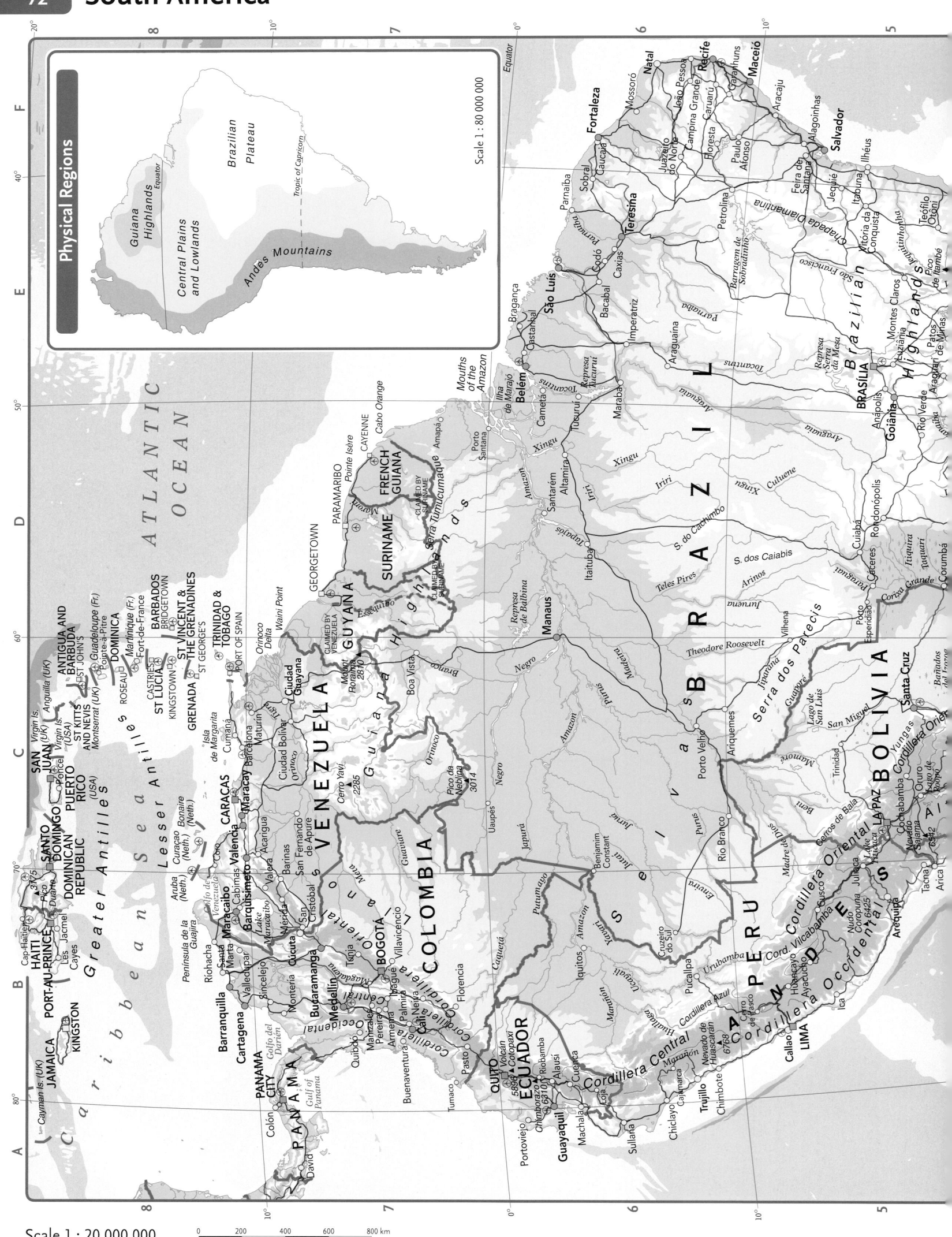

**Physical Regions**

Guiana Highlands

Brazilian Plateau

Central Plains and Lowlands

Andes Mountains

Equator

Tropic of Capricorn

Scale 1 : 80 000 000

ATLANTIC OCEAN

Cayman Is. (UK)

JAMAICA
KINGSTON

HAITI
Cap-Haïtien
PORT-AU-PRINCE
Les Cayes
Jacmel
Pico Duarte 3175

DOMINICAN REPUBLIC
SANTO DOMINGO

SAN JUAN (USA)
PUERTO RICO (USA)
Ponce

Virgin Is. (UK)
Anguilla (UK)
Virgin Is. (USA)

ST KITTS AND NEVIS
ANTIGUA AND BARBUDA
ST JOHN'S
Montserrat (UK)
Guadeloupe (Fr.)
Pointe-à-Pitre
DOMINICA
ROSEAU
Martinique (Fr.)
Fort-de-France
ST LUCIA
CASTRIES
BARBADOS
BRIDGETOWN
ST VINCENT & THE GRENADINES
KINGSTOWN
GRENADA
ST GEORGE'S
TRINIDAD & TOBAGO
PORT OF SPAIN

Greater Antilles

Caribbean Sea

Lesser Antilles

Aruba (Neth.)
Curaçao (Neth.)
Bonaire (Neth.)

Isla de Margarita

Peninsula de la Guajira

PANAMA
PANAMA CITY
Colón
David
Gulf of Panama

Riohacha
Barranquilla
Cartagena
Santa Marta
Valledupar
Sincelejo
Montería
Gulfo del Darién

Golfo de Venezuela
Maracaibo
Cabimas
Lake Maracaibo
Valera
Mérida
San Cristóbal
Cúcuta
Bucaramanga
Medellín
Quibdó
Manizales
Pereira
Armenia
Ibagué
Palmira
Cali
Buenaventura
Pasto
Tumaco

COLOMBIA
BOGOTÁ
Villavicencio
Neiva
Florencia

Cordillera Occidental
Cordillera Central
Cordillera Oriental

Magdalena

VENEZUELA
CARACAS
Maracay
Valencia
Barquisimeto
Acarigua
Barinas
San Fernando de Apure
Coro
Barcelona
Maturín
Ciudad Bolívar
Cumaná
Ciudad Guayana

Orinoco
Orinoco Delta
Waini Point

GUYANA
GEORGETOWN
Essequibo
Mount Roraima 2810

CLAIMED BY VENEZUELA

SURINAME
PARAMARIBO
Pointe Isère
CAYENNE
FRENCH GUIANA
Cabo Orange

CLAIMED BY SURINAME
Serra Tumucumaque

Guiana Highlands

CLAIMED BY SURINAME

Cerro Yaví 2285
Pico da Neblina 3014

Guaviare
Meta
Guainía

Vaupés
Caquetá
Putumayo
Napo
Mocoa

ECUADOR
QUITO
Volcán Cotopaxi 5896
Riobamba
Volcán Chimborazo 6310
Ambato
Cuenca
Alausí
Loja
Machala
Portoviejo
Guayaquil
Sullana

Marañón
Iquitos
Cruzeiro do Sul
Benjamin Constant

PERU
LIMA
Callao
Cerro de Pasco
Huánuco
Pucallpa
Cordillera Azul
Ayacucho
Cusco
Nevado de Huascarán 6768
Trujillo
Chimbote
Chiclayo
Cajamarca
Huancayo
Ica
Arequipa
Tacna
Arica

Cordillera Blanca
Cordillera Central
Cordillera Occidental
Cordillera Oriental
ANDES

Ucayali
Huallaga
Urubamba
Cord. Vilcabamba
Nudo Coropuna
Juliaca
Lake Titicaca

BOLIVIA
LA PAZ
Santa Cruz
Cochabamba
Oruro
Potosí
Sucre
Sajama 6542
Yungas
Cordillera Oriental
Cordillera Orient.
Mamoré
Beni
Trinidad
Lago de San Luis
San Miguel

Equator

Mouths of the Amazon

Ilha de Marajó

Belém
Castanhal
Bragança
São Luís
Bacabal
Imperatriz
Araguaína
Marabá
Cametá
Porto Santana
Amapá

Amazon
Xingu
Iriri
Tapajós
Teles Pires
Arinos
Juruena
Madeira
Negro
Branco
Boa Vista
Manaus
Represa de Balbina
Represa Tucuruí
Tocantins
Araguaia

Purus
Juruá
Madre de Dios
Porto Velho
Ariquemes
Theodore Roosevelt
Vilhena
Serra dos Parecis
Porto Esperidião
Cáceres
Cuiabá
S. do Cachimbo
S. dos Caiabis
Guaporé
Corixa Grande
Corumbá
Bañados del Izozog

BRASIL

Fortaleza
Caucaia
Sobral
Parnaíba
Teresina
Codó
Caxias
Parnaíba

Natal
Mossoró
João Pessoa
Campina Grande
Caruaru
Recife
Garanhuns
Maceió
Arcoverde
Paulo Afonso
Petrolina
Floresta
Juazeiro do Norte
Alagoinhas
Feira de Santana
Salvador
Ilhéus
Jequié
Itabuna

São Francisco
Barragem de Sobradinho

Brazilian Highlands

Chapada Diamantina
Vitória da Conquista
Montes Claros
Teófilo Otoni
Pico da Bandeira
Pico da Pedra
Araguari de Minas

Represa Serra da Mesa
BRASÍLIA
Anápolis
Goiânia
Rio Verde
Rondonópolis

Scale 1 : 20 000 000

0    200    400    600    800 km

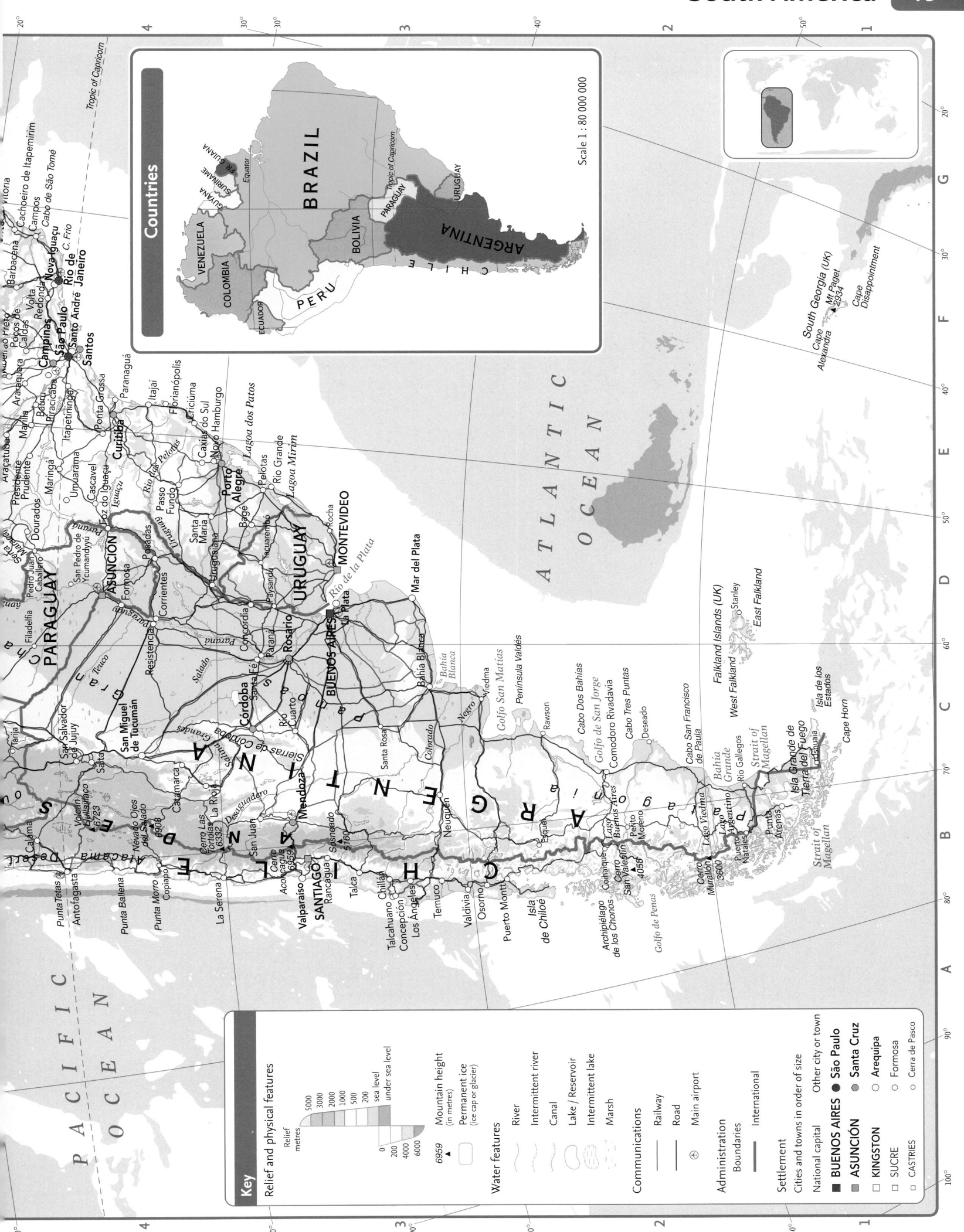

Scale 1 : 80 000 000

## Countries

BRAZIL
FR. GUIANA
SURINAME
GUYANA
VENEZUELA
COLOMBIA
ECUADOR
PERU
BOLIVIA
PARAGUAY
URUGUAY
ARGENTINA
CHILE

South Georgia (UK)
Cape Alexandra
Mt Paget 2934▲
Cape Disappointment

Tropic of Capricorn

Cachoeiro de Itapemirim
Campos
Cabo de São Tomé
Barbacena
Volta Redonda
Rio de C. Frio
Nova Iguaçu
Rio de Janeiro
Poços de Caldas
Campinas
São Paulo
Santo André
Santos
Araxá
Araraquara
Marília
Bauru
Piracicaba
Itapetininga
Presidente Prudente
Maringá
Umuarama
Cascavel
Ponta Grossa
Foz do Iguaçu
Curitiba
Paranaguá
Dourados
Itajaí
Florianópolis
Criciúma
Caxias do Sul
Novo Hamburgo
Passo Fundo
Porto Alegre
Pelotas
Rio Grande
Lagoa dos Patos
Lagoa Mirim
Santa Maria
Bagé
Uruguaiana
Jaguarão
Rocha
Rio los Pelotas
Rio los Patos
San Pedro de Ycumandyyú
Filadelfia
Pedro Juan Caballero
Concepción
ASUNCIÓN
PARAGUAY
Formosa
Posadas
Corrientes
Resistencia
Santa Fe
Paraná
Rosario
Concordia
Paysandú
MONTEVIDEO
URUGUAY
Mar del Plata
La Plata
BUENOS AIRES
Córdoba
Río Cuarto
Santa Rosa
Bahía Blanca
Bahía Blanca
Viedma
Península Valdés
Golfo San Matías
ATLANTIC OCEAN
Falkland Islands (UK)
Stanley
East Falkland
West Falkland
Cabo Dos Bahías
Golfo de San Jorge
Comodoro Rivadavia
Cabo Tres Puntas
Deseado
Cabo San Francisco de Paula
Puerto Deseado
Bahía Grande
Río Gallegos
Strait of Magellan
Isla de los Estados
Cape Horn
Isla Grande de Tierra del Fuego
Ushuaia
Punta Arenas
Puerto Natales
Strait of Magellan
Cerro Murallón 3600
Lago Argentino
Lago Viedma
Lago Buenos Aires
Perito Moreno
Coihaique
Cerro San Valentín 4058▲
Archipiélago de los Chonos
Golfo de Penas
Isla de Chiloé
Puerto Montt
Osorno
Valdivia
Temuco
Los Ángeles
Concepción
Talcahuano
Chillán
Talca
Rancagua
SANTIAGO
Valparaíso
La Serena
Copiapó
Punta Morro
Punta Ballena
Antofagasta
PuntaTetas
Calama
Atacama Desert
Volcán Llullaillaco 6723
Nevado Ojos del Salado 6908
Cerro Las Tórtolas 6332
Cerro Aconcagua 6959
San Juan
Mendoza
San Rafael
Desaguadero
La Rioja
Catamarca
San Miguel de Tucumán
Santiago del Estero
Salta
San Salvador de Jujuy
Tarija
Sierras de Córdoba
Salado
Teuco
Gran Chaco
Pilcomayo
Bermejo
Paraguay
Paraná
Uruguay
Salado
Negro
Colorado
Río Grandes
Neuquén
Santa Rosa
Equel
ANDES
ARGENTINA
PATAGONIA
PACIFIC OCEAN

## Key

### Relief and physical features

Relief
metres
5000
3000
2000
1000
500
200
sea level
under sea level
200
4000
6000
0

Mountain height (in metres)
6959 ▲

Permanent ice (ice cap or glacier)

### Water features

River
Intermittent river
Canal
Lake / Reservoir
Intermittent lake
Marsh

### Communications

Railway
Road
⊕ Main airport

### Administration

Boundaries
International

### Settlement

National capital
■ BUENOS AIRES
● ASUNCIÓN
□ KINGSTON
□ SUCRE
□ CASTRIES

Cities and towns in order of size
● São Paulo
● Santa Cruz
○ Arequipa
□ Formosa
□ Cerra de Pasco

Other city or town

Lambert Azimuthal Equal Area projection

## 1 Temperature and Pressure : January

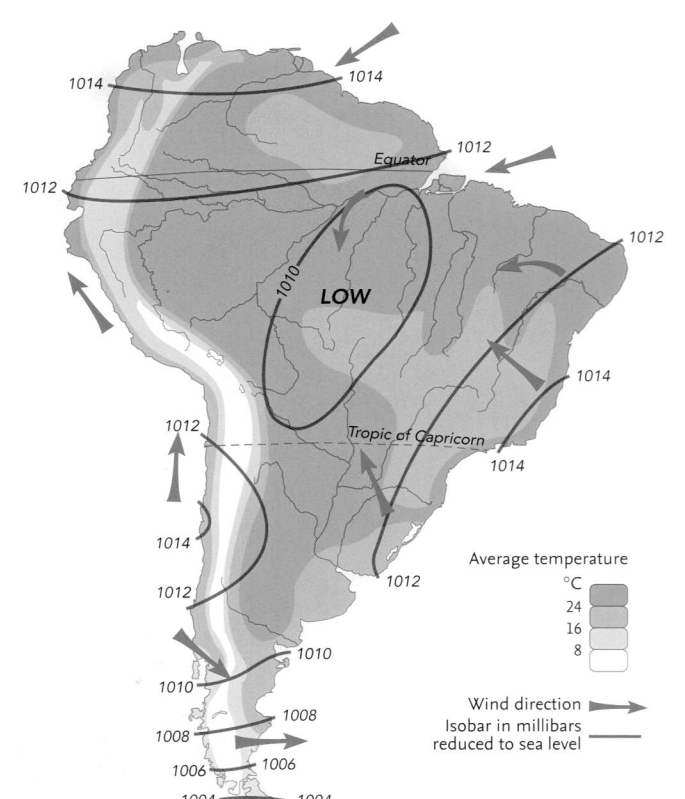

1014
1014
1012
1012
Equator
1010
LOW
1012
1014
Tropic of Capricorn
1012
1014
1014
1012
1010
1010
1008
1008
1006  1006
1004  1004

**Average temperature**
°C
24
16
8

Wind direction
Isobar in millibars
reduced to sea level

## 2 Temperature and Pressure : July

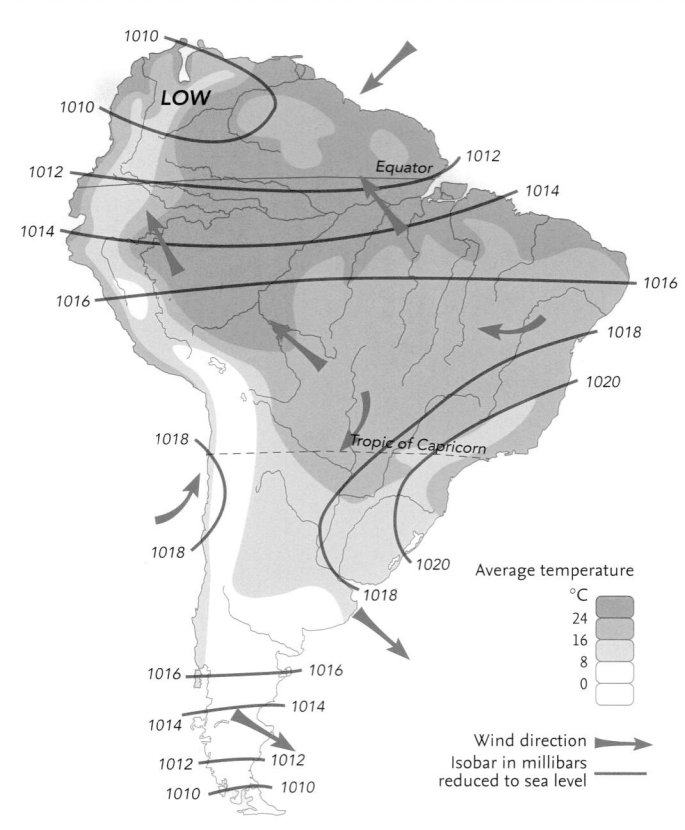

1010
LOW
1010
1012
Equator
1012
1014
1014
1016
1016
1018
1020
1018
1018
1020
1018
1016  1016
1014
1014
1012  1012
1010  1010

**Average temperature**
°C
24
16
8
0

Wind direction
Isobar in millibars
reduced to sea level

## 3 Annual Rainfall

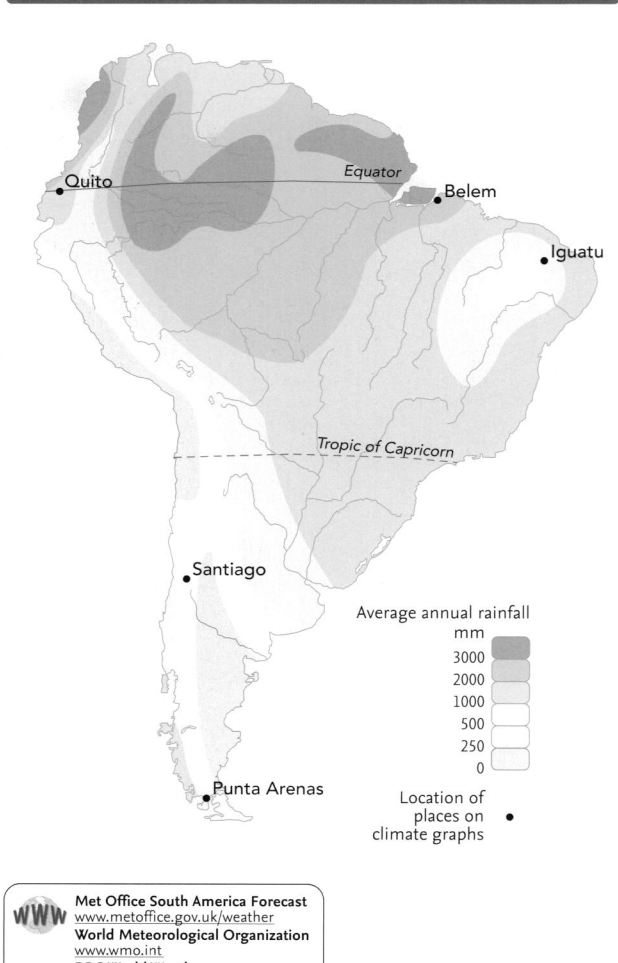

Quito
Equator
Belem
Iguatu
Tropic of Capricorn
Santiago
Punta Arenas

**Average annual rainfall**
mm
3000
2000
1000
500
250
0

Location of
places on
climate graphs  •

## 4 Climate Statistics

| Quito | Jan | Feb | Mar | Apr | May | Jun | Jul | Aug | Sep | Oct | Nov | Dec |
|---|---|---|---|---|---|---|---|---|---|---|---|---|
| Temperature - max. (°C) | 22 | 22 | 22 | 21 | 21 | 22 | 22 | 23 | 23 | 22 | 22 | 22 |
| Temperature - min. (°C) | 8 | 8 | 8 | 8 | 8 | 7 | 7 | 7 | 7 | 8 | 7 | 8 |
| Rainfall - (mm) | 99 | 112 | 142 | 175 | 137 | 43 | 20 | 31 | 69 | 112 | 97 | 79 |

| Belem | Jan | Feb | Mar | Apr | May | Jun | Jul | Aug | Sep | Oct | Nov | Dec |
|---|---|---|---|---|---|---|---|---|---|---|---|---|
| Temperature - max. (°C) | 31 | 30 | 31 | 31 | 31 | 31 | 31 | 31 | 32 | 32 | 32 | 32 |
| Temperature - min. (°C) | 22 | 22 | 23 | 23 | 23 | 22 | 22 | 22 | 22 | 22 | 22 | 22 |
| Rainfall - (mm) | 318 | 358 | 358 | 320 | 259 | 170 | 150 | 112 | 89 | 84 | 66 | 155 |

| Iguatu | Jan | Feb | Mar | Apr | May | Jun | Jul | Aug | Sep | Oct | Nov | Dec |
|---|---|---|---|---|---|---|---|---|---|---|---|---|
| Temperature - max. (°C) | 34 | 33 | 32 | 31 | 31 | 31 | 32 | 32 | 35 | 36 | 36 | 36 |
| Temperature - min. (°C) | 23 | 23 | 23 | 23 | 22 | 22 | 21 | 22 | 22 | 23 | 23 | 23 |
| Rainfall - (mm) | 89 | 173 | 185 | 160 | 61 | 61 | 36 | 5 | 18 | 18 | 10 | 33 |

| Santiago | Jan | Feb | Mar | Apr | May | Jun | Jul | Aug | Sep | Oct | Nov | Dec |
|---|---|---|---|---|---|---|---|---|---|---|---|---|
| Temperature - max. (°C) | 29 | 29 | 27 | 23 | 18 | 14 | 15 | 17 | 19 | 22 | 26 | 28 |
| Temperature - min. (°C) | 12 | 11 | 9 | 7 | 5 | 3 | 3 | 4 | 6 | 7 | 9 | 11 |
| Rainfall - (mm) | 3 | 3 | 5 | 13 | 64 | 84 | 76 | 56 | 31 | 15 | 8 | 5 |

| Punta Arenas | Jan | Feb | Mar | Apr | May | Jun | Jul | Aug | Sep | Oct | Nov | Dec |
|---|---|---|---|---|---|---|---|---|---|---|---|---|
| Temperature - max. (°C) | 14 | 14 | 12 | 10 | 7 | 5 | 4 | 6 | 8 | 11 | 12 | 14 |
| Temperature - min. (°C) | 7 | 7 | 5 | 4 | 2 | 1 | -1 | 1 | 2 | 3 | 4 | 6 |
| Rainfall - (mm) | 38 | 23 | 33 | 36 | 33 | 41 | 28 | 31 | 23 | 28 | 18 | 36 |

**Town**
°C 40 / mm 400
Altitude in metres
above sea level
30 / 300
Temperature range
shows the average
daily max. and min.
20 / 200
Average
monthly
rainfall
in mm
10 / 100
0 / 0
-10
J F M A M J J A S O N D

**Quito**
°C 40 / mm 400
Altitude 2879 m
30 / 300
20 / 200
10 / 100
0 / 0
-10
J F M A M J J A S O N D

**Belem**
°C 40 / mm 400
Altitude 13 m
30 / 300
20 / 200
10 / 100
0 / 0
-10
J F M A M J J A S O N D

**Iguatu**
°C 40 / mm 400
Altitude 209 m
30 / 300
20 / 200
10 / 100
0 / 0
-10
J F M A M J J A S O N D

**Santiago**
°C 40 / mm 400
Altitude 520 m
30 / 300
20 / 200
10 / 100
0 / 0
-10
J F M A M J J A S O N D

**Punta Arenas**
°C 40 / mm 400
Altitude 8 m
30 / 300
20 / 200
10 / 100
0 / 0
-10
J F M A M J J A S O N D

www  **Met Office South America Forecast**
www.metoffice.gov.uk/weather
**World Meteorological Organization**
www.wmo.int
**BBC World Weather**
news.bbc.co.uk/weather

Scale 1 : 70 000 000

0    1000    2000    3000 km

Lambert Azimuthal Equal Area projection

## 1 Land Cover

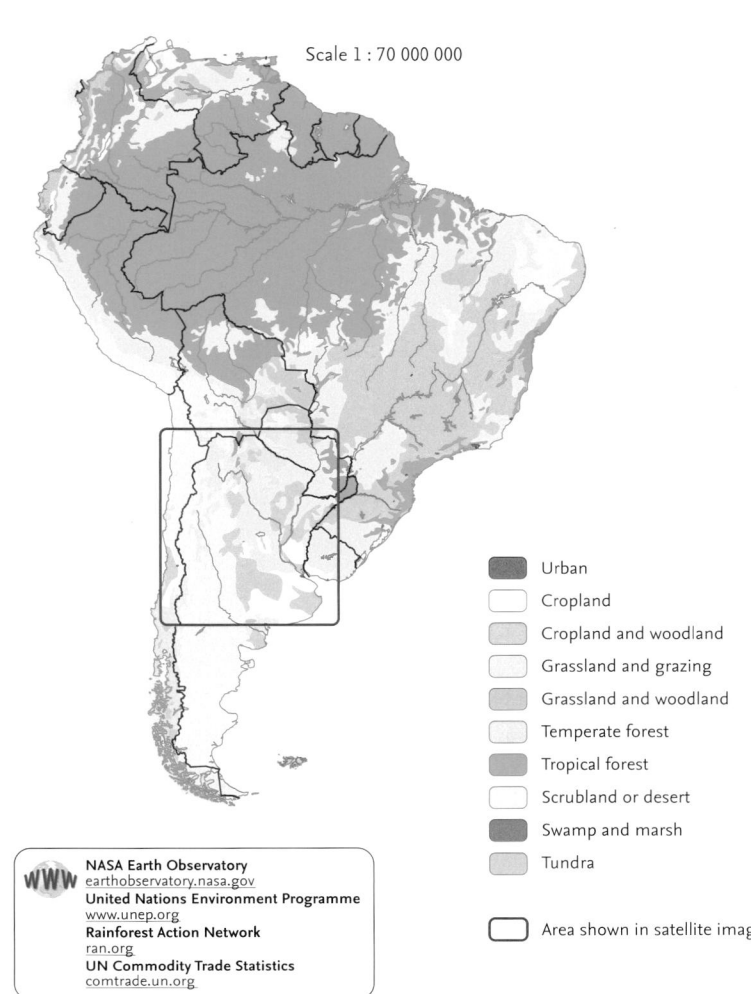

Scale 1 : 70 000 000

The highest mountains, the Andes, run along the left hand side of this true colour image. The range narrows in the south where a strip of snow can be seen on the highest peaks. Green featureless areas are the vast wetlands of Argentina and Paraguay. In the east the Uruguay river flows along the border between Argentina and Uruguay and into the Rio de La Plata. Sediment dumped by both the Uruguay and Paraná river shows as a murky brown colour in the bay.

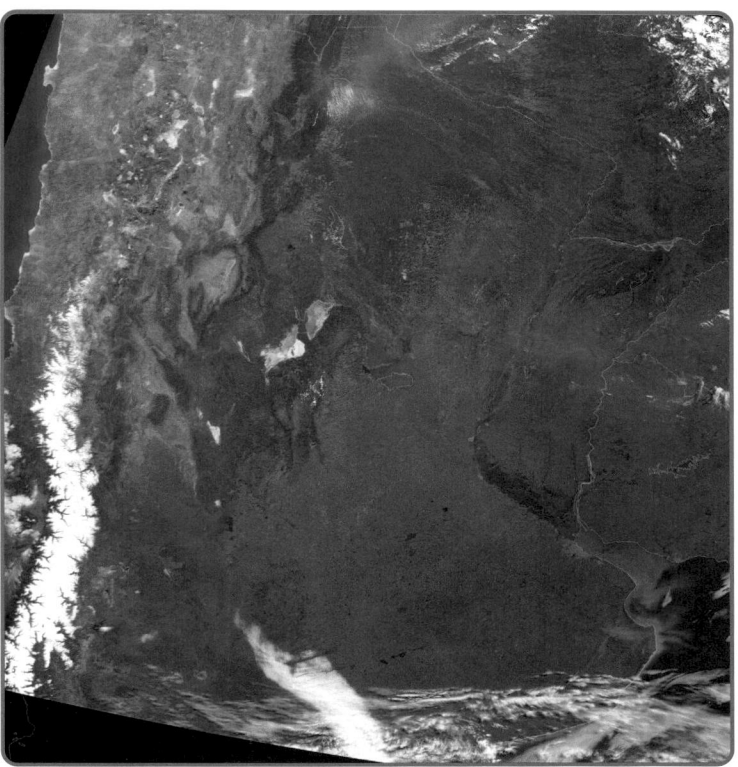

- Urban
- Cropland
- Cropland and woodland
- Grassland and grazing
- Grassland and woodland
- Temperate forest
- Tropical forest
- Scrubland or desert
- Swamp and marsh
- Tundra

- Area shown in satellite image

**www** NASA Earth Observatory
earthobservatory.nasa.gov
**United Nations Environment Programme**
www.unep.org
**Rainforest Action Network**
ran.org
**UN Commodity Trade Statistics**
comtrade.un.org

## 2 Population

Persons per sq. km
- over 1000
- 501 – 1000
- 101 – 500
- 11 – 100
- 1 – 10
- less than 1

Cities
- over 10 000 000
- 5 000 000 – 10 000 000
- 1 000 000 – 5 000 000

| Urban agglomeration | 2015 (projected) |
|---|---|
| **São Paulo** Brazil | 21 300 000 |
| **Buenos Aires** Argentina | 13 401 000 |
| **Rio de Janeiro** Brazil | 12 404 000 |
| **Lima** Peru | 9 659 000 |
| **Bogotá** Colombia | 9 521 000 |
| **Belo Horizonte** Brazil | 6 260 000 |
| **Santiago** Chile | 6 237 000 |

Scale 1 : 70 000 000

## 3 Trade

### Argentina
**GDP by sector, 2009**

Agriculture 8%
Industry 32%
Services 60%

**Main trading partners, 2009**

Imports
Others 38.6%
Brazil 29.3%
USA 13.4%
China 13.4%
Germany 5.3%
Total : US$ 40.3 billion

Exports
Brazil 20.4%
Chile 7.9%
USA 6.6%
China 6.6%
Netherlands 4.3%
Others 54.2%
Total : US$ 55.7 billion

### Colombia
**GDP by sector, 2009**

Agriculture 7%
Industry 34%
Services 59%

**Main trading partners, 2009**

Imports
USA 25.9%
Others 41.2%
China 13.5%
Mexico 9.5%
Brazil 5.8%
Germany 4.1%
Total : US$ 32.9 billion

Exports
USA 43.1%
Others 39.7%
China 4.9%
Ecuador 4.6%
Netherlands 4.1%
Venezuela 3.6%
Total : US$ 32.9 billion

### Chile
**GDP by sector, 2009**

Agriculture 3%
Industry 42%
Services 55%

**Main trading partners, 2009**

Imports
Others 53.8%
USA 16.8%
China 11.8%
Argentina 10.9%
Brazil 6.7%
Total : US$ 42.4 billion

Exports
China 23.2%
Others 45.4%
USA 11.3%
Japan 9.2%
S.Korea 5.8%
Brazil 5.1%
Total : US$ 53.7 billion

## Map labels

**Grid references (top):** B 90° · C 85° · D 80° · E 75° · F 70° · G 65°

**COLOMBIA**

Orinoco
Negro
Pico da Neblina 3014
Uaupés
Negro
Barcel
Nevado de Huila 5750
Neiva
Popayán
Tumaco
Florencia
Caquetá
Esmeraldas
Cabo de San Francisco
Pasto
Apaporis
Japurá
Nevado de Cumbal 4764
Ibarra
QUITO
Volcán Cotopaxi 5896
Cabo Pasado
Manta
Latacunga
Tena
Napo
Cabo Pantoja
Putumayo
Portoviejo
Chimborazo 6310
Ambato
Riobamba
**ECUADOR**
Curaray
AMAZ
Galapagos Islands (Ecuador)
Isla Santa Cruz
Isla San Cristóbal
Baquerizo Moreno
Isla Isabela
Bahía de Santa Elena
**Guayaquil**
Alausí
Macas
Tigre
Pastaza
Iquitos
Amazon
Tefé
Golfo de Guayaquil
Cuenca
Azogues
Marañón
Coari
Tumbes
Machala
Loja
Benjamim Constant
Jutaí
A M A Z
Talara
Macará
Cord. del Condor
Tarapoto
Juruá
Tapauá
Sullana
Catacaos
Marañón
Huallaga
**PACIFIC**
Bahía de Sechura
Punta Negra
Olmos
Cruzeiro do Sul
Purus
Huma
Chiclayo
Cajamarca
Pucallpa
Tarauacá
**OCEAN**
Pacasmayo
Cordillera Central
Cordillera Oriental
Cordillera Azul
**A C R E**
Ituxi
Sena Madureira
Rio Branco
Abuná
Po Ve
**Trujillo**
Nevado de Huascarán 6768
Huánuco
Ucayali
Abancay
Cobija
Acre
Abuná
Ariqueme
Chimbote
Cordillera Negra
**P E R U**
Cerro de Pasco
Urubamba
Cordillera de Carabaya
Madre de Dios
R O N
Huarmey
Huancayo
Cordillera Vilcabamba
Apurimac
Puerto Maldonado
Riberalta
Mo
Huacho
Cusco
Inambari
Madidi
Beni
Gu
**Callao**
Huancavelica
Ayacucho
Cerros de Yácuma
Laguna Rogagua
**LIMA**
Cordillera Occidental
Lago de San Luis
Pisco
Ica
Abancay
Juliaca
San Borja
Llanos de Mojos
Yungas
Nazca
Nudo Coropuna 6425
Cordillera Oriental
6402
Trinidad
Chala
**Arequipa**
Lake Titicaca
**LA PAZ**
**B O L I**
Moquegua
**SUCRE**
Tacna
Nevado Sajama 6542
Oruro
Cochabamba
Sant Cr
Arica
Altiplano
Cabeza
**SUCRE**
Iquique
Nevado Sajama
Potosí
Boyui
Tocopilla
Salar de Coipasa
Lago de Poopó
Uyuni
Monte
Salar de Uyuni
Tupiza
Cordillera Central
Calama
Tarija
Pichanal
Antofagasta
Punta Tetas
Salar de Atacama
San Salvador de Jujuy
Taltal
Volcán Llullaillaco 6723
Nevados de Cachi 6720
Salta
Punta Ballena
**D A R G E**
Chañaral
Nevado Ojos del Salado 6908
San Miguel de Tucumán
Punta Morro
Copiapó
Cerro Bonete 6872
Concepción
La Banda
Catamarca
**C H I L E**
Sierra de Mejicana 6250
La Rioja
La Serena
Cerro de Olivares
Cerro Las Tortolas
Patquía
Coquimbo
Salir Gran
San Juan
Cord
Los Vilos
Sierras de Córd
Cerro Champaquí 2880
Cerro Aconcagua 6959
**Mendoza**
Viña del Mar
**Valparaíso**
**SANTIAGO**
San
San Bernardo
Rancagua
San Luis
Desaguadero

**São Paulo** (inset map)

Res. Juqueri
Juqueri
Caieiras
Res. Pirapora
Guarulhos
Tietê
Tietê
Suzano
Osasco
**São Paulo**
Cotia
Cotia
Pinheiros
São Caetano do Sul
Embu-Mirim
Tamanduatej
Res. Guarapiranga
**Santo André**
Tatuapeba
Res. Pedro Beicht
Res. Billinos
Res. Rio das Pedras

| | Land use |
|---|---|
| | Residential |
| | Industrial |
| | Commercial |
| | Commercial/Residential |
| | Government |
| | Recreation |
| | Parks |
| | Other use |
| —— | Road |
| —— | Railway |

Scale 1 : 750 000
0 5 10 15 km

## Key

### Relief and physical features

Relief metres
5000
3000
2000
1000
500
200
sea level
0 sea level
200 under sea level
4000
6000

6959 ▲ Mountain height (in metres)

### Water features

River
Intermittent river
Canal
Lake / Reservoir
Intermittent lake
Marsh

### Communications

—— Railway
—— Road
⊕ Main airport

### Administration

**Boundaries**

—— International
—— Internal
--- Disputed

**Settlement**

Cities and towns in order of size

National capital
■ **BUENOS AIRES**
■ **BRASÍLIA**
□ SUCRE

Other city or town
● **São Paulo**
● **Recife**
○ **Teresina**
○ Vitória
○ Salto

Scale 1 : 15 000 000
0 200 400 600 800 km

Lambert Azimuthal Equal Area projection

## 1 Population Density

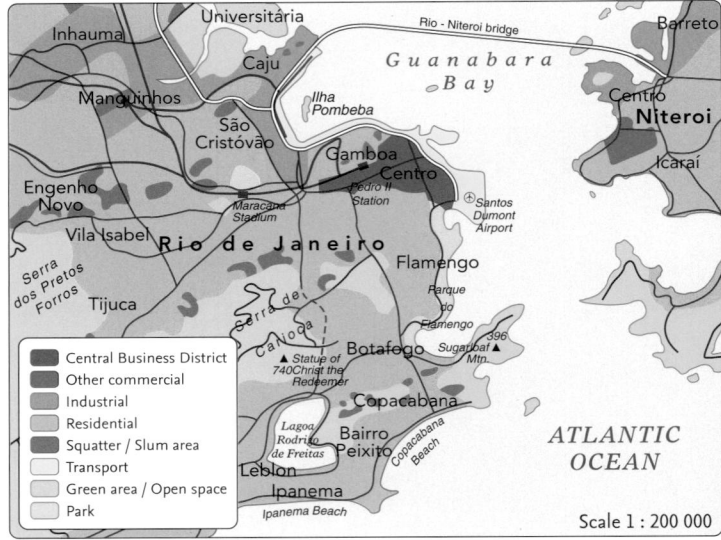

Persons per sq. km

- over 50
- 11 – 50
- 1 – 10
- less than 1

Cities

- ● over 10 000 000
- ◐ 5 000 000 – 10 000 000
- ◔ 1 000 000 – 5 000 000
- ○ 500 000 – 1 000 000
- ○ 100 000 – 500 000

Scale 1 : 45 000 000

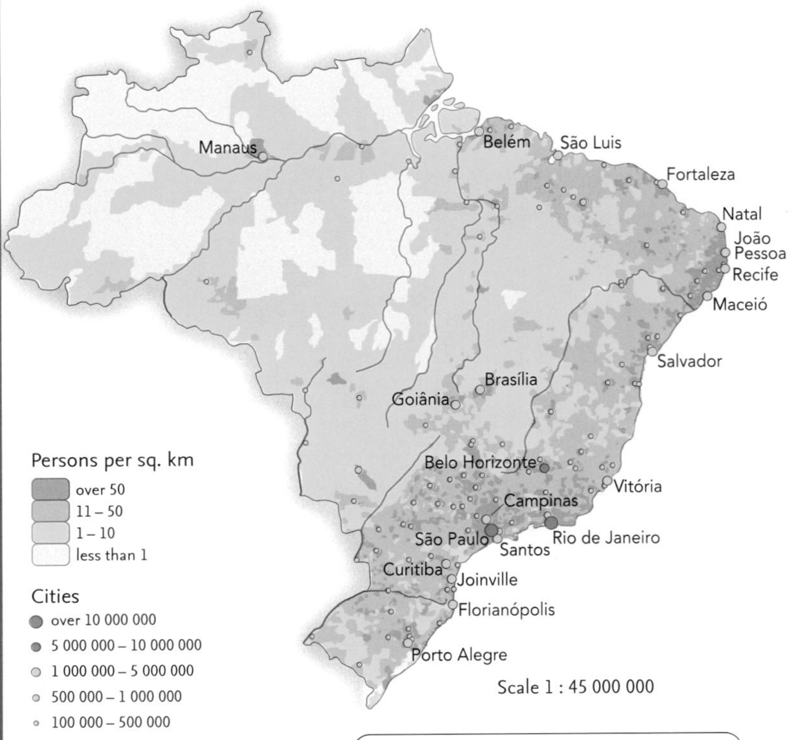

**WWW** Brazilian Institute of Geography and Statistics
www.ibge.gov.br

## 2 Population Structure

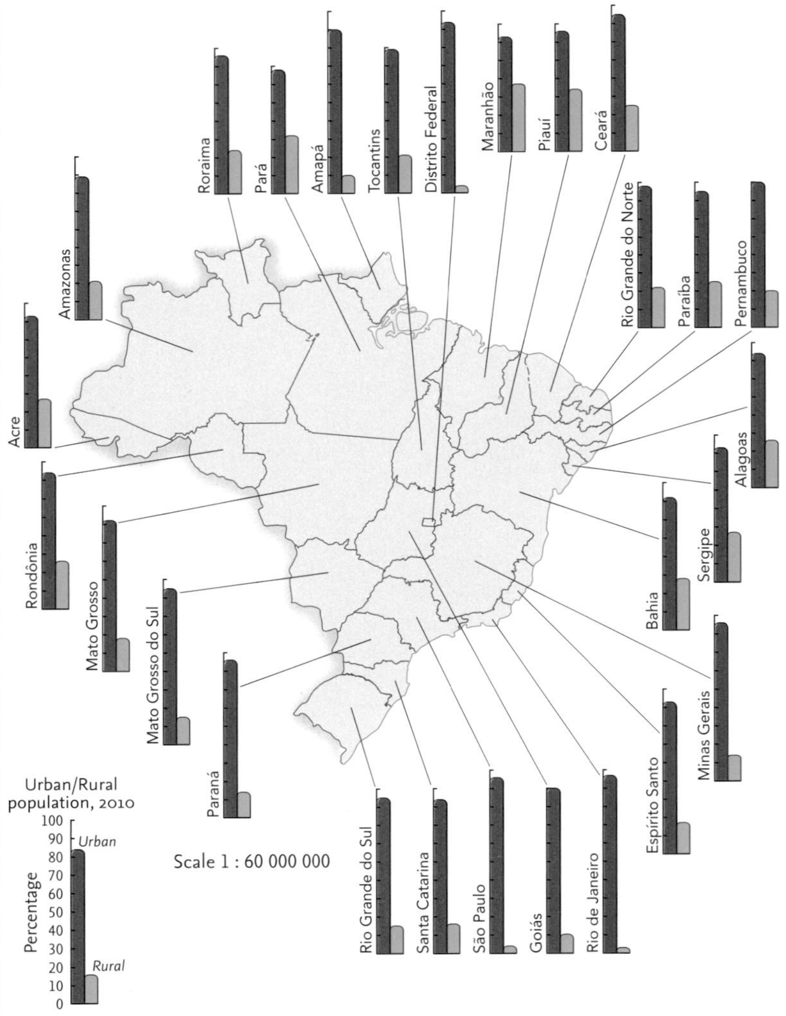

Urban/Rural
population, 2010

Urban

Rural

Scale 1 : 60 000 000

Brazil urban population, 2010 (% of total) : 84%

## 3 Main Urban Agglomerations

| Urban agglomeration | 1980 | 1995 | 2005 | 2015 (projected) |
|---|---|---|---|---|
| São Paulo | 12 497 000 | 16 417 000 | 18 333 000 | 21 300 000 |
| Rio de Janeiro | 8 741 000 | 9 888 000 | 11 469 000 | 12 404 000 |
| Belo Horizonte | 2 588 000 | 3 899 000 | 5 304 000 | 6 260 000 |
| Porto Alegre | 2 273 000 | 3 349 000 | 3 795 000 | 4 316 000 |
| Brasília | 1 162 000 | 1 778 000 | 3 341 000 | 4 296 000 |
| Salvador | 1 754 000 | 2 819 000 | 3 331 000 | 4 243 000 |
| Recife | 2 337 000 | 3 168 000 | 3 527 000 | 4 107 000 |
| Fortaleza | 1 569 000 | 2 660 000 | 3 261 000 | 4 011 000 |
| Curitiba | 1 427 000 | 2 270 000 | 2 871 000 | 3 791 000 |
| Campinas | 926 000 | 1 607 000 | 2 640 000 | 3 018 000 |
| Belém | 992 000 | 1 574 000 | 2 097 000 | 2 351 000 |
| Goiânia | 707 000 | 1 006 000 | 1 878 000 | 2 327 000 |

## 4 Rio de Janeiro Urban Land Use

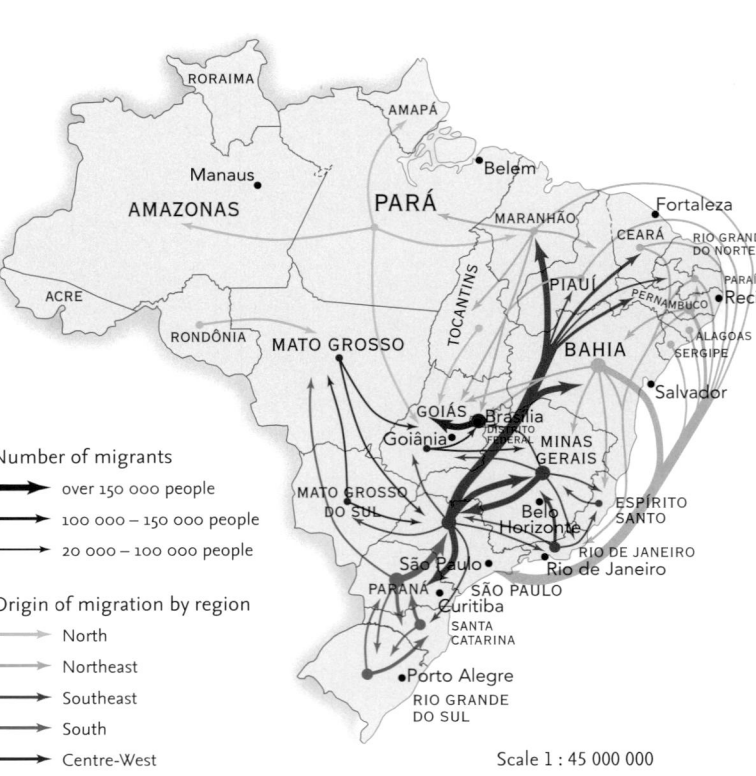

- Central Business District
- Other commercial
- Industrial
- Residential
- Squatter / Slum area
- Transport
- Green area / Open space
- Park

Scale 1 : 200 000

## 5 Internal Migration

Number of migrants

- → over 150 000 people
- → 100 000 – 150 000 people
- → 20 000 – 100 000 people

Origin of migration by region

- → North
- → Northeast
- → Southeast
- → South
- → Centre-West

Scale 1 : 45 000 000

## 6 Regional Comparisons

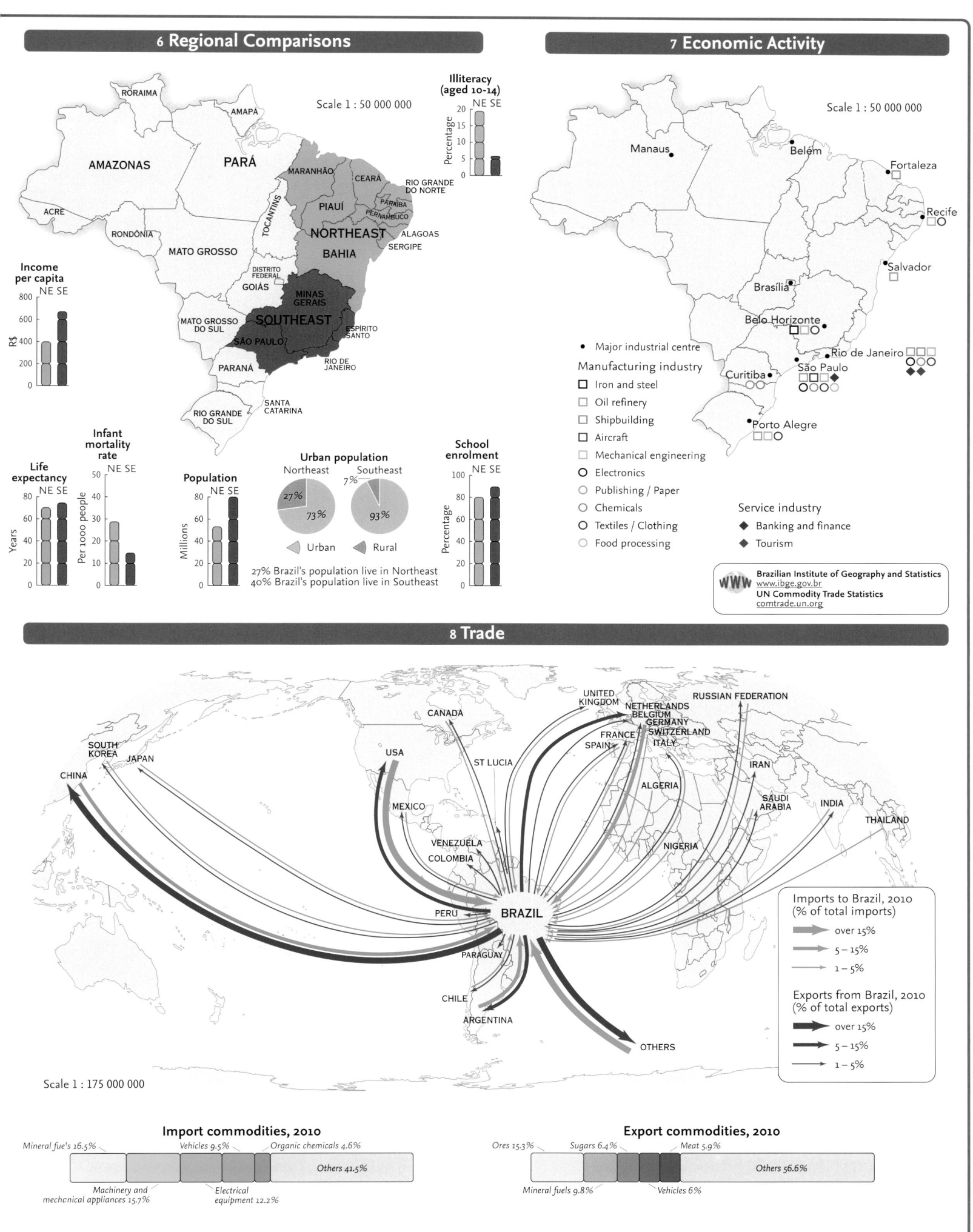

Scale 1 : 50 000 000

Illiteracy (aged 10-14)

Income per capita
NE SE
R$

Life expectancy
NE SE
Years

Infant mortality rate
NE SE
Per 1000 people

Population
NE SE
Millions

### Urban population

Northeast
27%
73%

Southeast
7%
93%

▷ Urban   ▷ Rural

27% Brazil's population live in Northeast
40% Brazil's population live in Southeast

School enrolment
NE SE
Percentage

## 7 Economic Activity

Scale 1 : 50 000 000

Manaus · Belém
Fortaleza
Recife
Salvador
Brasília
Belo Horizonte
Rio de Janeiro
Curitiba   São Paulo
Porto Alegre

· Major industrial centre

Manufacturing industry
□ Iron and steel
□ Oil refinery
□ Shipbuilding
□ Aircraft
□ Mechanical engineering
○ Electronics
○ Publishing / Paper
○ Chemicals
○ Textiles / Clothing
○ Food processing

Service industry
◆ Banking and finance
◆ Tourism

**www** Brazilian Institute of Geography and Statistics
www.ibge.gov.br
**UN Commodity Trade Statistics**
comtrade.un.org

## 8 Trade

Scale 1 : 175 000 000

Imports to Brazil, 2010 (% of total imports)
→ over 15%
→ 5 – 15%
→ 1 – 5%

Exports from Brazil, 2010 (% of total exports)
➡ over 15%
➡ 5 – 15%
→ 1 – 5%

### Import commodities, 2010

Mineral fue's 16.5% | Vehicles 9.5% | Organic chemicals 4.6% | Others 41.5%
Machinery and mechcnical appliances 15.7% | Electrical equipment 12.2%

### Export commodities, 2010

Ores 15.3% | Sugars 6.4% | Meat 5.9% | Others 56.6%
Mineral fuels 9.8% | Vehicles 6%

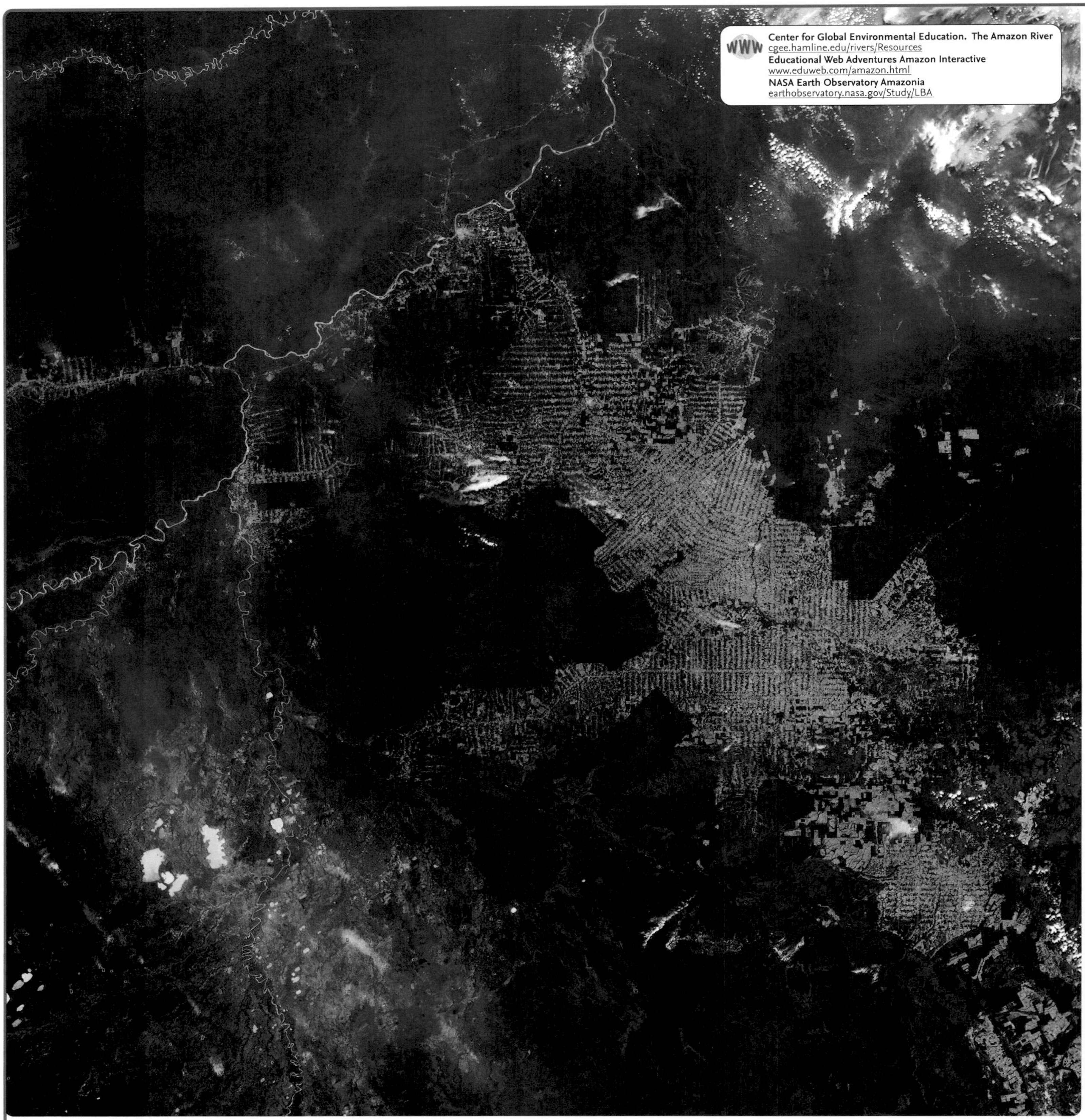

**Deforested areas**
Yellowish green coloured lines mark land cleared of forest for commercial logging. Most of the deforestation has taken place in Rondônia state which covers most of the right hand side of the image.

**Forest**
Areas of forest appear deep green on the image. Left of centre the forests of the Pando region of Bolivia remain undisturbed.

**Rivers**
The course of the Madeira river is clearly visible where it flows through forest, top centre.

**Highland**
The highland areas of the Serra dos Parecis, in Rondônia state, appear dark brown.

**Fires**
Numerous smoke plumes from forest fires suggest the practice of slash and burn farming is still underway.

**Water bodies**
Deep reservoirs are almost black in the image, however the outlines of shallower lagoons on the Bolivian side of the border show clearly in pale green.

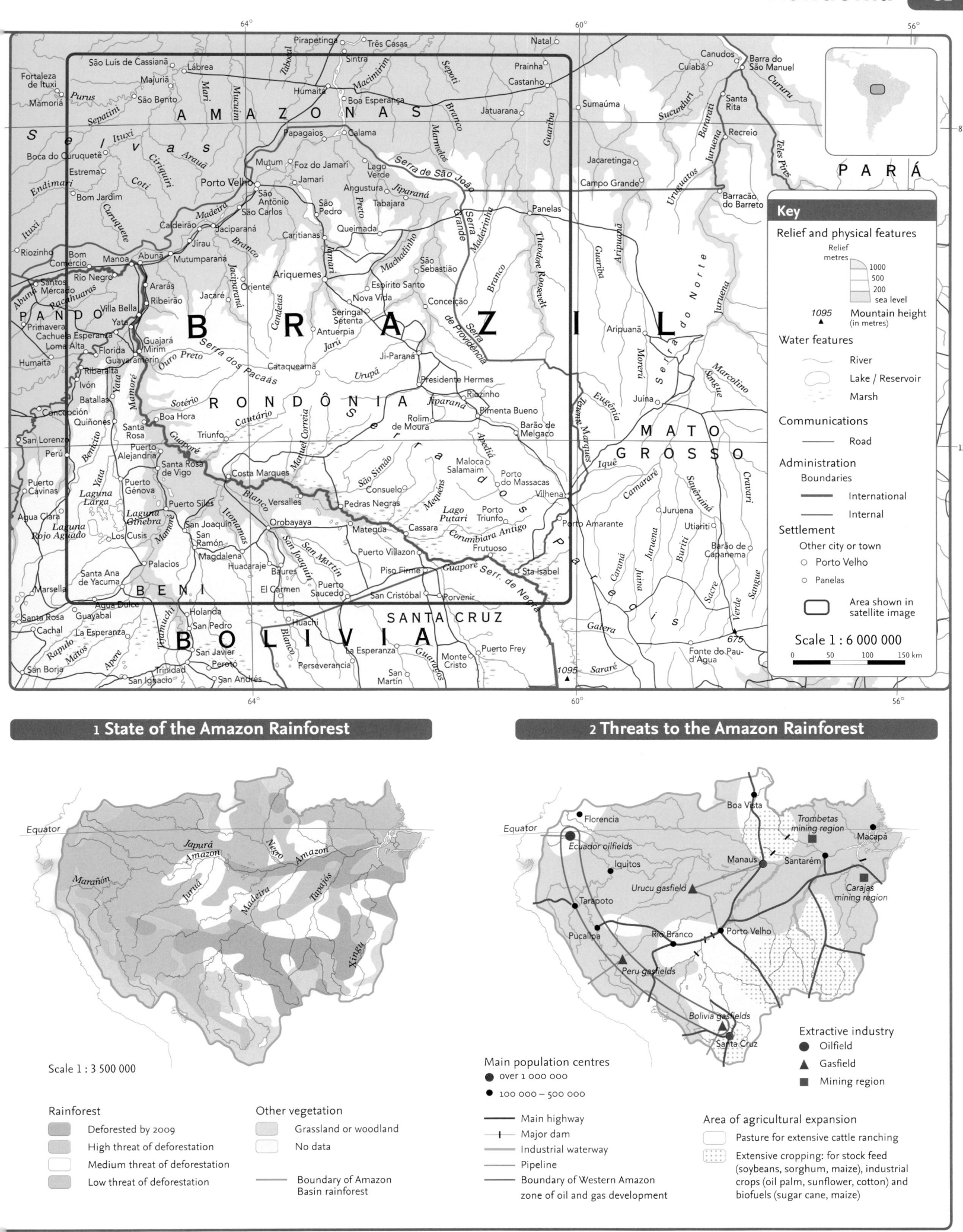

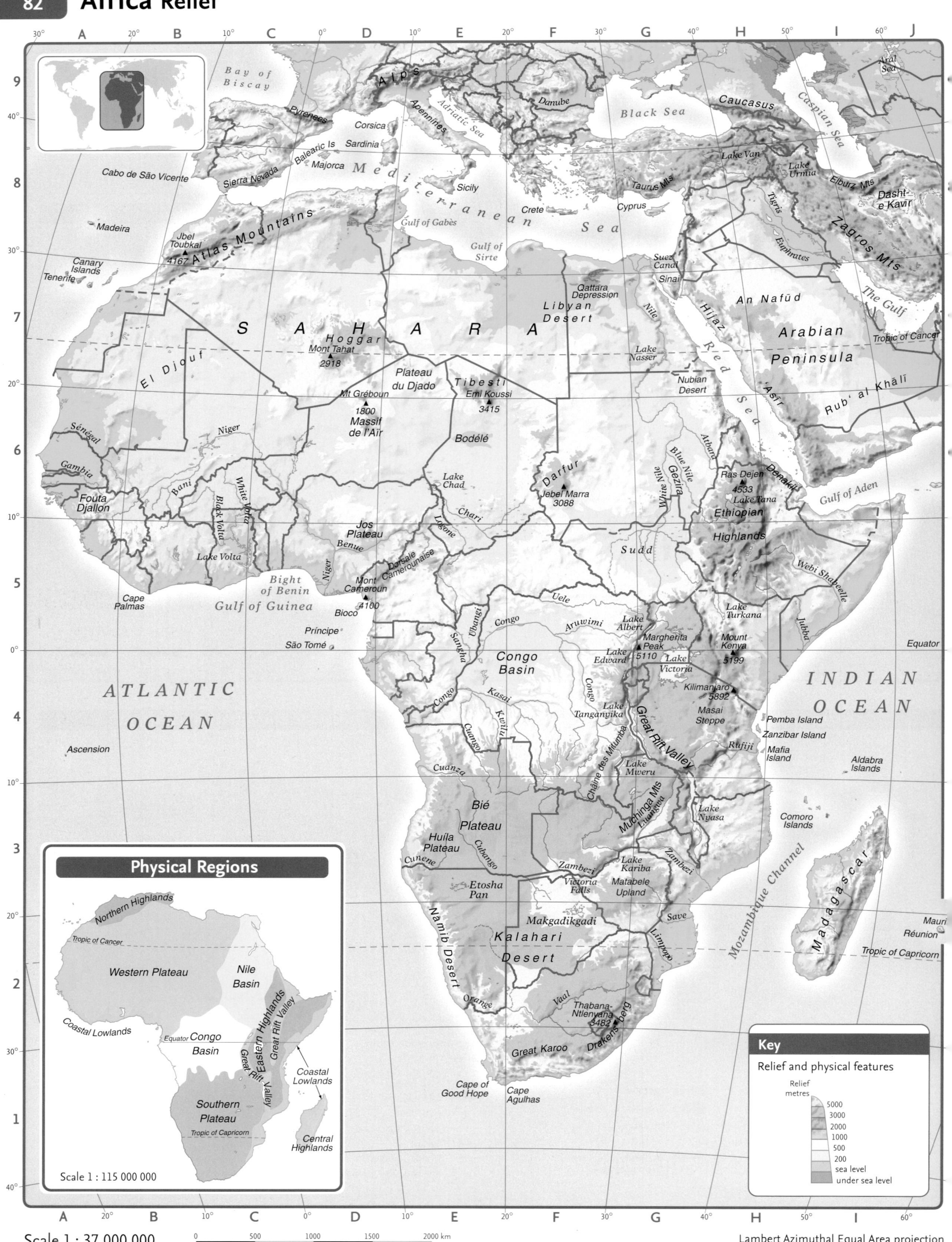

ATLANTIC OCEAN

INDIAN OCEAN

S A H A R A

Mediterranean Sea

Black Sea

Caspian Sea

Arabian Peninsula

**Physical Regions**

Northern Highlands

Western Plateau

Nile Basin

Eastern Highlands

Congo Basin

Great Rift Valley

Coastal Lowlands

Southern Plateau

Central Highlands

Scale 1 : 115 000 000

**Key**

Relief and physical features

Relief
metres

5000
3000
2000
1000
500
200
sea level
under sea level

Scale 1 : 37 000 000

0    500    1000    1500    2000 km

Lambert Azimuthal Equal Area projection

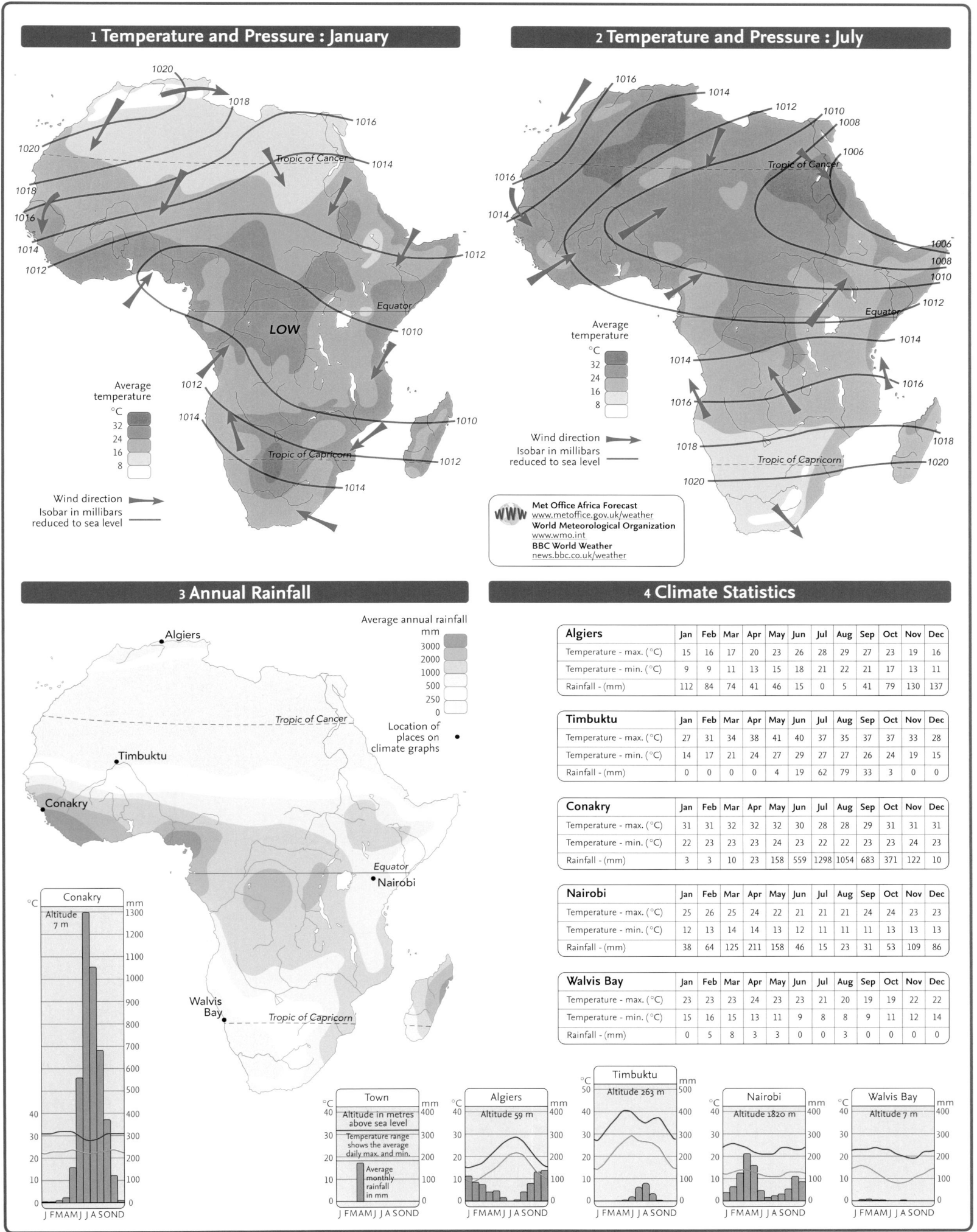

## 1 Temperature and Pressure : January

Average temperature
°C
32
24
16
8

Wind direction
Isobar in millibars
reduced to sea level

## 2 Temperature and Pressure : July

Average temperature
°C
32
24
16
8

Wind direction
Isobar in millibars
reduced to sea level

WWW **Met Office Africa Forecast**
www.metoffice.gov.uk/weather
**World Meteorological Organization**
www.wmo.int
**BBC World Weather**
news.bbc.co.uk/weather

## 3 Annual Rainfall

Average annual rainfall
mm
3000
2000
1000
500
250
0

Location of
places on
climate graphs •

## 4 Climate Statistics

| **Algiers** | Jan | Feb | Mar | Apr | May | Jun | Jul | Aug | Sep | Oct | Nov | Dec |
|---|---|---|---|---|---|---|---|---|---|---|---|---|
| Temperature - max. (°C) | 15 | 16 | 17 | 20 | 23 | 26 | 28 | 29 | 27 | 23 | 19 | 16 |
| Temperature - min. (°C) | 9 | 9 | 11 | 13 | 15 | 18 | 21 | 22 | 21 | 17 | 13 | 11 |
| Rainfall - (mm) | 112 | 84 | 74 | 41 | 46 | 15 | 0 | 5 | 41 | 79 | 130 | 137 |

| **Timbuktu** | Jan | Feb | Mar | Apr | May | Jun | Jul | Aug | Sep | Oct | Nov | Dec |
|---|---|---|---|---|---|---|---|---|---|---|---|---|
| Temperature - max. (°C) | 27 | 31 | 34 | 38 | 41 | 40 | 37 | 35 | 37 | 37 | 33 | 28 |
| Temperature - min. (°C) | 14 | 17 | 21 | 24 | 27 | 29 | 27 | 27 | 26 | 24 | 19 | 15 |
| Rainfall - (mm) | 0 | 0 | 0 | 0 | 4 | 19 | 62 | 79 | 33 | 3 | 0 | 0 |

| **Conakry** | Jan | Feb | Mar | Apr | May | Jun | Jul | Aug | Sep | Oct | Nov | Dec |
|---|---|---|---|---|---|---|---|---|---|---|---|---|
| Temperature - max. (°C) | 31 | 31 | 32 | 32 | 32 | 30 | 28 | 28 | 29 | 31 | 31 | 31 |
| Temperature - min. (°C) | 22 | 23 | 23 | 23 | 24 | 23 | 22 | 22 | 23 | 23 | 24 | 23 |
| Rainfall - (mm) | 3 | 3 | 10 | 23 | 158 | 559 | 1298 | 1054 | 683 | 371 | 122 | 10 |

| **Nairobi** | Jan | Feb | Mar | Apr | May | Jun | Jul | Aug | Sep | Oct | Nov | Dec |
|---|---|---|---|---|---|---|---|---|---|---|---|---|
| Temperature - max. (°C) | 25 | 26 | 25 | 24 | 22 | 21 | 21 | 21 | 24 | 24 | 23 | 23 |
| Temperature - min. (°C) | 12 | 13 | 14 | 14 | 13 | 12 | 11 | 11 | 11 | 13 | 13 | 13 |
| Rainfall - (mm) | 38 | 64 | 125 | 211 | 158 | 46 | 15 | 23 | 31 | 53 | 109 | 86 |

| **Walvis Bay** | Jan | Feb | Mar | Apr | May | Jun | Jul | Aug | Sep | Oct | Nov | Dec |
|---|---|---|---|---|---|---|---|---|---|---|---|---|
| Temperature - max. (°C) | 23 | 23 | 23 | 24 | 23 | 23 | 21 | 20 | 19 | 19 | 22 | 22 |
| Temperature - min. (°C) | 15 | 16 | 15 | 13 | 11 | 9 | 8 | 8 | 9 | 11 | 12 | 14 |
| Rainfall - (mm) | 0 | 5 | 8 | 3 | 3 | 0 | 0 | 3 | 0 | 0 | 0 | 0 |

Conakry
Altitude 7 m

Town
Altitude in metres
above sea level
Temperature range
shows the average
daily max. and min.
Average
monthly
rainfall
in mm

Algiers
Altitude 59 m

Timbuktu
Altitude 263 m

Nairobi
Altitude 1820 m

Walvis Bay
Altitude 7 m

Scale 1 : 77 000 000          0    1000    2000    3000 km          Lambert Azimuthal Equal Area projection

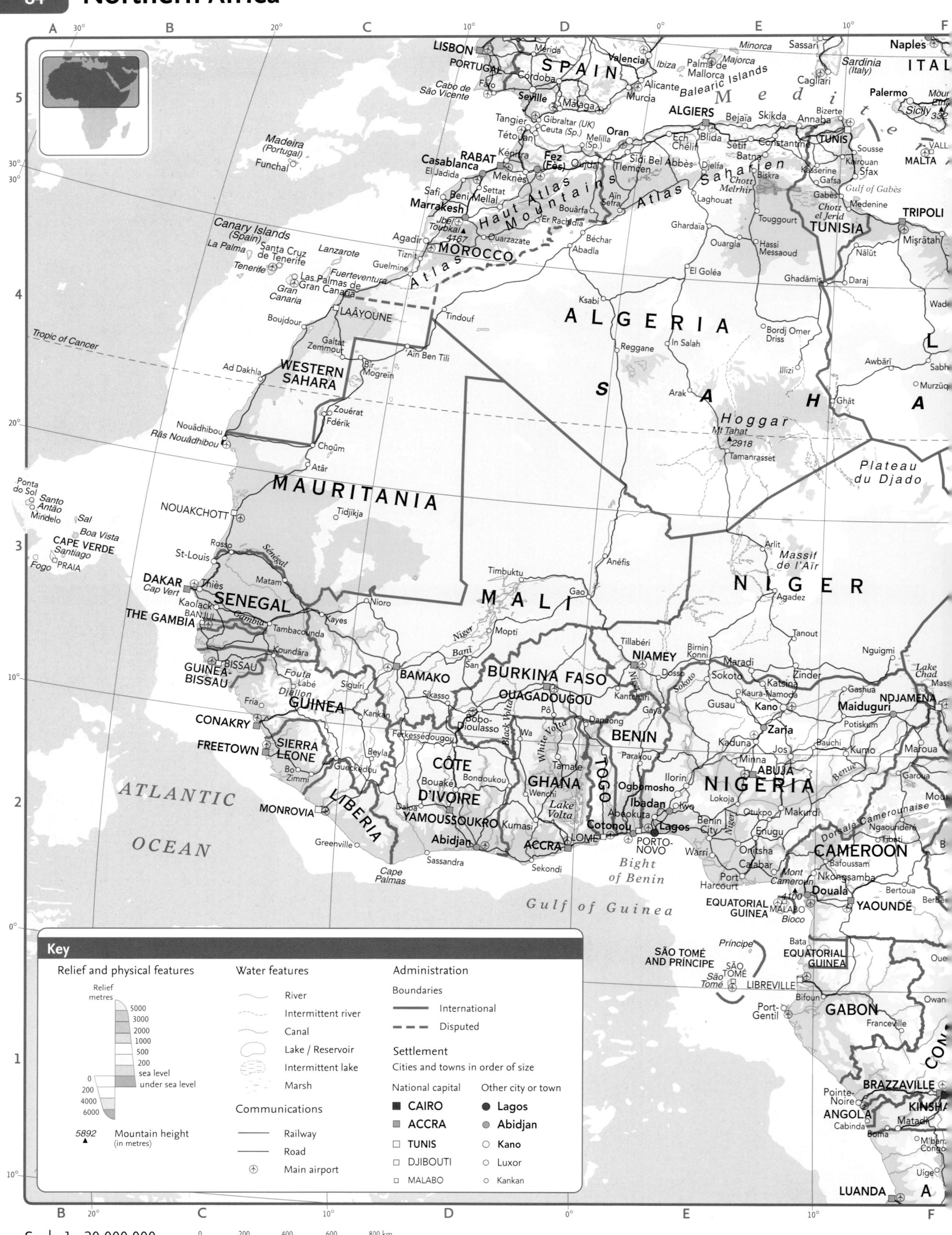

Scale 1 : 20 000 000

| 0 | 200 | 400 | 600 | 800 km |

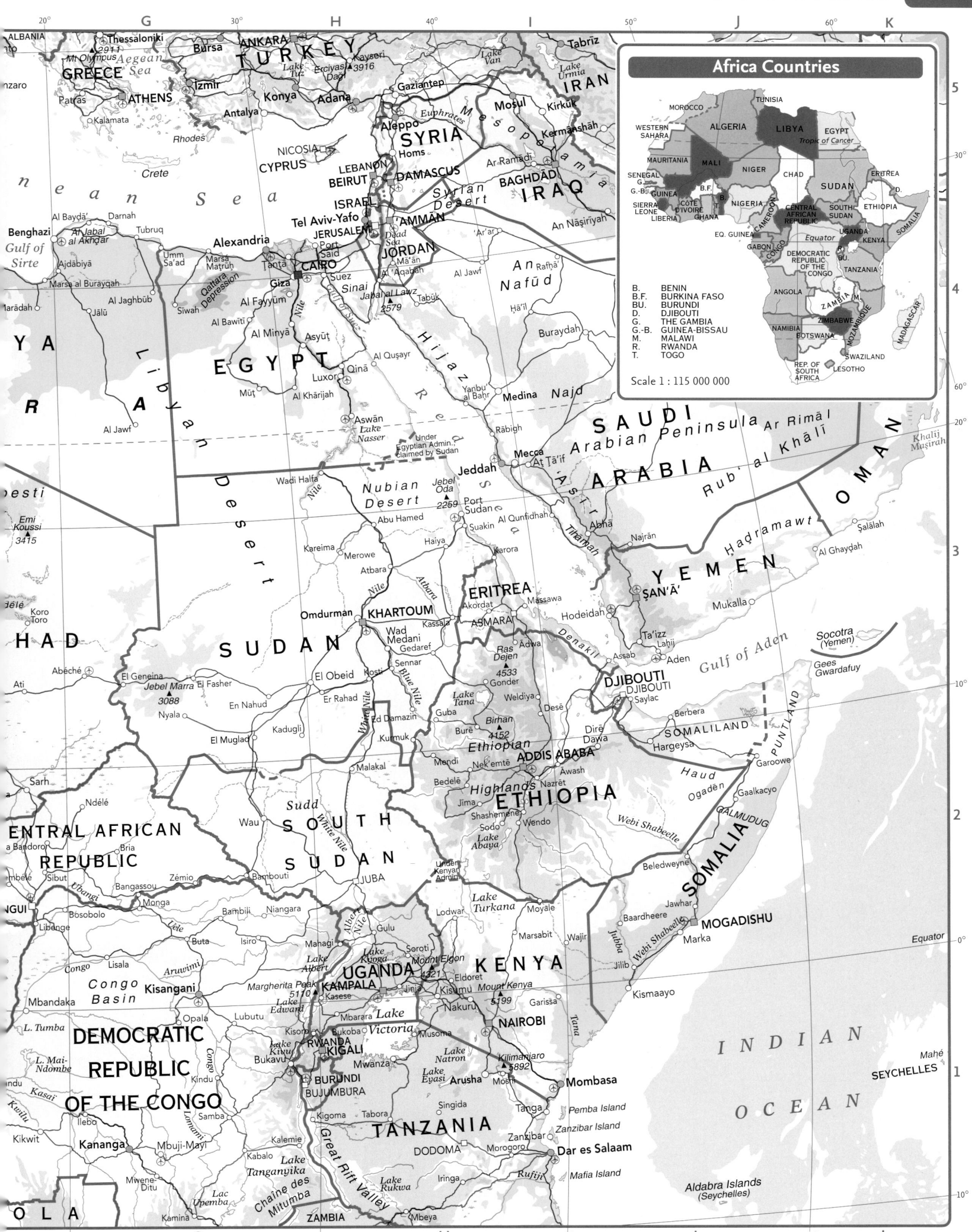

## Africa Countries

| | |
|---|---|
| B. | BENIN |
| B.F. | BURKINA FASO |
| BU. | BURUNDI |
| D. | DJIBOUTI |
| G. | THE GAMBIA |
| G.-B. | GUINEA-BISSAU |
| M. | MALAWI |
| R. | RWANDA |
| T. | TOGO |

Scale 1 : 115 000 000

Lambert Azimuthal Equal Area projection

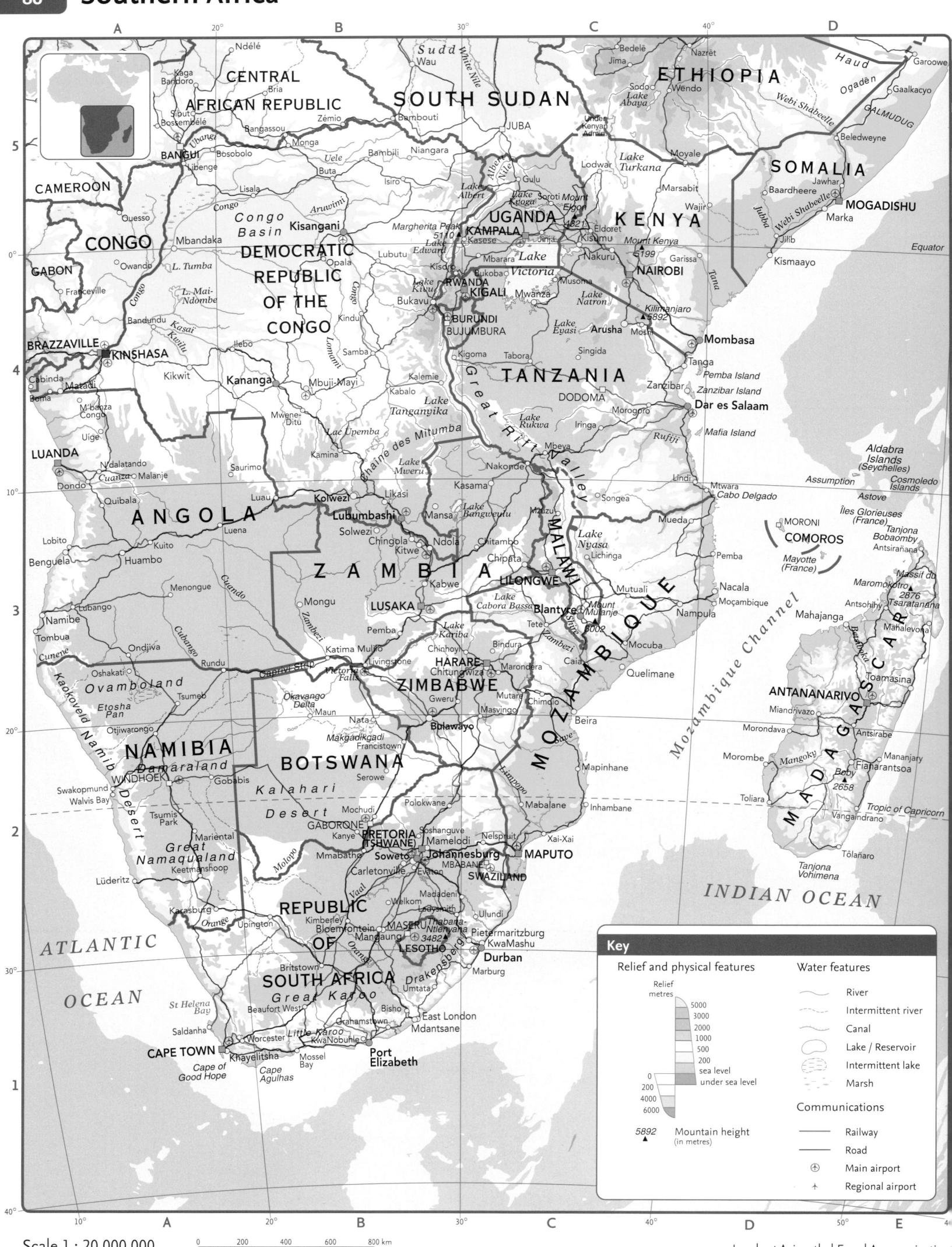

Lambert Azimuthal Equal Area projection

Key

**Administration**

Boundaries

———— International

- - - - Disputed

———— Internal

.......... National Park / Reserve

**Settlement**

Cities and towns in order of size

National capital    Other city or town

■ **NAIROBI**    ● **Durban**

□ **BANGUI**    ○ **Arusha**

□ **DODOMA**    ○ Namibe

□ MORONI    ○ Walvis Bay

## 1 Population Density

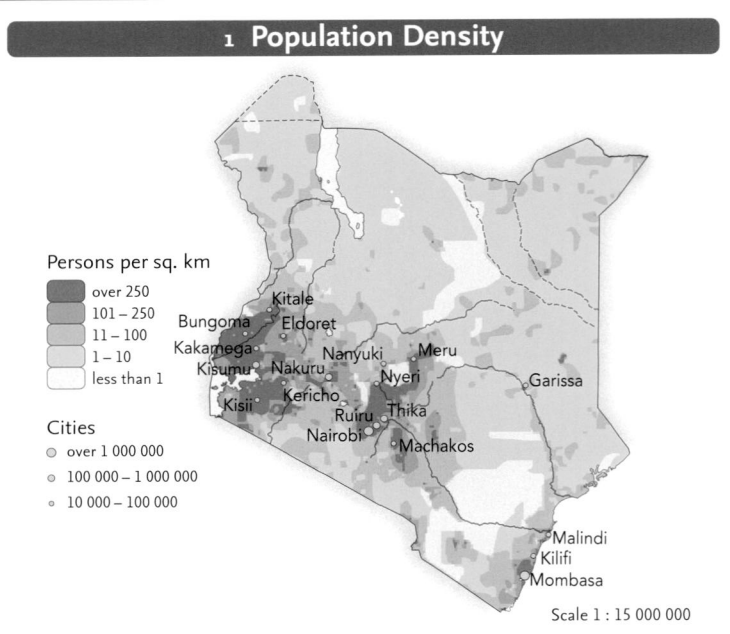

Persons per sq. km
- over 250
- 101 – 250
- 11 – 100
- 1 – 10
- less than 1

Cities
- ⦿ over 1 000 000
- ⊙ 100 000 – 1 000 000
- ∘ 10 000 – 100 000

Scale 1 : 15 000 000

## 2 Population Change

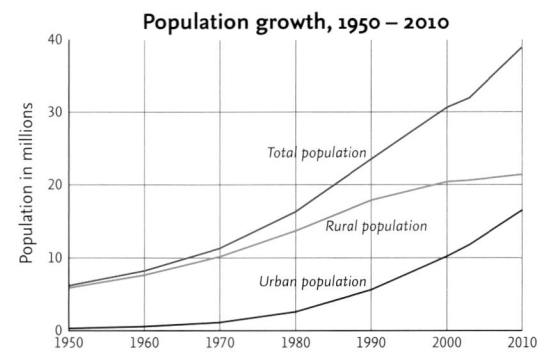

Percentage change, 1999 – 2006
- 30 – 40
- 20 – 30
- 10 – 20
- 0 – 10

Scale 1 : 15 000 000

## 3 Urban Agglomerations

| Urban agglomeration | 1969 census | 1989 census | 1999 census | 2009 census |
|---|---|---|---|---|
| Nairobi | 509 286 | 1 324 570 | 2 143 254 | 3 138 369 |
| Mombasa | 247 073 | 461 753 | 665 018 | 939 370 |

**www** Government of Kenya
www.statehousekenya.go.ke
Kenya Tourist Board
www.magicalkenya.com
Central Bureau of Statistics
http://www.knbs.or.ke

## 4 Population Growth

**Population growth, 1950 – 2010**

Total population

Rural population

Urban population

## 5 Tourism

**Tourist arrivals 2000 – 2009**

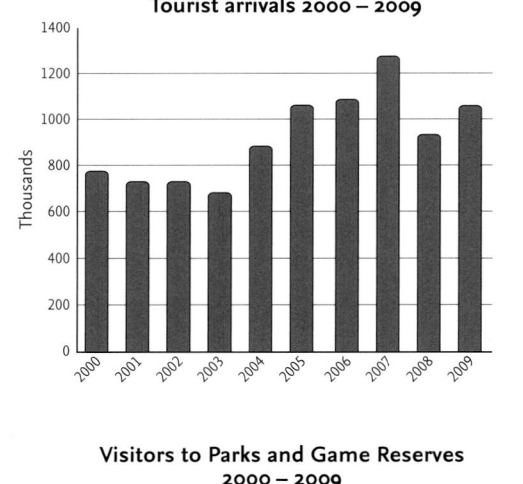

**Visitors to Parks and Game Reserves 2000 – 2009**

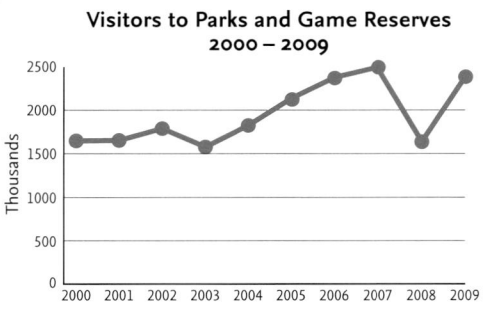

- National Park
- National Reserve
- • Hotel
- ∘ Lodge

Scale 1 : 10 500 000

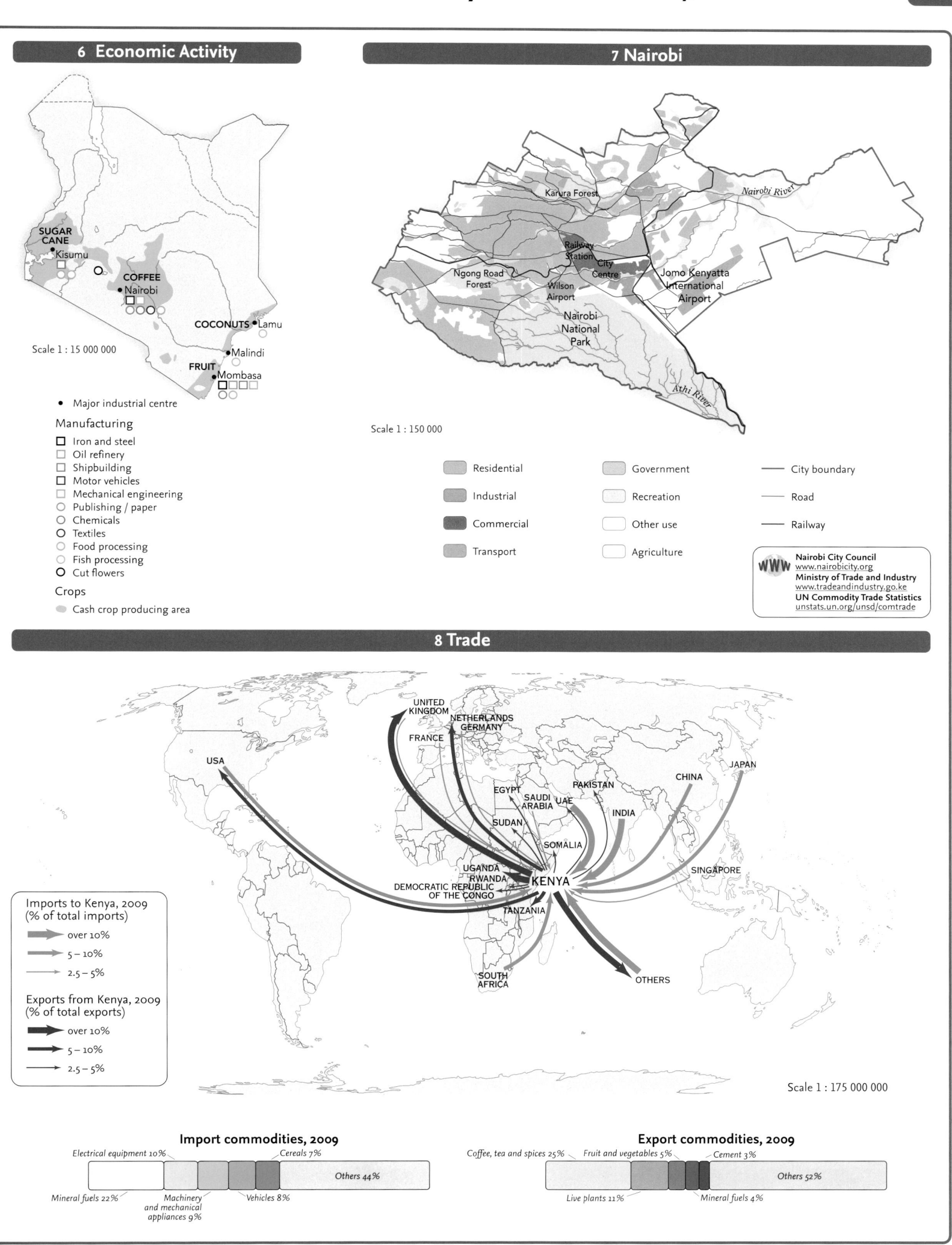

## 6 Economic Activity

SUGAR
CANE
Kisumu

COFFEE
Nairobi

COCONUTS Lamu

Scale 1 : 15 000 000

Malindi

FRUIT
Mombasa

- Major industrial centre

Manufacturing
- Iron and steel
- Oil refinery
- Shipbuilding
- Motor vehicles
- Mechanical engineering
- Publishing / paper
- Chemicals
- Textiles
- Food processing
- Fish processing
- Cut flowers

Crops
- Cash crop producing area

## 7 Nairobi

Karura Forest

Nairobi River

Railway
Station
City
Centre

Ngong Road
Forest

Wilson
Airport

Jomo Kenyatta
International
Airport

Nairobi
National
Park

Athi River

Scale 1 : 150 000

| | |
|---|---|
| Residential | Government |
| Industrial | Recreation |
| Commercial | Other use |
| Transport | Agriculture |

— City boundary
— Road
— Railway

WWW **Nairobi City Council**
www.nairobicity.org
**Ministry of Trade and Industry**
www.tradeandindustry.go.ke
**UN Commodity Trade Statistics**
unstats.un.org/unsd/comtrade

## 8 Trade

UNITED
KINGDOM
NETHERLANDS
GERMANY
FRANCE

USA

EGYPT
SAUDI
ARABIA UAE
SUDAN
SOMALIA

PAKISTAN

CHINA

JAPAN

INDIA

SINGAPORE

UGANDA
RWANDA
DEMOCRATIC REPUBLIC
OF THE CONGO
KENYA

TANZANIA

SOUTH
AFRICA

OTHERS

Imports to Kenya, 2009
(% of total imports)
→ over 10%
→ 5 – 10%
→ 2.5 – 5%

Exports from Kenya, 2009
(% of total exports)
→ over 10%
→ 5 – 10%
→ 2.5 – 5%

Scale 1 : 175 000 000

### Import commodities, 2009

Electrical equipment 10%
Cereals 7%
Others 44%
Mineral fuels 22%
Machinery
and mechanical
appliances 9%
Vehicles 8%

### Export commodities, 2009

Coffee, tea and spices 25%
Fruit and vegetables 5%
Cement 3%
Others 52%
Live plants 11%
Mineral fuels 4%

ARCTIC OCEAN

Norwegian Sea

North Sea

Baltic Sea

Barents Sea

North European Plain

Central Russian Upland

West Siberian Plain

Central Siberian Plateau

S I B E R I A

Laptev Sea

Sea of Okh

Ural Mountains

Volga

Caspian Sea

Black Sea

Caucasus

El'brus 5642

Mount Ararat 5165

Aral Sea

Lake Balkhash

Lake Zaysan

Altai Mountains

Lake Baikal

Stanovoy Khrebet

Yablonovyy Khrebet

Da Hinggan Ling

Manchuria

Tien Shan

Gobi

Turpan Pendi

Lop Nur

Taklimakan Desert

Kunlun Shan

North China Plain

Huang He

Yellow Sea

Zagros Mts

Iranian Plateau

Dasht-e Kavir

Hindu Kush

Karakoram Ra.

K2 8611

Plateau of Tibet

H i m a l a y a

Gongga Shan 7514

Chang Jiang

Arabian Peninsula

An Nafūd

Rub' al Khālī

Makran

Thar Desert

Indus

Sutlej

Dhaulagiri 8167

Annapurna 8091

Mount Everest 8848

Ganges

Brahmaputra

Nan Ling

Xi Jiang

Taiwan

Gulf of Aden

Socotra

Arabian Sea

Deccan

Western Ghats

Eastern Ghats

Godavari

Narmada

Yamuna

Bay of Bengal

Mouths of the Ganges

Arakan Yoma

Irrawaddy

Salween

Mekong

Hainan

South China Sea

Palawan

Luzon

Philipp

Laccadive Islands

Cape Comorin

Sri Lanka

Maldives

Andaman Islands

Andaman Sea

Nicobar Islands

Gulf of Thailand

Strait of Malacca

Peninsular Malaysia

Sumatra

Borneo

Sulu Se

INDIAN OCEAN

Chagos Archipelago

Java Sea

Java

Bali

Lombok

Flores

**Key**

Relief and physical features

Relief metres

5000
3000
2000
1000
500
200
sea level
under sea level

Permanent ice (ice cap or glacier)

0    500    1000    1500    2000 km

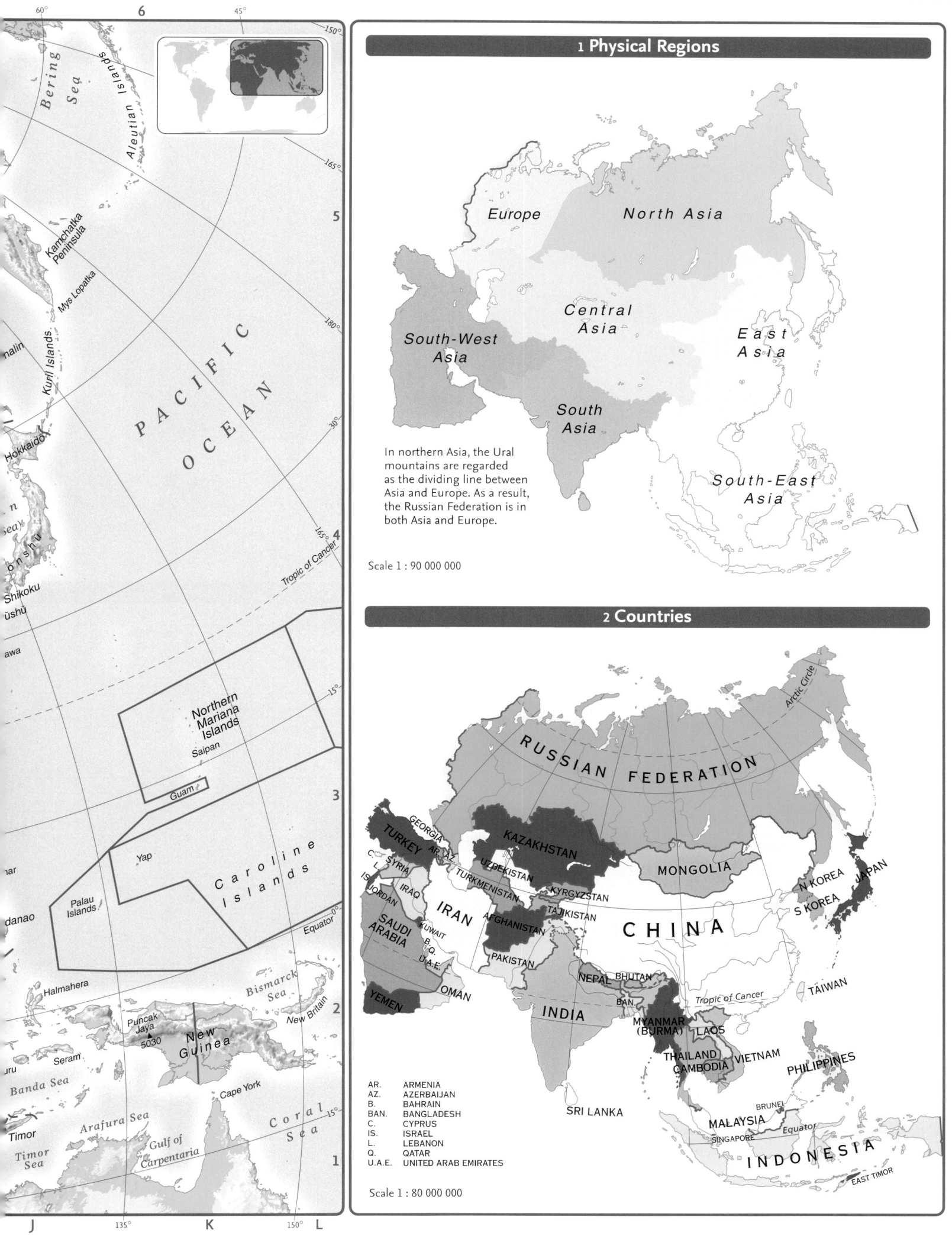

## 1 Physical Regions

Europe

North Asia

Central Asia

South-West Asia

East Asia

South Asia

South-East Asia

In northern Asia, the Ural mountains are regarded as the dividing line between Asia and Europe. As a result, the Russian Federation is in both Asia and Europe.

Scale 1 : 90 000 000

## 2 Countries

RUSSIAN FEDERATION

GEORGIA
TURKEY    AR  AZ
KAZAKHSTAN
C.
L.  SYRIA    UZBEKISTAN
IS.            TURKMENISTAN
JORDAN  IRAQ    KYRGYZSTAN
IRAN    AFGHANISTAN    TAJIKISTAN
KUWAIT
SAUDI    B.Q.
ARABIA    U.A.E.    PAKISTAN
YEMEN    OMAN    NEPAL  BHUTAN
BAN.
INDIA
MYANMAR
(BURMA)    LAOS
THAILAND
CAMBODIA  VIETNAM

MONGOLIA

CHINA

N KOREA    JAPAN
S KOREA

TAIWAN

Tropic of Cancer

PHILIPPINES

SRI LANKA

BRUNEI
MALAYSIA
SINGAPORE    Equator

INDONESIA

EAST TIMOR

| AR. | ARMENIA |
| AZ. | AZERBAIJAN |
| B. | BAHRAIN |
| BAN. | BANGLADESH |
| C. | CYPRUS |
| IS. | ISRAEL |
| L. | LEBANON |
| Q. | QATAR |
| U.A.E. | UNITED ARAB EMIRATES |

Scale 1 : 80 000 000

60°    6    45°    150°

Bering Sea
Aleutian Islands
165°

Kamchatka Peninsula
Mys Lopatka

5

PACIFIC OCEAN
180°

Kuril Islands

30°

Hokkaido

165°    4

Honshu
Tropic of Cancer

Shikoku
Kyushu

Northern Mariana Islands
Saipan

15°    3

Guam

Yap

Caroline Islands

Palau Islands

Equator  0°

danao

Halmahera
Bismarck Sea
New Britain

2

Seram
Puncak Jaya
5030
New Guinea

15°    1

Banda Sea
Timor
Arafura Sea
Cape York
Gulf of Carpentaria
Coral Sea

J    135°    K    150°    L

Lambert Azimuthal Equal Area projection

## 1 Temperature : January

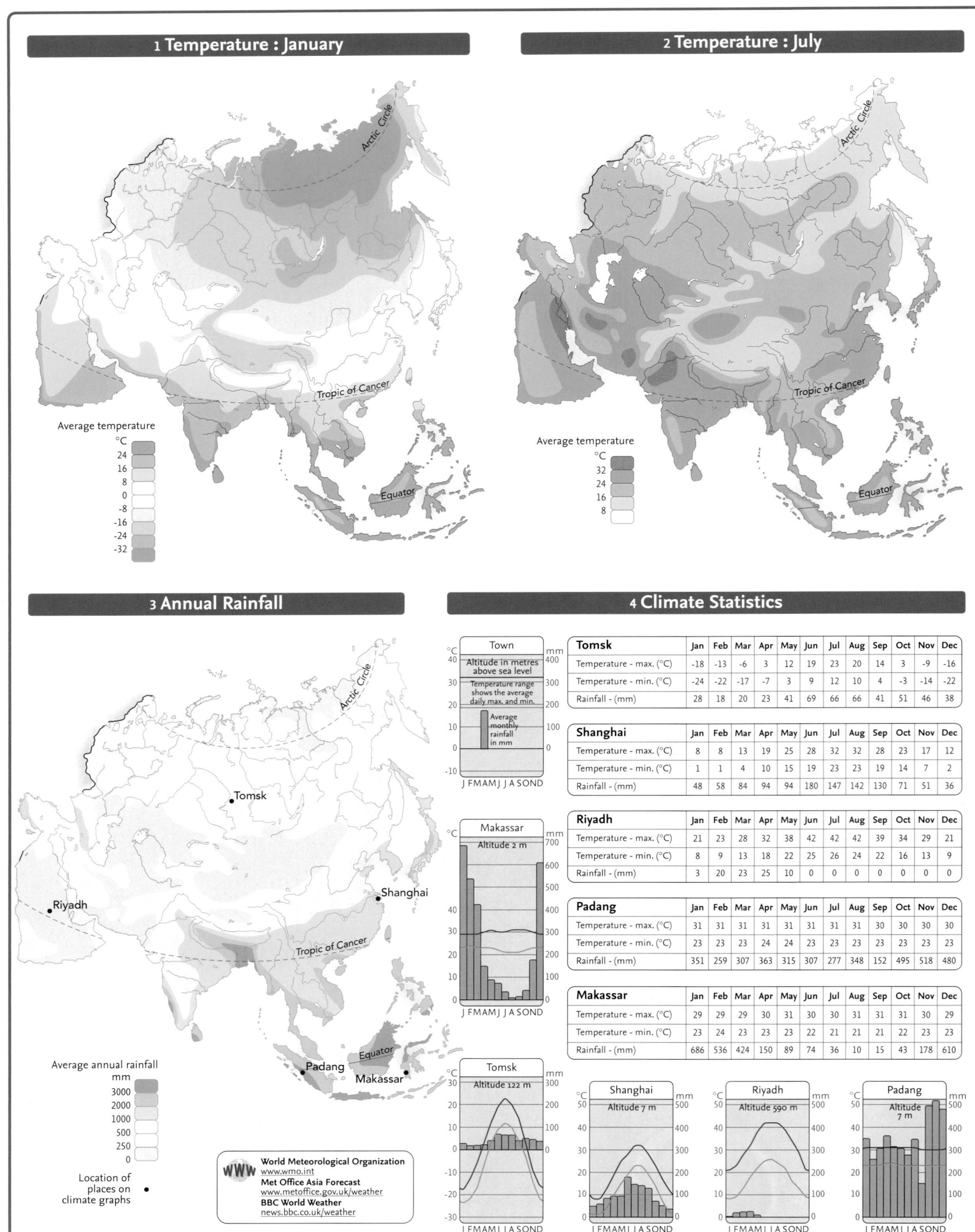

Average temperature
°C
24
16
8
0
-8
-16
-24
-32

## 2 Temperature : July

Average temperature
°C
32
24
16
8

## 3 Annual Rainfall

Average annual rainfall
mm
3000
2000
1000
500
250
0

Location of places on climate graphs •

WWW **World Meteorological Organization**
www.wmo.int
**Met Office Asia Forecast**
www.metoffice.gov.uk/weather
**BBC World Weather**
news.bbc.co.uk/weather

## 4 **Climate Statistics**

Town

Altitude in metres above sea level

Temperature range shows the average daily max. and min.

Average monthly rainfall in mm

J F M A M J J A S O N D

Makassar
Altitude 2 m
J F M A M J J A S O N D

| Tomsk | Jan | Feb | Mar | Apr | May | Jun | Jul | Aug | Sep | Oct | Nov | Dec |
|---|---|---|---|---|---|---|---|---|---|---|---|---|
| Temperature - max. (°C) | -18 | -13 | -6 | 3 | 12 | 19 | 23 | 20 | 14 | 3 | -9 | -16 |
| Temperature - min. (°C) | -24 | -22 | -17 | -7 | 3 | 9 | 12 | 10 | 4 | -3 | -14 | -22 |
| Rainfall - (mm) | 28 | 18 | 20 | 23 | 41 | 69 | 66 | 66 | 41 | 51 | 46 | 38 |

| Shanghai | Jan | Feb | Mar | Apr | May | Jun | Jul | Aug | Sep | Oct | Nov | Dec |
|---|---|---|---|---|---|---|---|---|---|---|---|---|
| Temperature - max. (°C) | 8 | 8 | 13 | 19 | 25 | 28 | 32 | 32 | 28 | 23 | 17 | 12 |
| Temperature - min. (°C) | 1 | 1 | 4 | 10 | 15 | 19 | 23 | 23 | 19 | 14 | 7 | 2 |
| Rainfall - (mm) | 48 | 58 | 84 | 94 | 94 | 180 | 147 | 142 | 130 | 71 | 51 | 36 |

| Riyadh | Jan | Feb | Mar | Apr | May | Jun | Jul | Aug | Sep | Oct | Nov | Dec |
|---|---|---|---|---|---|---|---|---|---|---|---|---|
| Temperature - max. (°C) | 21 | 23 | 28 | 32 | 38 | 42 | 42 | 42 | 39 | 34 | 29 | 21 |
| Temperature - min. (°C) | 8 | 9 | 13 | 18 | 22 | 25 | 26 | 24 | 22 | 16 | 13 | 9 |
| Rainfall - (mm) | 3 | 20 | 23 | 25 | 10 | 0 | 0 | 0 | 0 | 0 | 0 | 0 |

| Padang | Jan | Feb | Mar | Apr | May | Jun | Jul | Aug | Sep | Oct | Nov | Dec |
|---|---|---|---|---|---|---|---|---|---|---|---|---|
| Temperature - max. (°C) | 31 | 31 | 31 | 31 | 31 | 31 | 31 | 31 | 30 | 30 | 30 | 30 |
| Temperature - min. (°C) | 23 | 23 | 23 | 24 | 24 | 23 | 23 | 23 | 23 | 23 | 23 | 23 |
| Rainfall - (mm) | 351 | 259 | 307 | 363 | 315 | 307 | 277 | 348 | 152 | 495 | 518 | 480 |

| Makassar | Jan | Feb | Mar | Apr | May | Jun | Jul | Aug | Sep | Oct | Nov | Dec |
|---|---|---|---|---|---|---|---|---|---|---|---|---|
| Temperature - max. (°C) | 29 | 29 | 29 | 30 | 31 | 30 | 30 | 31 | 31 | 31 | 30 | 29 |
| Temperature - min. (°C) | 23 | 24 | 23 | 23 | 23 | 22 | 21 | 21 | 21 | 22 | 23 | 23 |
| Rainfall - (mm) | 686 | 536 | 424 | 150 | 89 | 74 | 36 | 10 | 15 | 43 | 178 | 610 |

Tomsk
Altitude 122 m
J F M A M J J A S O N D

Shanghai
Altitude 7 m
J F M A M J J A S O N D

Riyadh
Altitude 590 m
J F M A M J J A S O N D

Padang
Altitude 7 m
J F M A M J J A S O N D

0  1000  2000  3000  4000 km

Lambert Azimuthal Equal Area projection

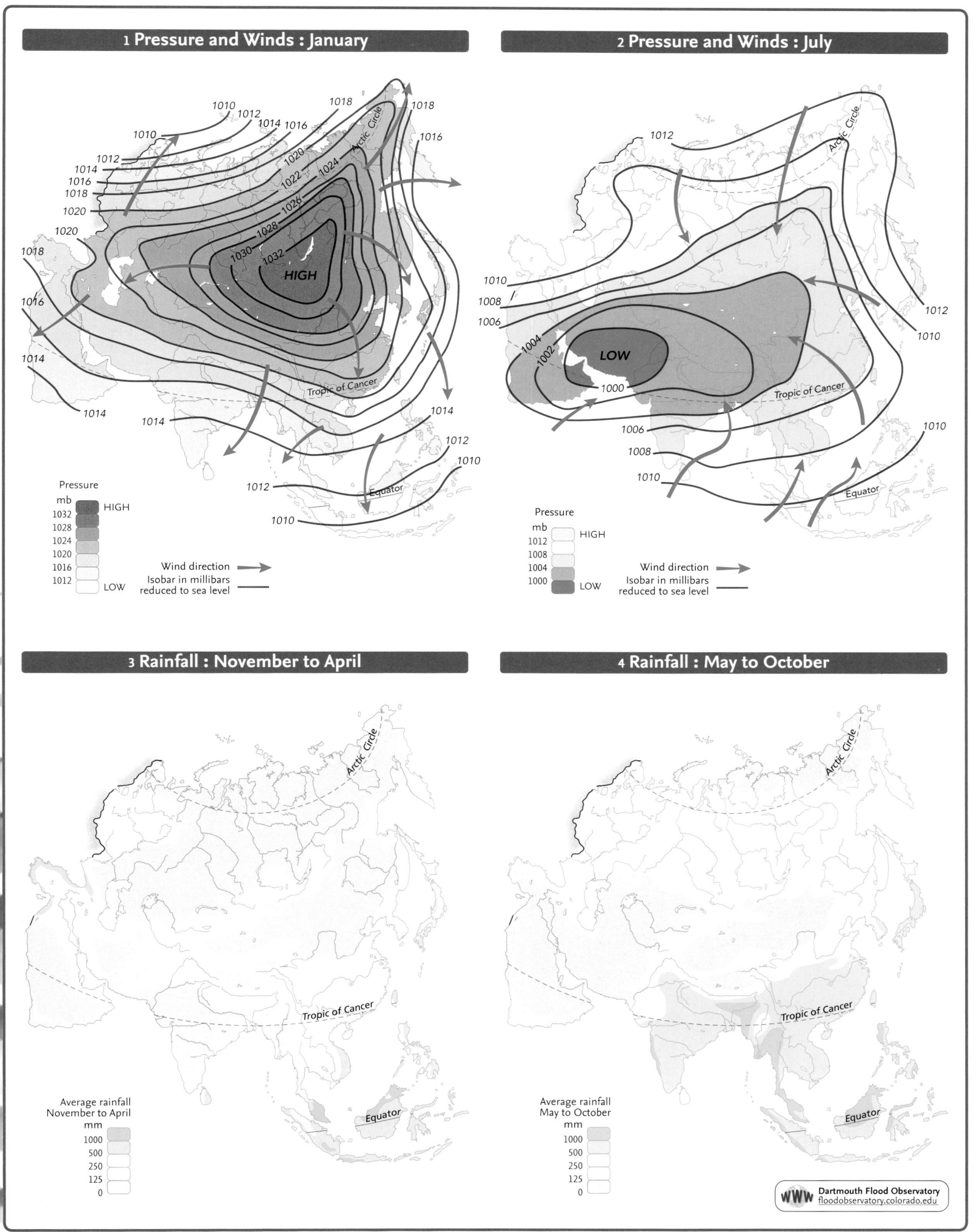

## 1 Pressure and Winds : January

1010 1012 1014 1016
1010
1012
1014
1016
1018
1020
1020
1018
1016
1014
1018
1020
1022
1024
1026
1028
1030 1028 1026
1032
1032
**HIGH**
Arctic Circle
1018
1018
1016
1014
Tropic of Cancer
1014
1012
1014
1012
1010
1012
Equator
1010

**Pressure**
mb
1032 — HIGH
1028
1024
1020
1016
1012 — LOW

Wind direction →
Isobar in millibars
reduced to sea level ——

## 2 Pressure and Winds : July

1012
Arctic Circle
1012
1010
1010
1008
1006
1004
1002
1000
**LOW**
Tropic of Cancer
1006
1008
1010
1010
Equator

**Pressure**
mb
1012 — HIGH
1008
1004
1000 — LOW

Wind direction →
Isobar in millibars
reduced to sea level ——

## 3 Rainfall : November to April

Arctic Circle
Tropic of Cancer
Equator

Average rainfall
November to April
mm
1000
500
250
125
0

## 4 Rainfall : May to October

Arctic Circle
Tropic of Cancer
Equator

Average rainfall
May to October
mm
1000
500
250
125
0

Scale 1 : 100 000 000

0   1000   2000   3000   4000 km

Lambert Azimuthal Equal Area projection

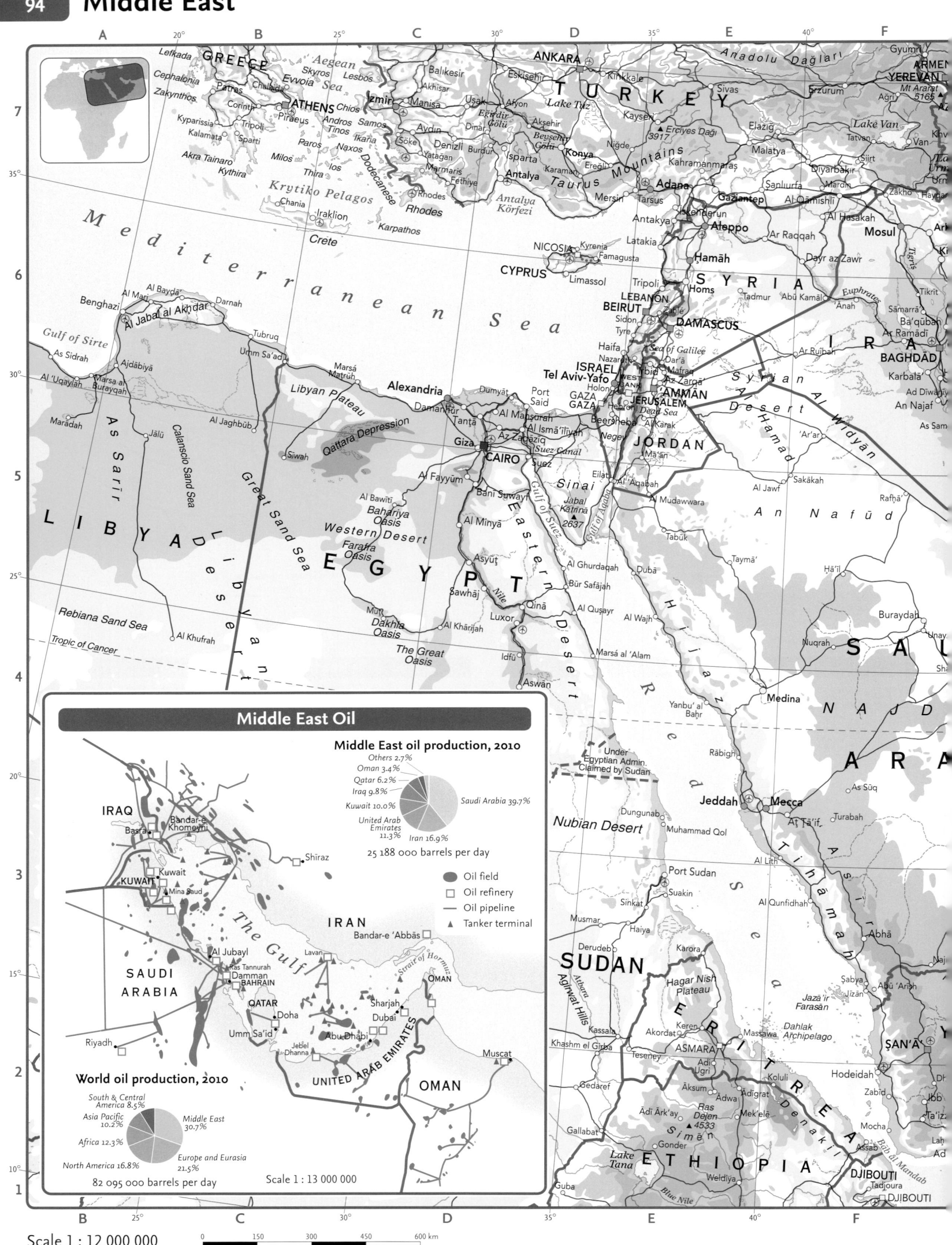

# Middle East

GREECE
Aegean

**Lefkada**
**Cephalonia**
Skyros
Lesbos
Balıkesir
Akhisar
**ANKARA**
Kırıkkale
**Anadolu** Dağları
Gyumri
**ARMEN**
**YEREVAN**

Patras
Chalkida
Izmir
Manisa
Uşak
Afyon
Eskişehir
Lake Tuz
**T U R K E Y**
Kayseri
Sivas
Erzurum
Mt Ararat 5165
Ağrı

**ATHENS**
Chios
Aydın
Denizli
Burdur
Isparta
Niğde
Ercıyes Dağı 3917
Kahramanmaraş
Malatya
Elazığ
Lake Van
Tatvan
Van

Milos
Ios
Dodecanese
Söke
Yatağan
Marmaris
Fethiye
Antalya
Karaman
Ereğli
Konya
T a u r u s
M o u n t a i n s
Adana
Tarsus
Mersin
Antakya
İskenderun
Gaziantep
Şanlıurfa
Diyarbakır
Mardin
Siirt
Zakho

**Crete**
Rhodes
Antalya Körfezi
NICOSIA
Kyrenia
Latakia
Aleppo
Ar Raqqah
Al Qāmishlī
Al Hasakah
**Mosul**

M e d i t e r r a n e a n  S e a
CYPRUS
Limassol
Famagusta
Tripoli
Homs
Ḥamāh
S Y R I A
Dayr az Zawr
Euphrates
Tikrit

Benghazi
Al Bayḍā'
Darnah
Al Jabal al Akhḍar
**BEIRUT**
LEBANON
Sidon
Zahlé
**DAMASCUS**
Tadmur
Abū Kamāl
Ānah
Sāmarrā'
Ar Ramādī
**IRA**
**BAGHDAD**

Gulf of Sirte
As Sidrah
Ajdābiyā
Umm Sa'ad
Haifa
Nazareth
Sea of Galilee
Dar'ā
Ar Ruṭbah
Karbalā'
Ad Dīwān

Marādah
Al 'Uqaylah
Marsa al Burayqah
Libyan Plateau
Alexandria
Damanhūr
Port Said
ISRAEL
WEST BANK
AMMAN
JORDAN
An Najaf

Marsá Matrūḥ
Tanṭā
Tel Aviv-Yafo
Holon
GAZA
JERUSALEM
Hebron
Dead Sea
Al Karak
Ma'ān
Ar'ar
As Sam

**L I B Y A**
As Sarīr
Jālū
Calanscio Sand Sea
Siwah
Qattâra Depression
Al Manṣūrah
Az Zaqāzīq
Suez Canal
GAZA
Beersheba
Negev
Sinai
Jabal Kātrīnā 2637
Al Mudawwara
Al Jawf
Sakākah
Rafḥā'

Western Desert
Baḥarīya Oasis
Al Fayyūm
Al Minyā
Suez
Eilat
Al 'Aqaba
Tabūk
An Nafūd

Rebiana Sand Sea
Farâfra Oasis
Bani Suwayf
Asyūṭ
Taymā'
Ḥā'il
Buraydah

Tropic of Cancer
Al Khufrah
Dākhla Oasis
Al Khārijah
Luxor
Al Ghurdaqah
Dubā
Al Qusayr
Al Wajh
Nuqrah
Unay

The Great Oasis
Ṣawhāj
Qinā
Idfū
Marsá al 'Alam
Yanbu' al Bahr
Medina
**SAU**
**NAJD**

Aswān
Under Egyptian Admin. Claimed by Sudan
Rābigh
Shar

Red Sea
**A R A B**

Nubian Desert
Dungunab
Jeddah
Mecca
As Sūq
Muhammad Qol
At Ṭā'if
Jurabah

Port Sudan
Al Lith
Al Qunfidhah
Abhā

Derudeb
Suakin
Sinkat
Haiya
Musmar
Jāzā'ir Farasān
Jīzān
Najr

**SUDAN**
Aq̱iwat Hills
Karora
Al Jubayl
Lavan
Bandar-e 'Abbās
Strait of Hormuz
**OMAN**

## Middle East Oil

**IRAQ**
Bandar-e Khomeyni
Baṣra
Shīrāz

### Middle East oil production, 2010

Others 2.7%
Oman 3.4%
Qatar 6.2%
Iraq 9.8%
Kuwait 10.0%
United Arab Emirates 11.3%
Iran 16.9%
Saudi Arabia 39.7%

**25 188 000 barrels per day**

Kuwait
**KUWAIT**
Mina Saud

◯ Oil field
□ Oil refinery
— Oil pipeline
▲ Tanker terminal

Al Jubayl
Ras Tannurah
Dammam
BAHRAIN
QATAR
Doha
**IRAN**

**SAUDI ARABIA**
Umm Sa'id
Jebel Dhanna
Abu Dhabi
Sharjah
Dubai
**OMAN**
Muscat

Riyadh
**UNITED ARAB EMIRATES**

### World oil production, 2010

South & Central America 8.5%
Asia Pacific 10.2%
Africa 12.3%
North America 16.8%
Middle East 30.7%
Europe and Eurasia 21.5%

**82 095 000 barrels per day**

Scale 1 : 13 000 000

The Gulf

**OMAN**

**ERITREA**
**ASMARA**
Kassala
Khashm el Girba
Teseney
Keren
Massawa
Dahlak Archipelago
Hagar Nish Plateau
Akordat
Adi Ugri
Koluli
Hodeidah
Zabid

Gedaref
Mek'elē
Ras Dejen 4533
Simēn
**Ta'iz**
Mocha

**SUDAN**
Akṣum
Ādwa
Adigrat
Ādī Ārk'ay
Gonder
Lake Tana
Blue Nile
**ETHIOPIA**
Weldiya
Gonder
Assab
Bāb al Mandab
**DJIBOUTI**
Tadjoura
**DJIBOUTI**

Gallabat
Guba

**ŞAN'Ā'**

Scale 1 : 12 000 000

0   150   300   450   600 km

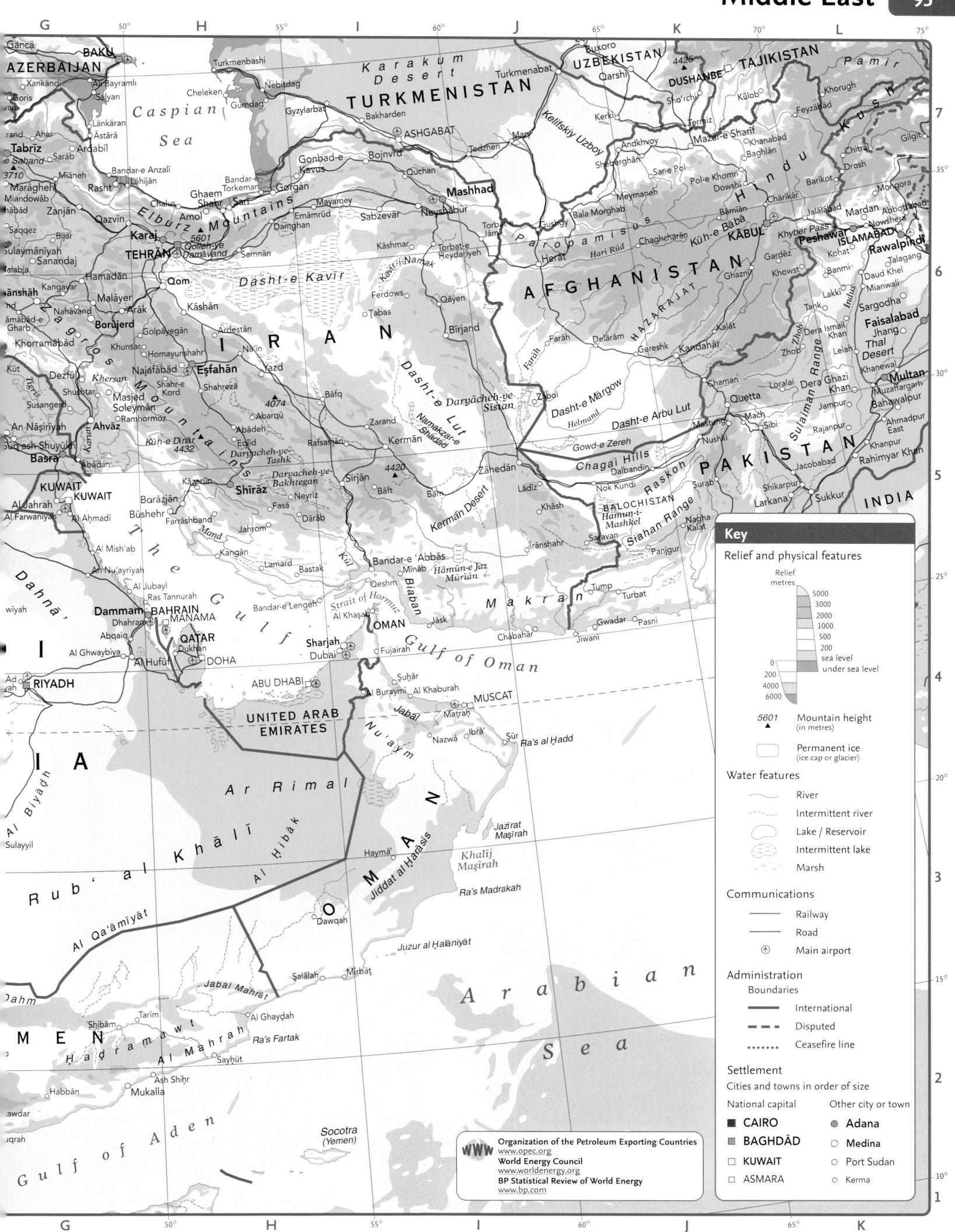

Albers Conic Equal Area projection

**Key**

**Relief and physical features**

Relief
metres

5000
3000
2000
1000
500
200
0 sea level
under sea level
200
4000
6000

5601 ▲ Mountain height
(in metres)

Permanent ice
(ice cap or glacier)

**Water features**

River

Intermittent river

Lake / Reservoir

Intermittent lake

Marsh

**Communications**

Railway

Road

⊕ Main airport

**Administration**

Boundaries

International

Disputed

Ceasefire line

**Settlement**

Cities and towns in order of size

National capital    Other city or town

■ CAIRO          ● Adana

■ BAGHDĀD        ○ Medina

□ KUWAIT         ○ Port Sudan

□ ASMARA         ○ Kerma

Organization of the Petroleum Exporting Countries
www.opec.org
World Energy Council
www.worldenergy.org
BP Statistical Review of World Energy
www.bp.com

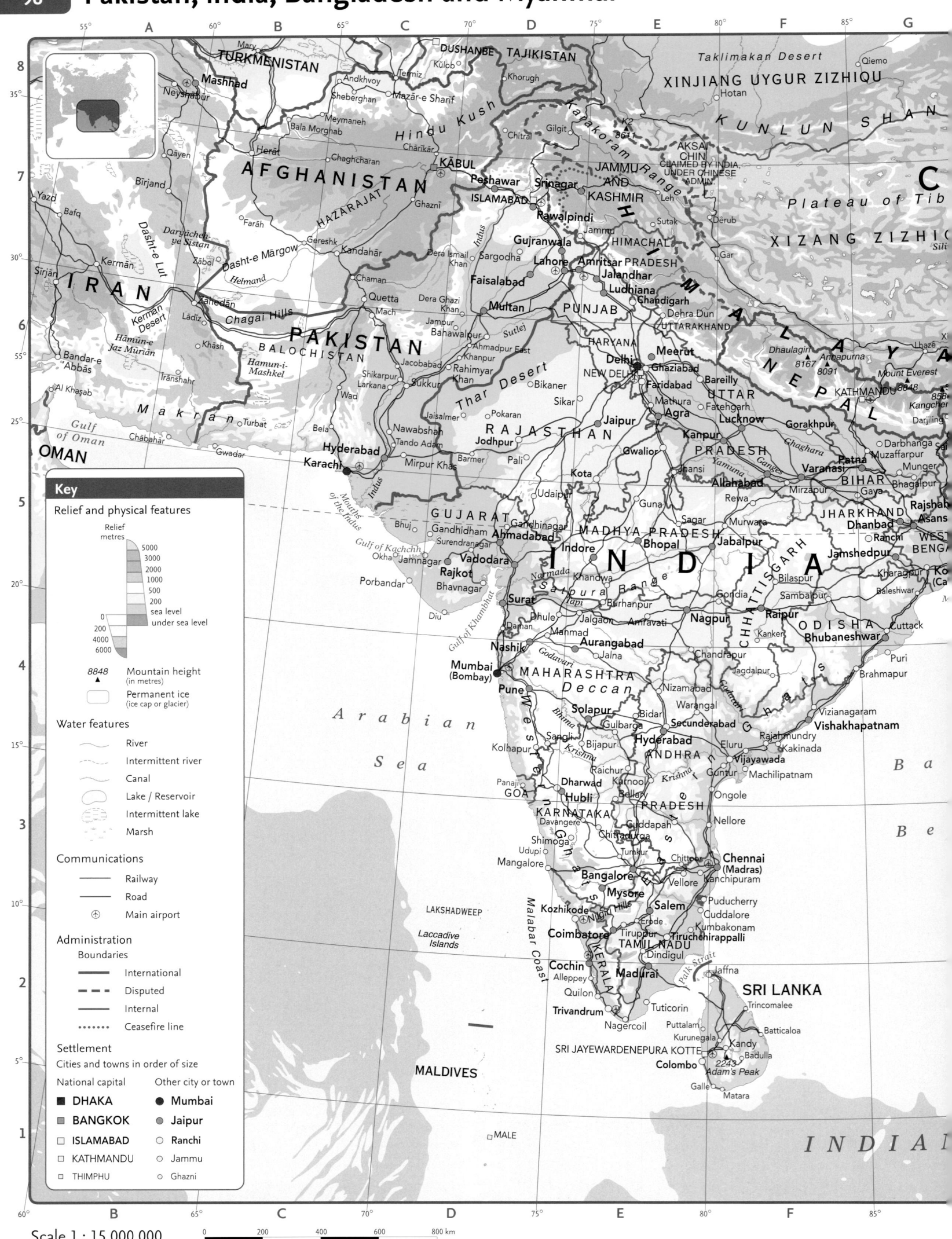

Scale 1 : 15 000 000

0    200    400    600    800 km

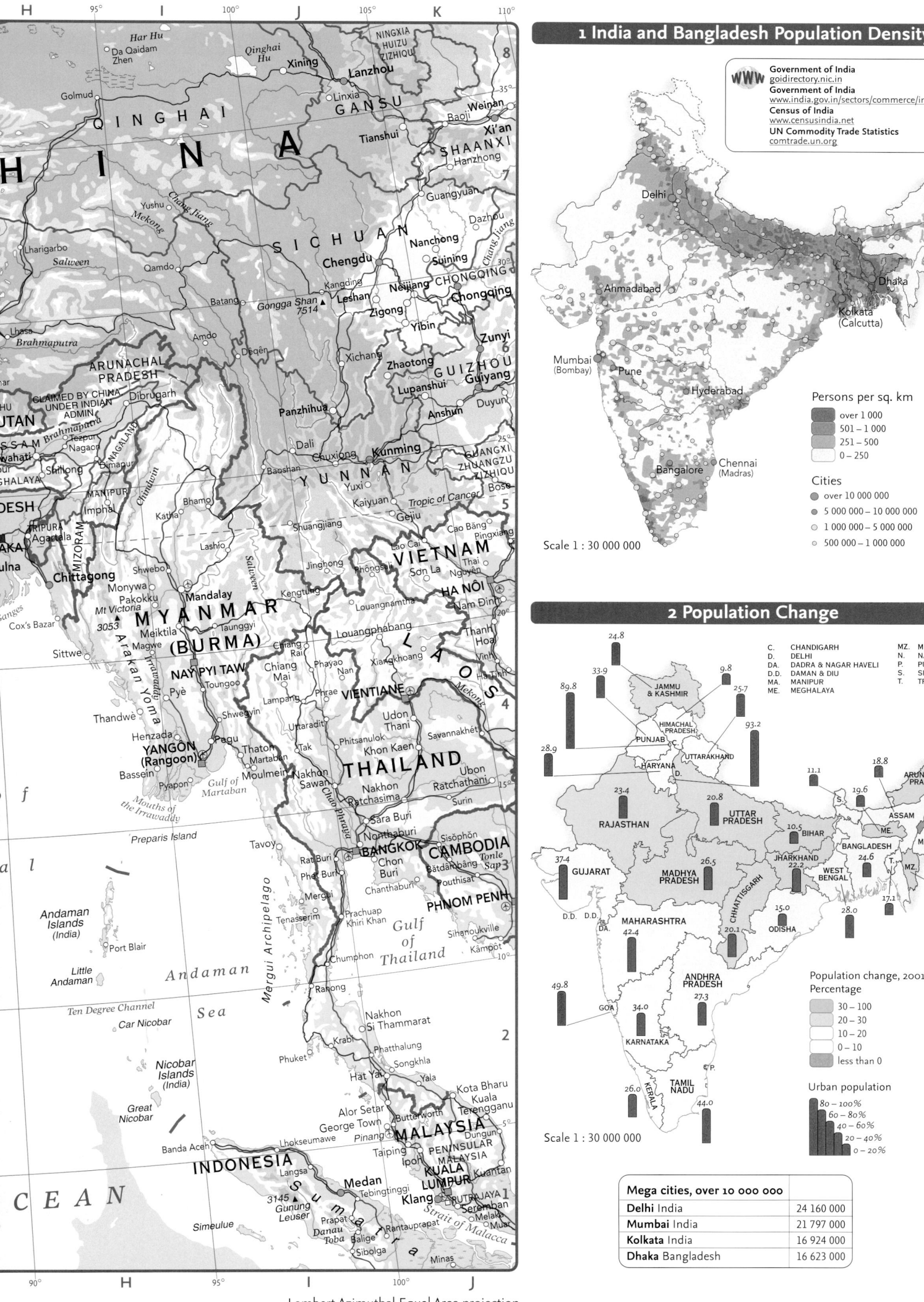

## 1 India and Bangladesh Population Density

WWW  Government of India
goidirectory.nic.in
Government of India
www.india.gov.in/sectors/commerce/index.php
Census of India
www.censusindia.net
UN Commodity Trade Statistics
comtrade.un.org

**Persons per sq. km**
- over 1 000
- 501 – 1 000
- 251 – 500
- 0 – 250

**Cities**
- over 10 000 000
- 5 000 000 – 10 000 000
- 1 000 000 – 5 000 000
- 500 000 – 1 000 000

Scale 1 : 30 000 000

## 2 Population Change

| | |
|---|---|
| C. | CHANDIGARH |
| D. | DELHI |
| DA. | DADRA & NAGAR HAVELI |
| D.D. | DAMAN & DIU |
| MA. | MANIPUR |
| ME. | MEGHALAYA |
| MZ. | MIZORAM |
| N. | NAGALAND |
| P. | PUDUCHERRY |
| S. | SIKKIM |
| T. | TRIPURA |

**Population change, 2001-2011**
**Percentage**
- 30 – 100
- 20 – 30
- 10 – 20
- 0 – 10
- less than 0

**Urban population**
- 80 – 100%
- 60 – 80%
- 40 – 60%
- 20 – 40%
- 0 – 20%

Scale 1 : 30 000 000

| Mega cities, over 10 000 000 | |
|---|---|
| **Delhi** India | 24 160 000 |
| **Mumbai** India | 21 797 000 |
| **Kolkata** India | 16 924 000 |
| **Dhaka** Bangladesh | 16 623 000 |

Lambert Azimuthal Equal Area projection

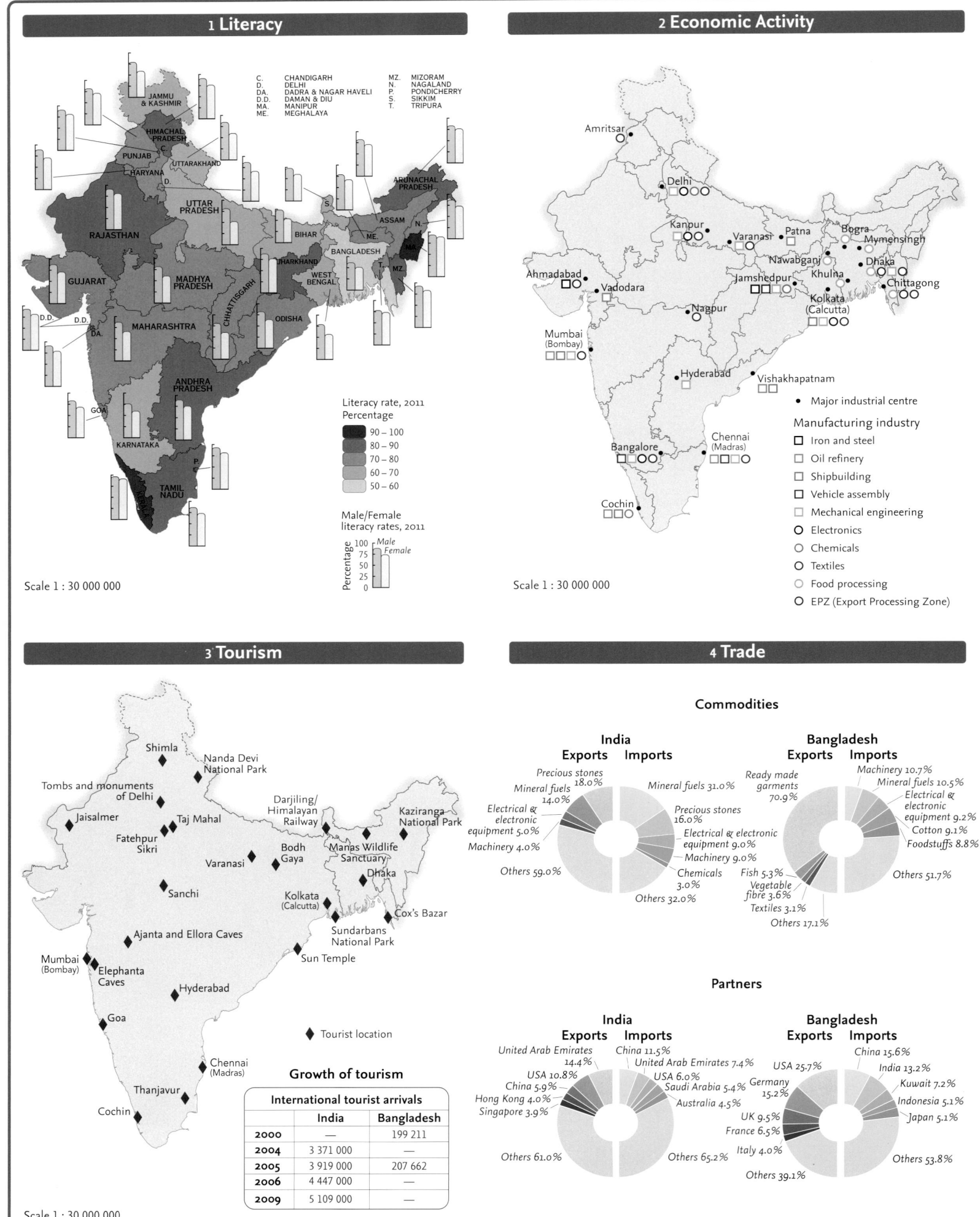

## 1 Literacy

| | | | |
|---|---|---|---|
| C. | CHANDIGARH | MZ. | MIZORAM |
| D. | DELHI | N. | NAGALAND |
| DA. | DADRA & NAGAR HAVELI | P. | PONDICHERRY |
| D.D. | DAMAN & DIU | S. | SIKKIM |
| MA. | MANIPUR | T. | TRIPURA |
| ME. | MEGHALAYA | | |

Literacy rate, 2011
Percentage
- 90 – 100
- 80 – 90
- 70 – 80
- 60 – 70
- 50 – 60

Male/Female literacy rates, 2011
Percentage 100 Male / Female
75
50
25
0

Scale 1 : 30 000 000

## 2 Economic Activity

- • Major industrial centre

Manufacturing industry
- ☐ Iron and steel
- ☐ Oil refinery
- ☐ Shipbuilding
- ☐ Vehicle assembly
- ☐ Mechanical engineering
- ○ Electronics
- ○ Chemicals
- ○ Textiles
- ○ Food processing
- ◎ EPZ (Export Processing Zone)

Scale 1 : 30 000 000

## 3 Tourism

◆ Tourist location

Scale 1 : 30 000 000

### Growth of tourism

| International tourist arrivals | | |
|---|---|---|
| | India | Bangladesh |
| 2000 | — | 199 211 |
| 2004 | 3 371 000 | — |
| 2005 | 3 919 000 | 207 662 |
| 2006 | 4 447 000 | — |
| 2009 | 5 109 000 | — |

## 4 Trade

### Commodities

**India**
Exports / Imports

Exports:
- Precious stones 18.0%
- Mineral fuels 14.0%
- Electrical & electronic equipment 5.0%
- Machinery 4.0%
- Others 59.0%

Imports:
- Mineral fuels 31.0%
- Precious stones 16.0%
- Electrical & electronic equipment 9.0%
- Machinery 9.0%
- Chemicals 3.0%
- Others 32.0%

**Bangladesh**
Exports / Imports

Exports:
- Ready made garments 70.9%
- Fish 5.3%
- Vegetable fibre 3.6%
- Textiles 3.1%
- Others 17.1%

Imports:
- Machinery 10.7%
- Mineral fuels 10.5%
- Electrical & electronic equipment 9.2%
- Cotton 9.1%
- Foodstuffs 8.8%
- Others 51.7%

### Partners

**India**
Exports / Imports

Exports:
- United Arab Emirates 14.4%
- USA 10.8%
- China 5.9%
- Hong Kong 4.0%
- Singapore 3.9%
- Others 61.0%

Imports:
- China 11.5%
- United Arab Emirates 7.4%
- USA 6.0%
- Saudi Arabia 5.4%
- Australia 4.5%
- Others 65.2%

**Bangladesh**
Exports / Imports

Exports:
- USA 25.7%
- Germany 15.2%
- UK 9.5%
- France 6.5%
- Italy 4.0%
- Others 39.1%

Imports:
- China 15.6%
- India 13.2%
- Kuwait 7.2%
- Indonesia 5.1%
- Japan 5.1%
- Others 53.8%

## 1 Satellite Image

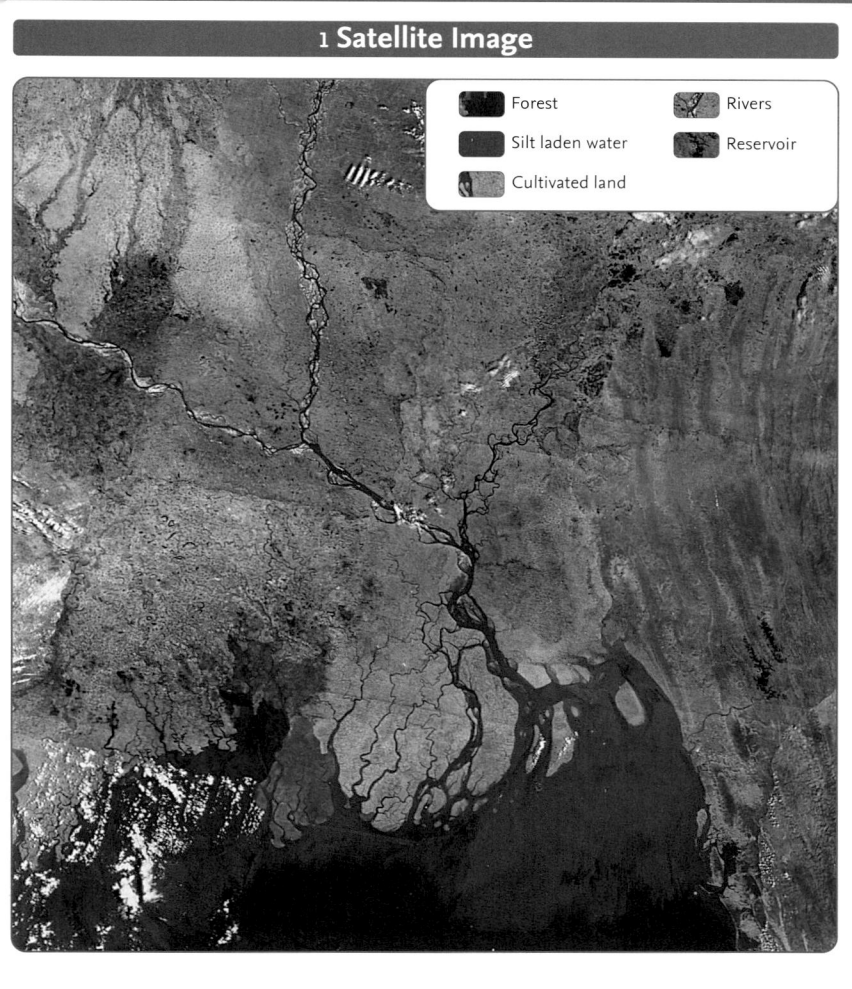

| | | | |
|---|---|---|---|
| | Forest | | Rivers |
| | Silt laden water | | Reservoir |
| | Cultivated land | | |

## 2 Bangladesh

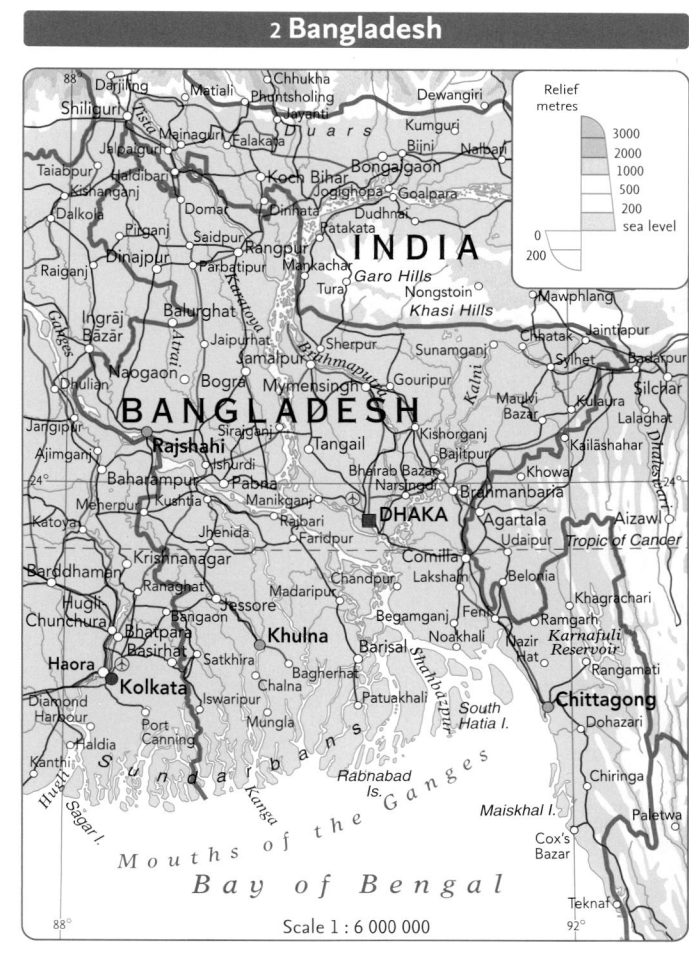

Relief
metres
3000
2000
1000
500
200
0
200
sea level

Scale 1 : 6 000 000

## 3 Annual Rainfall

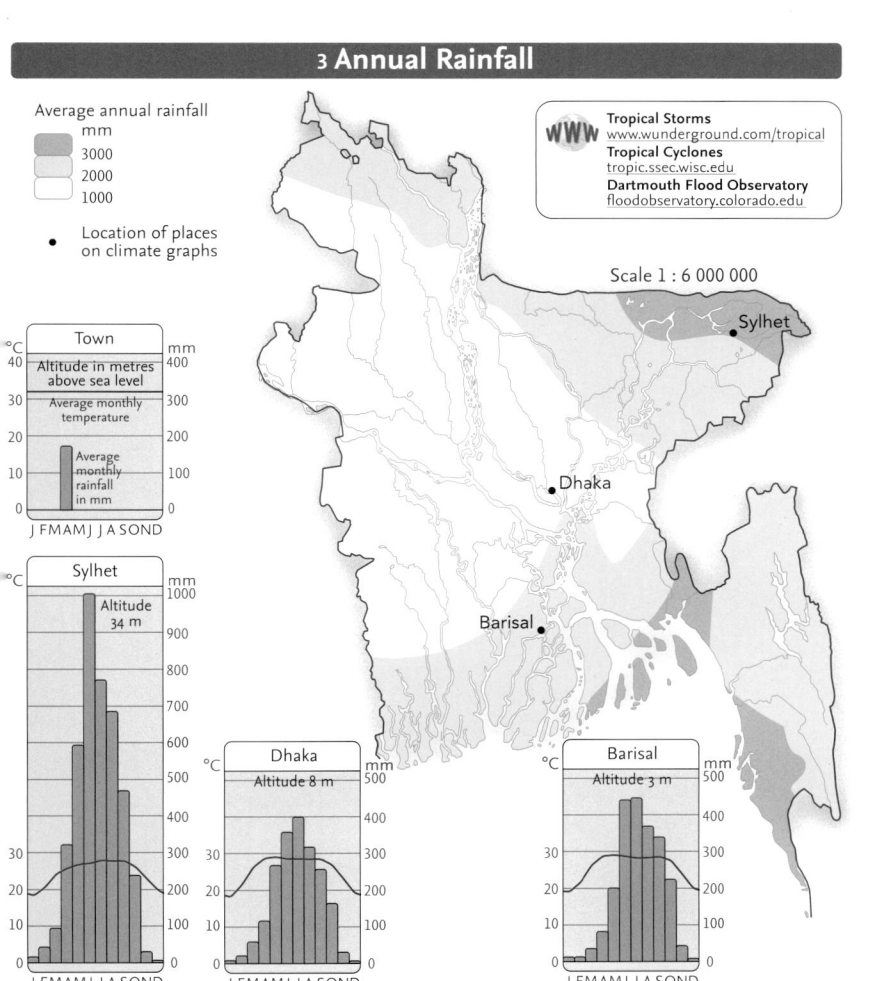

Average annual rainfall
mm
3000
2000
1000

• Location of places
  on climate graphs

**Tropical Storms**
www.wunderground.com/tropical
**Tropical Cyclones**
tropic.ssec.wisc.edu
**Dartmouth Flood Observatory**
floodobservatory.colorado.edu

Scale 1 : 6 000 000

Town
Altitude in metres
above sea level
Average monthly
temperature
Average
monthly
rainfall
in mm

Sylhet — Altitude 34 m

Dhaka — Altitude 8 m

Barisal — Altitude 3 m

## 4 Flood Control Projects

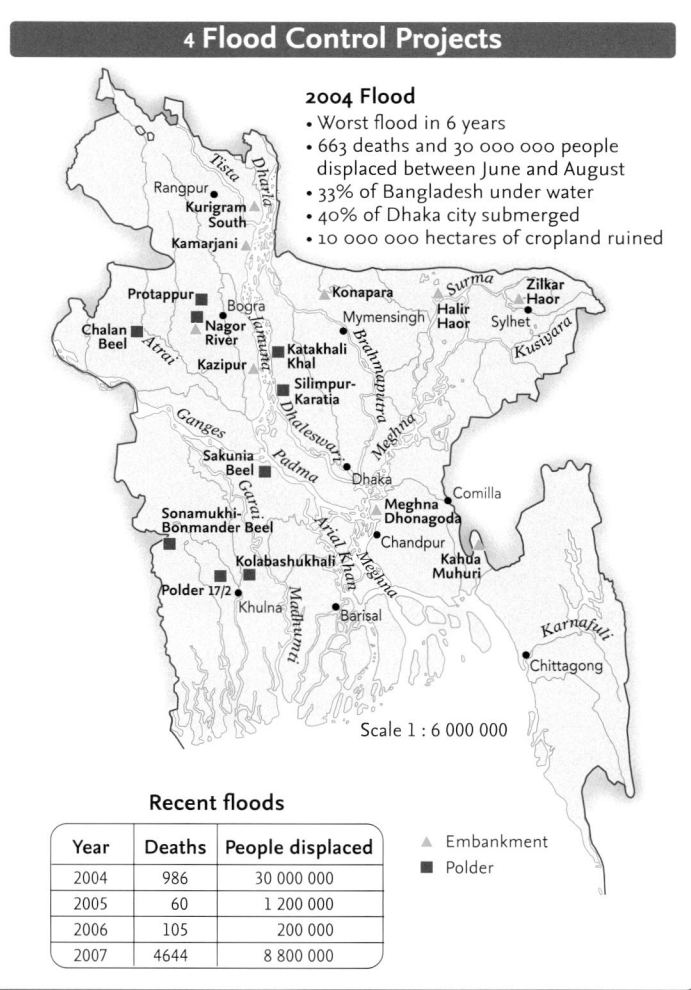

**2004 Flood**
• Worst flood in 6 years
• 663 deaths and 30 000 000 people
  displaced between June and August
• 33% of Bangladesh under water
• 40% of Dhaka city submerged
• 10 000 000 hectares of cropland ruined

Scale 1 : 6 000 000

### Recent floods

| Year | Deaths | People displaced |
|---|---|---|
| 2004 | 986 | 30 000 000 |
| 2005 | 60 | 1 200 000 |
| 2006 | 105 | 200 000 |
| 2007 | 4644 | 8 800 000 |

▲ Embankment
■ Polder

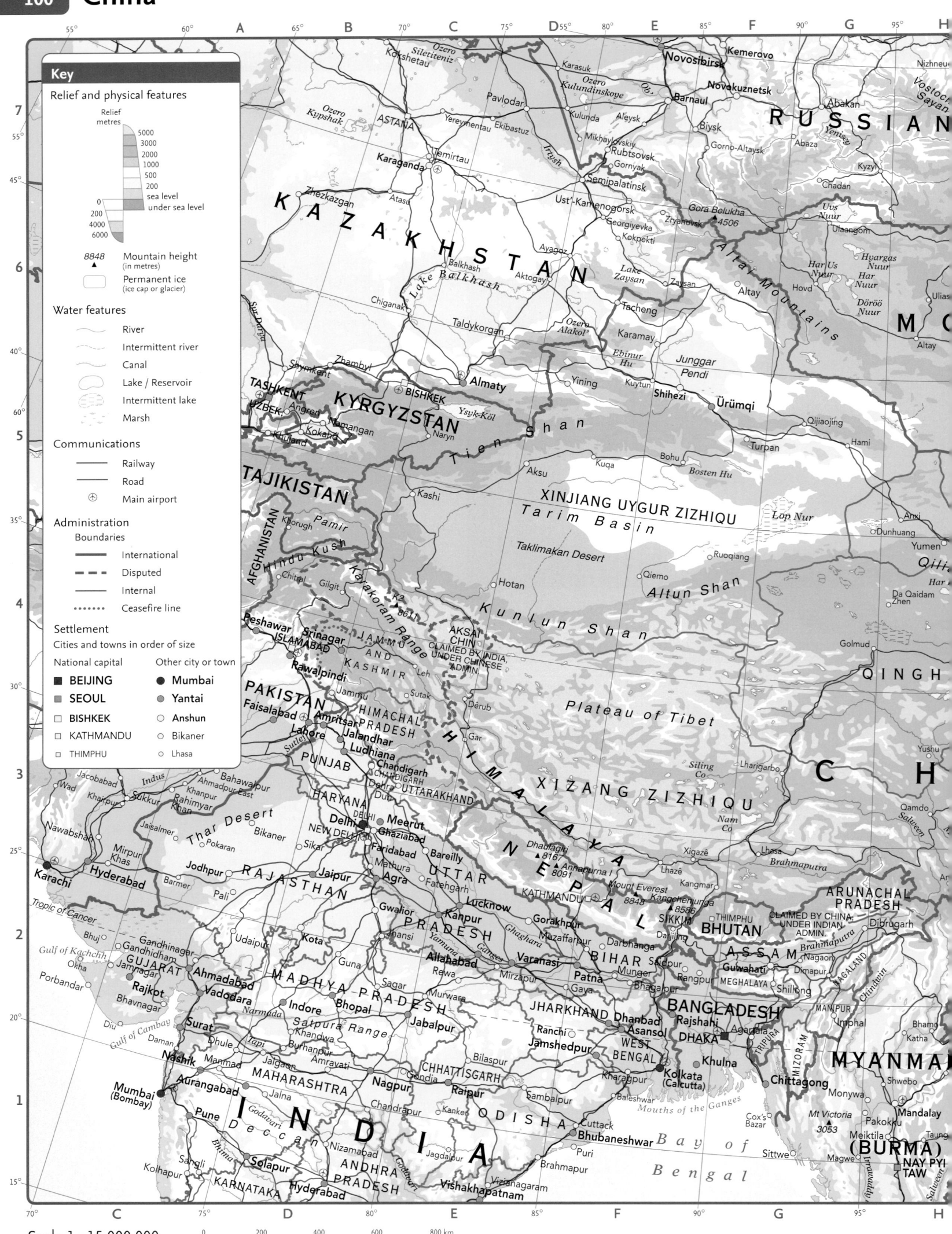

## Key

**Relief and physical features**

Relief
metres
5000
3000
2000
1000
500
200
sea level
under sea level
0
200
4000
6000

▲ 8848  Mountain height
(in metres)

Permanent ice
(ice cap or glacier)

**Water features**

~~~ River

~~~ Intermittent river

~~~ Canal

Lake / Reservoir

Intermittent lake

Marsh

**Communications**

Railway

Road

⊕ Main airport

**Administration**

Boundaries

International

Disputed

Internal

Ceasefire line

**Settlement**

Cities and towns in order of size

National capital          Other city or town

■ BEIJING          ● Mumbai

■ SEOUL          ● Yantai

□ BISHKEK          ○ Anshun

□ KATHMANDU          ○ Bikaner

□ THIMPHU          ○ Lhasa

Scale 1 : 15 000 000

0    200    400    600    800 km

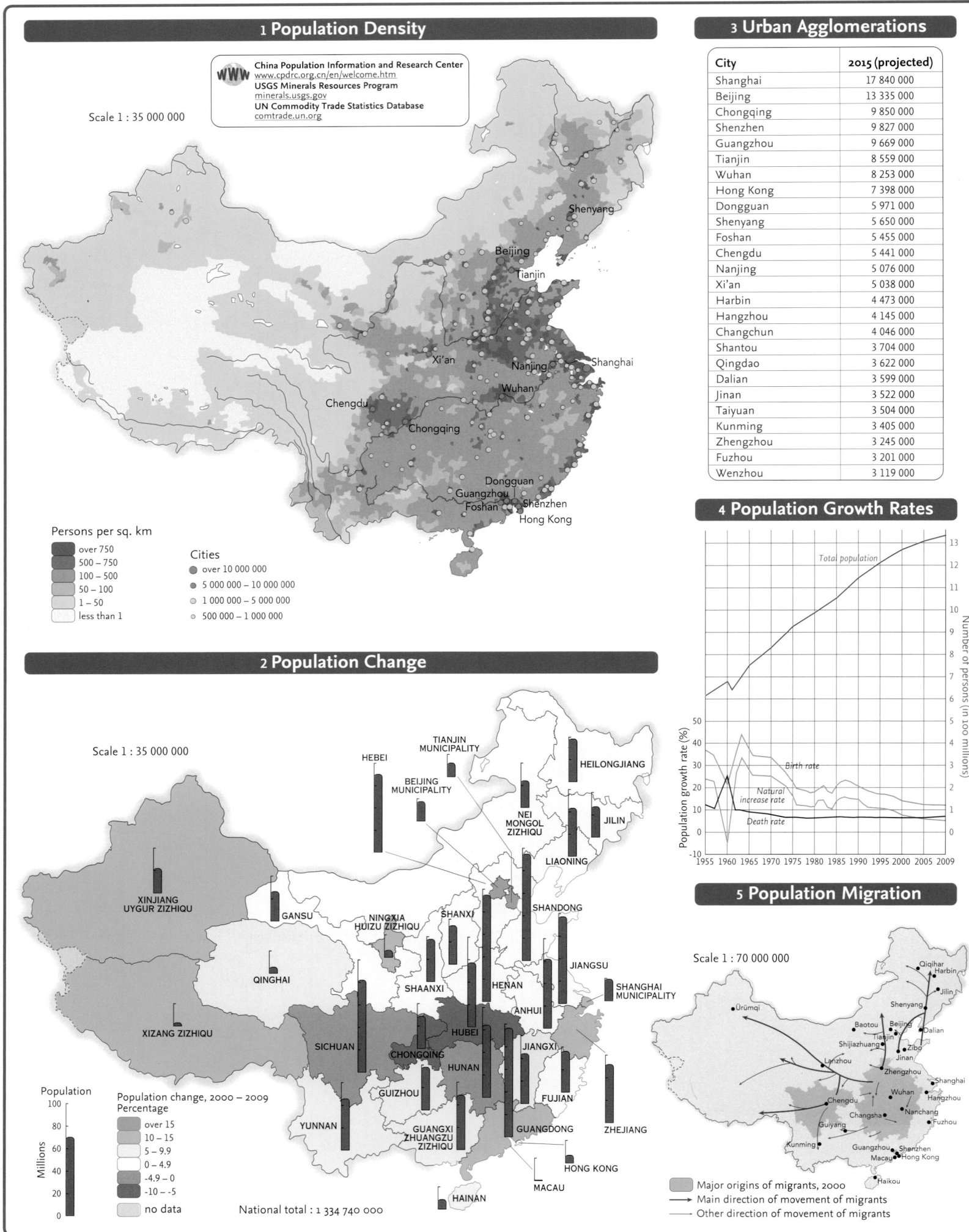

## 1 Population Density

China Population Information and Research Center
www.cpdrc.org.cn/en/welcome.htm
USGS Minerals Resources Program
minerals.usgs.gov
UN Commodity Trade Statistics Database
comtrade.un.org

Scale 1 : 35 000 000

Persons per sq. km

- over 750
- 500 – 750
- 100 – 500
- 50 – 100
- 1 – 50
- less than 1

Cities
- over 10 000 000
- 5 000 000 – 10 000 000
- 1 000 000 – 5 000 000
- 500 000 – 1 000 000

## 2 Population Change

Scale 1 : 35 000 000

Population
Millions
100
80
60
40
20
0

Population change, 2000 – 2009
Percentage
- over 15
- 10 – 15
- 5 – 9.9
- 0 – 4.9
- -4.9 – 0
- -10 – -5
- no data

National total : 1 334 740 000

## 3 Urban Agglomerations

| City | 2015 (projected) |
| --- | --- |
| Shanghai | 17 840 000 |
| Beijing | 13 335 000 |
| Chongqing | 9 850 000 |
| Shenzhen | 9 827 000 |
| Guangzhou | 9 669 000 |
| Tianjin | 8 559 000 |
| Wuhan | 8 253 000 |
| Hong Kong | 7 398 000 |
| Dongguan | 5 971 000 |
| Shenyang | 5 650 000 |
| Foshan | 5 455 000 |
| Chengdu | 5 441 000 |
| Nanjing | 5 076 000 |
| Xi'an | 5 038 000 |
| Harbin | 4 473 000 |
| Hangzhou | 4 145 000 |
| Changchun | 4 046 000 |
| Shantou | 3 704 000 |
| Qingdao | 3 622 000 |
| Dalian | 3 599 000 |
| Jinan | 3 522 000 |
| Taiyuan | 3 504 000 |
| Kunming | 3 405 000 |
| Zhengzhou | 3 245 000 |
| Fuzhou | 3 201 000 |
| Wenzhou | 3 119 000 |

## 4 Population Growth Rates

## 5 Population Migration

Scale 1 : 70 000 000

- Major origins of migrants, 2000
- → Main direction of movement of migrants
- → Other direction of movement of migrants

## 6 Mineral Resources

**Non-metallic ore**
◇ Phosphorus
◇ Iron pyrites
◇ Asbestos

**Metallic ore**
▢ Iron
▢ Manganese
▢ Copper
▢ Lead and zinc
▢ Bauxite
▢ Tungsten

○ Tin
○ Antimony
○ Mercury
○ Gold
○ Silver

Scale 1 : 45 000 000

### Mineral production, 2009

| Mineral | Thousand tonnes |
|---|---|
| Antimony | 140 |
| Asbestos | 380 |
| Bauxite | 40 000 |
| Copper | 873 |
| Iron Ore | 880 000 |
| Lead | 1600 |
| Manganese | 2400 |
| Tin | 115 |
| Tungsten | 51 |
| Zinc | 3400 |

## 7 East China Manufacturing Industry

• Major industrial centre

**Manufacturing industry**
▢ Iron and steel
▢ Oil refining and petro-chemicals
▢ Shipbuilding
▢ Aircraft and aerospace
▢ Motor vehicles
▢ Engineering
○ Electronic and electrical goods
○ Chemicals
○ Textiles

Shenyang   Fushun
Liaoyang   Benxi
Jinzhou    Anshan
Huludao    Yingkou    Dandong
Tianjin    Dalian
           Yantai
Jinan
           Qingdao
           Lianyungang
Nanjing    Nantong
           Shanghai
Hangzhou
           Ningbo
           Wenzhou
           Fuzhou
           Xiamen
Guangzhou  Shantou
Zhuhai     Shenzhen
Beihai
Zhanjiang
Hainan

Scale 1 : 25 000 000

## 8 Trade

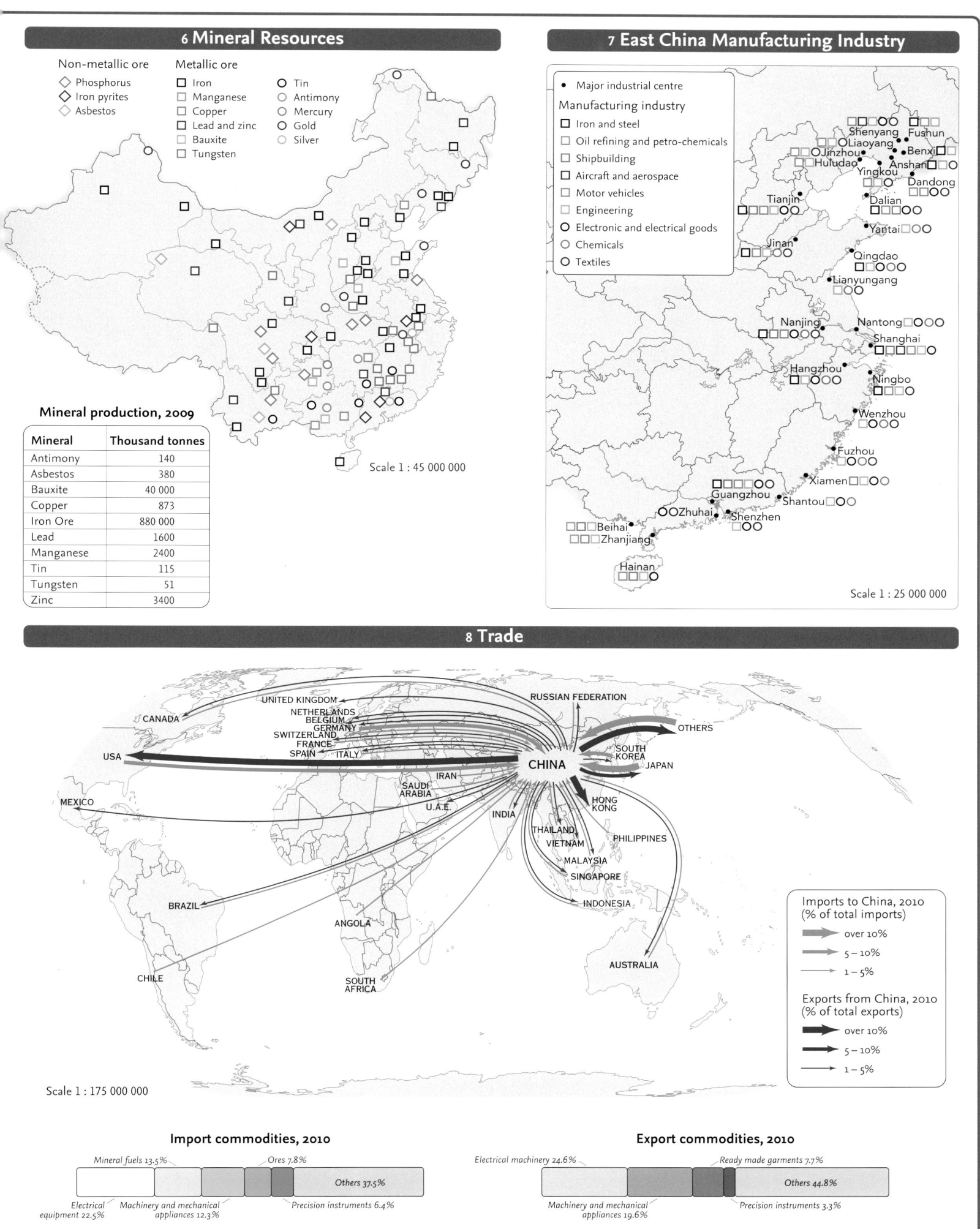

RUSSIAN FEDERATION
UNITED KINGDOM
CANADA
NETHERLANDS
BELGIUM
GERMANY
SWITZERLAND
FRANCE
SPAIN      ITALY
USA
MEXICO
IRAN
SAUDI
ARABIA
U.A.E.
INDIA
BRAZIL
ANGOLA
CHILE
SOUTH
AFRICA
OTHERS
SOUTH
KOREA
JAPAN
CHINA
HONG
KONG
THAILAND
VIETNAM
PHILIPPINES
MALAYSIA
SINGAPORE
INDONESIA
AUSTRALIA

Scale 1 : 175 000 000

**Imports to China, 2010**
(% of total imports)
→ over 10%
→ 5 – 10%
→ 1 – 5%

**Exports from China, 2010**
(% of total exports)
→ over 10%
→ 5 – 10%
→ 1 – 5%

### Import commodities, 2010

Mineral fuels 13.5%   Ores 7.8%   Others 37.5%
Electrical equipment 22.5%   Machinery and mechanical appliances 12.3%   Precision instruments 6.4%

### Export commodities, 2010

Electrical machinery 24.6%   Ready made garments 7.7%   Others 44.8%
Machinery and mechanical appliances 19.6%   Precision instruments 3.3%

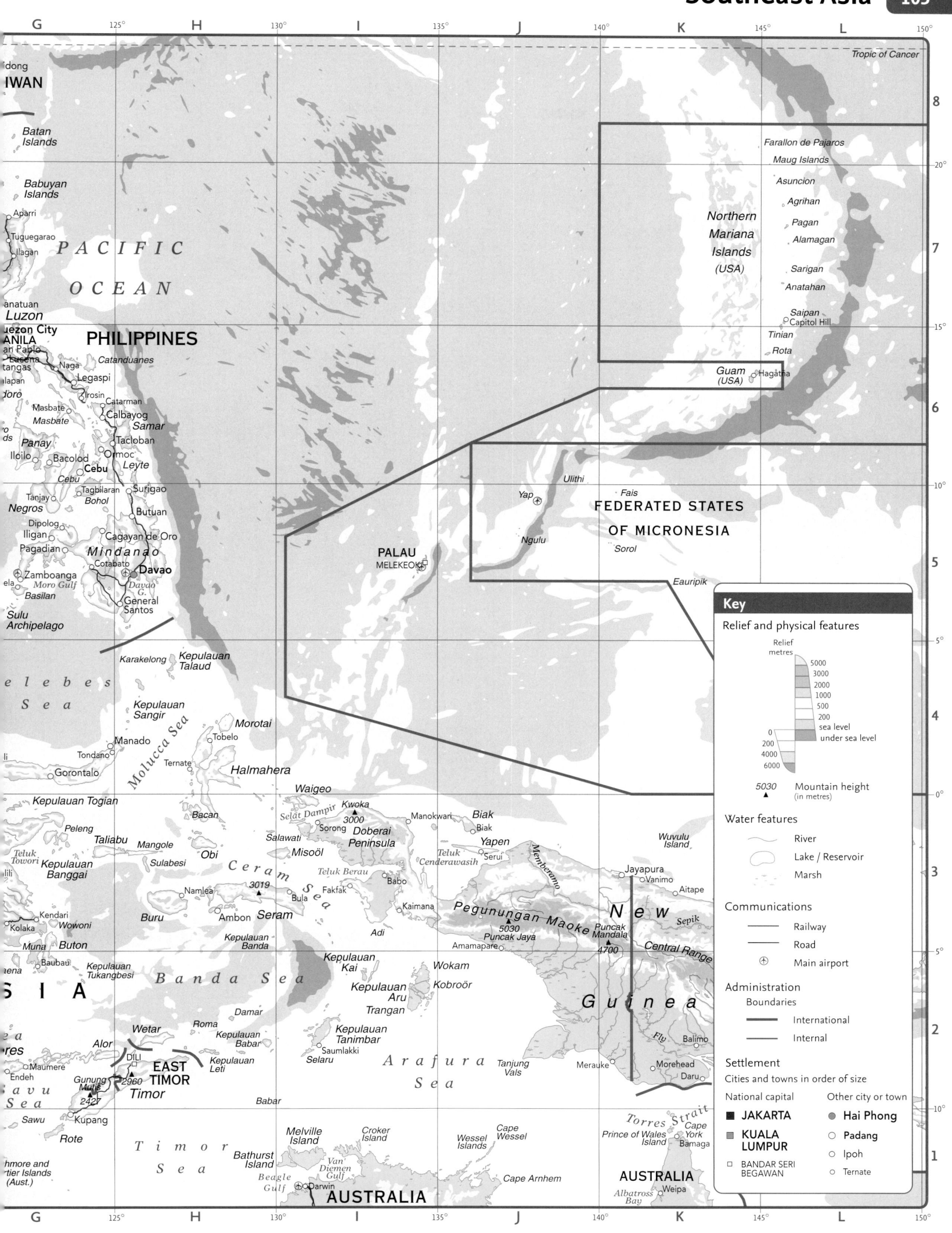

G  125°  H  130°  I  135°  J  140°  K  145°  L  150°

Tropic of Cancer

8

IWAN

Batan
Islands

Babuyan
Islands

Aparri
Tuguegarao
Ilagan

Farallon de Pajaros
Maug Islands

Asuncion
Agrihan
Pagan
Alamagan

Northern
Mariana
Islands
(USA)

Sarigan
Anatahan

7

PACIFIC

OCEAN

anatuan
Luzon

uezon City
ANILA
an Pablo

Lucena
tangas

Naga
Legaspi
Irosin

Catanduanes

PHILIPPINES

Saipan
Capitol Hill

Tinian

Rota

15°

Guam
(USA)

Hagåtña

6

Catarman
Calbayog
Samar
Tacloban
Leyte
Ormoc

Masbate
Masbate

Panay
Iloilo
Bacolod  Cebu
Cebu

Tagbilaran
Bohol

Surigao
Butuan

Ulithi

Fais
Yap

FEDERATED STATES
OF MICRONESIA

10°

Negros
Tanjay
Dipolog
Iligan
Pagadian

Cagayan de Oro

Mindanao

Ngulu

Sorol

5

Zamboanga
ela
Basilan
Moro Gulf

Cotabato

Davao
Davao
G.
General
Santos

PALAU
MELEKEOK

Eauripik

Sulu
Archipelago

Karakelong

Kepulauan
Talaud

5°

elebes

Sea

Kepulauan
Sangir

Molucca Sea

Morotai
Tobelo

Manado
Tondano
Ternate

Gorontalo

Halmahera

Waigeo

Kwoka
3000
Sorong
Salawati
Misoöl

Doberai
Peninsula

Manokwari

Biak
Biak

Yapen
Serui

Wuvulu
Island

0°

Kepulauan Togian
Peleng

Taliabu
Mangole
Obi

Selat Dampir

Teluk
Cenderawasih

Jayapura
Vanimo

New

4

Teluk
Towori
lili
Kepulauan
Banggai

Sulabesi

Ceram

Namlea
3019

Bula

Fakfak

Babo

Memberamo

Aitape

Sepik

Kendari
Kolaka
Wowoni

Buru
Ambon
Seram

Adi

Kaimana

Pegunungan Maoke

Puncak
Mandala
4700

Guinea

3

Muna
Buton

Baubau

Kepulauan
Tukangbesi

Kepulauan
Banda

Banda Sea

Kepulauan
Kai

Wokam

Kobroör

Pegunungan Maoke
5030
Puncak Jaya
Amamapare

Central Range

5°

SIA

Damar

Kepulauan
Aru
Trangan

Fly
Balimo

2

Wetar
Alor

Roma

Kepulauan
Babar

Kepulauan
Tanimbar
Saumlakki
Selaru

Arafura

Morehead
Daru

Endeh
res

DILI
Gunung
Mutis
2960  Timor
2427

EAST
TIMOR

Kepulauan
Leti

Sea

Tanjung
Vals

Merauke

Torres Strait

Cape
York
Bamaga

10°

avu
Sea
Sawu

Kupang

Rote

Babar

Timor

Melville
Island

Croker
Island

Cape
Wessel
Wessel
Islands

Prince of Wales
Island

AUSTRALIA

Weipa

1

hmore and
rtier Islands
(Aust.)

Sea

Bathurst
Island

Van
Diemen
Gulf
Darwin

Beagle
Gulf

AUSTRALIA

Cape Arnhem

Albatross
Bay

G  125°  H  130°  I  135°  J  140°  K  145°  L  150°

**Key**

**Relief and physical features**

Relief
metres

5000
3000
2000
1000
500
200
sea level
under sea level

0
200
4000
6000

5030  ▲  Mountain height
(in metres)

**Water features**

~  River

◯  Lake / Reservoir

Marsh

**Communications**

———  Railway

———  Road

⊕  Main airport

**Administration**
Boundaries

———  International

———  Internal

**Settlement**
Cities and towns in order of size

National capital    Other city or town

■ JAKARTA      ● Hai Phong

■ KUALA      ◯ Padang
  LUMPUR

□ BANDAR SERI   ◯ Ipoh
  BEGAWAN

◯ Ternate

Mercator projection

## Relief and physical features / Water features / Administration

A  130°  B  135°  C  140°  D  145°  E

5  45°

**HEILONGJIANG**
Dongfanghong
Qitaihe
Hulin
Linkou
Mudan
**Jixi**
Iman
*Iesozavodsk*
*Sakhalin*
*La Pérouse Strait*
*Sea of Okhotsk*

Jiaohe
**Mudanjiang**
Suifenhe
Spassk-Dal'niy
Ussuri
*Sikhote-Alin'*
Dal'negorsk
Amgu
Wakkanai
*Ostrov Kunashir*

**CHINA**
Wangqing
**Ussuriysk**
*Zaliv Petra Velikogo*
Rudnaya Pristan'
Monbetsu
Abashiri
Yuzhno-Kuril'sk

Dunhua
Helong
Yanji
Tumen
Hunchun
**Vladivostok**
Nakhodka
Asahikawa
Kitami
Nemuro

Fusong
**JILIN**
Helong
Hunchun
Yanji
*Hokkaidō*
Asahi-dake 2290

Changbai
*Baotou Shan 2750*
Unggi
Najin
Otaru
Bibai
Yūbari
*Hidaka-sanmyaku*
Obihiro
Kushiro

Hyesan
**Ch'ŏngjin**
**Sapporo**
*Ishikari-wan*
Yakumo
Tomakomai
Samani

4  40°

**NORTH KOREA**
*Puksubaek-san 2522*
Pukch'ŏng
Kimch'aek
Yakumo
Muroran
Samani

**Hamhŭng**
Hakodate
*Tsugaru-kaikyō*
Mutsu

Goshogawara
Aomori

Hirosaki
Towada
Hachinohe

Noshiro
Ōdate

**Akita**
Morioka
Miyako

*Ch'unch'ŏn*
Kangnŭng
*Ullŭng-do*
Hanamaki
Kamaishi

*Sea of Japan (East Sea)*
*Ōno*
Ichinoseki
Kesennuma

3  35°

**SOUTH KOREA**
Ulchin
Sakata
Ishinomaki

Andong
*Sadoga-shima*
Ryōtsu
Yamagata
Tendō
**Sendai**

**P'ohang**
Suzu
*J A P A N*
**Niigata**
Fukushima

**Taegu**
*Oki-shotō*
Nanao
*Toyama-wan*
Nagaoka
Aizuwakamatsu
Kōriyama
Iwaki

**Masan**
**Pusan**
Takaoka
Toyama
Jōetsu
Kashiwazaki
Utsunomiya
Hitachi

Chinju
*Korea Strait*
Kanazawa
Nagano
Ueda
Maebashi
Mito

Komatsu
Matsumoto
Oyama
Tsuchiura
Chōshi

*Higashi-suidō*
*Tsushima*
*Iki*
Fukui
Okaya
*Shirane-san 3192*
Saitama
Sakura

Matsue
Tsuruga
Maizuru
Gifu
Kōfu
**TŌKYŌ**
**Chiba**

Masuda
Tottori
*Biwa-ko*
**Kyōto**
Suzuka
*Fuji-san 3776*
**Kawasaki**
**Yokohama**

2

**Hiroshima**
Okayama
**Kōbe**
**Ōsaka**
Toyota
Numazu
Ise
Shizuoka
*O-shima*

*Chūgoku-sanchi*
Ōgaki
**Nagoya**
Tsu
**Hamamatsu**

Shimonoseki
Sakai
Matsusaka

**Kita-Kyūshū**
Takamatsu
Tokushima
Wakayama
*Izu-shotō*

**Fukuoka**
Matsuyama
*Shikoku-sanchi*
Kōchi
Shingū

Sasebo
Kurume
Ōmuta
*Kujū-san 1788*
Ōita
Uwajima
*Shikoku*

Nagasaki
**Kumamoto**
Nobeoka
*Hachijō-jima*

**Kyūshū**
Miyazaki

1  30°

*Tokara-rettō*
**Kagoshima**
*Osumi-kaikyō*
*Ōsumi-shotō*
Tanega-shima
Yaku-shima

*Amami-Ō-shima*

*PACIFIC OCEAN*

---

## Key

### Relief and physical features
Relief metres
5000
3000
2000
1000
500
200
sea level
under sea level
200
4000
6000

*3776* Mountain height (in metres)

### Water features
~ River
Lake / Reservoir
Marsh

### Communications
Railway
Road
⊕ Main airport

### Administration
**Boundaries**
— International  --- Disputed
— Internal  ····· Ceasefire line

**Settlement**
Cities and towns in order of size

National capital
■ **TŌKYŌ**

Other city or town
● Ōsaka
● Yokohama
○ Hamamatsu
○ Morioka
○ Yakumo

---

Scale 1 : 7 500 000

0  100  200  300  400 km

Albers Equal Area Conic projection

## 1 Economic Activity and Trade

### Exports, 2009

Vehicles 21.9%
Electrical equipment 19.9%
Machinery 17.8%
Chemicals 10.7%
Iron and steel products 5.4%
Others 24.3%

### Imports, 2009

Mineral fuels 27.6%
Electrical equipment 12.6%
Chemicals 8.9%
Machinery 8.2%
Others 42.7%

- Major industrial centre

Manufacturing industry
□ Iron and steel
□ Oil refinery
□ Shipbuilding
■ Motor vehicles
□ Mechanical engineering
○ Electrical engineering
◐ Publishing / Paper
○ Chemicals
● Textiles
○ Food processing

Service industry
◆ Banking and finance

Scale 1 : 20 000 000

Sapporo
Niigata
Toyama
Tōkyō
Kyōto
Nagoya
Yokohama
Okayama
Kōbe  Osaka
Kita-Kyūshū
Ōita
Nagasaki

## 2 Population Density

Persons per sq. km
■ over 250
■ 101 – 250
■ 11 – 100
■ 1 – 10
□ 0

Cities
● over 10 000 000
● 5 000 000 – 10 000 000
○ 1 000 000 – 5 000 000
○ 100 000 – 1 000 000

Scale 1 : 15 000 000

Sapporo
Sendai
Tōkyō
Yokohama
Kawasaki
Kyōto  Nagoya
Kōbe
Hiroshima
Osaka
Fukuoka

Ministry of Economy, Trade and Industry
www.meti.go.jp
Statistics Bureau
www.stat.go.jp/english
Japan Information Network
jin.jcic.or.jp
USGS National Earthquake Information Center
earthquake.usgs.gov

## 3 Energy

### Primary energy supply

2003    2010

Oil 50%    Oil 41%
Coal 20%    Coal 18%
Natural gas 14%    Natural gas 14%
Nuclear 12%    Nuclear 15%
Hydro 2%    Hydro 4%
Others 2%    Others 8%

### Sources of fuels by country

**Coal**
Others 2%
Russian Federation 5%
Canada 5%
China 11%
Indonesia 18%
Australia 59%

**Oil**
Others 7%
Indonesia 3%
Other Middle East 3%
Russian Federation 4%
Kuwait 8%
Qatar 10%
Iran 12%
Saudi Arabia 28%
United Arab Emirates 25%

**Natural Gas**
Others 4%
Oman 5%
United Arab Emirates 8%
Brunei 10%
Qatar 12%
Malaysia 19%
Indonesia 22%
Australia 20%

**Uranium**
Others 15%
Russian Federation 4%
Niger 5%
Brazil 6%
Namibia 6%
South Africa 7%
USA 7%
Canada 9%
Kazakhstan 17%
Australia 24%

### New energy - solar power generation, 2006

Japan produces 30.6% of world solar power energy

Thousand MW
Germany
Japan
USA
Rest of the World

## 4 Tectonics

■ Volcanic rocks
▨ Volcanic zones
▲ Volcano
● Earthquakes greater than M6 since 1900
▰▰▰ Convergent/subducting plate boundary
←60 Direction and speed of plate movement, mm/year

Scale 1:15 000 000

Okhotsk Plate
Tokachi-dake
Akan
Hokkaidō
Sapporo
Usu-zan  Tarumae-san
Komaga-take
Eurasian Plate
Chōkai-san
Zao-zan
Azuma-san  Adatara-san
Honshū
M9.0 earthquake and tsunami, 11 March 2011
Iwate-san
Niigata-yake-yama
Hiuchiga-take
Tate-yama  Iwasuge-yama
Yake-dake  Asama
Tōkyō
Nagoya  Fuji-san
Kōbe  Izu-tōbu
Shikoku
Japan Trench
Pacific Plate
Unzen-dake  Aso-san
Kyūshū
Kagoshima  Kirishima-yama
Sakura-jima
Nankai Trench
44
60
Philippine Sea Plate

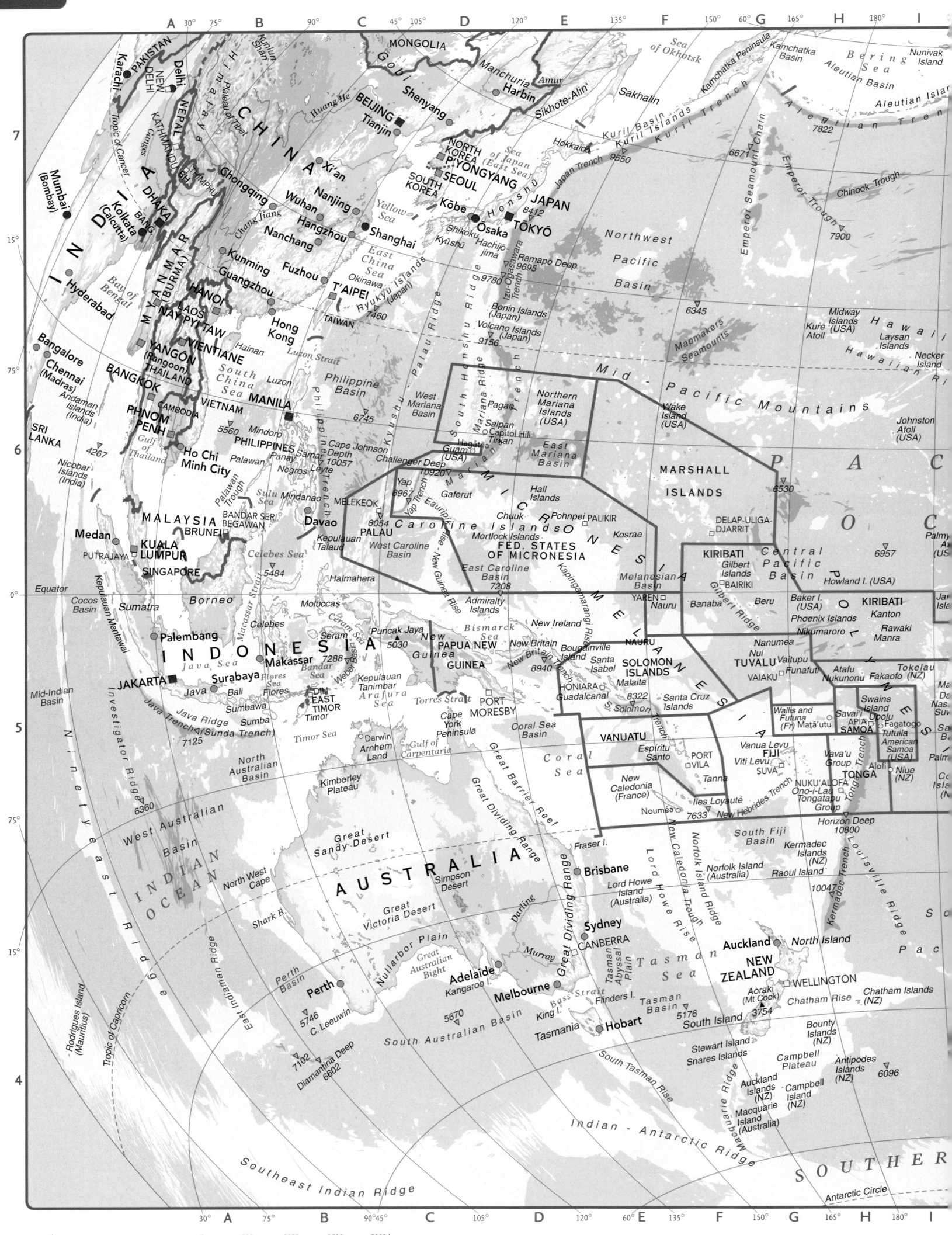

0    500    1000    1500    2000 km

## Key

### Relief and physical features

Relief metres
5000
3000
2000
1000
500
200
0   sea level
    under sea level
200
4000
6000

▲ 6959  Mountain height (in metres)

▽ 10920  Ocean depth (in metres)

### Water features

~ River
~ Intermittent river
Canal
Lake / Reservoir
Intermittent lake
Marsh

### Settlement

Cities and towns in order of size

National capital          Other city or town

■ MEXICO CITY            ● Los Angeles

■ BANGKOK                ● Adelaide

□ KINGSTON               ○ Honolulu

□ CANBERRA

□ VAIAKU

### Administration

Boundaries

——— International

– – – Disputed

········· Ceasefire line

Lambert Azimuthal Equal Area projection

## Key

**Relief and physical features**

Relief metres
5000
3000
2000
1000
500
200
sea level
under sea level
0
200
4000
6000

▲ 5030 Mountain height (in metres)

**Water features**

~ River
Intermittent river
Lake / Reservoir
Intermittent lake
Marsh
Coral reef

**Communications**

Railway
Road
⊕ Main airport

**Administration**

Boundaries

International
Internal

**Settlement**

Cities and towns in order of size

National capital
□ CANBERRA
□ SUVA

Other city or town
● **Sydney**
○ Newcastle
○ Darwin

Scale 1 : 20 000 000

0    200    400    600    800 km

---

*Major labels on map:*

INDONESIA, PAPUA NEW GUINEA, NEW GUINEA, AUSTRALIA, WESTERN AUSTRALIA, NORTHERN TERRITORY, SOUTH AUSTRALIA, QUEENSLAND, NEW SOUTH WALES, VICTORIA, TASMANIA, AUST. CAP. TER.

Molucca Sea, Banda Sea, Ceram Sea, Flores Sea, Savu Sea, Timor Sea, Arafura Sea, Gulf of Carpentaria, Coral Sea, Bismarck Sea, Solomon Sea, Coral Sea Islands Territory (Australia), Gulf of Papua

Makassar, Darwin, Katherine, Wyndham, Derby, Broome, Port Hedland, Barrow Island, Dampier, Hamersley Range, Geraldton, Dongara, Perth, Fremantle, Bunbury, Albany, Esperance, Norseman, Kalgoorlie, Alice Springs, Mount Isa, Normanton, Cooktown, Cairns, Townsville, Mackay, Rockhampton, Gladstone, Bundaberg, Maryborough, Brisbane, Gold Coast, Coolangatta, Lismore, Grafton, Coffs Harbour, Port Macquarie, Newcastle, Gosford, Sydney, Wollongong, Canberra, Broken Hill, Dubbo, Bourke, Moree, Toowoomba, Dirranbandi, Armidale, Tamworth, Bathurst, Goulburn, Wagga Wagga, Albury, Bendigo, Ballarat, Geelong, Melbourne, Sale, Bairnsdale, Horsham, Mildura, Port Augusta, Port Pirie, Whyalla, Adelaide, Murray Bridge, Port Lincoln, Mount Gambier, Portland, Launceston, Devonport, Burnie, Hobart

Great Sandy Desert, Great Victoria Desert, Gibson Desert, Tanami Desert, Simpson Desert, Sturt Stony Desert, Nullarbor Plain, Great Australian Bight, Kimberley Plateau, Macdonnell Ranges, Musgrave Ranges, Flinders Ranges, Great Dividing Range, Darling Downs, Barkly Tableland, Arnhem Land, Cape York Peninsula, Nullarbor Plain

Lake Eyre (North), Lake Eyre (South), Lake Torrens, Lake Gairdner, Lake Frome, Lake Blanche, Lake Amadeus, Lake Mackay, Lake Disappointment, Lake Carnegie, Lake Wells, Lake Barlee, Lake Moore, Lake Cowan, Lake MacLeod, Lake Argyle, Lake Wills, Lake White, Cooper Creek, Darling, Murray, Murrumbidgee, Lachlan, Warrego, Diamantina, Georgina, Flinders, Mitchell

Mount Kosciuszko 2229, Mount Ossa 1617, Mount William 1167, Uluru (Ayers Rock) 867, Mount Zeil 1531, Round Mountain 1615, Mount Dalrymple 1277, Ashburton 1250, Mount Ord 936

Bass Strait, Torres Strait, King Island, Flinders Island, Kangaroo Island, Fraser Island, Melville Island, Bathurst Island, Groote Eylandt, Wessel Islands, Cape York, Cape Arnhem, Cape Wessel, Cape Leeuwin, Cape Carnot, North West Cape, Wilson's Promontory, South East Cape

Kwoka 3000, Doberai Peninsula, Biak, Yapen, Jayapura, Aitape, Lae, Mt Wilhelm 4509, Puncak Jaya 5030, Puncak Mandala 4700, Mount Victoria 4073, Port Moresby, Owen Stanley Ra, Admiralty Islands, New Ireland, New Britain, Bougainville Island, Woodlark Island, Trobriand Islands, D'Entrecasteaux Islands, Rossel Is, Tagula Island

Seram 3019, Timor 2960, East Timor, Dili, Kupang, Makassar

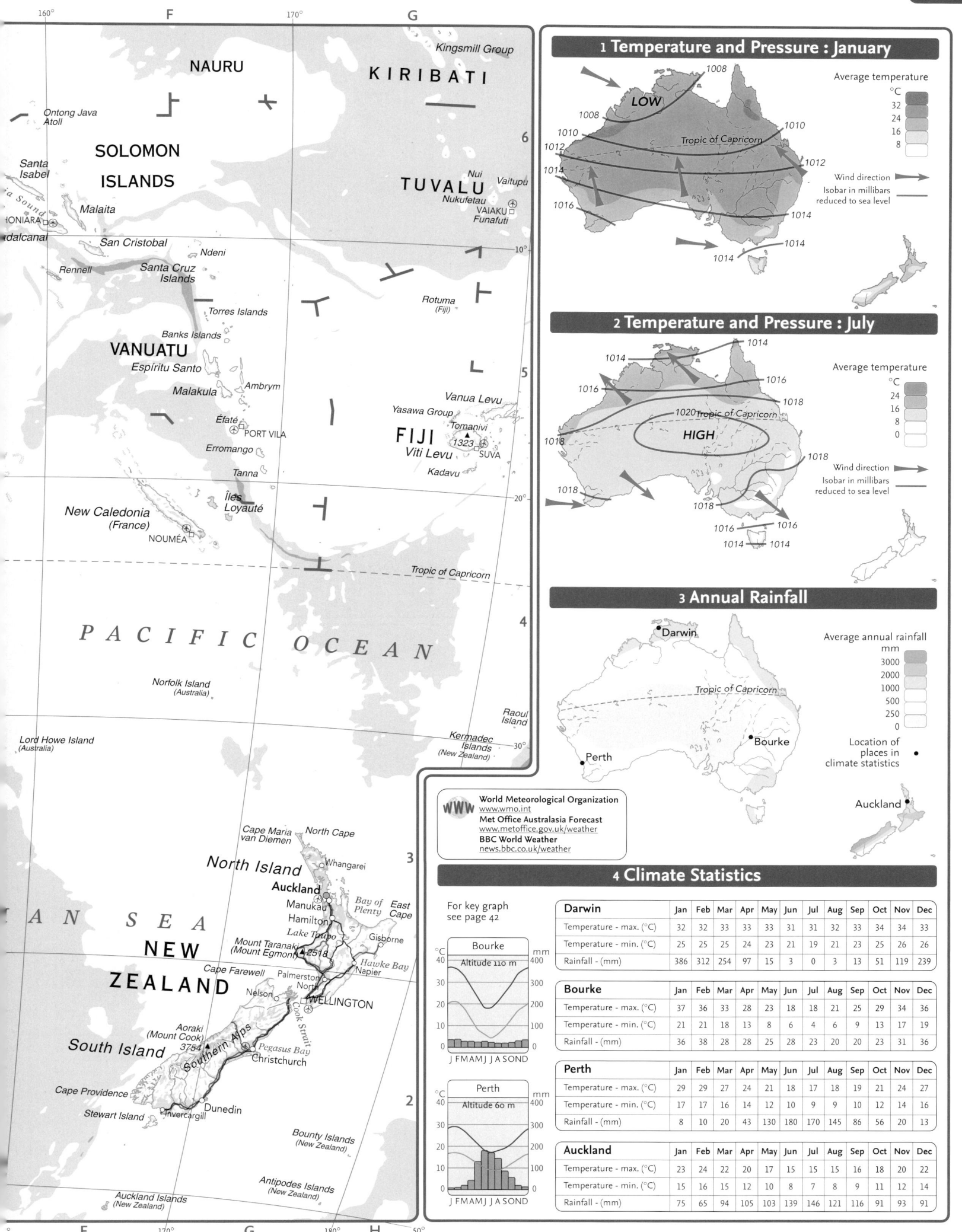

## 1 Temperature and Pressure : January

Average temperature
°C
32
24
16
8

Wind direction →
Isobar in millibars
reduced to sea level

LOW

## 2 Temperature and Pressure : July

Average temperature
°C
24
16
8
0

Wind direction →
Isobar in millibars
reduced to sea level

HIGH

## 3 Annual Rainfall

Average annual rainfall
mm
3000
2000
1000
500
250
0

Location of
places in
climate statistics

WWW
World Meteorological Organization
www.wmo.int
Met Office Australasia Forecast
www.metoffice.gov.uk/weather
BBC World Weather
news.bbc.co.uk/weather

## 4 Climate Statistics

For key graph
see page 42

Bourke
Altitude 110 m

Perth
Altitude 60 m

| Darwin | Jan | Feb | Mar | Apr | May | Jun | Jul | Aug | Sep | Oct | Nov | Dec |
|---|---|---|---|---|---|---|---|---|---|---|---|---|
| Temperature - max. (°C) | 32 | 32 | 33 | 33 | 33 | 31 | 31 | 32 | 33 | 34 | 34 | 33 |
| Temperature - min. (°C) | 25 | 25 | 25 | 24 | 23 | 21 | 19 | 21 | 23 | 25 | 26 | 26 |
| Rainfall - (mm) | 386 | 312 | 254 | 97 | 15 | 3 | 0 | 3 | 13 | 51 | 119 | 239 |

| Bourke | Jan | Feb | Mar | Apr | May | Jun | Jul | Aug | Sep | Oct | Nov | Dec |
|---|---|---|---|---|---|---|---|---|---|---|---|---|
| Temperature - max. (°C) | 37 | 36 | 33 | 28 | 23 | 18 | 18 | 21 | 25 | 29 | 34 | 36 |
| Temperature - min. (°C) | 21 | 21 | 18 | 13 | 8 | 6 | 4 | 6 | 9 | 13 | 17 | 19 |
| Rainfall - (mm) | 36 | 38 | 28 | 28 | 25 | 28 | 23 | 20 | 20 | 23 | 31 | 36 |

| Perth | Jan | Feb | Mar | Apr | May | Jun | Jul | Aug | Sep | Oct | Nov | Dec |
|---|---|---|---|---|---|---|---|---|---|---|---|---|
| Temperature - max. (°C) | 29 | 29 | 27 | 24 | 21 | 18 | 17 | 18 | 19 | 21 | 24 | 27 |
| Temperature - min. (°C) | 17 | 17 | 16 | 14 | 12 | 10 | 9 | 9 | 10 | 12 | 14 | 16 |
| Rainfall - (mm) | 8 | 10 | 20 | 43 | 130 | 180 | 170 | 145 | 86 | 56 | 20 | 13 |

| Auckland | Jan | Feb | Mar | Apr | May | Jun | Jul | Aug | Sep | Oct | Nov | Dec |
|---|---|---|---|---|---|---|---|---|---|---|---|---|
| Temperature - max. (°C) | 23 | 24 | 22 | 20 | 17 | 15 | 15 | 15 | 16 | 18 | 20 | 22 |
| Temperature - min. (°C) | 15 | 16 | 15 | 12 | 10 | 8 | 7 | 8 | 9 | 11 | 12 | 14 |
| Rainfall - (mm) | 75 | 65 | 94 | 105 | 103 | 139 | 146 | 121 | 116 | 91 | 93 | 91 |

Lambert Azimuthal Equal Area projection

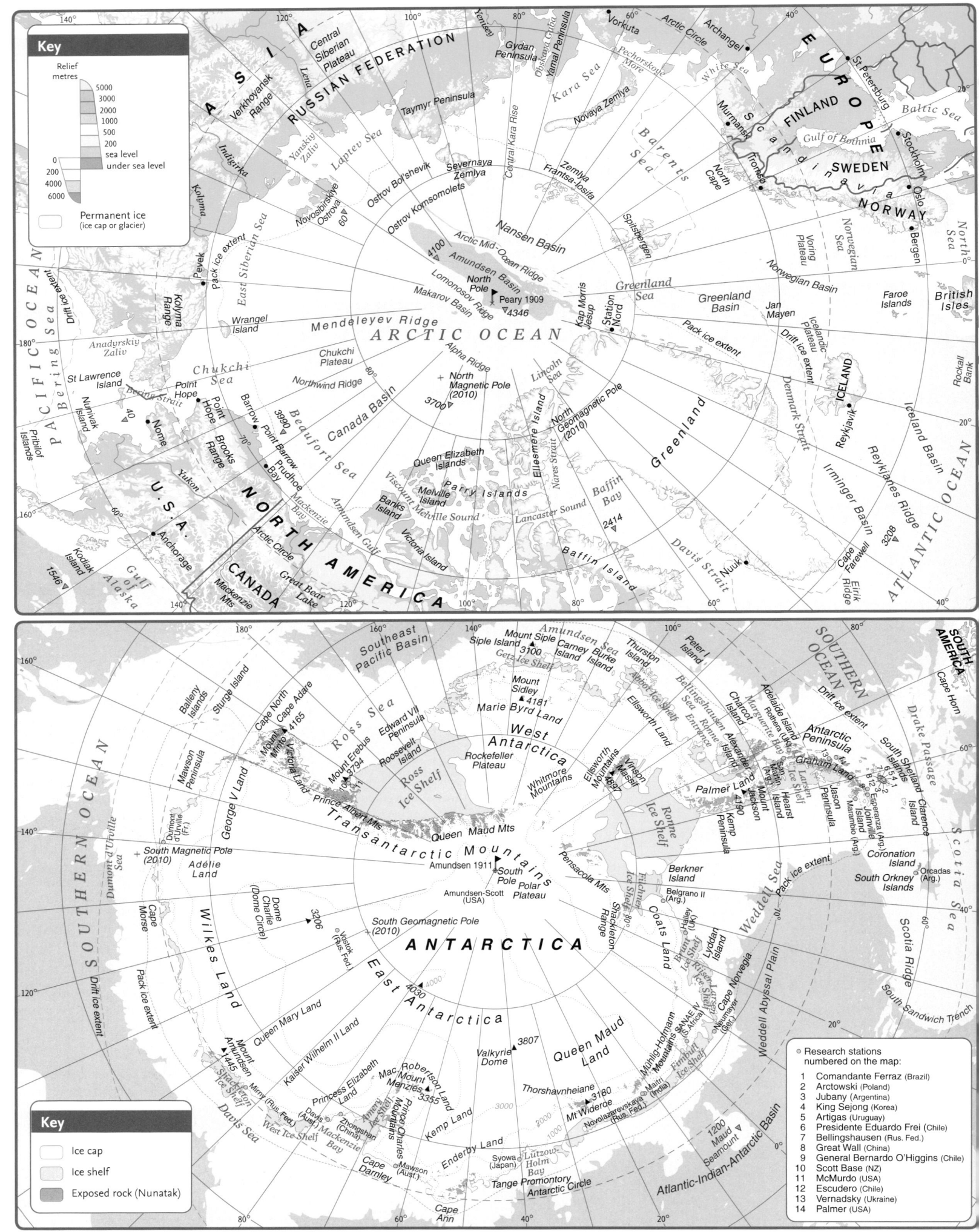

**Key**

Relief
metres

5000
3000
2000
1000
500
200
0 sea level
200 under sea level
4000
6000

Permanent ice
(ice cap or glacier)

**Key**

Ice cap

Ice shelf

Exposed rock (Nunatak)

Research stations
numbered on the map:

1  Comandante Ferraz (Brazil)
2  Arctowski (Poland)
3  Jubany (Argentina)
4  King Sejong (Korea)
5  Artigas (Uruguay)
6  Presidente Eduardo Frei (Chile)
7  Bellingshausen (Rus. Fed.)
8  Great Wall (China)
9  General Bernardo O'Higgins (Chile)
10  Scott Base (NZ)
11  McMurdo (USA)
12  Escudero (Chile)
13  Vernadsky (Ukraine)
14  Palmer (USA)

Scale 1 : 36 000 000

0        500        1000        1500 km

Polar Stereographic projection

## 1 International Organizations - Political

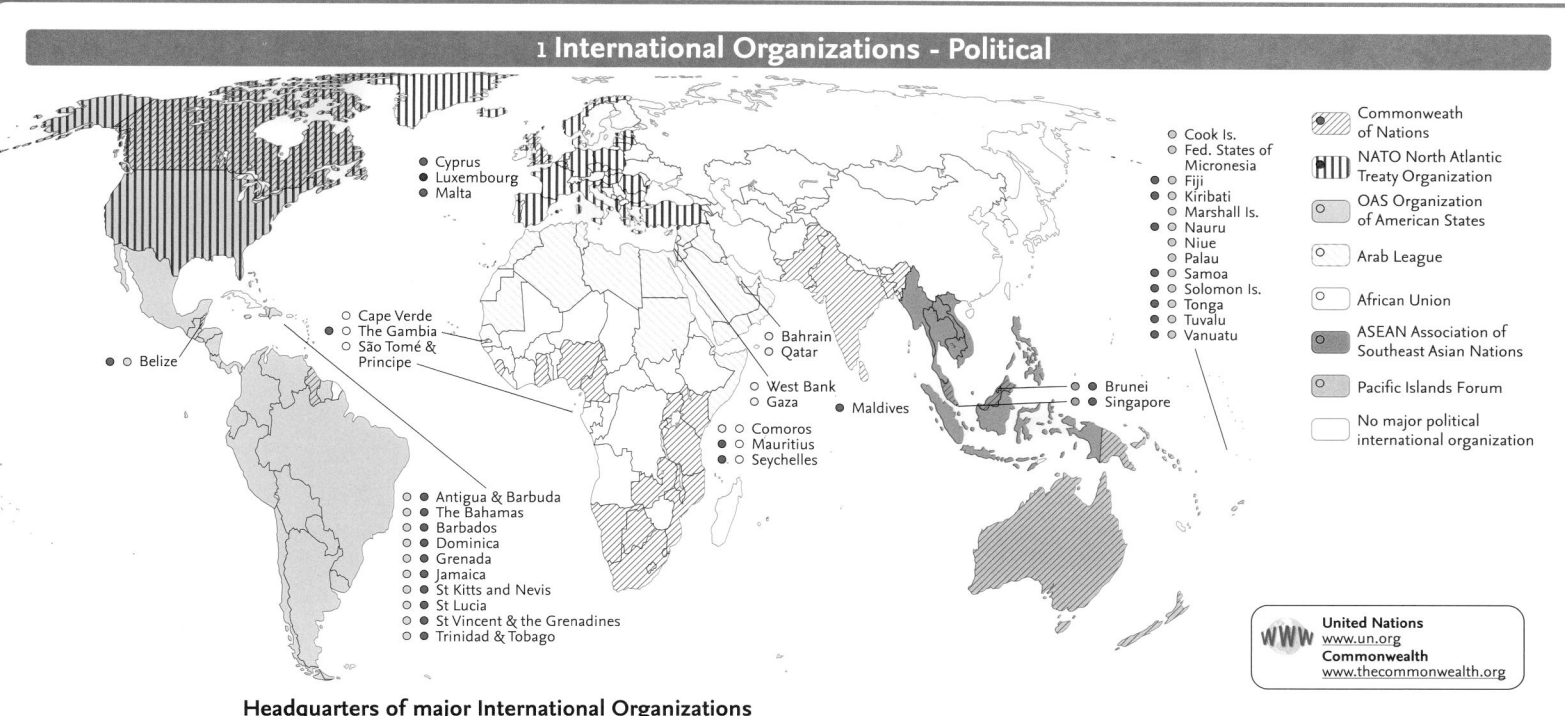

**Legend:**
- Commonweath of Nations
- NATO North Atlantic Treaty Organization
- OAS Organization of American States
- Arab League
- African Union
- ASEAN Association of Southeast Asian Nations
- Pacific Islands Forum
- No major political international organization

Cook Is.
Fed. States of Micronesia
Fiji
Kiribati
Marshall Is.
Nauru
Niue
Palau
Samoa
Solomon Is.
Tonga
Tuvalu
Vanuatu

Cyprus
Luxembourg
Malta

Belize

Cape Verde
The Gambia
São Tomé & Principe

Bahrain
Qatar

West Bank
Gaza

Maldives

Brunei
Singapore

Comoros
Mauritius
Seychelles

Antigua & Barbuda
The Bahamas
Barbados
Dominica
Grenada
Jamaica
St Kitts and Nevis
St Lucia
St Vincent & the Grenadines
Trinidad & Tobago

www **United Nations** www.un.org
**Commonwealth** www.thecommonwealth.org

### Headquarters of major International Organizations

| City | Organisation | Abbreviation |
|---|---|---|
| **Addis Ababa** Ethiopia | African Union | AU |
| **Bangui** Central African Republic | Economic and Monetary Community of Central Africa | EMCCA |
| **Brussels** Belgium | North Atlantic Treaty Organization | NATO |
| **Brussels** Belgium | European Union | EU |
| **Cairo** Egypt | Arab League | |
| **Colombo** Sri Lanka | Colombo Plan | |
| **Gaborone** Botswana | Southern African Development Community | SADC |
| **Geneva** Switzerland | World Trade Organization | WTO |
| **Geneva** Switzerland | World Health Organization | WHO |
| **Georgetown** Guyana | Caribbean Community | CARICOM |
| **Jakarta** Indonesia | Association of Southeast Asian Nations | ASEAN |
| **Lima** Peru | Andean Community | |
| **Lomé** Togo | Economic Community of West African States | ECOWAS |
| **London** UK | Commonwealth of Nations | |
| **Montevideo** Uruguay | Latin American Integration Association | LAIA |
| **New York** USA | United Nations | UN |
| **Paris** France | Organisation for Economic Co-operation and Development | OECD |
| **Singapore** Singapore | Asia-Pacific Economic Cooperation | APEC |
| **Suva** Fiji | Pacific Islands Forum | |
| **Vienna** Austria | Organization of Petroleum Exporting Countries | OPEC |
| **Washington DC** USA | Organization of American States | OAS |

**United Nations Factfile**

| | |
|---|---|
| **Established:** | 24th October 1945 |
| **Headquarters:** | New York, USA |
| **Purpose:** | Maintain international peace and security. Develop friendly relations among nations. Help to solve international, economic, social, cultural and humanitarian problems. Help to promote respect for human rights. To be a centre for harmonizing the actions of nations in attaining these ends. |
| **Structure:** | The 6 principal organs of the UN are: General Assembly, Security Council, Economic and Social Council, Trusteeship Council, International Court of Justice, Secretariat |
| **Members:** | There are 193 members. Vatican City and Kosovo are the only non member countries. |

## 2 International Organizations - Economic

**Legend:**
- Colombo Plan
- OPEC Organization of Petroleum Exporting Countries
- OECD Organisation for Economic Co-operation and Development
- EU European Union
- CARICOM Caribbean Community
- LAIA Latin American Integration Association
- APEC Asia-Pacific Economic Cooperation
- Andean Community
- ECOWAS Economic Community of West African States
- EMCCA Economic and Monetary Community of Central Africa
- SADC Southern African Development Community
- No major economic international organization

Luxembourg
Malta
Cape Verde
Qatar
Brunei
Maldives
Singapore
Mauritius
Fiji

Canada, United States and Mexico constitute the North American Free Trade Agreement (NAFTA).

Antigua & Barbuda
The Bahamas
Barbados
Dominica
Grenada
Jamaica
Montserrat
St Kitts and Nevis
St Lucia
St Vincent & the Grenadines
Trinidad & Tobago

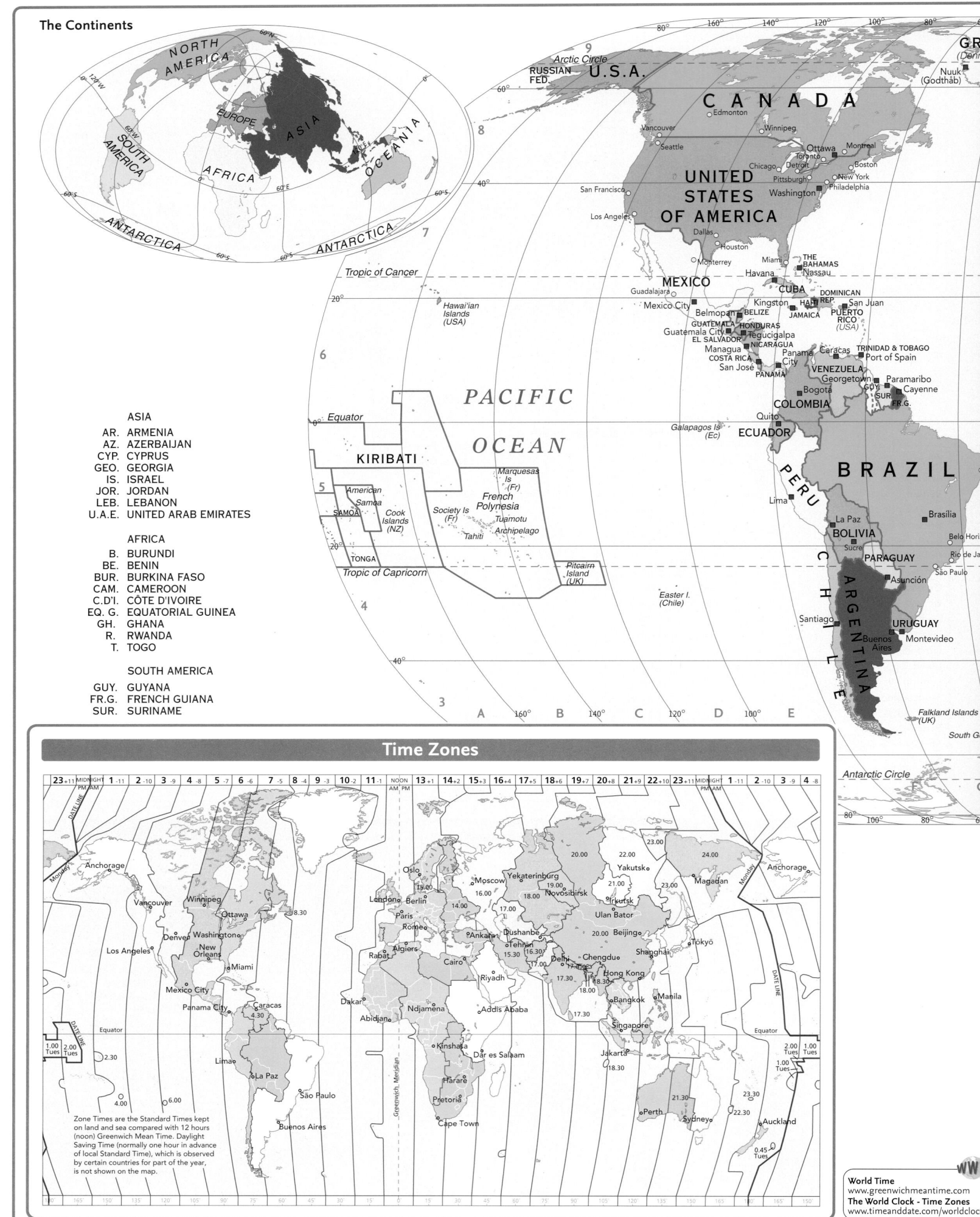

## The Continents

NORTH AMERICA
SOUTH AMERICA
EUROPE
ASIA
AFRICA
OCEANIA
ANTARCTICA
ANTARCTICA

### ASIA
AR. ARMENIA
AZ. AZERBAIJAN
CYP. CYPRUS
GEO. GEORGIA
IS. ISRAEL
JOR. JORDAN
LEB. LEBANON
U.A.E. UNITED ARAB EMIRATES

### AFRICA
B. BURUNDI
BE. BENIN
BUR. BURKINA FASO
CAM. CAMEROON
C.D'I. CÔTE D'IVOIRE
EQ. G. EQUATORIAL GUINEA
GH. GHANA
R. RWANDA
T. TOGO

### SOUTH AMERICA
GUY. GUYANA
FR.G. FRENCH GUIANA
SUR. SURINAME

## Time Zones

Zone Times are the Standard Times kept on land and sea compared with 12 hours (noon) Greenwich Mean Time. Daylight Saving Time (normally one hour in advance of local Standard Time), which is observed by certain countries for part of the year, is not shown on the map.

World Time
www.greenwichmeantime.com
The World Clock - Time Zones
www.timeanddate.com/worldcloc

Scale 1 : 93 000 000

0    1000    2000    3000    4000 km

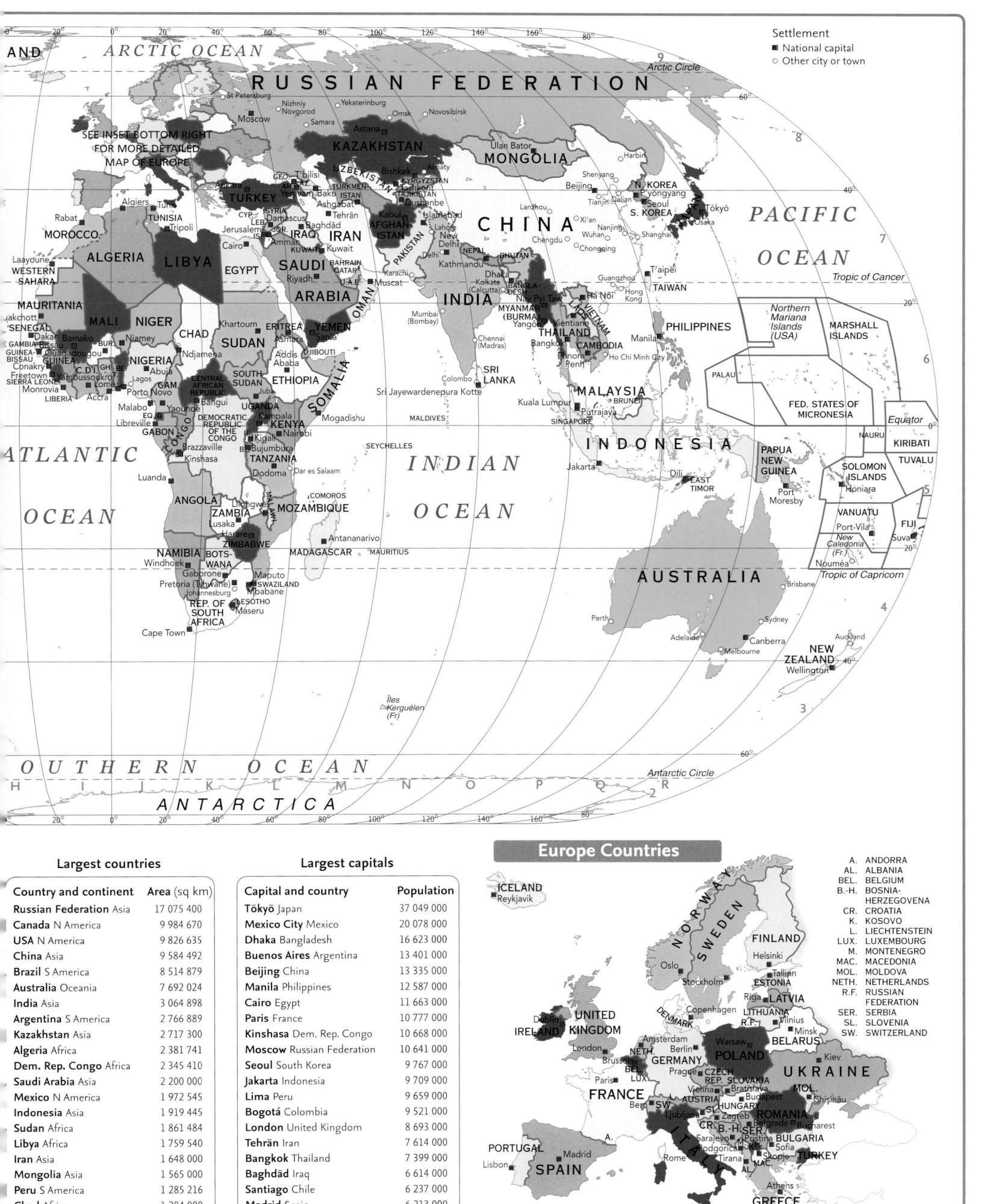

Settlement
- ■ National capital
- ○ Other city or town

**Largest countries**

| Country and continent | Area (sq km) |
|---|---|
| **Russian Federation** Asia | 17 075 400 |
| **Canada** N America | 9 984 670 |
| **USA** N America | 9 826 635 |
| **China** Asia | 9 584 492 |
| **Brazil** S America | 8 514 879 |
| **Australia** Oceania | 7 692 024 |
| **India** Asia | 3 064 898 |
| **Argentina** S America | 2 766 889 |
| **Kazakhstan** Asia | 2 717 300 |
| **Algeria** Africa | 2 381 741 |
| **Dem. Rep. Congo** Africa | 2 345 410 |
| **Saudi Arabia** Asia | 2 200 000 |
| **Mexico** N America | 1 972 545 |
| **Indonesia** Asia | 1 919 445 |
| **Sudan** Africa | 1 861 484 |
| **Libya** Africa | 1 759 540 |
| **Iran** Asia | 1 648 000 |
| **Mongolia** Asia | 1 565 000 |
| **Peru** S America | 1 285 216 |
| **Chad** Africa | 1 284 000 |

**Largest capitals**

| Capital and country | Population |
|---|---|
| **Tōkyō** Japan | 37 049 000 |
| **Mexico City** Mexico | 20 078 000 |
| **Dhaka** Bangladesh | 16 623 000 |
| **Buenos Aires** Argentina | 13 401 000 |
| **Beijing** China | 13 335 000 |
| **Manila** Philippines | 12 587 000 |
| **Cairo** Egypt | 11 663 000 |
| **Paris** France | 10 777 000 |
| **Kinshasa** Dem. Rep. Congo | 10 668 000 |
| **Moscow** Russian Federation | 10 641 000 |
| **Seoul** South Korea | 9 767 000 |
| **Jakarta** Indonesia | 9 709 000 |
| **Lima** Peru | 9 659 000 |
| **Bogotá** Colombia | 9 521 000 |
| **London** United Kingdom | 8 693 000 |
| **Tehrān** Iran | 7 614 000 |
| **Bangkok** Thailand | 7 399 000 |
| **Baghdād** Iraq | 6 614 000 |
| **Santiago** Chile | 6 237 000 |
| **Madrid** Spain | 6 213 000 |

**Europe Countries**

A. ANDORRA
AL. ALBANIA
BEL. BELGIUM
B.-H. BOSNIA-HERZEGOVENA
CR. CROATIA
K. KOSOVO
L. LIECHTENSTEIN
LUX. LUXEMBOURG
M. MONTENEGRO
MAC. MACEDONIA
MOL. MOLDOVA
NETH. NETHERLANDS
R.F. RUSSIAN FEDERATION
SER. SERBIA
SL. SLOVENIA
SW. SWITZERLAND

Eckert IV projection

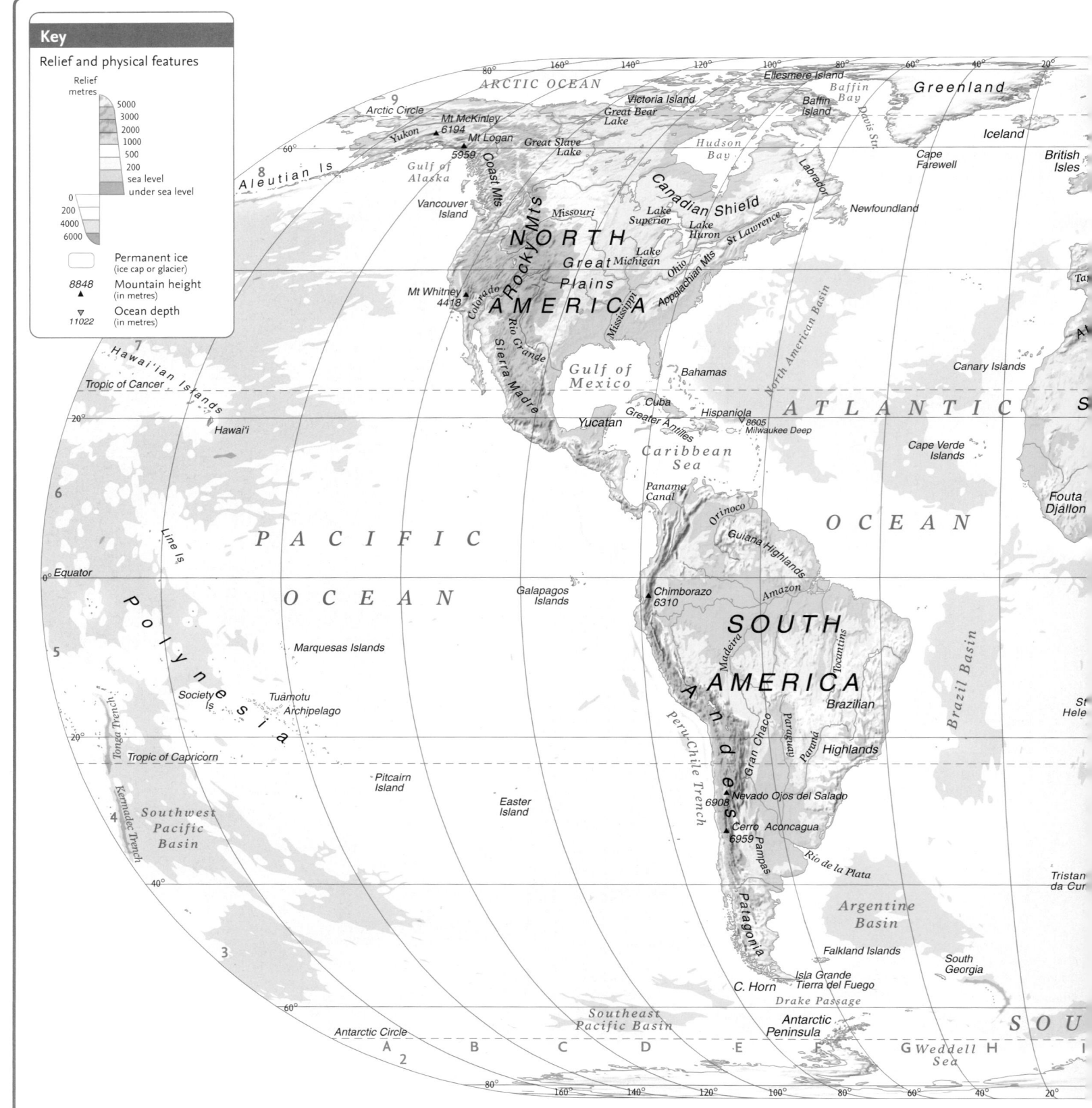

**Key**

Relief and physical features

Relief
metres
5000
3000
2000
1000
500
200
sea level
under sea level

0
200
4000
6000

Permanent ice
(ice cap or glacier)

8848 ▲ Mountain height
(in metres)

11022 ▽ Ocean depth
(in metres)

| Mountain heights | metres |
|---|---|
| Mt Everest (Nepal/China) | 8848 |
| K2 (Jammu & Kashmir/China) | 8611 |
| Kangchenjunga (Nepal/India) | 8586 |
| Dhaulagiri (Nepal) | 8167 |
| Annapurna (Nepal) | 8091 |
| Cerro Aconcagua (Argentina) | 6959 |
| Nevado Ojos del Salado (Arg./Chile) | 6908 |
| Chimborazo (Ecuador) | 6310 |
| Mt McKinley (USA) | 6194 |
| Mt Logan (Canada) | 5959 |

| Island areas | sq km |
|---|---|
| Greenland | 2 175 600 |
| New Guinea | 808 510 |
| Borneo | 745 561 |
| Madagascar | 587 040 |
| Baffin Island | 507 451 |
| Sumatra | 473 606 |
| Honshū | 227 414 |
| Great Britain | 218 476 |
| Victoria Island | 217 291 |
| Ellesmere Island | 196 236 |

| Continents | sq km |
|---|---|
| Asia | 45 036 492 |
| Africa | 30 343 578 |
| North America | 24 680 331 |
| South America | 17 815 420 |
| Antarctica | 12 093 000 |
| Europe | 9 908 599 |
| Oceania | 8 923 000 |

Scale 1 : 80 000 000

0    800    1600    2400    3200 km

| Oceans | sq km |
|---|---|
| Pacific Ocean | 166 241 000 |
| Atlantic Ocean | 86 557 000 |
| Indian Ocean | 73 427 000 |
| Arctic Ocean | 9 485 000 |

| Lake areas | sq km |
|---|---|
| Caspian Sea | 371 000 |
| Lake Superior | 82 100 |
| Lake Victoria | 68 800 |
| Lake Huron | 59 600 |
| Lake Michigan | 57 800 |
| Lake Tanganyika | 32 900 |
| Great Bear Lake | 31 328 |
| Lake Baikal | 30 500 |
| Lake Nyasa | 30 044 |

| River lengths | km |
|---|---|
| Nile (Africa) | 6695 |
| Amazon (S. America) | 6516 |
| Chang Jiang (Asia) | 6380 |
| Mississippi-Missouri (N. America) | 5969 |
| Ob'-Irtysh (Asia) | 5568 |
| Yenisey-Angara-Selenga (Asia) | 5500 |
| Huang He (Asia) | 5464 |
| Congo (Africa) | 4667 |
| Río de la Plata-Paraná (S. America) | 4500 |
| Mekong (Asia) | 4425 |

## 1 Continental Drift

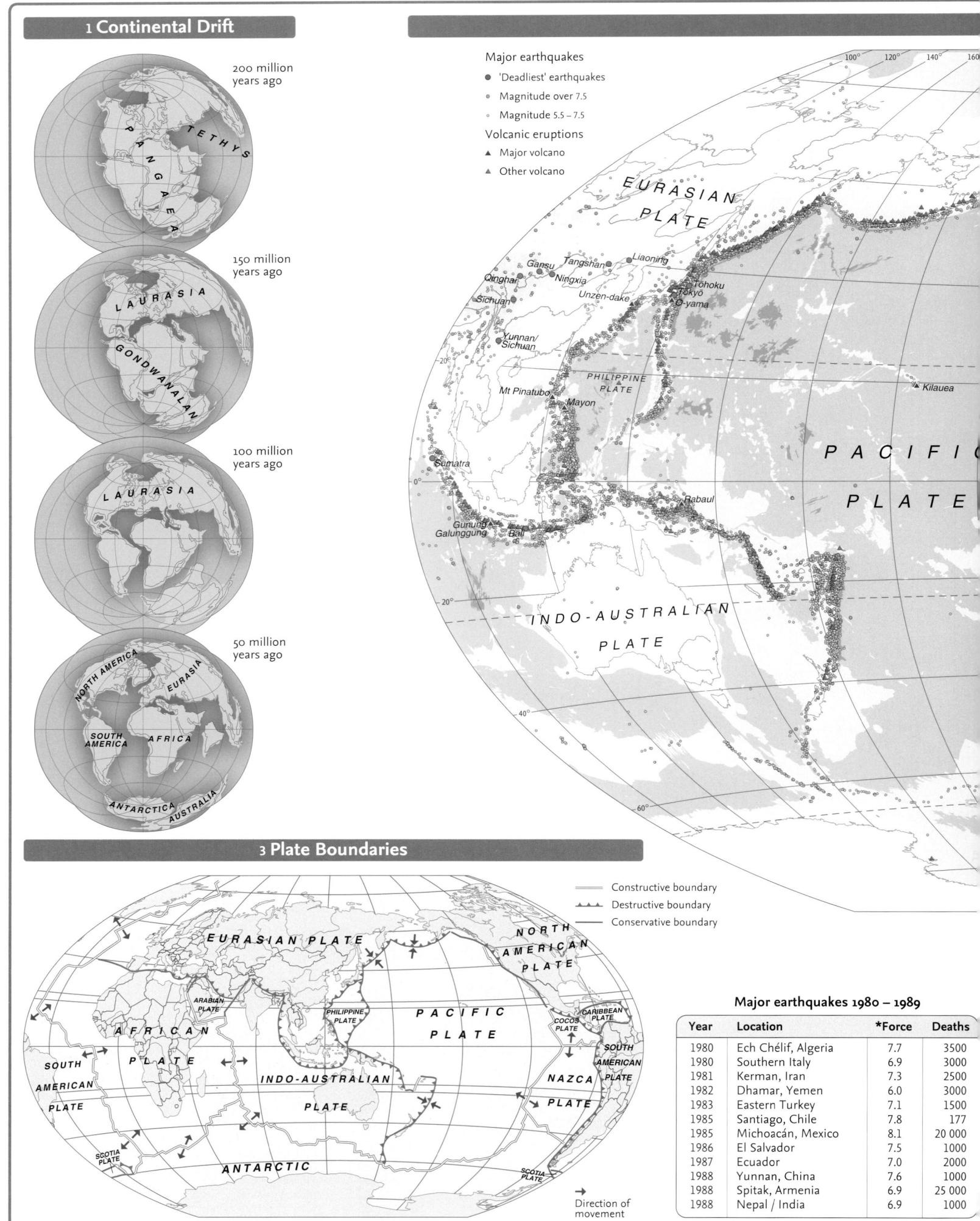

200 million
years ago

150 million
years ago

100 million
years ago

50 million
years ago

## 3 Plate Boundaries

Major earthquakes
- ● 'Deadliest' earthquakes
- ● Magnitude over 7.5
- ● Magnitude 5.5 – 7.5

Volcanic eruptions
- ▲ Major volcano
- ▲ Other volcano

━━ Constructive boundary
▲▲▲ Destructive boundary
━━ Conservative boundary

→ Direction of
movement

### Major earthquakes 1980 – 1989

| Year | Location | *Force | Deaths |
|------|----------|--------|--------|
| 1980 | Ech Chélif, Algeria | 7.7 | 3500 |
| 1980 | Southern Italy | 6.9 | 3000 |
| 1981 | Kerman, Iran | 7.3 | 2500 |
| 1982 | Dhamar, Yemen | 6.0 | 3000 |
| 1983 | Eastern Turkey | 7.1 | 1500 |
| 1985 | Santiago, Chile | 7.8 | 177 |
| 1985 | Michoacán, Mexico | 8.1 | 20 000 |
| 1986 | El Salvador | 7.5 | 1000 |
| 1987 | Ecuador | 7.0 | 2000 |
| 1988 | Yunnan, China | 7.6 | 1000 |
| 1988 | Spitak, Armenia | 6.9 | 25 000 |
| 1988 | Nepal / India | 6.9 | 1000 |

## 2 Earthquakes and Volcanoes

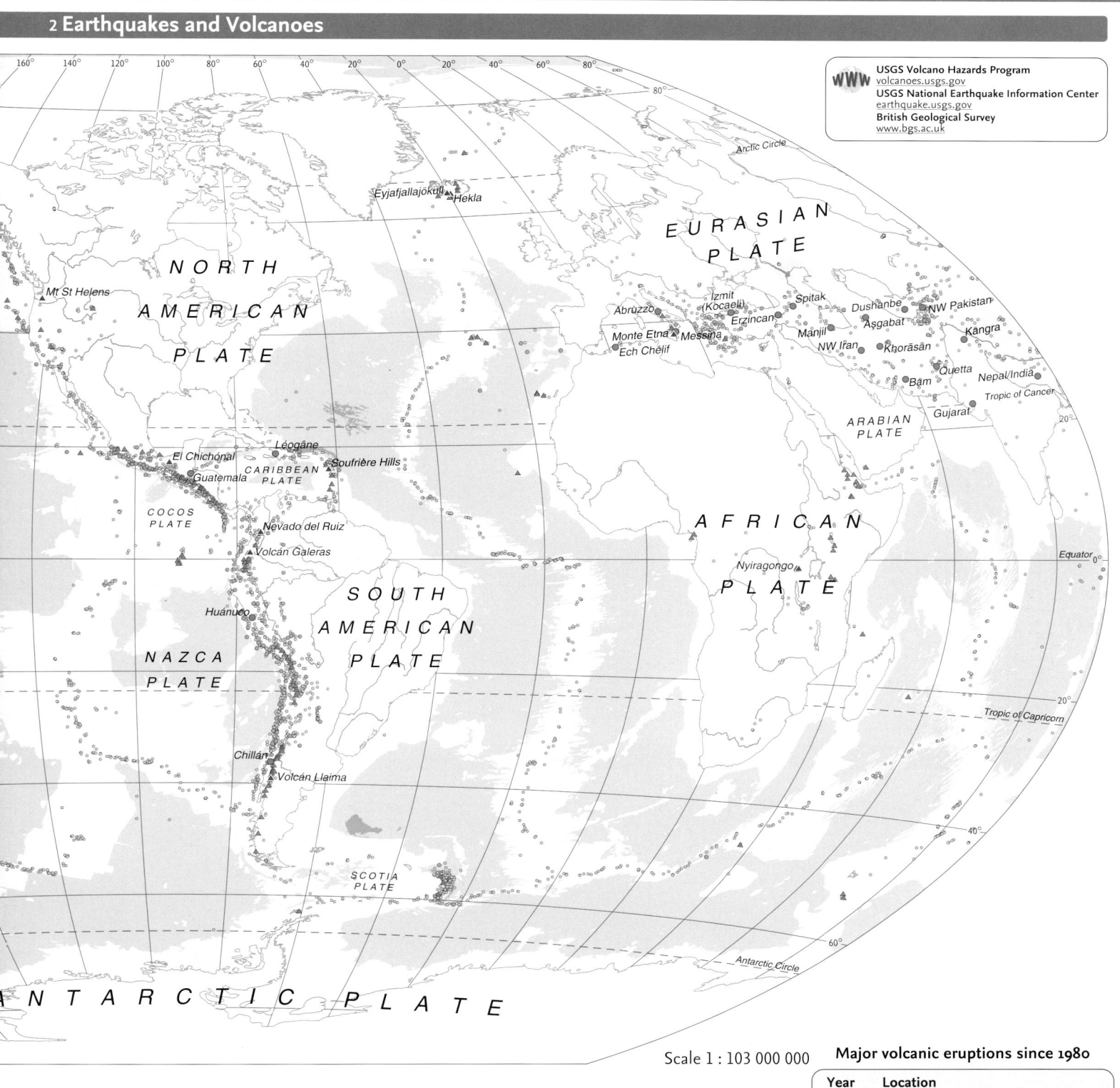

**WWW** USGS Volcano Hazards Program
volcanoes.usgs.gov
USGS National Earthquake Information Center
earthquake.usgs.gov
British Geological Survey
www.bgs.ac.uk

Scale 1 : 103 000 000

### Major earthquakes 1990 – 1996

| Year | Location | *Force | Deaths |
|------|----------|--------|--------|
| 1990 | Manjil, Iran | 7.7 | 50 000 |
| 1990 | Luzon, Philippines | 7.7 | 1600 |
| 1991 | Georgia | 7.1 | 114 |
| 1991 | Uttar Pradesh, India | 6.1 | 1600 |
| 1992 | Flores, Indonesia | 7.5 | 2500 |
| 1992 | Erzincan, Turkey | 6.8 | 500 |
| 1992 | Cairo, Egypt | 5.9 | 550 |
| 1993 | Northern Japan | 7.8 | 185 |
| 1993 | Maharashtra, India | 6.4 | 9748 |
| 1994 | Kuril Islands, Japan | 8.3 | 10 |
| 1995 | Kōbe, Japan | 7.2 | 5502 |
| 1995 | Sakhalin, Russian Fed. | 7.6 | 2500 |
| 1996 | Yunnan, China | 7.0 | 251 |

### Major earthquakes 1997 – 2011

| Year | Location | *Force | Deaths |
|------|----------|--------|--------|
| 1998 | Papua New Guinea | | 2183 |
| 1999 | İzmit, Turkey | 7.4 | 17 118 |
| 1999 | Chi-Chi, Taiwan | | 2400 |
| 2001 | Gujarat, India | 6.9 | 20 085 |
| 2002 | Hindu Kush, Afghanistan | 6.0 | 1000 |
| 2003 | Boumerdes, Algeria | 5.8 | 2266 |
| 2003 | Bam, Iran | 6.6 | 26 271 |
| 2004 | Sumatra, Indonesia | 9.0 | 283 106 |
| 2005 | Northern Sumatra, Indonesia | 8.7 | 1313 |
| 2005 | Muzzafarabad, Pakistan | 7.6 | 80 361 |
| 2008 | Sichuan Province | 8.0 | 87 476 |
| 2010 | Léogâne, Haiti | 7.0 | 222 570 |
| 2011 | Tōhoku, Japan | 9.0 | 14 500 |

* Earthquake force measured on the Richter scale

### Major volcanic eruptions since 1980

| Year | Location |
|------|----------|
| 1980 | Mount St Helens, USA |
| 1982 | El Chichónal, Mexico |
| 1982 | Gunung Galunggung, Indonesia |
| 1983 | Kilauea, Hawaii |
| 1983 | Ō-yama, Japan |
| 1985 | Nevado del Ruiz, Colombia |
| 1986 | Lake Nyos, Cameroon |
| 1991 | Hekla, Iceland |
| 1991 | Mount Pinatubo, Philippines |
| 1991 | Unzen-dake, Japan |
| 1993 | Mayon, Philippines |
| 1993 | Volcán Galeras, Colombia |
| 1994 | Volcán Llaima, Chile |
| 1994 | Rabaul, PNG |
| 1997 | Soufrière Hills, Montserrat |
| 2000 | Hekla, Iceland |
| 2001 | Mt Etna, Italy |
| 2002 | Nyiragongo, Dem. Rep. of the Congo |
| 2010 | Eyjafjallajökull, Iceland |

## 1 Climatic Regions and Ocean Currents

**Climatic regions**

Ice cap

Tundra climate, warmest month below 10°C

Sub-arctic, rainy climate with severe cold winters and less than 4 months over 10°C

Continental climate, rainy with warmest month below 22°C

Continental climate, rainy with warmest month above 22°C

Temperate, rainy climate with mild winter, coolest month above 0°C

Wet subtropical, coolest month above 0°C, warmest month above 22°C

Mediterranean, rainy with mild wet winter, dry summer

Semi-arid, dry climate

Desert climate

Rainy tropical climate with no winter, coolest month above 18°C

Rainy tropical climate, constantly wet throughout the year

**Ocean currents**

→ Cold

→ Warm

→ Seasonal

WWW
World Meteorological Organization
www.wmo.ch
Met Office
www.metoffice.com/weather
United Nations Environment Programme
www.unep.org
World Conservation Monitoring Centre
www.unep-wcmc.org
World Resources Institute Earthtrends
earthtrends.wri.org

Scale 1 : 133 000 000

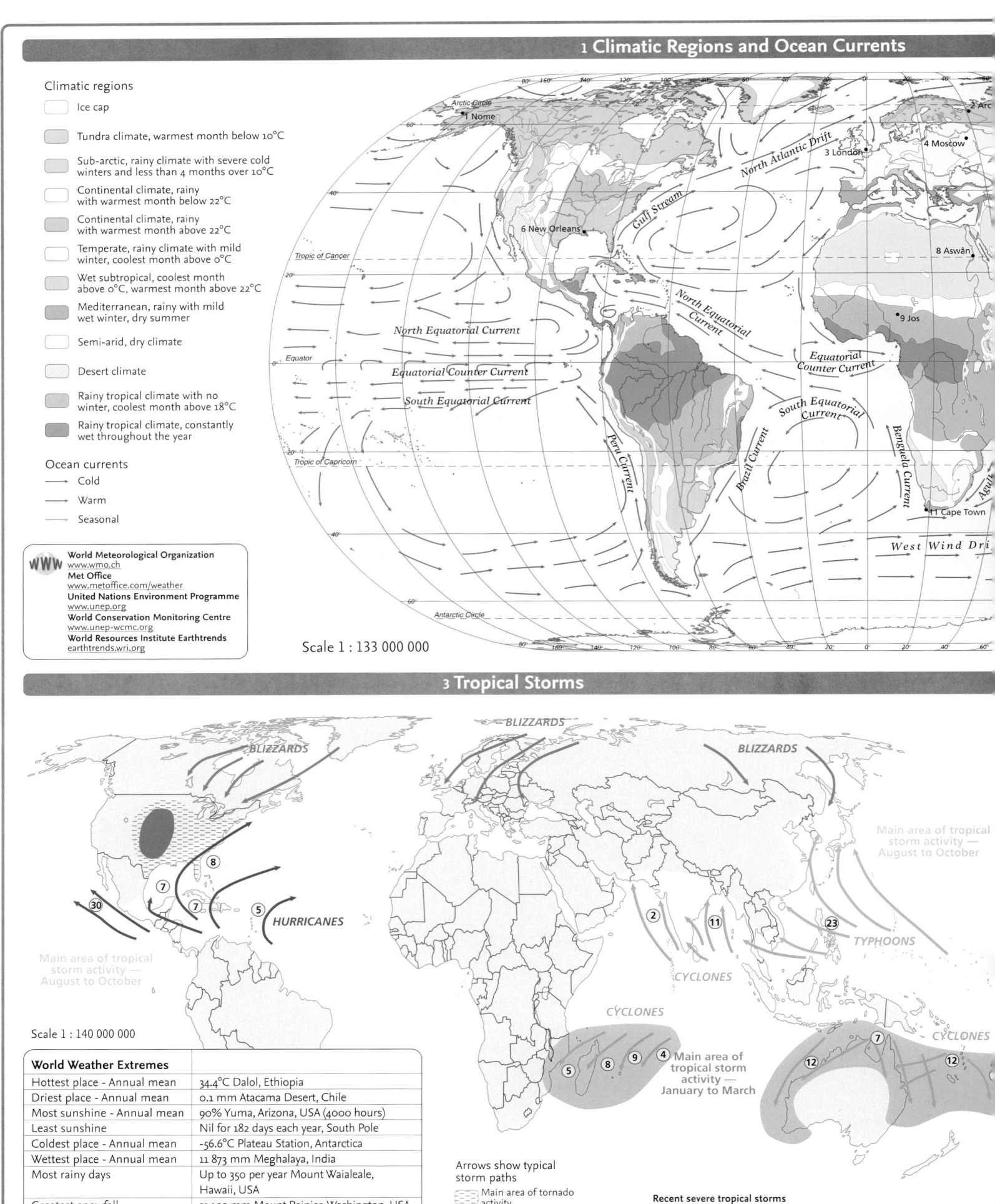

## 3 Tropical Storms

Scale 1 : 140 000 000

**Arrows show typical storm paths**

Main area of tornado activity

Tornado Alley – highest concentration of tornadoes

(8) Likely number of severe tropical storms in 10 years

| World Weather Extremes | |
|---|---|
| Hottest place - Annual mean | 34.4°C Dalol, Ethiopia |
| Driest place - Annual mean | 0.1 mm Atacama Desert, Chile |
| Most sunshine - Annual mean | 90% Yuma, Arizona, USA (4000 hours) |
| Least sunshine | Nil for 182 days each year, South Pole |
| Coldest place - Annual mean | -56.6°C Plateau Station, Antarctica |
| Wettest place - Annual mean | 11 873 mm Meghalaya, India |
| Most rainy days | Up to 350 per year Mount Waialeale, Hawaii, USA |
| Greatest snowfall | 31 102 mm Mount Rainier, Washington, USA (19th February 1971 - 18th February 1972) |
| Windiest place | 322 km per hour in gales, Commonwealth Bay, Antarctica |

**Recent severe tropical storms**

| Year | Location | Deaths | Year | Location | Death |
|---|---|---|---|---|---|
| 1995 Angela | Philippines | 1050 | 2000 | Madagascar | 15 |
| 1997 Linda | Vietnam | 4300 | 2004 Rananim | China | 13 |
| 1998 Mitch | Honduras, Nicaragua | 12 000 | 2005 Katrina | Louisiana, USA | over 100 |
| 1999 | Odisha, India | 2000 | 2008 Nargis | Myanmar | 138 36 |

## 2 Climatic Graphs

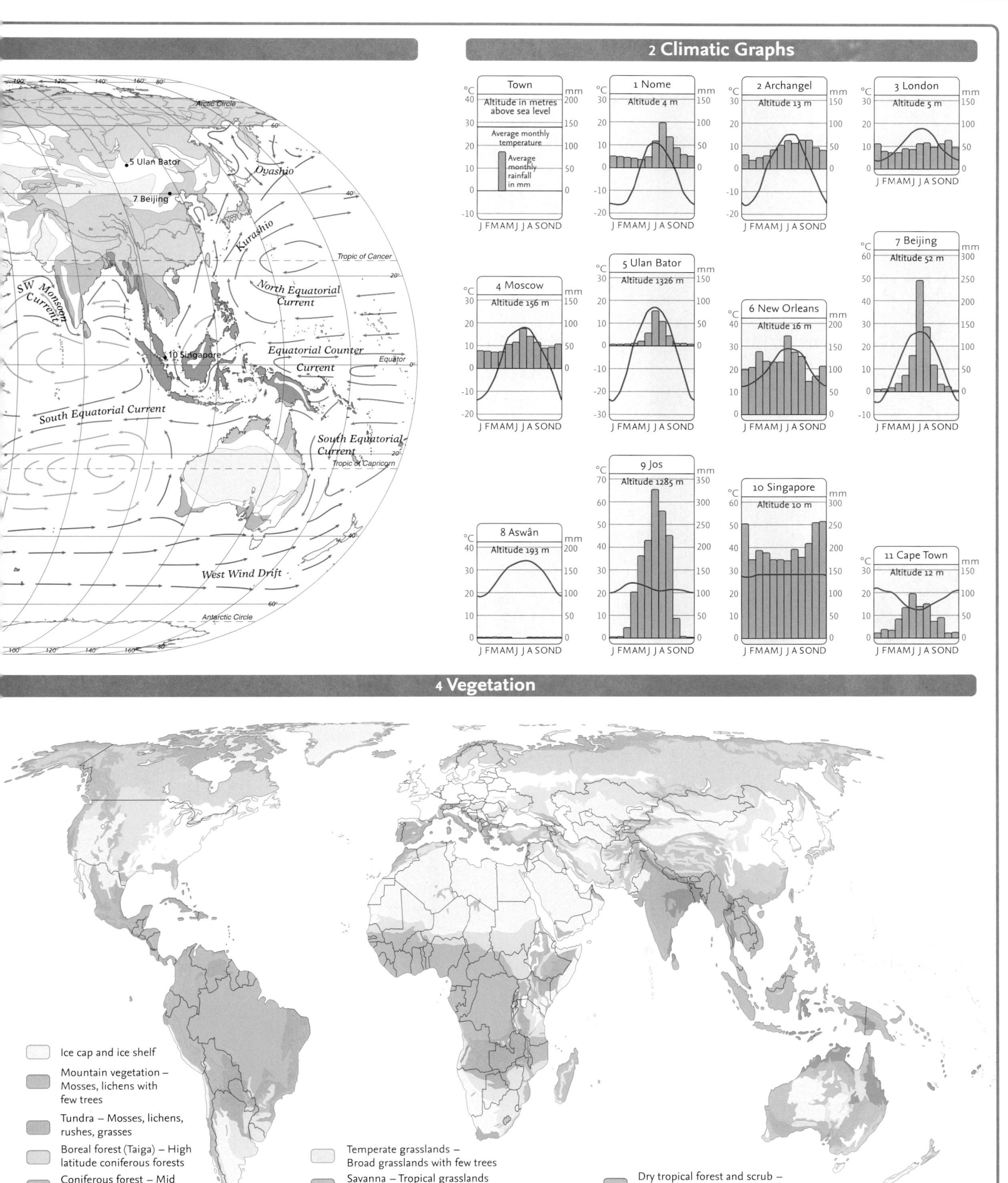

## 4 Vegetation

Ice cap and ice shelf

Mountain vegetation –
Mosses, lichens with
few trees

Tundra – Mosses, lichens,
rushes, grasses

Boreal forest (Taiga) – High
latitude coniferous forests

Coniferous forest – Mid
latitude coniferous forests

Mixed forest – Broadleaf and
coniferous forests

Mediterranean scrub –
Drought-hardy shrubs and trees

Temperate grasslands –
Broad grasslands with few trees

Savanna – Tropical grasslands
with few trees

Tropical rain forest – Tall dense
multi-layered forests

Monsoon forest – Tropical wet
and dry deciduous forests

Dry tropical forest and scrub –
Semi deciduous forests and shrubs

Sub tropical forest – Hardleaf evergreen
forests

Desert vegetation – Drought-tolerant
trees, shrubs and grasses

Scale 1 : 140 000 000

# 1 Agriculture

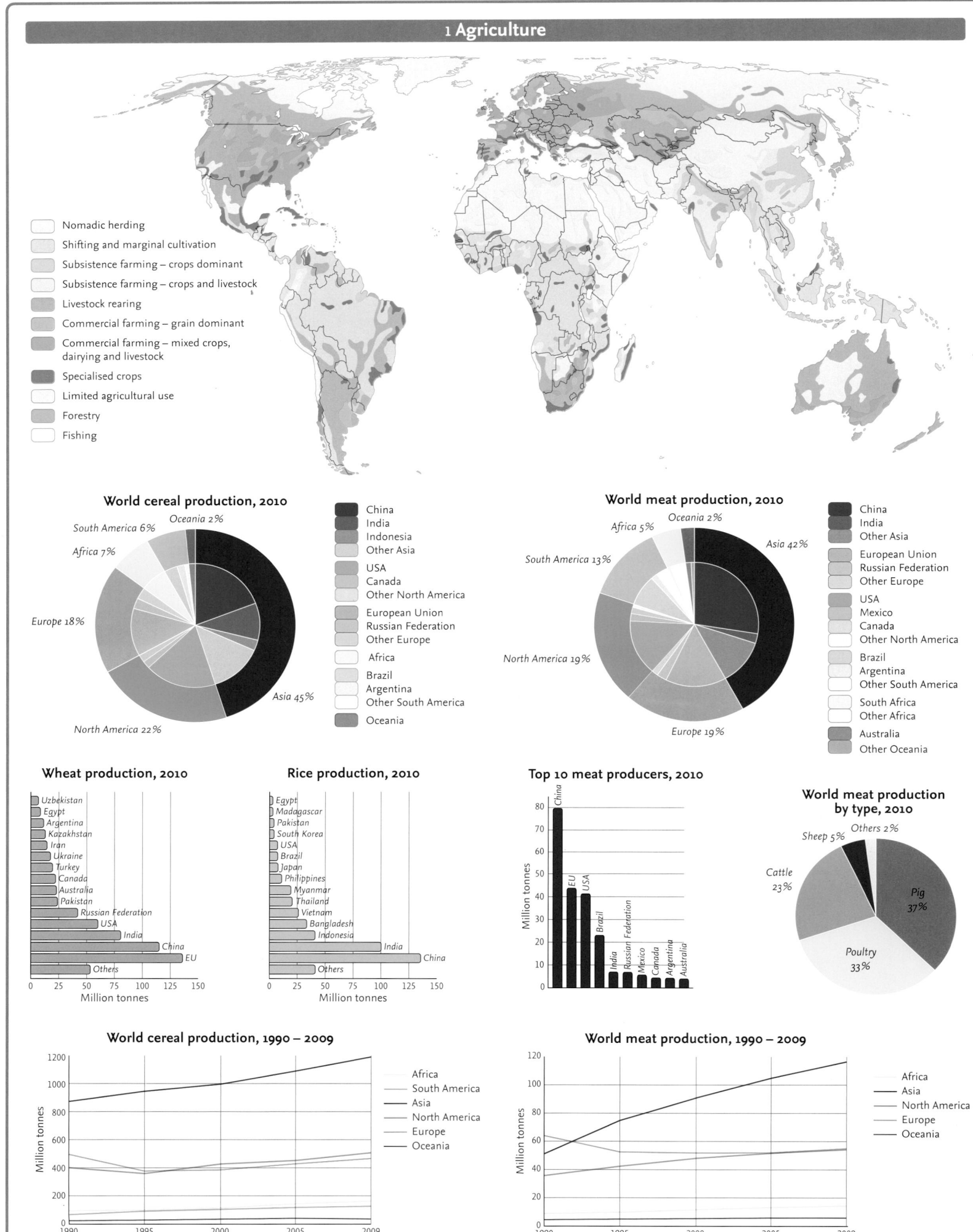

Nomadic herding
Shifting and marginal cultivation
Subsistence farming – crops dominant
Subsistence farming – crops and livestock
Livestock rearing
Commercial farming – grain dominant
Commercial farming – mixed crops, dairying and livestock
Specialised crops
Limited agricultural use
Forestry
Fishing

**World cereal production, 2010**

South America 6%
Oceania 2%
Africa 7%
Europe 18%
North America 22%
Asia 45%

China
India
Indonesia
Other Asia
USA
Canada
Other North America
European Union
Russian Federation
Other Europe
Africa
Brazil
Argentina
Other South America
Oceania

**World meat production, 2010**

Oceania 2%
Africa 5%
South America 13%
North America 19%
Europe 19%
Asia 42%

China
India
Other Asia
European Union
Russian Federation
Other Europe
USA
Mexico
Canada
Other North America
Brazil
Argentina
Other South America
South Africa
Other Africa
Australia
Other Oceania

**Wheat production, 2010**

Uzbekistan
Egypt
Argentina
Kazakhstan
Iran
Ukraine
Turkey
Canada
Australia
Pakistan
Russian Federation
USA
India
China
EU
Others

Million tonnes
0   25   50   75   100   125   150

**Rice production, 2010**

Egypt
Madagascar
Pakistan
South Korea
USA
Brazil
Japan
Philippines
Myanmar
Thailand
Vietnam
Bangladesh
Indonesia
India
China
Others

Million tonnes
0   25   50   75   100   125   150

**Top 10 meat producers, 2010**

China
EU
USA
Brazil
India
Russian Federation
Mexico
Canada
Argentina
Australia

Million tonnes
0 10 20 30 40 50 60 70 80

**World meat production by type, 2010**

Others 2%
Sheep 5%
Cattle 23%
Pig 37%
Poultry 33%

**World cereal production, 1990 – 2009**

Million tonnes
1200
1000
800
600
400
200
0
1990   1995   2000   2005   2009

Africa
South America
Asia
North America
Europe
Oceania

**World meat production, 1990 – 2009**

Million tonnes
120
100
80
60
40
20
0
1990   1995   2000   2005   2009

Africa
Asia
North America
Europe
Oceania

Scale 1 : 140 000 000

Eckert IV projection

## 1 Global Inequalities

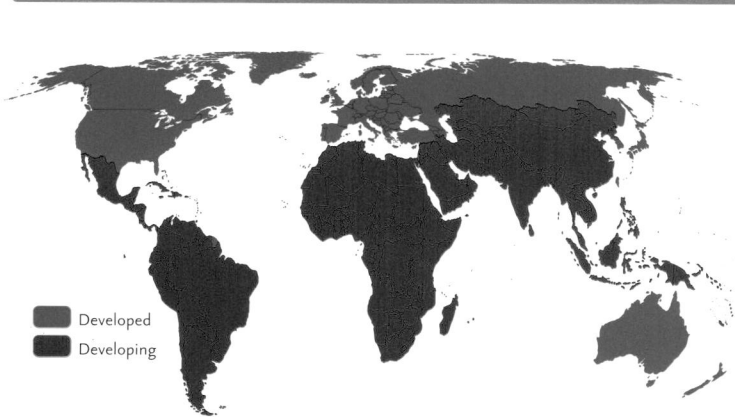

Developed
Developing

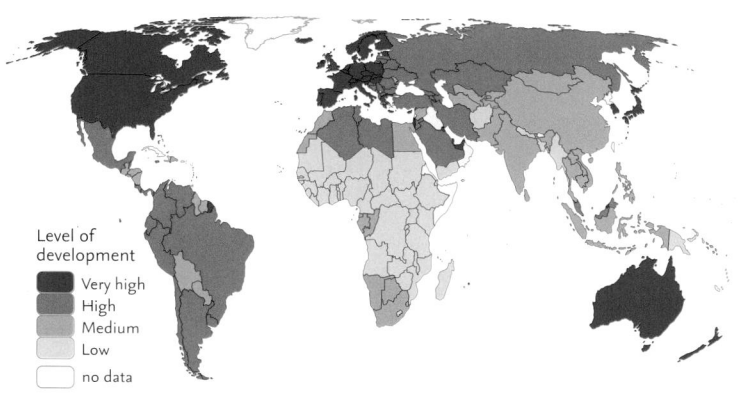

Level of development
- Very high
- High
- Medium
- Low
- no data

International organizations generally agree that countries can be categorized into more economically developed countries (MEDCs) and less economically developed countries (LEDCs). The group of MEDCs includes the following countries/regions: Canada; United States; Israel; Japan; Singapore; South Korea; Andorra; Greece; Hungary; Norway; Austria; Iceland; Portugal; Belgium; Bulgaria; Cyprus; Czech Republic; Denmark; Estonia; Finland; France; Germany; Gibraltar; Ireland; Italy; Latvia; Poland; Romania; San Marino; Slovakia; Slovenia; Spain; Sweden; Switzerland; United Kingdom; Vatican City; Australia; New Zealand; Russian Federation.

This map categorizes countries by their stage of development: Very high; High; Medium; Low. Indicators, such as life expectancy as an index of population health and longevity, education as measured by adult literacy and school enrolment, and standards of living based on the GDP per capita, are used to measure the level of development. The development of regions, cities or villages can also be assessed using these indicators.

### Kenya

| Health | |
|---|---|
| Under-5 mortality rate (per 1000 live births) | 84 |
| Life expectancy at birth | 55 |
| **Education** | |
| Adult literacy | 87% |
| School enrolment, primary | 84% |
| **Income** | |
| GDP per capita | $1573 |
| GNI per capita | $760 |
| Poverty line (% of population) | 45.9% |

### China

| Health | |
|---|---|
| Under-5 mortality rate (per 1000 live births) | 19 |
| Life expectancy at birth | 73 |
| **Education** | |
| Adult literacy | 94% |
| School enrolment, primary | 94% |
| **Income** | |
| GDP per capita | $6828 |
| GNI per capita | $3650 |
| Poverty line (% of population) | 2.8% |

### Brazil

| Health | |
|---|---|
| Under-5 mortality rate (per 1000 live births) | 21 |
| Life expectancy at birth | 73 |
| **Education** | |
| Adult literacy | 90% |
| School enrolment, primary | 95% |
| **Income** | |
| GDP per capita | $10 367 |
| GNI per capita | $8070 |
| Poverty line (% of population) | 21.4% |

### Australia

| Health | |
|---|---|
| Under-5 mortality rate (per 1000 live births) | 5 |
| Life expectancy at birth | 82 |
| **Education** | |
| Adult literacy | no data |
| School enrolment, primary | no data |
| **Income** | |
| GDP per capita | $39 539 |
| GNI per capita | $43 770 |
| Poverty line (% of population) | no data |

## 2 World Indicators

### GDP per capita, 1980 – 2009
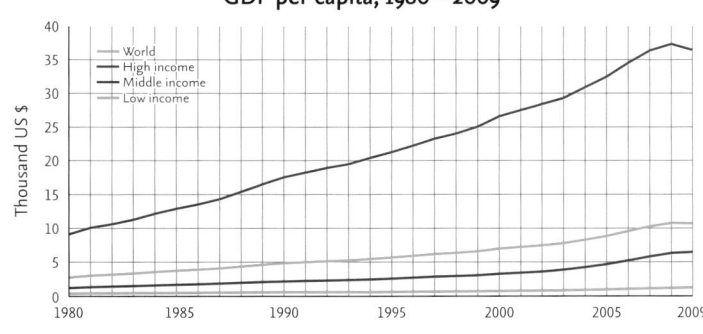

World
High income
Middle income
Low income

### GNI per capita, 1980 – 2009
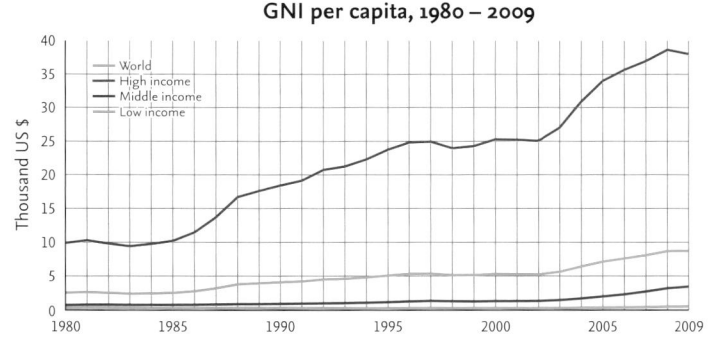

World
High income
Middle income
Low income

### Primary school enrolment, 1999 – 2009
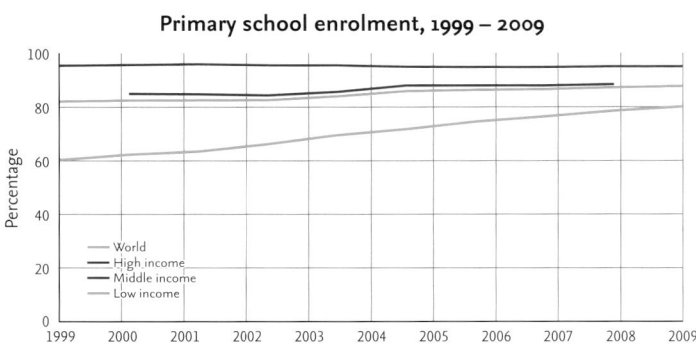

World
High income
Middle income
Low income

### Life expectancy, 1980 – 2009
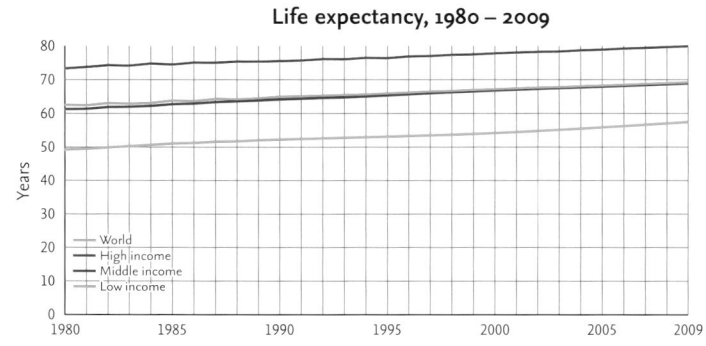

World
High income
Middle income
Low income

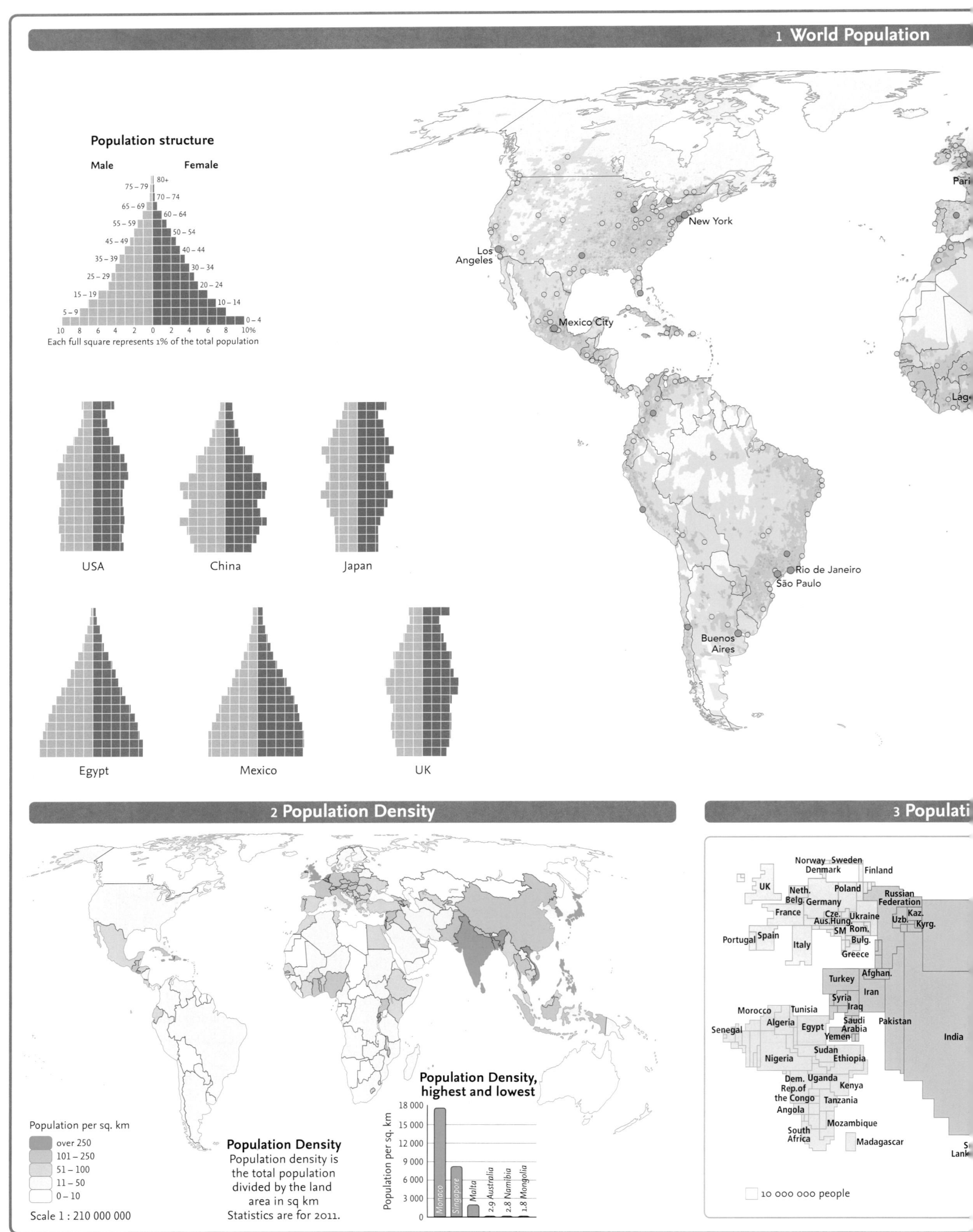

**1 World Population**

**Population structure**

Male    Female

80+
75 – 79    70 – 74
65 – 69    60 – 64
55 – 59    50 – 54
45 – 49    40 – 44
35 – 39    30 – 34
25 – 29    20 – 24
15 – 19    10 – 14
5 – 9    0 – 4

10  8  6  4  2  0  2  4  6  8  10%

Each full square represents 1% of the total population

USA    China    Japan

Egypt    Mexico    UK

New York
Los Angeles
Mexico City
Rio de Janeiro
São Paulo
Buenos Aires

Pari
Lag

**2 Population Density**

Population per sq. km
- over 250
- 101 – 250
- 51 – 100
- 11 – 50
- 0 – 10

Scale 1 : 210 000 000

**Population Density**
Population density is the total population divided by the land area in sq km
Statistics are for 2011.

**Population Density, highest and lowest**

Population per sq. km

18 000
15 000
12 000
9 000
6 000
3 000
0

Monaco  Singapore  Malta  2.9 Australia  2.8 Namibia  1.8 Mongolia

**3 Populati**

Norway  Sweden
Denmark  Finland
UK
Neth.  Poland
Belg.  Germany  Russian Federation
France  Cze.  Ukraine  Kaz.
Aus.Hung.  Uzb.  Kyrg.
Portugal  Spain  SM  Rom.
Italy  Bulg.
Greece
Turkey  Afghan.
Syria  Iran
Morocco  Tunisia  Iraq
Algeria  Egypt  Saudi  Pakistan  India
Senegal  Arabia
Yemen
Nigeria  Sudan  Ethiopia
Dem.  Uganda
Rep.of  Kenya
the Congo  Tanzania
Angola
Mozambique
South  Madagascar
Africa  S
Lank

10 000 000 people

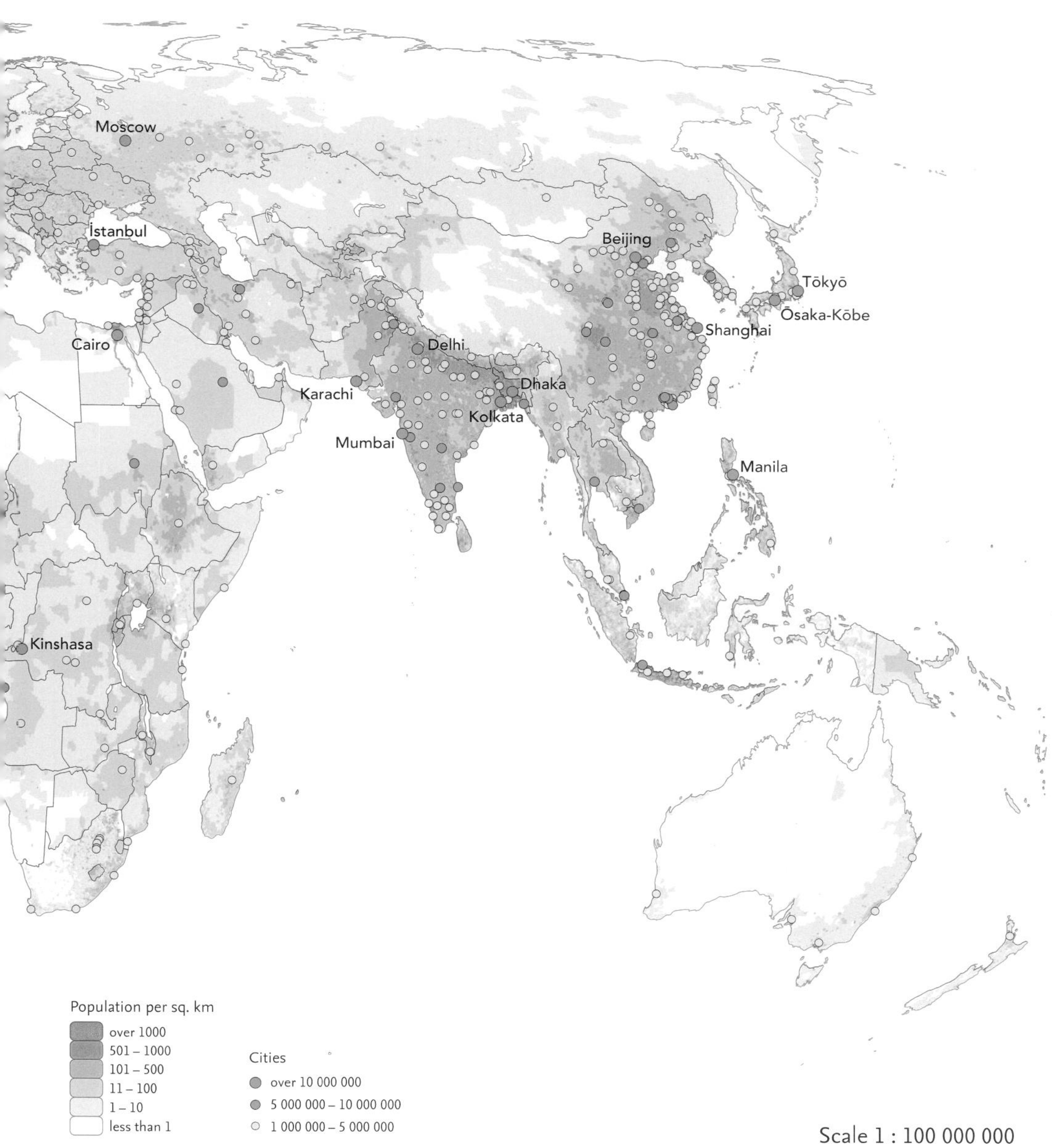

## Largest countries by population, 2011

| Country and continent | Population |
|---|---|
| **China** Asia | 1 332 079 000 |
| **India** Asia | 1 241 492 000 |
| **United States of America** N America | 313 085 000 |
| **Indonesia** Asia | 242 326 000 |
| **Brazil** S America | 196 655 000 |
| **Pakistan** Asia | 176 745 000 |
| **Nigeria** Africa | 162 471 000 |
| **Bangladesh** Asia | 150 494 000 |
| **Russian Federation** Asia/Europe | 142 836 000 |
| **Japan** Asia | 126 497 000 |
| **Mexico** N America | 114 793 000 |
| **Philippines** Asia | 94 852 000 |
| **Vietnam** Asia | 88 792 000 |
| **Ethiopia** Africa | 84 734 000 |
| **Egypt** Africa | 82 537 000 |
| **Germany** Europe | 82 163 000 |
| **Iran** Asia | 74 799 000 |
| **Turkey** Asia | 73 640 000 |
| **Thailand** Asia | 69 519 000 |
| **Dem. Rep. of the Congo** Africa | 67 758 000 |

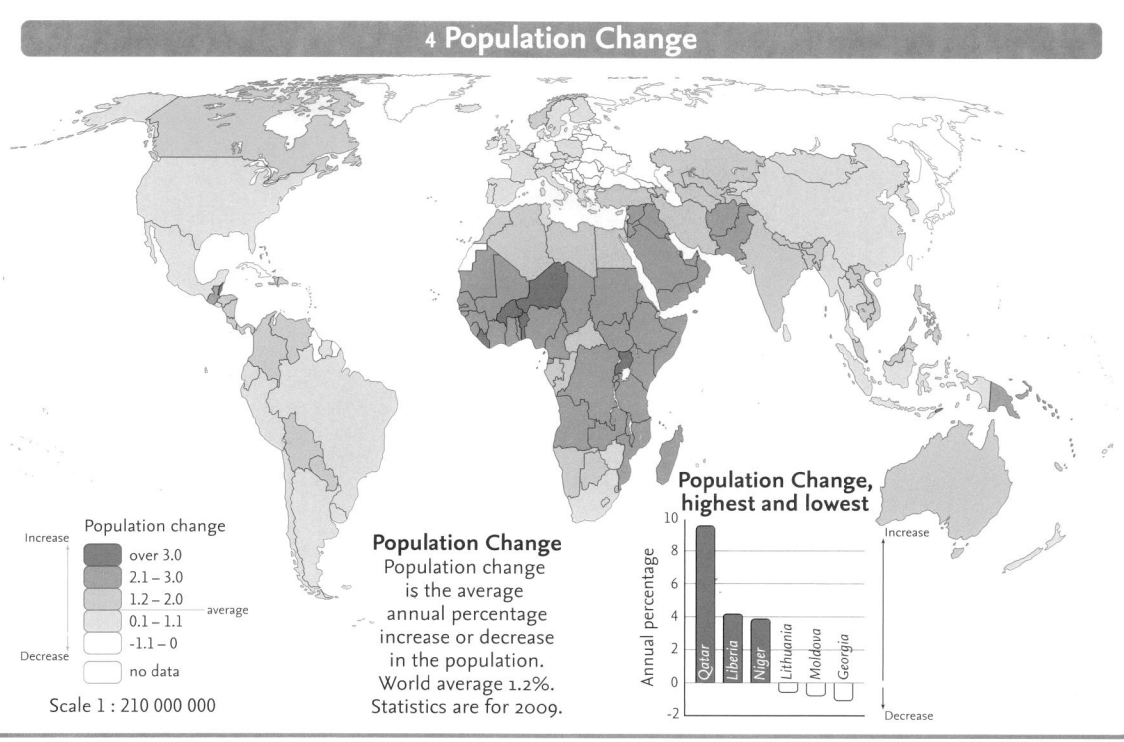

**Population per sq. km**

- over 1000
- 501 – 1000
- 101 – 500
- 11 – 100
- 1 – 10
- less than 1

**Cities**

- over 10 000 000
- 5 000 000 – 10 000 000
- 1 000 000 – 5 000 000

Scale 1 : 100 000 000

**United Nations Statistics Division**
unstats.un.org
**UN Population Information Network**
www.un.org/popin
**Population Reference Bureau**
www.prb.org
**World Bank**
www.worldbank.org

## mparisons

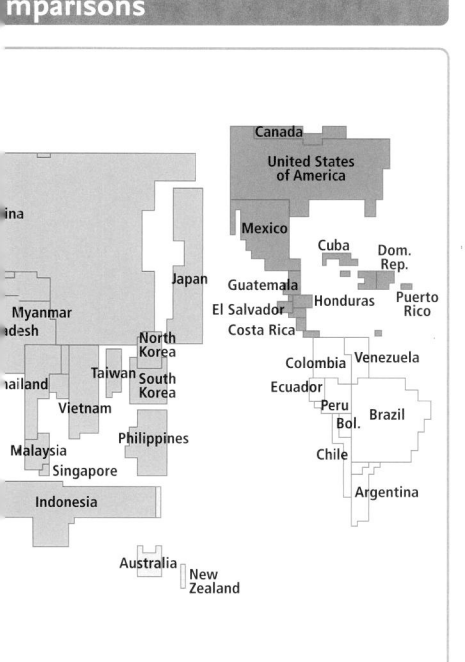

## 4 Population Change

**Population change**

Increase
- over 3.0
- 2.1 – 3.0
- 1.2 – 2.0 } average
- 0.1 – 1.1
Decrease
- -1.1 – 0
- no data

Scale 1 : 210 000 000

**Population Change**
Population change
is the average
annual percentage
increase or decrease
in the population.
World average 1.2%.
Statistics are for 2009.

**Population Change,
highest and lowest**

Annual percentage (highest): Qatar, Liberia, Niger
Annual percentage (lowest): Lithuania, Moldova, Georgia

# World Urbanization

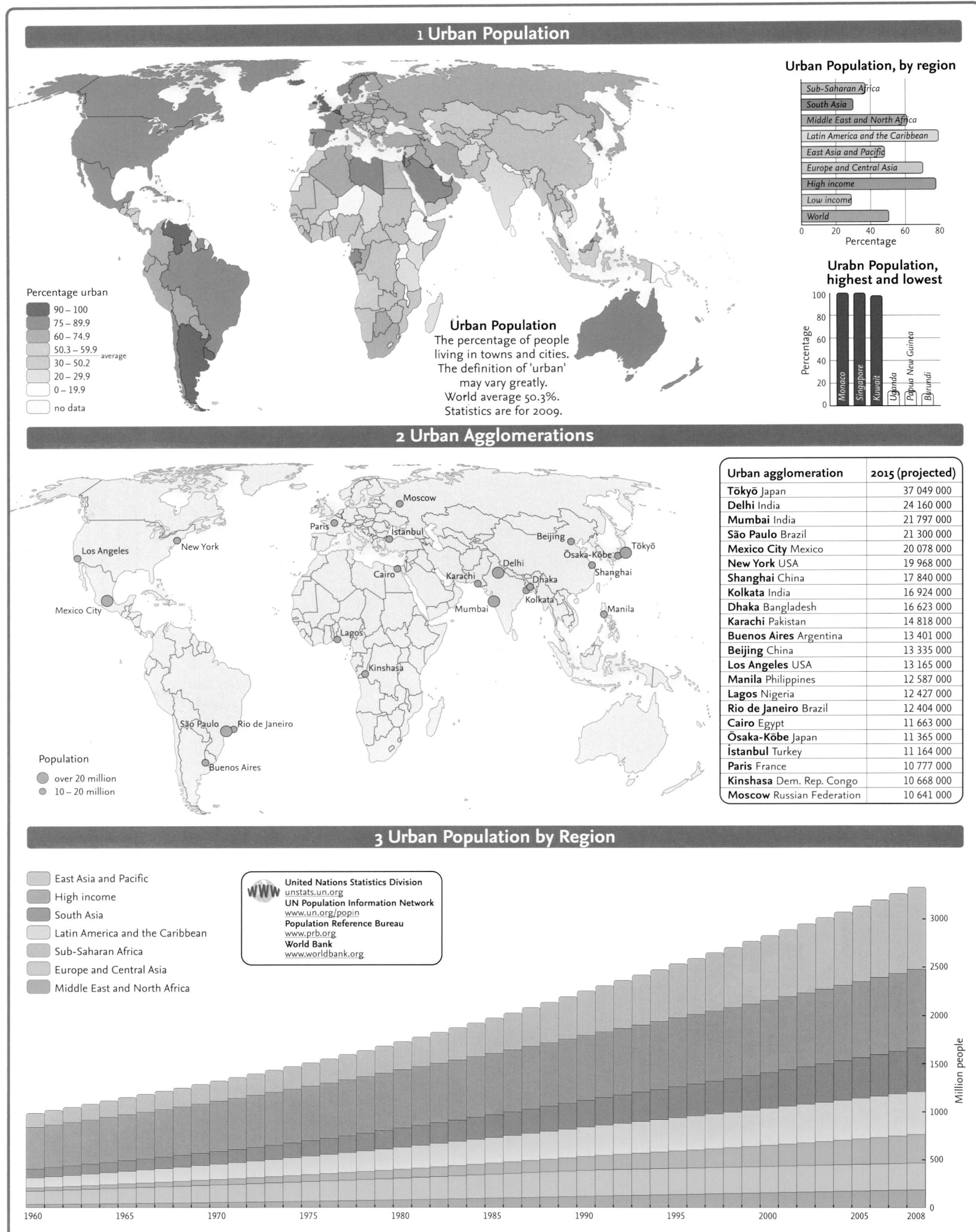

## 1 Urban Population

### Urban Population, by region

Sub-Saharan Africa
South Asia
Middle East and North Africa
Latin America and the Caribbean
East Asia and Pacific
Europe and Central Asia
High income
Low income
World

Percentage: 0  20  40  60  80

### Urabn Population, highest and lowest

Percentage: 0 20 40 60 80 100

Monaco, Singapore, Kuwait, Uganda, Papua New Guinea, Burundi

**Percentage urban**

- 90 – 100
- 75 – 89.9
- 60 – 74.9
- 50.3 – 59.9  average
- 30 – 50.2
- 20 – 29.9
- 0 – 19.9
- no data

**Urban Population**
The percentage of people living in towns and cities. The definition of 'urban' may vary greatly. World average 50.3%. Statistics are for 2009.

## 2 Urban Agglomerations

Moscow, Paris, İstanbul, Beijing, Ōsaka-Kōbe, Tōkyō, Los Angeles, New York, Cairo, Karachi, Delhi, Shanghai, Dhaka, Mexico City, Kolkata, Manila, Mumbai, Lagos, Kinshasa, São Paulo, Rio de Janeiro, Buenos Aires

**Population**
- over 20 million
- 10 – 20 million

| Urban agglomeration | 2015 (projected) |
|---|---|
| **Tōkyō** Japan | 37 049 000 |
| **Delhi** India | 24 160 000 |
| **Mumbai** India | 21 797 000 |
| **São Paulo** Brazil | 21 300 000 |
| **Mexico City** Mexico | 20 078 000 |
| **New York** USA | 19 968 000 |
| **Shanghai** China | 17 840 000 |
| **Kolkata** India | 16 924 000 |
| **Dhaka** Bangladesh | 16 623 000 |
| **Karachi** Pakistan | 14 818 000 |
| **Buenos Aires** Argentina | 13 401 000 |
| **Beijing** China | 13 335 000 |
| **Los Angeles** USA | 13 165 000 |
| **Manila** Philippines | 12 587 000 |
| **Lagos** Nigeria | 12 427 000 |
| **Rio de Janeiro** Brazil | 12 404 000 |
| **Cairo** Egypt | 11 663 000 |
| **Ōsaka-Kōbe** Japan | 11 365 000 |
| **İstanbul** Turkey | 11 164 000 |
| **Paris** France | 10 777 000 |
| **Kinshasa** Dem. Rep. Congo | 10 668 000 |
| **Moscow** Russian Federation | 10 641 000 |

## 3 Urban Population by Region

- East Asia and Pacific
- High income
- South Asia
- Latin America and the Caribbean
- Sub-Saharan Africa
- Europe and Central Asia
- Middle East and North Africa

**United Nations Statistics Division**
unstats.un.org
**UN Population Information Network**
www.un.org/popin
**Population Reference Bureau**
www.prb.org
**World Bank**
www.worldbank.org

Million people: 500, 1000, 1500, 2000, 2500, 3000

1960  1965  1970  1975  1980  1985  1990  1995  2000  2005  2008

Scale 1 : 210 000 000

Eckert IV projection

## 5 City Density

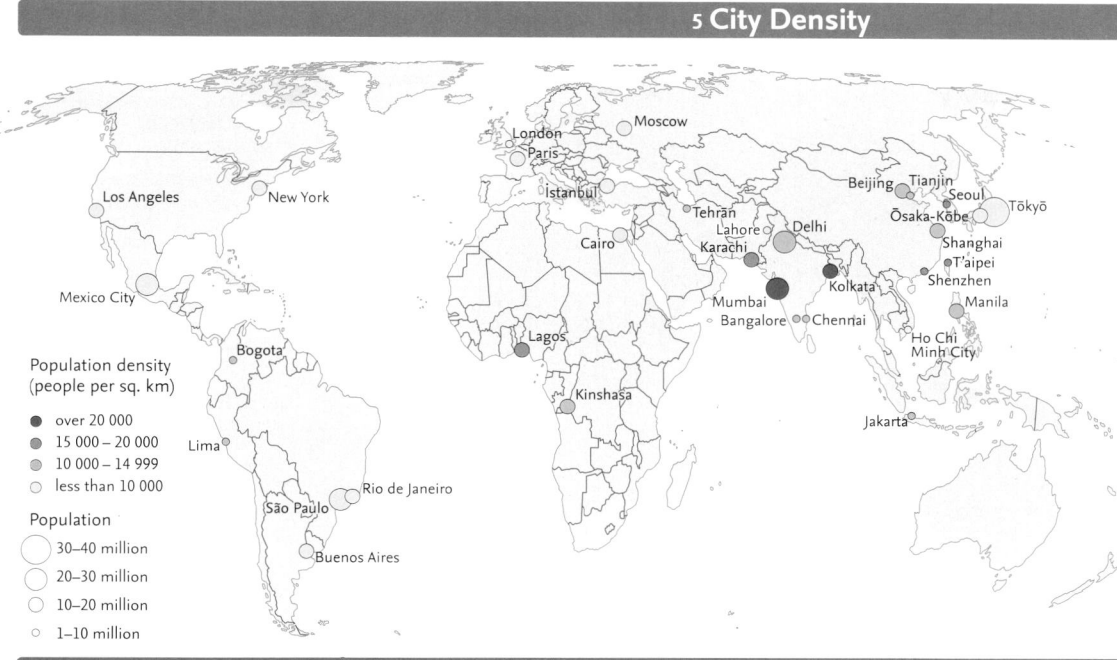

**Population density (people per sq. km)**
- ● over 20 000
- ● 15 000 – 20 000
- ● 10 000 – 14 999
- ○ less than 10 000

**Population**
- ○ 30–40 million
- ○ 20–30 million
- ○ 10–20 million
- ○ 1–10 million

**Top 20 densest cities**

| City | People per sq. km |
|------|-------------------|
| **Mumbai** India | 29 650 |
| **Kolkata** India | 23 900 |
| **Karachi** Pakistan | 18 900 |
| **Lagos** Nigeria | 18 150 |
| **Shenzhen** China | 17 150 |
| **Seoul** South Korea | 16 700 |
| **T'aipei** Taiwan | 15 200 |
| **Chennai** India | 14 350 |
| **Bogota** Colombia | 13 500 |
| **Shanghai** China | 13 400 |
| **Lima** Peru | 11 750 |
| **Beijing** China | 11 500 |
| **Delhi** India | 11 050 |
| **Kinshasa** Dem. Rep. Congo | 10 650 |
| **Manila** Philippines | 10 550 |
| **Tehrān** Iran | 10 550 |
| **Jakarta** Indonesia | 10 500 |
| **Tianjin** China | 10 500 |
| **Bangalore** India | 10 100 |
| **Ho Chi Minh City** Vietnam | 9450 |

## 5 City Growth

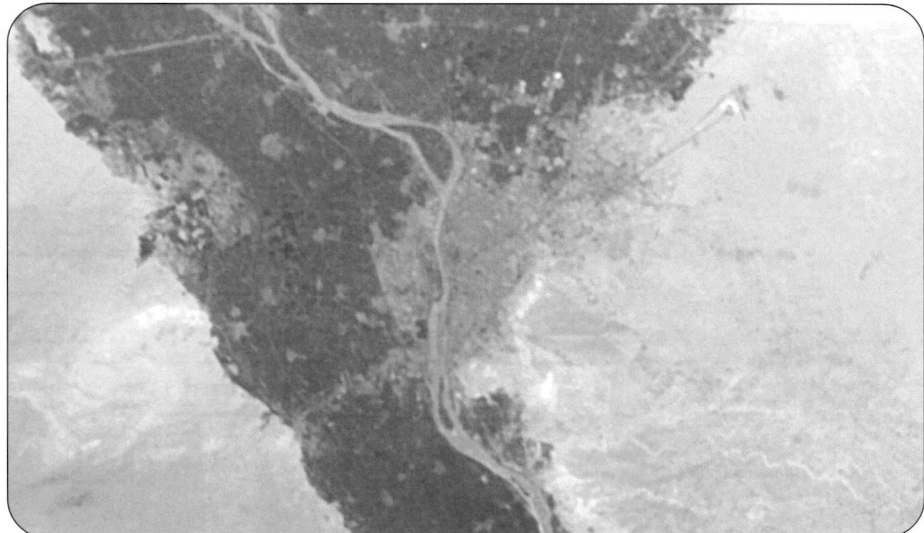

Cairo, 1965

Cairo, 1998

The metropolitan area of Cairo has doubled, to more than 400 square kilometres, between 1965 and 1998. In this same period of time the population has increased by over 4 million.

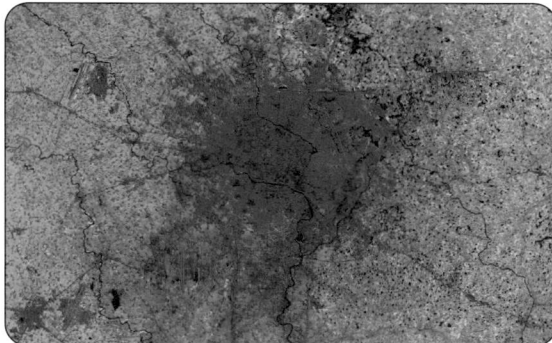

Chengdu, 1990

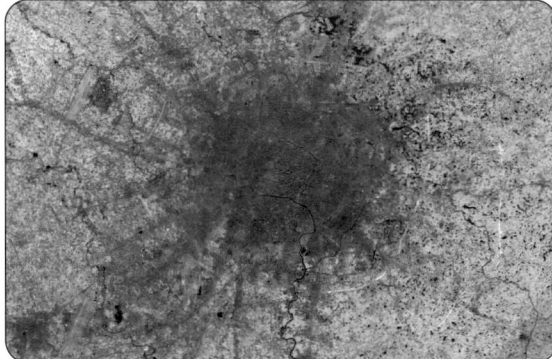

Chengdu, 2000

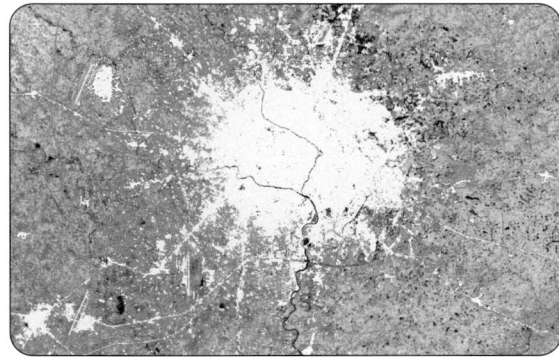

Chengdu urban growth

This sequence of images shows rapid urban growth in Chengdu, China. Orange areas represent expansion from the 1990 extent shown in yellow.

Scale 1 : 210 000 000

# World Birth Rates, Death Rates and Infant Mortality Rate

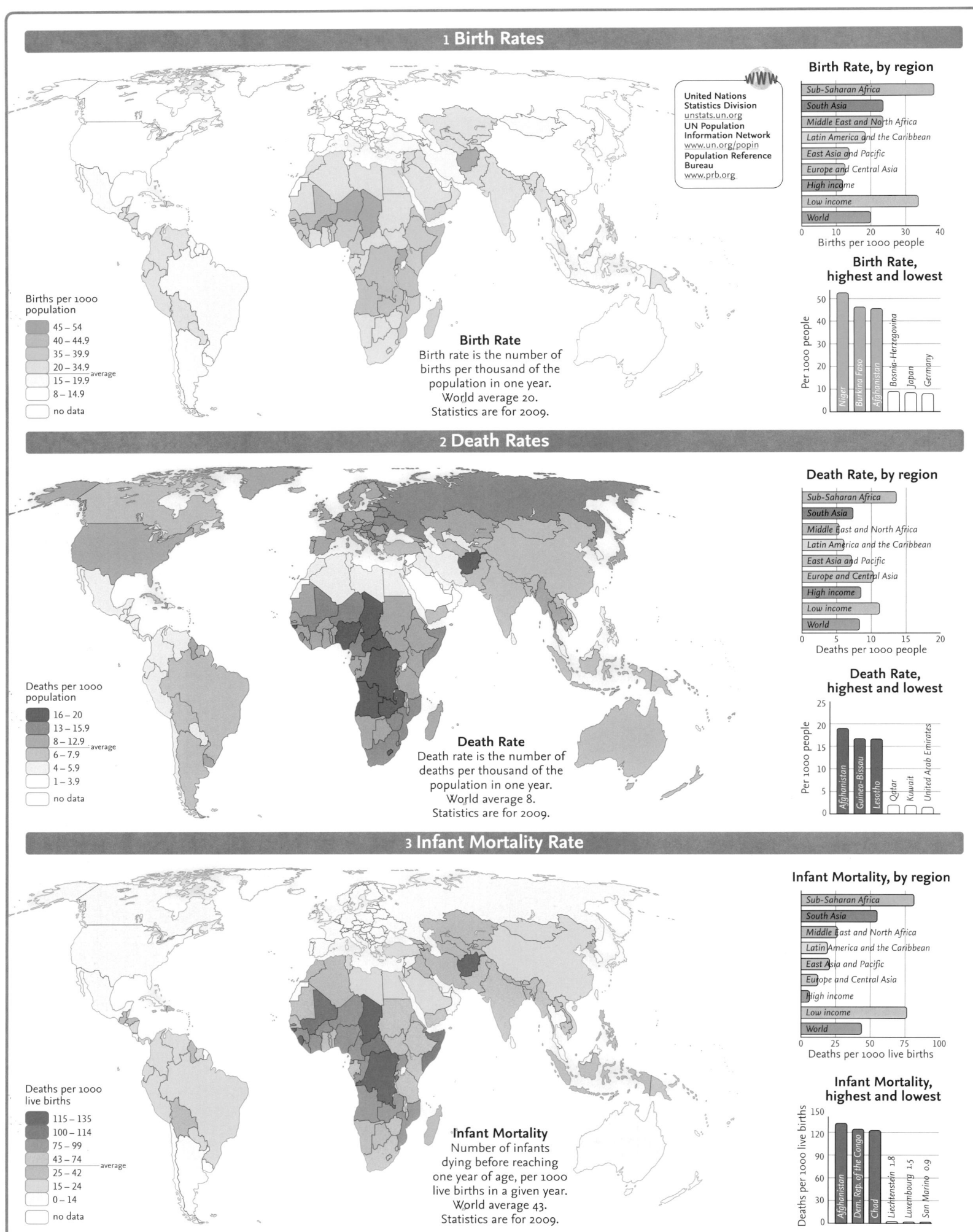

## 1 Birth Rates

United Nations
Statistics Division
unstats.un.org
UN Population
Information Network
www.un.org/popin
Population Reference
Bureau
www.prb.org

### Birth Rate, by region

Sub-Saharan Africa
South Asia
Middle East and North Africa
Latin America and the Caribbean
East Asia and Pacific
Europe and Central Asia
High income
Low income
World

Births per 1000 people
0   10   20   30   40

**Births per 1000 population**
- 45 – 54
- 40 – 44.9
- 35 – 39.9
- 20 – 34.9 — average
- 15 – 19.9
- 8 – 14.9
- no data

### Birth Rate
Birth rate is the number of
births per thousand of the
population in one year.
World average 20.
Statistics are for 2009.

### Birth Rate, highest and lowest

Per 1000 people
Niger, Burkina Faso, Afghanistan, Bosnia-Herzegovina, Japan, Germany

## 2 Death Rates

### Death Rate, by region

Sub-Saharan Africa
South Asia
Middle East and North Africa
Latin America and the Caribbean
East Asia and Pacific
Europe and Central Asia
High income
Low income
World

Deaths per 1000 people
0   5   10   15   20

**Deaths per 1000 population**
- 16 – 20
- 13 – 15.9
- 8 – 12.9 — average
- 6 – 7.9
- 4 – 5.9
- 1 – 3.9
- no data

### Death Rate
Death rate is the number of
deaths per thousand of the
population in one year.
World average 8.
Statistics are for 2009.

### Death Rate, highest and lowest

Per 1000 people
Afghanistan, Guinea-Bissau, Lesotho, Qatar, Kuwait, United Arab Emirates

## 3 Infant Mortality Rate

### Infant Mortality, by region

Sub-Saharan Africa
South Asia
Middle East and North Africa
Latin America and the Caribbean
East Asia and Pacific
Europe and Central Asia
High income
Low income
World

Deaths per 1000 live births
0   25   50   75   100

**Deaths per 1000 live births**
- 115 – 135
- 100 – 114
- 75 – 99
- 43 – 74 — average
- 25 – 42
- 15 – 24
- 0 – 14
- no data

### Infant Mortality
Number of infants
dying before reaching
one year of age, per 1000
live births in a given year.
World average 43.
Statistics are for 2009.

### Infant Mortality, highest and lowest

Deaths per 1000 live births
Afghanistan, Dem. Rep. of the Congo, Chad, Liechtenstein 1.8, Luxembourg 1.5, San Marino 0.9

Eckert IV projection

## 1 Life Expectancy

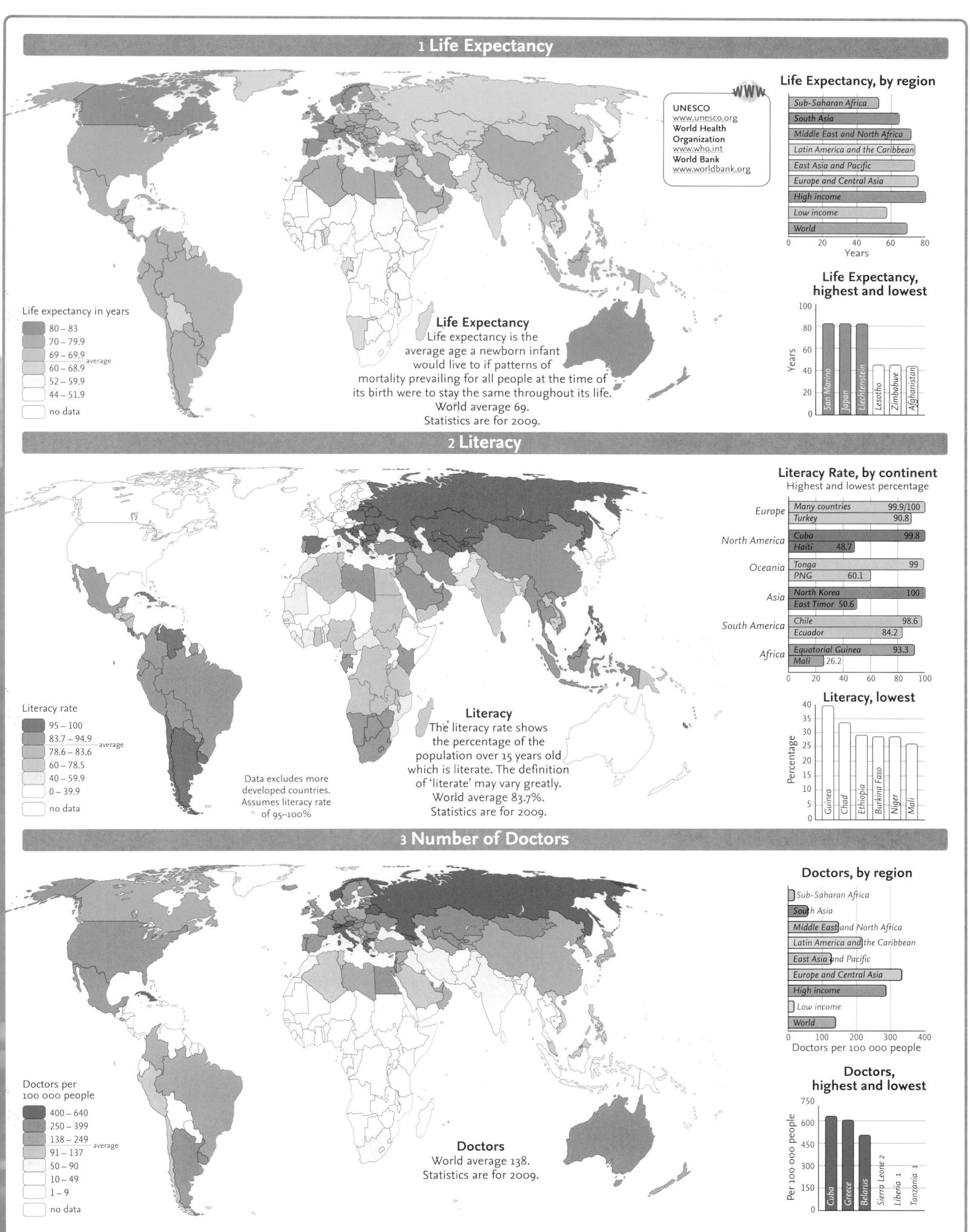

UNESCO
www.unesco.org
**World Health Organization**
www.who.int
**World Bank**
www.worldbank.org

**Life expectancy in years**
- 80 – 83
- 70 – 79.9
- 69 – 69.9 average
- 60 – 68.9
- 52 – 59.9
- 44 – 51.9
- no data

**Life Expectancy**
Life expectancy is the average age a newborn infant would live to if patterns of mortality prevailing for all people at the time of its birth were to stay the same throughout its life. World average 69.
Statistics are for 2009.

**Life Expectancy, by region**
- Sub-Saharan Africa
- South Asia
- Middle East and North Africa
- Latin America and the Caribbean
- East Asia and Pacific
- Europe and Central Asia
- High income
- Low income
- World

Years: 0 20 40 60 80

**Life Expectancy, highest and lowest**
San Marino, Japan, Liechtenstein, Lesotho, Zimbabwe, Afghanistan
Years: 0 20 40 60 80 100

## 2 Literacy

**Literacy rate**
- 95 – 100
- 83.7 – 94.9 average
- 78.6 – 83.6
- 60 – 78.5
- 40 – 59.9
- 0 – 39.9
- no data

Data excludes more developed countries. Assumes literacy rate of 95–100%

**Literacy**
The literacy rate shows the percentage of the population over 15 years old which is literate. The definition of 'literate' may vary greatly. World average 83.7%.
Statistics are for 2009.

**Literacy Rate, by continent**
Highest and lowest percentage

| Continent | Country | Value |
|---|---|---|
| Europe | Many countries | 99.9/100 |
| | Turkey | 90.8 |
| North America | Cuba | 99.8 |
| | Haiti | 48.7 |
| Oceania | Tonga | 99 |
| | PNG | 60.1 |
| Asia | North Korea | 100 |
| | East Timor | 50.6 |
| South America | Chile | 98.6 |
| | Ecuador | 84.2 |
| Africa | Equatorial Guinea | 93.3 |
| | Mali | 26.2 |

0 20 40 60 80 100

**Literacy, lowest**
Guinea, Chad, Ethiopia, Burkina Faso, Niger, Mali
Percentage: 0 5 10 15 20 25 30 35 40

## 3 Number of Doctors

**Doctors per 100 000 people**
- 400 – 640
- 250 – 399
- 138 – 249 average
- 91 – 137
- 50 – 90
- 10 – 49
- 1 – 9
- no data

**Doctors**
World average 138.
Statistics are for 2009.

**Doctors, by region**
- Sub-Saharan Africa
- South Asia
- Middle East and North Africa
- Latin America and the Caribbean
- East Asia and Pacific
- Europe and Central Asia
- High income
- Low income
- World

Doctors per 100 000 people: 0 100 200 300 400

**Doctors, highest and lowest**
Cuba, Greece, Belarus, Sierra Leone 2, Liberia 1, Tanzania 1
Per 100 000 people: 0 150 300 450 600 750

Scale 1 : 190 000 000

Eckert IV projection

# World Human Development Index, Access to Safe Water and Nutrition

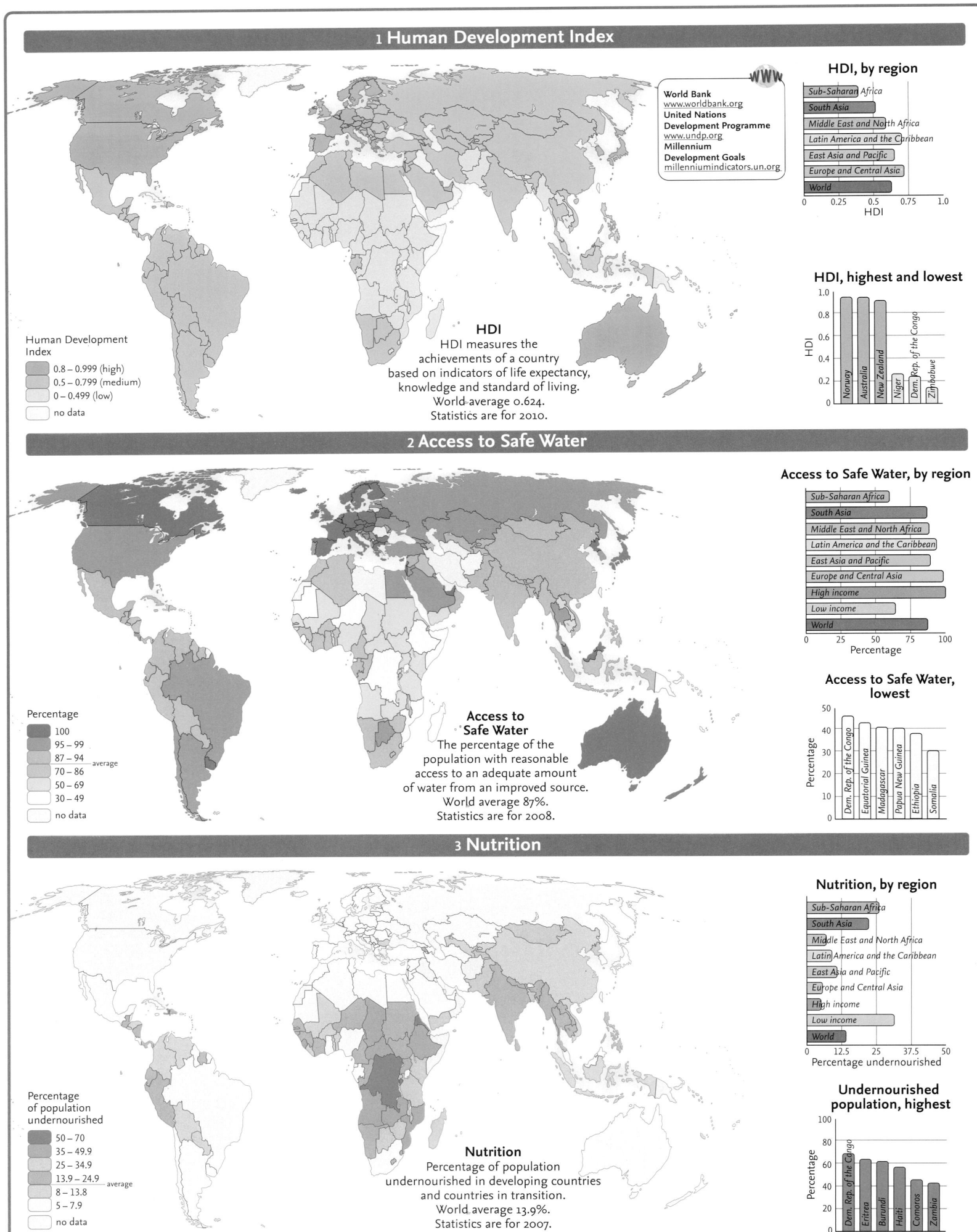

## 1 Human Development Index

World Bank
www.worldbank.org
United Nations
Development Programme
www.undp.org
Millennium
Development Goals
millenniumindicators.un.org

### HDI, by region

Sub-Saharan Africa
South Asia
Middle East and North Africa
Latin America and the Caribbean
East Asia and Pacific
Europe and Central Asia
World

0    0.25    0.5    0.75    1.0
HDI

### HDI, highest and lowest

**HDI**
HDI measures the
achievements of a country
based on indicators of life expectancy,
knowledge and standard of living.
World average 0.624.
Statistics are for 2010.

Human Development
Index
0.8 – 0.999 (high)
0.5 – 0.799 (medium)
0 – 0.499 (low)
no data

HDI
1.0
0.8
0.6
0.4
0.2
0

Norway
Australia
New Zealand
Niger
Dem. Rep. of the Congo
Zimbabwe

## 2 Access to Safe Water

### Access to Safe Water, by region

Sub-Saharan Africa
South Asia
Middle East and North Africa
Latin America and the Caribbean
East Asia and Pacific
Europe and Central Asia
High income
Low income
World

0    25    50    75    100
Percentage

**Access to
Safe Water**
The percentage of the
population with reasonable
access to an adequate amount
of water from an improved source.
World average 87%.
Statistics are for 2008.

Percentage
100
95 – 99
87 – 94    average
70 – 86
50 – 69
30 – 49
no data

### Access to Safe Water, lowest

Percentage
50
40
30
20
10
0

Dem. Rep. of the Congo
Equatorial Guinea
Madagascar
Papua New Guinea
Ethiopia
Somalia

## 3 Nutrition

### Nutrition, by region

Sub-Saharan Africa
South Asia
Middle East and North Africa
Latin America and the Caribbean
East Asia and Pacific
Europe and Central Asia
High income
Low income
World

0    12.5    25    37.5    50
Percentage undernourished

**Nutrition**
Percentage of population
undernourished in developing countries
and countries in transition.
World average 13.9%.
Statistics are for 2007.

Percentage
of population
undernourished
50 – 70
35 – 49.9
25 – 34.9
13.9 – 24.9    average
8 – 13.8
5 – 7.9
no data

### Undernourished population, highest

Percentage
100
80
60
40
20
0

Dem. Rep. of the Congo
Eritrea
Burundi
Haiti
Comoros
Zambia

Scale 1 : 190 000 000

Eckert IV projection

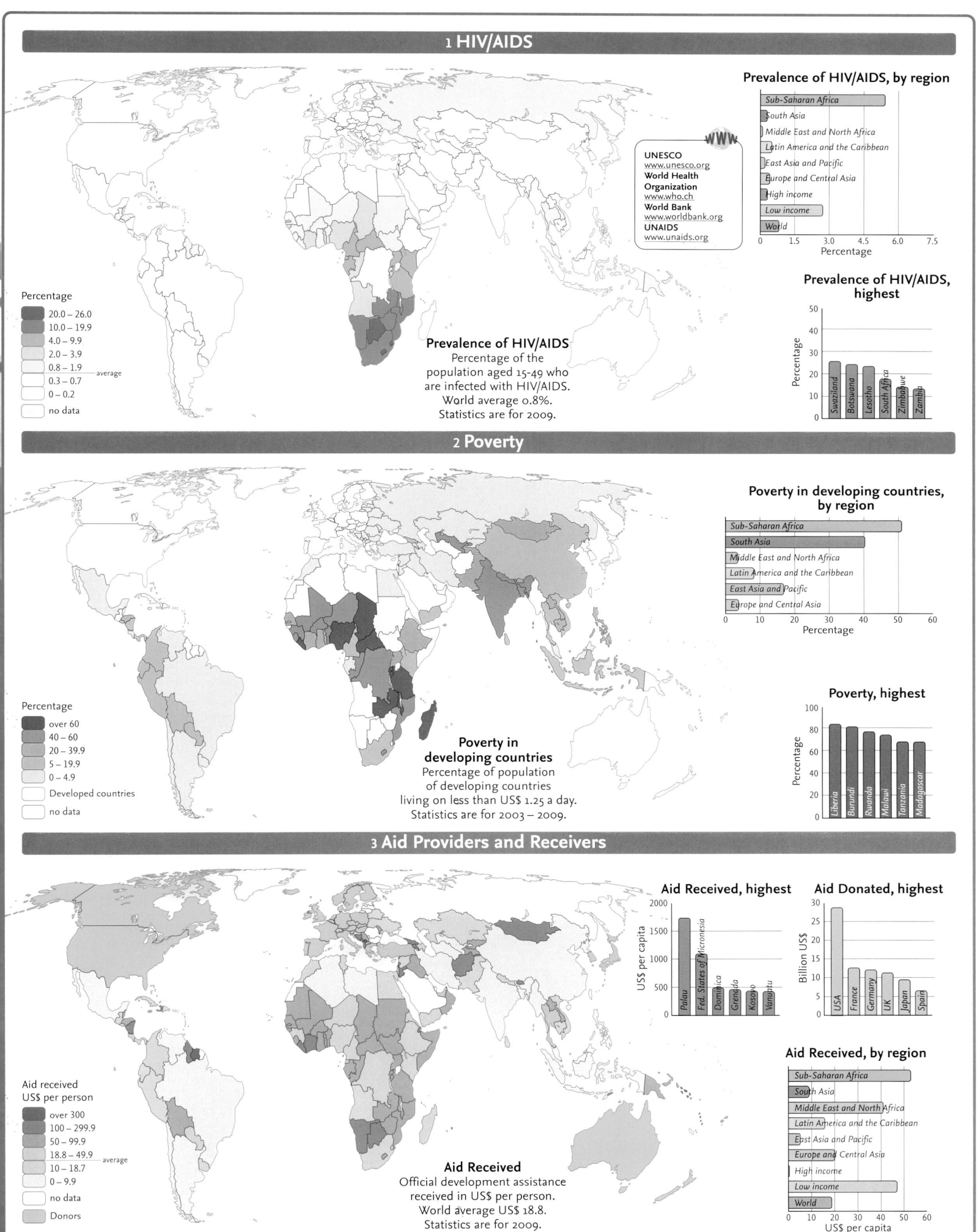

## 1 HIV/AIDS

**Prevalence of HIV/AIDS, by region**

Sub-Saharan Africa
South Asia
Middle East and North Africa
Latin America and the Caribbean
East Asia and Pacific
Europe and Central Asia
High income
Low income
World

Percentage: 0   1.5   3.0   4.5   6.0   7.5

UNESCO
www.unesco.org
**World Health Organization**
www.who.ch
**World Bank**
www.worldbank.org
**UNAIDS**
www.unaids.org

**Prevalence of HIV/AIDS, highest**

Percentage: 0, 10, 20, 30, 40, 50
Swaziland, Botswana, Lesotho, South Africa, Zimbabwe, Zambia

**Prevalence of HIV/AIDS**
Percentage of the population aged 15-49 who are infected with HIV/AIDS. World average 0.8%. Statistics are for 2009.

Percentage
20.0 – 26.0
10.0 – 19.9
4.0 – 9.9
2.0 – 3.9
0.8 – 1.9     average
0.3 – 0.7
0 – 0.2
no data

## 2 Poverty

**Poverty in developing countries, by region**

Sub-Saharan Africa
South Asia
Middle East and North Africa
Latin America and the Caribbean
East Asia and Pacific
Europe and Central Asia

Percentage: 0   10   20   30   40   50   60

**Poverty, highest**

Percentage: 0, 20, 40, 60, 80, 100
Liberia, Burundi, Rwanda, Malawi, Tanzania, Madagascar

**Poverty in developing countries**
Percentage of population of developing countries living on less than US$ 1.25 a day. Statistics are for 2003 – 2009.

Percentage
over 60
40 – 60
20 – 39.9
5 – 19.9
0 – 4.9
Developed countries
no data

## 3 Aid Providers and Receivers

**Aid Received, highest**

US$ per capita: 0, 500, 1000, 1500, 2000
Palau, Fed. States of Micronesia, Dominica, Grenada, Kosovo, Vanuatu

**Aid Donated, highest**

Billion US$: 0, 5, 10, 15, 20, 25, 30
USA, France, Germany, UK, Japan, Spain

**Aid Received, by region**

Sub-Saharan Africa
South Asia
Middle East and North Africa
Latin America and the Caribbean
East Asia and Pacific
Europe and Central Asia
High income
Low income
World

US$ per capita: 0   10   20   30   40   50   60

**Aid Received**
Official development assistance received in US$ per person. World average US$ 18.8. Statistics are for 2009.

Aid received
US$ per person
over 300
100 – 299.9
50 – 99.9
18.8 – 49.9     average
10 – 18.7
0 – 9.9
no data
Donors

Scale 1 : 190 000 000

Eckert IV projection

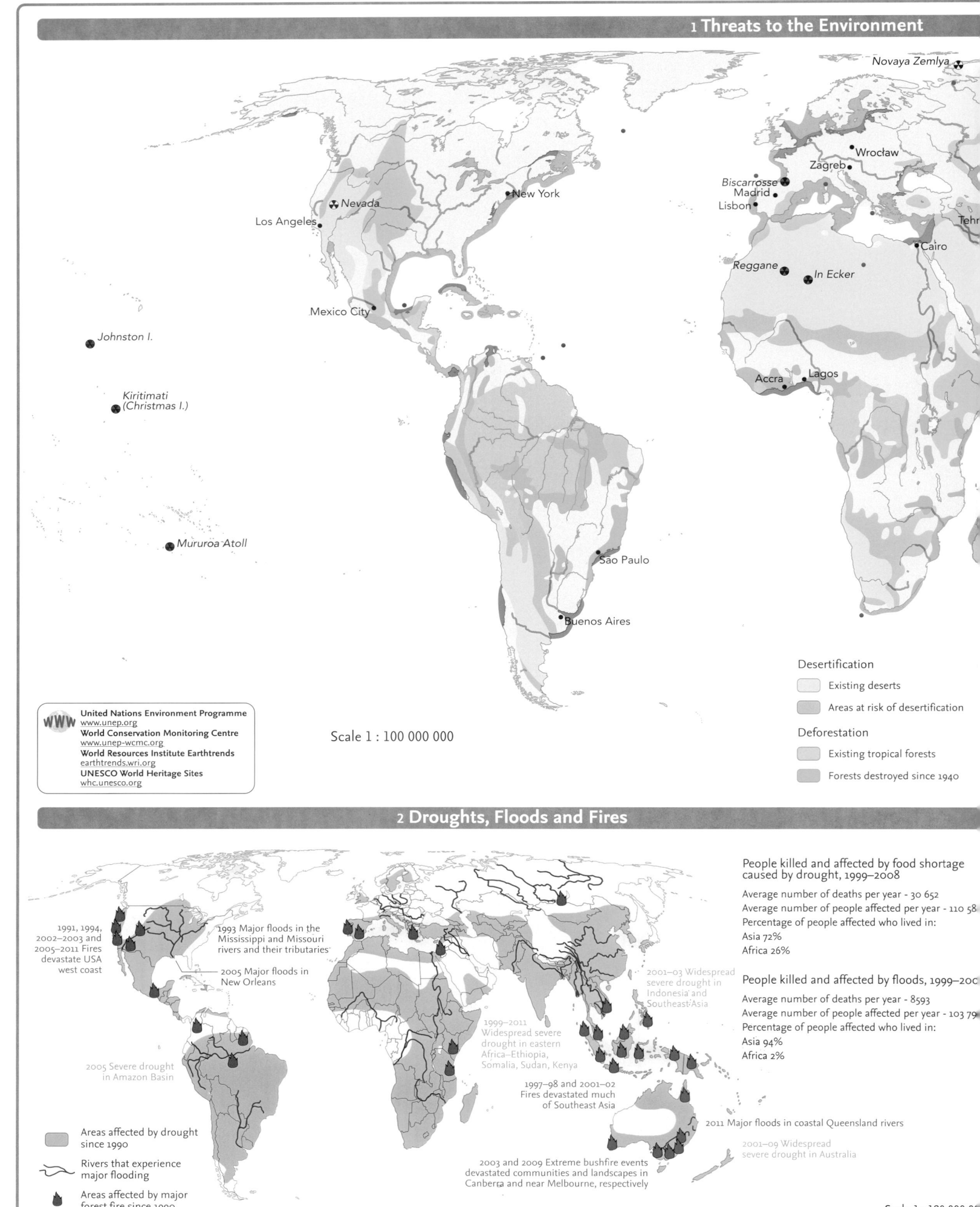

**1 Threats to the Environment**

Novaya Zemlya

Wrocław
Zagreb
Biscarrosse
Madrid
Lisbon
Tehr

Nevada
New York
Los Angeles

Cairo

Mexico City
Reggane        In Ecker

Johnston I.

Accra    Lagos

Kiritimati
(Christmas I.)

Mururoa Atoll

São Paulo

Buenos Aires

United Nations Environment Programme
www.unep.org
World Conservation Monitoring Centre
www.unep-wcmc.org
World Resources Institute Earthtrends
earthtrends.wri.org
UNESCO World Heritage Sites
whc.unesco.org

Scale 1 : 100 000 000

**Desertification**

Existing deserts

Areas at risk of desertification

**Deforestation**

Existing tropical forests

Forests destroyed since 1940

**2 Droughts, Floods and Fires**

1991, 1994, 2002–2003 and 2005–2011 Fires devastate USA west coast

1993 Major floods in the Mississippi and Missouri rivers and their tributaries

2005 Major floods in New Orleans

2005 Severe drought in Amazon Basin

2001–03 Widespread severe drought in Indonesia and Southeast Asia

1999–2011 Widespread severe drought in eastern Africa–Ethiopia, Somalia, Sudan, Kenya

1997–98 and 2001–02 Fires devastated much of Southeast Asia

2011 Major floods in coastal Queensland rivers

2001–09 Widespread severe drought in Australia

2003 and 2009 Extreme bushfire events devastated communities and landscapes in Canberra and near Melbourne, respectively

People killed and affected by food shortage caused by drought, 1999–2008

Average number of deaths per year - 30 652
Average number of people affected per year - 110 58
Percentage of people affected who lived in:
Asia 72%
Africa 26%

People killed and affected by floods, 1999–200

Average number of deaths per year - 8593
Average number of people affected per year - 103 79
Percentage of people affected who lived in:
Asia 94%
Africa 2%

Areas affected by drought since 1990

Rivers that experience major flooding

Areas affected by major forest fire since 1990

Scale 1 : 190 000 0

Semipalatinsk
Lop Nur
Amchitka I.
Shenyang
North Korea
Beijing
Seoul
Tōkyō
Xi'an
Ōsaka
Lahore
Shanghai
stan
Rajasthan
Guangzhou
Kolkata (Calcutta)
Hong Kong
Mumbai (Bombay)
Bangkok
Eniwetok
Bikini Atoll
Monte Bello Is.
Woomera
Maralinga
ater pollution
Severe coastal pollution
Persistent coastal pollution
Significant oil spill
River pollution
Current nuclear test site
Former nuclear test site
Major city with air pollution. Problem due to industry and vehicle exhaust

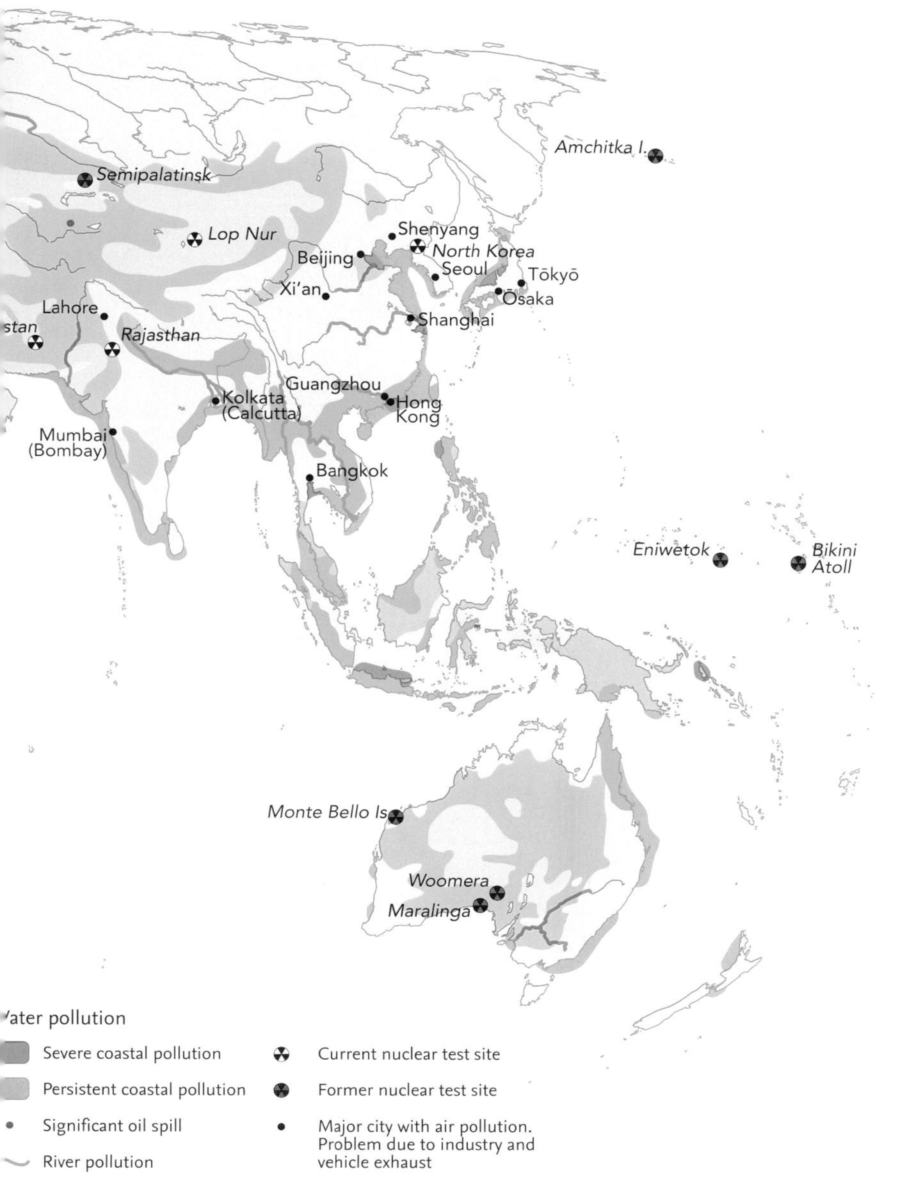

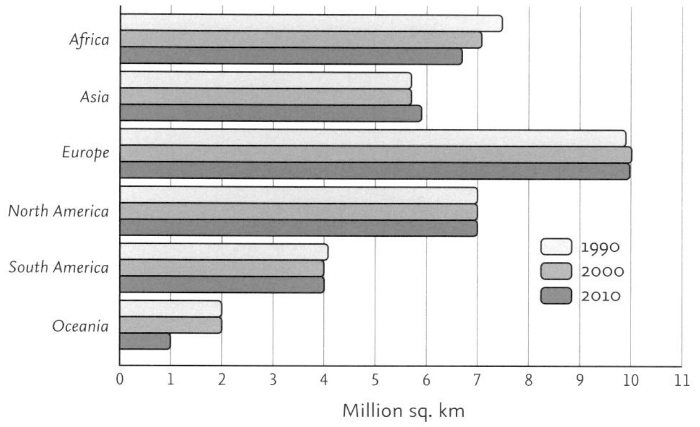

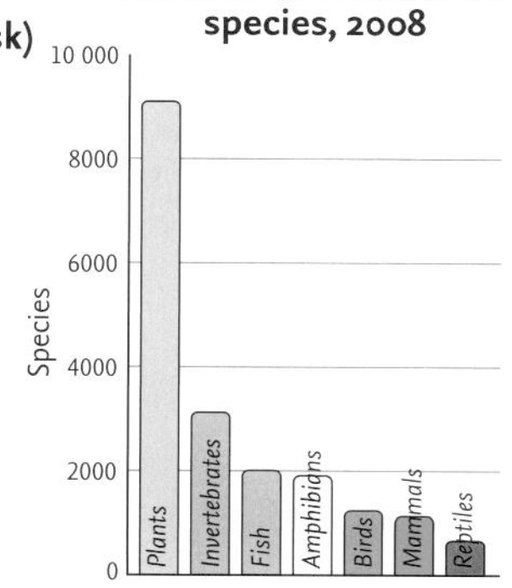

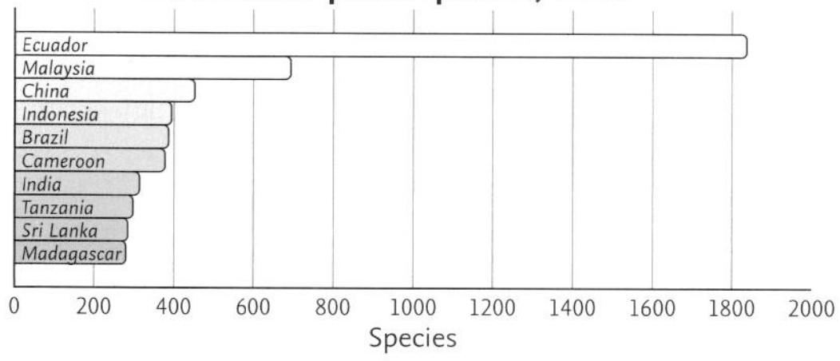

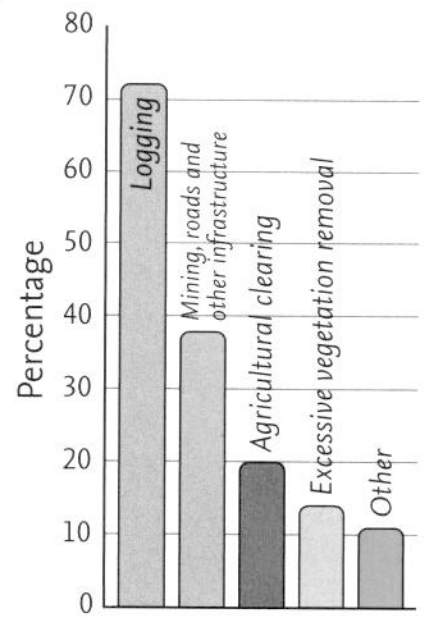

Threats to forests (% of world's forests at risk)
Percentage
80
70
60
50
40
30
20
10
0
Logging
Mining, roads and other infrastructure
Agricultural clearing
Excessive vegetation removal
Other

Number of threatened species, 2008
Species
10 000
8000
6000
4000
2000
0
Plants
Invertebrates
Fish
Amphibians
Birds
Mammals
Reptiles

Countries with the most threatened plant species, 2008
Ecuador
Malaysia
China
Indonesia
Brazil
Cameroon
India
Tanzania
Sri Lanka
Madagascar
0 200 400 600 800 1000 1200 1400 1600 1800 2000
Species

Total forest area, by region, 1990–2010
Africa
Asia
Europe
North America
South America
Oceania
1990
2000
2010
0 1 2 3 4 5 6 7 8 9 10 11
Million sq. km

## 3 Forest and Coral Reefs at Risk

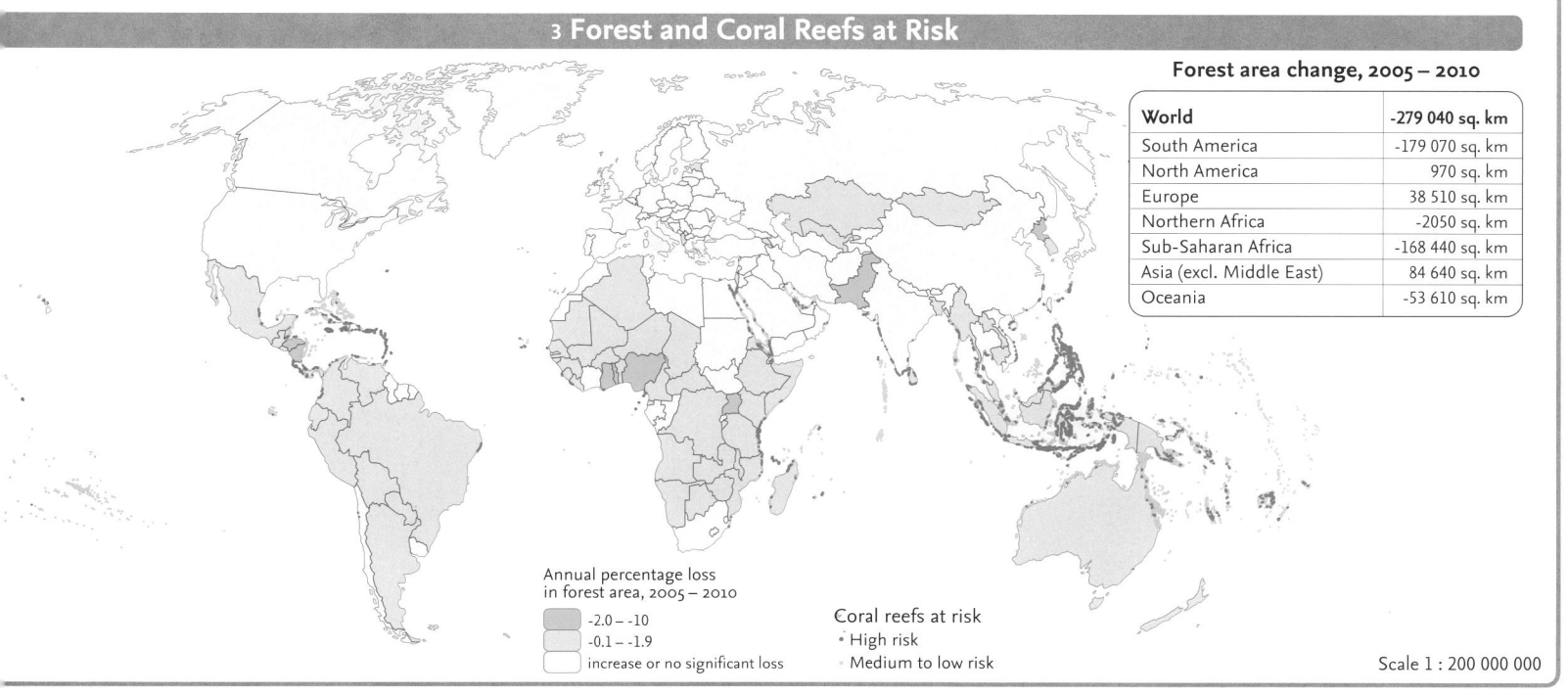

**Forest area change, 2005 – 2010**

| | |
|---|---|
| **World** | **-279 040 sq. km** |
| South America | -179 070 sq. km |
| North America | 970 sq. km |
| Europe | 38 510 sq. km |
| Northern Africa | -2050 sq. km |
| Sub-Saharan Africa | -168 440 sq. km |
| Asia (excl. Middle East) | 84 640 sq. km |
| Oceania | -53 610 sq. km |

Annual percentage loss in forest area, 2005 – 2010
-2.0 – -10
-0.1 – -1.9
increase or no significant loss
Coral reefs at risk
High risk
Medium to low risk
Scale 1 : 200 000 000

## 1 Global Warming, 1910–2010

Temperature anomaly (°C)

— Annual mean temperature
— 5-year mean temperature –
  smooths out annual variation

0.6
0.5
0.4
0.3
0.2
0.1
0
-0.1
-0.2
-0.3
-0.4

1910 1920 1930 1940 1950 1960 1970 1980 1990 2000 2010

World Meteorological
Organization
www.wmo.int
Met Office
www.metoffice.gov.uk/weather
Intergovernmental Panel on Climate Change
www.ipcc.ch

## 2 The Impact of Climate Change

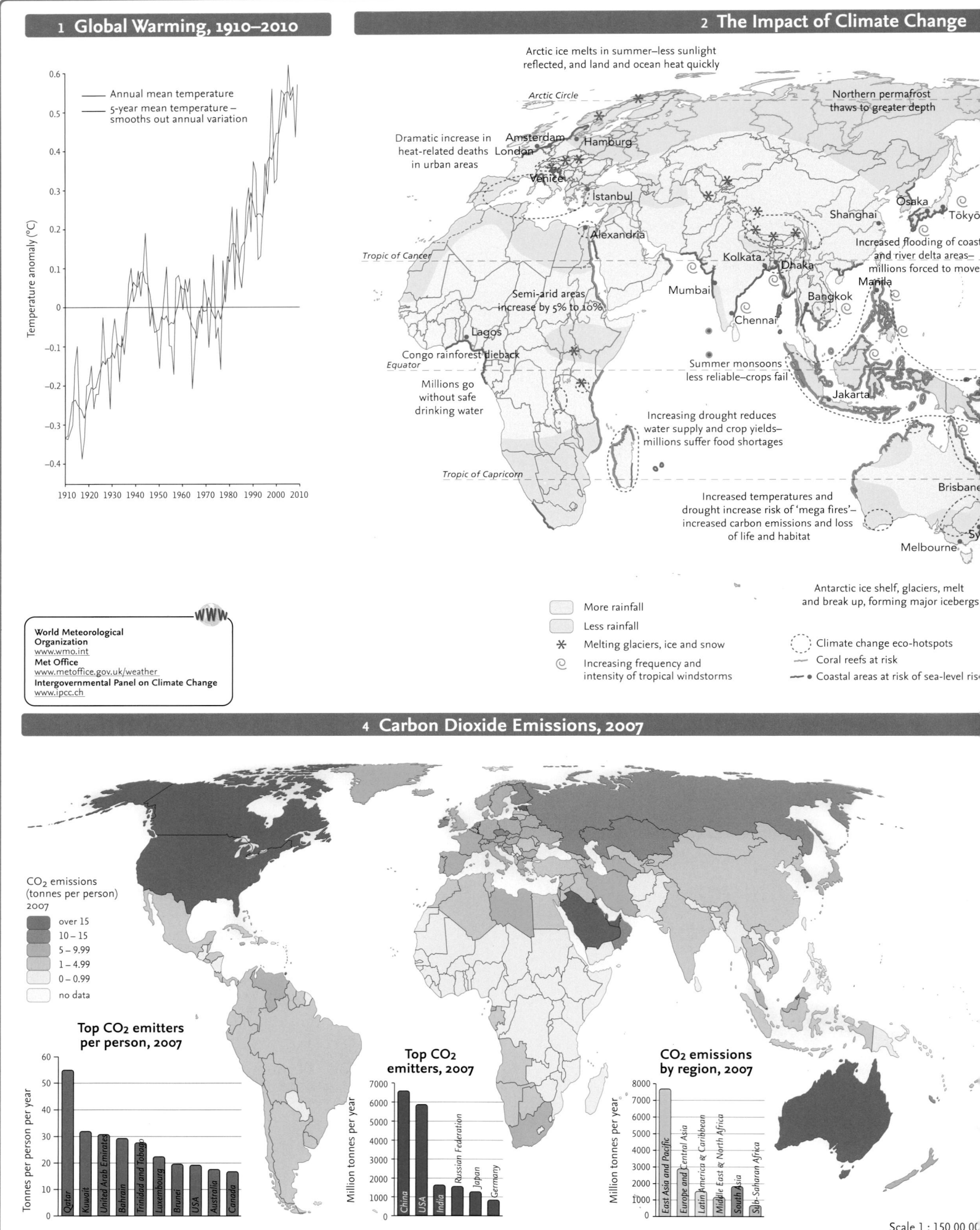

Arctic ice melts in summer—less sunlight
reflected, and land and ocean heat quickly

Arctic Circle

Northern permafrost
thaws to greater depth

Dramatic increase in
heat-related deaths
in urban areas

Amsterdam
London
Hamburg

Venice
İstanbul
Osaka
Tōkyō
Shanghai

Alexandria

Tropic of Cancer

Kolkata
Dhaka
Mumbai
Chennai
Bangkok
Manila

Increased flooding of coast
and river delta areas—
millions forced to move

Semi-arid areas
increase by 5% to 10%

Lagos

Congo rainforest dieback

Equator

Millions go
without safe
drinking water

Summer monsoons
less reliable—crops fail

Jakarta

Increasing drought reduces
water supply and crop yields—
millions suffer food shortages

Tropic of Capricorn

Increased temperatures and
drought increase risk of 'mega fires'—
increased carbon emissions and loss
of life and habitat

Brisbane

Sy

Melbourne

Antarctic ice shelf, glaciers, melt
and break up, forming major icebergs

More rainfall
Less rainfall
* Melting glaciers, ice and snow
Increasing frequency and
intensity of tropical windstorms

Climate change eco-hotspots
Coral reefs at risk
Coastal areas at risk of sea-level ris

## 4 Carbon Dioxide Emissions, 2007

CO₂ emissions
(tonnes per person)
2007

over 15
10 – 15
5 – 9.99
1 – 4.99
0 – 0.99
no data

### Top CO₂ emitters per person, 2007

Tonnes per person per year

60
50
40
30
20
10
0

Qatar
Kuwait
United Arab Emirates
Bahrain
Trinidad and Tobago
Luxembourg
Brunei
USA
Australia
Canada

### Top CO₂ emitters, 2007

Million tonnes per year

7000
6000
5000
4000
3000
2000
1000
0

China
USA
India
Russian Federation
Japan
Germany

### CO₂ emissions by region, 2007

Million tonnes per year

8000
7000
6000
5000
4000
3000
2000
1000
0

East Asia and Pacific
Europe and Central Asia
Latin America & Caribbean
Middle East & North Africa
South Asia
Sub-Saharan Africa

Scale 1 : 150 00 00

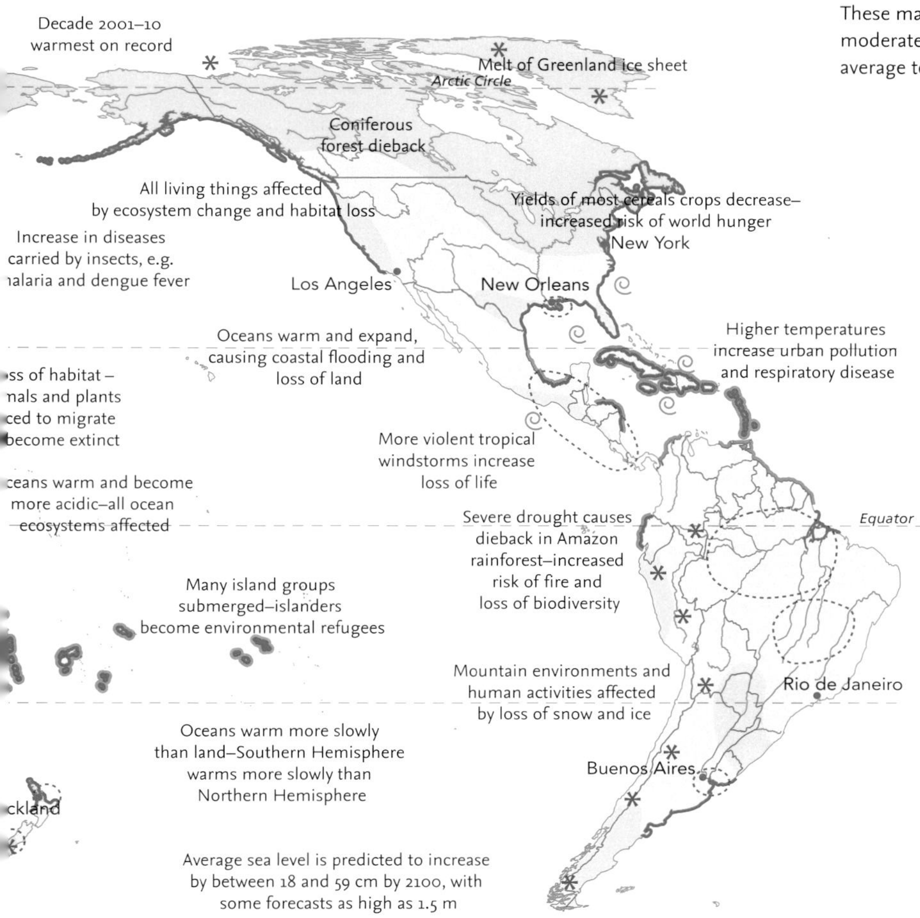

Decade 2001–10 warmest on record

Melt of Greenland ice sheet
*Arctic Circle*

Coniferous forest dieback

All living things affected by ecosystem change and habitat loss

Yields of most cereals crops decrease– increased risk of world hunger

New York

Increase in diseases carried by insects, e.g. malaria and dengue fever

Los Angeles

New Orleans

Oceans warm and expand, causing coastal flooding and loss of land

Higher temperatures increase urban pollution and respiratory disease

ss of habitat – nals and plants ed to migrate become extinct

More violent tropical windstorms increase loss of life

ceans warm and become more acidic–all ocean ecosystems affected

Severe drought causes dieback in Amazon rainforest–increased risk of fire and loss of biodiversity

*Equator*

Many island groups submerged–islanders become environmental refugees

Mountain environments and human activities affected by loss of snow and ice

Rio de Janeiro

Oceans warm more slowly than land–Southern Hemisphere warms more slowly than Northern Hemisphere

ckland

Buenos Aires

Average sea level is predicted to increase by between 18 and 59 cm by 2100, with some forecasts as high as 1.5 m

## 3 Projected Annual Mean Temperature Change

These maps show projected change in annual mean surface air temperature given moderate growth in $CO_2$ emissions, for three time periods, compared with the average temperature for 1980–99.

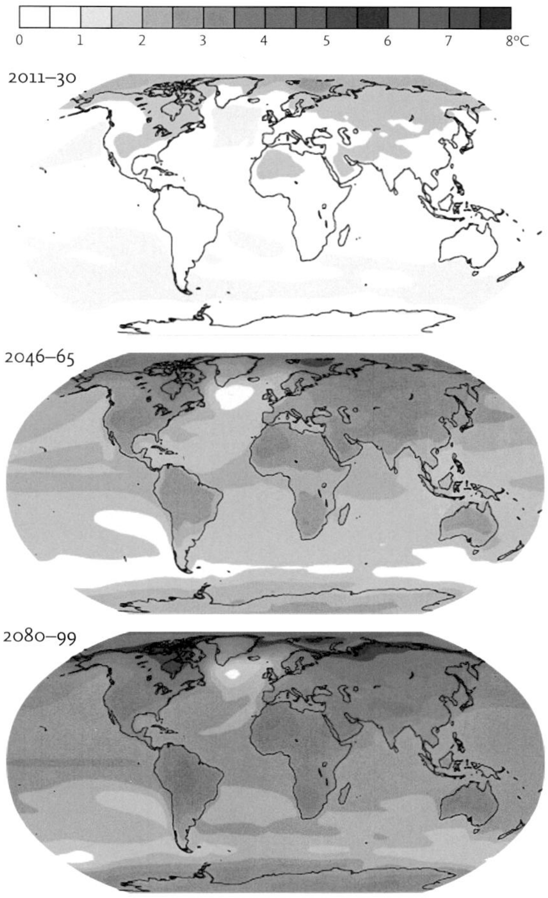

0   1   2   3   4   5   6   7   8°C

2011–30

2046–65

2080–99

## 5 Climate Change Vulnerability Index, 2010

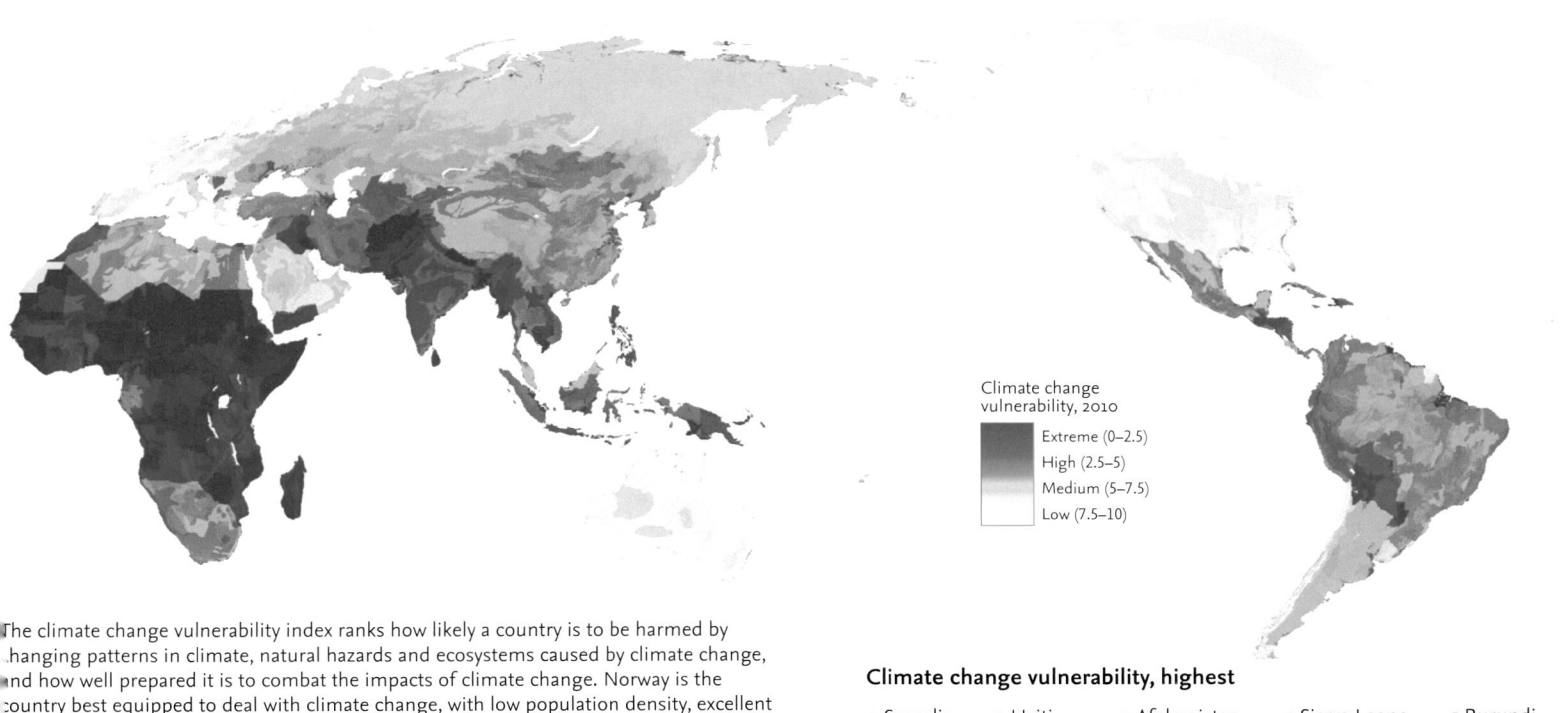

Climate change vulnerability, 2010

Extreme (0–2.5)
High (2.5–5)
Medium (5–7.5)
Low (7.5–10)

The climate change vulnerability index ranks how likely a country is to be harmed by changing patterns in climate, natural hazards and ecosystems caused by climate change, and how well prepared it is to combat the impacts of climate change. Norway is the country best equipped to deal with climate change, with low population density, excellent healthcare and communication systems and high overall food, water and energy security. n contrast Somalia, with scarce natural resources, low food security, political violence and human rights risk, is extremely vulnerable to the impacts of climate change.

**Climate change vulnerability, highest**

| 1 Somalia | 2 Haiti | 3 Afghanistan | 4 Sierra Leone | 5 Burundi |
| 6 Guinea | 7 Rwanda | 8 The Gambia | 9 Chad | 10 Nigeria |

Of the 28 countries most at risk, 22 are in Africa.

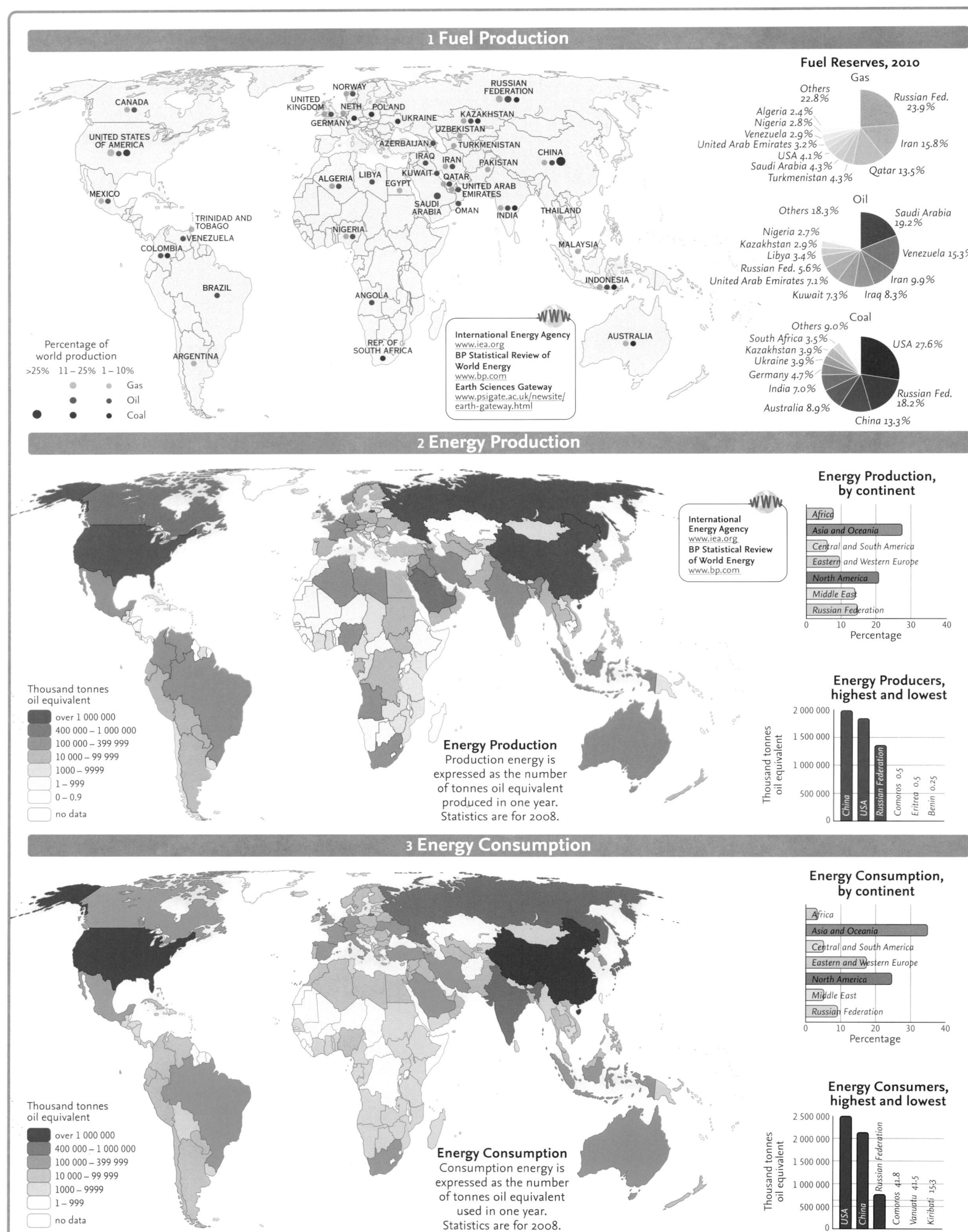

## 1 Fuel Production

### Fuel Reserves, 2010

**Gas**

Others 22.8%
Russian Fed. 23.9%
Algeria 2.4%
Nigeria 2.8%
Venezuela 2.9%
United Arab Emirates 3.2%
USA 4.1%
Saudi Arabia 4.3%
Turkmenistan 4.3%
Iran 15.8%
Qatar 13.5%

**Oil**

Others 18.3%
Saudi Arabia 19.2%
Nigeria 2.7%
Kazakhstan 2.9%
Libya 3.4%
Russian Fed. 5.6%
United Arab Emirates 7.1%
Venezuela 15.3%
Kuwait 7.3%
Iran 9.9%
Iraq 8.3%

**Coal**

Others 9.0%
USA 27.6%
South Africa 3.5%
Kazakhstan 3.9%
Ukraine 3.9%
Germany 4.7%
India 7.0%
Russian Fed. 18.2%
Australia 8.9%
China 13.3%

Percentage of
world production
>25%  11 – 25%  1 – 10%
Gas
Oil
Coal

International Energy Agency
www.iea.org
BP Statistical Review of
World Energy
www.bp.com
Earth Sciences Gateway
www.psigate.ac.uk/newsite/
earth-gateway.html

## 2 Energy Production

International
Energy Agency
www.iea.org
BP Statistical Review
of World Energy
www.bp.com

### Energy Production, by continent

Africa
Asia and Oceania
Central and South America
Eastern and Western Europe
North America
Middle East
Russian Federation

0  10  20  30  40
Percentage

### Energy Producers, highest and lowest

Thousand tonnes oil equivalent

China
USA
Russian Federation
Comoros 0.5
Eritrea 0.5
Benin 0.25

Thousand tonnes
oil equivalent
over 1 000 000
400 000 – 1 000 000
100 000 – 399 999
10 000 – 99 999
1000 – 9999
1 – 999
0 – 0.9
no data

**Energy Production**
Production energy is
expressed as the number
of tonnes oil equivalent
produced in one year.
Statistics are for 2008.

## 3 Energy Consumption

### Energy Consumption, by continent

Africa
Asia and Oceania
Central and South America
Eastern and Western Europe
North America
Middle East
Russian Federation

0  10  20  30  40
Percentage

### Energy Consumers, highest and lowest

Thousand tonnes oil equivalent

USA
China
Russian Federation
Comoros 41.8
Vanuatu 41.5
Kiribati 153

Thousand tonnes
oil equivalent
over 1 000 000
400 000 – 1 000 000
100 000 – 399 999
10 000 – 99 999
1000 – 9999
1 – 999
no data

**Energy Consumption**
Consumption energy is
expressed as the number
of tonnes oil equivalent
used in one year.
Statistics are for 2008.

Scale 1 : 190 000 000

Eckert IV projection

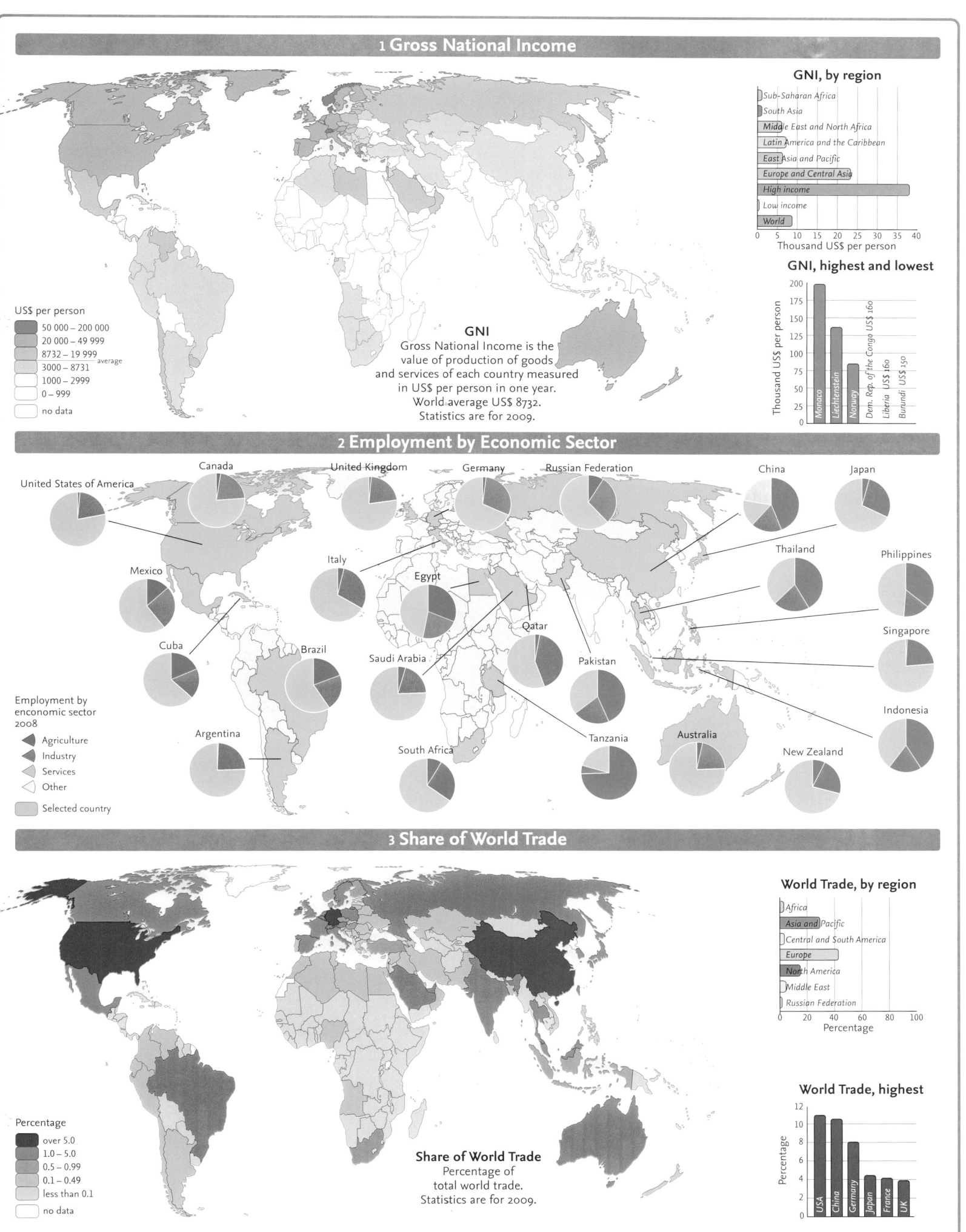

## 1 Gross National Income

**GNI, by region**

Sub-Saharan Africa
South Asia
Middle East and North Africa
Latin America and the Caribbean
East Asia and Pacific
Europe and Central Asia
High income
Low income
World

0 5 10 15 20 25 30 35 40
Thousand US$ per person

**GNI, highest and lowest**

Thousand US$ per person
200
175
150
125
100
75
50
25
0

Monaco
Liechtenstein
Norway
Dem. Rep. of the Congo US$ 160
Liberia US$ 160
Burundi US$ 150

**US$ per person**
- 50 000 – 200 000
- 20 000 – 49 999
- 8732 – 19 999 average
- 3000 – 8731
- 1000 – 2999
- 0 – 999
- no data

**GNI**
Gross National Income is the value of production of goods and services of each country measured in US$ per person in one year. World average US$ 8732. Statistics are for 2009.

## 2 Employment by Economic Sector

United States of America
Canada
United Kingdom
Germany
Russian Federation
China
Japan
Mexico
Italy
Egypt
Thailand
Philippines
Cuba
Brazil
Qatar
Saudi Arabia
Pakistan
Singapore
Argentina
South Africa
Tanzania
Australia
Indonesia
New Zealand

**Employment by economic sector 2008**
- Agriculture
- Industry
- Services
- Other
- Selected country

## 3 Share of World Trade

**World Trade, by region**

Africa
Asia and Pacific
Central and South America
Europe
North America
Middle East
Russian Federation

0 20 40 60 80 100
Percentage

**World Trade, highest**

Percentage
12
10
8
6
4
2
0

USA
China
Germany
Japan
France
UK

**Percentage**
- over 5.0
- 1.0 – 5.0
- 0.5 – 0.99
- 0.1 – 0.49
- less than 0.1
- no data

**Share of World Trade**
Percentage of total world trade. Statistics are for 2009.

## 1 Ecological Footprint

### World Ecological Footprint compared with biocapacity, 1961–2007

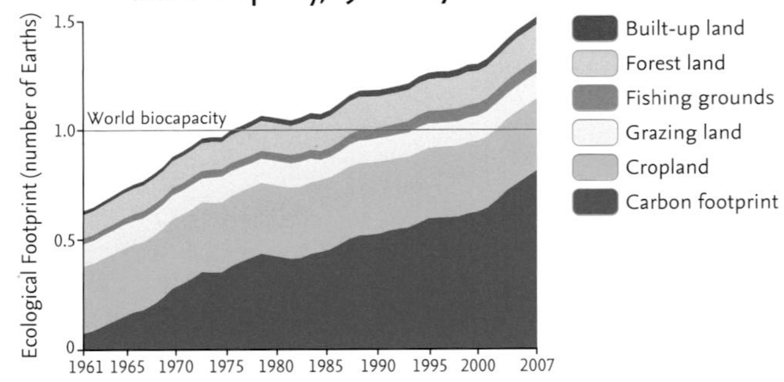

Legend:
- Built-up land
- Forest land
- Fishing grounds
- Grazing land
- Cropland
- Carbon footprint

The Ecological Footprint measures the area of biologically productive land and water required to produce the resources an individual or a population consumes and to absorb the waste it generates. A country's Ecological Footprint is usually expressed in global hectares (gha) per person—the average area of land required to support each of that country's inhabitants.

Since 1961, when the data from which the Ecological Footprint is calculated first became available, there has been a marked increase in the contribution made by the carbon footprint—that is, the amount of forest land needed to absorb emissions of carbon dioxide ($CO_2$). Most $CO_2$ emissions come from the burning of fossil fuels.

Ecological Footprint is often compared with biocapacity, or the ability of the land to supply resources and absorb waste. A country's biocapacity, which can also be expressed in global hectares per person, is its total amount of biologically productive land divided by its population.

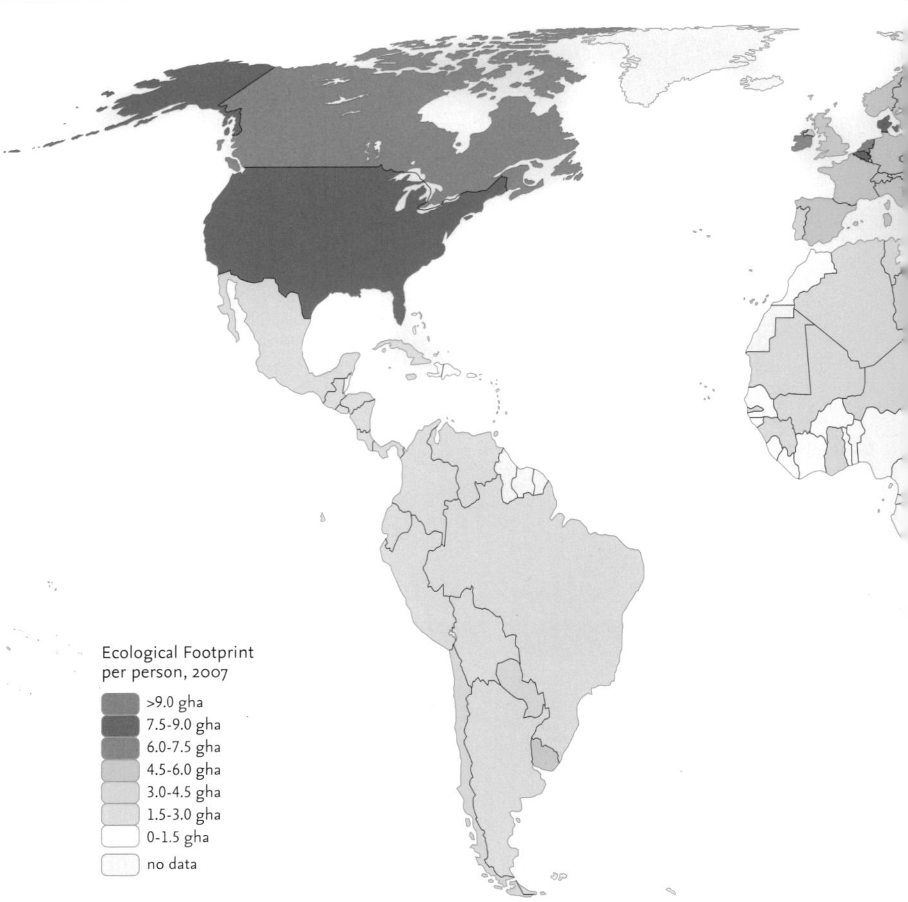

Ecological Footprint per person, 2007
- >9.0 gha
- 7.5-9.0 gha
- 6.0-7.5 gha
- 4.5-6.0 gha
- 3.0-4.5 gha
- 1.5-3.0 gha
- 0-1.5 gha
- no data

## 2 Ecological Footprint of Nations

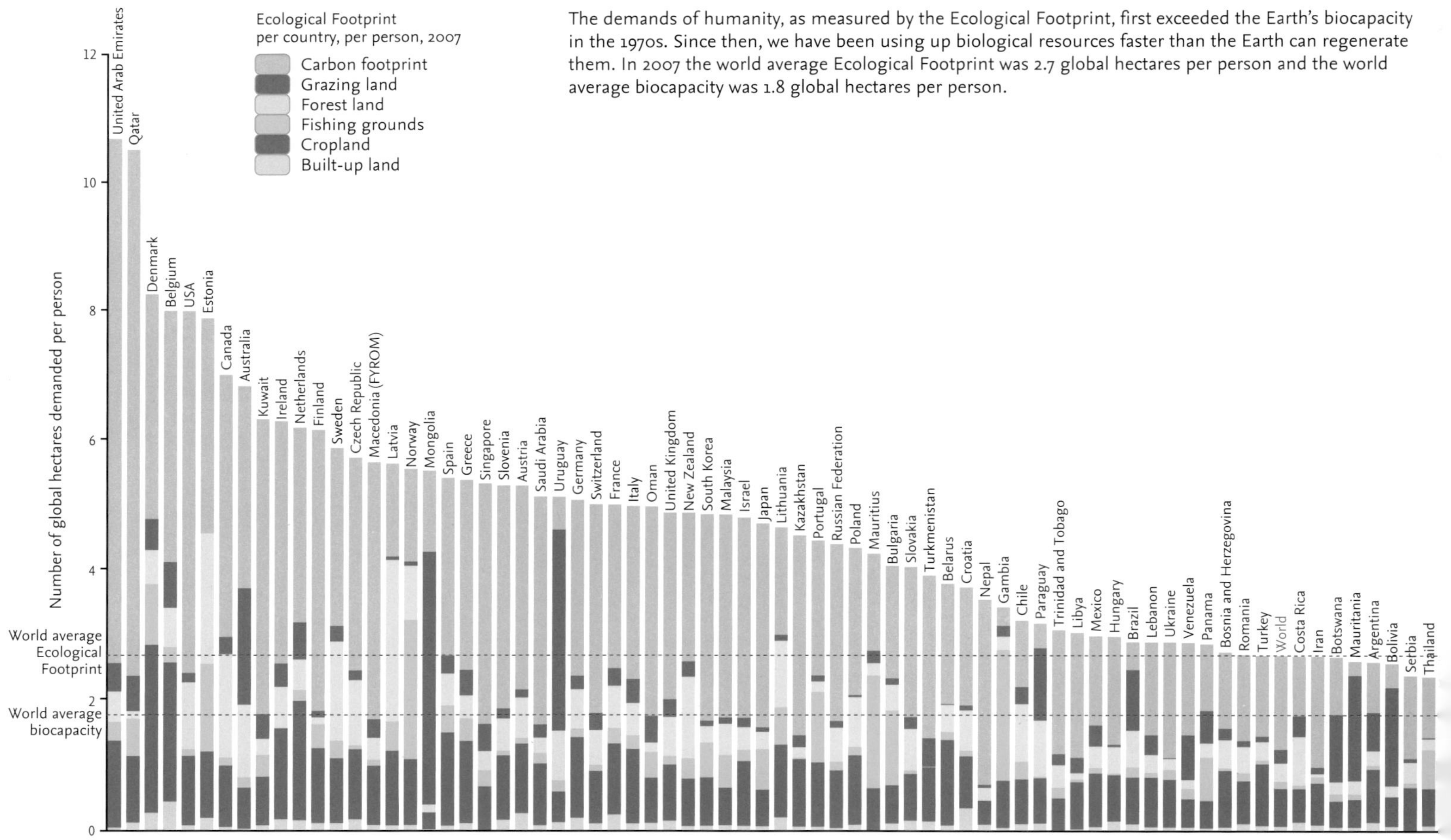

Ecological Footprint per country, per person, 2007
- Carbon footprint
- Grazing land
- Forest land
- Fishing grounds
- Cropland
- Built-up land

The demands of humanity, as measured by the Ecological Footprint, first exceeded the Earth's biocapacity in the 1970s. Since then, we have been using up biological resources faster than the Earth can regenerate them. In 2007 the world average Ecological Footprint was 2.7 global hectares per person and the world average biocapacity was 1.8 global hectares per person.

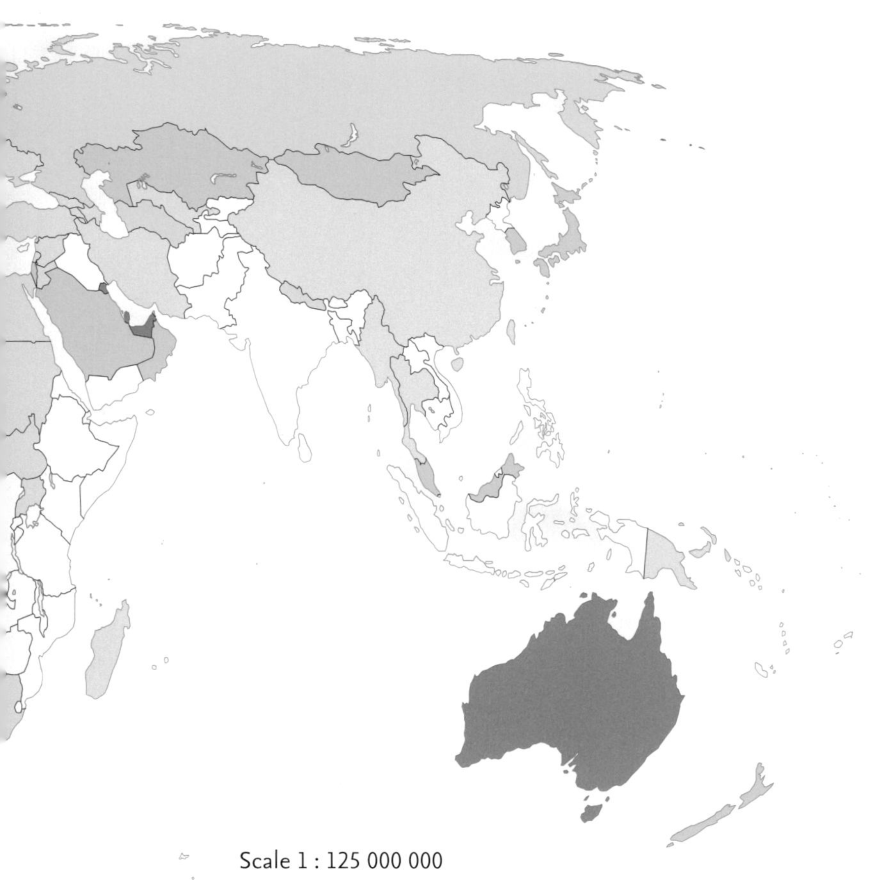

## Top 10 national biocapacities, 2007

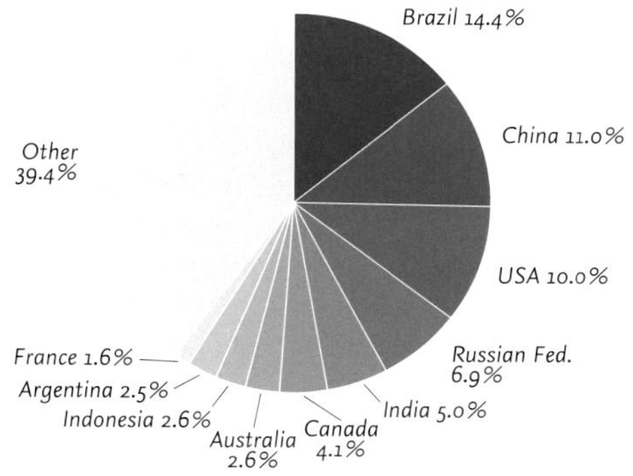

- Brazil 14.4%
- China 11.0%
- USA 10.0%
- Russian Fed. 6.9%
- India 5.0%
- Canada 4.1%
- Australia 2.6%
- Indonesia 2.6%
- Argentina 2.5%
- France 1.6%
- Other 39.4%

## Return to sustainability

Number of planet Earths

- World Ecological Footprint 1961–2007
- Biocapacity
- Projected Ecological Footprint, 'business as usual' scenario
- Biocapacity reserve
- Ecological debt
- Projected Ecological Footprint, 'return to sustainability' scenario

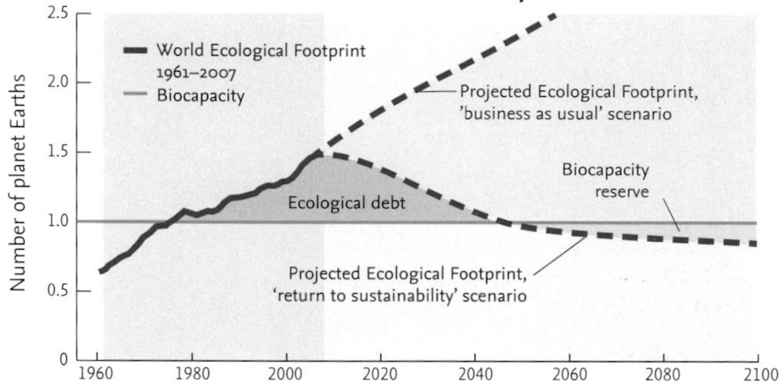

The world's Ecological Footprint is exceeding its biocapacity by an increasing margin. Rapid steps could end this so-called 'overshoot' by the middle of the 21st century, lessen the risk of ecological collapse and create a biocapacity reserve.

Scale 1 : 125 000 000

## 3 Ecological Debtors and Creditors

**Ecological debtor countries, 2007**
- Footprint more than 150% larger than biocapacity
- Footprint 100–150% larger than biocapacity
- Footprint 50–100% larger than biocapacity
- Footprint 0–50% larger than biocapacity

**Ecological creditor countries, 2007**
- Biocapacity 0–50% larger than Footprint
- Biocapacity 50–100% larger than Footprint
- Biocapacity 100–150% larger than Footprint
- Biocapacity more than 150% larger than Footprint

- no data

Ecological debtor countries have an Ecological Footprint greater than their biocapacity; ecological creditors have an Ecological Footprint smaller than their biocapacity.

Scale 1 : 200 000 000

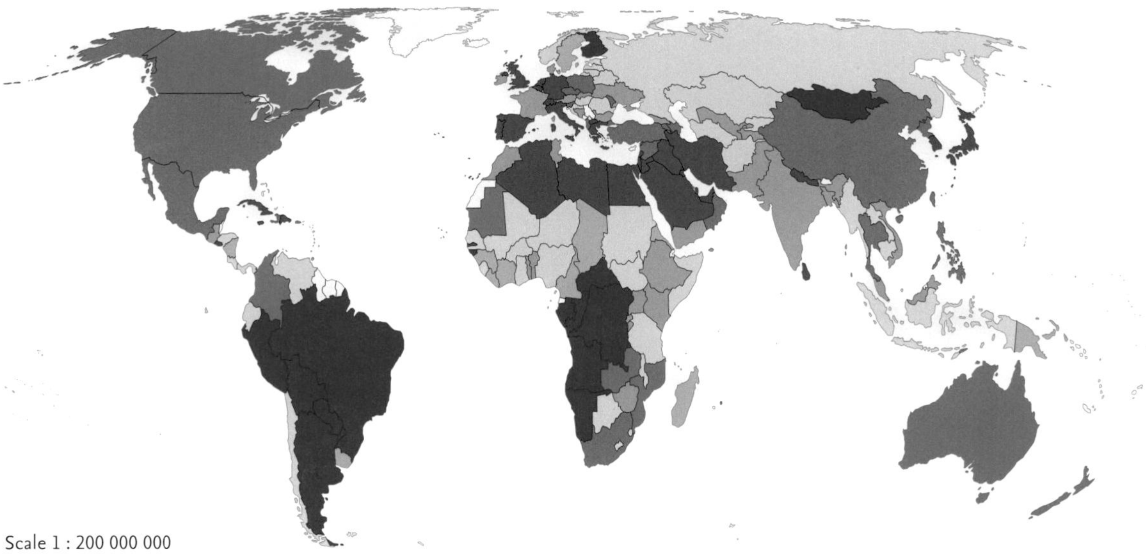

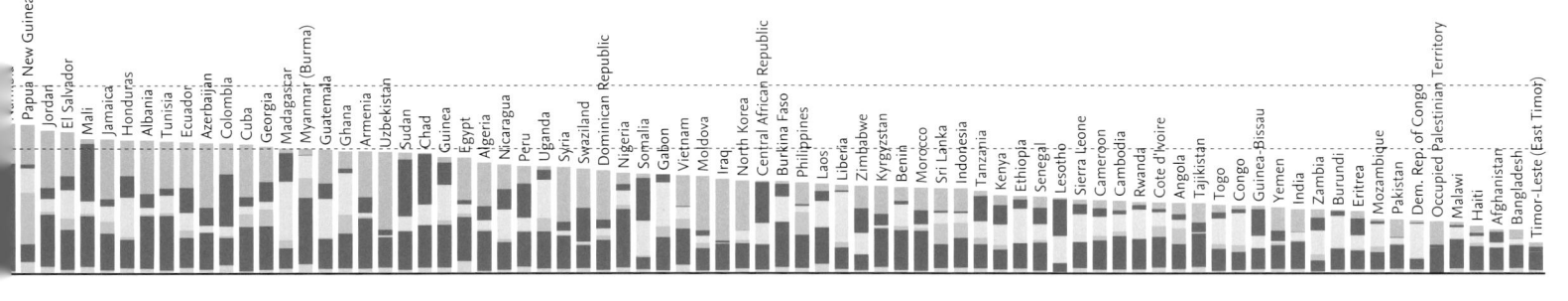

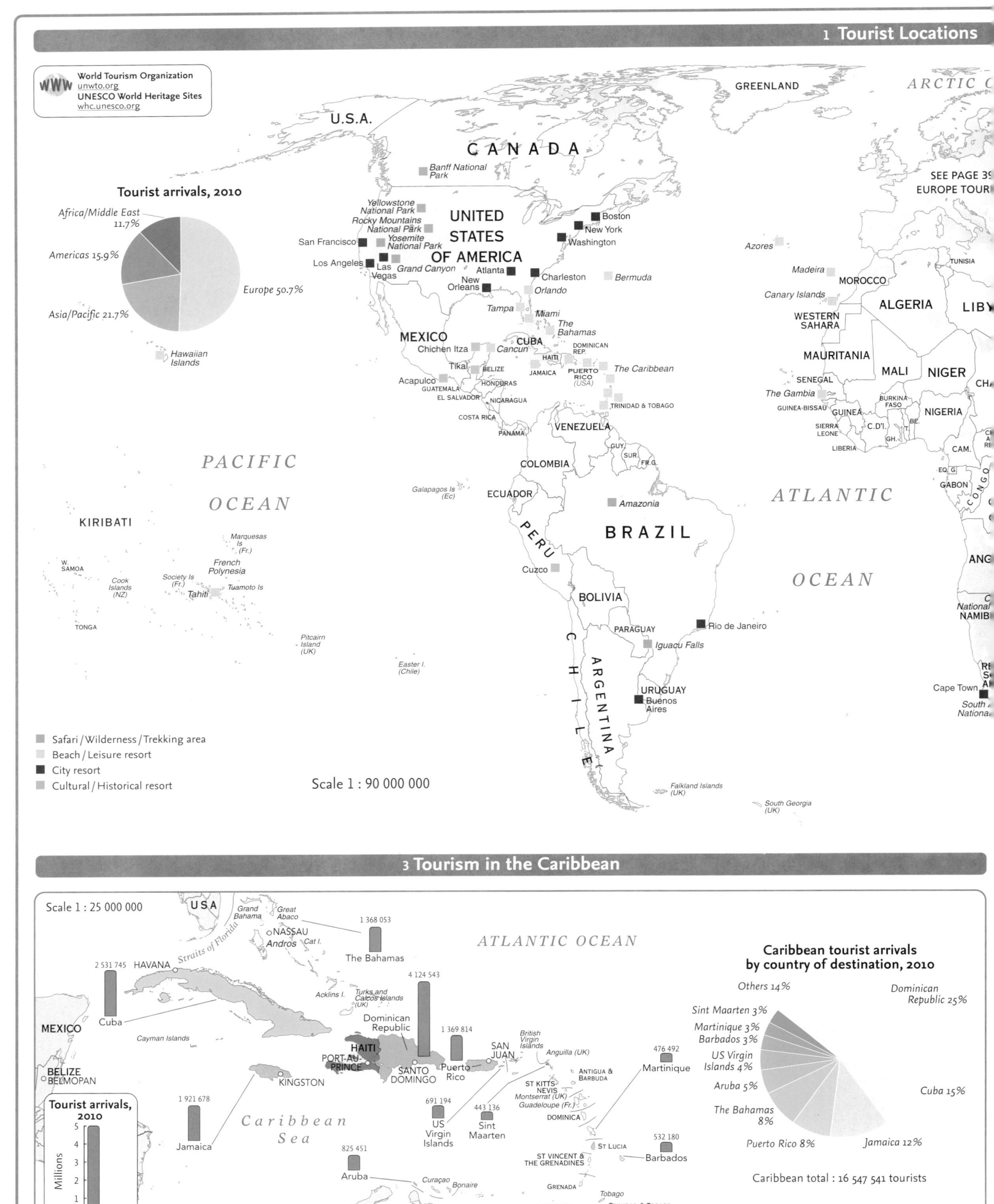

**1 Tourist Locations**

World Tourism Organization
unwto.org
UNESCO World Heritage Sites
whc.unesco.org

**Tourist arrivals, 2010**

- Africa/Middle East 11.7%
- Americas 15.9%
- Asia/Pacific 21.7%
- Europe 50.7%

SEE PAGE 39
EUROPE TOUR

■ Safari/Wilderness/Trekking area
▫ Beach/Leisure resort
■ City resort
▪ Cultural/Historical resort

Scale 1 : 90 000 000

**3 Tourism in the Caribbean**

Scale 1 : 25 000 000

**Tourist arrivals, 2010**
Millions
5
4
3
2
1
0

The Bahamas 1 368 053
Cuba 2 531 745
Dominican Republic 4 124 543
Puerto Rico 1 369 814
Jamaica 1 921 678
US Virgin Islands 691 194
Sint Maarten 443 136
Aruba 825 451
Martinique 476 492
Barbados 532 180

**Caribbean tourist arrivals
by country of destination, 2010**

- Others 14%
- Sint Maarten 3%
- Martinique 3%
- Barbados 3%
- US Virgin Islands 4%
- Aruba 5%
- The Bahamas 8%
- Puerto Rico 8%
- Dominican Republic 25%
- Cuba 15%
- Jamaica 12%

Caribbean total : 16 547 541 tourists

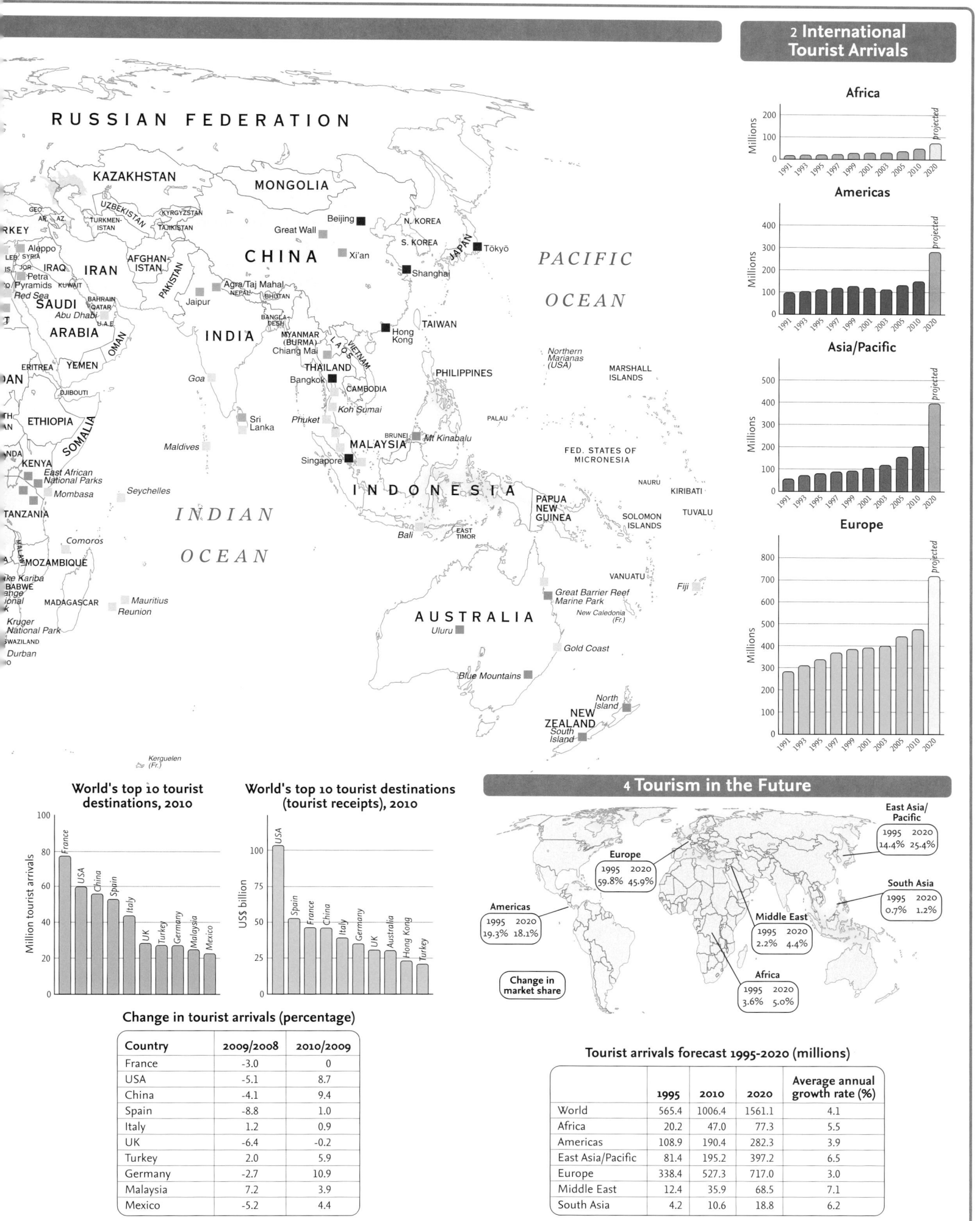

## 2 International Tourist Arrivals

### Africa

Millions

### Americas

Millions

### Asia/Pacific

Millions

### Europe

Millions

## World's top 10 tourist destinations, 2010

Million tourist arrivals

France, USA, China, Spain, Italy, UK, Turkey, Germany, Malaysia, Mexico

## World's top 10 tourist destinations (tourist receipts), 2010

US$ billion

USA, Spain, France, China, Italy, Germany, UK, Australia, Hong Kong, Turkey

## Change in tourist arrivals (percentage)

| Country | 2009/2008 | 2010/2009 |
|---------|-----------|-----------|
| France | -3.0 | 0 |
| USA | -5.1 | 8.7 |
| China | -4.1 | 9.4 |
| Spain | -8.8 | 1.0 |
| Italy | 1.2 | 0.9 |
| UK | -6.4 | -0.2 |
| Turkey | 2.0 | 5.9 |
| Germany | -2.7 | 10.9 |
| Malaysia | 7.2 | 3.9 |
| Mexico | -5.2 | 4.4 |

## 4 Tourism in the Future

East Asia/Pacific
1995: 14.4%  2020: 25.4%

Europe
1995: 59.8%  2020: 45.9%

South Asia
1995: 0.7%  2020: 1.2%

Americas
1995: 19.3%  2020: 18.1%

Middle East
1995: 2.2%  2020: 4.4%

Africa
1995: 3.6%  2020: 5.0%

Change in market share

## Tourist arrivals forecast 1995-2020 (millions)

|  | 1995 | 2010 | 2020 | Average annual growth rate (%) |
|---|------|------|------|-------------------------------|
| World | 565.4 | 1006.4 | 1561.1 | 4.1 |
| Africa | 20.2 | 47.0 | 77.3 | 5.5 |
| Americas | 108.9 | 190.4 | 282.3 | 3.9 |
| East Asia/Pacific | 81.4 | 195.2 | 397.2 | 6.5 |
| Europe | 338.4 | 527.3 | 717.0 | 3.0 |
| Middle East | 12.4 | 35.9 | 68.5 | 7.1 |
| South Asia | 4.2 | 10.6 | 18.8 | 6.2 |

# World Communications

## 1 Telephone Lines

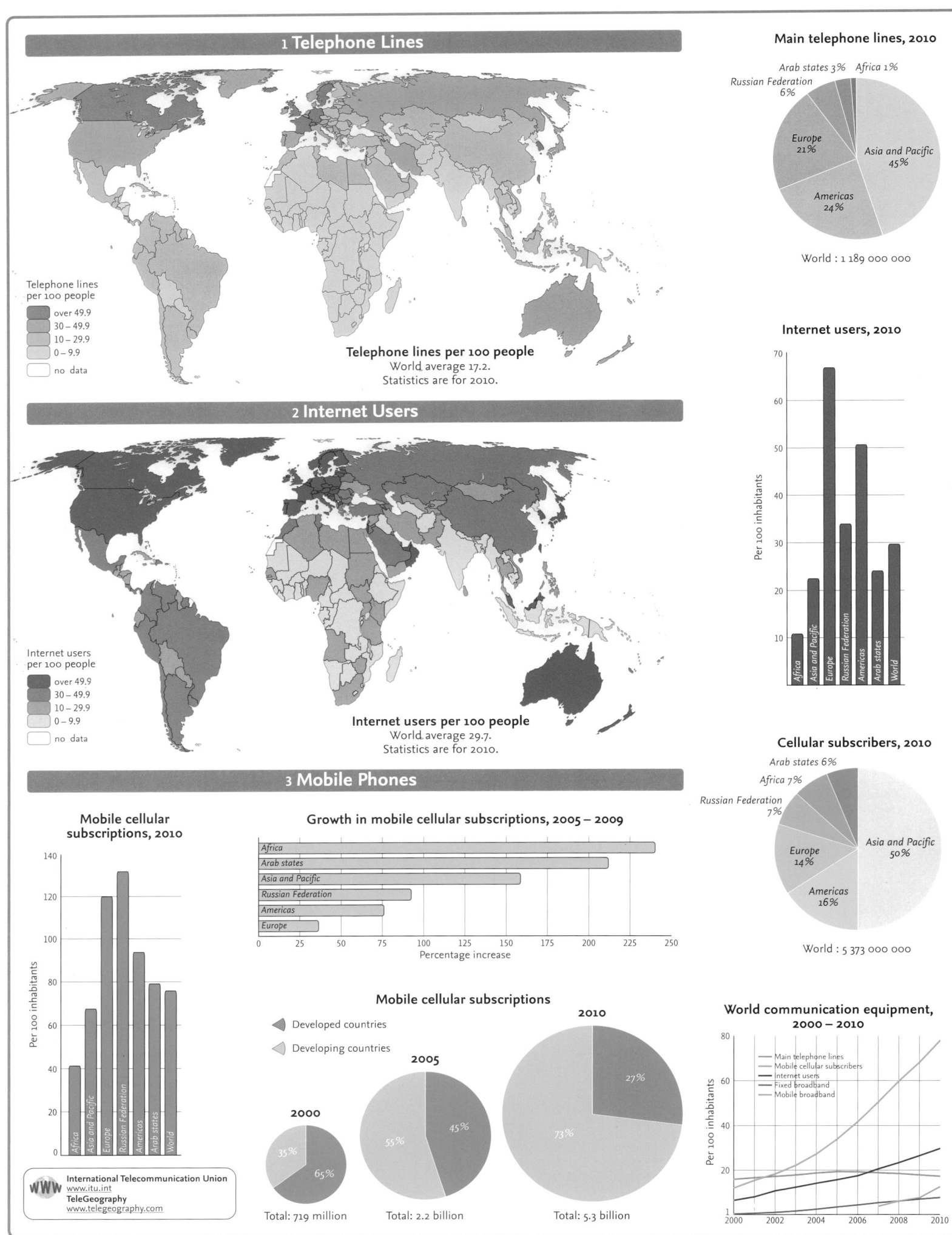

**Telephone lines per 100 people**
World average 17.2.
Statistics are for 2010.

Telephone lines per 100 people
- over 49.9
- 30 – 49.9
- 10 – 29.9
- 0 – 9.9
- no data

### Main telephone lines, 2010

Arab states 3% · Africa 1%
Russian Federation 6%
Europe 21%
Asia and Pacific 45%
Americas 24%

World : 1 189 000 000

## 2 Internet Users

**Internet users per 100 people**
World average 29.7.
Statistics are for 2010.

Internet users per 100 people
- over 49.9
- 30 – 29.9
- 10 – 29.9
- 0 – 9.9
- no data

### Internet users, 2010

Per 100 inhabitants
- Africa
- Asia and Pacific
- Europe
- Russian Federation
- Americas
- Arab states
- World

## 3 Mobile Phones

### Mobile cellular subscriptions, 2010

Per 100 inhabitants
- Africa
- Asia and Pacific
- Europe
- Russian Federation
- Americas
- Arab states
- World

### Growth in mobile cellular subscriptions, 2005 – 2009

- Africa
- Arab states
- Asia and Pacific
- Russian Federation
- Americas
- Europe

Percentage increase

### Cellular subscribers, 2010

Arab states 6%
Africa 7%
Russian Federation 7%
Europe 14%
Asia and Pacific 50%
Americas 16%

World : 5 373 000 000

### Mobile cellular subscriptions

- Developed countries
- Developing countries

**2000**
35%
65%
Total: 719 million

**2005**
55%
45%
Total: 2.2 billion

**2010**
27%
73%
Total: 5.3 billion

### World communication equipment, 2000 – 2010

Per 100 inhabitants
- Main telephone lines
- Mobile cellular subscribers
- Internet users
- Fixed broadband
- Mobile broadband

2000  2002  2004  2006  2008  2010

**WWW** International Telecommunication Union
www.itu.int
TeleGeography
www.telegeography.com

Scale 1 : 210 000 000

Eckert IV projectio

## 1 Air Transport

### Top 20 busiest airports, 2010

| | Airport | Passengers carried |
|---|---|---|
| 1 | Atlanta | 89 331 622 |
| 2 | Beijing | 73 948 113 |
| 3 | Chicago | 66 774 738 |
| 4 | London Heathrow | 65 884 143 |
| 5 | Tōkyō | 64 211 074 |
| 6 | Los Angeles | 59 070 127 |
| 7 | Paris | 58 167 062 |
| 8 | Dallas/Fort Worth | 56 906 610 |
| 9 | Frankfurt | 53 009 221 |
| 10 | Denver | 52 209 377 |
| 11 | Hong Kong | 50 348 960 |
| 12 | Madrid | 49 844 596 |
| 13 | Dubai | 47 180 628 |
| 14 | New York | 46 514 154 |
| 15 | Amsterdam | 45 211 749 |
| 16 | Jakarta | 44 355 998 |
| 17 | Bangkok | 42 784 967 |
| 18 | Singapore | 42 038 777 |
| 19 | Guangzhou | 40 975 673 |
| 20 | Shanghai | 40 578 621 |

**Passengers carried**
Air passengers carried include both domestic and international aircraft passengers. Statistics are for 2009.

Passengers carried in millions
- over 100
- 25 – 100
- 10 – 25
- 1 – 10
- less than 1
- no data

● Main airport
· Other airport
— Main air route

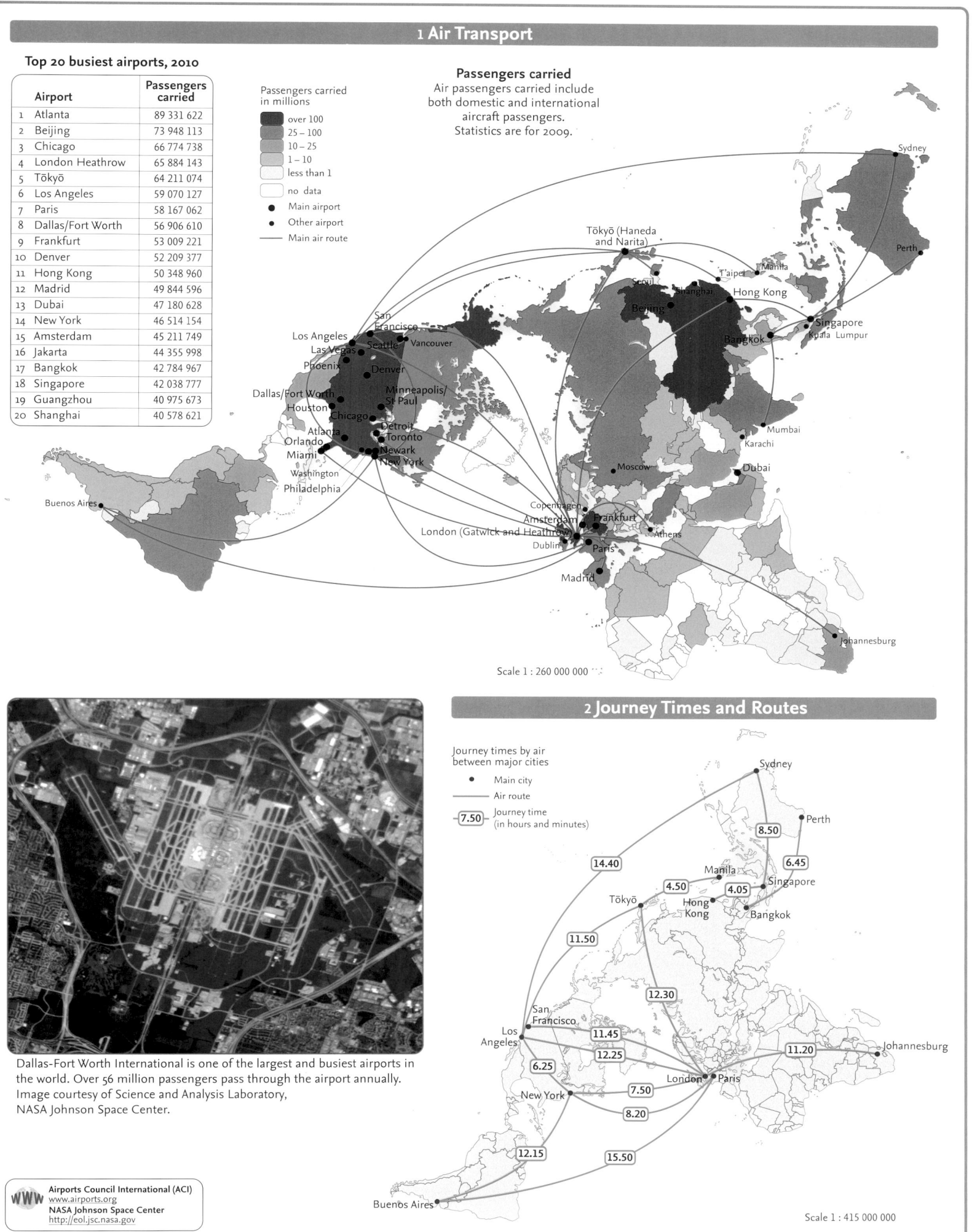

Scale 1 : 260 000 000

Dallas-Fort Worth International is one of the largest and busiest airports in the world. Over 56 million passengers pass through the airport annually.
Image courtesy of Science and Analysis Laboratory, NASA Johnson Space Center.

## 2 Journey Times and Routes

Journey times by air between major cities
● Main city
— Air route
7.50 Journey time (in hours and minutes)

Scale 1 : 415 000 000

Airports Council International (ACI)
www.airports.org
NASA Johnson Space Center
http://eol.jsc.nasa.gov

Fuller projection

| | Key Information | | Population | | | | | | |
|---|---|---|---|---|---|---|---|---|---|
| Flag | Country | Capital city | Population total 2011 | Density persons per sq km 2011 | Birth rate per 1000 population 2009 | Death rate per 1000 population 2009 | Life expectancy in years 2009 | Population change annual % per annum 2009 | Urban population % 2009 |
| | Afghanistan | Kābul | 32 358 000 | 50 | 46 | 19 | 44 | 2.7 | 24 |
| | Albania | Tirana | 3 216 000 | 112 | 15 | 6 | 77 | 0.4 | 47 |
| | Algeria | Algiers | 35 980 000 | 15 | 21 | 5 | 73 | 1.5 | 66 |
| | Andorra | Andorra la Vella | 86 000 | 185 | 10 | 3 | .. | 1.6 | 89 |
| | Angola | Luanda | 19 618 000 | 16 | 42 | 17 | 48 | 2.6 | 58 |
| | Antigua & Barbuda | St John's | 90 000 | 204 | .. | .. | .. | 1.1 | 30 |
| | Argentina | Buenos Aires | 40 765 000 | 15 | 17 | 8 | 76 | 1.0 | 92 |
| | Armenia | Yerevan | 3 100 000 | 104 | 15 | 9 | 74 | 0.2 | 64 |
| | Australia | Canberra | 22 606 000 | 3 | 14 | 6 | 82 | 2.0 | 89 |
| | Austria | Vienna | 8 413 000 | 100 | 9 | 9 | 80 | 0.3 | 67 |
| | Azerbaijan | Baku | 9 306 000 | 108 | 17 | 6 | 70 | 1.2 | 52 |
| | Bahamas, The | Nassau | 347 000 | 25 | 17 | 6 | 74 | 1.2 | 84 |
| | Bahrain | Manama | 1 324 000 | 1 916 | 18 | 3 | 76 | 2.0 | 89 |
| | Bangladesh | Dhaka | 150 494 000 | 1 045 | 21 | 7 | 67 | 1.4 | 28 |
| | Barbados | Bridgetown | 274 000 | 637 | 11 | 8 | 77 | 0.3 | 40 |
| | Belarus | Minsk | 9 559 000 | 46 | 12 | 14 | 70 | -0.2 | 74 |
| | Belgium | Brussels | 10 754 000 | 352 | 12 | 10 | 81 | 0.7 | 97 |
| | Belize | Belmopan | 318 000 | 14 | 24 | 4 | 77 | 3.4 | 52 |
| | Benin | Porto-Novo | 9 100 000 | 81 | 39 | 9 | 62 | 3.1 | 42 |
| | Bhutan | Thimphu | 738 000 | 16 | 21 | 7 | 67 | 1.5 | 36 |
| | Bolivia | La Paz/Sucre | 10 088 000 | 9 | 27 | 7 | 66 | 1.7 | 66 |
| | Bosnia-Herzegovina | Sarajevo | 3 752 000 | 73 | 9 | 10 | 75 | -0.2 | 48 |
| | Botswana | Gaborone | 2 031 000 | 4 | 24 | 12 | 55 | 1.5 | 60 |
| | Brazil | Brasília | 196 655 000 | 23 | 16 | 6 | 73 | 0.9 | 86 |
| | Brunei | Bandar Seri Begawan | 406 000 | 70 | 20 | 3 | 78 | 1.9 | 75 |
| | Bulgaria | Sofia | 7 446 000 | 67 | 11 | 14 | 73 | -0.5 | 71 |
| | Burkina Faso | Ouagadougou | 16 968 000 | 62 | 47 | 13 | 53 | 3.4 | 20 |
| | Burundi | Bujumbura | 8 575 000 | 308 | 34 | 14 | 51 | 2.8 | 11 |
| | Cambodia | Phnom Penh | 14 305 000 | 79 | 25 | 8 | 62 | 1.7 | 22 |
| | Cameroon | Yaoundé | 20 030 000 | 42 | 36 | 14 | 51 | 2.2 | 58 |
| | Canada | Ottawa | 34 350 000 | 3 | 12 | 7 | 81 | 1.3 | 81 |
| | Cape Verde | Praia | 501 000 | 124 | 24 | 5 | 71 | 1.4 | 60 |
| | Central African Republic | Bangui | 4 487 000 | 7 | 35 | 17 | 47 | 1.9 | 39 |
| | Chad | Ndjamena | 11 525 000 | 9 | 45 | 17 | 49 | 2.6 | 27 |
| | Chile | Santiago | 17 270 000 | 23 | 15 | 6 | 79 | 1.0 | 89 |
| | China | Beijing (Peking) | 1 332 079 000 | 139 | 12 | 7 | 73 | 0.5 | 44 |
| | Colombia | Bogotá | 46 927 000 | 41 | 20 | 6 | 73 | 1.4 | 75 |
| | Comoros | Moroni | 754 000 | 405 | 32 | 7 | 66 | 2.4 | 28 |
| | Congo | Brazzaville | 4 140 000 | 12 | 34 | 13 | 54 | 1.9 | 62 |
| | Congo, Dem. Rep. of the | Kinshasa | 67 758 000 | 29 | 44 | 17 | 48 | 2.7 | 35 |
| | Costa Rica | San José | 4 727 000 | 93 | 17 | 4 | 79 | 1.3 | 64 |
| | Côte d'Ivoire | Yamoussoukro | 20 153 000 | 63 | 35 | 11 | 58 | 2.3 | 49 |
| | Croatia | Zagreb | 4 396 000 | 78 | 10 | 12 | 76 | 0.0 | 58 |
| | Cuba | Havana | 11 254 000 | 102 | 10 | 7 | 79 | 0.0 | 76 |
| | Cyprus | Nicosia | 1 117 000 | 121 | 12 | 7 | 80 | 1.0 | 70 |
| | Czech Republic | Prague | 10 534 000 | 134 | 11 | 10 | 77 | 0.6 | 74 |
| | Denmark | Copenhagen | 5 573 000 | 129 | 11 | 10 | 79 | 0.6 | 87 |
| | Djibouti | Djibouti | 906 000 | 39 | 28 | 11 | 56 | 1.7 | 88 |
| | Dominica | Roseau | 68 000 | 91 | .. | .. | .. | 0.5 | 74 |

| Land | | Education and Health | | | Development | | Communications | | | Country | Time Zones |
|---|---|---|---|---|---|---|---|---|---|---|---|
| Area sq km | Forest 'ooo sq km 2010 | Adult literacy % 2009 | Doctors per 100 000 population 2009 | Nutrition population under-nourished % 2007 | Energy consumption million tonnes oil equivalent 2008 | GNI per capita US$ 2009 | Telephone lines per 100 population 2010 | Cell phones per 100 population 2010 | Internet users per 100 population 2010 | | + or - GMT |
| 652 225 | 14 | .. | 21 | .. | 0.4 | 310 | 0.5 | 41.4 | 4.0 | Afghanistan | +4½ |
| 28 748 | 8 | 95.9 | 115 | ≤5 | 2.8 | 4 000 | 10.4 | 141.9 | 45.0 | Albania | +1 |
| 2 381 741 | 15 | 72.6 | 121 | ≤5 | 42.7 | 4 420 | 8.2 | 92.4 | 12.5 | Algeria | +1 |
| 465 | <1 | .. | 372 | .. | .. | 41 130 | 45.0 | 77.2 | 81.0 | Andorra | +1 |
| 1 246 700 | 585 | 70.0 | 8 | 41 | 5.0 | 3 750 | 1.6 | 46.7 | 10.0 | Angola | +1 |
| 442 | <1 | 99.0 | .. | 22 | 0.2 | 12 130 | 47.1 | 184.7 | 80.0 | Antigua & Barbuda | -4 |
| 2 766 889 | 294 | 97.7 | 321 | ≤5 | 82.4 | 7 550 | 24.7 | 141.8 | 36.0 | Argentina | -3 |
| 29 800 | 3 | 99.5 | 370 | 22 | 5.4 | 3 100 | 19.1 | 125.0 | 37.0 | Armenia | +4 |
| 7 692 024 | 1 493 | .. | 299 | ≤5 | 143.8 | 43 770 | 38.9 | 101.0 | 76.0 | Australia | +8 to +10½ |
| 83 855 | 39 | .. | 475 | ≤5 | 38.0 | 46 450 | 38.7 | 145.8 | 72.7 | Austria | +1 |
| 86 600 | 9 | 99.5 | 379 | ≤5 | 17.0 | 4 840 | 16.3 | 99.0 | 36.0 | Azerbaijan | +4 |
| 13 939 | 5 | .. | .. | 6 | 1.7 | 21 390 | 37.7 | 124.9 | 43.0 | Bahamas, The | -5 |
| 691 | <1 | 91.4 | 144 | .. | 13.7 | 25 420 | 18.1 | 124.2 | 55.0 | Bahrain | +3 |
| 143 998 | 14 | 55.9 | 30 | 27 | 21.8 | 580 | 0.6 | 46.2 | 3.7 | Bangladesh | +6 |
| 430 | <1 | .. | 181 | ≤5 | 0.5 | .. | 50.3 | 128.1 | 70.2 | Barbados | -4 |
| 207 600 | 86 | 99.7 | 511 | ≤5 | 29.0 | 5 560 | 43.1 | 107.7 | 31.7 | Belarus | +2 |
| 30 520 | 7 | .. | 299 | ≤5 | 72.8 | 45 270 | 43.3 | 113.5 | 79.3 | Belgium | +1 |
| 22 965 | 14 | .. | 83 | ≤5 | 0.4 | 3 740 | 9.7 | 62.3 | 14.0 | Belize | -6 |
| 112 620 | 46 | 41.7 | 6 | 12 | 1.2 | 750 | 1.5 | 79.9 | 3.1 | Benin | +1 |
| 46 620 | 32 | 52.8 | 2 | .. | 1.4 | 2 020 | 3.6 | 54.3 | 13.6 | Bhutan | +6 |
| 1 098 581 | 572 | 90.7 | .. | 27 | 6.3 | 1 630 | 8.5 | 72.3 | 20.0 | Bolivia | -4 |
| 51 130 | 22 | 97.8 | 142 | ≤5 | 7.4 | 4 700 | 26.6 | 80.1 | 52.0 | Bosnia-Herzegovina | +1 |
| 581 370 | 114 | 84.1 | 34 | 25 | 1.6 | 6 260 | 6.9 | 117.8 | 6.0 | Botswana | +2 |
| 8 514 879 | 5 195 | 90.0 | 172 | 6 | 265.7 | 8 070 | 21.6 | 104.1 | 40.7 | Brazil | -2 to -4 |
| 5 765 | 4 | 95.3 | 142 | ≤5 | 4.7 | 27 050 | 20.0 | 109.1 | 50.0 | Brunei | +8 |
| 110 994 | 39 | 98.3 | 364 | 10 | 20.8 | 6 060 | 29.4 | 141.2 | 46.2 | Bulgaria | +2 |
| 274 200 | 56 | 28.7 | 6 | 9 | 0.5 | 510 | 0.9 | 34.7 | 1.4 | Burkina | GMT |
| 27 835 | 2 | 66.6 | 3 | 62 | 0.2 | 150 | 0.4 | 13.7 | 2.1 | Burundi | +2 |
| 181 035 | 101 | 77.6 | 23 | 22 | 1.7 | 650 | 2.5 | 57.7 | 1.3 | Cambodia | +7 |
| 475 442 | 199 | 70.7 | 19 | 21 | 2.5 | 1 190 | 2.5 | 41.6 | 4.0 | Cameroon | +1 |
| 9 984 670 | 3 101 | .. | 191 | ≤5 | 350.7 | 41 980 | 50.0 | 70.7 | 81.6 | Canada | -3½ to -8 |
| 4 033 | 1 | 84.8 | 57 | 10 | 0.1 | 3 010 | 14.5 | 75.0 | 30.0 | Cape Verde | -1 |
| 622 436 | 226 | 55.2 | 8 | 40 | 0.2 | 450 | 0.3 | 23.2 | 2.3 | Central African Republic | +1 |
| 1 284 000 | 115 | 33.6 | 4 | 37 | 0.1 | 600 | 0.5 | 23.3 | 1.7 | Chad | +1 |
| 756 945 | 162 | 98.6 | 128 | ≤5 | 30.4 | 9 470 | 20.2 | 116.0 | 45.0 | Chile | -4 |
| 9 584 492 | 2 069 | 94.0 | 142 | 10 | 2 126.5 | 3 650 | 22.0 | 64.0 | 34.3 | China | +8 |
| 1 141 748 | 605 | 93.2 | 143 | 10 | 34.3 | 4 990 | 14.7 | 93.8 | 36.5 | Colombia | -5 |
| 1 862 | <1 | 74.2 | 15 | 46 | <0.1 | 810 | 2.9 | 22.5 | 5.1 | Comoros | +3 |
| 342 000 | 224 | .. | 10 | 15 | 2.6 | 2 080 | 0.2 | 94.0 | 5.0 | Congo | +1 |
| 2 345 410 | 1 541 | 67.0 | 11 | 69 | 0.9 | 160 | 0.1 | 17.2 | 0.7 | Congo, Dem. Rep. of the | +1 to +2 |
| 51 100 | 26 | 96.1 | .. | ≤5 | 4.9 | 6 260 | 31.8 | 65.1 | 36.5 | Costa Rica | -6 |
| 322 463 | 104 | 55.3 | 14 | 14 | 3.1 | 1 070 | 1.1 | 75.5 | 2.6 | Côte d'Ivoire | GMT |
| 56 538 | 19 | 98.8 | 268 | ≤5 | 10.2 | 13 770 | 42.4 | 144.5 | 60.3 | Croatia | +1 |
| 110 860 | 29 | 99.8 | 640 | ≤5 | 10.4 | 5 550 | 10.3 | 8.9 | 15.1 | Cuba | -5 |
| 9 251 | 2 | 97.9 | 230 | ≤5 | 3.3 | 30 480 | 37.6 | 93.7 | 53.0 | Cyprus | +2 |
| 78 864 | 27 | .. | 363 | ≤5 | 40.4 | 17 310 | 21.0 | 136.6 | 68.8 | Czech Republic | +1 |
| 43 075 | 5 | .. | 342 | ≤5 | 20.9 | 59 060 | 47.3 | 124.4 | 88.7 | Denmark | +1 |
| 23 200 | <1 | .. | 23 | 28 | 0.6 | 1 280 | 2.1 | 18.6 | 6.5 | Djibouti | +3 |
| 750 | <1 | .. | .. | ≤5 | 0.1 | 4 900 | 22.9 | 144.9 | 47.5 | Dominica | -4 |

.. no data available

| Flag | Country | Capital city | Population total 2011 | Density persons per sq km 2011 | Birth rate per 1000 population 2009 | Death rate per 1000 population 2009 | Life expectancy in years 2009 | Population change annual % per annum 2009 | Urban population % 2009 |
|---|---|---|---|---|---|---|---|---|---|
| | Dominican Republic | Santo Domingo | 10 056 000 | 208 | 22 | 6 | 73 | 1.4 | 70 |
| | East Timor | Dili | 1 154 000 | 78 | 40 | 9 | 62 | 3.2 | 28 |
| | Ecuador | Quito | 14 666 000 | 54 | 20 | 5 | 75 | 1.1 | 66 |
| | Egypt | Cairo | 82 537 000 | 82 | 24 | 6 | 70 | 1.8 | 43 |
| | El Salvador | San Salvador | 6 227 000 | 296 | 20 | 7 | 72 | 0.5 | 61 |
| | Equatorial Guinea | Malabo | 720 000 | 26 | 38 | 15 | 51 | 2.6 | 40 |
| | Eritrea | Asmara | 5 415 000 | 46 | 36 | 8 | 60 | 2.9 | 21 |
| | Estonia | Tallinn | 1 341 000 | 30 | 12 | 12 | 75 | 0.0 | 70 |
| | Ethiopia | Addis Ababa | 84 734 000 | 75 | 38 | 12 | 56 | 2.6 | 17 |
| | Fiji | Suva | 868 000 | 47 | 21 | 7 | 69 | 0.6 | 53 |
| | Finland | Helsinki | 5 385 000 | 16 | 11 | 9 | 80 | 0.5 | 64 |
| | France | Paris | 63 126 000 | 116 | 13 | 9 | 81 | 0.5 | 78 |
| | Gabon | Libreville | 1 534 000 | 6 | 27 | 10 | 61 | 1.8 | 86 |
| | Gambia, The | Banjul | 1 776 000 | 157 | 36 | 11 | 56 | 2.7 | 57 |
| | Georgia | T'bilisi | 4 329 000 | 62 | 12 | 12 | 72 | -1.1 | 53 |
| | Germany | Berlin | 82 163 000 | 230 | 8 | 10 | 80 | -0.3 | 74 |
| | Ghana | Accra | 24 966 000 | 105 | 32 | 11 | 57 | 2.1 | 51 |
| | Greece | Athens | 11 390 000 | 86 | 11 | 10 | 80 | 0.4 | 61 |
| | Grenada | St George's | 105 000 | 278 | 20 | 6 | 76 | 0.4 | 31 |
| | Guatemala | Guatemala City | 14 757 000 | 136 | 33 | 6 | 71 | 2.5 | 49 |
| | Guinea | Conakry | 10 222 000 | 42 | 39 | 11 | 58 | 2.4 | 35 |
| | Guinea-Bissau | Bissau | 1 547 000 | 43 | 41 | 17 | 48 | 2.2 | 30 |
| | Guyana | Georgetown | 756 000 | 4 | 17 | 8 | 68 | -0.1 | 28 |
| | Haiti | Port–au–Prince | 10 124 000 | 365 | 27 | 9 | 61 | 1.6 | 48 |
| | Honduras | Tegucigalpa | 7 755 000 | 69 | 27 | 5 | 72 | 2.0 | 48 |
| | Hungary | Budapest | 9 966 000 | 107 | 10 | 13 | 74 | -0.2 | 68 |
| | Iceland | Reykjavík | 324 000 | 3 | 16 | 6 | 82 | 0.5 | 92 |
| | India | New Delhi | 1 241 492 000 | 405 | 23 | 7 | 64 | 1.3 | 30 |
| | Indonesia | Jakarta | 242 326 000 | 126 | 18 | 6 | 71 | 1.1 | 53 |
| | Iran | Tehrān | 74 799 000 | 45 | 19 | 6 | 72 | 1.3 | 69 |
| | Iraq | Baghdād | 32 665 000 | 75 | 31 | 6 | 68 | 2.5 | 67 |
| | Ireland | Dublin | 4 526 000 | 64 | 17 | 7 | 80 | 0.6 | 62 |
| | Israel | [1]Jerusalem | 7 562 000 | 364 | 22 | 5 | 82 | 1.8 | 92 |
| | Italy | Rome | 60 789 000 | 202 | 10 | 10 | 81 | 0.6 | 68 |
| | Jamaica | Kingston | 2 751 000 | 250 | 16 | 7 | 72 | 0.5 | 54 |
| | Japan | Tōkyō | 126 497 000 | 335 | 9 | 9 | 83 | -0.1 | 67 |
| | Jordan | 'Ammān | 6 330 000 | 71 | 25 | 4 | 73 | 2.4 | 79 |
| | Kazakhstan | Astana | 16 207 000 | 6 | 22 | 9 | 68 | 1.4 | 58 |
| | Kenya | Nairobi | 41 610 000 | 71 | 38 | 11 | 55 | 2.6 | 22 |
| | Kiribati | Bairiki | 101 000 | 141 | .. | .. | .. | 1.5 | 44 |
| | Kosovo | Priština | 2 180 686 | 200 | 19 | 7 | 70 | 0.6 | .. |
| | Kuwait | Kuwait | 2 818 000 | 158 | 18 | 2 | 78 | 2.4 | 98 |
| | Kyrgyzstan | Bishkek | 5 393 000 | 27 | 25 | 7 | 67 | 0.8 | 36 |
| | Laos | Vientiane | 6 288 000 | 27 | 27 | 7 | 65 | 1.8 | 32 |
| | Latvia | Rīga | 2 243 000 | 35 | 10 | 13 | 73 | -0.5 | 68 |
| | Lebanon | Beirut | 4 259 000 | 408 | 16 | 7 | 72 | 0.7 | 87 |
| | Lesotho | Maseru | 2 194 000 | 72 | 29 | 17 | 45 | 0.8 | 26 |
| | Liberia | Monrovia | 4 129 000 | 37 | 38 | 10 | 59 | 4.2 | 61 |
| | Libya | Tripoli | 6 423 000 | 4 | 23 | 4 | 75 | 2.0 | 78 |

[1] Jerusalem - not internationally recognised.

| Land | | Education and Health | | | Development | | Communications | | | Country | Time Zones |
|---|---|---|---|---|---|---|---|---|---|---|---|
| Area sq km | Forest 'ooo sq km 2010 | Adult literacy % 2009 | Doctors per 100 000 population 2009 | Nutrition population under-nourished % 2007 | Energy consumption million tonnes oil equivalent 2008 | GNI per capita US$ 2009 | Telephone lines per 100 population 2010 | Cell phones per 100 population 2010 | Internet users per 100 population 2010 | | + or - GMT |
| 48 442 | 20 | 88.2 | .. | 24 | 7.4 | 4 550 | 10.2 | 89.6 | 39.5 | Dominican Republic | -4 |
| 14 874 | 7 | 50.6 | 10 | 31 | 0.1 | 2 460 | 0.2 | 53.4 | 0.2 | East Timor | +9 |
| 272 045 | 99 | 84.2 | .. | 15 | 12.4 | 3 970 | 14.4 | 102.2 | 24.0 | Ecuador | -5 |
| 1 001 450 | 1 | 66.4 | 283 | ≤5 | 79.2 | 2 070 | 11.9 | 87.1 | 26.7 | Egypt | +2 |
| 21 041 | 3 | 84.1 | 160 | 9 | 3.4 | 3 370 | 16.2 | 124.3 | 15.0 | El Salvador | -6 |
| 28 051 | 16 | 93.3 | 30 | .. | 1.5 | 12 420 | 1.9 | 57.0 | 6.0 | Equatorial Guinea | +1 |
| 117 400 | 15 | 66.6 | 5 | 64 | 0.3 | 320 | 1.0 | 3.5 | 5.4 | Eritrea | +3 |
| 45 200 | 22 | 99.8 | 341 | ≤5 | 6.1 | 14 060 | 36.0 | 123.2 | 74.1 | Estonia | +2 |
| 1 133 880 | 123 | 29.8 | 2 | 41 | 3.0 | 330 | 1.1 | 7.9 | 0.8 | Ethiopia | +3 |
| 18 330 | 10 | .. | 45 | ≤5 | 1.0 | 3 840 | 15.9 | 116.2 | 14.8 | Fiji | +12 |
| 338 145 | 222 | .. | 274 | ≤5 | 32.3 | 45 940 | 23.3 | 156.4 | 86.9 | Finland | +2 |
| 543 965 | 160 | .. | 350 | ≤5 | 282.3 | 42 620 | 56.1 | 99.7 | 80.1 | France | +1 |
| 267 667 | 220 | 87.7 | 29 | ≤5 | 1.2 | 7 370 | 2.0 | 106.9 | 7.2 | Gabon | +1 |
| 11 295 | 5 | 46.5 | 4 | 19 | 0.1 | 440 | 2.8 | 85.5 | 9.2 | Gambia, The | GMT |
| 69 700 | 27 | 99.7 | 454 | ≤5 | 4.2 | 2 530 | 13.7 | 73.4 | 27.0 | Georgia | +4 |
| 357 022 | 111 | .. | 353 | ≤5 | 358.9 | 42 450 | 55.4 | 127.0 | 81.9 | Germany | +1 |
| 238 537 | 49 | 66.6 | 9 | ≤5 | 4.1 | 1 190 | 1.1 | 71.5 | 8.6 | Ghana | GMT |
| 131 957 | 39 | 97.2 | 604 | ≤5 | 36.7 | 29 040 | 45.8 | 108.2 | 44.4 | Greece | +2 |
| 378 | <1 | 96.0 | .. | 20 | 0.1 | 5 580 | 27.2 | 116.7 | 33.5 | Grenada | -4 |
| 108 890 | 37 | 74.5 | .. | 21 | 5.2 | 2 650 | 10.4 | 125.6 | 10.5 | Guatemala | -6 |
| 245 857 | 65 | 39.5 | 10 | 17 | 0.6 | 370 | 0.2 | 40.1 | 1.0 | Guinea | GMT |
| 36 125 | 20 | 52.2 | 5 | 22 | 0.2 | 510 | 0.3 | 39.2 | 2.5 | Guinea-Bissau | GMT |
| 214 969 | 152 | .. | .. | 7 | 0.5 | 2 660 | 19.9 | 73.6 | 29.9 | Guyana | -4 |
| 27 750 | 1 | 48.7 | .. | 57 | 0.7 | .. | 0.5 | 40.0 | 8.4 | Haiti | -5 |
| 112 088 | 52 | 83.6 | .. | 12 | 3.3 | 1 800 | 8.8 | 125.1 | 11.1 | Honduras | -6 |
| 93 030 | 20 | 99.4 | 310 | ≤5 | 27.7 | 12 980 | 29.8 | 120.3 | 65.3 | Hungary | +1 |
| 102 820 | <1 | .. | 393 | ≤5 | 6.2 | 43 430 | 63.7 | 108.7 | 95.0 | Iceland | GMT |
| 3 064 898 | 684 | 62.8 | 60 | 21 | 498.9 | 1 220 | 2.9 | 61.4 | 7.5 | India | +5½ |
| 1 919 445 | 944 | 92.2 | 29 | 13 | 145.6 | 2 050 | 15.8 | 91.7 | 9.1 | Indonesia | +7 to +9 |
| 1 648 000 | 111 | 85.0 | 89 | ≤5 | 203.0 | 4 530 | 36.3 | 91.2 | 13.0 | Iran | +3½ |
| 438 317 | 8 | 78.1 | 69 | .. | 34.0 | 2 210 | 5.1 | 75.8 | 5.6 | Iraq | +3 |
| 70 282 | 7 | .. | 319 | ≤5 | 17.2 | 44 280 | 46.5 | 105.2 | 69.9 | Ireland | GMT |
| 20 770 | 2 | .. | 363 | ≤5 | 21.5 | 25 790 | 44.2 | 133.1 | 67.2 | Israel | +2 |
| 301 245 | 91 | 98.9 | 424 | ≤5 | 197.4 | 35 110 | 35.7 | 135.4 | 53.7 | Italy | +1 |
| 10 991 | 3 | 86.4 | 85 | ≤5 | 4.3 | 4 590 | 9.6 | 113.2 | 26.1 | Jamaica | -5 |
| 377 727 | 250 | .. | 206 | ≤5 | 546.7 | 38 080 | 31.9 | 95.4 | 80.0 | Japan | +9 |
| 89 206 | 1 | 92.2 | 245 | ≤5 | 54.2 | 3 980 | 7.8 | 107.0 | 38.0 | Jordan | +2 |
| 2 717 300 | 33 | 99.7 | 380 | ≤5 | .. | 6 920 | 25.0 | 123.3 | 34.0 | Kazakhstan | +5 to +6 |
| 582 646 | 35 | 87.0 | 14 | 31 | 5.2 | 760 | 1.1 | 61.6 | 21.0 | Kenya | +3 |
| 717 | <1 | .. | 30 | ≤5 | <0.1 | 1 830 | 4.1 | 10.0 | 9.0 | Kiribati | +12 to +14 |
| 10 908 | .. | .. | .. | .. | .. | 3 240 | .. | .. | .. | Kosovo | +1 |
| 17 818 | <1 | 93.9 | 179 | ≤5 | 29.8 | 43 930 | 20.7 | 160.8 | 38.3 | Kuwait | +3 |
| 198 500 | 10 | 99.2 | 230 | 10 | 4.6 | 870 | 9.4 | 91.9 | 20.0 | Kyrgyzstan | +6 |
| 236 800 | 158 | 72.7 | 27 | 23 | 1.1 | 880 | 1.7 | 64.6 | 7.0 | Laos | +7 |
| 64 589 | 34 | 99.8 | 299 | ≤5 | 4.1 | 12 390 | 23.6 | 102.4 | 68.4 | Latvia | +2 |
| 10 452 | 1 | 89.6 | 354 | ≤5 | 5.1 | 8 060 | 21.0 | 68.0 | 31.0 | Lebanon | +2 |
| 30 355 | <1 | 89.7 | 5 | 14 | 0.1 | 980 | 1.8 | 32.2 | 3.9 | Lesotho | +2 |
| 111 369 | 43 | 59.1 | 1 | 33 | 0.2 | 160 | 0.2 | 39.3 | 0.1 | Liberia | GMT |
| 1 759 540 | 2 | 88.9 | 190 | ≤5 | 19.6 | 12 020 | 19.3 | 171.5 | 14.0 | Libya | +2 |

no data available

| Flag | Key Information | | Population | | | | | | |
|---|---|---|---|---|---|---|---|---|---|
| | Country | Capital city | Population total 2011 | Density persons per sq km 2011 | Birth rate per 1000 population 2009 | Death rate per 1000 population 2009 | Life expectancy in years 2009 | Population change annual % per annum 2009 | Urban population % 2009 |
| | Liechtenstein | Vaduz | 36 000 | 225 | 11 | 6 | 83 | 0.8 | 14 |
| | Lithuania | Vilnius | 3 307 000 | 51 | 11 | 13 | 73 | -0.6 | 67 |
| | Luxembourg | Luxembourg | 516 000 | 200 | 11 | 7 | 80 | 1.9 | 82 |
| | Macedonia (FYROM)[2] | Skopje | 2 064 000 | 80 | 11 | 9 | 74 | 0.1 | 67 |
| | Madagascar | Antananarivo | 21 315 000 | 36 | 35 | 9 | 61 | 2.7 | 30 |
| | Malawi | Lilongwe | 15 381 000 | 130 | 40 | 12 | 54 | 2.8 | 19 |
| | Malaysia | Kuala Lumpur/Putrajaya | 28 859 000 | 87 | 20 | 5 | 75 | 1.7 | 71 |
| | Maldives | Male | 320 000 | 1 074 | 19 | 5 | 72 | 1.4 | 39 |
| | Mali | Bamako | 15 840 000 | 13 | 42 | 15 | 49 | 2.4 | 33 |
| | Malta | Valletta | 418 000 | 1 323 | 10 | 8 | 80 | 0.7 | 95 |
| | Marshall Islands | Dalap-Uliga-Darrit | 55 000 | 304 | .. | .. | .. | 2.3 | 71 |
| | Mauritania | Nouakchott | 3 542 000 | 3 | 33 | 10 | 57 | 2.3 | 41 |
| | Mauritius | Port Louis | 1 307 000 | 641 | 12 | 7 | 73 | 0.5 | 43 |
| | Mexico | Mexico City | 114 793 000 | 58 | 18 | 5 | 75 | 1.0 | 78 |
| | Micronesia, Fed. States of | Palikir | 112 000 | 160 | 25 | 6 | 69 | 0.3 | 23 |
| | Moldova | Chişinău | 3 545 000 | 105 | 13 | 13 | 69 | -0.8 | 42 |
| | Monaco | Monaco-Ville | 35 000 | 17 500 | .. | .. | .. | 0.3 | 100 |
| | Mongolia | Ulan Bator | 2 800 000 | 2 | 19 | 7 | 67 | 1.1 | 57 |
| | Montenegro | Podgorica | 632 000 | 46 | 12 | 10 | 74 | 0.3 | 60 |
| | Morocco | Rabat | 32 273 000 | 72 | 20 | 6 | 72 | 1.2 | 56 |
| | Mozambique | Maputo | 23 930 000 | 30 | 38 | 16 | 48 | 2.3 | 38 |
| | Myanmar (Burma) | Nay Pyi Taw/Yangôn | 48 337 000 | 71 | 20 | 10 | 62 | 0.9 | 33 |
| | Namibia | Windhoek | 2 324 000 | 3 | 27 | 8 | 62 | 1.9 | 37 |
| | Nauru | Yaren | 10 000 | 476 | .. | .. | .. | .. | .. |
| | Nepal | Kathmandu | 30 486 000 | 207 | 25 | 6 | 67 | 1.8 | 18 |
| | Netherlands | Amsterdam/The Hague | 16 665 000 | 401 | 11 | 8 | 81 | 0.5 | 82 |
| | New Zealand | Wellington | 4 415 000 | 16 | 15 | 7 | 80 | 1.1 | 87 |
| | Nicaragua | Managua | 5 870 000 | 45 | 24 | 5 | 74 | 1.3 | 57 |
| | Niger | Niamey | 16 069 000 | 13 | 53 | 15 | 52 | 3.9 | 17 |
| | Nigeria | Abuja | 162 471 000 | 176 | 39 | 16 | 48 | 2.3 | 49 |
| | North Korea | P'yŏngyang | 24 451 000 | 203 | 14 | 10 | 67 | 0.4 | 63 |
| | Norway | Oslo | 4 925 000 | 15 | 13 | 9 | 81 | 1.2 | 78 |
| | Oman | Muscat | 2 846 000 | 9 | 22 | 3 | 76 | 2.1 | 72 |
| | Pakistan | Islamabad | 176 745 000 | 220 | 30 | 7 | 67 | 2.1 | 37 |
| | Palau | Melekeok | 21 000 | 42 | .. | .. | .. | 0.6 | 82 |
| | Panama | Panama City | 3 571 000 | 46 | 20 | 5 | 76 | 1.6 | 74 |
| | Papua New Guinea | Port Moresby | 7 014 000 | 15 | 31 | 8 | 61 | 2.3 | 13 |
| | Paraguay | Asunción | 6 568 000 | 16 | 24 | 6 | 72 | 1.8 | 61 |
| | Peru | Lima | 29 400 000 | 23 | 21 | 5 | 74 | 1.1 | 72 |
| | Philippines | Manila | 94 852 000 | 316 | 24 | 5 | 72 | 1.8 | 66 |
| | Poland | Warsaw | 38 299 000 | 123 | 11 | 10 | 76 | 0.1 | 61 |
| | Portugal | Lisbon | 10 690 000 | 120 | 9 | 10 | 79 | 0.1 | 60 |
| | Qatar | Doha | 1 870 000 | 164 | 12 | 2 | 76 | 9.6 | 96 |
| | Romania | Bucharest | 21 436 000 | 90 | 10 | 12 | 73 | -0.1 | 54 |
| | Russian Federation | Moscow | 142 836 000 | 8 | 12 | 14 | 69 | -0.1 | 73 |
| | Rwanda | Kigali | 10 943 000 | 416 | 41 | 14 | 51 | 2.8 | 19 |
| | St Kitts & Nevis | Basseterre | 53 000 | 203 | .. | .. | .. | 0.8 | 32 |
| | St Lucia | Castries | 176 000 | 286 | .. | .. | .. | 1.1 | 28 |
| | St Vincent & the Grenadines | Kingstown | 109 000 | 280 | 17 | 7 | 72 | 0.1 | 47 |

[2] FYROM - Former Yugoslav Republic of Macedonia.

| Land | | Education and Health | | | Development | | Communications | | | Country | Time Zones |
|---|---|---|---|---|---|---|---|---|---|---|---|
| Area sq km | Forest 'ooo sq km 2010 | Adult literacy % 2009 | Doctors per 100 000 population 2009 | Nutrition population under-nourished % 2007 | Energy consumption million tonnes oil equivalent 2008 | GNI per capita US$ 2009 | Telephone lines per 100 population 2010 | Cell phones per 100 population 2010 | Internet users per 100 population 2010 | | + or - GMT |
| 160 | <1 | .. | .. | .. | .. | 136 630 | 54.4 | 98.5 | 80.0 | Liechtenstein | +1 |
| 65 200 | 22 | 99.7 | 366 | ≤5 | 9.8 | 11 410 | 22.1 | 147.2 | 62.1 | Lithuania | +2 |
| 2 586 | 1 | .. | 286 | ≤5 | 4.9 | 76 710 | 53.7 | 143.3 | 90.6 | Luxembourg | +1 |
| 25 713 | 10 | 97.1 | 255 | ≤5 | 3.1 | 4 400 | 20.1 | 104.5 | 51.9 | Macedonia (FYROM)[2] | +1 |
| 587 041 | 126 | 64.5 | 16 | 25 | 1.2 | 430 | 0.8 | 39.8 | 1.7 | Madagascar | +3 |
| 118 484 | 32 | 73.7 | 2 | 28 | 0.8 | 290 | 1.1 | 20.4 | 2.3 | Malawi | +2 |
| 332 965 | 205 | 92.5 | 94 | ≤5 | 61.3 | 7 350 | 16.1 | 121.3 | 55.3 | Malaysia | +8 |
| 298 | <1 | 98.4 | 160 | 7 | 0.3 | 3 970 | 15.2 | 156.5 | 28.3 | Maldives | +5 |
| 1 240 140 | 125 | 26.2 | 5 | 12 | 0.3 | 680 | 0.7 | 47.7 | 2.7 | Mali | GMT |
| 316 | .. | 92.4 | 307 | ≤5 | 1.1 | 18 360 | 59.4 | 109.3 | 63.0 | Malta | +1 |
| 181 | <1 | .. | 56 | .. | .. | 3 060 | 8.1 | 7.0 | 3.6 | Marshall Islands | +12 |
| 1 030 700 | 2 | 57.5 | 13 | 7 | 1.0 | 990 | 2.1 | 79.3 | 3.0 | Mauritania | GMT |
| 2 040 | <1 | 87.9 | 106 | ≤5 | 1.6 | 7 250 | 29.8 | 91.7 | 24.9 | Mauritius | +4 |
| 1 972 545 | 648 | 93.4 | 289 | ≤5 | 182.7 | 8 960 | 17.5 | 80.6 | 31.0 | Mexico | -6 to -8 |
| 701 | 1 | .. | 56 | .. | .. | 2 500 | 7.6 | 24.8 | 20.0 | Micronesia, F. S. of | +10 to +11 |
| 33 700 | 4 | 98.5 | 267 | 6 | 3.4 | 1 560 | 32.5 | 88.6 | 40.0 | Moldova | +2 |
| 2 | 0 | .. | .. | .. | .. | 197 590 | 96.4 | 74.3 | 80.0 | Monaco | +1 |
| 1 565 000 | 109 | 97.5 | 276 | 26 | 2.2 | 1 630 | 7.0 | 91.1 | 10.2 | Mongolia | +8 |
| 13 812 | 5 | .. | 199 | .. | .. | 6 650 | 26.8 | 185.3 | 52.0 | Montenegro | +1 |
| 446 550 | 51 | 56.1 | 62 | ≤5 | 14.0 | 2 770 | 11.7 | 100.1 | 49.0 | Morocco | GMT |
| 799 380 | 390 | 55.1 | 3 | 38 | 4.2 | 440 | 0.4 | 30.9 | 4.2 | Mozambique | +2 |
| 676 577 | 318 | 92.0 | 46 | 16 | 6.6 | .. | 1.3 | 1.2 | 0.2 | Myanmar (Burma) | +6½ |
| 824 292 | 73 | 88.5 | 37 | 19 | 1.9 | 4 270 | 6.7 | 67.2 | 6.5 | Namibia | +1 |
| 21 | .. | .. | .. | .. | .. | .. | 0.0 | 60.5 | 6.0 | Nauru | +12 |
| 147 181 | 36 | 59.1 | 21 | 16 | 1.9 | 440 | 2.8 | 30.7 | 6.8 | Nepal | +5¾ |
| 41 526 | 4 | .. | 392 | ≤5 | 103.4 | 48 460 | 43.2 | 116.2 | 90.7 | Netherlands | +1 |
| 270 534 | 83 | .. | 238 | ≤5 | 22.1 | 28 810 | 42.8 | 114.9 | 83.0 | New Zealand | +12 to +12¾ |
| 130 000 | 31 | 78.0 | 37 | 19 | 1.9 | 1 000 | 4.5 | 65.1 | 10.0 | Nicaragua | -6 |
| 1 267 000 | 12 | 28.7 | 2 | 20 | 0.4 | 340 | 0.5 | 24.5 | 0.8 | Niger | +1 |
| 923 768 | 90 | 60.8 | 40 | 6 | 27.2 | 1 190 | 0.7 | 55.1 | 28.4 | Nigeria | +1 |
| 120 538 | 57 | 100.0 | 329 | 33 | 22.1 | .. | 4.9 | 1.8 | 0.0 | North Korea | +9 |
| 323 878 | 101 | .. | 408 | ≤5 | 48.6 | 84 640 | 34.9 | 113.1 | 93.4 | Norway | +1 |
| 309 500 | <1 | 86.6 | 190 | .. | 17.8 | 17 890 | 10.2 | 165.5 | 62.6 | Oman | +4 |
| 803 940 | 17 | 55.5 | 81 | 26 | 62.0 | 1 000 | 2.0 | 59.2 | 16.8 | Pakistan | +5 |
| 497 | <1 | .. | 130 | .. | .. | 6 220 | 34.1 | 70.9 | 27.0 | Palau | +9 |
| 77 082 | 33 | 93.6 | .. | 15 | 6.0 | 6 570 | 15.7 | 184.7 | 42.8 | Panama | -5 |
| 462 840 | 287 | 60.1 | 5 | .. | 1.8 | 1 180 | 1.8 | 27.8 | 1.3 | Papua New Guinea | +10 |
| 406 752 | 176 | 94.6 | .. | 11 | 10.9 | 2 250 | 6.3 | 91.6 | 23.6 | Paraguay | -4 |
| 1 285 216 | 680 | 89.6 | 92 | 15 | 17.4 | 4 200 | 10.9 | 100.1 | 34.3 | Peru | -5 |
| 300 000 | 77 | 95.4 | 115 | 15 | 32.3 | 2 050 | 7.3 | 85.7 | 25.0 | Philippines | +8 |
| 312 683 | 93 | 99.5 | 214 | ≤5 | 97.2 | 12 260 | 24.7 | 120.2 | 62.3 | Poland | +1 |
| 88 940 | 35 | 94.9 | 376 | ≤5 | 26.5 | 21 910 | 42.0 | 142.3 | 51.1 | Portugal | GMT |
| 11 437 | 0 | 94.7 | 276 | .. | 25.1 | .. | 17.0 | 132.4 | 69.0 | Qatar | +3 |
| 237 500 | 66 | 97.7 | 192 | ≤5 | 41.9 | 8 330 | 20.9 | 114.7 | 39.9 | Romania | +2 |
| 7 075 400 | 8 091 | 99.6 | 431 | ≤5 | 760.6 | 9 340 | 31.5 | 166.3 | 43.0 | Russian Federation | +2 to +11 |
| 26 338 | 4 | 70.7 | 2 | 34 | 0.3 | 460 | 0.4 | 33.4 | 7.7 | Rwanda | +2 |
| 261 | <1 | .. | .. | 16 | 0.1 | 10 150 | 39.3 | 161.4 | 32.9 | St Kitts & Nevis | -4 |
| 616 | <1 | .. | .. | 8 | 0.2 | 5 190 | 23.6 | 102.9 | 36.0 | St Lucia | -4 |
| 389 | <1 | .. | .. | ≤5 | 0.1 | 5 130 | 19.9 | 120.5 | 69.6 | St Vincent & the Grenadines | -4 |

no data available

| | Key Information | | Population | | | | | | |
|---|---|---|---|---|---|---|---|---|---|
| Flag | Country | Capital city | Population total 2011 | Density persons per sq km 2011 | Birth rate per 1000 population 2009 | Death rate per 1000 population 2009 | Life expectancy in years 2009 | Population change annual % per annum 2009 | Urban population % 2009 |
| | Samoa | Apia | 184 000 | 65 | 23 | 5 | 72 | 0.0 | 23 |
| | San Marino | San Marino | 32 000 | 525 | 11 | 6 | 83 | 1.3 | 94 |
| | São Tomé & Príncipe | São Tomé | 169 000 | 175 | 32 | 7 | 66 | 1.6 | 61 |
| | Saudi Arabia | Riyadh | 28 083 000 | 13 | 24 | 4 | 73 | 2.3 | 82 |
| | Senegal | Dakar | 12 768 000 | 65 | 38 | 11 | 56 | 2.6 | 43 |
| | Serbia | Belgrade | 7 306 677 | 94 | 10 | 14 | 74 | -0.4 | 52 |
| | Seychelles | Victoria | 87 000 | 191 | 17 | 7 | 74 | 1.2 | 55 |
| | Sierra Leone | Freetown | 5 997 000 | 84 | 40 | 15 | 48 | 2.4 | 38 |
| | Singapore | Singapore | 5 188 000 | 8 119 | 10 | 4 | 81 | 3.0 | 100 |
| | Slovakia | Bratislava | 5 472 000 | 112 | 11 | 10 | 75 | 0.2 | 57 |
| | Slovenia | Ljubljana | 2 035 000 | 101 | 11 | 9 | 79 | 1.1 | 48 |
| | Solomon Islands | Honiara | 552 000 | 20 | 30 | 6 | 67 | 2.4 | 18 |
| | Somalia | Mogadishu | 9 557 000 | 15 | 44 | 16 | 50 | 2.3 | 37 |
| | South Africa, Republic of | Pretoria/Cape Town | 50 460 000 | 41 | 22 | 15 | 52 | 1.1 | 61 |
| | South Korea | Seoul | 48 391 000 | 487 | 10 | 5 | 80 | 0.3 | 82 |
| | South Sudan | Juba | 8 260 490 | 13 | .. | .. | .. | .. | .. |
| | Spain | Madrid | 46 455 000 | 92 | 11 | 8 | 82 | 0.9 | 77 |
| | Sri Lanka | Sri Jayewardenepura Kotte | 21 045 000 | 321 | 19 | 5 | 74 | 0.7 | 15 |
| | Sudan | Khartoum | 36 371 510 | 20 | 31 | 10 | 59 | 2.2 | 44 |
| | Suriname | Paramaribo | 529 000 | 3 | 19 | 8 | 69 | 0.9 | 75 |
| | Swaziland | Mbabane | 1 203 000 | 69 | 30 | 15 | 46 | 1.5 | 25 |
| | Sweden | Stockholm | 9 441 000 | 21 | 12 | 10 | 81 | 0.9 | 85 |
| | Switzerland | Bern | 7 702 000 | 187 | 10 | 8 | 82 | 1.1 | 74 |
| | Syria | Damascus | 20 766 000 | 112 | 28 | 3 | 74 | 2.5 | 55 |
| | Taiwan | T'aipei | 23 164 000 | 640 | .. | .. | .. | .. | .. |
| | Tajikistan | Dushanbe | 6 977 000 | 49 | 28 | 6 | 67 | 1.7 | 27 |
| | Tanzania | Dodoma | 46 218 000 | 49 | 41 | 11 | 56 | 2.9 | 26 |
| | Thailand | Bangkok | 69 519 000 | 136 | 14 | 9 | 69 | 0.6 | 34 |
| | Togo | Lomé | 6 155 000 | 108 | 32 | 8 | 63 | 2.4 | 43 |
| | Tonga | Nuku'alofa | 105 000 | 140 | 27 | 6 | 72 | 0.4 | 25 |
| | Trinidad & Tobago | Port of Spain | 1 346 000 | 262 | 15 | 8 | 70 | 0.4 | 14 |
| | Tunisia | Tunis | 10 594 000 | 65 | 18 | 6 | 75 | 1.0 | 67 |
| | Turkey | Ankara | 73 640 000 | 95 | 18 | 6 | 72 | 1.2 | 69 |
| | Turkmenistan | Ashgabat | 5 105 000 | 11 | 22 | 8 | 65 | 1.3 | 49 |
| | Tuvalu | Vaiaku | 10 000 | 400 | .. | .. | .. | .. | 50 |
| | Uganda | Kampala | 34 509 000 | 143 | 46 | 12 | 53 | 3.3 | 13 |
| | Ukraine | Kiev | 45 190 000 | 75 | 11 | 15 | 69 | -0.5 | 68 |
| | United Arab Emirates | Abu Dhabi | 7 891 000 | 102 | 14 | 2 | 78 | 2.5 | 78 |
| | United Kingdom | London | 62 417 000 | 256 | 13 | 9 | 80 | 0.7 | 90 |
| | United States of America | Washington | 313 085 000 | 32 | 14 | 8 | 79 | 0.9 | 82 |
| | Uruguay | Montevideo | 3 380 000 | 19 | 15 | 9 | 76 | 0.3 | 92 |
| | Uzbekistan | Tashkent | 27 760 000 | 62 | 22 | 5 | 68 | 1.6 | 37 |
| | Vanuatu | Port Vila | 246 000 | 20 | 30 | 5 | 71 | 2.5 | 25 |
| | Vatican City | Vatican City | 800 | 1 600 | .. | .. | .. | .. | .. |
| | Venezuela | Caracas | 29 437 000 | 32 | 21 | 5 | 74 | 1.6 | 94 |
| | Vietnam | Ha Nôi | 88 792 000 | 269 | 17 | 5 | 75 | 1.2 | 28 |
| | Yemen | Şan'ā' | 24 800 000 | 47 | 36 | 7 | 63 | 2.9 | 31 |
| | Zambia | Lusaka | 13 475 000 | 18 | 42 | 17 | 46 | 2.5 | 36 |
| | Zimbabwe | Harare | 12 754 000 | 33 | 30 | 15 | 45 | 0.5 | 38 |

| Land | | Education and Health | | | Development | | Communications | | | Country | Time Zones |
|---|---|---|---|---|---|---|---|---|---|---|---|
| Area sq km | Forest 'ooo sq km 2010 | Adult literacy % 2009 | Doctors per 100 000 population 2009 | Nutrition population under-nourished % 2007 | Energy consumption million tonnes oil equivalent 2008 | GNI per capita US$ 2009 | Telephone lines per 100 population 2010 | Cell phones per 100 population 2010 | Internet users per 100 population 2010 | | + or - GMT |
| 2 831 | 2 | 98.8 | 27 | ≤5 | 0.1 | 2 840 | 19.3 | 91.4 | 7.0 | Samoa | -11 |
| 61 | 0 | .. | .. | .. | .. | 50 670 | 68.8 | 76.1 | 54.2 | San Marino | +1 |
| 964 | <1 | 88.8 | 49 | ≤5 | <0.1 | 1 130 | 4.6 | 62.0 | 18.8 | São Tomé & Príncipe | GMT |
| 2 200 000 | 10 | 86.1 | 94 | ≤5 | 168.2 | 17 210 | 15.2 | 187.9 | 41.0 | Saudi Arabia | +3 |
| 196 720 | 85 | 49.7 | 6 | 17 | 2.2 | 1 040 | 2.8 | 67.1 | 16.0 | Senegal | GMT |
| 77 453 | 27 | .. | 204 | .. | .. | 6 000 | 40.5 | 129.2 | 40.9 | Serbia | +1 |
| 455 | <1 | 91.8 | 151 | 7 | 0.4 | 8 480 | 25.5 | 135.9 | 41.0 | Seychelles | +4 |
| 71 740 | 27 | 40.9 | 2 | 35 | 0.5 | 340 | 0.2 | 34.1 | 0.3 | Sierra Leone | GMT |
| 639 | <1 | 94.7 | 183 | .. | 59.4 | 37 220 | 39.0 | 143.7 | 70.0 | Singapore | +8 |
| 49 035 | 19 | .. | 300 | ≤5 | 20.1 | 16 130 | 20.1 | 108.5 | 79.4 | Slovakia | +1 |
| 20 251 | 13 | 99.7 | 247 | ≤5 | 8.2 | 23 520 | 45.0 | 104.5 | 70.0 | Slovenia | +1 |
| 28 370 | 22 | .. | 19 | 10 | 0.1 | 910 | 1.6 | 5.6 | 5.0 | Solomon Islands | +11 |
| 637 657 | 67 | .. | 4 | .. | 0.3 | .. | 1.1 | 6.9 | 1.2 | Somalia | +3 |
| 1 219 090 | 57 | 88.7 | 77 | ≤5 | 142.9 | 5 760 | 8.4 | 100.5 | 12.3 | South Africa, Republic of | +2 |
| 99 274 | 62 | .. | 197 | ≤5 | 247.2 | 19 830 | 59.2 | 105.4 | 83.7 | South Korea | +9 |
| 644 329 | .. | .. | .. | .. | .. | .. | .. | .. | .. | South Sudan | +3 |
| 504 782 | 182 | 97.7 | 371 | ≤5 | 162.6 | 32 120 | 43.2 | 111.8 | 66.5 | Spain | +1 |
| 65 610 | 19 | 90.6 | 49 | 19 | 5.4 | 1 990 | 17.2 | 83.2 | 12.0 | Sri Lanka | +5½ |
| 1 861 484 | 699 | 70.2 | 28 | 22 | 4.7 | 1 220 | 0.9 | 40.5 | 10.2 | Sudan | +3 |
| 163 820 | 148 | 94.6 | .. | 14 | 0.9 | 4 760 | 16.2 | 169.6 | 31.6 | Suriname | -3 |
| 17 364 | 6 | 86.9 | 16 | 18 | 0.5 | 2 470 | 3.7 | 61.8 | 8.0 | Swaziland | +2 |
| 449 964 | 282 | .. | 358 | ≤5 | 55.5 | 48 840 | 53.5 | 113.5 | 90.0 | Sweden | +1 |
| 41 293 | 12 | .. | 407 | ≤5 | 33.0 | 65 430 | 58.6 | 123.6 | 83.9 | Switzerland | +1 |
| 185 180 | 5 | 84.2 | 150 | ≤5 | 20.9 | 2 410 | 19.9 | 57.3 | 20.7 | Syria | +2 |
| 36 179 | .. | .. | .. | .. | .. | .. | 70.8 | 119.9 | 71.5 | Taiwan | +8 |
| 143 100 | 4 | 99.7 | 201 | 30 | 6.4 | 700 | 5.4 | 86.4 | 11.6 | Tajikistan | +5 |
| 945 087 | 334 | 72.9 | 1 | 34 | 2.9 | 500 | 0.4 | 46.8 | 11.0 | Tanzania | +3 |
| 513 115 | 190 | 93.5 | 30 | 16 | 99.0 | 3 760 | 10.1 | 100.8 | 21.2 | Thailand | +7 |
| 56 785 | 3 | 56.9 | 5 | 30 | 1.0 | 440 | 3.6 | 40.7 | 5.4 | Togo | GMT |
| 748 | <1 | 99.0 | .. | .. | 0.1 | 3 260 | 29.8 | 52.2 | 12.0 | Tonga | +13 |
| 5 130 | 2 | 98.7 | 118 | 11 | 22.2 | 16 700 | 21.9 | 141.2 | 48.5 | Trinidad & Tobago | -4 |
| 164 150 | 10 | 77.6 | 119 | ≤5 | 8.7 | 3 720 | 12.3 | 106.0 | 36.8 | Tunisia | +1 |
| 779 452 | 113 | 90.8 | 164 | ≤5 | 107.6 | 8 720 | 22.3 | 84.9 | 39.8 | Turkey | +2 |
| 488 100 | 41 | 99.6 | 244 | 6 | 24.9 | 3 420 | 10.3 | 63.4 | 2.2 | Turkmenistan | +5 |
| 25 | <1 | .. | 64 | .. | .. | .. | 16.5 | 25.4 | 25.0 | Tuvalu | +12 |
| 241 038 | 30 | .. | 12 | 21 | 1.1 | 460 | 1.0 | 38.4 | 12.5 | Uganda | +3 |
| 603 700 | 97 | 99.7 | 313 | ≤5 | 157.5 | 2 800 | 28.5 | 118.7 | 23.0 | Ukraine | +2 |
| 77 700 | 3 | 90.0 | 193 | ≤5 | 81.4 | ... | 19.7 | 145.5 | 78.0 | United Arab Emirates | +4 |
| 243 609 | 29 | .. | 274 | ≤5 | 233.7 | 41 370 | 53.7 | 130.2 | 85.0 | United Kingdom | GMT |
| 9 826 635 | 3 040 | .. | 267 | ≤5 | 2 485.1 | 46 360 | 48.7 | 89.9 | 79.0 | United States | -5 to -10 |
| 176 215 | 17 | 98.3 | 374 | ≤5 | 4.2 | 9 010 | 28.6 | 131.7 | 43.4 | Uruguay | -3 |
| 447 400 | 33 | 99.3 | 262 | 11 | 58.8 | 1 100 | 6.8 | 76.3 | 20.0 | Uzbekistan | +5 |
| 12 190 | 4 | 82.0 | 12 | 7 | <0.1 | 2 620 | 2.1 | 119.0 | 8.0 | Vanuatu | +11 |
| 0.5 | .. | .. | .. | .. | .. | .. | .. | .. | .. | Vatican City | +1 |
| 912 050 | 463 | 95.2 | .. | 8 | 79.8 | 10 090 | 24.4 | 96.2 | 35.6 | Venezuela | -4½ |
| 329 565 | 138 | 92.8 | 122 | 11 | 40.1 | 1 000 | 18.7 | 175.3 | 27.6 | Vietnam | +7 |
| 527 968 | 5 | 62.4 | 30 | 31 | 7.9 | 1 060 | 4.4 | 46.1 | 10.9 | Yemen | +3 |
| 752 614 | 495 | 70.9 | 6 | 43 | 3.2 | 960 | 0.7 | 37.8 | 6.7 | Zambia | +2 |
| 390 759 | 156 | 91.9 | 16 | 30 | 4.1 | 360 | 3.0 | 59.7 | 11.5 | Zimbabwe | +2 |

no data available

## Using the Dictionary

Geographical terms in the dictionary are arranged alphabetically. **Bold** words in an entry identify key terms which are explained in greater detail within separate entries of their own. Important terms which do not have separate entries are shown in *italic* and are explained in the entry in which they occur.

# A

**abrasion** The wearing away of the landscape by rivers, **glaciers**, the sea or wind, caused by the load of debris that they carry. *See also* **corrasion**.

**abrasion platform** *See* **wave-cut platform**.

**accuracy** A measure of the degree of correctness.

**acid rain** Rain that contains a high concentration of pollutants, notably sulphur and nitrogen oxides. These pollutants are produced from factories, power stations burning **fossil fuels**, and car exhausts. Once in the **atmosphere**, the sulphur and nitrogen oxides combine with moisture to give sulphuric and nitric acids which fall as corrosive rain.

**administrative region** An area in which organizations carry out administrative functions; for example, the regions of local health authorities and water companies, and commercial sales regions.

**adult literacy rate** A percentage measure which shows the proportion of an adult population able to read. It is one of the measures used to assess the level of development of a country.

**aerial photograph** A photograph taken from above the ground. There are two types of aerial photograph – a vertical photograph (or 'bird's-eye view') and an oblique photograph where the camera is held at an angle. Aerial photographs are often taken from aircraft and provide useful information for map-making and surveys. *Compare* **satellite image**.

**afforestation** The conversion of open land to forest; especially, in Britain, the planting of coniferous trees in upland areas for commercial gain. *Compare* **deforestation**.

**agglomerate** A mass of coarse rock fragments or blocks of lava produced during a volcanic eruption.

**agribusiness** Modern **intensive farming** which uses machinery and artificial fertilizers to increase **yield** and output. Thus agriculture resembles an industrial process in which the general running and managing of the farm could parallel that of large-scale industry.

**agriculture** Human management of the **environment** to produce food. The numerous forms of agriculture fall into three groups: **commercial agriculture**, **subsistence agriculture** and **peasant agriculture**. *See also* **agribusiness**.

**aid** The provision of finance, personnel and equipment for furthering economic development and improving standards of living in the **Third World**. Most aid is organized by international institutions (e.g. the United Nations), by charities (e.g. Oxfam) (*see* **non-governmental organizations** (NGOs); or by national governments. Aid to a country from the international institutions

is called *multilateral aid*. Aid from one country to another is called *bilateral aid*.

**air mass** A large body of air with generally the same temperature and moisture conditions throughout. Warm or cold and moist air masses usually develop over large bodies of water (**oceans**). Hot or cold and dry air masses develop over large land areas (**continents**).

**alluvial fan** A cone of **sediment** deposited at an abrupt change of slope; for example, where a post-glacial stream meets the flat floor of a **U-shaped valley**. Alluvial fans are also common in arid regions where streams flowing off **escarpments** may periodically carry large loads of sediment during **flash floods**.

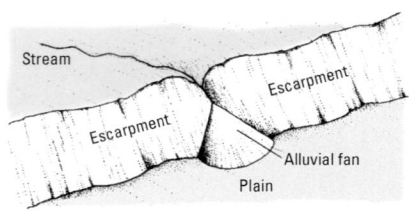

*alluvial fan*

**alluvium** Material deposited by a river in its middle and lower course. Alluvium comprises **silt**, sand and coarser debris eroded from the river's upper course and transported downstream. Alluvium is deposited in a graded sequence: coarsest first (heaviest) and finest last (lightest). Regular floods in the lower course create extensive layers of alluvium which can build up to a considerable depth on the **flood plain**.

**alp** A gentle slope above the steep sides of a glaciated valley, often used for summer grazing. *See also* **transhumance**.

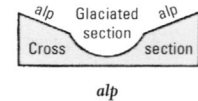

*alp*

**analysis** The examination of the constituent parts of a complex entity.

**anemometer** An instrument for measuring the velocity of the wind. An anemometer should be fixed on a post at least 5 m above ground level. The wind blows the cups around and the speed is read off the dial in km/hr (or knots).

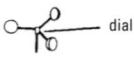

*anemometer*

**annotation** Labels in the form of text or graphics that can be individually selected, positioned or stored in a database.

**antarctic circle** Imaginary line that encircles the South Pole at **latitude** 66° 32'S.

**anthracite** A hard form of **coal** with a high carbon content and few impurities.

**anticline** An arch in folded **strata**; the opposite of **syncline**. *See* **fold**.

**anticyclone** An area of high atmospheric pressure with light winds, clear skies and settled **weather**. In summer, anticyclones are associated with warm and sunny conditions; in winter, they bring frost and fog as well as sunshine.

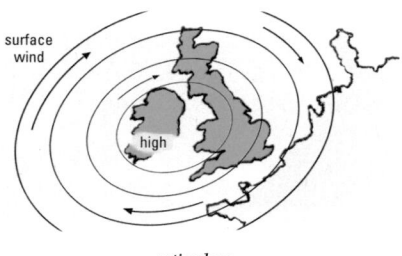

*anticyclone*

**API (application programming interface)** A set of interfaces, methods, procedures and tools used to build or customise a software program.

**aquifer** *See* **artesian basin**.

**arable farming** The production of cereal and root crops – as opposed to the keeping of livestock.

**arc** A coverage feature class representing lines and polygon boundaries.

**archipelago** A group or chain of islands.

**arctic circle** Imaginary line that encircles the North Pole at **latitude** 66° 32'N.

**arête** A knife-edged ridge separating two **corries** in a glaciated upland. The arête is formed by the progressive enlargement of corries by **weathering** and **erosion**. *See also* **pyramidal peak**.

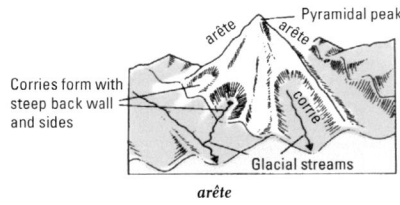

*arête*

**artesian basin** This consists of a shallow **syncline** with a layer of **permeable rock**, e.g. chalk, sandwiched between two impermeable layers, e.g. clay. Where the permeable rock is exposed at the surface, rainwater will enter the rock and the rock will become saturated. This is known as an *aquifer*. Boreholes can be sunk into the structure to tap the water in the aquifer.

**asymmetrical fold** Folded **strata** where the two limbs are at different angles to the horizontal.

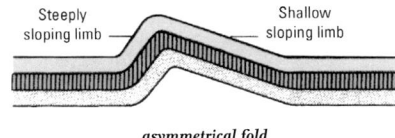

*asymmetrical fold*

**atlas** A collection of maps.

**atmosphere** The air which surrounds the Earth, and consists of three layers: the *troposphere* (6 to 10km from the Earth's surface), the *stratosphere* (50km from the Earth's surface), and the *mesosphere* and *ionosphere*, an ionised region of rarefied gases (1000km from the Earth's surface). The atmosphere comprises oxygen (21%), nitrogen (78%), carbon dioxide, argon, helium and other gases in minute quantities.

**attrition** The process by which a river's load is eroded through particles, such as pebbles and boulders, striking each other.

# B

**backwash** The return movement of seawater off the beach after a wave has broken. *See also* **longshore drift** and **swash**.

**bar graph** A graph on which the values of a certain variable are shown by the length of shaded columns, which are numbered in sequence. *Compare* **histogram**.

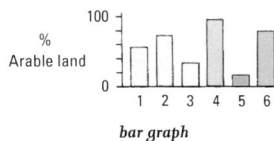

*bar graph*

**barchan** A type of crescent-shaped sand dune formed in desert regions where the wind direction is very constant. Wind blowing round the edges of the dune causes the crescent shape, while the dune may advance in a downwind direction as particles are blown over the crest.

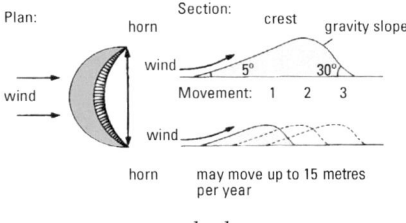

*barchan*

**barograph** An aneroid **barometer** connected to an arm and inked pen which records pressure changes continuously on a rotating drum. The drum usually takes a week to make one rotation.

**barometer** An instrument for measuring atmospheric pressure. There are two types, the *mercury barometer* and the *aneroid barometer*. The mercury barometer consists of a glass tube containing mercury which fluctuates in height as pressure varies. The aneroid barometer is a small metal box from which some of the air has been removed. The box expands and contracts as the air pressure changes. A series of levers joined to a pointer shows pressure on a dial.

**barrage** A type of dam built across a wide stretch of water, e.g. an estuary, for the purposes of water management. Such a dam may be intended to provide water supply, to harness wave energy or to control flooding, etc. There is a large barrage across Cardiff Bay in South Wales.

**basalt** A dark, fine-grained extrusive **igneous rock** formed when **magma** emerges onto the Earth's surface and cools rapidly. A succession of basalt **lava flows** may lead to the formation of a **lava plateau**.

**base flow** The water flowing in a stream which is fed only by **groundwater**. During dry periods it is only the base flow which passes through the stream channel.

**base map** Map on which thematic information can be placed.

**batholith** A large body of igneous material intruded into the Earth's **crust**. As the batholith slowly cools, large-grained **rocks** such as **granite** are formed. Batholiths may eventually be exposed at the Earth's surface by the removal of overlying rocks through **weathering** and **erosion**.

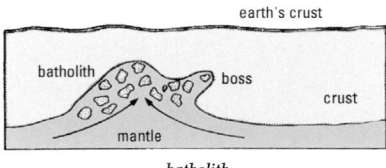

*batholith*

**bay** An indentation in the coastline with a **headland** on either side. Its formation is due to the more rapid **erosion** of softer rocks.

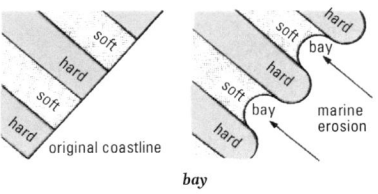

*bay*

**beach** A strip of land sloping gently towards the sea, usually recognized as the area lying between high and low tide marks.

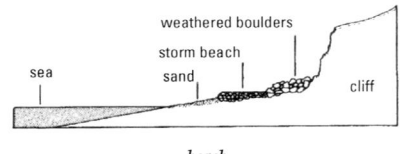

*beach*

**bearing** A compass reading between 0 and 360 degrees, indicating direction of one location from another.

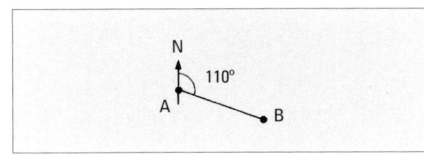

*bearing* *The bearing from A to B is 110°.*

**Beaufort wind scale** An international scale of wind velocities, ranging from 0 (calm) to 12 (hurricane).

**bedrock** The solid rock which usually lies beneath the soil.

**bergschrund** A large **crevasse** located at the rear of a **corrie** icefield in a glaciated region, formed by the weight of the ice in the corrie dragging away from the rear wall as the **glacier** moves downslope. *See* diagram overleaf.

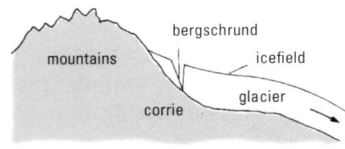

*bergschrund*

**biodiversity** The existence of a wide variety of plant and animal species in their natural environment.

**biogas** The production of methane and carbon dioxide, which can be obtained from plant or crop waste. Biogas is an example of a renewable source of energy (*see* **renewable resources**, **nonrenewable resources**).

**biomass** The total number of living organisms, both plant and animal, in a given area.

**biome** A complex community of plants and animals in a specific physical and climatic region. *See* **climate**.

**biosphere** The part of the Earth which contains living organisms. The biosphere contains a variety of **habitats**, from the highest mountains to the deepest oceans.

**birth rate** The number of live births per 1000 people in a population per year.

**bituminous coal** Sometimes called house coal – a medium-quality **coal** with some impurities; the typical domestic coal. It is also the major fuel source for **thermal power stations**.

**block mountain** *or* **horst** A section of the Earth's **crust** uplifted by faulting. Mt Ruwenzori in the East African Rift System is an example of a block mountain.

**blowhole** A crevice, **joint** or **fault** in coastal rocks, enlarged by marine **erosion**. A blowhole often leads from the rear of a cave (formed by wave action at the foot of a **cliff**) up to the cliff top. As waves break in the cave they erode the roof at the point of weakness and eventually a hole is formed. Air and sometimes spray are forced up the blowhole to erupt at the surface.

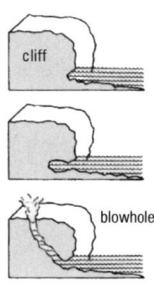

*blowhole*

**bluff** *See* **river cliff**.
**boreal forest** *See* **taiga**.
**boulder clay** *or* **till** The unsorted mass of debris dragged along by a **glacier** as *ground moraine* and dumped as the glacier melts. Boulder clay may be several metres thick and may comprise any combination of finely ground 'rock flour', sand, pebbles or boulders.

**breakwater** *or* **groyne** A wall built at right angles to a beach in order to prevent sand loss due to **longshore drift**.

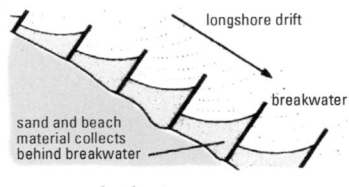

*breakwater or groyne*

**breccia** Rock fragments cemented together by a matrix of finer material; the fragments are angular and unsorted. An example of this is volcanic breccia, which is made up of coarse angular fragments of **lava** and **crust** rocks welded by finer material such as ash and **tuff**.

**buffers** Memory devices for temporarily storing data.

**bush fallowing** *or* **shifting cultivation** A system of **agriculture** in which there are no permanent fields. For example in the **tropical rainforest**, remote societies cultivate forest clearings for one year and then move on. The system functions successfully when forest **regeneration** occurs over a sufficiently long period to allow the soil to regain its fertility.

**bushfire** An uncontrolled fire in forests and grasslands.

**business park** An out-of-town site accommodating offices, high-technology companies and light industry. *Compare* **science park**.

**butte** An outlier of a **mesa** in arid regions.

# C

**cache** A small high-speed memory that improves computer performance.

**caldera** A large crater formed by the collapse of the summit cone of a **volcano** during an eruption. The caldera may contain subsidiary cones built up by subsequent eruptions, or a crater lake if the volcano is extinct or dormant.

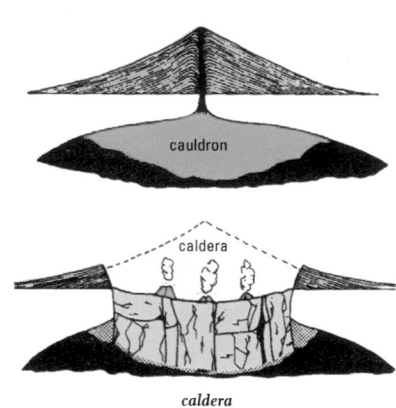

*caldera*

**canal** An artificial waterway, usually connecting existing **rivers**, **lakes** or

oceans, constructed for navigation and transportation.

**canyon** A deep and steep-sided river valley occurring where rapid vertical **corrasion** takes place in arid regions. In such an **environment** the rate of **weathering** of the valley sides is slow. If the **rocks** of the region are relatively soft then the canyon profile becomes even more pronounced. The Grand Canyon of the Colorado River in the USA is the classic example.

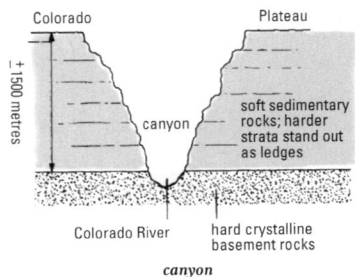

*canyon*

**capital city** Seat of government of a country or political unit.

**cartogram** A map showing statistical data in diagrammatic form.

**cartography** The technique of drawing maps or charts.

**catchment** **1.** In **physical geography**, an alternative term to **river basin**.
**2.** In **human geography**, an area around a town or city – hence 'labour catchment' means the area from which an urban workforce is drawn.

**cavern** In **limestone** country, a large underground cave formed by the dissolving of limestone by subterranean streams. *See also* **stalactite**, **stalagmite**.

**cay** A small low **island** or bank composed of sand and coral fragments. Commonly found in the Caribbean Sea.

**CBD (Central Business District)** This is the central zone of a town or city, and is characterized by high accessibility, high land values and limited space. The visible result of these factors is a concentration of high-rise buildings at the city centre. The CBD is dominated by retail and business functions, both of which require maximum accessibility.

**CFCs (Chlorofluorocarbons)** Chemicals used in the manufacture of some aerosols, the cooling systems of refrigerators and fast-food cartons. These chemicals are harmful to the **ozone** layer.

**chalk** A soft, whitish **sedimentary rock** formed by the accumulation of small fragments of skeletal matter from marine organisms; the rock may be almost pure calcium carbonate. Due to the **permeable** and soluble nature of the rock, there is little surface **drainage** in chalk landscapes.

**channel** *See* **strait**.

**chernozem** A deep, rich soil of the plains of southern Russia. The upper **horizons** are rich in lime and other plant nutrients; in the dry **climate** the predominant movement

of **soil** moisture is upwards (*contrast* with **leaching**), and lime and other chemical nutrients therefore accumulate in the upper part of the **soil profile**.

**chloropleth map** *See* **shading map**.

**choropleth** A symbol or marked area on a map which denotes the distribution of some property.

**cirrus** High, wispy or strand-like, thin **cloud** associated with the advance of a **depression**.

**clay** A soil composed of very small particles of **sediment**, less than 0.002 mm in diameter. Due to the dense packing of these minute particles, clay is almost totally impermeable, i.e. it does not allow water to drain through. Clay soils very rapidly waterlog in wet weather.

**cliff** A steep rockface between land and sea, the profile of which is determined largely by the nature of the coastal rocks. For example, resistant rocks such as **granite** (e.g. at Land's End, England) will produce steep and rugged cliffs.

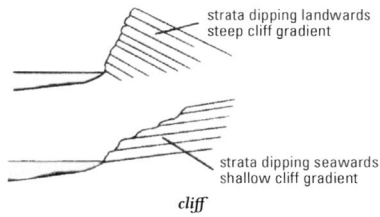
*cliff*

**climate** The average atmospheric conditions prevailing in a region, as distinct from its **weather**. A statement of climate is concerned with long-term trends. Thus the climate of, for example, the Amazon Basin is described as hot and wet all the year round; that of the Mediterranean Region as having hot dry summers and mild wet winters. *See* **extreme climate**, **maritime climate**.

**clint** A block of **limestone**, especially when part of a **limestone pavement**, where the surface is composed of clints and **grykes**.

**cloud** A mass of small water drops or ice crystals formed by the **condensation** of water vapour in the **atmosphere**, usually at a considerable height above the Earth's surface. There are three main types of cloud: **cumulus**, **stratus** and **cirrus**, each of which has many variations.

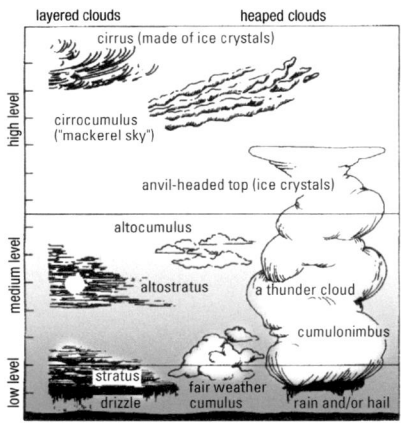
*cloud*

**CMYK** A colour model that combines cyan, magenta, yellow and black to create a range of colours.

**coal** A **sedimentary rock** composed of decayed and compressed vegetative matter. Coal is usually classified according to a scale of hardness and purity ranging from **anthracite** (the hardest), through **bituminous coal** and **lignite** to **peat**.

**cold front** *See* **depression**.

**commercial agriculture** A system of **agriculture** in which food and materials are produced specifically for sale in the market, in contrast to **subsistence agriculture**. Commercial agriculture tends to be capital intensive. *See also* **agribusiness**.

**Common Agricultural Policy (CAP)** The policy of the European Union to support and subsidize certain crops and methods of animal husbandry.

**common land** Land which is not in the ownership of an individual or institution, but which is historically available to any member of the local community.

**communications** The contacts and linkages in an **environment**. For example, roads and railways are communications, as are telephone systems, newspapers, and radio and television.

**commuter zone** An area on or near to the outskirts of an urban area. Commuters are among the most affluent and mobile members of the urban community and can afford the greatest physical separation of home and work.

**concordant coastline** A coastline that is parallel to mountain ranges immediately inland. A rise in sea level or a sinking of the land cause the valleys to be flooded by the sea and the mountains to become a line of islands. *Compare* **discordant coastline**.

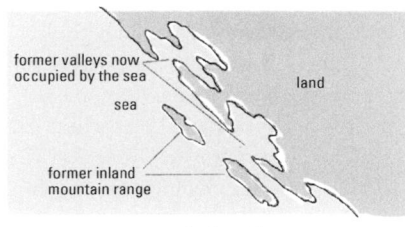
*concordant coastline*

**condensation** The process by which cooling vapour turns into a liquid. **Clouds**, for example, are formed by the condensation of water vapour in the **atmosphere**.

**coniferous forest** A forest of **evergreen** trees such as pine, spruce and fir. Natural coniferous forests occur considerably further north than forests of broad-leaved **deciduous** species, as coniferous trees are able to withstand harsher climatic conditions. The **taiga** areas of the northern hemisphere consist of coniferous forests.

**conservation** The preservation and management of the natural **environment**.

In its strictest form, conservation may mean total protection of endangered species and habitats, as in nature reserves. In some cases, conservation of the man-made environment, e.g. ancient buildings, is undertaken.

**continent** One of the earth's large land masses. The world's continents are generally defined as Asia, Africa, North America, South America, Europe, Oceania and Antarctica.

**continental climate** The climate at the centre of large landmasses, typified by a large annual range in temperature, with precipitation most likely in the summer.

**continental drift** The theory that the Earth's continents move gradually over a layer of semi-molten rock underneath the Earth's **crust**. It is thought that the present-day continents once formed the supercontinent, **Pangaea**, which existed approximately 200 million years ago. *See also* **Gondwanaland**, **Laurasia** *and* **plate tectonics**.

**continental shelf** The seabed bordering the continents, which is covered by shallow water – usually of less than 200 metres. Along some coastlines the continental shelf is so narrow it is almost absent.

**contour** A line drawn on a map to join all places at the same height above sea level.

**conurbation** A continuous built-up urban area formed by the merging of several formerly separate towns or cities. Twentieth-century **urban sprawl** has led to the merging of towns.

**coombe** *See* **dry valley**.

**cooperative** A system whereby individuals pool their **resources** in order to optimize individual gains.

**coordinates** A set of numbers that defines the location of a point with reference to a system of axes.

**core** **1.** In **physical geography**, the core is the innermost zone of the Earth. It is probably solid at the centre, and composed of iron and nickel.
**2.** In **human geography**, a central place or central region, usually the centre of economic and political activity in a region or nation.

**corrasion** The abrasive action of an agent of **erosion** (rivers, ice, the sea) caused by its load. For example the pebbles and boulders carried along by a river wear away the channel bed and the river bank. *Compare* with **hydraulic action**.

**corrie, cirque** *or* **cwm** A bowl-shaped hollow on a mountainside in a glaciated region; the area where a valley **glacier** originates. In glacial times the corrie contained an icefield, which in cross section appears as in diagram *a* overleaf. The shape of the corrie is determined by the rotational erosive force of ice as the glacier moves downslope (diagram *b*). *See* diagrams overleaf.

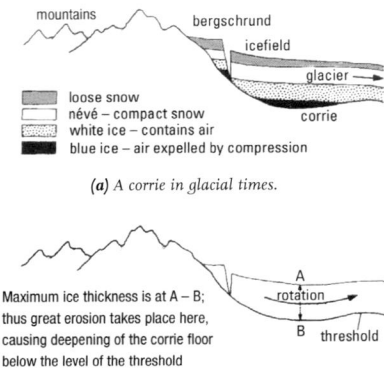

*(a) A corrie in glacial times.*

Maximum ice thickness is at A – B; thus great erosion takes place here, causing deepening of the corrie floor below the level of the threshold

*(b) Erosion of a corrie.*

**corrosion** **Erosion** by solution action, such as the dissolving of **limestone** by running water.

**crag** Rocky outcrop on a valley side formed, for example, when a **truncated spur** exists in a glaciated valley.

**crag and tail** A feature of lowland **glaciation**, where a resistant rock outcrop withstands **erosion** by a **glacier** and remains as a feature after the **Ice Age**. Rocks of volcanic or metamorphic origin are likely to produce such a feature. As the ice advances over the crag, material will be eroded from the face and sides and will be deposited as a mass of boulder clay and debris on the leeward side, thus producing a 'tail'.

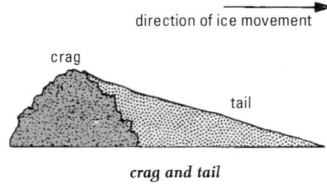

*crag and tail*

**crevasse** A crack or fissure in a **glacier** resulting from the stressing and fracturing of ice at a change in **gradient** or valley shape.

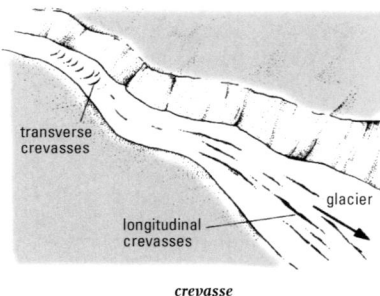

*crevasse*

**cross section** A drawing of a vertical section of a line of ground, deduced from a map. It depicts the **topography** of a system of **contours**.

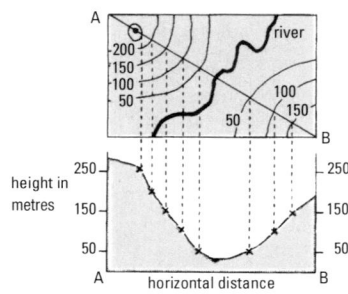

*cross section* Map and corresponding cross section.

**crust** The outermost layer of the Earth, representing only 0.1% of the Earth's total volume. It comprises continental crust and oceanic crust, which differ from each other in age as well as in physical and chemical characteristics. The crust, together with the uppermost layer of the **mantle**, is also known as the *lithosphere*.

**culvert** An artificial drainage channel for transporting water quickly from place to place.

**cumulonimbus** A heavy, dark **cloud** of great vertical height. It is the typical thunderstorm cloud, producing heavy showers of rain, snow or hail. Such clouds form where intense solar radiation causes vigorous convection.

**cumulus** A large **cloud** (smaller than a **cumulonimbus**) with a 'cauliflower' head and almost horizontal base. It is indicative of fair or, at worst, showery **weather** in generally sunny conditions.

**cut-off** *See* **oxbow lake**.

**cyclone** *See* **hurricane**.

# D

**dairying** A **pastoral farming** system in which dairy cows produce milk that is used by itself or used to produce dairy products such as cheese, butter, cream and yoghurt.

**dam** A barrier built across a stream, river or **estuary** to create a body of water.

**data** A series of observations, measurements or facts which can be operated on by a computer programme.

**data capture** Any process for converting information into a form that can be handled by a computer.

**database** A large store of information. A GIS database includes data about spatial locations and shapes of geographical features.

**datum** A single piece of information.

**death rate** The number of deaths per 1000 people in a population per year.

**deciduous woodland** Trees which are generally of broad-leaved rather than **coniferous** habit, and which shed their leaves during the cold season.

**deflation** The removal of loose sand by wind **erosion** in desert regions. It often exposes a bare rock surface beneath.

**deforestation** The practice of clearing trees. Much deforestation is a result of development pressures, e.g. trees are cut down to provide land for agriculture and industry. *Compare* **afforestation**.

**delta** A fan-shaped mass consisting of the deposited load of a river where it enters the sea. A delta only forms where the river deposits material at a faster rate than can be removed by coastal currents. While deltas may take almost any shape and size, three types are generally recognized, as shown in the following diagrams.

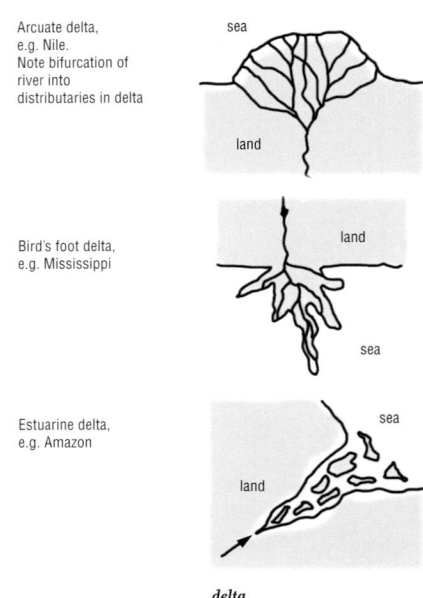

Arcuate delta, e.g. Nile. Note bifurcation of river into distributaries in delta

Bird's foot delta, e.g. Mississippi

Estuarine delta, e.g. Amazon

*delta*

**DEM (Digital elevation model)** Representation of the relief of a topographic surface.

**denudation** The wearing away of the Earth's surface by the processes of **weathering** and **erosion**.

**depopulation** A long-term decrease in the population of any given area, frequently caused by economic migration to other areas.

**deposition** The laying down of **sediments** resulting from **denudation**.

**depression** An area of low atmospheric pressure occurring where warm and cold air masses come into contact. The passage of a depression is marked by thickening cloud, rain, a period of dull and drizzly weather and then clearing skies with showers. A depression develops as in the diagrams on the right.

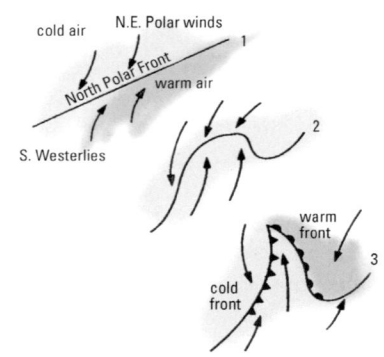

*depression* The development of a depression.

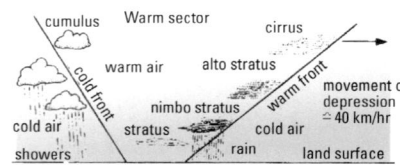

**desert** An area where all forms of **precipitation** are so low that very little, if anything, can grow.

Deserts can be broadly divided into three types, depending upon average temperatures:

(a) *hot deserts:* occur in tropical latitudes in regions of high pressure where air is sinking and therefore making rainfall unlikely. *See* **cloud**.

(b) *temperate deserts:* occur in mid-latitudes in areas of high pressure. They are far inland, so moisture-bearing winds rarely deposit rainfall in these areas.

(c) *cold deserts:* occur in the northern latitudes, again in areas of high pressure. Very low temperatures throughout the year mean the air is unable to hold much moisture.

**desertification** The encroachment of **desert** conditions into areas which were once productive. Desertification can be due partly to climatic change, i.e. a move towards a drier climate in some parts of the world (possibly due to **global warming**), though human activity has also played a part through bad farming practices. The problem is particularly acute along the southern margins of the Sahara desert in the Sahel region between Mali and Mauritania in the west, and Ethiopia and Somalia in the east.

**developing countries** A collective term for those nations in Africa, Asia and Latin America which are undergoing the complex processes of modernization, **industrialization** and **urbanization**. *See also* **Third World**.

**dew point** The temperature at which the **atmosphere**, being cooled, becomes saturated with water vapour. This vapour is then deposited as drops of dew.

**digitising** Translating into a digital format for computer processing.

**dip slope** The gentler of the two slopes on either side of an escarpment crest; the dip slope inclines in the direction of the dipping **strata**; the steep slope in front of the crest is the **scarp slope**.

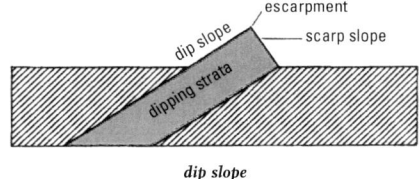
*dip slope*

**discharge** The volume of run-off in the channels of a **river basin**.

**discordant coastline** A coastline that is at right angles to the mountains and valleys immediately inland. A rise in sea level or a sinking of the land will cause the valleys to be flooded. A flooded river valley is known as a **ria**, whilst a flooded glaciated valley is known as a **fjord**. *Compare* **concordant coastline**.

*discordant coastline*

**distributary** An outlet stream which drains from a larger river or stream. Often found in a **delta** area. *Compare* **tributary**.

**doldrums** An equatorial belt of low atmospheric pressure where the **trade winds** converge. Winds are light and variable but the strong upward movement of air caused by this convergence produces frequent thunderstorms and heavy rains.

**domain name** That part of an internet address which identifies a group of computers by country or institution.

**dormitory settlement** A village located beyond the edge of a city but inhabited by residents who work in that city (*see* **commuter zone**).

**drainage** The removal of water from the land surface by processes such as streamflow and infiltration.

**drainage basin** *See* **river basin**.

**drift** Material transported and deposited by glacial action on the Earth's surface. *See also* **boulder clay**.

**drought** A prolonged period where rainfall falls below the requirement for a region.

**dry valley** *or* **coombe** A feature of **limestone** and **chalk** country, where valleys have been eroded in dry landscapes.

**dune** A mound or ridge of drifted sand, occurring on the sea coast and in deserts.

**dyke** **1.** An artificial **drainage** channel. **2.** An artificial bank built to protect low-lying land from flooding. **3.** A vertical or semi-vertical igneous intrusion occurring where a stream of **magma** has extended through a line of weakness in the surrounding **rock**. *See* **igneous rock**.

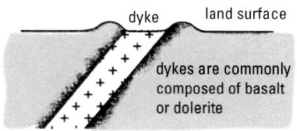
*dyke* Cross section of eroded dyke, showing how metamorphic margins, harder than dyke or surrounding rocks, resist erosion.

# E

**earthquake** A movement or tremor of the Earth's crust. Earthquakes are associated with plate boundaries (*see* **plate tectonics**) and especially with subduction zones, where one plate plunges beneath another. Here the crust is subjected to tremendous stress. The rocks are forced to bend, and eventually the stress is so great that the rocks 'snap' along a **fault** line.

**eastings** The first element of a **grid reference**. *See* **northing**.

**ecology** The study of living things, their interrelationships and their relationships with the **environment**.

**ecosystem** A natural system comprising living organisms and their **environment**. The concept can be applied at the global scale or in the context of a smaller defined environment. The principle of the ecosystem is constant: all elements are intricately linked by flows of energy and nutrients.

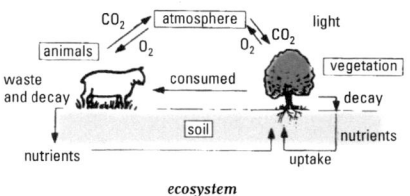
*ecosystem*

**El Niño** The occasional development of warm ocean surface waters along the coast of Ecuador and Peru. Where this warming occurs the tropical Pacific trade winds weaken and the usual up-welling of cold, deep ocean water is reduced. El Niño normally occurs late in the calendar year and lasts for a few weeks to a few months and can have a dramatic impact on weather patterns throughout the world.

**emigration** The movement of population out of a given area or country.

**employment structure** The distribution of the workforce between the **primary**, **secondary**, **tertiary** and **quaternary sectors** of the economy. Primary employment is in **agriculture**, mining, forestry and fishing; secondary in manufacturing; tertiary in the retail, service and administration category; quaternary in information and expertise.

**environment** Physical surroundings: **soil**, vegetation, wildlife and the **atmosphere**.

**equator** The great circle of the Earth with a **latitude** of 0°, lying equidistant from the poles.

**erosion** The wearing away of the Earth's surface by running water (rivers and streams), moving ice (**glaciers**), the sea and the wind. These are called the *agents* of erosion.

**erratic** A boulder of a certain rock type resting on a surface of different geology. For example, blocks of **granite** resting on a surface of carboniferous **limestone**.

**escarpment** A ridge of high ground as, for example, the **chalk** escarpments of southern England (the Downs and the Chilterns).

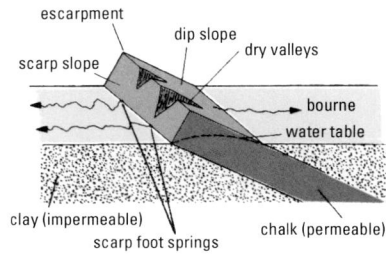
*escarpment*

**esker** A low, winding ridge of pebbles and finer **sediment** on a glaciated lowland.

**estuary** The broad mouth of a river where it enters the sea. An estuary forms where opposite conditions to those favourable for **delta** formation exist: deep water offshore, strong marine currents and a smaller **sediment** load.

**ethnic group** A group of people with a common identity such as culture, religion or skin colour.

**evaporation** The process whereby a substance changes from a liquid to a vapour. Heat from the sun evaporates water from seas, lakes, rivers, etc., and this process produces water vapour in the **atmosphere**.

**evergreen** A vegetation type in which leaves are continuously present. *Compare* **deciduous woodland**.

**exfoliation** A form of **weathering** whereby the outer layers of a **rock** or boulder shear off due to the alternate expansion and contraction produced by diurnal heating and cooling. Such a process is especially active in **desert** regions.

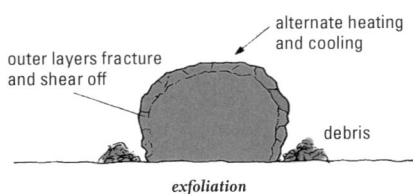

*exfoliation*

**exports** Goods and services sold to a foreign country (*compare* **imports**).

**extensive farming** A system of **agriculture** in which relatively small amounts of capital or labour investment are applied to relatively large areas of land. For example, sheep ranching is an extensive form of farming, and yields per unit area are low.

**external processes** Landscape-forming processes such as **weather** and **erosion**, in contrast to internal processes.

**extreme climate** A climate that is characterized by large ranges of temperature and sometimes of rainfall. *Compare* **temperate climate**, **maritime climate**.

# F

**fault** A fracture in the Earth's crust on either side of which the **rocks** have been relatively displaced. Faulting occurs in response to stress in the Earth's crust; the release of this stress in fault movement is experienced as an **earthquake**. *See also* **rift valley**.

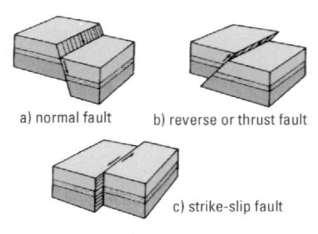

a) normal fault  b) reverse or thrust fault

c) strike-slip fault

*fault The main types.*

**feature class** A collection of features with the same properties, attributes and spatial reference.

**fell** Upland rough grazing in a **hill farming** system, for example in the English Lake District.

**fjord** A deep, generally straight inlet of the sea along a glaciated coast. A fjord is a glaciated valley which has been submerged either by a post-glacial rise in sea level or a subsidence of the land.

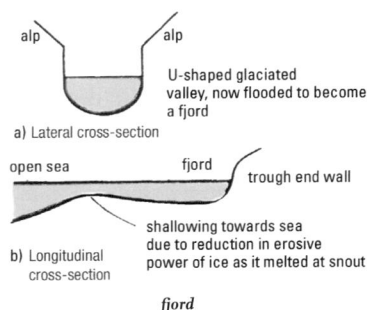

alp  alp

U-shaped glaciated valley, now flooded to become a fjord

a) Lateral cross-section

open sea  fjord  trough end wall

shallowing towards sea due to reduction in erosive power of ice as it melted at snout

b) Longitudinal cross-section

*fjord*

**flash flood** A sudden increase in river **discharge** and overland flow due to a violent rainstorm in the upper **river basin**.

**flood plain** The broad, flat valley floor of the lower course of a river, levelled by annual flooding and by the lateral and downstream movement of **meanders**.

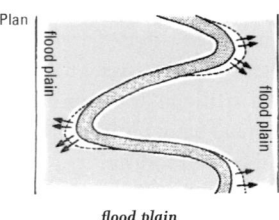

Plan

flood plain

flood plain

*flood plain*

**flow line** A diagram showing volumes of movement, e.g. of people, goods or information between places. The width of the flow line is proportional to the amount of movement, for example in portraying commuter flows into an urban centre from surrounding towns and villages.

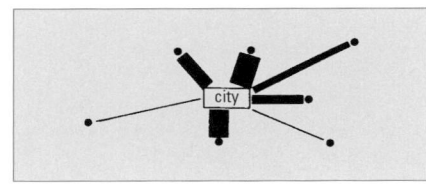

city

***Flow line*** *Commuter flows into a city.*

**fodder crop** A crop grown for animal feed.

**fold** A bending or buckling of once horizontal rock **strata**. Many folds are the result of rocks being crumpled at plate boundaries (*see* **plate tectonics**), though **earthquakes** can also cause rocks to fold, as can igneous **intrusions**.

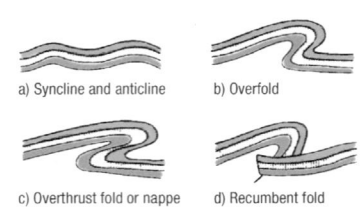

a) Syncline and anticline  b) Overfold

c) Overthrust fold or nappe  d) Recumbent fold

*fold*

**fold mountains** Mountains which have been formed by large-scale and complex folding. Studies of typical fold mountains (the Himalayas, Andes, Alps and Rockies) indicate that folding has taken place deep inside the Earth's **crust** and upper **mantle** as well as in the upper layers of the crust.

**fossil fuel** Any naturally occurring carbon or hydrocarbon fuel, notably coal, oil, peat and natural gas. These fuels have been formed by decomposed prehistoric organisms.

**free trade** The movement of goods and services between countries without any restrictions (such as quotas, tariffs or taxation) being imposed.

**freeze-thaw** A type of physical **weathering** whereby **rocks** are denuded by the freezing of water in cracks and crevices on the rock face. Water expands on freezing, and this process causes stress and fracture along any line of weakness in the rock. **Nivation** debris accumulates at the bottom of a rock face as **scree**.

**front** A boundary between two air masses. *See also* **depression**.

# G

**gazetteer** A list of place names with their geographical coordinates.

**GDP** *See* **Gross Domestic Product**.

**geosyncline** A basin (a large **syncline**) in which thick marine sediments have accumulated.

**geothermal energy** A method of producing power from heat contained in the lower layers of the Earth's **crust**. New Zealand and Iceland both use superheated water or steam from geysers and volcanic **springs** to heat buildings and for hothouse cultivation and also to drive steam turbines to generate electricity. Geothermal energy is an example of a renewable resource of energy (*see* **renewable resources**, **nonrenewable resources**).

**glaciation** A period of cold **climate** during which time **ice sheets** and **glaciers** are the dominant forces of **denudation**.

**glacier** A body of ice occupying a valley and originating in a **corrie** or icefield. A glacier moves at a rate of several metres per day, the precise speed depending upon climatic and **topographic** conditions in the area in question.

**global warming** *or* **greenhouse effect** The warming of the Earth's atmosphere caused by an excess of carbon dioxide, which acts like a blanket, preventing the natural escape of heat. This situation has been developing over the last 150 years because of (a) the burning of **fossil fuels**, which releases vast amounts of carbon dioxide into the **atmosphere**, and (b) **deforestation**, which results in fewer trees

being available to take up carbon dioxide (*see* **photosynthesis**).

**globalization** The process that enables financial markets and companies to operate internationally (as a result of deregulation and improved communications). **Transnational corporations** now locate their manufacturing in places that best serve their global market at the lowest cost.

**GNI (gross national income)** *formerly* **GNP (gross national product)** The total value of the goods and services produced annually by a nation, plus net property income from abroad.

**Gondwanaland** The southern-hemisphere super-continent, consisting of the present South America, Africa, India, Australasia and Antarctica, which split from **Pangaea** *c.*200 million years ago. Gondwanaland is part of the theory of **continental drift**. *See also* **plate tectonics**.

**GPS (global positioning system)** A system of earth-orbiting satellites, transmitting signals continuously towards earth, which enable the position of a receiving device on the earth's surface to be accurately estimated from the difference in arrival of the signals.

**gradient** **1.** The measure of steepness of a line or slope. In mapwork, the average gradient between two points can be calculated as:

$$\frac{\textit{difference in altitude}}{\textit{distance apart}}$$

**2.** The measure of change in a property such as density. In **human geography** gradients are found in, for example, **population density**, land values and **settlement** ranking.

**granite** An **igneous rock** having large crystals due to slow cooling at depth in the Earth's **crust**.

**green belt** An area of land, usually around the outskirts of a town or city on which building and other developments are restricted by legislation.

**greenfield site** A development site for industry, retailing or housing that has previously been used only for agriculture or recreation. Such sites are frequently in the **green belt**.

**greenhouse effect** *See* **global warming**.

**Greenwich Meridian** *See* **prime meridian**.

**grid reference** A method for specifying position on a map. *See* **eastings** and **northings**.

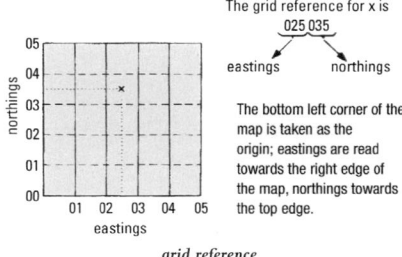

*grid reference*

**Gross Domestic Product (GDP)** The total value of all goods and services produced domestically by a nation during a year. It is equivalent to **Gross National Income (GNI)** minus investment incomes from foreign nations.

**groundwater** Water held in the bedrock of a region, having percolated through the **soil** from the surface. Such water is an important **resource** in areas where **surface run-off** is limited or absent.

**groyne** *See* **breakwater**.

**gryke** An enlarged joint between blocks of **limestone** (**clints**), especially in a **limestone pavement**.

**gulf** A large coastal indentation, similar to a **bay** but larger in extent. Commonly formed as a result of rising sea levels.

# H

**habitat** A preferred location for particular species of plants and animals to live and reproduce.

**hanging valley** A tributary valley entering a main valley at a much higher level because of deepening of the main valley, especially by glacial erosion.

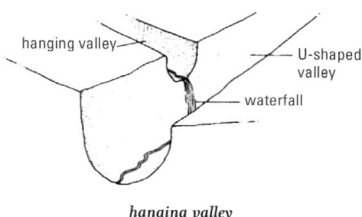

*hanging valley*

**HDI (human development index)** A measurement of a country's achievements in three areas: longevity, knowledge and standard of living. Longevity is measured by life expectancy at birth; knowledge is measured by a combination of the adult literacy rate and the combined gross primary, secondary and tertiary school enrolment ratio; standard of living is measured by **GDP** per capita.

**headland** A promontory of resistant **rock** along the coastline. *See* **bay**.

**hemisphere** Any half of a globe or sphere. The earth has traditionally been divided into hemispheres by the **equator** (northern and southern hemispheres) and by the **prime meridian** and **International Date Line** (eastern and western hemispheres).

**hill farming** A system of **agriculture** where sheep (and to a lesser extent cattle) are grazed on upland rough pasture.

**hill shading** Shadows drawn on a map to create a 3-dimensional effect and a sense of visual relief.

**histogram** A graph for showing values of classed data as the areas of bars.

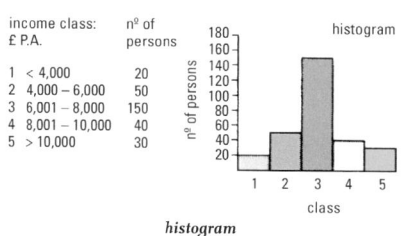

*histogram*

**horizon** The distinct layers found in the **soil profile**. Usually three horizons are identified – A, B and C, as in the diagram below.

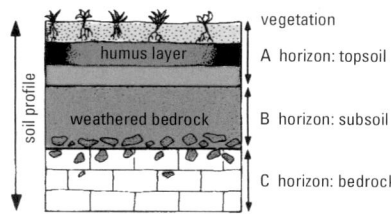

*horizon A typical soil profile.*

**horst** *See* **block mountain**.

**horticulture** The growing of plants and flowers for commercial sale. It is now an international trade, for example, orchids are grown in Southeast Asia for sale in Europe.

**human geography** The study of people and their activities in terms of patterns and processes of population, **settlement**, economic activity and **communications**. *Compare* **physical geography**.

**hunter/gatherer economy** A pre-agricultural phase of development in which people survive by hunting and gathering the animal and plant **resources** of the natural **environment**. No cultivation or herding is involved.

**hurricane, cyclone** *or* **typhoon** A wind of force 12 on the **Beaufort wind scale**, i.e. one having a velocity of more than 118 km per hour. Hurricanes can cause great damage by wind as well as from the storm waves and floods that accompany them.

**hydraulic action** The erosive force of water alone, as distinct from **corrasion**. A river or the sea will erode partially by the sheer force of moving water and this is termed 'hydraulic action'.

**hydroelectric power** The generation of electricity by turbines driven by flowing water. Hydroelectricity is most efficiently generated in rugged **topography** where a head of water can most easily be created, or on a large river where a dam can create similar conditions. Whatever the location, the principle remains the same – that water descending via conduits from an upper storage area passes through turbines and thus creates electricity.

**hydrological cycle** The cycling of water through sea, land and **atmosphere**. *See* diagram overleaf.

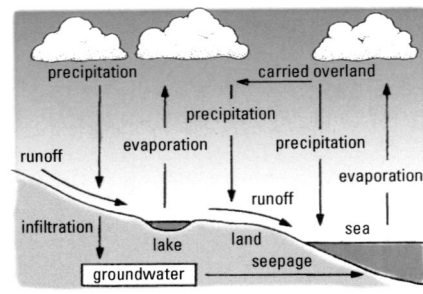

*hydrological cycle*

**hydrosphere** All the water on Earth, including that present in the **atmosphere** as well as in oceans, seas, **ice sheets**, etc.

**hygrometer** An instrument for measuring the relative humidity of the **atmosphere**. It comprises two thermometers, one of which is kept moist by a wick inserted in a water reservoir. Evaporation from the wick reduces the temperature of the 'wet bulb' thermometer, and the difference between the dry and the wet bulb temperatures is used to calculate relative humidity from standard tables.

# I

**Ice Age** A period of **glaciation** in which a cooling of **climate** leads to the development of **ice sheets**, **ice caps** and valley **glaciers**.

**ice cap** A covering of permanent ice over a relatively small land mass, e.g. Iceland.

**ice sheet** A covering of permanent ice over a substantial continental area such as Antarctica.

**iceberg** A large mass of ice which has broken off an **ice sheet** or **glacier** and left floating in the sea.

**ID (Identifier)** A unique value given to a particular object.

**igneous rock** A **rock** which originated as **magma** (molten rock) at depth in or below the Earth's **crust**. Igneous rocks are generally classified according to crystal size, colour and mineral composition. *See also* **plutonic rock.**

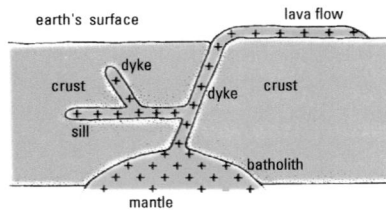

*igneous rock*

**immigration** The movement of people into a country or region from other countries or regions.

**impermeable rock** A rock that is non-porous and therefore incapable of taking in water or of allowing it to pass through between the grains. *Compare* **impervious rock**. *See also* **permeable rock.**

**impervious rock** A non-porous rock with no cracks or fissures through which water might pass.

**imports** Goods or services bought into one country from another (*compare* **exports**).

**industrialization** The development of industry on an extensive scale.

**infiltration** The gradual movement of water into the ground.

**infrastructure** The basic structure of an organization or system. The infrastructure of a city includes, for example, its roads and railways, schools, factories, power and water supplies and drainage systems.

**inner city** The ring of buildings around the **Central Business District (CBD)** of a town or city.

**intensive farming** A system of **agriculture** where relatively large amounts of capital and/or labour are invested on relatively small areas of land.

**interglacial** A warm period between two periods of **glaciation** and cold **climate**. The present interglacial began about 10,000 years ago.

**interlocking spurs** Obstacles of hard **rock** round which a river twists and turns in a V-shaped valley. **Erosion** is pronounced on the concave banks, and this ultimately causes the development of spurs which alternate on either side of the river and interlock as shown in the diagram top right.

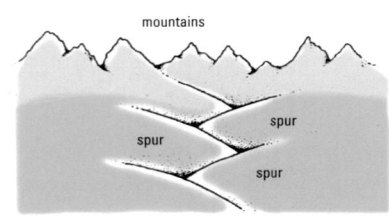

**interlocking spurs** *A V-shaped valley with interlocking spurs.*

**International Date Line** An imaginary line which approximately follows 180° **longitude**. The area of the world just east of the line is one day ahead of the area just west of the line.

**international trade** The exchange of goods and services between countries.

**intrusion** A body of **igneous rock** injected into the Earth's **crust** from the **mantle** below. *See* **dyke**, **sill**, **batholith**.

**ionosphere** *See* **atmosphere**.

**irrigation** A system of artificial watering of the land in order to grow crops. Irrigation is particularly important in areas of low or unreliable rainfall.

**island** A mass of land, smaller than a continent, which is completely surrounded by water.

**isobar** A line joining points of equal atmospheric pressure, as on the meteorological map below.

**isohyet** A line on a meteorological map joining places of equal rainfall.

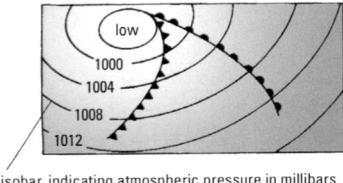

*isobar, indicating atmospheric pressure in millibars*

*isobar*

**isotherm** A line on a meteorological map joining places of equal temperature.

# J

**joint** A vertical or semi-vertical fissure in a **sedimentary rock**, contrasted with roughly horizontal bedding planes. In **igneous rocks** jointing may occur as a result of contraction on cooling from the molten state. Joints should be distinguished from **faults** in that they are on a much smaller scale and there is no relative displacement of the rocks on either side of the joint. Joints, being lines of weakness are exploited by **weathering**.

# K

**kame** A short ridge of sand and gravel deposited from the water of a melted glacier.

**karst topography** An area of **limestone** scenery where **drainage** is predominantly subterranean.

**kettle hole** A small depression or hollow in a glacial outwash plain, formed when a block of ice embedded in the outwash deposits eventually melts, causing the **sediment** above to subside.

# L

**laccolith** An igneous **intrusion**, domed and often of considerable dimensions, caused where a body of viscous **magma** has been intruded into the **strata** of the Earth's **crust**. These strata are buckled upwards over the laccolith.

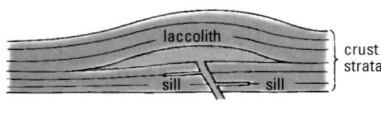

*laccolith*

**lagoon** **1.** An area of sheltered coastal water behind a bay bar or **tombolo**. **2.** The calm water behind a coral reef.

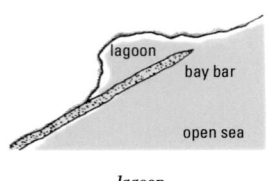

*lagoon*

**lahar** A landslide of volcanic debris mixed with water down the sides of a volcano,

caused either by heavy rain or the heat of the volcano melting snow and ice.

**lake** A body of water completely surrounded by land.

**land tenure** A system of land ownership or allocation.

**land use** The function of an area of land. For example, the land use in rural areas could be farming or forestry, whereas urban land use could be housing or industry.

**landform** Any natural feature of the Earth's surface, such as mountains or valleys.

**laterite** A hard (literally 'brick-like') soil in tropical regions caused by the baking of the upper **horizons** by exposure to the sun.

**latitude** Distance north or south of the equator, as measured by degrees of the angle at the Earth's centre:

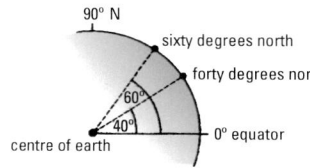

*latitude*

**Laurasia** The northern hemisphere supercontinent, consisting of the present North America, Europe and Asia (excluding India), which split from **Pangaea** *c.* 200 million years ago. Laurasia is part of the theory of **continental drift**. *See also* **plate tectonics**.

**lava** **Magma** extruded onto the Earth's surface via some form of volcanic eruption. Lava varies in viscosity (*see* **viscous lava**), colour and chemical composition. Acidic lavas tend to be viscous and flow slowly; basic lavas tend to be nonviscous and flow quickly. Commonly, **lava flows** comprise basaltic material, as for example in the process of sea-floor spreading (*see* **plate tectonics**).

**lava flow** A stream of **lava** issuing from some form of volcanic eruption. *See also* **viscous lava**.

**lava plateau** A relatively flat upland composed of layer upon layer of approximately horizontally bedded lavas. An example of this is the Deccan Plateau of India.

**leaching** The process by which soluble substances such as mineral salts are washed out of the upper soil layer into the lower layer by rain water.

**levée** The bank of a river, raised above the general level of the **flood plain** by **sediment** deposition during flooding. When the river bursts its banks, relatively coarse sediment is deposited first, and recurrent flooding builds up the river's banks accordingly.

**lignite** A soft form of **coal**, harder than **peat** but softer than **bituminous coal**.

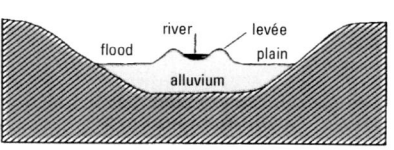

*levée*

**limestone** Calcium-rich **sedimentary rock** formed by the accumulation of the skeletal matter of marine organisms.

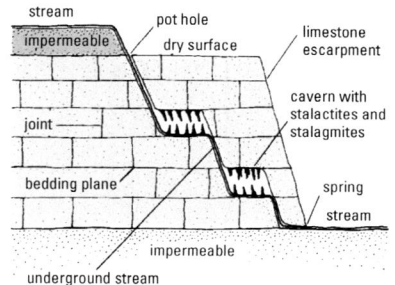

*limestone*

**limestone pavement** An exposed **limestone** surface on which the joints have been enlarged by the action of rainwater dissolving the limestone to form weak carbonic acid. These enlarged joints, or **grykes**, separate roughly rectangular blocks of limestone called **clints**.

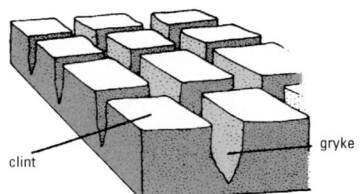

*limestone pavement*

**location** The position of population, settlement and economic activity in an area or areas. Location is a basic theme in **human geography**.

**loess** A very fine **silt** deposit, often of considerable thickness, transported by the wind prior to **deposition**. When irrigated, loess can be very fertile and, consequently, high **yields** can be obtained from crops grown on loess deposits.

**longitude** A measure of distance on the Earth's surface east or west of the Greenwich Meridian, an imaginary line running from pole to pole through Greenwich in London. Longitude, like **latitude**, is measured in degrees of an angle taken from the centre of the Earth.

The precise location of a place can be given by a **grid reference** comprising longitude and latitude. *See also* **map projection**, **prime meridian**.

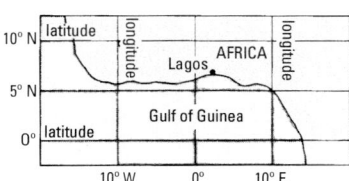

*longitude* A grid showing the location of Lagos, Nigeria.

**longshore drift** The net movement of material along a beach due to the oblique approach of waves to the shore. Beach deposits move in a zig-zag fashion, as shown in the diagram. Longshore drift is especially active on long, straight coastlines.

As waves approach, sand is carried up the beach by the **swash**, and retreats back down the beach with the **backwash**. Thus a single representative grain of sand will migrate in the pattern A, B, C, D, E, F in the diagram.

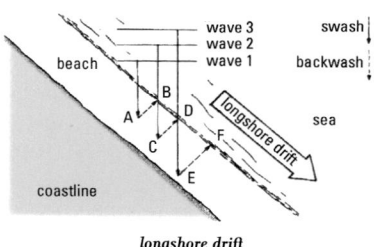

*longshore drift*

# M

**magma** Molten rock originating in the Earth's **mantle**; it is the source of all **igneous rocks**.

**malnutrition** The condition of being poorly nourished, as contrasted with **undernutrition**, which is lack of a sufficient quantity of food. The diet of a malnourished person may be high in starchy foods but is invariably low in protein and essential minerals and vitamins.

**mantle** The largest of the concentric zones of the Earth's structure, overlying the **core** and surrounded in turn by the **crust**.

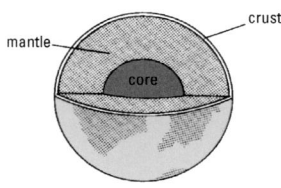

*mantle*

**manufacturing industry** The making of articles using physical labour or machinery, especially on a large scale. *See* **secondary sector**.

**map** Diagrammatic representation of an area – for example part of the earth's surface.

**map projection** A method by which the curved surface of the Earth is shown on a flat surface map. As it is not possible to show all the Earth's features accurately on a flat surface, some projections aim to show direction accurately at the expense of area, some the shape of the land and oceans, while others show correct area at the expense of accurate shape.

One of the projections most commonly used is the *Mercator projection*, devised in 1569, in which all lines of **latitude** are the same length as the equator. This results in increased distortion of area, moving from the equator towards the poles. This projection is suitable for navigation charts.

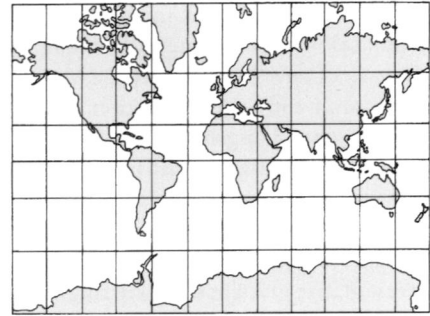

***map projection*** *Mercator projection.*

The *Mollweide projection* shows the land masses the correct size in relation to each other but there is distortion of shape. As the Mollweide projection has no area distortion it is useful for showing distributions such as population distribution.

The only true representation of the Earth's surface is a globe.

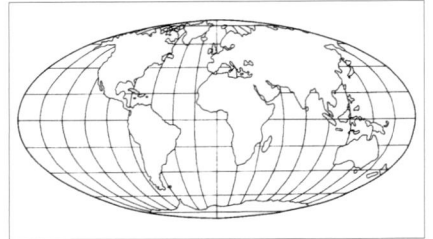

***map projection*** *Mollweide projection.*

**marble** A whitish, crystalline **metamorphic rock** produced when **limestone** is subjected to great heat or pressure (or both) during Earth movements.

**maritime climate** A **temperate climate** that is affected by the closeness of the sea, giving a small annual range of temperatures – a coolish summer and a mild winter – and rainfall throughout the year. Britain has a maritime climate. *Compare* **extreme climate**.

**market gardening** An intensive type of **agriculture** traditionally located on the margins of urban areas to supply fresh produce on a daily basis to the city population. Typical market-garden produce includes salad crops, such as tomatoes, lettuce, cucumber, etc., cut flowers, fruit and some green vegetables.

**mask** A method of hiding features on a map to improve legibility.

**maximum and minimum thermometer** An instrument for recording the highest and lowest temperatures over a 24-hour period.

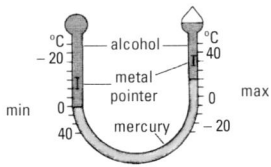

***maximum and minimum thermometer***

**meander** A large bend, especially in the middle or lower stages of a river's course. *See* **flood plain**. A meander is the result

of lateral **corrasion**, which becomes dominant over vertical corrasion as the **gradient** of the river's course decreases. The characteristic features of a meander are summarized in the diagrams below. *See also* **oxbow lake**.

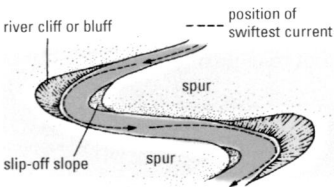

***meander*** *A river meander.*

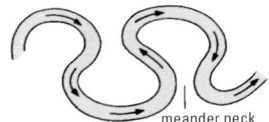

***meander*** *Fully formed meanders.*

**mesa** A flat-topped, isolated hill in arid regions. A mesa has a protective cap of hard **rock** underlain by softer, more readily eroded **sedimentary rock**. A **butte** is a relatively small outlier of a mesa.

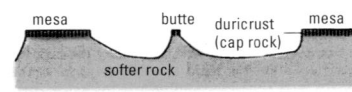

***mesa***

**mesosphere** *See* **atmosphere**.

**metadata** All Information used to describe content, quality, condition, origin and other characteristics of data.

**metamorphic rock** A **rock** which has been changed by intensive heat or pressure. Metamorphism implies an increase in hardness and resistance to **erosion**. Shale, for example, may be metamorphosed by pressure into **slate**; **sandstone** by heat into **quartzite**, **limestone** into **marble**. Metamorphism of pre-existing rocks is associated with the processes of **folding**, **faulting** and **vulcanicity**.

**migration** A permanent or semipermanent change of residence.

**monoculture** The growing of a single crop.

**monsoon** The term strictly means 'seasonal wind' and is used generally to describe a situation where there is a reversal of wind direction from one season to another. This is especially the case in South and Southeast Asia, where two monsoon winds occur, both related to the extreme pressure gradients created by the large land mass of the Asian continent.

**moraine** A collective term for debris deposited on or by **glaciers** and ice bodies in general. Several types of moraine are recognized: *lateral* moraine forms along the edges of a valley glacier where debris eroded from the valley sides, or weathered from the slopes above the glacier, collects;

*medial* moraine forms where two lateral moraines meet at a glacier junction; *englacial* moraine is material which is trapped within the body of the glacier; and *ground* moraine is material eroded from the floor of the valley and used by the glacier as an abrasive tool. A *terminal* moraine is material bulldozed by the glacier during its advance and deposited at its maximum down-valley extent. *Recessional* moraines may be deposited at standstills during a period of general glacial retreat.

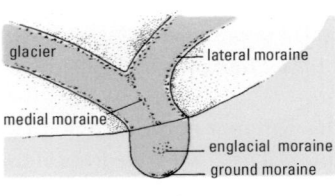

***moraine***

**mortlake** *See* **oxbow lake**.

**mountain** A natural upward projection of the Earth's surface, higher and steeper than a hill, and often having a rocky summit.

# N

**national park** An area of scenic countryside protected by law from uncontrolled development. A national park has two main functions:
(a) to conserve the natural beauty of the landscape;
(b) to enable the public to visit and enjoy the countryside for leisure and recreation.

**natural hazard** A natural event which, in extreme cases, can lead to loss of life and destruction of property. Some natural hazards result from geological events, such as **earthquakes** and the eruption of **volcanoes**, whilst others are due to weather events such as **hurricanes**, floods and droughts.

**natural increase** The increase in population due to the difference between **birth rate** and **death rate**.

**neap tides** *See* **tides**.

**névé** Compact snow. In a **corrie** icefield, for example, four layers are recognized: blue and white ice at the bottom of the ice mass; névé overlying the ice and powder snow on the surface.

**new town** A new urban location created
(a) to provide overspill accommodation for a large city or **conurbation**;
(b) to provide a new focus for industrial development.

**newly industrialized country (NIC)** A **developing country** which is becoming industrialized, for example Malaysia and Thailand. Some NICs have successfully used large-scale development to move into the industrialized world. Usually the capital for such developments comes from outside the country.

**nivation** The process of **weathering** by snow and ice, particularly through **freeze-thaw** action. Particularly active in cold **climates** and high altitudes – for example on exposed slopes above a **glacier**.

**node** A point representing the beginning or ending point of an edge or arc.

**nomadic pastoralism** A system of **agriculture** in dry grassland regions. People and stock (cattle, sheep, goats) are continually moving in search of pasture and water. The pastoralists subsist on meat, milk and other animal products.

**non-governmental organizations (NGOs)** Independent organizations, such as charities (Oxfam, Water Aid) which provide aid and expertise to economically developing countries.

**nonrenewable resources** Resources of which there is a fixed supply, which will eventually be exhausted. Examples of these are metal ores and **fossil fuels**. *Compare* **renewable resources**.

**North and South** A way of dividing the industrialized nations, found predominantly in the North from those less developed nations in the South. The gap which exists between the rich 'North' and the poor 'South' is called the *development gap*.

**northings** The second element of a **grid reference**. *See* **eastings**.

**nuclear power station** An electricity-generating plant using nuclear fuel as an alternative to the conventional **fossil fuels** of **coal**, oil and gas.

**nuée ardente** A very hot and fast-moving cloud of gas, ash and rock that flows close to the ground after a violent ejection from a volcano. It is very destructive.

**nunatak** A mountain peak projecting above the general level of the ice near the edge of an **ice sheet**.

**nutrient cycle** The cycling of nutrients through the **environment**.

# O

**ocean** A large area of sea. The world's oceans are the Pacific, Atlantic, Indian and Arctic. The Southern Ocean is made up of the areas of the Pacific, Atlantic and Indian Oceans south of latitude 60°S.

**ocean current** A movement of the surface water of an ocean.

**opencast mining** A type of mining where the mineral is extracted by direct excavation rather than by shaft or drift methods.

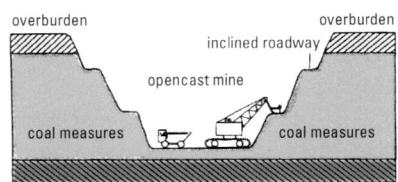
*opencast mining*

**organic farming** A system of farming that avoids the use of any artificial fertilizers or chemical pesticides, using only organic fertilizers and pesticides derived directly from animal or vegetable matter. Yields from organic farming are lower, but the products are sold at a premium price.

**overfold** *See* **fold**.

**oxbow lake, mortlake** *or* **cut-off** A crescent-shaped lake originating in a **meander** that was abandoned when **erosion** breached the neck between bends, allowing the stream to flow straight on, bypassing the meander. The ends of the meander rapidly silt up and it becomes separated from the river.

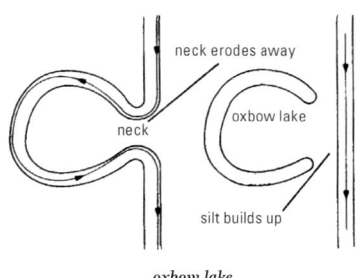
*oxbow lake*

**ozone** A form of oxygen found in a layer in the **stratosphere**, where it protects the Earth's surface from ultraviolet rays.

# P

**Pangaea** The supercontinent or universal land mass in which all continents were joined together approximately 200 million years ago. *See* **continental drift**.

**passage** *See* **strait**.

**pastoral farming** A system of farming in which the raising of livestock is the dominant element. *See also* **nomadic pastoralism**.

**peasant agriculture** The growing of crops or raising of animals, partly for subsistence needs and partly for market sale. Peasant agriculture is thus an intermediate stage between subsistence and commercial farming.

**peat** Partially decayed and compressed vegetative matter accumulating in areas of high rainfall and/or poor **drainage**.

**peneplain** A region that has been eroded until it is almost level. The more resistant rocks will stand above the general level of the land.

**per capita income** The **GNI** (gross national income) of a country divided by the size of its population. It gives the average income per head of the population if the national income were shared out equally. Per capita income comparisons are used as one indicator of levels of economic development.

**periglacial features** A periglacial landscape is one which has not been glaciated *per se*, but which has been affected by the severe **climate** prevailing around the ice margin.

**permafrost** The permanently frozen subsoil that is a feature of areas of **tundra**.

**permeable rock** Rock through which water can pass via a network of pores between the grains. *Compare* **pervious rock**. *See also* **impermeable rock**.

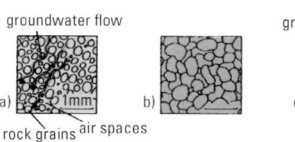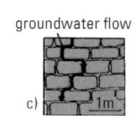
*permeable rock* (**a**) *Permeable rock,* (**b**) *impermeable rock,* (**c**) *pervious rock.*

**pervious rock** Rock which, even if non-porous, can allow water to pass through via interconnected joints, bedding planes and fissures. An example is **limestone**. *Compare* **permeable rock**. *See also* **impervious rock**.

**photosynthesis** The process by which green plants make carbohydrates from carbon dioxide and water, and give off oxygen. Photosynthesis balances **respiration**.

**physical feature** *See* **topography**.

**physical geography** The study of our **environment**, comprising such elements as geomorphology, hydrology, pedology, meteorology, climatology and biogeography.

**pie chart** A circular graph for displaying values as proportions:

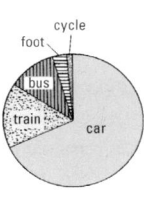
*pie chart*

**plain** A level or almost level area of land.

**plantation agriculture** A system of **agriculture** located in a tropical or semi-tropical **environment**, producing commodities for export to Europe, North America and other industrialized regions. Coffee, tea, bananas, rubber and sisal are examples of plantation crops.

**plateau** An upland area with a fairly flat surface and steep slopes. Rivers often dissect plateau surfaces.

**plate tectonics** The theory that the Earth's **crust** is divided into seven large, rigid plates, and several smaller ones, which are moving relative to each other over the upper layers of the Earth's **mantle**. *See* **continental drift**. **Earthquakes** and volcanic activity occur at the boundaries between the plates. *See* diagrams overleaf.

**plucking** A process of glacial **erosion** whereby, during the passage of a valley **glacier** or other ice body, ice forming in cracks and fissures drags out material from a **rock** face. This is particularly the case with the backwall of a **corrie**.

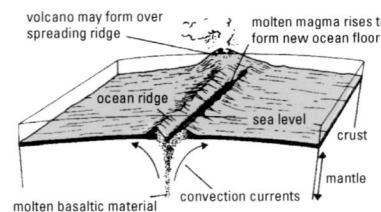

*a) Constructive plate boundary*

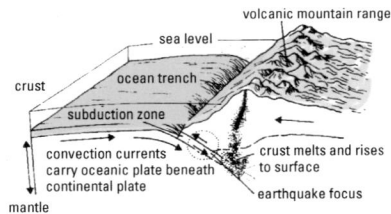

*b) Destructive plate boundary*

**plate tectonics**

**plug** The solidified material which seals the vent of a **volcano** after an eruption.

**plutonic rock** **Igneous rock** formed at depth in the Earth's **crust**; its crystals are large due to the slow rate of cooling. **Granite**, such as is found in **batholiths** and other deep-seated intrusions, is a common example.

**podzol** The characteristic **soil** of the **taiga** coniferous forests of Canada and northern Russia. Podzols are leached, greyish soils: iron and lime especially are leached out of the upper horizons, to be deposited as *hardpan* in the B **horizon**.

**pollution** Environmental damage caused by improper management of **resources**, or by careless human activity.

**polygons** Closed shapes defined by a connected sequences of coordinate pairs, where the first and last coordinate pair are the same.

**polyline** A series of connected segments which form a path to define a shape.

**population change** The increase of a population, the components of which are summarized in the following diagram.

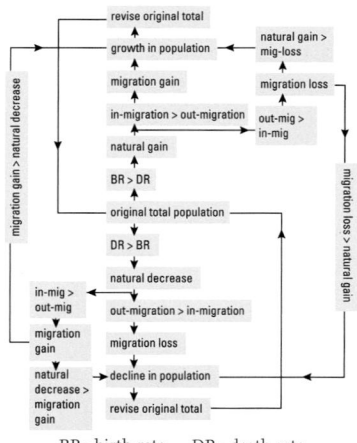

BR= birth rate    DR= death rate

*population change*

**population density** The number of people per unit area. Population densities are usually expressed per square kilometre.

**population distribution** The pattern of population location at a given **scale**.

**population explosion** On a global **scale**, the dramatic increase in population during the 20th century. The graph below shows world **population growth**.

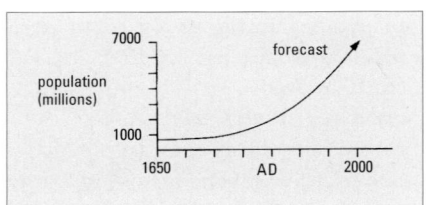

*population explosion*

**population growth** An increase in the population of a given region. This may be the result of natural increase (more births than deaths) or of in-migration, or both.

**population pyramid** A type of **bar graph** used to show population structure, i.e. the age and sex composition of the population for a given region or nation.

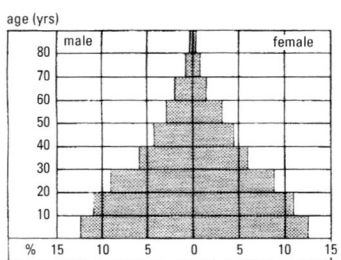

*a) population pyramid Pyramid for India, showing high birth rates and death rates.*

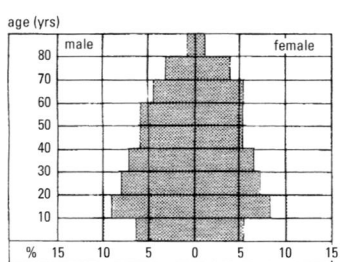

*b) population pyramid Pyramid for England and Wales, showing low birth and death rates.*

**pothole** **1.** A deep hole in limestone, caused by the enlargement of a **joint** through the dissolving effect of rainwater.
**2.** A hollow scoured in a river bed by the swirling of pebbles and small boulders in eddies.

**precipitation** Water deposited on the Earth's surface in the form of e.g. rain, snow, sleet, hail and dew.

**prevailing wind** The dominant wind direction of a region. Prevailing winds are named by the direction from which they blow.

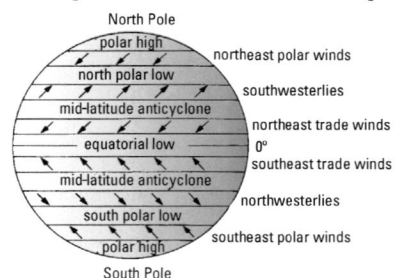

**primary keys** A set of properties in a database that uniquely identifies each record.

**primary sector** That sector of the national economy which deals with the production of primary materials: **agriculture**, mining, forestry and fishing. Primary products such as these have had no processing or manufacturing involvement. The total economy comprises the primary sector, the **secondary sector**, the **tertiary sector** and the **quaternary sector**.

**primary source** *See* **secondary source**.

**prime meridian** or **Greenwich Meridian** The line of 0° longitude passing through Greenwich in London.

**pumped storage** Water pumped back up to the storage lake of a **hydroelectric power** station, using surplus 'off-peak' electricity.

**pyramidal peak** A pointed mountain summit resulting from the headward extension of **corries** and **arêtes**. Under glacial conditions a given summit may develop corries on all sides, especially those facing north and east. As these erode into the summit, a formerly rounded profile may be changed into a pointed, steep-sided peak.

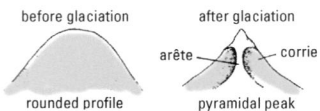

*pyramidal peak*

**pyroclasts** Rocky debris emitted during a volcanic eruption, usually following a previous emission of gases and prior to the outpouring of **lava** – although many eruptions do not reach the final lava stage.

# Q

**quality of life** The level of wellbeing of a community and of the area in which the community lives.

**quartz** One of the commonest minerals found in the Earth's **crust**, and a form of silica (silicon+oxide). Most **sandstones** are composed predominantly of quartz.

**quartzite** A very hard and resistant **rock** formed by the metamorphism of **sandstone**.

**quaternary sector** That sector of the economy providing information and expertise. This includes the microchip and microelectronics industries. Highly developed economies are seeing an increasing number of their workforce employed in this sector. *Compare* **primary sector**, **secondary sector**, **tertiary sector**.

**query** A request to select features or records from a database.

# R

**rain gauge** An instrument used to measure rainfall. Rain passes through a funnel into the jar below and is then transferred to a measuring cylinder. The reading is in millimetres and indicates the depth of rain which has fallen over an area.

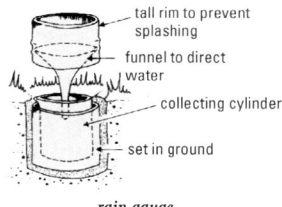

*rain gauge*

**raised beach** *See* **wave-cut platform**.

**range** A long series or chain of mountains.

**rapids** An area of broken, turbulent water in a river channel, caused by a stratum of resistant **rock** that dips downstream. The softer rock immediately upstream and downstream erodes more quickly, leaving the resistant rock sticking up, obstructing the flow of the water. *Compare* **waterfall**.

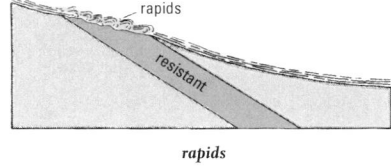

*rapids*

**raster** A pattern of closely spaced rows of dots that form an image.

**raw materials** The **resources** supplied to industries for subsequent manufacturing processes.

**reef** A ridge of rock, sand or coral whose top lies close to the sea's surface.

**regeneration** Renewed growth of, for example, forest after felling. Forest regeneration is crucial to the long-term stability of many **resource** systems, from **bush fallowing** to commercial forestry.

**region** An area of land which has marked boundaries or unifying internal characteristics. Geographers may identify regions according to physical, climatic, political, economic or other factors.

**rejuvenation** Renewed vertical **corrasion** by rivers in their middle and lower courses, caused by a fall in sea level, or a rise in the level of land relative to the sea.

**relative humidity** The relationship between the actual amount of water vapour in the air and the amount of vapour the air could hold at a particular temperature. This is usually expressed as a percentage. Relative humidity gives a measure of dampness in the **atmosphere**, and this can be determined by a **hygrometer**.

**relief** The differences in height between any parts of the Earth's surface. Hence a relief map will aim to show differences in the height of land by, for example, **contour** lines or by a colour key.

**remote sensing** The gathering of information by the use of electronic or other sensing devices in satellites.

**renewable resources** Resources that can be used repeatedly, given appropriate management and conservation. *Compare* **non-renewable resources**.

**representative fraction** The fraction of real size to which objects are reduced on a map; for example, on a 1:50 000 map, any object is shown at 1/50 000 of its real size.

**reserves** Resources which are available for future use.

**reservoir** A natural or artificial lake used for collecting or storing water, especially for water supply or **irrigation**.

**resolution** The smallest allowable separation between two coordinate values in a feature class.

**resource** Any aspect of the human and physical **environments** which people find useful in satisfying their needs.

**respiration** The release of energy from food in the cells of all living organisms (plants as well as animals). The process normally requires oxygen and releases carbon dioxide. It is balanced by **photosynthesis**.

**revolution** The passage of the Earth around the sun; one revolution is completed in 365.25 days. Due to the tilt of the Earth's axis ($23\frac{1}{2}°$ from the vertical), revolution results in the sequence of seasons experienced on the Earth's surface.

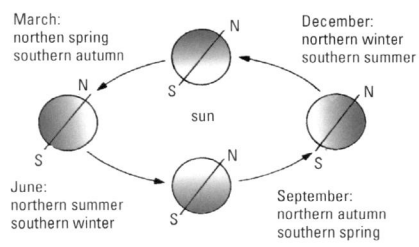

*revolution The seasons of the year.*

**ria** A submerged river valley, caused by a rise in sea level or a subsidence of the land relative to the sea.

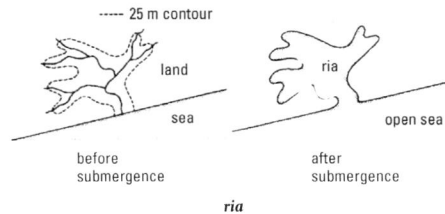

*ria*

**ribbon lake** A long, relatively narrow lake, usually occupying the floor of a U-shaped glaciated valley. A ribbon lake may be caused by the *overdeepening* of a section of the valley floor by glacial **abrasion**.

**Richter scale** A scale of **earthquake** measurement that describes the magnitude of an earthquake according to the amount of energy released, as recorded by **seismographs**.

**rift valley** A section of the Earth's **crust** which has been downfaulted. The **faults** bordering the rift valley are approximately parallel. There are two main theories related to the origin of rift valleys. The first states that tensional forces within the Earth's crust have caused a block of land to sink between parallel faults. The second theory states that compression within the Earth's crust has caused faulting in which two side blocks have risen up towards each other over a central block.

The most complex rift valley system in the world is that ranging from Syria in the Middle East to the river Zambezi in East Africa.

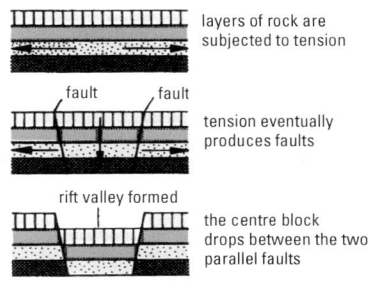

*rift valley*

**river** A large natural stream of fresh water flowing along a definite course, usually into the sea.

**river basin** The area drained by a river and its tributaries, sometimes referred to as a **catchment** area.

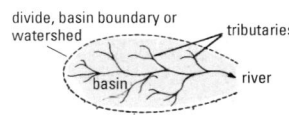

*river basin*

**river cliff** *or* **bluff** The outer bank of a **meander**. The cliff is kept steep by undercutting since river **erosion** is concentrated on the outer bank. *See* **meander** and **river's course**.

**river's course** The route taken by a river from its source to the sea. There are three major sections: the upper course, the middle course and the lower course.

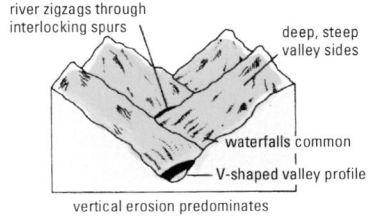

*river's course Upper course.*

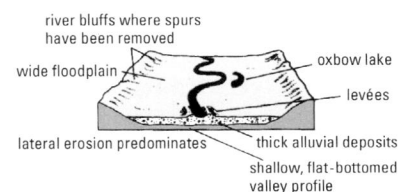

*river's course Lower course.*

**river terrace** A platform of land beside a river. This is produced when a river is **rejuvenated** in its middle or lower courses. The river cuts down into its **flood plain**, which then stands above the new general level of the river as paired terraces.

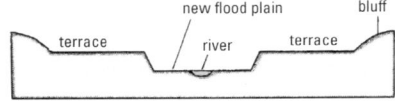

*river terrace* Paired river terraces above a flood plain.

**roche moutonnée** An outcrop of resistant **rock** sculpted by the passage of a **glacier**.

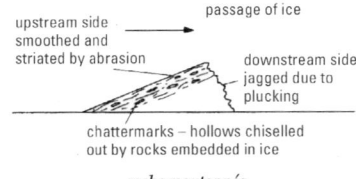

*roche moutonnée*

**rock** The solid material of the Earth's **crust**. *See* **igneous rock**, **sedimentary rock**, **metamorphic rock**.

**rotation** The movement of the Earth about its own axis. One rotation is completed in 24 hours. Due to the tilt of the Earth's axis, the length of day and night varies at different points on the Earth's surface. Days become longer with increasing latitude north; shorter with increasing latitude south. The situation is reversed during the northern midwinter (= the southern midsummer).

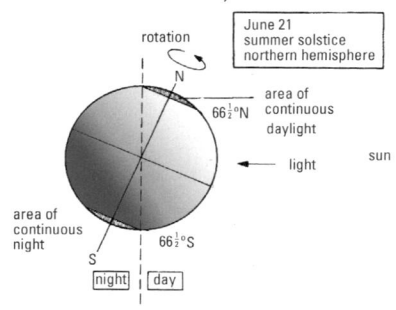

*rotation* The tilt of the Earth at the northern summer and southern winter solstice.

**rural depopulation** The loss of population from the countryside as people move away from rural areas towards cities and **conurbations**.

**rural–urban migration** The movement of people from rural to urban areas. *See* **migration** and **rural depopulation**.

# S

**saltpan** A shallow basin, usually in a desert region, containing salt which has been deposited from an evaporated salt lake.

**sandstone** A common **sedimentary rock** deposited by either wind or water.
Sandstones vary in texture from fine- to coarse-grained, but are invariably composed of grains of **quartz**, cemented by such substances as calcium carbonate or silica.

**satellite image** An image giving information about an area of the Earth or another planet, obtained from a satellite. Instruments on an Earth-orbiting satellite, such as Landsat, continually scan the Earth and sense the brightness of reflected light. When the information is sent back to Earth, computers turn it into *false-colour images* in which built-up areas appear in one colour (perhaps blue), vegetation in another (often red), bare ground in a third, and water in a fourth colour, making it easy to see their distribution and to monitor any changes. *Compare* **aerial photograph**.

**savanna** The grassland regions of Africa which lie between the **tropical rainforest** and the hot **deserts**. In South America, the *Llanos* and *Campos* regions are representative of the savanna type.

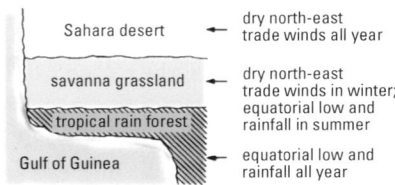

*savanna* The position of the savanna in West Africa.

**scale** The size ratio represented by a map; for example, on a map of scale 1:25 000, the real landscape is portrayed at 1/25 000 of its actual size.

**scarp slope** The steeper of the two slopes which comprise an **escarpment** of inclined **strata**. *Compare* **dip slope**.

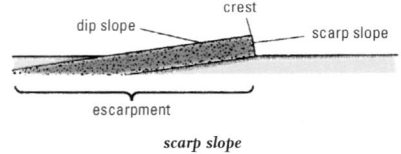

*scarp slope*

**science park** A site accommodating several companies involved in scientific work or research. Science parks are linked to universities and tend to be located on **greenfield** and/or landscaped sites. *Compare* **business park**.

**scree** *or* **talus** The accumulated **weathering** debris below a **crag** or other exposed rock face. Larger boulders will accumulate at the base of the scree, carried there by greater momentum.

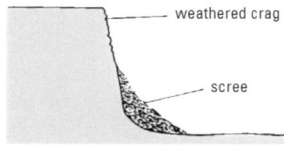

*scree or talus*

**sea level** The average height of the surface of the oceans and seas.

**secondary sector** The sector of the economy which comprises manufacturing and processing industries, in contrast with the **primary sector** which produces **raw materials**, the **tertiary sector** which provides **services**, and the **quaternary sector** which provides information.

**secondary source** A supply of information or data that has been researched or collected by an individual or group of people and made available for others to use; census data is an example of this. A *primary source* of data or information is one collected at first hand by the researcher who needs it; for example, a traffic count in an area, undertaken by a student for his or her own project.

**sediment** The material resulting from the **weathering** and **erosion** of the landscape, which has been deposited by water, ice or wind. It may be reconsolidated to form **sedimentary rock**.

**sedimentary rock** A rock which has been formed by the consolidation of **sediment** derived from pre-existing rocks. **Sandstone** is a common example of a rock formed in this way. **Chalk** and **limestone** are other types of sedimentary rock, derived from organic and chemical precipitations.

**seif dune** A linear sand dune, the ridge of sand lying parallel to the prevailing wind direction. The eddying movement of the wind keeps the sides of the dune steep.

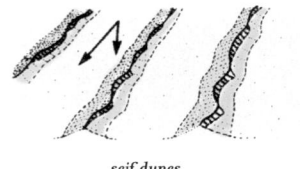

*seif dunes*

**seismograph** An instrument which measures and records the seismic waves which travel through the Earth during an **earthquake**.

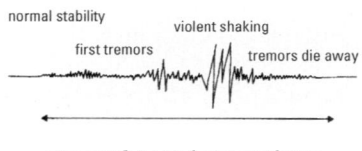

*seismograph* A typical seismograph trace.

**seismology** The study of **earthquakes**.

**serac** A pinnacle of ice formed by the tumbling and shearing of a **glacier** at an ice fall, i.e. the broken ice associated with a change in **gradient** of the valley floor.

**service industry** The people and organizations that provide a service to the public.

**settlement** Any location chosen by people as a permanent or semi-permanent dwelling place.

**shading map** *or* **choropleth map** A map in which shading of varying intensity is used. For example, the pattern of **population densities** in a region.

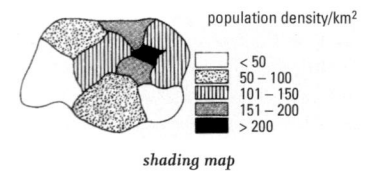

*shading map*

**shanty town** An area of unplanned, random, urban development often around the edge of a city. The shanty town is a major element of the structure of many **Third World** cities such as São Paulo, Mexico City, Nairobi, Kolkata and Lagos. The shanty town is characterized by high-density/low-quality dwellings, often constructed from the simplest materials such as scrap wood, corrugated iron and plastic sheeting – and by the lack of standard services such as sewerage and water supply, power supplies and refuse collection.

**shape files** A storage format for storing the location, shape and attributes of geographic features.

**shifting cultivation** *See* **bush fallowing**.

**shoreface terrace** A bank of **sediment** accumulating at the change of slope which marks the limit of a marine **wave-cut platform**.

Material removed from the retreating cliff base is transported by the undertow off the wave-cut platform to be deposited in deeper water offshore.

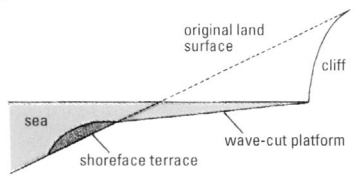

*shoreface terrace*

**silage** Any **fodder crop** harvested whilst still green. The crop is kept succulent by partial fermentation in a *silo*. It is used as animal feed during the winter.

**sill** **1.** An igneous intrusion of roughly horizontal disposition. *See* **igneous rock**. **2.** (Also called **threshold**) the lip of a **corrie**.

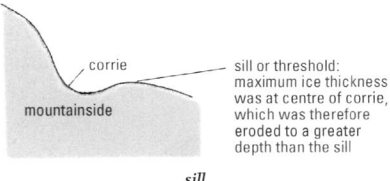

*sill*

**silt** Fine **sediment**, the component particles of which have a mean diameter of between 0.002 mm and 0.02 mm.

**sinkhole** *See* **pothole**.

**slash and burn** *See* **tropical rainforest**.

**slate** Metamorphosed shale or **clay**. Slate is a dense, fine-grained **rock** distinguished by the characteristic of *perfect cleavage*, i.e. it can be split along a perfectly smooth plane.

**slip** The amount of vertical displacement of **strata** at a **fault**.

**smog** A mixture of smoke and fog associated with urban and industrial areas, that creates an unhealthy **atmosphere**.

**snow line** The altitude above which permanent snow exists, and below which any snow that falls will not persist during the summer months.

**socioeconomic group** A group defined by particular social and economic characteristics, such as educational qualifications, type of job, and earnings.

**soil** The loose material which forms the uppermost layer of the Earth's surface, composed of the *inorganic fraction*, i.e. material derived from the **weathering** of bedrock, and the *organic fraction* – that is material derived from the decay of vegetable matter.

**soil erosion** The accelerated breakdown and removal of soil due to poor management. Soil erosion is particularly a problem in harsh **environments**.

**soil profile** The sequence of layers or **horizons** usually seen in an exposed soil section.

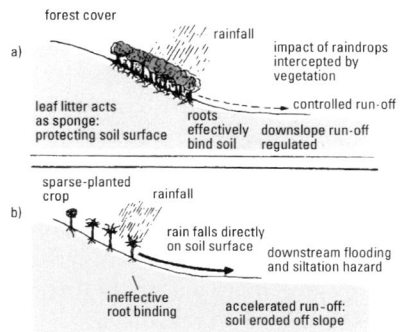

*soil erosion* a) *Stable environment,* b) *unstable environment.*

**solar power** Heat radiation from the sun converted into electricity or used directly to provide heating. Solar power is an example of a renewable source of energy (*see* **renewable resources**).

**solifluction** A process whereby thawed surface soil creeps downslope over a permanently frozen **subsoil (permafrost)**.

**spatial distribution** The pattern of locations of, for example, population or **settlement** in a region.

**spit** A low, narrow bank of sand and shingle built out into an **estuary** by the process of **longshore drift**.

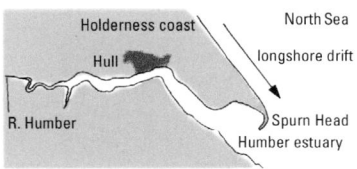

*spit Spurn Head, a coastal spit.*

**spring** The emergence of an underground stream at the surface, often occurring where **impermeable rock** underlies **permeable rock** or **pervious rock** or **strata**.

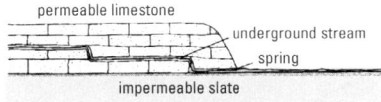

*spring Rainwater enters through the fissures of the limestone and the stream springs out where the limestone meets slate.*

**spring tides** *See* **tides**.

**squatter settlement** An area of peripheral urban settlement in which the residents occupy land to which they have no legal title. *See* **shanty town**.

**stack** A coastal feature resulting from the collapse of a natural arch. The stack remains after less resistant **strata** have been worn away by **weathering** and marine **erosion**.

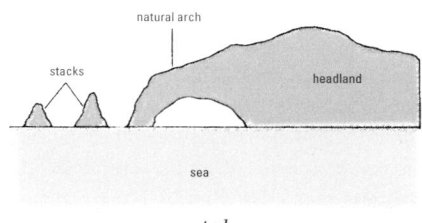

*stack*

**stalactite** A column of calcium carbonate hanging from the roof of a **limestone** cavern. As water passes through the limestone it dissolves a certain proportion, which is then precipitated by **evaporation** of water droplets dripping from the cavern roof. The drops splashing on the floor of a cavern further evaporate to precipitate more calcium carbonate as a **stalagmite**.

**stalagmite** A column of calcium carbonate growing upwards from a cavern floor. *Compare* **stalactite**. Stalactites and stalagmites may meet, forming a column or pillar.

**staple diet** The basic foodstuff which comprises the daily meals of a given people.

**stereoplotter** An instrument used for projecting an aerial photograph and converting locations of objects on the image to x-, y-, and z-coordinates. It plots these coordinates as a map.

**Stevenson's screen** A shelter used in weather stations, in which thermometers and other instruments may be hung.

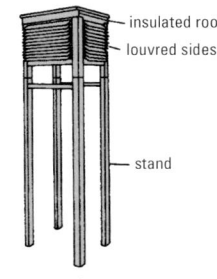

*Stevenson's screen*

**strait, channel** *or* **passage** A narrow body of water, between two land masses, which links two larger bodies of water.

**strata** Layers of **rock** superimposed one upon the other.

**stratosphere** The layer of the **atmosphere** which lies immediately above the troposphere and below the mesosphere and ionosphere. Within the stratosphere, temperature increases with altitutude.

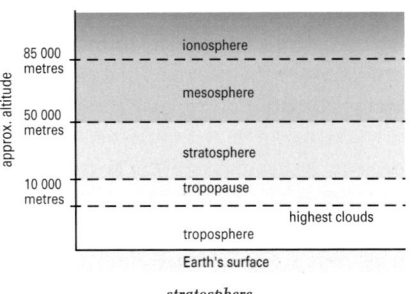

*stratosphere*

**stratus** Layer-cloud of uniform grey appearance, often associated with the warm sector of a **depression**. Stratus is a type of low **cloud** which may hang as mist over mountain tops.

**striations** The grooves and scratches left on bare **rock** surfaces by the passage of a **glacier**.

**strip cropping** A method of **soil** conservation whereby different crops are planted in a series of strips, often following **contours** around a hillside. The purpose of such a sequence of cultivation is to arrest the downslope movement of soil. *See* **soil erosion**.

**subduction zone** *See* **plate tectonics**.

**subsistence agriculture** A system of **agriculture** in which farmers produce exclusively for their own consumption, in contrast to **commercial agriculture** where farmers produce purely for sale at the market.

**subsoil** *See* **soil profile**.

**suburbs** The outer, and largest, parts of a town or city.

**surface run-off** That proportion of rainfall received at the Earth's surface which runs off either as channel flow or overland flow. It is distinguished from the rest of the rainfall, which either percolates into the soil or evaporates back into the **atmosphere**.

**sustainable development** The ability of a country to maintain a level of economic development, thus enabling the majority of the population to have a reasonable standard of living.

**swallow hole** *See* **pothole**.

**swash** The rush of water up the beach as a wave breaks. *See also* **backwash** and **longshore drift**.

**syncline** A trough in folded **strata**; the opposite of **anticline**. *See* **fold**.

# T

**taiga** The extensive **coniferous forests** of Siberia and Canada, lying immediately south of the arctic **tundra**.

**talus** *See* **scree**.

**tarn** The postglacial lake which often occupies a **corrie**.

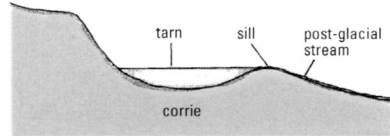

**temperate climate** A climate typical of mid-latitudes. Such a climate is intermediate between the extremes of hot (tropical) and cold (polar) climates. *Compare* **extreme climate**. *See also* **maritime climate**.

**terminal moraine** *See* **moraine**.

**terracing** A means of **soil** conservation and land utilization whereby steep hillsides are engineered into a series of flat ledges which can be used for **agriculture**, held in places by stone banks to prevent **soil erosion**.

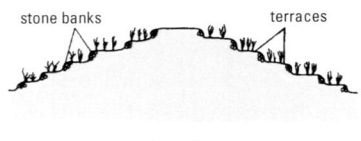

*terracing*

**tertiary sector** That sector of the economy which provides **services** such as transport, finance and retailing, as opposed to the **primary sector** which provides **raw materials**, the **secondary sector** which processes and manufactures products, and the **quaternary sector** which provides information and expertise.

**thermal power station** An electricity-generating plant which burns **coal**, oil or natural gas to produce steam to drive turbines.

**Third World** A collective term for the poor nations of Africa, Asia and Latin America, as opposed to the 'first world' of capitalist, developed nations and the 'second world' of formerly communist, developed nations. The terminology is far from satisfactory as there are great social and political variations within the 'Third World'. Indeed, there are some countries where such extreme poverty prevails that these could be regarded as a fourth group. Alternative terminology includes '**developing countries**', 'economically developing countries' and 'less economically developed countries' (LEDC). **Newly industrialized countries** are those showing greatest economic development.

**threshold** *See* **sill** (sense 2).

**tidal range** The mean difference in water level between high and low tides at a given location. *See* **tides**.

**tides** The alternate rise and fall of the surface of the sea, approximately twice a day, caused by the gravitational pull of the moon and, to a lesser extent, of the sun.

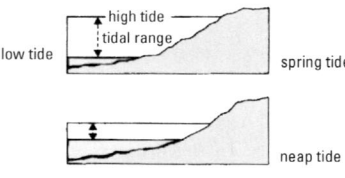

*tides Tidal ranges.*

**till** *See* **boulder clay**.

**tombolo** A **spit** which extends to join an island to the mainland.

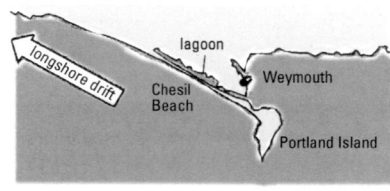

*tombolo Chesil Beach, England.*

**topography** The composition of the visible landscape, comprising both physical features and those made by people.

**topsoil** The uppermost layer of **soil**, more rich in organic matter than the underlying **subsoil**. *See* **horizon**, **soil profile**.

**tornado** A violent storm with winds circling around a small area of extremely low pressure. Characterized by a dark funnel-shaped cloud. Winds associated with tornadoes can reach speeds of over 300 mph (480 km/h).

**trade winds** Winds which blow from the subtropical belts of high pressure towards the equatorial belt of low pressure. In the northern hemisphere, the winds blow from the northeast and in the southern hemisphere from the southeast.

**transhumance** The practice whereby herds of farm animals are moved between regions of different climates. Pastoral farmers (*see* **pastoral farming**) take their herds from valley pastures in the winter to mountain pastures in the summer. *See also* **alp**.

**transnational corporation (TNC)** A company that has branches in many countries of the world, and often controls the production of the primary product and the sale of the finished article.

**tributary** A stream or river which feeds into a larger one. *Compare* **distributary**.

**tropical rainforest** The dense forest cover of the equatorial regions, reaching its greatest extent in the Amazon Basin of South America, the Congo Basin of Africa, and in parts of South East Asia and Indonesia. There has been much concern in recent years about the rate at which the world's rainforests are being cut down and burnt. The burning of large tracts of rainforest is thought to be contributing to **global warming**. Many governments and **conservation** bodies are now examining ways of protecting the remaining rainforests, which are unique **ecosystems** containing millions of plant and animal species.

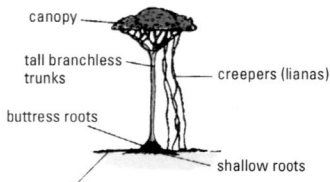

*a forest giant in the tropical rainforest*

**tropics** The region of the Earth lying between the *tropics of Cancer* ($23\frac{1}{2}°$N) and *Capricorn* ($23\frac{1}{2}°$S). *See* **latitude**.

**troposphere** *See* **atmosphere**.

**trough** An area of low pressure, not sufficiently well-defined to be regarded as a **depression**.

**truncated spur** A spur of land that previously projected into a valley and has been completely or partially cut off by a moving **glacier**.

**tsunami** A very large, and often destructive, sea wave produced by a submarine **earthquake**. Tsunamis tend to occur along the coasts of Japan and parts of the Pacific Ocean, and can be the cause of large numbers of deaths.

**tuff** Volcanic ash or dust which has been consolidated into **rock**.

**tundra** The barren, often bare-rock plains of the far north of North America and Eurasia where subarctic conditions prevail and where, as a result, vegetation is restricted to low-growing, hardy shrubs and mosses and lichens.

**typhoon** *See* **hurricane**.

# U

**undernutrition** A lack of a sufficient quantity of food, as distinct from **malnutrition** which is a consequence of an unbalanced diet.

**urban decay** The process of deterioration in the **infrastructure** of parts of the city. It is the result of long-term shifts in patterns of economic activity, residential **location** and **infrastructure**.

**urban sprawl** The growth in extent of an urban area in response to improvements in transport and rising incomes, both of which allow a greater physical separation of home and work.

**urbanization** The process by which a national population becomes predominantly urban through a **migration** of people from the countryside to cities, and a shift from agricultural to industrial employment.

**U-shaped valley** A glaciated valley, characteristically straight in plan and U-shaped in **cross section**. *See* diagram. *Compare* **V-shaped valley**.

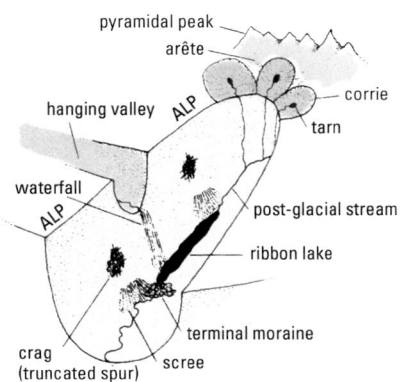

*U-shaped valley*

# V

**valley** A long depression in the Earth's surface, usually containing a river, formed by **erosion** or by movements in the Earth's **crust**.

**vector** A quantity that has both magnitude and direction.

**vegetation** The plant life of a particular region.

**viscous lava** **Lava** that resists the tendency to flow. It is sticky, flows slowly and congeals

rapidly. *Non-viscous* lava is very fluid, flows quickly and congeals slowly.

**volcanic rock** A category of **igneous rock** which comprises those rocks formed from **magma** which has reached the Earth's surface. **Basalt** is an example of a volcanic rock.

**volcano** A fissure in the Earth's **crust** through which **magma** reaches the Earth's surface. There are four main types of volcano:
(a) *Acid lava cone* – a very steep-sided cone composed entirely of acidic, **viscous lava** which flows slowly and congeals very quickly.
(b) *Composite volcano* – a single cone comprising alternate layers of ash (or other **pyroclasts**) and lava.

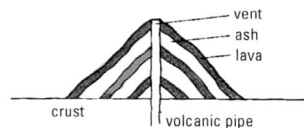

*volcano Composite volcano.*

(c) *Fissure volcano* – a volcano that erupts along a linear fracture in the crust, rather than from a single cone.
(d) *Shield volcano* – a volcano composed of very basic, non-viscous lava which flows quickly and congeals slowly, producing a very gently sloping cone.

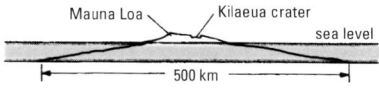

*volcano Shield volcano.*

**V-shaped valley** A narrow, steep-sided valley made by the rapid erosion of rock by streams and rivers. It is V-shaped in cross-section. *Compare* **U-shaped valley**.

**vulcanicity** A collective term for those processes which involve the intrusion of **magma** into the **crust**, or the extrusion of such molten material onto the Earth's surface.

# W

**wadi** A dry watercourse in an arid region; occasional rainstorms in the desert may cause a temporary stream to appear in a wadi.

**warm front** *See* **depression**.

**waterfall** An irregularity in the long profile of a **river's course**, usually located in the upper course. *Compare* **rapids**.

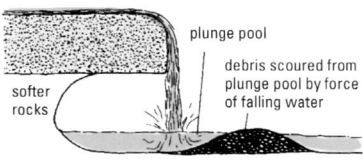

*waterfall*

**watershed** The boundary, often a ridge of high ground, between two **river basins**.

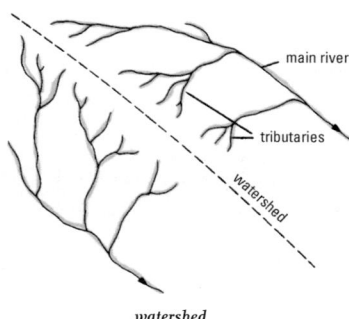

*watershed*

**water table** The level below which the ground is permanently saturated. The water table is thus the upper level of the **groundwater**. In areas where **permeable rock** predominates, the water table may be at some considerable depth.

**wave-cut platform** *or* **abrasion platform** A gently sloping surface eroded by the sea along a coastline.

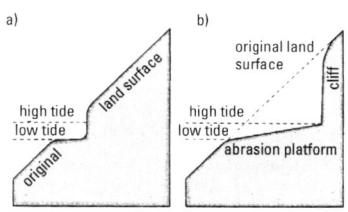

*wave-cut platform a) Early in formation, b) later in formation.*

**weather** The day-to-day conditions of e.g. rainfall, temperature and pressure, as experienced at a particular location.

**weather chart** A map or chart of an area giving details of **weather** experienced at a particular time of day. Weather charts are sometimes called *synoptic charts*, as they give a synopsis of the weather at a particular time.

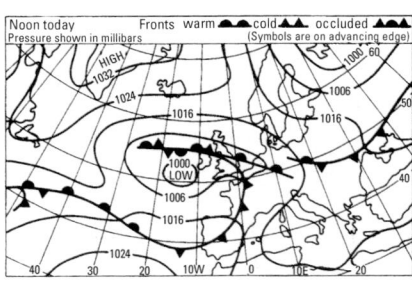

*weather chart*

**weather station** A place where all elements of the weather are measured and recorded. Each station will have a **Stevenson's screen** and a variety of instruments such as a **maximum and minimum thermometer**, a **hygrometer**, a **rain gauge**, a **wind vane** and an **anemometer**.

**weathering** The breakdown of rocks *in situ*; contrasted with **erosion** in that no large-scale transport of the denuded material is involved.

**wet and dry bulb thermometer**
  *See* **hygrometer**.
**wind vane**   An instrument used to indicate wind direction. It consists of a rotating arm which always points in the direction from which the wind blows.

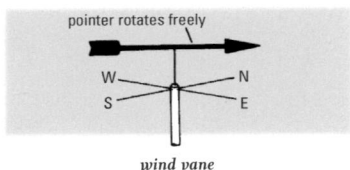

*wind vane*

# Y

**yardang**   Long, roughly parallel ridges of **rock** in arid and semi-arid regions. The ridges are undercut by wind **erosion** and the corridors between them are swept clear of sand by the wind. The ridges are oriented in the direction of the prevailing wind.

**yield**   The productivity of land as measured by the weight or volume of produce per unit area.

# Z

**Zeugen**   *Pedestal rocks* in arid regions; wind **erosion** is concentrated near the ground, where **corrasion** by wind-borne sand is most active. This leads to undercutting and the pedestal profile emerges.

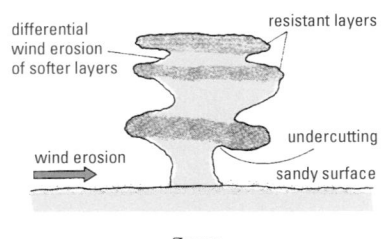

*Zeugen*

## How to use the Index

All the names on the maps in this atlas, except some of those on the special topic maps, are included in the index.

The names are arranged in **alphabetical order.** Where the name has more than one word the separate words are considered as one to decide the position of the name in the index:

**Thetford**
**The Trossachs**
**The Wash**
**The Weald**
**Thiers**
**Thiès**

Where there is more than one place with the same name, the country name is used to decide the order:

**London** Canada
**London** England

If both places are in the same country, the county or state name is also used:

**Avon** *r.* Bristol England
**Avon** *r.* Dorset England

Each entry in the index starts with the name of the place or feature, followed by the name of the country or region in which it is located. This is followed by the number of the most appropriate page on which the name appears, usually the largest scale map. Next comes the alphanumeric reference followed by the latitude and longitude.

Names of physical features such as rivers, capes, mountains etc are followed by a description. The descriptions are usually shortened to one or two letters, these abbreviations are keyed below. Town names are followed by a description only when the name may be confused with that of a physical feature:

**Big Spring** *town*

## Abbreviations

To help to distinguish the different parts of each entry, different styles of type are used:

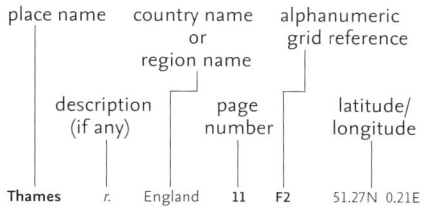

place name    country name        alphanumeric
                  or            grid reference
              region name

description       page          latitude/
  (if any)       number         longitude

**Thames**   *r.*   England   **11**   F2      51.27N 0.21E

To use the **alphanumeric grid reference** to find a feature on the map, first find the correct page and then look at the coloured letters printed outside the frame along the top, bottom and sides of the map.
When you have found the correct letter and number follow the grid boxes up and along until you find the correct grid box in which the feature appears. You must then search the grid box until you find the name of the feature.

The **latitude and longitude reference** gives a more exact description of the position of the feature.

Page 2 of the atlas describes lines of latitude and lines of longitude, and explains how they are numbered and divided into degrees and minutes. Each name in the index has a different latitude and longitude reference, so the feature can be located accurately. The lines of latitude and lines of longitude shown on each map are numbered in degrees. These numbers are printed in black along the top, bottom and sides of the map frame.

The drawing above shows part of the map on page 41 and the lines of latitude and lines of longitude.

The index entry for Wexford is given as follows

**Wexford** Ireland **41** E2   52.20N 6.28W

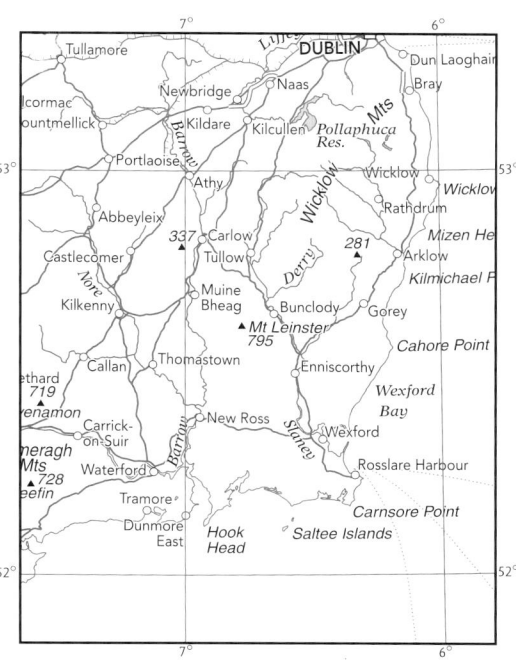

To locate Wexford, first find latitude 52N and estimate 20 minutes north from 52 degrees to find 52.20N, then find longitude 6W and estimate 28 minutes west from 6 degrees to find 6.28W. The symbol for the town of Wexford is where latitude 52.20N and longitude 6.28W meet.

On maps at a smaller scale than the map of Ireland, it is not possible to show every line of latitude and longitude. Only every 5 or 10 degrees of latitude and longitude may be shown. On these maps you must estimate the degrees and minutes to find the exact location of a feature.

| | |
|---|---|
| A. and B | Argyll and Bute |
| Afgh. | Afghanistan |
| Ala. | Alabama |
| Ang. | Angus |
| *b.* | bay |
| Baja Calif. | Baja California |
| Bangl. | Bangladesh |
| Bos.-Herz. | Bosnia-Herzegovina |
| Brist. | Bristol |
| *c.* | cape |
| Cambs. | Cambridgeshire |
| C.A.R. | Central African Republic |
| Colo. | Colorado |
| Corn. | Cornwall |
| Cumb. | Cumbria |
| Czech Rep. | Czech Republic |
| *d.* | internal division e.g. county, state |
| Del. | Delaware |
| Dem. Rep. Congo | Democratic Republic of the Congo |
| Derbys. | Derbyshire |
| *des.* | desert |
| Dev. | Devon |
| Dom. Rep. | Dominican Republic |
| Don. | Donegal |
| Dor. | Dorset |
| Dur. | Durham |
| Equat. Guinea | Equatorial Guinea |
| Ess. | Essex |
| *est.* | estuary |
| E. Sussex | East Sussex |
| E. Yorks. | East Riding of Yorkshire |
| *f.* | physical feature, e.g. valley, plain, geographic area |
| Falk. | Falkirk |
| *for.* | forest |
| *g.* | gulf |
| Ga. | Georgia |
| Glos. | Gloucestershire |
| Hants. | Hampshire |
| High. | Highland |

| | |
|---|---|
| *hd* | headland |
| *i.* | island |
| Ill. | Illinois |
| I. o. W. | Isle of Wight |
| *is* | islands |
| *l.* | lake |
| La. | Louisiana |
| Lancs. | Lancashire |
| Leics. | Leicestershire |
| Lincs. | Lincolnshire |
| Lux. | Luxembourg |
| Man. | Manitoba |
| Mass. | Massachusetts |
| Me. | Maine |
| Mich. | Michigan |
| Minn. | Minnesota |
| Miss. | Mississippi |
| Mo. | Missouri |
| Mor. | Moray |
| *mt.* | mountain |
| *mts* | mountains |
| N. Africa | North Africa |
| N. America | North America |
| N. Atlantic Oc. | North Atlantic Ocean |
| *nat. park* | National Park |
| *nature res.* | Nature Reserve |
| N. C. | North Carolina |
| Neth. | Netherlands |
| Neth. Antilles | Netherlands Antilles |
| Nev. | Nevada |
| New. | Newport |
| Nfld. and Lab. | Newfoundland and Labrador |
| N. Korea | North Korea |
| N. M. | New Mexico |
| N. Mariana Is | Northern Marianas Islands |
| Norf. | Norfolk |
| Northum. | Northumberland |
| Notts. | Nottinghamshire |
| N. Pacific Oc. | North Pacific Ocean |
| N. Y. | New York |
| Oh. | Ohio |
| Oreg. | Oregon |

| | |
|---|---|
| Orkn. | Orkney |
| Oxon. | Oxfordshire |
| Pacific Oc. | Pacific Ocean |
| P. and K. | Perth and Kinross |
| P'boro. | Peterborough |
| Pem. | Pembrokeshire |
| *pen.* | peninsula |
| P.N.G. | Papua New Guinea |
| *pt* | point |
| *r.* | river |
| *r. mouth* | river mouth |
| *resr* | reservoir |
| Rus. Fed. | Russian Federation |
| S. Africa | South Africa |
| S. America | South America |
| S. Atlantic Oc. | South Atlantic Ocean |
| S. C. | South Carolina |
| S. China Sea | South China Sea |
| Shetl. | Shetland |
| S. Korea | South Korea |
| Som. | Somerset |
| Southern Oc. | Southern Ocean |
| S. Pacific Oc. | South Pacific Ocean |
| *str.* | strait |
| Suff. | Suffolk |
| Switz. | Switzerland |
| T. and W. | Tyne and Wear |
| Tel. Wre. | Telford and Wrekin |
| Tex. | Texas |
| Tipp. | Tipperary |
| U.A.E. | United Arab Emirates |
| U.K. | United Kingdom |
| U.S.A. | United States of America |
| Va. | Virginia |
| *vol.* | volcano |
| Vt. | Vermont |
| Water. | Waterford |
| Warwicks. | Warwickshire |
| Wick. | Wicklow |
| W. Isles | Western Isles |
| W. Va. | West Virginia |
| Wyo. | Wyoming |

## A

Aa r. France 11 H2 .......... 51.00N 2.07E
Aabenraa Denmark 40 B1 .......... 55.02N 9.25E
Aachen Germany 54 B4 .......... 50.46N 6.05E
Aalborg Denmark 40 B2 .......... 57.03N 9.55E
Aalen Germany 54 D3 .......... 48.50N 10.06E
Aalst Belgium 42 D4 .......... 50.56N 4.03E
Ābādān Iran 95 G6 .......... 30.20N 48.15E
Ābādeh Iran 95 H6 .......... 31.08N 52.36E
Abadla Algeria 84 D5 .......... 31.00N 2.43W
Abakan Rus. Fed. 59 K3 .......... 53.42N 91.25E
Abancay Peru 76 G6 .......... 13.39S 72.52W
Abarqū Iran 95 H6 .......... 31.06N 53.13E
Abashiri Japan 106 D4 .......... 44.01N 144.15E
Abaya, Lake Ethiopia 85 H2 .......... 6.19N 37.53E
Abaza Rus. Fed. 100 G8 .......... 52.40N 90.06E
Abbeville France 44 D7 .......... 50.06N 1.50E
Abbeyfeale Ireland 41 B2 .......... 52.23N 9.18W
Abbey Head Scotland 17 F2 .......... 54.46N 3.58W
Abbeyleix Ireland 41 D2 .......... 52.55N 7.21W
Abbottabad Pakistan 95 L6 .......... 34.13N 73.17E
Abéché Chad 85 G3 .......... 13.50N 20.49E
Abeokuta Nigeria 84 E2 .......... 7.07N 3.18E
Aberaeron Wales 12 C4 .......... 52.15N 4.15W
Aberchirder Scotland 19 G2 .......... 57.34N 2.38W
Aberdare Wales 12 D3 .......... 51.43N 3.27W
Aberdare Range mts Kenya 87 B2 .......... 0.21S 36.19E
Aberdaron Wales 12 C4 .......... 52.48N 4.43W
Aberdeen Scotland 19 G2 .......... 57.09N 2.06W
Aberdeen d. Scotland 8 D5 .......... 57.10N 2.11W
Aberdeen U.S.A. 64 G6 .......... 45.28N 98.31W
Aberdeenshire d. Scotland 8 D5 .......... 57.21N 2.32W
Aberfeldy Scotland 19 F1 .......... 56.37N 3.52W
Aberford England 15 F2 .......... 53.50N 1.21W
Aberfoyle Scotland 16 E4 .......... 56.11N 4.23W
Abergavenny Wales 12 D3 .......... 51.49N 3.01W
Abergele Wales 12 D5 .......... 53.17N 3.35W
Aberlour Scotland 19 F2 .......... 57.29N 3.13W
Aberporth Wales 12 C4 .......... 52.08N 4.33W
Abersoch Wales 12 C4 .......... 52.50N 4.30W
Abertillery Wales 12 D3 .......... 51.44N 3.08W
Aberystwyth Wales 12 C4 .......... 52.25N 4.05W
Abhā Saudi Arabia 94 F3 .......... 18.14N 42.27E
Abidjan Côte d'Ivoire 84 D2 .......... 5.21N 4.02W
Abilene U.S.A. 64 G3 .......... 32.26N 99.45W
Abingdon England 10 D2 .......... 51.40N 1.17W
Abington Scotland 17 F3 .......... 55.30N 3.41W
Abitibi, Lake Canada 65 J6 .......... 48.55N 80.01W
Aboyne Scotland 19 G2 .......... 57.05N 2.47W
Abqaiq Saudi Arabia 95 G5 .......... 25.56N 49.42E
Abrolhos Bank f. S. Atlantic Oc. 109 R4 .......... 19.28S 38.59W
Abū 'Arīsh Saudi Arabia 94 F3 .......... 16.59N 42.45E
Abu Dhabi U.A.E. 95 H4 .......... 24.28N 54.20E
Abū Hamed Sudan 85 H3 .......... 19.30N 33.24E
Abuja Nigeria 84 E2 .......... 9.06N 7.19E
Abū Kamāl Syria 94 F6 .......... 34.26N 40.56E
Abunã r. Bolivia 76 G6 .......... 9.43S 65.26W
Abunã Brazil 76 G6 .......... 9.44S 65.20W
Abū Nujaym Libya 53 G3 .......... 30.28N 15.27E
Abū Sunbul Egypt 94 D4 .......... 22.22N 31.37E
Abyad Sudan 94 C2 .......... 13.46N 26.26E
A Cañiza Spain 48 A5 .......... 42.13N 8.16W
Acaponeta Mexico 70 C5 .......... 22.30N 105.25W
Acapulco Mexico 70 E4 .......... 16.55N 99.52W
Acarigua Venezuela 72 C7 .......... 9.33N 69.11W
Accra Ghana 84 D2 .......... 5.35N 0.14W
Accrington England 15 E2 .......... 53.45N 2.22W
Acheloös r. Greece 56 D4 .......... 38.20N 21.06E
Achill Island Ireland 41 A3 .......... 53.56N 10.00W
Achinsk Rus. Fed. 59 K3 .......... 56.17N 90.34E
A'Chralaig mt. Scotland 18 D2 .......... 57.11N 5.09W
Acklins Island Bahamas 71 J5 .......... 22.18N 74.08W
Acle England 11 G3 .......... 52.38N 1.33E
Aconcagua, Cerro mt. Argentina 73 B3 .......... 32.38S 70.01W
A Coruña Spain 48 A5 .......... 43.22N 8.23W
Acre d. Brazil 76 F6 .......... 9.06S 70.25W
Acre r. Brazil 76 G5 .......... 10.07S 67.52W
Actéon, Groupe is French Polynesia 109 K4 .......... 21.20S 135.57W
Adaja r. Spain 48 C4 .......... 41.33N 4.51W
Adam's Peak Sri Lanka 96 F2 .......... 6.49N 80.28E
Adana Turkey 57 K3 .......... 36.59N 35.19E
Adapazarı Turkey 57 I5 .......... 40.47N 30.23E
Ada Terra Ethiopia 87 C4 .......... 6.37N 40.56E
Adda r. Italy 50 C6 .......... 45.08N 9.53E
Ad Dahnā' des. Saudi Arabia 95 G5 .......... 20.40N 46.52E
Ad Dakhla Western Sahara 84 C4 .......... 23.42N 15.56W
Adderbury England 10 D3 .......... 52.01N 1.19W
Ad Dir'īyah Saudi Arabia 95 G5 .......... 24.45N 46.34E
Addis Ababa Ethiopia 85 H2 .......... 9.01N 38.45E
Ad Dīwānīyah Iraq 94 F6 .......... 31.59N 44.59E
Adelaide Australia 110 C3 .......... 34.56S 138.40E
Aden Yemen 94 F2 .......... 12.49N 44.59E
Aden, Gulf of Somalia/Yemen 85 I3 .......... 11.44N 45.16E
Adi i. Indonesia 105 I3 .......... 4.15S 133.27E
Ādī Ārk'ay Ethiopia 94 E2 .......... 13.24N 38.03E
Adige r. Italy 50 F6 .......... 45.08N 12.18E
Ādīgrat Ethiopia 94 E2 .......... 14.16N 39.29E
Adilanga Uganda 87 A3 .......... 2.43N 33.28E
Adi Ugri Eritrea 94 E2 .......... 14.52N 38.48E
Adıyaman Turkey 57 M3 .......... 37.46N 38.17E
Admiralty Islands P.N.G. 110 D6 .......... 1.44S 146.17E
Adour r. France 44 C3 .......... 43.32N 1.31W
Adriatic Sea Europe 50 E6 .......... 44.19N 13.24E
Ādwa Ethiopia 85 H3 .......... 14.09N 38.52E
Adwick le Street England 15 F2 .......... 53.34N 1.12W
Adycha r. Rus. Fed. 59 O4 .......... 66.42N 136.32E
Aegean Sea Greece/Turkey 56 F4 .......... 39.00N 24.51E
Afghanistan Asia 95 K6 .......... 33.53N 65.52E
Afmadow Somalia 87 C3 .......... 0.32N 42.04E
Africa 82
Afyon Turkey 57 I4 .......... 38.46N 30.33E
Agadez Niger 84 E3 .......... 16.57N 7.59E
Agadir Morocco 84 D5 .......... 30.27N 9.37W
Agano r. Japan 106 C3 .......... 37.58N 139.02E
Agartala India 97 H5 .......... 23.50N 91.16E
Agde France 44 E3 .......... 43.18N 3.28E
Agen France 44 D4 .......... 44.12N 0.38E
Āgere Maryam Ethiopia 87 B4 .......... 5.38N 38.13E
Agios Dimitrios Greece 56 E3 .......... 37.49N 23.51E
Agios Efstratios i. Greece 56 F4 .......... 39.30N 25.01E
Agios Konstantinos Greece 56 E4 .......... 38.45N 22.51E
Agios Nikolaos Greece 56 F2 .......... 35.12N 25.43E
Agirwat Hills Sudan 94 E3 .......... 18.23N 36.41E
Agra India 96 E6 .......... 27.09N 78.02E
Ağrı Turkey 94 F7 .......... 39.43N 43.04E
Agrigento Italy 50 E2 .......... 37.18N 13.35E
Agrihan i. N. Mariana Is 105 L7 .......... 18.46N 145.42E
Aguadulce Panama 71 H2 .......... 8.12N 80.33W
Aguascalientes Mexico 70 D5 .......... 21.51N 102.21W
Aguascalientes d. Mexico 70 D5 .......... 21.57N 102.11W
Aguilar de Campóo Spain 48 C5 .......... 42.47N 4.14W
Águilas Spain 48 E2 .......... 37.25N 1.35W

Agulhas, Cape S. Africa 86 B1 .......... 34.50S 20.03E
Ahar Iran 95 G7 .......... 38.27N 47.02E
Ahaus Germany 42 G5 .......... 52.05N 7.01E
Ahmadabad India 96 D5 .......... 23.03N 72.37E
Ahmadpur East Pakistan 96 D6 .......... 29.10N 71.22E
Ahvāz Iran 95 G6 .......... 31.15N 48.40E
Aigialousa Cyprus 57 K2 .......... 35.31N 34.11E
Aigina i. Greece 56 E3 .......... 37.41N 23.31E
Ailsa Craig i. Scotland 16 D3 .......... 55.15N 5.06W
'Aïn Beïda Algeria 52 E4 .......... 35.47N 7.25E
'Aïn Ben Tili Mauritania 84 D4 .......... 25.58N 9.31W
Aïn Sefra Algeria 84 D5 .......... 32.42N 0.35W
Aïr, Massif de l' mts Niger 84 E3 .......... 18.46N 8.15E
Airdrie Canada 62 G3 .......... 51.17N 114.01W
Airdrie Scotland 17 F3 .......... 55.52N 3.58W
Aisne r. France 44 E6 .......... 49.26N 2.51E
Aitape P.N.G. 105 K3 .......... 3.09S 142.22E
Aitutaki i. Cook Is 109 J4 .......... 18.52S 159.44W
Aix-en-Provence France 44 F3 .......... 43.32N 5.27E
Aizkraukle Latvia 46 F7 .......... 56.36N 25.15E
Aizu-wakamatsu Japan 106 C3 .......... 37.29N 139.56E
Ajaccio France 44 H2 .......... 41.55N 8.44E
Ajdābiyā Libya 85 G4 .......... 30.45N 20.13E
Akçakale Turkey 57 M3 .......... 36.43N 38.57E
Akdağmadeni Turkey 57 K4 .......... 39.39N 35.54E
Akhdar, Al Jabal al mts Libya 53 H3 .......... 31.46N 20.46E
Akhdar, Jabal mts Oman 95 I4 .......... 23.22N 57.00E
Akhisar Turkey 57 G4 .......... 38.55N 27.50E
Akimiski Island Canada 63 J3 .......... 53.08N 81.17W
Akita Japan 106 D3 .......... 39.43N 140.07E
Akkajaure l. Sweden 40 D4 .......... 67.41N 17.29E
Aknoul Morocco 48 D1 .......... 34.38N 3.51W
Akordat Eritrea 85 H3 .......... 15.31N 37.54E
Akpatok Island Canada 63 L4 .......... 60.24N 67.45W
Akranes Iceland 40 X2 .......... 64.19N 22.05W
Akron U.S.A. 65 J5 .......... 41.07N 81.33W
Aksai Chin Asia 96 E8 .......... 35.08N 79.11E
Aksaray Turkey 57 K4 .......... 38.23N 34.02E
Akşehir Turkey 57 I4 .......... 38.21N 31.24E
Aksu China 100 E6 .......... 41.06N 80.21E
Aktau Kazakhstan 58 G2 .......... 43.39N 51.12E
Aktobe Kazakhstan 58 G3 .......... 50.13N 57.10E
Aktogay Kazakhstan 58 I2 .......... 47.06N 79.42E
Akureyri Iceland 40 Y2 .......... 65.41N 18.07W
Alabama d. U.S.A. 65 I3 .......... 32.41N 86.42W
Alabama r. U.S.A. 65 I3 .......... 31.09N 87.57W
Alagoas d. Brazil 77 M6 .......... 9.33S 36.46W
Alagoinhas Brazil 77 M5 .......... 12.07S 38.17W
Al Aḥmadī Kuwait 95 G5 .......... 29.04N 48.02E
Alakol', Ozero l. Kazakhstan 100 E7 .......... 46.03N 81.30E
Alamagan i. N. Mariana Is 105 L7 .......... 17.35N 145.52E
Åland Islands Finland 40 D3 .......... 60.28N 19.53E
Alanya Turkey 57 J3 .......... 36.33N 32.00E
Al 'Aqabah Jordan 94 E5 .......... 29.31N 35.01E
Al Arṭāwīyah Saudi Arabia 95 G5 .......... 26.30N 45.21E
Alaşehir Turkey 57 H4 .......... 38.21N 28.30E
Alaska d. U.S.A. 62 D4 .......... 63.41N 143.45W
Alaska, Gulf of U.S.A. 62 D3 .......... 58.10N 147.57W
Alaska Peninsula U.S.A. 62 C3 .......... 55.18N 162.25W
Alaska Range mts U.S.A. 62 D4 .......... 63.19N 148.01W
Alausí Ecuador 76 F7 .......... 2.10S 78.52W
Alavus Finland 40 E3 .......... 62.35N 23.37E
Alaw, Llyn resr Wales 12 C5 .......... 53.21N 4.25W
Albacete Spain 48 E3 .......... 39.00N 1.50W
Alba Iulia Romania 56 E8 .......... 46.05N 23.36E
Albania Europe 56 C5 .......... 41.56N 19.58E
Albany Australia 110 A3 .......... 34.58S 117.54E
Albany r. Canada 63 J3 .......... 52.08N 81.59W
Albany U.S.A. 65 L5 .......... 42.40N 73.46W
Albatross Bay Australia 105 K1 .......... 12.41S 141.44E
Al Bawītī Egypt 85 G4 .......... 28.21N 28.50E
Al Baydā' Libya 85 G5 .......... 32.44N 21.44E
Albenga Italy 50 C6 .......... 44.03N 8.13E
Alberche r. Spain 48 C3 .......... 39.58N 4.46W
Albert France 42 B2 .......... 49.59N 2.39E
Albert, Lake Dem. Rep. Congo/Uganda 86 C5 .......... 1.43N 30.52E
Alberta d. Canada 62 G3 .......... 52.45N 113.59W
Albert Lea U.S.A. 65 H5 .......... 43.39N 93.22W
Albert Nile r. South Sudan/Uganda 85 H2 .......... 3.36N 32.02E
Albi France 44 E3 .......... 43.56N 2.08E
Al Biyāḍh f. Saudi Arabia 95 G5 .......... 20.57N 46.14E
Alborán, Isla de i. Spain 48 D1 .......... 35.56N 3.02W
Albuquerque U.S.A. 64 E4 .......... 35.07N 106.38W
Al Buraymī Oman 95 I4 .......... 24.14N 55.46E
Albury Australia 110 D3 .......... 36.03S 146.54E
Alcalá de Henares Spain 48 D4 .......... 40.29N 3.21W
Alcalá la Real Spain 48 D2 .......... 37.28N 3.55W
Alcañiz Spain 48 E4 .......... 41.03N 0.07W
Alcázar de San Juan Spain 48 D3 .......... 39.23N 3.11W
Alcester England 10 D3 .......... 52.13N 1.52W
Alcoy-Alcoi Spain 48 E3 .......... 38.42N 0.27W
Alcúdia Spain 48 G3 .......... 39.52N 3.08E
Aldabra Islands Seychelles 85 I1 .......... 9.16S 46.30E
Aldan Rus. Fed. 59 N3 .......... 58.36N 125.25E
Aldan r. Rus. Fed. 59 N4 .......... 63.32N 128.46E
Aldbrough England 15 G2 .......... 53.50N 0.07W
Aldeburgh England 11 G3 .......... 52.09N 1.36E
Alderley Edge England 15 E2 .......... 53.18N 2.14W
Alderney i. Channel Is 13 Z9 .......... 49.42N 2.15W
Aldershot England 10 E2 .......... 51.15N 0.45W
Aldingham England 14 D3 .......... 54.08N 3.06W
Aldridge England 10 D3 .......... 52.36N 1.55W
Aleksandrovsk-Sakhalinskiy Rus. Fed. 59 P3 .......... 51.08N 142.21E
Aleksin Rus. Fed. 55 Q6 .......... 54.31N 37.05E
Alençon France 44 D6 .......... 48.26N 0.06E
Aleppo Syria 94 E7 .......... 36.12N 37.09E
Alès France 44 F4 .......... 44.08N 4.05E
Aleşd Romania 46 F1 .......... 47.03N 22.25E
Alessandria Italy 50 C6 .......... 44.55N 8.38E
Ålesund Norway 40 A3 .......... 62.28N 6.12E
Aleutian Basin f. Bering Sea 108 H9 .......... 57.54N 179.12E
Aleutian Islands U.S.A. 62 A3 .......... 53.03N 176.15W
Aleutian Range mts U.S.A. 62 C3 .......... 56.10N 159.17W
Aleutian Trench f. N. Pacific Oc. 108 I9 .......... 49.44N 178.54W
Alexander Archipelago is U.S.A. 62 E3 .......... 57.59N 137.33W
Alexandra L. S. Atlantic Oc. 73 F1 .......... 54.05S 37.56W
Alexandria Egypt 85 G5 .......... 31.13N 29.56E
Alexandria Romania 56 F6 .......... 43.58N 25.20E
Alexandria Scotland 16 E3 .......... 55.59N 4.35W
Alexandria La. U.S.A. 65 H3 .......... 31.17N 92.28W
Alexandria Va. U.S.A. 65 K4 .......... 38.48N 77.05W
Aleysk Rus. Fed. 100 E8 .......... 52.30N 82.51E
Al Fayyūm Egypt 85 H4 .......... 29.18N 30.51E
Alfreton England 15 F2 .......... 53.06N 1.23W
Algarve f. Portugal 48 A2 .......... 37.16N 8.07W
Algeciras Spain 48 C2 .......... 36.07N 5.27W
Algeria Africa 84 E4 .......... 30.15N 3.31E
Al Ghaydah Yemen 95 H3 .......... 16.14N 52.13E
Alghero Italy 50 C4 .......... 40.34N 8.20E
Al Ghurdaqah Egypt 53 J2 .......... 27.12N 33.48E

Al Ghwaybiyah Saudi Arabia 95 G5 .......... 25.14N 49.43E
Algiers Algeria 84 E5 .......... 36.46N 3.04E
Algorta Spain 48 D5 .......... 43.21N 2.59W
Al Ḥasakah Syria 94 F7 .......... 36.30N 40.44E
Al Hoceima Morocco 52 C4 .......... 35.15N 3.56W
Al Hufūf Saudi Arabia 95 G5 .......... 25.22N 49.35E
Aliağa Turkey 56 G4 .......... 38.47N 26.58E
Aliakmonas r. Greece 56 E5 .......... 40.28N 22.38E
Alicante Spain 48 E3 .......... 38.21N 0.28W
Alice Springs town Australia 110 C4 .......... 23.42S 133.52E
Alingsås Sweden 40 C2 .......... 57.56N 12.33E
Al Ismā'īlīyah Egypt 53 J3 .......... 30.35N 32.17E
Al Jaghbūb Libya 85 G4 .......... 29.43N 24.31E
Al Jahrah Kuwait 95 G5 .......... 29.20N 47.41E
Al Jawf Libya 85 G4 .......... 24.14N 23.24E
Al Jawf Saudi Arabia 94 E5 .......... 29.47N 39.55E
Al Jawsh Libya 52 F3 .......... 32.01N 11.42E
Al Jubayl Saudi Arabia 95 G5 .......... 27.02N 49.38E
Aljustrel Portugal 48 A2 .......... 37.53N 8.10W
Al Karak Jordan 94 E6 .......... 31.10N 35.42E
Al Khābūrah Oman 95 I4 .......... 23.58N 57.06E
Al Khārijah Egypt 85 H4 .......... 25.24N 30.33E
Al Khaşab Oman 95 I5 .......... 26.11N 56.14E
Al Khums Libya 52 F3 .......... 32.35N 14.22E
Alkmaar Neth. 42 D5 .......... 52.38N 4.45E
Al Kūt Iraq 95 G6 .......... 32.31N 45.47E
Allahabad India 96 F6 .......... 25.25N 81.52E
Allakh-Yun' Rus. Fed. 59 O4 .......... 61.05N 138.03E
Allegheny r. U.S.A. 65 K5 .......... 40.27N 79.59W
Allegheny Mountains U.S.A. 65 J4 .......... 38.46N 82.22W
Allen, Lough l. Ireland 41 C4 .......... 54.09N 8.03W
Allendale Town England 15 E3 .......... 54.54N 2.15W
Allentown U.S.A. 65 K5 .......... 40.37N 75.30W
Alleppey India 96 E2 .......... 9.30N 76.21E
Aller r. Germany 54 C5 .......... 52.57N 9.11E
Allinge-Sandvig Denmark 46 B5 .......... 55.16N 14.49E
Al Lith Saudi Arabia 94 F4 .......... 20.10N 40.16E
Alloa Scotland 17 F4 .......... 56.07N 3.47W
Almansa Spain 48 E3 .......... 38.52N 1.05W
Al Manşūrah Egypt 53 J3 .......... 31.02N 31.23E
Almanzor mt. Spain 48 C4 .......... 40.15N 5.18W
Al Marj Libya 53 H3 .......... 32.29N 20.50E
Almaty Kazakhstan 58 I2 .......... 43.16N 77.01E
Almeirim Brazil 77 J7 .......... 1.30S 52.35W
Almelo Neth. 42 F5 .......... 52.21N 6.40E
Almendra, Embalse de resr Spain 48 B4 .......... 41.17N 6.14W
Almería Spain 48 D2 .......... 36.50N 2.27W
Almina, Punta pt Spain 48 C1 .......... 35.54N 5.16W
Al Minyā Egypt 85 H4 .......... 28.05N 30.45E
Almodôvar Portugal 48 A2 .......... 37.31N 8.04W
Almond r. Scotland 17 F4 .......... 56.25N 3.28W
Al Mudawwara Jordan 94 E5 .......... 29.19N 36.02E
Almuñécar Spain 48 D2 .......... 36.44N 3.41W
Alnwick England 15 F4 .......... 55.25N 1.42W
Alofi Niue 108 I4 .......... 19.03S 169.54W
Aloi Uganda 87 A3 .......... 2.17N 33.09E
Alor i. Indonesia 105 G2 .......... 8.17S 124.45E
Alor Setar Malaysia 104 C5 .......... 6.08N 100.22E
Alpena U.S.A. 65 J6 .......... 45.03N 83.27W
Alpine U.S.A. 64 F3 .......... 30.18N 103.35W
Alps mts Europe 52 F6 .......... 46.00N 7.30E
Al Qa'āmīyāt f. Saudi Arabia 95 G3 .......... 17.59N 47.47E
Al Qaddāḥīyah Libya 53 G3 .......... 31.22N 15.12E
Al Qāmishlī Syria 94 F7 .......... 37.03N 41.13E
Al Qaryatayn Syria 57 L2 .......... 34.13N 37.14E
Al Qunfidhah Saudi Arabia 94 F3 .......... 19.09N 41.04E
Al Quşayr Egypt 85 H4 .......... 26.07N 34.13E
Alsace d. France 42 G1 .......... 48.22N 7.24E
Alsager England 15 E2 .......... 53.06N 2.18W
Alston England 15 E3 .......... 54.49N 2.26W
Altaelva r. Norway 40 E5 .......... 69.57N 23.20E
Altai Mountains Asia 100 F7 .......... 48.55N 87.16E
Altamira Brazil 77 J7 .......... 3.14S 52.14W
Altamura Italy 50 G4 .......... 40.49N 16.34E
Altay China 101 I4 .......... 47.48N 88.10E
Altay Mongolia 100 H7 .......... 46.18N 96.15E
Altiplano f. Bolivia 76 G4 .......... 16.24S 69.39W
Altiplano Mexicano mts N. America 60 I5 .......... 24.00N 105.00W
Alton England 10 E2 .......... 51.09N 0.58W
Altoona U.S.A. 65 K5 .......... 40.30N 78.24W
Altötting Germany 54 E3 .......... 48.14N 12.41E
Altrincham England 15 E2 .......... 53.23N 2.21W
Altun Shan mts China 100 F5 .......... 37.45N 86.38E
Alturas U.S.A. 64 B5 .......... 41.30N 120.31W
Al 'Uqaylah Libya 53 G3 .......... 30.13N 19.12E
Al 'Uwaynāt Libya 94 B4 .......... 22.10N 24.00E
Älvdalen Sweden 40 C3 .......... 61.13N 14.04E
Alveley England 10 C3 .......... 52.27N 2.21W
Älvsbyn Sweden 40 E4 .......... 65.40N 21.00E
Al Wajh Saudi Arabia 94 E5 .......... 26.17N 36.25E
Alwen Reservoir Wales 12 D5 .......... 53.05N 3.35W
Al Widyān f. Iraq/Saudi Arabia 94 F6 .......... 32.09N 40.22E
Alyth Scotland 19 F1 .......... 56.38N 3.14W
Alytus Lithuania 46 F6 .......... 54.23N 24.03E
Amadeus, Lake Australia 110 C4 .......... 24.50S 131.09E
Amadjuak Lake Canada 63 K4 .......... 64.57N 71.09W
Amadora Portugal 48 A3 .......... 38.46N 9.14W
Åmål Sweden 40 C2 .......... 59.03N 12.44E
Amamapare Indonesia 105 J3 .......... 4.54S 136.58E
Amami-Ō-shima i. Japan 106 A1 .......... 28.13N 129.08E
Amapá Brazil 77 J8 .......... 2.02N 50.50W
Amapá d. Brazil 77 J8 .......... 1.29N 51.50W
Amarillo U.S.A. 64 F4 .......... 35.15N 101.50W
Amasya Turkey 57 K5 .......... 40.39N 35.50E
Amazon r. S. America 72 D7 .......... 0.01N 50.37W
Amazon, Mouths of the Brazil 77 K8 .......... 0.41N 49.28W
Amazonas d. Brazil 77 H6 .......... 4.38S 65.10W
Ambarchik Rus. Fed. 59 R4 .......... 69.35N 162.13E
Ambato Ecuador 76 F7 .......... 1.16S 78.39W
Ambergate England 15 F2 .......... 53.04N 1.29W
Ambergris Cay i. Belize 70 G4 .......... 18.08N 87.52W
Amble England 15 F4 .......... 55.20N 1.35W
Ambleside England 14 E3 .......... 54.26N 2.58W
Ambon Indonesia 105 H3 .......... 3.43S 128.11E
Amboseli National Park Kenya 87 B2 .......... 2.37S 37.14E
Ambrym i. Vanuatu 111 F5 .......... 16.12S 168.13E
Ameland i. Neth. 42 E6 .......... 53.28N 5.48E
American Samoa is S. Pacific Oc. 108 I5 .......... 12.00S 170.00W
Amersfoort Neth. 42 E5 .......... 52.09N 5.23E
Amersham England 10 E2 .......... 51.41N 0.36W
Amesbury England 10 D2 .......... 51.10N 1.47W
Amfissa Greece 56 E4 .......... 38.32N 22.22E
Amgu Rus. Fed. 106 C5 .......... 45.46N 137.32E
Amgun' r. Rus. Fed. 59 O3 .......... 53.01N 139.38E
Amiens France 44 E6 .......... 49.54N 2.18E
Amino Ethiopia 87 C4 .......... 4.21N 41.51E
Amlwch Wales 12 C5 .......... 53.25N 4.21W
'Ammān Jordan 94 E6 .......... 31.57N 35.56E
Ammanford Wales 12 D3 .......... 51.48N 3.59W
Amol Iran 95 H7 .......... 36.27N 52.20E
Amorgos i. Greece 56 F3 .......... 36.49N 25.54E
Amos Canada 63 K2 .......... 48.34N 78.08W

Ampthill England 11 E3 .......... 52.02N 0.30W
Amravati India 96 E5 .......... 20.56N 77.51E
Amritsar India 96 D7 .......... 31.34N 74.56E
Amstelveen Neth. 42 D5 .......... 52.19N 4.52E
Amsterdam Neth. 42 D5 .......... 52.23N 4.54E
Amstetten Austria 54 F3 .......... 48.08N 14.52E
Amu Darya r. Asia 58 H2 .......... 43.50N 59.00E
Amund Ringnes Island Canada 63 I5 .......... 78.17N 96.35W
Amundsen Gulf Canada 62 F5 .......... 70.25N 121.26W
Amuntai Indonesia 104 F3 .......... 2.25S 115.13E
Amur r. Rus. Fed. 59 P3 .......... 53.17N 140.37E
Anabar r. Rus. Fed. 59 M5 .......... 73.13N 113.31E
Anadolu Dağları mts Turkey 57 L5 .......... 40.59N 36.11E
Anadyr' Rus. Fed. 59 T4 .......... 64.44N 177.20E
Anadyrskiy Zaliv b. Rus. Fed. 59 T4 .......... 63.56N 177.42W
'Ānah Iraq 94 F6 .......... 34.25N 41.56E
Anambas, Kepulauan is Indonesia 104 D4 .......... 3.17N 105.55E
Anamur Turkey 57 J3 .......... 36.06N 32.50E
Anapa Rus. Fed. 57 L7 .......... 44.54N 37.20E
Anápolis Brazil 77 K4 .......... 16.20S 48.55W
Anatahan i. N. Mariana Is 105 L7 .......... 16.21N 145.42E
Anatolia f. Turkey 57 J4 .......... 38.58N 33.19E
Anchorage U.S.A. 62 D4 .......... 61.12N 149.52W
Ancona Italy 50 E5 .......... 43.37N 13.31E
Åndalsnes Norway 40 A3 .......... 62.34N 7.42E
Andaman Islands India 97 H3 .......... 12.46N 93.11E
Andaman Sea Indian Oc. 97 I3 .......... 11.33N 95.19E
Anderlecht Belgium 42 D4 .......... 50.49N 4.18E
Andermatt Switz. 54 C2 .......... 46.38N 8.36E
Anderson r. Canada 62 F4 .......... 69.41N 128.56W
Anderson U.S.A. 62 D4 .......... 64.22N 149.12W
Andes mts S. America 73 B6 .......... 9.10S 77.03W
Andfjorden str. Norway 40 D5 .......... 68.53N 16.04E
Andhra Pradesh d. India 96 E4 .......... 16.03N 79.11E
Andkhvoy Afgh. 95 K7 .......... 36.59N 65.08E
Andong S. Korea 106 A3 .......... 36.33N 128.43E
Andorra Europe 48 F5 .......... 42.31N 1.35E
Andorra la Vella Andorra 48 F5 .......... 42.31N 1.32E
Andover England 10 D2 .......... 51.12N 1.29W
Andøya i. Norway 40 C5 .......... 69.11N 15.48E
Andreas Isle of Man 14 C3 .......... 54.22N 4.27W
Andria Italy 50 G4 .......... 41.14N 16.18E
Andros i. Bahamas 71 I5 .......... 24.25N 78.09W
Andros i. Greece 56 F3 .......... 37.53N 24.57E
Andújar Spain 48 C3 .......... 38.02N 4.03W
Anéfis Mali 84 E3 .......... 18.02N 0.32E
Anegada i. Virgin Is (U.K.) 71 L4 .......... 18.44N 64.19W
Aneto mt. Spain 48 F5 .......... 42.37N 0.39E
Angara r. Rus. Fed. 59 K3 .......... 58.05N 92.59E
Angarsk Rus. Fed. 101 I8 .......... 52.24N 103.45E
Änge Sweden 40 C3 .......... 62.32N 15.40E
Ángel de la Guarda, Isla i. Mexico 70 B6 .......... 29.25N 113.24W
Ångelholm Sweden 40 C2 .......... 56.15N 12.51E
Angers France 44 C5 .......... 47.28N 0.33W
Anglesey i. Wales 12 C5 .......... 53.18N 4.23W
Angola Africa 86 A3 .......... 11.40S 17.34E
Angola Basin f. Atlantic Oc. 117 J5 .......... 15.00S 0.00E
Angoulême France 44 D4 .......... 45.39N 0.10E
Angren Uzbekistan 100 C6 .......... 41.02N 70.07E
Anguilla i. Central America 71 L4 .......... 18.14N 63.02W
Angus d. Scotland 8 D5 .......... 56.43N 2.55W
Anhui d. China 101 L4 .......... 32.10N 117.07E
Ankara Turkey 57 J4 .......... 39.56N 32.50E
Annaba Algeria 84 E5 .......... 36.54N 7.46E
An Nabk Syria 57 L2 .......... 34.01N 36.44E
An Nafūd des. Saudi Arabia 94 F5 .......... 28.28N 41.17E
An Najaf Iraq 94 F6 .......... 31.59N 44.19E
Annalee r. Ireland 41 D4 .......... 54.02N 7.23W
Annalong Northern Ireland 16 D2 .......... 54.06N 5.54W
Annan Scotland 17 F2 .......... 54.59N 3.15W
Annan r. Scotland 17 F2 .......... 54.59N 3.16W
Annapurna mt. Nepal 96 F6 .......... 28.34N 83.49E
Ann Arbor U.S.A. 65 J5 .......... 42.17N 83.45W
An Nāşirīyah Iraq 95 G6 .......... 31.01N 46.14E
An Nawfalīyah Libya 53 G3 .......... 30.51N 17.52E
Annecy France 44 G4 .......... 45.54N 6.08E
Anniston U.S.A. 65 I3 .......... 33.39N 85.43W
An Nu'ayrīyah Saudi Arabia 95 G5 .......... 27.29N 48.26E
An Nuşayrīyah, Jabal mts Syria 57 L2 .......... 35.15N 36.05E
Ansbach Germany 54 D3 .......... 49.18N 10.36E
Anshan China 101 M6 .......... 41.06N 123.02E
Anshun China 101 J3 .......... 26.15N 105.57E
Anstruther Scotland 17 G4 .......... 56.13N 2.42W
Antakya Turkey 57 L3 .......... 36.11N 36.07E
Antalya Turkey 57 I3 .......... 36.53N 30.41E
Antalya Körfezi g. Turkey 57 I3 .......... 36.40N 30.58E
Antananarivo Madagascar 86 D3 .......... 18.54S 47.33E
Antarctica 112
Antarctic Peninsula f. Antarctica 116 F2 .......... 65.00S 64.00W
An Teallach mt. Scotland 18 D2 .......... 57.48N 5.16W
Antequera Spain 48 C2 .......... 37.02N 4.33W
Antibes France 44 G3 .......... 43.35N 7.07E
Anticosti, Île d' i. Canada 63 L2 .......... 49.27N 62.59W
Antigua i. Antigua 71 L4 .......... 17.02N 61.43W
Antigua and Barbuda Central America 71 L4 .......... 17.20N 61.20W
Antikythira i. Greece 56 E2 .......... 35.51N 23.18E
Antipodes Islands New Zealand 111 G2 .......... 49.39S 178.44E
Antofagasta Chile 73 B4 .......... 23.37S 70.22W
Antrim Northern Ireland 16 C2 .......... 54.43N 6.12W
Antrim d. Northern Ireland 9 B4 .......... 54.43N 6.16W
Antrim f. Northern Ireland 16 C2 .......... 54.43N 6.16W
Antrim Hills Northern Ireland 16 C3 .......... 55.05N 6.16W
Antsirabe Madagascar 86 D3 .......... 19.53S 47.03E
Antsiranana Madagascar 86 D3 .......... 12.19S 49.17E
Antsohihy Madagascar 86 D3 .......... 14.53S 47.59E
Antwerp Belgium 42 D4 .......... 51.12N 4.26E
Antwerpen d. Belgium 42 D4 .......... 51.17N 4.46E
Anxi China 100 H6 .......... 40.27N 95.48E
Anyang China 101 K5 .......... 36.04N 114.22E
Anzhero-Sudzhensk Rus. Fed. 58 J3 .......... 56.08N 86.01E
Aomori Japan 106 D4 .......... 40.49N 140.45E
Aoraki mt. New Zealand 111 G2 .......... 43.37S 170.09E
Aosta Italy 50 B6 .......... 45.44N 7.20E
Apa r. Brazil 77 I3 .......... 22.07S 57.57W
Apalachee Bay U.S.A. 65 J2 .......... 29.50N 84.40W
Apaporis r. Colombia 76 G7 .......... 1.04S 69.26W
Aparri Phil. 105 G7 .......... 18.21N 121.40E
Apatity Rus. Fed. 40 H4 .......... 67.34N 33.23E
Apeldoorn Neth. 42 E5 .......... 52.12N 5.68E
Apennines mts Italy 50 D6 .......... 44.37N 9.47E
Apia Samoa 108 I5 .......... 13.48S 171.44W
Aporé r. Brazil 77 J4 .......... 19.25S 50.59W
Apostolos Andreas, Cape Cyprus 57 K2 .......... 35.41N 34.35E
Appalachian Mountains U.S.A. 65 J4 .......... 38.08N 83.01W
Appleby-in-Westmorland England 15 E3 .......... 54.35N 2.29W
Appledore England 13 C3 .......... 51.03N 4.12W
Apucarana Brazil 77 J3 .......... 23.34S 51.27W
Apurímac r. Peru 76 F5 .......... 12.16S 73.54W
Aqaba, Gulf of Asia 94 D5 .......... 29.19N 34.54E
Åra Ārba Ethiopia 87 C4 .......... 5.53N 41.26E
Arabian Peninsula Asia 85 I4 .......... 24.00N 45.00E
Arabian Sea Indian Oc. 90 F4 .......... 18.08N 66.38E
Aracaju Brazil 77 M5 .......... 10.52S 37.03W

Aracati Brazil 77 M7 .................................4.33S 37.42W
Araçatuba Brazil 77 J3 ............................21.12S 50.22W
Aracena, Sierra de hills Spain 48 B2 ...........37.51N 7.07W
Arad Romania 56 D8 ...............................46.11N 21.21E
Arafura Sea Australia/Indonesia 110 C6 ......9.04S 132.58E
Aragón r. Spain 48 E5 ............................42.13N 1.45W
Araguaia r. Brazil 77 K6 .........................5.24S 48.41W
Araguaína Brazil 77 K6 ...........................7.20S 48.15W
Araguari Brazil 77 K4 .............................18.38S 48.09W
Arak Algeria 84 E4 ...............................25.18N 3.39E
Arāk Iran 95 G6 ...................................34.05N 49.42E
Arakan Yoma mts Myanmar 97 H5 .............20.18N 94.07E
Aral Sea Kazakhstan/Uzbekistan 58 H2 .......45.07N 60.05E
Aral'sk Kazakhstan 58 H2 ........................46.46N 61.43E
Aranda de Duero Spain 48 D4 ..................41.41N 3.40W
Aran Island Ireland 41 C3 ........................54.59N 8.35W
Aran Islands Ireland 41 B3 .......................53.07N 9.44W
Aranjuez Spain 48 D4 .............................40.02N 3.36W
Arapgir Turkey 57 M4 ............................39.02N 38.29E
Arapiraca Brazil 77 M6 ...........................9.44S 36.37W
Arapis, Akra pt Greece 56 F5 ....................40.27N 24.00E
'Ar'ar Saudi Arabia 94 F6 ........................30.58N 40.58E
Araraquara Brazil 77 K3 ..........................21.47S 48.06W
Ararat, Mount Turkey 58 F1 .....................39.45N 44.15E
Árba Minch Ethiopia 87 B4 ......................5.59N 37.32E
Arbīl Iraq 94 F7 ...................................36.11N 44.01E
Arbroath Scotland 17 G4 .........................56.34N 2.35W
Arbu Lut, Dasht-e des. Afgh. 95 J5 ............29.57N 63.56E
Arcachon France 44 C4 ...........................44.40N 1.10W
Archangel Rus. Fed. 34 H4 .......................64.33N 40.33E
Arctic Bay town Canada 63 J5 ...................72.55N 85.10W
Arctic Ocean 112
Arctic Red r. Canada 62 E4 ......................67.27N 133.44W
Ardabīl Iran 95 G7 ................................38.14N 48.15E
Ardas r. Greece 56 G5 ............................41.40N 26.30E
Ardèche r. France 44 F4 ..........................44.16N 4.39E
Ardestān Iran 95 H6 ..............................33.20N 52.21E
Ardglass Northern Ireland 16 D2 ................54.15N 5.36W
Ardila r. Portugal 48 B3 ..........................38.10N 7.28W
Ardnamurchan, Point of Scotland 18 C1 ......56.43N 6.13W
Ardrishaig Scotland 16 D4 ........................56.01N 5.27W
Ardrossan Scotland 16 E3 ........................55.39N 4.49W
Ards d. Northern Ireland 9 C4 ...................54.28N 5.37W
Ards Peninsula Northern Ireland 16 D2 ........54.30N 5.25W
Ardvasar Scotland 18 D2 .........................57.03N 5.55W
Arena, Point U.S.A. 64 B4 .......................38.57N 123.44W
Arendal Norway 40 B2 ............................58.27N 8.46E
Arenig Fawr hill Wales 12 D4 ....................52.55N 3.45W
Arequipa Peru 76 F4 ..............................16.23S 71.32W
Arezzo Italy 50 D5 ................................43.27N 11.53E
Arganda Spain 48 D4 .............................40.18N 3.25W
Argentan France 44 C6 ...........................48.45N 0.01W
Argentina S. America 73 C3 .....................35.00S 68.00W
Argentine Rise f. S. Atlantic Oc. 109 Q3 ......39.32S 53.02W
Argentino, Lago l. Argentina 73 B1 .............50.20S 72.51W
Argenton-sur-Creuse France 44 D5 ............46.36N 1.31E
Argeş r. Romania 56 G7 ..........................44.04N 26.37E
Argun' r. China/Rus. Fed. 101 M8 ..............53.18N 121.20E
Argyle, Lake Australia 110 B5 ...................16.37S 128.41E
Argyll f. Scotland 16 D4 ..........................56.08N 5.19W
Argyll and Bute d. Scotland 8 C4 ...............55.46N 5.25W
Århus Denmark 40 B2 ............................56.09N 10.12E
Arica Chile 72 B5 ..................................18.29S 70.20W
Arienas, Loch l. Scotland 16 D4 .................56.35N 5.46W
Arinos r. Brazil 77 I5 ..............................10.25S 58.13W
Aripuanã r. Brazil 77 H6 ..........................5.07S 60.22W
Ariquemes Brazil 76 H6 ..........................9.59S 63.05W
Arisaig Scotland 18 D1 ...........................56.55N 5.50W
Arisaig, Sound of str. Scotland 18 D1 ..........56.51N 5.56W
Arizona d. U.S.A. 64 D3 ..........................34.11N 111.37W
Arkadelphia U.S.A. 65 H3 ........................34.09N 93.03W
Arkaig, Loch l. Scotland 18 D1 ..................56.58N 5.13W
Arkansas d. U.S.A. 65 H4 .......................35.49N 92.00W
Arkansas r. U.S.A. 65 H3 ........................33.49N 91.08W
Arkansas City U.S.A. 64 G4 .....................37.04N 97.03W
Arklow Ireland 41 E2 .............................52.48N 6.10W
Arkona, Kap c. Germany 54 E6 .................54.41N 13.27E
Arles France 44 F3 ................................43.41N 4.38E
Arlit Niger 84 E3 .................................18.42N 7.21E
Arlon Belgium 42 E2 ..............................49.41N 5.49E
Armagh Northern Ireland 16 C2 ................54.20N 6.39W
Armagh d. Northern Ireland 9 B4 ...............54.18N 6.39W
Armagh f. Northern Ireland 41 E4 ..............54.18N 6.39W
Armant Egypt 53 J2 ..............................25.37N 32.32E
Armavir Rus. Fed. 53 L6 .........................45.01N 41.06E
Armenia Asia 58 F2 ..............................40.26N 44.30E
Armenia Colombia 72 B7 ........................4.33N 75.39W
Armidale Australia 110 E3 .......................30.32S 151.41E
Armyans'k Ukraine 53 J3 .........................46.07N 33.41E
Arnhem Neth. 42 E4 .............................51.59N 5.55E
Arnhem, Cape Australia 110 C5 ................12.19S 136.58E
Arnhem Land f. Australia 110 C5 ...............13.26S 133.57E
Arno r. Italy 50 D5 ...............................43.41N 10.16E
Arnsberg Germany 54 C4 .........................51.23N 8.04E
ar Ramādī Iraq 94 F6 .............................33.23N 43.16E
arran i. Scotland 16 D3 ...........................55.35N 5.20W
ar Raqqah Syria 94 F7 ...........................35.57N 39.01E
Arras France 44 E7 ...............................50.17N 2.46E
Arrecife Canary Islands 48 Z2 ..................28.57N 13.33W
arriagá Mexico 70 F4 .............................16.16N 93.52W
arrieta Canary Islands 48 Z2 ....................29.08N 13.28W
ar Rimāl f. Saudi Arabia 95 H4 .................21.43N 52.53E
Arrochar Scotland 16 E4 .........................56.12N 4.44W
ar Ruţbah Iraq 94 F6 ............................33.01N 40.17E
Arta Greece 56 D4 ................................39.10N 20.59E
Artesia U.S.A. 64 F3 ..............................32.52N 104.25W
Artigas Uruguay 77 I1 ............................30.24S 56.29W
Artois f. France 42 A3 ............................50.40N 1.55E
Artois, Collines de l' hills France 11 G1 ........50.33N 1.54E
Artsyz Ukraine 53 H7 .............................45.59N 29.27E
aru, Kepulauan is Indonesia 105 I2 .............6.09S 134.05E
aruba i. Central America 71 K3 .................12.30N 69.56W
arunachal Pradesh d. India 97 H6 ..............27.28N 92.48E
arundel England 11 E1 ...........................50.51N 0.33W
arusha Tanzania 86 C4 ...........................3.22S 36.67E
arusha d. Tanzania 87 B2 ........................3.51S 36.39E
aruwimi r. Dem. Rep. Congo 86 B5 ...........1.14N 23.38E
arvayheer Mongolia 101 I7 ......................46.08N 102.47E
arviat Canada 63 I4 ...............................61.12N 94.09W
arvidsjaur Sweden 40 D4 ........................65.35N 19.12E
arvika Sweden 40 C2 .............................59.39N 12.37E
arzamas Rus. Fed. 58 F3 .........................55.23N 43.49E
asad, Buḥayrat al resr Syria 57 M3 .............36.05N 38.03E
asahi-dake mt. Japan 106 D4 ...................43.41N 142.54E
asahikawa Japan 106 D4 .........................43.46N 142.22E
asansol India 96 G5 ..............................23.41N 87.01E
ascension Island Atlantic Oc. 82 B4 ...........8.00S 14.00W
ascoli Piceno Italy 50 E5 ........................42.52N 13.34E
asele Sweden 40 D4 ...............................64.10N 17.22E
asenovgrad Bulgaria 56 F6 ......................42.00N 24.52E
asfordby England 10 E3 ..........................52.46N 0.57W

Ashbourne England 15 F2 .......................53.01N 1.44W
Ashbourne Ireland 41 E3 .........................53.31N 6.23W
Ashburton watercourse Australia 110 A4 ......21.43S 114.54E
Ashburton England 13 D2 .......................50.31N 3.45W
Ashby de la Zouch England 10 D3 .............52.45N 1.28W
Ashford England 11 F2 ...........................51.09N 0.53E
Ashington England 15 F4 ........................55.11N 1.34W
Ashland U.S.A. 65 H6 .............................46.35N 90.53W
Ashmyany Belarus 46 G5 .........................54.25N 25.56E
Ash Shiḥr Yemen 95 G3 ..........................14.49N 49.45E
Ashton-under-Lyne England 15 E2 .............53.30N 2.06W
Asia 90
Asilah Morocco 48 B1 .............................35.28N 6.02W
Asinara, Golfo dell' b. Italy 50 C4 ..............40.59N 8.31E
Asipovichy Belarus 55 M5 ........................53.18N 28.38E
'Asīr f. Saudi Arabia 94 F4 ......................20.53N 40.14E
Askern England 15 F2 ............................53.37N 1.09W
Askim Norway 40 B2 ..............................59.35N 11.10E
Asmara Eritrea 85 H3 ............................15.20N 38.56E
Åsnen l. Sweden 40 C2 ...........................56.37N 14.50E
Aspang-Markt Austria 54 G2 ....................47.33N 16.05E
Aspatria England 14 D3 ...........................54.46N 3.20W
Aspen U.S.A. 64 E4 ...............................39.11N 106.49W
Assab Eritrea 85 I3 ................................12.59N 42.43E
Assam d. India 97 H6 ............................26.14N 91.22E
As Samāwah Iraq 94 G6 ..........................31.15N 45.19E
As Sarīr f. Libya 53 H2 ...........................27.02N 21.36E
As Sidrah Libya 53 G3 ............................30.38N 18.18E
As Sulaymānīyah Iraq 95 G7 ....................35.32N 45.27E
Assumption i. Seychelles 86 D4 ................9.30S 47.20E
As Sūq Saudi Arabia 94 F4 ......................21.57N 41.59E
Assynt, Loch l. Scotland 18 D3 ..................58.11N 5.05W
Astana Kazakhstan 58 I3 .........................51.09N 71.27E
Astārā Iran 95 G7 .................................38.27N 48.52E
Asti Italy 50 C6 ...................................44.54N 8.13E
Astorga Spain 48 B5 .............................42.28N 6.03W
Astoria U.S.A. 64 B6 .............................46.08N 123.46W
Astove i. Seychelles 86 D4 .......................10.05S 47.40E
Astrakhan' Rus. Fed. 58 F2 ......................46.20N 48.03E
Astravyets Belarus 46 G5 ........................54.36N 25.56E
Asunción i. N. Mariana Is 105 L7 ...............19.40N 145.25E
Asunción Paraguay 77 I2 ........................25.16S 57.39W
Aswān Egypt 85 H4 ...............................24.02N 32.56E
Asyūţ Egypt 85 H4 ...............................27.07N 31.08E
Atacama, Salar de l. Chile 76 G3 ...............23.23S 68.18W
Atacama Desert Chile 73 C4 ....................26.13S 69.39W
Atafu i. Tokelau 108 I5 ...........................8.33S 172.30W
Atār Mauritania 84 C4 ...........................20.32N 13.03W
Atasu Kazakhstan 58 J2 .........................48.42N 71.37E
Atbara Sudan 85 H3 ..............................17.43N 33.55E
Atbara r. Sudan 85 H3 ...........................17.40N 33.58E
Ath Belgium 42 C3 ................................50.38N 3.47E
Athabasca r. Canada 62 G3 ....................58.28N 111.09W
Athabasca, Lake Canada 62 H3 ................59.17N 109.24W
Athboy Ireland 41 E3 ............................53.37N 6.55W
Athenry Ireland 41 C3 ............................53.18N 8.45W
Athens Greece 56 E3 .............................37.59N 23.43E
Atherstone England 10 D3 ......................52.35N 1.33W
Athi r. Kenya 87 B2 ..............................2.57S 38.31E
Athi Plains f. Kenya 87 B2 ......................1.30S 36.50E
Athi River town Kenya 87 B2 ...................1.27S 36.58E
Athlone Ireland 41 D3 ...........................53.25N 7.57W
Atholl, Forest of Scotland 19 E1 ...............56.51N 4.10W
Athos mt. Greece 56 F5 ..........................40.10N 24.19E
Athy Ireland 41 E2 ...............................52.59N 6.59W
Ati Chad 85 F3 ....................................13.14N 18.20E
Atikokan Canada 65 H6 .........................48.45N 91.37W
Atiu i. Cook Is 109 J4 ............................19.59S 158.07W
Atlanta U.S.A. 65 J3 ..............................33.46N 84.22W
Atlantic City U.S.A. 65 L4 .......................39.21N 74.26W
Atlantic Ocean 116 G7
Atlas Mountains Africa 84 D5 ..................30.13N 7.41W
Atlas Saharien mts Algeria 84 E5 ..............32.41N 0.20E
Aţ Ţā'if Saudi Arabia 94 F4 .....................21.15N 40.20E
Attleborough England 11 G3 ....................52.31N 1.01E
Atyrau Kazakhstan 58 G2 ........................47.08N 51.56E
Aube r. France 44 E6 .............................48.34N 3.43E
Auchterarder Scotland 17 F4 ....................56.18N 3.42W
Auchtermuchty Scotland 17 F4 .................56.18N 3.14W
Auckland New Zealand 111 G3 ..................36.52S 174.46E
Auckland Islands New Zealand 111 F1 ........50.43S 166.12E
Auderville France 13 Z9 ..........................49.43N 1.55W
Audlem England 10 C3 ............................52.59N 2.31W
Audo mts Ethiopia 87 C4 .........................6.46N 41.15E
Audruicq France 11 H1 ...........................50.52N 2.05E
Aughton England 15 F2 ..........................53.22N 1.19W
Augsburg Germany 54 D3 ........................48.22N 10.52E
Augusta G. U.S.A. 65 J3 .........................33.28N 82.02W
Augusta Me. U.S.A. 65 M5 ......................44.19N 69.46W
Aulnoye-Aymeries France 42 C3 ...............50.12N 3.51E
Aurangabad India 96 E4 .........................19.53N 75.24E
Aurich Germany 42 G6 ...........................53.28N 7.30E
Aurora U.S.A. 64 F4 ..............................39.43N 104.53W
Auskerry i. Scotland 19 G4 ......................59.02N 2.33W
Aus Maduli Kenya 87 C3 .........................2.16N 40.36E
Austin U.S.A. 64 G3 ..............................30.16N 97.42W
Australia Oceania 110 B4 .........................27.11S 129.18E
Australian Capital Territory d. Australia 110 J .35.27S 148.52E
Austria Europe 54 E2 .............................47.12N 13.26E
Authie r. France 11 G1 ...........................50.22N 1.37E
Auvergne, Monts d' mts France 44 E4 .........45.45N 2.59E
Auxerre France 44 E5 ............................47.48N 3.35E
Avallon France 44 E5 .............................47.30N 3.54E
Avanos Turkey 57 K4 .............................38.43N 34.51E
Avarua Cook Is 109 J4 ...........................21.13S 159.46W
Aveiro Portugal 48 A4 ............................40.39N 8.38W
Avellino Italy 50 F4 ..............................40.55N 14.48E
Avesta Sweden 40 D3 ............................60.09N 16.10E
Aveyron r. France 44 D4 .........................44.05N 1.16E
Avezzano Italy 50 E5 .............................42.02N 13.25E
Aviemore Scotland 19 F2 ........................57.12N 3.49W
Avignon France 44 F3 ............................43.57N 4.49E
Avilés Spain 48 C5 ...............................43.33N 5.54W
Avon r. Brist. England 10 C2 ....................51.29N 2.40W
Avon r. Dor. England 10 D1 .....................50.44N 1.46W
Avon r. Glos. England 10 C3 .....................52.00N 2.10W
Avon r. Scotland 19 F2 ..........................57.25N 3.22W
Avonmore r. Ireland 12 A4 .....................52.48N 6.08W
Avonmouth England 10 C2 ......................51.30N 2.42W
Awara Plain f. Kenya 87 C3 .....................3.39N 40.54E
Awasa Ethiopia 87 B4 ............................6.57N 38.28E
Awash Ethiopia 85 I2 .............................8.59N 40.10E
Awe, Loch l. Scotland 16 D4 ....................56.16N 5.14W
Awjilah Libya 84 F4 ..............................29.06N 21.18E
Axe r. England 13 D2 ............................50.43N 3.04W
Axel Heiberg Island Canada 63 I5 ..............79.47N 91.17W
Axminster England 10 C1 ........................50.47N 2.59W

Ayacucho Peru 76 F5 ............................13.10S 74.13W
Ayagoz Kazakhstan 58 J2 ........................47.56N 80.23E
Ayan Rus. Fed. 59 O3 ............................56.26N 138.12E
Aydarko'l ko'li l. Uzbekistan 58 H2 ............41.02N 66.33E
Aydın Turkey 57 G3 ..............................37.50N 27.49E
Aylesbury England 10 E2 .........................51.49N 0.48W
Aylesham England 11 G2 ........................51.14N 1.12E
Aylsham England 11 G3 ..........................52.48N 1.15E
Ayr Scotland 16 E3 ...............................55.28N 4.38W
Ayr r. Scotland 16 E3 .............................55.28N 4.38W
Ayr, Point of Wales 12 D5 .......................53.21N 3.18W
Ayre, Point of Isle of Man 14 C3 ...............54.25N 4.22W
Ayvalık Turkey 56 G4 .............................39.17N 26.41E
Azerbaijan Asia 58 F1 ...........................40.23N 48.09E
Azogues Ecuador 76 E7 .........................2.44S 78.50W
Azov, Sea of Rus. Fed./Ukraine 58 E2 .........46.03N 36.47E
Azrou Morocco 52 D2 ............................33.26N 5.11W
Azuero, Península de pen. Panama 71 H2 .....7.39N 80.41W
Azul Argentina 73 D3 ............................36.45N 59.50W
Azul, Cordillera mts Peru 76 E6 ...............8.31S 75.56W
Az Zaqāzīq Egypt 53 J3 .........................30.35N 31.30E
Az Zarqā' Jordan 94 E6 ..........................32.04N 36.05E

## B

Baardheere Somalia 85 I2 .......................2.19N 42.18E
Bābā, Kūh-e mts Afgh. 95 K6 ..................34.48N 68.27E
Babadag Romania 57 H7 .........................44.54N 28.42E
Babaeski Turkey 56 G5 ...........................41.26N 27.06E
Bāb al Mandab str. Africa/Asia 94 F2 ..........12.21N 43.26E
Babar i. Indonesia 105 H2 .......................7.57S 129.51E
Babati Tanzania 87 A1 ...........................4.15S 35.44E
Babbacombe Bay England 13 D2 ..............50.31N 3.28W
Babia Góra mt. Poland 46 D2 ..................49.35N 19.32E
Babo Indonesia 105 I3 ...........................2.35S 133.21E
Babruysk Belarus 55 M5 .........................53.09N 29.14E
Bab-Termas hill Morocco 48 D1 ...............34.29N 3.53W
Babuyan Islands Phil. 105 G7 ..................19.13N 121.59E
Bacabal Brazil 77 L7 ..............................4.16S 44.47W
Bacan i. Indonesia 105 H3 .......................0.44S 127.35E
Bacău Romania 55 L2 ............................46.34N 26.55E
Back r. Canada 63 I4 .............................66.32N 95.51W
Backwater Reservoir Scotland 19 F1 ..........56.44N 3.13W
Bac Liêu Vietnam 104 D5 .......................9.15N 105.45E
Bacolod Phil. 105 G6 ............................10.37N 122.57E
Badajoz Spain 48 B3 .............................38.53N 6.57W
Baden Austria 50 G6 ..............................48.00N 16.15E
Baden-Baden Germany 54 C3 ..................48.45N 8.15E
Bad Neuenahr-Ahrweiler Germany 42 G3 ....50.33N 7.07E
Badulla Sri Lanka 96 F2 .........................7.00N 81.01E
Baffin Bay sea Canada/Greenland 63 L5 ......72.51N 66.20W
Baffin Island Canada 63 L4 .....................64.57N 68.47W
Bafoussam Cameroon 84 F2 ...................5.28N 10.26E
Bāfq Iran 95 I6 ....................................31.34N 55.21E
Bafra Turkey 57 K5 ...............................41.34N 35.55E
Bāft Iran 95 I5 ....................................29.14N 56.36E
Bagé Brazil 77 J1 .................................31.20S 54.06W
Baggy Point England 13 C3 .....................51.08N 4.16W
Baghdad Iraq 94 F6 ..............................33.18N 44.22E
Baghlān Afgh. 95 K7 .............................36.11N 68.47E
Bagrationovsk Rus. Fed. 46 E5 .................54.23N 20.38E
Bahariya Oasis Egypt 94 C5 ....................27.56N 28.51E
Bahawalpur Pakistan 96 D6 .....................29.23N 71.45E
Bahia d. Brazil 77 L5 .............................14.28S 40.45W
Bahía, Islas de la is Honduras 71 G4 ..........16.13N 86.56W
Bahía Blanca Argentina 73 C3 ..................38.43S 62.18W
Bahía Negra Paraguay 77 I3 ....................20.11S 58.10W
Bahrain Asia 95 H5 ...............................26.29N 50.51E
Baía Mare Romania 55 J2 .......................47.39N 23.35E
Baicheng China 101 M7 ........................45.29N 122.50E
Baie-Comeau Canada 63 L2 ....................49.13N 68.10W
Baikal, Lake Rus. Fed. 59 L3 ...................52.37N 107.12E
Bailieborough Ireland 41 E3 ....................53.55N 6.58W
Bain r. England 15 G2 ............................53.05N 0.12W
Bainbridge U.S.A. 65 J3 .........................30.54N 84.40W
Bairiki Kiribati 108 H5 ...........................1.21N 172.57E
Bairnsdale Australia 110 D3 ....................37.51S 147.37E
Baiyuda Desert Sudan 94 D3 ..................18.03N 32.59E
Baja Hungary 54 H2 ..............................46.12N 18.57E
Baja California d. Mexico 70 A6 ...............29.49N 115.07W
Baja California pen. Mexico 70 B6 ............30.40N 115.41W
Baja California Sur d. Mexico 70 B6 ..........25.19N 112.09W
Baker, Mount vol. U.S.A. 64 B6 ...............48.46N 121.47W
Baker Island N. Pacific Oc. 108 I5 ............0.13N 176.28W
Baker Lake Canada 63 I4 ........................64.09N 95.23W
Bakersfield U.S.A. 64 C4 ........................35.22N 118.59W
Bakharden Turkmenistan 95 I7 ................38.27N 57.24E
Bakhtegan, Daryācheh-ye l. Iran 95 H5 ......29.18N 53.52E
Bakırköy Turkey 57 H5 ..........................40.58N 28.51E
Bako Ethiopia 87 B4 .............................5.49N 36.37E
Baku Azerbaijan 58 F2 ...........................40.22N 49.50E
Bala Wales 12 D4 ................................52.55N 3.36W
Bala, Cerros de mts Bolivia 76 G5 ............13.49S 68.25W
Balabac Strait Malaysia/Phil. 104 F5 ..........7.36N 116.45E
Bala Lake Wales 12 D4 ..........................52.52N 3.39W
Bālā Morghāb Afgh. 95 J7 ......................35.35N 63.21E
Balashikha Rus. Fed. 55 Q6 ....................55.49N 37.57E
Balaton, Lake Hungary 54 G2 ..................46.46N 17.32E
Balbina, Represa de resr Brazil 77 I7 .........1.34S 59.27W
Balbriggan Ireland 41 E3 ........................53.36N 6.11W
Baldock England 11 E2 ..........................51.59N 0.11W
Baldy Peak U.S.A. 64 E3 ........................33.54N 109.34W
Balearic Islands Spain 48 F3 ...................39.28N 1.30E
Baleia, Ponta da pt Brazil 77 M4 ...............17.41S 39.09W
Baleine, Rivière à la r. Canada 63 L3 .........57.57N 67.37W
Baleshwar India 96 G5 ..........................21.30N 86.56E
Balestrieri, Punta mt. Italy 50 C4 ..............40.51N 9.10E
Bali i. Indonesia 104 E2 .........................8.41S 114.55E
Balige Indonesia 104 B4 .........................2.20N 99.03E
Balikesir Turkey 56 G4 ..........................39.39N 27.52E
Balıkh r. Syria/Turkey 57 M2 ...................35.56N 39.03E
Balikpapan Indonesia 104 F3 ...................1.12S 116.49E
Balimo P.N.G. 105 K2 ...........................7.59S 143.01E
Balintore Scotland 19 F2 ........................57.45N 3.54W
Bali Sea Indonesia 104 F2 .......................7.31S 114.31E
Balivanich Scotland 18 B2 ......................57.28N 7.22W
Balkan Mountains Bulgaria/Serbia 56 E6 .....43.23N 22.47E
Balkhash Kazakhstan 58 I2 .....................46.50N 74.59E
Balkhash, Lake Kazakhstan 58 I2 ..............46.07N 74.57E
Ballagan Point Ireland 16 C1 ...................53.59N 6.06W
Ballantrae Scotland 16 D3 .......................55.06N 5.00W
Ballarat Australia 110 D3 ........................37.35S 143.52E
Ballater Scotland 19 F2 ..........................57.03N 3.02W
Ballena, Punta pt Chile 73 B4 ..................25.47S 70.47W
Ballencleuch Law hill Scotland 17 F3 .........55.20N 3.41W
Ballina Ireland 41 C4 .............................54.07N 9.09W
Ballinasloe Ireland 41 C3 ........................53.20N 8.13W
Ballybay Ireland 41 E4 ...........................54.07N 6.54W
Ballybunnion Ireland 41 B2 .....................52.31N 9.40W
Ballycastle Northern Ireland 16 C3 ............55.12N 6.14W
Ballyclare Northern Ireland 16 D2 .............54.45N 5.59W

Ballyhaunis Ireland 41 C3 .......................53.46N 8.46W
Ballymena Northern Ireland 16 C2 .............54.52N 6.16W
Ballymena d. Northern Ireland 8 B4 ...........54.53N 6.14W
Ballymoney Northern Ireland 16 C3 ...........55.04N 6.31W
Ballymoney d. Northern Ireland 8 B4 ..........54.58N 6.28W
Ballynahinch Northern Ireland 16 D2 ..........54.24N 5.53W
Ballyquintin Point Northern Ireland 16 D2 ....54.19N 5.29W
Ballyshannon Ireland 41 C4 ....................54.30N 8.12W
Balochistan f. Pakistan 96 B6 ..................27.30N 63.31E
Balsas Brazil 77 K6 ...............................7.31S 46.00W
Balsas r. Mexico 70 D4 ..........................17.57N 102.09W
Balta Ukraine 55 M2 .............................47.56N 29.37E
Baltasound Scotland 19 I5 ......................60.46N 0.52W
Bălţi Moldova 53 I6 ...............................47.47N 27.56E
Baltic Sea g. Europe 40 D1 .....................55.28N 16.46E
Baltimore U.S.A. 65 K4 ..........................39.17N 76.37W
Baltiysk Rus. Fed. 46 D5 ........................54.39N 19.53E
Bam Iran 95 I5 ...................................29.07N 58.22E
Bamaga Australia 110 D5 .......................10.53S 142.23E
Bamako Mali 84 D3 ..............................12.38N 7.59W
Bambari Dem. Rep. Congo 86 B5 .............3.38N 26.07E
Bambouti C.A.R. 85 G2 ..........................5.22N 27.12E
Bāmiān Afgh. 95 K6 .............................34.52N 67.49E
Bampton Dev. England 13 D2 .................50.59N 3.29W
Bampton Oxon. England 10 D2 ................51.43N 1.33W
Banaba i. Kiribati 108 H5 ........................0.49S 169.35E
Bañados del Izozog f. Bolivia 77 H4 ...........18.20S 61.45W
Banagher Ireland 41 D3 .........................53.11N 7.59W
Bananal, Ilha do i. Brazil 77 J5 ................11.26S 50.19W
Banaz Turkey 57 H4 ..............................38.44N 29.44E
Banbridge Northern Ireland 16 C2 .............54.21N 6.16W
Banbridge d. Northern Ireland 9 B4 ...........54.20N 6.09W
Banbury England 10 D3 .........................52.04N 1.20W
Banchory Scotland 19 G2 .......................57.03N 2.29W
Banda, Kepulauan is Indonesia 105 H3 ........4.33S 129.53E
Banda Aceh Indonesia 104 B5 .................5.30N 95.18E
Bandar-e 'Abbās Iran 95 I5 .....................27.11N 56.18E
Bandar-e Anzalī Iran 95 G7 ....................37.26N 49.26E
Bandar-e Lengeh Iran 95 H5 ...................26.34N 54.53E
Bandar-e Torkeman Iran 95 H7 ................36.54N 53.59E
Bandar Lampung Indonesia 104 C2 ...........5.27S 105.17E
Bandar Seri Begawan Brunei 104 E4 .........4.57N 114.58E
Banda Sea Indonesia 105 H2 ...................5.40S 130.07E
Bandeiras, Pico de mt. Brazil 77 L3 ..........20.26S 41.48W
Bandırma Turkey 57 G5 ..........................40.21N 27.57E
Bandon Ireland 41 C1 ...........................51.45N 8.44W
Bandon r. Ireland 41 C1 ........................51.45N 8.38W
Bandundu Dem. Rep. Congo 86 A4 ...........3.17S 17.23E
Bandung Indonesia 104 D2 .....................6.56S 107.35E
Banff Canada 62 G3 .............................51.11N 115.35W
Banff Scotland 19 G2 ............................57.40N 2.31W
Bangalore India 96 E3 ...........................12.57N 77.34E
Bangassou C.A.R. 85 G2 ........................4.44N 22.50E
Banggai, Kepulauan is Indonesia 105 G3 ......1.59S 123.27E
Bangka i. Indonesia 104 D3 ....................2.07S 106.17E
Bangkok Thailand 104 C6 .......................13.44N 100.33E
Bangladesh Asia 97 H5 ..........................23.47N 89.49E
Bangor Northern Ireland 16 D2 ................54.39N 5.40W
Bangor U.S.A. 65 M5 ............................44.48N 68.47W
Bangor Wales 12 C5 .............................53.14N 4.08W
Bangui C.A.R. 85 F2 ..............................4.23N 18.36E
Bangweulu, Lake Zambia 86 B3 ...............11.13S 29.39E
Bani r. Mali 84 D3 ................................14.30N 4.13W
Banī Mazār Egypt 53 J2 .........................28.29N 30.49E
Banī Suwayf Egypt 53 J2 ........................29.05N 31.06E
Banī Walīd Libya 52 F3 ..........................31.47N 14.00E
Bāniyās Syria 57 K2 ..............................35.11N 35.57E
Banja Luka Bos.-Herz. 56 B7 ...................44.46N 17.12E
Banjarmasin Indonesia 104 E3 ................3.23S 114.33E
Banjul Gambia 84 C3 ............................13.27N 16.36W
Banks Island Canada 62 F5 .....................73.06N 121.26W
Banks Islands Vanuatu 111 F5 ..................13.46S 167.13E
Banmi Pakistan 95 L6 ............................33.00N 70.40E
Bann r. Northern Ireland 16 C3 ................55.09N 6.42W
Bann r. Ireland 12 A4 ...........................52.33N 6.33W
Bantry Ireland 41 B1 .............................51.41N 9.27W
Bantry Bay Ireland 41 B1 .......................51.34N 9.53W
Baoding China 101 L5 ...........................38.46N 115.34E
Baoji China 101 J4 ...............................34.21N 107.09E
Baoshan China 101 H3 ..........................25.07N 99.05E
Baotou China 101 K6 ............................40.31N 110.08E
Baotou Shan mt. China/N. Korea 106 A4 .....41.57N 128.08E
Ba'qūbah Iraq 94 F6 .............................33.42N 44.38E
Baquerizo Moreno Ecuador 76 C7 ............0.54S 89.37W
Bar Montenegro 56 C6 ..........................42.05N 19.05E
Bara Sudan 94 D2 ...............................13.40N 30.21E
Baracoa Cuba 71 J5 ..............................20.21N 74.29W
Baranavichy Belarus 55 L5 ......................53.08N 26.02E
Baranīs Egypt 53 K1 .............................23.53N 35.27E
Barbacena Brazil 77 L3 ..........................21.13S 43.45W
Barbados Central America 71 M3 ..............13.09N 59.25W
Barbuda i. Antigua 71 L4 .......................17.39N 61.47W
Barcaldine Australia 110 D4 ....................23.32S 145.19E
Barcelona Spain 48 G4 ..........................41.25N 2.13E
Barcelona Venezuela 72 C8 .....................10.06N 64.41W
Barcelos Brazil 76 H7 ...........................0.58S 62.58W
Bárðarbunga mt. Iceland 40 Y2 ...............64.38N 17.32W
Bardejov Slovakia 46 E2 ........................49.18N 21.17E
Bardney England 15 G2 .........................53.13N 0.19W
Bardsey Island Wales 12 C4 ....................52.45N 4.46W
Bardsey Sound str. Wales 12 C4 ...............52.47N 4.48W
Bareilly India 96 F6 ..............................28.22N 79.27E
Barentsburg Arctic Oc. 58 C5 ..................77.49N 14.26E
Barents Sea Arctic Oc. 58 F5 ...................75.18N 42.14E
Barham England 11 G2 ..........................51.12N 1.10E
Bari Italy 50 G4 ..................................41.07N 16.52E
Barinas Venezuela 72 B7 ........................8.34N 70.11W
Baringo, Lake Kenya 87 B3 .....................0.33N 36.05E
Barisan, Pegunungan mts Indonesia 104 C3 .1.12S 100.37E
Barkly Tableland f. Australia 110 C5 ...........18.06S 135.25E
Bârlad Romania 56 G8 ...........................46.13N 27.39E
Barlee, Lake Australia 110 A4 ..................28.58S 119.40E
Barletta Italy 50 G4 ..............................41.19N 16.17E
Barmer India 96 D6 ..............................25.44N 71.26E
Barmouth Wales 12 C4 ..........................52.43N 4.03W
Barmouth Bay Wales 12 C4 ....................52.43N 4.10W
Barnard Castle England 15 F3 .................54.33N 1.55W
Barnaul Rus. Fed. 58 J3 .........................53.22N 83.49E
Barnet England 11 E2 ............................51.39N 0.12W
Barnoldswick England 15 E2 ...................53.55N 2.11W
Barnsley England 15 F2 .........................53.33N 1.29W
Barnstaple England 13 C3 ......................51.05N 4.03W
Barnstaple or Bideford Bay England 13 C3 ..51.05N 4.23W
Barquisimeto Venezuela 72 C8 ................10.04N 69.18W
Barra i. Scotland 18 B1 ..........................56.59N 7.30W
Barra, Sound of str. Scotland 18 B2 ..........57.04N 7.27W
Barra do Corda Brazil 77 K6 ...................5.29S 45.10W
Barra do Garças Brazil 77 J4 ...................15.53S 52.16W
Barranquilla Colombia 72 B8 ..................10.59N 74.51W
Barreiras Brazil 77 L5 ...........................12.07S 44.53W
Barretos Brazil 77 K3 ............................20.35S 48.34W
Barrhead Scotland 16 E3 ........................55.48N 4.24W
Barrow r. Ireland 41 E2 ..........................52.23N 6.57W

Barrow U.S.A. 62 C5 .......71.18N 156.43W
Barrow, Point U.S.A. 62 C5 .......71.23N 156.22W
Barrow-in-Furness England 14 D3 .......54.07N 3.13W
Barry Wales 13 D3 .......51.24N 3.17W
Barstow U.S.A. 64 C3 .......34.54N 117.01W
Bartın Turkey 57 J5 .......41.38N 32.21E
Barton-upon-Humber England 15 G2 .......53.41N 0.27W
Bartoszyce Poland 46 E5 .......54.15N 20.49E
Baruun-Urt Mongolia 101 K7 .......46.31N 113.22E
Barysaw Belarus 55 M6 .......54.14N 28.31E
Basel Switz. 50 B7 .......47.33N 7.35E
Basilan i. Phil. 105 G5 .......6.32N 121.52E
Basildon England 11 F2 .......51.35N 0.29E
Basingstoke England 10 D2 .......51.16N 1.06W
Basra Iraq 95 G6 .......30.29N 47.48E
Bassein Myanmar 97 H4 .......16.45N 94.44E
Bassenthwaite Lake England 14 D3 .......54.40N 3.14W
Basse-Terre Guadeloupe 71 L4 .......16.01N 61.44W
Bass Rock i. Scotland 17 G4 .......56.05N 2.38W
Bass Strait Australia 110 D3 .......39.43S 146.11E
Bastak Iran 95 H5 .......27.12N 54.21E
Bastia France 44 H3 .......42.42N 9.27E
Bastogne Belgium 42 E2 .......50.00N 5.43E
Bata Equat. Guinea 84 E2 .......1.50N 9.48E
Batabanó, Golfo de b. Cuba 71 H5 .......22.16N 82.38W
Batang China 101 H4 .......30.01N 99.08E
Batang Indonesia 97 I6 .......6.57S 109.43E
Batangas Phil. 105 G6 .......13.46N 121.01E
Batan Islands Phil. 105 G8 .......20.46N 122.05E
Bătdâmbâng Cambodia 104 C6 .......13.06N 103.14E
Bath England 10 C2 .......51.23N 2.22W
Bath and North East Somerset d. England 9 D2
.......51.21N 2.28W
Bathgate Scotland 17 F3 .......55.54N 3.39W
Bathurst Australia 110 D3 .......33.25S 149.34E
Bathurst Canada 63 L2 .......47.36N 65.39W
Bathurst Inlet Canada 62 H4 .......66.50N 108.10W
Bathurst Island Australia 110 C5 .......11.29S 130.11E
Bathurst Island Canada 63 I5 .......75.49N 98.59W
Batley England 15 F2 .......53.43N 1.38W
Batna Algeria 84 E5 .......35.32N 6.13E
Baton Rouge U.S.A. 65 H3 .......30.27N 91.11W
Batticaloa Sri Lanka 96 F2 .......7.42N 81.39E
Battle England 11 F1 .......50.55N 0.29E
Batu mt. Ethiopia 87 B4 .......6.51N 39.50E
Batu, Pulau-pulau is Indonesia 104 B3 .......0.14S 98.16E
Bat'umi Georgia 58 F2 .......41.39N 41.38E
Baubau Indonesia 105 G2 .......5.29S 122.37E
Bauchi Nigeria 84 E3 .......10.19N 9.50E
Bauru Brazil 77 K3 .......22.20S 49.05W
Bauska Latvia 55 K7 .......56.25N 24.13E
Bautzen Germany 54 F4 .......51.11N 14.26E
Bawean i. Indonesia 104 E2 .......5.48S 112.34E
Bayamo Cuba 71 I5 .......20.22N 76.38W
Bayanhongor Mongolia 101 I7 .......46.09N 100.41E
Bayburt Turkey 57 N5 .......40.15N 40.14E
Bay City Mich. U.S.A. 65 J5 .......43.35N 83.53W
Bay City Tex. U.S.A. 64 G2 .......28.59N 96.02W
Baydaratskaya Guba Rus. Fed. 58 H4 .......69.29N 66.01E
Bayonne France 44 C3 .......43.29N 1.29W
Bayreuth Germany 54 D3 .......49.56N 11.36E
Bayy al Kabīr, Wādī watercourse Libya 52 G3 .......31.11N 15.53E
Baza Spain 48 D2 .......37.30N 2.46W
Beachy Head England 11 F1 .......50.44N 0.15E
Beaconsfield England 10 E2 .......51.36N 0.39W
Beagle Gulf Australia 105 H1 .......12.04S 129.55E
Beaminster England 10 C1 .......50.49N 2.45W
Beardmore Canada 65 I6 .......49.36N 87.58W
Beata, Cabo c. Dom. Rep. 71 J4 .......17.38N 71.23W
Beata, Isla i. Dom. Rep. 71 J4 .......17.36N 71.30W
Beaufort Sea Canada/U.S.A. 62 F5 .......73.19N 129.52W
Beaufort West S. Africa 86 B1 .......32.20S 22.36E
Beauly Scotland 19 E2 .......57.29N 4.28W
Beauly r. Scotland 19 E2 .......57.29N 4.27W
Beauly Firth est. Scotland 19 E2 .......57.29N 4.23W
Beaumaris Wales 12 C5 .......53.16N 4.05W
Beaumont France 42 D3 .......49.40N 1.50W
Beaumont U.S.A. 65 H3 .......30.05N 94.09W
Beaune France 44 E5 .......47.01N 4.50E
Beauvais France 44 E6 .......49.26N 2.05E
Beaver r. Canada 62 H3 .......55.22N 107.45W
Beaver Creek town Canada 62 D4 .......62.23N 140.49W
Bebington England 14 D2 .......53.21N 3.00W
Beccles England 11 G3 .......52.28N 1.34E
Becerreá Spain 48 B5 .......42.51N 7.09W
Béchar Algeria 84 D5 .......31.36N 2.13W
Beckingham England 15 G2 .......53.24N 0.49W
Beckley U.S.A. 65 J4 .......37.47N 81.11W
Bedale England 15 F3 .......54.17N 1.35W
Bedelē Ethiopia 85 H2 .......8.28N 36.21E
Bedford England 11 E3 .......52.08N 0.28W
Bedford d. England 9 E3 .......52.10N 0.28W
Bedlington England 15 F4 .......55.08N 1.36W
Bedworth England 10 D3 .......52.29N 1.28W
Beersheba Israel 53 J3 .......31.15N 34.48E
Beeville U.S.A. 64 G2 .......28.25N 97.45W
Beg, Lough l. Northern Ireland 16 C2 .......54.47N 6.27W
Bei'an China 101 N7 .......48.11N 126.31E
Beihai China 101 J2 .......21.27N 109.08E
Beijing China 101 L5 .......39.52N 116.27E
Beinn an Oir hill Scotland 16 D3 .......55.54N 5.59W
Beinn Dearg mt. High. Scotland 18 E2 .......57.47N 4.56W
Beinn Dearg mt. P. and K. Scotland 19 F1 .......56.53N 3.53W
Beinn Heasgarnich mt. Scotland 16 E4 .......56.31N 4.35W
Beira Mozambique 86 C3 .......19.50S 34.52E
Beirut Lebanon 53 K3 .......33.52N 35.30E
Beith Scotland 16 E3 .......55.45N 4.38W
Beiuş Romania 55 J2 .......46.40N 22.23E
Beja Portugal 48 B3 .......38.01N 7.52W
Bejaïa Algeria 84 E5 .......36.44N 5.03E
Béjar Spain 48 C4 .......40.24N 5.46W
Békés Hungary 46 E1 .......46.46N 21.07E
Békéscsaba Hungary 54 I2 .......46.41N 21.05E
Bela Pakistan 96 C6 .......26.12N 66.21E
Belarus Europe 55 L5 .......54.01N 28.39E
Belaya r. Rus. Fed. 59 S4 .......65.32N 173.15E
Bełchatów Poland 46 D3 .......51.22N 19.22E
Belcher Islands Canada 63 K3 .......56.10N 78.47W
Beledweyne Somalia 85 I2 .......4.44N 45.13E
Belém Brazil 77 K7 .......1.26S 48.29W
Belev Rus. Fed. 55 Q5 .......53.48N 36.10E
Belfast Northern Ireland 16 D2 .......54.36N 5.55W
Belfast d. Northern Ireland 9 C4 .......54.36N 5.55W
Belfast Lough inlet Northern Ireland 16 D2 .......54.40N 5.52W
Belford England 15 F4 .......55.36N 1.50W
Belgium Europe 42 D3 .......50.55N 4.14E
Belgorod Rus. Fed. 58 E3 .......50.36N 36.37E
Belgrade Serbia 56 D7 .......44.48N 20.29E
Belitung i. Indonesia 104 D3 .......2.47S 108.14E
Belize town Belize 70 G4 .......17.31N 88.14W
Belize Central America 70 G4 .......17.10N 88.18W
Bellac France 44 D5 .......46.08N 1.03E

Bellary India 96 E4 .......15.10N 76.53E
Belle-Île i. France 44 B5 .......47.19N 3.15W
Belle Isle, Strait of Canada 63 M3 .......51.16N 56.57W
Bellingham England 15 E4 .......55.09N 2.15W
Bellingham U.S.A. 64 B6 .......48.45N 122.28W
Bellinzona Switz. 50 C7 .......46.12N 9.01E
Belluno Italy 50 E7 .......46.08N 12.13E
Belmopan Belize 70 G4 .......17.14N 88.46W
Belmullet Ireland 41 B4 .......54.14N 9.59W
Belo Horizonte Brazil 77 L4 .......19.55S 43.56W
Belper England 15 F2 .......53.02N 1.29W
Belukha, Gora mt. Kazakhstan/Rus. Fed. 58 J2 .......49.50N 86.41E
Belyy Rus. Fed. 55 O6 .......55.50N 32.57E
Bembridge England 10 D1 .......50.41N 1.05W
Bemidji U.S.A. 65 H6 .......47.27N 94.52W
Ben Alder mt. Scotland 19 E1 .......56.49N 4.28W
Benavente Spain 48 C5 .......42.00N 5.40W
Benbane Head Northern Ireland 16 C3 .......55.15N 6.30W
Benbecula i. Scotland 18 B2 .......57.27N 7.23W
Ben Cleuch hill Scotland 17 F4 .......56.11N 3.46W
Ben Cruachan mt. Scotland 16 D4 .......56.25N 5.08W
Bend U.S.A. 64 B5 .......44.04N 121.17W
Bendigo Australia 110 D3 .......36.46S 144.18E
Benešov Czech Rep. 54 F3 .......49.47N 14.42E
Bengal, Bay of sea Indian Oc. 96 G4 .......17.51N 88.40E
Bengbu China 101 L4 .......32.54N 117.23E
Benghazi Libya 85 G5 .......32.06N 20.04E
Bengkulu Indonesia 104 C3 .......3.45S 102.18E
Benguela Angola 86 A3 .......12.36S 13.21E
Ben Hope hill Scotland 19 E3 .......58.25N 4.36W
Beni r. Bolivia 76 E5 .......11.01S 66.07W
Benidorm Spain 48 E3 .......38.32N 0.08W
Beni Mellal Morocco 84 D5 .......32.17N 6.25W
Benin Africa 84 E2 .......8.26N 2.11E
Benin, Bight of g. Africa 84 E2 .......5.17N 3.27E
Beni-Saf Algeria 52 C4 .......35.20N 1.21W
Benjamim Constant Brazil 76 E7 .......4.23S 69.58W
Ben Klibreck hill Scotland 19 E3 .......58.15N 4.24W
Ben Lawers mt. Scotland 16 E4 .......56.33N 4.13W
Ben Lomond hill Scotland 16 E4 .......56.11N 4.38W
Ben Loyal hill Scotland 19 E3 .......58.24N 4.27W
Ben Lui mt. Scotland 16 E4 .......56.24N 4.49W
Ben Macdui mt. Scotland 19 F2 .......57.05N 3.40W
Ben More mt. Scotland 16 D4 .......56.25N 6.00W
Ben More mt. Scotland 16 E4 .......56.23N 4.32W
Ben More Assynt hill Scotland 18 E3 .......58.08N 4.51W
Ben Nevis mt. Scotland 18 D1 .......56.48N 5.00W
Bentley England 15 F2 .......53.33N 1.09W
Benue r. Nigeria 84 E2 .......7.49N 6.48E
Ben Vorlich hill Scotland 16 E4 .......56.21N 4.13W
Ben Wyvis mt. Scotland 19 E2 .......57.41N 4.35W
Benxi China 101 M6 .......41.16N 123.45E
Beoraid, Loch l. Scotland 18 D1 .......56.54N 5.36W
Berat Albania 56 C5 .......40.42N 19.58E
Berau, Teluk b. Indonesia 105 I3 .......2.28S 132.36E
Berber Sudan 94 D3 .......18.00N 34.02E
Berbera Somalia 85 I3 .......10.24N 45.02E
Berbérati C.A.R. 84 F2 .......4.14N 15.47E
Berck France 11 G1 .......50.25N 1.35E
Berdyans'k Ukraine 53 K6 .......46.46N 36.48E
Berdychiv Ukraine 55 M3 .......49.53N 28.36E
Berehove Ukraine 46 E2 .......48.13N 22.38E
Berens River town Canada 62 I3 .......52.21N 97.01W
Berezhany Ukraine 46 G2 .......49.27N 24.56E
Berezivka Ukraine 55 N2 .......47.12N 30.55E
Berezniki Rus. Fed. 58 G3 .......59.25N 56.48E
Bergama Turkey 56 G4 .......39.07N 27.11E
Bergamo Italy 50 C6 .......45.42N 9.41E
Bergen Norway 40 A3 .......60.23N 5.22E
Bergerac France 44 D4 .......44.51N 0.29E
Bergisch Gladbach Germany 54 B4 .......50.58N 7.08E
Bering Sea N. Pacific Oc. 60 A7 .......60.00N 170.00E
Bering Strait Rus. Fed./U.S.A. 59 U4 .......66.18N 168.40W
Berkel r. Neth. 42 F5 .......52.08N 6.11E
Berkeley England 10 C2 .......51.41N 2.27W
Berkshire Downs hills England 10 D2 .......51.30N 1.20W
Berlin Germany 54 E5 .......52.31N 13.23E
Bermuda i. N. Atlantic Oc. 71 L7 .......32.24N 64.56W
Bern Switz. 50 B7 .......46.57N 7.27E
Berneray i. W. Isles Scotland 18 B1 .......56.47N 7.38W
Berneray i. W. Isles Scotland 18 B2 .......57.44N 7.18W
Beroun Czech Rep. 46 B2 .......49.58N 14.04E
Berounka r. Czech Rep. 46 B2 .......49.59N 14.22E
Berry Head England 13 D2 .......50.24N 3.29W
Bertoua Cameroon 84 F2 .......4.35N 13.41E
Beru atoll Kiribati 108 H5 .......1.17S 176.00E
Berwick-upon-Tweed England 15 E4 .......55.46N 2.00W
Besançon France 44 G5 .......47.15N 6.01E
Bessbrook Northern Ireland 16 C2 .......54.12N 6.23W
Betanzos Spain 48 A5 .......43.17N 8.12W
Beth, Oued r. Morocco 48 B1 .......34.25N 6.26W
Bethesda Wales 12 C5 .......53.11N 4.03W
Béthune France 42 B3 .......50.31N 2.38E
Betsiboka r. Madagascar 86 D3 .......15.58S 46.27E
Bettystown Ireland 12 A5 .......53.42N 6.15W
Beult r. England 11 F2 .......51.13N 0.25E
Beverley England 15 G2 .......53.51N 0.26W
Bewdley England 10 C3 .......52.23N 2.19W
Bewl Water resr England 11 F2 .......51.04N 0.23E
Bexhill England 11 F1 .......50.50N 0.29E
Beykoz Turkey 57 H5 .......41.07N 29.05E
Beyla Guinea 84 D2 .......8.41N 8.41W
Beyneu Kazakhstan 58 G2 .......45.18N 55.11E
Beypazarı Turkey 57 I5 .......40.10N 31.56E
Beyşehir Turkey 57 I3 .......37.42N 31.43E
Beyşehir Gölü l. Turkey 57 I3 .......37.42N 31.33E
Béziers France 44 E3 .......43.21N 3.13E
Bhagalpur India 96 G6 .......25.15N 86.56E
Bhamo Myanmar 97 I5 .......24.18N 97.17E
Bhavnagar India 96 D5 .......21.46N 72.14E
Bhima r. India 96 E4 .......16.26N 77.13E
Bhopal India 96 E5 .......23.15N 77.23E
Bhubaneshwar India 96 G5 .......20.13N 85.53E
Bhuj India 96 C5 .......23.11N 69.44E
Bhutan Asia 97 H6 .......27.38N 90.33E
Biak Indonesia 105 J3 .......1.12S 136.05E
Biak i. Indonesia 105 J3 .......0.59S 135.59E
Biała Podlaska Poland 46 F4 .......52.02N 23.07E
Białogard Poland 46 F4 .......53.59N 15.59E
Białystok Poland 46 F4 .......53.08N 23.10E
Biarritz France 44 C3 .......43.29N 1.33W
Bibai Japan 106 D4 .......43.18N 141.52E
Biberach an der Riß Germany 54 C3 .......48.06N 9.47E
Bicester England 10 D2 .......51.54N 1.09W
Bidar India 96 E4 .......17.54N 77.34E
Biddulph England 15 E2 .......53.07N 2.10W
Bidean nam Bian mt. Scotland 18 D1 .......56.39N 5.02W
Bideford England 13 C3 .......51.01N 4.12W
Biel Switz. 50 B7 .......47.09N 7.15E
Bielefeld Germany 54 C5 .......52.01N 8.32E
Biella Italy 50 C6 .......45.34N 8.04E
Bielsko-Biała Poland 46 D2 .......49.49N 19.03E

Bié Plateau f. Angola 82 E3 .......13.00S 16.00E
Bifoun Gabon 84 F1 .......0.15S 10.25E
Biga Turkey 56 G5 .......40.13N 27.13E
Bigbury Bay England 13 D2 .......50.15N 3.54W
Biggar Scotland 17 F3 .......55.37N 3.31W
Biggleswade England 11 E3 .......52.05N 0.16W
Bighorn r. U.S.A. 64 E6 .......46.10N 107.30W
Bighorn Mountains U.S.A. 64 E5 .......44.06N 106.55W
Big Spring U.S.A. 64 F3 .......32.16N 101.24W
Big Trout Lake town Canada 63 J3 .......53.49N 89.50W
Bihać Bos.-Herz. 56 A7 .......44.49N 15.53E
Bihar d. India 96 G5 .......24.13N 85.37E
Bihor, Vârful mt. Romania 55 J2 .......46.27N 22.44E
Bijapur India 96 E4 .......16.49N 75.48E
Bijār Iran 95 G7 .......35.51N 47.37E
Bijeljina Bos.-Herz. 56 C7 .......44.46N 19.14E
Bijelo Polje Montenegro 56 C6 .......43.02N 19.45E
Bikaner India 96 D6 .......28.00N 73.23E
Bilaspur India 96 F5 .......22.05N 82.09E
Bilaspur India 96 E7 .......31.17N 76.49E
Bila Tserkva Ukraine 55 N3 .......49.48N 30.07E
Bilbao Spain 48 D5 .......43.15N 2.54W
Bilecik Turkey 57 H5 .......40.09N 29.57E
Biłgoraj Poland 46 F3 .......50.33N 22.43E
Bilhorod-Dnistrovs'kyy Ukraine 53 J6 .......46.11N 30.20E
Billericay England 11 F2 .......51.38N 0.25E
Billingham England 15 F3 .......54.37N 1.17W
Billinghay England 15 G2 .......53.05N 0.17W
Billings U.S.A. 64 E6 .......45.48N 108.27W
Billingshurst England 11 E2 .......51.01N 0.27W
Bill of Portland hd England 10 C1 .......50.30N 2.30W
Bilopillya Ukraine 55 P4 .......51.09N 34.20E
Biloxi U.S.A. 65 I3 .......30.24N 88.57W
Bilston Scotland 17 F3 .......55.52N 3.11W
Bilton England 15 G2 .......53.47N 0.15W
Bimini Islands Bahamas 71 I6 .......25.46N 79.14W
Bindura Zimbabwe 86 C3 .......17.18S 31.19E
Bingham England 10 E3 .......52.57N 0.57W
Binghamton U.S.A. 65 K5 .......42.06N 75.55W
Bingley England 15 F2 .......53.51N 1.50W
Bintulu Malaysia 104 E4 .......3.12N 113.03E
Bioco i. Equat. Guinea 84 E2 .......3.16N 8.31E
Birāk Libya 52 F2 .......27.33N 14.16E
Birao C.A.R. 94 B2 .......10.15N 22.48E
Birecik Turkey 57 L3 .......37.01N 37.59E
Birhan mt. Ethiopia 85 H3 .......10.43N 37.52E
Bīrjand Iran 95 I6 .......32.53N 59.08E
Birkenhead England 14 D2 .......53.23N 3.01W
Birmingham England 10 D3 .......52.29N 1.53W
Birmingham U.S.A. 65 I3 .......33.32N 86.47W
Bîr Mogreïn Mauritania 84 C4 .......25.14N 11.34W
Birnin Konni Niger 84 E3 .......13.48N 5.14E
Birobidzhan Rus. Fed. 101 O7 .......48.45N 132.52E
Birr Ireland 41 D3 .......53.06N 7.55W
Birsay Scotland 19 F4 .......59.08N 3.18W
Birstall England 10 D3 .......52.41N 1.07W
Biržai Lithuania 46 G6 .......56.12N 24.45E
Biscay, Bay of sea France/Spain 48 C6 .......45.40N 5.07W
Bischofshofen Austria 54 E2 .......47.25N 13.13E
Bishkek Kyrgyzstan 100 C6 .......42.54N 74.32E
Bisho S. Africa 86 B1 .......32.51S 27.24E
Bishop Auckland England 15 F3 .......54.40N 1.41W
Bishop's Lydeard England 13 D3 .......51.04N 3.11W
Bishop's Stortford England 11 F2 .......51.52N 0.10E
Bishop's Waltham England 10 D1 .......50.57N 1.13W
Bisina, Lake Uganda 87 A3 .......1.38N 33.57E
Biskra Algeria 84 E5 .......34.49N 5.44E
Bismarck U.S.A. 64 F6 .......46.50N 100.46W
Bismarck Sea P.N.G. 110 D6 .......4.01S 149.01E
Bissau Guinea-Bissau 84 C3 .......11.53N 15.38W
Bistra mt. Serbia 56 D6 .......42.09N 20.59E
Bistriţa Romania 55 K2 .......47.09N 24.30E
Bistriţa r. Romania 55 L2 .......46.30N 26.58E
Bitburg Germany 42 F2 .......49.58N 6.32E
Bitola Macedonia 56 D5 .......41.01N 21.20E
Bitterroot Range mts U.S.A. 64 D6 .......47.16N 115.41W
Biwa-ko l. Japan 106 C3 .......35.09N 135.59E
Biysk Rus. Fed. 58 J3 .......52.33N 85.17E
Bizerte Tunisia 52 E4 .......37.16N 9.52E
Bjørnøya i. Arctic Oc. 58 C5 .......74.24N 19.07E
Blackburn England 15 E2 .......53.45N 2.29W
Blackburn with Darwen d. England 9 D3 .......53.41N 2.27W
Black Combe hill England 14 D3 .......54.15N 3.20W
Blackfield England 10 D1 .......50.49N 1.22W
Black Forest mts Germany 54 C2 .......47.56N 8.08E
Black Head England 13 B2 .......50.00N 5.07W
Black Hill England 15 F2 .......53.32N 1.53W
Black Isle pen. Scotland 19 E2 .......57.35N 4.19W
Black Mountains hills Wales 12 D3 .......51.58N 3.08W
Blackpool England 14 D2 .......53.49N 3.03W
Blackpool d. England 9 D3 .......53.50N 3.01W
Black Sea Asia/Europe 57 M6 .......42.31N 38.22E
Blacksod Bay Ireland 41 A4 .......54.03N 10.03W
Black Volta r. Africa 84 D2 .......8.29N 0.51W
Blackwater r. England 11 F2 .......51.44N 0.41E
Blackwater r. Northern Ireland 16 C2 .......54.16N 6.34W
Blackwater r. Meath Ireland 41 E3 .......53.39N 6.41W
Blackwater r. Water. Ireland 41 D2 .......51.58N 7.52W
Blackwood Wales 12 D3 .......51.40N 3.12W
Blaenau Ffestiniog Wales 12 D4 .......52.59N 3.57W
Blaenau Gwent d. Wales 9 D2 .......51.46N 3.12W
Blaenavon Wales 12 D3 .......51.47N 3.06W
Blagdon England 10 C2 .......51.20N 2.43W
Blagoevgrad Bulgaria 56 D6 .......42.01N 23.06E
Blagoveshchensk Rus. Fed. 59 N3 .......50.17N 127.29E
Blair Atholl Scotland 19 F1 .......56.46N 3.51W
Blairgowrie Scotland 19 F1 .......56.35N 3.21W
Blanc, Mont mt. France/Italy 44 G4 .......45.50N 6.51E
Blanca, Bahía b. Argentina 73 C3 .......39.08S 61.47W
Blanche, Lake Australia 110 C4 .......29.15S 139.42E
Blanc Nez, Cap c. France 11 G1 .......50.56N 1.44E
Blanco, Cape U.S.A. 64 B5 .......42.51N 124.34W
Blandford Forum England 10 C1 .......50.51N 2.10W
Blanquilla, Isla i. Venezuela 71 L3 .......11.51N 64.35W
Blansko Czech Rep. 46 C2 .......49.21N 16.39E
Blantyre Malawi 86 C3 .......15.47S 35.02E
Blarney Ireland 41 C1 .......51.56N 8.34W
Bletchley England 10 E2 .......51.59N 0.45W
Blida Algeria 84 E5 .......36.33N 2.55E
Bloemfontein S. Africa 86 B2 .......29.05S 26.13E
Blois France 44 D5 .......47.35N 1.20E
Bloody Foreland pt Ireland 41 C5 .......55.10N 8.18W
Bloomington U.S.A. 65 I5 .......40.29N 88.59W
Blue Mountains U.S.A. 64 C6 .......45.27N 118.38W
Blue Nile r. Sudan 85 H3 .......15.38N 32.30E
Blue Stack hill Ireland 16 A2 .......54.45N 8.05W
Blue Stack Mountains hills Ireland 41 C4
.......54.42N 8.14W
Blumenau Brazil 77 K2 .......26.52S 49.04W
Blyth Northum. England 15 F4 .......55.08N 1.30W
Blyth Notts. England 15 F2 .......53.22N 1.03W
Blytheville U.S.A. 65 I4 .......35.56N 89.52W
Bo Sierra Leone 84 C2 .......7.55N 11.45W
Boa Esperança, Açude resr Brazil 77 L6 .......6.58S 43.47W

Boa Vista Brazil 77 H8 .......2.51N 60.43W
Boa Vista i. Cape Verde 84 B3 .......16.05N 22.40W
Bobaomby, Tanjona c. Madagascar 86 D3 .......11.57S 49.15E
Bobo-Dioulasso Burkina Faso 84 D3 .......11.11N 4.18W
Bóbr r. Poland 46 B4 .......52.03N 15.04E
Boby mt. Madagascar 86 D2 .......22.13S 46.54E
Bochnia Poland 46 E2 .......49.58N 20.26E
Bocholt Germany 54 B4 .......51.50N 6.36E
Boddam Scotland 19 H2 .......57.28N 1.47W
Bodélé f. Chad 85 F3 .......16.12N 16.17E
Boden Sweden 40 E4 .......65.49N 21.41E
Bodenham England 10 C3 .......52.09N 2.41W
Bodmin England 13 C2 .......50.28N 4.43W
Bodmin Moor f. England 13 C2 .......50.34N 4.36W
Bodø Norway 40 C4 .......67.17N 14.23E
Bodrum Turkey 56 G3 .......37.02N 27.25E
Boğazlıyan Turkey 57 K4 .......39.11N 35.15E
Boggeragh Mountains hills Ireland 41 B2 .......52.01N 9.01E
Bogie r. Scotland 19 G2 .......57.27N 2.46W
Bognor Regis England 10 E1 .......50.47N 0.40W
Bogor Indonesia 104 D2 .......6.35S 106.45E
Bogotá Colombia 72 B7 .......4.35N 74.04W
Bo Hai g. China 101 L5 .......38.32N 119.14E
Bohain-en-Vermandois France 42 C2 .......49.59N 3.28E
Bohemian Forest mts Germany 54 E3 .......49.42N 12.27E
Bohol i. Phil. 105 G5 .......9.55N 124.16E
Bohu China 100 F6 .......41.55N 86.35E
Boise U.S.A. 64 C5 .......43.38N 116.11W
Bojnūrd Iran 95 I7 .......37.27N 57.19E
Bolhrad Ukraine 53 I6 .......45.41N 28.37E
Bolívar, Pico mt. Venezuela 71 J2 .......8.33N 70.59W
Bolivia S. America 76 H4 .......16.23S 64.00W
Bollnäs Sweden 40 D3 .......61.21N 16.24E
Bolmen l. Sweden 40 C2 .......56.52N 13.43E
Bologna Italy 50 D6 .......44.30N 11.20E
Bolsena, Lago di l. Italy 50 D5 .......42.36N 11.56E
Bol'shakovo Rus. Fed. 46 E5 .......54.53N 21.39E
Bol'shevik, Ostrov i. Rus. Fed. 59 L5 .......78.39N 102.16E
Bol'shoy Aluy r. Rus. Fed. 59 Q4 .......66.29N 159.26E
Bol'shoy Lyakhovskiy, Ostrov i. Rus. Fed. 59 P5
.......73.26N 142.14E
Bolsover England 15 F2 .......53.14N 1.17W
Bolt Head England 13 D2 .......50.12N 3.47W
Bolton England 15 E2 .......53.35N 2.26W
Bolu Turkey 57 I5 .......40.44N 31.36E
Bolus Head Ireland 41 A1 .......51.47N 10.20W
Bolzano Italy 50 D7 .......46.29N 11.21E
Boma Dem. Rep. Congo 86 A4 .......5.48S 13.03E
Bømlo i. Norway 40 A2 .......59.45N 5.13E
Bon, Cap c. Tunisia 52 F4 .......37.04N 11.04E
Bonaire i. Neth. Antilles 71 K3 .......12.02N 68.12W
Bonar Bridge Scotland 19 E2 .......57.54N 4.21W
Bonavista Canada 63 M2 .......48.33N 52.43W
Bondoukou Côte d'Ivoire 84 D2 .......8.03N 2.48W
Bo'ness Scotland 17 F4 .......56.01N 3.37W
Bonete, Cerro mt. Bolivia 76 G2 .......21.46S 66.29W
Bonifacio France 44 H2 .......41.23N 9.10E
Bonifacio, Strait of France/Italy 44 H2 .......41.15N 8.45E
Bonin Islands Japan 108 F7 .......27.13N 141.44E
Bonn Germany 54 B4 .......50.44N 7.04E
Bonnyrigg Scotland 17 F3 .......55.52N 3.06W
Bontosunggu Indonesia 104 F2 .......5.41S 119.43E
Boothia, Gulf of Canada 63 I5 .......68.48N 86.41W
Boothia Peninsula Canada 63 I5 .......70.35N 95.10W
Bootle England 14 D2 .......53.27N 2.59W
Bor Serbia 56 D7 .......44.05N 22.07E
Borås Sweden 40 C2 .......57.44N 12.57E
Borāzjān Iran 95 H5 .......29.16N 51.12E
Bordeaux France 44 C4 .......44.51N 0.34W
Borden Island Canada 62 G5 .......78.31N 111.01W
Borden Peninsula Canada 63 J5 .......72.45N 82.32W
Bordj Messaouda Algeria 52 E3 .......30.10N 9.25E
Bordj Omer Driss Algeria 84 E4 .......28.11N 6.47E
Boreray i. Scotland 18 B2 .......57.42N 7.16W
Borgarnes Iceland 40 X2 .......64.32N 21.55W
Borken Germany 42 F4 .......51.50N 6.51E
Borkum i. Germany 42 F6 .......53.37N 6.44E
Borlänge Sweden 40 C3 .......60.29N 15.26E
Borneo i. Asia 104 E4 .......0.08N 113.25E
Bornholm i. Denmark 40 C1 .......55.09N 14.38E
Bornova Turkey 56 G4 .......38.27N 27.11E
Borodyanka Ukraine 55 M4 .......50.39N 29.56E
Boroughbridge England 15 F3 .......54.06N 1.24W
Borūjerd Iran 95 G6 .......33.53N 48.43E
Boryspil' Ukraine 55 N4 .......50.21N 30.58E
Borzna Ukraine 55 O4 .......51.15N 32.26E
Borzya Rus. Fed. 59 M3 .......50.11N 116.31E
Bosanska Dubica Bos.-Herz. 56 B7 .......45.11N 16.48E
Bose China 101 J2 .......23.54N 106.37E
Bosna r. Bos.-Herz. 56 C7 .......45.04N 18.29E
Bosnia-Herzegovina Europe 56 B7 .......44.23N 17.40E
Bosobolo Dem. Rep. Congo 86 A5 .......4.10N 19.52E
Bosporus str. Turkey 57 H5 .......41.20N 29.06E
Bossembélé C.A.R. 85 F2 .......5.15N 17.38E
Bosten Hu l. China 100 F6 .......41.53N 87.24E
Boston England 11 E3 .......52.58N 0.01W
Boston U.S.A. 65 L5 .......42.23N 71.06W
Boston Spa England 15 F2 .......53.54N 1.20W
Botevgrad Bulgaria 56 E6 .......42.54N 23.47E
Bothnia, Gulf of Finland/Sweden 40 D3 .......61.09N 19.15E
Botoşani Romania 55 L2 .......47.45N 26.39E
Botswana Africa 86 B2 .......24.56S 22.47E
Botte Donato, Monte mt. Italy 50 G3 .......39.17N 16.28E
Bottesford England 15 G2 .......53.33N 0.38W
Bouaké Côte d'Ivoire 84 D2 .......7.42N 5.03W
Bouar C.A.R. 84 F2 .......5.56N 15.35E
Bouârfa Morocco 84 D5 .......32.34N 1.56W
Bougainville Island P.N.G. 110 E6 .......6.04S 154.53E
Bouillon Belgium 42 E2 .......49.48N 5.06E
Boujdour Western Sahara 84 C4 .......26.08N 14.28W
Boulder U.S.A. 64 E5 .......40.02N 105.16W
Boulogne-Billancourt France 44 E6 .......48.50N 2.15E
Boulogne-sur-Mer France 44 D7 .......50.43N 1.37E
Bounty Islands New Zealand 111 G2 .......47.40S 179.02E
Bourg-en-Bresse France 44 F5 .......46.12N 5.14E
Bourges France 44 E5 .......47.05N 2.24E
Bourke Australia 110 D3 .......30.07S 145.54E
Bourne England 11 E3 .......52.46N 0.23W
Bournemouth England 10 D1 .......50.43N 1.53W
Bournemouth d. England 9 E2 .......50.43N 1.53W
Bou Saâda Algeria 52 D4 .......35.13N 4.11E
Bow r. Canada 64 D6 .......49.58N 111.41W
Bowes England 15 E3 .......54.31N 2.00W
Bowland, Forest of England 14 E2 .......53.59N 2.33W
Boxtel Neth. 42 E4 .......51.35N 5.20E
Boyabat Turkey 57 K5 .......41.28N 34.46E
Boyle Ireland 41 C3 .......53.58N 8.18W
Boyne r. Ireland 41 E3 .......53.43N 6.18W
Boyuibe Bolivia 76 H3 .......20.27S 63.17W
Bozeman U.S.A. 64 D6 .......45.42N 111.02W
Bozüyük Turkey 57 I4 .......39.55N 30.01E
Braan r. Scotland 17 F4 .......56.34N 3.36W
Brabant Wallon d. Belgium 42 D3 .......50.39N 4.35E
Brač i. Croatia 56 B6 .......43.17N 16.51E

Bracadale, Loch *b.* Scotland 18 C2........................57.21N 6.33W
Bräcke Sweden 40 C3.....................................62.46N 15.26E
Brackley England 10 D3..................................52.02N 1.08W
Bracknell England 9 E2..................................51.25N 0.45W
Bracknell Forest *d.* England 9 E2......................51.24N 0.45W
Brad Romania 56 E8......................................46.07N 22.48E
Bradano *r.* Italy 50 G4.................................40.23N 16.51E
Bradford England 15 F2..................................53.48N 1.45W
Bradford-on-Avon England 10 C2..........................51.21N 2.15W
Braemar Scotland 19 F2..................................57.00N 3.24W
Braga Portugal 48 A4....................................41.33N 8.26W
Bragança Brazil 77 K7...................................1.00S 46.49W
Bragança Portugal 48 B4.................................41.49N 6.45W
Brahmapur India 96 F4...................................19.21N 84.52E
Brahmaputra *r.* China/India 100 G2.....................23.36N 90.31E
Brăila Romania 57 G2....................................45.17N 27.58E
Braintree England 11 F2.................................51.53N 0.33E
Brämön *i.* Sweden 40 D3................................62.13N 17.45E
Brampton England 14 E3..................................54.57N 2.44W
Branco *r.* Brazil 77 H7................................1.18S 61.52W
Brandenburg Germany 54 E5...............................52.25N 12.34E
Brandesburton England 15 G2.............................53.55N 0.18W
Brandon Canada 62 I2....................................49.51N 99.57W
Brandon England 11 F3...................................52.27N 0.37E
Brandon Head Ireland 41 A2..............................52.17N 10.13W
Brandon Mountain *hill* Ireland 41 A2...................52.14N 10.15W
Braniewo Poland 46 D5...................................54.23N 19.49E
Bransgore England 10 D1.................................50.47N 1.44W
Brasília Brazil 77 K4...................................15.49S 47.55W
Braşov Romania 56 F7....................................45.40N 25.36E
Bratislava Slovakia 54 G3...............................48.09N 17.06E
Bratsk Rus. Fed. 59 L3..................................56.16N 101.41E
Braunau am Inn Austria 54 E3............................48.16N 13.02E
Braunschweig Germany 54 D5..............................52.17N 10.32E
Braunton England 13 C3..................................51.06N 4.10W
Brawley U.S.A. 64 C3....................................32.58N 115.32W
Bray Ireland 41 E3......................................53.12N 6.07W
Bray Head Ireland 41 A1.................................51.52N 10.25W
Brazil S. America 77 I5.................................29.58S 54.33W
Brazil Basin *f.* Atlantic Oc. 116 H5...................15.00S 30.00W
Brazilian Highlands *mts* Brazil 77 K5..................17.00S 48.00W
Brazos *r.* U.S.A. 64 G2................................28.52N 95.25W
Brazzaville Congo 84 F1.................................4.17S 15.11E
Breamish *r.* England 15 E4.............................55.41N 2.13W
Breckland England 11 F3.................................52.28N 0.39E
Břeclav Czech Rep. 54 G3................................48.46N 16.53E
Brecon Wales 12 D3......................................51.57N 3.24W
Brecon Beacons *f.* Wales 12 D3.........................51.53N 3.26W
Breda Neth. 42 D4.......................................51.35N 4.46E
Breiðafjörður *b.* Iceland 40 W2........................65.03N 24.07W
Breiðdalsvík Iceland 40 Z2..............................64.48N 14.02W
Bremen Germany 54 C5....................................53.05N 8.51E
Bremerhaven Germany 54 C5...............................53.33N 8.35E
Brenner Pass Austria/Italy 50 D7........................46.59N 11.32E
Brentwood England 11 F2.................................51.37N 0.19E
Brescia Italy 50 D6.....................................45.32N 10.13E
Bressanone Italy 50 D7..................................46.43N 11.40E
Bressay *i.* Scotland 19 H5.............................60.16N 1.18W
Bressuire France 44 C5..................................46.50N 0.30W
Brest Belarus 55 J5.....................................52.05N 23.40E
Brest France 44 A6......................................48.24N 4.29W
Bretton Wales 12 E5.....................................53.10N 2.58W
Bria C.A.R. 85 G2.......................................6.32N 21.59E
Briançon France 44 G4...................................44.54N 6.38E
Brianne, Llyn *resr* Wales 12 D4........................52.08N 3.45W
Bride *r.* Ireland 41 D2................................52.04N 7.52W
Bridgend Wales 13 D3....................................51.30N 3.35W
Bridgend *d.* Wales 9 D2................................51.34N 3.33W
Bridgeport U.S.A. 65 L5.................................41.12N 73.12W
Bridgetown Barbados 71 M3...............................13.05N 59.36W
Bridgnorth England 10 C3................................52.32N 2.25W
Bridgwater England 13 D3................................51.08N 3.00W
Bridgwater Bay England 13 D3............................51.16N 3.19W
Bridlington England 15 G3...............................54.05N 0.12W
Bridlington Bay England 15 G3...........................54.03N 0.07W
Bridport England 10 C1..................................50.44N 2.45W
Brig Switz. 50 B7.......................................46.19N 7.59E
Brigg England 15 G2.....................................53.33N 0.29W
Brighstone England 10 D1................................50.39N 1.23W
Brightlingsea England 11 G2.............................51.49N 1.01E
Brighton England 11 E1..................................50.49N 0.08W
Brighton and Hove *d.* England 9 E2.....................50.51N 0.08W
Brindisi Italy 50 H5....................................40.38N 17.56E
Brisbane Australia 110 E4...............................27.33S 153.03E
Bristol England 10 C2...................................51.27N 2.35W
Bristol *d.* England 9 D2...............................51.28N 2.36W
Bristol U.S.A. 65 J4....................................36.36N 82.10W
Bristol Bay U.S.A. 62 B3................................57.22N 161.29W
Bristol Channel *est.* England 10 B2....................51.20N 4.16W
British Columbia *d.* Canada 62 F3......................51.49N 121.48W
British Empire Range *mts* Canada 63 J6.................82.22N 80.08W
British Isles Europe 34 D3..............................54.00N 5.00W
Briton Ferry Wales 12 D3................................51.38N 3.49W
Britstown S. Africa 86 B1...............................30.35S 23.30E
Brittany *f.* France 44 B6..............................48.10N 3.22W
Brittas Bay Ireland 12 A4...............................52.52N 6.03W
Brive-la-Gaillarde France 44 D4.........................45.10N 1.32E
Brixham England 13 C2...................................50.24N 3.31W
Brno Czech Rep. 54 G3...................................49.11N 16.37E
Broad *r.* U.S.A. 65 J3.................................34.00N 81.04W
Broadback *r.* Canada 65 K7.............................51.21N 78.50W
Broad Bay Scotland 18 C3................................58.15N 6.15W
Broad Law *hill* Scotland 17 F3.........................55.30N 3.21W
Broadstairs England 11 G2...............................51.22N 1.26E
Broadway England 10 D3..................................52.02N 1.51W
Broadwey England 10 C1..................................50.39N 2.28W
Broadwindsor England 10 C1..............................50.49N 2.48W
Brockenhurst England 10 D1..............................50.49N 1.34W
Brock Island Canada 62 G5...............................77.53N 114.21W
Brodeur Peninsula Canada 63 J5..........................71.50N 88.32W
Brodick Scotland 16 D3..................................55.35N 5.09W
Brodnica Poland 46 D4...................................53.16N 19.24E
Brody Ukraine 55 K4.....................................50.05N 25.09E
Broken Hill *town* Australia 110 D3.....................31.55S 141.27E
Bromley England 11 F2...................................51.24N 0.01E
Bromsgrove England 10 C3................................52.20N 2.04W
Bromyard England 10 C3..................................52.11N 2.30W
Brønderslev Denmark 40 B2...............................57.17N 9.58E
Brønnøysund Norway 40 C4................................65.28N 12.12E
Brooke England 11 G3....................................52.33N 1.23E
Brooke's Point *town* Phil. 104 F5......................8.50N 117.51E
Brookings U.S.A. 64 F5..................................44.19N 96.44W
Brooks Canada 64 D7.....................................50.35N 111.54W
Brooks Range *mts* U.S.A. 62 D4.........................69.18N 144.41W
Broom, Loch *inlet* Scotland 18 D2......................57.56N 5.19W
Broome Australia 110 B5.................................17.57S 122.14E
Brora Scotland 19 F3....................................58.01N 3.51W
Brora *r.* Scotland 19 F3...............................58.01N 3.50W
Brosna *r.* Ireland 41 D3...............................53.13N 7.57W
Brotton England 15 G3...................................54.34N 0.56W
Brough Cumb. England 15 E3..............................54.32N 2.19W
Brough E. Yorks. England 15 G2..........................53.44N 0.34W
Brough Head Scotland 19 F4..............................59.08N 3.21W

Brough Ness *pt* Scotland 19 G3.........................58.44N 2.58W
Broughshane Northern Ireland 16 C2......................54.54N 6.12W
Brownhills England 10 D3................................52.39N 1.56W
Broxburn Scotland 17 F3.................................55.56N 3.28W
Bruay-la-Bussière France 42 B3..........................50.29N 2.33E
Brue *r.* England 10 C2.................................51.13N 2.59W
Brugge Belgium 42 C4....................................51.12N 3.15E
Brumado Brazil 77 L5....................................14.12S 41.34W
Brunei Asia 104 E4......................................5.06N 114.18E
Brunflo Sweden 40 C3....................................63.05N 14.51E
Brunswick U.S.A. 65 J3..................................31.09N 81.30W
Bruntál Czech Rep. 46 C2................................49.59N 17.28E
Brussels Belgium 42 D3..................................50.50N 4.21E
Bruton England 10 C2....................................51.07N 2.27W
Bryansk Rus. Fed. 58 E3.................................53.15N 34.23E
Bryher *i.* England 13 A1...............................49.57N 6.23W
Brynamman Wales 12 D3...................................51.49N 3.52W
Brynmawr Wales 12 D3....................................51.48N 3.10W
Brzeg Poland 46 C3......................................50.51N 17.28E
Buca Turkey 56 G4.......................................38.22N 27.11E
Bucaramanga Colombia 72 B7..............................7.05N 73.09W
Bucharest Romania 56 G2.................................44.26N 26.06E
Buckhaven Scotland 17 F4................................56.11N 3.02W
Buckie Scotland 19 G2...................................57.41N 2.58W
Buckingham England 10 E2................................51.59N 0.59W
Buckinghamshire *d.* England 9 E2.......................51.47N 0.56W
Buckley Wales 12 D5.....................................53.10N 3.05W
Budapest Hungary 54 H2..................................47.30N 19.04E
Buddon Ness *pt* Scotland 17 G4.........................56.28N 2.43W
Bude England 13 C2......................................50.50N 4.32W
Bude Bay England 13 C2..................................50.50N 4.38W
Buenaventura Colombia 72 B7.............................3.52N 77.00W
Buenos Aires Argentina 73 D3............................34.36S 58.24W
Buenos Aires, Lago *l.* Argentina/Chile 73 B2...........46.31S 72.13W
Buffalo N. Y. U.S.A. 65 K5..............................42.53N 78.52W
Buffalo Wyo. U.S.A. 64 E5...............................44.20N 106.41W
Bug *r.* Poland 46 F3...................................51.30N 23.39E
Buhu *r.* Tanzania 87 A1................................6.03S 35.20E
Builth Wells Wales 12 D4................................52.09N 3.24W
Buir Nur *l.* Mongolia 101 L7...........................47.47N 117.53E
Bujumbura Burundi 85 G1.................................3.24S 29.22E
Bukavu Dem. Rep. Congo 86 B4............................2.30S 28.49E
Bukittinggi Indonesia 104 C3............................0.15S 100.20E
Bukoba Tanzania 86 C4...................................1.18S 31.48E
Bula Indonesia 105 I3...................................3.06S 130.28E
Bulawayo Zimbabwe 86 B2.................................20.09S 28.36E
Bulgan Mongolia 101 I7..................................48.44N 103.28E
Bulgaria Europe 56 F6...................................42.51N 25.15E
Bulun Rus. Fed. 59 N5...................................70.59N 127.16E
Buna Kenya 87 B3........................................2.47N 39.31E
Bunbury Australia 110 A3................................33.20S 115.36E
Bunclody Ireland 41 E2..................................52.39N 6.39W
Buncrana Ireland 41 D5..................................55.09N 7.27W
Bunda Tanzania 87 A2....................................2.04S 33.56E
Bundaberg Australia 110 E4..............................24.52S 152.22E
Bundoran Ireland 41 C4..................................54.28N 8.18W
Bungay England 11 G3....................................52.27N 1.27E
Bungoma Kenya 87 A3.....................................0.34N 34.34E
Buôn Ma Thuôt Vietnam 104 D6............................12.38N 108.05E
Bura Kenya 87 B2........................................1.06S 39.57E
Buraydah Saudi Arabia 94 F5.............................26.20N 43.57E
Burbage England 10 D2...................................51.21N 1.40W
Burdur Turkey 57 I3.....................................37.43N 30.17E
Bure *r.* England 11 G3.................................52.37N 1.43E
Burē Ethiopia 85 H3.....................................10.50N 36.57E
Burford England 10 D2...................................51.48N 1.38W
Burgas Bulgaria 56 G6...................................42.30N 27.28E
Burgess Hill *town* England 11 E1.......................50.57N 0.08W
Burghausen Germany 54 E3................................48.10N 12.50E
Burghead Scotland 19 F2.................................57.42N 3.29W
Burgh le Marsh England 15 H2............................53.10N 0.14E
Burgos Spain 48 D5......................................42.21N 3.41W
Burhanpur India 96 E5...................................21.18N 76.14E
Burkina Faso Africa 84 D3...............................11.39N 1.18W
Burlington Colo. U.S.A. 64 F4...........................39.19N 102.17W
Burlington Iowa U.S.A. 65 H5............................40.49N 91.06W
Burlington Vt. U.S.A. 65 L5.............................44.28N 73.13W
Burma *see* Myanmar
Burnham England 10 E2...................................51.32N 0.39W
Burnham Market England 11 F3............................52.57N 0.44E
Burnham-on-Crouch England 11 F2.........................51.38N 0.49E
Burnham-on-Sea England 10 C2............................51.14N 2.59W
Burnie Australia 110 D2.................................41.03S 145.57E
Burniston England 15 G3.................................54.19N 0.27W
Burnley England 15 E2...................................53.47N 2.15W
Burns U.S.A. 64 C5......................................43.36N 119.01W
Burns Lake *town* Canada 62 F3..........................54.15N 125.46W
Burntisland Scotland 17 F4..............................56.04N 3.14W
Burntwood Green England 10 D3...........................52.41N 1.54W
Burra Australia 110 C3..................................33.42S 138.56E
Burray *i.* Scotland 19 H5..............................60.05N 1.22W
Burro, Serranías del *mts* Mexico 70 D6.................29.02N 102.00W
Burrow Head Scotland 16 E2..............................54.41N 4.23W
Burry Inlet Wales 12 C3.................................51.38N 4.18W
Burry Port Wales 12 C3..................................51.41N 4.16W
Bursa Turkey 57 H4......................................40.14N 29.03E
Bûr Safâjah Egypt 53 J2.................................26.45N 33.55E
Burscough Bridge England 14 E2..........................53.36N 2.51W
Burton-in-Kendal England 14 E3..........................54.11N 2.43W
Burton Latimer England 10 E3............................52.22N 0.41W
Burton upon Trent England 10 D3.........................52.48N 1.39W
Buru *i.* Indonesia 105 H3..............................3.24S 126.35E
Burundi Africa 85 H1....................................3.36S 30.03E
Burwash Landing Canada 62 E4............................61.21N 138.58W
Burwell England 11 F3...................................52.16N 0.20E
Burwick Scotland 19 G3..................................58.45N 2.58W
Bury England 15 E2......................................53.36N 2.18W
Bury St Edmunds England 11 F3...........................52.15N 0.44E
Bush *r.* Northern Ireland 16 C3........................55.13N 6.31W
Bushbush *r.* Kenya/Somalia 87 C2.......................1.11S 41.49E
Büsseher Iran 95 H5.....................................28.58N 50.51E
Bushmills Northern Ireland 16 C3........................55.12N 6.31W
Buta Dem. Rep. Congo 86 B5..............................2.49N 24.45E
Bute *i.* Scotland 16 D3................................55.49N 5.06W
Bute, Sound of *str.* Scotland 16 D3....................55.44N 5.19W
Buton *i.* Indonesia 105 G3.............................4.55S 123.00E
Butte U.S.A. 64 D6......................................46.01N 112.32W
Butterworth Malaysia 104 C5.............................5.22N 100.22E
Buttevant Ireland 41 C2.................................52.14N 8.40W
Butt of Lewis *hd* Scotland 18 C3.......................58.32N 6.17W
Butuan Phil. 105 H5.....................................8.56N 125.32E
Buur Gaabo Somalia 87 C2................................1.15S 41.49E
Buvuma Island Uganda 87 A3..............................0.10N 33.18E
Buxoro Uzbekistan 58 H1.................................39.46N 64.25E
Buxton England 15 F2....................................53.16N 1.55W
Büyük Ağrı Dağı *mt.* Turkey 94 F7......................39.44N 44.15E
Büyükmenderes *r.* Turkey 57 G3.........................37.28N 27.11E
Buzău Romania 56 G7.....................................45.09N 26.48E
Byarezina *r.* Belarus 55 K5............................53.48N 26.58E
Byaroza Belarus 55 K5...................................52.32N 24.59E
Bydgoszcz Poland 46 D4..................................53.08N 18.02E
Byfield England 10 E3...................................52.11N 1.14W
Bylot Island Canada 63 K5...............................73.07N 79.01W
Byrranga, Gory *mts* Rus. Fed. 59 K5....................74.25N 99.53E

Bytom Poland 46 D3......................................50.21N 18.55E

# C

Caacupé Paraguay 77 I2..................................25.20S 57.05W
Cabanatuan Phil. 105 G7.................................15.31N 120.58E
Caban Coch Reservoir Wales 12 D4........................52.15N 3.35W
Cabezas Bolivia 76 H4...................................18.46S 63.23W
Cabimas Venezuela 72 B8.................................10.23N 71.26W
Cabo Frio Brazil 73 E4..................................22.51S 42.02W
Cabonga, Réservoir Canada 65 K6.........................47.21N 76.32W
Cabo Pantoja Peru 76 E7.................................0.58S 75.13W
Cabora Bassa, Lake *resr* Mozambique 86 C3..............15.46S 31.11E
Caborca Mexico 70 B7....................................30.44N 112.09W
Cabot Strait Canada 63 L2...............................47.39N 60.16W
Cabrera, Sierra de la *mts* Spain 48 B5.................42.13N 6.51W
Cabriel *r.* Spain 48 E3................................39.16N 1.04W
Cáceres Brazil 77 I4....................................16.03S 57.41W
Cáceres Spain 48 B3.....................................39.29N 6.21W
Cachi, Nevados de *mts* Argentina 76 G3.................24.48S 66.25W
Cachimbo, Serra do *hills* Brazil 77 J6.................9.18S 54.11W
Cachoeiro de Itapemirim Brazil 77 L3....................20.51S 41.08W
Čadca Slovakia 46 D2....................................49.26N 18.48E
Cadillac U.S.A. 65 I5...................................44.14N 85.23W
Cádiz Spain 48 B2.......................................36.32N 6.17W
Cádiz, Golfo de *g.* Spain 48 B2........................36.44N 7.14W
Caen France 44 C6.......................................49.11N 0.21W
Caerleon Wales 12 E3....................................51.37N 2.57W
Caernarfon Wales 12 C5..................................53.08N 4.16W
Caernarfon Bay Wales 12 C5..............................53.06N 4.34W
Caerphilly Wales 12 D3..................................51.35N 3.13W
Caerphilly *d.* Wales 9 D2..............................51.38N 3.11W
Caerwent Wales 12 E3....................................51.37N 2.46W
Cagayan de Oro Phil. 105 G5.............................8.29N 124.39E
Cagliari Italy 50 C3....................................39.13N 9.08E
Cagliari, Golfo di *b.* Italy 50 C3.....................39.07N 9.13E
Caha Mountains Ireland 41 B1............................51.41N 9.44W
Cahirciveen Ireland 41 A1...............................51.57N 10.13W
Cahore Point Ireland 41 E2..............................52.33N 6.11W
Cahors France 44 D4.....................................44.28N 1.26E
Cahul Moldova 57 H7.....................................45.54N 28.12E
Caia Mozambique 86 C3...................................17.50S 35.19E
Caiabis, Serra dos *hills* Brazil 77 I5.................12.46S 56.21W
Caiapó, Serra do *hills* Brazil 77 J4...................17.19S 52.31W
Caicos Islands Turks and Caicos Is 71 J5................21.45N 71.53W
Caimodorro *mt.* Spain 48 E4............................40.32N 1.40W
Cairn Gorm *mt.* Scotland 19 F2.........................57.07N 3.39W
Cairngorm Mountains Scotland 19 F2......................57.08N 3.45W
Cairnryan Scotland 16 D2................................54.59N 5.02W
Cairns Australia 110 D5.................................16.54S 145.45E
Cairn Toul *mt.* Scotland 19 F2.........................57.03N 3.43W
Cairo Egypt 85 H5.......................................30.01N 31.15E
Caister-on-Sea England 11 G3............................52.39N 1.44E
Caistor England 15 G2...................................53.30N 0.19W
Caithness *f.* Scotland 19 F3...........................58.24N 3.22W
Cajamarca Peru 76 E6....................................7.11S 78.31W
Calabar Nigeria 84 E2...................................4.59N 8.19E
Calafat Romania 56 E6...................................43.59N 22.57E
Calais France 44 D6.....................................50.57N 1.51E
Calais U.S.A. 65 M6.....................................45.10N 67.18W
Calama Chile 73 C4......................................22.29S 68.56W
Calamian Group *is* Phil. 104 F6........................11.59N 119.29E
Calamocha Spain 48 E4...................................40.56N 1.17W
Calanscio Sand Sea *des.* Libya 53 H3...................30.11N 22.22E
Calapan Phil. 105 G6....................................13.24N 121.11E
Cǎlǎraşi Romania 56 G7..................................44.12N 27.19E
Calatayud Spain 48 E4...................................41.21N 1.37W
Calbayog Phil. 105 G6...................................12.05N 124.37E
Calcanhar, Ponta do *pt* Brazil 77 M6...................5.07S 35.34W
Caldas da Rainha Portugal 48 A3.........................39.24N 9.08W
Caldey Island Wales 12 C3...............................51.38N 4.40W
Calf of Man *i.* Isle of Man 14 C3......................54.04N 4.50W
Calgary Canada 62 G3....................................51.02N 114.04W
Cali Colombia 72 B7.....................................3.22N 76.28W
Caliente U.S.A. 64 D4...................................37.37N 114.31W
California *d.* U.S.A. 64 B5.............................41.35N 122.50W
California, Gulf of Mexico 70 B7.........................30.51N 113.58W
Callan Ireland 41 D2....................................52.33N 7.24W
Callander Scotland 16 E4................................56.15N 4.13W
Callanish Scotland 18 C3................................58.12N 6.45W
Callao Peru 76 E5.......................................12.04S 77.08W
Callington England 13 C2................................50.30N 4.19W
Calne England 10 C2.....................................51.26N 2.00W
Caltanissetta Italy 50 F2...............................37.30N 14.03E
Calvi France 44 H3......................................42.34N 8.45E
Cam *r.* England 11 F3..................................52.20N 0.15E
Camaçari Brazil 77 M5...................................12.43S 38.15W
Camagüey Cuba 71 I5.....................................21.23N 77.54W
Camagüey, Archipiélago de *is* Cuba 71 I5...............22.44N 78.34W
Ca Mau, Mui *c.* Vietnam 104 C5.........................8.35N 104.45E
Camberley England 10 E2.................................51.20N 0.44W
Camborne England 13 B2..................................50.13N 5.18W
Cambrai France 42 C3....................................50.10N 3.14E
Cambrian Mountains Wales 12 D4..........................52.37N 3.40W
Cambridge England 11 F3.................................52.12N 0.07E
Cambridge Bay *town* Canada 62 H4.......................69.02N 105.14W
Cambridgeshire *d.* England 9 F3........................52.25N 0.02E
Camelford England 13 C2.................................50.37N 4.41W
Cameroon Africa 84 F2...................................5.45N 12.41E
Cameroun, Mont *vol.* Cameroon 84 E2....................4.12N 9.12E
Cametá Brazil 77 K7.....................................2.13S 49.30W
Campbell Island New Zealand 108 H2......................52.31S 169.01E
Campbell Plateau *f.* S. Pacific Oc. 108 H2.............49.32S 170.53E
Campbell River *town* Canada 62 F3......................50.01N 125.14W
Campbeltown Scotland 16 D3..............................55.25N 5.36W
Campeche Mexico 70 F4...................................19.51N 90.30W
Campeche *d.* Mexico 70 F4..............................18.53N 90.28W
Campeche, Bahía de *g.* Mexico 70 F4....................19.30N 93.30W
Campina Grande Brazil 77 M6.............................7.14S 35.49W
Campinas Brazil 77 K2...................................22.55S 47.04W
Campobasso Italy 50 F4..................................41.34N 14.39E
Campo Grande Brazil 77 J3...............................20.24S 54.34W
Campos Brazil 77 L3.....................................21.45S 41.20W
Câmpulung Moldovenesc Romania 55 K2.....................47.32N 25.30E
Camrose Wales 12 B3.....................................51.50N 5.01W
Çan Turkey 56 G5........................................40.02N 27.02E
Canada N. America 62 F4.................................46.44N 81.59W
Canadian *r.* U.S.A. 64 G4..............................35.11N 95.52W
Canadian Shield *f.* N. America 60 K7...................50.00N 80.00W
Çanakkale Turkey 56 G5..................................40.08N 26.23E
Canarreos, Archipiélago de los *is* Cuba 71 H5..........21.44S 82.00W
Canary Islands N. Atlantic Oc. 48 X2....................30.08N 18.27W
Canaveral, Cape U.S.A. 65 J2............................28.26N 80.36W
Canberra Australia 110 D3...............................35.19S 149.09E
Cancún Mexico 70 G5.....................................21.10N 86.50W
Canelones Uruguay 77 I1.................................34.32S 56.17W
Caniapiscau *r.* Canada 63 L3...........................57.39N 69.25W
Caniapiscau, Lac *l.* Canada 63 K3......................54.21N 70.31W
Canindé *r.* Brazil 77 L6...............................6.17S 42.49W
Canisp *hill* Scotland 18 D3............................58.07N 5.03W

Çankaya Turkey 57 J4....................................39.53N 32.49E
Çankırı Turkey 57 J5....................................40.36N 33.36E
Canna *i.* Scotland 18 C2...............................57.04N 6.34W
Cannes France 44 G3.....................................43.33N 7.01E
Cannock England 10 C3...................................52.41N 2.02W
Canoas Brazil 77 J2.....................................29.54S 51.10W
Canora Canada 64 F7.....................................51.39N 102.26W
Cantabrian Mountains Spain 48 C5........................43.07N 4.13W
Canterbury England 11 G2................................51.17N 1.05E
Cân Thơ Vietnam 104 D6..................................10.01N 105.46E
Canvey Island England 11 F2.............................51.31N 0.35E
Cao Bằng Vietnam 104 D8.................................22.41N 106.17E
Capbreton France 44 C3..................................43.39N 1.26W
Cape Breton Island Canada 63 L2.........................46.45N 60.24W
Cape Johnson Depth *f.* N. Pacific Oc. 108 E6...........10.26N 126.39E
Capel St Mary England 11 G3.............................52.00N 1.03E
Cape Town S. Africa 86 A1...............................33.57S 18.28E
Cape Verde N. Atlantic Oc. 84 B3........................15.47N 24.31W
Cape York Peninsula Australia 110 D5....................12.33S 142.33E
Cap-Haïtien Haiti 71 J4.................................19.46N 72.15W
Capim *r.* Brazil 77 K7.................................1.30S 48.30W
Capitol Hill *town* N. Mariana Is 108 F7................15.12N 145.45E
Capraia, Isola di *i.* Italy 50 C5......................43.03N 9.49E
Caprera, Isola *i.* Italy 50 C4.........................41.13N 9.29E
Capri, Isola di *i.* Italy 50 F4........................40.32N 14.13E
Capricorn Channel Australia 110 E4......................22.20S 151.46E
Caprivi Strip *f.* Namibia 86 B3........................18.11S 21.64E
Caquetá *r.* Colombia 72 C6.............................1.27S 69.25W
Carabaya, Cordillera de *mts* Peru 76 F5................13.57S 71.27W
Caracal Romania 56 F7...................................44.07N 24.21E
Caracas Venezuela 72 C8.................................10.35N 66.59W
Carajás, Serra dos *hills* Brazil 77 J6.................5.43S 51.27W
Caransebeş Romania 56 E7................................45.25N 22.14E
Caratasca, Laguna de *lagoon* Honduras 71 H4............15.20N 83.58W
Caratinga Brazil 77 L4..................................19.45S 42.04W
Caravaca de la Cruz Spain 48 E3.........................38.07N 1.51W
Carbonara, Capo *c.* Italy 50 C3........................39.06N 9.32E
Carcassonne France 44 E3................................43.13N 2.22E
Cardiff Wales 13 D3.....................................51.29N 3.11W
Cardiff *d.* Wales 9 D2.................................51.30N 3.12W
Cardigan Wales 12 C4....................................52.05N 4.40W
Cardigan Bay Wales 12 C4................................52.30N 4.30W
Carei Romania 55 J2.....................................47.41N 22.28E
Carey, Lake Australia 110 B4............................28.57S 122.21E
Caribbean Sea N. Atlantic Oc. 71 H4.....................19.03N 83.05W
Caribou Mountains Canada 62 G3..........................59.02N 115.22W
Cark Mountain *hill* Ireland 16 B2......................54.53N 7.52W
Carletonville S. Africa 86 B2...........................26.21S 27.24E
Carlingford Lough *inlet* Ireland/U.K. 41 E4............54.05N 6.14W
Carlisle England 14 E3..................................54.54N 2.56W
Carlow Ireland 41 E2....................................52.50N 6.56W
Carlow *d.* Ireland 41 E2...............................52.47N 6.52W
Carluke Scotland 17 F3..................................55.44N 3.50W
Carmacks Canada 62 E4...................................62.05N 136.17W
Carmarthen Wales 12 C3..................................51.51N 4.19W
Carmarthen Bay Wales 12 C3..............................51.38N 4.32W
Carmarthenshire *d.* Wales 9 C2.........................51.57N 4.19W
Carmel Head Wales 12 C5.................................53.25N 4.34W
Carmen, Isla *i.* Mexico 70 B6..........................25.59N 111.09W
Carnac France 44 B5.....................................47.35N 3.04W
Carn Dearg *hill* Scotland 19 E2........................57.06N 4.16W
Carndonagh Ireland 16 B3................................55.15N 7.15W
Carnedd Llywelyn *mt.* Wales 12 D5......................53.10N 3.58W
Carnedd y Filiast *hill* Wales 12 D4....................52.59N 3.41W
Carnegie, Lake Australia 110 B4.........................26.10S 122.54E
Carn Eighe *mt.* Scotland 18 D2.........................57.17N 5.07W
Carnforth England 14 E3.................................54.08N 2.46W
Carnic Alps *mts* Italy 50 E7...........................46.40N 12.48E
Car Nicobar *i.* India 97 H2............................9.10N 92.47E
Carnlough Northern Ireland 16 D2........................54.59N 5.59W
Carn Mòr *hill* Scotland 19 F2..........................57.15N 3.13W
Carn nan Gabhar *mt.* Scotland 19 F1....................56.50N 3.41W
Carnot, Cape Australia 110 C3...........................34.55S 135.37E
Carnoustie Scotland 17 G4...............................56.30N 2.42W
Carnsore Point Ireland 41 E2............................52.10N 6.22W
Caroline Island *atoll* Kiribati 109 J5.................9.58S 150.11W
Caroline Islands N. Pacific Oc. 108 F6..................6.35N 144.24E
Carpathian Mountains Europe 55 J3.......................48.45S 23.45E
Carpentaria, Gulf of Australia 110 C5...................14.06S 139.04E
Carpentras France 44 F4.................................44.04N 5.03E
Carra, Lough *l.* Ireland 41 B3.........................53.44N 9.14W
Carrantuohill *mt.* Ireland 41 B1.......................51.59N 9.44W
Carrara Italy 50 D6.....................................44.04N 10.06E
Carrickfergus Northern Ireland 16 D2....................54.43N 5.48W
Carrickfergus *d.* Northern Ireland 9 C4................54.44N 5.49W
Carrickmacross Ireland 41 E3............................53.59N 6.43W
Carrick-on-Shannon Ireland 41 C3........................53.56N 8.05W
Carrick-on-Suir Ireland 41 D2...........................52.21N 7.25W
Carron *r.* Falk. Scotland 17 F4........................56.02N 3.44W
Carron *r.* High. Scotland 18 E2........................57.53N 4.22W
Carrowmore Lake Ireland 41 B4...........................54.11N 9.47W
Carson City U.S.A. 64 C4................................39.10N 119.46W
Carsphairn Scotland 16 E3...............................55.13N 4.16W
Cartagena Colombia 72 B8................................10.23N 75.33W
Cartagena Spain 48 E2...................................37.36N 0.59W
Carteret France 13 Z9...................................49.23N 1.47W
Carteret, Cap de *c.* France 13 Z9......................49.22N 1.48W
Carterton England 10 D2.................................51.45N 1.35W
Cartmel England 14 E3...................................54.12N 2.57W
Caruarú Brazil 77 M6....................................8.15S 35.52W
Carvin France 42 B3.....................................50.29N 2.57E
Casablanca Morocco 84 D5................................33.35N 7.34W
Casa Grande U.S.A. 64 D3................................32.53N 111.45W
Cascade Range *mts* Canada/U.S.A. 62 F2.................41.49N 122.21W
Cascavel Brazil 77 J3...................................24.55S 53.28W
Caserta Italy 50 F4.....................................41.04N 14.20E
Cashel Ireland 41 D2....................................52.31N 7.53W
Casper U.S.A. 64 E5.....................................42.52N 106.20W
Caspian Lowland *f.* Kazakhstan/Rus. Fed. 58 F2........44.15N 45.47E
Caspian Sea *l.* Asia/Europe 58 G2......................42.00N 51.00E
Cassai *r.* Scotland 18 E2..............................59.40N 130.31W
Cassley *r.* Scotland 18 E2.............................57.58N 4.34W
Castanhal Brazil 77 K7..................................1.18S 47.54W
Castelló de la Plana Spain 48 E3........................39.59N 0.02W
Castlebar Ireland 41 B3.................................53.51N 9.17W
Castlebay Scotland 18 B1................................56.57N 7.29W
Castleblayney Ireland 41 E4.............................54.07N 6.43W
Castle Cary England 10 C2...............................51.05N 2.31W
Castlecomer Ireland 41 D2...............................52.48N 7.13W
Castleconnell Ireland 41 C2.............................52.43N 8.30W
Castlederg Northern Ireland 16 B2.......................54.42N 7.35W
Castle Donington England 10 D3..........................52.50N 1.19W
Castle Douglas Scotland 17 F2...........................54.56N 3.56W
Castleford England 15 F2................................53.43N 1.21W
Castleisland Ireland 41 B2..............................52.14N 9.27W
Castlereagh *d.* Northern Ireland 9 C4..................54.35N 5.53W
Castletown Isle of Man 14 C3............................54.05N 4.39W
Castres France 44 E3....................................43.36N 2.14E
Castries St Lucia 71 L3.................................14.00N 60.59W
Castro Verde Portugal 48 A2.............................37.42N 8.05W
Catacaos Peru 76 D6.....................................5.18S 80.42W
Catalão Brazil 77 K4....................................18.09S 47.52W
Catamarca Argentina 73 C4...............................28.26S 65.45W
Catanduanes *i.* Phil. 105 G6...........................13.46N 124.14E

Catania Italy 50 F2 ......37.30N 15.05E
Catanzaro Italy 50 G3 ......38.55N 16.36E
Catarman Phil. 105 G6 ......12.29N 124.38E
Caterham England 11 E2 ......51.17N 0.05W
Cat Island Bahamas 71 I5 ......24.28N 75.30W
Catoche, Cabo c. Mexico 70 G5 ......21.37N 87.06W
Catterick England 15 F3 ......54.23N 1.38W
Cauca r. Colombia 71 J2 ......8.54N 74.29W
Caucaia Brazil 77 M7 ......3.42S 38.42W
Caucasus mts Asia/Europe 58 F2 ......43.53N 40.00E
Caudry France 42 C3 ......50.07N 3.25E
Cavan Ireland 41 D3 ......53.59N 7.22W
Cavan d. Ireland 41 D3 ......53.57N 7.15W
Cawston England 11 G3 ......52.46N 1.10E
Caxias Brazil 77 L7 ......4.54S 43.19W
Caxias do Sul Brazil 77 J2 ......29.13S 51.11W
Cayenne French Guiana 72 D7 ......4.53N 52.21W
Cayman Brac i. Cayman Is 71 I4 ......19.43N 79.48W
Cayman Islands Central America 71 H4 ......19.31N 81.15W
Ceará d. Brazil 77 M7 ......4.51S 39.03W
Cebu Phil. 105 G6 ......10.17N 123.55E
Cebu i. Phil. 105 G6 ......10.26N 123.53E
Cedar r. U.S.A. 65 J5 ......43.40N 84.23W
Cedar City U.S.A. 64 D4 ......37.41N 113.04W
Cedar Rapids town U.S.A. 65 H5 ......41.59N 91.40W
Cedros, Isla i. Mexico 70 A6 ......28.11N 115.20W
Cefalù Italy 50 F3 ......38.02N 14.02E
Cegléd Hungary 54 H2 ......47.10N 19.48E
Celebes i. Indonesia 104 G3 ......2.01S 120.29E
Celebes Sea Indonesia/Phil. 104 G4 ......3.03N 121.10E
Celje Slovenia 54 F2 ......46.14N 15.15E
Celle Germany 54 D5 ......52.38N 10.05E
Celtic Sea Ireland/U.K. 13 A2 ......50.54N 6.33W
Celyn, Llyn l. Wales 12 D4 ......52.57N 3.43W
Cenderawasih, Teluk b. Indonesia 105 J3 ......2.05S 135.33E
Central r. Kenya 87 B2 ......0.42S 36.55E
Central, Cordillera mts Bolivia 76 G4 ......18.27S 66.22W
Central, Cordillera mts Colombia 72 B7 ......1.38N 76.51W
Central, Cordillera mts Peru 76 E5 ......10.02S 76.25W
Central African Republic Africa 85 G2 ......6.25N 20.12E
Central Bedfordshire d. England 9 E3 ......51.59N 0.30W
Central Pacific Basin f. Pacific Oc. 108 H6 ......3.53N 179.43E
Central Range mts P.N.G. 105 K3 ......4.57S 142.36E
Central Russian Upland hills Rus. Fed. 55 Q6 ......54.27N 36.28E
Central Siberian Plateau f. Rus. Fed. 59 M4 ......67.03N 110.35E
Cephalonia i. Greece 56 D4 ......38.14N 20.21E
Ceram Sea Indonesia 105 I3 ......2.33S 130.11E
Ceredigion d. Wales 9 D3 ......52.19N 3.58W
Cernavodă Romania 57 H7 ......44.21N 28.02E
Cerralvo, Isla i. Mexico 70 C5 ......24.10N 109.48W
Cerro de Pasco Peru 76 E5 ......10.42S 76.14W
Cervo Spain 48 B5 ......43.41N 7.26W
České Budějovice Czech Rep. 54 F3 ......48.59N 14.29E
Cetinje Montenegro 56 C6 ......42.23N 18.55E
Ceuta N. Africa 52 B4 ......35.53N 5.20W
Cévennes mts France 44 E3 ......43.50N 3.17E
Ceyhan Turkey 57 K3 ......37.01N 35.47E
Ceyhan r. Turkey 57 K3 ......36.42N 35.37E
Chābahār Iran 95 J5 ......25.18N 60.38E
Chad Africa 85 F3 ......15.07N 18.13E
Chad, Lake Africa 84 F3 ......13.27N 14.24E
Chadan Rus. Fed. 100 G8 ......51.18N 91.31E
Chadron U.S.A. 64 F5 ......42.50N 102.57W
Chagai Hills Afgh./Pakistan 96 B6 ......29.17N 63.23E
Chaghcharān Afgh. 95 K6 ......34.28N 65.03E
Chagos Archipelago is. Indian Oc. 90 F2 ......7.00S 72.00E
Chake Chake Tanzania 87 B1 ......5.15S 39.47E
Chala Peru 76 F4 ......15.49S 74.12W
Chalbi Desert Kenya 87 B3 ......3.13N 37.14E
Chale England 10 D1 ......50.36N 1.19W
Chalkida Greece 56 E4 ......38.27N 23.37E
Challenger Deep f. N. Pacific Oc. 117 Q6 ......11.17N 142.30E
Challenger Fracture Zone f. S. Pacific Oc. 108 M3 ......34.26S 113.31W
Châlons-en-Champagne France 44 F6 ......48.58N 4.22E
Chalon-sur-Saône France 44 F5 ......46.48N 4.51E
Chālus Iran 95 H7 ......36.37N 51.26E
Chaman Pakistan 96 C7 ......30.55N 66.28E
Chambéry France 44 F4 ......45.34N 5.55E
Ch'amo Hāyk' l. Ethiopia 87 B4 ......5.49N 37.32E
Chamonix-Mont-Blanc France 44 G4 ......45.55N 6.52E
Champagne-Ardenne d. France 42 D1 ......48.43N 4.15E
Champaign U.S.A. 65 I5 ......40.06N 88.17W
Champaqui, Cerro mt. Argentina 76 H1 ......31.59S 64.56W
Champlain, Lake Canada/U.S.A. 65 L5 ......44.23N 73.22W
Chañaral Chile 76 F2 ......26.19S 70.41W
Chandalar r. U.S.A. 62 D4 ......66.36N 145.51W
Chandigarh India 96 E7 ......30.42N 76.48E
Chandigarh d. India 100 D4 ......30.43N 76.52E
Chandrapur India 96 E4 ......19.57N 79.21E
Changbai China 106 A4 ......41.25N 128.10E
Changchun China 101 N6 ......43.53N 125.20E
Changde China 101 K3 ......29.03N 111.42E
Chang Jiang r. China 101 M4 ......31.24N 121.48E
Changsha China 101 K3 ......28.10N 112.59E
Changzhi China 101 K5 ......36.06N 113.09E
Changzhou China 101 M4 ......31.47N 119.59E
Chania Greece 56 F2 ......35.30N 24.02E
Channel Islands English Channel 13 Z9 ......49.20N 2.37W
Channel Islands U.S.A. 64 C3 ......33.41N 119.26W
Channel-Port-aux-Basques Canada 63 M2 ......47.33N 59.01W
Channel Tunnel France/U.K. 11 G2 ......51.04N 1.24E
Chanthaburi Thailand 104 C6 ......12.37N 102.08E
Chantilly France 42 B2 ......49.12N 2.28E
Chao Phraya r. Thailand 104 C6 ......13.40N 100.36E
Chaouèn Morocco 52 B4 ......35.11N 5.16W
Chapala, Laguna de l. Mexico 70 D5 ......20.15N 103.04W
Chapecó Brazil 77 J2 ......27.09S 52.39W
Chapel-en-le-Frith England 15 F2 ......53.20N 1.54W
Chapeltown England 15 F2 ......53.28N 1.28W
Chapleau Canada 63 J2 ......47.51N 83.24W
Chard England 10 C1 ......50.52N 2.58W
Chari r. Chad 82 E6 ......13.00N 14.30E
Chārīkār Afgh. 95 K7 ......35.02N 69.15E
Charlbury England 10 D2 ......51.52N 1.29W
Charleroi Belgium 42 D3 ......50.25N 4.27E
Charles, Cape U.S.A. 65 K4 ......37.10N 75.58W
Charleston S. Carolina U.S.A. 65 K3 ......32.48N 79.58W
Charleston W. Va. U.S.A. 65 J4 ......38.21N 81.39W
Charlestown Ireland 41 C3 ......53.57N 8.47W
Charleville-Mézières France 44 F6 ......49.46N 4.44E
Charlotte U.S.A. 65 J4 ......35.14N 80.50W
Charlottesville U.S.A. 65 K4 ......38.01N 78.30W
Charlottetown Canada 63 L2 ......46.16N 63.09W
Chartres France 44 D6 ......48.27N 1.30E
Chassiron, Pointe de pt France 44 C5 ......46.03N 1.24W
Châteaubriant France 44 C5 ......47.43N 1.22W
Châteaudun France 44 D6 ......48.04N 1.20E
Châteauroux France 44 D5 ......46.48N 1.41E
Château-Thierry France 44 E6 ......49.03N 3.25E
Châtellerault France 44 D5 ......46.49N 0.33E
Chatham England 11 F2 ......51.23N 0.31E
Chatham Islands New Zealand 108 I3 ......43.24S 176.11W
Chatham Rise f. S. Pacific Oc. 108 I3 ......42.18S 176.14W

Chattahoochee r. U.S.A. 65 J3 ......30.55N 84.58W
Chattanooga U.S.A. 65 I4 ......35.02N 85.21W
Chatteris England 11 F3 ......52.27N 0.03E
Chaumont France 44 F6 ......48.07N 5.08E
Chauny France 42 C2 ......49.37N 3.13E
Chaves Brazil 77 K7 ......0.11S 49.58W
Cheadle England 10 D3 ......52.59N 1.59W
Cheboksary Rus. Fed. 58 F3 ......56.09N 47.13E
Cheboygan U.S.A. 65 J6 ......45.39N 84.28W
Cheddar England 10 C2 ......51.17N 2.47W
Cheju-do i. S. Korea 101 N4 ......33.34N 126.43E
Chekhov Rus. Fed. 55 Q6 ......55.09N 37.28E
Cheleken Turkmenistan 95 H7 ......39.25N 53.01E
Chełm Poland 55 J4 ......51.08N 23.29E
Chelmer r. England 11 F2 ......51.45N 0.40E
Chełmno Poland 46 D4 ......53.21N 18.26E
Chelmsford England 11 F2 ......51.44N 0.29E
Cheltenham England 10 C2 ......51.54N 2.04W
Chelyabinsk Rus. Fed. 58 H3 ......55.11N 61.24E
Chen'ch'a Ethiopia 87 B4 ......6.17N 37.38E
Chengde China 101 L6 ......40.52N 117.58E
Chengdu China 101 I4 ......30.43N 104.04E
Chennai India 96 F3 ......13.06N 80.16E
Chenzhou China 101 K3 ......25.44N 113.00E
Chepstow Wales 12 E3 ......51.38N 2.40W
Cher r. France 44 D5 ......47.20N 0.29E
Cherbourg France 44 C6 ......49.38N 1.37W
Cherchell Algeria 48 G2 ......36.32N 2.06E
Cherepovets Rus. Fed. 58 E3 ......59.08N 37.55E
Chergui, Chott ech l. Algeria 52 C3 ......34.03N 0.16W
Cherkasy Ukraine 55 O3 ......49.26N 32.05E
Cherkessk Rus. Fed. 53 L5 ......44.13N 42.03E
Chernihiv Ukraine 55 N4 ......51.29N 31.19E
Chernivtsi Ukraine 55 K3 ......48.19N 25.56E
Chernyakhovsk Rus. Fed. 46 E5 ......54.38N 21.49E
Chernyshevskiy Rus. Fed. 59 M4 ......62.56N 112.36E
Cherskogo, Khrebet mts Rus. Fed. 59 P4 ......63.42N 146.57E
Chervonohrad Ukraine 55 K4 ......50.23N 24.14E
Cherwell r. England 10 D2 ......51.44N 1.15W
Chesapeake Bay U.S.A. 65 K4 ......38.05N 76.14W
Chesham England 11 E2 ......51.43N 0.37W
Cheshire East d. England 9 D3 ......53.09N 2.18W
Cheshire West and Chester d. England 9 D3 ......53.11N 2.46W
Cheshskaya Guba b. Russian Fed. 35 I4 ......67.20N 46.30E
Cheshunt England 11 E2 ......51.42N 0.02W
Chesil Beach f. England 10 C1 ......50.38N 2.36W
Chester England 14 E2 ......53.12N 2.54W
Chesterfield England 15 F2 ......53.14N 1.25W
Chester-le-Street England 15 F3 ......54.52N 1.34W
Chetumal Mexico 70 G4 ......18.30N 88.18W
Cheviot Hills England 15 E4 ......55.12N 2.39W
Che'w Bahir l. Ethiopia 87 B4 ......4.40N 36.56E
Che'w Bahir Wildlife Reserve Ethiopia 87 B4 ......4.51N 36.51E
Chew Magna England 10 C2 ......51.20N 2.37W
Chew Valley Lake resr England 10 C2 ......51.20N 2.38W
Cheyenne U.S.A. 64 F5 ......41.09N 104.49W
Cheyenne r. U.S.A. 64 F5 ......44.44N 101.09W
Chhattisgarh d. India 96 F5 ......21.29N 81.46E
Chiang Mai Thailand 104 B7 ......18.47N 98.59E
Chiang Rai Thailand 104 B7 ......19.55N 99.53E
Chiapas d. Mexico 70 F4 ......16.23N 92.17W
Chiba Japan 106 D3 ......35.37N 140.07E
Chibougamau Canada 63 K2 ......49.55N 74.22W
Chicago U.S.A. 65 I5 ......41.55N 87.38W
Chichester England 10 E1 ......50.50N 0.46W
Chiclayo Peru 76 E6 ......6.44S 79.51W
Chicoutimi Canada 63 K2 ......48.26N 71.03W
Chidley, Cape Canada 63 L4 ......60.26N 64.20W
Chiemsee l. Germany 54 E2 ......47.52N 12.28E
Chieti Italy 50 F5 ......42.21N 14.10E
Chifeng China 101 L6 ......42.11N 119.02E
Chiganak Kazakhstan 100 E2 ......45.10N 73.57E
Chihuahua Mexico 70 C6 ......28.38N 106.07W
Chihuahua d. Mexico 70 C6 ......29.10N 106.11W
Chile S. America 73 B3 ......34.06S 71.23W
Chile Basin f. S. Pacific Oc. 109 O3 ......31.51S 80.03W
Chile Rise f. S. Pacific Oc. 109 O2 ......41.37S 89.56W
Chilham England 11 F2 ......51.15N 0.58E
Chillán Chile 73 B3 ......36.37S 72.07W
Chiloé, Isla de i. Chile 73 B2 ......42.26S 74.29W
Chilpancingo Mexico 70 E4 ......17.33N 99.30W
Chiltern Hills England 10 E2 ......51.39N 0.50W
Chimborazo mt. Ecuador 76 E7 ......1.27S 78.50W
Chimbote Peru 76 E6 ......9.03S 78.35W
Chimoio Mozambique 86 C3 ......19.07S 33.28E
China Asia 100 H3 ......38.39N 78.40E
Chindwin r. Myanmar 97 I5 ......21.27N 95.15E
Chingola Zambia 86 B3 ......12.33S 27.54E
Chinhoyi Zimbabwe 86 C3 ......17.21S 30.11E
Chinju S. Korea 106 A3 ......35.10N 128.05E
Chinook Trough f. N. Pacific Oc. 108 I8 ......41.53N 179.40W
Chioggia Italy 50 E6 ......45.12N 12.16E
Chios Greece 56 G4 ......38.22N 26.08E
Chios i. Greece 56 F4 ......38.24N 25.58E
Chipata Zambia 86 C3 ......13.37S 32.38E
Chippenham England 10 C2 ......51.27N 2.07W
Chipping Campden England 10 D3 ......52.03N 1.47W
Chipping Norton England 10 D2 ......51.57N 1.32W
Chipping Ongar England 11 F2 ......51.42N 0.15E
Chipping Sodbury England 10 C2 ......51.32N 2.23W
Chiriquí, Golfo de b. Panama 71 H2 ......8.02N 82.04W
Chirk Wales 12 D4 ......52.56N 3.03W
Chirnside Scotland 17 G3 ......55.48N 2.12W
Chirripó mt. Costa Rica 71 H2 ......9.30N 83.30W
Chisasibi Canada 63 K3 ......53.49N 78.59W
Chișinău Moldova 53 I6 ......47.02N 28.50E
Chita Rus. Fed. 59 M3 ......51.54N 113.27E
Chitambo Zambia 86 C3 ......12.54S 30.37E
Chitradurga India 96 E3 ......14.14N 76.22E
Chitral Pakistan 96 D8 ......35.53N 71.47E
Chittagong Bangl. 97 H5 ......22.20N 91.49E
Chittoor India 96 E3 ......13.12N 79.05E
Chitungwiza Zimbabwe 86 C3 ......18.01S 31.04E
Chojnice Poland 46 C4 ......53.42N 17.34E
Cholet France 44 C5 ......47.04N 0.53W
Chomutov Czech Rep. 54 E4 ......50.28N 13.24E
Chon Buri Thailand 104 C6 ......13.22N 101.02E
Ch'ŏngjin N. Korea 101 N6 ......41.46N 129.45E
Chongqing China 101 J3 ......29.36N 106.32E
Chongqing d. China 101 J3 ......30.04N 107.39E
Chŏnju S. Korea 101 N5 ......35.51N 127.09E
Chonos, Archipiélago de los is Chile 73 B2 ......44.59S 75.31W
Chorley England 14 E2 ......53.39N 2.38W
Chornobyl' Ukraine 55 N4 ......51.16N 30.14E
Chornomors'ke Ukraine 57 J7 ......45.30N 32.43E
Chortkiv Ukraine 55 K3 ......49.01N 25.47E
Chōshi Japan 106 D3 ......35.44N 140.49E
Choszczno Poland 46 B4 ......53.10N 15.26E
Choûm Mauritania 84 C4 ......21.20N 12.59W
Choybalsan Mongolia 101 K7 ......47.57N 114.34E
Chřiby hills Czech Rep. 46 C2 ......49.05N 17.11E
Christchurch England 10 D1 ......50.44N 1.47W

Christchurch New Zealand 111 G2 ......43.31S 172.37E
Christmas Island Indian Oc. 104 D1 ......10.30S 105.44E
Chūgoku-sanchi mts Japan 106 B3 ......34.45N 132.19E
Chukchi Sea Rus. Fed./U.S.A. 59 T4 ......69.12N 171.31W
Chukotskiy Poluostrov pen. Rus. Fed. 59 S4 ......65.58N 175.16W
Chulmleigh England 13 D2 ......50.55N 3.52W
Chumba Ethiopia 87 B4 ......4.30N 38.15E
Chumphon Thailand 104 B6 ......10.31N 99.13E
Ch'unch'ŏn S. Korea 101 N5 ......37.52N 127.46E
Chunya r. Rus. Fed. 59 K4 ......61.36N 96.31E
Chur Switz. 50 C7 ......46.51N 9.32E
Churchill Canada 63 I3 ......58.44N 94.05W
Churchill r. Man. Canada 63 I3 ......58.11N 94.23W
Churchill r. Nfld. and Lab. Canada 63 L3 ......53.16N 60.14W
Churchill, Cape Canada 63 I3 ......58.45N 93.16W
Church Stretton England 10 C3 ......52.32N 2.48W
Chuuk is Micronesia 108 G6 ......7.22N 151.37E
Chuxiong China 101 I3 ......25.02N 101.32E
Chyulu Range mts Kenya 87 B2 ......2.34S 37.41E
Ciechanów Poland 46 E4 ......52.53N 20.38E
Ciego de Ávila Cuba 71 I5 ......21.50N 78.45W
Cienfuegos Cuba 71 H5 ......22.10N 80.25W
Cigüela r. Spain 48 D3 ......39.08N 3.43W
Cihanbeyli Turkey 57 J3 ......38.40N 32.56E
Cilacap Indonesia 104 D2 ......7.41S 109.00E
Cinca r. Spain 48 F4 ......41.26N 0.21E
Cincinnati U.S.A. 65 J4 ......39.06N 84.32W
Cinderford England 10 C2 ......51.49N 2.30W
Ciney Belgium 42 E3 ......50.18N 5.06E
Cinto, Monte mt. France 44 H3 ......42.23N 8.56E
Cirebon Indonesia 104 D2 ......6.45S 108.34E
Cirencester England 10 D2 ......51.43N 1.58W
Ciudad Bolívar Venezuela 72 C7 ......8.01N 63.35W
Ciudad del Carmen Mexico 70 F4 ......18.39N 91.51W
Ciudad Delicias Mexico 70 C6 ......28.10N 105.30W
Ciudad de Valles Mexico 70 E5 ......21.59N 99.00W
Ciudad Guayana Venezuela 72 C7 ......8.20N 62.37W
Ciudad Ixtepec Mexico 70 E4 ......16.35N 95.06W
Ciudad Juárez Mexico 70 C7 ......31.44N 106.28W
Ciudad Madero Mexico 70 E5 ......22.19N 97.51W
Ciudad Obregón Mexico 70 C6 ......27.28N 109.57W
Ciudad Real Spain 48 D3 ......38.59N 3.54W
Ciudad Rodrigo Spain 48 B4 ......40.36N 6.31W
Ciudad Victoria Mexico 70 E5 ......23.45N 99.08W
Ciutadella de Menorca Spain 48 G4 ......40.00N 3.52E
Civitavecchia Italy 50 D5 ......42.05N 11.48E
Çivril Turkey 57 H3 ......38.18N 29.43E
Cixi China 101 M4 ......30.10N 121.14E
Clackmannanshire d. Scotland 8 D5 ......56.09N 3.45W
Clacton-on-Sea England 11 G2 ......51.47N 1.10E
Claonaig Scotland 16 D3 ......55.45N 5.24W
Clara Ireland 41 D3 ......53.20N 7.37W
Clare d. Ireland 41 C2 ......52.53N 8.50W
Clare r. Ireland 41 B3 ......53.19N 9.03W
Clare Island Ireland 41 A3 ......53.49N 10.01W
Claremorris Ireland 41 C3 ......53.43N 8.59W
Clarksville U.S.A. 65 I4 ......36.32N 87.20W
Claro r. Brazil 77 J4 ......19.07S 50.39W
Clay Cross England 15 F2 ......53.10N 1.25W
Claydon England 11 G3 ......52.06N 1.07E
Clay Head Isle of Man 14 C3 ......54.12N 4.23W
Clayton U.S.A. 64 F4 ......36.28N 103.12W
Clear, Cape Ireland 41 B1 ......51.25N 9.31W
Clear Island Ireland 41 B1 ......51.26N 9.28W
Cleator Moor England 14 D3 ......54.31N 3.31W
Cleethorpes England 15 G2 ......53.33N 0.02W
Cleobury Mortimer England 10 C3 ......52.23N 2.29W
Clermont Canada 42 B2 ......49.23N 2.24E
Clermont-Ferrand France 44 E4 ......45.46N 3.05E
Clevedon England 10 C2 ......51.26N 2.51W
Cleveland U.S.A. 65 J5 ......41.30N 81.41W
Cleveland Hills England 15 F3 ......54.22N 1.13W
Cleveleys England 14 D2 ......53.53N 3.02W
Clew Bay Ireland 41 B3 ......53.48N 9.47W
Cliffe England 11 F2 ......51.28N 0.30E
Clinton U.S.A. 64 G4 ......35.32N 98.58W
Clipperton, Île i. N. Pacific Oc. 109 M6 ......10.21N 109.19W
Clisham hill Scotland 18 C2 ......57.58N 6.49W
Clitheroe England 15 E2 ......53.52N 2.23W
Clogher Head Ireland 41 E3 ......53.48N 6.13W
Clonakilty Ireland 41 C1 ......51.36N 8.53W
Clones Ireland 41 D4 ......54.10N 7.13W
Clonmel Ireland 41 D2 ......52.21N 7.43W
Cloud Peak U.S.A. 64 E5 ......44.24N 107.01W
Clovis U.S.A. 64 F3 ......34.27N 103.12W
Cluanie, Loch l. Scotland 18 D2 ......57.09N 5.07W
Cluj-Napoca Romania 55 J2 ......46.46N 23.36E
Clun England 10 B3 ......52.25N 3.02W
Clwydach Wales 12 D3 ......51.42N 3.54W
Clyde r. Scotland 16 E3 ......55.56N 4.29W
Clyde, Firth of est. Scotland 16 E3 ......55.25N 4.59W
Clydebank Scotland 16 E3 ......55.54N 4.24W
Clyde River town Canada 63 L5 ......70.23N 68.31W
Coahuila d. Mexico 70 D6 ......27.30N 102.24W
Coalville England 10 D3 ......52.43N 1.22W
Coari Brazil 76 H7 ......4.08S 63.07W
Coari r. Brazil 76 H7 ......4.26S 63.30W
Coast r. Kenya 87 C2 ......2.40S 40.07E
Coastal Plain f. U.S.A. 65 H3 ......30.25N 94.23W
Coast Mountains Canada 62 F3 ......52.40N 127.48W
Coast Ranges mts U.S.A. 64 B5 ......40.40N 123.39W
Coatbridge Scotland 17 F3 ......55.52N 4.01W
Coats Island Canada 63 J4 ......62.41N 82.53W
Coatzacoalcos Mexico 70 F4 ......18.08N 94.26W
Cobh Ireland 41 C1 ......51.51N 8.18W
Cobija Bolivia 76 G5 ......11.03S 68.47W
Cochabamba Bolivia 76 G4 ......17.25S 66.11W
Cochin India 96 E2 ......10.00N 76.18E
Cochrane Canada 65 J6 ......49.04N 81.03W
Cockburnspath Scotland 17 G3 ......55.56N 2.22W
Cockermouth England 14 D3 ......54.40N 3.22W
Coco r. Honduras/Nicaragua 71 H3 ......14.59N 83.15W
Coco, Isla de i. N. Pacific Oc. 60 K2 ......5.32N 87.04W
Cocos Basin f. Indian Oc. 108 C5 ......0.02N 91.02E
Cocos Islands Indian Oc. 104 B1 ......11.56S 96.54E
Cocos Ridge f. N. Pacific Oc. 109 O6 ......0.42N 89.55W
Cocuy, Sierra Nevada del mt. Colombia 71 J2 ......6.28N 72.19W
Cod, Cape U.S.A. 65 L5 ......41.58N 70.01W
Coddington England 15 G2 ......53.05N 0.45W
Codó Brazil 77 L7 ......4.28S 43.50W
Codsall England 10 C3 ......52.38N 2.11W
Coeur d'Alene U.S.A. 64 C6 ......47.41N 116.47W
Coffs Harbour Australia 110 E3 ......30.19S 153.06E
Coggeshall England 11 F2 ......51.52N 0.42E
Coiba, Isla de i. Panama 71 H2 ......7.27N 81.51W
Coigeach, Rubha pt Scotland 18 D3 ......58.06N 5.28W
Coihaique Chile 73 B2 ......45.36S 72.05W
Coimbatore India 96 E3 ......10.59N 76.57E
Coimbra Portugal 48 A4 ......40.13N 8.25W
Coipasa, Salar de f. Bolivia 76 G4 ......19.26S 68.07W
Colatina Brazil 77 L4 ......19.32S 40.37W
Colchester England 11 F2 ......51.53N 0.54E
Coldstream Scotland 17 G3 ......55.39N 2.15W

Coleford England 10 C2 ......51.48N 2.37W
Coleraine Northern Ireland 16 C3 ......55.08N 6.40W
Coleraine d. Northern Ireland 8 B4 ......54.58N 6.41W
Colima Mexico 70 D4 ......19.14N 103.45W
Colima d. Mexico 70 D4 ......19.03N 103.59W
Colima, Nevado de vol. Mexico 70 D4 ......19.33N 103.37W
Coll i. Scotland 18 C4 ......56.36N 6.36W
Collier Bay Australia 110 B5 ......16.15S 124.15E
Colmar France 44 G6 ......48.05N 7.21E
Colne England 15 E2 ......53.51N 2.11W
Colne r. England 11 F2 ......51.51N 0.57E
Cologne Germany 54 B4 ......50.56N 6.57E
Colombia S. America 72 B7 ......3.45N 72.22W
Colombo Sri Lanka 96 E2 ......6.56N 79.50E
Colón Panama 71 I2 ......9.22N 79.55W
Colonsay i. Scotland 16 C4 ......56.05N 6.15W
Colorado r. Argentina 73 C3 ......39.42S 62.07W
Colorado r. Mexico/U.S.A. 64 C3 ......31.56N 115.01W
Colorado r. U.S.A. 64 E4 ......39.02N 105.31W
Colorado d. U.S.A. 64 G2 ......28.40N 96.01W
Colorado Plateau f. U.S.A. 64 E4 ......37.27N 109.54W
Colorado Springs U.S.A. 64 F4 ......38.52N 104.47W
Coltishall England 11 G3 ......52.44N 1.22E
Columbia U.S.A. 65 J3 ......33.59N 81.01W
Columbia r. U.S.A. 64 B6 ......46.11N 123.23W
Columbia, Mount Canada 62 G3 ......52.08N 117.25W
Columbus d. U.S.A. 65 J3 ......32.32N 84.59W
Columbus Miss. U.S.A. 65 I3 ......33.33N 88.25W
Columbus Oh. U.S.A. 65 J4 ......39.58N 83.00W
Colville U.S.A. 62 C5 ......70.20N 150.32W
Colwyn Bay town Wales 12 D5 ......53.18N 3.43W
Comacchio Italy 50 E6 ......44.41N 12.11E
Combe Martin England 13 C3 ......51.12N 4.01W
Comber Northern Ireland 16 D2 ......54.33N 5.44W
Comeragh Mountains Ireland 41 D2 ......52.18N 7.39W
Como Italy 50 C6 ......45.48N 9.05E
Como, Lake Italy 50 C6 ......45.57N 9.11E
Comodoro Rivadavia Argentina 73 C2 ......45.56S 67.30W
Comorin, Cape India 90 G3 ......8.04N 77.35E
Comoros Africa 86 D3 ......11.50S 44.17E
Compiègne France 42 B2 ......49.25N 2.50E
Comrat Moldova 57 H8 ......46.18N 28.40E
Comrie Scotland 17 F4 ......56.23N 3.59W
Conakry Guinea 84 C2 ......9.33N 13.42W
Concarneau France 44 B5 ......47.53N 3.55W
Concepción Argentina 76 G2 ......27.20S 65.37W
Concepción Chile 73 B3 ......36.50S 73.04W
Conception, Point U.S.A. 64 B3 ......34.27N 120.26W
Conchos r. Mexico 70 D6 ......29.35N 104.29W
Concord U.S.A. 65 L5 ......43.12N 71.33W
Concordia Argentina 73 D3 ......31.23S 57.59W
Condor, Cordillera del mts Ecuador/Peru 76 E7 ......4.17S 78.34W
Congleton England 15 E2 ......53.10N 2.13W
Congo Africa 84 F1 ......2.24S 15.10E
Congo r. Congo/Dem. Rep. Congo 86 A4 ......6.05S 12.26E
Congo, Democratic Republic of the Africa 86 B4 ......3.43S 22.17E
Congo Basin f. Africa 82 F4 ......1.00S 20.00E
Coningsby England 15 G2 ......53.07N 0.10W
Coniston England 14 D3 ......54.22N 3.05W
Coniston Water l. England 14 D3 ......54.19N 3.04W
Conn, Lough l. Ireland 41 B4 ......54.01N 9.16W
Connah's Quay Wales 12 D5 ......53.13N 3.04W
Connecticut d. U.S.A. 65 L5 ......41.41N 72.36W
Connecticut r. U.S.A. 65 L5 ......41.16N 72.22W
Connemara f. Ireland 41 B3 ......53.28N 9.52W
Conon Bridge Scotland 19 E2 ......57.34N 4.26W
Consett England 15 F3 ......54.51N 1.50W
Con Son i. Vietnam 104 D5 ......8.42N 106.40E
Constance, Lake Germany/Switz. 54 C2 ......47.40N 9.17E
Constanța Romania 57 H7 ......44.11N 28.37E
Constantine Algeria 84 E5 ......36.23N 6.38E
Conwy Wales 12 D5 ......53.17N 3.50W
Conwy d. Wales 9 D3 ......53.10N 3.43W
Conwy r. Wales 12 D5 ......53.14N 3.48W
Conwy Bay Wales 12 D5 ......53.16N 4.02W
Cook, Mount New Zealand 111 G2 ......43.37S 170.08E
Cook Islands S. Pacific Oc. 108 J4 ......20.05S 160.06W
Cookstown Northern Ireland 16 C2 ......54.38N 6.44W
Cookstown d. Northern Ireland 9 B4 ......54.39N 6.44W
Cook Strait New Zealand 111 G2 ......40.32S 174.01E
Cooktown Australia 110 D5 ......15.28S 145.17E
Coolangatta Australia 110 E4 ......28.10S 153.31E
Cooper Creek watercourse Australia 110 C4 ......28.29S 137.43E
Coos Bay town U.S.A. 64 B5 ......43.22N 124.12W
Copenhagen Denmark 40 C1 ......55.40N 12.34E
Copiapó Chile 73 B4 ......27.18S 70.23W
Copinsay i. Scotland 19 G3 ......58.54N 2.40W
Coquimbo Chile 73 B4 ......29.58S 71.20W
Corabia Romania 56 F6 ......43.47N 24.29E
Coral Harbour Canada 63 J4 ......64.12N 83.19W
Coral Sea S. Pacific Oc. 110 E5 ......13.27S 151.06E
Coral Sea Basin f. S. Pacific Oc. 108 G5 ......13.23S 152.14E
Coral Sea Islands Territory Australia 110 E5 ......15.01S 150.43E
Corbie France 42 B2 ......49.55N 2.31E
Corbridge England 15 E3 ......54.58N 2.01W
Corby England 10 E3 ......52.29N 0.41W
Córdoba Argentina 73 C3 ......31.24S 64.11W
Córdoba Mexico 70 E4 ......18.55N 96.53W
Córdoba Spain 48 C2 ......37.53N 4.46W
Córdoba, Sierras de mts Argentina 73 C3 ......31.25S 64.50W
Corfe Castle England 10 C1 ......50.38N 2.03W
Corfu i. Greece 56 C4 ......39.36N 19.47E
Corigliano Calabro Italy 50 G3 ......39.35N 16.32E
Corinth Greece 56 E3 ......37.56N 22.55E
Corixa Grande r. Bolivia/Brazil 77 I4 ......17.30S 57.56W
Cork Ireland 41 C1 ......51.54N 8.28W
Cork d. Ireland 41 C2 ......52.01N 8.39W
Çorlu Turkey 57 G5 ......41.09N 27.48E
Corner Brook Canada 63 M2 ......48.54N 57.47W
Corno, Monte mt. Italy 50 E5 ......42.28N 13.34E
Cornwall d. England 9 C2 ......50.32N 4.33W
Cornwall, Cape England 13 B2 ......50.08N 5.47W
Cornwallis Island Canada 63 I5 ......75.08N 94.56W
Coro Venezuela 72 C8 ......11.23N 69.40W
Coronado, Bahía de b. Costa Rica 71 H2 ......8.55N 83.48W
Coronation Gulf Canada 62 G4 ......68.08N 112.23W
Coronel Oviedo Paraguay 77 I2 ......25.21S 56.27W
Corpus Christi U.S.A. 64 G2 ......27.44N 97.27W
Corral de Cantos mt. Spain 48 C3 ......39.34N 4.27W
Corrente Brazil 77 K5 ......10.28S 45.07S
Corrib, Lough l. Ireland 41 B3 ......53.27N 9.19W
Corrientes Argentina 73 D4 ......27.27S 58.46W
Corrientes r. Argentina 73 D3 ......30.25S 59.35W
Corrientes, Cabo c. Mexico 70 C5 ......20.26N 105.42W
Corse, Cap c. France 44 H3 ......43.00N 9.23E
Corserine hill Scotland 16 E3 ......55.09N 4.21W
Corsham England 10 C2 ......51.26N 2.11W
Corsica i. France 44 H3 ......42.20N 8.29E
Corte France 44 H3 ......42.18N 9.09E
Cortegana Spain 48 B2 ......37.55N 6.49W
Cortina d'Ampezzo Italy 50 E7 ......46.32N 12.09E
Corton England 11 G3 ......52.31N 1.45E
Çorum Turkey 57 K5 ......40.33N 34.57E
Corumbá Brazil 77 I4 ......19.00S 57.39W

Corwen Wales 12 D4.....52.59N 3.22W
Cosenza Italy 50 G3.....39.18N 16.15E
Cosmoledo Islands Seychelles 86 D4.....9.30S 49.00E
Cosne-Cours-sur-Loire France 44 E5.....47.25N 2.56E
Costa Blanca f. Spain 48 E3.....38.03N 0.20W
Costa Brava f. Spain 48 G4.....41.28N 3.05E
Costa del Sol f. Spain 48 C2.....36.25N 5.06W
Costa de Mosquitos f. Nicaragua 71 H3.....12.08N 83.52W
Costa Rica Central America 71 H3.....10.08N 84.19W
Cotabato Phil. 105 G5.....7.13N 124.14E
Côte d'Azur f. France 44 G3.....43.33N 7.13E
Côte d'Ivoire Africa 84 D2.....7.35N 4.22W
Cothi r. Wales 12 C3.....51.52N 4.10W
Cotonou Benin 84 E2.....6.21N 2.27E
Cotopaxi, Volcán vol. Ecuador 76 E7.....0.39S 78.26W
Cotswold Hills England 10 C2.....51.36N 2.15W
Cottbus Germany 54 F4.....51.45N 14.21E
Cottenham England 11 F3.....52.17N 0.08E
Cottesmore England 10 E3.....52.43N 0.40W
Coulogne France 42 A3.....50.55N 1.53E
Coupar Angus Scotland 17 F4.....56.33N 3.16W
Courland Lagoon b. Lithuania/Rus. Fed. 40 E1.....55.16N 21.06E
Coutances France 44 C4.....49.03N 1.27W
Coventry England 10 D3.....52.24N 1.31W
Covilhã Portugal 48 B4.....40.17N 7.29W
Cowan, Lake Australia 110 B3.....31.45S 121.59E
Cowbridge Wales 13 D3.....51.28N 3.27W
Cowdenbeath Scotland 17 F4.....56.07N 3.20W
Cowes England 10 D1.....50.46N 1.18W
Cowfold England 11 E2.....50.59N 0.16W
Cow Green Reservoir England 15 E3.....54.40N 2.20W
Coxim Brazil 77 J4.....18.30S 54.44W
Cox's Bazar Bangl. 97 H5.....21.27N 91.59E
Cozumel, Isla de i. Mexico 70 G5.....20.22N 86.53W
Craig U.S.A. 64 E5.....40.31N 107.32W
Craigavon Northern Ireland 16 C2.....54.26N 6.21W
Craigavon d. Northern Ireland 9 B4.....54.29N 6.22W
Craig Goch Reservoir Wales 12 D4.....52.19N 3.37W
Craignure Scotland 16 D4.....56.28N 5.43W
Crail Scotland 17 G4.....56.16N 2.38W
Craiova Romania 56 E7.....44.19N 23.48E
Cramlington England 15 F4.....55.05N 1.35W
Cranbrook Canada 62 G2.....49.32N 115.45W
Cranleigh England 11 E2.....51.08N 0.29W
Crawley England 11 E2.....51.07N 0.11W
Creag Meagaidh mt. Scotland 19 E1.....56.57N 4.36W
Credenhill England 10 C3.....52.05N 2.48W
Crediton England 13 D2.....50.48N 3.39W
Cree Lake Canada 62 H3.....57.31N 106.29W
Creil France 42 B2.....49.16N 2.29E
Cremona Italy 50 D6.....45.08N 10.01E
Crépy-en-Valois France 42 B2.....49.14N 2.53E
Cres i. Croatia 56 A7.....44.51N 14.28E
Crescent City U.S.A. 64 B5.....41.47N 124.09W
Creston U.S.A. 65 H5.....41.03N 94.22W
Creswell England 15 F2.....53.16N 1.13W
Crete i. Greece 56 F2.....35.28N 24.41E
Creuse r. France 44 D5.....47.00N 0.34E
Crewe England 15 E2.....53.06N 2.26W
Crewkerne England 10 C1.....50.53N 2.48W
Crianlarich Scotland 16 E4.....56.24N 4.37W
Criccieth Wales 12 C4.....52.55N 4.14W
Criciúma Brazil 77 K2.....28.45S 49.25W
Crickhowell Wales 12 D3.....51.51N 3.08W
Crieff Scotland 17 F4.....56.23N 3.50W
Criffel hill Scotland 17 F2.....54.57N 3.38W
Crimea pen. Ukraine 53 J6.....45.20N 34.05E
Crimond Scotland 19 H2.....57.36N 1.55W
Croatia Europe 56 B7.....45.02N 15.14E
Croisilles France 11 H1.....50.12N 2.53E
Croker Island Australia 105 I1.....11.04S 132.38E
Cromarty Scotland 19 E2.....57.41N 4.02W
Cromarty Firth est. Scotland 19 E2.....57.38N 4.19W
Cromdale, Hills of Scotland 19 F2.....57.19N 3.31W
Cromer England 11 G3.....52.56N 1.18E
Cronamuck Mountain hill Ireland 16 B2.....54.54N 7.51W
Crook England 15 F3.....54.43N 1.45W
Crooked Island Bahamas 71 J5.....22.48N 74.14W
Crooked Island Passage str. Bahamas 71 J5.....22.29N 74.55W
Croom Ireland 41 C2.....52.31N 8.43W
Crosby England 14 D2.....53.29N 3.02W
Cross Fell hill England 15 E3.....54.42N 2.29W
Crossgar Northern Ireland 16 D2.....54.24N 5.45W
Crossmaglen Northern Ireland 16 C2.....54.04N 6.36W
Crotone Italy 50 G3.....39.05N 17.08E
Crouch r. England 11 F2.....51.38N 0.36E
Crowborough England 11 F2.....51.04N 0.10E
Crowland England 11 E3.....52.41N 0.10W
Crowle England 15 G2.....53.37N 0.50W
Crowthorne England 10 E2.....51.22N 0.48W
Croyde England 13 C3.....51.08N 4.13W
Croydon England 11 E2.....51.23N 0.06W
Crozet Islands Indian Oc. 117 L3.....47.00S 52.00E
Cruden Bay town Scotland 19 H2.....57.25N 1.51W
Crumlin Northern Ireland 16 C2.....54.38N 6.13W
Cruz, Cabo c. Cuba 71 I4.....19.51N 77.43W
Cruzeiro do Sul Brazil 76 F6.....7.41S 72.40W
Cuando r. Angola/Zambia 86 B3.....17.39S 23.24E
Cuanza r. Angola 86 A4.....9.21S 13.08E
Cuauhtémoc Mexico 70 C6.....28.24N 106.53W
Cuba Central America 71 H5.....21.28N 80.06W
Cubango r. Angola/Namibia 86 B3.....18.01S 21.26E
Cuckfield England 11 E2.....51.00N 0.09W
Cúcuta Colombia 72 B7.....7.53N 72.31W
Cuddalore India 96 E3.....11.42N 79.43E
Cuddapah India 96 E3.....14.29N 78.48E
Cuenca Ecuador 76 E7.....2.53S 79.00W
Cuenca Spain 48 D4.....40.04N 2.08W
Cuenca, Serranía de mts Spain 48 D4.....40.38N 2.08W
Cuernavaca Mexico 70 E4.....18.56N 99.11W
Cuiabá Brazil 77 I4.....15.33S 56.04W
Cuiabá r. Brazil 77 I4.....17.19S 56.41W
Cuilcagh hill Ireland/U.K. 16 B2.....54.12N 7.49W
Cuillin Hills Scotland 18 C2.....57.14N 6.17W
Cuillin Sound str. Scotland 18 C2.....57.08N 6.21W
Culiacán Mexico 70 C5.....24.47N 107.27W
Cullen Scotland 19 G2.....57.41N 2.49W
Cullera Spain 48 E3.....39.10N 0.13W
Cullompton England 13 D2.....50.51N 3.23W
Cullybackey Northern Ireland 16 C2.....54.53N 6.21W
Cul Mòr hill Scotland 18 D3.....58.03N 5.07W
Culuene r. Brazil 77 J5.....11.11S 53.09W
Culzean Bay Scotland 16 E3.....55.22N 4.49W
Cumaná Venezuela 72 C8.....10.24N 64.09W
Cumbal, Nevado de vol. Colombia 76 E8.....0.57N 77.51W
Cumberland r. U.S.A. 65 I4.....36.30N 87.49W
Cumberland Sound str. Canada 63 L4.....64.08N 63.14W
Cumbernauld Scotland 17 F3.....55.57N 3.59W
Cumbria d. England 9 D4.....54.42N 3.17W
Cumnock Scotland 16 E3.....55.27N 4.16W
Cunene r. Angola 86 A3.....17.15S 11.46E
Cuneo Italy 50 B6.....44.24N 7.33E
Cupar Scotland 17 F4.....56.19N 3.01W
Cupica, Golfo de b. Colombia 71 I2.....6.25N 77.46W

Curaçao i. Neth. Antilles 71 K3.....12.12N 69.04W
Curaray r. Ecuador 76 F7.....2.25S 74.06W
Curitiba Brazil 77 K2.....25.28S 49.17W
Curuá r. Brazil 77 J6.....5.25S 54.21W
Cusco Peru 76 F5.....13.31S 71.59W
Cushendall Northern Ireland 16 C3.....55.05N 6.04W
Cuttack India 96 G5.....20.27N 85.55E
Cuxhaven Germany 54 C5.....53.52N 8.42E
Cuyo Islands Phil. 105 G6.....11.11N 121.10E
Cwmbrân Wales 12 D3.....51.39N 3.02W
Cyclades is Greece 56 F3.....37.14N 24.37E
Cyprus Asia 57 J2.....35.38N 33.17E
Cyrenaica f. Libya 53 H3.....31.06N 22.24E
Czech Republic Europe 54 F3.....49.38N 15.37E
Czersk Poland 46 C4.....53.48N 17.59E
Częstochowa Poland 46 D3.....50.48N 19.07E

## D

Dąbrowa Górnicza Poland 46 D3.....50.21N 19.15E
Dachau Germany 54 D3.....48.15N 11.27E
Dagupan Phil. 104 G7.....16.04N 120.21E
Da Hinggan Ling mts China 101 L6.....43.33N 117.52E
Dahlak Archipelago is Eritrea 94 F3.....15.58N 40.04E
Dahm, Ramlat des. Saudi Arabia/Yemen 94 G3.....17.09N 45.00E
Dailly Scotland 16 E3.....55.17N 4.43W
Dakar Senegal 84 C3.....14.43N 17.28W
Dakhla Oasis Egypt 94 C5.....25.25N 28.53E
Dakol'ka r. Belarus 55 M5.....52.08N 28.52E
Dalaman Turkey 57 H3.....36.47N 28.48E
Đa Lat Vietnam 104 D6.....11.56N 108.26E
Dalbandin Pakistan 95 J5.....28.56N 64.30E
Dalbeattie Scotland 17 F2.....54.56N 3.49W
Dali China 101 I3.....25.33N 100.13E
Dalian China 101 M5.....38.51N 121.37E
Dalkeith Scotland 17 F3.....55.54N 3.04W
Dallas U.S.A. 64 G3.....32.46N 96.48W
Dalmally Scotland 16 E4.....56.24N 4.58W
Dalmatia f. Bos.-Herz./Croatia 56 A7.....44.01N 15.30E
Dalmellington Scotland 16 E3.....55.19N 4.24W
Dal'negorsk Rus. Fed. 106 D3.....44.28N 135.30E
Daloa Côte d'Ivoire 84 D2.....6.54N 6.28W
Dalry Scotland 16 E3.....55.43N 4.43W
Dalrymple Scotland 16 E3.....55.24N 4.35W
Dalrymple, Mount Australia 110 D4.....20.59S 148.37E
Dalton U.S.A. 65 J3.....34.49N 84.56W
Dalton-in-Furness England 14 D3.....54.09N 3.11W
Daly r. Australia 110 C5.....13.31S 130.28E
Daman India 96 D5.....20.24N 72.58E
Damanhûr Egypt 53 J3.....31.02N 30.28E
Damar i. Indonesia 105 H2.....7.08S 128.32E
Damaraland f. Namibia 86 A2.....21.58S 17.06E
Damascus Syria 94 E6.....33.30N 36.20E
Damāvand, Qolleh-ye mt. Iran 95 H7.....35.58N 52.07E
Damghan Iran 95 H7.....36.09N 54.19E
Dammam Saudi Arabia 95 H5.....26.24N 50.10E
Dampier Australia 110 A4.....20.41S 116.47E
Dampir, Selat str. Indonesia 105 I3.....0.40S 130.43E
Đa Năng Vietnam 104 D7.....16.01N 108.12E
Dande Ethiopia 87 B4.....4.44N 36.25E
Dandong China 101 M6.....40.06N 124.22E
Dane r. England 15 E2.....53.15N 2.31W
Danger Island Indian Oc. 108 A5.....6.24S 71.17E
Danube r. Bulgaria/Croatia/Serbia 53 I6.....45.26N 29.38E
Danube Delta Romania/Ukraine 57 H7.....45.11N 29.13E
Danville U.S.A. 65 K4.....36.35N 79.24W
Dapaong Togo 84 E3.....10.53N 0.15E
Da Qaidam Zhen China 100 H5.....37.49N 95.18E
Daqing China 101 N7.....46.28N 125.01E
Dar'ā Syria 94 E6.....32.38N 36.07E
Dārāb Iran 95 H5.....28.45N 54.32E
Darabani Romania 55 L3.....48.11N 26.36E
Daraj Libya 53 H3.....30.10N 10.29E
Darbhanga India 96 G6.....26.10N 85.57E
Dardanelles str. Turkey 56 G5.....40.12N 26.25E
Dar es Salaam Tanzania 84 C4.....6.48S 39.16E
Darhan Mongolia 101 J7.....49.23N 105.49E
Darién, Golfo del g. Colombia 72 B7.....8.56N 77.01W
Darjiling India 96 G6.....27.02N 88.19E
Darling r. Australia 110 D3.....34.05S 141.56E
Darling Downs hills Australia 110 D4.....27.58S 149.54E
Darlington England 15 F3.....54.31N 1.33W
Darlington d. England 9 E4.....54.33N 1.34W
Darmstadt Germany 44 H6.....49.52N 8.38E
Darnah Libya 85 G5.....32.42N 22.40E
Dart r. England 13 D2.....50.25N 3.39W
Dartford England 11 F2.....51.27N 0.13E
Dartmoor hills England 13 C2.....50.36N 4.01W
Dartmouth Canada 63 M2.....44.41N 63.35W
Dartmouth England 13 D2.....50.21N 3.35W
Darton England 15 F2.....53.35N 1.31W
Daru P.N.G. 105 K2.....9.03S 143.12E
Darwen England 14 E2.....53.42N 2.28W
Darwin Australia 110 C5.....12.27S 130.51E
Datong China 101 K6.....40.03N 113.20E
Daud Khel Pakistan 95 L6.....32.51N 71.37E
Daugava r. Latvia 40 F2.....57.03N 24.04E
Daugavpils Latvia 40 F1.....55.53N 26.31E
Dauphin Canada 62 H3.....51.09N 100.02W
Dauphiné f. France 44 F4.....45.22N 5.07E
Davangere India 96 E3.....14.27N 75.51E
Davao Phil. 105 H5.....7.05N 125.34E
Davao Gulf Phil. 105 H5.....6.22N 125.49E
Davenport U.S.A. 65 H5.....41.32N 90.33W
Daventry England 10 D3.....52.15N 1.10W
David Panama 71 H2.....8.27N 82.25W
Davis Strait Canada/Greenland 63 M4.....63.48N 56.19W
Davos Switz. 50 C7.....46.48N 9.49E
Dawa Wenz r. Ethiopia 87 C4.....4.09N 42.04E
Dawlish England 13 D2.....50.35N 3.28W
Dawqah Oman 95 H3.....18.37N 54.04E
Dawson r. Australia 110 D4.....24.04N 139.24W
Dawson Creek town Canada 62 F3.....55.46N 120.17W
Daxian China 101 J4.....31.05N 107.26E
Dayr az Zawr Syria 94 F7.....35.19N 40.06E
Dayton U.S.A. 65 J4.....39.45N 84.11W
Daytona Beach town U.S.A. 65 J2.....29.08N 81.05W
Dazhou China 101 J4.....31.12N 107.28E
Dead Sea l. Asia 94 E6.....31.08N 35.27E
Deal England 11 G2.....51.13N 1.24E
Dean, Forest of England 10 C2.....51.48N 2.32W
Dearne r. England 15 F2.....53.29N 1.14W
Death Valley f. U.S.A. 64 C4.....36.34N 117.01W
Debak Malaysia 104 E4.....1.31N 111.29E
Debar Macedonia 56 D5.....41.31N 20.31E
Debenham England 11 G3.....52.14N 1.11E
Debrecen Hungary 55 I2.....47.32N 21.37E
Debre Zeyit Ethiopia 87 B4.....8.45N 38.57E
Decatur U.S.A. 65 I3.....34.37N 86.59W
Deccan f. India 96 E4.....18.40N 77.05E
Děčín Czech Rep. 54 F4.....50.47N 14.13E
Dee r. Scotland 19 G2.....57.09N 2.05W

Dee r. Wales 12 D5.....53.13N 3.01W
Dee est. Scotland 16 D5.....53.18N 3.09W
Deele r. Ireland 16 B2.....54.51N 7.28W
Degodia f. Ethiopia 87 C4.....4.13N 41.24E
De Grey r. Australia 110 A4.....20.19S 119.14E
Dehra Dun India 96 E7.....30.20N 78.05E
Dej Romania 55 J2.....47.09N 23.53E
Delano Peak U.S.A. 64 D4.....38.23N 112.21W
Delap-Uliga-Djarrit Marshall Is 108 H6.....7.07N 171.22E
Delārām Afgh. 95 J6.....32.11N 63.28E
Delaware d. U.S.A. 65 K4.....38.58N 75.28W
Delft Neth. 42 D5.....52.01N 4.21E
Delfzijl Neth. 42 F6.....53.20N 6.55E
Delgado, Cabo c. Mozambique 86 D3.....10.41S 40.36E
Delhi India 96 E6.....28.38N 77.17E
Delhi d. India 100 D3.....28.38N 77.08E
Delice r. Turkey 57 K5.....40.31N 34.13E
Del Rio U.S.A. 64 F2.....29.21N 100.58W
Demanda, Sierra de la mts Spain 48 D5.....42.13N 3.27W
Deming U.S.A. 64 E3.....32.16N 107.45W
Demirci Turkey 57 H4.....39.02N 28.39E
Demirkazık Tepe mt. Turkey 57 K3.....37.48N 35.09E
Demmin Germany 46 A4.....53.54N 13.03E
Dempo, Gunung vol. Indonesia 104 C3.....4.02S 103.06E
Denakil f. Africa 85 I3.....14.27N 40.44E
Denbigh Wales 12 D5.....53.11N 3.25W
Denbighshire d. Wales 9 D3.....53.06N 3.20W
Den Burg Neth. 42 D6.....53.03N 4.49E
Dendermonde Belgium 42 D4.....51.01N 4.07E
Den Helder Neth. 42 D5.....52.58N 4.46E
Denizli Turkey 57 H3.....37.45N 29.05E
Denmark Europe 40 B2.....56.13N 10.09E
Denmark Strait Greenland/Iceland 63 P4.....67.00N 25.00W
Denny Scotland 17 F4.....56.01N 3.54W
Denpasar Indonesia 104 F2.....8.41S 115.10E
Denton U.S.A. 64 G3.....33.15N 97.08W
D'Entrecasteaux Islands P.N.G. 110 E6.....9.38S 151.02E
Denver U.S.A. 64 E4.....39.45N 105.02W
Dêqên China 101 H3.....28.26N 98.50E
Dera Ghazi Khan Pakistan 96 D7.....30.05N 70.44E
Dera Ismail Khan Pakistan 96 D7.....31.51N 70.56E
Derby Australia 110 B5.....17.19S 123.38E
Derby England 10 D3.....52.55N 1.28W
Derby d. England 9 E3.....52.55N 1.28W
Derbyshire d. England 9 E3.....53.11N 1.36W
Dereham England 11 F3.....52.41N 0.56E
Derg r. Ireland/U.K. 41 E4.....54.44N 7.26W
Derg, Lough l. Don. Ireland 41 D4.....54.37N 7.51W
Derg, Lough l. Tipp. Ireland 41 C3.....52.54N 8.28W
Derry r. Northern Ireland 8 B4.....54.56N 7.10W
Derry r. Ireland 41 C2.....52.41N 6.40W
Derryveagh Mountains Ireland 41 C4.....54.56N 8.14W
Dersingham England 11 F3.....52.51N 0.31E
Dêrub China 100 D4.....33.25N 79.46E
Derudeb Sudan 94 E3.....17.38N 36.05E
Derwent r. England 15 F2.....53.45N 0.58W
Derwent Reservoir Derbys. England 15 F2.....53.25N 1.44W
Derwent Reservoir Dur. England 15 F3.....54.50N 2.00W
Derwent Water l. England 14 D3.....54.34N 3.10W
Desaguadero r. Argentina 73 C3.....34.03S 66.43W
Desaguadero r. Bolivia 76 G4.....16.40S 69.01W
Désappointement, Îles du is French Polynesia 109 K5.....13.59S 141.06W
Desē Ethiopia 85 H3.....11.07N 39.38E
Deseado Argentina 73 C2.....47.45S 65.55W
Des Moines U.S.A. 65 H5.....41.36N 93.37W
Des Moines r. U.S.A. 65 H5.....40.23N 91.28W
Desna r. Rus. Fed./Ukraine 55 M3.....49.19N 28.31E
Desna r. Rus. Fed./Ukraine 55 N4.....50.32N 30.33E
Dessau Germany 54 E4.....51.50N 12.15E
Detroit U.S.A. 65 J5.....42.19N 83.04W
Deva Romania 56 E7.....45.54N 22.55E
Deventer Neth. 42 F5.....52.15N 6.10E
Deveron r. Scotland 19 G2.....57.40N 2.31W
Devét Skal hill Czech Rep. 46 C2.....49.40N 16.02E
Devil's Bit Mountain hill Ireland 41 D2.....52.49N 7.55E
Devil's Bridge Wales 12 D4.....52.23N 3.51W
Devil's Lake town U.S.A. 64 G6.....48.02N 98.46W
Devizes England 10 D2.....51.21N 1.59W
Devon d. England 13 D2.....50.32N 3.51W
Devon r. England 15 G2.....53.04N 0.50W
Devon r. Scotland 17 F4.....56.10N 3.40W
Devon Island Canada 63 I5.....75.20N 91.06W
Devonport Australia 110 D2.....41.11S 146.20E
Devrez r. Turkey 57 K5.....41.27N 35.01E
Dewsbury England 15 F2.....53.41N 1.38W
Dezfūl Iran 95 G6.....32.22N 48.24E
Dezhou China 101 L5.....37.25N 116.19E
Dhahran Saudi Arabia 95 H5.....26.19N 50.07E
Dhaka Bangl. 97 H5.....23.43N 90.24E
Dhamār Yemen 94 F2.....14.34N 44.26E
Dhanbad India 96 G5.....23.47N 86.25E
Dharwad India 96 E4.....15.27N 75.04E
Dhaulagiri mt. Nepal 96 F6.....28.40N 83.28E
Dhule India 96 D5.....20.53N 74.52E
Diablo, Picacho del mt. Mexico 70 A7.....30.59N 115.24W
Diamantina watercourse Australia 110 C4.....26.30S 139.22E
Diamantina, Chapada f. Brazil 77 L5.....14.21S 43.09W
Diamantina Deep f. Indian Oc. 108 C3.....35.42S 104.20E
Dibrugarh India 97 H6.....27.27N 94.55E
Dickinson U.S.A. 64 F6.....46.53N 102.48W
Dida Galgalu f. Kenya 87 B3.....3.11N 38.06E
Didcot England 10 D2.....51.36N 1.15W
Diekirch d. Lux. 42 F2.....49.59N 5.59E
Dieppe France 44 D6.....49.55N 1.05E
Diest Belgium 42 E3.....50.59N 5.03E
Digne-les-Bains France 44 G4.....44.06N 6.15E
Dijon France 44 F5.....47.20N 5.03E
Diksmuide Belgium 42 B4.....51.02N 2.52E
Dili East Timor 105 H2.....8.35S 125.36E
Dillon U.S.A. 64 D6.....45.13N 112.37W
Dimapur India 97 H6.....25.54N 93.47E
Dimitrovgrad Bulgaria 56 F6.....42.03N 25.36E
Dinan France 44 B6.....48.27N 2.03W
Dinant Belgium 42 D3.....50.16N 4.56E
Dinar Turkey 56 I3.....38.04N 30.10E
Dīnār, Kūh-e mt. Iran 95 H6.....30.49N 51.32E
Dinaric Alps mts Bos.-Herz./Croatia 56 B7.....44.13N 16.16E
Dindigul India 96 E3.....10.22N 77.58E
Dingle Ireland 41 A2.....52.08N 10.16W
Dingle Bay Ireland 41 A2.....52.00N 10.16W
Dingwall Scotland 19 E2.....46.54N 60.29W
Dipolog Phil. 105 G5.....8.39N 123.26E
Dir Pakistan 95 L7.....35.12N 71.50E
Dirē Dawa Ethiopia 85 I3.....9.34N 41.53E
Dirranbandi Australia 110 D4.....28.35S 148.14E
Disappointment, Cape S. Atlantic Oc. 73 F1.....54.51S 36.07W
Disappointment, Lake Australia 110 B4.....23.30S 122.50E
Disko I. Greenland 63 M4.....69.44N 53.33W
Diss England 11 G3.....52.23N 1.07E
Distington England 14 D3.....54.36N 3.32W
Distrito Federal d. Brazil 77 K4.....15.56S 47.39W
Distrito Federal d. Mexico 70 E4.....19.15N 99.08W

Diu India 96 D5.....20.40N 71.03E
Divinópolis Brazil 77 L3.....20.09S 44.53W
Divnoye Rus. Fed. 53 L6.....45.55N 43.20E
Divriği Turkey 57 M4.....39.22N 38.06E
Dixon Entrance str. Canada/U.S.A. 62 E3.....54.18N 133.28W
Diyarbakır Turkey 53 L4.....37.55N 40.14E
Djado, Plateau du f. Niger 84 F4.....21.30N 12.53E
Djelfa Algeria 84 E5.....34.38N 3.16E
Djibouti Africa 85 I3.....11.34N 42.25E
Djibouti town Djibouti 85 I3.....11.32N 43.09E
Djouce Mountain hill Ireland 12 A5.....53.11N 6.17E
Dnieper r. Belarus 55 N4.....51.16N 30.34E
Dnieper r. Ukraine 55 O2.....46.30N 32.19E
Dniester r. Moldova 55 N2.....46.25N 30.11E
Dniester r. Ukraine 55 M3.....48.30N 28.30E
Dniprodzerzhyns'k Ukraine 55 P3.....48.30N 34.39E
Dnipropetrovs'k Ukraine 55 P3.....48.30N 35.05E
Dniprorudne Ukraine 55 P2.....47.23N 34.58E
Doba Chad 85 F2.....8.40N 16.51E
Doberai Peninsula Indonesia 105 I3.....1.19S 132.27E
Doboj Bos.-Herz. 56 C7.....44.44N 18.06E
Dobrich Bulgaria 57 G6.....43.34N 27.49E
Dobskie, Jezioro l. Poland 46 E5.....54.04N 21.36E
Dochart r. Scotland 16 E4.....56.28N 4.18W
Docking England 11 F3.....52.54N 0.38E
Dodecanese is Greece 56 G2.....35.57N 27.47E
Dodge City U.S.A. 64 F4.....37.46N 100.02W
Dodman Point England 13 C2.....50.13N 4.48W
Dodoma Tanzania 86 C4.....6.10S 35.45E
Doetinchem Neth. 42 F4.....51.58N 6.17E
Doha Qatar 95 H5.....25.17N 51.33E
Dokkum Neth. 42 E6.....53.19N 5.59E
Dolbenmaen Wales 12 C4.....52.58N 4.14W
Dole France 44 F5.....47.06N 5.30E
Dolgellau Wales 12 D4.....52.45N 3.53W
Dolomites mts Italy 50 D6.....46.42N 11.37E
Dolo Odo Ethiopia 87 C4.....4.09N 42.03E
Dolyna Ukraine 55 J3.....48.58N 23.59E
Dolyns'ka Ukraine 55 O3.....48.07N 32.46E
Dominica Central America 71 L4.....15.18N 61.15W
Dominican Republic Central America 71 J4.....18.57N 70.23W
Don r. Rus. Fed. 35 H2.....47.06N 39.16E
Don r. Scotland 19 G2.....57.10N 2.05W
Donaghadee Northern Ireland 16 D2.....54.38N 5.32W
Donegal Ireland 41 C4.....54.39N 8.07W
Donegal d. Ireland 41 C4.....54.56N 8.07W
Donegal Bay Ireland 41 C4.....54.31N 8.21W
Donegal Point Ireland 41 B2.....52.44N 9.39W
Donets'k Ukraine 53 K6.....47.59N 37.47E
Dongara Australia 110 A4.....29.17S 114.54E
Dongfang China 101 J1.....19.03N 108.39E
Dongfanghong China 106 B5.....46.10N 133.02E
Đông Hơi Vietnam 104 D7.....17.26N 106.36E
Dongotona Mountains South Sudan 87 A4.....4.12N 33.08E
Dongting Hu l. China 101 K3.....29.20N 112.57E
Dongying China 101 L5.....37.25N 118.41E
Donostia-San Sebastián Spain 48 E5.....43.19N 1.59W
Doon r. Scotland 16 E3.....55.26N 4.39W
Doon, Loch l. Scotland 16 E3.....55.15N 4.24W
Dorchester England 10 C1.....50.43N 2.26W
Dordogne r. France 44 C4.....45.00N 0.29W
Dordrecht Neth. 42 D4.....51.48N 4.41E
Dorking England 11 E2.....51.14N 0.20W
Dornbirn Austria 54 C2.....47.26N 9.45E
Dornoch Scotland 19 E2.....57.53N 4.02W
Dornoch Firth est. Scotland 19 E2.....57.51N 4.04W
Döröö Nuur l. Mongolia 100 G7.....47.33N 93.37E
Dorsale Camerounaise f. Cameroon/Nigeria 84 F2.....5.59N 10.49E
Dorset d. England 9 D2.....50.53N 2.18W
Dortmund Germany 54 B4.....51.30N 7.27E
Dos Bahías, Cabo c. Argentina 73 C2.....44.56S 65.32W
Dosso Niger 84 E3.....13.03N 3.12E
Dothan U.S.A. 65 I3.....31.14N 85.24W
Douai France 42 C4.....50.22N 3.05E
Douala Cameroon 84 E2.....4.03N 9.42E
Douglas Isle of Man 14 C3.....54.09N 4.29W
Douglas Scotland 17 F3.....55.33N 3.51W
Douglas U.S.A. 64 E5.....31.20N 109.33W
Doullens France 42 B3.....50.09N 2.21E
Doune Scotland 17 E4.....56.11N 4.03W
Dounreay Scotland 19 F3.....58.35N 3.45W
Dourados Brazil 77 J3.....22.13S 54.49W
Douro r. Portugal 48 A4.....41.09N 8.34W
Dove r. Derbys. England 10 D4.....52.50N 1.35W
Dove r. Suff. England 11 G3.....52.21N 1.11E
Dover England 11 G2.....51.08N 1.19E
Dover U.S.A. 65 K4.....39.09N 75.32W
Dover, Strait of France/U.K. 11 G1.....50.53N 1.23E
Down d. Northern Ireland 9 C4.....54.17N 5.32W
Downham Market England 11 F3.....52.36N 0.23E
Downpatrick Northern Ireland 16 D2.....54.19N 5.42W
Downpatrick Head Ireland 41 B4.....54.20N 9.20W
Downton England 10 D1.....50.59N 1.45W
Dowshī Afgh. 95 K7.....35.38N 68.46E
Drâa, Hammada du f. Algeria 52 B2.....28.29N 8.17W
Drachten Neth. 42 F6.....53.06N 6.06E
Draguignan France 44 G3.....43.32N 6.28E
Drahichyn Belarus 55 K5.....52.11N 25.08E
Drakensberg mts Lesotho/S. Africa 86 B2.....29.59S 28.56E
Drama Greece 56 F5.....41.09N 24.08E
Drammen Norway 40 B2.....59.45N 10.12E
Draperstown Northern Ireland 16 C2.....54.48N 6.46W
Drau r. Austria 54 E2.....46.38N 14.57E
Drava r. Europe 56 D7.....45.33N 18.56E
Drenthe d. Neth. 42 F5.....52.53N 6.43E
Dresden Germany 54 E4.....51.03N 13.45E
Dreux France 44 D6.....48.44N 1.23E
Drina r. Bos.-Herz./Serbia 56 C7.....44.55N 19.22E
Drobeta-Turnu Severin Romania 56 E7.....44.37N 22.40E
Drogheda Ireland 41 E3.....53.43N 6.21W
Drohobych Ukraine 55 J3.....49.30N 23.30E
Droitwich Spa England 10 C3.....52.16N 2.09W
Dromore Northern Ireland 16 C2.....54.25N 6.08W
Dronfield England 15 F2.....53.18N 1.28W
Drosh Pakistan 95 L7.....35.33N 71.50E
Drumheller Canada 62 G3.....51.27N 112.42W
Drummore Scotland 16 E2.....54.41N 4.54W
Druskininkai Lithuania 46 G4.....53.59N 24.01E
Druts' r. Belarus 55 N5.....53.03N 30.03E
Drygarn Fawr hill Wales 12 D4.....52.13N 3.40W
Drymen Scotland 16 E4.....56.04N 4.27W
Duarte, Pico mt. Dom. Rep. 71 J4.....19.03N 70.59W
Đuba Saudi Arabia 94 E5.....27.20N 35.45E
Dubai U.A.E. 95 I5.....25.13N 55.17E
Dubawnt Lake Canada 62 H4.....63.05N 101.38W
Dubbo Australia 110 D3.....32.16S 148.39E
Dublin Ireland 41 E3.....53.20N 6.16W
Dublin d. Ireland 41 E3.....53.24N 6.18W
Dublin Bay Ireland 41 E3.....53.21N 6.10W

Dubno Ukraine 55 K4 .............................................50.25N 25.43E
Dubrovnik Croatia 56 C6 .........................................42.39N 18.06E
Dubrovytsya Ukraine 55 L4 ......................................51.34N 26.34E
Dubysa r. Lithuania 46 F5 .........................................55.04N 23.25E
Ducie Island atoll S. Pacific Oc. 109 L4 ........................24.40S 124.48W
Dudinka Rus. Fed. 59 J4 ...........................................69.22N 86.11E
Dudley England 10 C3 ..............................................52.31N 2.05W
Duero r. Spain 48 B4 ...............................................41.02N 6.56W
Dufftown Scotland 19 F2 ..........................................57.27N 3.08W
Dufourspitze mt. Italy/Switz. 50 B6 .............................45.57N 7.53E
Dugi Otok i. Croatia 56 A7 ........................................44.01N 15.01E
Duisburg Germany 54 B4 ..........................................51.28N 6.47E
Dukhān Qatar 95 H5 ................................................25.25N 50.47E
Dulce r. Argentina 72 H1 ..........................................30.33S 62.34W
Duluth U.S.A. 65 H6 ................................................46.45N 92.07W
Dulverton England 13 D3 ..........................................51.02N 3.33W
Dumas U.S.A. 64 F4 .................................................35.53N 101.59W
Dumbarton Scotland 16 E3 ........................................55.57N 4.34W
Ďumbier mt. Slovakia 46 D2 .......................................48.57N 19.39E
Dumfries Scotland 17 F3 ...........................................55.04N 3.36W
Dumfries and Galloway d. Scotland 8 D4 ......................55.09N 3.46W
Dumyāṭ Egypt 53 J2 ................................................31.25N 31.49E
Dunaff Head Ireland 16 B3 ........................................55.18N 7.31W
Dunany Point Ireland 41 E3 .......................................53.52N 6.14W
Dunaújváros Hungary 54 H2 ......................................46.59N 18.56E
Dunbar Scotland 17 G4 ............................................56.00N 2.31W
Dunblane Scotland 17 F4 ..........................................56.11N 3.58W
Duncansby Head Scotland 19 F3 .................................58.39N 3.01W
Dunchurch England 10 D3 .........................................52.20N 1.17W
Dundalk Ireland 41 E4 ..............................................54.00N 6.24W
Dundalk Bay Ireland 41 E3 ........................................53.57N 6.13W
Dundee Scotland 17 G4 ............................................56.28N 2.58W
Dundee d. Scotland 8 D5 ..........................................56.29N 2.59W
Dundonald Northern Ireland 16 D2 .............................54.36N 5.48W
Dundrum Bay Northern Ireland 16 D2 .........................54.13N 5.46W
Dunedin New Zealand 111 H2 ....................................45.53S 170.30E
Dunfermline Scotland 17 F4 ......................................56.04N 3.27W
Dungannon Northern Ireland 16 C2 .............................54.30N 6.46W
Dungannon and South Tyrone d. Northern Ireland 9 B4 ...54.28N 6.52W
Dungarvan Ireland 41 D2 ..........................................52.05N 7.38W
Dungeness hd England 11 F1 .....................................50.55N 0.59E
Dungiven Northern Ireland 16 C2 ...............................54.55N 6.55W
Dungun Malaysia 104 C4 ...........................................4.46N 103.23E
Dungunab Sudan 94 E4 ............................................21.04N 37.04E
Dunholme England 15 G2 ..........................................53.18N 0.28W
Dunhua China 106 A4 ...............................................43.22N 128.14E
Dunhuang China 100 G6 ...........................................40.07N 94.40E
Dunkerque France 42 C3 ...........................................51.02N 2.22E
Dunkery Beacon hill England 13 D3 ............................51.10N 3.35W
Dunkirk France 44 E7 ..............................................51.02N 2.22E
Dún Laoghaire Ireland 41 E3 .....................................53.17N 6.08W
Dunleer Ireland 41 E3 ..............................................53.50N 6.23W
Dunloy Northern Ireland 16 C3 ..................................55.00N 6.24W
Dunmore East Ireland 41 E2 ......................................52.09N 6.59W
Dunmurry Northern Ireland 16 D2 ..............................54.33N 5.59W
Dunnet Bay Scotland 19 F3 ........................................58.37N 3.24W
Dunnet Head Scotland 19 F3 .....................................58.41N 3.23W
Dunoon Scotland 16 E3 .............................................55.57N 4.56W
Duns Scotland 17 G3 ...............................................55.47N 2.21W
Dunstable England 11 E2 ...........................................51.53N 0.31W
Dunvegan, Loch b. Scotland 18 C2 .............................57.31N 6.41W
Durance r. France 44 F3 ...........................................43.55N 4.45E
Durango Mexico 70 D5 .............................................24.02N 104.43W
Durango d. Mexico 70 D5 ..........................................24.44N 104.59W
Durango U.S.A. 64 E4 ..............................................37.16N 107.52W
Durazno Uruguay 77 I1 .............................................33.25S 56.31W
Durban S. Africa 86 C2 ............................................29.51S 31.02E
Düren Germany 42 F3 ..............................................50.48N 6.29E
Durham England 15 F3 ............................................54.47N 1.35W
Durham d. England 9 E4 ...........................................54.42N 1.45W
Durham U.S.A. 65 K4 ...............................................35.59N 78.54W
Durmitor mt. Montenegro 56 C6 ................................43.07N 19.03E
Durness Scotland 18 E3 ............................................58.34N 4.45W
Durness, Kyle of inlet Scotland 18 E3 ..........................58.34N 4.49W
Durrës Albania 56 C5 ...............................................41.19N 19.27E
Dursey Head Ireland 41 A1 ........................................51.34N 10.13W
Dursley England 10 C2 .............................................51.41N 2.21W
Dushanbe Tajikistan 96 C8 ........................................38.38N 68.51E
Düsseldorf Germany 54 B4 ........................................51.13N 6.47E
Duyun China 101 J3 .................................................26.13N 107.32E
Düzce Turkey 57 I5 ..................................................40.50N 31.09E
Dyat'kovo Rus. Fed. 55 P5 ........................................53.36N 34.21E
Dyce Scotland 19 G2 ...............................................57.12N 2.11W
Dyer, Cape Canada 63 L4 .........................................66.39N 61.16W
Dyfi r. Wales 12 D4 ................................................52.33N 3.56W
Dylewska Góra hill Poland 46 D4 ...............................53.34N 19.57E
Dymchurch England 11 F2 .........................................51.01N 0.59E
Dymock England 10 C2 .............................................51.59N 2.26W
Dzerzhinsk Rus. Fed. 58 F3 ......................................56.14N 43.28E
Dzhankoy Ukraine 55 R2 ..........................................45.43N 34.24E
Dzhugdzhur, Khrebet mts Rus. Fed. 59 O3 .................59.35N 135.07E
Działdowo Poland 46 E4 ...........................................53.15N 20.11E
Dzisna r. Belarus 55 M6 ...........................................55.33N 28.13E

**E**

Ealing England 11 E2 ...............................................51.31N 0.18W
Earlston Scotland 17 G3 ...........................................55.38N 2.41W
Earn r. Scotland 17 F4 .............................................56.20N 3.20W
Earn, Loch l. Scotland 16 E4 .....................................56.23N 4.15W
Easington England 15 F3 ..........................................54.47N 1.21W
Easingwold England 11 E2 ........................................54.07N 1.11W
East Anglian Heights hills England 11 F3 .....................52.03N 0.15E
East Ayrshire d. Scotland 8 C4 ..................................55.29N 4.15W
Eastbourne England 11 F1 ........................................50.46N 0.18E
East Cape New Zealand 111 G3 .................................37.40S 178.33E
East Caroline Basin f. N. Pacific Oc. 108 F6 ................2.08N 148.16E
East China Sea N. Pacific Oc. 101 N4 ........................31.00N 127.22E
East Dunbartonshire d. Scotland 8 C4 .......................55.58N 4.12W
Easter Island S. Pacific Oc. 109 M4 ...........................27.05S 109.17W
Eastern d. Kenya 87 B3 ............................................0.23S 37.55E
Eastern Desert Egypt 53 J2 .......................................26.39N 32.50E
Eastern Equatoria d. South Sudan 87 A4 .....................4.55N 33.19E
Eastern Ghats mts India 96 E3 ..................................11.54N 77.22E
Easter Ross f. Scotland 18 E2 ....................................57.49N 4.24W
East Falkland i. Falkland Is 73 D1 ..............................52.11S 57.55W
East Fen f. England 15 H2 .........................................53.05N 0.02E
Eastfield England 15 G3 ...........................................54.15N 0.24W
East Frisian Islands Germany 54 B5 ...........................53.45N 7.00E
East Grinstead England 11 E2 ...................................51.08N 0.01W
East Indiaman Ridge f. Indian Oc. 108 C4 ..................23.28S 91.17E
East Kilbride Scotland 16 E3 .....................................55.46N 4.10W
East Linton Scotland 17 G3 .......................................56.00N 2.39W
East Loch Tarbert inlet Scotland 18 C2 .......................57.51N 6.46W
East London S. Africa 86 B1 .....................................33.01S 27.56E
East Looe England 13 C2 ..........................................50.21N 4.27W
East Lothian d. Scotland 8 D4 ...................................55.57N 2.45W
Eastmain Canada 63 K3 ............................................52.14N 78.30W
Eastmain r. Canada 63 K3 .........................................52.14N 78.34W
East Mariana Basin f. N. Pacific Oc. 108 G6 ...............14.07N 152.36E

Easton England 10 C1 ..............................................50.33N 2.26W
East Pacific Rise f. N. Pacific Oc. 109 M4 ...................18.04N 107.07W
East Renfrewshire d. Scotland 8 C4 ...........................55.46N 4.21W
East Riding of Yorkshire d. England 9 E3 ...................53.55N 0.19W
Eastry England 11 G2 ..............................................51.15N 1.18E
East Sea N. Pacific Oc. 106 C3 .................................39.13N 133.37E
East Siberian Sea Rus. Fed. 59 P5 ............................72.59N 148.21E
East Timor Asia 105 H2 ...........................................8.57S 125.59E
Eastwood England 15 F2 ..........................................53.01N 1.18W
Eaton Socon England 11 E3 .......................................52.13N 0.17W
Eau Claire U.S.A. 65 H5 ...........................................44.49N 91.30W
Eau Claire, Lac à l' l. Canada 63 K3 ...........................56.13N 74.07W
Eauripik atoll Micronesia 105 K5 ................................6.43N 143.04E
Eauripik Rise-New Guinea Rise f. N. Pacific Oc. 108 F6 ...8.13N 141.00E
Ebbw Vale Wales 12 D3 ...........................................51.47N 3.12W
Eberswalde-Finow Germany 54 E5 .............................52.50N 13.49E
Ebinur Hu l. China 100 E6 ........................................44.46N 82.51E
Ebro r. Spain 48 F4 .................................................40.43N 0.51E
Ecclefechan Scotland 17 F3 ......................................55.04N 3.16W
Eccleshall England 10 C3 .........................................52.52N 2.15W
Éch Chélif Algeria 84 E5 ..........................................36.09N 1.17E
Écija Spain 48 C2 ..................................................37.33N 5.04W
Eck, Loch l. Scotland 16 E4 ......................................56.04N 4.59W
Eckington England 10 C3 .........................................52.04N 2.07W
Ecuador S. America 76 E7 ........................................1.08S 78.05W
Eday i. Scotland 19 G4 ............................................59.11N 2.50W
Ed Da'ein Sudan 94 C2 ............................................11.27N 26.09E
Ed Damazin Sudan 85 H3 .........................................11.47N 34.20E
Ed Damer Sudan 94 D3 ............................................17.26N 33.58E
Ed Debba Sudan 94 D3 ............................................18.00N 30.55E
Ed Dueim Sudan 94 D2 ............................................13.57N 32.17E
Eden r. England 14 D3 .............................................54.57N 3.01W
Edessa Greece 56 E5 ...............................................40.48N 22.04E
Edgeøya i. Arctic Oc. 58 D5 ......................................77.32N 22.45E
Edinburgh Scotland 17 F3 ........................................55.57N 3.11W
Edinburgh d. Scotland 8 D4 ......................................55.56N 3.17W
Edirne Turkey 56 G5 ...............................................41.39N 26.34E
Edmonton Canada 62 G3 ..........................................53.33N 113.33W
Edmundston Canada 63 L2 .......................................47.23N 68.20W
Edremit Turkey 56 G4 ..............................................39.35N 27.00E
Edson Canada 62 G3 ...............................................53.35N 116.25W
Edward, Lake Dem. Rep. Congo/Uganda 86 B4 ..........0.17S 29.40E
Edwards Plateau f. U.S.A. 64 F3 ...............................30.28N 100.22W
Éfaté i. Vanuatu 111 F5 ............................................17.38S 168.30E
Effingham U.S.A. 65 I4 ............................................39.07N 88.33W
Eger Hungary 54 I2 .................................................47.54N 20.22E
Egilsay i. Scotland 19 G4 .........................................59.09N 2.55W
Egilsstaðir Iceland 40 Y1 .........................................65.16N 14.25W
Eğirdir Turkey 57 I3 ................................................37.51N 30.51E
Eğirdir Gölü l. Turkey 57 I3 ......................................37.59N 30.53E
Eglinton Northern Ireland 16 B3 ...............................55.02N 7.11W
Egremont England 14 D3 ..........................................54.29N 3.32W
Egvekinot Rus. Fed. 59 T4 .......................................66.20N 179.17W
Egypt Africa 85 G4 .................................................29.53N 31.16E
Eifel hills Germany 54 B4 .........................................50.10N 6.39E
Eigg i. Scotland 18 C1 .............................................56.54N 6.10W
Eighty Mile Beach f. Australia 110 B5 ........................19.54S 120.10E
Eilat Israel 53 J2 ...................................................29.33N 34.56E
Eilean Siar d. Scotland 8 B6 .....................................58.15N 6.33W
Eindhoven Neth. 42 E4 ............................................51.26N 5.29E
Eisenhüttenstadt Germany 54 F5 ..............................52.09N 14.38E
Eishort, Loch inlet Scotland 18 D2 ............................57.09N 5.59W
Ekibastuz Kazakhstan 100 D8 ...................................51.46N 75.27E
Ekostrovskaya Imandra, Ozero l. Rus. Fed. 40 H4 .......67.29N 32.23E
Eksjö Sweden 40 C2 ................................................57.40N 14.59E
Elazığ Turkey 57 M4 ...............................................38.39N 39.15E
Elba, Isola d' i. Italy 50 D5 .......................................42.50N 10.16E
El'ban Rus. Fed. 101 P8 ...........................................50.03N 136.26E
El Bayadh Algeria 84 E5 ..........................................33.41N 0.56E
Elbe r. Germany 54 C5 ............................................53.53N 9.05E
Elbert, Mount U.S.A. 64 E4 ......................................39.05N 106.25W
Elbistan Turkey 57 L4 .............................................38.12N 37.11E
Elbląg Poland 46 D5 ...............................................54.10N 19.24E
El'brus mt. Rus. Fed. 53 K5 .....................................43.22N 42.25E
Elburz Mountains Iran 95 G7 ...................................36.52N 49.43E
El Callao Venezuela 71 L2 ........................................7.17N 61.47W
El Cerro Bolivia 77 H4 .............................................17.32S 61.36W
Elche-Elx Spain 48 E3 .............................................38.16N 0.41W
Elda Spain 48 E3 ...................................................38.29N 0.47W
Eldama Ravine Kenya 87 A3 .....................................0.05N 35.44E
El Dera Kenya 87 B3 ...............................................0.39N 38.43E
El Djouf des. Africa 82 C7 ........................................21.00N 8.00W
El Dorado U.S.A. 65 H3 ...........................................33.13N 92.36W
Eldoret Kenya 87 A3 ...............................................0.31N 35.15E
Eleanora r. Algeria 52 E4 .........................................36.07N 5.48E
Eleuthera i. Bahamas 71 I6 .......................................25.21N 76.22W
El Fasher Sudan 85 G3 .............................................13.36N 25.20E
El Geneina Sudan 85 G3 ..........................................13.26N 22.26E
Elgin Scotland 19 F2 ...............................................57.39N 3.19W
El'ginskiy Rus. Fed. 59 P4 ........................................64.32N 141.40E
El Goléa Algeria 84 E5 ............................................30.34N 2.58E
Elgon, Mount Kenya/Uganda 87 A3 ..........................1.08N 34.34E
El Hierro i. Canary Islands 48 X1 ...............................27.40N 17.56W
El Jadida Morocco 84 D5 .........................................33.12N 8.27W
Ełk Poland 46 F4 ...................................................53.50N 22.22E
Elkhovo Bulgaria 56 G6 ...........................................42.11N 26.34E
Elko U.S.A. 64 C5 ..................................................40.51N 115.46W
Ellef Ringnes Island Canada 63 H5 ...........................78.38N 101.56W
Ellensburg U.S.A. 64 B6 ..........................................46.59N 120.32W
Ellesmere England 10 C3 .........................................52.54N 2.54W
Ellesmere Island Canada 63 J5 .................................77.10N 83.03W
Ellesmere Port England 14 E2 ..................................53.17N 2.54W
Ellice r. Canada 62 H4 ............................................67.56N 103.59W
Ellon Scotland 19 G2 ..............................................57.22N 2.04W
Elmalı Turkey 57 H3 ...............................................36.44N 29.55E
El Meghaïer Algeria 52 E3 ........................................33.56N 5.56E
El Muglad Sudan 85 G3 ...........................................11.01N 27.44E
El Obeid Sudan 85 H3 .............................................13.10N 30.11E
El Oued Algeria 84 E5 .............................................33.18N 6.54E
El Paso U.S.A. 64 E3 ...............................................31.46N 106.24W
El Puerto de Santa María Spain 48 B2 ........................36.36N 6.13W
El Salvador Central America 70 G3 ............................13.22N 88.59W
El Tigre Venezuela 71 L2 ..........................................8.52N 64.16W
Eluru India 96 F4 ..................................................16.44N 81.09E
Elvas Portugal 48 B3 ...............................................38.53N 7.10W
Elverum Norway 40 B3 .............................................60.53N 11.33E
El Wak Kenya 87 C3 ...............................................2.47N 40.56E
Ely England 11 F3 ..................................................52.24N 0.15E
Ely, U.S.A. 64 D4 ..................................................39.15N 114.53W
Ely, Isle of f. England 11 F3 .....................................52.25N 0.14E
Emāmrūd Iran 95 H7 ...............................................36.24N 54.56E
Embu Kenya 87 B2 .................................................0.31S 37.26E
Emden Germany 54 B5 ............................................53.22N 7.13E
Emerald Australia 110 D4 ........................................23.32S 148.10E
Emi Koussi mt. Chad 85 F3 ......................................19.46N 18.34E
Emirdağ Turkey 57 I4 ..............................................39.01N 31.09E
Emmeloord Neth. 42 E5 ...........................................52.43N 5.45E
Emmen Neth. 42 F5 ................................................52.47N 6.54E
Emory Peak U.S.A. 64 F2 .........................................29.15N 103.18W

Emperor Seamount Chain f. N. Pacific Oc. 108 H9 .......52.16N 167.06E
Emperor Trough f. N. Pacific Oc. 108 H9 ...................46.06N 173.14E
Ems r. Germany 54 B5 .............................................53.18N 7.22E
Encarnación Paraguay 77 I2 ......................................27.17S 55.49W
Endeh Indonesia 105 G2 ...........................................8.47S 121.38E
Endicott Mountains U.S.A. 62 C4 .............................67.50N 152.33W
Enfield England 11 E2 ..............................................51.39N 0.05W
Engel's Rus. Fed. 58 F3 ...........................................51.29N 46.06E
Enggano i. Indonesia 104 C2 ....................................5.25S 102.20E
England U.K. 9 E3 ..................................................52.48N 1.24W
English Channel France/U.K. 11 E1 ...........................49.59N 1.24W
Enköping Sweden 40 D2 ...........................................59.38N 17.06E
En Nahud Sudan 85 G3 ............................................12.42N 28.25E
Ennedi, Massif mts Chad 85 F3 .................................16.59N 22.58E
Ennerdale Water l. England 14 D3 .............................54.30N 3.22W
Ennis Ireland 41 C2 ................................................52.51N 8.59W
Enniscorthy Ireland 41 E2 ........................................52.30N 6.34W
Enniskerry Ireland 12 A5 ..........................................53.11N 6.10W
Enniskillen Northern Ireland 16 B2 ...........................54.20N 7.37W
Ennistymon Ireland 41 B2 ........................................52.56N 9.17W
Enns r. Austria 54 F3 ..............................................48.14N 14.31E
Enschede Neth. 42 F5 ..............................................52.13N 6.54E
Ensenada Mexico 70 A7 ...........................................31.52N 116.37W
Enshi China 101 J4 .................................................30.13N 109.28E
Enugu Nigeria 84 E2 ...............................................6.24N 7.31E
Envira r. Brazil 76 F6 ..............................................7.31S 70.14W
Épernay France 42 C2 .............................................49.03N 3.58E
Épinal France 44 G6 ...............................................48.11N 6.27E
Epomeo, Monte vol. Italy 50 E4 ...............................40.44N 13.53E
Epping England 11 F2 ..............................................51.42N 0.07E
Eppynt, Mynydd hills Wales 12 D4 ............................52.05N 3.28W
Epsom England 11 E2 ..............................................51.20N 0.16W
Epworth England 15 G2 ...........................................53.32N 0.49W
Eqlid Iran 95 H6 ....................................................30.53N 52.42E
Equatorial Guinea Africa 84 E2 .................................3.00N 8.36E
Équeurdreville-Hainneville France 13 Z9 .....................49.39N 1.39W
Erbeskopf hill Germany 42 G2 ..................................49.43N 7.04E
Erciyes Dağı mt. Turkey 57 K4 ..................................38.32N 35.27E
Erdemli Turkey 57 K3 ..............................................36.36N 34.19E
Erdi f. Chad 94 B3 .................................................19.02N 21.36E
Ereğli Konya Turkey 57 K3 .......................................37.30N 34.03E
Ereğli Zonguldak Turkey 57 I5 ..................................41.17N 31.25E
Erfurt Germany 54 D4 .............................................50.59N 11.02E
Ergani Turkey 57 M4 ...............................................38.15N 39.46E
Ergene r. Turkey 56 G5 ...........................................40.59N 26.22E
Ericht r. Scotland 17 F5 ..........................................56.34N 3.15W
Ericht, Loch l. Scotland 19 E1 ..................................56.48N 4.25W
Erie U.S.A. 65 J5 ...................................................42.07N 80.06W
Erie, Lake Canada/U.S.A. 63 J2 ................................42.14N 80.53W
Eriskay i. Scotland 18 B2 .........................................57.04N 7.16W
Eritrea Africa 85 H3 ...............................................15.57N 37.33E
Erlangen Germany 54 D3 .........................................49.35N 11.01E
Ermenek Turkey 57 J3 .............................................36.37N 32.54E
Ermoupoli Greece 56 F3 ..........................................37.26N 24.56E
Erode India 96 E3 ..................................................11.21N 77.43E
Er Rachidia Morocco 84 D5 ......................................31.54N 4.29W
Er Rahad Sudan 85 H3 ............................................12.44N 30.38E
Errigal hill Ireland 41 C5 ..........................................55.02N 8.07W
Erris Head Ireland 41 A4 ..........................................54.19N 10.01W
Errochty, Loch l. Scotland 19 E1 ..............................56.45N 4.11W
Erromango i. Vanuatu 111 F5 ...................................18.49S 168.58E
Erzgebirge mts Czech Rep./Germany 54 E4 ...............50.33N 13.07E
Erzincan Turkey 57 M4 ...........................................39.45N 39.29E
Erzurum Turkey 94 F7 ............................................39.53N 41.17E
Esbjerg Denmark 40 B1 ...........................................55.28N 8.27E
Escanaba U.S.A. 65 I6 ............................................45.45N 87.03W
Escárcega Mexico 70 F4 ..........................................18.39N 90.43W
Esch-sur-Alzette Lux. 42 E2 .....................................49.30N 5.59E
Eschweiler Germany 42 F3 .......................................50.49N 6.18E
Esfahān Iran 95 H6 ................................................32.41N 51.39E
Esha Ness hd Scotland 19 H5 ...................................60.30N 1.37W
Esk r. Scotland 17 F3 .............................................55.56N 3.04W
Eske, Lough l. Ireland 16 A2 .....................................54.42N 8.04W
Eski Gediz Turkey 57 H4 .........................................39.03N 29.25E
Eskilstuna Sweden 40 D2 .........................................59.22N 16.32E
Eskişehir Turkey 57 I4 ............................................39.47N 30.31E
Esla r. Spain 48 B4 ................................................41.30N 6.01W
Eslāmābād-e Gharb Iran 95 G6 ...............................34.06N 46.31E
Esmeraldas Ecuador 76 E8 ......................................0.55N 79.41W
Esperance Australia 110 B3 ......................................33.49S 121.52E
Espigüete mt. Spain 48 C5 ......................................42.57N 4.47W
Espinaço, Serra do mts Brazil 77 L4 .........................17.59S 43.59W
Espinosa Brazil 77 L5 .............................................14.54S 42.46W
Espírito Santo d. Brazil 77 L4 ..................................19.31S 40.33W
Espíritu Santo i. Vanuatu 111 F5 ..............................15.16S 166.35E
Espoo Finland 40 F3 ...............................................60.12N 24.40E
Esquel Argentina 73 B2 ...........................................42.55S 71.20W
Essen Germany 54 B4 .............................................51.28N 7.03E
Essequibo r. Guyana 72 D7 ......................................6.23N 58.36W
Essex d. England 9 F2 ............................................51.51N 0.42E
Estados, Isla de los i. Argentina 73 C1 ......................54.44S 64.16W
Estats, Pic d' mt. France/Spain 48 F5 ........................42.40N 1.24E
Estevan Canada 62 H2 ............................................49.08N 102.59W
Estonia Europe 40 F2 .............................................58.44N 25.26E
Estrela, Serra da mts Portugal 48 B4 ........................40.17N 7.57W
Estrella mt. Spain 48 D3 ..........................................38.24N 3.36W
Estrondo, Serra hills Brazil 77 K6 ..............................9.08S 48.42W
Étaples France 44 D7 ..............................................50.31N 1.39E
Ethiopia Africa 85 H2 .............................................6.30N 39.41E
Ethiopian Highlands f. Ethiopia 85 H2 ........................8.49N 36.39E
Etimesğut Turkey 57 J4 ...........................................39.56N 32.39E
Etive, Loch inlet Scotland 16 D4 ...............................56.27N 5.12W
Etna, Mount vol. Italy 50 F3 .....................................37.45N 15.00E
Etosha Pan f. Namibia 86 A3 ....................................18.52S 16.19E
Ettelbruck Lux. 42 F2 .............................................49.51N 6.06E
Ettrick Forest f. Scotland 17 F3 ................................55.31N 3.05W
Ettrick Water r. Scotland 17 G3 ................................55.34N 2.49W
Etwall England 10 D2 .............................................52.53N 1.36W
Eugene U.S.A. 64 B5 ..............................................44.04N 123.05W
Eugenia, Punta pt Mexico 70 A6 ...............................27.51N 115.04W
Euphrates r. Asia 94 F6 ..........................................30.59N 47.24E
Eureka U.S.A. 64 B5 ...............................................40.48N 124.09W
Europa, Picos de mts Spain 48 C5 .............................43.07N 5.01W
Europe 34
Evans, Lac l. Canada 63 K3 ......................................50.49N 77.07W
Evanston U.S.A. 64 D5 ............................................41.17N 110.56W
Evansville U.S.A. 65 I4 ............................................37.59N 87.32W
Evaton S. Africa 86 B2 ............................................26.32S 27.49E
Everest, Mount China/Nepal 100 F3 ..........................27.59N 86.55E
Everglades f. U.S.A. 65 J2 ........................................26.15N 81.02W
Evesham England 10 D3 ..........................................52.06N 1.57W
Evesham, Vale of f. England 10 D3 ............................52.05N 1.57W
Évora Portugal 48 B3 ..............................................38.34N 7.54W
Évreux France 44 D6 ..............................................49.01N 1.09E
Evvoia i. Greece 56 F4 ............................................38.19N 24.14E
Ewaso Ngiro r. North Eastern Kenya 87 B3 ................0.31N 41.04E
Ewaso Ngiro r. Rift Valley Kenya 87 B3 .....................2.02S 36.07E
Ewe, Loch b. Scotland 18 D2 ...................................57.50N 5.40W
Exe r. England 13 D2 .............................................50.41N 3.29W
Exeter England 13 D2 .............................................50.43N 3.32W
Exminster England 10 D2 ........................................50.41N 3.30W
Exmoor hills England 13 D3 .....................................51.10N 3.46W
Exmouth England 13 D2 ..........................................50.37N 3.25W

Exuma Cays is Bahamas 71 I5 ..................................24.35N 76.34W
Exuma Sound str. Bahamas 71 I5 ..............................24.17N 75.59W
Eyasi, Lake Tanzania 86 C4 ......................................3.38S 35.05E
Eye P'boro. England 11 E3 ........................................52.37N 0.11W
Eye Suff. England 11 G3 ..........................................52.19N 1.09E
Eyemouth Scotland 17 G3 ........................................55.52N 2.05W
Eye Peninsula Scotland 18 C3 ...................................58.14N 6.14W
Eyre, Lake (North) Australia 110 C4 ...........................28.24S 137.16E
Eyre, Lake (South) Australia 110 C4 ...........................28.30S 137.25E
Ezine Turkey 56 G4 ................................................39.46N 26.19E

**F**

Faafxadhuun Somalia 87 C3 .....................................2.11N 41.37E
Faenza Italy 50 D6 .................................................44.11N 11.53E
Făgăraş Romania 56 F7 ............................................45.51N 24.59E
Fagatogo American Samoa 108 I5 ..............................14.17S 170.41W
Fagersta Sweden 40 C2 ...........................................59.59N 15.49E
Fairbanks U.S.A. 62 D4 ...........................................64.50N 147.47W
Fair Head Northern Ireland 16 C3 ..............................55.14N 6.08W
Fair Isle i. Scotland 19 H4 ........................................59.34N 1.38W
Fairmont U.S.A. 65 H5 ............................................43.39N 94.28W
Fairweather, Mount Canada/U.S.A. 62 E3 ..................58.54N 137.29W
Fais i. Micronesia 105 K5 .........................................9.45N 140.33E
Faisalabad Pakistan 96 D7 .......................................31.24N 73.09E
Fakaofo atoll Tokelau 108 I5 ....................................9.23S 171.08W
Fakenham England 11 F3 .........................................52.50N 0.51E
Fakfak Indonesia 105 I3 ...........................................2.55S 132.17E
Fal r. England 13 C2 ...............................................50.14N 4.58W
Falcon Lake Mexico/U.S.A. 70 E6 .............................26.53N 99.20W
Falkenberg Sweden 40 C2 .......................................56.55N 12.31E
Falkirk Scotland 17 F4 ............................................56.00N 3.47W
Falkirk d. Scotland 8 D4 ..........................................55.59N 3.48W
Falkland Islands S. Atlantic Oc. 73 D1 ......................50.55S 59.36W
Falköping Sweden 40 C2 .........................................58.10N 13.33E
Falmouth England 13 B2 ..........................................50.08N 5.04W
Falmouth Bay England 13 B2 ....................................50.08N 5.04W
Falso, Cabo c. Mexico 70 C5 ....................................22.53N 109.59W
Falster i. Denmark 40 B1 .........................................54.49N 11.58E
Falun Sweden 40 C3 ...............................................60.36N 15.38E
Famagusta Cyprus 57 J2 .........................................35.06N 33.57E
Famatina, Sierra de mts Argentina 76 G2 ..................28.03S 68.06W
Fanad Head Ireland 16 B3 .......................................55.17N 7.38W
Fane r. Ireland 41 E3 ..............................................53.57N 6.22W
Fannich, Loch l. Scotland 18 D2 ...............................57.39N 5.03W
Farafra Oasis Egypt 94 C5 .......................................26.43N 28.09E
Farāh Afgh. 95 J6 ..................................................32.22N 62.07E
Farallon de Pajaros vol. N. Mariana Is 105 K8 ............20.32N 144.55E
Farasān, Jazā'ir is Saudi Arabia 94 F3 .......................16.48N 41.54E
Fareham England 10 D1 ...........................................50.51N 1.11W
Farewell, Cape New Zealand 111 G2 .........................40.29S 172.40E
Fargo U.S.A. 64 G6 ................................................46.52N 96.49W
Faridabad India 96 E6 .............................................28.25N 77.19E
Farnborough England 10 E2 .....................................51.17N 0.45W
Farndon England 14 E2 ...........................................53.05N 2.53W
Farne Islands England 15 F4 .....................................55.38N 1.37W
Farnham England 10 E2 ..........................................51.13N 0.48W
Faro Portugal 48 B2 ...............................................37.01N 7.56W
Fårö i. Sweden 40 D2 .............................................57.58N 19.22E
Faroe Islands Europe 34 D4 ......................................62.02N 7.00W
Farrāshband Iran 95 H5 ...........................................28.52N 52.05E
Fasā Iran 95 H5 ....................................................28.56N 53.38E
Fastiv Ukraine 55 M4 ..............................................50.04N 29.55E
Fatehgarh India 96 E6 .............................................27.22N 79.36E
Faulquemont France 42 F2 .......................................49.03N 6.36E
Faversham England 11 F2 ........................................51.19N 0.53E
Faxaflói b. Iceland 40 X2 .........................................64.27N 22.58W
Fayetteville U.S.A. 65 K4 .........................................35.02N 78.53W
Fdérik Mauritania 84 C4 ..........................................22.42N 12.44W
Feale r. Ireland 41 B2 .............................................52.28N 9.38W
Fear, Cape U.S.A. 65 K3 ..........................................33.51N 77.58W
Fehmarn i. Germany 54 D6 ......................................54.29N 11.07E
Feira de Santana Brazil 77 M5 ..................................12.12S 38.57W
Feldkirch Austria 54 C2 ...........................................47.15N 9.36E
Felixstowe England 11 G2 ........................................51.58N 1.21E
Femunden l. Norway 40 B3 ......................................62.05N 11.48E
Feniton England 13 D2 ............................................50.47N 3.16W
Feodosiya Ukraine 53 K6 .........................................45.02N 35.23E
Ferdows Iran 95 I6 .................................................33.59N 58.10E
Fergus Falls town U.S.A. 64 G6 ................................46.17N 96.07W
Ferkessédougou Côte d'Ivoire 84 D2 .........................9.35N 5.13W
Fermanagh d. Northern Ireland 9 A4 .........................54.27N 8.04W
Fermanagh f. Northern Ireland 41 D4 .......................54.16N 7.35W
Fermo Italy 50 E5 ..................................................43.09N 13.43E
Fermoy Ireland 41 C2 .............................................52.08N 8.17W
Ferndown England 10 D1 .........................................50.48N 1.54W
Ferrara Italy 50 D6 .................................................44.50N 11.38E
Ferrol Spain 48 A5 .................................................43.29N 8.13W
Ferryhill England 15 F3 ...........................................54.41N 1.33W
Fès Morocco 84 D5 ................................................34.04N 4.57W
Fethaland, Point of Scotland 19 H5 ...........................60.39N 1.18W
Fethard Ireland 41 D2 .............................................52.28N 7.42W
Fethiye Turkey 57 H3 ..............................................36.37N 29.06E
Fetlar i. Scotland 19 I5 ............................................60.37N 0.51W
Feuilles, Rivière aux r. Canada 63 K3 ........................58.46N 70.13W
Feyzābād Afgh. 95 L7 .............................................37.05N 70.41E
Fez Morocco 84 D5 ................................................34.04N 4.57W
Ffestiniog Wales 12 D4 ...........................................52.58N 3.56W
Fianarantsoa Madagascar 86 D2 ...............................21.27S 47.07E
Fife d. Scotland 8 D5 ..............................................56.16N 2.58W
Fife Ness pt Scotland 17 G4 .....................................56.16N 2.35W
Figeac France 44 E4 ...............................................44.37N 2.01E
Figueira da Foz Portugal 48 A4 ................................40.10N 8.51W
Figueres Spain 48 G5 .............................................42.16N 2.58E
Figuig Morocco 52 C3 .............................................32.09N 1.17W
Fiji S. Pacific Oc. 111 G5 .........................................17.51S 177.08E
Filadelfia Paraguay 77 H3 .........................................22.22S 60.03W
Filey England 15 G3 ...............................................54.13N 0.18W
Filtu Ethiopia 87 C4 ...............................................5.06N 40.38E
Findhorn r. Scotland 19 F2 .......................................57.38N 3.38W
Finisterre, Cape Spain 48 A5 ....................................42.53N 9.15W
Finland Europe 40 F3 ..............................................63.43N 26.54E
Finland, Gulf of Europe 40 E2 ..................................59.31N 22.42E
Finlay r. Canada 62 F3 ............................................56.41N 124.49W
Finn r. Ireland 41 D4 ..............................................54.50N 7.28W
Finspång Sweden 40 C2 ..........................................58.42N 15.46E
Finstown Scotland 19 F4 .........................................59.00N 3.07W
Fintona Northern Ireland 16 B2 ................................54.30N 7.19W
Fionn Loch l. Scotland 18 D2 ...................................57.46N 5.28W
Fionnphort Scotland 16 C4 ......................................56.19N 6.22W
Fisher Strait Canada 63 J4 .......................................63.14N 83.06W
Fishguard Wales 12 C3 ...........................................51.59N 4.58W
Fishguard Bay Wales 12 C4 ......................................52.01N 4.58W
Fismes France 42 C2 ..............................................49.18N 3.42E
Flagstaff U.S.A. 64 D4 ............................................35.12N 111.39W
Flamborough England 15 G3 ....................................54.07N 0.07W
Flamborough Head England 15 G3 ............................54.07N 0.03W
Flannan Isles Scotland 18 B3 ...................................58.18N 7.39W
Flåsjön l. Sweden 40 C4 ..........................................64.06N 15.53E
Flathead Lake U.S.A. 64 D6 .....................................47.52N 114.03W
Flat Holm i. Wales 13 D3 .........................................51.23N 3.07W
Fleet England 10 E2 ...............................................51.17N 0.50W

Fleetwood England 14 D2.....53.55N 3.02W
Flensburg Germany 54 C6.....54.47N 9.25E
Flevoland d. Neth. 42 E5.....52.17N 5.07E
Flinders r. Australia 110 D5.....17.37S 140.35E
Flinders Island Australia 110 D3.....39.56S 148.04E
Flinders Ranges mts Australia 110 C3.....32.24S 137.57E
Flin Flon Canada 62 H3.....54.46N 101.51W
Flint U.S.A. 65 J5.....43.01N 83.42W
Flint Wales 12 D5.....53.15N 3.08W
Flintshire d. Wales 9 D3.....53.11N 3.07W
Florence Italy 50 D5.....43.46N 11.16E
Florence U.S.A. 65 K3.....34.11N 79.45W
Florencia Colombia 72 B7.....1.36N 75.36W
Flores i. Indonesia 105 G2.....8.29S 121.14E
Flores Sea Indonesia 104 F2.....7.41S 119.59E
Floresta Brazil 77 M6.....8.31S 38.32W
Florianópolis Brazil 77 K2.....27.32S 48.32W
Florida d. U.S.A. 65 J3.....30.12N 83.39W
Florida, Straits of Bahamas/U.S.A. 71 H5.....23.59N 81.35W
Florida Keys is U.S.A. 65 J1.....24.41N 81.38W
Florina Greece 56 D5.....40.46N 21.24E
Florø Norway 40 A3.....61.36N 5.01E
Flotta i. Scotland 19 F3.....58.50N 3.05W
Fly r. P.N.G. 105 K2.....8.18S 142.36E
Foča Bos.-Herz. 56 C6.....43.29N 18.45E
Fochabers Scotland 19 F2.....57.37N 3.06W
Focşani Romania 56 G7.....45.42N 27.11E
Foggia Italy 50 F4.....41.28N 15.33E
Fogo i. Cape Verde 84 B3.....14.59N 24.18W
Foinaven hill Scotland 18 E3.....58.25N 4.53W
Foix France 44 D3.....42.58N 1.36E
Foligno Italy 50 E5.....42.57N 12.42E
Folkestone England 11 G2.....51.05N 1.10E
Fonseca, Golfo de b. Central America 70 G3.....13.03N 88.12W
Fontainebleau France 44 E6.....48.25N 2.43E
Fontur pt Iceland 40 Z2.....66.23N 14.32W
Førde Norway 40 A3.....61.27N 5.52E
Fordingbridge England 10 D1.....50.56N 1.47W
Foreland hd England 10 D1.....50.41N 1.04W
Foreland Point England 13 D3.....51.15N 3.47W
Forfar Scotland 19 G1.....56.39N 2.53W
Forlì Italy 50 E6.....44.14N 12.02E
Formby England 14 D2.....53.34N 3.04W
Formentera i. Spain 48 F3.....38.40N 1.24E
Formosa Argentina 73 D4.....26.07S 58.12W
Formosa, Serra hills Brazil 77 I5.....12.31S 55.28W
Forres Scotland 19 F2.....57.37N 3.37W
Forssa Finland 40 E3.....60.49N 23.39E
Fort Albany Canada 63 J3.....52.13N 81.41W
Fortaleza Brazil 77 M7.....3.43S 38.32W
Fort Augustus Scotland 18 E2.....57.09N 4.41W
Fort Chipewyan Canada 62 G3.....58.42N 111.07W
Fort Collins U.S.A. 64 E5.....40.35N 105.05W
Fort-de-France Martinique 71 L3.....14.37N 61.05W
Fortescue r. Australia 110 A4.....21.02S 116.06E
Fort Frances Canada 63 I2.....48.37N 93.24W
Fort Good Hope Canada 62 F4.....66.16N 128.39W
Forth r. Scotland 16 F4.....56.07N 3.52W
Forth, Firth of est. Scotland 17 F4.....56.01N 3.13W
Fort Lauderdale U.S.A. 65 J2.....26.04N 80.11W
Fort Liard Canada 62 F4.....60.14N 123.24W
Fort McMurray Canada 62 G3.....56.43N 111.21W
Fort McPherson Canada 62 E4.....67.33N 134.44W
Fort Nelson Canada 62 F3.....58.45N 122.39W
Fort Peck Reservoir U.S.A. 64 E6.....47.47N 106.55W
Fort Pierce U.S.A. 65 J2.....27.18N 80.24W
Fortrose Scotland 19 E2.....57.35N 4.08W
Fort St John Canada 62 F3.....56.15N 120.49W
Fort Severn Canada 63 J3.....56.00N 87.39W
Fort-Shevchenko Kazakhstan 58 G2.....44.29N 50.17E
Fort Simpson Canada 62 F4.....61.52N 121.22W
Fort Smith Canada 62 G4.....60.00N 112.13W
Fort Smith U.S.A. 65 H4.....35.26N 94.24W
Fortuneswell England 10 C1.....50.34N 2.27W
Fort Wayne U.S.A. 65 I5.....41.04N 85.08W
Fort William Scotland 18 D1.....56.49N 5.06W
Fort Worth U.S.A. 64 G3.....32.46N 97.19W
Fort Yukon U.S.A. 62 D4.....66.35N 145.13W
Foshan China 101 K2.....23.03N 113.06E
Fossano Italy 50 B6.....44.33N 7.43E
Fougères France 44 C6.....48.21N 1.12W
Foula i. Scotland 19 Q6.....60.10N 2.10W
Foulness Point England 11 F2.....51.37N 0.57E
Fouta Djallon f. Guinea 84 C3.....11.26N 12.34W
Fowey r. England 13 C2.....50.26N 4.41W
Foxe Basin g. Canada 63 K4.....66.53N 78.58W
Foxe Channel Canada 63 J4.....64.56N 81.03W
Foxe Peninsula Canada 63 K4.....64.48N 77.03W
Foxford Ireland 41 B3.....53.58N 9.07W
Fox Islands U.S.A. 62 B3.....52.45N 168.53W
Foyle r. Ireland/U.K. 41 D4.....54.53N 7.26W
Foyle, Lough inlet Ireland/U.K. 41 D5.....55.07N 7.07W
Foz do Iguaçu Brazil 77 J2.....25.30S 54.32W
Framlingham England 11 G3.....52.13N 1.21E
Franca Brazil 77 K3.....20.32S 47.23W
France Europe 44 E5.....46.57N 2.11E
Franceville Gabon 84 F1.....1.37S 13.37E
Francistown Botswana 86 B2.....21.10S 27.29E
Frankfort U.S.A. 65 J4.....38.12N 84.53W
Frankfurt am Main Germany 54 C4.....50.07N 8.41E
Frankfurt an der Oder Germany 54 F5.....52.21N 14.33E
Franklin D. Roosevelt Lake resr U.S.A. 64 C6.....48.16N 118.09W
Frantsa-Iosifa, Zemlya is Rus. Fed. 58 G5.....79.40N 58.29E
Frasca, Capo della c. Italy 50 C3.....39.46N 8.26E
Fraser r. Canada 62 F2.....49.19N 121.38W
Fraserburgh Scotland 19 G2.....57.42N 2.01W
Fraser Island Australia 110 E4.....25.12S 153.11E
Freckleton England 14 E2.....53.45N 2.52W
Fredericia Denmark 40 B1.....55.34N 9.45E
Fredericton Canada 63 L2.....45.57N 66.39W
Frederikshavn Denmark 40 B2.....57.27N 10.32E
Fredrikstad Norway 40 B2.....59.13N 10.56E
Freeport City Bahamas 71 I6.....26.30N 78.45W
Freetown Sierra Leone 84 C2.....8.28N 13.12W
Freiburg im Breisgau Germany 54 B3.....48.00N 7.50E
Fréjus France 44 G3.....43.26N 6.45E
Fremantle Australia 110 A3.....32.05S 115.42E
French Guiana is S. America 109 Q6.....4.25N 53.03W
French Polynesia is S. Pacific Oc. 109 K4.....18.43S 147.32W
Freshwater England 10 D1.....50.40N 1.31W
Fresno U.S.A. 64 C4.....36.46N 119.46W
Frévent France 11 H1.....50.16N 2.17E
Freyming-Merlebach France 42 F2.....49.09N 6.48E
Fria Guinea 84 C3.....10.24N 13.35W
Friedrichshafen Germany 54 C2.....47.39N 9.31E
Friesland d. Neth. 42 E6.....53.08N 5.48E
Frinton-on-Sea England 11 G2.....51.50N 1.15E
Frisa, Loch l. Scotland 16 C4.....56.34N 6.06W
Frisian Islands Europe 44 H6.....54.00N 7.00E
Frizington England 14 D3.....54.32N 3.30W
Frobisher Bay Canada 63 L4.....63.18N 67.31W
Frodsham England 14 E2.....53.18N 2.44W
Frohavet b. Norway 40 B3.....63.52N 9.12E
Frome England 10 C2.....51.14N 2.19W

Frome r. England 10 C1.....50.41N 2.05W
Frome, Lake Australia 110 C3.....30.43S 139.48E
Frosinone Italy 50 E4.....41.39N 13.21E
Frøya i. Norway 40 B3.....63.41N 8.39E
Fruges France 11 H1.....50.31N 2.08E
Frýdek-Místek Czech Rep. 54 H3.....49.41N 18.21E
Fuenlabrada Spain 48 D4.....40.17N 3.47W
Fuerteventura i. Canary Islands 48 Y2.....28.36N 14.04W
Fujairah U.A.E. 95 I5.....25.06N 56.21E
Fujian d. China 101 L3.....25.52N 117.59E
Fuji-san vol. Japan 106 C3.....35.22N 138.43E
Fukui Japan 106 C3.....36.04N 136.13E
Fukuoka Japan 106 B2.....33.35N 130.24E
Fukushima Japan 106 D3.....37.45N 140.28E
Fulda Germany 54 C4.....50.33N 9.41E
Fulford England 15 F2.....53.56N 1.04W
Fulham England 11 E2.....51.29N 0.13W
Fumay France 42 D2.....49.59N 4.42E
Funafuti atoll Tuvalu 111 G6.....8.25S 179.13E
Funchal Atlantic Oc. 84 C5.....32.39N 16.54W
Fundy, Bay of Canada 63 L2.....44.06N 67.03W
Fürth Germany 54 D3.....49.29N 10.57E
Fushun China 101 M6.....41.51N 123.50E
Fusong China 106 A4.....42.20N 127.17E
Fuxin China 101 M6.....42.02N 121.41E
Fuyang China 101 L4.....32.51N 115.52E
Fuyu China 101 M7.....47.44N 124.26E
Fuzhou Fujian China 101 L3.....26.07N 119.21E
Fuzhou Jiangxi China 101 L3.....27.58N 116.17E
Fyn i. Denmark 40 B1.....55.38N 10.17E

G

Gaalkacyo Somalia 85 I2.....6.46N 47.25E
Gabès Tunisia 52 F3.....33.53N 10.07E
Gabès, Golfe de g. Tunisia 52 F3.....34.08N 10.40E
Gabon Africa 84 F1.....0.56S 11.32E
Gaborone Botswana 86 B2.....24.38S 25.56E
Gabrovo Bulgaria 56 F6.....42.53N 25.20E
Gadsden U.S.A. 65 I3.....34.03N 86.04W
Gaer Wales 12 D3.....51.53N 3.12W
Gaeta Italy 50 E4.....41.13N 13.34E
Gaeta, Golfo di g. Italy 50 E4.....41.06N 13.33E
Gaferut i. Micronesia 108 F6.....9.15N 145.25E
Gafsa Tunisia 52 E3.....34.26N 8.51E
Gagarin Rus. Fed. 55 P6.....55.33N 35.01E
Gagnon Canada 63 L3.....51.52N 68.07W
Gagra Georgia 57 N6.....43.18N 40.16E
Gainesville U.S.A. 65 J2.....29.36N 82.20W
Gainsborough England 15 G2.....53.24N 0.46W
Gairdner, Lake Australia 110 C3.....31.17S 135.38E
Gairloch Scotland 18 D2.....57.44N 5.42W
Gair Loch b. Scotland 18 D2.....57.43N 5.44W
Galana r. Kenya 87 C2.....3.10S 40.08E
Galapagos Islands Ecuador 72 C7.....0.03S 89.05W
Galapagos Rise f. Pacific Oc. 109 N5.....8.25S 96.06W
Galashiels Scotland 17 G3.....55.37N 2.49W
Galaţi Romania 57 H7.....45.27N 28.03E
Gala Water r. Scotland 17 G3.....55.36N 2.47W
Galdhøpiggen mt. Norway 40 B3.....61.38N 8.19E
Galilee, Sea of l. Israel 53 K3.....32.49N 35.37E
Gallabat Sudan 94 E2.....12.57N 36.06E
Galle Sri Lanka 96 F2.....6.04N 80.09E
Gallego Rise f. Pacific Oc. 109 M5.....2.20S 117.59W
Galley Head Ireland 41 C1.....51.32N 8.57W
Gallinas, Punta pt Colombia 71 J3.....12.27N 71.42W
Gallipoli Italy 50 H4.....40.03N 18.00E
Gallipoli Turkey 56 G5.....40.25N 26.39E
Gällivare Sweden 40 E4.....67.08N 20.40E
Gallup U.S.A. 64 E4.....35.32N 108.45W
Galole Kenya 87 C2.....1.34S 40.01E
Galston Scotland 16 E3.....55.36N 4.23W
Galtat Zemmour Western Sahara 84 C4.....25.08N 12.24W
Galtee Mountains hills Ireland 41 C2.....52.19N 8.16W
Galveston U.S.A. 65 H2.....29.15N 94.54W
Galveston Bay U.S.A. 65 H2.....29.19N 94.46W
Galway Ireland 41 B3.....53.16N 9.03W
Galway d. Ireland 41 B3.....53.22N 9.16W
Galway Bay Ireland 41 B3.....53.12N 9.16W
Gambia r. Gambia 84 C3.....13.28N 16.35W
Gambier, Îles is French Polynesia 109 L4.....22.56S 134.51W
Gamud mt. Ethiopia 87 B4.....4.08N 38.07E
Gäncä Azerbaijan 58 F2.....40.41N 46.22E
Gandadiwata, Bukit mt. Indonesia 104 F3.....2.43S 119.25E
Gander Canada 63 M2.....48.54N 54.17W
Gandhidham India 96 D5.....23.06N 70.08E
Gandhinagar India 96 D5.....23.14N 72.44E
Gandía Spain 48 E3.....38.58N 0.10W
Ganges r. Bangl./India 96 H5.....23.32N 90.08E
Ganges, Mouths of the Bangl./India 96 G5.....21.17N 88.23E
Gannett Peak U.S.A. 64 E5.....43.12N 109.39W
Gansu d. China 100 H6.....40.01N 97.56E
Gantamaa Somalia 87 C3.....2.25N 41.50E
Ganzhou China 101 K3.....25.50N 114.53E
Gao Mali 84 D3.....16.16N 0.02W
Gaoxiong Taiwan 101 M2.....22.39N 120.20E
Gap France 44 G4.....44.34N 6.05E
Gar China 100 E4.....32.33N 80.05E
Gara, Lough l. Ireland 41 C3.....53.57N 8.28W
Garanhuns Brazil 77 M6.....8.52S 36.22W
Garbahaarey Somalia 87 C3.....3.14N 42.16E
Garba Tula Kenya 87 C3.....0.30N 38.31E
Garcia Sola, Embalse de resr Spain 48 C3.....39.14N 5.02W
Gard r. France 44 F3.....43.51N 4.37E
Garda, Lake Italy 50 D6.....45.28N 10.33E
Garden City U.S.A. 64 F4.....37.59N 100.53W
Gardēz Afgh. 95 K6.....33.38N 69.09E
Garelochhead Scotland 16 E4.....56.05N 4.50W
Garforth England 15 F2.....53.48N 1.23W
Gargždai Lithuania 40 E1.....55.43N 21.24E
Garissa Kenya 87 B2.....0.25S 39.40E
Garmisch-Partenkirchen Germany 54 D2.....47.30N 11.06E
Garonne r. France 44 C4.....44.53N 0.32W
Garoowe Somalia 87 C3.....8.23N 48.28E
Garoua Cameroon 84 F2.....9.19N 13.23E
Garron Point Northern Ireland 16 D3.....55.03N 5.57W
Garry r. Scotland 19 E1.....57.04N 4.46W
Garry, Loch l. Scotland 19 E1.....56.48N 4.15W
Garsen Kenya 87 C2.....2.16S 40.06E
Garstang England 14 E2.....53.54N 2.46W
Garvagh Northern Ireland 16 C2.....54.59N 6.41W
Gary U.S.A. 65 I5.....41.35N 87.20W
Gascony, Gulf of France 44 B3.....43.43N 2.00W
Gascoyne r. Australia 110 A4.....24.44S 114.03E
Gashua Nigeria 84 F3.....12.51N 11.04E
Gaspé Canada 63 L2.....48.48N 64.32W
Gaspé, Péninsule de pen. Canada 63 L2.....48.35N 65.31W
Gastonia U.S.A. 65 J4.....35.17N 81.13W
Gata, Cabo de c. Spain 48 D2.....36.43N 2.11E
Gatehouse of Fleet Scotland 16 E2.....54.53N 4.11W
Gateshead England 15 F3.....54.57N 1.36W
Gatineau r. Canada 65 K6.....45.27N 75.42W

Gävle Sweden 40 D3.....60.41N 17.08E
Gaya India 96 G5.....24.48N 85.00E
Gaya Niger 84 E3.....11.54N 3.27E
Gaza Asia 53 J3.....31.22N 34.19E
Gaza town Gaza 94 D6.....31.31N 34.26E
Gaziantep Turkey 57 L3.....37.03N 37.21E
Gdańsk Poland 46 D5.....54.21N 18.39E
Gdańsk, Gulf of Poland/Rus. Fed. 46 D5.....54.32N 19.12E
Gdynia Poland 46 D5.....54.31N 18.33E
Geal Charn hill Scotland 19 F2.....57.12N 3.30W
Gedaref Sudan 85 H3.....14.02N 35.23E
Gediz r. Turkey 57 G4.....38.35N 26.48E
Gedo d. Somalia 87 C3.....2.52N 41.47E
Geel Belgium 42 E4.....51.09N 5.00E
Geelong Australia 110 D3.....38.08S 144.21E
Gejiu China 101 I2.....23.22N 103.09E
Gela Italy 50 F2.....37.04N 14.15E
Gelderland d. Neth. 42 F5.....52.04N 6.08E
Gelibolu Turkey 57 H5.....40.25N 29.09E
Gelincik Dağı mt. Turkey 57 I4.....38.03N 30.42E
Gelligaer Wales 12 D3.....51.40N 3.15W
Gelsenkirchen Germany 54 B4.....51.33N 7.06E
Gemlik Turkey 57 H5.....40.25N 29.09E
Genalê Wenz r. Ethiopia 87 C4.....4.10N 42.05E
General Santos Phil. 105 H5.....6.08N 125.15E
Geneva Switz. 50 B7.....46.13N 6.09E
Geneva, Lake France/Switz. 44 G5.....46.22N 6.16E
Genil r. Spain 48 C2.....37.42N 5.18W
Genk Belgium 42 E3.....50.57N 5.31E
Genoa Italy 50 C6.....44.25N 8.56E
Genoa, Gulf of Italy 50 C6.....44.08N 8.57E
George r. Canada 63 L3.....58.19N 65.55W
Georgetown Guyana 72 D7.....6.49N 58.09W
George Town Malaysia 104 C5.....5.26N 100.17E
Georgia Asia 58 F2.....41.49N 43.59E
Georgia d. U.S.A 65 J3.....32.35N 83.28W
Georgian Bay Canada 63 J2.....45.17N 80.51W
Georgina watercourse Australia 110 C4.....24.54S 139.35E
Georgiyevka Kazakhstan 100 E7.....49.16N 81.34E
Gera Germany 54 E4.....50.53N 12.06E
Geral de Goiás, Serra hills Brazil 77 K5.....11.38S 46.01W
Geraldton Australia 110 A4.....28.46S 114.37E
Gerede Turkey 57 J5.....40.48N 32.12E
Gereshk Afgh. 95 J6.....31.51N 64.37E
Gerlachovský štít mt. Slovakia 54 I3.....49.10N 20.07E
Germany Europe 54 D4.....51.18N 10.22E
Gevgelija Macedonia 56 E5.....41.09N 22.30E
Geyik Dağ mt. Turkey 57 J3.....36.52N 32.11E
Geyve Turkey 57 I5.....40.30N 30.15E
Gezira f. Sudan 82 G6.....14.30N 33.00E
Ghadāmis Libya 84 E5.....30.05N 9.34E
Ghaem Shahr Iran 95 H7.....36.32N 52.39E
Ghaghara r. India 96 F6.....25.42N 84.51E
Ghana Africa 84 D2.....8.23N 0.47W
Ghardaïa Algeria 84 E5.....32.20N 3.49E
Gharyān Libya 52 F3.....32.11N 13.01E
Ghāt Libya 84 F4.....25.10N 10.13E
Ghazaouet Algeria 52 C4.....35.06N 1.51W
Ghaziabad India 96 E6.....28.40N 77.25E
Ghazni Afgh. 95 K6.....33.33N 68.27E
Ghent Belgium 42 C4.....51.03N 3.43E
Gherla Romania 46 F1.....47.03N 23.55E
Giant's Causeway f. Northern Ireland 16 C3.....55.14N 6.31W
Gibraltar Gibraltar 48 C2.....36.08N 5.21W
Gibraltar, Strait of Morocco/Spain 48 B1.....35.50N 6.05W
Gibson Desert Australia 110 B4.....24.46S 123.25E
Gīdolē Ethiopia 87 B4.....5.36N 37.23E
Gien France 44 E5.....47.41N 2.38E
Gießen Germany 54 C4.....50.35N 8.41E
Gifu Japan 106 C3.....35.25N 136.46E
Gigha i. Scotland 16 D3.....55.41N 5.46W
Gijón-Xixón Spain 48 C5.....43.32N 5.39W
Gila r. U.S.A. 64 D3.....32.45N 114.31W
Gilbert Islands Kiribati 108 H6.....1.31N 170.43E
Gilbert Ridge f. Pacific Oc. 108 H5.....0.07S 172.43E
Gilgil Kenya 87 B2.....0.29S 36.21E
Gilgit Jammu and Kashmir 96 D8.....35.54N 74.21E
Gill, Lough l. Ireland 41 C4.....54.15N 8.25W
Gillette U.S.A. 64 E5.....44.18N 105.29W
Gillingham Dor. England 10 C2.....51.02N 2.17W
Gillingham Medway England 11 F2.....51.23N 0.33E
Gilwern Wales 12 D3.....51.49N 3.06W
Gimbala, Jebel mt. Sudan 94 B2.....13.00N 24.20E
Giresun Turkey 57 M5.....40.55N 38.23E
Girona Spain 48 G4.....41.58N 2.49E
Gironde est. France 44 C4.....45.31N 0.59W
Girvan Scotland 16 E3.....55.15N 4.51W
Gisborne New Zealand 111 H3.....38.39S 178.01E
Giurgiu Romania 56 F6.....43.54N 25.57E
Giza Egypt 85 H4.....29.59N 31.12E
Gizhiga Rus. Fed. 59 R4.....62.01N 160.28E
Gjirokastër Albania 56 D5.....40.04N 20.09E
Gjøvik Norway 40 B3.....60.48N 10.41E
Gladstone Australia 110 E4.....23.51S 151.18E
Glan r. Germany 42 G2.....49.47N 7.42E
Glanton England 15 F4.....55.25N 1.53W
Glasgow Scotland 16 E3.....55.52N 4.15W
Glasgow d. Scotland 8 C4.....55.52N 4.15W
Glasgow U.S.A. 64 E6.....48.10N 106.34W
Glass, Loch l. Scotland 19 E2.....57.44N 4.31W
Glastonbury England 10 C2.....51.09N 2.43W
Glenarm Northern Ireland 16 D2.....54.58N 5.56W
Glen Coe f. Scotland 18 D1.....56.41N 5.05W
Glendale U.S.A. 64 D3.....33.32N 112.12W
Glengad Head Ireland 41 D5.....55.20N 7.10W
Glen Garry f. Scotland 18 D2.....57.03N 5.05W
Glenluce Scotland 16 E2.....54.53N 4.49W
Glen More f. Scotland 19 E2.....57.09N 4.44W
Glen Moriston f. Scotland 18 E2.....57.09N 4.52W
Glennallen U.S.A. 62 D4.....62.09N 145.32W
Glenrothes Scotland 17 F4.....56.12N 3.10W
Glen Shee f. Scotland 19 F1.....56.48N 3.29W
Glinton England 11 E3.....52.38N 0.18W
Gliwice Poland 46 H4.....50.18N 18.40E
Głogów Poland 46 G4.....51.40N 16.05E
Glomfjord Norway 40 C4.....66.49N 13.57E
Glorieuses, Îles is Indian Oc. 86 D3.....11.34S 47.18E
Glossop England 15 F2.....53.27N 1.57W
Gloucester England 10 C2.....51.52N 2.14W
Gloucestershire d. England 9 C2.....51.49N 2.11W
Glusburn England 15 F2.....53.56N 2.00W
Glyder Fawr hill Wales 12 C5.....53.06N 4.02W
Glynneath Wales 12 D3.....51.45N 3.37W
Gmünd Austria 54 F3.....48.47N 14.59E
Gniezno Poland 46 G4.....52.32N 17.36E
Goa d. India 96 D4.....15.24N 74.11E
Gobabis Namibia 86 A2.....22.27S 18.58E
Gobi des. China/Mongolia 101 J6.....44.59N 107.19E
Gobowen England 10 B3.....52.54N 3.02W
Goch Germany 42 F4.....51.40N 6.09E
Godalming England 11 E2.....51.11N 0.37W
Godavari r. India 96 F4.....16.57N 81.49E
Godmanchester England 11 E3.....52.19N 0.10W
Goes Neth. 42 C4.....51.30N 3.54E

Goiânia Brazil 77 K4.....16.41S 49.16W
Goiás Brazil 77 J4.....15.54S 50.04W
Goiás d. Brazil 77 J4.....16.19S 50.03W
Gökçeada i. Turkey 56 F5.....40.12N 25.48E
Göksun Turkey 57 L4.....38.02N 36.30E
Gölcük Turkey 57 H5.....40.43N 29.49E
Gołdap Poland 46 F5.....54.18N 22.12E
Gold Coast town Australia 110 E4.....28.03S 153.26E
Golmud China 100 G5.....36.21N 94.50E
Golpāyegān Iran 95 H6.....33.23N 50.13E
Golspie Scotland 19 F2.....57.58N 3.59W
Gómez Palacio Mexico 70 D6.....25.35N 103.32W
Gonaïves Haiti 71 J4.....19.27N 72.42W
Gonbad-e Kavus Iran 95 I7.....37.14N 55.07E
Gonder Ethiopia 85 H3.....12.39N 37.28E
Gondia India 96 F5.....21.28N 80.12E
Gongga Shan mt. China 101 I3.....29.57N 101.55E
Good Hope, Cape of S. Africa 86 A1.....34.22S 18.29E
Goodwick Wales 12 C4.....52.00N 4.59W
Goole England 15 G2.....53.42N 0.53W
Göppingen Germany 54 C3.....48.43N 9.39E
Gora mt. Rus. Fed. 58 H4.....64.59N 60.03E
Góra Kalwaria Poland 46 E4.....51.59N 21.13E
Gorakhpur India 96 F6.....26.45N 83.25E
Gorebridge Scotland 17 F3.....55.50N 3.03W
Gorey Ireland 41 E2.....52.40N 6.18E
Gorgān Iran 95 H7.....36.50N 54.24E
Goris Armenia 95 G7.....39.30N 46.20E
Gorizia Italy 50 E6.....45.57N 13.36E
Gorlice Poland 46 E3.....49.40N 21.10E
Görlitz Germany 54 F4.....51.09N 14.59E
Gornji Vakuf Bos.-Herz. 56 B6.....43.55N 17.36E
Gorno-Altaysk Rus. Fed. 100 F8.....51.59N 85.53E
Gornyak Rus. Fed. 100 E8.....50.59N 81.23E
Gorontalo Indonesia 105 G4.....0.34N 123.01E
Gort Ireland 41 C3.....53.04N 8.49W
Gory mts Rus. Fed. 59 K4.....69.06N 95.00E
Gorzów Wielkopolski Poland 46 B4.....52.44N 15.14E
Gosberton England 11 E3.....52.52N 0.10W
Gosford Australia 110 E3.....33.25S 151.20E
Gosforth Cumb. England 14 D3.....54.25N 3.27W
Gosforth T. and W. England 15 F4.....55.00N 1.37W
Goshogawara Japan 106 D4.....40.48N 140.26E
Gospić Croatia 56 A7.....44.33N 15.23E
Gosport England 10 D1.....50.48N 1.08W
Gostivar Macedonia 56 D5.....41.47N 20.54E
Gotha Germany 54 D4.....50.57N 10.42E
Gothenburg Sweden 40 B2.....57.43N 11.58E
Gotland i. Sweden 40 D2.....57.36N 18.52E
Göttingen Germany 54 C4.....51.32N 9.56E
Gouda Neth. 42 D5.....52.00N 4.42E
Gouin, Réservoir resr Canada 63 K2.....48.39N 74.39W
Goulburn Australia 110 D3.....34.47S 149.45E
Gourdon France 44 D4.....44.45N 1.23E
Governador Valadares Brazil 77 L4.....18.49S 41.57W
Gower pen. Wales 12 C3.....51.36N 4.15W
Gowna, Lough l. Ireland 41 D3.....53.53N 7.35W
Goya Argentina 77 I2.....29.08S 59.15W
Göynük Turkey 57 I5.....40.24N 30.46E
Gozo i. Malta 50 F2.....36.05N 14.15E
Gradaús, Serra dos hills Brazil 77 J6.....8.30S 50.40W
Grafham Water resr England 11 E3.....52.18N 0.19W
Grafton Australia 110 E4.....29.41S 152.57E
Grafton U.S.A. 64 G6.....48.25N 97.25W
Grahamstown S. Africa 86 B1.....33.19S 26.32E
Grain England 11 F2.....51.27N 0.43E
Grampian Mountains Scotland 19 E1.....56.47N 4.37W
Granada Spain 48 D2.....37.11N 3.36W
Gran Canaria i. Canary Islands 48 Y1.....27.47N 15.23W
Gran Chaco f. Argentina/Paraguay 73 C4.....27.08S 62.24W
Grand Bahama i. Bahamas 71 I6.....26.34N 78.29W
Grand Canyon f. U.S.A. 64 D4.....36.03N 112.09W
Grand Canyon town U.S.A. 64 D4.....36.03N 112.09W
Grand Cayman i. Cayman Is 71 H4.....19.23N 81.06W
Grande r. Brazil 77 L5.....11.08S 43.10W
Grande, Bahía b. Argentina 73 C1.....50.40S 68.18W
Grande Prairie Canada 62 G3.....55.11N 118.47W
Grandes, Salinas f. Argentina 73 C3.....30.24S 65.31W
Grand Falls - Windsor Canada 63 M2.....48.53N 55.25W
Grand Forks U.S.A. 64 G6.....47.55N 97.06W
Grand Island U.S.A. 64 G5.....40.56N 98.23W
Grand Junction U.S.A. 64 E4.....39.04N 108.33W
Grândola Portugal 48 A3.....38.11N 8.34W
Grand Rapids town U.S.A. 65 I5.....42.57N 85.40W
Grand Turk Turks and Caicos Is 71 J5.....21.28N 71.08W
Grangemouth Scotland 17 F4.....56.01N 3.43W
Grange-over-Sands England 14 E3.....54.11N 2.55W
Gran Paradiso mt. Italy 50 B6.....45.31N 7.16E
Gran Tarajal Canary Islands 48 Y2.....28.12N 14.01W
Grantham England 10 E3.....52.55N 0.39W
Grantown-on-Spey Scotland 19 F2.....57.20N 3.36W
Grants Pass U.S.A. 64 B5.....42.29N 123.19W
Grasse France 44 G3.....43.40N 6.55E
Grassington England 15 F3.....54.04N 1.59W
Grave, Pointe de pt France 44 C4.....45.35N 1.04W
Gravelines France 11 H1.....50.59N 2.08E
Gravesend England 11 F2.....51.26N 0.22E
Grays England 11 F2.....51.28N 0.20E
Graz Austria 54 F2.....47.04N 15.27E
Great Abaco i. Bahamas 71 I6.....26.08N 77.12W
Great Australian Bight g. Australia 110 B3.....33.06S 129.50E
Great Baddow England 11 F2.....51.43N 0.30E
Great Barrier Reef Australia 110 D5.....11.25S 144.09E
Great Basin U.S.A. 64 C4.....39.25N 116.09W
Great Bear Lake Canada 62 G4.....66.03N 119.59W
Great Belt str. Denmark 54 D6.....55.34N 10.52E
Great Bend U.S.A. 64 G4.....38.23N 98.47W
Great Bernera i. Scotland 18 C3.....58.14N 6.52W
Great Blasket Island Ireland 41 A2.....52.06N 10.32W
Great Clifton England 14 D3.....54.39N 3.29W
Great Cumbrae i. Scotland 16 E3.....55.47N 4.58W
Great Dividing Range mts Australia 110 D3.....37.30S 144.27E
Great Driffield England 15 G3.....54.00N 0.27W
Great Dunmow England 11 F2.....51.52N 0.22E
Greater Antilles is Caribbean Sea 71 H5.....21.05N 81.40W
Greater London d. England 9 E2.....51.30N 0.11W
Greater Manchester d. England 9 D3.....53.31N 2.22W
Great Exuma i. Bahamas 71 I5.....23.35N 75.54W
Great Falls town U.S.A. 64 D6.....47.30N 111.17W
Great Gonerby England 10 E3.....52.56N 0.40W
Greatham England 15 F3.....54.38N 1.14W
Great Harwood England 14 E2.....53.47N 2.24W
Great Inagua i. Bahamas 71 J5.....21.13N 73.26W
Great Karoo f. S. Africa 86 B1.....32.29S 23.21E
Great Linford England 10 E3.....52.04N 0.46W
Great Malvern England 10 C3.....52.07N 2.19W
Great Namaqualand f. Namibia 86 A2.....26.29S 16.25E
Great Nicobar i. India 97 H1.....7.06N 94.08E
Great Ormes Head Wales 12 D5.....53.21N 3.52W
Great Ouse r. England 11 F3.....52.46N 0.23E
Great Plains f. N. America 60 I7.....45.00N 100.00W
Great Rhos hill Wales 12 D4.....52.16N 3.12W
Great Rift Valley f. Africa 82 G4.....7.00S 33.00E
Great St Bernard Pass Italy/Switz. 50 B6.....45.53N 7.11E

Great Salt Lake U.S.A. 64 D5 ............40.58N 112.26W
Great Sand Sea des. Egypt/Libya 53 H2 .....28.55N 24.22E
Great Sandy Desert Australia 110 B4 ......20.35S 123.36E
Great Shelford England 11 F3 ...............52.09N 0.08E
Great Slave Lake Canada 62 G4 ...........61.26N 114.35W
Great Stour r. England 11 G2 ..............51.20N 1.14E
Great Torrington England 13 C2 ...........50.57N 4.08W
Great Victoria Desert Australia 110 B4 ....28.43S 128.38E
Great Whernside hill England 15 F3 ........54.10N 1.59W
Great Yarmouth England 11 G3 ............52.36N 1.44E
Greco, Monte mt. Italy 50 E4 ..............41.48N 13.59E
Gredos, Sierra de mts Spain 48 C4 .........40.08N 5.43W
Greece Europe 56 D4 ......................39.03N 21.56E
Greeley U.S.A. 64 F5 ......................40.25N 104.41W
Green r. U.S.A. 64 E4 .....................38.12N 109.53W
Green Bay town U.S.A. 65 I5 ...............44.30N 88.02W
Greenland i. N. America 63 N5 ...........72.21N 41.01W
Greenlaw Scotland 17 G3 .................55.42N 2.28W
Greenock Scotland 16 E3 .................55.57N 4.46W
Greenore Point Ireland 12 A4 .............52.14N 6.18W
Green River town U.S.A. 64 E5 ...........41.36N 109.29W
Greensboro U.S.A. 65 K4 .................36.04N 79.48W
Greenstone Point Scotland 18 D2 .........57.56N 5.40W
Greenville Liberia 84 D2 .................5.01N 9.02W
Greenville Miss. U.S.A. 65 H3 ............33.22N 91.01W
Greenville S. C. U.S.A. 65 J3 .............34.50N 82.27W
Greenwich England 11 E2 ................51.29N 0.00W
Greifswald Germany 54 E6 ...............54.05N 13.24E
Grená Denmark 40 B2 ....................56.24N 10.54E
Grenada Central America 71 L3 ..........12.03N 61.38W
Grenade France 44 D3 ....................43.46N 1.18E
Grenoble France 44 F4 ...................45.11N 5.44E
Greta r. England 15 E3 ...................54.09N 2.37W
Gretna Scotland 17 F2 ...................54.59N 3.04W
Greven Germany 42 G5 ...................52.06N 7.38E
Grevena Greece 56 D5 ....................40.05N 21.25E
Grevenmacher d. Lux. 42 F2 ..............49.42N 6.21E
Grey Range hills Australia 110 D4 ........28.13S 142.35E
Grimmen Germany 46 A5 ................54.07N 13.02E
Grimsby England 15 G2 ..................53.34N 0.04W
Grímsey i. Iceland 40 Y2 .................66.32N 17.59W
Gris Nez, Cap c. France 11 G1 ...........50.52N 1.36E
Gritley Scotland 19 G3 ...................58.56N 2.45W
Grodzisk Wielkopolski Poland 46 C4 ......52.13N 16.22E
Groningen Neth. 42 F6 ...................53.13N 6.34E
Groningen d. Neth. 42 F6 .................53.16N 6.40E
Groote Eylandt i. Australia 110 C5 ........13.58S 137.09E
Grosser Speikkogel mt. Austria 54 F2 .....46.48N 14.58E
Grosseto Italy 50 D5 .....................42.46N 11.07E
Großglockner mt. Austria 54 E2 ..........47.05N 12.41E
Groundhog r. Canada 63 J2 ...............49.40N 81.56W
Groznyy Rus. Fed. 58 F2 .................43.19N 45.42E
Grudziądz Poland 46 D4 .................53.30N 18.46E
Gruinard Bay Scotland 18 D2 .............57.53N 5.32W
Gryfice Poland 46 B4 .....................53.54N 15.12E
Gryfino Poland 46 B4 .....................53.15N 14.29E
Gryfów Śląski Poland 46 B3 ..............51.01N 15.25E
Guacanayabo, Golfo de b. Cuba 71 I5 .....20.31N 77.38W
Guadajoz r. Spain 48 C2 .................37.51N 4.51W
Guadalajara Mexico 70 D5 ...............20.40N 103.24W
Guadalajara Spain 48 D4 .................40.38N 3.09W
Guadalcanal i. Solomon Is 111 F6 ........9.38S 160.05E
Guadalete r. Spain 48 B2 .................36.32N 6.14W
Guadalope r. Spain 48 E4 ................41.15N 0.02W
Guadalquivir r. Spain 48 B2 ..............36.48N 6.21W
Guadalupe i. Mexico 64 C2 ...............29.09N 118.23W
Guadalupe, Sierra de mts Spain 48 C3 ....39.20N 5.49W
Guadarrama, Sierra de mts Spain 48 C4 ...40.40N 4.10W
Guadeloupe i. Central America 71 L4 .....16.30N 61.29W
Guadiana r. Portugal/Spain 48 B2 ........37.11N 7.24W
Guadix Spain 48 D2 ......................37.18N 3.07W
Guajira, Península de la pen. Colombia 72 B8 ...11.59N 71.45W
Guam i. N. Pacific Oc. 105 K6 ............13.29N 144.58E
Guanajuato Mexico 70 D5 ...............21.01N 101.15W
Guanajuato d. Mexico 70 D5 .............21.16N 100.47W
Guanare Venezuela 71 K2 ................9.03N 69.44W
Guane Cuba 71 H5 ......................22.13N 84.05W
Guangdong d. China 101 K2 ..............23.49N 114.45E
Guangxi Zhuangzu Zizhiqu d. China 101 J2 ...23.52N 108.27E
Guangyuan China 101 J4 .................32.24N 105.51E
Guangzhou China 101 K2 ................23.09N 113.21E
Guanipa r. Venezuela 71 L2 ..............9.53N 62.26W
Guantánamo Cuba 71 I5 .................20.07N 75.13W
Guaporé r. Bolivia/Brazil 76 G5 ...........11.57S 65.04W
Guara, Sierra de mts Spain 48 E5 .........42.15N 0.20W
Guarapuava Brazil 77 J2 .................25.24S 51.29W
Guarda Portugal 48 B4 ...................40.33N 7.16W
Guasave Mexico 70 C6 ...................25.33N 108.30W
Guatemala Central America 70 F3 ........15.43N 90.16W
Guatemala City Guatemala 70 F3 ........14.37N 90.31W
Guaviare r. Colombia 72 C7 ..............4.02N 67.45W
Guayaquil Ecuador 76 E7 ................2.10S 79.56W
Guayaquil, Golfo de g. Ecuador 76 D7 ....3.10S 80.53W
Guaymas Mexico 70 B6 ..................27.57N 110.53W
Guba Ethiopia 85 H3 .....................11.16N 35.17E
Gudbrandsdalen v. Norway 40 B3 ........61.58N 9.20E
Gudong r. China 106 A4 .................42.31N 128.03E
Guéckédou Guinea 84 C2 ................8.33N 10.11W
Guelma Algeria 52 E4 ....................36.27N 7.29E
Guelmine Morocco 84 C4 ................28.59N 10.02W
Guéret France 44 D5 .....................46.10N 1.53E
Guernsey i. Channel Is 13 Y9 ............49.29N 2.36W
Guerrero d. Mexico 70 D4 ...............17.41N 100.48W
Gugē mt. Ethiopia 87 B4 .................6.15N 37.28E
Guiana Highlands mts Guyana/Venezuela 72 C7 ...6.18N 63.41W
Guildford England 11 E2 .................51.14N 0.34W
Guilin China 101 K3 .....................25.17N 110.19E
Guinea Africa 84 C3 .....................10.50N 11.28W
Guinea, Gulf of Africa 84 E2 .............2.31N 4.26E
Guinea-Bissau Africa 84 C3 ..............11.54N 14.45W
Guînes France 42 A3 .....................50.52N 1.52E
Güiria Venezuela 71 L3 ..................10.33N 62.19W
Guisborough England 15 F3 .............54.32N 1.03W
Guise France 42 C2 ......................49.54N 3.38E
Guiyang China 101 J3 ....................26.33N 106.39E
Guizhou d. China 101 J3 .................26.59N 106.45E
Gujarat d. India 96 D5 ...................22.51N 72.32E
Gujranwala Pakistan 96 D7 ..............32.07N 74.13E
Gulbarga India 96 E4 ....................17.20N 76.47E
Gullane Scotland 17 G4 ..................56.02N 2.50W
Gulu Uganda 85 H2 ......................2.44N 32.17E
Gumdag Turkmenistan 95 H7 ...........39.11N 54.29E
Gümüşhane Turkey 57 M5 ...............40.29N 39.28E
Guna India 96 E5 .........................24.39N 77.18E
Guntur India 96 F4 ......................16.19N 80.26E
Gurgueia r. Brazil 77 L6 .................6.51S 43.23W
Guri, Embalse de resr Venezuela 71 L2 ...7.38N 62.47W
Gurupi r. Brazil 77 K7 ...................1.19S 46.11W
Gusau Nigeria 84 E3 .....................12.11N 6.40E
Gusev Rus. Fed. 46 F5 ...................54.36N 22.12E
Gushgy Turkmenistan 95 J7 .............35.18N 62.21E
Güstrow Germany 54 E5 .................53.48N 12.11E
Guwahati India 97 H6 ...................26.09N 91.46E
Guyana S. America 72 D7 ...............5.59N 59.59W

Gwadar Pakistan 96 B6 ..................25.09N 62.23E
Gwalior India 96 E6 ......................26.15N 78.10E
Gwardafuy, Gees c. Somalia 85 J3 .......11.49N 51.16E
Gweebarra Bay Ireland 41 C4 ...........54.53N 8.30W
Gweru Zimbabwe 86 B3 .................19.27S 29.50E
Gwynedd d. Wales 9 D3 .................53.00N 4.02W
Gydan Peninsula Rus. Fed. 58 I5 ........70.08N 77.30E
Gyöngyös Hungary 54 H2 ................47.46N 19.56E
Győr Hungary 54 G2 .....................47.41N 17.38E
Gypsumville Canada 62 I3 ..............51.47N 98.37W
Gyula Hungary 54 H2 ....................46.39N 21.16E
Gyumri Armenia 94 F8 ..................40.47N 43.51E
Gyzylarbat Turkmenistan 58 G1 ........38.59N 56.17E

# H

Haapajärvi Finland 40 F3 ................63.45N 25.20E
Haapsalu Estonia 40 E2 .................58.56N 23.33E
Haarlem Neth. 42 D5 ....................52.22N 4.38E
Habaswein Kenya 87 B3 .................1.01N 39.30E
Habbān Yemen 95 G3 ...................14.20N 47.05E
Hachijō-jima i. Japan 106 C2 ...........33.07N 139.50E
Hachinohe Japan 106 D4 ...............40.32N 141.31E
Ḩadd, Ra's al pt Oman 95 I4 ...........22.30N 59.50E
Haddington Scotland 17 G3 ............55.58N 2.46W
Haderslev Denmark 40 B1 ..............55.15N 9.29E
Had Kourt Morocco 48 C1 ..............34.31N 5.48W
Hadleigh England 11 F3 .................52.03N 0.57E
Ḩaḑramawt f. Yemen 95 G3 ...........15.07N 47.48E
Hadyach Ukraine 55 O4 .................50.22N 33.59E
Haeju N. Korea 101 N5 .................38.02N 125.45E
Hagadera Kenya 87 C3 ..................0.02N 40.22E
Hagar Nish Plateau f. Eritrea 94 E3 .....17.03N 37.58E
Hagåtña Guam 108 F6 ..................13.29N 144.45E
Hagen Germany 54 B4 ...................51.22N 7.28E
Hag's Head Ireland 41 B2 ...............52.56N 9.29W
Hague, Cap de la c. France 13 Z9 .......49.44N 1.55W
Hai Tanzania 87 B2 ......................3.25S 37.06E
Haifa Israel 53 J3 ........................32.50N 34.58E
Haikou China 101 K2 ....................20.01N 110.18E
Ḩā'il Saudi Arabia 94 F5 ................27.33N 41.41E
Hailsham England 11 F1 ................50.52N 0.15E
Hainan i. China 101 J1 ..................19.09N 109.33E
Hainan i. China 108 D7 .................18.51N 110.29E
Hainaut d. Belgium 42 D3 ..............50.29N 4.00E
Haines U.S.A. 62 E3 .....................59.13N 135.25W
Hai Phong Vietnam 104 D8 ............20.50N 106.41E
Haiti Central America 71 J4 ............19.19N 73.30W
Haiya Sudan 85 H3 ......................18.20N 36.23E
Hakodate Japan 106 D4 ................41.47N 140.44E
Halabja Iraq 95 G7 ......................35.11N 45.56E
Ḩalāniyāt, Juzur al is Oman 95 I3 ......17.30N 56.11E
Halden Norway 40 B2 ...................59.07N 11.25E
Halesowen England 10 C3 ..............52.27N 2.03W
Halesworth England 11 G3 .............52.21N 1.30E
Halifax Canada 63 L2 ....................44.39N 63.36W
Halifax England 15 F2 ..................53.44N 1.51W
Halkirk Scotland 19 F3 .................58.31N 3.29W
Halladale r. Scotland 19 F3 .............58.33N 3.54W
Hall Beach town Canada 63 J4 .........68.42N 81.17W
Halle Belgium 42 D3 ....................50.44N 4.14E
Halle Germany 54 D4 ...................51.29N 11.59E
Hall Islands Micronesia 108 G6 ........8.55N 151.52E
Halls Creek town Australia 110 B5 .....18.15S 127.40E
Halmahera i. Indonesia 105 H4 ........1.06N 128.32E
Halmstad Sweden 40 C2 ...............56.40N 12.52E
Halstead England 11 F2 ................51.57N 0.39E
Halton d. England 9 D3 .................53.20N 2.43W
Haltwhistle England 15 E3 .............54.58N 2.27W
Ham France 42 C2 .......................49.45N 3.04E
Hamadān Iran 95 G6 ....................34.46N 48.30E
Ḩamāh Syria 94 E7 ......................35.08N 36.45E
Hamamatsu Japan 106 C2 .............34.42N 137.44E
Hamar Norway 40 B3 ...................60.48N 11.05E
Hambleton Hills England 15 F3 ........54.19N 1.14W
Hamburg Germany 54 C5 ..............53.34N 9.59E
Hämeenlinna Finland 40 F3 ............60.59N 24.27E
Hamersley Range mts Australia 110 A4 ...22.11S 116.31E
Hamhŭng N. Korea 101 N5 ............39.55N 127.33E
Hami China 100 G6 .....................42.47N 93.32E
Hamilton Bermuda 71 L7 ..............32.18N 64.46W
Hamilton Canada 63 K2 ................43.15N 79.51W
Hamilton New Zealand 111 G3 ........37.48S 175.16E
Hamilton Scotland 16 E3 ..............55.47N 4.03W
Hamīm, Wādī al watercourse Libya 53 H3 ...30.04N 21.35E
Hamina Finland 40 F3 ..................60.34N 27.12E
Hammamet, Golfe de g. Tunisia 52 F4 ...36.09N 10.50E
Hammerdal Sweden 40 C3 .............63.35N 15.21E
Hammerfest Norway 40 E5 .............70.40N 23.40E
Hampshire d. England 9 E2 .............51.10N 1.13W
Hampshire Downs hills England 10 D2 ...51.20N 1.35W
Ḩamrā', Al Ḩamādah al f. Libya 52 F2 ...29.40N 11.48E
Hamstreet England 11 F2 ...............51.04N 0.52E
Hanamaki Japan 106 D3 ................39.23N 141.07E
Hanang mt. Tanzania 87 A1 ...........4.26S 35.23E
Hancock U.S.A. 65 I6 ...................47.08N 88.36W
Handa Island Scotland 18 D3 ..........58.23N 5.13W
Handan China 101 K5 ..................36.35N 114.32E
Handeni Tanzania 87 B1 ...............5.26S 38.00E
Hangzhou China 101 M4 ...............30.15N 120.10E
Hanna Canada 64 D7 ...................51.38N 111.56W
Hannover Germany 54 C5 ..............52.23N 9.44E
Hanöbukten b. Sweden 54 F6 ..........55.48N 14.37E
Ha Nôi Vietnam 104 D8 ................21.01N 105.51E
Hantsavichy Belarus 55 L5 .............52.46N 26.27E
Hanzhong China 101 J4 .................33.04N 107.03E
Happy Valley-Goose Bay town Canada 63 L3 ...53.19N 60.07W
Harare Zimbabwe 86 C3 ...............17.49S 31.04E
Ḩarāsīs, Jiddat al des. Oman 95 I3 .....19.45N 56.11E
Harbin China 101 N7 ...................45.40N 126.37E
Harderwijk Neth. 42 E5 ................52.21N 5.38E
Haren Germany 42 G5 ..................52.48N 7.15E
Hargele Ethiopia 87 C4 .................5.11N 42.10E
Hargeysa Somalia 87 C3 ...............9.32N 44.05E
Har Hu l. China 100 H5 ................38.18N 97.23E
Har Rūd r. Afgh./Iran 95 J7 ...........36.50N 60.58E
Harlech Wales 12 C4 ....................52.52N 4.06W
Harleston England 11 G3 ..............52.24N 1.18E
Harlingen Neth. 42 E6 ..................53.10N 5.25E
Harlow England 11 F2 ..................51.46N 0.05E
Harney Basin f. U.S.A. 64 C5 ..........43.23N 119.55W
Härnösand Sweden 40 D3 .............62.38N 17.56E
Harpenden England 11 E2 .............51.49N 0.21W
Harray, Loch of l. Scotland 19 F4 .....58.57N 3.15W
Harricanaw r. Canada 63 K3 ..........50.58N 79.33W
Harris, Sound of str. Scotland 18 B2 ...57.44N 7.03W
Harrisburg U.S.A. 65 K5 ...............40.17N 76.54W
Harrison, Cape Canada 63 M3 .........54.56N 57.42W
Harrogate England 15 F2 ..............53.59N 1.32W

Hârşova Romania 57 G7 ................44.41N 27.57E
Harstad Norway 40 D5 .................68.47N 16.32E
Harteigen mt. Norway 40 A3 ..........60.12N 7.05E
Harter Fell hill England 14 E3 ..........54.29N 2.52E
Hart Fell hill Scotland 17 F3 ...........55.24N 3.24W
Hartford U.S.A. 65 L5 ..................41.46N 72.42W
Hartland England 13 C2 ...............50.59N 4.29W
Hartland Point England 13 C3 .........51.01N 4.33W
Hartlepool England 15 F3 .............54.41N 1.13W
Hartlepool d. England 9 E4 ...........54.40N 1.15W
Har Us Nuur l. Mongolia 100 G7 ......47.53N 92.19E
Harwich England 11 G2 ................51.56N 1.16E
Haryana d. India 96 E6 .................29.11N 76.12E
Haslemere England 10 E2 ..............51.05N 0.43W
Hasselt Belgium 42 E3 .................50.56N 5.20E
Hassi Messaoud Algeria 84 E5 ........31.41N 6.10E
Hässleholm Sweden 40 C2 ............56.10N 13.46E
Hastings England 11 F1 ................50.51N 0.35E
Hatfield England 15 G2 ................53.35N 0.59W
Hatteras, Cape U.S.A. 65 K4 ..........35.14N 75.34W
Hattiesburg U.S.A. 65 I3 ...............31.23N 89.19W
Hat Yai Thailand 104 C5 ...............7.01N 100.26E
Haud f. Ethiopia 85 I2 .................8.37N 44.15E
Haugesund Norway 40 A2 .............59.24N 5.18E
Haukivesi l. Finland 40 G3 ............62.06N 28.28E
Haut Atlas mts Morocco 84 D5 ........30.51N 8.03W
Haut-Folin hill France 44 F5 ..........46.59N 4.01E
Hauts Plateaux f. Algeria 52 C3 .......33.42N 0.42W
Havana Cuba 71 H5 ....................23.07N 82.22W
Havant England 11 E1 .................50.52N 0.59W
Haverfordwest Wales 12 C3 ...........51.48N 4.58W
Haverhill England 11 F3 ...............52.05N 0.26E
Havlíčkův Brod Czech Rep. 46 B2 .....49.36N 15.34E
Havre U.S.A. 64 E6 ......................48.32N 109.41W
Havre-St-Pierre Canada 63 L3 ........50.14N 63.28W
Hawaii i. U.S.A. 109 J7 .................20.02N 155.17W
Hawaiian Islands N. Pacific Oc. 108 I7 ...28.26N 174.25W
Hawaiian Ridge f. N. Pacific Oc. 108 I7 ...26.19N 178.56W
Hawarden Wales 12 D5 ................53.11N 3.02W
Hawes England 15 E3 ...................54.18N 2.12W
Haweswater Reservoir England 14 E3 ...54.30N 2.48W
Hawick Scotland 17 G3 ................55.26N 2.47W
Hawke Bay New Zealand 111 G3 ......39.24S 177.23E
Hawkhurst England 11 F2 .............51.03N 0.31E
Haxby England 15 F3 ...................54.01N 1.04W
Hay Australia 110 D3 ...................34.31S 144.48E
Hay r. Canada 62 G4 ...................60.48N 115.47W
Haydarābād Iran 94 G7 ................37.04N 45.05E
Haydon Bridge England 15 E3 ........54.59N 2.15W
Hayle England 13 B2 ...................50.11N 5.25W
Haymā' Oman 95 I3 ....................19.54N 56.13E
Hay-on-Wye Wales 12 D4 .............52.04N 3.08W
Hay River town Canada 62 G4 ........60.51N 115.40W
Hayshah, Sabkhat al f. Libya 53 G3 ...31.55N 15.19E
Haywards Heath England 11 E1 .......50.59N 0.06W
Hazārajat f. Afgh. 95 K6 ...............32.29N 65.07E
Hazebrouck France 42 B3 .............50.43N 2.32E
Heacham England 11 F3 ...............52.54N 0.30E
Headcorn England 11 F2 ...............51.10N 0.38E
Heanor England 15 F2 .................53.01N 1.21W
Hearst Canada 65 J6 ...................49.41N 83.41W
Heathfield England 11 F1 ..............50.58N 0.16E
Hebei d. China 101 L5 .................38.33N 115.69E
Hebron Israel 53 J3 .....................31.53N 34.49E
Hecate Strait Canada 62 E3 ...........52.36N 130.27W
Hechi China 101 J2 .....................24.38N 108.04E
Heckington England 11 E3 ............52.59N 0.18W
Hede Sweden 40 C3 ....................62.25N 13.32E
Heerenveen Neth. 42 E5 ...............52.58N 5.56E
Heerlen Neth. 42 E3 ...................50.53N 5.59E
Hefei China 101 L4 .....................31.51N 117.19E
Hegang China 101 O7 ..................47.13N 130.13E
Heidelberg Germany 54 C3 ...........49.24N 8.41E
Heighington England 15 G2 ..........53.37N 0.16W
Heilbronn Germany 54 C3 .............49.08N 9.12E
Heilen, Loch l. Scotland 19 F3 ........58.36N 3.17W
Heilongjiang d. China 101 N7 ........46.55N 128.30E
Heilong Jiang r. China 101 O7 ........48.25N 134.59E
Heinola Finland 40 F3 ..................61.12N 26.02E
Hekla vol. Iceland 40 Y1 ...............63.59N 19.41W
Helena U.S.A. 64 D6 ...................46.36N 112.01W
Helensburgh Scotland 16 E4 ..........56.00N 4.44W
Helgoländer Bucht g. Germany 54 C6 ...54.10N 8.14E
Hellín Spain 48 E3 .....................38.31N 1.41W
Helmand r. Afgh. 95 J6 ................31.13N 61.35E
Helmond Neth. 42 E4 ..................51.28N 5.40E
Helmsdale Scotland 19 F3 .............58.07N 3.39W
Helmsdale r. Scotland 19 F3 ..........58.07N 3.38W
Helmsley England 15 F3 ...............54.15N 1.04W
Helong China 106 B4 ..................42.33N 128.59E
Helsingborg Sweden 40 C2 ...........56.03N 12.42E
Helsingør Denmark 54 E7 ............56.02N 12.36E
Helsinki Finland 40 F3 .................60.10N 24.57E
Helston England 13 B2 ................50.06N 5.16W
Helvellyn hill England 14 D3 .........54.32N 3.01W
Hemel Hempstead England 11 E2 ....51.45N 0.27W
Henan d. China 101 K4 ................33.59N 112.54E
Henares r. Spain 48 D4 ................40.25N 3.29W
Henderson Island S. Pacific Oc. 109 L4 ...24.20S 128.20W
Hendon England 11 E2 .................51.35N 0.13W
Henfield England 11 E1 ................50.56N 0.16W
Hengelo Neth. 42 F5 ...................52.16N 6.48E
Hengoed Wales 12 D3 .................51.39N 3.14W
Hengyang China 101 K3 ...............26.53N 112.32E
Heniches'k Ukraine 53 J6 .............46.10N 34.48E
Henley-on-Thames England 10 E2 ....51.32N 0.54W
Hennef Germany 42 G3 ...............50.47N 7.18E
Henrietta Maria, Cape Canada 63 J3 ...55.21N 82.13W
Henzada Myanmar 97 I4 ..............17.36N 95.26E
Herāt Afgh. 95 J6 .......................34.22N 62.11E
Hereford England 10 C3 ...............52.03N 2.43W
Herefordshire d. England 9 D3 .......52.07N 2.40W
Herm i. Channel Is 13 Y9 ...............49.28N 2.26W
Herma Ness hd Scotland 19 I5 ........60.51N 0.54W
Hermosillo Mexico 70 B6 .............29.04N 110.58W
Herne Germany 42 G4 .................51.32N 7.13E
Herne Bay town England 11 G2 ......51.22N 1.08E
Herning Denmark 40 B2 ..............56.08N 8.58E
Hertford England 11 E2 ...............51.48N 0.05W
Hertfordshire d. England 9 F2 ........51.55N 0.09E
Hesdin France 11 H1 ..................50.22N 2.03E
Heswall England 14 D2 ................53.20N 3.06W
Hetton England 15 E3 .................54.01N 2.07W
Hexham England 15 E3 ................54.58N 2.06W
Heysham England 14 E3 ...............54.02N 2.54W
Heywood England 15 E2 ..............53.35N 2.13W
Heze China 101 L5 .....................35.17N 115.32E
Hidaka-sanmyaku mts Japan 106 D4 ...42.49N 142.38E
Hidalgo d. Mexico 70 E5 ..............20.35N 99.07W
Hidalgo del Parral Mexico 70 C6 .....26.56N 105.41W
Higashi-suidō str. Japan 106 A2 .....33.55N 129.23E
Higham Ferrers England 11 E3 .......52.18N 0.36W
Highbridge England 10 C2 ............51.13N 2.59W

Highclere England 10 D2 ..............51.20N 1.22W
Highland d. Scotland 8 C5 ............57.38N 4.59W
High Peak hills England 15 F2 ........53.23N 1.54W
High Seat hill England 15 E3 ..........54.24N 2.18W
Highworth England 10 D2 ............51.38N 1.43W
High Wycombe England 10 E2 .......51.38N 0.45W
Hiiumaa i. Estonia 40 E2 ...............58.50N 22.24E
Hijaz f. Saudi Arabia 94 E5 ...........26.08N 37.01E
Hilāl, Ra's al pt Libya 53 H3 ..........32.54N 22.09E
Hildesheim Germany 54 C5 ...........52.09N 9.57E
Hillah Iraq 94 F6 .......................32.27N 44.24E
Hillerød Denmark 40 C1 ..............55.56N 12.18E
Hillside Scotland 17 G4 ...............56.45N 2.29W
Hillswick Scotland 19 H5 .............60.29N 1.29W
Hilpsford Point England 14 D3 .......54.02N 3.12W
Hilversum Neth. 42 E5 .................52.13N 5.11E
Himachal Pradesh d. India 96 E7 .....31.59N 77.23E
Himalaya mts Asia 96 F6 ..............33.06N 76.46E
Hinckley England 10 D3 ...............52.33N 1.23W
Hinderwell England 15 G3 ............54.32N 0.46W
Hindhead England 10 E2 ..............51.07N 0.44W
Hindley England 14 E2 .................53.32N 2.35W
Hindu Kush mts Afgh./Pakistan 95 K6 ...34.58N 67.52E
Hinnøya i. Norway 40 C5 ..............68.37N 15.58E
Hiraman watercourse Kenya 87 B2 ...1.08S 39.54E
Hirosaki Japan 106 D4 .................40.36N 140.28E
Hiroshima Japan 106 B2 ...............34.22N 132.27E
Hirson France 42 D2 ...................49.55N 4.05E
Hirwaun Wales 12 D3 .................51.44N 3.31W
Hispaniola i. Caribbean Sea 71 J5 ....20.18N 72.57W
Hitachi Japan 106 D3 ..................36.35N 140.39E
Hitchin England 11 E2 .................51.57N 0.17W
Hitra i. Norway 40 B3 ..................63.31N 8.49E
Hiva Oa i. French Polynesia 109 K5 ...9.47S 138.57W
Hjälmaren l. Sweden 40 C2 ...........59.14N 15.51E
Hjørring Denmark 40 B2 ..............57.28N 10.01E
Hlybokaye Belarus 55 L6 ..............55.08N 27.40E
Hobart Australia 110 D2 ...............42.52S 147.19E
Hobro Denmark 40 B2 .................56.38N 9.48E
Ho Chi Minh City Vietnam 104 D6 ...10.45N 106.42E
Hochschwab mt. Austria 54 F2 .......47.38N 15.09E
Hoddesdon England 11 E2 ............51.46N 0.01W
Hodeidah Yemen 94 F2 ................14.50N 42.54E
Hódmezővásárhely Hungary 54 H2 ...46.25N 20.21E
Hodna, Chott el f. Algeria 52 D4 .....35.27N 4.55E
Hodnet England 10 C3 .................52.51N 2.35W
Hoek van Holland Neth. 42 D4 .......51.58N 4.08E
Hof Germany 54 D4 ....................50.19N 11.55E
Höfn Iceland 40 Z2 .....................64.16N 15.13W
Hofsjökull ice cap Iceland 40 Y2 .....64.49N 18.52W
Hoggar f. Algeria 84 E4 ................23.10N 4.23E
Hohhot China 101 K6 ..................40.43N 111.44E
Hokkaidō i. Japan 106 D4 .............43.33N 143.27E
Holbæk Denmark 40 B1 ...............55.43N 11.44E
Holbeach England 11 F3 ...............52.48N 0.01E
Holbeach Marsh England 11 F3 ......52.51N 0.02E
Holderness pen. England 15 G2 ......53.52N 0.18W
Holguín Cuba 71 I5 ....................20.54N 76.14W
Hollabrunn Austria 54 G3 .............48.34N 16.05E
Holland Fen f. England 11 E3 .........53.00N 0.13W
Hollesley Bay England 11 G3 .........52.02N 1.28E
Hollington England 11 F1 .............50.53N 0.33E
Hollingworth England 15 F2 ..........53.28N 1.59W
Holme-on-Spalding-Moor England 15 G2 ...53.50N 0.47W
Holmfirth England 15 F2 ..............53.34N 1.47W
Holstebro Denmark 40 B2 .............56.21N 8.37E
Holsworthy England 13 C2 ...........50.49N 4.21W
Holt England 11 G3 ....................52.55N 1.05E
Holyhead Wales 12 C5 .................53.19N 4.38W
Holyhead Bay Wales 12 C5 ...........53.22N 4.40W
Holy Island England 17 G4 ...........55.41N 1.47W
Holy Island Wales 12 C5 ..............53.15N 4.41W
Holywell Wales 12 D5 .................53.17N 3.13W
Homa Bay town Kenya 87 A2 .........0.32S 34.27E
Homāyunshahr Iran 95 H6 ............32.59N 50.23E
Homburg Germany 42 G2 ............49.19N 7.20E
Home Bay Canada 63 L4 ..............68.52N 67.27W
Homs Syria 94 E7 ......................34.44N 36.44E
Homyel' Belarus 55 N5 ................52.25N 31.01E
Honduras Central America 70 G3 ....14.47N 86.43W
Honduras, Gulf of Belize/Honduras 60 K3 ...16.20N 87.30W
Hønefoss Norway 40 B3 ...............60.10N 10.14E
Hong Kong China 101 K2 .............22.16N 114.11E
Hong Kong d. China 101 K2 ..........22.21N 114.19E
Honiara Solomon Is 111 E6 ...........9.26S 159.57E
Honiton England 13 D2 ...............50.48N 3.11W
Honley England 15 F2 .................53.36N 1.48W
Honolulu U.S.A. 109 J7 ...............21.19N 157.52W
Honshū i. Japan 106 B3 ...............35.42N 133.20E
Hood, Mount vol. U.S.A. 64 B6 .......45.23N 121.42W
Hood Point Australia 110 A3 .........34.19S 119.33E
Hoogeveen Neth. 42 F5 ...............52.43N 6.30E
Hook England 10 E2 ...................51.17N 0.58W
Hook Head Ireland 41 E2 .............52.07N 6.56W
Hoorn Neth. 42 E5 .....................52.39N 5.04E
Hope, Loch l. Scotland 19 E3 .........58.27N 4.40W
Hope, Point U.S.A. 62 B4 .............68.21N 166.49W
Hopedale Canada 63 L3 ...............55.27N 60.00W
Hörby Sweden 54 E6 ...................55.51N 13.40E
Horizon Deep f. S. Pacific Oc. 108 I4 ...23.23S 174.48W
Horley England 11 E2 ..................51.10N 0.10W
Hormuz, Strait of Iran/Oman 95 I5 ...26.35N 56.57E
Horn Austria 46 B2 .....................48.40N 15.40E
Horn c. Iceland 40 X2 ..................66.28N 22.29W
Horn, Cape Chile 73 C1 ...............56.04S 67.17W
Hornavan l. Sweden 40 D4 ...........66.11N 17.44E
Horncastle England 15 G2 ............53.12N 0.07W
Hornepayne Canada 65 J6 ............49.13N 84.47W
Hornsea England 15 G2 ...............53.55N 0.10W
Horodnya Ukraine 55 N4 ..............51.53N 31.36E
Horodok Ukraine 55 J3 ................49.47N 23.39E
Horokhiv Ukraine 46 G3 ..............50.30N 24.46E
Horrabridge England 13 C2 ..........50.30N 4.05W
Horsens Denmark 40 B1 ..............55.52N 9.51E
Horsham Australia 110 D3 ...........36.43S 142.13E
Horsham England 11 E2 ..............51.04N 0.19W
Horten Norway 40 B2 .................59.25N 10.28E
Horwich England 14 E2 ...............53.36N 2.33W
Hotan China 100 E5 ...................37.07N 80.02E
Houffalize Belgium 42 E3 .............50.08N 5.48E
Houghton le Spring England 15 F3 ...54.50N 1.28W
Houghton Regis England 11 E2 ......51.54N 0.31W
Hourn, Loch inlet Scotland 18 D2 ....57.08N 5.42W
Houston U.S.A. 65 G2 .................29.43N 95.19W
Hovd Mongolia 100 G7 ...............47.59N 91.41E
Hove England 11 E1 ...................50.50N 0.10W
Hoveton England 11 G3 ...............52.43N 1.25E
Hövsgöl Nuur l. Mongolia 101 I8 ....50.59N 100.42E
Howden England 15 G2 ...............53.45N 0.52W
Howland Island N. Pacific Oc. 108 I6 ...0.48N 176.38W
Hoy i. Scotland 19 F3 ..................58.49N 3.17W
Høyanger Norway 40 A3 ..............61.13N 6.04E
Hoyerswerda Germany 54 F4 ........51.27N 14.16E
Höytiäinen l. Finland 40 G3 ..........62.46N 29.43E

Hradec Králové Czech Rep. 54 F4 ...... 50.13N 15.50E
Hrebinka Ukraine 55 O4 ...... 50.06N 32.26E
Hrodna Belarus 55 J5 ...... 53.41N 23.49E
Huacho Peru 76 E5 ...... 11.09S 77.35W
Huaibei China 101 L4 ...... 33.57N 116.51E
Huainan China 101 L4 ...... 32.36N 117.02E
Huallaga r. Peru 76 E6 ...... 5.06S 75.40W
Huambo Angola 86 A3 ...... 12.46S 15.64E
Huancayo Peru 76 E5 ...... 12.03S 75.11W
Huang He r. China 101 L5 ...... 37.46N 118.57E
Huangshi China 101 L4 ...... 30.10N 115.08E
Huánuco Peru 76 E6 ...... 9.57S 76.14W
Huarmey Peru 76 E5 ...... 10.03S 78.11W
Huascarán, Nevado de mt. Peru 76 E6 ...... 9.09S 77.36W
Hubei d. China 101 K4 ...... 31.09N 113.06E
Hubli India 96 E4 ...... 15.18N 75.15E
Hucknall England 15 F2 ...... 53.02N 1.12W
Huddersfield England 15 F2 ...... 53.39N 1.47W
Hudiksvall Sweden 40 D3 ...... 61.43N 17.06E
Hudson r. U.S.A. 65 L5 ...... 40.54N 73.56W
Hudson Bay sea Canada 63 J3 ...... 59.05N 86.00W
Hudson Strait Canada 63 K4 ...... 63.31N 74.25W
Huê Vietnam 104 D7 ...... 16.26N 107.33E
Huelva Spain 48 B2 ...... 37.16N 6.55W
Huércal-Overa Spain 48 E2 ...... 37.23N 1.55W
Huesca Spain 48 E5 ...... 42.09N 0.25W
Huila, Nevado de vol. Colombia 76 E8 ...... 2.59N 75.57W
Huizhou China 101 K2 ...... 23.05N 114.25E
Hulin China 106 B5 ...... 45.42N 132.52E
Hull Canada 65 K6 ...... 45.27N 75.45W
Hulun Buir China 101 L7 ...... 49.04N 119.46E
Hulun Nur l. China 101 L7 ...... 48.32N 117.11E
Hulwan Egypt 53 J2 ...... 29.55N 31.18E
Humaitá Brazil 76 H6 ...... 7.33S 63.02W
Humber, Mouth of the England 15 H2 ...... 53.30N 0.06E
Humboldt r. U.S.A. 64 C5 ...... 40.04N 118.36W
Humenné Slovakia 46 E2 ...... 48.56N 21.54E
Humphreys Peak U.S.A. 64 D4 ...... 35.21N 111.40W
Húnaflói b. Iceland 40 X2 ...... 65.46N 20.50W
Hunan d. China 101 K3 ...... 27.26N 111.22E
Hunchun China 106 B4 ...... 42.52N 130.21E
Hunchun r. China 106 B4 ...... 42.18N 130.17E
Hungarian Plain f. Hungary 34 F2 ...... 46.30N 19.00E
Hungary Europe 54 H2 ...... 47.01N 18.59E
Hungerford England 10 D2 ...... 51.25N 1.31W
Hunish, Rubha pt Scotland 18 C2 ...... 57.42N 6.24W
Hunmanby England 15 G2 ...... 54.11N 0.19W
Hunsrück hills Germany 54 B3 ...... 49.47N 7.00E
Hunstanton England 11 F3 ...... 52.56N 0.30E
Huntingdon England 11 F3 ...... 52.20N 0.11W
Huntington U.S.A. 65 J4 ...... 38.25N 82.18W
Huntly Scotland 19 G2 ...... 57.27N 2.47W
Huntsville Ala. U.S.A. 65 I3 ...... 34.46N 86.34W
Huntsville Tex. U.S.A. 65 G3 ...... 30.42N 95.34W
Huri Hills Kenya 87 B3 ...... 4.04N 37.40E
Huron U.S.A. 64 G5 ...... 44.23N 98.13W
Huron, Lake Canada/U.S.A. 63 J2 ...... 44.39N 82.23W
Hurstpierpoint England 11 E1 ...... 50.56N 0.11W
Husum Germany 54 C6 ...... 54.29N 9.04E
Hutton Rudby England 15 F3 ...... 54.26N 1.17W
Huzhou China 101 M4 ...... 30.50N 120.08E
Hvannadalshnúkur vol. Iceland 40 Y2 ...... 64.01N 16.41W
Hvar i. Croatia 56 B6 ...... 43.08N 16.33E
Hyargas Nuur l. Mongolia 100 G7 ...... 49.17N 93.18E
Hyderabad India 96 E4 ...... 17.21N 78.25E
Hyderabad Pakistan 96 C6 ...... 25.21N 68.23E
Hyères France 44 G3 ...... 43.07N 6.08E
Hyesan N. Korea 106 A4 ...... 41.24N 128.11E
Hyrynsalmi Finland 40 G4 ...... 64.40N 28.29E
Hythe Hants. England 10 D1 ...... 50.52N 1.24W
Hythe Kent England 11 G2 ...... 51.04N 1.05E
Hyvinkää Finland 40 F3 ...... 60.38N 24.51E

I
Ialomiţa r. Romania 56 G7 ...... 44.43N 27.51E
Iar Connaught f. Ireland 41 B3 ...... 53.21N 9.19W
Iaşi Romania 53 I6 ...... 47.10N 27.35E
Ibadan Nigeria 84 E2 ...... 7.24N 3.55E
Ibagué Colombia 72 B7 ...... 4.24N 75.13W
Ibarra Ecuador 76 E8 ...... 0.23N 78.04W
Ibb Yemen 94 F2 ...... 14.03N 44.09E
Ibiapaba, Serra da hills Brazil 77 L7 ...... 3.38S 41.10W
Ibiza Spain 48 F3 ...... 38.54N 1.27E
Ibiza i. Spain 48 F3 ...... 39.10N 1.39E
Ibrā' Oman 95 I4 ...... 22.44N 58.33E
Ibstock England 10 D3 ...... 52.42N 1.24W
Ica Peru 76 E5 ...... 14.04S 75.43W
Iceland Europe 40 X2 ...... 64.42N 18.19W
Ichinoseki Japan 106 D3 ...... 38.55N 141.07E
Icklesham England 11 F1 ...... 50.55N 0.40E
Idaho d. U.S.A. 64 D5 ...... 44.08N 114.08W
Idaho Falls town U.S.A. 64 D5 ...... 43.32N 112.01W
Idar-Oberstein Germany 42 G2 ...... 49.42N 7.18E
Idfū Egypt 53 J1 ...... 24.55N 32.49E
Idi mt. Greece 56 F2 ...... 35.13N 24.47E
Idlib Syria 57 J7 ...... 35.56N 36.38E
Ieper Belgium 42 B3 ...... 50.51N 2.53E
Iešjávri l. Norway 40 F5 ...... 69.39N 24.28E
Igan Malaysia 104 E4 ...... 2.51N 111.44E
Iganga Uganda 87 A3 ...... 0.37N 33.28E
Iggesund Sweden 40 D3 ...... 61.39N 17.05E
Iglesias Italy 50 C3 ...... 39.19N 8.32E
Igneada Burnu pt Turkey 57 H5 ...... 41.53N 28.03E
Igoumenitsa Greece 56 D4 ...... 39.30N 20.17E
Iguaçu r. Brazil 77 J2 ...... 25.36S 54.35W
Iguaçu Falls Argentina/Brazil 77 J2 ...... 25.38S 54.26W
Iguatu Brazil 77 M6 ...... 6.22S 39.17W
Iisalmi Finland 40 F3 ...... 63.34N 27.11E
Ijmuiden Neth. 42 D5 ...... 52.27N 4.37E
IJssel r. Neth. 42 E5 ...... 52.35N 5.50E
IJsselmeer l. Neth. 42 E5 ...... 52.48N 5.22E
IJzer r. Belgium 11 H2 ...... 51.09N 2.44E
Ikaahuk Canada 62 F5 ...... 71.55N 125.05W
Ikaria i. Greece 56 G2 ...... 37.39N 26.13E
Iki i. Japan 106 A2 ...... 33.45N 129.39E
Ilagan Phil. 105 G7 ...... 17.06N 121.53E
Ilaisamis Kenya 87 B3 ...... 1.36N 37.47E
Ilchester England 10 C2 ...... 51.00N 2.41W
Ilebo Dem. Rep. Congo 86 B4 ...... 4.21S 20.36E
Ile-de-France d. France 42 B1 ...... 48.39N 2.36E
Ilemi Triangle Africa 87 A4 ...... 4.53N 35.15E
Ileret Kenya 87 B4 ...... 4.18N 36.14E
Ilford England 11 F2 ...... 51.32N 0.05E
Ilfracombe England 13 C3 ...... 51.12N 4.07W
Ilhéus Brazil 77 L5 ...... 14.46S 39.02W
Iligan Phil. 105 G5 ...... 8.13N 124.15E
Ilkeston England 10 D3 ...... 52.58N 1.18W
Ilkley England 15 F2 ...... 53.56N 1.49W
Illinois d. U.S.A. 65 I4 ...... 39.52N 89.07W
Illinois r. U.S.A. 65 H4 ...... 38.56N 90.30W

Illizi Algeria 84 E4 ...... 26.29N 8.30E
Ilminster England 10 C1 ...... 50.56N 2.54W
Iloilo Phil. 105 G6 ...... 10.41N 122.32E
Ilorin Nigeria 84 E2 ...... 8.30N 4.34E
Iman r. Rus. Fed. 106 B5 ...... 45.57N 133.45E
Imatra Finland 40 G3 ...... 61.11N 28.47E
Immingham England 15 G2 ...... 53.37N 0.13W
Imola Italy 50 D6 ...... 44.21N 11.42E
Imperatriz Brazil 77 K6 ...... 5.33S 47.26W
Imphal India 97 H5 ...... 24.46N 93.56E
İmroz Turkey 56 F5 ...... 40.10N 25.55E
Inambari r. Peru 76 G5 ...... 12.44S 69.47W
Inarijärvi l. Finland 40 F5 ...... 68.57N 27.37E
Inchard, Loch b. Scotland 18 D3 ...... 58.27N 5.04W
Inch'ini Terara mt. Ethiopia 87 B4 ...... 4.35N 37.07E
Inchkeith i. Scotland 17 F4 ...... 56.02N 3.08W
Inch'ŏn S. Korea 101 N5 ...... 37.28N 126.39E
Indalsälven r. Sweden 40 D3 ...... 62.32N 17.24E
Independence U.S.A. 65 H4 ...... 39.07N 94.26W
India Asia 96 E5 ...... 22.00N 79.00E
Indiana d. U.S.A. 65 I5 ...... 40.09N 86.01W
Indian-Antarctic Ridge f. Southern Oc. 108 D2 ...... 49.49S 117.01E
Indianapolis U.S.A. 65 I4 ...... 39.46N 86.10W
Indian Ocean 117 M5
Indigirka r. Rus. Fed. 59 P5 ...... 71.28N 149.53E
Indonesia Asia 104 E2 ...... 4.12S 112.02E
Indore India 96 E5 ...... 22.40N 75.53E
Indre r. France 44 D5 ...... 47.14N 0.12E
Indus r. China/Pakistan 100 B3 ...... 23.56N 67.38E
Indus, Mouths of the Pakistan 96 C5 ...... 24.36N 66.36E
İnebolu Turkey 57 J5 ...... 41.58N 33.45E
İnegöl Turkey 57 H5 ...... 40.04N 29.30E
Infiernillo, Presa resr Mexico 70 D4 ...... 18.41N 101.57W
Infiesto Spain 48 C5 ...... 43.21N 5.20W
Ingatestone England 11 F2 ...... 51.40N 0.23E
Ingleborough hill England 15 E3 ...... 54.10N 2.24W
Ingleton England 15 E3 ...... 54.09N 2.28W
Ingoldmells England 15 H2 ...... 53.12N 0.20E
Ingolstadt Germany 54 D3 ...... 48.46N 11.27E
Inhambane Mozambique 86 C2 ...... 23.47S 35.31E
Inhul r. Ukraine 55 N2 ...... 46.58N 31.58E
Inhulets' r. Ukraine 55 N2 ...... 46.41N 32.49E
Inishbofin i. Ireland 41 A3 ...... 53.38N 10.14W
Inisheer i. Ireland 41 B3 ...... 53.04N 9.30W
Inishmaan i. Ireland 41 B3 ...... 53.05N 9.33W
Inishmore i. Ireland 41 B3 ...... 53.09N 9.47W
Inishmurray i. Ireland 41 C4 ...... 54.26N 8.40W
Inishowen pen. Ireland 41 D5 ...... 55.13N 7.17W
Inishowen Head Ireland 16 C3 ...... 55.14N 6.55W
Inishtrahull i. Ireland 41 D5 ...... 55.28N 7.13W
Inishtrahull Sound str. Ireland 16 B3 ...... 55.27N 7.28W
Inishturk i. Ireland 41 A3 ...... 53.42N 10.08W
Inn r. Europe 50 D7 ...... 48.35N 13.28E
Inner Mongolia r. China 101 I6 ...... 40.12N 103.26E
Inner Sound str. Scotland 18 D2 ...... 57.21N 5.57W
Innsbruck Austria 54 D2 ...... 47.16N 11.24E
Inny r. Ireland 41 D3 ...... 53.33N 7.50W
Inowrocław Poland 46 D4 ...... 52.48N 18.16E
In Salah Algeria 84 E4 ...... 27.13N 2.25E
Insch Scotland 19 G2 ...... 57.20N 2.37W
International Falls town U.S.A. 65 H6 ...... 48.36N 93.25W
Inukjuak Canada 63 K3 ...... 58.28N 78.04W
Inuvik Canada 62 E4 ...... 68.24N 133.43W
Inveraray Scotland 16 D4 ...... 56.14N 5.04W
Inverbervie Scotland 19 G1 ...... 56.51N 2.17W
Invercargill New Zealand 111 F2 ...... 46.25S 168.22E
Inverclyde d. Scotland 16 E3 ...... 55.54N 4.44W
Invergordon Scotland 19 E2 ...... 57.42N 4.10W
Inverkeithing Scotland 17 F4 ...... 56.02N 3.24W
Inverness Scotland 19 E2 ...... 57.29N 4.13W
Inverurie Scotland 19 G2 ...... 57.17N 2.22W
Investigator Ridge f. Indian Oc. 108 C5 ...... 7.10S 98.15E
Ioannina Greece 56 D4 ...... 39.40N 20.51E
Iona i. Scotland 16 C4 ...... 56.19N 6.25W
Ionian Islands Greece 56 C4 ...... 39.26N 19.33E
Ionian Sea Greece/Italy 56 C4 ...... 38.11N 18.29E
Ios i. Greece 56 F3 ...... 36.44N 25.22E
Iowa d. U.S.A. 65 H5 ...... 42.12N 92.47W
Iowa City U.S.A. 65 H5 ...... 41.40N 91.32W
Ipatinga Brazil 77 L4 ...... 19.25S 42.28W
Ipoh Malaysia 104 C4 ...... 4.40N 101.04E
Ipswich England 11 G3 ...... 52.03N 1.09E
Iput' r. Rus. Fed. 55 N5 ...... 52.30N 31.37E
Iput' r. Belarus 55 N5 ...... 52.26N 31.04E
Iqaluit Canada 63 L4 ...... 63.45N 68.36W
Iquique Chile 76 E4 ...... 20.14S 70.07W
Iquitos Peru 76 F7 ...... 3.50S 73.13W
Iraklion Greece 56 F2 ...... 35.19N 25.08E
Iran Asia 95 H6 ...... 31.28N 55.05E
Iran, Pegunungan mts Indonesia 104 E4 ...... 1.47N 114.46E
Iranian Plateau f. Iran 90 E5 ...... 32.00N 55.00E
İranshahr Iran 95 J5 ...... 27.13N 60.42E
Irapuato Mexico 70 D5 ...... 20.41N 101.23W
Iraq Asia 94 F6 ...... 32.50N 42.21E
Irbid Jordan 94 E6 ...... 32.34N 35.51E
Ireland Europe 41 D3 ...... 53.33N 7.43W
Ireland's Eye i. Ireland 41 E3 ...... 53.24N 6.03W
Irgiz Kazakhstan 58 H4 ...... 48.36N 61.18E
Iringa Tanzania 86 C4 ...... 7.48S 35.43E
Iriri r. Brazil 77 J7 ...... 3.52S 52.37W
Irish Sea Ireland/U.K. 41 F3 ...... 53.40N 5.11W
Irkutsk Rus. Fed. 59 L3 ...... 52.11N 104.09E
Iron Mountain U.S.A. 65 I6 ...... 45.49N 88.04W
Ironwood U.S.A. 65 H6 ...... 46.28N 90.09W
Irosin Phil. 105 G6 ...... 12.42N 124.00E
Irrawaddy r. Myanmar 97 I4 ...... 15.48N 95.05E
Irrawaddy, Mouths of the Myanmar 97 H4 ...... 15.35N 94.02E
Irsha r. Ukraine 55 M4 ...... 50.46N 29.35E
Irtysh r. Kazakhstan/Rus. Fed. 58 H4 ...... 61.07N 68.50E
Irún Spain 48 E5 ...... 43.20N 1.48W
Irvine Scotland 16 E3 ...... 55.37N 4.40W
Isabela Phil. 105 G5 ...... 6.40N 121.59E
Isabela, Isla i. Ecuador 76 B7 ...... 0.41S 91.03W
Isabelia, Cordillera mts Nicaragua 71 G3 ...... 13.13N 85.03W
Ísafjörður Iceland 40 X2 ...... 66.05N 23.10W
Isar r. Germany 54 E3 ...... 48.49N 12.59E
Isbister Scotland 19 H5 ...... 60.36N 1.19W
Ischia, Isola d' i. Italy 50 E4 ...... 40.42N 13.51E
Ise Japan 106 C2 ...... 34.29N 136.43E
Isère, Pointe pt French Guiana 72 D7 ...... 5.47N 53.57W
Ishikari-wan b. Japan 106 D4 ...... 43.17N 140.58E
Ishim r. Kazakhstan/Rus. Fed. 58 I3 ...... 57.40N 71.13E
Ishinomaki Japan 106 D3 ...... 38.25N 141.17E
Isiolo Kenya 87 B3 ...... 0.21N 37.38E
Isiro Dem. Rep. Congo 86 B5 ...... 2.46N 27.36E
Iskenderun Turkey 57 L3 ...... 36.34N 36.08E
Iskenderun Körfezi g. Turkey 57 K3 ...... 36.38N 35.54E
Iskūr r. Bulgaria 56 F6 ...... 43.44N 24.27E
Isla r. Ang. Scotland 19 F1 ...... 56.32N 3.22W
Isla r. Mor. Scotland 19 F2 ...... 57.31N 2.47W
Islamabad Pakistan 96 D7 ...... 33.42N 73.08E
Island Magee pen. Northern Ireland 16 D2 ...... 54.50N 5.41W
Islay i. Scotland 16 C3 ...... 55.48N 6.20W

Isle of Anglesey d. Wales 9 C3 ...... 53.18N 4.23W
Isle of Wight d. England 9 E2 ...... 50.41N 1.18W
Isles of Scilly d. England 9 B1 ...... 49.55N 6.17W
Isna Egypt 53 J2 ...... 25.16N 32.30E
Isparta Turkey 57 I3 ...... 37.46N 30.32E
Israel Asia 53 J3 ...... 32.12N 34.48E
İstanbul Turkey 57 H5 ...... 41.07N 28.58E
Istra pen. Croatia 54 E1 ...... 45.12N 13.53E
Itaberaba Brazil 77 L5 ...... 12.31S 40.17W
Itabuna Brazil 77 M5 ...... 14.47S 39.17W
Itaituba Brazil 77 I7 ...... 4.16S 56.00W
Itajaí Brazil 77 K2 ...... 26.52S 48.41W
Italy Europe 50 D6 ...... 41.46N 14.35E
Itambé, Pico de mt. Brazil 77 L4 ...... 18.23S 43.20W
Itapetininga Brazil 77 K4 ...... 23.36S 48.03W
Itapicuru r. Maranhão Brazil 77 L7 ...... 2.55S 44.16W
Itapicuru r. Sergipe Brazil 77 M5 ...... 11.48S 37.30W
Itapicuru Mirim Brazil 77 L7 ...... 3.24S 44.21W
Itiquira r. Brazil 77 I5 ...... 17.18S 56.20W
Ituí r. Brazil 76 F7 ...... 4.23S 70.13W
Ituxi r. Brazil 76 H6 ...... 7.21S 64.52W
Iul'tin Rus. Fed. 59 T4 ...... 67.51N 178.47W
Ivaí r. Brazil 77 J3 ...... 23.14S 53.15W
Ivalo Finland 40 F5 ...... 68.39N 27.32E
Ivanava Belarus 46 G4 ...... 52.09N 25.32E
Ivano-Frankivs'k Ukraine 55 K3 ...... 48.55N 24.43E
Ivanovo Rus. Fed. 58 F3 ...... 56.59N 40.59E
Ivatsevichy Belarus 55 K5 ...... 52.43N 25.21E
Ivittuut Greenland 63 N4 ...... 61.13N 48.10W
Ivybridge England 13 D2 ...... 50.23N 3.55W
Iwaki Japan 106 D3 ...... 37.03N 140.53E
İwo Nigeria 84 E2 ...... 7.38N 4.10E
Iwye Belarus 46 G4 ...... 53.55N 25.47E
Ixworth England 11 F3 ...... 52.18N 0.50E
Izabal, Lago de l. Guatemala 70 G4 ...... 15.36N 89.08W
Izhevsk Rus. Fed. 58 G3 ...... 56.49N 53.10E
Izmayil Ukraine 53 I6 ...... 45.21N 28.51E
İzmir Turkey 56 G4 ...... 38.24N 27.10E
İzmir Körfezi g. Turkey 56 G4 ...... 38.30N 26.44E
Izu-Ogasawara Trench f. N. Pacific Oc. 108 F8 ...... 34.34N 141.53E
Izu-shotō is Japan 106 C2 ...... 34.24N 139.14E

J
Jabalón r. Spain 48 C3 ...... 38.53N 4.05W
Jabalpur India 96 E5 ...... 23.10N 79.57E
Jablah Syria 57 K3 ...... 35.21N 35.56E
Jaboatão Brazil 77 N6 ...... 8.03S 34.55W
Jaca Spain 48 E5 ...... 42.34N 0.34W
Jacareacanga Brazil 77 I6 ...... 5.59S 57.33W
Jackson U.S.A. 65 H3 ...... 32.19N 90.12W
Jacksonville U.S.A. 65 J3 ...... 30.18N 81.42W
Jacmel Haiti 71 J4 ...... 18.16N 72.32W
Jacobabad Pakistan 96 C6 ...... 28.15N 68.29E
Jacuí r. Brazil 77 J1 ...... 30.03S 51.15W
Jacuípe r. Brazil 77 M5 ...... 12.33S 39.04W
Jādū Libya 52 F3 ...... 31.58N 12.04E
Jaén Spain 48 D2 ...... 37.46N 3.47W
Jaffna Sri Lanka 96 F2 ...... 9.41N 79.59E
Jagdalpur India 96 F4 ...... 19.04N 82.07E
Jahrom Iran 95 H5 ...... 28.31N 53.33E
Jaipur India 96 E6 ...... 26.51N 75.50E
Jaisalmer India 96 D6 ...... 26.52N 70.56E
Jajce Bos.-Herz. 56 B7 ...... 44.21N 17.16E
Jakarta Indonesia 104 D2 ...... 6.07S 106.48E
Jakobstad Finland 40 E3 ...... 63.40N 22.42E
Jalālābād Afgh. 95 L6 ...... 34.26N 70.28E
Jalandhar India 96 E7 ...... 31.18N 75.40E
Jalgaon India 96 E5 ...... 21.01N 75.41E
Jalisco d. Mexico 70 D4 ...... 19.59N 104.18W
Jalna India 96 E5 ...... 19.49N 75.57E
Jalón r. Spain 48 E4 ...... 41.47N 1.02W
Jālū Libya 85 H4 ...... 29.03N 21.33E
Jamaica Central America 71 I4 ...... 17.30N 77.19W
Jamaica Channel Haiti/Jamaica 71 I4 ...... 18.29N 75.24W
Jamanxim r. Brazil 77 I7 ...... 4.43S 56.24W
Jambi Indonesia 104 C3 ...... 1.37S 103.37E
James r. U.S.A. 64 G5 ...... 42.53N 97.17W
James Bay Canada 63 J3 ...... 53.23N 80.25W
Jamestown U.S.A. 64 G6 ...... 46.53N 98.43W
Jammu India 96 D7 ...... 32.42N 74.56E
Jammu and Kashmir Asia 96 E7 ...... 34.06N 76.59E
Jamnagar India 96 D5 ...... 22.26N 70.06E
Jampur Pakistan 96 D6 ...... 29.37N 70.41E
Jāmsänkoski Finland 40 F3 ...... 61.56N 25.11E
Jamshedpur India 96 G5 ...... 22.46N 86.12E
Jandiá hill Canary Islands 48 Y2 ...... 28.06N 14.21W
Jan Mayen i. Arctic Oc. 34 D5 ...... 72.00N 8.00W
Januária Brazil 77 L4 ...... 15.26S 44.20W
Japan Asia 106 C3 ...... 34.48N 133.17E
Japan, Sea of N. Pacific Oc. 106 B3 ...... 39.13N 133.37E
Japan Trench f. N. Pacific Oc. 108 F8 ...... 34.52N 143.17E
Japurá r. Brazil 76 H7 ...... 3.06S 64.45W
Jardines de la Reina, Archipiélago de los is Cuba 71 I5 ...... 20.46N 79.01W
Jarocin Poland 46 C3 ...... 51.58N 17.31E
Jarosław Poland 46 F3 ...... 50.01N 22.40E
Järpen Sweden 40 C3 ...... 63.22N 13.28E
Järvenpää Finland 40 F3 ...... 60.29N 25.06E
Jarvis Island S. Pacific Oc. 108 J5 ...... 0.26S 160.02W
Jäsk Iran 95 I5 ...... 25.40N 57.47E
Jasło Poland 46 E2 ...... 49.45N 21.28E
Jasper Canada 62 G3 ...... 52.53N 118.05W
Jastrzębie-Zdrój Poland 46 D2 ...... 49.57N 18.35E
Jataí Brazil 77 J4 ...... 17.53S 51.44W
Jatapu r. Brazil 77 J4 ...... 2.22S 58.11W
Jaú Brazil 77 K3 ...... 22.16S 48.33W
Java i. Indonesia 104 D2 ...... 8.12S 107.16E
Java Ridge f. Indian Oc. 108 D5 ...... 8.53S 107.00E
Java Sea Indonesia 104 E3 ...... 4.56S 110.49E
Java Trench f. Indian Oc. 108 C5 ...... 8.48S 104.02E
Jawhar Somalia 85 I2 ...... 2.43N 45.27E
Jawor Poland 46 C3 ...... 51.03N 16.12E
Jaya, Puncak mt. Indonesia 105 J3 ...... 4.05S 137.12E
Jayapura Indonesia 105 K3 ...... 2.34S 140.42E
Jaz Mūrīān, Hāmūn-e l. Iran 95 I5 ...... 27.32N 58.47E
Jebel Abyad Plateau f. Sudan 94 C4 ...... 19.25N 28.59E
Jedburgh Scotland 17 G3 ...... 55.29N 2.33W
Jeddah Saudi Arabia 94 E4 ...... 21.30N 39.08E
Jefferson City U.S.A. 65 H4 ...... 38.37N 92.11W
Jelenia Góra Poland 46 B3 ...... 50.56N 15.44E
Jelgava Latvia 40 E2 ...... 56.39N 23.44E
Jember Indonesia 104 E2 ...... 8.05S 113.45E
Jena Germany 54 D4 ...... 50.56N 11.36E
Jendouba Tunisia 52 E4 ...... 36.28N 8.47E
Jequié Brazil 77 L5 ...... 13.48S 40.00W
Jequitinhonha r. Brazil 77 M4 ...... 15.51S 38.52W
Jérémie Haiti 71 I4 ...... 18.38N 74.09W
Jerez de la Frontera Spain 48 B2 ...... 36.41N 6.08W
Jerid, Chott el f. Tunisia 52 E3 ...... 33.38N 8.28E

Jersey i. Channel Is 13 Z8 ...... 49.16N 2.10W
Jerusalem Israel/West Bank 53 K3 ...... 31.47N 35.13E
Jesi Italy 50 E5 ...... 43.31N 13.15E
Jesup U.S.A. 65 J3 ...... 31.34N 81.59W
Jhang Pakistan 95 L6 ...... 31.17N 72.23E
Jhansi India 96 E6 ...... 25.27N 78.37E
Jharkhand d. India 96 G5 ...... 23.36N 85.06E
Jiamusi China 101 O7 ...... 46.47N 130.15E
Ji'an China 101 K3 ...... 27.09N 114.56E
Jiangmen China 101 K2 ...... 22.35N 113.06E
Jiangsu d. China 101 L4 ...... 33.10N 119.42E
Jiangxi d. China 101 L3 ...... 27.21N 115.22E
Jiaohe China 106 A4 ...... 43.43N 127.20E
Jiaozuo China 101 K5 ...... 35.12N 113.15E
Jiaxing China 101 M4 ...... 30.46N 120.49E
Jiayi Taiwan 101 M2 ...... 23.29N 120.27E
Jiehkkevárri mt. Norway 40 D5 ...... 69.28N 19.51E
Jieyang China 101 L2 ...... 23.34N 116.19E
Jieznas Lithuania 46 G5 ...... 54.36N 24.10E
Jihlava Czech Rep. 54 F3 ...... 49.24N 15.36E
Jilf al Kabīr, Haḍabat al f. Egypt 94 C4 ...... 23.12N 25.56E
Jilib Somalia 85 I2 ...... 0.30N 42.47E
Jilin China 101 N6 ...... 43.53N 126.33E
Jilin d. China 101 N6 ...... 43.33N 125.10E
Jilong Taiwan 101 M3 ...... 25.07N 121.43E
Jima Ethiopia 85 H2 ...... 7.40N 36.49E
Jiménez Mexico 70 D6 ...... 27.08N 104.57W
Jinan China 101 L5 ...... 36.38N 117.01E
Jindřichův Hradec Czech Rep. 46 B2 ...... 49.09N 15.01E
Jingdezhen China 101 L3 ...... 29.21N 117.21E
Jinghong China 101 I2 ...... 21.57N 100.52E
Jingmen China 101 K4 ...... 30.58N 112.02E
Jingzhou China 101 K4 ...... 30.17N 112.17E
Jinhua China 101 L3 ...... 29.10N 119.41E
Jining Nei Mongol China 101 K6 ...... 40.54N 113.06E
Jining Shandong China 101 L5 ...... 35.22N 116.29E
Jinja Uganda 85 H3 ...... 0.28N 33.14E
Jinjiang China 101 L2 ...... 24.49N 118.36E
Jinka Ethiopia 87 B4 ...... 5.40N 36.39E
Jinzhou China 101 M6 ...... 41.02N 121.10E
Jiparaná r. Brazil 77 H6 ...... 8.09S 62.50W
Jipe, Lake Kenya/Tanzania 87 B2 ...... 3.35S 37.45E
Jiu r. Romania 56 E6 ...... 43.47N 23.48E
Jiujiang China 101 L3 ...... 29.43N 116.00E
Jiwani Pakistan 95 J5 ...... 25.07N 61.48E
Jixi China 101 O7 ...... 45.13N 130.53E
Jīzān Saudi Arabia 94 F3 ...... 16.56N 42.32E
João Pessoa Brazil 77 N6 ...... 7.05S 34.50W
Jodhpur India 96 D6 ...... 26.16N 73.07E
Joensuu Finland 40 G3 ...... 62.36N 29.46E
Jōetsu Japan 106 C3 ...... 37.10N 138.14E
Johannesburg S. Africa 86 B2 ...... 26.09S 27.59E
John o'Groats Scotland 19 F3 ...... 58.38N 3.04W
Johnston Atoll N. Pacific Oc. 108 I7 ...... 16.42N 169.30W
Johnstone Scotland 16 E3 ...... 55.50N 4.31W
Johor Bahru Malaysia 104 C4 ...... 1.29N 103.46E
Joinville Brazil 77 K2 ...... 26.17S 48.51W
Jonava Lithuania 46 G5 ...... 55.04N 24.17E
Jones Sound str. Canada 63 J5 ...... 75.58N 88.58W
Jonglei d. Sudan 87 A2 ...... 7.17N 32.12E
Jönköping Sweden 40 C2 ...... 57.46N 14.09E
Jonquière Canada 63 K2 ...... 48.25N 71.14W
Joplin U.S.A. 65 H4 ...... 37.12N 94.31W
Jordan Asia 94 F6 ...... 31.17N 36.26E
Jörn Sweden 40 E4 ...... 65.03N 20.03E
Jos Nigeria 84 E2 ...... 9.55N 8.53E
Joseph Bonaparte Gulf Australia 110 B5 ...... 14.08S 128.39E
Jos Plateau f. Nigeria 82 D5 ...... 10.00N 9.00E
Juan Fernández, Archipiélago is S. Pacific Oc. 109 O3 ...... 33.24S 80.02W
Juàzeiro Brazil 77 L6 ...... 9.25S 40.26W
Juàzeiro do Norte Brazil 77 M6 ...... 7.11S 39.14W
Juba South Sudan 85 H2 ...... 4.53N 31.38E
Jubba r. Somalia 85 I1 ...... 0.15S 42.37E
Jubbada Hoose d. Somalia 87 C2 ...... 1.41S 41.53E
Júcar r. Spain 48 E3 ...... 39.09N 0.13W
Juchitán Mexico 70 F4 ...... 16.29N 95.02W
Judenburg Austria 54 F2 ...... 47.11N 14.41E
Juist i. Germany 42 G6 ...... 53.41N 7.01E
Juiz de Fora Brazil 77 L3 ...... 21.46S 43.21W
Juliaca Peru 76 F4 ...... 15.28S 70.11W
Junction City U.S.A. 64 G4 ...... 39.03N 96.50W
Juneau U.S.A. 62 E3 ...... 58.19N 134.23W
Jungfrau mt. Switz. 50 B7 ...... 46.33N 7.58E
Junggar Pendi basin China 100 F7 ...... 45.02N 87.38E
Jura mts France/Switz. 44 F4 ...... 46.35N 5.26E
Jura i. Scotland 16 D3 ...... 56.02N 5.56W
Jura, Sound of str. Scotland 16 D3 ...... 55.51N 5.49W
Jurbarkas Lithuania 46 F5 ...... 55.05N 22.46E
Jūrmala Latvia 55 J7 ...... 56.57N 23.40E
Juruá r. Brazil 76 G7 ...... 2.39S 65.48W
Juruena r. Brazil 77 I6 ...... 7.21S 58.08W
Jutaí r. Brazil 76 G7 ...... 2.45S 66.58W
Jutland pen. Denmark 40 B2 ...... 56.13N 9.08E
Juventud, Isla de la i. Cuba 71 H5 ...... 21.27N 82.50W
Jyväskylä Finland 40 F3 ...... 62.14N 25.44E

K
K2 mt. China/Jammu and Kashmir 100 D5 ...... 35.52N 76.34E
Kaambooni Somalia 87 C2 ...... 1.41S 41.34E
Kaambooni, Raas pt Somalia 87 C2 ...... 1.40S 41.34E
Kabaena i. Indonesia 105 G2 ...... 5.15S 121.50E
Kabalo Dem. Rep. Congo 86 B4 ...... 6.02S 26.57E
Kabarnet Kenya 87 B3 ...... 0.31N 35.45E
Kābul Afgh. 95 K6 ...... 34.30N 69.11E
Kabwe Zambia 86 B3 ...... 14.27S 28.26E
Kachalagu mt. Kenya 87 A3 ...... 2.20N 35.04E
Kachchh, Gulf of India 96 C5 ...... 22.35N 68.57E
Kachug Rus. Fed. 59 L3 ...... 53.54N 105.47E
Kadam mt. Uganda 87 A3 ...... 1.45N 34.43E
Kadavu i. Fiji 111 G5 ...... 19.00S 178.10E
Kadıköy Turkey 57 H5 ...... 40.59N 29.01E
Kadirli Turkey 57 L3 ...... 37.22N 36.05E
Kadugli Sudan 94 C3 ...... 11.01N 29.43E
Kaduna Nigeria 84 E3 ...... 10.30N 7.25E
Kaesŏng N. Korea 101 N5 ...... 37.58N 126.33E
Kafireas, Akra pt Greece 56 F4 ...... 38.10N 24.36E
Kaga Bandoro C.A.R. 85 F2 ...... 6.57N 19.11E
Kagoshima Japan 106 B2 ...... 31.35N 130.33E
Kahramanmaraş Turkey 57 L3 ...... 37.35N 36.55E
Kai, Kepulauan is Indonesia 105 I2 ...... 5.35S 132.45E
Kaifeng China 101 K4 ...... 34.43N 114.24E
Kaimana Indonesia 105 I3 ...... 3.42S 133.49E
Kairouan Tunisia 52 F4 ...... 35.41N 10.06E
Kaiserslautern Germany 54 B3 ...... 49.27N 7.46E
Kaiyuan China 101 I2 ...... 23.42N 103.12E
Kajaani Finland 40 F4 ...... 64.13N 27.43E
Kajiado Kenya 87 B2 ...... 1.50S 36.47E

Kakamega Kenya 87 A3......................0.17N 34.45E
Kakhovs'ke Vodoskhovyshche resr Ukraine 55 O2
....................................................47.00N 33.42E
Kakinada India 96 F4........................16.57N 82.19E
Kaktovik U.S.A. 62 D5..................70.04N 143.44W
Kakuma Kenya 87 A3..........................3.40N 34.53E
Kalacha Dida Kenya 87 A3..................3.07N 37.36E
Kalahari Desert Africa 86 B2............23.28S 22.18E
Kalajoki Finland 40 E4......................64.15N 23.57E
Kalamaria Greece 56 E5......................40.36N 22.57E
Kalamata Greece 56 E3........................37.02N 22.07E
Kalāt Afgh. 95 K6...............................32.05N 66.58E
Kalecik Turkey 57 J5..........................40.05N 33.26E
Kalemie Dem. Rep. Congo 86 B4...........5.56S 29.08E
Kalgoorlie Australia 110 B3............30.50S 121.30E
Kaliakra, Nos pt Bulgaria 57 H6.........43.22N 28.28E
Kalimantan f. Indonesia 104 E3............2.10S 111.35E
Kaliningrad Rus. Fed. 55 M5...............54.42N 20.31E
Kalinkavichy Belarus 55 M5...............52.08N 29.15E
Kalispell U.S.A. 64 D6....................48.11N 114.19W
Kalisz Poland 46 G5..........................51.46N 18.05E
Kalixälven r. Sweden 40 E4...............65.51N 23.08E
Kallavesi l. Finland 40 F3..................62.47N 27.47E
Kallsjön l. Sweden 40 D3....................63.37N 13.00E
Kalmar Sweden 40 D2........................56.40N 16.22E
Kaltag U.S.A. 62 C4......................64.20N 158.52W
Kaluga Rus. Fed. 55 Q6......................54.31N 36.16E
Kalundborg Denmark 40 B1................55.41N 11.06E
Kalush Ukraine 55 K3..........................49.02N 24.22E
Kama r. Rus. Fed. 58 G3....................56.01N 53.46E
Kamaishi Japan 106 D3......................39.16N 141.53E
Kaman Turkey 57 J4...........................39.22N 33.43E
Kamchatka Basin f. Bering Sea 108 H9....57.09N 166.28E
Kamchatka Peninsula Rus. Fed. 59 Q3....56.10N 159.12E
Kamenskoye Rus. Fed. 59 R4...............62.33N 166.10E
Kamensk-Ural'skiy Rus. Fed. 58 H3.....56.28N 61.48E
Kamina Dem. Rep. Congo 86 B4.............8.44S 24.57E
Kamin'-Kashyrs'kyy Ukraine 55 K4.......51.38N 24.58E
Kamloops Canada 62 F3....................50.41N 120.21W
Kampala Uganda 85 H2........................0.20N 32.34E
Kampen Neth. 42 E5..........................52.33N 5.55E
Kâmpóng Cham Cambodia 104 D6.......11.59N 105.26E
Kâmpôt Cambodia 104 C6..................10.36N 104.12E
Kamuli Uganda 87 A3..........................0.54N 33.06E
Kam"yanets'-Podil's'kyy Ukraine 55 L3....48.41N 26.35E
Kam"yanka-Buz'ka Ukraine 46 G4.......50.06N 24.21E
Kamyshin Rus. Fed. 53 F3..................50.06N 45.25E
Kananga Dem. Rep. Congo 86 B4...........5.51S 22.22E
Kanazawa Japan 106 C3......................36.34N 136.39E
Kanchipuram India 96 E3..................12.51N 79.43E
Kandahār Afgh. 95 K6........................31.37N 65.47E
Kandalaksha Rus. Fed. 40 H4...............67.10N 32.23E
Kandalakshskiy Zaliv g. Rus. Fed. 40 H4....66.38N 33.25E
Kandıra Turkey 57 I5..........................41.04N 30.08E
Kandy Sri Lanka 96 F2........................7.19N 80.34E
Kandyagash Kazakhstan 58 G2.............49.27N 57.21E
Kangal Turkey 57 L4..........................39.14N 37.23E
Kangān Iran 95 H5.............................27.50N 52.05E
Kangaroo Island Australia 110 C3......35.48S 137.11E
Kangāvar Iran 95 G6..........................34.29N 47.51E
Kangchenjunga mt. India/Nepal 96 G6....27.41N 88.12E
Kangding China 97 J7........................30.03N 101.56E
Kangean, Kepulauan is Indonesia 104 E2....6.56S 115.13E
Kangertittivaq str. Greenland 63 P5....70.31N 24.44W
Kangetet Kenya 87 B3........................1.58N 36.03E
Kangiqsualujjuaq Canada 63 L3...........58.35N 65.45W
Kangiqsujuaq Canada 63 K4...............61.34N 71.56W
Kangmar China 100 F3........................28.30N 89.33E
Kangnŭng S. Korea 106 A3..................37.46N 128.52E
Kanin, Poluostrov pen. Rus. Fed. 58 F4....66.50N 44.50E
Kankaanpää Finland 40 E3..................61.47N 22.22E
Kankakee U.S.A. 65 I5......................41.07N 87.51W
Kankan Guinea 84 D3..........................10.23N 9.19W
Kanker India 96 F5............................20.16N 81.32E
Kano Nigeria 84 E3...........................12.01N 8.31E
Kanpur India 96 F6...........................26.27N 80.24E
Kansas d. U.S.A. 64 G4......................38.35N 98.34W
Kansas r. U.S.A. 64 H4......................39.07N 94.40W
Kansas City U.S.A. 65 H4..................39.11N 94.45W
Kansk Rus. Fed. 59 L3........................56.10N 95.43E
Kanta mt. Ethiopia 87 A4....................6.10N 35.35E
Kantchari Burkina Faso 84 E3...........12.29N 1.30E
Kanton atoll Kiribati 108 I5...............2.44S 171.42W
Kanye Botswana 86 B2........................24.58S 25.21E
Kaokoveld f. Namibia 86 A3...............17.41S 12.33E
Kaolack Senegal 84 C3......................14.09N 16.04W
Kapchorwa Uganda 87 A3....................1.27N 34.29E
Kapenguria Kenya 87 A3......................1.21N 35.05E
Kapingamarangi Rise f. N. Pacific Oc. 108 G6....6.41N 150.16E
Kapoeta South Sudan 87 A4..................4.47N 33.35E
Kaposvár Hungary 54 G2......................46.22N 17.48E
Kapsabet Kenya 87 A3........................0.13N 35.08E
Kapuskasing Canada 63 J2..................49.26N 82.26W
Kaputir Kenya 87 A3..........................2.05N 35.28E
Kara-Bogaz-Gol, Zaliv b. Turkmenistan 58 G2....41.24N 53.32E
Karabük Turkey 57 J5........................41.12N 32.37E
Karabutak Kazakhstan 58 H2...............49.55N 60.09E
Karachi Pakistan 96 C4......................24.51N 67.03E
Karaganda Kazakhstan 58 I2...............49.52N 73.04E
Karaginskiy Zaliv b. Rus. Fed. 59 R3....59.32N 164.48E
Karaj Iran 95 H7.............................35.45N 50.54E
Karakelong i. Indonesia 105 H4...........4.22N 126.43E
Karakoram Range mts Asia 96 D8.........36.18N 74.54E
Karakum Desert Turkmenistan 58 G2....38.58N 60.05E
Karaman Turkey 57 J3........................37.11N 33.13E
Karamay China 100 E7........................45.31N 84.54E
Karand Iran 95 G6............................34.14N 46.16E
Karapınar Turkey 57 J3......................37.43N 33.33E
Karasburg Namibia 86 A2....................28.01S 18.45E
Kara Sea Rus. Fed. 58 I5..................75.13N 71.44E
Karasuk Rus. Fed. 58 I3....................53.43N 78.03E
Karbalā' Iraq 94 F6..........................32.36N 44.01E
Karcag Hungary 54 I2........................47.19N 20.55E
Karditsa Greece 56 D4......................39.21N 21.55E
Kärdla Estonia 40 E2........................58.59N 22.45E
Kareima Sudan 85 H3..........................18.31N 31.49E
Kariba, Lake resr Zambia/Zimbabwe 86 B3....17.37S 27.17E
Karimata, Selat str. Indonesia 104 D3....1.50S 108.08E
Karkinits'ka Zatoka b. Ukraine 53 J6....45.27N 32.11E
Karlovac Croatia 40 F1......................45.29N 15.33E
Karlovo Bulgaria 56 F6......................42.39N 24.48E
Karlovy Vary Czech Rep. 54 E4............50.14N 12.53E
Karlshamn Sweden 40 C2....................56.11N 14.52E
Karlskoga Sweden 40 C2......................59.20N 14.33E
Karlskrona Sweden 40 C2....................56.12N 15.38E
Karlsruhe Germany 54 C3....................49.01N 8.24E
Karlstad Sweden 40 C2......................59.23N 13.31E
Karmøy i. Norway 40 A2......................59.11N 5.15E
Karnataka d. India 96 E3....................15.37N 75.29E
Karnobat Bulgaria 56 G6....................42.38N 26.59E
Karora Eritrea 85 H3........................17.41N 38.23E
Karpathos i. Greece 56 G2..................35.36N 27.09E
Karpenisi Greece 56 D4......................38.55N 21.48E
Kärsava Latvia 55 L7..........................56.47N 27.41E

Karşıyaka Turkey 56 G4......................38.27N 27.06E
Karstula Finland 40 F3......................62.53N 24.48E
Kartal Turkey 57 H5..........................40.54N 29.11E
Karungu Bay Kenya 87 A2......................0.55S 33.59E
Karymskoye Rus. Fed. 59 M3...............51.30N 114.25E
Kaş Turkey 57 H3............................36.12N 29.37E
Kasai r. Dem. Rep. Congo 86 A4............3.02S 16.58E
Kasama Zambia 86 C3........................10.12S 31.12E
Kasese Uganda 85 H2..........................0.10N 30.05E
Kāshān Iran 95 H6............................33.58N 51.30E
Kashi China 100 D5..........................39.29N 76.03E
Kashiwazaki Japan 106 C3..................37.22N 138.34E
Kāšmar Iran 95 I7............................35.10N 58.22E
Kasos i. Greece 56 G2........................35.23N 26.52E
Kassala Sudan 85 H3........................15.24N 36.20E
Kassel Germany 54 C4........................51.19N 9.30E
Kasserine Tunisia 52 E4....................35.11N 8.50E
Kastamonu Turkey 57 J5......................41.22N 33.46E
Kastelli Greece 56 E2........................35.30N 23.38E
Kastoria Greece 56 D5......................40.31N 21.16E
Kastsyukovichy Belarus 55 O5...........53.21N 32.09E
Kataxwi Uganda 87 A3..........................1.54N 33.56E
Katerini Greece 56 E5........................40.16N 22.31E
Katesh Tanzania 87 A1..........................4.32S 35.20E
Kate's Needle mt. Canada/U.S.A. 62 E3....57.02N 132.02W
Katha Myanmar 97 I5........................24.11N 96.20E
Katherine Australia 110 C5...............14.28S 132.18E
Kathmandu Nepal 96 G6......................27.42N 85.18E
Kathua watercourse Kenya 87 B2............1.23S 39.09E
Katima Mulilo Namibia 86 B3...............17.32S 24.15E
Katowice Poland 46 D3........................50.16N 19.01E
Katrīnā, Jabal mt. Egypt 53 J2...........28.31N 33.58E
Katrine, Loch l. Scotland 16 E4.........56.15N 4.34W
Katrineholm Sweden 40 D2..................58.59N 16.14E
Katsina Nigeria 84 E3......................12.59N 7.36E
Kattegat str. Denmark/Sweden 40 B2....56.49N 11.21E
Kauai i. U.S.A. 109 J7....................22.10N 159.43W
Kauhajoki Finland 40 E3....................62.25N 22.11E
Kaunas Lithuania 40 E1......................54.54N 23.55E
Kaura-Namoda Nigeria 84 E3...............12.37N 6.35E
Kavala Greece 56 F5..........................40.56N 24.23E
Kavarna Bulgaria 57 H6......................43.26N 28.19E
Kavīr, Dasht-e des. Iran 95 H6...........34.36N 54.41E
Kawasaki Japan 106 C3......................35.32N 139.43E
Kawm Umbū Egypt 53 J1......................24.26N 32.55E
Kayes Mali 84 C3.............................14.26N 11.27W
Kayseri Turkey 57 L4..........................38.43N 35.29E
Kazach'ye Rus. Fed. 59 O5..................70.45N 136.09E
Kazakhstan Asia 58 H2......................49.18N 62.53E
Kazan' Rus. Fed. 58 F3......................55.47N 49.07E
Kazanlŭk Bulgaria 56 F6....................42.37N 25.23E
Kāzerūn Iran 95 H5..........................29.37N 51.39E
Kazincbarcika Hungary 46 E2...............48.16N 20.39E
Kea i. Greece 56 F3..........................37.38N 24.24E
Keady Northern Ireland 16 C2.............54.15N 6.42W
Kearney U.S.A. 64 G5........................40.43N 99.05W
Keban Barajı resr Turkey 57 M4..........38.53N 38.55E
Kebkabiya Sudan 94 E3......................13.37N 24.06E
Kebnekaise mt. Sweden 40 D4...............67.55N 18.31E
Kebock Head Scotland 18 C3...............58.03N 6.21W
Keçiören Turkey 57 J5........................40.00N 32.50E
Kecskemét Hungary 54 H2..................46.55N 19.42E
Kėdainiai Lithuania 40 E1..................55.17N 23.59E
Kędzierzyn-Koźle Poland 46 D3...........50.20N 18.13E
Keen, Mount hill Scotland 19 G1.........56.58N 2.59W
Keetmanshoop Namibia 86 A2.............26.35S 18.09E
Keewatin Canada 65 H6......................49.46N 94.34W
Keflavík Iceland 40 X2......................64.00N 22.34W
Kegworth England 10 D3....................52.50N 1.17W
Keighley England 15 F2....................53.52N 1.55W
Keitele l. Finland 40 F3....................62.52N 26.00E
Keith Scotland 19 G2........................57.33N 2.57W
Kelibia Tunisia 52 F4......................36.51N 11.04E
Kelifskiy Uzboy f. Turkmenistan 95 J7....38.07N 63.33E
Kelkit r. Turkey 57 L5......................40.51N 36.26E
Kellett, Cape Canada 62 F5...............71.59N 125.59W
Kells Ireland 41 E3..........................53.44N 6.52W
Kelmė Lithuania 46 F5......................55.38N 22.56E
Kelo Chad 84 F2.............................9.18N 15.49E
Kelowna Canada 62 G2....................49.53N 119.29W
Kelso Scotland 17 G3........................55.36N 2.26W
Keluang Malaysia 104 C4..................1.59N 103.19E
Kelvedon England 11 F2....................51.50N 0.42E
Kem' Rus. Fed. 58 E4........................64.57N 34.34E
Kemerovo Rus. Fed. 58 J3..................55.23N 86.01E
Kemi Finland 40 F4..........................65.46N 24.33E
Kemijärvi Finland 40 F4....................66.43N 27.23E
Kemijärvi l. Finland 40 F4................66.35N 27.25E
Kemijoki r. Finland 40 F4..................65.47N 24.32E
Kemnay Scotland 19 G2......................57.14N 2.27W
Kempston England 11 E3....................52.07N 0.30W
Kempten Germany 54 D2....................47.43N 10.18E
Kenai U.S.A. 62 C4..........................60.35N 151.16W
Kenamuke Swamp f. South Sudan 87 A4....5.25N 34.00E
Kendal England 14 E3........................54.20N 2.45W
Kendari Indonesia 105 G3..................3.59S 122.35E
Kendawangan Indonesia 104 E3...........2.30S 110.14E
Kengtung Myanmar 97 I5....................21.18N 99.38E
Kenilworth England 10 D3..................52.21N 1.35W
Kénitra Morocco 84 D5......................34.16N 6.33W
Kenmare Ireland 41 B1......................51.53N 9.35W
Kenmare River inlet Ireland 41 A1........51.43N 10.03W
Kennet r. England 10 D2....................51.27N 0.57W
Kenora Canada 63 I2........................49.47N 94.30W
Kent d. England 11 F2......................51.12N 0.37E
Kent r. England 14 E3........................54.15N 2.48W
Kentucky d. U.S.A. 65 J4..................37.24N 84.54W
Kentucky r. U.S.A. 65 I4....................38.41N 85.10W
Kenya Africa 87 B3..........................0.59N 37.32E
Kenya, Mount Kenya 87 B2..................0.08S 37.18E
Kępno Poland 46 C3..........................51.17N 17.59E
Kerala d. India 96 E3........................11.31N 75.51E
Kerch Ukraine 53 K6........................45.22N 36.29E
Kerema P.N.G. 110 D6........................7.56S 145.48E
Keren Eritrea 94 E3..........................15.46N 38.28E
Kerinci, Gunung vol. Indonesia 104 C3....1.42S 101.15E
Kerio watercourse Kenya 87 B3.............2.56N 36.11E
Kerio Valley f. Kenya 87 A3...............1.10N 35.45E
Kerki Turkmenistan 95 K7..................37.51N 65.13E
Kerkyra Greece 56 C4........................39.37N 19.55E
Kerma Sudan 94 D3..........................19.37N 30.26E
Kermadec Islands S. Pacific Oc. 108 I3....29.41S 178.19W
Kermadec Trench f. S. Pacific Oc. 108 I3....34.29S 177.56W
Kermān Iran 95 I6..........................30.17N 57.04E
Kermān Desert Iran 95 I5..................28.27N 59.19E
Kermānshāh Iran 95 G6......................34.19N 47.02E
Kerry d. Ireland 41 B2......................52.09N 9.28W
Kerry Head Ireland 41 B2..................52.25N 9.57W
Keşan Turkey 56 G5..........................40.51N 26.37E
Kesennuma Japan 106 D3..................38.54N 141.33E
Kessingland England 11 G3................52.25N 1.43E
Keswick England 14 D3......................54.36N 3.07W
Ketapang Indonesia 104 E3................1.50S 110.00E

Ketchikan U.S.A. 62 E3..................55.20N 131.38W
Kettering England 10 E3....................52.24N 0.44W
Keweenaw Bay U.S.A. 65 I6...............46.52N 88.26W
Key, Lough l. Ireland 41 C4...............54.01N 8.15W
Keyala South Sudan 87 A4..................4.29N 32.51E
Keynsham England 10 C2....................51.25N 2.30W
Kežmarok Slovakia 46 E2..................49.08N 20.26E
Khabarovsk Rus. Fed. 59 O2...............48.30N 135.08E
Khadyzhensk Rus. Fed. 57 M7.............44.25N 39.32E
Khairpur Pakistan 100 D3..................27.31N 68.49E
Khambhat, Gulf of India 96 D4...........19.59N 71.29E
Khānābād Afgh. 95 K7........................36.42N 69.09E
Khandwa India 96 E5..........................21.49N 76.21E
Khanewal Pakistan 95 L6....................30.19N 71.59E
Khanka, Lake China/Rus. Fed. 101 O6....44.54N 132.45E
Khanpur Pakistan 96 D6....................28.37N 70.41E
Khantayskoye, Ozero l. Rus. Fed. 59 K4....68.25N 91.57E
Khanty-Mansiysk Rus. Fed. 58 H4.......61.05N 69.01E
Kharagpur India 96 G5......................22.20N 87.20E
Kharkiv Ukraine 55 N3......................49.59N 36.16E
Khartoum Sudan 85 H3......................15.32N 32.32E
Khāsh Iran 95 J5............................28.12N 61.14E
Khashm el Girba Sudan 94 E2.............14.56N 35.51E
Khaskovo Bulgaria 56 F5..................41.56N 25.32E
Khatanga Rus. Fed. 59 L5..................71.57N 102.24E
Khatangskiy Zaliv b. Rus. Fed. 59 L5....73.19N 107.17E
Khayelitsha S. Africa 86 A1...............34.05S 18.39E
Khenchela Algeria 52 E4....................35.26N 7.10E
Khenifra Morocco 52 B3....................32.58N 5.37W
Kherson Ukraine 53 J6......................46.39N 32.37E
Kheta r. Rus. Fed. 59 L5..................71.55N 102.04E
Khimki Rus. Fed. 55 Q6....................55.53N 37.26E
Khmel'nyts'kyy Ukraine 55 L3...........49.25N 26.59E
Khon Kaen Thailand 104 C7...............16.27N 102.52E
Khorinsk Rus. Fed. 101 J8................52.09N 109.48E
Khorramābād Iran 95 G6....................33.27N 48.19E
Khorugh Tajikistan 95 L7..................37.29N 71.35E
Khouribga Morocco 52 B3..................32.53N 6.55W
Khowst Afgh. 95 K6..........................33.21N 69.59E
Khŭjand Tajikistan 100 B6................40.15N 69.38E
Khulna Bangl. 97 G5........................22.50N 89.33E
Khunsar Iran 95 H6..........................33.10N 50.17E
Khust Ukraine 55 J3........................48.10N 23.18E
Khvoy Iran 94 F7...........................38.33N 44.58E
Khyber Pass Afgh./Pakistan 95 L6.......34.08N 71.12E
Kiambu Kenya 87 B2..........................1.13S 36.45E
Kiantajärvi l. Finland 40 G4.............64.58N 29.06E
Kibaya Tanzania 87 B1......................5.17S 36.33E
Kibre Mengist Ethiopia 87 B4.............5.52N 38.57E
Kičevo Macedonia 56 D5....................41.30N 20.58E
Kidderminster England 10 C3.............52.23N 2.15W
Kidepo Valley National Park Uganda 87 A3....3.51N 33.48E
Kidsgrove England 15 E2..................53.05N 2.14W
Kidwelly Wales 12 C3........................51.44N 4.18W
Kiel Germany 54 D6..........................54.19N 10.08E
Kiel Canal Germany 40 B1................54.10N 9.27E
Kielce Poland 46 E3..........................50.51N 20.37E
Kielder Water resr England 15 E4.......55.12N 2.34W
Kieler Bucht b. Germany 54 D6...........54.27N 10.41E
Kiev Ukraine 55 N4..........................50.26N 30.34E
Kigali Rwanda 85 H1..........................1.59S 30.05E
Kigoma Tanzania 86 B4......................4.51S 29.40E
Kii-suidō str. Japan 106 B2...............33.57N 134.49E
Kikinda Serbia 56 D7........................45.50N 20.28E
Kikori P.N.G. 110 D6........................7.22S 144.14E
Kikwit Dem. Rep. Congo 86 A4.............5.03S 18.50E
Kilbrannan Sound str. Scotland 16 D3....55.25S 5.27W
Kilcoole Ireland 12 A5......................53.06N 6.03W
Kilcormac Ireland 41 D3....................53.10N 7.44W
Kilcullen Ireland 41 E3....................53.08N 6.45W
Kildare Ireland 41 E3........................53.09N 6.55W
Kildare d. Ireland 41 E3..................53.17N 6.47W
Kilifi Kenya 87 B2..........................3.36S 39.51E
Kilimanjaro d. Tanzania 87 B2...........3.15S 37.23E
Kilimanjaro vol. Tanzania 86 C4.........3.03S 37.21E
Kilimanjaro National Park Tanzania 87 B2....3.01S 37.13E
Kilis Turkey 57 L3..........................36.43N 37.07E
Kilkee Ireland 41 B2........................52.41N 9.38W
Kilkeel Northern Ireland 16 D2...........54.04N 5.59W
Kilkenny Ireland 41 D2....................52.39N 7.15W
Kilkenny d. Ireland 41 D2................52.41N 7.14W
Kilkis Greece 56 E5..........................40.59N 22.52E
Killala Bay Ireland 41 B4..................54.16N 9.08W
Killarney Ireland 41 B2....................52.03N 9.30W
Killeen U.S.A. 64 G3........................31.08N 97.44W
Killin Scotland 16 E4........................56.28N 4.19W
Killorglin Ireland 41 B2..................52.06N 9.47W
Killybegs Ireland 41 C4....................54.38N 8.27W
Kilmallock Ireland 41 C2..................52.24N 8.35W
Kilmarnock Scotland 16 E3...............55.37N 4.30W
Kilmelford Scotland 16 D4................56.16N 5.28W
Kilmichael Point Ireland 41 E2...........52.44N 6.08W
Kilrea Northern Ireland 16 C2...........54.57N 6.33W
Kilrush Ireland 41 B2......................52.39N 9.29W
Kilsyth Scotland 17 E3....................55.59N 4.03W
Kilwinning Scotland 16 E3................55.39N 4.42W
Kimberley S. Africa 86 B2................28.44S 24.46E
Kimberley Plateau f. Australia 110 B5....17.26S 127.05E
Kimch'aek N. Korea 101 N6...............40.41N 129.12E
Kinabalu, Gunung mt. Malaysia 104 F5....6.04N 116.33E
Kinango Kenya 87 B1..........................4.08S 39.20E
Kinder Scout hill England 15 F2.........53.23N 1.52W
Kindersley Canada 64 F7..................51.28N 109.10W
Kindia Guinea 84 C3........................10.04N 12.51W
Kindu Dem. Rep. Congo 86 B4.............2.57S 25.53E
King Island Australia 110 D3.............39.50S 143.58E
Kingman U.S.A. 64 D4......................35.14N 114.02W
Kingsbridge England 13 D2...............50.17N 3.47W
Kingsclere England 10 D2..................51.19N 1.14W
Kingscourt Ireland 41 E3..................53.54N 6.48W
King's Lynn England 11 F3................52.45N 0.24E
Kingsmill Group is Kiribati 111 G6......1.37S 175.52E
Kingsnorth England 11 F2................51.07N 0.52E
Kings Peak U.S.A. 64 D5..................40.45N 110.23W
Kingston Canada 63 K2....................44.14N 76.30W
Kingston Jamaica 71 I4....................18.00N 76.47W
Kingston upon Hull England 15 G2.......53.45N 0.20W
Kingston upon Hull d. England 9 E3....53.46N 0.19W
Kingston upon Thames England 11 E2....51.25N 0.18W
Kingstown St Vincent 71 L3...............13.10N 61.15W
Kingsville U.S.A. 64 G2..................27.27N 97.47W
Kingswood England 10 C2................51.28N 2.30W
Kington England 10 C3....................52.12N 3.02W
Kingussie Scotland 19 E2................57.05N 4.03W
King William Island Canada 63 I4.......69.10N 97.45W
Kinlochbervie Scotland 18 D3...........58.28N 5.03W
Kinlochleven Scotland 18 E1............56.43N 4.58W
Kinloss Scotland 19 F2..................57.58N 3.34W
Kinna Sweden 40 C2........................57.31N 12.40E
Kinnegad Ireland 41 D3..................53.27N 7.06W
Kinross Scotland 17 F4..................56.12N 3.25W
Kinsale Ireland 41 C1......................51.42N 8.31W
Kinshasa Dem. Rep. Congo 86 A4.......4.22S 15.23E
Kintore Scotland 19 G2..................57.14N 2.21W

Kintyre pen. Scotland 16 D3...............55.30N 5.39W
Kipini Kenya 87 C2..........................2.30S 40.32E
Kircubbin Northern Ireland 16 D2.......54.29N 5.31W
Kiribati Pacific Oc. 108 I5...............6.00S 164.59W
Kırıkhan Turkey 57 L3......................36.29N 36.22E
Kırıkkale Turkey 57 J4....................39.50N 33.30E
Kiritimati atoll Kiribati 109 J6.........1.44N 157.13W
Kirkbean Scotland 17 F2..................54.55N 3.36W
Kirkby England 14 E2......................53.29N 2.53W
Kirkby in Ashfield England 15 F2.......53.06N 1.16W
Kirkby Lonsdale England 14 E3...........54.12N 2.36W
Kirkbymoorside England 15 G3...........54.16N 0.56W
Kirkby Stephen England 15 E3...........54.29N 2.21W
Kirkcaldy Scotland 17 F4................56.07N 3.09W
Kirkcolm Scotland 16 D2..................54.58N 5.03W
Kirkconnel Scotland 17 E3...............55.23N 4.00W
Kirkcudbright Scotland 17 E2...........54.50N 4.03W
Kirkenes Norway 40 G5....................69.43N 30.01E
Kirkham England 14 E2....................53.47N 2.52W
Kirkintilloch Scotland 16 E3...........55.56N 4.09W
Kirkland Lake town Canada 63 J2.......48.10N 80.02W
Kırklareli Turkey 56 G5..................41.44N 27.13E
Kirk Michael Isle of Man 14 C3.........54.17N 4.35W
Kirkūk Iraq 94 F6..........................35.24N 44.24E
Kirkwall Scotland 19 G3..................58.59N 2.58W
Kirov Rus. Fed. 55 P6......................54.04N 34.20E
Kirovohrad Ukraine 55 O3................48.30N 32.16E
Kirovsk Rus. Fed. 40 H2..................59.52N 30.59E
Kirovsk Rus. Fed. 40 H4..................67.37N 33.40E
Kirriemuir Scotland 19 F1...............56.41N 3.00W
Kırşehir Turkey 57 K4....................39.09N 34.09E
Kirtlington England 10 D2...............51.53N 1.16W
Kirton in Lindsey England 15 G2.......53.29N 0.35W
Kiruna Sweden 40 E4......................67.51N 20.14E
Kisangani Dem. Rep. Congo 86 B5.......0.34N 25.11E
Kisii Kenya 87 A2..........................0.42S 34.46E
Kislovodsk Rus. Fed. 53 L5...............43.55N 42.44E
Kismaayo Somalia 85 I1..................0.19S 42.31E
Kisoro Uganda 87 A2........................1.17S 29.45E
Kisumu Kenya 87 A2..........................0.04S 34.47E
Kita-Kyūshū Japan 106 B2................33.50N 130.50E
Kitale Kenya 87 A3..........................1.01N 35.00E
Kitami Japan 106 D4......................43.49N 143.53E
Kitgum Uganda 87 A3........................3.16N 32.53E
Kitimat Canada 62 F3....................54.03N 128.39W
Kittilä Finland 40 F4......................67.38N 24.54E
Kitui Kenya 87 B2..........................1.22S 38.00E
Kitwe Zambia 86 B3........................12.48S 28.12E
Kiuruvesi Finland 40 F4..................63.39N 26.38E
Kivu, Lake Dem. Rep. Congo/Rwanda 86 B4....1.55S 29.09E
Kızıl Dağı mt. Turkey 57 M4.............39.57N 38.12E
Kızılırmak r. Turkey 57 K5..............41.43N 35.58E
Kladno Czech Rep. 54 F4..................50.09N 14.08E
Klagenfurt Austria 54 F2................46.38N 14.19E
Klaipėda Lithuania 40 E1................55.43N 21.09E
Klamath r. U.S.A. 64 B5..................41.27N 124.02W
Klamath Falls town U.S.A. 64 B5.......42.15N 121.46W
Klang Malaysia 104 C4....................3.02N 101.25E
Klazienaveen Neth. 42 F5................52.44N 6.59E
Kleve Germany 42 F4......................51.47N 6.08E
Klimovo Rus. Fed. 55 O5..................52.23N 32.12E
Klintsy Rus. Fed. 55 O5..................52.45N 32.15E
Kłodzko Poland 46 C3......................50.26N 16.39E
Kluczbork Poland 46 D3..................50.58N 18.13E
Klyuchevskaya, Sopka vol. Rus. Fed. 59 R3....56.01N 160.41E
Knaresborough England 15 F3...........54.01N 1.28W
Knighton Wales 12 D4......................52.20N 3.03W
Knin Croatia 56 B7........................44.03N 16.12E
Knockaboy hill Ireland 41 B1...........51.48N 9.26W
Knockadoon Head Ireland 41 D1.........51.53N 7.52W
Knockalongy hill Ireland 41 C4.........54.12N 8.46W
Knock Hill Scotland 19 G2................57.35N 2.46W
Knocklayd hill Northern Ireland 16 C3....55.10N 6.15W
Knockmealdown Mountains hills Ireland 41 C2
....................................................52.14N 8.04W
Knottingley England 15 F2................53.42N 1.15W
Knowle England 10 D3......................52.23N 1.44W
Knoxville U.S.A. 65 J4....................35.59N 83.56W
Knutsford England 15 E2..................53.18N 2.22W
Kōbe Japan 106 C2..........................34.41N 135.11E
Koblenz Germany 54 B4....................50.21N 7.36E
Kobroör i. Indonesia 105 I2.............6.07S 134.30E
Kobryn Belarus 55 K5......................52.13N 24.20E
Kočani Macedonia 56 E5..................41.55N 22.23E
Kōchi Japan 106 B2........................33.33N 133.32E
Kodiak U.S.A. 62 C3......................57.46N 152.30W
Kodiak Island U.S.A. 62 C3.............57.26N 153.20W
Kōfu Japan 106 C3........................35.39N 138.34E
Køge Denmark 40 C1........................55.27N 12.11E
Kohat Pakistan 95 L6......................33.34N 71.24E
Kokand Uzbekistan 100 C6...............40.31N 70.57E
Kokkola Finland 40 E4....................63.50N 23.08E
Kokpekti Kazakhstan 100 E7.............48.46N 82.21E
Kokshetau Kazakhstan 58 H3...........53.18N 69.24E
Kola Rus. Fed. 40 H5......................68.52N 33.03E
Kolaka Indonesia 105 G3................4.03S 121.38E
Kola Peninsula Rus. Fed. 58 E4........67.29N 36.37E
Kolding Denmark 40 B1..................55.30N 9.28E
Kolguyev, Ostrov i. Rus. Fed. 58 F4....69.11N 49.00E
Kolhapur India 96 D4......................16.40N 74.19E
Kolkata India 96 G5........................22.32N 88.21E
Kołobrzeg Poland 46 B5..................54.11N 15.35E
Kolomyya Ukraine 55 K3..................48.32N 25.02E
Koluli Eritrea 94 F2........................14.24N 40.20E
Kolvitskoye, Ozero l. Rus. Fed. 40 H4....67.04N 33.36E
Kolwezi Dem. Rep. Congo 86 B3.........10.42S 25.28E
Kolyma r. Rus. Fed. 59 R4...............69.22N 161.24E
Kolymskiy, Khrebet mts Rus. Fed. 59 R4....66.50N 167.12E
Komatsu Japan 106 C3....................36.23N 136.28E
Kome Island Uganda 87 A2...............0.06S 32.49E
Komotini Greece 56 F5....................41.07N 25.24E
Komsomolets, Ostrov i. Rus. Fed. 59 K6....80.42N 94.20E
Komsomol'sk Rus. Fed. 55 O5...........49.01N 33.39E
Komsomol'sk-na-Amure Rus. Fed. 59 O3....50.36N 136.55E
Kondoa Tanzania 87 B1..................4.55S 35.47E
Kong Christian IX Land f. Greenland 63 O4....66.49N 37.44W
Kongsberg Norway 40 B2..................59.40N 9.38E
Kongsvinger Norway 40 C3...............60.12N 12.01E
Konin Poland 46 D4........................52.13N 18.15E
Konotop Ukraine 55 O4....................51.14N 33.12E
Konso Ethiopia 87 B4....................5.17N 37.29E
Konstanz Germany 54 C2................47.40N 9.10E
Konya Turkey 57 J3........................37.52N 32.29E
Köping Sweden 40 D2......................59.31N 16.00E
Koprivnica Croatia 54 G2................46.10N 16.50E
Kora National Park Kenya 87 B2.........0.30S 39.08E
Korçë Albania 56 D5......................40.37N 20.47E
Korčula i. Croatia 56 B6................42.56N 16.50E
Korea Bay China/N. Korea 101 M5.......39.05N 124.20E
Korea Strait Japan/S. Korea 106 A2....34.12N 128.36E
Körfez Turkey 57 I4........................40.46N 29.46E
Korinthiakos Kolpos str. Greece 56 E4....38.16N 22.11E
Kōriyama Japan 106 D3....................37.24N 140.22E

Korkuteli Turkey 57 I3 ............................37.04N 30.11E
Köroğlu Tepesi mt. Turkey 57 J5 ..............40.30N 32.01E
Korogwe Tanzania 87 B1..............................5.09S 38.30E
Körös r. Hungary 46 E1 ...........................46.42N 20.11E
Korosten' Ukraine 55 M4.........................50.57N 28.39E
Koro Toro Chad 85 F3 .............................16.05N 18.30E
Korsakov Rus. Fed. 59 P2........................46.38N 142.45E
Kortrijk Belgium 42 C3.............................50.49N 3.16E
Koryakskiy Khrebet mts Rus. Fed. 59 S4....62.59N 177.49E
Kos i. Greece 56 G3 .................................36.46N 27.07E
Kościan Poland 46 C4...............................52.05N 16.39E
Kościerzyna Poland 46 C5........................54.07N 17.59E
Kosciuszko, Mount Australia 110 D3.........36.28S 148.15E
Košice Slovakia 54 I3................................48.43N 21.16E
Kosovo Europe 56 D6...............................42.35N 21.00E
Kosovska Mitrovica Kosovo 56 D6.............42.52N 20.52E
Kosrae atoll Micronesia 108 G6 ................5.19N 163.04E
Kostanay Kazakhstan 58 H3.....................53.12N 63.40E
Kosti Sudan 85 H3...................................13.09N 32.38E
Kostroma Rus. Fed. 58 F3.........................57.46N 40.58E
Kostrzyn Poland 46 B4.............................52.35N 14.39E
Koszalin Poland 46 C5..............................54.11N 16.11E
Kota India 96 E6......................................25.10N 75.57E
Kota Bharu Malaysia 104 C5......................6.08N 102.16E
Kotabumi Indonesia 104 C3.......................4.51S 104.55E
Kota Kinabalu Malaysia 104 F5.................6.00N 116.05E
Kotel'nyy Rus. Fed. 59 O5.......................76.00N 137.59E
Kotel'nyy, Ostrov i. Rus. Fed. 59 O5........75.07N 139.31E
Kotido Uganda 87 A3................................2.59N 34.06E
Kotlas Rus. Fed. 58 F4.............................61.16N 46.38E
Kötlutangi pt Iceland 40 Y1 .....................63.24N 18.45W
Kotuy r. Rus. Fed. 59 L5...........................71.55N 102.06E
Kotzebue U.S.A. 62 B4............................66.53N 162.32W
Kotzebue Sound str. U.S.A. 62 B4............66.33N 163.11W
Koundâra Guinea 84 C3............................12.30N 13.19W
Kouvola Finland 40 F3..............................60.52N 26.42E
Kovel' Ukraine 55 K4................................51.13N 24.43E
Kowloon China 104 E8.............................22.20N 114.13E
Koyang South Korea 101 N5......................37.38N 126.49E
Kozan Turkey 57 K3.................................37.28N 35.48E
Kozani Greece 56 D5................................40.18N 21.48E
Kozhikode India 96 E3.............................11.15N 75.45E
Kozyatyn Ukraine 55 M3..........................49.42N 28.49E
Krabi Thailand 104 B5................................8.05N 98.56E
Krâchéh Cambodia 104 D6.......................12.27N 106.03E
Kragujevac Serbia 56 D7...........................44.01N 20.55E
Kraków Poland 46 D3................................50.03N 19.56E
Kraljevo Serbia 53 H5...............................43.43N 20.41E
Kramfors Sweden 40 D3...........................62.56N 17.46E
Kranj Slovenia 54 F2................................46.15N 14.21E
Krasino Rus. Fed. 58 G2...........................70.44N 54.28E
Krasnoarmiys'k Ukraine 53 K6.................48.17N 37.10E
Krasnodar Rus. Fed. 58 E2.......................45.02N 38.59E
Krasnohrad Ukraine 55 P3........................49.22N 35.28E
Krasnoperekops'k Ukraine 57 J7...............45.57N 33.49E
Krasnoyarsk Rus. Fed. 59 K3....................56.03N 92.50E
Kremenchuk Ukraine 55 O3......................49.04N 33.25E
Kremenchuts'ka Vodoskhovyshche resr Ukraine 55 O3
                                                                      49.18N 32.42E
Křemešník hill Czech Rep. 46 B2..............49.24N 15.20E
Kretinga Lithuania 46 E1..........................55.53N 21.14E
Krishna r. India 96 F4...............................16.01N 80.53E
Kristiansand Norway 40 A2.......................58.08N 7.59E
Kristianstad Sweden 40 D2.......................56.02N 14.10E
Kristiansund Norway 40 A3.......................63.07N 7.45E
Kristinehamn Sweden 40 C2.....................59.19N 14.07E
Krk i. Croatia 56 A7.................................45.02N 14.47E
Kropotkin Rus. Fed. 53 L6........................45.26N 40.34E
Krosno Poland 46 E2.................................49.41N 21.46E
Krotoszyn Poland 46 C3...........................51.42N 17.27E
Kruševac Serbia 56 D6.............................43.35N 21.19E
Krychaw Belarus 55 N5.............................53.44N 31.43E
Krymsk Rus. Fed. 57 L7............................44.55N 37.59E
Krytiko Pelagos sea Greece 56 F3............36.11N 25.24E
Kryvyy Rih Ukraine 55 O2........................47.54N 33.21E
Ksabi Algeria 84 D4.................................28.54N 0.47W
Ksar el Boukhari Algeria 52 D4.................35.52N 2.45E
Ksar el Kebir Morocco 52 B4.....................35.01N 5.54W
Kuala Lumpur Malaysia 104 C4..................3.06N 101.42E
Kuala Terengganu Malaysia 104 C5............5.19N 103.07E
Kuantan Malaysia 104 C4...........................3.50N 103.21E
Kuban' r. Rus. Fed. 57 L7.........................45.19N 37.22E
Kuching Malaysia 104 E4............................1.32N 110.20E
Kugluktuk Canada 62 G4.........................67.46N 115.07W
Kuhmo Finland 40 G4...............................64.07N 29.30E
Kuito Angola 86 B3....................................12.23S 16.57E
Kujū-san vol. Japan 106 B2.....................33.05N 131.16E
Kül r. Iran 95 I5.......................................27.04N 55.44E
Kulal, Mount Kenya 87 B3..........................2.42N 36.58E
Kuldiga Latvia 40 E2................................56.58N 21.59E
Kŭlob Tajikistan 95 K7.............................37.54N 69.51E
Kulunda Rus. Fed. 100 D8........................52.33N 78.56E
Kulundinskoye, Ozero l. Rus. Fed. 100 D8....53.08N 79.46E
Kumamoto Japan 106 B2..........................32.47N 130.43E
Kumanovo Macedonia 56 D6....................42.08N 21.43E
Kumasi Ghana 84 D2..................................6.42N 1.38W
Kumbakonam India 96 E3........................10.58N 79.23E
Kumertau Rus. Fed. 58 G3........................52.44N 55.46E
Kumla Sweden 40 C2................................59.07N 15.10E
Kumo Nigeria 84 F3.................................10.03N 11.11E
Kunashir, Ostrov i. Rus. Fed. 106 E4.......44.13N 146.23E
Kunlun Shan mts China 100 D5................36.11N 78.10E
Kunming China 101 I3..............................25.02N 102.44E
Kuohijärvi l. Finland 40 F3.......................61.12N 24.59E
Kuopio Finland 40 F3...............................62.53N 27.41E
Kupa r. Croatia/Slovenia 56 B7................45.28N 16.25E
Kupang Indonesia 105 G1.......................10.12S 123.35E
Kupiškis Lithuania 40 F1..........................55.49N 24.59E
Kuqa China 100 C4..................................41.38N 83.01E
Kŭrdzhali Bulgaria 56 F5.........................41.39N 25.22E
Kure Atoll U.S.A. 108 I7.........................28.20N 178.17W
Kuressaare Estonia 40 E2........................58.16N 22.29E
Kurgan Rus. Fed. 58 H3...........................55.28N 65.23E
Kurikka Finland 40 E3..............................62.37N 22.25E
Kuril Basin f. N. Pacific Oc. 108 F9...........46.04N 145.16E
Kuril Islands Rus. Fed. 59 P2....................46.04N 148.33E
Kuril Trench f. N. Pacific Oc. 117 Q8........41.44N 146.31E
Kuril'sk Rus. Fed. 59 P2...........................45.13N 147.57E
Kurmuk Sudan 85 H3...............................10.31N 34.16E
Kurnool India 96 E4.................................15.49N 77.59E
Kursk Rus. Fed. 58 E3..............................51.45N 36.12E
Kuršumlija Serbia 56 D6...........................43.08N 21.17E
Kurume Japan 106 B2..............................33.18N 130.31E
Kurun r. South Sudan 87 A4.......................5.37N 34.33E
Kurunegala Sri Lanka 96 F3........................7.30N 80.19E
Kuşadası Turkey 56 G3............................37.52N 27.15E
Kushiro Japan 106 D4.............................42.59N 144.23E
Kuskokwim Mountains U.S.A. 62 C4.........64.24N 155.17W
Kütahya Turkey 57 H4.............................39.25N 29.59E
Kutno Poland 46 D4.................................52.14N 19.22E
Kuujjuaq Canada 63 L3............................58.10N 68.13W

Kuusamo Finland 40 G4...........................65.58N 29.09E
Kuwait Asia 95 G5...................................29.22N 47.08E
Kuwait town Kuwait 95 G5.......................29.18N 47.55E
Kuytun China 100 E6...............................44.20N 84.55E
Kuznetsk Rus. Fed. 58 F3.........................53.07N 46.37E
Kvaløya i. Norway 40 D5..........................69.38N 18.30E
Kwale Kenya 87 B1...................................4.12S 39.27E
KwaMashu S. Africa 86 C2......................29.44S 30.59E
Kwa Mtoro Tanzania 87 A1........................5.13S 35.26E
Kwangju S. Korea 101 N5.........................35.09N 126.54E
Kwania, Lake Uganda 87 A3......................1.46N 32.43E
KwaNobuhle S. Africa 86 B1....................33.48S 25.24E
Kwilu r. Angola/Dem. Rep. Congo 86 A4.....3.23S 17.22E
Kyakhta Rus. Fed. 59 L3..........................50.21N 106.30E
Kybartai Lithuania 46 F5...........................54.38N 22.46E
Kyle of Lochalsh Scotland 18 D2...............57.17N 5.43W
Kyle of Tongue inlet Scotland 19 E3.........58.28N 4.27W
Kyllini mt. Greece 56 E3...........................37.56N 22.24E
Kyoga, Lake Uganda 85 H2........................1.28N 32.53E
Kyōto Japan 106 C3................................34.59N 135.46E
Kyparissia Greece 56 D3...........................37.15N 21.41E
Kypshak, Ozero l. Kazakhstan 58 H3.........50.09N 68.23E
Kyrenia Cyprus 57 J2...............................35.20N 33.19E
Kyrgyzstan Asia 100 C5............................41.47N 74.37E
Kythira i. Greece 56 E3............................36.16N 22.55E
Kythnos i. Greece 56 E3..........................37.26N 24.27E
Kyūshū i. Japan 106 B2...........................31.30N 131.45E
Kyushu-Palau Ridge f. N. Pacific Oc. 108 F7....27.44N 135.16E
Kyustendil Bulgaria 56 E6........................42.17N 22.41E
Kyyivs'ke Vodoskhovyshche resr Ukraine 55 N4....50.54N 30.30E
Kyzyl Rus. Fed. 59 K3..............................51.43N 94.24E
Kyzylorda Kazakhstan 58 H2.....................44.51N 65.30E

L

Laâyoune Western Sahara 84 C4...............27.09N 13.12W
La Banda Argentina 76 H2........................27.41S 64.15W
Labé Guinea 84 C3...................................11.20N 12.18W
Labrador f. Canada 63 L3..........................54.04N 62.29W
Labrador City Canada 63 L3......................52.59N 66.54W
Labrador Sea Canada/Greenland 63 M4.....60.07N 56.06W
Laccadive Islands India 96 D3..................10.59N 72.11E
Laceby England 15 G2...............................53.32N 0.10W
Lachlan r. Australia 110 D3........................34.21S 143.57E
La Crosse U.S.A. 65 H5............................43.48N 91.12W
Ladhar Bheinn mt. Scotland 18 D2............57.05N 5.35W
Ladoga, Lake Rus. Fed. 58 E4...................60.48N 31.37E
Ladybank Scotland 17 F4.........................56.17N 3.08W
Ladybower Reservoir England 15 F2...........53.23N 1.45W
Ladysmith S. Africa 86 B2........................28.34S 29.47E
Lae P.N.G. 110 D6.....................................6.43S 147.00E
Læsø i. Denmark 40 B2.............................57.15N 11.05E
Lafayette U.S.A. 65 H3.............................30.14N 92.03W
Lagan r. Northern Ireland 16 D2................54.37N 5.54W
Laggan, Loch l. Scotland 19 E1.................56.56N 4.31W
Lagh Bogal watercourse Kenya/Somalia 87 C3....0.42N 40.57E
Lagh Bor watercourse Kenya/Somalia 87 C3....0.31N 42.04E
Lagh Dima watercourse Kenya/Somalia 87 C3....0.31N 41.03E
Lagh Kutulo watercourse Kenya/Somalia 87 C3....2.04N 40.58E
Laghouat Algeria 84 E5............................33.42N 2.53E
Lagh Walde watercourse Ethiopia/Kenya 87 B3....2.38N 38.53E
La Gomera i. Canary Islands 48 X2............28.14N 17.18W
Lagos Nigeria 84 E2...................................6.26N 3.20E
Lagos Portugal 48 A2...............................37.06N 8.41W
La Grande U.S.A. 64 C6...........................45.19N 118.02W
La Grande 2, Réservoir Canada 63 K3........53.52N 76.54W
La Grande 3, Réservoir Canada 63 K3........53.36N 75.18W
La Grande 4, Réservoir Canada 63 K3........54.13N 73.17W
La Gran Sabana f. Venezuela 71 L2............5.13N 61.40W
Lahad Datu Malaysia 104 F5.......................5.02N 118.20E
Lahat Indonesia 104 C3.............................3.46S 103.34E
Lahij Yemen 94 F2...................................13.02N 44.50E
Lāhījān Iran 95 G7..................................37.11N 49.56E
Lahore Pakistan 96 D7.............................31.33N 74.23E
Lahti Finland 40 F3...................................60.59N 25.41E
Laidon, Loch l. Scotland 19 E3.................56.39N 4.39W
Laihia Finland 40 E3.................................62.58N 22.01E
Lainioälven r. Sweden 40 E4......................67.22N 22.39E
Lairg Scotland 19 E3................................58.01N 4.24W
Lajes Brazil 77 J2.....................................27.44S 50.19W
Lake City U.S.A. 65 J3..............................30.10N 82.39W
Lake District f. England 14 D3...................54.30N 3.10W
Lakeland U.S.A. 65 J2..............................27.59N 81.58W
Lakki Pakistan 95 L6................................32.35N 70.58E
Lakonikos Kolpos b. Greece 56 E3.............36.32N 22.42E
Laksefjorden str. Norway 40 F5................70.52N 27.00E
Lakshadweep d. India 96 D3....................10.35N 73.13E
La Línea de la Concepción Spain 48 C2......36.10N 5.21W
La Louvière Belgium 42 D3........................50.28N 4.11E
La Mancha f. Spain 48 D3.........................39.06N 2.59W
Lamar U.S.A. 64 F4.................................38.06N 102.38W
Lamard Iran 95 H5...................................27.22N 53.08E
La Marmora, Punta mt. Italy 50 C3...........39.59N 9.20E
La Martre, Lac l. Canada 62 G4................63.19N 118.02W
Lambay Island Ireland 41 F3.......................53.29N 5.59W
Lambourn England 10 D2.........................51.30N 1.32W
Lambourn Downs hills England 10 D2........51.32N 1.32W
Lamego Portugal 48 B4.............................41.06N 7.48W
Lamia Greece 56 E4..................................38.54N 22.25E
Lamlash Scotland 16 D3...........................55.32N 5.08W
Lammermuir Hills Scotland 17 G3..............55.49N 2.50W
Lampang Thailand 104 B8........................18.16N 99.32E
Lampeter Wales 12 C4.............................52.07N 4.05W
Lamu Kenya 87 C2.....................................2.18S 40.52E
Lamu Island Kenya 87 C2..........................2.19S 40.50E
Lanark Scotland 17 F3..............................55.40N 3.47W
Lancashire d. England 9 D3......................53.57N 2.51W
Lancaster England 14 E3..........................54.03N 2.48W
Lancaster Canal England 14 E2.................53.59N 2.48W
Lancaster Sound str. Canada 63 J5...........74.15N 89.18W
Landeck Austria 54 D2.............................47.08N 10.34E
Lander U.S.A. 64 E5................................42.50N 108.42W
Landes f. France 44 C4.............................44.48N 0.55W
Landguard Point England 11 G2................51.56N 1.19E
Land's End England 13 B2.........................50.03N 5.46W
Landshut Germany 54 E3..........................48.33N 12.10E
Landskrona Sweden 54 E6........................55.52N 12.50E
Lanesborough Ireland 41 D3.....................53.40N 7.59W
Langavat, Loch l. Scotland 18 C2.............57.48N 6.59W
Langavat, Loch l. W. Isles Scotland 18 C3....58.02N 6.49W
Langeland i. Denmark 40 B1.....................55.02N 10.55E
Langeoog i. Germany 42 G6......................53.46N 7.36E
Langholm Scotland 17 G3.........................55.09N 2.59W
Langøya i. Norway 40 C4...........................68.44N 14.27E
Langport England 10 C2...........................51.02N 2.50W
Langres France 44 F5................................47.52N 5.20E
Langsa Indonesia 104 B4..........................4.25N 97.57E
Langstrothdale Chase hills England 15 E3....54.12N 2.11W
Languedoc f. France 44 E3........................43.10N 1.57E
Lanivet England 13 C2..............................50.26N 4.46W

Länkäran Azerbaijan 95 G7.......................38.45N 48.51E
Lannion France 44 B6..............................48.44N 3.27W
Lanzarote i. Canary Islands 48 Z2............29.09N 13.35W
Lanzhou China 101 I5..............................36.04N 103.43E
Laoag Phil. 104 G7..................................18.14N 120.36E
Lao Cai Vietnam 104 C8...........................22.26N 103.59E
Laois d. Ireland 41 D2..............................52.57N 7.23W
Laon France 44 E6...................................49.34N 3.38E
Laos Asia 104 C7.....................................19.30N 103.01E
La Palma i. Canary Islands 48 X2..............28.33N 17.44W
La Palma Panama 71 I2..............................8.21N 78.11W
La Palma del Condado Spain 48 B2............37.23N 6.33W
La Paragua Venezuela 71 L2........................6.50N 63.19W
La Paz Bolivia 76 N5................................16.30S 68.10W
La Paz Mexico 70 B5................................24.08N 110.17W
La Pérouse Strait Japan/Rus. Fed. 106 D5....45.35N 141.33E
La Plata Argentina 73 D3.........................34.55S 57.58W
La Plata, Río de str. Argentina/Uruguay 73 D3....34.39S 57.53W
Lappajärvi l. Finland 40 G3.......................63.07N 23.41E
Lappeenranta Finland 40 G3.....................61.03N 28.11E
Laptev Sea Rus. Fed. 59 N5.....................76.05N 125.40E
Lapua Finland 40 F3.................................62.58N 23.00E
L'Aquila Italy 50 E5.................................42.22N 13.24E
Larache Morocco 52 B4............................35.12N 6.09W
Laramie U.S.A. 64 E5.............................41.20N 105.36W
Laredo U.S.A. 64 G2...............................27.30N 99.30W
La Rioja Argentina 73 C4.........................29.25S 66.51W
Larisa Greece 56 E4.................................39.38N 22.25E
Larkana Pakistan 96 C6.............................27.31N 68.15E
Larnaca Cyprus 57 J2...............................34.55N 33.38E
Larne Northern Ireland 16 D2...................54.51N 5.49W
Larne d. Northern Ireland 8 C4.................54.55N 5.43W
Larne Lough inlet Northern Ireland 16 D2....54.49N 5.47W
La Rochelle France 44 C5.........................46.10N 1.09W
La Roche-sur-Yon France 44 C5...............46.40N 1.25W
La Ronge Canada 62 H3..........................55.06N 105.17W
Larvik Norway 40 B2................................59.03N 10.05E
La Sagra r. Spain 48 D4.............................40.05N 3.56W
La Sagra mt. Spain 48 D3.........................37.58N 2.33W
Las Cruces U.S.A. 64 E3.........................32.19N 106.47W
La Serena Chile 73 B4..............................29.53S 71.16W
Lashio Myanmar 97 I5..............................22.57N 97.44E
Las Marismas marsh Spain 48 B2..............37.07N 6.35W
Las Palmas de Gran Canaria Canary Islands 48 Y2
                                                                      28.06N 15.26W
La Spezia Italy 50 C6................................44.07N 9.45E
Las Tórtolas, Cerro mt. Chile 73 C4..........29.56S 69.52W
Las Tunas Cuba 71 J5..............................20.57N 76.57W
Las Vegas U.S.A. 64 C4..........................36.10N 115.09W
Las Villuercas mt. Spain 48 C3.................39.29N 5.23W
Latacunga Ecuador 76 E7...........................0.58S 78.37W
Latakia Syria 94 E7..................................35.31N 35.47E
Latheron Scotland 19 F3...........................58.17N 3.22W
Latina Italy 50 E4....................................41.28N 12.54E
La Tortuga, Isla i. Venezuela 71 K3...........10.58N 65.17W
La Tuque Canada 65 L6............................47.27N 72.47W
Latvia Europe 40 F2.................................56.47N 23.45E
Lauchhammer Germany 54 E4..................51.30N 13.46E
Launceston Australia 110 D2....................41.27S 147.05E
Launceston England 13 C2.......................50.38N 4.21W
Laurencekirk Scotland 19 G1....................56.50N 2.28W
Lausanne Switz. 50 B7.............................46.32N 6.35E
Laut i. Indonesia 104 F3............................3.39S 116.18E
Laval France 44 C6..................................48.04N 0.46W
Lavenham England 11 F3..........................52.06N 0.48E
Lawton U.S.A. 64 G3..............................34.37N 98.24W
Lawz, Jabal al mt. Saudi Arabia 53 K2........28.39N 35.18E
Laxey Isle of Man 14 C3...........................54.14N 4.24W
Laxford, Loch inlet Scotland 18 D3...........58.25N 5.06W
Laysan Island U.S.A. 108 I7.....................25.47N 171.43W
Lázaro Cárdenas Baja Calif. Mexico 70 A7....30.30N 115.56W
Lázaro Cárdenas Michoacán Mexico 70 D4....17.57N 102.12W
Leader Water r. Scotland 17 G3................55.36N 2.40W
Leane, Lough l. Ireland 41 B2...................52.02N 9.34W
Leatherhead England 11 E2......................51.17N 0.19W
Lebanon Asia 53 K3.................................33.17N 35.22E
Lębork Poland 46 C5...............................54.32N 17.45E
Łebsko, Jezioro lagoon Poland 46 C5........54.43N 17.30E
Lecce Italy 50 H4....................................40.20N 18.11E
Lech r. Austria/Germany 54 D2.................47.36N 10.50E
Lechlade England 10 D2...........................51.42N 1.41W
Le Crotoy France 11 G1...........................50.13N 1.38E
Ledbury England 10 C3............................52.02N 2.25W
Lee r. Ireland 41 C1.................................51.54N 8.25W
Leeds England 15 F2................................53.48N 1.33W
Leek England 15 E2.................................53.07N 2.01W
Leeming England 15 F3............................54.18N 1.32W
Lee Moor England 13 C2..........................50.26N 4.01W
Leer Germany 42 G6................................53.14N 7.26E
Leeuwarden Neth. 42 E6..........................53.12N 5.48E
Leeuwin, Cape Australia 110 A3...............34.23S 115.09E
Leeward Islands Caribbean Sea 71 L4.......18.59N 64.04W
Lefkada i. Greece 56 D4...........................38.45N 20.35E
Legaspi Phil. 105 G6...............................13.08N 123.44E
Legionowo Poland 46 E4...........................52.25N 20.58E
Legnica Poland 46 C3..............................51.13N 16.10E
Leh India 96 E7.......................................34.09N 77.36E
Le Havre France 44 D6.............................49.30N 0.08E
Leiah Pakistan 95 L6...............................30.58N 70.58E
Leicester England 10 D3..........................52.38N 1.08W
Leicester d. England 9 E3.........................52.37N 1.05W
Leicestershire d. England 9 E3..................52.37N 0.59W
Leichhardt r. Australia 110 C5..................17.35S 139.48E
Leiden Neth. 42 D5..................................52.10N 4.30E
Leigh England 14 E2................................53.30N 2.31W
Leighton Buzzard England 10 E2...............51.55N 0.40W
Leinster, Mount hill Ireland 41 E2.............52.37N 6.46W
Leipzig Germany 54 E4............................51.21N 12.23E
Leiston England 11 G3.............................52.13N 1.35E
Leith Scotland 17 F3................................55.59N 3.10W
Leith Hill England 11 E2...........................51.11N 0.22W
Leitrim d. Ireland 41 C4...........................54.07N 8.04W
Leixlip Ireland 41 E3................................53.22N 6.29W
Leizhou Bandao pen. China 101 J2...........21.03N 109.41E
Lek r. Neth. 42 D4...................................51.54N 4.34E
Leka Norway 40 B4..................................65.05N 11.35E
Leksozero, Ozero l. Rus. Fed. 40 G3.........63.51N 30.48E
Lelystad Neth. 42 E5................................52.32N 5.29E
Le Mans France 44 D6..............................48.00N 0.12E
Lena r. Rus. Fed. 59 N5............................72.20N 126.37E
Lens France 44 E7...................................50.26N 2.50E
Lensk Rus. Fed. 59 M4...........................60.44N 114.53E
Leoben Austria 54 F2...............................47.23N 15.06E
Leominster England 10 C3........................52.14N 2.44W
León Mexico 70 D5.................................21.07N 101.44W
León Spain 48 C5....................................42.36N 5.34W
Le Puy-en-Velay France 44 E4..................45.03N 3.53E
Lerum Sweden 40 C2...............................57.46N 12.18E
Lerwick Scotland 19 H5...........................60.09N 1.09W
Lesatima mt. Kenya 87 B2..........................0.21S 36.39E
Lesbos i. Greece 87 B2.............................39.08N 25.56E
Les Cayes Haiti 71 J4...............................18.14N 73.47W

Leshan China 101 I3...............................29.37N 103.44E
Leskovac Serbia 56 D6.............................42.59N 21.56E
Lesotho Africa 86 B2................................29.38S 28.26E
Lesozavodsk Rus. Fed. 106 B5................45.23N 133.23E
Les Pieux France 13 Z9............................49.31N 1.48W
Les Sables-d'Olonne France 44 C5............46.30N 1.46W
Lesser Antilles is Caribbean Sea 71 K3.....12.28N 67.56W
Lesser Slave Lake Canada 62 G3...............55.28N 115.29W
Lestijärvi l. Finland 40 F3........................63.30N 24.47E
Leszno Poland 46 C3................................51.51N 16.35E
Letchworth Garden City England 11 E2.....51.59N 0.13W
Lethbridge Canada 62 G2........................49.41N 112.49W
Leti, Kepulauan is Indonesia 105 H2...........8.18S 127.58E
Letterkenny Ireland 41 D4........................54.57N 7.43W
Leuchars Scotland 17 G4..........................56.23N 2.53W
Leuser, Gunung mt. Indonesia 104 B4.........3.46N 97.11E
Leuven Belgium 42 D3.............................50.52N 4.43E
Levadeia Greece 56 E4.............................38.26N 22.52E
Leven England 15 G2...............................53.54N 0.18W
Leven Scotland 17 G4..............................56.12N 2.59W
Leven, Loch inlet Scotland 18 D1..............56.41N 5.06W
Leven, Loch l. Scotland 17 F4..................56.12N 3.23W
Levens England 14 E3..............................54.16N 2.47W
Leverkusen Germany 54 B4......................51.03N 6.59E
Lewes England 11 F1...............................50.52N 0.01E
Lewis, Isle of i. Scotland 18 C3................58.09N 6.59W
Lexington U.S.A. 65 J4............................38.02N 84.31W
Leyburn England 15 F3............................54.19N 1.50W
Leyland England 14 E2............................53.42N 2.42W
Leyte i. Phil. 105 G6...............................11.05N 124.31E
Lezhë Albania 56 C5................................41.46N 19.39E
L'gov Rus. Fed. 55 P4.............................51.39N 35.16E
Lharigarbo China 100 G4.........................32.15N 91.43E
Lhasa China 100 G3................................29.39N 91.05E
Lhazê China 100 F3.................................29.08N 87.36E
Lhokseumawe Indonesia 104 B5................5.09N 97.08E
Lianshan China 101 M6...........................40.41N 120.55E
Lianyungang China 101 L4.......................34.37N 119.11E
Liaoning d. China 101 M6.......................41.30N 122.43E
Liaoyuan China 101 N6............................42.54N 125.08E
Liard r. Canada 62 F4.............................61.51N 121.17W
Libenge Dem. Rep. Congo 86 A5................3.37N 18.42E
Liberal U.S.A. 64 F4...............................37.03N 100.57W
Liberec Czech Rep. 54 F4.........................50.45N 15.03E
Liberia Africa 84 C2...................................6.52N 9.55W
Libin Belgium 42 E2.................................49.59N 5.16E
Liboi Kenya 87 C3.....................................0.20N 40.54E
Libourne France 44 C4............................44.55N 0.14W
Libreville Gabon 84 E2..............................0.28N 9.27E
Libya Africa 84 F4...................................26.07N 17.09E
Libyan Desert Egypt/Libya 85 G4.............24.51N 25.00E
Libyan Plateau f. Egypt/Libya 53 I3..........30.59N 25.49E
Lichfield England 10 D3...........................52.41N 1.50W
Lichinga Mozambique 86 C3.....................13.17S 35.14E
Lida Belarus 55 K5..................................53.53N 25.19E
Liddel r. Scotland 17 G3...........................55.04N 2.57W
Lidköping Sweden 40 C2.........................58.30N 13.11E
Liechtenstein Europe 44 H5......................47.07N 9.36E
Liège Belgium 42 E3................................50.38N 5.35E
Liège d. Belgium 42 E3.............................50.29N 5.42E
Lieksa Finland 40 G3...............................63.19N 30.02E
Lienz Austria 54 E2.................................46.50N 12.46E
Liepāja Latvia 40 E2................................56.31N 21.01E
Liévin France 42 B3.................................50.25N 2.47E
Liezen Austria 50 F7...............................47.35N 14.15E
Liffey r. Ireland 41 E3..............................53.21N 6.14W
Lifford Ireland 41 D4...............................54.50N 7.29W
Ligurian Sea France/Italy 44 H3................43.30N 8.50E
Likasi Dem. Rep. Congo 86 B3..................10.58S 26.47E
Lilla Edet Sweden 40 C2..........................58.08N 12.08E
Lille France 42 D4...................................51.14N 4.50E
Lille France 44 E7...................................50.38N 3.04E
Lillehammer Norway 40 B3......................61.06N 10.29E
Lilleshall England 10 C3...........................52.44N 2.24W
Lillestrøm Norway 40 B2..........................59.59N 11.02E
Lilongwe Malawi 86 C3............................13.57S 33.47E
Lima Peru 76 E5...................................12.04S 77.03W
Limassol Cyprus 57 J2.............................34.41N 33.02E
Limavady Northern Ireland 16 C3..............55.03N 6.57W
Limavady d. Northern Ireland 8 B4............54.57N 6.58W
Limburg d. Belgium 42 E4........................51.04N 5.27E
Limburg d. Neth. 42 E4...........................51.15N 5.54E
Limerick Ireland 41 C2............................52.40N 8.37W
Limerick d. Ireland 41 C2.........................52.29N 8.50W
Limingen l. Norway 40 C4........................64.48N 13.33E
Limnos i. Greece 56 F4............................39.51N 25.21E
Limoges France 44 D4.............................45.50N 1.15E
Limousin f. France 44 D4.........................45.34N 1.17E
Limoux France 44 E3...............................43.04N 2.13E
Limpopo r. S. Africa/Zimbabwe 86 C2........25.13S 33.32E
Linares Spain 48 D3................................38.06N 3.37W
Lincoln England 15 G2.............................53.14N 0.32W
Lincoln U.S.A. 64 G5..............................40.51N 96.40W
Lincolnshire d. England 9 E3....................53.07N 0.14W
Lincolnshire Wolds hills England 15 G2.....53.30N 0.19W
Lindesnes c. Norway 40 A2......................58.00N 7.06E
Lindfield England 11 E2...........................51.01N 0.05W
Lindi Tanzania 86 C3.................................9.59S 39.40E
Lindos Greece 56 H3...............................36.05N 28.04E
Line Islands Kiribati 109 J6........................5.19N 161.36W
Linfen China 101 K5................................36.05N 111.34E
Lingen Germany 54 B5.............................52.32N 7.19E
Lingfield England 11 E2...........................51.11N 0.01W
Lingga, Kepulauan is Indonesia 104 C3......0.02S 105.19E
Linhares Brazil 77 L4...............................19.27S 40.08W
Linköping Sweden 40 C2..........................58.25N 15.37E
Linkou China 101 O6...............................45.11N 130.11E
Linlithgow Scotland 17 F3........................55.58N 3.36W
Linney Head Wales 12 B3.........................51.37N 5.05W
Linnhe, Loch inlet Scotland 16 D4.............56.31N 5.33W
Linosa, Isola di i. Italy 50 E1....................35.52N 12.53E
Linqing China 101 L5...............................36.49N 115.40E
Linxia China 101 I5................................35.29N 102.55E
Linz Austria 54 F3...................................48.19N 14.18E
Lions, Gulf of France 44 E3......................43.00N 3.31E
Lipari, Isole is Italy 50 F3.........................38.39N 14.43E
Lipetsk Rus. Fed. 58 E3...........................52.37N 39.36E
Liphook England 10 E2............................51.04N 0.48W
Lippe r. Germany 42 F4............................51.39N 6.36E
Lisala Dem. Rep. Congo 86 B5...................2.10N 21.32E
Lisbon Portugal 48 A3.............................38.44N 9.08W
Lisburn Northern Ireland 16 C2.................54.31N 6.02W
Lisburn d. Northern Ireland 9 B4...............54.31N 6.04W
Liscannor Bay Ireland 41 B2.....................52.55N 9.26W
Liskeard England 13 C2...........................50.27N 4.28W
Lismore Australia 110 E4.........................28.47S 153.19E
Lismore Ireland 41 D2.............................52.08N 7.56W
Lisnaskea Northern Ireland 16 B2.............54.15N 7.26W
Liss England 10 E2..................................51.03N 0.53W
Listowel Ireland 41 B2.............................52.27N 9.29W
Litani r. Lebanon 53 K3...........................33.22N 35.14E
Lithuania Europe 55 J6.............................55.29N 23.45E
Little Abaco i. Bahamas 71 I6...................26.54N 77.50W

Little Andaman *i.* India 97 H3 ......10.38N 92.31E
Little Belt *str.* Denmark 40 B1 ......55.15N 9.47E
Littleborough England 15 E2 ......53.39N 2.06W
Little Cayman *i.* Cayman Is 71 H4 ......19.42N 80.04W
Littlehampton England 11 E1 ......50.49N 0.32W
Little Inagua Island Bahamas 71 J5 ......21.31N 72.59W
Little Karoo *f.* S. Africa 86 B1 ......33.43S 20.46E
Little Minch *str.* Scotland 18 B2 ......57.32N 7.00W
Little Ouse *r.* England 11 F3 ......52.30N 0.22E
Littleport England 11 F3 ......52.27N 0.19E
Little Rock *town* U.S.A. 65 H3 ......34.46N 92.18W
Liuzhou China 101 J3 ......24.21N 109.22E
Liverpool Canada 65 N5 ......44.02N 64.43W
Liverpool England 14 E2 ......53.25N 2.59W
Livingston Scotland 17 F3 ......55.54N 3.31W
Livingstone Zambia 86 B3 ......17.52S 25.52E
Livorno Italy 50 D5 ......43.32N 10.19E
Lizard England 13 B1 ......49.58N 5.12W
Lizard Point England 13 B1 ......49.57N 5.17W
Ljubljana Slovenia 54 F2 ......46.03N 14.30E
Ljungan *r.* Sweden 40 D3 ......62.18N 17.23E
Ljungby Sweden 40 C2 ......56.51N 13.59E
Ljusdal Sweden 40 D3 ......61.50N 16.06E
Llanarth Wales 12 C4 ......52.12N 4.18W
Llanbadarn Fawr Wales 12 C4 ......52.24N 4.04W
Llanberis Wales 12 C5 ......53.07N 4.08W
Llandeilo Wales 12 C3 ......51.53N 3.59W
Llandovery Wales 12 D3 ......51.59N 3.48W
Llandrindod Wells Wales 12 D4 ......52.14N 3.23W
Llandudno Wales 12 D5 ......53.19N 3.50W
Llandwrog Wales 12 C5 ......53.05N 4.19W
Llandysul Wales 12 C4 ......52.03N 4.18W
Llanegwad Wales 12 C3 ......51.52N 4.09W
Llanelli Wales 12 C3 ......51.41N 4.10W
Llanes Spain 48 C5 ......43.25N 4.44W
Llanfair Caereinion Wales 12 D4 ......52.39N 3.20W
Llanfairfechan Wales 12 D5 ......53.15N 3.58W
Llanfairpwllgwyngyll Wales 12 C5 ......53.13N 4.12W
Llanfair-yn-neubwll Wales 12 C5 ......53.16N 4.33W
Llanfyllin Wales 12 D4 ......52.46N 3.16W
Llangadog Wales 12 D3 ......51.56N 3.53W
Llangefni Wales 12 C5 ......53.15N 4.19W
Llangeler Wales 12 C4 ......52.02N 4.22W
Llangelynin Wales 12 C4 ......52.39N 4.07W
Llangoed Wales 12 C5 ......53.18N 4.05W
Llangollen Wales 12 D4 ......52.58N 3.10W
Llangurig Wales 12 D4 ......52.24N 3.36W
Llanidloes Wales 12 D4 ......52.27N 3.32W
Llanllwchaiarn Wales 12 D4 ......52.32N 3.17W
Llanllyfni Wales 12 C5 ......53.03N 4.17W
Llanos *f.* Col./Venez. 72 C7 ......5.54N 69.50W
Llanrhystud Wales 13 D3 ......51.31N 3.07W
Llanrwst Wales 12 D5 ......53.08N 3.48W
Llansannan Wales 12 D5 ......53.11N 3.36W
Llantrisant Wales 12 D3 ......51.33N 3.22W
Llantwit Major Wales 13 D3 ......51.25N 3.29W
Llanwnda Wales 12 C5 ......53.05N 4.17W
Llanwnog Wales 12 D4 ......52.32N 3.27W
Llanybydder Wales 12 C4 ......52.04N 4.09W
Llay Wales 12 D5 ......53.06N 3.00W
Lleida Spain 48 F4 ......41.36N 0.38E
Llerena Spain 48 B3 ......38.15N 6.01W
Lleyn Peninsula Wales 12 C4 ......52.51N 4.34W
Lloyd George, Mount Canada 62 F3 ......57.50N 124.57W
Lloydminster Canada 62 G3 ......53.17N 110.00W
Llullaillaco, Volcán *vol.* Chile 73 C4 ......24.42S 68.33W
Lobito Angola 86 A3 ......12.24S 13.32E
Lochaline Scotland 16 D4 ......56.32N 5.47W
Lochboisdale Scotland 18 B2 ......57.09N 7.19W
Lochgelly Scotland 17 F4 ......56.08N 3.18W
Lochgilphead Scotland 16 D4 ......56.03N 5.26W
Lochinver Scotland 18 D3 ......58.09N 5.14W
Lochmaben Scotland 17 F3 ......55.08N 3.26W
Lochmaddy Scotland 18 B2 ......57.36N 7.10W
Lochnagar *mt.* Scotland 19 F1 ......56.58N 3.15W
Lochranza Scotland 16 D3 ......55.42N 5.17W
Lochy, Loch Scotland 18 E1 ......56.56N 4.58W
Lockerbie Scotland 17 F3 ......55.07N 3.21W
Loddon England 11 G3 ......52.32N 1.29E
Lodwar Kenya 87 A3 ......3.06N 35.34E
Łódź Poland 46 D3 ......51.46N 19.27E
Lofoten *is* Norway 40 C4 ......68.06N 12.44E
Lofusa South Sudan 87 A3 ......3.50N 33.10E
Logan, Mount Canada 62 D4 ......60.40N 140.02W
Loggerheads England 12 D5 ......52.55N 2.23W
Logone *r.* Cameroon/Chad 82 E6 ......12.10N 15.00E
Logroño Spain 48 D5 ......42.28N 2.26W
Loire *r.* France 44 B5 ......47.17N 2.07W
Loja Ecuador 76 E7 ......4.00S 79.14W
Loja Spain 48 C2 ......37.10N 4.09W
Lokan tekojärvi *resr* Finland 40 F4 ......67.45N 27.35E
Lokeren Belgium 42 C4 ......51.06N 4.00E
Lokichar Kenya 87 A3 ......2.22N 35.37E
Lokichokio Kenya 87 A4 ......4.14N 34.21E
Løkken Norway 40 B3 ......63.07N 9.42E
Lokoja Nigeria 84 E2 ......7.49N 6.44E
Lokwa Kangole Kenya 87 A3 ......3.32N 35.50E
Lolland *i.* Denmark 40 B1 ......54.47N 11.21E
Lollondo Tanzania 87 A2 ......2.01S 35.38E
Lom Bulgaria 56 E6 ......43.49N 23.14E
Lomami *r.* Dem. Rep. Congo 86 B5 ......0.47N 24.17E
Lombok *i.* Indonesia 104 F2 ......9.07S 116.13E
Lomé Togo 84 E2 ......6.09N 1.13E
Lommel Belgium 42 E4 ......51.14N 5.19E
Lomond, Loch *l.* Scotland 16 E4 ......56.04N 4.37W
Łomża Poland 46 F4 ......53.11N 22.05E
London Canada 63 J2 ......42.59N 81.14W
London England 11 E2 ......51.30N 0.07W
Londonderry Northern Ireland 16 B2 ......54.59N 7.20W
Londonderry *d.* Northern Ireland 41 E4 ......54.59N 6.51W
Londonderry, Cape Australia 110 B5 ......13.47S 126.53E
Long, Loch *inlet* Scotland 16 E4 ......56.06N 4.51W
Longa, Proliv *str.* Rus. Fed. 59 S5 ......70.10N 178.17E
Long Ashton England 10 C2 ......51.26N 2.39W
Long Bennington England 10 E3 ......52.59N 0.46W
Long Beach *town* U.S.A. 64 C3 ......33.47N 118.20W
Long Eaton England 10 D3 ......52.54N 1.16W
Longford Ireland 41 D3 ......53.43N 7.48W
Longford *d.* Ireland 41 D3 ......53.45N 7.41W
Longhorsley England 15 F4 ......55.15N 1.46W
Longhoughton England 15 F4 ......55.26N 1.37W
Longido Tanzania 87 B2 ......2.47S 36.42E
Long Island Bahamas 71 I5 ......23.18N 75.06W
Long Island U.S.A. 65 L5 ......40.49N 72.36W
Longlac Canada 63 J2 ......49.47N 86.33W
Longridge England 14 E2 ......53.50N 2.36W
Long Stratton England 11 G3 ......52.29N 1.14E
Longton England 14 E2 ......53.44N 2.48W
Longtown England 14 E4 ......55.01N 2.58W
Longuyon France 42 E2 ......49.27N 5.37E
Longview U.S.A. 65 H3 ......32.32N 94.44W
Long Xuyên Vietnam 104 D6 ......10.20N 105.25E
Longyearbyen Arctic Oc. 58 C5 ......77.59N 15.44E
Lons-le-Saunier France 44 F5 ......46.41N 5.33E

Lookout, Cape U.S.A. 65 K3 ......34.37N 76.33W
Loolmalasin *vol.* Tanzania 87 A2 ......3.02S 35.48E
Loop Head Ireland 41 B2 ......52.33N 9.56W
Lop Nur *f.* China 100 G6 ......40.28N 90.20E
Lopphavet *b.* Norway 40 E5 ......70.21N 21.03E
Loralai Pakistan 95 K6 ......30.21N 68.43E
Lorca Spain 48 E2 ......37.41N 1.41W
Lord Howe Island Australia 111 E3 ......31.26S 158.57E
Lord Howe Rise *f.* S. Pacific Oc. 108 G4 ......27.06S 160.37E
Lorient France 44 B5 ......47.45N 3.22W
Lorn, Firth of *est.* Scotland 16 D4 ......56.15N 5.54W
Lorraine *d.* France 42 F1 ......48.48N 6.06E
Losai National Reserve Kenya 87 B3 ......1.33N 37.39E
Los Ángeles Chile 73 B3 ......37.28S 72.21W
Los Angeles U.S.A. 64 C3 ......34.01N 118.15W
Los Mochis Mexico 70 C6 ......25.48N 108.59W
Los Roques, Islas *is* Venezuela 71 K3 ......11.55N 66.39W
Lossie *r.* Scotland 19 F2 ......57.43N 3.17W
Lossiemouth Scotland 19 F2 ......57.43N 3.17W
Lostwithiel England 13 C2 ......50.24N 4.40W
Los Vilos Chile 76 F1 ......31.56S 71.29W
Lot *r.* France 44 D4 ......44.19N 0.20E
Lotagipi Swamp *f.* Kenya/South Sudan 87 A4 ......4.44N 34.42E
Loth Scotland 19 G4 ......59.12N 2.41W
Lotikipi Plain *f.* Kenya/South Sudan 87 A4 ......4.36N 34.38E
Lotta *r.* Finland/Rus. Fed. 40 G5 ......68.40N 30.14E
Lotuke *mt.* South Sudan 87 A4 ......4.08N 33.51E
Louangnamtha Laos 104 C8 ......21.03N 101.29E
Louangphabang Laos 104 C7 ......19.54N 102.10E
Loughborough England 10 D3 ......52.46N 1.12W
Loughor *r.* Wales 12 C3 ......51.42N 4.03W
Loughrea Ireland 41 C3 ......53.12N 8.35W
Loughton England 11 F2 ......51.39N 0.04E
Louisiana *d.* U.S.A. 65 H3 ......30.40N 91.56W
Louisville U.S.A. 65 I4 ......38.15N 85.46W
Louisville Ridge *f.* S. Pacific Oc. 108 I3 ......30.29S 173.10W
Loukhi Rus. Fed. 40 H4 ......66.04N 33.03E
Louny Czech Rep. 46 A3 ......50.21N 13.49E
Lourdes France 44 C3 ......43.06N 0.02W
Louth England 15 G2 ......53.22N 0.01W
Louth *d.* Ireland 41 E3 ......53.53N 6.31W
Lovech Bulgaria 56 F6 ......43.09N 24.42E
Lovozero Rus. Fed. 40 H5 ......68.01N 34.59E
Lowell U.S.A. 65 L5 ......42.39N 71.19W
Lower Lough Erne *l.* Northern Ireland 16 B2 ......54.29N 7.51W
Lowestoft England 11 G3 ......52.29N 1.45E
Łowicz Poland 46 D4 ......52.07N 19.57E
Loyal, Loch *l.* Scotland 19 E3 ......58.25N 4.22W
Loyauté, Îles *is* New Caledonia 111 F4 ......20.23S 167.17E
Loyne, Loch *l.* Scotland 18 D2 ......57.06N 5.05W
Loznica Serbia 56 C7 ......44.33N 19.15E
Lu'an China 101 L4 ......31.45N 116.32E
Luanda Angola 86 A4 ......8.50S 13.14E
Luarca Spain 48 B5 ......43.32N 6.31W
Luau Angola 86 B3 ......10.42S 22.15E
Lubaczów Poland 46 F3 ......50.10N 23.08E
Lubango Angola 86 A3 ......14.55S 13.30E
Lubartów Poland 46 F3 ......51.28N 22.37E
Lubbock U.S.A. 64 F3 ......33.38N 101.51W
Lübeck Germany 54 D5 ......53.52N 10.42E
Lübecker Bucht *b.* Germany 54 D6 ......54.03N 10.47E
Lubin Poland 46 C3 ......51.24N 16.13E
Lublin Poland 46 F3 ......51.14N 22.35E
Lubnaig, Loch *l.* Scotland 16 E4 ......56.18N 4.19W
Lubny Ukraine 55 O4 ......50.01N 33.00E
Lubuklinggau Indonesia 104 C3 ......3.23S 102.56E
Lubumbashi Dem. Rep. Congo 86 B3 ......11.40S 27.29E
Lubutu Dem. Rep. Congo 86 B4 ......0.44S 26.35E
Lucan Ireland 41 E3 ......53.21N 6.27W
Luce Bay Scotland 16 E2 ......54.47N 4.52W
Lucena Phil. 105 G6 ......13.56N 121.36E
Lucena Spain 48 C2 ......37.25N 4.29W
Lučenec Slovakia 54 H3 ......48.21N 19.41E
Lucerne Switz. 54 C2 ......47.03N 8.18E
Lucknow India 96 F6 ......26.51N 80.58E
Lüderitz Namibia 86 A2 ......26.40S 15.09E
Ludgershall England 10 D2 ......51.15N 1.37W
Ludhiana India 96 E7 ......30.54N 75.53E
Ludlow England 10 C3 ......52.22N 2.43W
Ludvika Sweden 40 D3 ......60.09N 15.12E
Ludwigsburg Germany 54 C3 ......48.54N 9.12E
Ludwigshafen am Rhein Germany 54 C3 ......49.28N 8.26E
Ludwigslust Germany 54 D5 ......53.20N 11.30E
Luena Angola 86 A3 ......11.47S 19.54E
Lufeng China 101 L3 ......22.58N 115.41E
Lufkin U.S.A. 65 H3 ......31.21N 94.44W
Luga Rus. Fed. 40 G2 ......58.43N 29.51E
Luga *r.* Rus. Fed. 40 G2 ......59.40N 28.18E
Lugano Switz. 50 C7 ......46.01N 8.57E
Lugg *r.* Wales 12 E4 ......52.02N 2.38W
Lugo Spain 48 B5 ......43.00N 7.33W
Lugoj Romania 56 D7 ......45.42N 21.55E
Luichart, Loch *l.* Scotland 18 E2 ......57.37N 4.48W
Luing *i.* Scotland 16 D4 ......56.14N 5.39W
Łuków Poland 46 F3 ......51.56N 22.24E
Luleå Sweden 40 E4 ......65.35N 22.10E
Luleälven *r.* Sweden 40 E4 ......65.35N 22.03E
Lüleburgaz Turkey 56 G5 ......41.25N 27.21E
Lumberton U.S.A. 65 K3 ......34.36N 79.05W
Lunan Bay Scotland 19 G1 ......56.39N 2.30W
Lund Sweden 40 C1 ......55.42N 13.12E
Lundy *i.* England 13 C2 ......51.11N 4.39W
Lune *r.* England 14 E3 ......54.03N 2.49W
Lüneburg Germany 54 D5 ......53.15N 10.25E
Lunéville France 44 G6 ......48.36N 6.30E
Luninyets Belarus 55 L5 ......52.14N 26.48E
Luoyang China 101 K4 ......34.38N 112.27E
Lupanshui China 101 I3 ......26.40N 104.48E
Lure France 44 G5 ......47.41N 6.30E
Lurgainn, Loch *l.* Scotland 18 D3 ......58.02N 5.14W
Lurgan Northern Ireland 16 C2 ......54.27N 6.19W
Lusaka Zambia 86 B3 ......15.23S 28.16E
Lushnjë Albania 56 C5 ......40.57N 19.42E
Lushoto Tanzania 87 B1 ......4.47S 38.18E
Lut, Dasht-e *des.* Iran 95 I6 ......30.47N 58.45E
Lutherstadt Wittenberg Germany 54 E4 ......51.52N 12.39E
Luton England 11 E2 ......51.53N 0.25W
Luton *d.* England 9 E2 ......51.54N 0.25W
Luts'k Ukraine 55 K4 ......50.45N 25.21E
Lutterworth England 10 D3 ......52.27N 1.12W
Luxembourg *i.* Belgium 42 E3 ......50.03N 5.27E
Luxembourg Europe 42 F2 ......49.49N 6.01E
Luxembourg *town* Lux. 42 F2 ......49.36N 6.08E
Luxor Egypt 85 H4 ......25.43N 32.39E
Luziânia Brazil 77 J8 ......16.17S 47.53E
Luzon *i.* Phil. 105 G7 ......15.24N 122.02E
Luzon Strait Phil. 104 G8 ......20.11N 121.07E
L'viv Ukraine 55 K3 ......49.50N 24.02E
Lycksele Sweden 40 D4 ......64.36N 18.41E
Lydd England 11 F1 ......50.57N 0.55E
Lydford England 13 C2 ......50.39N 4.06W
Lydney England 10 C2 ......51.44N 2.32W
Lyepyel' Belarus 55 M6 ......54.53N 28.42E
Lyme Bay England 10 C1 ......50.40N 2.59W

Lyme Regis England 10 C1 ......50.43N 2.56W
Lymington England 10 D1 ......50.45N 1.33W
Lynchburg U.S.A. 65 K4 ......37.24N 79.09W
Lyndhurst England 10 D1 ......50.52N 1.35W
Lynmouth England 13 D3 ......51.14N 3.50W
Lynn Lake *town* Canada 62 H3 ......56.51N 101.03W
Lynton England 13 D3 ......51.14N 3.50W
Lyon France 44 F4 ......45.45N 4.52E
Lyon *r.* Scotland 19 F1 ......56.37N 3.58W
Lytchett Minster England 10 C1 ......50.44N 2.03W
Lytham St Anne's England 14 D2 ......53.45N 3.02W
Lyubeshiv Ukraine 46 G3 ......51.46N 25.31E

# M

Ma'an Jordan 94 E6 ......30.12N 35.43E
Ma'arrat an Nu'mān Syria 57 L2 ......35.39N 36.40E
Maas *r.* Neth. 42 D4 ......51.43N 4.53E
Maaseik Belgium 42 E4 ......51.05N 5.48E
Maastricht Neth. 42 E3 ......50.51N 5.42E
Mabalane Mozambique 86 C2 ......23.50S 32.37E
Mablethorpe England 15 H2 ......53.20N 0.16E
Macaé Brazil 77 L3 ......22.22S 41.50W
Macao China 101 K2 ......22.15N 113.34E
Macará Ecuador 76 E7 ......4.24S 79.58W
Macas Ecuador 76 E7 ......2.19S 78.10W
Macassar Strait Indonesia 104 F3 ......3.55S 117.24E
Macclesfield England 15 E2 ......53.16N 2.07W
Macdonnell Ranges *mts* Australia 110 C4 ......23.33S 131.18E
Macduff Scotland 19 G2 ......57.40N 2.30W
Macedo de Cavaleiros Portugal 48 B4 ......41.32N 6.57W
Macedonia Europe 56 D5 ......41.31N 21.46E
Maceió Brazil 77 M6 ......9.36S 35.40W
Macgillycuddy's Reeks *mts* Ireland 41 B1 ......51.57N 9.52W
Mach Pakistan 96 C6 ......29.52N 67.20E
Machakos Kenya 87 B2 ......1.31S 37.16E
Machala Ecuador 76 E7 ......3.17S 79.57W
Machilipatnam India 96 F4 ......16.11N 81.10E
Machrihanish Scotland 16 D3 ......55.25N 5.44W
Machynlleth Wales 12 D4 ......52.35N 3.51W
Mackay Australia 110 D4 ......21.10S 149.11E
Mackay, Lake Australia 110 B4 ......22.36S 128.28E
Mackenzie *r.* Canada 62 E4 ......69.15N 134.11W
Mackenzie King Island Canada 62 G5 ......77.42N 111.56W
Mackenzie Mountains Canada 62 E4 ......65.04N 133.03W
MacLeod, Lake Australia 110 A4 ......24.08S 113.43E
Macomer Italy 50 C4 ......40.16N 8.47E
Mâcon France 44 F5 ......46.19N 4.50E
Macon U.S.A. 65 J3 ......32.53N 83.37W
Macquarie Island S. Pacific Oc. 108 G2 ......54.36S 158.58E
Macquarie Ridge *f.* S. Pacific Oc. 108 G2 ......55.50S 157.21E
Macroom Ireland 41 C1 ......51.54N 8.58W
Madadeni S. Africa 86 C2 ......27.45S 30.02E
Madagascar Africa 86 D2 ......19.57S 46.27E
Madeira *r.* Brazil 77 I7 ......3.23S 58.47W
Madeira *is* N. Atlantic Oc. 84 C5 ......33.15N 16.57W
Madeley England 10 C3 ......52.38N 2.26W
Madera Mexico 70 C6 ......29.11N 108.11W
Madhya Pradesh *d.* India 96 E5 ......23.32N 78.56E
Madidi *r.* Bolivia 76 G5 ......12.34S 66.54W
Madīnat ath Thawrah Syria 57 M2 ......35.51N 38.33E
Madison U.S.A. 65 I5 ......43.04N 89.23W
Mado Gashi Kenya 87 B3 ......0.42N 39.09E
Madona Latvia 55 L7 ......56.51N 26.13E
Madrakah, Ra's *c.* Oman 95 I3 ......19.01N 57.51E
Madre, Laguna *lagoon* Mexico 70 E6 ......25.06N 97.37W
Madre, Sierra *mts* C. America 60 J4 ......15.00N 90.00W
Madre de Dios *r.* Peru 76 F5 ......12.34S 70.05W
Madre de Dios *r.* Peru 72 C6 ......10.59S 66.07W
Madre del Sur, Sierra *mts* Mexico 70 D4 ......18.07N 101.24W
Madre Occidental, Sierra *mts* Mexico 70 C6 ......28.46N 108.51W
Madre Oriental, Sierra *mts* Mexico 70 D6 ......26.41N 101.44W
Madrid Spain 48 D4 ......40.26N 3.40W
Madura *i.* Indonesia 104 E2 ......7.02S 113.11E
Madurai India 96 E2 ......9.55N 78.07E
Maebashi Japan 106 C3 ......36.23N 139.04E
Maesteg Wales 12 D3 ......51.36N 3.40W
Maestra, Sierra *mts* Cuba 71 I4 ......19.54N 77.33W
Mafia Island Tanzania 86 C4 ......7.48S 39.52E
Mafraq Jordan 94 E6 ......32.20N 36.13E
Magadan Rus. Fed. 59 Q3 ......59.38N 151.00E
Magadi Kenya 87 B2 ......1.52S 36.19E
Magdalena *r.* Colombia 72 B8 ......11.06N 74.52W
Magdalena Mexico 70 B7 ......30.38N 110.59W
Magdeburg Germany 54 D5 ......52.07N 11.38E
Magellan, Strait of Chile 73 B1 ......53.42S 71.59W
Magerøya *i.* Norway 40 F5 ......70.59N 25.40E
Maggiorasca, Monte *mt.* Italy 50 C6 ......44.33N 9.30E
Maggiore, Lake Italy 50 C6 ......45.56N 8.36E
Maghera Northern Ireland 16 C2 ......54.50N 6.40W
Magherafelt Northern Ireland 16 C2 ......54.45N 6.36W
Magherafelt *d.* Northern Ireland 9 B4 ......54.49N 6.39W
Maghull England 14 E2 ......53.31N 2.57W
Magilligan Point Northern Ireland 16 C3 ......55.12N 6.56W
Magnitogorsk Rus. Fed. 58 G3 ......53.24N 59.08E
Mago National Park Ethiopia 87 B4 ......5.29N 36.17E
Maguarinho, Cabo *c.* Brazil 77 K7 ......0.19S 48.27W
Magwe Myanmar 97 H5 ......20.09N 94.56E
Mahābād Iran 95 G7 ......36.44N 45.41E
Mahagi Dem. Rep. Congo 85 H2 ......1.26N 30.55E
Mahajanga Madagascar 86 D3 ......15.41S 46.21E
Mahalevona Madagascar 86 D3 ......15.24S 49.53E
Maharashtra *d.* India 96 E4 ......19.24N 75.18E
Mahé *i.* Seychelles 85 J1 ......4.36S 55.24E
Mahilyow Belarus 55 N5 ......53.55N 30.20E
Mahón Spain 48 H3 ......39.53N 4.17E
Mahrāt, Jabal *mt.* Yemen 95 H3 ......17.07N 51.07E
Maicao Colombia 71 J3 ......11.25N 72.23W
Maidenhead England 10 E2 ......51.31N 0.43W
Maidstone England 11 F2 ......51.16N 0.31E
Maiduguri Nigeria 84 F3 ......11.50N 13.08E
Main *r.* Northern Ireland 16 C2 ......54.43N 6.18W
Mai-Ndombe, Lac *l.* Dem. Rep. Congo 86 A4 ......2.15S 18.22E
Maine *d.* U.S.A. 65 M6 ......45.20N 69.21W
Mainland *i.* Orkn. Scotland 19 F4 ......59.04N 3.15W
Mainland *i.* Shetl. Scotland 19 H5 ......60.21N 1.17W
Mainz Germany 54 C4 ......50.00N 8.16E
Maiquetía Venezuela 71 K3 ......10.32N 66.56W
Maisons-Laffitte France 42 B1 ......48.57N 2.09E
Maíz, Islas del *is* Nicaragua 71 H3 ......12.10N 83.02W
Maizuru Japan 106 C3 ......35.28N 135.24E
Maja Jezercë *mt.* Albania 56 C6 ......42.26N 19.50E
Majene Indonesia 104 F3 ......3.30S 118.54E
Maji Ethiopia 87 A4 ......6.08N 35.37E
Major, Puig *mt.* Spain 48 G3 ......39.48N 2.49E
Majorca *i.* Spain 48 G3 ......39.57N 2.43E
Makale Indonesia 104 F3 ......3.06S 119.52E
Makarska Croatia 56 B6 ......43.18N 17.02E
Makassar Indonesia 104 F2 ......5.06S 119.27E
Makat Kazakhstan 58 G2 ......47.37N 53.14E
Makgadikgadi *f.* Botswana 86 B2 ......20.45S 25.35E
Makhachkala Rus. Fed. 58 F2 ......42.59N 47.30E

Makindu Kenya 87 B2 ......2.18S 37.50E
Makran *f.* Iran/Pakistan 95 J5 ......26.29N 60.27E
Makurdi Nigeria 84 E2 ......7.43N 8.33E
Makuyuni Tanzania 87 B2 ......3.33S 36.05E
Mala, Punta *pt* Panama 71 H2 ......7.27N 80.00W
Malabar Coast *f.* India 96 D3 ......12.16N 74.30E
Malabo Equat. Guinea 84 E2 ......3.45N 8.46E
Malacca, Strait of Indonesia/Malaysia 104 B5 ......5.41N 98.38E
Maladzyechna Belarus 55 L6 ......54.18N 26.52E
Málaga Spain 48 C2 ......36.43N 4.25W
Malahide Ireland 41 E3 ......53.27N 6.09W
Malaita *i.* Solomon Is 111 F6 ......8.58S 161.09E
Malakal South Sudan 85 H2 ......9.30N 31.40E
Malakula *i.* Vanuatu 111 F5 ......16.16S 167.19E
Malang Indonesia 104 E2 ......7.56S 112.46E
Malanje Angola 86 A4 ......9.33S 16.23E
Malären Sweden 40 D2 ......59.27N 17.13E
Malatya Turkey 57 M4 ......38.20N 38.20E
Malawi Africa 86 C3 ......11.32S 33.43E
Malåyer Iran 95 G6 ......34.17N 48.48E
Malaysia Asia 104 D5 ......3.39N 108.45E
Malbork Poland 46 D5 ......54.02N 19.02E
Malden Island Kiribati 109 J5 ......4.02S 154.57W
Maldives Indian Oc. 96 D2 ......6.09N 72.23E
Maldon England 11 F2 ......51.44N 0.40E
Male Maldives 96 D1 ......4.18N 73.29E
Maleas, Akra *pt* Greece 56 E3 ......36.26N 23.12E
Malgomaj *l.* Sweden 40 D4 ......64.44N 16.15E
Mali Africa 84 D3 ......13.54N 5.34W
Malili Indonesia 105 G3 ......2.37S 121.07E
Malindi Kenya 87 C2 ......3.14S 40.06E
Malin Head Ireland 41 D5 ......55.23N 7.24W
Malka Mari Kenya 87 C4 ......4.13N 40.47E
Mallaig Scotland 18 D2 ......57.00N 5.50W
Mallawī Egypt 53 J2 ......27.43N 30.50E
Mallow Ireland 41 C2 ......52.08N 8.39W
Malmédy Belgium 42 F3 ......50.26N 6.02E
Malmesbury England 10 C2 ......51.35N 2.06W
Malmö Sweden 40 C1 ......55.36N 13.01E
Måløy Norway 40 A3 ......61.56N 5.07E
Malpas England 14 E2 ......53.01N 2.46W
Malpaso *mt.* Canary Islands 48 W1 ......27.44N 18.01W
Malpelo, Isla de *i.* N. Pacific Oc. 109 O6 ......3.59N 81.34W
Malta Europe 50 F1 ......35.49N 14.18E
Maltby England 15 F2 ......53.25N 1.12W
Malton England 15 G3 ......54.08N 0.48W
Malvern Hills England 10 C3 ......52.04N 2.20W
Malyy Anyuy *r.* Rus. Fed. 59 R4 ......68.27N 161.01E
Mama *r.* Rus. Fed. 59 N4 ......66.28N 143.13E
Mamelodi S. Africa 86 B2 ......25.42S 28.23E
Mamoré *r.* Bolivia/Brazil 76 G5 ......10.23S 65.21W
Mamuju Indonesia 104 F3 ......2.40S 118.51E
Man, Isle of *i.* Irish Sea 9 C4 ......54.15N 4.39W
Man, Isle of *i.* Irish Sea 16 E2 ......54.16N 4.41W
Manacapuru Brazil 77 H7 ......3.14S 60.35W
Manacor Spain 48 G3 ......39.34N 3.14E
Manado Indonesia 105 G4 ......1.33N 124.52E
Managua Nicaragua 71 G2 ......12.07N 86.17W
Manama Bahrain 95 H5 ......26.12N 50.35E
Mananjary Madagascar 86 D2 ......21.14S 48.20E
Manaus Brazil 77 H7 ......3.04S 60.00W
Manavgat Turkey 57 J3 ......36.48N 31.26E
Manchester England 15 E2 ......53.29N 2.15W
Manchuria *f.* China 101 M7 ......46.27N 123.48E
Mand *r.* India 95 H5 ......21.42N 83.15E
Mandala, Puncak *mt.* Indonesia 105 K3 ......4.43S 140.21E
Mandalay Myanmar 97 I5 ......21.59N 96.06E
Mandalgovĭ Mongolia 101 J7 ......45.42N 106.19E
Mandera Kenya 87 C3 ......3.53N 41.50E
Mandioré, Lagoa *l.* Bolivia/Brazil 77 I4 ......18.08S 57.32W
Manevychi Ukraine 46 G3 ......51.17N 25.32E
Manfredonia Italy 50 F4 ......41.38N 15.55E
Manfredonia, Golfo di *g.* Italy 56 B5 ......41.31N 16.05E
Mangaia *i.* Cook Is 109 J4 ......21.52S 157.52W
Mangalia Romania 57 H6 ......43.49N 28.34E
Mangalore India 96 D3 ......12.53N 74.51E
Mangaung S. Africa 86 B2 ......29.09S 26.16E
Mangoky *r.* Madagascar 86 D2 ......23.25S 45.25E
Mangole *i.* Indonesia 105 H3 ......1.51S 125.49E
Mangotsfield England 10 C2 ......51.29N 2.31W
Mangu Kenya 87 B2 ......0.59S 36.57E
Manicouagan, Réservoir *l.* Canada 63 L3 ......51.18N 68.18W
Manihiki *atoll* Cook Is 108 J5 ......10.30S 160.55W
Maniitsoq Greenland 63 M4 ......65.26N 52.55W
Manila Phil. 105 G6 ......14.34N 120.59E
Manipur *d.* India 97 H5 ......24.53N 93.56E
Manisa Turkey 56 G4 ......38.36N 27.25E
Manitoba *d.* Canada 62 I3 ......53.40N 98.06W
Manitoba, Lake Canada 62 I3 ......51.34N 99.04W
Manizales Colombia 72 B7 ......5.00N 75.30W
Manmad India 96 D5 ......20.15N 74.30E
Mannheim Germany 54 C3 ......49.29N 8.28E
Manningtree England 11 G2 ......51.57N 1.04E
Manokwari Indonesia 105 I3 ......0.52S 134.06E
Manorbier Wales 12 C3 ......51.39N 4.48W
Manorhamilton Ireland 41 C4 ......54.18N 8.11W
Manra *i.* Kiribati 108 I5 ......4.26S 171.13W
Manresa Spain 48 F4 ......41.43N 1.50E
Mansa Zambia 86 B3 ......11.11S 28.53E
Mansel Island Canada 63 K4 ......62.05N 79.35W
Mansfield England 15 F2 ......53.09N 1.12W
Mansfield U.S.A. 65 J5 ......40.45N 82.32W
Manston England 10 C1 ......50.56N 2.16W
Manta Ecuador 76 D7 ......0.59S 80.42W
Mantua Italy 50 D6 ......45.09N 10.47E
Manukau New Zealand 111 G3 ......36.58S 174.50E
Manyara, Lake Tanzania 87 A2 ......3.42S 35.47E
Manzanares Spain 48 D3 ......39.00N 3.21W
Manzhouli China 101 L7 ......49.20N 117.29E
Maoke, Pegunungan *mts* Indonesia 105 J3 ......3.34S 135.25E
Mapinhane Mozambique 86 C2 ......22.17S 35.06E
Mapmakers Seamounts *f.* N. Pacific Oc. 108 H7 ......23.40N 165.39E
Mapuera *r.* Brazil 77 I7 ......1.05S 57.06W
Maputo Mozambique 86 C2 ......25.56S 32.34E
Mar, Serra do *mts* Brazil 77 J2 ......29.20S 50.12W
Mara *d.* Tanzania 87 A2 ......1.44S 34.21E
Maraba Brazil 77 K6 ......5.23S 49.08W
Maracá, Ilha de *i.* Brazil 77 J8 ......1.59N 50.22W
Maracaibo Venezuela 72 B8 ......10.40N 71.38W
Maracaibo, Lake *inlet* Venezuela 71 J2 ......9.45N 71.36W
Maracaju, Serra de *hills* Brazil 77 I3 ......21.59S 55.53W
Maracás, Chapada de *hills* Brazil 77 L5 ......13.22S 40.28W
Maracay Venezuela 72 C8 ......10.16N 67.35W
Marādah Libya 85 G4 ......29.12N 19.12E
Maradi Niger 84 E3 ......13.31N 7.07E
Marāgheh Iran 95 G7 ......37.23N 46.14E
Marajó, Ilha de *i.* Brazil 77 J7 ......0.45S 50.38W
Maralal Kenya 87 B3 ......1.06N 36.42E
Marand Iran 95 G7 ......38.26N 45.46E
Maranhão *d.* Brazil 77 K6 ......5.06S 45.19W
Marañón *r.* Peru 76 E7 ......4.27S 73.30W
Marathon Canada 63 I6 ......48.43N 86.23W
Marathonas Greece 56 E4 ......38.09N 23.58E
Marazion England 13 B2 ......50.07N 5.28W

Marbella Spain 48 C2 ........................................36.31N 4.52W
Marburg S. Africa 86 C1 ....................................30.43S 30.26E
Marburg an der Lahn Germany 54 C4 ........50.48N 8.46E
March England 11 F3 ..........................................52.33N 0.05E
Marche-en-Famenne Belgium 42 E3 ..........50.14N 5.21E
Mar Chiquita, Laguna l. Argentina 77 H1 ....30.43S 62.38W
Marchtrenk Austria 54 F3 ..................................48.12N 14.07E
Mardan Pakistan 95 L6 ......................................34.14N 72.04E
Mar del Plata Argentina 73 D3 ..........37.59S 57.35W
Mardin Turkey 94 F7 ..........................................37.18N 40.46E
Maree, Loch l. Scotland 18 D2 ..............57.38N 5.21W
Maresfield England 11 F1 ..................................50.59N 0.05E
Margarita, Isla de i. Venezuela 72 C8 ....11.06N 63.53W
Margate England 11 G2 ......................................51.23N 1.23E
Margery Hill England 15 F2 ................................53.28N 1.43W
Margherita Peak Dem. Rep. Congo/Uganda 86 B5 0.25N 29.56E
Märgow, Dasht-e des. Afgh. 95 J6 ..........30.27N 62.22E
Marhanets' Ukraine 55 P2 ..................................47.40N 34.37E
Mariana Ridge f. N. Pacific Oc. 108 F7 ....20.44N 144.30E
Mariana Trench f. N. Pacific Oc. 108 F6 ....11.20N 141.08E
Marías, Islas is Mexico 70 C5 ..............21.25N 106.33W
Maria van Diemen, Cape New Zealand 111 G3 .. 34.29S 172.38E
Ma'rib Yemen 95 G3 ..........................................15.32N 45.26E
Maribor Slovenia 54 F2 ......................................46.32N 15.40E
Mariehamn Finland 40 D3 ..................................60.06N 19.57E
Mariental Namibia 86 A2 ....................................24.39S 17.58E
Mariestad Sweden 40 C2 ....................................58.43N 13.50E
Marijampolė Lithuania 46 F5 ............54.33N 23.22E
Marília Brazil 77 K3 ..........................................22.13S 49.57W
Mar''ina Horka Belarus 55 M5 ............53.31N 28.08E
Maringá Brazil 77 J3 ..........................................23.27S 51.59W
Maritime Alps mts France/Italy 44 G4 ....44.16N 6.56E
Maritsa r. Bulgaria 56 G5 ..................................41.43N 26.20E
Mariupol' Ukraine 53 K6 ....................................47.06N 37.33E
Marka Somalia 85 I2 ..........................................1.43N 44.44E
Markermeer l. Neth. 42 E5 ..............52.34N 5.14E
Market Deeping England 11 E3 ..........52.41N 0.19W
Market Drayton England 10 C3 ..........52.54N 2.29W
Market Harborough England 10 E3 ......52.29N 0.55W
Markethill Northern Ireland 16 C2 ......54.17N 6.31W
Market Rasen England 15 G2 ..............53.23N 0.20W
Market Warsop England 15 F2 ..............53.12N 1.09W
Market Weighton England 15 G2 ..........53.52N 0.40W
Markha r. Rus. Fed. 59 M4 ................63.29N 118.52E
Marlborough England 10 D2 ..............51.25N 1.44W
Marlborough Downs hills England 10 D2 ....51.29N 1.48W
Marlow England 10 E2 ......................................51.34N 0.46W
Marmande France 44 D4 ....................................44.31N 0.10E
Marmara, Sea of g. Turkey 57 H5 ......40.43N 28.26E
Marmaris Turkey 57 H3 ......................................36.50N 28.15E
Marmolada mt. Italy 50 D7 ..............46.26N 11.51E
Marne r. France 44 E6 ......................................48.49N 2.25E
Marne-la-Vallée France 44 E6 ..........48.51N 2.36E
Maromokotro mt. Madagascar 86 D3 ....14.01S 48.58E
Marondera Zimbabwe 86 C3 ..............18.13S 31.34E
Maroni r. French Guiana 72 D7 ..........5.44N 54.01W
Maroua Cameroon 84 F3 ....................................10.37N 14.19E
Marple England 15 E2 ........................................53.24N 2.04W
Marquesas Islands French Polynesia 109 K5 ....8.39S 139.15W
Marquette U.S.A. 65 I6 ......................................46.32N 87.25W
Marra, Jebel mt. Sudan 85 G3 ..........12.54N 24.11E
Marrakesh Morocco 84 C5 ..................................31.39N 7.58W
Marra Plateau f. Sudan 94 B2 ..........13.24N 24.25E
Marsá al 'Alam Egypt 53 J2 ..............25.04N 34.50E
Marsa al Burayqah Libya 85 F5 ..........30.22N 19.35E
Marsabit Kenya 87 B3 ........................................2.20N 37.59E
Marsabit National Reserve Kenya 87 B3 ....2.11N 37.58E
Marsala Italy 50 E2 ............................................37.48N 12.26E
Marsá Maţrūḩ Egypt 85 G5 ................31.20N 27.16E
Marseille France 44 F3 ......................................43.18N 5.23E
Marsfjället mt. Sweden 40 C4 ............65.06N 15.23E
Marshall Islands N. Pacific Oc. 108 H6 ....13.59N 164.53E
Märsta Sweden 40 D2 ........................................59.37N 17.53E
Martaban Myanmar 97 I4 ..................................16.34N 97.34E
Martaban, Gulf of Myanmar 97 I4 ......16.20N 96.57E
Martapura Indonesia 104 C3 ............4.20S 104.21E
Martin Slovakia 54 H3 ......................................49.04N 18.55E
Martinique i. Central America 71 L3 ..14.36N 60.56W
Martock England 10 C1 ....................................50.58N 2.46W
Mary Turkmenistan 95 J7 ..................................37.34N 61.52E
Maryborough Australia 110 E4 ........25.32S 152.41E
Maryland d. U.S.A. 65 K4 ..................................38.39N 76.30W
Maryport England 14 D3 ....................................54.43N 3.30W
Masai Mara National Reserve Kenya 87 A2 ....1.20S 35.04E
Masai Steppe f. Tanzania 87 B1 ........4.47S 36.53E
Masan S. Korea 101 N5 ....................................35.14N 128.36E
Masbate Phil. 105 G6 ........................................12.20N 123.37E
Masbate i. Phil. 105 G6 ....................................12.20N 123.36E
Mascara Algeria 52 D4 ......................................35.23N 0.08E
Maseno Kenya 87 A2 ........................................0.01N 34.36E
Maseru Lesotho 86 B2 ......................................29.19S 27.29E
Mashhad Iran 95 I7 ............................................36.18N 59.35E
Mashkel, Hamun-i- f. Pakistan 96 B6 ....28.15N 63.02E
Masinga Reservoir Kenya 87 B2 ........0.54S 37.26E
Maşirah, Jazirat i. Oman 95 I4 ..........20.16N 58.58E
Maşirah, Khalij b. Oman 95 I3 ..........19.47N 58.22E
Masjed Soleymān Iran 95 G6 ............31.57N 49.17E
Mask, Lough l. Ireland 41 B3 ..............53.37N 9.21W
Mason City U.S.A. 65 H5 ..................................43.09N 93.12W
Massachusetts d. U.S.A. 65 L5 ........42.23N 72.18W
Massachusetts Bay U.S.A. 65 L5 ......42.25N 70.51W
Massakory Chad 84 F3 ......................................12.59N 15.43E
Massawa Eritrea 85 H3 ......................................15.36N 39.27E
Massif Central f. France 44 E4 ..........45.16N 3.25E
Mastung Pakistan 95 K5 ....................................29.45N 66.56E
Masty Belarus 46 G4 ..........................................53.25N 24.33E
Masuda Japan 106 B2 ......................................34.40N 131.50E
Masvingo Zimbabwe 86 C2 ................................20.04S 30.48E
Matadi Dem. Rep. Congo 86 A4 ..........5.49S 13.29E
Matagami Canada 65 K6 ....................................49.46N 77.38W
Matam Senegal 84 C3 ........................................15.40N 13.16W
Matamoros Mexico 70 E6 ................................25.53N 97.34W
Matanzas Cuba 71 H5 ......................................23.04N 81.34W
Matara Sri Lanka 96 F1 ....................................5.58N 80.29E
Mataram Indonesia 104 F2 ..............8.35S 116.10E
Mataró Spain 48 G4 ..........................................41.33N 2.26E
Matā'utu Wallis and Futuna Is 108 I5 ....13.17S 176.07W
Matehuala Mexico 64 F1 ..................................23.40N 100.38W
Matera Italy 50 G4 ............................................40.40N 16.37E
Mathura India 96 E6 ........................................27.26N 77.43E
Matlock England 15 F2 ....................................53.08N 1.33W
Mato Grosso d. Brazil 77 J5 ..............12.17S 54.47W
Mato Grosso do Sul d. Brazil 77 J3 ..20.42S 53.59W
Maţraḩ Oman 95 I4 ..........................................23.37N 58.32E
Matsue Japan 106 B3 ......................................35.28N 133.03E
Matsumoto Japan 106 C3 ..............36.15N 137.58E
Matsusaka Japan 106 C2 ................34.34N 136.33E
Matsu Tao i. Taiwan 101 M3 ..........26.13N 120.03E
Matsuyama Japan 106 B2 ..............33.49N 132.46E
Matterhorn mt. Italy/Switz. 50 B6 ....45.59N 7.40E
Maturín Venezuela 72 C7 ..................................9.44N 63.09W
Mau mt. Kenya 87 A2 ......................................0.29S 35.52E
Maubeuge France 42 C3 ....................................50.17N 3.58E

Mauchline Scotland 16 E3 ................55.31N 4.23W
Maughold Head Isle of Man 14 C3 ....54.18N 4.18W
Maug Islands N. Mariana Is 105 L8 ....20.02N 145.16E
Maui i. U.S.A. 109 J7 ........................................20.48N 156.00W
Mauke i. Cook Is 109 J4 ..................................20.11S 157.18W
Maumere Indonesia 105 G2 ............8.40S 122.13E
Maun Botswana 86 B3 ....................................19.57S 23.25E
Mauritania Africa 84 C3 ..................................19.51N 11.35W
Mauritius country Indian Oc. 115 L4 ..20.10S 58.00E
May, Isle of i. Scotland 17 G4 ..........56.11N 2.33W
Maya r. Rus. Fed. 59 O4 ..................................60.26N 134.33E
Mayaguana i. Bahamas 71 J5 ..........22.23N 72.56W
Mayagüez Puerto Rico 71 K4 ..........18.12N 67.08W
Mayamey Iran 95 H7 ........................................36.27N 55.40E
Mayar hill Scotland 19 F1 ..............56.51N 3.15W
Maybole Scotland 16 E3 ..................................55.21N 4.41W
Mayen Germany 42 G3 ....................................50.19N 7.13E
Mayenne France 44 C5 ....................................48.18N 0.37W
Maykop Rus. Fed. 57 N7 ..................................44.36N 40.07E
Mayo Canada 62 E4 ..........................................63.37N 135.54W
Mayo d. Ireland 41 B3 ......................................53.46N 9.13W
Mayotte i. Africa 86 D3 ....................................12.59S 45.09E
Mazār-e Sharif Afgh. 95 K7 ............36.43N 67.07E
Mazatlán Mexico 70 C5 ....................................23.14N 106.27W
Mažeikiai Lithuania 40 E2 ................56.18N 22.22E
Mazyr Belarus 55 M5 ........................................52.03N 29.15E
Mbabane Swaziland 86 C2 ..............26.20S 31.09E
Mbala Uganda 87 A3 ........................................1.05N 34.08E
Mbandaka Dem. Rep. Congo 86 A4 ..0.00S 18.17E
M'banza Congo Angola 86 A4 ..........6.14S 14.15E
Mbarara Uganda 85 H1 ....................................0.35S 30.37E
Mbeya Tanzania 86 C4 ....................................8.53S 33.26E
Mbuji-Mayi Dem. Rep. Congo 86 B4 ....6.06S 23.36E
Mbulu Tanzania 87 A2 ......................................3.50S 35.31E
McClintock Channel Canada 62 H5 ....71.10N 101.39W
McClure Strait Canada 62 G5 ..........74.09N 114.57W
McCook U.S.A. 64 F5 ........................................40.14N 100.39W
McGrath U.S.A. 62 C4 ......................................62.52N 155.37W
McKinley, Mount U.S.A. 62 C4 ..........63.05N 150.20W
Mdantsane S. Africa 86 B1 ..............32.58S 27.48E
Mead, Lake resr U.S.A. 64 D4 ..........36.12N 114.24W
Mealasta Island i. Scotland 18 B3 ....58.05N 7.10W
Meall a' Bhuiridh mt. Scotland 18 E1 ....56.37N 4.51W
Meath d. Ireland 41 E3 ....................................53.41N 6.35W
Meaux France 44 E6 ..........................................48.58N 2.53E
Mecca Saudi Arabia 94 E4 ..............21.25N 39.47E
Mechelen Belgium 42 D4 ..................................51.01N 4.29E
Mecheria Algeria 52 C3 ....................................33.33N 0.19W
Meckenheim Germany 42 G3 ..........50.37N 7.02E
Medan Indonesia 104 B4 ..................................3.38N 98.40E
Medellín Colombia 72 B7 ................6.13N 75.35W
Meden r. England 15 G2 ..................................53.25N 0.59W
Medenine Tunisia 52 F3 ....................................33.21N 10.31E
Medetsiz Tepe mt. Turkey 57 K3 ......37.24N 34.37E
Mediaş Romania 56 F8 ....................................46.10N 24.22E
Medicine Hat Canada 62 G3 ..........50.03N 110.41W
Medina Saudi Arabia 94 E4 ............24.31N 39.32E
Medina del Campo Spain 48 C4 ......41.19N 4.54W
Mediterranean Sea World 52 D4 ......33.25N 22.44E
Medvezh'yegorsk Rus. Fed. 58 E4 ....63.00N 34.25E
Medway r. England 9 F2 ..................................51.22N 0.34E
Medway r. England 11 F2 ................................51.21N 0.27E
Meerut India 96 E6 ..........................................29.02N 77.45E
Mēga Ethiopia 87 B4 ........................................4.01N 38.20E
Mega Escarpment f. Ethiopia/Kenya 87 B4 ....4.21N 37.29E
Megara Greece 56 E4 ......................................38.00N 23.21E
Meghalaya d. India 97 H6 ..............25.36N 91.22E
Meiktila Myanmar 97 I5 ....................................20.50N 95.53E
Meiningen Germany 54 D4 ..............50.34N 10.25E
Meißen Germany 54 F4 ....................................51.10N 13.28E
Meizhou China 101 L2 ....................................24.17N 116.09E
Mejicana mt. Argentina 76 G2 ........29.01S 67.50W
Mek'elē Ethiopia 94 E2 ....................................13.31N 39.28E
Meknès Morocco 84 C5 ....................................33.53N 5.30W
Mekong r. Asia 97 K3 ......................................10.53N 105.14E
Mekong, Mouths of the Vietnam 104 D5 ....9.03N 106.31E
Melaka Malaysia 104 C4 ..................................2.09N 102.17E
Melanesia f. Pacific Oc. 108 G6 ......10.00S 165.00E
Melanesian Basin f. Pacific Oc. 108 G6 ....0.19N 164.50E
Melbourn England 11 F3 ..................................52.05N 0.02E
Melbourne Australia 110 D3 ............37.49S 144.59E
Melbourne U.S.A. 65 J2 ....................................28.01N 80.43W
Melby Scotland 19 H5 ......................................60.18N 1.40W
Melekeok Palau 105 I5 ....................................7.30N 134.39E
Melilla N. Africa 52 C4 ....................................35.18N 2.57W
Melitopol' Ukraine 55 P2 ..................................46.51N 35.22E
Melka Guba Ethiopia 87 B4 ............4.41N 39.13E
Melksham England 10 C2 ..................................51.22N 2.08W
Melo Uruguay 77 I1 ..........................................32.22S 54.10W
Melrhir, Chott l. Algeria 84 E5 ........34.15N 6.23E
Melrose Scotland 17 G3 ..................................55.36N 2.43W
Meltham England 15 F2 ....................................53.36N 1.51W
Melton Mowbray England 10 E3 ......52.46N 0.53W
Melun France 44 E6 ..........................................48.32N 2.39E
Melvich Scotland 19 F3 ....................................58.33N 3.55W
Melville Canada 62 H3 ......................................50.56N 102.49W
Melville Bay Greenland 63 L4 ..........76.00N 64.00W
Melville Island Australia 110 C5 ......11.37S 130.55E
Melville Island Canada 62 H5 ..........75.14N 109.26W
Melville Peninsula Canada 63 J4 ......68.09N 84.12W
Melvin, Lough l. Ireland/U.K. 41 C4 ....54.25N 8.09W
Memberamo r. Indonesia 105 J3 ......1.32S 137.52E
Memmingen Germany 54 D2 ............47.59N 10.11E
Memphis U.S.A. 65 H4 ......................................35.09N 90.04W
Mena Ukraine 55 N4 ........................................51.31N 32.14E
Menai Bridge Wales 12 C5 ..............53.13N 4.10W
Menai Strait Wales 12 C5 ..................................53.09N 4.17W
Mende France 44 E4 ........................................44.31N 3.30E
Mendebo mts Ethiopia 87 B4 ..........5.50N 38.39E
Mendī Ethiopia 85 H2 ......................................9.49N 35.03E
Mendip Hills England 10 C2 ............51.19N 2.46W
Mendoza Argentina 73 C3 ..............32.53S 68.50W
Menongue Angola 86 A3 ................14.38S 17.41E
Mentawai, Kepulauan is Indonesia 104 B3 ....2.01S 105.12E
Mentok Indonesia 104 D3 ..............2.01S 105.12E
Menzel Bourguiba Tunisia 52 E4 ......37.09N 9.46E
Meppel Neth. 42 F5 ..........................................52.42N 6.11E
Meppen Germany 42 G5 ................52.41N 7.18E
Merano Italy 50 D7 ..........................................46.41N 11.10E
Merauke Indonesia 105 K2 ............8.31S 140.25E
Mercedes Uruguay 77 I1 ..................................33.16S 58.01W
Mere England 10 C2 ........................................51.05N 2.16W
Merefa Ukraine 55 Q3 ......................................49.49N 36.04E
Mergui Myanmar 97 I5 ......................................12.27N 98.37E
Mergui Archipelago is Myanmar 97 I3 ....11.38N 97.41E
Mérida Mexico 70 G5 ........................................20.59N 89.37W
Mérida Spain 48 B3 ..........................................38.56N 6.20W
Mérida Venezuela 72 B7 ..................................8.36N 71.07W
Mérida, Cordillera de mts Venezuela 71 J2 ....7.59N 71.35W
Meridian U.S.A. 65 I3 ......................................32.23N 88.40W
Merkys r. Lithuania 46 G5 ................54.08N 24.12E
Merowe Sudan 85 H3 ......................................18.27N 31.51E
Merrick hill Scotland 16 E3 ..............55.08N 4.28W
Mersch Lux. 42 F2 ............................................49.45N 6.07E

Mersey est. England 14 E2 ..............53.21N 2.56W
Merseyside d. England 9 D3 ..........53.28N 3.06W
Mersin Turkey 57 K3 ........................................36.49N 34.37E
Merthyr Tydfil Wales 12 D3 ............51.45N 3.23W
Merthyr Tydfil d. Wales 9 D2 ..........51.44N 3.20W
Merti Kenya 87 B3 ..........................................1.02N 38.39E
Mértola Portugal 48 B2 ....................................37.38N 7.39W
Méru France 42 B2 ..........................................49.14N 2.08E
Meru Kenya 87 B3 ............................................0.05N 37.38E
Meru vol. Tanzania 87 B2 ................3.15S 36.44E
Merzifon Turkey 57 K5 ....................................40.52N 35.27E
Merzig Germany 42 F2 ......................................49.27N 6.39E
Mesolongi Greece 56 D4 ................38.22N 21.26E
Mesopotamia f. Iraq 85 I5 ............35.42N 42.19E
Messina Italy 50 F3 ..........................................38.11N 15.33E
Messiniakos Kolpos b. Greece 56 E3 ....36.51N 22.03E
Mesta r. Bulgaria 56 F5 ..................................41.26N 24.02E
Meta r. Col./Venez. 72 C7 ..............6.10N 67.24W
Metheringham England 15 G2 ........53.08N 0.24W
Methwold England 11 F3 ..................................52.31N 0.33E
Metković Croatia 56 B6 ....................................43.03N 17.40E
Metlika Slovenia 54 F1 ......................................45.39N 15.19E
Metz France 44 G6 ............................................49.07N 6.11E
Meuse r. Belgium/France 42 E4 ......51.08N 5.51E
Mevagissey England 13 C2 ..............50.16N 4.47W
Mexborough England 15 F2 ............53.30N 1.17W
Mexicali Mexico 70 A7 ..................................32.39N 115.28W
Mexico Central America 70 C5 ......31.47N 114.01W
México d. Mexico 70 E4 ................19.38N 99.46W
Mexico, Gulf of Mexico/U.S.A. 70 F5 ..22.09N 95.51W
Mexico City Mexico 70 E4 ............19.24N 99.12W
Meymaneh Afgh. 95 J7 ....................................35.56N 64.45E
Mezen' Rus. Fed. 35 I4 ....................................65.51N 44.18E
Mezha r. Rus. Fed. 55 N6 ................55.43N 31.30E
Mezőtúr Hungary 46 E1 ................46.59N 20.39E
Mezquital r. Mexico 70 C5 ............21.52N 105.29W
Mfangano Island Uganda 87 A2 ......0.27S 34.00E
Miami U.S.A. 65 J2 ..........................................25.41N 80.18W
Miandowāb Iran 95 G7 ....................................36.58N 46.07E
Miandrivazo Madagascar 86 D3 ......19.30S 45.29E
Miāneh Iran 95 G7 ............................................37.24N 47.40E
Mianwali Pakistan 95 L6 ................32.32N 71.34E
Miass Rus. Fed. 58 H3 ......................................54.58N 60.05E
Michalovce Slovakia 46 E2 ..............48.45N 21.55E
Michigan d. U.S.A. 65 I6 ..................................46.12N 88.00W
Michigan, Lake U.S.A. 65 I5 ............43.02N 87.18W
Michipicoten Island Canada 65 I6 ....47.41N 85.48W
Michipicoten River town Canada 65 J6 ....47.57N 84.50W
Michoacán d. Mexico 70 D4 ..........18.21N 102.59W
Michurinsk Rus. Fed. 58 F3 ............52.55N 40.30E
Micronesia is Pacific Oc. 108 F6 ....9.00N 147.31E
Micronesia, Federated States of N. Pacific Oc. 105 K5
 ........................................................................3.37N 153.49E
Mid-Atlantic Ridge f. Atlantic Ocean 109 Q7 ....16.18N 49.57W
Middlesbrough England 15 F3 ........54.34N 1.14W
Middlesbrough d. England 9 E4 ....54.34N 1.14W
Middleton England 15 E2 ..................................53.33N 2.12W
Middleton in Teesdale England 15 E3 ....54.38N 2.05W
Middleton St George England 15 F3 ....54.31N 1.28W
Middlewich England 15 E2 ..............53.12N 2.27W
Midhurst England 10 E1 ....................................50.59N 0.44W
Midi, Canal du France 44 E3 ..........43.14N 2.22E
Midland U.S.A. 64 F3 ........................................32.01N 101.38W
Midleton Ireland 41 C1 ....................................51.55N 8.10W
Midlothian d. Scotland 8 D4 ..........55.50N 3.06W
Mid-Pacific Mountains f. N. Pacific Oc. 108 G7 .. 23.27N 150.34E
Midway Islands N. Pacific Oc. 108 I7 ....28.18N 177.17W
Miekojärvi l. Finland 40 F4 ............66.33N 24.25E
Mielec Poland 46 E3 ........................................50.17N 21.26E
Miercurea-Ciuc Romania 56 F8 ......46.22N 25.48E
Mikhaylovskiy Rus. Fed. 100 D3 ......51.40N 79.45E
Mikkeli Finland 40 F3 ........................................61.41N 27.17E
Milan Italy 50 C6 ..............................................45.28N 9.11E
Milas Turkey 57 G3 ..........................................37.18N 27.46E
Milborne Port England 10 C1 ..........50.58N 2.28W
Mildenhall England 11 F3 ..................................52.21N 0.31E
Mildura Australia 110 D3 ................34.12S 142.11E
Miles City U.S.A. 64 E6 ....................................46.25N 105.47W
Milford Haven Wales 12 B3 ..............51.43N 5.02W
Milk r. U.S.A. 64 E6 ..........................................48.03N 106.19W
Millárs r. Spain 48 E4 ......................................39.57N 0.04W
Millau France 44 E4 ..........................................44.06N 3.05E
Mille Lacs lakes U.S.A. 65 H6 ........46.14N 93.39W
Milleur Point Scotland 16 D3 ..........55.01N 5.07W
Millom England 14 D3 ......................................54.13N 3.16W
Millport Scotland 16 E3 ....................................55.45N 4.56W
Milnthorpe England 14 E3 ..............54.14N 2.46W
Milos i. Greece 56 F3 ......................................36.39N 24.25E
Milton Keynes England 10 E3 ..........52.01N 0.44W
Milton Keynes d. England 9 E3 ......52.01N 0.44W
Milwaukee U.S.A. 65 I5 ....................................43.01N 87.55W
Mimizan France 44 C4 ......................................44.12N 1.14W
Mināb Iran 95 I5 ..............................................27.09N 57.04E
Minas Indonesia 97 J1 ....................................0.52N 101.30E
Minas Gerais d. Brazil 77 L4 ..........18.31S 44.00W
Minatitlán Mexico 70 F4 ................18.01N 94.33W
Mindanao i. Phil. 105 H5 ..................................7.48N 125.06E
Mindelo Cape Verde 84 B3 ............16.52N 24.59W
Mindoro i. Phil. 105 G6 ....................................13.05N 120.52E
Mindoro Strait Phil. 104 F6 ............12.47N 119.59E
Minehead England 13 D3 ..................................51.12N 3.29W
Mingulay i. Scotland 18 B1 ..............56.49N 7.37W
Minna Nigeria 84 E2 ........................................9.38N 6.32E
Minneapolis U.S.A. 65 H5 ..............44.55N 93.18W
Minnesota d. U.S.A. 65 H6 ............47.08N 92.44W
Miño r. Portugal/Spain 48 A4 ........41.56N 8.45W
Minorca i. Spain 48 G4 ....................................40.06N 3.51E
Minot U.S.A. 64 F6 ..........................................48.13N 101.18W
Minsk Belarus 55 L5 ........................................53.51N 27.34E
Mińsk Mazowiecki Poland 46 E4 ......52.11N 21.34E
Minsterley England 10 C3 ..............52.38N 2.55W
Mintlaw Scotland 19 H2 ..................................57.31N 1.59W
Miranda Brazil 77 I3 ........................................20.11S 56.21W
Miranda de Ebro Spain 48 D5 ........42.42N 2.56W
Mirandela Portugal 48 B4 ..............41.29N 7.10W
Mirbāţ Oman 95 H3 ..........................................17.02N 54.43E
Miri Malaysia 104 E4 ........................................4.23N 113.59E
Mirim, Lagoa l. Brazil/Uruguay 77 J1 ....32.40S 52.59W
Mirnyy Rus. Fed. 59 M4 ..................................62.25N 114.10E
Mirpur Khas Pakistan 96 C6 ..........25.32N 69.04E
Mirzapur India 96 F6 ......................................25.06N 82.39E
Miskitos, Cayos is Nicaragua 71 H3 ....14.30N 82.45W
Miskolc Hungary 54 I3 ......................................48.06N 20.48E
Misoöl i. Indonesia 105 I3 ..............1.53S 130.06E
Mişrātah Libya 85 F5 ......................................32.21N 15.06E
Missinaibi r. Canada 63 J3 ..............50.43N 81.29W
Mississippi d. U.S.A. 65 I3 ..............32.33N 89.45W
Mississippi r. U.S.A. 65 I2 ..............29.07N 89.17W
Mississippi Delta U.S.A. 65 I2 ......29.05N 89.06W
Missoula U.S.A. 64 D6 ......................................46.53N 113.58W
Missouri d. U.S.A. 65 H4 ..................................38.27N 92.10W

Missouri r. U.S.A. 65 H4 ..................................38.50N 90.09W
Mistassini, Lac l. Canada 63 K3 ......51.01N 73.34W
Mistissini Canada 63 K3 ..................................50.13N 73.48W
Mitchell r. Australia 110 D5 ............15.14S 141.37E
Mitchell U.S.A. 64 G5 ......................................43.42N 98.02W
Mitchell, Mount U.S.A. 65 J4 ..........35.51N 82.20W
Mitchelstown Ireland 41 C2 ..........52.16N 8.16W
Mito Japan 106 D3 ..........................................36.23N 140.28E
Mittimatalik Canada 63 K5 ..............72.35N 77.46W
Mitumba, Chaîne des mts Dem. Rep. Congo 86 B3
 ........................................................................11.46S 26.06E
Miyako Japan 106 D3 ......................................39.38N 141.57E
Miyazaki Japan 106 B2 ....................................31.54N 131.25E
Mizdah Libya 52 F3 ..........................................31.25N 12.59E
Mizen Head Cork Ireland 41 B1 ......51.26N 9.49W
Mizen Head Wick. Ireland 41 E2 ....52.51N 6.03W
Mizhhir''ya Ukraine 46 F2 ..............48.31N 23.31E
Mizoram d. India 97 H5 ..................................23.29N 92.50E
Mjölby Sweden 40 C2 ......................................58.20N 15.08E
Mkoani Tanzania 87 B1 ....................................5.23S 39.39E
Mkomazi Tanzania 87 B1 ..................................4.40S 38.06E
Mkomazi Game Reserve Tanzania 87 B2 ....3.53S 37.53E
Mladá Boleslav Czech Rep. 46 B3 ....50.25N 14.55E
Mława Poland 46 E4 ........................................53.07N 20.23E
Mljet i. Croatia 56 B6 ......................................42.44N 17.27E
Mmabatho S. Africa 86 B2 ..............25.47S 25.37E
Mobile U.S.A. 65 I3 ..........................................30.40N 88.04W
Mobile Bay U.S.A. 65 I3 ..................................30.24N 88.01W
Mobridge U.S.A. 64 F6 ....................................45.32N 100.25W
Moçambique Mozambique 86 D3 ....15.05S 40.41E
Mocha Yemen 94 F2 ........................................13.20N 43.12E
Mochudi Botswana 86 B2 ................................24.25S 26.08E
Mocuba Mozambique 86 C3 ..........16.53S 36.58E
Modbury England 13 D2 ....................................50.21N 3.53W
Modena Italy 50 D6 ..........................................44.39N 10.56E
Moelfre Wales 12 C5 ........................................53.21N 4.14W
Moel Sych hill Wales 12 D4 ..............52.53N 3.23W
Moffat Scotland 17 F3 ....................................55.20N 3.26W
Mogadishu Somalia 85 I2 ................................2.04N 45.20E
Mohawk r. U.S.A. 65 L5 ..................................42.46N 73.44W
Mohyliv Podil's'kyy Ukraine 55 L3 ..48.27N 27.48E
Mo i Rana Norway 40 C4 ................66.19N 14.10E
Moji das Cruzes Brazil 77 K3 ..........23.32S 46.10W
Mojos, Llanos de f. Bolivia 76 G5 ..14.42S 66.08W
Mold Wales 12 D5 ..........................................53.10N 3.08W
Molde Norway 40 A3 ......................................62.44N 7.10E
Moldova Europe 55 L3 ....................................46.59N 28.55E
Moldoveanu, Vârful mt. Romania 56 F7 ....45.36N 24.45E
Molėtai Lithuania 46 G5 ..................................55.14N 25.25E
Molfetta Italy 56 B5 ........................................41.12N 16.36E
Molopo watercourse Botswana/S. Africa 86 B2 ....28.32S 20.13E
Moluccas is Indonesia 108 E5 ..........0.30S 127.26E
Molucca Sea Indonesia 105 H3 ........1.08S 125.11E
Mombasa Kenya 87 B1 ....................................3.59S 39.40E
Møn i. Denmark 40 C1 ....................................55.00N 12.22E
Mona, Isla i. Puerto Rico 71 K4 ......18.04N 67.52W
Monach Islands Scotland 18 B2 ......57.32N 7.41W
Monach, Sound of str. Scotland 18 B2 ....57.33N 7.39W
Monaco Europe 44 G3 ......................................43.44N 7.26E
Monadhliath Mountains Scotland 19 E2 ....57.04N 4.31W
Monaghan Ireland 41 E4 ..................................54.15N 6.57W
Monaghan d. Ireland 41 E4 ............54.13N 7.00W
Mona Passage str. Dom. Rep./Puerto Rico 71 K4 ....18.01N 68.06W
Monar, Loch l. Scotland 18 D2 ........57.25N 5.08W
Monbetsu Japan 106 D4 ....................................44.21N 143.21E
Monchegorsk Rus. Fed. 40 H4 ........67.57N 32.56E
Mönchengladbach Germany 42 F4 ....51.12N 6.25E
Monclova Mexico 70 D6 ..................................26.53N 101.30W
Moncton Canada 63 L2 ....................................46.04N 64.47W
Mondego r. Portugal 48 A4 ..............40.10N 8.39W
Mondoví Italy 50 B6 ..........................................44.23N 7.49E
Moneymore Northern Ireland 16 C2 ....54.41N 6.40W
Monforte de Lemos Spain 48 B5 ......42.32N 7.30W
Monga Dem. Rep. Congo 86 B5 ........4.11N 22.50E
Mongolia Asia 101 I7 ......................................46.59N 103.48E
Mongora Pakistan 95 L6 ..................................34.45N 72.08E
Mongu Zambia 86 B3 ......................................15.15S 23.08E
Moniaive Scotland 17 F3 ................55.12N 3.55W
Monmouth Wales 12 E3 ....................................51.49N 2.43W
Monmouthshire d. Wales 9 D2 ......51.47N 2.58W
Monnow r. U.K. 10 C2 ......................................51.49N 2.43W
Monroe U.S.A. 65 H3 ......................................32.30N 92.06W
Monrovia Liberia 84 C2 ..................................6.20N 10.46W
Mons Belgium 42 C3 ......................................50.27N 3.57E
Montana Bulgaria 56 E6 ..................................43.25N 23.13E
Montana d. U.S.A. 64 E6 ..................................46.44N 109.17W
Montargis France 44 E5 ....................................47.59N 2.44E
Montauban France 44 D4 ..................................44.01N 1.21E
Montbéliard France 44 G5 ..............47.30N 6.49E
Mont-de-Marsan France 44 C3 ......43.53N 0.30W
Montdidier France 42 B2 ..................................49.39N 2.35E
Monte Alegre Brazil 77 J7 ..............1.58S 54.04W
Monte-Carlo Monaco 44 G3 ..........43.44N 7.25E
Montecristo, Isola di i. Italy 50 D5 ..42.19N 10.18E
Montego Bay town Jamaica 71 I4 ....18.28N 77.54W
Montélimar France 44 F4 ................44.33N 4.45E
Monte Lindo r. Paraguay 77 I3 ........23.57S 57.16W
Montemorelos Mexico 70 E6 ........25.11N 99.49W
Montenegro Europe 56 C6 ................................43.01N 19.05E
Montería Colombia 72 B7 ..............8.43N 75.53W
Monterrey Mexico 70 D6 ..................................25.42N 100.18W
Monte Santu, Capo di c. Italy 50 C4 ....40.04N 9.44E
Montes Claros Brazil 77 L4 ..............16.42S 43.49W
Montevideo Uruguay 73 D3 ............34.52S 56.13W
Monte Vista U.S.A. 64 E4 ..................................37.36N 106.09W
Montgomery U.S.A. 65 I3 ................................32.23N 86.19W
Montgomery Wales 12 D4 ................52.33N 3.09W
Mont-Joli Canada 65 M6 ..................................48.35N 68.12W
Montluçon France 44 E5 ..................................46.20N 2.36E
Montmagny Canada 65 L6 ..............46.59N 70.34W
Montpelier U.S.A. 65 L5 ..................................44.16N 72.35W
Montpellier France 44 E3 ..................................43.37N 3.53E
Montréal Canada 63 K2 ..................................45.32N 73.39W
Montreuil France 11 G1 ..................................50.28N 1.46E
Montrose Scotland 19 G1 ..............56.42N 2.28W
Montserrat i. Central America 71 L4 ....16.44N 62.12W
Monywa Myanmar 97 I5 ..................................22.05N 95.13E
Monzón Spain 48 F4 ........................................41.55N 0.11E
Moore, Lake Australia 110 A4 ..........29.43S 117.28E
Moose r. Canada 63 J3 ....................................51.20N 80.31W
Moose Jaw Canada 62 H3 ..............50.26N 105.33W
Moosomin Canada 64 F7 ..................................50.09N 101.41W
Moosonee Canada 63 J3 ..................................51.16N 80.40W
Mopti Mali 84 D3 ............................................14.30N 4.11W
Moquegua Peru 76 F4 ......................................17.09S 70.55W
Mora Sweden 40 C3 ........................................61.00N 14.32E
Moray d. Scotland 8 D5 ..................................57.30N 3.16W
Moray Firth b. Scotland 19 E2 ........57.31N 4.11W
Morbach Germany 42 G2 ..................................49.48N 7.06E
Morden Canada 64 F7 ......................................49.12N 98.07W
More, Loch l. Scotland 18 E3 ..........58.18N 4.53W
Morecambe England 14 E3 ..............54.04N 2.52W

Morecambe Bay England 14 D3....54.07N 3.04W
Moree Australia 110 D4....29.28S 149.52E
Morehead P.N.G. 105 K2....8.44S 141.39E
Morelia Mexico 70 D4....19.39N 101.12W
Morelos d. Mexico 70 E4....18.47N 98.59W
Morena, Sierra mts Spain 48 B2....37.57N 6.06W
Moretonhampstead England 13 D2....50.40N 3.46W
Morgan City U.S.A. 65 H2....29.43N 91.25W
Mori Japan 106 D4....42.06N 140.34E
Morioka Japan 106 D3....39.42N 141.08E
Moriston r. Scotland 18 E2....57.13N 4.36W
Morlaix France 44 B6....48.35N 3.50W
Morley England 15 F2....53.45N 1.36W
Mornington Abyssal Plain f. S. Atlantic Oc. 109 O2....
50.59S 89.12W
Morocco Africa 84 D5....31.57N 5.40W
Morogoro Tanzania 86 C4....6.47S 37.40E
Moro Gulf Phil. 105 G5....6.59N 123.21E
Morombe Madagascar 86 D2....21.46S 43.21E
Mörön Mongolia 101 I7....49.28N 100.08E
Morondava Madagascar 86 D2....20.18S 44.17E
Morón de la Frontera Spain 48 C2....37.08N 5.27W
Moroni Comoros 86 D3....11.39S 43.14E
Morotai i. Indonesia 105 H4....2.23N 128.27E
Moroto Uganda 87 A3....2.31N 34.40E
Moroto, Mount Uganda 87 A3....2.30N 34.47E
Morpeth England 15 F4....55.10N 1.41W
Morriston Wales 12 D3....51.40N 3.56W
Morro, Punta pt Chile 73 B4....27.07S 70.59W
Morrosquillo, Golfo de b. Colombia 71 I2....9.33N 75.39W
Morte Bay England 13 C3....51.10N 4.14W
Mortehoe England 13 C3....51.11N 4.12W
Mortes, Rio das r. Brazil 77 J5....11.49S 50.37W
Mortlock Islands Micronesia 108 G6....5.07N 153.51E
Morungole mt. Uganda 87 A3....3.48N 34.02E
Moruroa atoll French Polynesia 109 K4....21.50S 138.44W
Morvern f. Scotland 18 D1....56.36N 5.53W
Mosborough England 15 F2....53.20N 1.22W
Moscow Rus. Fed. 58 E5....55.45N 37.38E
Moscow U.S.A. 64 C6....46.44N 116.58W
Mosel r. Germany 42 G5....50.22N 7.36E
Moselle r. France 44 G6....49.27N 6.22E
Moshi Tanzania 86 C4....3.23S 37.20E
Mosina Poland 46 C4....52.14N 16.51E
Mosjøen Norway 40 C4....65.51N 13.12E
Mosquitos, Golfo de los b. Panama 71 H2....8.56N 81.17W
Moss Norway 40 B2....59.26N 10.39E
Mossel Bay town S. Africa 86 B1....34.11S 22.08E
Mossoró Brazil 76 M6....5.08S 37.15W
Most Czech Rep. 46 A3....50.32N 13.39E
Mostaganem Algeria 52 D4....35.55N 0.06E
Mostar Bos.-Herz. 56 B6....43.20N 17.49E
Mosul Iraq 94 F7....36.18N 43.05E
Møsvatnet l. Norway 40 B2....59.51N 8.06E
Motala Sweden 40 C2....58.32N 15.02E
Motherwell Scotland 17 F3....55.48N 3.59W
Motril Spain 48 D2....36.45N 3.31W
Moulins France 44 E5....46.34N 3.20E
Moulmein Myanmar 97 I4....16.30N 97.40E
Moundou Chad 84 F2....8.35N 16.05E
Mount Gambier town Australia 110 D3....37.52S 140.48E
Mount Isa town Australia 110 C4....20.45S 139.29E
Mountmellick Ireland 41 D3....53.07N 7.20W
Mountrath Ireland 41 D3....53.00N 7.28W
Mount's Bay England 13 B2....50.05N 5.29W
Mountsorrel England 10 D3....52.44N 1.08W
Mourdi, Dépression du f. Chad 94 B3....18.01N 21.06E
Mourne r. Northern Ireland 16 C2....54.50N 7.28W
Mourne Mountains Northern Ireland 16 C2....54.06N 6.11W
Mousa i. Scotland 19 H5....60.00N 1.11W
Mouscron Belgium 42 C3....50.44N 3.13E
Mouzon France 42 E2....49.37N 5.05E
Moy r. Northern Ireland 16 B2....54.07N 9.08W
Moyale Ethiopia 85 H2....3.32N 39.03E
Moyen Atlas mts Morocco 52 B3....32.25N 5.37W
Moyle d. Northern Ireland 8 B4....54.59N 6.06W
Mozambique Africa 86 C2....20.09S 34.14E
Mozambique Channel Africa 86 D2....20.15S 40.16E
M'Saken Tunisia 52 F4....35.43N 10.35E
Msambweni Kenya 87 B1....4.25S 39.31E
Mtelo Kenya 87 A3....1.41S 35.22E
Mtsensk Rus. Fed. 55 Q5....53.17N 36.36E
Mtwara Tanzania 86 D1....10.19S 40.09E
Muar Malaysia 104 C4....2.02N 102.34E
Muarabungo Indonesia 104 C3....1.27S 102.08E
Muchinga Mountains Zambia 82 G3....12.00S 31.00E
Much Wenlock England 10 C3....52.36N 2.33W
Muck i. Scotland 18 C1....56.50N 6.14W
Muckish Mountain hill Ireland 16 A3....55.06N 8.00W
Muckle Roe i. Scotland 19 H5....60.21N 1.25W
Mudan r. China 106 A5....46.15N 129.31E
Mudanjiang China 101 N6....44.32N 129.34E
Mudukani Tanzania 87 A2....3.54S 35.38E
Mudurnu Turkey 57 I5....40.27N 31.13E
Mueda Mozambique 86 C3....11.38S 39.34E
Muğla Turkey 57 H3....37.12N 28.21E
Muhammad Qol Sudan 94 E4....20.54N 37.07E
Mühlhausen Germany 54 D4....51.12N 10.27E
Muhos Finland 40 F4....64.48N 25.58E
Mui Ethiopia 87 A4....5.59N 35.33E
Muine Bheag Ireland 41 E2....52.42N 6.58W
Muirkirk Scotland 17 E3....55.31N 4.04W
Muirneag hill Scotland 18 C3....58.22N 6.18W
Mukacheve Ukraine 55 J3....48.27N 22.43E
Mukalla Yemen 95 G2....14.34N 49.06E
Mukono Uganda 87 A3....0.21N 32.45E
Mulanje, Mount Malawi 86 C3....15.54S 35.35E
Mulde r. Germany 54 E4....51.52N 12.15E
Mulhacén mt. Spain 48 D2....37.03N 3.18W
Mulhouse France 44 G5....47.45N 7.20E
Muling r. China 106 B5....45.51N 133.26E
Mull i. Scotland 16 D4....56.27N 5.58W
Mull, Sound of str. Scotland 16 D4....56.37N 6.01W
Mullaghareirk Mountains Ireland 41 B2....52.22N 9.17W
Mullaghcleevaun hill Ireland 12 A5....53.06N 6.24W
Mull Head Scotland 19 G4....59.23N 2.53W
Mullingar Ireland 41 D3....53.31N 7.20W
Mull of Galloway c. Scotland 16 E2....54.38N 4.52W
Mull of Kintyre hd Scotland 16 D3....55.17N 5.50W
Mull of Oa hd Scotland 16 C3....55.35N 6.20W
Multan Pakistan 96 D7....30.12N 71.35E
Mumbai India 96 D4....18.56N 72.51E
Muna i. Indonesia 105 G2....5.02S 122.30E
Muna r. Rus. Fed. 59 N4....67.51N 123.04E
Mundesley England 11 G3....52.53N 1.26E
Mundford England 11 F3....52.31N 0.39E
Munger India 96 G6....25.22N 86.28E
Munich Germany 54 D3....48.08N 11.35E
Munim r. Brazil 77 L7....2.49S 44.04W
Münster Germany 54 C4....51.57N 7.38E
Muojärvi l. Finland 40 G4....65.56N 29.38E
Muonio Finland 40 F4....67.57N 23.40E
Muonioälven r. Finland/Sweden 40 E4....67.10N 23.33E
Murallón, Cerro mt. Chile 73 B2....49.50S 73.27W

Muranga Kenya 87 B2....0.43S 37.09E
Murchison watercourse Australia 110 A4....27.39S 114.09E
Murcia Spain 48 E2....37.59N 1.06W
Mureșul r. Romania 56 D8....46.11N 20.29E
Muret France 44 D3....43.28N 1.20E
Muriaé Brazil 77 L3....21.08S 42.23W
Müritz l. Germany 54 E5....53.25N 12.43E
Murmansk Rus. Fed. 58 E4....68.57N 33.07E
Muroran Japan 106 D4....42.06N 140.34E
Murray r. Australia 110 C3....35.22S 139.18E
Murray Bridge Australia 110 C3....35.07S 139.17E
Murrumbidgee r. Australia 110 D3....34.42S 143.13E
Murwara India 96 F5....23.50N 80.23E
Murzūq Libya 84 F4....25.54N 13.55E
Mürzzuschlag Austria 54 F2....47.37N 15.41E
Musala mt. Bulgaria 56 E6....42.11N 23.35E
Muscat Oman 95 I4....23.36N 58.35E
Musgrave Ranges mts Australia 110 C4....26.17S 131.01E
Musmar Sudan 94 E3....18.13N 35.40E
Musoma Tanzania 86 C4....1.32S 33.47E
Musselburgh Scotland 17 F3....55.57N 3.03W
Mustafakemalpaşa Turkey 57 H5....40.02N 28.23E
Müt Egypt 85 G4....25.28N 28.58E
Mut Turkey 57 J3....36.39N 33.26E
Mutare Zimbabwe 86 C3....18.58S 32.39E
Mutis, Gunung mt. Indonesia 105 G2....9.35S 124.14E
Mutsu Japan 106 D4....41.17N 141.10E
Mutuali Mozambique 86 C3....14.52S 37.01E
Muzaffargarh Pakistan 95 L6....30.03N 71.14E
Muzaffarpur India 96 G6....26.05N 85.28E
Mwanza Tanzania 86 C4....2.30S 32.56E
Mwene-Ditu Dem. Rep. Congo 86 B4....7.01S 23.27E
Mweru, Lake Dem. Rep. Congo/Zambia 86 B4....8.57S 28.46E
Myanmar Asia 97 I5....22.37N 95.02E
Mykolayiv Ukraine 53 J6....46.57N 32.02E
Myronivka Ukraine 55 N3....49.39N 30.59E
Myrtle Beach town U.S.A. 65 K3....33.43N 78.54W
Myślibórz Poland 46 B4....52.55N 14.52E
Mysore India 96 E3....12.16N 76.36E
My Tho Vietnam 104 D6....10.20N 106.23E
Mytilini Greece 56 G4....39.07N 26.33E
Mzuzu Malawi 86 C3....11.27S 34.00E

## N

Naas Ireland 41 E3....53.13N 6.40W
Naberera Tanzania 87 B1....4.12S 36.55E
Naberezhnyye Chelny Rus. Fed. 58 G3....55.42N 52.21E
Nabeul Tunisia 52 F4....36.29N 10.45E
Nacala Mozambique 86 D3....14.34S 40.40E
Nador Morocco 52 C4....35.11N 2.56W
Nadvirna Ukraine 46 G2....48.38N 24.35E
Nadym Rus. Fed. 58 I4....65.29N 72.34E
Nafplio Greece 56 E3....37.34N 22.49E
Naga Phil. 105 G6....13.35N 123.11E
Nagaland d. India 97 H6....26.03N 94.37E
Nagano Japan 106 C3....36.38N 138.11E
Nagaoka Japan 106 C3....37.26N 138.51E
Nagaon India 97 H6....26.19N 92.42E
Nagasaki Japan 106 A2....32.46N 129.52E
Nagercoil India 96 E2....8.10N 77.28E
Nagha Kalat Pakistan 95 K5....27.23N 65.13E
Nagichot South Sudan 87 A4....4.14N 33.37E
Nagoya Japan 106 C3....35.10N 136.53E
Nagpur India 96 F5....21.09N 79.05E
Nagurskoye Rus. Fed. 58 F6....80.31N 47.57E
Nagykanizsa Hungary 54 G2....46.28N 16.59E
Naha Japan 101 N3....26.12N 127.39E
Nahāvand Iran 95 H6....34.12N 48.22E
Nailsworth England 10 C2....51.42N 2.13W
Nain Canada 63 L3....56.31N 61.31W
Na'in Iran 95 H6....32.50N 53.03E
Nairn Scotland 19 F2....57.35N 3.52W
Nairn r. Scotland 19 F2....57.35N 3.52W
Nairobi Kenya 87 B2....1.17S 36.48E
Naivasha Kenya 87 B2....0.44S 36.27E
Naivasha, Lake Kenya 87 B2....0.45S 36.19E
Najafābād Iran 95 H6....32.37N 51.20E
Najd f. Saudi Arabia 94 F4....26.14N 40.21E
Najin N. Korea 106 B4....42.15N 130.18E
Najrān Saudi Arabia 94 F3....17.34N 44.17E
Nakhodka Rus. Fed. 59 O2....42.48N 132.54E
Nakhon Ratchasima Thailand 104 C6....14.57N 102.08E
Nakhon Sawan Thailand 104 C7....15.40N 100.06E
Nakhon Si Thammarat Thailand 104 B5....8.25N 99.58E
Nakina Canada 63 I7....50.10N 86.43W
Nakonde Zambia 86 C4....9.21S 32.42E
Nakskov Denmark 40 B1....54.49N 11.09E
Nakuru Kenya 87 B2....0.16S 36.05E
Nalubaale Dam Uganda 87 A3....0.29N 33.14E
Nālūt Libya 84 F5....31.49N 10.57E
Namak, Kavīr-e f. Iran 95 I6....34.26N 57.32E
Namakzar-e Shadad f. Iran 95 I6....30.44N 58.01E
Namanga Kenya 87 B2....2.31S 36.49E
Namangan Uzbekistan 100 C6....40.59N 71.38E
Nam Co l. China 100 G4....30.41N 90.35E
Nam Đinh Vietnam 104 D8....20.22N 106.11E
Namib Desert Namibia 86 A2....25.21S 15.06E
Namibe Angola 86 A3....15.11S 12.10E
Namibia Africa 86 A2....23.22S 15.55E
Namlea Indonesia 105 H3....3.14S 127.05E
Nampʻo N. Korea 101 N5....38.43N 125.23E
Nampula Mozambique 86 C3....15.10S 39.13E
Namsos Norway 40 B4....64.28N 11.31E
Namur Belgium 42 D3....50.28N 4.52E
Namur d. Belgium 42 D3....50.16N 4.53E
Nan Thailand 104 C7....18.48N 100.47E
Nanaimo Canada 64 B4....49.10N 123.56W
Nanao Japan 106 C3....37.03N 136.58E
Nanchang China 101 L3....28.42N 115.58E
Nanchong China 101 J4....30.46N 106.04E
Nancy France 44 G6....48.42N 6.11E
Nanjing China 101 L4....32.04N 118.50E
Nan Ling mts China 101 K2....24.59N 111.08E
Nanning China 101 J2....22.49N 108.24E
Nanortalik Greenland 63 N4....60.08N 45.19W
Nanping China 101 L3....26.41N 118.09E
Nansio Tanzania 87 A2....2.06S 33.03E
Nantes France 44 C5....47.13N 1.33W
Nantes à Brest, Canal de France 44 B5....47.42N 2.07W
Nantong China 101 M4....32.00N 120.52E
Nantucket Island U.S.A. 65 M5....41.17N 69.59W
Nant-y-moch Reservoir Wales 12 D4....52.28N 3.54W
Nanumea atoll Tuvalu 108 H5....5.38S 176.08E
Nanyang China 101 K4....33.01N 112.35E
Nanyuki Kenya 87 B3....0.00S 37.04E
Nao, Cabo de la c. Spain 48 F3....38.44N 0.15E
Napaimiut U.S.A. 62 C4....61.38N 158.24W
Napier New Zealand 111 G3....39.30S 176.53E

Naples Italy 50 F4....40.51N 14.15E
Napo r. Ecuador 76 F7....3.18S 72.37W
Narberth Wales 12 C3....51.48N 4.45W
Narbonne France 44 E3....43.11N 3.01E
Narborough Leics. England 10 D3....52.34N 1.13W
Narborough Norf. England 11 F3....52.41N 0.35E
Nares Strait Canada/Greenland 63 K5....79.12N 71.28W
Narmada r. India 96 D5....21.43N 73.06E
Naro-Fominsk Rus. Fed. 55 Q6....55.22N 36.45E
Narok Kenya 87 A2....1.06S 35.51E
Närpes Finland 40 E3....62.29N 21.21E
Narva Estonia 40 G2....59.22N 28.11E
Narvik Norway 40 D5....68.26N 17.25E
Nar'yan-Mar Rus. Fed. 58 G4....67.40N 53.10E
Naryn Kyrgyzstan 100 D6....41.19N 75.56E
Nashik India 96 D5....20.00N 73.52E
Nashville U.S.A. 65 I4....36.11N 86.46W
Näsijärvi l. Finland 40 E3....61.35N 23.44E
Nassau Bahamas 71 I6....25.05N 77.23W
Nassau r. Cook Is 108 I5....11.32S 165.22W
Nasser, Lake resr Egypt 85 H4....23.09N 33.02E
Nässjö Sweden 40 C2....57.39N 14.43E
Nata Botswana 86 B2....20.12S 26.10E
Nata Tanzania 87 A2....2.01S 34.22E
Natal Brazil 77 M6....5.44S 35.10W
Natchez U.S.A. 65 H3....31.35N 91.24W
Natron, Lake Tanzania 86 C4....2.18S 36.02E
Natuna, Kepulauan is Indonesia 104 D4....4.12N 107.23E
Natuna Besar i. Indonesia 104 D4....4.04N 108.28E
Naturaliste Plateau f. Indian Oc. 108 D3....34.04S 111.21E
Nauru S. Pacific Oc. 108 H5....0.30S 166.56E
Navahrudak Belarus 46 G4....53.36N 25.50E
Navalmoral de la Mata Spain 48 C3....39.53N 5.32W
Navan Ireland 41 E3....53.39N 6.41W
Navapolatsk Belarus 55 M6....55.32N 28.40E
Naver r. Scotland 19 E3....58.31N 4.13W
Naver, Loch l. Scotland 19 E3....58.17N 4.24W
Navlya Rus. Fed. 55 P5....52.49N 34.31E
Navojoa Mexico 70 C6....27.04N 109.32W
Nawabshah Pakistan 96 C6....26.13N 68.25E
Naxçıvan Azerbaijan 95 G7....39.13N 45.24E
Naxos i. Greece 56 F3....37.05N 25.28E
Nayarit d. Mexico 70 D5....22.07N 104.45W
Nay Pyi Taw Myanmar 97 I4....19.44N 96.13E
Nazas r. Mexico 70 D6....25.34N 104.55W
Nazca Peru 76 F5....14.51S 74.54W
Nazca Ridge f. S. Pacific Oc. 109 O4....22.54S 83.41W
Nazilli Turkey 57 H3....37.55N 28.19E
Nazrēt Ethiopia 85 H2....8.32N 39.15E
Nazwá Oman 95 I4....22.57N 57.27E
N'dalatando Angola 86 A4....9.18S 14.56E
Ndélé C.A.R. 85 G2....8.24N 20.38E
Ndeni i. Solomon Is 111 F5....10.41S 166.07E
Ndjamena Chad 84 F3....12.08N 15.03E
Ndola Zambia 86 B3....12.57S 28.39E
Ndoto mt. Kenya 87 B3....1.46N 37.09E
Neagh, Lough l. Northern Ireland 16 C2....54.40N 6.24W
Nea Liosia Greece 56 E3....38.04N 23.42E
Neapoli Greece 56 E3....36.31N 23.04E
Neath Wales 12 D3....51.39N 3.48W
Neath r. Wales 12 D3....51.39N 3.49W
Neath Port Talbot d. Wales 9 D2....51.43N 3.49W
Nebitdag Turkmenistan 95 H7....39.27N 54.17E
Neblina, Pico da mt. Brazil 76 G8....0.49N 66.13W
Nebraska d. U.S.A. 64 F5....41.30N 100.06W
Nebrodi, Monti mts Italy 50 F2....37.43N 14.02E
Neckar r. Germany 44 H6....49.31N 8.27E
Necker Island U.S.A. 108 J7....23.34N 164.42W
Needham Market England 11 G3....52.09N 1.03E
Needles U.S.A. 64 D3....34.50N 114.36W
Nefyn Wales 12 C4....52.56N 4.31W
Negēlē Ethiopia 87 B4....5.20N 39.34E
Negotin Serbia 56 E7....44.13N 22.33E
Negra, Cordillera mts Peru 76 E6....9.19S 78.15W
Negra, Punta pt Peru 76 D6....6.05S 81.21W
Negro r. Argentina 73 C2....41.01S 62.48W
Negro r. Brazil 77 I4....19.17S 57.15W
Negro r. S. America 77 H7....3.08S 59.57W
Negro r. Uruguay 77 I1....33.24S 58.21W
Negro, Cabo c. Morocco 48 C1....35.41N 5.17W
Negros i. Phil. 105 G5....9.43N 122.50E
Neijiang China 101 J3....29.35N 105.04E
Nei Mongol Zizhiqu d. China 101 I6....40.12N 103.26E
Neiße r. Germany/Poland 54 F5....52.04N 14.46E
Neiva Colombia 72 B7....2.55N 75.15W
Nek'emtē Ethiopia 85 H2....9.06N 36.32E
Nekso Denmark 46 E5....55.03N 15.08E
Nelidovo Rus. Fed. 55 O7....56.14N 32.47E
Nellore India 96 E3....14.28N 79.59E
Nelson Canada 62 G2....49.29N 117.17W
Nelson r. Canada 63 I3....56.58N 92.45W
Nelson England 15 E2....53.50N 2.13W
Nelson New Zealand 111 G2....41.17S 173.15E
Nelspruit S. Africa 86 C2....25.28S 30.59E
Neman Rus. Fed. 46 F5....55.02N 22.02E
Neman r. Rus. Fed. 55 J6....55.03N 22.14E
Nementcha, Monts des mts Algeria 52 E3....34.48N 6.23E
Nemuro Japan 106 E4....43.17N 145.30E
Nenagh Ireland 41 C2....52.52N 8.12W
Nene r. England 11 G3....52.49N 0.13E
Nenjiang China 101 N7....49.04N 125.12E
Nepal Asia 96 F6....29.50N 82.06E
Nephin hill Ireland 41 B4....54.01N 9.22W
Neris r. Lithuania 40 F1....54.55N 23.53E
Ness r. Scotland 19 E2....57.29N 4.14W
Ness, Loch l. Scotland 19 E2....57.10N 4.37W
Neston England 14 D2....53.17N 3.04W
Nestos r. Greece 56 F5....40.51N 24.48E
Netherlands Europe 42 E5....52.35N 5.33E
Netley England 10 D1....50.52N 1.19W
Nettilling Lake Canada 63 K4....66.30N 70.39W
Neubari r. South Sudan 87 A4....7.05N 33.14E
Neubrandenburg Germany 54 E5....53.33N 13.15E
Neuchâtel Switz. 50 B7....46.59N 6.56E
Neuchâtel, Lac de l. Switz. 50 B7....46.51N 6.48E
Neufchâteau Belgium 42 E2....49.51N 5.27E
Neumünster Germany 54 C6....54.05N 9.59E
Neunkirchen Germany 42 G2....49.21N 7.10E
Neuquén Argentina 73 C2....38.57S 68.03W
Neuruppin Germany 54 E5....52.56N 12.48E
Neustrelitz Germany 54 E5....53.22N 13.04E
Neuwied Germany 54 B4....50.26N 7.28E
Nevada d. U.S.A. 64 C4....39.03N 117.06W
Nevada, Sierra mts Spain 48 D2....37.04N 3.20W
Nevada, Sierra mts U.S.A. 64 B5....40.07N 121.00W
Nevel' Rus. Fed. 55 M7....56.01N 29.55E
Nevers France 44 E5....47.00N 3.09E
Nevinnomyssk Rus. Fed. 53 L5....44.38N 41.56E
Nevis, Loch inlet Scotland 18 D2....57.00N 5.42W
Nevşehir Turkey 57 K4....38.37N 34.43E
New Addington England 11 E2....51.21N 0.01W
New Alresford England 10 D2....51.05N 1.10W

Newark U.S.A. 65 L5....40.44N 74.24W
Newark-on-Trent England 15 G2....53.04N 0.48W
New Bern U.S.A. 65 K4....35.05N 77.03W
Newbiggin-by-the-Sea England 15 F4....55.11N 1.31W
Newbridge Ireland 41 E3....53.11N 6.48W
Newbridge Wales 12 D3....51.40N 3.09W
New Britain i. P.N.G. 110 D6....5.42S 148.56E
New Britain Trench f. S. Pacific Oc. 108 G5....6.35S 150.51E
New Brunswick d. Canada 63 L2....46.41N 66.28W
Newburgh Scotland 17 F4....56.21N 3.14W
Newbury England 10 D2....51.24N 1.19W
New Caledonia is S. Pacific Oc. 111 F4....21.41S 164.17E
New Caledonia Trough f. Tasman Sea 108 G4....22.53S 164.54E
Newcastle Australia 110 E3....32.56S 151.44E
Newcastle Northern Ireland 16 D2....54.12N 5.54W
Newcastle Emlyn Wales 12 C4....52.02N 4.28W
Newcastleton Scotland 17 G3....55.11N 2.49W
Newcastle-under-Lyme England 15 E2....53.01N 2.13W
Newcastle upon Tyne England 15 F3....54.59N 1.37W
Newcastle West Ireland 41 B2....52.27N 9.03W
New Cumnock Scotland 16 E3....55.23N 4.11W
New Delhi India 96 E6....28.36N 77.17E
Newent England 10 C2....51.56N 2.24W
New Forest nature res. England 10 D1....50.52N 1.37W
Newfoundland i. Canada 63 M2....48.30N 56.04W
Newfoundland and Labrador d. Canada 63 M3....55.44N 56.53W
New Galloway Scotland 16 E3....55.05N 4.08W
New Georgia Sound str. Solomon Is 110 E6....7.21S 156.36E
New Glasgow Canada 65 N6....45.35N 62.35W
New Guinea i. Indonesia/P.N.G. 105 K2....5.26S 140.49E
New Hampshire d. U.S.A. 65 L5....44.02N 71.34W
Newhaven England 11 F1....50.48N 0.03E
New Haven U.S.A. 65 L5....41.18N 72.56W
New Hebrides Trench f. S. Pacific Oc. 108 H4....22.43S 170.39E
New Ireland i. P.N.G. 110 E6....3.33S 152.14E
New Jersey d. U.S.A. 65 L4....39.57N 74.26W
New Liskeard Canada 63 K6....47.31N 79.41W
Newmarket England 11 F3....52.15N 0.25E
Newmarket-on-Fergus Ireland 41 C2....52.46N 8.53W
New Mexico d. U.S.A. 64 E3....34.32N 105.55W
New Milton England 10 D1....50.45N 1.40W
Newnham England 10 C2....51.48N 2.27W
New Orleans U.S.A. 65 H2....29.58N 90.03W
New Pitsligo Scotland 19 G2....57.35N 2.11W
Newport Ess. England 11 F2....51.59N 0.13E
Newport I. o. W. England 10 D1....50.42N 1.17W
Newport Tel. Wre. England 10 C3....52.46N 2.22W
Newport New. Wales 12 B3....51.35N 2.59W
Newport Pem. Wales 12 C4....52.01N 4.50W
Newport d. Wales 9 D2....51.35N 2.59W
Newport Bay Wales 12 C4....52.02N 4.53W
Newport News U.S.A. 65 K4....37.00N 76.26W
Newport Pagnell England 10 E3....52.05N 0.43W
New Providence i. Bahamas 71 I6....25.03N 77.25W
Newquay England 13 B2....50.25N 5.04W
New Quay Wales 12 C4....52.13N 4.22W
New Romney England 11 F1....50.59N 0.56E
New Ross Ireland 41 E2....52.24N 6.56W
Newry Northern Ireland 16 C2....54.10N 6.19W
Newry and Mourne d. Northern Ireland 9 B4....54.10N 6.18W
Newry Canal Northern Ireland 16 C2....54.16N 6.21W
New Siberia Islands Rus. Fed. 59 P5....76.08N 147.21E
New South Wales d. Australia 110 D3....32.42S 146.24E
Newton Abbot England 13 D2....50.32N 3.37W
Newton Aycliffe England 15 F3....54.37N 1.34W
Newtonhill Scotland 19 G2....57.02N 2.09W
Newton-le-Willows England 14 E2....53.27N 2.38W
Newton Mearns Scotland 16 E3....55.46N 4.20W
Newtonmore Scotland 19 E2....57.04N 4.07W
Newton St Cyres England 13 D2....50.46N 3.35W
Newton Stewart Scotland 16 E2....54.58N 4.29W
Newtown Wales 12 D4....52.31N 3.19W
Newtownabbey Northern Ireland 16 D2....54.39N 5.54W
Newtownabbey d. Northern Ireland 9 C4....54.44N 5.59W
Newtownards Northern Ireland 16 D2....54.35N 5.41W
Newtown St Boswells Scotland 17 G3....55.35N 2.40W
Newtownstewart Northern Ireland 16 B2....54.43N 7.22W
New York U.S.A. 65 L5....40.41N 73.59W
New York d. U.S.A. 65 K5....42.43N 75.14W
New Zealand Oceania 111 G2....42.54S 174.10E
Neyrīz Iran 95 H5....29.12N 54.19E
Neyshābūr Iran 95 I7....36.12N 58.46E
Ngaoundéré Cameroon 84 F2....7.19N 13.34E
Ngorongoro Conservation Area Tanzania 87 A2....3.06S 35.20E
Nguigmi Niger 84 F3....14.14N 13.05E
Ngulu atoll Micronesia 105 J5....8.28N 137.37E
Nha Trang Vietnam 104 D6....12.11N 109.11E
Niamey Niger 84 E3....13.31N 2.07E
Niangara Dem. Rep. Congo 86 B5....3.40N 27.52E
Nias i. Indonesia 104 B4....1.11N 97.04E
Nīca Latvia 46 E6....56.21N 21.04E
Nicaragua Central America 71 G3....13.13N 85.57W
Nicaragua, Lake Nicaragua 71 G3....11.31N 85.17W
Nice France 44 G3....43.42N 7.17E
Nicobar Islands India 97 H2....8.00N 93.59E
Nicosia Cyprus 57 J2....35.10N 33.22E
Nicoya, Golfo de b. Costa Rica 71 H2....9.42N 84.48W
Nidd r. England 15 F2....54.01N 1.12W
Nidzica Poland 46 E4....53.22N 20.26E
Niedersachsen d. Germany 42 G5....52.43N 8.53E
Nienburg Germany 54 C5....52.38N 9.13E
Niers r. Germany 42 F4....51.43N 5.57E
Nieuwpoort Belgium 42 B4....51.08N 2.45E
Nieves, Pico de las mt. Canary Islands 48 Y1....27.57N 15.34W
Niğde Turkey 57 K3....37.59N 34.41E
Niger Africa 84 E3....17.03N 10.05E
Niger r. Africa 84 E2....4.17N 6.05E
Nigeria Africa 84 E2....9.09N 7.54E
Nigg Bay Scotland 19 E2....57.43N 4.05W
Niigata Japan 106 C3....37.55N 139.03E
Nijmegen Neth. 42 E4....51.50N 5.52E
Nikel' Rus. Fed. 40 G5....69.24N 30.13E
Nikopol' Ukraine 55 P2....47.34N 34.24E
Niksar Turkey 57 L5....40.35N 36.57E
Nikšić Montenegro 56 C6....42.46N 18.56E
Nikumaroro atoll Kiribati 108 I5....4.43S 174.31W
Nile r. Africa 85 H5....30.11N 31.06E
Nilgiri Hills India 96 E3....11.08N 76.28E
Nîmes France 44 F3....43.51N 4.22E
Ninetyeast Ridge f. Indian Oc. 108 B3....34.14S 86.15E
Ningbo China 101 M3....29.54N 121.34E
Ningxia Huizu Zizhiqu d. China 101 J5....37.11N 105.28E
Niobrara r. U.S.A. 64 G5....42.46N 98.02W
Nioro Mali 84 D3....15.14N 9.36W
Niort France 44 C5....46.20N 0.28W
Nipigon Canada 63 J2....49.00N 88.17W
Nipigon, Lake Canada 63 J2....49.43N 88.33W
Nipissing, Lake Canada 65 K6....46.15N 79.39W
Niš Serbia 56 D6....43.19N 21.54E
Niterói Brazil 77 L3....22.54S 43.06W
Nith r. Scotland 17 F3....55.00N 3.36W
Nitra Slovakia 54 H3....48.19N 18.05E
Niue i. S. Pacific Oc. 108 I4....19.03S 169.45W
Nivelles Belgium 42 D3....50.36N 4.20E

Nizamabad India 96 E4 .................................18.40N 78.07E
Nizhneudinsk Rus. Fed. 59 K3 .................54.55N 98.58E
Nizhnevartovsk Rus. Fed. 58 I4 ...............60.56N 76.38E
Nizhniy Novgorod Rus. Fed. 58 F3 .........56.17N 43.54E
Nizhnyaya Tunguska r. Rus. Fed. 59 J4 ....65.47N 87.59E
Nizhyn Ukraine 55 N4 ...............................51.02N 31.53E
Nizip Turkey 57 L3 .....................................36.59N 37.48E
Nkongsamba Cameroon 84 E2 ..................4.58N 9.57E
Nobeoka Japan 106 B2 ...............................32.34N 131.41E
Nogales Mexico 70 B7 ...............................31.19N 110.57W
Nogent-le-Rotrou France 44 D6 ...............48.19N 0.49E
Nogent-sur-Oise France 42 B2 ...................49.17N 2.28E
Nohfelden Germany 42 G2 .........................49.35N 7.08E
Noirmoutier, Île de i. France 44 B5 ........46.58N 2.16W
Nok Kundi Pakistan 95 J5 ..........................28.49N 62.50E
Nome U.S.A. 62 B4 ......................................64.32N 165.28W
Nonthaburi Thailand 104 C6 ....................13.51N 100.32E
Noord-Brabant d. Neth. 42 E4 ...................51.32N 5.01E
Noord-Holland d. Neth. 42 D5 ..................52.46N 4.54E
Nordaustlandet i. Arctic Oc. 58 D5 .........79.36N 22.37E
Norden Germany 42 G6 ..............................53.36N 7.12E
Norderney i. Germany 42 G6 .....................53.44N 7.19E
Norderstedt Germany 54 D5 .....................53.44N 10.00E
Nordhausen Germany 54 D4 .....................51.30N 10.47E
Nordhorn Germany 42 G5 ..........................52.26N 7.05E
Nord-Pas-de-Calais d. France 42 B3 .......50.14N 2.43E
Nordrhein-Westfalen d. Germany 42 G4 .51.04N 7.25E
Nordvik Rus. Fed. 59 M5 ...........................74.01N 111.20E
Nore r. Ireland 41 E2 ..................................52.25N 6.58W
Norfolk d. England 9 F3 .............................52.44N 0.59E
Norfolk U.S.A. 65 K4 ..................................36.53N 76.16W
Norfolk Broads f. England 11 G3 ............52.43N 1.28E
Norfolk Island S. Pacific Oc. 111 F4 .......28.59S 167.59E
Norfolk Island Ridge f. Tasman Sea 108 H4 ..23.55S 167.20E
Noril'sk Rus. Fed. 59 J4 .............................69.19N 88.08E
Normandy f. France 44 C6 .........................48.53N 0.32W
Normanton Australia 110 D5 .....................17.41S 141.05E
Norra Storfjället mts Sweden 40 C4 ........65.53N 15.07E
Norrköping Sweden 40 D2 .........................58.36N 16.12E
Norrtälje Sweden 40 D2 .............................59.45N 18.41E
Norseman Australia 110 B3 .......................32.14S 121.47E
Norte, Cabo c. Brazil 77 K8 ......................1.40N 49.59W
Northallerton England 15 F3 ....................54.20N 1.26W
North America 60
North American Basin f. Atlantic Oc. 116 G7 ..30.00N 60.00W
Northampton England 10 E3 .....................52.14N 0.54W
Northamptonshire d. England 9 E3 ........52.12N 0.57W
North Australian Basin f. Indian Oc. 108 D5 ..14.09S 114.44E
North Ayrshire d. Scotland 8 C4 .............55.44N 4.44W
North Battleford Canada 62 H3 ...............52.46N 108.17W
North Bay town Canada 63 K2 ................46.19N 79.28W
North Berwick Scotland 17 G4 .................56.04N 2.43W
North Cape New Zealand 111 G3 ...........34.25S 173.03E
North Cape Norway 40 F5 ..........................71.10N 25.47E
North Carolina d. U.S.A. 65 K4 ...............36.13N 79.52W
North Cave England 15 G2 ........................53.47N 0.39W
North Channel U.K. 16 C3 ........................55.23N 6.13W
North China Plain f. China 90 I4 ............34.30N 117.00E
North Dakota d. U.S.A. 64 F6 ..................47.19N 100.24W
North Dorset Downs hills England 10 C1 ..50.46N 2.32W
North Down d. Northern Ireland 9 C4 ....54.39N 5.43W
North Downs hills England 11 E2 ...........51.14N 0.58E
North Eastern d. Kenya 87 C3 .................1.16N 40.02E
North East Lincolnshire d. England 9 E3 ..53.37N 0.13W
Northeast Pacific Basin f. N. Pacific Oc. 109 J7 ..27.45N 154.35W
Northern Dvina r. Rus. Fed. 58 F4 ..........64.31N 40.33E
Northern Ireland d. U.K. 9 B4 .................54.38N 6.49W
Northern Mariana Islands N. Pacific Oc. 105 K7 ..17.15N 143.32E
Northern Territory d. Australia 110 C5 ..17.40S 133.30E
North Esk r. Scotland 19 G1 .....................56.45N 2.26W
North European Plain f. Europe 34 G3 ....56.00N 27.00E
North Foreland c. England 11 G2 .............51.23N 1.27E
North Frisian Islands Germany 54 C6 .....54.52N 8.02E
North Harris f. Scotland 18 C2 ................57.59N 6.48W
North Hykeham England 15 G2 ...............53.11N 0.35W
North Island New Zealand 111 G3 .........38.11S 173.23E
North Korea Asia 101 N6 ...........................40.01N 126.39E
North Lanarkshire d. Scotland 8 D4 .......55.51N 3.57W
North Lincolnshire d. England 9 E3 ........53.37N 0.35W
North Platte U.S.A. 64 F5 ..........................41.09N 100.46W
North Platte r. U.S.A. 64 F5 ......................41.10N 100.48W
North Ronaldsay i. Scotland 19 G4 .........59.24N 2.26W
North Ronaldsay Firth str. Scotland 19 G4 ..59.20N 2.29W
North Saskatchewan r. Canada 62 H3 .....53.13N 105.11W
North Sea Europe 34 E3 ..............................56.00N 4.00E
North Shields England 15 F4 ....................55.01N 1.27W
North Siberian Lowland f. Rus. Fed. 59 L5 ..73.26N 103.17E
North Somercotes England 15 H2 ...........53.27N 0.09E
North Somerset d. England 9 D2 ..............51.24N 2.48W
North Sunderland England 15 F4 ............55.35N 1.39W
North Tidworth England 10 D2 ................51.14N 1.40W
North Tyne r. England 15 E3 ....................54.59N 2.08W
North Uist i. Scotland 19 H2 ....................57.32N 1.55W
North Uist i. Scotland 18 B2 ....................57.37N 7.26W
Northumberland d. England 8 D4 ...........55.09N 2.35W
Northumberland Strait Canada 65 N6 ....46.50N 64.43W
North Walsham England 11 G3 ................52.49N 1.23E
North West Cape Australia 110 A4 ..........21.49S 114.12E
Northwest Pacific Basin f. N. Pacific Oc. 108 G8 ..35.59N 154.41E
Northwest Territories d. Canada 62 H4 ..63.48N 105.17W
Northwich England 15 E2 ..........................53.16N 2.31W
North York Moors f. England 15 G3 .........54.23N 0.50W
North Yorkshire d. England 9 E3 .............54.12N 1.59W
Norton England 15 G3 ................................54.08N 0.47W
Norton Fitzwarren England 13 D3 ..........51.02N 3.08W
Norton Sound str. U.S.A. 62 B4 ...............63.58N 163.01W
Norway Europe 40 B3 .................................62.46N 10.30E
Norway House Canada 62 I3 ....................53.56N 97.52W
Norwegian Sea N. Atlantic Oc. 34 D4 ....66.00N 2.00E
Norwich England 11 G3 .............................52.38N 1.18E
Noshiro Japan 106 D4 ................................40.12N 140.01E
Noss, Isle of i. Scotland 19 H5 ................60.09N 1.00W
Noteć r. Poland 46 B4 ................................52.43N 15.26E
Nottingham England 10 D3 ......................52.57N 1.09W
Nottingham d. England 9 E3 ...................52.58N 1.10W
Nottinghamshire d. England 9 E3 ...........53.03N 0.59W
Nouâdhibou Mauritania 84 C4 ...............21.04N 17.00W
Nouâdhibou, Râs c. Mauritania 84 C4 ....20.51N 17.04W
Nouakchott Mauritania 84 C3 .................18.06N 15.58W
Nouméa New Caledonia 111 F4 ...............22.18S 166.26E
Noup Head Scotland 19 F4 .......................59.20N 3.04W
Nova Friburgo Brazil 77 L3 .......................22.18S 42.32W
Nova Gradiška Croatia 56 B7 ..................45.16N 17.23E
Nova Iguaçu Brazil 77 L3 .........................22.44S 43.29W
Novara Italy 50 C6 ......................................45.27N 8.37E
Nova Scotia d. Canada 63 L2 ..................45.53N 65.45W
Novaya Sibir', Ostrov i. Rus. Fed. 59 P5 ..75.04N 148.22E
Novaya Zemlya is Rus. Fed. 58 G5 ...........71.41N 55.45E
Nové Zámky Slovakia 54 H2 .....................47.59N 18.09E
Novi Pazar Serbia 56 D6 ...........................43.08N 20.30E
Novi Sad Serbia 56 C7 ...............................45.16N 19.51E
Novo Aripuanã Brazil 76 F5 ......................5.07S 60.20W
Novodvinsk Rus. Fed. 58 F4 .....................64.25N 40.50E
Novo Hamburgo Brazil 77 J2 ...................29.40S 51.09W

Novohrad-Volyns'kyy Ukraine 55 L4 .......50.36N 27.37E
Novokuznetsk Rus. Fed. 58 J3 .................53.45N 87.09E
Novo Mesto Slovenia 54 F1 ......................45.48N 15.10E
Novomoskovsk Rus. Fed. 58 E3 ...............54.01N 38.19E
Novomoskovs'k Ukraine 55 P3 ................48.38N 35.14E
Novooleksiyivka Ukraine 57 K8 ..............46.14N 34.39E
Novorossiysk Rus. Fed. 58 E2 ..................44.43N 37.47E
Novosibirsk Rus. Fed. 58 J3 .....................55.03N 83.02E
Novovolyns'k Ukraine 55 K4 ....................50.43N 24.11E
Nový Jičín Czech Rep. 46 D6 ....................49.36N 17.59E
Novyy Port Rus. Fed. 58 I4 .......................68.13N 73.02E
Nowogard Poland 46 B4 ............................53.40N 15.07E
Nowshera Pakistan 95 L6 .........................34.00N 72.01E
Nowy Sącz Poland 46 E2 ..........................49.38N 20.42E
Nowy Targ Poland 46 E2 ...........................49.29N 20.03E
Noyabr'sk Rus. Fed. 58 I4 .........................63.13N 75.32E
Noyon France 42 B2 ...................................49.35N 2.59E
Npitamaiong mt. Kenya 87 A3 ...............3.08N 35.01E
Nu'aym f. Oman 95 I4 ...............................23.14N 55.59E
Nuba Mountains Sudan 94 D2 .................11.28N 30.33E
Nubian Desert Sudan 85 H4 .....................20.25N 34.58E
Nudo Coropuna mt. Peru 76 F4 ...............15.29S 72.43W
Nueva Casas Grandes Mexico 70 C7 ........30.23N 107.56W
Nuevo Laredo Mexico 70 E6 .....................27.29N 99.31W
Nuevo León d. Mexico 70 E6 ...................25.51N 99.56W
Nui atoll Tuvalu 111 G6 ..........................7.12S 177.12E
Nuku'alofa Tonga 108 I4 ...........................21.07S 175.12W
Nukufetau atoll Tuvalu 111 G6 ...............8.03S 178.25E
Nuku Hiva i. French Polynesia 109 K5 ....8.52S 140.06W
Nukunonu atoll Tokelau 108 I5 ..............9.05S 171.50W
Nukus Uzbekistan 58 G2 ...........................42.27N 59.36E
Nullarbor Plain f. Australia 110 B3 ........31.01S 129.03E
Numazu Japan 106 C3 ................................35.05N 138.52E
Nunavut d. Canada 63 I4 ..........................66.30N 89.54W
Nuneaton England 10 D3 ..........................52.31N 1.28W
Nunivak Island U.S.A. 62 B3 ...................59.58N 166.18W
Nuoro Italy 50 C4 .......................................40.19N 9.20E
Nuqrah Saudi Arabia 94 F5 ......................25.36N 41.26E
Nuremberg Germany 54 D3 ......................49.27N 11.06E
Nurmes Finland 40 G3 ...............................63.33N 29.07E
Nushki Pakistan 95 K5 ..............................29.34N 66.02E
Nuuk Greenland 63 M4 .............................64.11N 51.45W
Nyahururu Kenya 87 B3 ............................0.04N 36.23E
Nyala Sudan 85 G3 .....................................12.03N 24.55E
Nyambeni Hills Kenya 87 B3 ....................0.18N 37.54E
Nyanza d. Kenya 87 A2 ..............................0.26S 34.29E
Nyasa, Lake Africa 86 C4 .........................9.59S 34.05E
Nyborg Denmark 40 B1 ..............................55.19N 10.47E
Nybro Sweden 40 C2 ..................................56.44N 15.55E
Nyeri Kenya 87 B2 ......................................0.23S 36.57E
Nyíregyháza Hungary 55 I2 ......................47.57N 21.43E
Nyiru, Mount Kenya 87 B3 .......................2.09N 36.50E
Nykarleby Finland 40 E3 ...........................63.31N 22.33E
Nykøbing Denmark 40 B1 .........................54.46N 11.53E
Nyköping Sweden 40 D2 ...........................58.45N 17.01E
Nynäshamn Sweden 40 D2 .......................58.54N 17.57E
Nysa Poland 46 C3 ......................................50.29N 17.20E
Nyurba Rus. Fed. 59 M4 ............................63.17N 118.17E
Nyzhn'ohirs'kyy Ukraine 57 K7 ..............45.27N 34.45E
Nzoia r. Kenya 87 A3 .................................0.05N 33.57E

## O

Oadby England 10 D3 .................................52.36N 1.05W
Oahe, Lake U.S.A. 64 F5 ...........................44.49N 100.32W
Oahu i. U.S.A. 109 J7 .................................21.34N 157.54W
Oakengates England 10 C3 .......................52.42N 2.26W
Oakham England 10 E3 ..............................52.40N 0.44W
Oakland U.S.A. 64 B4 .................................37.50N 122.15W
Oaxaca Mexico 70 E4 .................................17.05N 96.40W
Oaxaca d. Mexico 70 E4 ............................17.22N 96.20W
Ob' r. Rus. Fed. 58 H4 ................................66.47N 69.08E
Oban Scotland 16 D4 .................................56.25N 5.28W
Obi i. Indonesia 105 H3 ...........................1.33S 127.41E
Óbidos Brazil 77 I7 ....................................1.50S 55.32W
Obihiro Japan 106 D4 ................................42.55N 143.11E
Obninsk Rus. Fed. 55 Q6 ..........................55.04N 36.38E
Oborniki Poland 46 C4 ..............................52.38N 16.49E
Oboyan' Rus. Fed. 55 Q4 ..........................51.13N 36.16E
Obskaya Guba str. Rus. Fed. 58 I4 ..........67.13N 72.49E
Occidental, Cordillera mts Colombia 72 B7 ..1.36N 77.47W
Occidental, Cordillera mts Peru 76 F4 ....16.07S 71.46W
Ocean Falls town Canada 62 F3 ..............52.21N 127.41W
Oceania 117
Oceanside U.S.A. 64 C3 .............................33.12N 117.23W
Ochil Hills Scotland 17 F4 ........................56.12N 3.49W
Oda, Jebel mt. Sudan 85 H4 .....................20.20N 36.39E
Ódáðahraun f. Iceland 40 Y2 ...................64.48N 17.37W
Ódate Japan 106 D4 ...................................40.16N 140.34E
Ödemiş Turkey 57 H3 ................................38.13N 27.58E
Odense Denmark 40 B1 .............................55.24N 10.23E
Oder r. Germany 54 C4 ..............................51.43N 9.56E
Odesa Ukraine 53 J6 ..................................46.28N 30.39E
Odessa U.S.A. 64 F3 ...................................31.50N 102.20W
Odintsovo Rus. Fed. 55 Q6 .......................55.40N 37.18E
Odisha d. India 96 F5 ................................20.57N 84.15E
Odra r. Germany/Poland 54 H3 ...............49.54N 18.19E
Ofanto r. Italy 50 F4 ..................................41.21N 16.13E
Offaly d. Ireland 41 D3 ..............................53.15N 7.35W
Offenbach am Main Germany 54 C4 ........50.06N 8.46E
Offenburg Germany 54 B3 ........................48.29N 7.57E
Ogadēn f. Ethiopia 85 I2 ...........................7.09N 45.27E
Ōgaki Japan 106 C3 ...................................35.21N 136.37E
Ogbomosho Nigeria 84 E2 ........................8.08N 4.14E
Ogden U.S.A. 64 D5 ...................................41.14N 111.57W
Ogilvie r. Canada 62 E4 .............................65.50N 137.13W
Oglio r. Italy 50 D6 ....................................45.01N 10.48E
Ogoki r. Canada 65 I7 ................................51.40N 85.58W
Ogulin Croatia 56 A7 ................................45.16N 15.14E
Ohio d. U.S.A. 65 J5 ..................................40.27N 82.28W
Ohio r. U.S.A. 65 J4 ...................................37.05N 89.12W
Ohrid Macedonia 56 D5 ............................41.07N 20.49E
Ohrid, Lake Albania/Macedonia 56 D5 ..41.02N 20.43E
Oich r. Scotland 18 E2 ...............................57.04N 4.46W
Oich, Loch l. Scotland 18 E2 ...................57.04N 4.46W
Oise r. France 42 B2 ..................................48.59N 2.04E
Ōita Japan 106 B2 .....................................33.13N 131.37E
Oiti mt. Greece 56 E4 ................................38.48N 22.16E
Ojinaga Mexico 70 D6 ...............................29.33N 104.25W
Ojos del Salado, Nevado mt. Argentina/Chile 73 C4 ..27.06S 68.35W
Oka r. Rus. Fed. 55 Q5 ...............................56.20N 43.59E
Okanogan r. U.S.A. 64 C6 .........................48.06N 119.41W
Okavango Delta f. Botswana 86 B3 .........19.42S 23.02E
Okaya Japan 106 C3 ...................................36.03N 138.00E
Okayama Japan 106 B2 ..............................34.39N 133.55E
Okeechobee, Lake U.S.A. 65 J2 ...............26.56N 81.00W
Okehampton England 13 C2 ....................50.44N 4.00W
Okha India 96 C5 ........................................22.26N 69.08E
Okha Rus. Fed. 59 P3 .................................53.33N 143.01E
Okhotsk Rus. Fed. 59 P3 ...........................59.22N 143.22E
Okhotsk, Sea of Japan/Rus. Fed. 106 D4 ..54.58N 144.06E

Okhtyrka Ukraine 55 P4 ...........................50.19N 34.54E
Okinawa i. Japan 101 N3 ..........................26.27N 127.58E
Oki-shotō is Japan 106 B3 .......................36.07N 133.26E
Oklahoma d. U.S.A. 64 G4 ........................35.41N 97.24W
Oklahoma City U.S.A. 64 G4 ...................35.31N 97.31W
Oksskolten mt. Norway 40 C4 .................66.01N 14.20E
Oktyabr'skoy Revolyutsii, Ostrov i. Rus. Fed. 59 K5 ..79.09N 96.42E
Öland i. Sweden 40 D2 ..............................56.57N 17.02E
Oława Poland 46 C3 ...................................50.56N 17.17E
Olbia Italy 50 C4 ........................................40.55N 9.30E
Old Crow Canada 62 E4 ............................67.36N 139.54W
Oldenburg Germany 54 C5 .......................53.09N 8.14E
Oldenzaal Neth. 42 F5 ...............................52.19N 6.56E
Oldham England 15 E2 ..............................53.33N 2.07W
Old Head of Kinsale Ireland 41 C1 .........51.36N 8.31W
Old Leake England 11 G2 ..........................53.02N 0.06E
Oldmeldrum Scotland 19 G2 ...................57.20N 2.19W
Olean U.S.A. 65 K5 .....................................42.05N 78.26W
Olecko Poland 46 F5 ..................................54.02N 22.31E
Olekma r. Rus. Fed. 59 N4 .......................60.05N 121.07E
Olekminsk Rus. Fed. 59 N4 .......................60.24N 120.21E
Oleksandriya Ukraine 55 O3 ....................48.41N 33.07E
Olenek Rus. Fed. 59 M4 ............................68.28N 112.26E
Olenek r. Rus. Fed. 59 M5 ........................72.58N 119.45E
Olenekskiy Zaliv b. Rus. Fed. 59 N5 .......73.22N 121.09E
Oléron, Île d' i. France 44 C4 ..................45.55N 1.20W
Olevs'k Ukraine 55 L4 ...............................51.13N 27.39E
Olinda Brazil 77 N6 ...................................7.58S 34.46W
Oliva, Cordillera de mts Argentina/Chile 76 G2 ..29.56S 69.57W
Olmos Peru 76 E6 .......................................5.59S 79.46W
Olney England 10 E3 ..................................52.09N 0.42W
Olomouc Czech Rep. 54 G3 ......................49.35N 17.16E
Oloron-Ste-Marie France 44 C3 ..............43.12N 0.36W
Olsztyn Poland 46 E4 ................................53.48N 20.29E
Olteț r. Romania 56 F7 ..............................44.22N 24.07E
Olympia U.S.A. 64 B6 ................................47.02N 122.53W
Olympus, Mount Greece 56 E5 ...............40.05N 22.21E
Olympus, Mount U.S.A. 64 B6 ................47.45N 123.47W
Olyutorskiy Zaliv b. Rus. Fed. 59 R3 ......59.51N 168.08E
Omagh Northern Ireland 16 B2 ...............54.36N 7.17W
Omagh d. Northern Ireland 9 B4 .............54.37N 7.16W
Omaha U.S.A. 64 G5 ..................................41.17N 95.58W
Oman Asia 95 H3 ........................................21.00N 57.00E
Oman, Gulf of Asia 95 I5 ..........................25.37N 56.49E
Ombersley England 10 C3 ........................52.16N 2.14W
Ombrone r. Italy 50 D5 ..............................42.39N 11.01E
Omdurman Sudan 85 H3 ...........................15.38N 32.28E
Ommen Neth. 42 F5 ...................................52.32N 6.25E
Omolon r. Rus. Fed. 59 Q4 .......................68.44N 158.43E
Omo National Park Ethiopia 87 A4 .........6.00N 35.51E
Omono r. Japan 106 D3 .............................39.41N 140.04E
Omo Wenz r. Ethiopia 87 B4 ...................4.36N 36.01E
Omsk Rus. Fed. 58 I3 .................................55.00N 73.22E
Omsukchan Rus. Fed. 59 Q4 ....................62.25N 155.43E
Omulew r. Poland 46 E4 ............................53.04N 21.33E
Ōmuta Japan 106 B2 ..................................33.02N 130.28E
Onchan Isle of Man 14 C3 .......................54.11N 4.27W
Ondjiva Angola 86 A3 ...............................17.04S 15.44E
Onega, Lake Rus. Fed. 58 E4 ....................62.05N 35.21E
Oneşti Romania 56 G8 ..............................46.16N 26.46E
Ongole India 96 F4 ....................................15.32N 80.02E
Onitsha Nigeria 84 E2 ..............................6.08N 6.48E
Ono-i-Lau i. Fiji 108 I4 ............................20.39S 178.43W
Ontario d. Canada 63 I3 ...........................51.51N 91.22W
Ontario, Lake Canada/U.S.A. 63 K2 .......43.41N 77.57W
Ontong Java Atoll Solomon Is 111 E6 ....5.24S 159.34E
Oosterschelde est. Neth. 42 C4 ...............51.38N 3.35E
Oost-Vlaanderen d. Belgium 42 C3 ........50.56N 3.44E
Opala Dem. Rep. Congo 86 B4 ................0.36S 24.22E
Opava Czech Rep. 54 G3 ...........................49.56N 17.54E
Opochka Rus. Fed. 40 G2 ..........................56.43N 28.41E
Opole Poland 46 C3 ....................................50.41N 17.56E
Oporto Portugal 48 A4 ..............................41.11N 8.36W
Oradea Romania 55 I2 ...............................47.03N 21.57E
Oran Algeria 84 D5 ....................................35.42N 0.38W
Orange France 44 F4 ..................................44.09N 4.49E
Orange r. Namibia/S. Africa 86 A2 ..........28.36S 16.28E
Orange, Cabo c. Brazil 72 D7 ..................4.22N 51.17W
Oranmore Ireland 41 C3 ...........................53.16N 8.55W
Orchila, Isla i. Venezuela 71 K3 .............11.45N 66.09W
Orchy r. Scotland 16 D4 ............................56.25N 5.01W
Ord, Mount hill Australia 110 B5 ...........17.19S 125.29E
Ordu Turkey 57 L5 .....................................40.59N 37.53E
Örebro Sweden 40 C2 ................................59.16N 15.14E
Oregon d. U.S.A. 64 B5 ..............................43.43N 120.32W
Orel Rus. Fed. 58 E3 ...................................52.58N 36.05E
Orenburg Rus. Fed. 58 G3 ........................51.46N 55.05E
Orford Ness hd England 11 G3 ...............52.05N 1.35E
Orhei Moldova 55 M2 ...............................47.22N 28.50E
Oriental, Cordillera mts Bolivia 76 G4 ..16.47S 65.35W
Oriental, Cordillera mts Colombia 72 B7 ..7.42N 72.45W
Oriental, Cordillera mts Peru 76 F5 .......10.29S 74.41W
Orillia Canada 65 K5 .................................44.36N 79.25W
Orinoco r. Col./Venez. 72 C7 ...................8.35N 61.50W
Orinoco Delta Venezuela 72 C7 .............9.22N 60.44W
Oristano Italy 50 C3 ..................................39.55N 8.35E
Oristano, Golfo di b. Italy 50 C3 ...........39.49N 8.30E
Orivesi l. Finland 40 G3 ............................62.14N 29.27E
Orizaba Mexico 70 E4 ...............................18.49N 97.06W
Örkelljunga Sweden 40 C2 .......................56.17N 13.17E
Orkney d. Scotland 8 F6 ...........................59.00N 3.00W
Orkney Islands Scotland 19 F4 ...............59.06N 3.20W
Orlando U.S.A. 65 J2 ..................................28.31N 81.21W
Orléans France 44 D5 ................................47.55N 1.54E
Ormoc Phil. 105 G6 ..................................11.00N 124.37E
Ormskirk England 14 E2 ...........................53.34N 2.53W
Orne r. France 44 C6 ..................................49.16N 0.14W
Örnsköldsvik Sweden 40 D3 ...................63.17N 18.43E
Oromiya d. Ethiopia 87 B5 .......................9.03N 37.33E
Oransay i. Scotland 16 C4 ........................56.01N 6.12W
Orosei Italy 50 C4 ......................................40.23N 9.42E
Orosei, Golfo di b. Italy 50 C4 ...............40.15N 9.44E
Orrin r. Scotland 19 E2 .............................57.33N 4.29W
Orrin Reservoir Scotland 18 E2 ..............57.30N 4.45W
Orsha Belarus 55 N6 ..................................54.30N 30.23E
Orsk Rus. Fed. 58 G3 .................................51.07N 58.33E
Orşova Romania 56 E7 ..............................44.42N 22.24E
Oruro Bolivia 76 G4 ..................................17.59S 67.09W
Osa, Península de pen. Costa Rica 71 H2 ..8.30N 83.32W
Ōsaka Japan 106 C2 ...................................34.42N 135.30E
Oshakati Namibia 86 A3 ...........................17.45S 15.43E
Oshawa Canada 63 K2 ...............................43.54N 78.51W
O-shima i. Japan 106 C2 ..........................34.44N 139.28E
Osijek Croatia 56 C7 ..................................45.33N 18.42E
Oskarshamn Sweden 40 D2 .....................57.16N 16.26E
Oslo Norway 40 B2 .....................................59.55N 10.46E
Osmancık Turkey 57 K5 .............................40.58N 34.47E
Osmaniye Turkey 57 L3 .............................37.04N 36.15E
Osnabrück Germany 54 C5 .......................52.17N 8.04E
Osorno Chile 73 B2 ...................................40.35S 73.09W
Osorno Spain 48 C5 ...................................42.25N 4.21W
Oss Neth. 42 E4 ..........................................51.45N 5.32E

Ossa mt. Greece 56 E4 ...............................39.48N 22.41E
Ossa, Mount Australia 110 D2 .................41.56S 146.12E
Ostend Belgium 42 B4 ...............................51.13N 2.55E
Österdalälven l. Sweden 40 C3 ...............61.40N 13.15E
Østerdalen f. Norway 40 B3 .....................62.05N 10.36E
Östersund Sweden 40 C3 ..........................63.11N 14.39E
Ostrava Czech Rep. 54 H3 .........................49.51N 18.17E
Ostróda Poland 46 D4 ...............................53.42N 19.59E
Ostrov Rus. Fed. 58 D3 ..............................57.21N 28.21E
Ostrowiec Świętokrzyski Poland 46 E3 ..50.56N 21.24E
Ostrów Mazowiecka Poland 46 E4 .........52.48N 21.53E
Ostrów Wielkopolski Poland 46 C3 ........51.39N 17.49E
Ostrzeszów Poland 54 G4 .........................51.25N 17.56E
Osüm r. Bulgaria 56 F6 .............................43.42N 24.50E
Osumi-kaiko str. Japan 106 B2 ...............30.50N 130.52E
Ōsumi-shotō is Japan 106 B2 .................30.32N 130.36E
Osuna Spain 48 C2 ....................................37.14N 5.06W
Oswestry England 10 B3 ...........................52.51N 3.03W
Otaru Japan 106 D4 ...................................43.12N 140.59E
Otjiwarongo Namibia 86 A2 .....................20.28S 16.40E
Otley England 15 F2 ..................................53.54N 1.41W
Otranto Italy 50 H4 ...................................40.09N 18.30E
Otranto, Strait of Albania/Italy 56 C5 ....40.36N 18.42E
Otta Norway 40 B3 .....................................61.46N 9.31E
Ottawa Canada 63 K2 ...............................45.25N 75.40W
Ottawa r. Canada 63 K2 ...........................45.28N 74.16W
Ottawa Islands Canada 63 J3 ..................59.57N 80.09W
Otter r. England 13 D2 ..............................50.38N 3.18W
Otterburn England 15 E4 .........................55.14N 2.11W
Ottery r. England 13 C2 .............................50.39N 4.20W
Ottignies Belgium 42 D3 ..........................50.39N 4.34E
Otukpo Nigeria 84 E2 ...............................7.13N 8.05E
Ouachita r. U.S.A. 65 H3 ..........................31.50N 91.49W
Ouagadougou Burkina Faso 84 D3 ........12.22N 1.31W
Ouargla Algeria 84 E5 ...............................31.59N 5.22E
Ouarzazate Morocco 84 D5 .....................30.56N 6.54W
Oudenaarde Belgium 42 C3 .....................50.51N 3.36E
Ouesso Congo 84 F2 ..................................1.36N 16.04E
Ouezzane Morocco 52 B3 .........................34.46N 5.32W
Oughter, Lough l. Ireland 41 D4 .............54.01N 7.28W
Ouistreham France 44 C6 .........................49.17N 0.16W
Oujda Morocco 84 D5 ...............................34.41N 1.54W
Oulainen Finland 40 F4 ............................64.16N 24.49E
Oulton England 11 G3 ..............................52.30N 1.43E
Oulu Finland 40 F4 ....................................65.01N 25.30E
Oulujärvi l. Finland 40 F4 ........................64.17N 27.15E
Oundle England 11 E3 ...............................52.29N 0.28W
Oupeye Belgium 42 E3 ...............................50.42N 5.39E
Ourense Spain 48 B5 .................................42.21N 7.51W
Ouse r. E. Sussex England 11 F1 .............50.48N 0.03E
Ouse r. E. Yorks. England 15 G2 ..............53.44N 0.54W
Outer Hebrides is Scotland 18 B2 ...........57.53N 7.21W
Outokumpu Finland 40 G3 .......................62.43N 29.01E
Out Skerries is Scotland 19 I5 ................60.26N 0.47W
Ovamboland f. Namibia 86 A3 .................17.50S 15.41E
Overijssel d. Neth. 42 F5 ..........................52.25N 6.32E
Overton Wales 12 E4 .................................52.58N 2.56W
Övertorneå Sweden 40 E4 ........................66.24N 23.37E
Oviedo Spain 48 C5 ...................................43.22N 5.50W
Ovruch Ukraine 55 M4 ..............................51.20N 28.49E
Owando Congo 84 F1 ................................0.29S 15.55E
Owen Stanley Range mts P.N.G. 110 D6 ..8.59S 147.57E
Owyhee r. U.S.A. 64 C5 .............................43.48N 117.04W
Öxarfjörður b. Iceland 40 Y2 ...................66.12N 16.47W
Oxelösund Sweden 40 D2 .........................58.40N 17.05E
Oxford England 10 D2 ...............................51.45N 1.15W
Oxfordshire d. England 9 E2 ...................51.54N 1.27W
Oxnard U.S.A. 64 C3 ..................................34.12N 119.12W
Oxted England 11 F2 .................................51.16N 0.01E
Oyama Japan 106 C3 .................................36.18N 139.48E
Oykel r. Scotland 18 E2 ............................57.55N 4.24W
Ozark Plateau f. U.S.A. 65 H4 .................36.58N 93.31W
Ozarks, Lake of the U.S.A. 65 H4 ...........38.14N 93.08W
Ózd Hungary 54 I3 ....................................48.13N 20.19E
Ozernovskiy Rus. Fed. 59 Q3 ...................51.30N 156.35E

## P

Paamiut Greenland 63 N4 ........................62.01N 49.40W
Pabbay i. W. Isles Scotland 18 B1 ...........56.51N 7.34W
Pabbay i. W. Isles Scotland 18 B2 ...........57.46N 7.18W
Pabianice Poland 46 D3 ............................51.40N 19.22E
Pacasmayo Peru 76 E6 ..............................7.26S 79.36W
Pachuca Mexico 70 E5 ..............................20.09N 98.44W
Pacific Ocean 108
Paczków Poland 46 C3 ..............................50.28N 17.00E
Padang Indonesia 104 C3 .........................0.58S 100.23E
Paderborn Germany 54 C4 ......................51.43N 8.45E
Padiham England 15 E2 ...........................53.48N 2.19W
Padre Island U.S.A. 64 G2 ........................26.57N 97.22W
Padstow England 13 C2 ............................50.32N 4.56W
Padua Italy 50 D6 .......................................45.24N 11.53E
Pag i. Croatia 56 A7 ...................................44.31N 14.53E
Pagadian Phil. 105 G5 ..............................7.50N 123.29E
Pagai Selatan i. Indonesia 104 C3 .........2.58S 100.24E
Pagai Utara i. Indonesia 104 C3 .............2.42S 100.15E
Pagan i. N. Mariana Is 108 F7 .................18.08N 145.49E
Page U.S.A. 64 D4 .......................................36.53N 111.28W
Paget, Mount S. Atlantic Oc. 73 F1 .......54.23S 36.44W
Paignton England 13 D2 ...........................50.26N 3.34W
Päijänne l. Finland 40 F3 ..........................61.30N 25.26E
Painswick England 10 C2 .........................51.47N 2.12W
Paisley Scotland 16 E3 ..............................55.51N 4.26W
Pakanbura Indonesia 104 C4 ...................0.34N 101.30E
Pakaraima Mountains S. America 71 L1 ..3.47N 63.40W
Pakistan Asia 96 C6 ...................................28.01N 64.37E
Pakokku Myanmar 97 I5 ...........................21.21N 95.07E
Pakxé Laos 104 D7 .....................................15.04N 105.50E
Palana Rus. Fed. 59 Q3 .............................59.05N 159.52E
Palangkaraya Indonesia 104 E3 ..............2.18S 113.55E
Palatka Rus. Fed. 59 Q4 ............................60.08N 150.56E
Palau N. Pacific Oc. 105 I5 ......................7.23N 134.07E
Palawan i. Phil. 104 F5 .............................8.50N 117.43E
Palembang Indonesia 104 C3 ..................2.56S 104.46E
Palencia Spain 48 C5 .................................42.01N 4.31W
Palermo Italy 50 E3 ...................................38.07N 13.21E
Pali India 96 D6 .........................................25.46N 73.26E
Palikir Micronesia 108 G6 .......................6.55N 158.10E
Palk Strait India/Sri Lanka 96 E2 ...........9.36N 79.18E
Pallisa Uganda 87 A3 ...............................1.10N 33.43E
Palma de Mallorca Spain 48 G3 .............39.35N 2.40E
Palmas, Cape Liberia 84 D2 ....................4.22N 7.32W
Palmerston atoll Cook Is 108 J4 .............18.01S 163.03W
Palmerston North New Zealand 111 G2 ..40.22S 175.37E
Palmi Italy 50 F3 .......................................38.21N 15.51E
Palmira Colombia 72 B7 ..........................3.31N 76.16W
Palmyra Atoll N. Pacific Oc. 108 J6 ........5.51N 162.06W
Palojoensuu Finland 40 E5 ......................68.17N 23.09E
Palopo Indonesia 104 G3 .........................3.01S 120.11E
Palos, Cabo de c. Spain 48 E2 .................37.37N 0.41W
Palu Indonesia 104 F3 ..............................0.54S 119.54E
Pamiers France 44 D3 ...............................43.07N 1.37E

Pamir mts Asia 95 L7 .....38.39N 72.48E
Pampas f. Argentina 73 C3 .....36.23S 64.07W
Pamplona Spain 48 E5 .....42.49N 1.39W
Panagyurishte Bulgaria 56 F6 .....42.30N 24.10E
Panaji India 96 D4 .....15.30N 73.50E
Panama Central America 71 H2 .....8.22N 81.33W
Panama, Gulf of Panama 71 I2 .....7.38N 79.19W
Panama, Isthmus of f. C. America 60 K3 .....9.00N 80.00W
Panama Canal Panama 71 I2 .....9.07N 79.45W
Panamá City Panama 71 I2 .....8.56N 79.36W
Panama City U.S.A. 65 I3 .....30.10N 85.40W
Panay i. Phil. 105 G6 .....11.10N 122.30E
Pančevo Serbia 56 D7 .....44.52N 20.39E
Panevėžys Lithuania 40 F1 .....55.44N 24.23E
Pangani Tanzania 87 B1 .....5.29S 38.56E
Pangkalanbuun Indonesia 104 D3 .....2.40S 111.38E
Pangkalpinang Indonesia 104 D3 .....2.08S 106.06E
Pangnirtung Canada 63 L4 .....66.03N 65.48W
Panjgur Pakistan 95 J5 .....26.58N 64.07E
Pantanal f. Brazil 77 H4 .....18.00S 57.00W
Pantelleria, Isola di i. Italy 50 E2 .....36.47N 12.04E
Panzhihua China 101 I3 .....26.35N 101.43E
Paola Italy 50 G3 .....39.21N 16.03E
Papa Stour i. Scotland 19 H5 .....60.21N 1.42W
Papa Westray i. Scotland 19 G4 .....59.22N 2.52W
Papeete French Polynesia 109 K4 .....17.30S 149.31W
Papenburg Germany 42 G6 .....53.05N 7.24E
Paphos Cyprus 57 J2 .....34.47N 32.25E
Papua, Gulf of P.N.G. 110 D6 .....8.34S 144.45E
Papua New Guinea Oceania 110 D6 .....6.05S 146.34E
Par England 13 C2 .....50.21N 4.42W
Paracel Islands S. China Sea 104 E7 .....16.46N 112.39E
Paragua r. Bolivia 76 F5 .....13.31S 61.50W
Paraguai r. Brazil 77 I3 .....22.06S 57.57W
Paraguay r. Argentina/Paraguay 73 D4 .....27.12S 58.39W
Paraguay S. America 77 I3 .....22.45S 58.44W
Paraíba d. Brazil 77 M6 .....7.06S 36.43W
Parakou Benin 84 E2 .....9.22N 2.36E
Paramaribo Suriname 72 D7 .....5.11N 55.17W
Paraná Argentina 73 C3 .....31.44S 60.31W
Paraná d. Brazil 77 J3 .....24.50S 51.01W
Paraná r. Brazil 77 K5 .....12.31S 48.12W
Paraná r. S. America 77 I1 .....33.52S 59.12W
Paranaguá Brazil 77 K2 .....25.32S 48.33W
Paranaíba r. Brazil 77 J3 .....20.04S 51.00W
Paranapanema r. Brazil 77 J3 .....22.36S 53.01W
Paranapiacaba, Serra mts Brazil 77 J3 .....24.58S 50.21W
Parângul Mare, Vârful mt. Romania 56 E7 .....45.21N 23.33E
Pardo r. Bahia Brazil 77 M4 .....15.41S 38.59W
Pardo r. Mato Grosso do Sul Brazil 77 J3 .....21.39S 52.14W
Pardubice Czech Rep. 54 F4 .....50.03N 15.47E
Parecis, Serra dos hills Brazil 77 H5 .....11.28S 63.12W
Parepare Indonesia 104 F3 .....4.01S 119.40E
Paria, Península de pen. Venezuela 71 L3 .....10.43N 62.58W
Parima, Serra mts Brazil 71 L1 .....2.57N 64.15W
Parintins Brazil 77 I7 .....2.38S 56.46W
Paris France 44 D6 .....48.52N 2.21E
Parma Italy 50 D6 .....44.48N 10.19E
Parnaíba r. Brazil 77 L7 .....2.56S 41.45W
Parnaíba r. Brazil 77 L7 .....3.02S 41.51W
Parnassos mt. Greece 56 E4 .....38.32N 22.38E
Pärnu Estonia 40 F2 .....58.23N 24.30E
Paropamisus mts Afgh. 95 J7 .....35.06N 61.20E
Paros i. Greece 56 F3 .....37.06N 25.08E
Parrett r. England 13 D3 .....51.08N 3.00W
Parry, Cape Canada 63 F5 .....70.12N 124.31W
Parry Islands Canada 62 G5 .....76.50N 111.03W
Parsęta r. Poland 46 B5 .....54.11N 15.34E
Parthenay France 44 C5 .....46.39N 0.15W
Partry Mountains hills Ireland 41 B3 .....53.36N 9.39W
Paru r. Brazil 77 J7 .....1.31S 52.41W
Pasadena U.S.A. 64 C3 .....34.11N 118.08W
Pasado, Cabo c. Ecuador 76 D7 .....0.22S 80.28W
Pașcani Romania 55 L2 .....47.15N 26.44E
Pasewalk Germany 46 B4 .....53.30N 14.00E
Pasłęka r. Poland 46 D5 .....54.26N 19.46E
Pasni Pakistan 95 J5 .....25.13N 63.31E
Passau Germany 54 E3 .....48.34N 13.25E
Passero, Capo c. Italy 50 F2 .....36.40N 15.08E
Passo Fundo Brazil 77 J2 .....28.18S 52.24W
Pastavy Belarus 55 L6 .....55.07N 26.50E
Pastaza r. Peru 76 E7 .....4.56S 76.24W
Pasto Colombia 72 B7 .....1.11N 77.17W
Pasvalys Lithuania 46 G6 .....56.03N 24.25E
Patagonia f. Argentina 73 B1 .....51.45S 71.19W
Patchway England 10 C2 .....51.32N 2.34W
Pate Island Kenya 87 C2 .....2.06S 41.08E
Paterson U.S.A. 65 L5 .....40.54N 74.09W
Patna India 96 G6 .....25.35N 85.16E
Patos Albania 56 C5 .....40.40N 19.39E
Patos, Lagoa dos l. Brazil 77 J1 .....30.39S 50.58W
Patos de Minas Brazil 77 K4 .....18.36S 46.30W
Patquía Argentina 76 G1 .....30.03S 66.53W
Patraïkos Kolpos b. Greece 56 D4 .....38.15N 21.26E
Patras Greece 56 D4 .....38.14N 21.45E
Patrington England 15 G2 .....53.41N 0.01W
Pau France 44 C3 .....43.18N 0.22W
Paulo Afonso Brazil 77 M6 .....9.20S 38.13W
Pavia Italy 50 C6 .....45.11N 9.09E
Pavlodar Kazakhstan 58 I3 .....52.18N 77.02E
Pavlohrad Ukraine 55 P3 .....48.31N 35.53E
Pavlovskaya Rus. Fed. 53 K6 .....46.09N 39.47E
Payapon Myanmar 97 I4 .....16.16N 95.41E
Paysandú Uruguay 73 D3 .....32.19S 58.05W
Pazardzhik Bulgaria 56 F6 .....42.12N 24.20E
Peace r. Canada 62 G3 .....58.54N 111.50W
Peacehaven England 11 E1 .....50.48N 0.00W
Peace River town Canada 62 G3 .....56.15N 117.17W
Peale, Mount U.S.A. 64 E4 .....38.26N 109.13W
Pearl r. U.S.A. 65 I3 .....30.10N 89.37W
Peć Kosovo 56 D6 .....42.39N 20.17E
Pechora r. Rus. Fed. 58 G4 .....68.13N 53.54E
Pecos U.S.A. 64 F3 .....31.23N 103.30W
Pecos r. U.S.A. 64 F2 .....29.50N 101.28W
Pécs Hungary 54 H2 .....46.05N 18.13E
Pedro Juan Caballero Paraguay 77 I3 .....22.29S 55.44W
Peebles Scotland 17 F3 .....55.39N 3.12W
Peel r. Canada 62 E4 .....68.03N 134.26W
Peel Isle of Man 14 C3 .....54.13N 4.41W
Pegasus Bay New Zealand 111 G2 .....43.20S 172.49E
Pegu Myanmar 97 I4 .....17.18N 96.28E
Pegwell Bay England 11 G2 .....51.19N 1.21E
Peipus, Lake Estonia/Rus. Fed. 40 F2 .....58.38N 27.28E
Pekalongan Indonesia 104 D2 .....6.54S 109.38E
Pelat, Mont mt. France 44 G4 .....44.16N 6.43E
Peleng i. Indonesia 105 G3 .....1.15S 123.29E
Pello Finland 40 E4 .....66.47N 23.59E
Pelotas Brazil 73 D2 .....31.46S 52.19W
Pelotas, Rio das r. Brazil 73 D4 .....27.35S 51.24W
Pemba Mozambique 86 D3 .....12.59S 40.32E
Pemba Zambia 86 B3 .....16.33S 27.22E
Pemba Channel Tanzania 87 B1 .....5.33S 39.19E
Pemba Island Tanzania 86 C4 .....5.25S 39.46E

Pembrey Wales 12 C3 .....51.41N 4.17W
Pembroke Canada 65 K6 .....45.49N 77.06W
Pembroke Wales 12 C3 .....51.40N 4.55W
Pembroke Dock Wales 12 C3 .....51.41N 4.57W
Pembrokeshire d. Wales 9 C2 .....51.55N 4.48W
Pembury England 11 F2 .....51.09N 0.19E
Peñalara mt. Spain 48 D4 .....40.51N 3.56W
Peña Nevada, Cerro mt. Mexico 70 E5 .....23.46N 99.50W
Peñaranda de Bracamonte Spain 48 C4 .....40.55N 5.11W
Penarth Wales 13 D3 .....51.26N 3.10W
Penas, Golfo de g. Chile 73 B2 .....47.18S 75.35W
Pendine Wales 12 C3 .....51.45N 4.34W
Pendlebury England 15 E2 .....53.30N 2.19W
Pendle Hill England 15 E2 .....53.52N 2.18W
Pendleton U.S.A. 64 C6 .....45.39N 118.48W
Penicuik Scotland 17 F3 .....55.50N 3.13W
Peninsular Malaysia Malaysia 104 C4 .....3.59N 102.43E
Penitente, Serra do hills Brazil 77 K6 .....9.20S 46.41W
Penkridge England 10 C3 .....52.43N 2.07W
Pennines hills England 15 E3 .....54.23N 2.18W
Pennsylvania d. U.S.A. 65 K5 .....41.18N 78.00W
Penny Icecap Canada 63 L4 .....67.10N 66.02W
Penrhyn atoll Cook Is 109 J5 .....8.58S 157.53W
Penrhyn Basin f. S. Pacific Oc. 109 J5 .....7.12S 157.13W
Penrhyn Mawr pt Wales 12 C4 .....52.51N 4.43W
Penrith England 14 E3 .....54.40N 2.45W
Penryn England 13 B2 .....50.10N 5.06W
Pensacola U.S.A. 65 I3 .....30.27N 87.13W
Penticton Canada 64 C6 .....49.30N 119.35W
Pentire Point England 13 B2 .....50.35N 5.00W
Pentland Firth str. Scotland 19 F3 .....58.43N 3.16W
Pentland Hills Scotland 17 F3 .....55.43N 3.30W
Pentland Skerries is Scotland 19 G3 .....58.41N 2.54W
Penygadair hill Wales 12 D4 .....52.42N 3.55W
Pen-y-Ghent hill England 15 E3 .....54.10N 2.15W
Penza Rus. Fed. 58 F3 .....53.12N 45.01E
Penzance England 13 B2 .....50.07N 5.32W
Penzhinskaya Guba b. Rus. Fed. 59 R4 .....62.05N 163.30E
Peoria U.S.A. 65 I5 .....40.41N 89.37W
Pereira Colombia 72 B7 .....4.45N 75.41W
Peremyshlyany Ukraine 46 G2 .....49.40N 24.34E
Périgueux France 44 D4 .....45.11N 0.43E
Perija, Sierra de mts Venezuela 71 J2 .....9.09N 73.12W
Perito Moreno Argentina 73 B2 .....46.36S 71.02W
Perlas, Punta de pt Nicaragua 71 H3 .....12.24N 83.31W
Perm' Rus. Fed. 58 G3 .....58.01N 56.14E
Pernambuco d. Brazil 77 M6 .....8.23S 37.51W
Pernik Bulgaria 56 E6 .....42.36N 23.02E
Péronne France 42 B2 .....49.56N 2.56E
Perpignan France 44 E3 .....42.42N 2.54E
Perranporth England 13 B2 .....50.21N 5.09W
Pershore England 10 C3 .....52.07N 2.04W
Perth Australia 110 A3 .....31.56S 115.47E
Perth Scotland 17 F4 .....56.24N 3.26W
Perth and Kinross d. Scotland 8 C5 .....56.37N 4.07W
Peru Basin f. Indian Oc. 108 D4 .....29.52S 109.00E
Peru S. America 76 .....5.50S 77.14W
Peru-Chile Trench f. S. Pacific Oc. 109 O5 .....9.16S 81.56W
Perugia Italy 50 E5 .....43.07N 12.23E
Pervomays'k Ukraine 55 N3 .....48.03N 30.51E
Pesaro Italy 50 E5 .....43.55N 12.53E
Pescara Italy 50 F5 .....42.27N 14.12E
Pescara r. Italy 50 F5 .....42.28N 14.13E
Pesebre, Punta pt Canary Islands 48 Y2 .....28.07N 14.29W
Peshawar Pakistan 96 D7 .....34.01N 71.40E
Peshkopi Albania 56 D5 .....41.41N 20.26E
Peterborough England 11 E3 .....52.34N 0.14W
Peterborough d. England 9 E3 .....52.36N 0.16W
Peterhead Scotland 19 H2 .....57.31N 1.47W
Peterlee England 15 F3 .....54.46N 1.20W
Petersfield England 10 E2 .....51.00N 0.56W
Petersville U.S.A. 62 C4 .....62.33N 150.50W
Petit Mécatina r. Canada 63 M3 .....50.40N 59.25W
Petra Velikogo, Zaliv b. Rus. Fed. 106 B4 .....42.41N 131.50E
Petrich Bulgaria 56 E5 .....41.24N 23.12E
Petrolina Brazil 77 L6 .....9.22S 40.25W
Petropavlovsk Kazakhstan 58 H3 .....54.51N 69.06E
Petropavlovsk-Kamchatskiy Rus. Fed. 59 Q3 .....53.01N 158.44E
Petroșani Romania 56 E7 .....45.25N 23.23E
Petrozavodsk Rus. Fed. 58 E4 .....61.48N 34.19E
Petworth England 11 E1 .....50.59N 0.36W
Pevensey England 11 F1 .....50.49N 0.21E
Pewsey England 10 D2 .....51.20N 1.46W
Pforzheim Germany 54 C3 .....48.53N 8.42E
Phan Thiết Vietnam 104 D6 .....10.55N 108.06E
Phatthalung Thailand 104 C5 .....7.39N 100.06E
Phayao Thailand 104 B7 .....19.10N 99.57E
Phet Buri Thailand 104 B6 .....13.06N 99.56E
Philadelphia U.S.A. 65 K4 .....39.57N 75.10W
Philippeville Belgium 42 D3 .....50.12N 4.33E
Philippine Basin f. N. Pacific Oc. 108 E7 .....16.41N 126.12E
Philippines Asia 105 G6 .....15.36N 122.55E
Philippine Trench f. N. Pacific Oc. 108 E6 .....15.40N 123.45E
Phitsanulok Thailand 104 C7 .....16.50N 100.18E
Phnom Penh Cambodia 104 C6 .....11.33N 104.57E
Phoenix U.S.A. 64 D3 .....33.31N 112.07W
Phoenix Islands Kiribati 108 I5 .....2.45S 173.22W
Phôngsali Laos 104 C8 .....21.41N 102.08E
Phrae Thailand 104 C7 .....18.07N 100.12E
Phuket Thailand 104 B5 .....7.53N 98.23E
Piacenza Italy 50 C6 .....45.03N 9.42E
Pianosa, Isola i. Italy 50 D5 .....42.34N 10.06E
Piatra Neamț Romania 55 L2 .....46.56N 26.22E
Piauí d. Brazil 77 L6 .....7.39S 42.52W
Piave r. Italy 50 E6 .....45.32N 12.44E
Picardie d. France 44 D6 .....49.42N 2.54E
Picardy d. France 44 D6 .....49.47N 1.35E
Pichanal Argentina 76 H3 .....23.18S 64.11W
Pickering England 15 G3 .....54.15N 0.47W
Pickering, Vale of f. England 15 G3 .....54.10N 0.45W
Piedras Negras Mexico 70 D6 .....28.40N 100.34W
Pieksämäki Finland 40 F3 .....62.18N 27.10E
Pielinen l. Finland 40 G3 .....63.14N 29.41E
Pierre U.S.A. 64 F5 .....44.23N 100.23W
Pietermaritzburg S. Africa 86 C2 .....29.36S 30.23E
Pietrosa mt. Romania 55 M2 .....47.34N 24.41E
Pihlajavesi l. Finland 40 G3 .....61.45N 28.46E
Pijijiapan Mexico 70 F4 .....15.46N 93.14W
Piła Poland 46 C4 .....53.09N 16.45E
Pilar Paraguay 77 I2 .....26.49S 58.19W
Pilcomayo r. Bolivia/Paraguay 77 I2 .....25.18S 57.43W
Pilica r. Poland 46 E3 .....51.52N 21.17E
Pimperne England 10 C1 .....50.53N 2.08W
Pinang d. Malaysia 104 C5 .....5.21N 100.11E
Pinar del Río Cuba 71 H5 .....22.25N 83.43W
Pińczów Poland 46 E3 .....50.31N 20.32E
Pindaré r. Brazil 77 L7 .....3.17S 44.50W
Pindus Mountains Greece 56 D4 .....39.56N 20.56E
Pine Bluff U.S.A. 65 H3 .....34.16N 92.02W
Pinega r. Rus. Fed. 58 F4 .....64.41N 43.24E
Pineios r. Greece 56 E4 .....39.53N 22.43E
Pinerolo Italy 50 B6 .....44.53N 7.20E

Pingdingshan China 101 K4 .....33.45N 113.18E
Pingxiang Guangxi China 101 J2 .....22.03N 106.50E
Pingxiang Jiangxi China 101 K3 .....27.42N 113.52E
Pinsk Belarus 55 L5 .....52.08N 26.06E
Pionki Poland 46 E3 .....51.29N 21.28E
Piotrków Trybunalski Poland 46 D3 .....51.25N 19.41E
Pipmuacan, Réservoir Canada 65 L6 .....49.37N 70.33W
Piracicaba Brazil 77 K3 .....22.44S 47.38W
Piraeus Greece 56 E3 .....37.56N 23.38E
Pirot Serbia 56 E6 .....43.09N 22.34E
Pisa Italy 50 D5 .....43.42N 10.24E
Pisco Peru 76 E5 .....13.43S 76.12W
Písek Czech Rep. 54 F3 .....49.19N 14.10E
Pisuerga r. Spain 48 C4 .....41.34N 4.50W
Pisz Poland 46 E4 .....53.38N 21.48E
Pitcairn Island S. Pacific Oc. 109 L4 .....25.03S 130.06W
Pitcairn Islands S. Pacific Oc. 109 L4 .....23.35S 126.31W
Piteå Sweden 40 E4 .....65.19N 21.30E
Pitești Romania 56 F7 .....44.52N 24.53E
Pitlochry Scotland 19 F1 .....56.42N 3.44W
Pittsburgh U.S.A. 65 K5 .....40.26N 79.59W
Piz Bernina mt. Italy/Switz. 50 C7 .....46.23N 9.54E
Plasencia Spain 48 B4 .....40.02N 6.05W
Platinum U.S.A. 62 B3 .....58.59N 161.48W
Platte r. U.S.A. 64 G5 .....41.04N 95.53W
Plauen Germany 54 E4 .....50.30N 12.08E
Plavsk Rus. Fed. 55 Q5 .....53.42N 37.18E
Playa Blanca Canary Islands 48 Z2 .....28.52N 13.50W
Plenty, Bay of g. New Zealand 111 G3 .....37.37S 176.56E
Pleven Bulgaria 56 F6 .....43.25N 24.37E
Płock Poland 46 D4 .....52.33N 19.43E
Pločno mt. Bos.-Herz. 56 B6 .....43.36N 17.35E
Ploiești Romania 56 G7 .....44.56N 26.02E
Plomb du Cantal mt. France 44 E4 .....45.03N 2.46E
Płoty Poland 46 B4 .....53.49N 15.16E
Plovdiv Bulgaria 56 F6 .....42.10N 24.44E
Plungė Lithuania 46 E5 .....55.55N 21.51E
Plymouth England 13 C2 .....50.22N 4.08W
Plymouth d. England 9 C2 .....50.24N 4.08W
Plympton England 13 C2 .....50.23N 4.03W
Plymstock England 13 C2 .....50.21N 4.06W
Plynlimon hill Wales 12 D4 .....52.28N 3.47W
Plzeň Czech Rep. 54 E3 .....49.45N 13.23E
Pô r. Burkina Faso 84 D3 .....11.12N 1.08W
Po r. Italy 50 E6 .....45.02N 12.11E
Pobeda, Gora mt. Rus. Fed. 59 P4 .....65.12N 145.54E
Pocatello U.S.A. 64 D5 .....42.54N 112.25W
Pochep Rus. Fed. 55 O5 .....52.56N 33.27E
Pocklington England 15 G2 .....53.56N 0.47W
Poços de Caldas Brazil 77 K3 .....21.48S 46.31W
Podgorica Montenegro 56 C6 .....42.27N 19.15E
Podkamennaya Tunguska r. Rus. Fed. 59 K4 .....61.36N 90.08E
Podol'sk Rus. Fed. 55 Q6 .....55.25N 37.34E
P'ohang S. Korea 106 A3 .....36.01N 129.22E
Pohnpei atoll Micronesia 108 G6 .....6.53N 158.22E
Pointe-à-Pitre Guadeloupe 72 C8 .....16.15N 61.32W
Pointe-Noire Congo 84 F1 .....4.44S 11.53E
Poitiers France 44 D5 .....46.35N 0.20E
Pokaran India 96 D6 .....26.53N 71.57E
Poland Europe 46 D4 .....52.07N 19.27E
Polatlı Turkey 57 J4 .....39.35N 32.08E
Polatsk Belarus 55 M6 .....55.29N 28.48E
Polegate England 11 F1 .....50.49N 0.15E
Pol-e Khomrī Afgh. 95 K7 .....35.56N 68.46E
Policastro, Golfo di b. Italy 50 F3 .....39.57N 15.33E
Police Poland 46 B4 .....53.33N 14.35E
Polis Cyprus 57 J2 .....35.01N 32.25E
Polkowice Poland 46 C3 .....51.30N 16.04E
Pollaphuca Reservoir Ireland 41 E3 .....53.08N 6.30W
Pollino, Monte mt. Italy 50 G3 .....39.54N 16.12E
Polokwane S. Africa 86 B2 .....23.54S 29.27E
Polperro England 13 C2 .....50.20N 4.31W
Poltava Ukraine 55 P3 .....49.36N 34.34E
Polygyros Greece 56 E5 .....40.23N 23.27E
Polykastro Greece 56 E5 .....40.59N 22.34E
Polynesia is Pacific Oc. 108 I6 .....8.00S 170.00E
Pombal Portugal 48 A3 .....39.55N 8.37W
Ponce Puerto Rico 71 K4 .....18.00N 66.37W
Ponferrada Spain 48 B5 .....42.33N 6.36W
Ponta do Sol Cape Verde 84 B3 .....17.10N 25.05W
Ponta Grossa Brazil 77 J2 .....25.03S 50.07W
Pont-à-Mousson France 42 F1 .....48.54N 6.03E
Pontardawe Wales 12 D3 .....51.43N 3.51W
Pontefract England 15 F2 .....53.41N 1.18W
Ponteland England 15 F4 .....55.03N 1.44W
Pontevedra Spain 48 A5 .....42.27N 8.37W
Pontianak Indonesia 104 D3 .....0.03S 109.18E
Pontine Islands Italy 50 E4 .....40.59N 12.59E
Pontoise France 44 E6 .....49.03N 2.06E
Pont-Ste-Maxence France 42 B2 .....49.18N 2.37E
Pontycymer Wales 12 D3 .....51.37N 3.35W
Pontypool Wales 12 D3 .....51.42N 3.02W
Pontypridd Wales 12 D3 .....51.36N 3.20W
Poole England 10 D1 .....50.43N 1.59W
Poole d. England 9 D2 .....50.44N 1.57W
Poole Bay England 10 D1 .....50.40N 1.55W
Pooley Bridge England 14 E3 .....54.37N 2.49W
Poopó, Lago de l. Bolivia 76 G4 .....18.50S 67.05W
Popayán Colombia 76 B7 .....2.24N 76.37W
Popigay r. Rus. Fed. 59 L5 .....72.56N 106.10E
Poplar Bluff U.S.A. 65 H4 .....36.47N 90.23W
Popocatépetl, Volcán vol. Mexico 70 E4 .....19.02N 98.38W
Poprad Slovakia 54 I3 .....49.04N 20.18E
Porbandar India 96 C5 .....21.39N 69.40E
Pori Finland 40 E3 .....61.29N 21.48E
Porlock England 13 D3 .....51.13N 3.36W
Poronaysk Rus. Fed. 59 P2 .....49.16N 143.03E
Porsangerfjorden str. Norway 40 F5 .....70.19N 25.18E
Porsangerhalvøya pen. Norway 40 F5 .....70.45N 25.01E
Porsgrunn Norway 40 B2 .....59.08N 9.39E
Porsuk r. Turkey 57 I4 .....39.41N 31.58E
Portadown Northern Ireland 16 C2 .....54.25N 6.26W
Portaferry Northern Ireland 16 D2 .....54.23N 5.32W
Portage la Prairie Canada 62 I2 .....49.58N 98.19W
Portalegre Portugal 48 B3 .....39.18N 7.25W
Port Angeles U.S.A. 64 B6 .....48.06N 123.25W
Port Arthur U.S.A. 65 H2 .....29.51N 93.58W
Port Askaig Scotland 16 C3 .....55.51N 6.06W
Port Augusta Australia 110 C3 .....32.29S 137.45E
Port-au-Prince Haiti 71 J4 .....18.33N 72.19W
Portavogie Northern Ireland 16 D2 .....54.27N 5.26W
Port Blair India 97 H3 .....11.41N 92.42E
Port-de-Paix Haiti 71 J4 .....19.57N 72.50W
Port Ellen Scotland 16 C3 .....55.38N 6.11W
Port Erin Isle of Man 14 C3 .....54.05N 4.45W
Port-Gentil Gabon 84 E1 .....0.46S 8.49E
Port Glasgow Scotland 16 E3 .....55.56N 4.41W
Port Harcourt Nigeria 84 E2 .....4.46N 7.01E
Porthcawl Wales 12 D3 .....51.29N 3.42W
Port Hedland Australia 110 A4 .....20.23S 118.37E
Porthleven England 13 B2 .....50.05N 5.19W
Porthmadog Wales 12 C4 .....52.56N 4.08W
Port Hope Simpson Canada 63 M3 .....52.31N 55.47W

Portimão Portugal 48 A2 .....37.08N 8.32W
Port Isaac Bay England 13 C2 .....50.36N 4.49W
Portishead England 10 C2 .....51.29N 2.46W
Portknockie Scotland 19 G2 .....57.42N 2.51W
Portland Australia 110 D3 .....38.21S 141.34E
Portland Me. U.S.A. 65 L5 .....43.41N 70.17W
Portland Oreg. U.S.A. 64 B6 .....45.29N 122.38W
Portland, Isle of pen. England 10 C1 .....50.33N 2.25W
Portlaoise Ireland 41 D3 .....53.02N 7.18W
Portlethen Scotland 19 G2 .....57.04N 2.08W
Port Lincoln Australia 110 C3 .....34.43S 135.49E
Port Macquarie Australia 110 E3 .....31.25S 152.53E
Port Moresby P.N.G. 110 D6 .....9.28S 147.13E
Portnahaven Scotland 16 C3 .....55.41N 6.30W
Port Ness Scotland 18 C3 .....58.30N 6.14W
Porto Alegre Brazil 77 J1 .....30.03S 51.11W
Porto Esperidião Brazil 77 I4 .....15.50S 58.32W
Port of Spain Trinidad and Tobago 71 L3 .....10.37N 61.30W
Portogruaro Italy 50 E6 .....45.46N 12.50E
Porto-Novo Benin 84 E2 .....6.28N 2.40E
Porto Primavera, Represa resr Brazil 77 J3 .....21.27S 52.03W
Porto Santana Brazil 77 J7 .....0.01S 51.09W
Porto Torres Italy 50 C4 .....40.50N 8.25E
Porto-Vecchio France 44 H2 .....41.35N 9.16E
Porto Velho Brazil 76 H6 .....8.47S 63.54W
Portoviejo Ecuador 76 D7 .....1.06S 80.28W
Portpatrick Scotland 16 D2 .....54.51N 5.07W
Port Pirie Australia 110 C3 .....33.10S 138.02E
Portree Scotland 18 C2 .....57.25N 6.12W
Portrush Northern Ireland 16 C3 .....55.12N 6.39W
Port Said Egypt 85 H5 .....31.16N 32.18E
Portsmouth England 10 D1 .....50.48N 1.06W
Portsmouth d. England 9 E2 .....50.50N 1.04W
Portsmouth U.S.A. 65 J4 .....38.44N 82.59W
Portsoy Scotland 19 G2 .....57.41N 2.41W
Portstewart Northern Ireland 16 C3 .....55.11N 6.43W
Port Sudan Sudan 85 H3 .....19.36N 37.12E
Port Talbot Wales 12 D3 .....51.36N 3.47W
Portugal Europe 48 B3 .....39.41N 7.57W
Portumna Ireland 41 C3 .....53.06N 8.13W
Port Vila Vanuatu 108 H4 .....17.44S 168.17E
Port William Scotland 16 E2 .....54.46N 4.35W
Posadas Argentina 73 D4 .....27.23S 55.52W
Poso Indonesia 105 G3 .....1.25S 120.47E
Posse Brazil 77 K5 .....14.06S 46.22W
Potenza Italy 50 F4 .....40.38N 15.48E
P'ot'i Georgia 53 L5 .....42.09N 41.40E
Potiskum Nigeria 84 F3 .....11.42N 11.04E
Potosí Bolivia 76 G4 .....19.36S 65.47W
Potsdam Germany 54 E5 .....52.24N 13.04E
Poulton-le-Fylde England 14 E2 .....53.51N 2.59W
Poūthīsăt Cambodia 104 C6 .....12.32N 103.57E
Považská Bystrica Slovakia 46 D2 .....49.07N 18.27E
Powell, Lake resr U.S.A. 64 D4 .....37.34N 110.37W
Powick England 10 C3 .....52.10N 2.15W
Powys d. Wales 9 D3 .....52.23N 3.25W
Poyang Hu l. China 101 L3 .....29.05N 116.22E
Požarevac Serbia 56 D7 .....44.37N 21.11E
Poza Rica Mexico 70 E5 .....20.35N 97.26W
Poznań Poland 46 C4 .....52.24N 16.55E
Pozoblanco Spain 48 C3 .....38.23N 4.50W
Prabumulih Indonesia 104 C3 .....3.26S 104.13E
Prachatice Czech Rep. 46 B2 .....49.01N 14.00E
Prachuap Khiri Khan Thailand 104 B6 .....11.49N 99.49E
Prague Czech Rep. 54 F4 .....50.04N 14.26E
Praia Cape Verde 84 B3 .....14.55N 23.29W
Prapat Indonesia 104 B4 .....2.41N 98.57E
Prato Italy 50 D5 .....43.52N 11.06E
Pravdinsk Rus. Fed. 46 E5 .....54.27N 21.01E
Prawle Point England 13 D2 .....50.12N 3.44W
Pregolya r. Rus. Fed. 46 E5 .....54.39N 20.22E
Prenzlau Germany 46 A4 .....53.19N 13.52E
Preparis Cocos Is 97 H3 .....14.51N 93.39E
Přerov Czech Rep. 54 G3 .....49.27N 17.27E
Presidencia Roque Sáenz Peña Argentina 77 H2 .....26.44S 60.27W
Presidente Prudente Brazil 77 J3 .....22.10S 51.23W
Prešov Slovakia 54 I3 .....48.59N 21.16E
Prespa, Lake Europe 56 D5 .....40.52N 21.03E
Presque Isle town U.S.A. 65 M6 .....46.41N 68.01W
Prestatyn Wales 12 D5 .....53.20N 3.24W
Presteigne Wales 12 D4 .....52.16N 3.00W
Preston Dor. England 10 C1 .....50.39N 2.25W
Preston Lancs. England 14 E2 .....53.46N 2.42W
Prestonpans Scotland 17 G3 .....55.58N 2.59W
Prestwick Scotland 16 E3 .....55.30N 4.37W
Pretoria S. Africa 86 B2 .....25.44S 28.13E
Preveza Greece 56 D4 .....38.57N 20.45E
Prienai Lithuania 46 F5 .....54.38N 23.57E
Prievidza Slovakia 54 H3 .....48.47N 18.38E
Prijedor Bos.-Herz. 56 B7 .....44.59N 16.43E
Prijepolje Serbia 56 C6 .....43.23N 19.39E
Prilep Macedonia 56 D5 .....41.21N 21.33E
Primorsko-Akhtarsk Rus. Fed. 57 M8 .....46.03N 38.10E
Prince Albert Canada 62 H3 .....53.12N 105.44W
Prince Alfred, Cape Canada 62 F5 .....74.20N 124.47W
Prince Charles Island Canada 63 K4 .....67.48N 76.12W
Prince Edward Island d. Canada 63 L2 .....46.41N 63.09W
Prince Edward Islands Indian Oc. 117 K3 .....47.00S 37.00E
Prince George Canada 62 F3 .....53.55N 122.46W
Prince of Wales Island Australia 110 D5 .....10.43S 142.09E
Prince of Wales Island Canada 63 I5 .....72.27N 99.08W
Prince of Wales Island U.S.A. 62 E3 .....55.38N 132.45W
Prince Patrick Island Canada 62 G5 .....76.57N 118.47W
Prince Rupert Canada 62 E3 .....54.19N 130.19W
Princes Risborough England 10 E2 .....51.43N 0.49W
Príncipe i. São Tomé and Príncipe 84 E2 .....1.39N 7.22E
Pripet r. Ukraine 55 N4 .....51.16N 30.16E
Pripet Marshes Belarus/Ukraine 55 K4 .....51.39N 24.34E
Priština Kosovo 56 D6 .....42.40N 21.10E
Privas France 44 F4 .....44.44N 4.36E
Prizren Kosovo 56 D6 .....42.13N 20.43E
Probolinggo Indonesia 104 E2 .....7.47S 113.13E
Probus England 13 C2 .....50.18N 4.57W
Providence U.S.A. 65 L5 .....41.50N 71.25W
Providence, Cape New Zealand 111 F2 .....46.01S 166.28E
Providencia, Isla de i. Caribbean Sea 71 H3 .....13.21N 81.20W
Provins France 44 E6 .....48.34N 3.18E
Provo U.S.A. 64 D5 .....40.17N 111.41W
Prudhoe Bay town U.S.A. 62 D5 .....70.18N 148.10W
Prüm Germany 42 F3 .....50.13N 6.25E
Pruszków Poland 46 E4 .....52.10N 20.49E
Prut r. Europe 55 M1 .....45.28N 28.12E
Pryluky Ukraine 55 O4 .....50.35N 32.24E
Przemyśl Poland 46 F2 .....49.47N 22.46E
Psara i. Greece 56 F4 .....38.37N 25.35E
Psebay Rus. Fed. 57 N7 .....44.07N 40.47E
Psel r. Rus. Fed./Ukraine 55 P4 .....49.35N 33.15E
Pskov Rus. Fed. 40 G2 .....57.49N 28.19E
Pskov, Lake Estonia/Rus. Fed. 40 F2 .....58.02N 27.56E
Pucallpa Peru 76 F6 .....8.22S 74.35W
Pudsey England 15 F2 .....53.48N 1.40W
Puducherry India 96 F3 .....11.57N 79.48E
Puebla Mexico 70 E4 .....19.02N 98.12W
Puebla d. Mexico 70 E4 .....18.04N 98.39W

Pueblo U.S.A. 64 F4....38.17N 104.38W
Puente-Genil Spain 48 C2....37.23N 4.46W
Puerto Ángel Mexico 70 E4....15.42N 96.31W
Puerto de la Estaca Canary Islands 48 X1....27.47N 17.54W
Puerto del Rosario Canary Islands 48 Z2....28.30N 13.52W
Puertollano Spain 48 C3....38.41N 4.06W
Puerto Maldonado Peru 76 G5....12.39S 69.14W
Puerto Montt Chile 73 B2....41.27S 72.58W
Puerto Natales Chile 73 B1....51.35S 72.24W
Puerto Peñasco Mexico 70 B7....31.19N 113.32W
Puerto Princesa Phil. 104 F5....9.45N 118.45E
Puerto Rico i. Central America 71 K4....17.45N 66.34W
Puerto Vallarta Mexico 70 C5....20.40N 105.14W
Pukch'ŏng N. Korea 106 A4....40.14N 128.19E
Puksubaek-san mt. N. Korea 106 A4....40.38N 127.47E
Pula Croatia 54 E1....44.53N 13.51E
Pulborough England 11 E1....50.57N 0.30W
Puttusk Poland 54 I5....52.42N 21.05E
Pune India 96 D4....18.32N 73.57E
Puning China 101 L2....23.17N 116.09E
Punjab d. India 96 E7....30.17N 75.18E
Punta Arenas Chile 73 B1....53.09S 70.57W
Punto Fijo Venezuela 71 J3....11.39N 70.11W
Pur r. Rus. Fed. 58 J3....67.33N 77.53E
Purari r. P.N.G. 110 D6....7.46S 144.54E
Purbeck, Isle of pen. England 10 C1....50.39N 2.01W
Puri India 96 G4....19.48N 85.55E
Purmerend Neth. 42 D5....52.31N 4.57E
Purus r. Brazil/Peru 77 H7....3.42S 61.28W
Pusan S. Korea 101 N5....35.09N 129.03E
Pustoshka Rus. Fed. 55 M7....56.20N 29.22E
Putian China 101 L3....25.26N 119.00E
Puting, Tanjung pt Indonesia 104 E3....3.35S 111.50E
Putrajaya Malaysia 104 C4....2.55N 101.39E
Puttalam Sri Lanka 96 E2....8.01N 79.50E
Putumayo r. Colombia 72 B6....2.43S 70.03W
Puvurnituq Canada 63 K4....60.02N 77.17W
Puy de Dôme mt. France 44 E4....45.46N 2.58E
Puy de Sancy mt. France 44 E4....45.31N 2.49E
Pwllheli Wales 12 C4....52.53N 4.25W
Pyaozero, Ozero l. Rus. Fed. 40 G4....66.11N 30.47E
Pyasina r. Rus. Fed. 59 J5....73.35N 86.19E
Pyè Myanmar 97 I4....18.48N 95.13E
Pyhäjoki r. Finland 40 F4....64.28N 24.15E
Pyhäselkä l. Finland 40 G3....62.31N 29.41E
Pyinmana Myanmar 97 I4....19.44N 96.13E
Pyle Wales 13 D3....51.32N 3.42W
Pylos Greece 56 D3....36.55N 21.42E
P'yŏngyang N. Korea 101 N5....39.01N 125.44E
Pyramid Lake U.S.A. 64 C5....40.09N 119.37W
Pyrenees mts Europe 48 G5....42.30N 2.00E
Pyrgos Greece 56 D3....37.40N 21.27E
Pyryatyn Ukraine 55 O4....50.14N 32.30E
Pyrzyce Poland 46 B4....53.08N 14.54E

Q
Qamanittuaq Canada 63 I4....64.17N 95.43W
Qamdo China 100 H4....31.13N 97.08E
Qarshi Uzbekistan 95 K7....38.52N 65.48E
Qasigiannguit Greenland 63 M4....68.48N 51.11W
Qatar Asia 95 H5....25.25N 51.57E
Qattara Depression f. Egypt 85 G4....29.48N 27.06E
Qāyen Iran 95 I6....33.42N 59.05E
Qazvīn Iran 95 H7....36.17N 49.58E
Qeshm Iran 95 I5....26.57N 56.15E
Qiemo China 100 F5....38.05N 85.33E
Qijiaojing China 100 G6....43.25N 91.38E
Qilian Shan mts China 100 H5....39.21N 97.06E
Qinā Egypt 85 H4....26.08N 32.45E
Qingdao China 101 M5....36.05N 120.24E
Qinghai d. China 100 H5....36.07N 96.31E
Qinghai Hu l. China 100 H5....36.49N 100.00E
Qinhuangdao China 101 L5....39.56N 119.38E
Qinzhou China 101 J2....21.57N 108.31E
Qionghai China 101 K1....19.13N 110.29E
Qiqihar China 101 M7....47.13N 123.58E
Qitaihe China 106 B5....45.41N 130.46E
Qom Iran 95 H6....34.38N 50.51E
Qornet es Saouda mt. Lebanon 57 L2....34.18N 36.06E
Quang Ngai Vietnam 104 D7....15.04N 108.50E
Quantock Hills England 13 D3....51.10N 3.15W
Quanzhou China 101 K3....25.57N 111.05E
Quchan Iran 95 I7....36.59N 58.29E
Québec d. Canada 63 K2....46.48N 71.15W
Québec d. Canada 63 K3....54.45N 74.31W
Queenborough England 11 F2....51.25N 0.45E
Queen Charlotte Islands Canada 62 E3....53.59N 133.20W
Queen Charlotte Sound str. Canada 62 F3....51.24N 129.09W
Queen Elizabeth Islands Canada 63 I4....76.31N 107.31W
Queen Maud Gulf Canada 62 H4....68.13N 102.08W
Queensland d. Australia 110 D4....22.37S 144.17E
Quelimane Mozambique 86 C3....17.53S 36.53E
Querétaro Mexico 70 D5....20.37N 100.22W
Querétaro d. Mexico 70 E5....20.51N 99.50W
Quetta Pakistan 96 C7....30.14N 67.03E
Quetzaltenango Guatemala 70 F3....14.50N 91.30W
Quezon City Phil. 105 G6....14.36N 121.01E
Quibala Angola 86 A3....10.44S 14.59E
Quibdó Colombia 72 B7....5.39N 76.38W
Quilon India 96 E2....8.53N 76.36E
Quimper France 44 A5....47.59N 4.06W
Quintana Roo d. Mexico 70 G4....18.44N 88.47W
Quito Ecuador 76 E7....0.14S 78.30W
Quixadá Brazil 77 M7....4.55S 38.59W
Quoich, Loch l. Scotland 18 D2....57.03N 5.18W
Quoile r. Northern Ireland 16 D2....54.21N 5.42W
Quy Nhơn Vietnam 104 D6....13.44N 109.13E
Quzhou China 101 L3....28.57N 118.52E

R
Raahe Finland 40 F4....64.41N 24.29E
Raalte Neth. 42 F5....52.23N 6.17E
Raasay i. Scotland 18 C2....57.23N 6.02W
Raasay, Sound of str. Scotland 18 C2....57.26N 6.06W
Raba Indonesia 104 F2....8.32S 118.46E
Rabat Morocco 84 D5....34.01N 6.47W
Rābigh Saudi Arabia 94 E4....22.50N 39.00E
Race, Cape Canada 63 M2....46.38N 53.09W
Rach Gia Vietnam 104 D5....9.59N 105.06E
Racibórz Poland 46 D3....50.06N 18.13E
Radom Poland 46 E3....51.24N 21.09E
Radomsko Poland 46 D3....51.04N 19.27E
Radstock England 10 C2....51.17N 2.27W
Radun' Belarus 46 G5....54.03N 24.59E
Radviliškis Lithuania 46 F5....55.49N 23.32E
Radyvyliv Ukraine 46 G3....50.08N 25.15E
Rafḥā' Saudi Arabia 94 F5....29.33N 43.25E
Rafsanjān Iran 95 I6....30.24N 55.59E

Raglan Wales 12 E3....51.46N 2.51W
Ragusa Italy 50 F2....36.55N 14.44E
Rahachow Belarus 55 N5....53.05N 30.03E
Rahimyar Khan Pakistan 96 D6....28.22N 70.19E
Raichur India 96 E4....16.13N 77.18E
Rainier, Mount vol. U.S.A. 64 B6....46.54N 121.44W
Raipur India 96 F5....21.14N 81.39E
Raivavae i. French Polynesia 109 K4....23.51S 147.39W
Rajahmundry India 96 F4....17.00N 81.52E
Rajanpur Pakistan 96 L5....29.05N 70.24E
Rajasthan d. India 96 D6....26.40N 73.31E
Rajkot India 96 D5....22.14N 70.53E
Rajshahi Bangladesh 96 G5....24.22N 88.36E
Rakhiv Ukraine 55 K3....48.03N 24.12E
Rakitnoye Rus. Fed. 55 P4....50.50N 35.50E
Rakvere Estonia 40 F2....59.21N 26.22E
Raleigh U.S.A. 65 K4....35.47N 78.37W
Ramapo Deep f. N. Pacific Oc. 108 F8....30.59N 142.13E
Rame Head England 13 C2....50.19N 4.15W
Rāmhormoz Iran 95 G6....31.10N 49.35E
Râmnicu Vâlcea Romania 56 F7....45.07N 24.22E
Ramsbottom England 15 E2....53.39N 2.19W
Ramsey England 11 E3....52.27N 0.06W
Ramsey Isle of Man 14 C3....54.19N 4.23W
Ramsey Bay Isle of Man 14 C3....54.20N 4.22W
Ramsey Island Wales 12 B3....51.51N 5.22W
Ramsgate England 11 G2....51.20N 1.25E
Ramu Kenya 87 C3....3.53N 41.14E
Rancagua Chile 73 B3....34.11S 70.44W
Ranchi India 96 G5....23.22N 85.20E
Randers Denmark 40 B2....56.27N 10.03E
Rangiroa atoll French Polynesia 109 K5....14.59S 147.42W
Rangoon Myanmar 97 I4....16.49N 96.08E
Rangpur Bangl. 97 G6....25.46N 89.16E
Rankin Inlet Canada 63 I4....62.52N 92.03W
Rannoch, Loch l. Scotland 19 E1....56.41N 4.23W
Rannoch Moor f. Scotland 18 E1....56.38N 4.46W
Ranong Thailand 104 B5....9.57N 98.38E
Rantauprapat Indonesia 104 B4....2.06N 99.47E
Raoul Island Pacific Oc. 111 H4....29.16S 177.57W
Rapa i. French Polynesia 109 K4....27.35S 144.21W
Rapallo Italy 50 C6....44.21N 9.14E
Raphoe Ireland 16 B2....54.52N 7.35W
Rapid City U.S.A. 64 F5....44.04N 103.14W
Raroia atoll French Polynesia 109 K4....16.05S 142.23W
Rarotonga i. Cook Is 109 J4....21.12S 159.46W
Ras Dejen mt. Ethiopia 85 H3....13.12N 38.23E
Rasht Iran 95 G7....37.16N 49.34E
Raskoh mts Pakistan 95 K5....28.54N 65.26E
Ras Tannūrah Saudi Arabia 95 H5....26.38N 50.10E
Rat Buri Thailand 104 B6....13.31N 99.50E
Rathdrum Ireland 41 E2....52.56N 6.14W
Rathenow Germany 54 E5....52.37N 12.20E
Rathfriland Northern Ireland 16 C2....54.14N 6.09W
Rathkeale Ireland 41 C2....52.31N 8.56W
Rathlin Island Northern Ireland 16 C3....55.17N 6.10W
Rathluirc Ireland 41 C2....52.21N 8.41W
Ratne Ukraine 55 K4....51.40N 24.52E
Rattray Head Scotland 19 H2....57.37N 1.49W
Rättvik Sweden 40 C3....60.53N 15.08E
Rauma Finland 40 E3....61.08N 21.31E
Raunds England 11 E3....52.20N 0.32W
Ravenna Italy 50 E6....44.25N 12.13E
Ravensthorpe Australia 110 B3....33.34S 120.01E
Rawaki i. Kiribati 108 I5....3.42S 170.40W
Rawalpindi Pakistan 96 D7....33.38N 73.08E
Rawicz Poland 46 C3....51.37N 16.51E
Rawlins U.S.A. 64 E5....41.48N 107.13W
Rawson Argentina 73 C2....43.15S 65.06W
Rawtenstall England 15 E2....53.42N 2.17W
Rayleigh England 11 F2....51.35N 0.36E
Razgrad Bulgaria 56 G6....43.32N 26.30E
Ré, Île de i. France 44 C5....46.10N 1.22W
Reading England 10 E2....51.27N 0.58W
Reading d. England 9 E2....51.27N 0.59W
Rebiana Sand Sea des. Libya 94 B4....24.42N 21.18E
Reboly Rus. Fed. 40 G3....63.50N 30.48E
Rechytsa Belarus 55 N5....52.22N 30.26E
Recife Brazil 77 N6....8.02S 34.48W
Reconquista Argentina 77 I2....29.09S 59.38W
Red r. U.S.A. 65 H3....31.05N 91.44W
Red Bluff U.S.A. 64 B5....40.11N 122.14W
Redcar England 15 F3....54.37N 1.03W
Redcar and Cleveland d. England 9 E4....54.33N 1.02W
Red Deer Canada 62 G3....52.16N 113.49W
Redding U.S.A. 64 B5....40.36N 122.29W
Redditch England 10 D3....52.19N 1.56W
Redhill England 11 E2....51.14N 0.10W
Red Lake town Canada 63 I3....51.01N 93.50W
Red Lakes U.S.A. 65 H6....48.03N 94.44W
Redruth England 13 B2....50.14N 5.14W
Red Sea Africa/Asia 94 E4....26.30N 34.42E
Red Wharf Bay Wales 12 C5....53.19N 4.11W
Ree, Lough l. Ireland 41 D3....53.32N 7.59W
Regensburg Germany 54 E3....49.01N 12.06E
Reggane Algeria 84 E4....26.46N 0.09E
Reggio di Calabria Italy 50 F3....38.06N 15.39E
Reggio nell'Emilia Italy 50 D6....44.41N 10.38E
Regina Canada 62 H3....50.27N 104.37W
Reidh, Rubha pt Scotland 18 D2....57.52N 5.51W
Reigate England 11 E2....51.14N 0.12W
Reims France 44 F6....49.15N 4.03E
Reindeer Lake Canada 62 H3....57.24N 102.23W
Reinosa Spain 48 C5....42.59N 4.07W
Reiphólsfjöll hill Iceland 40 X2....65.41N 22.20W
Reliance Canada 62 H4....62.43N 109.06W
Relizane Algeria 52 D4....35.44N 0.40E
Rena Norway 40 B3....61.08N 11.22E
Renfrewshire d. Scotland 8 C4....55.52N 4.31W
Reni Ukraine 57 H7....45.27N 28.18E
Rennell i. Solomon Is 111 F5....11.40S 160.18E
Rennes France 44 C6....48.07N 1.41W
Reno r. Italy 50 E6....44.35N 12.17E
Reno U.S.A. 64 C4....39.32N 119.48W
Republican r. U.S.A. 64 G4....39.06N 96.52W
Repulse Bay town Canada 63 J4....66.32N 86.08W
Resistencia Argentina 73 D4....27.24S 58.59W
Reşiţa Romania 56 D7....45.18N 21.53E
Resolute Canada 63 I5....74.41N 94.46W
Resolution Island Canada 63 L4....61.30N 64.50W
Retford England 15 G2....53.19N 0.57W
Rethel France 42 D2....49.31N 4.23E
Rethymno Greece 56 F2....35.21N 24.28E
Réunion i. Indian Oc. 117 L4....20.00S 55.00E
Reus Spain 48 F4....41.09N 1.06E
Reutlingen Germany 54 C3....48.30N 9.12E
Revillagigedo, Islas is Mexico 70 B4....18.34N 112.24W
Rewa India 96 F5....24.32N 81.18E
Reykjavík Iceland 40 X2....64.08N 21.55W
Reynosa Mexico 70 E6....26.04N 98.17W
Rēzekne Latvia 40 F2....56.31N 27.20E
Rhayader Wales 12 D4....52.18N 3.31W
Rheine Germany 42 G5....52.17N 7.28E
Rheinland-Pfalz d. Germany 42 G2....49.46N 7.27E

Rhine r. Germany 34 E3....51.53N 6.03E
Rhode Island U.S.A. 65 L5....41.40N 71.35W
Rhodes Greece 57 H3....36.26N 28.13E
Rhodes i. Greece 57 H3....36.15N 28.10E
Rhodope Mountains Bulgaria/Greece 56 E5....41.52N 23.41E
Rhondda Wales 12 D3....51.39N 3.30W
Rhondda Cynon Taff d. Wales 9 D2....51.36N 3.23W
Rhône r. France/Switz. 44 F3....43.37N 4.40E
Rhyl Wales 12 D5....53.19N 3.29W
Riau, Kepulauan is Indonesia 104 C4....0.34N 104.11E
Ribble r. England 15 E2....53.45N 2.45W
Ribe Denmark 40 B1....55.20N 8.46E
Ribeira r. Brazil 79 E5....24.39S 47.25W
Ribeirão Preto Brazil 77 K3....21.12S 47.48W
Riberalta Bolivia 76 G6....11.01S 66.05W
Ribnita Moldova 55 M2....47.46N 29.00E
Říčany Czech Rep. 46 B2....49.59N 14.40E
Richfield U.S.A. 64 D4....38.47N 112.05W
Richland U.S.A. 64 C6....46.19N 119.17W
Richmond England 15 F3....54.24N 1.44W
Richmond U.S.A. 65 K4....37.34N 77.28W
Riesa Germany 54 E4....51.19N 13.17E
Rietavas Lithuania 46 E5....55.43N 21.56E
Rīftangi pt Iceland 40 Y2....66.33N 16.13W
Rift Valley d. Kenya 87 A3....0.50N 35.34E
Rīga Latvia 40 F2....56.56N 24.07E
Riga, Gulf of Estonia/Latvia 40 E2....57.24N 23.45E
Rigside Scotland 17 F3....55.36N 3.47W
Riihimäki Finland 40 F3....60.44N 24.47E
Rijeka Croatia 56 A7....45.20N 14.26E
Rimini Italy 50 E6....44.04N 12.34E
Rimouski Canada 63 L2....48.27N 68.32W
Rimsdale, Loch l. Scotland 19 E3....58.17N 4.10W
Ringkøbing Denmark 40 B2....56.05N 8.15E
Ringvassøya i. Norway 40 D5....69.55N 19.15E
Ringwood England 10 D1....50.51N 1.47W
Riobamba Ecuador 76 E7....1.41S 78.42W
Rio Branco Brazil 76 G5....10.01S 67.48W
Río Cuarto Argentina 73 C3....33.08S 64.21W
Rio de Janeiro Brazil 77 L3....22.55S 43.17W
Rio de Janeiro d. Brazil 77 L3....21.58S 42.12W
Río Gallegos Argentina 73 C1....51.39S 69.15W
Rio Grande town Brazil 77 J1....32.04S 52.08W
Rio Grande r. Mexico/U.S.A. 70 F6....25.57N 97.10W
Rio Grande do Norte d. Brazil 77 M6....5.49S 36.21W
Rio Grande do Sul d. Brazil 77 J1....30.39S 54.07W
Riohacha Colombia 72 B8....11.32N 72.58W
Rio Verde Brazil 77 J4....17.48S 50.55W
Ripley England 15 F2....53.03N 1.24W
Ripon England 15 F3....54.08N 1.32W
Risca Wales 12 D3....51.37N 3.06W
Rishton England 15 E2....53.46N 2.25W
Riva del Garda Italy 50 D6....45.53N 10.50E
Rivera Uruguay 77 I1....31.00S 55.33W
Riverside U.S.A. 64 C3....33.57N 117.24W
Rivière-du-Loup Canada 63 L2....47.50N 69.32W
Rivne Ukraine 55 L4....50.37N 26.14E
Riyadh Saudi Arabia 95 G4....24.43N 46.41E
Rize Turkey 57 N5....41.02N 40.30E
Rizhao China 101 L5....35.19N 119.33E
Rjukan Norway 40 B2....59.52N 8.34E
Rjuvbrokkene mt. Norway 40 A2....59.11N 7.10E
Roadford Reservoir England 13 C2....50.42N 4.13W
Roanne France 44 F4....46.03N 4.05E
Roanoke U.S.A. 65 K4....37.16N 79.58W
Roanoke r. U.S.A. 65 K4....36.02N 76.22W
Robertsfors Sweden 40 E4....64.12N 20.52E
Roberval Canada 63 K2....48.31N 72.14W
Robson, Mount Canada 62 G3....53.07N 119.06W
Roca, Cabo da c. Portugal 48 A3....38.47N 9.29W
Rocca Busambra mt. Italy 50 E2....37.51N 13.24E
Rocha Uruguay 73 D3....34.30S 54.19W
Rochdale England 15 E2....53.37N 2.10W
Rochefort Belgium 42 E3....50.10N 5.13E
Rochefort France 44 C4....45.57N 0.58W
Rochester England 11 F2....51.23N 0.30E
Rochester Minn. U.S.A. 65 H5....44.02N 92.27W
Rochester N. Y. U.S.A. 65 K5....43.09N 77.38W
Rochford England 11 F2....51.35N 0.42E
Rockford U.S.A. 65 I5....42.17N 89.04W
Rockhampton Australia 110 E4....23.23S 150.34E
Rockingham Forest England 11 E3....52.31N 0.32W
Rocky Mountains Canada/U.S.A. 62 F3....40.57N 107.58W
Rodel Scotland 18 C2....57.45N 6.58W
Rodez France 44 E4....44.22N 2.34E
Rodrigues Island Mauritius 108 A4....19.37S 63.40E
Roe r. Northern Ireland 16 C3....55.06N 6.58W
Roermond Neth. 42 E4....51.12N 5.59E
Roeselare Belgium 42 C3....50.56N 3.08E
Rogagua, Laguna l. Bolivia 76 G5....14.03S 67.05W
Roggeveen Basin f. S. Pacific Oc. 109 O3....32.50S 89.54W
Rokiškis Lithuania 40 F1....55.57N 25.35E
Rolla U.S.A. 65 H4....37.56N 91.46W
Rom mt. Uganda 87 A3....3.23N 33.32E
Roma i. Indonesia 105 H2....7.31S 127.25E
Romain, Cape U.S.A. 65 K3....32.59N 79.27W
Roman Romania 55 L2....46.55N 26.55E
Romania Europe 53 H6....46.07N 24.36E
Romanzof, Cape U.S.A. 62 B4....61.49N 166.06W
Rombas France 42 F2....49.15N 6.05E
Rome Italy 50 E4....41.54N 12.30E
Romford England 11 F2....51.35N 0.11E
Romney Marsh f. England 11 F2....51.03N 0.54E
Romny Ukraine 55 O4....50.45N 33.28E
Romsey England 10 D1....50.59N 1.30W
Rona i. Scotland 18 D2....57.33N 5.57W
Ronas Hill Scotland 19 H5....60.32N 1.27W
Ronda Spain 48 C2....36.45N 5.10W
Rondônia d. Brazil 76 H5....11.18S 62.19W
Rondonópolis Brazil 77 J4....16.29S 54.38W
Rønne Denmark 40 C1....55.06N 14.43E
Ronse Belgium 42 C3....50.45N 3.36E
Roosendaal Neth. 42 D4....51.31N 4.28E
Roque de los Muchachos vol. Canary Islands 48 X2....28.45N 17.51W
Roquefort France 44 C4....44.02N 0.19W
Roraima, Brazil 77 H8....1.27N 60.48W
Roraima, Mount Guyana 72 C7....5.15N 60.44W
Røros Norway 40 B3....62.36N 11.23E
Rosario Argentina 73 C3....32.56S 60.41W
Roscoff France 44 B6....48.43N 3.59W
Roscommon Ireland 41 C3....53.38N 8.11W
Roscommon d. Ireland 41 C3....53.49N 8.16W
Roscrea Ireland 41 D2....52.57N 7.48W
Roseau Dominica 71 L4....15.17N 61.23W
Roseburg U.S.A. 64 B5....43.13N 123.21W
Roseires Reservoir Sudan 94 D2....11.33N 34.31E
Rosenheim Germany 54 E2....47.51N 12.08E
Roşiori de Vede Romania 56 F7....44.07N 25.00E
Roslavl' Rus. Fed. 55 N6....53.57N 32.51E
Rossan Point Ireland 41 C4....54.42N 8.48W
Rossel Island P.N.G. 110 E5....11.24S 154.10E
Rossington England 15 F2....53.29N 1.03W
Rosslare Harbour Ireland 41 E2....52.15N 6.20W
Rosso Mauritania 84 C3....16.29N 15.47W

Ross of Mull pen. Scotland 16 C4....56.18N 6.19W
Ross-on-Wye England 10 C3....51.55N 2.35W
Røssvatnet l. Norway 40 C4....65.46N 14.19E
Rostock Germany 54 E6....54.05N 12.07E
Rostov-na-Donu Rus. Fed. 58 E2....47.13N 39.44E
Roswell U.S.A. 64 F3....33.21N 104.32W
Rota i. N. Mariana Is 105 L6....14.09N 145.17E
Rote i. Indonesia 105 G1....10.29S 123.24E
Rothbury England 15 F4....55.19N 1.54W
Rother r. England 10 E1....50.57N 0.32W
Rotherham England 15 F2....53.26N 1.21W
Rothes Scotland 19 F2....57.32N 3.12W
Rothesay Scotland 16 D3....55.50N 5.03W
Rothwell England 10 E3....52.25N 0.48W
Rotterdam Neth. 42 D4....51.55N 4.30E
Rotuma i. Fiji 111 G5....12.29S 177.05E
Roubaix France 44 E7....50.42N 3.10E
Rouen France 44 D6....49.26N 1.06E
Round Hill England 15 F3....54.24N 1.05W
Round Mountain Australia 110 E3....30.24S 152.15E
Rousay i. Scotland 19 F4....59.11N 3.08W
Rouyn-Noranda Canada 65 K6....48.14N 79.02W
Rovaniemi Finland 40 F4....66.29N 25.42E
Rovigo Italy 50 D6....45.04N 11.47E
Rovinj Croatia 54 E1....45.05N 13.38E
Royale, Isle i. U.S.A. 65 I6....48.02N 88.38W
Royal Leamington Spa England 10 D3....52.17N 1.32W
Royal Tunbridge Wells England 11 F2....51.08N 0.16E
Royan France 44 C4....45.38N 1.01W
Roye France 42 B2....49.42N 2.48E
Royston England 11 E3....52.03N 0.01W
Royton England 15 E2....53.34N 2.07W
Ruabon Wales 12 D4....52.59N 3.02W
Rub' al Khālī des. Saudi Arabia 95 G3....19.01N 46.30E
Rubtsovsk Rus. Fed. 58 J3....51.33N 81.09E
Rudnaya Pristan' Rus. Fed. 106 C4....43.43N 135.20E
Rudnya Rus. Fed. 55 N6....54.57N 31.06E
Rudnyy Kazakhstan 58 H3....52.57N 63.07E
Rufiji r. Tanzania 86 C4....8.02S 39.17E
Rugby England 10 D3....52.22N 1.16W
Rugby U.S.A. 64 F6....48.20N 100.01W
Rugeley England 10 D3....52.46N 1.56W
Rügen i. Germany 54 E6....54.23N 13.27E
Ruhr r. Germany 42 G4....51.26N 6.43E
Rukwa, Lake Tanzania 86 C4....8.09S 32.25E
Rum i. Scotland 18 C1....56.59N 6.22W
Ruma Serbia 56 C7....45.01N 19.50E
Rum Cay i. Bahamas 71 J5....23.42N 74.48W
Runcorn England 14 E2....53.20N 2.42W
Rundu Namibia 86 A3....17.54S 19.47E
Ruoqiang China 100 F5....38.58N 88.08E
Rururu i. French Polynesia 109 J4....22.28S 151.21W
Ruse Bulgaria 56 F6....43.49N 25.57E
Rushden England 11 E3....52.17N 0.36W
Russian Federation Asia/Europe 58 I4....57.12N 40.44E
Ruteng Indonesia 104 G2....8.33S 120.25E
Ruthin Wales 12 D5....53.07N 3.19W
Rutland d. England 9 E3....52.42N 0.38W
Rutland Water resr England 10 E3....52.39N 0.40W
Ruza Rus. Fed. 55 P6....55.42N 36.13E
Ružomberok Slovakia 54 H3....49.05N 19.17E
Rwanda Africa 85 G1....2.16S 29.58E
Ryan, Loch b. Scotland 16 D3....55.01N 5.05W
Ryazan' Rus. Fed. 58 E3....54.37N 39.44E
Rybinsk Rus. Fed. 58 E3....58.03N 38.51E
Rybinskoye Vodokhranilishche resr Rus. Fed. 58 E3....58.21N 38.27E
Rybnik Poland 46 D3....50.06N 18.33E
Ryde England 10 D1....50.44N 1.10W
Rye England 11 F1....50.57N 0.44E
Rye r. England 15 G3....54.10N 0.44W
Rye Bay England 11 F1....50.55N 0.47E
Ryōtsu Japan 106 C3....38.04N 138.25E
Ryukyu Islands Japan 101 M2....24.13N 124.52E
Rzeszów Poland 46 E3....50.02N 22.01E
Rzhev Rus. Fed. 55 P7....56.16N 34.20E

S
Saale r. Germany 54 D4....51.57N 11.56E
Saarbrücken Germany 54 B3....49.15N 6.58E
Saaremaa i. Estonia 40 E2....58.14N 22.46E
Saarland d. Germany 42 F2....49.28N 6.53E
Saarlouis Germany 42 F2....49.20N 6.46E
Sab' Ābār Syria 57 L1....33.42N 37.47E
Šabac Serbia 56 C7....44.46N 19.42E
Sabadell Spain 48 G4....41.33N 2.05E
Sabah d. Malaysia 104 F5....5.27N 116.59E
Sabana, Archipiélago de is Cuba 71 H5....23.18N 80.46W
Sabinas Mexico 70 D6....27.52N 101.07W
Sable, Cape Canada 63 L2....43.25N 65.39W
Sable, Cape U.S.A. 65 J2....25.08N 81.10W
Sable Island Canada 63 M2....43.57N 59.55W
Şabyā Saudi Arabia 94 F3....17.07N 42.35E
Sabzevār Iran 95 I7....36.12N 57.37E
Sacramento U.S.A. 64 B4....38.34N 121.25W
Sacramento Mountains U.S.A. 64 E3....34.23N 106.04W
Sado r. Portugal 48 A3....38.25N 8.36W
Sadoga-shima i. Japan 106 C3....37.56N 138.33E
Säffle Sweden 40 C2....59.08N 12.56E
Saffron Walden England 11 F3....52.02N 0.15E
Safi Morocco 84 D5....32.22N 9.15W
Safonovo Rus. Fed. 55 O6....55.07N 33.14E
Sagar India 96 E5....23.50N 78.45E
Sagres Portugal 48 A2....37.01N 8.57W
Sahand, Küh-e mt. Iran 95 G7....37.38N 46.28E
Sahara des. Africa 84 E4....19.01N 4.03E
Saidpur Bangl. 96 G6....25.46N 88.58E
Saimaa l. Finland 40 G3....61.15N 28.21E
St Abb's Head Scotland 17 G3....55.55N 2.09W
St Agnes England 13 B2....50.19N 5.12W
St Agnes i. England 13 A1....49.53N 6.21W
St Albans England 11 E2....51.45N 0.20W
St Alban's Head England 10 C1....50.35N 2.03W
St-Amand-les-Eaux France 42 C3....50.26N 3.25E
St-Amand-Montrond France 44 E5....46.44N 2.30E
St Andrews Scotland 17 G4....56.20N 2.48W
St Ann's Head Wales 12 B3....51.41N 5.12W
St Anthony Canada 63 M3....51.20N 55.23W
St Asaph Wales 12 D5....53.15N 3.27W
St Austell England 13 C2....50.20N 4.47W
St Austell Bay England 13 C2....50.19N 4.45W
St-Barthélemy i. Central America 71 L4....17.54N 62.49W
St Bees England 14 D3....54.30N 3.35W
St Bees Head England 14 D3....54.31N 3.38W
St Brelade Channel Is 13 Z8....49.11N 2.12W
St Bride's Bay Wales 12 B3....51.48N 5.18W
St-Brieuc France 44 B6....48.31N 2.45W
St Catherine's Point England 10 D1....50.34N 1.17W
St Clears Wales 12 C3....51.49N 4.30W

St Cloud U.S.A. 65 H6 ....45.34N 94.10W
St Columb Major England 13 C2....50.26N 4.56W
St David's Wales 12 B3....51.53N 5.16W
St David's Head Wales 12 B3....51.54N 5.20W
St-Denis France 42 B1....48.57N 2.22E
St-Dié France 44 G6....48.17N 6.57E
St-Dizier France 44 F6....48.39N 4.57E
Saintes France 44 C4....45.45N 0.37W
St-Étienne France 44 F4....45.26N 4.24E
Saintfield Northern Ireland 16 D2....54.27N 5.49W
St Gallen Switz. 50 C7....47.26N 9.23E
St-Gaudens France 44 D3....43.07N 0.44E
St George's Grenada 71 L3....12.04N 61.45W
St George's Channel Ireland/U.K. 41 E1....51.58N 6.08W
St Germans England 13 C2....50.24N 4.19W
St Govan's Head Wales 12 C3....51.36N 4.55W
St Helena i. Atlantic Oc. 116 I5....16.00S 6.00W
St Helena Bay S. Africa 86 A1....32.43S 18.07E
St Helens England 14 E2....53.27N 2.44W
St Helens, Mount vol. U.S.A. 64 B6....46.08N 122.13W
St Helier Channel Is 13 Z8....49.11N 2.06W
St Ives Cambs. England 11 E3....52.20N 0.04W
St Ives Corn. England 13 B2....50.13N 5.29W
St Ives Bay England 13 B2....50.13N 5.28W
St-Jean, Lac l. Canada 65 L6....48.37N 72.07W
St Joe r. U.S.A. 64 C6....47.25N 116.45W
Saint John Canada 65 L2....45.16N 66.04W
St John Channel Is 13 Z8....49.15N 2.08W
St John r. U.S.A. 65 M6....45.46N 66.12W
St John's Antigua 71 L4....17.05N 61.51W
St John's Canada 63 M2....47.28N 52.18W
St John's Point Northern Ireland 16 D2....54.13N 5.39W
St John's Town of Dalry Scotland 16 E3....55.06N 4.10W
St Joseph U.S.A. 64 C6....39.48N 94.51W
St Joseph, Lake Canada 65 H7....50.59N 90.57W
St Just England 13 B2....50.08N 5.41W
St Keverne England 13 B2....50.03N 5.05W
St Kilda i. Scotland 18 A2....57.49N 8.33W
St Kitts and Nevis Central America 71 L4....17.17N 62.35W
St Lawrence inlet Canada 63 L2....48.16N 69.06W
St Lawrence, Gulf of Canada 63 L2....48.20N 61.29W
St Lawrence Island U.S.A. 62 B4....63.05N 169.50W
St-Lô France 44 C6....49.07N 1.05W
St-Louis Senegal 84 C3....16.00N 16.29W
St Louis U.S.A. 65 H4....38.43N 90.14W
St Lucia Central America 71 L3....13.57N 60.53W
St Magnus Bay Scotland 19 H5....60.24N 1.37W
St-Malo France 44 B6....48.39N 2.00W
St-Malo, Golfe de g. France 44 B6....48.48N 2.16W
St Margaret's Hope Scotland 19 G3....58.49N 2.57W
St Martin Channel Is 13 Y9....49.26N 2.33W
St Martin Channel Is 13 Z8....49.13N 2.03W
St-Martin i. Central America 71 L4....18.08N 62.59W
St Martin's England 13 A1....49.58N 6.17W
St Mary's i. England 13 A1....49.56N 6.19W
St Matthew Island U.S.A. 62 A4....60.27N 172.49W
St-Maurice r. Canada 65 L6....46.22N 72.32W
St Mawes England 13 B2....50.09N 5.01W
St Moritz Switz. 50 C7....46.30N 9.50E
St-Nazaire France 44 C5....47.17N 2.13W
St Neots England 11 E3....52.14N 0.16W
St-Niklaas Belgium 42 D4....51.10N 4.10E
St-Omer France 42 B3....50.45N 2.16E
St Ouen Channel Is 13 Z8....49.14N 2.12W
St Paul U.S.A. 65 H5....44.57N 93.05W
St Peter Port Channel Is 13 Y9....49.27N 2.32W
St Petersburg Rus. Fed. 58 E3....59.56N 30.18E
St Petersburg U.S.A. 65 J2....27.45N 82.42W
St Pierre and Miquelon is N. America 63 M2....46.42N 56.29W
St-Pol-sur-Ternoise France 11 G1....50.23N 2.20E
St Pölten Austria 54 F3....48.12N 15.38E
St-Quentin France 44 E6....49.51N 3.17E
St Sampson Channel Is 13 Y9....49.29N 2.31W
St Vincent and the Grenadines Central America 71 L3....12.50N 60.52W
St-Vith Belgium 42 F3....50.17N 6.07E
St Wendel Germany 42 G2....49.28N 7.09E
Saipan i. N. Mariana Is 108 F7....15.15N 145.49E
Saitama Japan 106 C3....35.51N 139.39E
Saittanulkki hill Finland 40 F4....66.57N 25.48E
Sajama, Nevado mt. Bolivia 76 G4....18.09S 68.52W
Saka Morocco 48 D1....34.37N 3.23W
Sakai Japan 106 C2....34.34N 135.29E
Sakākah Saudi Arabia 94 F5....29.59N 40.05E
Sakakawea, Lake U.S.A. 64 F6....47.45N 102.15W
Sakarya r. Turkey 57 I5....41.07N 30.38E
Sakata Japan 106 C3....38.54N 139.49E
Sakhalin i. Rus. Fed. 59 P2....48.10N 142.40E
Sakura Japan 106 D3....35.44N 140.13E
Sal i. Cape Verde 84 B3....16.49N 22.59W
Sala Sweden 40 D2....59.55N 16.36E
Salado r. Argentina 73 C3....32.27S 60.49W
Salado r. Mexico 70 E6....26.45N 99.26W
Şalālah Oman 95 H3....17.02N 54.10E
Salamanca Spain 48 C4....40.58N 5.39W
Salantai Lithuania 46 E6....56.04N 21.35E
Salawati i. Indonesia 105 I3....1.05S 130.53E
Salayar i. Indonesia 104 G2....6.08S 120.30E
Sala y Gómez, Isla i. S. Pacific Oc. 109 M4....26.31S 105.42W
Šalčininkai Lithuania 46 G5....54.18N 25.23E
Salcombe England 13 D2....50.14N 3.46W
Saldana S. Africa 86 A1....33.01S 17.57E
Sale Australia 110 D3....38.06S 147.06E
Sale England 15 E2....53.26N 2.19W
Salehurst England 11 F1....50.59N 0.30E
Salekhard Rus. Fed. 58 H4....66.31N 66.63E
Salem India 96 E3....11.37N 78.08E
Salem U.S.A. 64 B5....44.54N 122.58W
Salerno Italy 50 F4....40.40N 14.47E
Salerno, Golfo di g. Italy 50 F4....40.25N 14.43E
Salford England 15 E2....53.29N 2.18W
Salgado r. Brazil 77 M7....4.27S 37.46W
Salihli Turkey 57 M4....38.29N 28.08E
Salihorsk Belarus 55 L5....52.47N 27.32E
Salinas r. U.S.A. 64 B4....36.41N 121.39W
Salinas U.S.A. 64 B4....36.41N 121.39W
Salisbury England 10 D2....51.04N 1.48W
Salisbury U.S.A. 65 K4....38.22N 75.36W
Salisbury Plain f. England 10 C2....51.15N 2.03W
Salitre r. Brazil 77 L6....9.30S 40.33W
Salluit Canada 63 K4....62.11N 75.42W
Salmon r. U.S.A. 64 C6....45.52N 116.45W
Salmon Arm Canada 64 C7....50.42N 119.17W
Salmon River Mountains U.S.A. 64 C5....44.46N 115.01W
Salo Finland 40 E3....60.23N 23.08E
Sal'sk Rus. Fed. 53 L6....46.28N 41.33E
Salt r. U.S.A. 64 D4....33.22N 112.17W
Salta Argentina 73 C4....24.45S 65.25W
Saltash England 13 C2....50.24N 4.13W
Saltcoats Scotland 16 E3....55.38N 4.47W
Saltee Islands Ireland 41 E2....52.07N 6.36W
Saltillo Mexico 70 D6....25.25N 101.01W
Salt Lake City U.S.A. 64 D5....40.42N 111.54W
Salto Uruguay 77 I1....31.23S 57.57W

Salton Sea l. U.S.A. 64 C3....33.28N 115.58W
Salvador Brazil 77 M5....12.57S 38.25W
Salween r. China/Myanmar 97 I5....24.06N 98.35E
Salyan Azerbaijan 95 G7....39.35N 48.58E
Salzburg Austria 54 E2....47.48N 13.03E
Salzgitter Germany 54 D5....52.10N 10.24E
Samandağı Turkey 57 K3....36.04N 35.58E
Samani Japan 106 D4....42.08N 142.54E
Samar i. Phil. 105 H6....11.54N 125.43E
Samarinda Indonesia 104 F3....0.29S 117.11E
Samara Rus. Fed. 58 G3....53.11N 50.09E
Sāmarrā' Iraq 94 F6....34.12N 43.54E
Samba Dem. Rep. Congo 86 B4....4.38S 26.20E
Sambalpur India 96 F5....21.27N 83.59E
Sambas Indonesia 104 D4....1.22N 109.19E
Sambir Ukraine 55 J3....49.31N 23.12E
Sambre r. Belgium/France 42 D3....50.17N 4.06E
Same Tanzania 87 B1....4.05S 37.45E
Samer France 11 G1....50.38N 1.45E
Samoa S. Pacific Oc. 108 I5....13.58S 173.23W
Samoa Basin f. S. Pacific Oc. 108 I4....15.26S 165.38W
Samos i. Greece 56 G3....37.49N 26.44E
Samothraki i. Greece 56 F5....40.24N 25.34E
Sampit Indonesia 104 E3....2.34S 112.55E
Samsun Turkey 57 L5....41.17N 36.19E
San Mali 84 D3....13.18N 4.54W
Şan'a' Yemen 94 F3....15.23N 44.11E
Sanandaj Iran 95 G7....35.16N 46.58E
San Andrés, Isla de i. Caribbean Sea 71 H3....12.33N 81.41W
San Angelo U.S.A. 64 F3....31.28N 100.23W
San Antonio U.S.A. 64 G2....29.22N 98.27W
San Antonio, Cabo c. Cuba 71 H5....21.51N 84.55W
San Benedicto, Isla i. Mexico 70 B4....19.19N 110.47W
San Bernardo Chile 76 F1....33.36S 70.41W
San Borja Bolivia 76 G5....14.49S 66.54W
San Cristobal i. Solomon Is 111 F5....10.38S 161.38E
San Cristóbal Venezuela 72 B7....7.45N 72.15W
San Cristóbal, Isla i. Ecuador 76 C7....0.48S 89.20W
San Cristóbal de la Laguna Canary Islands 48 X2....28.28N 16.19W
Sancti Spíritus Cuba 71 I5....21.56N 79.26W
Sanda Island Scotland 16 D3....55.16N 5.35W
Sandakan Malaysia 104 F5....5.51N 118.05E
Sandane Norway 40 A3....61.47N 6.14E
Sandanski Bulgaria 56 E5....41.34N 23.16E
Sanday i. Scotland 19 G4....59.15N 2.29W
Sanday Sound str. Scotland 19 G4....59.12N 2.34W
Sandbach England 15 E2....53.09N 2.22W
Sandhurst England 10 E2....51.21N 0.48W
San Diego U.S.A. 64 C3....32.43N 117.05W
Sandıklı Turkey 57 I4....38.28N 30.16E
Sandnes Norway 40 A2....58.51N 5.44E
Sandnessjøen Norway 40 C4....66.01N 12.39E
Sandomierz Poland 46 I4....50.41N 21.45E
Sandoway Myanmar 97 H4....18.27N 94.22E
Sandown England 10 D1....50.40N 1.09W
Sandpoint U.S.A. 64 C6....48.16N 116.33W
Sandray i. Scotland 18 B1....56.54N 7.30W
Sandviken Sweden 40 D3....60.37N 16.46E
Sandwich England 11 G2....51.16N 1.20E
Sandy England 11 E3....52.08N 0.18W
Sandy Cape Australia 110 E4....24.42S 153.15E
Sandy Lake town Canada 63 I3....53.03N 93.18W
San Felipe Mexico 70 B7....31.02N 114.50W
San Fernando Argentina 77 I1....34.27S 58.32W
San Fernando Chile 73 B2....34.36S 71.00W
San Fernando Phil. 104 G7....16.38N 120.18E
San Fernando Spain 48 B2....36.28N 6.11W
San Fernando de Apure Venezuela 72 C7....7.49N 67.28W
San Francisco U.S.A. 64 B4....37.45N 122.25W
San Francisco, Cabo de c. Ecuador 76 D8....0.40N 80.03W
San Francisco de Paula, Cabo c. Argentina 73 C2....49.42S 67.40W
Sangha r. Congo 82 E4....1.10S 16.47E
Sangir, Kepulauan is Indonesia 105 G4....2.15N 124.57E
Sangkulirang Indonesia 104 F4....0.55N 117.58E
Sangli India 96 D4....16.53N 74.38E
Sangre de Cristo Range mts U.S.A. 64 E4....38.19N 106.01W
Sangue r. Brazil 77 I5....11.02S 58.32W
San Jorge, Golfo de g. Argentina 73 C2....45.57S 65.55W
San Jose Costa Rica 71 H2....9.57N 84.02W
San Jose U.S.A. 64 B4....37.18N 121.57W
San José, Isla i. Mexico 70 B5....24.54N 110.33W
San José del Cabo Mexico 70 C5....23.04N 109.44W
San Juan Argentina 73 C3....31.33S 68.31W
San Juan r. Costa Rica/Nicaragua 71 H3....10.47N 83.44W
San Juan Puerto Rico 71 K4....18.26N 66.04W
San Juan r. U.S.A. 64 E4....37.15N 110.30W
San Juan Bautista Paraguay 77 I2....26.34S 57.06W
San Juan Mountains U.S.A. 64 E4....37.35N 107.17W
Şanlıurfa Turkey 57 M3....37.09N 38.49E
San Lorenzo r. Spain 48 D5....42.14N 2.58W
San Luis Argentina 76 G1....33.19S 66.21W
San Luis, Lago de l. Bolivia 76 H5....13.40S 64.00W
San Luis Obispo U.S.A. 64 B4....35.18N 120.40W
San Luis Potosí Mexico 70 D5....22.10N 100.57W
San Luis Potosí d. Mexico 70 D5....22.51N 100.48W
San Marcos U.S.A. 64 G2....29.51N 97.56W
San Marino Europe 50 E5....43.58N 12.27E
San Marino San Marino 50 E5....43.55N 12.27E
San Martín r. Bolivia 77 H5....13.05S 63.48W
San Matías, Golfo g. Argentina 73 C2....41.20S 64.35W
San Miguel r. Bolivia 76 H5....13.52S 63.43W
San Miguel El Salvador 70 G3....13.32N 88.08W
San Miguel de Tucumán Argentina 73 C4....26.48S 65.16W
Sanming China 101 L3....26.11N 117.39E
San Nicolás de los Arroyos Argentina 77 H1....33.20S 60.14W
Sanok Poland 46 F2....49.34N 22.11E
San Pablo Phil. 105 G6....14.04N 121.18E
San Pedro Paraguay 77 I3....24.08S 57.08W
San Pedro, Sierra de mts Spain 48 B3....39.31N 7.15W
San Pedro de Ycuamandyyú Paraguay 73 D4....24.07S 57.07W
San Pedro Sula Honduras 70 G4....15.28N 88.01W
San Pietro, Isola di i. Italy 50 G4....39.10N 8.14E
Sanquhar Scotland 17 F3....55.22N 3.56W
San Quintín, Cabo c. Mexico 64 C3....30.23N 116.01W
San Remo Italy 50 B5....43.49N 7.47E
San Salvador i. Bahamas 71 J5....24.07N 74.27W
San Salvador El Salvador 70 G3....13.43N 89.11W
San Salvador de Jujuy Argentina 73 C4....24.10S 65.20W
San Sebastián de la Gomera Canary Islands 48 X2....28.05N 17.06W
San Severo Italy 50 F4....41.41N 15.23E
Santa Ana El Salvador 70 G3....13.59N 89.31W
Santa Ana U.S.A. 64 C3....33.45N 117.56W
Santa Barbara U.S.A. 64 C3....34.27N 119.43W
Santa Catarina d. Brazil 77 J2....27.00S 50.57W
Santa Clara Cuba 71 I5....22.24N 79.56W
Santa Cruz, Isla i. Ecuador 76 B7....0.36S 90.10W
Santa Cruz de la Palma Canary Islands 48 X2....28.41N 17.46W
Santa Cruz de Tenerife Canary Islands 48 X2....28.27N 16.15W
Santa Cruz do Sul Brazil 77 J2....29.44S 52.25W
Santa Cruz Islands Solomon Is 111 F5....10.46S 167.21E

Santa Elena, Bahía de b. Ecuador 76 D7....2.07S 81.05W
Santa Fé Brazil 73 C3....31.37S 60.42W
Santa Fe U.S.A. 64 E4....35.42N 105.57W
Santa Isabel i. Solomon Is 111 E6....7.54S 159.11E
Santa Margarita, Isla i. Mexico 70 B5....24.25N 111.50W
Santa Maria Brazil 77 J2....29.41S 53.48W
Santa Maria U.S.A. 64 B3....34.58N 120.26W
Santa Maria di Leuca, Capo c. Italy 50 H3....39.47N 18.21E
Santa Marta Colombia 72 B8....11.16N 74.12W
Santander Spain 48 D5....43.28N 3.48W
Santarém Brazil 77 J7....2.27S 54.43W
Santarém Portugal 48 A3....39.15N 8.41W
Santa Rosa Argentina 73 C3....36.37S 64.17W
Santa Rosalía Mexico 70 B6....27.21N 112.18W
Santiago Chile 73 B3....33.28S 70.39W
Santiago Dom. Rep. 71 J4....19.29N 70.41W
Santiago i. Cape Verde 84 B3....15.19N 23.45W
Santiago de Compostela Spain 48 A5....42.53N 8.32W
Santiago de Cuba Cuba 71 I5....20.00N 75.49W
Sant Jordi, Golf de g. Spain 48 F4....40.49N 0.56E
Santo André Brazil 77 K3....23.38S 46.30W
Santo Antão i. Cape Verde 84 B3....17.01N 25.21W
Santo Domingo Dom. Rep. 71 K4....18.31N 69.52W
Santoña Spain 48 D5....43.27N 3.27W
Santos Brazil 77 K3....23.58S 46.20W
Santos Plateau f. S. Atlantic Oc. 109 Q4....27.20S 45.43W
Santo Tomé Argentina 77 I2....28.32S 56.05W
San Valentín, Cerro mt. Chile 73 B2....46.35S 73.27W
San Vincenzo Italy 50 D5....43.05N 10.32E
São Carlos Brazil 77 K3....22.02S 47.53W
São Francisco r. Brazil 77 M5....10.19S 36.31W
São José do Rio Preto Brazil 77 K3....20.49S 49.22W
São Luís Brazil 77 L7....2.35S 44.18W
São Marcos, Baía de b. Brazil 77 L7....2.31S 44.19W
São Mateus Brazil 77 M4....18.42S 39.51W
Saône r. France 44 F5....45.44N 4.49E
São Paulo Brazil 77 K3....23.35S 46.43W
São Paulo d. Brazil 77 K3....22.19S 48.23W
São Raimundo Nonato Brazil 77 L6....9.01S 42.37W
São Sebastião, Ilha do i. Brazil 77 K3....23.51S 45.17W
São Tomé São Tomé and Príncipe 84 E2....0.19N 6.44E
São Tomé i. São Tomé and Príncipe 84 E2....0.21N 6.35E
São Tomé, Cabo de c. Brazil 73 E4....22.05S 40.59W
São Tomé and Príncipe Africa 84 E2....1.00N 7.04E
São Vicente Brazil 77 K3....23.58S 46.22W
São Vicente, Cabo de c. Portugal 48 A2....37.01N 8.59W
Sapporo Japan 106 D4....43.04N 141.20E
Sapri Italy 50 F4....40.04N 15.38E
Saqqaq Greenland 63 M5....70.01N 51.56W
Saqqez Iran 95 G7....36.12N 46.15E
Sarāb Iran 95 G7....37.55N 47.31E
Sara Buri Thailand 104 C6....14.29N 100.57E
Sarajevo Bos.-Herz. 56 C6....43.51N 18.25E
Sarandë Albania 56 D4....39.53N 20.01E
Saransk Rus. Fed. 58 F3....54.11N 45.12E
Sarasota U.S.A. 65 J2....27.19N 82.33W
Saratov Rus. Fed. 58 F3....51.34N 45.59E
Saravan Iran 95 J5....27.20N 62.25E
Sarawak d. Malaysia 104 E4....1.46N 111.55E
Saray Turkey 57 G5....41.26N 27.55E
Sardindida Plain f. Kenya 87 B3....2.41N 39.59E
Sardinia i. Italy 50 C4....40.16N 8.04E
Sarektjåkkå mt. Sweden 40 D4....67.27N 17.43E
Sar-e Pol Afgh. 95 H7....36.15N 65.57E
Sargodha Pakistan 96 D7....32.01N 72.41E
Sarh Chad 85 F2....9.07N 18.23E
Sārī Iran 95 H7....36.33N 53.03E
Sarigan i. N. Mariana Is 105 L7....16.42N 145.48E
Sarıyer Turkey 57 H5....41.10N 29.03E
Sark i. Channel Is 13 Y9....49.24N 2.24W
Şarkışla Turkey 57 L4....39.21N 36.25E
Şarköy Turkey 56 G5....40.37N 27.06E
Särna Sweden 40 C3....61.42N 13.08E
Sarny Ukraine 55 L4....51.20N 26.37E
Saros Körfezi b. Turkey 56 G5....40.34N 26.36E
Sarpsborg Norway 40 B2....59.17N 11.08E
Sarrebourg France 44 G6....48.44N 7.03E
Sarreguemines France 42 G2....49.07N 7.04E
Sarria Spain 48 B5....42.47N 7.24W
Sarthe r. France 44 C5....47.34N 0.31W
Sasebo Japan 106 A2....33.09N 129.44E
Saskatchewan d. Canada 62 H3....53.08N 106.03W
Saskatchewan r. Canada 62 H3....53.40N 100.27W
Saskatoon Canada 62 H3....52.08N 106.39W
Sassandra Côte d'Ivoire 84 D2....4.57N 6.05W
Sassari Italy 50 C4....40.43N 8.34E
Sassnitz Germany 54 E6....54.31N 13.38E
Satpura Range mts India 96 D5....21.47N 74.23E
Satu Mare Romania 56 D7....47.47N 22.53E
Sauðárkrókur Iceland 40 Y2....65.45N 19.40W
Saudi Arabia Asia 94 F4....23.41N 44.13E
Sault Sainte Marie Canada 63 J2....46.31N 84.20W
Saumlakki Indonesia 105 I2....8.00S 131.20E
Saundersfoot Wales 12 C3....51.43N 4.42W
Saurimo Angola 86 B4....9.39S 20.25E
Sava r. Europe 56 D6....44.50N 20.28E
Savai'i i. Samoa 108 I5....13.25S 172.39W
Savannah U.S.A. 65 J3....32.04N 81.07W
Savannah r. U.S.A. 65 J3....32.02N 80.53W
Savannakhét Laos 104 C7....16.32N 104.46E
Save r. Mozambique/Zimbabwe 86 C2....20.56S 35.03E
Savona Italy 50 C6....44.19N 8.29E
Savu Sea Indonesia 105 G2....9.51S 121.22E
Sawel Mountain hill Northern Ireland 16 B2....54.49N 7.02W
Sawhāj Egypt 53 J2....26.31N 31.38E
Sawston England 11 F3....52.07N 0.10E
Sawtry England 11 E3....52.26N 0.17W
Sawu i. Indonesia 105 G1....10.32S 121.58E
Saxilby England 15 G2....53.16N 0.40W
Saxmundham England 11 G3....52.13N 1.29E
Sayhūt Yemen 95 H3....15.15N 51.19E
Saylac Somalia 85 I3....11.17N 43.28E
Saynshand Mongolia 101 K6....44.46N 110.12E
Scafell Pike hill England 14 D3....54.27N 3.13W
Scalasaig Scotland 16 C4....56.04N 6.11W
Scalby England 15 G3....54.18N 0.27W
Scalloway Scotland 19 H5....60.08N 1.17W
Scalp hill Ireland 41 C2....52.59N 8.29W
Scalpay i. High. Scotland 18 D2....57.18N 5.59W
Scalpay i. W. Isles Scotland 18 C2....57.52N 6.39W
Scalp Mountain hill Ireland 16 B3....55.06N 7.22W
Scampton England 15 G2....53.18N 0.34W
Scandinavia f. Europe 34 F4....65.00N 18.00E
Scapa Flow inlet Scotland 19 F3....58.54N 3.08W
Scarba i. Scotland 16 D4....56.10N 5.45W
Scarborough England 15 G3....54.17N 0.24W
Scarp i. Scotland 18 B3....58.01N 7.11W
Schaffhausen Switz. 50 C7....47.42N 8.38E
Schagen Neth. 42 D5....52.47N 4.48E
Schefferville Canada 63 L3....54.47N 66.48W
Scheldt r. Belgium 42 D4....51.21N 4.04E
Schiehallion mt. Scotland 19 E1....56.40N 4.06W
Schiermonnikoog i. Neth. 42 F6....53.31N 6.17E
Schleswig Germany 54 C6....54.31N 9.33E

Schwäbische Alb mts Germany 54 C2....47.59N 8.43E
Schwaner, Pegunungan mts Indonesia 104 E3....0.46S 112.84E
Schwarzer Mann hill Germany 42 F2....50.15N 6.21E
Schwedt an der Oder Germany 54 F5....53.04N 14.18E
Schweinfurt Germany 54 D4....50.03N 10.13E
Schwerin Germany 54 D5....53.38N 11.25E
Scilly, Isles of England 13 A1....49.53N 6.17W
Scioto r. U.S.A. 65 J4....38.44N 82.59W
Scole England 11 G3....52.22N 1.09E
Scone Scotland 17 F4....56.25N 3.24W
Scotland d. U.K. 8 D5....57.01N 3.53W
Scottish Borders d. Scotland 8 D4....55.40N 2.44W
Scottsbluff U.S.A. 64 F5....41.54N 103.41W
Scourie Scotland 18 D3....58.21N 5.09W
Scranton U.S.A. 65 K5....41.25N 75.39W
Scridain, Loch inlet Scotland 16 C4....56.21N 6.11W
Scunthorpe England 15 G2....53.35N 0.39W
Scuol Switz. 50 D7....46.48N 10.18E
Scutari, Lake Albania/Montenegro 56 C6....42.14N 19.23E
Seaford England 11 F1....50.46N 0.06E
Seaham England 15 F3....54.50N 1.20W
Seamer England 15 G3....54.14N 0.26W
Seascale England 14 D3....54.24N 3.29W
Seaton Cumb. England 14 D3....54.40N 3.31W
Seaton Dev. England 13 D2....50.42N 3.04W
Seaton Delaval England 15 F4....55.04N 1.31W
Seattle U.S.A. 64 B6....47.36N 122.20W
Sebastián Vizcaíno, Bahía b. Mexico 70 B6....28.08N 114.45W
Sebeş Romania 56 E7....45.58N 23.34E
Şebinkarahisar Turkey 57 M5....40.17N 38.25E
Sechura, Bahía de b. Peru 76 D6....5.42S 81.18W
Secunderabad India 96 E4....17.25N 78.27E
Sedan France 44 F6....49.42N 4.57E
Sedbergh England 15 E3....54.19N 2.31W
Sedlčany Czech Rep. 54 E4....49.39N 14.26E
Šeduva Lithuania 46 F5....55.46N 23.44E
Seefin hill Ireland 41 D2....52.14N 7.36W
Segen Wenz watercourse Ethiopia 87 B4....4.58N 36.54E
Segera Tanzania 87 B1....5.20S 38.34E
Segorbe Spain 48 E3....39.51N 0.28W
Segovia Spain 48 C4....40.57N 4.06W
Segura r. Spain 48 E3....38.06N 0.38W
Segura, Sierra de mts Spain 48 D2....37.59N 2.46W
Seiland i. Norway 40 E5....70.28N 23.18E
Seinäjoki Finland 40 E3....62.47N 22.51E
Seine r. France 44 D6....49.29N 0.32W
Seine, Baie de b. France 44 C6....49.29N 0.32W
Sejny Poland 46 I5....54.06N 23.21E
Sekondi Ghana 84 D2....4.58N 1.43W
Selaru i. Indonesia 105 I2....8.13S 130.55E
Selatan, Tanjung pt Indonesia 104 E3....4.09S 114.38E
Selattyn England 10 B3....52.54N 3.05W
Selawik U.S.A. 62 B4....66.36N 160.16W
Selby England 15 F2....53.47N 1.04W
Selkirk Canada 62 I3....50.09N 96.53W
Selkirk Scotland 17 G3....55.33N 2.50W
Sellindge England 11 F2....51.06N 0.59E
Selsey England 10 E1....50.44N 0.47W
Selsey Bill hd England 10 E1....50.43N 0.49W
Selvas f. Brazil 76 F6....6.29S 71.47W
Selwyn Mountains Canada 62 E4....64.16N 131.38W
Selwyn Range hills Australia 110 C4....21.14S 139.54E
Semarang Indonesia 104 E2....6.55S 110.29E
Semenivka Ukraine 55 O5....52.10N 32.35E
Seminoe Reservoir U.S.A. 64 E5....42.06N 106.51W
Semipalatinsk Kazakhstan 58 J3....50.25N 80.19E
Semnān Iran 95 H7....35.30N 53.21E
Semois r. Belgium/France 42 D2....49.53N 4.45E
Sena Madureira Brazil 76 G6....9.07S 68.42W
Sendai Japan 106 D3....38.15N 140.53E
Senegal Africa 84 C3....14.29N 14.41W
Sénégal r. Mauritania 84 C3....16.00N 16.31W
Senftenberg Germany 46 B3....51.31N 14.00E
Senja i. Norway 40 D5....69.20N 17.14E
Senlis France 42 B2....49.12N 2.36E
Sennar Sudan 85 H3....13.31N 33.36E
Sens France 44 E6....48.12N 3.17E
Seoul S. Korea 101 N5....37.32N 127.00E
Sepik r. P.N.G. 105 K3....3.53S 144.33E
Sept-Îles Canada 63 L3....50.13N 66.23W
Seram i. Indonesia 105 H3....3.03S 129.24E
Serang Indonesia 104 D2....6.04S 106.09E
Serbia Europe 56 D6....44.01N 20.58E
Şereflikoçhisar Turkey 57 J4....38.56N 33.33E
Seremban Malaysia 104 C4....2.41N 101.54E
Serengeti National Park Tanzania 87 A2....2.28S 34.46E
Serengeti Plains f. Kenya 87 B2....3.43S 38.05E
Serere Uganda 87 A3....1.30N 33.27E
Seret r. Ukraine 55 L3....48.36N 25.51E
Sergipe d. Brazil 77 M5....10.30S 37.14W
Serik Turkey 57 I3....36.57N 31.07E
Serov Rus. Fed. 58 H3....59.38N 60.34E
Serowe Botswana 86 B2....22.24S 26.42E
Serpukhov Rus. Fed. 58 E3....54.55N 37.25E
Serra da Mesa, Represa resr Brazil 77 K5....14.17S 48.30W
Serres Greece 56 E5....41.06N 23.33E
Serui Indonesia 105 J3....1.52S 136.17E
Sestroretsk Rus. Fed. 40 G3....60.09N 29.57E
Sète France 44 E3....43.24N 3.42E
Sete Lagoas Brazil 77 L4....19.28S 44.13W
Setesdal f. Norway 40 A2....59.15N 7.23E
Sétif Algeria 84 E5....36.11N 5.25E
Seto-naikai sea Japan 106 B2....33.38N 132.17E
Settat Morocco 84 D5....32.58N 7.36W
Settle England 15 E3....54.04N 2.17W
Setúbal Portugal 48 A3....38.32N 8.53W
Setúbal, Baía de b. Portugal 48 A3....38.20N 9.02W
Seul, Lac l. Canada 65 H7....50.21N 92.29W
Sevastopol' Ukraine 55 N2....44.36N 33.31E
Seven Heads Ireland 41 C1....51.34N 8.42W
Sevenoaks England 11 F2....51.16N 0.12E
Severn r. Canada 63 J3....55.59N 87.36W
Severn r. U.K. 10 C2....51.51N 2.21W
Severnaya Zemlya is Rus. Fed. 59 L6....80.09N 103.23E
Severo-Kuril'sk Rus. Fed. 59 Q3....50.40N 156.06E
Sevier Lake U.S.A. 64 D4....38.56N 113.09W
Seville Spain 48 C2....37.24N 5.58W
Seward U.S.A. 62 D4....60.09N 149.24W
Seward Peninsula U.S.A. 62 B4....65.29N 164.05W
Seychelles Indian Oc. 85 J1....4.40S 55.43E
Seydişehir Turkey 57 I3....37.25N 31.52E
Seyðisfjörður Iceland 40 Z2....65.16N 14.02W
Seyhan r. Turkey 57 K3....36.44N 34.54E
Seym r. Rus. Fed./Ukraine 55 P4....51.16N 34.16E
Seymchan Rus. Fed. 59 Q4....62.50N 152.20E
Sfântu Gheorghe Romania 56 F7....45.52N 25.48E
Sfax Tunisia 52 F3....34.45N 10.45E
Sgurr Alasdair hill Scotland 18 C2....57.12N 6.13W
Sgurr Dhomhnuill hill Scotland 18 D1....56.45N 5.27W
Sgurr Mòr mt. Scotland 18 D2....57.42N 5.01W
Shaanxi d. China 101 J4....34.43N 108.13E
Shaftesbury England 10 C2....51.00N 2.12W
Shahr-e Kord Iran 95 H6....32.19N 50.49E
Shahreẕā Iran 95 H6....32.00N 51.52E

Shakhovskaya Rus. Fed. 55 P7............................56.02N 35.30E
Shakhty Rus. Fed. 53 L6..................................47.42N 40.12E
Shalkar Kazakhstan 58 G2...............................47.47N 59.39E
Shandong d. China 101 L5...............................36.22N 117.45E
Shandong Bandao pen. China 101 M5...............37.05N 121.02E
Shanghai China 101 M4..................................31.15N 121.29E
Shangqiu China 101 L4....................................34.24N 115.38E
Shanklin England 10 D1..................................50.38N 1.10W
Shannon r. Ireland 41 C2................................52.40N 8.38W
Shannon, Mouth of the Ireland 41 B2..............52.31N 9.51W
Shantarskiye Ostrova is Rus. Fed. 59 O3..........55.20N 137.22E
Shantou China 101 L2....................................23.24N 116.42E
Shanxi d. China 101 K5..................................38.03N 111.48E
Shaoguan China 101 K2..................................24.48N 113.37E
Shaoxing China 101 M4..................................30.01N 120.38E
Shaoyang China 101 K3..................................27.14N 111.30E
Shap England 14 E3........................................54.32N 2.41W
Shapinsay i. Scotland 19 G4............................59.02N 2.48W
Shaqrā' Saudi Arabia 94 G5............................25.15N 45.16E
Sharjah U.A.E. 95 I5......................................25.21N 55.23E
Shark Bay Australia 110 A4.............................25.17S 113.32E
Shashemenē Ethiopia 85 H2............................7.12N 38.36E
Shasta, Mount vol. U.S.A. 64 B5.....................41.23N 122.10W
Shchigry Rus. Fed. 55 Q4...............................51.52N 36.56E
Shchuchyn Belarus 46 G4...............................53.37N 24.44E
Sheberghān Afgh. 95 K7.................................36.42N 65.45E
Sheboygan U.S.A. 65 I5..................................43.45N 87.43W
Sheelin, Lough l. Ireland 41 D3.......................53.49N 7.19W
Sheep Haven b. Ireland 16 B2.........................55.12N 7.55W
Sheerness England 11 F2................................51.26N 0.46E
Sheffield England 15 F2.................................53.23N 1.28W
Shelby U.S.A. 64 D6......................................48.29N 111.48W
Shelikhova, Zaliv g. Rus. Fed. 59 Q4...............60.40N 157.23E
Shelikof Strait U.S.A. 62 C3...........................57.27N 155.17W
Shengena mt. Tanzania 87 B1.........................4.16S 37.56E
Shenyang China 101 M6.................................41.46N 123.24E
Shenzhen China 101 K2.................................22.33N 114.09E
Shepetivka Ukraine 55 L4...............................50.11N 27.04E
Sheppey, Isle of i. England 11 F2.....................51.24N 0.46E
Shepshed England 10 D3...............................52.46N 1.18W
Shepton Mallet England 10 C2.......................51.11N 2.33W
Sherborne England 10 C1..............................50.57N 2.31W
Sherbrooke Canada 63 K2.............................45.24N 71.54W
Shereiq Sudan 94 D3.....................................18.42N 33.40E
Sheridan U.S.A. 64 E5...................................44.48N 106.55W
Sheringham England 11 G3............................52.57N 1.13E
's-Hertogenbosch Neth. 42 E4.......................51.41N 5.19E
Sherwood Forest England 15 F2.....................53.04N 1.07W
Shetland d. Scotland 8 E7..............................60.14N 0.57W
Shetland Islands Scotland 19 I5......................60.36N 0.47W
Sheyenne r. U.S.A. 64 G6..............................47.03N 96.50W
Shiant Islands Scotland 18 C2.........................57.53N 6.25W
Shibām Yemen 95 G3....................................15.59N 48.57E
Shiel, Loch l. Scotland 18 D1..........................56.47N 5.35W
Shieldaig Scotland 18 D2...............................57.31N 5.39W
Shifnal England 10 C3...................................52.40N 2.22W
Shihezi China 100 F6.....................................44.14N 86.03E
Shijiazhuang China 101 K5.............................38.00N 114.30E
Shikarpur India 96 E3....................................14.14N 75.18E
Shikarpur Pakistan 95 K5...............................27.56N 68.42E
Shikoku i. Japan 106 B2.................................33.08N 133.49E
Shikoku-sanchi mts Japan 106 B2...................33.26N 132.53E
Shildon England 15 F3...................................54.38N 1.39W
Shillong India 97 H6......................................25.33N 91.53E
Shimoga India 96 E3......................................13.54N 75.31E
Shimoni Kenya 87 B2.....................................4.39S 39.22E
Shimonoseki Japan 106 B2.............................33.57N 130.57E
Shin, Loch l. Scotland 19 E3............................58.09N 4.38W
Shingū Japan 106 C2.....................................33.43N 136.00E
Shining Tor hill England 15 E2.........................53.16N 2.00W
Shipley England 15 F2....................................53.50N 1.47W
Shipston on Stour England 10 D3.....................52.04N 1.37W
Shirane-san mt. Japan 106 C3..........................35.40N 138.13E
Shīrāz Iran 95 H5...........................................29.37N 52.31E
Shire r. Malawi 86 C3.....................................17.41S 35.19E
Shizuishan China 101 J5..................................38.58N 106.27E
Shizuoka Japan 106 C2..................................34.58N 138.23E
Shklow Belarus 55 N6....................................54.13N 30.17E
Shkodër Albania 56 C6...................................42.04N 19.31E
Shona, Eilean i. Scotland 18 D1.......................56.48N 5.53W
Sho'rchi Uzbekistan 95 K7..............................37.59N 67.46E
Shostka Ukraine 55 N4...................................51.51N 33.29E
Shpola Ukraine 55 N3....................................49.01N 31.23E
Shreveport U.S.A. 65 H3.................................32.29N 93.46W
Shrewsbury England 10 C3..............................52.42N 2.45W
Shropshire d. England 9 D3.............................52.45N 2.38W
Shuangjiang China 101 H2..............................23.28N 99.49E
Shumagin Islands U.S.A. 62 C3........................55.09N 161.01W
Shumen Bulgaria 56 G6..................................43.16N 26.56E
Shuqrah Yemen 95 G2....................................13.24N 45.40E
Shushtar Iran 95 H6.......................................32.01N 48.49E
Shwebo Myanmar 97 I5..................................22.34N 95.43E
Shwegyin Myanmar 97 I4...............................17.56N 96.52E
Shymkent Kazakhstan 58 H2...........................42.19N 69.38E
Siahan Range mts Pakistan 95 J5......................27.13N 63.38E
Šiauliai Lithuania 40 E1...................................55.56N 23.19E
Siaya Kenya 87 A3.........................................0.02N 34.15E
Šibenik Croatia 56 A6.....................................43.44N 15.54E
Siberia f. Rus. Fed. 59 M4...............................65.18N 115.57E
Siberut i. Indonesia 104 B3.............................1.23S 98.41E
Sibi Pakistan 95 K5........................................29.30N 67.55E
Sibiloi National Park Kenya 87 B3....................3.59N 36.24E
Sibiu Romania 56 F7......................................45.48N 24.10E
Sibolga Indonesia 104 B4...............................1.40N 98.48E
Sibsey England 15 H2....................................53.02N 0.01E
Sibu Malaysia 104 E4.....................................2.17N 111.51E
Sibut C.A.R. 85 F2.........................................5.44N 19.05E
Sichuan d. China 101 I4..................................30.05N 103.11E
Sicily i. Italy 50 F3.........................................38.21N 14.09E
Sidi Bel Abbès Algeria 84 D5..........................35.12N 0.38W
Sidi Kacem Morocco 52 B3.............................34.12N 5.39W
Sidlaw Hills Scotland 17 F4.............................56.26N 3.21W
Sidmouth England 13 D2................................50.41N 3.14W
Sidney U.S.A. 64 F5.......................................41.12N 103.09W
Sidon Lebanon 53 K3.....................................33.33N 35.23E
Siedlce Poland 46 F4......................................52.10N 22.17E
Siegen Germany 54 C4...................................50.52N 8.01E
Siena Italy 50 D5...........................................43.19N 11.20E
Sieradz Poland 46 D3.....................................51.36N 18.44E
Sierra Leone Africa 84 C2...............................8.35N 11.58W
Sighetu Marmaţiei Romania 55 J2....................47.56N 23.54E
Sighişoara Romania 56 F8...............................46.14N 24.47E
Siglufjörður Iceland 40 Y2...............................66.08N 18.52W
Sigüenza Spain 48 D4.....................................41.05N 2.37W
Siguiri Guinea 84 D3......................................11.25N 9.10W
Sihanoukville Cambodia 104 C6......................10.38N 103.34E
Siilinjärvi Finland 40 F3..................................63.05N 27.40E
Siirt Turkey 94 F7..........................................37.55N 41.58E
Sikar India 96 E6...........................................27.31N 75.13E
Sikasso Mali 84 D3........................................11.19N 5.40W
Sikeston U.S.A. 65 I4......................................36.51N 89.34W
Sikhote-Alin' mts Rus. Fed. 59 O2....................43.58N 133.53E
Sikkim d. India 96 G6.....................................27.31N 88.27E
Sil r. Spain 48 B5...........................................42.28N 7.42W

Šilalė Lithuania 46 F5.....................................55.29N 22.11E
Silesia f. Europe 46 C3...................................50.45N 17.01E
Siletiteniz, Ozero l. Kazakhstan 100 C8.............53.11N 72.53E
Silifke Turkey 57 J3........................................36.22N 33.56E
Siling Co l. China 100 F4................................31.47N 88.41E
Silistra Bulgaria 56 G7...................................44.07N 27.16E
Silivri Turkey 57 H5.......................................41.04N 28.16E
Siljan l. Sweden 40 C3...................................60.53N 14.44E
Šilutė Lithuania 46 E5.....................................55.21N 21.28E
Silver City U.S.A. 64 E3..................................32.45N 108.19W
Silverstone England 10 D3.............................52.05N 1.02W
Silverton England 13 D2................................50.49N 3.29W
Simav Turkey 57 H4......................................39.05N 28.58E
Simēn mts Ethiopia 94 E2...............................13.16N 37.50E
Simeulue i. Indonesia 104 B4..........................2.41N 96.08E
Simferopol' Ukraine 53 J5...............................44.57N 34.07E
Şimleu Silvaniei Romania 46 F1.......................47.14N 22.50E
Simojärvi l. Finland 40 F4...............................66.01N 27.15E
Simplon Pass Switz. 50 C7..............................46.15N 8.02E
Simpson Desert Australia 110 C4.....................24.59S 136.50E
Simrishamn Sweden 54 F6..............................55.33N 14.21E
Sinai f. Egypt 85 H4.......................................29.13N 33.47E
Sinai, Mont hill France 42 D3..........................49.09N 4.08E
Sinaloa d. Mexico 70 C6................................25.42N 108.11W
Sincelejo Colombia 72 B7...............................9.17N 75.24W
Sinclair's Bay Scotland 19 F3...........................58.30N 3.07W
Sines Portugal 48 A2......................................37.58N 8.52W
Singa Sudan 94 D2........................................13.09N 33.54E
Singapore Asia 104 C4...................................1.27N 104.32E
Singapore town Singapore 104 C4....................1.19N 103.51E
Singaraja Indonesia 104 F2.............................8.06S 115.06E
Singida Tanzania 86 C4..................................4.50S 34.45E
Singkawang Indonesia 104 D4........................0.57N 108.59E
Sinj Croatia 56 B6..........................................43.42N 16.38E
Sinkat Sudan 94 E3........................................18.45N 36.49E
Sinop Turkey 57 K6.......................................42.02N 35.08E
Sint Maarten i. Neth. Antilles 71 L4..................18.02N 63.04W
Sion Mills Northern Ireland 16 B2.....................54.47N 7.28W
Sioux City U.S.A. 64 G5..................................42.32N 96.23W
Sioux Falls U.S.A. 64 G5.................................43.32N 96.43W
Sioux Lookout Canada 63 I3............................50.06N 91.56W
Sipacate Guatemala 70 F3...............................13.59N 91.08W
Siping China 101 M6......................................43.04N 124.24E
Sipura i. Indonesia 104 B3...............................2.12S 99.42E
Sira r. Norway 40 A2......................................58.16N 6.24E
Siret r. Romania 56 H7...................................45.25N 28.02E
Sīrjān Iran 95 I5.............................................29.27N 55.40E
Sirrei Ethiopia 87 C4......................................6.43N 42.05E
Sirte Libya 85 F5............................................31.09N 16.40E
Sirte, Gulf of Libya 85 F5................................31.11N 18.03E
Širvintos Lithuania 46 G5...............................55.02N 24.58E
Sisak Croatia 56 B7........................................45.29N 16.23E
Sisimiut Greenland 63 M4..............................66.56N 53.40W
Sisophon Cambodia 104 C6...........................13.34N 102.59E
Sīstān, Daryācheh-ye marsh Afgh./Iran 95 J6....31.10N 61.10E
Sisteron France 44 F4.....................................44.12N 5.57E
Siteia Greece 56 G2.......................................35.12N 26.06E
Sitka U.S.A. 62 E3..........................................57.03N 135.18W
Sittard Neth. 42 E3.........................................50.59N 5.51E
Sittingbourne England 11 F2...........................51.20N 0.44E
Sittwe Myanmar 97 H5...................................20.08N 92.54E
Sivas Turkey 57 L4.........................................39.43N 37.00E
Siverek Turkey 57 M3.....................................37.44N 39.21E
Sivrihisar Turkey 57 I4....................................39.27N 31.32E
Siwah Egypt 85 G4........................................29.09N 25.30E
Skadovs'k Ukraine 57 J8.................................46.07N 32.54E
Skaftárós r. mouth Iceland 40 Y1......................63.41N 17.47W
Skagen Denmark 40 B2..................................57.43N 10.35E
Skagerrak str. Denmark/Norway 40 B2.............57.30N 8.13E
Skagway U.S.A. 62 E3....................................59.29N 135.18W
Skara Sweden 40 C2......................................58.23N 13.26E
Skarżysko-Kamienna Poland 46 E3..................51.07N 20.53E
Skegness England 15 H2................................53.09N 0.20E
Skellefteå Sweden 40 E4.................................64.45N 20.58E
Skellefteälven r. Sweden 40 E4........................64.42N 21.07E
Skelmersdale England 14 E2...........................53.33N 2.46W
Skerries Ireland 41 E3.....................................53.35N 6.06W
Ski Norway 40 B2..........................................59.43N 10.50E
Skibbereen Ireland 41 B1...............................51.33N 9.16W
Skiddaw hill England 14 D3.............................54.39N 3.09W
Skien Norway 40 B2.......................................59.12N 9.36E
Skierniewice Poland 46 E3..............................51.57N 20.09E
Skikda Algeria 84 E5......................................36.54N 6.57E
Skipton England 15 E2...................................53.58N 2.01W
Skive Denmark 40 B2.....................................56.34N 9.02E
Skokholm Island Wales 12 B3.........................51.41N 5.16W
Skomer Island Wales 12 B3.............................51.44N 5.20W
Skopje Macedonia 56 D5................................41.59N 21.27E
Skövde Sweden 40 C2....................................58.23N 13.51E
Skovorodino Rus. Fed. 59 N3..........................54.05N 123.52E
Skuodas Lithuania 46 E6................................56.16N 21.32E
Skwierzyna Poland 46 B4...............................52.36N 15.30E
Skye i. Scotland 18 C2....................................57.21N 6.20W
Skyros i. Greece 56 F4...................................38.53N 24.35E
Slagelse Denmark 40 B1.................................55.24N 11.22E
Slamet vol. Indonesia 104 D2..........................7.14S 109.10E
Slaney r. Ireland 41 E2....................................52.25N 6.34W
Slatina Romania 56 F7....................................44.26N 24.22E
Slave r. Canada 62 G4....................................61.17N 113.31W
Slave Lake town Canada 62 G3........................55.17N 114.47W
Slavonski Brod Croatia 56 C7..........................45.10N 18.01E
Slavyansk-na-Kubani Rus. Fed. 57 M7..............45.16N 38.08E
Slawharad Belarus 55 N5................................53.27N 31.00E
Sławno Poland 46 C5.....................................54.22N 16.41E
Sleaford England 11 E4..................................53.00N 0.24W
Sleat, Sound of str. Scotland 18 D2..................57.02N 5.53W
Sleights England 15 G3..................................54.27N 0.40W
Slieve Anierin hill Ireland 16 B2.......................54.05N 7.59W
Slieve Beagh hill Ireland/U.K. 16 B2.................54.20N 7.12W
Slievecallan hill Ireland 41 B2..........................52.51N 9.16W
Slieve Car hill Ireland 41 B4............................54.04N 9.40W
Slieve Donard hill Northern Ireland 16 D2.........54.11N 5.55W
Slievenamon hill Ireland 41 D2........................52.26N 7.34W
Slieve Snaght hill Ireland 41 D5.......................55.12N 7.20W
Sligo Ireland 41 C4........................................54.17N 8.28W
Sligo d. Ireland 41 C4....................................54.07N 8.30W
Sligo Bay Ireland 41 C4.................................54.18N 8.55W
Sliven Bulgaria 56 G6....................................42.41N 26.19E
Slobozia Romania 56 G7................................44.34N 27.23E
Slonim Belarus 55 K5....................................53.05N 25.19E
Slough England 11 E2....................................51.31N 0.36W
Slough d. England 9 E2..................................51.30N 0.35W
Slovakia Europe 54 H3...................................48.45N 19.35E
Slovenia Europe 54 F1...................................46.09N 14.37E
Slovyechna r. Ukraine 55 M4...........................51.39N 29.43E
Sluch r. Ukraine 55 L4....................................51.37N 26.39E
Słupsk Poland 46 C5......................................54.27N 17.02E
Slutsk Belarus 55 L5......................................53.01N 27.32E
Slyne Head Ireland 41 A3...............................53.24N 10.14W
Slyudyanka Rus. Fed. 101 I8...........................51.28N 103.36E
Smallwood Reservoir Canada 63 L3.................54.01N 64.50W
Smarhon' Belarus 55 L6.................................54.29N 26.25E
Smila Ukraine 55 N3......................................49.12N 31.54E
Smoky r. U.S.A. 62 G3...................................56.08N 117.20W

Smøla i. Norway 40 A3...................................63.23N 7.59E
Smolensk Rus. Fed. 55 N6..............................54.47N 32.04E
Smolikas mt. Greece 56 D5.............................40.05N 20.56E
Smolyan Bulgaria 56 F5..................................41.35N 24.41E
Snæfell mt. Iceland 40 Z2...............................64.48N 15.35W
Snaefell hill Isle of Man 14 C3.........................54.16N 4.28W
Snaith England 15 F2.....................................53.41N 1.01W
Snake r. U.S.A. 64 C6.....................................46.13N 118.59W
Snares Islands New Zealand 108 H2.................48.02S 166.37E
Snåsa Norway 40 C4......................................64.15N 12.23E
Sneek Neth. 42 E6.........................................53.02N 5.40E
Snettisham England 11 F3...............................52.53N 0.30E
Snežnik mt. Slovenia 54 F1.............................45.35N 14.26E
Śniardwy, Jezioro l. Poland 46 E4.....................53.46N 21.42E
Snizort, Loch b. Scotland 18 C2.......................57.33N 6.28W
Snøtinden mt. Norway 40 C4..........................66.38N 13.57E
Snov r. Ukraine 55 N4....................................51.32N 31.32E
Snowdon mt. Wales 12 C5.............................53.04N 4.04W
Soay i. Scotland 18 C2...................................57.09N 6.15W
Sobradinho, Barragem de resr Brazil 77 L5........10.14S 42.24W
Sobral Brazil 77 L7.........................................3.41S 40.19W
Sochi Rus. Fed. 58 E2.....................................43.36N 39.46E
Société, Archipel de la is French Polynesia 109 J4
...................................................................17.22S 152.28W
Socorro, Isla i. Mexico 70 B4...........................18.51N 110.58W
Socotra i. Yemen 95 H2.................................12.34N 54.30E
Sodankylä Finland 40 F4................................67.25N 26.34E
Söderhamn Sweden 40 D3.............................61.18N 17.04E
Södertälje Sweden 40 D2................................59.12N 17.38E
Sodo Ethiopia 85 H2......................................6.49N 37.42E
Sødra Kvarken str. Finland/Sweden 40 D3.........60.19N 19.02E
Sofia Bulgaria 56 E6.......................................42.41N 23.19E
Sognefjorden inlet Norway 40 A3....................61.05N 5.33E
Soham England 11 F3.....................................52.20N 0.20E
Soignies Belgium 42 D3.................................50.35N 4.04E
Soissons France 44 E6....................................49.23N 3.20E
Sokal' Ukraine 46 G3......................................50.29N 24.17E
Söke Turkey 56 G3........................................37.45N 27.23E
Sokhumi Georgia 58 F2.................................43.00N 41.02E
Sokółka Poland 46 F4.....................................53.24N 23.31E
Sokoto Nigeria 84 E3.....................................13.05N 5.15E
Sokoto r. Nigeria 84 E3..................................11.24N 4.07E
Solapur India 96 E4.......................................17.41N 75.55E
Solihull England 10 D3...................................52.25N 1.47W
Solikamsk Rus. Fed. 58 G3.............................59.42N 56.44E
Sollefteå Sweden 40 D3.................................63.10N 17.15E
Solomon Islands S. Pacific Oc. 111 F6.............7.13S 157.49E
Solomon Sea S. Pacific Oc. 110 E6..................7.01S 152.18E
Solway Firth est. Scotland 17 F2......................54.48N 3.33W
Solwezi Zambia 86 B3...................................12.10S 26.26E
Soma Turkey 56 G4......................................39.10N 27.36E
Somalia Africa 85 I2.......................................3.56N 46.23E
Sombor Serbia 56 C7....................................45.47N 19.07E
Somerset d. England 9 D2..............................51.04N 2.56W
Somerset Island Canada 63 I5.........................73.19N 93.22W
Somerton England 10 C2...............................51.03N 2.44W
Sønderborg Denmark 54 C6...........................54.55N 9.48E
Sondrio Italy 50 C7.......................................46.10N 9.52E
Songea Tanzania 86 C2.................................10.39S 35.38E
Songkhla Thailand 104 C5..............................7.10N 100.35E
Songyuan China 101 M7...............................45.05N 124.53E
Søn La Vietnam 104 C8.................................21.20N 103.57E
Sono r. Brazil 77 K6.......................................8.58S 48.07W
Sonora r. Mexico 70 B6.................................29.42N 110.36W
Sonora r. Mexico 70 B6.................................28.47N 111.54W
Soria Spain 48 D4..........................................41.47N 2.26W
Soroca Moldova 53 I6....................................48.09N 28.17E
Sorocaba Brazil 77 K3....................................23.30S 47.30W
Sorol atoll Micronesia 105 K5..........................8.10N 140.22E
Sorong Indonesia 105 I3.................................0.54S 131.17E
Soroti Uganda 85 H3.....................................1.42N 33.37E
Sørøya i. Norway 40 E5..................................70.34N 22.32E
Sorraia r. Portugal 48 A3................................39.02N 8.50W
Sorsele Sweden 40 D4...................................65.31N 17.33E
Sortavala Rus. Fed. 40 G3..............................61.42N 30.41E
Soshanguve S. Africa 86 B2............................25.31S 28.06E
Sosna r. Rus. Fed. 55 R5.................................52.41N 38.54E
Sosneado mt. Argentina 73 C3........................34.44S 69.59W
Sosnowiec Poland 46 D3................................50.17N 19.08E
Souk Ahras Algeria 52 E4...............................36.17N 7.59E
Souk el Arbaâ du Rharb Morocco 48 C1..........34.40N 5.58W
Souris r. Canada 64 G6..................................49.41N 99.40W
Sousse Tunisia 52 F4......................................35.47N 10.39E
Soustons France 44 C3..................................43.45N 1.20W
South Africa, Republic of Africa 86 B1..............30.06S 24.04E
Southam England 10 D3................................52.15N 1.22W
South America 72-73
Southampton England 10 D1..........................50.55N 1.24W
Southampton d. England 9 E2.........................50.56N 1.24W
Southampton Island Canada 63 J4...................64.01N 83.45W
South Anston England 15 F2...........................53.21N 1.13W
South Australia d. Australia 110 C3...................30.27S 132.43E
South Australian Basin f. Indian Oc. 108 D3.......37.58S 119.18E
South Ayrshire d. Scotland 8 C4......................55.09N 4.47W
South Bank England 15 F3..............................54.35N 1.10W
South Bend U.S.A. 65 I5.................................41.40N 86.13W
Southborough England 11 F2..........................51.09N 0.16E
South Carolina d. U.S.A. 65 J3.........................34.02N 80.47W
South Cave England 15 G2.............................53.46N 0.36W
South China Sea N. Pacific Oc. 104 F6.............12.00N 117.49E
South Dakota d. U.S.A. 64 F5..........................44.27N 100.14W
South Dorset Downs hills England 10 C1...........50.42N 2.37W
South Downs hills England 11 E1.....................50.52N 0.22W
South East Cape Australia 110 D2....................43.38S 146.55E
Southeast Indian Ridge f. Indian Oc. 108 A4.....31.15S 76.54E
Southeast Pacific Basin f. S. Pacific Oc. 116 D2..63.41S 112.50W
Southend d. England 9 F2...............................51.33N 0.42E
Southend-on-Sea England 11 F2......................51.33N 0.43E
Southern Alps mts New Zealand 111 G2...........43.26S 170.28E
Southern Ocean 116 H2
Southern Uplands hills Scotland 16 E3..............55.14N 4.32W
Southery England 11 F3.................................52.31N 0.24E
South Esk r. Scotland 19 G1............................56.43N 2.33W
South Fiji Basin f. S. Pacific Oc. 108 H4.............25.53S 175.02E
South Georgia i. S. Atlantic Oc. 73 F1...............54.32S 37.11W
South Gloucestershire d. England 9 D2.............51.33N 2.27W
South Harris f. Scotland 18 B2.........................57.49N 7.03W
South Honshu Ridge f. N. Pacific Oc. 108 F8.....31.09N 138.30E
South Horr Kenya 87 B3.................................2.07N 36.56E
South Island New Zealand 111 G2...................44.24S 172.31E
South Kirkby England 15 F2............................53.36N 1.19W
South Kitui National Reserve Kenya 87 B2.........1.43S 38.50E
South Korea Asia 101 N5...............................35.32N 128.04E
South Lanarkshire d. Scotland 8 D4.................55.38N 3.49W
South Molton England 13 D3..........................51.01N 3.50W
South Nahanni r. Canada 62 F4.......................61.03N 123.18W
South Ockendon England 11 F2......................51.31N 0.18E
South Platte r. U.S.A. 64 F5.............................41.08N 100.47W
Southport Australia 110 E4.............................27.56S 153.23E
Southport England 14 D2...............................53.39N 3.00W
South Ronaldsay i. Scotland 19 G3..................58.47N 2.54W
South Saskatchewan r. Canada 62 H3..............53.09N 105.08W

South Shields England 15 F3............................54.59N 1.26W
South Solomon Trench f. S. Pacific Oc. 108 G5...11.28S 162.19E
South Sudan Africa 85 G2...............................7.01N 30.00E
South Tasman Rise f. Southern Oc. 108 F2.........45.34S 146.08E
South Tyne r. England 15 E3............................54.59N 2.08W
South Uist i. Scotland 18 B2.............................57.17N 7.22W
South Walls pen. Scotland 19 F3......................58.47N 3.08W
Southwell England 15 G2................................53.05N 0.58W
Southwest Pacific Basin f. S. Pacific Oc. 116 A4..36.11S 158.10W
Southwest Peru Ridge f. S. Pacific Oc. 109 O4...22.54S 83.41W
Southwold England 11 G3...............................52.19N 1.41E
South Woodham Ferrers England 11 F2.............51.39N 0.37E
South Wootton England 11 F3..........................52.46N 0.26E
South Yorkshire d. England 9 E3.......................53.28N 1.16W
Sovetsk Rus. Fed. 46 E5..................................55.05N 21.53E
Soweto S. Africa 86 B2...................................26.15S 27.50E
Sozh r. Europe 55 N4......................................51.57N 30.49E
Spain Europe 48 D4.......................................39.32N 3.04W
Spalding England 11 E3..................................52.47N 0.09W
Span Head hill England 13 D3..........................51.07N 3.49W
Sparks U.S.A. 64 C4.......................................39.32N 119.46W
Sparti Greece 56 E3........................................37.04N 22.26E
Spartivento, Capo c. Italy 50 G2.......................37.56N 16.05E
Spas-Demensk Rus. Fed. 55 P6........................54.25N 34.03E
Spassk-Dal'niy Rus. Fed. 106 B4.......................44.32N 132.48E
Spatha, Akra pt Greece 56 E2..........................35.41N 23.44E
Speke Gulf Tanzania 87 A2...............................2.19S 32.57E
Spencer Gulf est. Australia 110 C3....................34.54S 136.27E
Spennymoor England 15 F3.............................54.42N 1.35W
Sperrin Mountains hills Northern Ireland 16 B2...54.47N 7.09W
Spey r. Scotland 19 F2....................................57.39N 3.06W
Speyer Germany 44 H6...................................49.19N 8.24E
Spijkenisse Neth. 42 D4..................................51.50N 4.19E
Spilsby England 15 H2....................................53.10N 0.06E
Spitsbergen i. Arctic Oc. 58 C5.........................78.37N 16.06E
Split Croatia 56 B6.........................................43.31N 16.27E
Spofforth England 15 F2.................................53.57N 1.27W
Spokane U.S.A. 64 C6....................................47.38N 117.22W
Spratly Islands S. China Sea 104 E6..................10.01N 114.21E
Spree r. Germany 54 E5..................................52.32N 13.13E
Springfield Ill. U.S.A. 65 I4..............................39.48N 89.39W
Springfield Mass. U.S.A. 65 L5.........................42.05N 72.35W
Springfield Mo. U.S.A. 65 H4...........................37.16N 93.18W
Sprowston England 11 G3..............................52.39N 1.19E
Spurn Head England 15 H2.............................53.34N 0.05E
Srebrenica Bos.-Herz. 56 C7............................44.07N 19.19E
Srednekolymsk Rus. Fed. 59 Q4.......................67.32N 153.38E
Sretensk Rus. Fed. 59 M3................................52.08N 117.41E
Sri Aman Malaysia 104 E4...............................1.12N 111.30E
Sri Jayewardenepura Kotte Sri Lanka 96 E2.......6.56N 79.54E
Sri Lanka Asia 96 F2.......................................7.29N 80.42E
Srinagar India 96 D7......................................34.08N 74.51E
Stadskanaal Neth. 42 F5.................................52.59N 6.59E
Staffa i. Scotland 16 C4..................................56.26N 6.20W
Stafford England 10 C3...................................52.48N 2.07W
Staffordshire d. England 9 D3..........................52.52N 2.04W
Staines England 11 E2.....................................51.26N 0.31W
Stalbridge England 10 C1...............................50.57N 2.23W
Stalham England 11 G3..................................52.46N 1.31E
Stalowa Wola Poland 46 F3.............................50.34N 22.03E
Stamford England 11 E3.................................52.39N 0.29W
Stamford Bridge England 15 G2.......................53.59N 0.55W
Standish England 14 E2...................................53.35N 2.40W
Stanley England 15 F3.....................................54.52N 1.42W
Stanley Falkland Is 73 D1................................51.43S 57.52W
Stannington England 15 F4..............................55.06N 1.40W
Stanovoy Khrebet mts Rus. Fed. 59 N3.............57.21N 120.44E
Stansted Mountfitchet England 11 F2................51.54N 0.12E
Stanton England 11 F3....................................52.19N 0.53E
Starachowice Poland 46 E3.............................51.02N 21.04E
Stara Zagora Bulgaria 56 F6............................42.26N 25.38E
Starbuck Island Kiribati 109 J5..........................5.36S 155.51W
Stargard Szczeciński Poland 46 B4....................53.20N 15.03E
Starogard Gdański Poland 46 D4......................53.58N 18.31E
Starokostyantyniv Ukraine 55 L3......................49.45N 27.13E
Start Bay England 13 D2.................................50.18N 3.37W
Start Point England 13 D2...............................50.13N 3.38W
Staryya Darohi Belarus 55 M5.........................53.02N 28.17E
Staryy Oskol Rus. Fed. 58 E3...........................51.18N 37.51E
Stavanger Norway 40 A2................................58.58N 5.44E
Staveley England 15 F2..................................53.16N 1.21W
Stavropol' Rus. Fed. 53 L6..............................45.03N 41.59E
Stavropol'skaya Vozvyshennost' hills Rus. Fed. 58 F2
...................................................................45.05N 42.35E
Steenwijk Neth. 42 F5....................................52.47N 6.07E
Steep Holm i. England 10 B2...........................51.20N 3.06W
Stefansson Island Canada 62 H5......................73.21N 105.34W
Steinfurt Germany 42 G5................................52.09N 7.21E
Steinkjer Norway 40 B4..................................64.01N 11.30E
Stenness, Loch of l. Scotland 19 F4..................59.00N 3.16W
Sterling U.S.A. 64 F5......................................40.39N 103.09W
Sterlitamak Rus. Fed. 58 G3............................53.36N 55.53E
Stevenage England 11 E2...............................51.54N 0.12W
Stewart Canada 62 F3.....................................55.57N 129.59W
Stewart r. Canada 62 E4..................................63.18N 139.26W
Stewart Island New Zealand 111 F2..................47.09S 167.55E
Stewarton Scotland 16 E3...............................55.41N 4.31W
Steyning England 11 E1..................................50.53N 0.20W
Steyr Austria 54 F3........................................48.02N 14.25E
Stikine r. Canada 62 E3...................................56.41N 132.19W
Stilton England 11 E3.....................................52.29N 0.17W
Stinchar r. Scotland 16 D3..............................55.06N 5.01W
Stirling Scotland 17 F4....................................56.07N 3.56W
Stirling d. Scotland 8 D5.................................56.17N 4.23W
Stjørdalshalsen Norway 40 B3.........................63.28N 10.55E
Stob Choire Claurigh mt. Scotland 18 E1...........56.50N 4.51W
Stockholm Sweden 40 D2...............................59.20N 18.04E
Stockport England 15 E2................................53.24N 2.09W
Stockton U.S.A. 64 B4....................................37.57N 121.17W
Stockton-on-Tees England 15 F3.....................54.34N 1.19W
Stockton-on-Tees d. England 9 E4....................54.33N 1.22W
Stœng Trêng Cambodia 104 D6.......................13.28N 105.59E
Stoer, Point of Scotland 18 D3.........................58.16N 5.23W
Stoke-on-Trent England 15 E2.........................53.00N 2.11W
Stoke-on-Trent d. England 9 D3.......................53.01N 2.10W
Stokesay England 10 C3.................................52.26N 2.50W
Stokesley England 15 F3.................................54.28N 1.11W
Stolin Belarus 55 L4.......................................51.53N 26.50E
Stone England 10 C3......................................52.54N 2.09W
Stonehaven Scotland 19 G2.............................56.58N 2.13W
Stony Rapids town Canada 62 H3......................59.15N 105.59W
Stora Lulevatten l. Sweden 40 D4.....................67.09N 19.28E
Storavan l. Sweden 40 D4...............................65.40N 18.16E
Støren Norway 40 B3......................................63.02N 10.17E
Stornoway Scotland 18 C3..............................58.13N 6.23W
Storsjön l. Sweden 40 C3................................63.13N 14.16E
Storrington England 11 E1..............................50.55N 0.27W
Storuman Sweden 40 D4................................65.05N 17.09E
Storuman l. Sweden 40 D4..............................65.11N 16.54E
Stotfold England 11 E3...................................52.01N 0.14W
Stour r. Dor. England 10 D1............................50.44N 1.46W
Stour r. Kent England 11 G2............................51.18N 1.21E
Stour r. Warwicks. England 10 D3....................52.11N 1.44W

Stourbridge England 10 C3.....................52.27N 2.09W
Stourport-on-Severn England 10 C3.........52.20N 2.17W
Stowbtsy Belarus 55 L5..........................53.28N 26.44E
Stowmarket England 11 F3......................52.11N 0.59E
Stow-on-the-Wold England 10 D2............51.56N 1.43W
Strabane Northern Ireland 16 B2...............54.50N 7.27W
Strabane d. Northern Ireland 9 B4..............54.47N 7.21W
Stradbroke England 11 G3.......................52.19N 1.16E
Strakonice Czech Rep. 46 A2...................49.15N 13.55E
Stralsund Germany 54 E6........................54.18N 13.05E
Stranda Norway 40 A3.............................62.18N 6.57E
Strangford Lough inlet Northern Ireland 16 D2...54.28N 5.35W
Stranraer Scotland 16 D2........................54.54N 5.02W
Strasbourg France 44 G6.........................48.35N 7.44E
Stratford-upon-Avon England 10 D3.........52.11N 1.43W
Strathaven Scotland 17 E3........................55.41N 4.04W
Strathbeg, Loch of l. Scotland 19 H2..........57.37N 1.54W
Strathbogie f. Scotland 19 G2...................57.26N 2.53W
Strathmore f. Scotland 18 E3....................58.25N 4.39W
Strathspey f. Scotland 19 F2.....................57.11N 3.47W
Strathy Point Scotland 19 E3....................58.36N 4.01W
Stratton England 13 C2...........................50.50N 4.31W
Stratton St Margaret England 10 D2...........51.35N 1.45W
Straubing Germany 54 E3.........................48.54N 12.35E
Straumnes pt Iceland 40 X2.....................66.26N 23.10W
Streatley England 10 D2..........................51.32N 1.09W
Street England 10 C2...............................51.07N 2.44W
Strelka Rus. Fed. 59 Q4...........................61.52N 152.11E
Stretham England 11 F3...........................52.21N 0.13E
Strimonas r. Greece 56 E5........................40.48N 23.51E
Stroma, Island of l. Scotland 19 F3............58.42N 3.08W
Stromboli, Isola i. Italy 50 F3...................38.45N 15.14E
Stromness Scotland 19 F3........................58.58N 3.18W
Strömsund Sweden 40 C3........................63.52N 15.34E
Stronsay i. Scotland 19 G4........................59.08N 2.33W
Stronsay Firth str. Scotland 19 G4.............59.06N 2.50W
Stroud England 10 C2..............................51.45N 2.13W
Struer Denmark 40 B2.............................56.29N 8.36E
Strule r. Northern Ireland 16 B2.................54.43N 7.21W
Struma r. Bulgaria 56 E5...........................41.23N 23.20E
Strumble Head Wales 12 B4.....................52.02N 5.08W
Strumica Macedonia 56 E5........................41.26N 22.38E
Stryy Ukraine 55 J3.................................49.15N 23.51E
Stryy r. Ukraine 46 G2..............................49.23N 24.13E
Studley England 10 D3............................52.16N 1.54W
Stupino Rus. Fed. 55 R6...........................54.54N 38.05E
Sturry England 11 G2...............................51.18N 1.07E
Sturt Stony Desert Australia 110 D4...........28.20S 141.15E
Stuttgart Germany 54 D3..........................48.47N 9.10E
Styr r. Belarus/Ukraine 55 L5....................52.08N 26.35E
Suakin Sudan 85 H3................................19.06N 37.18E
Subotica Serbia 56 C8.............................46.06N 19.41E
Suceava Romania 55 L2............................47.40N 26.16E
Suck r. Ireland 41 C3...............................53.16N 8.03W
Sucre Bolivia 76 G4................................19.06S 65.18W
Sudak Ukraine 57 K7................................44.51N 34.59E
Sudan Africa 85 G3.................................13.34N 30.02E
Sudbury Canada 63 J2.............................46.29N 80.59W
Sudbury England 11 F3.............................52.03N 0.44E
Sudd f. South Sudan 85 G2........................7.43N 29.41E
Sudety mts Czech Rep./Poland 54 F4.........50.46N 15.50E
Suez Egypt 85 H4...................................29.58N 32.33E
Suez, Gulf of Egypt 85 H4.........................28.03N 33.33E
Suez Canal Egypt 53 J3............................30.47N 32.19E
Suffolk d. England 11 F3............................52.10N 0.52E
Suguta r. Kenya 87 B3..............................2.01N 36.32E
Suguti Bay Tanzania 87 A2........................1.45S 33.33E
Şuḩār Oman 95 I4...................................24.22N 56.44E
Suhl Germany 54 D4................................50.36N 10.42E
Suifenhe China 106 B4............................44.20N 131.11E
Suining China 101 J4...............................30.29N 105.33E
Suir r. Ireland 41 D2................................52.20N 7.23W
Suizhou China 101 K4..............................31.42N 113.20E
Sukabumi Indonesia 104 D2......................6.58S 106.53E
Sukadana Indonesia 104 D3......................1.12S 109.59E
Sukhinichi Rus. Fed. 55 P6.......................54.07N 35.22E
Sukkur Pakistan 96 C6.............................27.42N 68.55E
Sula i. Norway 40 A3................................61.09N 4.55E
Sulabesi i. Indonesia 105 H3.....................2.12S 125.58E
Sulaiman Range mts Pakistan 90 F5..........30.00N 68.00E
Sulina Romania 57 H7..............................45.09N 29.39E
Sullana Peru 76 D7.................................4.56S 80.41W
Sully Wales 13 D3...................................51.24N 3.13W
Sulmona Italy 50 E5................................42.03N 13.55E
Sulu Archipelago is Phil. 105 G5................6.55N 123.10E
Sulu Sea N. Pacific Oc. 104 F5...................8.20N 119.46E
Sumalē d. Ethiopia 87 C4..........................6.59N 43.45E
Sumatra i. Indonesia 104 B4.......................3.05N 98.12E
Sumba i. Indonesia 104 G2........................9.49S 120.11E
Sumbawa i. Indonesia 104 F2......................8.54S 118.45E
Sumburgh Scotland 19 H4.........................59.52N 1.17W
Sumburgh Head Scotland 19 H4................59.51N 1.16W
Summer Isles Scotland 18 D3.....................58.01N 5.30W
Sumy Ukraine 55 P4................................50.55N 34.48E
Sunart, Loch inlet Scotland 18 D1...............56.40N 5.51W
Sunda, Selat str. Indonesia 104 C2...............6.32S 104.55E
Sunda Trench f. Indian Oc. 108 C5...............8.48S 104.02E
Sunderland England 15 F3.........................54.54N 1.23W
Sundsvall Sweden 40 D3..........................62.24N 17.17E
Sunga Tanzania 87 B1..............................4.27S 38.14E
Sungurlu Turkey 57 K5..............................40.11N 34.22E
Suolijärvet l. Finland 40 G4.......................66.14N 28.07E
Suonenjoki Finland 40 F3.........................62.37N 27.07E
Superior U.S.A. 65 H6..............................46.41N 92.01W
Superior, Lake Canada/U.S.A. 63 J2...........47.46N 87.14W
Sūq ash Shuyūkh Iraq 95 G6....................30.51N 46.20E
Suqian China 101 L4...............................33.55N 118.18E
Şūr Oman 95 I4.....................................22.34N 59.31E
Surab Pakistan 95 K5..............................28.29N 66.19E
Surabaya Indonesia 104 E2.......................7.13S 112.45E
Surakarta Indonesia 104 E2.......................7.35S 110.45E
Surat India 96 D5...................................21.11N 72.53E
Surendranagar India 96 D5.......................22.42N 71.41E
Surgut Rus. Fed. 58 I4..............................61.13N 73.22E
Surigao Phil. 105 H5...............................9.48N 125.29E
Surin Thailand 104 C6.............................14.52N 103.32E
Surrey d. England 9 E2.............................51.15N 0.29W
Surtsey i. Iceland 40 X1...........................63.18N 20.36W
Süsangerd Iran 95 G6.............................31.37N 48.04E
Suşehri Turkey 57 M5.............................40.10N 38.04E
Susuman Rus. Fed. 59 Q4........................62.47N 148.02E
Susurluk Turkey 57 H4.............................39.55N 28.09E
Sutak Jammu and Kashmir 96 E7...............33.07N 77.34E
Sutherland f. Scotland 19 E3.....................58.14N 4.24W
Sutlej r. India/Pakistan 96 D6....................29.24N 71.08E
Sutterton England 11 F3...........................52.54N 0.06W
Sutton England 11 F3..............................52.23N 0.07E
Sutton Bridge England 11 F3....................52.46N 0.11E
Sutton Coldfield England 10 D3................52.34N 1.49W
Sutton in Ashfield England 15 F2...............53.08N 1.16W
Suva Fiji 111 G5....................................18.07S 178.28E
Suvorov Rus. Fed. 55 Q6.........................54.07N 36.31E
Suwałki Poland 46 F5..............................54.06N 22.56E

Suwarrow atoll Cook Is 108 J5...................13.11S 162.57W
Suzhou Anhui China 101 L4......................33.34N 116.59E
Suzhou Jiangsu China 101 M4...................31.18N 120.40E
Suzu Japan 106 C3.................................37.26N 137.15E
Suzuka Japan 106 C2...............................34.53N 136.35E
Svalbard is Arctic Oc. 58 C5.....................79.47N 16.13E
Svapa r. Rus. Fed. 55 P4...........................51.44N 34.57E
Sveg Sweden 40 C3.................................62.02N 14.23E
Svendborg Denmark 40 B1......................55.04N 10.37E
Svetlograd Rus. Fed. 53 L6.......................45.20N 42.51E
Svetogorsk Rus. Fed. 40 G3.....................61.07N 28.51E
Svíahnúkar vol. Iceland 40 Y2..................64.25N 17.09W
Svitava r. Czech Rep. 46 C2......................48.54N 16.37E
Svitavy Czech Rep. 54 G3.........................49.45N 16.28E
Svitlovods'k Ukraine 55 O3......................49.03N 33.15E
Svobodnyy Rus. Fed. 59 N3.....................51.23N 128.04E
Svyetlahorsk Belarus 55 M5....................52.38N 29.46E
Swadlincote England 10 D3......................52.46N 1.33W
Swaffham England 11 F3...........................52.39N 0.41E
Swains Island atoll American Samoa 108 I5...11.01S 171.03W
Swakopmund Namibia 86 A2.....................22.41S 14.32E
Swale r. England 15 F3.............................54.05N 1.21W
Swanage England 10 D1..........................50.36N 1.58W
Swanley England 11 F2.............................51.24N 0.11E
Swan River town Canada 64 F7..................52.06N 101.16W
Swansea Wales 12 D3..............................51.37N 3.57W
Swansea d. Wales 9 D2.............................51.39N 3.57W
Swansea Bay Wales 12 D3........................51.34N 3.54W
Swaziland Africa 86 C2............................26.29S 31.30E
Sweden Europe 40 C3..............................61.48N 15.08E
Sweetwater r. U.S.A. 64 E5.......................42.27N 106.55W
Świdnica Poland 46 C3.............................50.50N 16.29E
Świdwin Poland 46 B4.............................53.47N 15.47E
Świebodzin Poland 46 B4.........................52.15N 15.32E
Świecie Poland 46 D4..............................53.25N 18.27E
Swift Current Canada 62 H3......................50.17N 107.47W
Swilly, Lough inlet Ireland 41 D5................55.15N 7.34W
Swindon England 10 D2...........................51.33N 1.47W
Swindon d. England 9 E2...........................51.35N 1.45W
Swineshead England 11 E3.......................52.57N 0.10W
Świnoujście Poland 46 B4........................53.54N 14.15E
Switzerland Europe 50 B7........................46.44N 8.18E
Swords Ireland 41 E3..............................53.27N 6.13W
Sybil Point Ireland 41 A2..........................52.11N 10.28W
Sychevka Rus. Fed. 55 P6.........................55.49N 34.17E
Sydney Australia 110 E3...........................33.54S 151.11E
Sydney r. Canada 63 M2...........................46.06N 60.08W
Syktyvkar Rus. Fed. 58 G4........................61.41N 50.48E
Sylarna mt. Norway/Sweden 40 C3.............63.01N 12.12E
Sylt i. Germany 40 B1..............................54.49N 8.15E
Syracuse Italy 50 F2................................37.04N 15.17E
Syracuse U.S.A. 65 K5.............................43.04N 76.11W
Syr Darya r. Asia 100 A7...........................46.05N 60.55E
Syria Asia 94 E6....................................35.25N 39.17E
Syrian Desert Asia 94 E6..........................32.02N 39.22E
Syros i. Greece 56 F3...............................37.27N 24.53E
Syzran' Rus. Fed. 58 F3.............................53.10N 48.29E
Szczecin Poland 46 B4.............................53.26N 14.34E
Szczecinek Poland 46 C4..........................53.42N 16.42E
Szczytno Poland 46 E4.............................53.34N 20.59E
Szeged Hungary 54 I2..............................46.15N 20.09E
Székesfehérvár Hungary 54 H2..................47.12N 18.25E
Szekszárd Hungary 54 H2.........................46.22N 18.42E
Szolnok Hungary 54 I2.............................47.10N 20.12E
Szombathely Hungary 54 G2....................47.15N 16.38E

# T

Ţabas Iran 95 I6.....................................33.35N 56.52E
Tabasco d. Mexico 70 F4..........................18.03N 92.59W
Tabatinga, Serra do hills Brazil 77 L5...........10.56S 44.37W
Tábor Czech Rep. 54 F3............................49.24N 14.42E
Tabora Tanzania 86 C4.............................5.00S 32.47E
Tabrīz Iran 95 G7...................................38.04N 46.17E
Tabuaeran atoll Kiribati 109 J6..................3.49N 159.16W
Tabūk Saudi Arabia 94 E5.........................28.22N 36.38E
Tacheng China 100 E7.............................46.43N 83.01E
Tacloban Phil. 105 H6.............................11.12N 125.01E
Tacna Peru 76 F4...................................18.01S 70.15W
Tacoma U.S.A. 64 B6..............................47.15N 122.27W
Tacuarembó Uruguay 73 D3.....................31.42S 55.59W
Tadcaster England 15 F2..........................53.53N 1.16W
Tadjoura Djibouti 94 F2...........................11.46N 42.48E
Tadmur Syria 94 E6................................34.34N 38.17E
Taegu S. Korea 101 N5............................35.52N 128.35E
Taejŏn S. Korea 101 N5...........................36.22N 127.24E
Taf r. Wales 12 C3...................................51.47N 4.27W
Taganrog Rus. Fed. 53 K6.........................47.14N 38.55E
Taganrog, Gulf of Rus. Fed./Ukraine 53 K6...47.00N 38.31E
Tagbilaran Phil. 105 G5............................9.38N 123.53E
Tagula Island P.N.G. 110 E5.......................11.33S 153.23E
Tagus r. Portugal 48 A3............................38.59N 8.56W
Tahat, Mont mt. Algeria 84 E4....................23.18N 5.37E
Tahiti i. French Polynesia 109 K4................17.49S 149.15W
Taidong Taiwan 101 M2...........................22.45N 121.08E
Tain Scotland 19 E2................................57.49N 4.03W
Taibei Taiwan 101 M2..............................23.01N 120.13E
T'aipei Taiwan 101 M3.............................25.04N 121.33E
Taiping Malaysia 104 C4...........................4.55N 100.42E
Taita Hills Kenya 87 B2............................3.26S 38.21E
Taiti mt. Kenya 87 A3...............................1.20N 35.57E
Taivalkoski Finland 40 G4.........................65.34N 28.14E
Taivaskero hill Finland 40 F5.....................68.04N 24.02E
Taiwan Asia 101 M2...............................23.34N 121.32E
Taiwan Strait China/Taiwan 101 L2..............25.19N 119.16E
Taiyuan China 101 K5..............................37.48N 112.38E
Taizhong Taiwan 101 M2..........................24.09N 120.42E
Taizhou China 101 M3.............................28.39N 121.31E
Ta'izz Yemen 94 F2.................................13.35N 43.59E
Tajikistan Asia 115 M7............................38.54N 71.08E
Tak Thailand 104 B7................................16.51N 99.08E
Takamatsu Japan 106 B2.........................34.19N 134.03E
Takaungu Kenya 87 B2............................3.41S 39.50E
Taklimakan Desert China 100 E5...............38.52N 80.50E
Talagang Pakistan 95 L6...........................32.55N 72.29E
Talara Peru 76 D7..................................4.37S 81.18W
Talaud, Kepulauan is Indonesia 105 H4......4.05N 127.24E
Talavera de la Reina Spain 48 C3................39.58N 4.49W
Talca Chile 73 B3...................................35.26S 71.39W
Talcahuano Chile 73 B3..........................36.44S 73.07W
Taldykorgan Kazakhstan 58 I2...................44.59N 78.22E
Talgarth Wales 12 D3..............................51.59N 3.14W
Taliabu i. Indonesia 105 G3.......................1.50S 124.43E
Tallahassee U.S.A. 65 J3.........................30.26N 84.17W
Tallinn Estonia 40 F2...............................59.22N 24.45E
Taloyoak Canada 63 I4.............................69.27N 93.22W
Talsi Latvia 40 E2...................................57.15N 22.35E
Taltal Chile 76 F2...................................25.24S 70.33W

Taltson r. Canada 62 G4...........................61.24N 112.43W
Tamale Ghana 84 D2...............................9.25N 0.51W
Tamanrasset Algeria 84 E4.......................22.48N 5.33E
Tamar r. England 13 C2.............................50.29N 4.13W
Tamaulipas d. Mexico 70 E5.......................24.41N 99.13W
Tama Wildlife Reserve Ethiopia 87 B4..........6.02N 36.12E
Tambach Kenya 87 B3.............................0.37N 35.31E
Tambacounda Senegal 84 C3....................13.47N 13.40W
Tambelan, Kepulauan is Indonesia 104 D4...1.03N 107.03E
Tambov Rus. Fed. 58 F3...........................52.43N 41.26E
Tambre r. Spain 48 A5.............................42.49N 8.51W
Tâmega r. Portugal 48 A4.........................41.05N 8.17W
Tamiahua, Laguna de lagoon Mexico 70 E5...21.39N 97.36W
Tamil Nadu d. India 96 E3.........................11.11N 78.08E
Tamiš r. Serbia 56 D7...............................44.50N 20.39E
Tampa U.S.A. 65 J2................................27.57N 82.29W
Tampere Finland 40 E3.............................61.30N 23.48E
Tampico Mexico 70 E5.............................22.16N 97.52W
Tamsweg Austria 54 E2............................47.08N 13.47E
Tamworth Australia 110 E3........................31.06S 150.56E
Tamworth England 10 D3.........................52.38N 1.41W
Tana r. Kenya 87 C2................................2.31S 40.30E
Tana r. Norway 40 G5..............................70.32N 28.13E
Tana, Lake Ethiopia 85 H3........................11.59N 37.16E
Tanafjorden inlet Norway 40 G5..................70.32N 28.13E
Tanami Desert Australia 110 C5..................19.26S 131.26E
Tanana U.S.A. 62 C4...............................65.12N 152.04W
Tanaro r. Italy 50 C6...............................45.01N 8.47E
Tando Adam Pakistan 96 C6.....................25.43N 68.40E
Tandragee Northern Ireland 16 C2..............54.21N 6.24W
Taneatua New Zealand 111 G4..................38.04N 177.00E
Tanega-shima i. Japan 106 B2...................30.28N 130.58E
Tanga Tanzania 86 C4.............................5.06S 39.05E
Tanga d. Tanzania 87 B1...........................5.59S 38.02E
Tanganyika, Lake Africa 86 B4...................5.00S 29.26E
Tangier Morocco 84 D5............................35.47N 5.49W
Tangshan China 101 L5............................39.34N 118.13E
Tanimbar, Kepulauan is Indonesia 105 I2.....7.29S 131.40E
Tanjay Phil. 105 G5.................................9.29N 123.09E
Tanjungpandan Indonesia 104 D3.............2.46S 107.37E
Tanjungredeb Indonesia 104 F4.................2.09N 117.27E
Tank Pakistan 95 L6................................32.14N 70.29E
Tanna i. Vanuatu 111 F5...........................19.32S 169.14E
Tanout Niger 84 E3.................................14.56N 8.53E
Ţanţā Egypt 85 H5..................................30.47N 31.00E
Tanzania Africa 86 C4..............................6.14S 34.03E
Taonan China 101 M7.............................45.12N 122.48E
Taourirt Morocco 52 C3...........................34.25N 2.55W
Tapachula Mexico 70 F3..........................14.56N 92.15W
Tapajós r. Brazil 77 J7.............................2.23S 54.48W
Tapauá r. Brazil 76 H6.............................5.52S 64.27W
Tapi r. India 96 D5..................................21.13N 72.58E
Taquarí r. Brazil 77 I4..............................19.05S 57.22W
Tar r. Ireland 41 D2................................52.17N 7.50W
Tara r. Bos.-Herz./Montenegro 56 C6...........43.20N 18.53E
Taran, Mys pt Rus. Fed. 46 D5...................54.58N 19.59E
Tarakan Indonesia 104 F4.........................3.20N 117.37E
Taranaki, Mount vol. New Zealand 111 G3...39.18S 174.03E
Tarancón Spain 48 D4.............................40.01N 3.00W
Tarangire National Park Tanzania 87 B1........4.05S 36.04E
Taransay i. Scotland 18 B2........................57.55N 7.02W
Taranto Italy 50 G4.................................40.28N 17.14E
Taranto, Gulf of Italy 50 G4.......................40.07N 17.20E
Tarapoto Peru 76 E6...............................6.31S 76.24W
Tarauacá Brazil 76 F6..............................8.10S 70.43W
Tarbat Ness pt Scotland 19 F2....................57.52N 3.46W
Tarbert A. and B. Scotland 16 D3................55.58N 5.50W
Tarbert A. and B. Scotland 16 D3................55.52N 5.25W
Tarbert W. Isles Scotland 18 C2..................57.54N 6.48W
Tarbes France 44 D3...............................43.14N 0.05E
Tärgoviște Romania 56 F7.........................44.56N 25.27E
Târgu Jiu Romania 56 F7..........................45.03N 23.17E
Târgu Mureş Romania 56 F2......................46.32N 24.34E
Târgu Secuiesc Romania 56 G8..................46.00N 26.08E
Tarija Bolivia 76 H3................................21.36S 64.47W
Tarim Yemen 95 G3...............................16.08N 49.23E
Tarim Basin China 100 E5.........................39.41N 80.53E
Tarime Tanzania 87 A2.............................1.21S 34.20E
Tarleton England 14 E2...........................53.41N 2.50W
Tarn r. France 44 D4...............................44.05N 1.03E
Tarnobrzeg Poland 46 E3.........................50.34N 21.40E
Tarnów Poland 46 E3..............................50.01N 20.59E
Tarnowskie Góry Poland 46 D3.................50.27N 18.52E
Tarragona Spain 48 F4.............................41.07N 1.15E
Tarsus Turkey 57 K3...............................36.54N 34.53E
Tartu Estonia 40 F2................................58.23N 26.43E
Ţarţūs Syria 57 K2..................................34.54N 35.53E
Tashk, Daryācheh-ye l. Iran 95 H5..............29.42N 53.29E
Tashkent Uzbekistan 58 H2.......................41.16N 69.15E
Tasiilaq Greenland 63 O4.........................65.37N 37.42W
Tasikmalaya Indonesia 104 D2..................7.19S 108.17E
Tasman Abyssal Plain f. Tasman Sea 108 G3...32.04S 154.18E
Tasman Bay Tasman Sea 108 G3................41.29S 158.18E
Tasmania d. Australia 110 D2.....................42.27S 145.20E
Tasman Sea S. Pacific Oc. 110 G2..............40.31S 170.54E
Tatabánya Hungary 54 H2.........................47.34N 18.26E
Tatarbunary Ukraine 57 H7.......................45.50N 29.37E
Tatarsk Rus. Fed. 58 I3............................55.13N 75.59E
Tatarskiy Proliv str. Rus. Fed. 59 P3............50.29N 141.05E
Tatvan Turkey 94 F7...............................38.29N 42.17E
Taua Brazil 77 L6...................................6.01S 40.23W
Taubaté Brazil 77 K3...............................22.59S 45.32W
Taunggyi Myanmar 97 I5.........................20.49N 97.05E
Taunton England 13 D3...........................51.01N 3.06W
Taunus hills Germany 54 C4......................50.10N 7.59E
Taupo, Lake New Zealand 111 G3..............38.48S 175.55E
Tauragė Lithuania 46 F5...........................55.15N 22.17E
Taurus Mountains Turkey 57 J3..................37.00N 32.09E
Taverham England 11 G3.........................52.41N 1.12E
Tavira Portugal 48 B2..............................37.08N 7.38W
Tavistock England 13 C2..........................50.33N 4.08W
Tavoy Myanmar 97 I3.............................14.06N 98.13E
Tavşanlı Turkey 57 H4.............................39.32N 29.28E
Tavy r. England 13 C2.............................50.27N 4.09W
Taw r. England 13 D3..............................51.04N 4.03W
Tawau Malaysia 104 F4...........................4.16N 117.54E
Tawe r. Wales 12 D3...............................51.37N 3.55W
Tawitawi i. Phil. 104 F5............................5.14N 119.57E
Tay r. Scotland 17 F4..............................56.23N 3.24W
Tay, Firth of est. Scotland 17 F4.................56.25N 3.07W
Tay, Loch l. Scotland 16 E4......................56.30N 4.11W
Taymā' Saudi Arabia 94 E5........................27.39N 38.28E
Taymura r. Rus. Fed. 59 L4.......................63.43N 98.05E
Taymyr, Ozero l. Rus. Fed. 59 L5................74.20N 101.51E
Taymyr Peninsula f. Rus. Fed. 59 J5............73.54N 89.12E
Tây Ninh Vietnam 104 D6........................11.17N 106.07E
Tayport Scotland 17 G4...........................56.27N 2.53W
Taytay Phil. 104 F6................................10.49N 119.30E
Taz r. Rus. Fed. 58 I4..............................67.34N 78.36E
Tazovskiy Rus. Fed. 58 I4.........................67.34N 78.42E
Tbilisi Georgia 58 F2...............................41.42N 44.48E
Tczew Poland 46 D5...............................54.06N 18.48E
Te Anau, Lake New Zealand 111 F2............45.18S 167.48E
Tébessa Algeria 52 E4.............................35.23N 8.12E
Tebingtinggi Indonesia 104 B4...................3.19N 99.08E

Tecuci Romania 56 G7.............................45.51N 27.26E
Tedzhen Turkmenistan 95 J7.....................37.22N 60.25E
Tees r. England 15 F3..............................54.35N 1.15W
Tees Bay England 15 F3...........................54.41N 1.09W
Tefé r. Brazil 76 H7................................3.41S 64.52W
Tegal Indonesia 104 D2...........................6.51S 109.07E
Tegucigalpa Honduras 70 G3....................14.05N 87.12W
Tehrān Iran 95 H7..................................35.39N 51.23E
Tehuantepec, Gulf of Mexico 70 F4.............15.47N 94.53W
Teide, Pico del vol. Canary Islands 48 X2.....28.16N 16.37W
Teifi r. Wales 12 C4................................52.05N 4.40W
Teign r. England 13 D2............................50.32N 3.35W
Teignmouth England 13 D2......................50.33N 3.30W
Teith r. Scotland 16 E4............................56.09N 3.59W
Tekirdağ Turkey 56 G5............................40.59N 27.30E
Tel Aviv-Yafo Israel 53 J3.........................32.04N 34.46E
Teles Pires r. Brazil 77 I6.........................7.20S 58.03W
Telford England 10 C3.............................52.41N 2.27W
Telford and Wrekin d. England 9 D3............52.43N 2.29W
Telšiai Lithuania 46 F5.............................55.59N 22.16E
Tembenchi r. Rus. Fed. 59 K4....................64.35N 99.49E
Teme r. England 10 C2............................52.10N 2.17W
Temirtau Kazakhstan 58 I3.......................50.03N 72.57E
Temple Ewell England 11 G2.....................51.09N 1.16E
Templemore Ireland 41 D2.......................52.48N 7.50W
Temryuk Rus. Fed. 57 L7..........................45.17N 37.23E
Temuco Chile 73 B3...............................38.44S 72.35W
Tena Ecuador 76 E7...............................0.59S 77.49W
Tenasserim Myanmar 97 I3......................12.02N 98.58E
Tenbury Wells England 10 C2...................52.18N 2.36W
Tenby Wales 12 C3.................................51.40N 4.42W
Ten Degree Channel India 97 H2...............9.57N 92.51E
Tendō Japan 106 D3..............................38.21N 140.22E
Tenerife i. Canary Islands 48 X2.................28.28N 16.39W
Tennessee d. U.S.A. 65 I4........................36.12N 85.01W
Tennessee r. U.S.A. 65 I4.........................37.08N 88.25W
Tenterden England 11 F2.........................51.04N 0.41E
Tentudia mt. Spain 48 B3.........................38.03N 6.19W
Teófilo Otôni Brazil 77 L4.........................17.52S 41.31W
Tepic Mexico 70 D5................................21.31N 104.55W
Teplice Czech Rep. 54 E4........................50.38N 13.50E
Teraina i. Kiribati 109 J6..........................4.42N 160.24W
Teramo Italy 50 E5.................................42.39N 13.42E
Terebovlya Ukraine 55 K3........................49.18N 25.42E
Teresina Brazil 77 L6..............................5.07S 42.44W
Tergnier France 42 C2............................49.40N 3.18E
Terme Turkey 57 L5...............................41.12N 36.59E
Terminillo, Monte mt. Italy 50 E5................42.29N 12.59E
Términos, Laguna de lagoon Mexico 70 F4...18.30N 91.37W
Termiz Uzbekistan 95 K7.........................37.15N 67.17E
Termoli Italy 50 F4.................................42.00N 15.00E
Tern r. England 10 C3.............................52.40N 2.40W
Ternate Indonesia 105 H4........................0.49N 127.20E
Terneuzen Neth. 42 C4...........................51.19N 3.50E
Terni Italy 50 E5....................................42.33N 12.39E
Ternopil' Ukraine 55 K3............................49.33N 25.36E
Terrace Canada 62 F3.............................54.32N 128.37W
Terrassa Spain 48 G4.............................41.34N 2.00E
Terre Haute U.S.A. 65 I4..........................39.28N 87.24W
Terrington Marsh England 11 F3................52.47N 0.16E
Terschelling i. Neth. 42 E6.......................53.27N 5.28E
Teseney Eritrea 94 E3.............................15.07N 36.39E
Teslin Canada 62 E4..............................60.12N 132.39W
Test r. England 10 D1.............................50.56N 1.29W
Tetas, Punta pt Chile 73 B4......................23.28S 70.34W
Tetbury England 10 C2............................51.38N 2.09W
Tete Mozambique 86 C3.........................16.10S 33.36E
Tetney England 15 G2.............................53.29N 0.01W
Tétouan Morocco 84 D5..........................35.34N 5.23W
Tetovo Macedonia 56 D6.........................42.00N 20.58E
Teuco r. Argentina 73 C4.........................25.29S 60.11W
Teviot r. Scotland 17 G3..........................55.36N 2.26W
Teviothead Scotland 17 G3......................55.19N 2.59W
Tewkesbury England 10 C2......................51.59N 2.09W
Texarkana U.S.A. 65 H3...........................33.25N 94.08W
Texas d. U.S.A. 64 G3.............................31.58N 99.13W
Texel i. Neth. 42 D6...............................53.09N 4.46E
Texoma, Lake U.S.A. 64 G3......................33.59N 96.53W
Tezpur India 97 H6................................26.36N 92.49E
Thabana-Ntlenyana mt. Lesotho 86 B2.......29.29S 29.16E
Thai Binh Vietnam 104 D8........................20.24N 106.19E
Thailand Asia 104 C7.............................16.14N 101.59E
Thailand, Gulf of Asia 104 C6....................11.08N 101.16E
Thai Nguyên Vietnam 104 D8...................21.31N 105.52E
Thal Desert Pakistan 95 L6.......................31.25N 71.33E
Thame England 10 D2............................51.45N 0.58W
Thame r. England 10 D2..........................51.38N 1.10W
Thames r. England 11 F2..........................51.30N 0.31E
Thames est. England 11 F2.......................51.30N 0.43E
Thames r. England 11 F2.........................51.27N 0.22E
Thanet, Isle of pen. England 11 G2.............51.22N 1.17E
Thanh Hoa Vietnam 104 D7......................19.47N 105.49E
Thar Desert India/Pakistan 96 C6..............25.48N 69.50E
Thasos i. Greece 56 F5............................40.40N 24.37E
Thatcham England 10 D2.........................51.24N 1.16W
Thaton Myanmar 97 I4............................16.54N 97.23E
Thaxted England 11 F2............................51.57N 0.21E
The Bahamas Central America 71 I6............24.55N 77.44W
The Calf hill England 15 E3.......................54.22N 2.31E
The Cheviot hill England 15 E4...................55.29N 2.09W
The Fens f. England 11 F3.........................52.42N 0.08W
The Gambia Africa 84 C3.........................13.22N 16.25W
The Great Oasis Egypt 94 D4....................24.52N 30.42E
The Gulf Asia 95 H5...............................28.03N 50.06E
The Hague Neth. 42 D5...........................52.05N 4.18E
Thelon r. Canada 62 I4............................64.17N 96.18W
The Marsh England 11 F3.........................52.50N 0.10E
The Minch str. Scotland 18 C3...................58.02N 6.02W
The Mullet b. Ireland 41 A4......................54.10N 10.07W
The Mumbles Wales 12 C3.......................51.34N 4.00W
The Naze pt England 11 G2.......................51.52N 1.17E
The Needles f. England 10 D1....................50.39N 1.35W
The North Sound str. Scotland 19 G4...........59.17N 2.43W
Theodore Roosevelt r. Brazil 77 H6.............7.35S 60.21W
The Old Man of Coniston hill England 14 D3...54.22N 3.07W
The Pas Canada 62 H3............................53.49N 101.16W
The Rinns of Galloway pen. Scotland 16 D2...54.55N 5.07W
Thermaïkos Kolpos g. Greece 56 E5...........40.11N 22.54E
The Solent str. England 10 D1...................50.21N 4.09W
Thessaloniki Greece 56 E5.......................40.38N 22.57E
The Storr hill Scotland 18 C2.....................57.31N 6.11W
Thet r. England 11 F3..............................52.24N 0.45E
Thetford England 11 F3...........................52.25N 0.45E
The Trossachs hills Scotland 16 E4..............56.13N 4.26W
The Wash b. England 11 F3.......................52.55N 0.18E
The Weald f. England 11 F2.......................51.05N 0.18E
Thiers France 44 E4...............................45.51N 3.33E
Thiès Senegal 84 C3...............................14.48N 16.56W
Thika Kenya 87 B2.................................1.03S 37.05E
Thimbu Bhutan 97 G6.............................27.29N 89.42E
Thionville France 46 G3...........................49.22N 6.10E
Thira i. Greece 56 F3...............................36.27N 25.27E
Thirlmere resr England 14 D3....................54.33N 3.04W
Thirsk England 15 F3..............................54.14N 1.20W

**Thisted** Denmark 40 B2 56.57N 8.41E
**Thomastown** Ireland 41 D2 52.31N 7.07W
**Thompson** Canada 62 I3 55.48N 97.55W
**Thornaby-on-Tees** England 15 F3 54.32N 1.17W
**Thornbury** England 10 C2 51.36N 2.31W
**Thorne** England 15 G2 53.37N 0.58W
**Thornhill** Scotland 17 F3 55.15N 3.46W
**Thornton** England 14 D2 53.52N 3.00W
**Thrakiko Pelagos** sea Greece 56 F5 40.22N 24.46E
**Thrapston** England 11 E3 52.24N 0.32W
**Thuin** Belgium 42 D3 50.20N 4.17E
**Thule** Greenland 63 L5 77.28N 69.11W
**Thun** Switz. 50 B7 46.45N 7.38E
**Thunder Bay** town Canada 63 J2 48.26N 89.15W
**Thurles** Ireland 41 D2 52.41N 7.49W
**Thurrock** d. England 9 F2 51.31N 0.22E
**Thursby** England 14 D3 54.51N 3.03W
**Thurso** Scotland 19 F3 58.36N 3.31W
**Thurso** r. Scotland 19 F3 58.36N 3.31W
**Thurso Bay** Scotland 19 F3 58.38N 3.32W
**Tianjin** China 101 L5 39.04N 117.15E
**Tianshui** China 101 J4 34.30N 105.37E
**Tiaret** Algeria 52 D4 35.20N 1.19E
**Tibagi** r. Brazil 77 J3 23.07S 50.57W
**Tibati** Cameroon 84 F2 6.26N 12.35E
**Tiber** r. Italy 50 E4 41.44N 12.14E
**Tibesti** mts Chad 85 F4 20.53N 17.03E
**Tibet, Plateau of** f. China 100 E4 33.48N 84.16E
**Tiburón, Isla** i. Mexico 70 B6 29.08N 112.29W
**Ticehurst** England 11 F2 51.03N 0.25E
**Tidjikja** Mauritania 84 C3 18.31N 11.26W
**Tiel** Neth. 42 E4 51.52N 5.25E
**Tielt** Belgium 42 C3 50.59N 3.20E
**Tienen** Belgium 42 D3 50.48N 4.56E
**Tien Shan** mts China/Kyrgyzstan 100 D6 40.48N 76.25E
**Tierra del Fuego, Isla Grande de** i. Argentina/Chile 73 C1 54.11S 68.48W
**Tiétar** r. Spain 48 C3 39.56N 5.54W
**Tighina** Moldova 53 I6 46.49N 29.29E
**Tigre** r. Ecuador/Peru 76 F7 4.27S 74.06W
**Tigre** r. Venezuela 72 C7 9.26N 62.25W
**Tigris** r. Iraq/Syria 95 G6 30.59N 47.25E
**Tihāmah** f. Saudi Arabia 85 I3 17.18N 42.25E
**Tijuana** Mexico 70 A7 32.29N 117.02W
**Tikhoretsk** Rus. Fed. 57 N7 45.52N 40.06E
**Tiki Basin** f. S. Pacific Oc. 109 L4 18.48S 129.30W
**Tikrīt** Iraq 94 F6 34.33N 43.37E
**Tiksi** Rus. Fed. 59 N5 71.38N 128.36E
**Tilburg** Neth. 42 E4 51.33N 5.05E
**Tilbury** England 11 F2 51.28N 0.22E
**Tilehurst** England 10 D2 51.27N 1.02W
**Tillabéri** Niger 84 E3 14.13N 1.29E
**Tillicoultry** Scotland 17 F4 56.09N 3.44W
**Tīmā** Egypt 53 J2 26.53N 31.25E
**Timashevsk** Rus. Fed. 57 M7 45.37N 38.56E
**Timbuktu** Mali 84 D3 16.46N 2.59W
**Timiş** r. Romania 56 D7 45.27N 20.52E
**Timişoara** Romania 56 D7 45.46N 21.14E
**Timmins** Canada 63 J2 48.29N 81.21W
**Timon** Brazil 77 L6 5.08S 42.48W
**Timor** i. East Timor/Indonesia 105 H2 8.49S 126.02E
**Timor Sea** Australia/Indonesia 110 B5 11.23S 126.22E
**Timrå** Sweden 40 D3 62.30N 17.20E
**Tindouf** Algeria 84 D4 27.42N 8.07W
**Tinian** i. N. Mariana Is 108 F6 14.58N 145.41E
**Tinos** i. Greece 56 F3 37.40N 25.12E
**Tintagel** England 13 C2 50.40N 4.45W
**Tinto** hill Scotland 17 F3 55.36N 3.40W
**Tipasa** Algeria 48 G2 36.33N 2.28E
**Tipperary** Ireland 41 C2 52.28N 8.10W
**Tipperary** d. Ireland 41 D2 52.43N 7.54W
**Tiptree** England 11 F2 51.49N 0.45E
**Tiracambu, Serra do** hills Brazil 77 K7 4.46S 47.10W
**Tirana** Albania 56 C5 41.19N 19.49E
**Tiraspol** Moldova 53 I6 46.51N 29.37E
**Tiree** i. Scotland 16 C4 56.30N 6.57W
**Tirga Mòr** hill Scotland 18 C2 57.59N 6.59W
**Tirso** r. Italy 50 C3 39.53N 8.32E
**Tiruchchirappalli** India 96 E3 10.49N 78.41E
**Tiruppur** India 96 E3 11.06N 77.18E
**Tisa** r. Serbia 56 D7 45.08N 20.17E
**Tisza** r. Hungary 55 I2 46.09N 20.04E
**Tiszafüred** Hungary 46 E1 47.36N 20.46E
**Titicaca, Lake** Bolivia/Peru 76 G4 15.49S 69.40W
**Tiverton** England 13 D2 50.54N 3.29W
**Tivoli** Italy 50 E4 41.58N 12.49E
**Tizi Ouzou** Algeria 52 D4 36.41N 4.05E
**Tiznit** Morocco 84 D4 29.41N 9.43W
**Tiztoutine** Morocco 48 D1 34.58N 3.09W
**Tlaxcala** Mexico 70 E4 19.21N 98.13W
**Tlaxcala** d. Mexico 70 E4 19.35N 98.20W
**Tlemcen** Algeria 84 D5 34.54N 1.19W
**Toamasina** Madagascar 86 D3 18.09S 49.22E
**Toba, Danau** l. Indonesia 104 B4 2.32N 98.59E
**Tobago** i. Trinidad and Tobago 71 L3 11.17N 60.38W
**Tobelo** Indonesia 105 H4 1.44N 127.57E
**Tobermory** Scotland 18 C1 56.38N 6.04W
**Toboali** Indonesia 104 D3 2.59S 106.30E
**Tobol** r. Kazakhstan/Rus. Fed. 58 H3 58.10N 68.13E
**Tobol'sk** Rus. Fed. 58 H3 58.14N 68.16E
**Tocantins** d. Brazil 77 K5 11.15S 48.38W
**Tocantins** r. Brazil 77 K7 1.49S 49.13W
**Tocopilla** Chile 76 F3 22.04S 70.10W
**Todmorden** England 15 E2 53.43N 2.06W
**Toft** Scotland 19 H5 60.28N 1.13W
**Togian, Kepulauan** is Indonesia 105 G3 0.06S 121.53E
**Togo** Africa 84 E2 8.27N 1.11E
**Tok** U.S.A. 62 D4 63.21N 143.01W
**Tokaj** Hungary 46 E2 48.06N 21.25E
**Tokara-rettō** is Japan 106 A1 28.34N 129.00E
**Tokat** Turkey 57 L5 40.19N 36.32E
**Tokelau** is S. Pacific Oc. 108 I5 8.30S 171.28W
**Tokushima** Japan 106 B2 34.04N 134.34E
**Tōkyō** Japan 106 C3 35.40N 139.46E
**Tōkyō** d. Japan 106 C3 35.22N 139.03E
**Tôlañaro** Madagascar 86 D2 25.02S 46.58E
**Toledo** Spain 48 C3 39.52N 4.01W
**Toledo** U.S.A. 65 J5 41.39N 83.33W
**Toledo, Montes de** mts Spain 48 C3 39.39N 4.54W
**Toledo Bend Reservoir** U.S.A. 65 H3 31.38N 93.43W
**Tolentino** Italy 50 E5 43.13N 13.19E
**Toliara** Madagascar 86 D2 23.22S 43.39E
**Tolitoli** Indonesia 105 G4 1.05N 120.50E
**Tollesbury** England 11 F2 51.45N 0.50E
**Tolsta Head** Scotland 18 C3 58.21N 6.10W
**Toluca** Mexico 70 E4 19.18N 99.39W
**Tol'yatti** Rus. Fed. 58 F3 53.31N 49.26E
**Tomakomai** Japan 106 D4 42.38N 141.36E
**Tomanivi** mt. Fiji 111 G5 17.37S 178.00E
**Tomaszów Lubelski** Poland 46 F3 50.28N 23.25E
**Tomaszów Mazowiecki** Poland 46 E3 51.32N 20.01E
**Tombigbee** r. U.S.A. 65 I3 31.11N 87.57W
**Tombua** Angola 86 A3 15.50S 11.50E
**Tomelloso** Spain 48 D3 39.09N 3.00W
**Tomini, Teluk** g. Indonesia 104 G3 0.21S 120.54E
**Tomsk** Rus. Fed. 58 J3 56.30N 85.01E
**Tomtabacken** hill Sweden 40 C2 57.30N 14.29E
**Tonbridge** England 11 F2 51.12N 0.17E
**Tondano** Indonesia 105 G4 1.21N 124.56E
**Tønder** Denmark 54 C6 54.57N 8.52E
**Tone** r. England 10 C2 51.04N 2.56W
**Tonelagee** hill Ireland 12 A5 53.03N 6.23W
**Tonga** S. Pacific Oc. 108 I4 20.05S 173.45W
**Tongatapu Group** is Tonga 108 I4 21.07S 174.45W
**Tonga Trench** f. S. Pacific Oc. 108 I4 21.47S 173.51W
**Tongeren** Belgium 42 E3 50.47N 5.28E
**Tonghua** China 101 N6 41.43N 125.57E
**Tongking, Gulf of** China/Vietnam 101 J2 20.29N 108.15E
**Tongliao** China 101 M6 43.31N 122.14E
**Tongling** China 101 L4 30.55N 117.52E
**Tongshan** China 101 L4 34.12N 117.14E
**Tongue** Scotland 19 E3 58.29N 4.25W
**Tonle Sap** l. Cambodia 104 C6 13.04N 103.51E
**Tonopah** U.S.A. 64 C4 38.04N 117.14W
**Tønsberg** Norway 40 B2 59.17N 10.23E
**Toowoomba** Australia 110 E4 27.33S 151.58E
**Topeka** U.S.A. 65 G4 39.04N 95.36W
**Topozero, Ozero** l. Rus. Fed. 40 H4 65.42N 32.00E
**Topsham** England 13 D2 50.41N 3.28W
**Torbat-e Heydarīyeh** Iran 95 I7 35.13N 59.06E
**Torbat-e Jām** Iran 95 J7 35.15N 60.34E
**Torbay** d. England 9 D2 50.26N 3.34W
**Tor Bay** England 13 D2 50.25N 3.32W
**Tordesillas** Spain 48 C4 41.31N 4.59W
**Torenberg** hill Neth. 42 E5 52.14N 5.52E
**Torfaen** d. Wales 9 D2 51.44N 3.05W
**Tormes** r. Spain 48 B4 41.18N 6.27W
**Torneälven** r. Sweden 40 F4 65.49N 24.09E
**Torneträsk** l. Sweden 40 D5 68.23N 18.56E
**Tornio** Finland 40 F4 65.50N 24.11E
**Toronto** Canada 63 K2 43.40N 79.23W
**Toropets** Rus. Fed. 55 N7 56.30N 31.38E
**Tororo** Uganda 87 A3 0.39N 34.10E
**Torpoint** England 13 C2 50.22N 4.12W
**Torquay** England 13 D2 50.28N 3.31W
**Torre** mt. Portugal 48 B4 40.20N 7.35W
**Torrecerredo** mt. Spain 48 C5 43.12N 4.49W
**Torre del Greco** Italy 50 F4 40.47N 14.23E
**Torremolinos** Spain 48 C2 36.36N 4.30W
**Torrens, Lake** Australia 110 C3 30.32S 137.28E
**Torreón** Mexico 70 D6 25.31N 103.27W
**Torres Islands** Vanuatu 111 F5 13.08S 166.17E
**Torres Strait** Australia 110 D6 9.50S 142.11E
**Torres Vedras** Portugal 48 A3 39.06N 9.15W
**Torrevieja** Spain 48 E2 37.59N 0.40W
**Torridge** r. England 13 C2 50.59N 4.11W
**Torridon** Scotland 18 D2 57.33N 5.31W
**Torridon, Loch** b. Scotland 18 D2 57.37N 5.50W
**Tortosa** Spain 48 F4 40.50N 0.32E
**Toruń** Poland 46 D4 53.01N 18.37E
**Tory Island** Ireland 41 C5 55.16N 8.13W
**Tosno** Rus. Fed. 40 G2 59.33N 30.54E
**Tosya** Turkey 57 K5 40.59N 34.04E
**Totland** England 10 D1 50.41N 1.32W
**Totnes** England 13 D2 50.26N 3.41W
**Totton** England 10 D1 50.55N 1.29W
**Tottori** Japan 106 B3 35.29N 134.14E
**Toubkal, Jbel** mt. Morocco 84 D5 31.03N 7.57W
**Touggourt** Algeria 84 E5 33.06N 6.04E
**Toulon** France 44 F3 43.08N 5.56E
**Toulouse** France 44 D3 43.37N 1.26E
**Toungoo** Myanmar 97 I4 18.55N 96.25E
**Touraine** f. France 44 D5 47.14N 0.21E
**Tournai** Belgium 42 C3 50.36N 3.24E
**Tournon-sur-Rhône** France 44 F4 45.04N 4.50E
**Tours** France 44 D5 47.23N 0.42E
**Tove** r. England 10 E3 52.05N 0.50W
**Towada** Japan 106 D4 40.36N 141.12E
**Towcester** England 10 E3 52.08N 0.59W
**Townsville** Australia 110 D5 19.15S 146.49E
**Towori, Teluk** b. Indonesia 105 G3 2.02S 121.57E
**Towot** South Sudan 87 A4 6.10N 34.23E
**Toyama** Japan 106 C3 36.41N 137.13E
**Toyama-wan** b. Japan 106 C3 36.54N 137.14E
**Toyota** Japan 106 C3 35.05N 137.10E
**Tozeur** Tunisia 52 E3 33.55N 8.07E
**Trabzon** Turkey 57 M5 40.59N 39.44E
**Trafalgar, Cabo** c. Spain 48 B2 36.11N 6.02W
**Trakai** Lithuania 46 G5 54.38N 24.56E
**Tralee** Ireland 41 B2 52.16N 9.42W
**Tralee Bay** Ireland 41 B2 52.18N 9.57W
**Tramore** Ireland 41 D2 52.10N 7.09W
**Tranås** Sweden 40 C2 58.02N 14.59E
**Trangan** i. Indonesia 105 I2 6.35S 134.16E
**Transylvanian Alps** mts Romania 55 J1 45.35N 24.40E
**Trapani** Italy 50 E3 38.01N 12.31E
**Trasimeno, Lago** l. Italy 50 E5 43.08N 12.06E
**Traunsee** l. Austria 54 E2 47.54N 13.47E
**Traverse City** U.S.A. 65 I5 44.46N 85.37W
**Travnik** Bos.-Herz. 56 B7 44.14N 17.40E
**Trawsfynydd, Llyn** resr Wales 12 D4 52.55N 3.59W
**Trebišov** Slovakia 55 I3 48.39N 21.44E
**Tredegar** Wales 12 D3 51.46N 3.15W
**Tregaron** Wales 12 D4 52.13N 3.56W
**Treig, Loch** l. Scotland 18 E1 56.48N 4.44W
**Trelleborg** Sweden 40 C1 55.22N 13.10E
**Tremadog Bay** Wales 12 C4 52.52N 4.16W
**Trenčín** Slovakia 54 H3 48.53N 18.02E
**Trent** r. England 15 G2 53.38N 0.43W
**Trento** Italy 50 D7 46.04N 11.08E
**Trenton** U.S.A. 65 L5 40.13N 74.47W
**Tresco** i. England 13 A1 49.57N 6.19W
**Tres Puntas, Cabo** c. Argentina 73 C2 47.08S 65.53W
**Treviso** Italy 50 E6 45.40N 12.15E
**Trevose Head** England 13 B2 50.33N 5.06W
**Trier** Germany 54 B3 49.45N 6.38E
**Trieste** Italy 50 E6 45.39N 13.46E
**Trikala** Greece 56 D4 39.33N 21.46E
**Trim** Ireland 41 E3 53.33N 6.47W
**Trincomalee** Sri Lanka 96 F2 8.37N 81.13E
**Tring** England 10 E2 51.48N 0.39W
**Trinidad** Bolivia 76 H5 14.44S 64.51W
**Trinidad** i. Trinidad and Tobago 71 L3 10.27N 61.13W
**Trinidad** U.S.A. 64 F4 37.11N 104.30W
**Trinidad and Tobago** Central America 71 L3 10.49N 61.00W
**Tripoli** Greece 56 E3 37.31N 22.23E
**Tripoli** Lebanon 53 K3 34.26N 35.52E
**Tripoli** Libya 84 F5 32.52N 13.08E
**Tripolitania** f. Libya 52 F3 30.39N 13.17E
**Tripura** d. India 97 H5 23.36N 91.35E
**Tristan da Cunha** i. Atlantic Oc. 116 I4 38.00S 12.00W
**Trivandrum** India 96 E2 8.30N 76.57E
**Trnava** Slovakia 54 G3 48.22N 17.36E
**Trobriand Islands** P.N.G. 110 E6 8.33S 151.09E
**Troisdorf** Germany 42 G3 50.49N 7.09E
**Trois-Rivières** Canada 63 K2 46.21N 72.35W
**Trollhättan** Sweden 40 C2 58.16N 12.18E
**Trombetas** r. Brazil 77 I7 1.31S 56.06W
**Tromsø** Norway 40 D5 69.39N 18.57E
**Trondheim** Norway 40 B3 63.25N 10.22E
**Troödos, Mount** Cyprus 57 J2 34.56N 32.51E
**Troon** Scotland 16 E3 55.32N 4.40W
**Trostan** hill Northern Ireland 16 C3 55.03N 6.09W
**Troup Head** Scotland 19 G2 57.42N 2.18W
**Trout Lake** Canada 65 H7 51.15N 93.06W
**Trowbridge** England 10 C2 51.19N 2.12W
**Troyes** France 44 F6 48.18N 4.05E
**Trubchevsk** Rus. Fed. 55 O5 52.35N 33.47E
**Trujillo** Peru 76 E6 8.07S 79.02W
**Truro** Canada 63 L2 45.22N 63.13W
**Truro** England 13 B2 50.16N 5.03W
**Trutnov** Czech Rep. 46 B3 50.33N 15.55E
**Trzebiatów** Poland 46 B5 54.04N 15.16E
**Tsaratanana, Massif du** mts Madagascar 86 D3 13.44S 48.59E
**Tsavo** r. Kenya 87 B2 2.58S 38.31E
**Tsavo East National Park** Kenya 87 B2 2.43S 38.45E
**Tsavo West National Park** Kenya 87 B2 3.18S 37.58E
**Tsetserleg** Mongolia 101 I7 47.19N 101.29E
**Tshchikskoye Vodokhranilishche** resr Rus. Fed. 57 M7 45.07N 39.28E
**Tshwane** S. Africa 86 B2 25.44S 28.13E
**Tsimlyanskoye Vodokhranilishche** resr Russian Fed. 35 I2 48.00N 43.00E
**Tsna** r. Belarus 55 L5 52.09N 27.01E
**Tsu** Japan 106 C2 34.43N 136.31E
**Tsuchiura** Japan 106 D3 36.04N 140.12E
**Tsugarū-kaikyō** str. Japan 106 D4 41.16N 140.21E
**Tsumeb** Namibia 86 A3 19.14S 17.43E
**Tsumis Park** Namibia 86 A2 23.47S 17.31E
**Tsuruga** Japan 106 C3 35.38N 136.04E
**Tsushima** is Japan 106 A2 34.24N 129.23E
**Tuam** Ireland 41 C3 53.31N 8.51W
**Tuamotu, Archipel des** is French Polynesia 109 K5 14.29S 142.50W
**Tuapse** Rus. Fed. 57 M7 44.06N 39.04E
**Tuban** Indonesia 104 E2 6.55S 112.02E
**Tubbercurry** Ireland 41 C4 54.03N 8.43W
**Tübingen** Germany 54 C3 48.31N 9.04E
**Tubruq** Libya 85 G5 32.04N 23.57E
**Tubuai** i. French Polynesia 109 K4 23.21S 149.30W
**Tubuai Islands** French Polynesia 109 J4 23.34S 153.12W
**Tucavaca** Bolivia 77 I4 18.37S 58.56W
**Tucson** U.S.A. 64 D3 32.14N 110.54W
**Tucumcari** U.S.A. 64 F4 35.12N 103.44W
**Tucuruí** Brazil 77 K7 3.42S 49.44W
**Tucuruí, Represa** resr Brazil 77 K7 4.26S 49.07W
**Tudela** Spain 48 E5 42.04N 1.36W
**Tuela** r. Portugal 48 B4 41.38N 7.08W
**Tufts Abyssal Plain** f. N. Pacific Oc. 109 K9 49.37N 146.59W
**Tuguegarao** Phil. 105 G7 17.37N 121.43E
**Tui** Spain 48 A5 42.03N 8.38W
**Tukangbesi, Kepulauan** is Indonesia 105 G2 5.40S 123.55E
**Tukums** Latvia 40 E2 56.58N 23.10E
**Tula** watercourse Kenya 87 B2 0.50S 39.48E
**Tula** Rus. Fed. 58 E3 54.12N 37.37E
**Tulcea** Romania 57 H7 45.10N 28.48E
**Tul'chyn** Ukraine 55 M3 48.41N 28.50E
**Tulít'a** Canada 62 F4 64.55N 125.31W
**Tullamore** Ireland 41 D3 53.17N 7.30W
**Tulle** France 44 D4 45.16N 1.46E
**Tullow** Ireland 41 E2 52.48N 6.44W
**Tullybrack** hill Northern Ireland 16 B2 54.23N 7.52W
**Tulsa** U.S.A. 64 G4 36.09N 95.58W
**Tumaco** Colombia 72 B7 1.48N 78.49W
**Tumba, Lac** l. Dem. Rep. Congo 86 A4 0.52S 18.05E
**Tumbes** Peru 76 D7 3.35S 80.27W
**Tumen** r. Asia 106 A4 42.14N 130.41E
**Tumen** China 106 A4 42.59N 129.51E
**Tumkur** India 96 E3 13.19N 77.06E
**Tummel** r. Scotland 19 F1 56.39N 3.40W
**Tummel, Loch** l. Scotland 19 F1 56.42N 3.58W
**Tump** Pakistan 95 J5 26.06N 62.26E
**Tumucumaque, Serra** hills Brazil 77 I8 1.59N 56.09W
**Tunceli** Turkey 57 M4 39.06N 39.33E
**Tundzha** r. Bulgaria 56 G5 41.39N 26.33E
**Tunis** Tunisia 52 F4 36.46N 10.16E
**Tunis, Golfe de** g. Tunisia 50 D2 37.08N 10.31E
**Tunisia** Africa 52 E3 34.52N 9.24E
**Tunja** Colombia 72 B7 5.30N 73.22W
**Tunnsjøen** l. Norway 40 C4 64.42N 13.24E
**Tuolumne** r. U.S.A. 64 B4 37.36N 121.10W
**Tupinambarana, Ilha** i. Brazil 77 I7 3.50S 58.55W
**Tupiza** Bolivia 76 G3 21.27S 65.45W
**Tura** Rus. Fed. 59 L4 64.16N 100.15E
**Turabah** Saudi Arabia 94 F4 21.14N 41.37E
**Turbat** Pakistan 96 B6 26.01N 63.07E
**Turbo** Colombia 71 I2 8.05N 76.43W
**Turda** Romania 55 J2 46.34N 23.47E
**Turgutlu** Turkey 56 G4 38.29N 27.42E
**Turhal** Turkey 57 L5 40.23N 36.04E
**Turia** r. Spain 48 E3 39.26N 0.18W
**Turin** Italy 50 B6 45.04N 7.41E
**Turiys'k** Ukraine 46 G3 51.05N 24.32E
**Turkana, Lake** Ethiopia/Kenya 85 H2 3.59N 35.57E
**Turkey** Asia/Europe 57 I4 39.19N 34.21E
**Turkmenabat** Turkmenistan 58 H1 39.05N 63.34E
**Turkmenbashi** Turkmenistan 58 G2 40.02N 52.59E
**Turkmenistan** Asia 115 L7 40.00N 60.00E
**Turks and Caicos Islands** Central America 71 J5 21.59N 71.36W
**Turks Islands** Turks and Caicos Is 71 J5 21.25N 71.09W
**Turku** Finland 40 E3 60.27N 22.15E
**Turkwel** watercourse Kenya 87 B3 3.03N 36.08E
**Turnhout** Belgium 42 D4 51.19N 4.57E
**Turnu Măgurele** Romania 56 F6 43.45N 24.51E
**Turpan** China 100 F6 42.52N 89.12E
**Turquino, Pico** mt. Cuba 71 I5 20.02N 76.51W
**Turriff** Scotland 19 G2 57.32N 2.28W
**Tuscaloosa** U.S.A. 65 I3 33.11N 87.30W
**Tutbury** England 10 D3 52.51N 1.41W
**Tuticorin** India 96 E2 8.48N 78.08E
**Tuttlingen** Germany 54 C2 47.59N 8.49E
**Tutuila** i. American Samoa 108 I5 14.16S 170.33W
**Tuvalu** S. Pacific Oc. 111 G6 7.24S 178.20E
**Tuxford** England 15 G2 53.14N 0.54W
**Tuxpan** Mexico 70 E5 20.58N 97.22W
**Tuxtla Gutiérrez** Mexico 70 F4 16.46N 93.08W
**Tuz, Lake** Turkey 57 J4 38.42N 33.24E
**Tuzla** Bos.-Herz. 56 C7 44.33N 18.42E
**Tver'** Rus. Fed. 58 E3 56.50N 35.54E
**Tweed** r. U.K. 15 E4 55.45N 2.06W
**Twin Falls** town U.S.A. 64 D5 42.35N 114.27W
**Twyford** England 10 E2 51.29N 0.52W
**Tyler** U.S.A. 65 G3 32.22N 95.18W
**Tynda** Rus. Fed. 59 N3 55.07N 124.44E
**Tyne** r. Scotland 17 G3 56.00N 2.36W
**Tyne and Wear** d. England 8 E4 54.56N 1.16W
**Tynemouth** England 15 F4 55.01N 1.25W
**Tynset** Norway 40 B3 62.16N 10.47E
**Tyre** Lebanon 53 K3 33.15N 35.14E
**Tyrrhenian Sea** France/Italy 50 D4 40.13N 10.15E
**Tyumen'** Rus. Fed. 58 H3 57.09N 65.28E
**Tywi** r. Wales 12 C3 51.48N 4.20W


## U


**Uaupés** Brazil 76 G7 0.06S 67.02W
**Ubangi** r. C.A.R./Dem. Rep. Congo 85 F1 0.25S 17.44E
**Úbeda** Spain 48 D3 38.01N 3.22W
**Uberaba** Brazil 77 K4 19.46S 47.53W
**Uberlândia** Brazil 77 K4 18.56S 48.14W
**Ubon Ratchathani** Thailand 104 C7 15.14N 104.53E
**Ucayali** r. Peru 76 F7 4.28S 73.29W
**Uchur** r. Rus. Fed. 59 O3 57.19N 131.17E
**Uckfield** England 11 F1 50.58N 0.06E
**Uda** r. Rus. Fed. 59 O3 54.41N 135.18E
**Udaipur** India 96 D5 24.35N 73.47E
**Uddevalla** Sweden 40 B2 58.21N 11.57E
**Uddjaure** l. Sweden 40 D4 65.56N 17.52E
**Udine** Italy 50 E7 46.04N 13.14E
**Udon Thani** Thailand 104 C7 17.22N 102.50E
**Udupi** India 96 D3 13.20N 74.46E
**Ueda** Japan 106 C3 36.24N 138.15E
**Uele** r. Dem. Rep. Congo 86 B5 3.32N 25.16E
**Uelzen** Germany 54 D5 52.58N 10.34E
**Ufa** Rus. Fed. 58 G3 54.44N 55.58E
**Uganda** Africa 85 H2 2.34N 32.37E
**Uglegorsk** Rus. Fed. 59 P2 49.02N 142.02E
**Uherské Hradiště** Czech Rep. 46 C2 49.04N 17.28E
**Uig** Scotland 18 C2 57.35N 6.21W
**Uíge** Angola 86 A4 7.36S 15.05E
**Uinta Mountains** U.S.A. 64 D5 40.36N 110.59W
**Ukerewe Island** Tanzania 87 A2 1.57S 32.53E
**Ukhta** Rus. Fed. 58 G4 63.33N 53.46E
**Ukiah** U.S.A. 64 B4 39.09N 123.13W
**Ukmergė** Lithuania 46 G5 55.15N 24.46E
**Ukraine** Europe 55 N3 49.23N 31.18E
**Ulaangom** Mongolia 100 G7 49.57N 92.09E
**Ulan Bator** Mongolia 101 J7 47.48N 106.58E
**Ulanhot** China 101 M7 46.04N 122.03E
**Ulan-Ude** Rus. Fed. 59 L3 51.49N 107.38E
**Ulchin** S. Korea 106 A3 36.59N 129.23E
**Uliastay** Mongolia 100 H7 47.36N 96.48E
**Ulithi** atoll Micronesia 105 J6 10.07N 139.40E
**Ullapool** Scotland 18 D2 57.54N 5.10W
**Ullswater** l. England 14 E3 54.34N 2.54W
**Ullŭng-do** i. S. Korea 106 B3 37.30N 130.55E
**Ulm** Germany 54 C3 48.25N 9.59E
**Ulster Canal** Ireland/U.K. 16 B2 54.14N 7.01W
**Uludağ** mt. Turkey 57 H5 40.06N 29.17E
**Ulundi** S. Africa 86 C2 28.19S 31.25E
**Uluṟu** hill Australia 110 C4 25.20S 131.05E
**Ulva** i. Scotland 16 C4 56.28N 6.13W
**Ulverston** England 14 D3 54.12N 3.05W
**Ul'yanovsk** Rus. Fed. 58 F3 54.18N 48.23E
**Uman'** Ukraine 55 N3 48.45N 30.14E
**Umboi** i. P.N.G. 110 D6 5.42S 147.50E
**Umeå** Sweden 40 E3 63.50N 20.17E
**Umeälven** r. Sweden 40 D4 63.46N 20.19E
**Umm Keddada** Sudan 94 C2 13.35N 26.42E
**Umm Ruwaba** Sudan 94 D2 12.52N 31.10E
**Umm Sa'ad** Libya 85 G5 31.34N 25.03E
**Umtata** S. Africa 86 B1 31.35S 28.47E
**Umuarama** Brazil 77 J3 23.46S 53.19W
**Una** r. Bos.-Herz./Croatia 56 B7 45.16N 16.56E
**'Unayzah** Saudi Arabia 94 F5 26.05N 43.57E
**Unecha** Rus. Fed. 55 O5 52.51N 32.41E
**Ungava, Péninsule d'** pen. Canada 63 K4 60.46N 74.25W
**Ungava Bay** Canada 63 L3 59.16N 67.29W
**Unggi** N. Korea 106 B4 42.21N 130.24E
**Ungwana Bay** Kenya 87 C2 2.47S 40.28E
**Unimak Island** U.S.A. 62 B3 54.58N 164.02W
**Unini** r. Brazil 76 H7 1.41S 61.43W
**United Arab Emirates** Asia 95 H4 23.30N 52.20E
**United Kingdom** Europe 8-19 54.35N 1.53W
**United States of America** N. America 64 G4 38.59N 99.57W
**Unst** i. Scotland 19 I5 60.46N 0.53W
**Upa** r. Rus. Fed. 55 Q6 54.01N 36.20E
**Upavon** England 10 D2 51.18N 1.48W
**Upemba, Lac** l. Dem. Rep. Congo 86 B4 8.39S 26.29E
**Upernavik** Greenland 63 M5 72.48N 56.09W
**Upington** S. Africa 86 B2 28.28S 21.15E
**Upolu** i. Samoa 108 I5 14.04S 171.39W
**Upper Klamath Lake** U.S.A. 64 B5 42.22N 121.53W
**Upper Lough Erne** l. Northern Ireland 16 B2 54.15N 7.34W
**Upper Tean** England 10 D3 52.57N 1.59W
**Uppingham** England 10 E3 52.35N 0.43W
**Uppsala** Sweden 40 D2 59.51N 17.38E
**Upton upon Severn** England 10 C3 52.04N 2.13W
**Ural** r. Kazakhstan/Rus. Fed. 58 G2 46.55N 51.46E
**Ural Mountains** Rus. Fed. 58 H4 66.50N 63.48E
**Ural'sk** Kazakhstan 58 G3 51.11N 51.24E
**Uranium City** Canada 62 H3 59.31N 108.43W
**Ure** r. England 15 F3 54.05N 1.20W
**Urengoy** Rus. Fed. 58 I4 65.55N 78.13E
**Urganch** Uzbekistan 58 H2 41.32N 60.39E
**Urie** r. Scotland 19 G2 57.16N 2.22W
**Urla** Turkey 56 G4 38.17N 26.46E
**Urmia, Lake** Iran 94 G7 37.57N 45.17E
**Uruaçu** Brazil 77 K5 14.31S 49.10W
**Uruapan** Mexico 70 D4 19.25N 102.04W
**Urubamba** r. Peru 76 F5 10.46S 73.47W
**Urucara** Brazil 77 I7 2.31S 57.45W
**Uruguaiana** Brazil 77 I2 29.45S 57.03W
**Uruguay** r. Argentina/Brazil/Uruguay 77 I1 33.52S 58.25W
**Uruguay** S. America 73 D3 32.45S 55.56W
**Ürümqi** China 100 F6 43.44N 87.34E
**Urziceni** Romania 56 G7 44.43N 26.37E
**Uşak** Turkey 57 H4 38.40N 29.24E
**Ushuaia** Argentina 73 C1 54.46S 68.19W
**Usk** Wales 12 E3 51.42N 2.54W
**Usk** r. Wales 12 E3 51.34N 2.59W
**Usk Reservoir** Wales 12 D3 51.56N 3.44W
**Usol'ye-Sibirskoye** Rus. Fed. 59 L3 52.40N 103.30E
**Ussuri** r. China/Rus. Fed. 106 C5 48.24N 135.01E
**Ussuriysk** Rus. Fed. 59 O2 43.48N 131.57E
**Ustica, Isola di** i. Italy 50 E3 38.41N 13.10E
**Ust'-Ilimsk** Rus. Fed. 59 L3 58.02N 102.42E
**Ústí nad Labem** Czech Rep. 54 F4 50.40N 14.03E
**Ustka** Poland 46 C5 54.35N 16.52E
**Ust'-Kamchatsk** Rus. Fed. 59 R3 56.15N 162.32E
**Ust'-Kamenogorsk** Kazakhstan 58 J2 49.52N 82.46E
**Ust'-Kut** Rus. Fed. 59 L3 56.45N 105.42E
**Ust'-Maya** Rus. Fed. 59 O4 60.27N 134.31E
**Ust'-Olenek** Rus. Fed. 59 M5 72.55N 119.44E
**Ustyurt Plateau** f. Kazakhstan/Uzbekistan 58 G2 43.29N 56.11E
**Utah** d. U.S.A. 64 D4 39.34N 111.34W
**Utena** Lithuania 46 G5 55.30N 25.36E
**Utica** U.S.A. 65 K5 43.06N 75.15W
**Utiel** Spain 48 E3 39.34N 1.11W
**Utrecht** Neth. 42 E5 52.05N 5.07E
**Utrecht** d. Neth. 42 E5 52.07N 5.12E
**Utrera** Spain 48 C2 37.11N 5.46W
**Utsunomiya** Japan 106 C3 36.34N 139.54E
**Uttaradit** Thailand 104 C7 17.37N 100.04E
**Uttarakhand** d. India 96 E7 30.11N 79.08E
**Uttar Pradesh** d. India 96 E6 27.37N 79.17E

Uttoxeter England 10 D3 ..................................52.54N 1.52W
Uusikaupunki Finland 40 E3 .........................60.48N 21.25E
Uvs Nuur l. Mongolia 100 G8 ......................50.20N 92.39E
Uwajima Japan 106 B2 ................................33.13N 132.34E
Uxbridge England 11 E2 ...............................51.33N 0.29W
Uyuni Bolivia 76 G3 .....................................20.30S 66.51W
Uyuni, Salar de r. Bolivia 76 G3 ................20.13S 67.36W
Uzbekistan Asia 115 M8 ..............................40.00N 60.00E
Uzhhorod Ukraine 55 J3 ..............................48.37N 22.17E
Užice Serbia 56 C6 .......................................43.51N 19.51E
Uzunköprü Turkey 56 G5 .............................41.15N 26.41E

## V

Vaal r. S. Africa 86 B2 ..................................29.05S 23.39E
Vaasa Finland 40 E3 .....................................63.06N 21.38E
Vác Hungary 54 H2 .......................................47.47N 19.09E
Vadodara India 96 D5 ..................................22.16N 73.14E
Vadsø Norway 40 G5 ...................................70.05N 29.44E
Vaduz Liechtenstein 54 C2 ..........................47.08N 9.32E
Værøy i. Norway 40 C4 ...............................67.39N 12.36E
Vaganski Vrh mt. Croatia 56 A7 .................44.22N 15.30E
Váh r. Slovakia 54 H2 ..................................47.46N 18.08E
Vaiaku Tuvalu 108 H5 ..................................8.28S 179.10E
Vaitupu i. Tuvalu 111 G6 ............................7.27S 178.43E
Valdai Hills Russian Fed. 34 H3 ................57.10N 33.00E
Valdepeñas Spain 48 D3 .............................38.46N 3.22W
Valdés, Península pen. Argentina 73 C2 ....42.31S 63.25W
Valdez U.S.A. 62 D4 .....................................61.07N 146.16W
Valdivia Chile 73 B3 ......................................39.50S 73.13W
Val-d'Or Canada 63 K2 ...............................48.06N 77.47W
Valdosta U.S.A. 65 J3 ...................................30.51N 83.18W
Valdres f. Norway 40 B3 ..............................60.56N 9.13E
Valea lui Mihai Romania 46 F1 ..................47.30N 22.09E
Valence France 44 F4 ...................................44.56N 4.54E
Valencia Spain 48 E3 ....................................39.29N 0.21W
Valencia Venezuela 72 C8 ...........................10.10N 67.59W
Valencia, Golfo de g. Spain 48 F3 ............39.28N 0.02E
Valencia de Alcántara Spain 48 B3 ..........39.25N 7.14W
Valenciennes France 44 E7 .........................50.21N 3.32E
Vale of Glamorgan d. Wales 9 D2 ...........51.26N 3.21V
Valera Venezuela 72 B7 ...............................9.14N 70.35W
Valier, Mont mt. France 44 D3 ...................42.48N 1.05E
Valinco, Golfe de b. France 50 C4 ............41.40N 8.52E
Valinco, Gulf of Italy 44 H2 .......................41.40N 8.50E
Valjevo Serbia 56 C7 ...................................44.17N 19.55E
Valka Latvia 40 F4 .......................................57.46N 26.00E
Valkeakoski Finland 40 F3 ..........................61.15N 24.03E
Valkenswaard Neth. 42 E4 .........................51.21N 5.27E
Valladolid Spain 48 C4 ................................41.39N 4.43W
Valle de la Pascua Venezuela 71 K2 ..........9.10N 65.57W
Valledupar Colombia 72 B8 ........................10.30N 73.16W
Valletta Malta 50 F1 ....................................35.54N 14.30E
Valley Wales 12 C5 ......................................53.17N 4.34W
Valparaíso Chile 73 B3 ................................33.03S 71.36W
Vals, Tanjung c. Indonesia 105 J2 ..............8.26S 137.40E
Vammala Finland 40 E3 ...............................61.20N 22.56E
Van Turkey 94 F7 ..........................................38.30N 43.22E
Van, Lake Turkey 94 F7 ...............................38.37N 42.47E
Vancouver Canada 62 F2 .............................49.16N 123.08W
Vancouver Island Canada 62 F2 ................49.28N 125.39W
Van Diemen Gulf Australia 105 I1 ............11.54S 132.00E
Vänern l. Sweden 40 C2 ..............................59.05N 13.36E
Vänersborg Sweden 40 C2 ..........................58.23N 12.20E
Vangaindrano Madagascar 86 D2 .............23.22S 47.34E
Vanimo P.N.G. 105 K3 .................................2.42S 141.20E
Vännäs Sweden 40 D3 .................................63.55N 19.46E
Vannes France 44 B5 ...................................47.39N 2.45W
Vantaa Finland 40 F3 ..................................60.18N 24.57E
Vanua Levu i. Fiji 111 G5 ............................16.10S 179.40E
Vanuatu S. Pacific Oc. 111 F5 ...................16.05S 167.04E
Varanasi India 96 F6 ...................................25.20N 83.04E
Varangerfjorden str. Norway 40 G5 ..........70.04N 29.07E
Varaždin Croatia 54 G2 ...............................46.19N 16.22E
Varberg Sweden 40 C2 ................................57.07N 12.16E
Vardar r. Macedonia 56 E5 .........................41.07N 22.32E
Varėna Lithuania 46 G5 ...............................54.13N 24.35E
Varese Italy 50 C6 ........................................45.49N 8.50E
Varkaus Finland 40 F3 ................................62.19N 27.54E
Varna Bulgaria 57 G6 ..................................43.12N 27.54E
Värnamo Sweden 40 C2 ..............................57.11N 14.03E
Várpalota Hungary 54 H2 ...........................47.12N 18.08E
Vasa Barris r. Brazil 77 M5 .........................11.02S 37.11W
Västerås Sweden 40 D2 ..............................59.37N 16.33E
Västerdalälven r. Sweden 40 C3 ...............60.32N 15.07E
Västervik Sweden 40 D2 .............................57.45N 16.39E
Vasyl'kiv Ukraine 55 N4 ..............................50.11N 30.19E
Vatersay i. Scotland 18 B1 .........................56.56N 7.38W
Vatnajökull ice cap Iceland 40 Y2 ............64.28N 16.37W
Vättern l. Sweden 40 C2 .............................58.05N 14.21E
Vava'u Group is Tonga 108 I4 ...................18.24S 174.21W
Vawkavysk Belarus 55 K5 ...........................53.09N 24.27E
Växjö Sweden 40 C2 ....................................56.53N 14.49E
Vechte r. Germany 42 F5 ............................52.37N 6.43E
Veendam Neth. 42 F6 ..................................53.06N 6.53E
Veenendaal Neth. 42 E5 .............................52.01N 5.33E
Vega i. Norway 40 B4 ..................................65.39N 11.53E
Vejle Denmark 40 B1 ...................................55.43N 9.32E
Velen Germany 42 F4 ..................................51.53N 6.59E
Veles Macedonia 56 D5 ...............................41.42N 21.47E
Vélez-Málaga Spain 48 C2 .........................36.47N 4.06W
Velhas r. Brazil 72 E5 ...................................17.13S 44.49W
Velika Morava canal Serbia 56 D7 ...........44.43N 21.03E
Velikaya r. Rus. Fed. 55 M7 ........................57.50N 28.15E
Velikiye Luki Rus. Fed. 58 E3 .....................56.20N 30.31E
Velikiy Novgorod Rus. Fed. 58 E3 .............58.33N 31.16E
Veliko Türnovo Bulgaria 56 F6 ..................43.05N 25.39E
Velino, Monte mt. Italy 50 E5 ...................42.09N 13.23E
Velizh Rus. Fed. 55 N6 ................................55.36N 31.12E
Vellore India 96 E3 ......................................12.56N 79.07E
Vel'sk Rus. Fed. 58 G4 .................................61.03N 42.05E
Velten Germany 46 A4 ................................52.41N 13.11E
Vendôme France 44 D5 ...............................47.48N 1.04E
Venezuela S. America 71 K2 .......................7.35N 66.30W
Venezuela, Golfo de g. Venezuela 72 B8 ...11.32N 71.03W
Venezuelan Basin f. Caribbean Sea 109 P7 ...15.44N 70.59W
Venice Italy 50 E6 ........................................45.26N 12.20E
Venice, Gulf of Europe 50 E6 .....................45.19N 12.43E
Venray Neth. 42 E4 ......................................51.31N 5.58E
Venta r. Latvia/Lithuania 40 E2 ...............56.24N 22.14E
Ventnor England 10 D1 ..............................50.36N 1.12W
Ventspils Latvia 40 E2 ................................57.23N 21.36E
Vera Spain 48 E2 ..........................................37.15N 1.52W
Veracruz Mexico 70 E4 ...............................19.11N 96.09W
Veracruz d. Mexico 70 E5 ...........................20.54N 97.46W
Vercelli Italy 50 C6 .......................................45.19N 8.26E
Verdalsøra Norway 40 B3 ............................63.47N 11.29E
Verde r. Brazil 77 J3 ....................................21.10S 51.58W
Verde r. Paraguay 77 I3 ..............................23.01S 57.94W
Verde r. U.S.A. 64 D4 .................................33.33N 111.39W
Verdun France 44 F6 ....................................49.10N 5.24E

Verín Spain 48 B4 .........................................41.56N 7.25W
Verkhnevilyuysk Rus. Fed. 59 N4 .............63.26N 120.12E
Verkhoyansk Rus. Fed. 59 O4 ...................67.32N 133.27E
Verkhoyanskiy Khrebet mts Rus. Fed. 59 N5 ...70.07N 128.50E
Vermont d. U.S.A. 65 L5 .............................44.03N 72.42W
Veroia Greece 56 E5 ....................................40.32N 22.13E
Verona Italy 50 D6 ......................................45.26N 10.59E
Versailles France 44 E6 ...............................48.48N 2.08E
Vert, Cap c. Senegal 84 C3 .........................14.44N 17.31W
Verviers Belgium 42 E3 ...............................50.35N 5.52E
Vervins France 42 C2 ..................................49.50N 3.54E
Verwood England 10 D1 .............................50.53N 1.52W
Vesoul France 44 G5 ...................................47.38N 6.09E
Vesterålen is Norway 40 C5 .......................68.43N 13.59E
Vestfjorden str. Norway 40 C4 ..................67.40N 13.54E
Vestmannaeyjar is Iceland 40 X1 .............63.24N 20.13W
Vesturhorn hd Iceland 40 Z2 .....................64.17N 14.59W
Vesuvius vol. Italy 50 E5 ............................40.50N 14.26E
Veszprém Hungary 54 G2 ...........................47.06N 17.54E
Vettore, Monte mt. Italy 50 E5 ..................42.49N 13.17E
Veurne Belgium 42 B4 ................................51.04N 2.40E
Vézère r. France 44 D4 ...............................44.53N 0.53E
Vezirköprü Turkey 57 K5 .............................41.09N 35.28E
Viana do Castelo Portugal 48 A4 ..............41.42N 8.49W
Viborg Denmark 40 B2 ...............................56.27N 9.24E
Vibo Valentia Italy 50 G3 ...........................38.40N 16.06E
Vic Spain 48 G4 ...........................................41.56N 2.15E
Vicenza Italy 50 D6 .....................................45.33N 11.33E
Vichy France 44 E5 ......................................46.08N 3.26E
Victoria d. Australia 110 D3 ......................36.56S 144.52E
Victoria i. Australia 110 C5 ........................15.23S 130.17E
Victoria Canada 62 F2 ................................48.25N 123.22W
Victoria U.S.A. 64 G2 ..................................28.49N 96.59W
Victoria, Lake Africa 86 C4 ........................0.59S 32.51E
Victoria, Mount Myanmar 97 H5 ..............21.11N 93.56E
Victoria, Mount P.N.G. 110 D6 .................8.49S 147.30E
Victoria Falls Zambia/Zimbabwe 86 B3 ...17.49S 25.42E
Victoria Island Canada 62 H5 ...................70.42N 106.38W
Victoria Nile r. Uganda 87 A3 ...................2.15N 31.21E
Viedma Argentina 73 C2 ............................40.50S 63.00W
Viedma, Lago l. Argentina 73 B2 .............49.35S 72.49W
Vienna Austria 54 G3 ..................................48.12N 16.23E
Vienne France 44 F4 ....................................45.31N 4.53E
Vienne r. France 44 D5 ...............................47.13N 0.05E
Vientiane Laos 104 C7 .................................17.58N 102.37E
Vierzon France 44 E5 ...................................47.14N 2.04E
Vieste Italy 50 G4 ........................................41.53N 16.10E
Vietnam Asia 104 D7 ...................................19.20N 104.48E
Vignemale mt. France 44 C3 ......................42.46N 0.09W
Vigo Spain 48 A5 ........................................42.14N 8.43W
Vijayawada India 96 F4 ..............................16.33N 80.39E
Vík Iceland 40 Y1 ........................................63.26N 19.02W
Vikna i. Norway 40 B4 ................................64.53N 10.50E
Vilagarcía de Arousa Spain 48 A5 ...........42.36N 8.45W
Vilaine r. France 44 B5 ...............................47.35N 2.16W
Vila Real Portugal 48 B4 ............................41.18N 7.44W
Vila Velha Brazil 77 L3 ................................20.22S 40.20W
Vilcabamba, Cordillera mts Peru 76 F5 ...12.30S 73.27W
Vilhelmina Sweden 40 D4 ..........................64.37N 16.41E
Vilhena Brazil 77 H5 ....................................12.42S 60.07W
Viljandi Estonia 40 F2 .................................58.22N 25.35E
Vilkaviškis Lithuania 46 F5 ........................54.39N 23.03E
Vilkija Lithuania 46 F5 ................................55.03N 23.35E
Vil'kitskogo, Proliv str. Rus. Fed. 59 K5 ...77.30N 98.42E
Villach Austria 54 E2 ...................................46.37N 13.50E
Villahermosa Mexico 70 F4 ........................18.00N 92.53W
Villa Insurgentes Mexico 70 B6 ................25.16N 111.47W
Villa Montes Bolivia 76 H3 .........................21.14S 63.30W
Villaputzu Italy 50 C3 .................................39.26N 9.35E
Villarrica Paraguay 77 I2 ...........................25.43S 56.25W
Villarrobledo Spain 48 D3 .........................39.16N 2.36W
Villavicencio Colombia 72 B7 ....................4.07N 73.36W
Villefranche-sur-Saône France 44 F4 ........45.59N 4.44E
Villena Spain 48 E3 .....................................38.38N 0.51W
Villeneuve-sur-Lot France 44 D4 ...............44.25N 0.42E
Villers-Cotterêts France 42 C2 ..................49.15N 3.06E
Villeurbanne France 44 F4 ..........................45.46N 4.54E
Vilnius Lithuania 40 F1 ...............................54.40N 25.16E
Vilvoorde Belgium 42 D3 ............................50.55N 4.27E
Vilyuy r. Rus. Fed. 59 N4 ............................64.24N 126.28E
Viña del Mar Chile 76 F1 ...........................33.02S 71.34W
Vindelälven r. Sweden 40 D3 .....................63.56N 19.51E
Vinh Vietnam 104 D7 ..................................18.38N 105.42E
Vinkovci Croatia 56 C7 ...............................45.17N 18.49E
Vinnytsya Ukraine 55 M3 ...........................49.14N 28.30E
Viranşehir Turkey 57 M3 ............................37.13N 39.47E
Virden Canada 62 F2 ..................................49.51N 100.56W
Vire France 44 C6 .........................................48.50N 0.53W
Virginia d. U.S.A. 65 K4 ...............................37.47N 78.19W
Virgin Islands (U.K.) Central America 71 L4 ...18.37N 64.37W
Virgin Islands (U.S.A.) Central America 71 L4 ...18.14N 64.53W
Virovitica Croatia 56 B7 ..............................45.50N 17.23E
Virton Belgium 42 E2 ..................................49.34N 5.33E
Vis i. Croatia 56 B6 .....................................43.05N 16.06E
Visaginas Lithuania 55 L6 ..........................55.36N 26.26E
Visby Sweden 40 D2 ...................................57.38N 18.18E
Viscount Melville Sound str. Canada 62 G5 ...73.50N 112.57W
Viseu Portugal 48 B4 ..................................40.40N 7.55W
Vishakhapatnam India 96 F4 ....................17.42N 83.22E
Viso, Monte mt. Italy 50 B6 .......................44.40N 7.06E
Vistula r. Poland 46 D5 ...............................54.18N 18.55E
Viterbo Italy 50 E5 ......................................42.24N 12.07E
Viti Levu i. Fiji 111 G5 ................................18.05S 177.19E
Vitim r. Rus. Fed. 59 M3 .............................59.26N 112.35E
Vitória Brazil 77 L3 ......................................20.19S 40.21W
Vitória da Conquista Brazil 77 L5 .............14.50S 40.47W
Vitoria-Gasteiz Spain 48 D5 ......................42.51N 2.39W
Vitsyebsk Belarus 55 N6 .............................55.12N 30.10E
Vittel France 44 F6 ......................................48.12N 5.57E
Vizianagaram India 96 F4 ..........................18.08N 83.31E
Vlaams-Brabant d. Belgium 42 D3 ..........50.56N 4.36E
Vlaardingen Neth. 42 D4 ............................51.54N 4.21E
Vlădeasa, Vârful mt. Romania 55 J2 ........46.45N 22.50E
Vladimir Rus. Fed. 58 F3 ............................56.08N 40.24E
Vladivostok Rus. Fed. 59 O2 ......................43.07N 131.56E
Vlieland i. Neth. 42 C6 ...............................53.16N 4.57E
Vlissingen Neth. 42 C4 ...............................51.27N 3.34E
Vlorë Albania 56 C5 ....................................40.28N 19.30E
Vltava r. Czech Rep. 54 F4 .........................50.19N 14.29E
Voe Scotland 19 H5 ....................................60.21N 1.16W
Vohimena, Tanjona c. Madagascar 86 D2 ...25.36S 45.12E
Voi Kenya 87 B2 ..........................................3.24S 38.35E
Volcano Islands Japan 108 F7 ...................24.53N 140.34E
Volda Norway 40 A3 ...................................62.08N 6.05E
Volga r. Rus. Fed. 58 G2 ............................45.47N 47.34E
Volga Uplands hills Russian Fed. 35 I3 ....53.15N 45.45E
Volgograd Rus. Fed. 58 F2 .........................48.44N 44.30E
Völklingen Germany 42 F2 .........................49.15N 6.51E
Volodymyr-Volyns'kyy Ukraine 55 K4 .......50.51N 24.20E
Vologda Rus. Fed. 58 F3 .............................59.13N 39.54E
Volos Greece 56 E4 .....................................39.22N 22.57E
Volta, Lake resr Ghana 84 E2 ....................6.23N 0.05E
Volta Redonda Brazil 77 L3 .......................22.30S 44.07W
Volzhskiy Rus. Fed. 58 G3 ..........................53.24N 50.05E

Voreioi Sporades is Greece 56 E4 .............39.15N 23.27E
Vorkuta Rus. Fed. 58 H4 ............................67.29N 64.05E
Voronezh Rus. Fed. 58 F3 ..........................51.38N 39.12E
Vorskla r. Rus. Fed. 55 P3 ..........................48.55N 34.08E
Vosges mts France 44 G5 ...........................47.46N 6.41E
Voss Norway 40 A3 .....................................60.38N 6.27E
Vostochnyy Sayan mts Rus. Fed. 59 K3 ...54.43N 94.48E
Vostok Island Kiribati 109 J5 ....................10.04S 152.25W
Vouziers France 42 D2 ................................49.24N 4.42E
Voznesens'k Ukraine 55 N2 .......................47.33N 31.21E
Vranje Serbia 56 D6 ...................................42.33N 21.54E
Vratsa Bulgaria 56 E6 .................................43.12N 23.33E
Vrbas r. Bos.-Herz. 56 B7 ...........................45.07N 17.31E
Vršac Serbia 56 D7 ......................................45.07N 21.17E
Vung Tau Vietnam 104 D6 .........................10.22N 107.05E
Vuollerim Sweden 40 E4 ............................66.26N 20.37E
Vyatka r. Rus. Fed. 58 F3 ...........................58.36N 49.41E
Vyaz'ma Rus. Fed. 55 P6 ............................55.13N 34.18E
Vyborg r. Russian Fed. 35 I4 .....................60.42N 28.46E
Vychegda r. Russian Fed. 35 I4 ................61.15N 46.28E
Vyrnwy, Lake Wales 12 D5 ........................52.46N 3.29W
Vyškov Czech Rep. 46 C2 ...........................49.16N 17.00E
Vyžuona r. Lithuania 46 G5 .......................55.34N 25.31E

## W

Wa Ghana 84 D3 .........................................10.04N 2.30W
Wabasca r. Canada 62 G3 ..........................58.18N 115.23W
Wabash r. U.S.A. 65 I4 ...............................37.50N 88.01W
Wabē Gestro r. Ethiopia 87 C4 ................4.19N 42.03E
Wabē Mena r. Ethiopia 87 C4 ..................5.32N 41.12E
Wabush Canada 63 L3 ................................52.51N 66.49W
Waco U.S.A. 64 G3 ......................................31.34N 97.08W
Wad Pakistan 96 C6 ....................................27.20N 66.30E
Waddān Libya 84 F4 ...................................29.09N 16.09E
Waddenzee str. Neth. 42 D5 .....................52.51N 4.51E
Waddington England 15 G2 ......................53.10N 0.32W
Waddington, Mount Canada 62 F3 .........51.21N 125.18W
Wadebridge England 13 C2 .......................50.31N 4.50W
Wadhurst England 11 F2 ............................51.04N 0.20E
Wadi Halfa Sudan 85 H4 ...........................21.48N 31.20E
Wad Medani Sudan 85 H3 .........................14.22N 33.30E
Wagga Wagga Australia 110 D3 ................35.08S 147.23E
Wāhāt Jālū Libya 53 H2 ............................29.14N 21.04E
Wahpeton U.S.A. 64 G6 .............................46.15N 96.50W
Waigeo i. Indonesia 105 I3 ........................0.11S 130.59E
Wainfleet All Saints England 15 H2 .........53.06N 0.14E
Waingapu Indonesia 104 G2 .....................9.38S 120.15E
Waini Point Guyana 72 D7 ........................8.22N 59.44W
Wainwright U.S.A. 62 C5 ............................70.39N 159.51W
Wajir Kenya 87 C3 .......................................1.44N 40.03E
Wakasa-wan b. Japan 106 C3 ...................35.45N 135.36E
Wakayama Japan 106 C2 ...........................34.13N 135.10E
Wakefield England 15 F2 ...........................53.41N 1.30W
Wake Island N. Pacific Oc. 108 H7 ..........19.18N 166.39E
Wakkanai Japan 106 D5 .............................45.24N 141.40E
Wałbrzych Poland 46 C3 .............................50.46N 16.18E
Wałcz Poland 46 C4 ....................................53.17N 16.29E
Wales d. U.K. 9 D3 ......................................52.04N 3.41W
Wallasey England 14 D2 .............................53.26N 3.04W
Wallingford England 10 D2 ........................51.36N 1.08W
Wallis and Futuna Islands S. Pacific Oc. 108 I5 ...13.24S 177.57W
Walls Scotland 19 H5 ...................................60.14N 1.33W
Walney, Isle of i. England 14 D3 ...............54.04N 3.16W
Walsall England 10 D3 ................................52.35N 1.59W
Waltham on the Wolds England 10 E3 ......52.49N 0.49W
Walton-on-Thames England 11 E2 ...........51.23N 0.25W
Walvis Bay town Namibia 86 A2 ...............22.58S 14.30E
Wandsworth England 11 E2 .......................51.27N 0.12W
Wangqing China 106 A4 ............................43.19N 129.44E
Wantage England 10 D2 .............................51.35N 1.25W
Wanzhou China 101 J4 ..............................30.47N 108.22E
Warangal India 96 E4 .................................17.59N 79.35E
Warboys England 11 E3 .............................52.24N 0.05W
Warburton watercourse Australia 110 C4 ...27.54S 137.19E
Ward Hill Scotland 19 F3 ............................58.54N 3.22W
Ward's Stone hill England 14 E3 ...............54.02N 2.38W
Wareham England 10 C1 ............................50.41N 2.07W
Waremme Belgium 42 E3 ...........................50.42N 5.15E
Warka Poland 46 E3 ....................................51.47N 21.11E
Warlingham England 11 E2 .......................51.19N 0.03W
Warrego r. Australia 110 D3 ......................30.24S 145.21E
Warrenpoint Northern Ireland 16 C2 .......54.06N 6.15W
Warri Nigeria 84 E2 .....................................5.35N 5.45E
Warrington England 14 E2 .........................53.23N 2.36W
Warrington d. England 9 E3 .......................53.24N 2.33W
Warsaw Poland 46 E4 .................................52.15N 21.01E
Warta r. Poland 46 B4 ................................52.35N 14.38E
Warwick England 10 D3 .............................52.17N 1.35W
Warwickshire d. England 9 E3 ...................52.19N 1.32W
Washington U.S.A. 65 K4 ...........................38.54N 77.01W
Washington d. U.S.A. 64 B6 .......................47.36N 120.19W
Washington, Mount U.S.A. 65 L5 .............44.18N 71.18W
Waskaganish Canada 63 K3 ......................51.28N 78.46W
Wast Water l. England 14 D3 .....................54.26N 3.18W
Watampone Indonesia 104 G2 ..................4.31S 120.21E
Watchet England 13 D3 .............................51.11N 3.20W
Waterford Ireland 41 D2 ............................52.15N 7.07W
Waterford d. Ireland 41 D2 .......................52.10N 7.53W
Watergate Bay England 13 B2 ..................50.27N 5.05W
Waterlooville England 10 D1 .....................50.53N 1.02W
Water of Saughs r. Scotland 19 G1 ..........56.47N 2.37W
Watertown U.S.A. 64 G5 ............................44.53N 97.07W
Watford England 11 E2 ...............................51.39N 0.23W
Watlington England 10 D2 .........................51.39N 1.01W
Watson Lake town Canada 62 F4 .............60.05N 128.42W
Watten, Loch l. Scotland 19 F3 ................58.29N 3.22W
Watton England 11 F3 ................................52.34N 0.50E
Wau South Sudan 85 G2 ............................7.40N 27.59E
Wausau U.S.A. 65 I5 ...................................44.58N 89.37W
Waveney r. England 11 G3 .........................52.29N 1.41E
Wear r. England 15 E3 ................................54.55N 1.23W
Weber Basin f. Indonesia 108 E5 .............5.42S 130.54E
Webi Shabeelle r. Somalia 85 I2 ..............0.10N 42.46E
Webuye Kenya 87 A3 ..................................0.37N 34.44E
Wedmore England 10 C2 ............................51.14N 2.49W
Weener Germany 42 G6 .............................53.10N 7.21E
Weert Neth. 42 E4 .......................................51.15N 5.43E
Węgorzewo Poland 46 E5 ..........................54.13N 21.44E
Weifang China 101 L5 ................................36.42N 119.03E
Weihai China 101 M5 .................................37.30N 122.07E
Weinan China 101 J4 ..................................34.27N 109.33E
Weipa Australia 105 K1 ..............................12.37S 141.55E
Wejherowo Poland 46 D5 ...........................54.36N 18.14E
Weldiya Ethiopia 85 H3 ..............................11.49N 39.36E
Welkom S. Africa 86 B2 ..............................27.59S 26.44E
Welland r. England 11 E3 ...........................52.52N 0.03W
Wellesley Islands Australia 110 C5 ...........16.18S 139.33E
Wellingborough England 10 E3 .................52.18N 0.42W
Wellington Som. England 13 D2 ...............50.59N 3.13W

Wellington Tel. Wre. England 10 C3 .........52.42N 2.31W
Wellington New Zealand 111 G2 ..............41.18S 174.46E
Wells England 10 C2 ...................................51.13N 2.39W
Wells, Lake Australia 110 B4 ....................26.40S 123.16E
Wells-next-the-Sea England 11 F3 ...........52.57N 0.51E
Wels Austria 54 F3 ......................................48.10N 14.01E
Welshpool Wales 12 D4 .............................52.40N 3.09W
Welwyn Garden City England 11 E2 .........51.48N 0.12W
Wem England 10 C3 ....................................52.51N 2.44W
Wembley England 11 E2 .............................51.33N 0.18W
Wemel Shet' r. Ethiopia 87 C4 ..................5.41N 40.58E
Wemyss Bay town Scotland 16 E3 ...........55.53N 4.53W
Wenchi Ghana 84 D2 .................................7.45N 2.07W
Wendo Ethiopia 85 H2 ...............................6.35N 38.25E
Wendover England 10 E2 ...........................51.46N 0.44W
Wenlock Edge f. England 10 C3 ...............52.27N 2.49W
Wensleydale f. England 15 E3 ...................54.09N 2.02W
Wensum r. England 11 G3 ..........................52.37N 1.20E
Wenzhou China 101 M3 .............................27.59N 120.41E
Wesel Germany 42 F4 .................................51.40N 6.38E
Weser r. Germany 54 C5 .............................53.15N 8.25E
Wessel, Cape Australia 110 C5 ..................11.03S 136.46E
Wessel Islands Australia 110 C5 ...............11.19S 136.26E
West Australian Basin f. Indian Oc. 117 O5 ...17.42S 102.36E
West Bank Asia 53 K3 ................................31.52N 35.19E
West Bengal d. India 96 G5 .......................22.34N 87.20E
West Berkshire d. England 9 E2 ................51.28N 1.20W
West Bridgford England 10 D3 ..................52.56N 1.08W
West Bromwich England 10 D3 .................52.31N 1.59W
Westbury England 10 C2 ............................51.15N 2.11W
West Calder Scotland 17 F3 ......................55.51N 3.34W
West Caroline Basin f. N. Pacific Oc. 108 F6 ...2.42N 136.26E
West Dunbartonshire d. Scotland 8 C4 ...55.59N 4.31W
Western r. Kenya 87 A3 ..............................0.22N 34.35E
Western Australia d. Australia 110 B4 .....24.24S 121.53E
Western Desert Egypt 53 I2 .......................26.42N 29.45E
Western Dvina r. Europe 55 N6 ................55.28N 30.54E
Western Ghats mts India 96 D3 ................14.19N 74.54E
Western Isles d. Scotland 8 B5 ..................57.39N 5.20W
Western Ross f. Scotland 18 D2 ................57.39N 5.20W
Western Sahara Africa 84 C4 ....................22.14N 15.05W
Wester Ross f. Scotland 18 D2 ..................57.39N 5.20W
Westerschelde est. Neth. 42 C4 ...............51.27N 3.27E
West Falkland i. Falkland Is 73 C1 ...........51.16S 61.32W
West Fen f. Cambs. England 11 F3 ............52.32N 0.00E
West Fen f. Lincs. England 15 G2 .............53.04N 0.05W
West Frisian Islands Neth. 42 D6 .............53.11N 4.37E
Westhill Scotland 19 G2 .............................57.09N 2.17W
West Kirby England 14 D2 .........................53.22N 3.11W
West Lavington England 10 D2 .................51.17N 1.59W
West Linton Scotland 17 F3 .......................55.45N 3.22W
West Loch Roag b. Scotland 18 C3 ..........58.15N 6.57W
West Lothian d. Scotland 8 D4 .................55.55N 3.30W
West Malling England 11 F2 ......................51.18N 0.25E
West Mariana Basin f. N. Pacific Oc. 108 F7 ...17.32N 140.09E
Westmeath d. Ireland 41 D3 .....................53.34N 7.24W
West Mersea England 11 F2 ......................51.47N 0.56E
West Midlands d. England 9 E3 ................52.28N 1.49W
Weston-super-Mare England 10 C2 .........51.21N 2.59W
West Palm Beach town U.S.A. 65 J2 ........26.40N 80.09W
Westport Ireland 41 B3 ..............................53.48N 9.31W
Westray i. Scotland 19 F4 ..........................59.18N 3.00W
Westray Firth str. Scotland 19 F4 ............59.16N 3.07W
West Siberian Plain f. Rus. Fed. 58 J4 .....62.39N 80.21E
West Sussex d. England 9 F2 ....................51.00N 0.18W
West-Terschelling Neth. 42 E6 ..................53.22N 5.13E
West Virginia d. U.S.A. 65 J4 ....................38.45N 80.27W
West-Vlaanderen d. Belgium 42 B3 .........50.59N 2.56E
Westward Ho! England 13 C3 ...................51.02N 4.14W
West Yorkshire d. England 9 E3 ................53.46N 2.04W
Wetar i. Indonesia 105 H2 .........................7.49S 126.13E
Wete Tanzania 87 B1 .................................5.04S 39.43E
Wetherby England 15 F2 ............................53.56N 1.23W
Wetzlar Germany 44 H7 ............................50.34N 8.30E
Wexford Ireland 41 E2 ...............................52.20N 6.28W
Wexford d. Ireland 41 E2 ...........................52.37N 6.32W
Wexford Bay Ireland 41 E2 ........................52.25N 6.19W
Weybridge England 11 E2 .........................51.22N 0.27W
Weymouth England 10 C1 .........................50.36N 2.27W
Whalsay i. Scotland 19 I5 ...........................60.21N 0.57W
Whangarei New Zealand 111 G3 ..............35.43S 174.17E
Wharfe r. England 15 F2 .............................53.50N 1.08W
Wheeler Peak N. M. U.S.A. 64 E4 ............36.33N 105.24W
Wheeler Peak Nev. U.S.A. 64 D4 .............38.57N 114.17W
Whernside hill England 15 E3 ...................54.14N 2.24W
Whitburn Scotland 17 F3 ...........................55.52N 3.41W
Whitby England 15 G3 ...............................54.29N 0.37W
Whitchurch England 10 C3 ........................52.58N 2.41W
Whitchurch Wales 13 D3 ...........................51.31N 3.13W
White r. U.S.A. 65 H3 .................................33.59N 91.09W
White, Lake Australia 110 B4 ....................21.03S 129.07E
Whitecourt Canada 62 G3 .........................54.08N 115.43W
Whitehaven England 14 D3 .......................54.33N 3.35W
Whitehead Northern Ireland 16 D2 .........54.45N 5.42W
Whitehill England 10 E2 ..............................51.06N 0.52W
Whitehorse Canada 62 E4 .........................60.44N 135.06W
White Nile r. Sudan/South Sudan/Uganda 85 H3 ...15.38N 32.30W
White Sea Rus. Fed. 58 E4 .........................65.51N 36.58E
White Volta r. Burkina Faso/Ghana 84 D2 ...9.07N 1.10W
Whitfield England 11 G2 ............................51.09N 1.17E
Whithorn Scotland 16 E2 ...........................54.44N 4.25W
Whitland Wales 12 C3 ................................51.49N 4.37W
Whitley Bay town England 15 F4 ..............55.03N 1.27W
Whitney, Mount U.S.A. 64 C4 ..................36.35N 118.16W
Whitsand Bay England 13 C2 ....................50.20N 4.20W
Whitstable England 11 G2 .........................51.22N 1.01E
Whittlesey England 11 E3 ..........................52.34N 0.08W
Whyalla Australia 110 C3 ...........................33.03S 137.31E
Wichita U.S.A. 64 G4 ..................................37.42N 97.20W
Wichita Falls town U.S.A. 64 G3 ..............33.55N 98.30W
Wick Scotland 19 F3 ...................................58.26N 3.06W
Wick r. Scotland 19 F3 ...............................58.26N 3.05W
Wickford England 11 F2 .............................51.37N 0.31E
Wickham England 10 D1 ............................50.54N 1.11W
Wickham Market England 11 G3 ..............52.09N 1.22E
Wicklow Ireland 41 E2 ...............................52.59N 6.02W
Wicklow d. Ireland 41 E2 ...........................52.58N 6.27W
Wicklow Head Ireland 41 E2 .....................52.58N 5.59W
Wicklow Mountains Ireland 41 E2 ...........53.02N 6.27W
Widecombe in the Moor England 13 D2 ...50.34N 3.49W
Wide Firth str. Scotland 19 F4 ..................59.01N 3.02W
Widnes England 14 E2 ...............................53.21N 2.44W
Wielka Sowa mt. Poland 46 C3 ................50.40N 16.29E
Wieluń Poland 46 D3 ..................................51.14N 18.34E
Wiener Neustadt Austria 54 G2 ...............47.49N 16.15E
Wieprz r. Poland 46 E3 ...............................51.34N 21.49E
Wiesbaden Germany 54 C4 .......................50.05N 8.14E
Wiesmoor Germany 42 G6 ........................53.24N 7.44E
Wieżyca hill Poland 46 D5 ..........................54.14N 18.08E
Wigan England 14 E2 .................................53.33N 2.38W
Wight, Isle of i. England 10 D1 ................50.39N 1.07W
Wigston England 10 D3 .............................52.35N 1.06W
Wigton Scotland 16 E2 ...............................54.52N 4.27W
Wigtown Scotland 16 E2 ............................54.52N 4.27W
Wigtown Bay Scotland 16 E2 ....................54.48N 4.19W

Wijchen Neth. 42 E4 ... 51.48N 5.43E
Wildhorn mt. Switz. 50 B7 ... 46.22N 7.22E
Wilhelm, Mount P.N.G. 110 D6 ... 5.46S 144.52E
Wilhelmshaven Germany 54 C5 ... 53.32N 8.08E
Willebroek Belgium 42 D4 ... 51.03N 4.22E
William, Mount Australia 110 D3 ... 37.19S 142.35E
Williams Lake town Canada 62 F3 ... 52.08N 122.09W
Willingdon England 11 F1 ... 50.48N 0.15E
Williston U.S.A. 64 F6 ... 48.10N 103.37W
Williston Lake Canada 62 F3 ... 55.51N 123.43W
Williton England 13 D3 ... 51.10N 3.19W
Wills, Lake Australia 110 B4 ... 21.20S 128.37E
Wilmington Del. U.S.A. 65 K4 ... 39.43N 75.38W
Wilmington N.C. U.S.A. 65 K3 ... 34.13N 77.58W
Wilmslow England 15 E2 ... 53.20N 2.14W
Wilson's Promontory pen. Australia 110 D3 ... 38.55S 146.27E
Wilton England 10 D2 ... 51.05N 1.52W
Wiltshire d. England 9 E2 ... 51.24N 1.53W
Wiltz Lux. 42 E2 ... 49.58N 5.56E
Wimblington England 11 F3 ... 52.31N 0.05E
Wimborne Minster England 10 D1 ... 50.48N 1.59W
Wimereux France 11 G1 ... 50.46N 1.37E
Winam Gulf Kenya 87 A2 ... 0.20S 34.24E
Wincanton England 10 C2 ... 51.03N 2.25W
Winchester England 10 D2 ... 51.04N 1.19W
Windermere England 14 E3 ... 54.23N 2.54W
Windermere l. England 14 E3 ... 54.18N 2.57W
Windhoek Namibia 86 A2 ... 22.34S 17.04E
Windrush r. England 10 D2 ... 51.43N 1.25W
Windsor Canada 65 J5 ... 42.18N 83.01W
Windsor England 11 E2 ... 51.29N 0.37W
Windsor and Maidenhead d. England 9 E2 ... 51.28N 0.40W
Windward Islands Caribbean Sea 71 L4 ... 15.42N 60.03W
Windward Passage str. Cuba/Haiti 71 J4 ... 19.40N 74.11W
Wingate England 15 F3 ... 54.44N 1.23W
Winisk r. Canada 63 J3 ... 55.01N 85.22W
Winkleigh England 13 D2 ... 50.51N 3.57W
Winnebago, Lake U.S.A. 65 I5 ... 44.00N 88.28W
Winnemucca U.S.A. 64 C5 ... 40.59N 117.44W
Winnipeg Canada 62 I2 ... 49.53N 97.10W
Winnipeg, Lake Canada 62 I3 ... 51.31N 96.40W
Winnipegosis, Lake Canada 62 H3 ... 53.05N 100.40W
Winsford Englanc 15 E2 ... 53.12N 2.31W
Winslow England 11 E2 ... 51.57N 0.53W
Winslow U.S.A. 64 D4 ... 35.02N 110.42W
Winston-Salem U.S.A. 65 J4 ... 36.07N 80.17W
Winterswijk Neth. 42 F4 ... 51.58N 6.42E
Winterthur Switz. 50 C7 ... 47.30N 8.43E
Winterton England 15 G2 ... 53.39N 0.36W
Wirksworth England 15 F2 ... 53.05N 1.34W
Wirral pen. England 14 D2 ... 53.22N 3.07W
Wisbech England 11 F3 ... 52.40N 0.10E
Wisconsin d. U.S.A. 65 I5 ... 44.30N 89.32W
Wishaw Scotland 17 F3 ... 55.46N 3.55W
Wismar Germany 54 D5 ... 53.53N 11.28E
Witham England 11 F2 ... 51.48N 0.38E
Witham r. England 11 F3 ... 52.56N 0.05E
Witheridge England 13 D2 ... 50.55N 3.42W
Withernsea England 15 H2 ... 53.44N 0.02E
Witney England 10 D2 ... 51.47N 1.29W
Wittenberge Germany 54 D5 ... 52.59N 11.45E
Wittlich Germany 42 F2 ... 49.59N 6.53E
Wittmund Germany 42 G6 ... 53.35N 7.47E
Witu Kenya 87 C2 ... 2.23S 40.27E
Wiveliscombe England 13 D3 ... 51.03N 3.19W
Wivenhoe England 11 F2 ... 51.51N 0.58E
Wkra r. Poland 46 E4 ... 52.27N 20.45E
Władysławowo Poland 46 D5 ... 54.47N 18.25E
Włocławek Poland 46 D4 ... 52.39N 19.05E
Włodawa Poland 46 F3 ... 51.33N 23.33E
Wokam i. Indonesia 105 I2 ... 5.45S 134.31E
Woking England 11 E2 ... 51.19N 0.34W
Wokingham England 10 E2 ... 51.25N 0.50W
Wokingham d. England 9 E2 ... 51.24N 0.53W
Wolfsberg Austria 54 F2 ... 46.50N 14.51E
Wolfsburg Germany 54 D5 ... 52.25N 10.48E
Wolgast Germany 46 A5 ... 54.03N 13.47E
Wolin Poland 46 B4 ... 53.51N 14.36E
Wollaston Lake Canada 62 H3 ... 58.16N 103.22W
Wollongong Australia 110 E3 ... 34.25S 150.51E
Wolsingham England 15 F3 ... 54.44N 1.53W
Wolvega Neth. 42 F5 ... 52.53N 6.00E
Wolverhampton England 10 C3 ... 52.35N 2.08W
Wombwell England 15 F2 ... 53.31N 1.24W
Wŏnsan N. Korea 101 N5 ... 39.09N 127.27E
Woodbridge England 11 G3 ... 52.06N 1.19E
Woodcote England 10 D2 ... 51.32N 1.04W
Woodhall Spa England 15 G2 ... 53.09N 0.13W
Woodlark Island P.N.G. 110 E6 ... 8.58S 152.47E
Woods, Lake of the Canada/U.S.A. 63 I2 ... 49.22N 94.50W
Woodstock England 10 D2 ... 51.51N 1.21W
Wooler England 15 E4 ... 55.33N 2.01W
Wootton Bassett England 10 D2 ... 51.32N 1.54W
Worcester England 10 C3 ... 52.12N 2.13W
Worcester S. Africa 86 A1 ... 33.38S 19.27E
Worcester U.S.A. 65 L5 ... 42.16N 71.48W
Worcestershire d. England 9 D3 ... 52.12N 2.12W
Wörgl Austria 54 E2 ... 47.29N 12.05E
Workington England 14 D3 ... 54.39N 3.32W
Worksop England 15 F2 ... 53.19N 1.07W
Worms Germany 44 H6 ... 49.38N 8.21E
Worms Head Wales 12 C3 ... 51.34N 4.21W

Worth England 11 E2 ... 51.07N 0.09W
Worthing England 11 E1 ... 50.49N 0.22W
Wowoni i. Indonesia 105 G3 ... 4.09S 123.13E
Wragby England 15 G2 ... 53.17N 0.18W
Wrangel Island Rus. Fed. 59 T5 ... 71.07N 178.56W
Wrangell U.S.A. 62 E3 ... 56.28N 132.22W
Wrangle England 15 H2 ... 53.02N 0.07E
Wrath, Cape Scotland 18 D3 ... 58.38N 5.00W
Wreake r. England 10 D3 ... 52.42N 1.06W
Wrexham Wales 12 E5 ... 53.03N 2.59W
Wrexham d. Wales 9 D3 ... 53.01N 2.59W
Wrigley Canada 62 F4 ... 63.12N 123.24W
Wrocław Poland 46 C3 ... 51.06N 17.02E
Września Poland 46 C4 ... 52.19N 17.34E
Wuhai China 101 J5 ... 39.36N 106.53E
Wuhan China 101 K4 ... 30.37N 114.18E
Wuhu China 101 L4 ... 31.21N 118.25E
Wuppertal Germany 42 G4 ... 51.16N 7.09E
Würzburg Germany 54 C3 ... 49.48N 9.55E
Wuvulu Island P.N.G. 105 K3 ... 1.43S 142.50E
Wuwei China 101 I5 ... 37.52N 102.38E
Wuxi China 101 L4 ... 31.31N 120.18E
Wuzhou China 101 K2 ... 23.28N 111.22E
Wye England 11 F2 ... 51.11N 0.56E
Wye r. Wales 12 E3 ... 51.37N 2.40W
Wylye r. England 10 D2 ... 51.04N 1.48W
Wymondham England 11 F3 ... 52.34N 1.07E
Wyndham Australia 110 B5 ... 15.29S 128.05E
Wynyard Canada 62 H3 ... 51.46N 104.12W
Wyoming d. U.S.A. 64 E5 ... 42.57N 107.30W
Wyszków Poland 46 E4 ... 52.36N 21.28E
Wythall England 10 D3 ... 52.23N 1.53W

## X

Xai-Xai Mozambique 86 C2 ... 25.02S 33.41E
Xankändi Azerbaijan 95 G7 ... 39.49N 46.46E
Xanthi Greece 56 F5 ... 41.09N 24.53E
Xavantes, Serra dos hills Brazil 77 K5 ... 12.34S 49.14W
Xiamen China 101 L2 ... 24.29N 118.11E
Xi'an China 101 J4 ... 34.12N 108.59E
Xiangfan China 101 K4 ... 32.03N 112.07E
Xiangkhoang Laos 104 C7 ... 19.21N 103.25E
Xiangtan China 101 K3 ... 27.52N 112.47E
Xichang China 101 I3 ... 27.55N 102.11E
Xigazê China 100 F3 ... 29.17N 88.45E
Xi Jiang r. China 90 I4 ... 22.23N 113.20E
Xilinhot China 101 L6 ... 43.54N 116.08E
Xingtai China 101 K5 ... 37.01N 114.33E
Xingu r. Brazil 77 J7 ... 1.37S 52.12W
Xining China 101 I5 ... 36.35N 101.40E
Xinjiang Uygur Zizhiqu d. China 100 D6 ... 40.15N 78.50E
Xintai China 101 L5 ... 35.55N 117.45E
Xinxiang China 101 K5 ... 35.14N 113.54E
Xinyang China 101 K4 ... 32.08N 114.04E
Xinzhu Taiwan 101 M2 ... 24.48N 120.58E
Xizang Zizhiqu d. China 100 F4 ... 31.26N 88.12E
Xun Jiang r. China 101 K2 ... 23.27N 111.25E
Xuwen China 104 E8 ... 20.18N 110.09E

## Y

Yabēlo Ethiopia 87 B4 ... 4.51N 38.08E
Yabēlo Wildlife Sanctuary nature res. Ethiopia 87 B4 ... 4.56N 38.22E
Yablonovyy Khrebet mts Rus. Fed. 59 L3 ... 50.48N 108.47E
Yacuma r. Bolivia 76 G5 ... 13.39S 65.25W
Yakima U.S.A. 64 B6 ... 46.36N 120.29W
Yakumo Japan 106 D4 ... 42.15N 140.15E
Yaku-shima i. Japan 106 B2 ... 30.15N 130.36E
Yakutsk Rus. Fed. 59 N4 ... 61.59N 129.40E
Yala Thailand 104 C5 ... 6.32N 101.17E
Yalova Turkey 57 H5 ... 40.39N 29.17E
Yalta Ukraine 57 K7 ... 44.30N 34.10E
Yamagata Japan 106 D3 ... 38.15N 140.20E
Yamal Peninsula Rus. Fed. 58 H5 ... 70.40N 69.23E
Yambol Bulgaria 56 G6 ... 42.29N 26.30E
Yamoussoukro Côte d'Ivoire 84 D2 ... 6.48N 5.15W
Yamuna r. India 96 F6 ... 25.26N 81.57E
Yana r. Rus. Fed. 59 O5 ... 71.09N 135.57E
Yanbu' al Bahr Saudi Arabia 94 E4 ... 24.05N 38.06E
Yancheng China 101 M4 ... 33.22N 120.09E
Yangôn Myanmar 97 I4 ... 16.49N 96.08E
Yangquan China 101 K5 ... 37.52N 113.33E
Yangzhou China 101 L4 ... 32.23N 119.25E
Yanji China 101 N6 ... 42.54N 129.31E
Yanskiy Zaliv g. Rus. Fed. 59 O5 ... 71.55N 135.13E
Yantai China 101 M5 ... 37.30N 121.21E
Yaoundé Cameroon 84 F2 ... 3.51N 11.30E
Yap i. Micronesia 105 J5 ... 9.30N 138.12E
Yapen i. Indonesia 105 J3 ... 1.46S 136.12E
Yap Trench f. N. Pacific Oc. 108 F6 ... 7.14N 136.38E
Yaqui r. Mexico 70 B6 ... 27.36N 110.36W
Yare r. England 11 G3 ... 52.35N 1.38E
Yaren Nauru 108 H5 ... 0.33S 166.55E
Yarm England 15 F3 ... 54.30N 1.21W
Yarmouth Canada 63 L2 ... 43.50N 66.07W
Yarmouth England 10 D1 ... 50.42N 1.30W

Yaroslavl' Rus. Fed. 58 E3 ... 57.37N 39.53E
Yartsevo Rus. Fed. 55 O6 ... 55.04N 32.41E
Yasawa Group is Fiji 111 G5 ... 16.56S 177.18E
Yasyel'da r. Belarus 55 L5 ... 52.08N 26.27E
Yatağan Turkey 57 H3 ... 37.20N 28.09E
Yate England 10 C2 ... 51.32N 2.25W
Yatton England 10 C2 ... 51.23N 2.49W
Yavari r. Brazil/Peru 76 G7 ... 4.18S 69.59W
Yaví, Cerro mt. Venezuela 72 C7 ... 5.32N 65.58W
Yavoriv Ukraine 46 F3 ... 49.57N 23.25E
Yawatahama Japan 106 B2 ... 33.27N 132.26E
Yazd Iran 95 H6 ... 31.53N 54.21E
Yealmpton England 13 D2 ... 50.21N 3.59W
YeDebub Bihēroch Bihēreseboch na Hizboch d. Ethiopia 87 B4 ... 6.14N 36.32E
Yekaterinburg Rus. Fed. 58 H3 ... 56.53N 60.35E
Yell i. Scotland 19 H5 ... 60.35N 1.06W
Yellowknife Canada 62 G4 ... 62.29N 114.19W
Yellow Sea N. Pacific Oc. 101 N5 ... 35.28N 125.29E
Yellowstone r. U.S.A. 64 F6 ... 47.59N 103.59W
Yell Sound str. Scotland 19 H5 ... 60.37N 1.15W
Yemen Asia 95 G3 ... 14.48N 45.46E
Yenisey r. Rus. Fed. 59 J5 ... 70.22N 82.59E
Yeniseysk Rus. Fed. 59 K3 ... 58.27N 92.13E
Yeovil England 10 C1 ... 50.56N 2.38W
Yerevan Armenia 58 F2 ... 40.11N 44.32E
Yereymentau Kazakhstan 100 C8 ... 51.36N 73.08E
Yeşilırmak r. Turkey 57 L5 ... 41.27N 36.36E
Yes Tor hill England 13 C2 ... 50.41N 4.01W
Yevpatoriya Ukraine 53 J6 ... 45.12N 33.22E
Yeysk Rus. Fed. 53 K6 ... 46.43N 38.17E
Yibin China 101 I3 ... 28.46N 104.36E
Yichang China 101 K4 ... 30.41N 111.19E
Yichun China 101 N7 ... 47.37N 128.52E
Yıldızeli Turkey 57 L4 ... 39.53N 36.35E
Yinchuan China 101 J5 ... 38.26N 106.18E
Yingkou China 101 M6 ... 40.40N 122.15E
Yining China 100 E6 ... 43.54N 81.22E
Yirga Alem Ethiopia 87 B4 ... 6.47N 38.22E
Yirga Ch'efē Ethiopia 87 B4 ... 6.06N 38.11E
Yli-Kitka l. Finland 40 G4 ... 66.10N 28.46E
Ylitornio Finland 40 E4 ... 66.20N 23.41E
Y Llethr hill Wales 12 D4 ... 52.49N 3.59W
Ylöjärvi Finland 40 E3 ... 61.34N 23.36E
Yogyakarta Indonesia 104 E2 ... 7.47S 110.23E
Yokohama Japan 106 C3 ... 35.26N 139.37E
Yongzhou China 101 K3 ... 26.25N 111.35E
Yonne r. France 44 E6 ... 48.23N 2.58E
York England 15 F2 ... 53.58N 1.05W
York d. England 9 E3 ... 53.57N 1.04W
York, Cape Australia 110 D5 ... 10.41S 142.36E
York, Cape Canada 63 J5 ... 73.47N 87.15W
York, Vale of f. England 15 F3 ... 54.13N 1.32W
Yorkshire Wolds hills England 15 G2 ... 53.53N 0.35W
Yorkton Canada 62 H3 ... 51.12N 102.27W
Youghal Ireland 41 D1 ... 51.58N 7.51W
Yozgat Turkey 57 K4 ... 39.49N 34.47E
Yser r. France 11 H1 ... 50.54N 2.37E
Ystad Sweden 40 C1 ... 55.26N 13.49E
Ystalyfera Wales 12 D3 ... 51.46N 3.47W
Ystwyth r. Wales 12 C4 ... 52.24N 4.05W
Ysyk-Köl l. Kyrgyzstan 100 D6 ... 42.25N 77.12E
Ythan r. Scotland 19 G2 ... 57.22N 2.01W
Yūbari Japan 106 D4 ... 43.04N 141.59E
Yucatán d. Mexico 70 G5 ... 20.35N 89.05W
Yucatán pen. Mexico 70 F4 ... 19.17N 90.15W
Yucatan Channel Cuba/Mexico 71 G5 ... 22.16N 86.46W
Yueyang China 101 K3 ... 29.23N 113.07E
Yukon d. Canada 62 E4 ... 63.59N 137.15W
Yukon r. Canada/U.S.A. 62 B4 ... 62.44N 164.41W
Yulin China 101 K2 ... 22.37N 110.12E
Yuma U.S.A. 64 D3 ... 32.43N 114.38W
Yumen China 100 H5 ... 39.46N 97.33E
Yunak Turkey 57 I4 ... 38.48N 31.44E
Yungas f. Bolivia 76 G4 ... 16.51S 65.20W
Yunnan d. China 101 I2 ... 24.45N 101.07E
Yushu China 100 H4 ... 32.59N 96.59E
Yuxi China 101 I2 ... 24.20N 102.33E
Yuzhno-Kuril'sk Rus. Fed. 106 E4 ... 44.04N 145.49E
Yuzhno-Sakhalinsk Rus. Fed. 59 P2 ... 46.57N 142.39E
Yuzhnoukrayinsk Ukraine 55 N2 ... 47.50N 31.11E

## Z

Zaandam Neth. 42 D5 ... 52.26N 4.51E
Zabid Yemen 94 F2 ... 14.11N 43.15E
Zabol Iran 95 J6 ... 30.59N 61.31E
Zacatecas Mexico 70 D5 ... 22.46N 102.38W
Zacatecas d. Mexico 70 D5 ... 23.56N 102.42W
Zadar Croatia 56 A7 ... 44.07N 15.14E
Zafra Spain 48 B3 ... 38.26N 6.25W
Zagreb Croatia 56 A7 ... 45.48N 15.58E
Zagros Mountains Iran 95 G6 ... 34.02N 47.10E
Zähedän Iran 95 J5 ... 29.30N 60.52E
Zahlé Lebanon 53 K3 ... 33.50N 35.55E
Zaječar Serbia 56 E6 ... 43.54N 22.16E
Zākhō Iraq 94 F7 ... 37.08N 42.42E
Zakynthos Greece 56 D3 ... 37.47N 20.54E

Zakynthos i. Greece 56 D3 ... 37.45N 20.42E
Zalaegerszeg Hungary 54 G2 ... 46.51N 16.53E
Zalău Romania 56 E2 ... 47.11N 23.04E
Zambezi r. Africa 86 C3 ... 15.41S 30.25E
Zambia Africa 86 B3 ... 14.13S 27.30E
Zamboanga Phil. 105 G5 ... 6.56N 122.05E
Zamora Spain 48 C4 ... 41.31N 5.44W
Zamość Poland 46 F3 ... 50.43N 23.16E
Zanjän Iran 95 G7 ... 36.40N 48.27E
Zanzibar Tanzania 86 C4 ... 6.08S 39.14E
Zanzibar Island Tanzania 86 C4 ... 6.17S 39.32E
Zaoyang China 101 K4 ... 32.10N 112.46E
Zaozhuang China 101 L4 ... 34.52N 117.34E
Zapadnaya Dvina r. Rus. Fed. 55 O7 ... 56.16N 32.06E
Zapadnyy Sayan f. Rus. Fed. 59 J3 ... 51.41N 88.08E
Zapolyarnyy Rus. Fed. 40 G5 ... 69.26N 30.50E
Zaporizhzhya Ukraine 55 P2 ... 47.50N 35.10E
Zara Turkey 57 L4 ... 39.54N 37.45E
Zaragoza Spain 48 E4 ... 41.40N 0.51W
Zarand Iran 95 I6 ... 30.49N 56.34E
Zarasai Lithuania 46 H5 ... 55.44N 26.15E
Zaraza Venezuela 71 K2 ... 9.21N 65.18W
Zaria Nigeria 84 E3 ... 11.07N 7.43E
Zarubino Rus. Fed. 106 B4 ... 42.39N 131.04E
Żary Poland 46 B3 ... 51.38N 15.08E
Zarzis Tunisia 52 F3 ... 33.30N 11.05E
Zawiercie Poland 46 D3 ... 50.29N 19.26E
Zawilah Libya 52 G2 ... 26.08N 15.08E
Zaysan Kazakhstan 100 E7 ... 47.27N 84.55E
Zaysan, Lake Kazakhstan 58 J2 ... 48.05N 83.34E
Zealand i. Denmark 40 B1 ... 55.23N 11.46E
Zeebrugge Belgium 42 C4 ... 51.20N 3.16E
Zeeland d. Neth. 42 C4 ... 51.31N 3.49E
Zeil, Mount Australia 110 C4 ... 23.24S 132.24E
Zelenograd Rus. Fed. 55 Q7 ... 56.00N 37.12E
Zelenogradsk Rus. Fed. 46 E5 ... 54.58N 20.29E
Zémio C.A.R. 85 G2 ... 5.00N 25.05E
Zenica Bos.-Herz. 56 B7 ... 44.11N 17.55E
Zereh, Gowd-e f. Afgh. 95 J5 ... 29.50N 62.27E
Zeya Rus. Fed. 59 N3 ... 53.47N 126.54E
Zêzere r. Portugal 48 A3 ... 39.28N 8.20W
Zgierz Poland 46 D3 ... 51.51N 19.24E
Zhabinka Belarus 46 G4 ... 52.11N 24.00E
Zhambyl Kazakhstan 100 C6 ... 42.50N 71.25E
Zhangjiakou China 101 K6 ... 40.41N 114.55E
Zhangping China 101 L3 ... 25.21N 117.28E
Zhangshu China 101 L3 ... 28.04N 115.30E
Zhanjiang China 101 K2 ... 21.10N 110.22E
Zhaotong China 101 I3 ... 27.22N 103.41E
Zhashkiv Ukraine 55 N3 ... 49.15N 30.08E
Zhejiang d. China 101 M3 ... 29.21N 120.06E
Zheleznogorsk Rus. Fed. 55 P5 ... 52.19N 35.23E
Zhengzhou China 101 K4 ... 34.41N 113.41E
Zhenjiang China 101 L4 ... 32.10N 119.25E
Zhezkazgan Kazakhstan 58 H2 ... 47.45N 67.44E
Zhlobin Belarus 55 N5 ... 52.54N 30.02E
Zhmerynka Ukraine 55 M3 ... 49.03N 28.06E
Zhob Pakistan 95 K6 ... 31.21N 69.32E
Zhongshan China 101 K2 ... 22.31N 113.26E
Zhovti Vody Ukraine 55 O3 ... 48.21N 33.30E
Zhukovskiy Rus. Fed. 55 R6 ... 55.35N 38.08E
Zhuzhou China 101 K3 ... 27.49N 113.07E
Zhydachiv Ukraine 46 G2 ... 49.23N 24.09E
Zhytkavichy Belarus 55 L5 ... 52.13N 27.52E
Zhytomyr Ukraine 55 M4 ... 50.15N 28.40E
Zibo China 101 L5 ... 36.47N 118.06E
Zielona Góra Poland 46 B3 ... 51.57N 15.30E
Zighan Libya 53 H2 ... 25.27N 22.07E
Zigong China 101 I3 ... 29.24N 104.49E
Žilina Slovakia 54 H3 ... 49.14N 18.44E
Zillah Libya 53 G2 ... 28.32N 17.33E
Zima Rus. Fed. 101 I8 ... 53.54N 101.59E
Zimbabwe Africa 86 B3 ... 22.06S 30.59E
Zimmi Sierra Leone 84 C2 ... 7.16N 11.17W
Zimnicea Romania 56 F6 ... 43.40N 25.22E
Zinder Niger 84 E3 ... 13.48N 8.59E
Zlín Czech Rep. 54 G3 ... 49.13N 17.41E
Złotów Poland 46 C4 ... 53.22N 17.04E
Zmiyevka Rus. Fed. 55 Q5 ... 52.40N 36.23E
Znam"yanka Ukraine 55 O3 ... 48.43N 32.41E
Znojmo Czech Rep. 54 G3 ... 48.51N 16.04E
Zolochiv Ukraine 55 K3 ... 49.48N 24.54E
Zolotonosha Ukraine 55 O3 ... 49.42N 32.02E
Zonguldak Turkey 57 I5 ... 41.27N 31.46E
Żory Poland 46 D3 ... 50.03N 18.42E
Zouar Chad 85 F4 ... 20.27N 16.35E
Zouérat Mauritania 84 C4 ... 22.46N 12.29W
Zrenjanin Serbia 56 D7 ... 45.23N 20.25E
Zugdidi Georgia 53 L5 ... 42.30N 41.52E
Zugspitze mt. Austria/Germany 54 D2 ... 47.26N 10.59E
Zuid-Holland d. Neth. 42 D4 ... 51.57N 4.28E
Zújar r. Spain 48 C3 ... 39.01N 5.46W
Zülpich Germany 42 F3 ... 50.41N 6.40E
Zunyi China 101 J3 ... 27.40N 106.54E
Zürich Switz. 50 C7 ... 47.23N 8.32E
Zutphen Neth. 42 F5 ... 52.09N 6.12E
Zuwärah Libya 52 F3 ... 32.56N 12.05E
Zvolen Slovakia 54 H3 ... 48.35N 19.08E
Zvornik Bos.-Herz. 56 C7 ... 44.24N 19.07E
Zwickau Germany 54 E4 ... 50.43N 12.30E
Zwolle Neth. 42 F5 ... 52.30N 6.06E
Zyryanovsk Kazakhstan 100 E7 ... 49.46N 84.21E

## References

BP Statistical Review of World Energy
British Geological Survey
Census 2001
Dartmouth Flood Observatory
Department of Trade and Industry, UK
Department of Transport, UK
Intergovernmental Panel on Climate Change
Met Office, UK
UK National Statistics
UN Commodity Trade Statistics
UNESCO World Heritage Sites
United Nations Population Information Network
US Census Bureau
USGS Earthquake Hazards Program
USGS Minerals Yearbook
World Bank Group
World Resources Institute
World Tourism Organization

## Photo credits

**University of Maryland Global Land Cover Facility:**
p4 Aral Sea 1989
**NASA/LAADS**
p4 Aral Sea 2009
**NASA/GSFC/METI/ERSDAC/JAROS and U.S./Japan ASTER Science Team:**
p4 Kitakami River, p5 Dubai 2002, Dubai 2008
**NASA/Landsat Project Science Office:**
p5 Dubai 1973
**NASA/GSFC:**
p5 World at night
**NASA/Johnson Space Center**
p5 Las Vegas, Brasilia, Milan, Dubai, Tokyo, p127 Cairo
**National Snow and Ice Data Center:**
p5 Larsen Ice Shelf

**MODIS Rapid Response Team, NASA/GSFC**
p75 Argentina and Paraguay, p80 Rondônia, p70 Hurricane Gustav
**Annemarie Schneider, Boston University and NASA Landsat Science Team**
p127 Chengdu
**NASA Johnson Space Center**
p143 Dalla-Fort Worth Airport
**Science Photo Library**
p43 Europoort CNES 1999 Distribution Spot Image, p68 San Francisco, p99 Bangladesh
**USGS Land Processes Data Center**

## Acknowledgements

General Bathymetric Chart of the Oceans (GEBCO)
Ministry of Planning and National Development, Nairobi, Kenya
Rotterdam Municipal Port Management, Rotterdam, Netherlands
Instituto Geográfico e Cartográfico, São Paulo, Brazil
International Hydrographic Organisation, Monaco
National Atlas and Thematic Mapping Organisation, Kolkata, India

Maps on the pages listed below are derived in part from material originally published in the **Collins Longman Student Atlas.**
Pp20-21, p23, p24 (part), p27 (part), p28 (part), p29, p30, p36, p38, p39, p61, p67 (part), pp68-69, p74, p76 (inset), p78 (part), p79 (part), p83, p88 (part), p89 (part), p92-93, p94 (inset), p97 (inset), p99 (part), p107 (part), p111 (part), p113, p114-115, p116-117, p120-121 (part)